Professional C#

Simon Robinson
Ollie Cornes
Jay Glynn
Burton Harvey
Craig McQueen
Jerod Moemeka
Christian Nagel
Morgan Skinner
Karli Watson

Wrox Press Ltd. ®

Professional C#

Reprinted with Corrections – November 2001

Published by Wrox Press Ltd,
Arden House, 1102 Warwick Road, Acocks Green,
Birmingham, B27 6BH, UK
Printed in USA
ISBN 1861004990

Trademark Acknowledgements

Wrox has endeavored to provide trademark information about all the companies and products mentioned in this book by the appropriate use of capitals. However, Wrox cannot guarantee the accuracy of this information.

Credits

Authors
Simon Robinson
Ollie Cornes
Jay Glynn
Burton Harvey
Craig McQueen
Jerod Moemeka
Christian Nagel
Morgan Skinner
Karli Watson

Additional Material
Julian Skinner
Adrian Young

Category Manager
Bruce Lawson

Technical Architect
Julian Skinner

Technical Editors
Helen Callaghan
Gary Evans
Allan Jones
M. K. L. Lau
Adrian Young

Author Agents
Sarah Bowers
Avril Corbin

Project Administrators
Rob Hesketh
Chandima Nethisinghe

Production Manager
Simon Hardware

Production Coordinator
Mark Burdett

Production Assistants
Abbie Forletta
Paul Grove
Shabnam Hussain

Technical Reviewers
Jonathan Allen
Martin Beaulieu
Christopher Blexrud
Richard Bonneau
Beth Breidenback
Ramu Choppa
Ollie Cornes
Steve Danielson
Mike Erickson
Jeff Gabriel
Zach Greenvoss
Jacob Hammer Pedersen
Scott Hanselman
Ben Hickman
Mark Horner
Michael Johnson
Deepak Kumar
Don Lee
Shaun McAravey
Duncan McIntosh
Jason Montgomery
Paul Murphy
Jan Narkiewicz
Maria Petitt
Jawaharlal Puvvala
Jon Reid
Scott Robertson
Kristy Saunders
David Schultz
Adwait Ullal
Stacey Wagoner
Helmut Watson
Donald Xie
Radomir Zaric

Cover
Dawn Chellingworth

Index
Martin Brooks
Alessandro Ansa
Bill Johncocks

Proof Readers
Miriam Robinson
Fiver Locker
Chris Smith

About the Authors

Simon Robinson

Simon Robinson lives in Lancaster in the UK, where he shares a house with some students. He first encountered serious programming when he was doing his PhD in physics, modeling all sorts of weird things to do with superconductors and quantum mechanics. The experience of programming was nearly enough to put him off computers for life (though, oddly, he seems to have survived all the quantum mechanics), and he tried for a while being a sports massage therapist instead. He then realized how much money was in computers compared to sports massage, and therefore, rapidly got a job as a C++ programmer/researcher instead. Simon is clearly the charitable, deep, spiritual type, who understands the true meaning of life.

His programming work eventually lead him into writing, and he now makes a living mostly from writing great books for programmers. He is a great enthusiast for C#, which he firmly believes is set to revolutionize programming. His spare time is spent either at dance classes (he loves performing arts) or on his pet project writing a computer strategy game. With what little time is left, he is an honorary research associate at Lancaster University, where he does research in computational fluid dynamics with the environmental science department. You can visit Simon's web site at http://www.SimonRobinson.com.

Dedications

Apart from the editors who've been great to work with, and who've worked incredibly hard to help bring this book out, I'd like to thank:

- ❑ Joe Crump at Microsoft, for some very useful technical input and getting a number of queries answered.
- ❑ Morgan Skinner for some useful suggestions for Chapter 7.
- ❑ Jason Sickler, a student at MIT, and alias Darrius, President of the Chinese, for agreeing to have details of his negotiations with me used in one of the samples in Chapter 14.

Ollie Cornes

Ollie has been working with the Internet and the Microsoft platform since the early 90's. In 1999 he co-founded a business-to-business Internet company and until recently, was their Chief Technical Officer.

Prior to that, his various roles involved programming, technical authoring, network management, writing, leading development projects, and consulting. He has worked with Demon Internet, Microsoft, Saab, Tesco, Travelstore, and Vodafone. Ollie has a degree in computer science and is Microsoft certified.

When he's not working he spends his time devouring books on human potential, practicing Chinese internal martial arts, meditating, and juggling fire.

Dedication

I want to say thank you to my friends and family for the support and love you've given me. Life throws the good and the bad at us all, and you have made the bad stuff much easier to get past.

Jay Glynn

Jay started developing software in the late 1980's, writing applications for the Pick operating system in Pick BASIC. Afterwhich he has created applications using Paradox PAL and Object PAL, Delphi, Pascal, C/C++, Java, VBA, and Visual Basic. Currently, Jay is a Project Coordinator and Architect for a large insurance company based in Nashville TN. For the past 5 years, he has been developing software for pen based computers and, more recently, for ASP and server based systems. When not sitting in front of a keyboard, Jay is busy restoring a house in Franklin TN, playing a round of golf whenever possible, and watching Disney movies with his wife and 3 year old son.

Burton Harvey

Burton Harvey builds software that elegantly fulfils users' needs. An MCSD with fifteen years' experience using Microsoft development tools, Burt is adept at a multitude of technologies including VB, COM, ASP, SQL, C#, C++, x86 assembler, UML, WML, and the Palm OS.

In 1998, Burt served as the founding editor of an online journal of scientific research, Scientia. His Master's thesis, "The Outlaw Method for Solving Multimodal Functions with Parallel Genetic Algorithms," was presented at the International Conference on Evolutionary Computation, and Burt has spoken on C# at Wrox conferences in Las Vegas and Amsterdam.

As a consultant, Burt provides services to healthcare companies, music publishers, financial institutions, and sports organizations. As the CEO of Promethean Personal Software, he develops handheld applications that empower the individual (http://www.propersonal.com).

Burt currently resides in Nashville, Tennessee, and can be reached at kbharvey@mindspring.com.

This is his third book.

Craig McQueen

Chief E-Business Architect, Sage Information Consultants Inc

As a strategic technology advisor at Sage, Craig plays a key role in educating clients about the latest trends in current and emerging IT industry standards (COM, .NET, Dynamic HTML, XML, and so on). This role is supported by Craig's active involvement in trade and industry publishing and speaking opportunities. He has been a contributor to six books related to web applications, as well as industry periodicals including Visual C++ Developer and ActiveWeb Developer. Craig was also a presenter at the 1999 and 2000 ASP Professional Web Developer Conferences.

Jerod Moemeka

Jerod Moemeka is an architect with Fujitsu Transaction services. At Fujitsu, he is responsible for opportunity identification and ownership, as well as full product life cycle inception, design, and implementation. Part of this charge involves project planning, UML design, software and hardware evaluation, resource acquisition, and project team mentoring. Jerod has also worked as a Java architect for SUN Microsystems, a senior IT specialist with IBM, and lead architect with JIS. In this capacity he has been part of the architecture team of such high profile sites as Priceline.com, MyFujiFilm.com, SonyStyle.com, and Volume.com.

Christian Nagel

Christian Nagel is working as a trainer and consultant for Global Knowledge, the largest independent information technology training provider. Having worked with PDP 11, VMS, and Unix platforms, he looks back to more than 15 years of experience in the field of software development. With his profound knowledge of Microsoft technologies - he's certified as Microsoft Certified Trainer (MCT), Solution Developer (MCSD), and Systems Engineer (MCSE) – he enjoys teaching others programming and architecting distributed solutions. As founder of what is now called .NET User Group Austria, and as MSDN Regional Director, he is speaker at European Developer conferences, and more and more addressed by many developers. You can contact Christian via his web site at http://christian.nagel.net.

Morgan Skinner

I started my computing at a tender age on a ZX80 at school, where I was underwhelmed by some code my teacher had put together and decided I could do better in assembly language. After getting hooked on Z80 (much better than those paltry 3 registers in 6502 land!) I graduated through the school ZX81's to my own ZX Spectrum.

Since then I've used all sorts of languages and platforms, including VAX Macro Assembler (way cool!), Pascal, Modula2, Smalltalk, x86 assembly language, PowerBuilder, C/C++, Visual Basic, and currently C#. I've managed to stay in the same company for nearly 12 years, largely down to the diversity of the job and a good working environment.

In my spare time I'm a bit of a DIY nut, I spend lots of money on Bicycles, and 'relax' by fighting weeds on my allotment.

I can be reached by email at morgan.skinner@totalise.co.uk.

Karli Watson

Karli Watson is an in-house author for Wrox Press with a penchant for multicolored clothing. He started out with the intention of becoming a world famous nanotechnologist, so perhaps one day you might recognize his name as he receives a Nobel Prize. For now, though, Karli's computing interests include all things mobile, and upcoming technologies such as C#. He can often be found preaching about these technologies at conferences, as well as after hours in drinking establishments. Karli is also a snowboading enthusiast, and wishes he had a cat.

Table of Contents

Table of Contents

Table of Contents

Table of Contents

vii

Table of Contents

Table of Contents

Chapter 21: Graphics with GDI+ 903

Table of Contents

Introduction

If we were to describe the C# language and its associated environment, the .NET framework, as the most important new technology for developers for many years, we would not be exaggerating. .NET is designed to provide a new environment within which you can develop almost any application to run on Windows, and possibly in the future on other platforms, while C# is a new programming language that has been designed specifically to work with .NET. Using C# you can, for example, write a dynamic web page, a component of a distributed application, a database access component, or a classic Windows desktop application.

Don't be fooled by the .NET label. The NET bit in the name is there to emphasize that Microsoft believe that distributed applications, in which the processing is distributed between client and server, are the way forward, but C# is not just a language for writing Internet or network-aware applications. It provides a means for you to code up almost any type of software or component that you might need to write for the Windows platform. Between them, C# and .NET are set to both revolutionize the way that you write programs, and to make programming on Windows much easier than it has ever been.

That's quite a substantial claim, and needs to be justified. After all, we all know how quickly computer technology changes. Every year Microsoft brings out new software, programming tools or versions of Windows, with the claim that these will be hugely beneficial to developers. So what's different about .NET and C#?

The Significance of .NET

In order to understand the significance of .NET it is useful to remind ourselves of the nature of many of the Windows technologies that have appeared in the last ten years or so. In that time, we've progressed on the home PC side from Windows 3.1 (introduced in 1992) through to Windows 95, 98, and most recently the Millennium Edition. On the business side, we've seen Windows NT 3.5, NT 4.0, and Windows 2000, while Windows XP is set to cater for both home and business users. Although Windows XP, Windows 2000, and Windows millennium edition look on the surface very different from Windows 3.1 (and indeed Windows 2000 has a very different kernel at its core), programming all these platforms is quite similar.

This is because they all have the same familiar Windows API at their core. As we've progressed through new versions of Windows, huge numbers of new functions have been added to the API, but this has been a process of evolving and extending the API rather than replacing it.

The same can be said for many of the technologies and frameworks that we've used to develop software for Windows. **COM (Component Object Model)**, for example, originated as **OLE (Object Linking and Embedding)**. At the time it was, to a large extent, simply a means by which different types of office documents could be linked together, so that for example you could place a small Excel spreadsheet in your Word document. From that it evolved into COM, **DCOM (Distributed COM)**, and eventually COM+ - a sophisticated technology that formed the basis of the way almost all components communicated, as well as implementing transactions, messaging services, and object pooling.

Similarly, Visual Basic started off as a way of placing ActiveX controls into an application and was gradually extended until it became the full-blown development language that you can use to write ActiveX controls, and compile to native executable code that VB6 is. On the other hand, C++ has gradually been extended with various attributes, as well as the big class and template libraries of **MFC (Microsoft Foundation Classes)**, and **ATL (Active Template Library)**.

Evolution vs Revolution

The point of these examples is that they all represent evolution. While some new technologies have appeared, the emphasis has been on existing technologies evolving and extending their capabilities. Microsoft has chosen this path for the very obvious reason that it is concerned about backward compatibility. Over the years a huge base of third-party software has been written for Windows, and Windows wouldn't have enjoyed the success it has had if every time Microsoft introduced a new technology it broke the existing code base!

While this backward compatibility issue has been a crucial feature of Windows technologies and one of the strengths of Windows, it does have a big disadvantage. Every time some technology evolves and adds new features, it ends up a bit more complicated than it was before. The result of this after a decade is that there are a large number of programming areas that are very obviously much harder to write code for than they need to be, because they were designed to be backwardly compatible with technology that is ten or more years old.

As an example, COM is based on some rather complex threading models that are basically there because of the need to match up current multithreaded technology with components written for Windows 3.1, in which multithreaded processes did not exist. COM is an extremely good example of a family of technologies whose usefulness has been badly dented by its complexity, with even experienced developers facing a learning curve of perhaps six months to a year to master the intricacies of interfaces, GUIDs (Globally Unique IDentifiers), marshalling, and all the other low level subtleties that COM uses.

Similarly, MFC is based on an object model that is there to be compatible with Windows 3.1, and does not make use of many great features of C++, simply because those features were not present when MFC was first designed.

It's true that Visual Basic does maintain considerable simplicity, and does successfully hide the user from the complexities of, for example, low level COM, but this comes at a cost. Calling the Windows API from VB code is difficult, and VB developers generally have access to only a small part of the functionality and flexibility offered by Windows and the Windows API.

A Clean Slate

It is clear that something had to change. Microsoft couldn't go on forever extending these same development tools and languages, always making them more and more complex in order to satisfy the conflicting demands of keeping up with the newest hardware, and maintaining backward compatibility with what was around when Windows first became popular in the early 1990s. There comes a point where you have to start with a clean slate if you want a simple yet sophisticated set of languages, environments and developer tools, which make it easy for developers to write state-of-the-art software.

This fresh start is what C# and .NET are all about. Roughly speaking, .NET is a new framework – a new API – for programming on Windows. And C# is a new language that has been designed from scratch to work with .NET, as well as to take advantage of all the progress in developer environments and in our understanding of object-oriented programming principles that has taken place over the last 20 years.

Before we continue, we should make it clear that backward compatibility has not been lost in the process. Existing programs will continue to work, and .NET was designed with the ability to work with existing software. Communication between software components on Windows now almost entirely takes place on Windows using COM. Taking account of this, .NET does have the ability to (a) provide wrappers around existing COM components so that .NET components can talk to them, and (b) provide COM wrappers around new .NET components that you write, so that legacy COM-aware clients can use your .NET components just as if they were actually COM components.

It is true that you don't need to learn C# in order to write code for .NET. Microsoft have extended C++, and made substantial changes to VB to turn it into the more powerful language VB.NET, in order to allow code written in either of these languages to target the .NET environment. Both of these languages however, are hampered by the legacy of having evolved over the years rather than being written from the start with today's technology in mind.

Visual J++, which has been beset by legal difficulties, and never really took off in the first place, has not been upgraded for .NET. It seems likely that that language will quietly disappear, though C# is sufficiently similar to J++ that in some ways C# can be viewed as a replacement for J++.

> **If you're prepared to take the trouble to learn the C# language and how the .NET framework works, you will find in many cases coding in C# is a far more pleasant and efficient business than using the older languages of C++ and VB ever was.**

This book will equip you to program in C#, while at the same time providing the necessary background in how the .NET architecture works. We will not only cover the fundamentals of the C# language, but also go on to give examples of applications that use a variety of related technologies, including database access, dynamic web pages, advanced graphics, and directory access. The only requirement is that you are familiar with at least one other high level language used on Windows – either C++, VB, or J++.

So What is .NET?

We can best answer the question, "what is .NET?" by comparing it with Windows and asking what Windows is to developers. The answer to that is twofold. In the first instance, Windows is a library; it is the set of all function calls in the Windows API, which are available for you to use in your program. These functions provide common features such as displaying dialog boxes, multiple-document-interface and single-document-interface windows, accessing base functions such as security features or component services, and so on. In the second instance, Windows is the environment in which your application runs, as well as the operating system itself.

In a similar way, .NET is two things. First, it is a library, one that is just as extensive as the Windows API. You can use it to call up all the same sorts of features that have traditionally been the role of the Windows operating system: displaying windows and dialog boxes, verifying security credentials, calling on base operating system services, creating threads, and so on, as well as newer areas such as accessing databases or connecting to the Internet or providing web services. Unlike the old Windows API however, which was basically a huge set of C function calls, the .NET library (known as the **.NET base classes**) is fully object-oriented. It is exposed as a set of objects, each of which implements a number of methods. For example, a `Thread` object allows you to create threads.

Second, .NET provides the environment in which your program is run. In this context we generally talk about the **.NET runtime** (also known as the **Common Language Runtime - CLR**), which really means the software that deals with the execution of your programs. When .NET-aware code (the usual term is **managed code**) is executed, it will be the .NET runtime which starts up your code, manages the running threads, provides various background services, and in a real sense is the immediate environment seen by the code. You can equivalently view .NET as something that provides a level of abstraction from the Operating System.

We should stress, however, that .NET is not itself an operating system. The operating system is still Windows at least until (and if) .NET gets ported to other systems, and the Windows API is still there behind the scenes. The .NET runtime sits as a layer between the Windows OS and other applications, providing a much more up to date, object-oriented, and easy to use framework for developing and running code. There will be cases in which you do want to by-pass the facilities offered by .NET and use the Windows API directly, and you can do so from C# code (or, for that matter, managed code written in C++ or VB.NET). Of course, older applications which are not .NET-aware (**unmanaged applications**), will continue to work with Windows and the Windows API directly just as they always have done. The scenario is represented in this diagram:

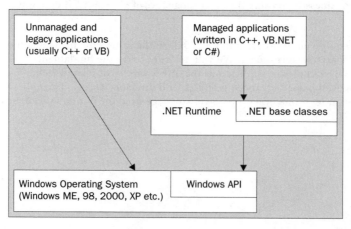

Advantages of .NET

We've talked in general terms about how great .NET is, but we haven't said much about how it helps to make your life as a developer easier. In this section, we'll discuss some of the improved features of .NET in brief.

Object-Oriented Programming

Object-oriented Programming (**OOP**) is a style of programming in which your code is broken up into units, known as **objects** or **classes**. Each object usually abstracts some real-world object that the application is concerned with. An object carries some state information as well as making methods (functions) available. OOP also allows you to base new objects on existing objects by a process known as **inheritance**.

OOP can be contrasted with procedural programming, in which your code is simply broken up into a large number of functions. Over the last 20 years, OOP has largely replaced procedural programming as the technique of choice, because it has been found that it leads to more maintainable programs and more code reuse. Of the languages currently in use, C++ and J++ fully support OOP, while VB supports a limited subset of OOP features. The old Windows API, however, was written in C and hence is entirely procedural.

That means the API literally consists of a list of literally thousands of functions. By contrast, both .NET and C# are entirely based on object-oriented principles right from the start. In particular, .NET's library is a library of classes rather than functions. You can instantiate the classes and in many cases inherit from them, as well as call up their member methods. This makes it easier to write intuitively well structured and maintainable client code, in a way that was not possible with the Windows API.

Good Design

What constitutes good design is, of course, subjective, but Microsoft has taken a lot of trouble with .NET to consult developers and to learn from previous mistakes. The result is a base class library, which is designed from the ground up in a highly intuitive way. In the vast majority of cases, you only have to look at the definition of a method to be able to see what it does and how to use it. That was certainly not true of the Windows API, for which functions are often not intuitive, and often require a number of parameters that have more to do with the intricacies of the internal operation of the API or backward compatibility than with the aim of that function.

As an example, creating and displaying a new window with .NET means instantiating a Form object, perhaps setting a few properties on it, and calling its Show() method. Using the Windows API this meant a complex process of registering a window class and setting up a message loop. It's true that in VB6, the controls that were available simplified this process in much the same way that .NET does, but that was at the expense of making many of the features of Windows unavailable. .NET makes creating a window easy, while still giving access to the full functionality of Windows.

Language Independence

Although in the past COM components could communicate with each other no matter which COM-aware languages each one had been written in, there was still a large gulf between Visual Basic, Visual J++, and Visual C++. The data types were different, and making a COM component available to any language meant putting severe restrictions on its method signatures, often in a way that would limit performance. And it was certainly not possible to mix the various languages in the same code module.

All that has now changed. With .NET, all of the languages VB.NET, C#, and managed C++ compile to a common subset called the **Intermediate Language**. This means that languages are interoperable in a way that has not been seen before. In the debugger, for example, you can step straight from C++ code into C# code, and from there into VB.NET code without any problems. Indeed all languages now even share the same developer environment.

It's important to understand that this language independence has not been achieved by going for the lowest common denominator in terms of functionality.

Instead, Microsoft has achieved this by adding features to the various languages in order to bring each language up to the standard of whatever language excelled in a particular area. VB.NET now boasts classes and inheritance, previously the preserve of C++. If you are coding in C++, the developer environment supports drag-and-drop controls in the same way that has always been the case in VB.

There are, however, some advanced features of C++, such as multiple inheritance and templates that are not supported in .NET, and are therefore, not available in managed code.

Better Support for Dynamic Web Pages

Up to now, the standard way of hosting dynamic web pages on Windows servers has been using ASP. While ASP offers a lot of flexibility, it is also inefficient due to its use of interpreted scripting languages, and the lack of object-oriented design often results in messy ASP code. .NET offers an integrated support for web pages, using a new technology – ASP.NET. With ASP.NET, code in your pages is compiled, and may be written in a .NET-aware high-level language such as C# or VB. This results in much more efficient processing of requests from browsers. Scripting languages for use in servers are now essentially obsolete (although still permitted), although client-side JScript for use in browsers is still current and has been upgraded to JScript.NET.

Not only that, but a number of other options with ASP.NET allow you to write better designed pages with a clearer separation of the background processing from the user interface. In addition, new server controls are able to deal with certain user interface elements, and are able, behind the scenes, to tailor their output to the capabilities of different browsers, so you largely don't need to be concerned about that aspect, freeing you up to concentrate more on the business logic behind your web pages.

Data Access

The .NET base class library is extremely extensive, and includes virtually full support for Windows base services, as well as for a number of component libraries. In particular, data access, something that was added to Windows later on, is a fundamental part of the base class library from the start. A set of .NET components, collectively known as ADO.NET, provide efficient access to relational databases and a variety of data sources. Components are also available to allow access to the file system, and to directories. In particular, XML support is built in to .NET, allowing you to manipulate data, which may be imported from or to non-Windows platforms.

No More DLL Hell

DLLs (**dynamic linked libraries**) were great when they were first introduced as a way of saving disk space and memory while allowing different processes to share code. With experience, however, it has become apparent that DLLs have also given rise to a number of problems, largely due to both their lack of any formal system for versioning, and the fact that newer versions of a DLL usually overwrite older versions.

The problem is most commonly that some software overwrites a shared DLL with an updated version. The updated version turns out not to be fully backward compatible, resulting in some existing software on the machine that used the same DLL no longer working. Such bugs are very hard to track down. With .NET this is no longer an issue. .NET has completely revamped the way that code is shared between applications, introducing the concept of the **assembly,** which replaces the traditional DLL. Assemblies have formal facilities for versioning, and different versions of assemblies can exist side by side.

Improved Security

This is another area that benefits from the way that assemblies are designed. Each assembly can also contain built-in security information that can indicate precisely who or what category of user or process is allowed to call which methods on which classes. This gives you a very fine degree of control over how the assemblies that you deploy can be used.

Zero Impact Installation

Since Windows 95, COM components have been registered in the registry. This system of registering software is great for providing centralized information about what software is installed on your system. However, along with COM's system of using type libraries, this has been shown to cause a number of problems because information about your software is stored in several different places. For example, the code that makes up your components will normally be in a DLL or an executable file. A description of the methods and interfaces will be in the type library somewhere else, while the GUIDs and so on will be detailed in the registry.

The fact that the information is spread out like this makes it very easy for some of information to get out of synchronization. Many developers who write COM components have at some point ended up having to fiddle with the registry to try to fix some inconsistency that has arisen. This is not a problem with .NET, since the assemblies are entirely self-describing.

At the same time, various efficient but sophisticated hashing algorithms provide runtime checks that ensure that each assembly has not been tampered with. It is also now possible to distinguish between public assemblies, which are intended to be available to other applications, and private assemblies, which are only intended to be used by the application they were installed with. This solves another existing problem with COM – that the registry would tend to get jam packed with information about thousands of components that were not really intended for public use in the first place

Support for Web Services

Web services are something that many people in the industry are convinced are going to be big business in the next few years. The idea is that various methods on an object can be called across the Internet via standard web protocols. This will bring a new aspect to distributed applications. It'll mean that companies will be able to provide services such as weather reports, parcel service status, and credit card validation via these methods, and charge clients to be able to call them over the Internet from the client's own software. Up to now, Microsoft provided limited support for Web services via the SOAP toolkit. .NET has fully integrated support for developing web services as easily as you'd develop any other type of application.

C#

The list of advantages of .NET wouldn't be complete without mentioning the fact that using .NET means you get to write to code in C# if you want to. C# is a very well designed language which corrects a number of flaws that were present in existing languages. If you want to find out exactly how great C# is, however, you'll need to read this book in its entirety!

Where C# Fits In

In one sense, C# can be seen as being the same thing to programming languages as .NET is to the Windows environment. Just as Microsoft has been adding more and more features to Windows and the Windows API over the last decade, VB and C++ have undergone expansion. Although VB and C++ have ended up as hugely powerful languages as a result of this, both languages also suffer from problems due to the legacies of how they have evolved.

In the case of Visual Basic, the main strength of the language is the fact that it is simple to understand, and does make many programming tasks easy, largely hiding the details of the Windows API and the COM component infrastructure from the developer. The downside to this is that Visual Basic has never truly been object-oriented, so that large applications quickly become disorganized and hard to maintain. As well as this, because VB's syntax was inherited from early versions of BASIC (which, in turn, was designed to be intuitively simple for beginning programmers to understand, rather than to write large commercial applications), it doesn't really lend itself to well-structured or object-oriented programs.

C++, on the other hand, has its roots in the ANSI C++ language definition. It isn't completely ANSI compliant for the simple reason that Microsoft first wrote their C++ compiler before the ANSI definition had become official, but it comes close. Unfortunately, this has lead to two problems. First, ANSI C++ has its roots in the state of technology over a decade ago and this shows up in a lack of support for modern concepts (such as Unicode strings and generating XML documentation), and in some archaic syntax structures designed for the compilers of yesteryear (such as the separation of declaration from definition of member functions). Secondly, Microsoft have been simultaneously trying to evolve C++ into a language that is designed for high-performance tasks on Windows, and in order to achieve that they've been forced to add a huge number of Microsoft-specific keywords as well as various libraries to the language. The result is that on Windows, the language has become a complete mess. Just ask a C++ developer how many definitions for a string he or she can think of: `char*`, `LPTSTR`, `string`, `CString` (MFC version), `CString` (WTL version), `wchar_t*`, `OLECHAR*` and so on.

Now enter .NET – a completely new environment, which is going to involve new extensions to both languages. Microsoft have got around this by adding yet more Microsoft-specific keywords to C++, and by completely revamping VB into VB.NET, a language which retains some of the basic VB syntax, but which is so different in design that we can consider it to be, for all practical purposes, a new language.

It's in this context that Microsoft have decided to give developers an alternative – a language designed specifically for .NET, and designed with a clean slate. C# is the result. Officially, Microsoft describe C# as a "simple, modern, object-oriented, and type safe programming language derived from C and C++." Most independent observers would probably change that to "derived from C, C++ and Java". Such descriptions are technically accurate, but do little to convey the beauty or elegance of the language. Syntactically, C# is very similar to both C++ and Java, to such an extent that many keywords are the same, and C# also shares the same block structure with braces ({}) to mark blocks of code, and semicolons to separate statements. The first impression of a piece of C# code is that it looks visually quite like C++ or Java code. Behind that initial similarity however, C# is a lot easier to learn than C++, and of comparable difficulty to Java. Its design is more in tune with modern developer tools than both of those other languages, and it has been designed to give us simultaneously, the ease of use of Visual Basic, and the high performance, low-level memory access of C++ if required. Some of the features of C# include:

❏ Full support for classes and object-oriented programming, including both interface and implementation inheritance, virtual functions, and operator overloading.

❏ A consistent and well-defined set of basic types.

❏ Inbuilt support for automatic generation of XML documentation.

❏ Automatic cleanup of dynamically allocated memory.

❏ The facility to mark classes or methods with user-defined attributes. This can be useful for documentation and can have some effects on compilation (for example, marking methods to be compiled only in debug builds).

❏ Full access to the .NET base class library, as well as easy access to the Windows API (if you really need it, which won't be all that often).

❏ Pointers and direct memory access are available if required, but the language has been designed in such a way that you can work without them in almost all cases.

❏ Support for properties and events in the style of VB.

❏ Just by changing the compiler options, you can compile either to an executable or to a library of .NET components that can be called up by other code in the same way as ActiveX controls (COM components).

❏ C# can be used to write ASP.NET dynamic web pages.

Most of the above statements it should be pointed out do apply to VB.NET and Managed C++. The fact that C# is designed from the start to work with .NET however, means that its support for the features of .NET is both more complete, and offered within the context of a more suitable syntax than for those other languages. Compared with Java, the C# language itself is very similar to Java, but there are some improvements. In particular, Java is not designed to work with the .NET environment.

The bottom line of all this is that C# is not only a highly powerful language that is not too hard to learn, but it is also arguably the only language on the market, which has been designed around today's technology and today's development tools. By learning from the experience of previous similar languages, Microsoft have been able to ensure the language is very well designed and allows rapid development of good quality code.

Before we leave the subject, we should point out a couple of limitations of C#. The one area the language is not designed for is time-critical or extremely high performance code – the kind where you really are worried about whether a loop takes 1000 or 1050 machine cycles to run through, and you need to clean up your resources the millisecond they are no longer needed. C++ is likely to continue to reign supreme amongst low-level languages in this area. C# lacks certain key facilities needed for extremely high performance apps, including inline functions and destructors that are guaranteed to run at particular points in the code. The proportion of applications that fall into this category however, are very low.

The New Developer Environment

Before concluding this introduction, we'll just say a couple of words about the new development environment, Visual Studio.NET. Up until now, each language has effectively had its own independent developer environment within the Visual Studio 6 package. C++ programmers have had their own environment (confusingly, also referred to simply as Visual Studio 6), while VB developers have coded using so-called the VB6 IDE, and the corresponding equivalent for J++ has been the Visual J++ environment, and all of these environments, while implementing many of the same features as each other, have looked completely different. Developers writing ASP pages had a raw deal, usually using Visual Interdev, an environment that offered only a tiny fraction of the code generation and debugging facilities that users of compiled languages had come to expect (on at least one occasion the author has heard Visual Interdev referred to as Visual Notepad). All of these environments (with the exception of Interdev) were very powerful in their own way, but they were obviously different environments, each with very different user interfaces.

Each developer environment before .NET had its strengths and weaknesses, which largely reflected those of the corresponding language. For example, Visual Studio (C++) has very powerful debugging and profiling facilities not available in the other environments, whereas the Visual Basic developer environment is extremely good when it comes to the visual side, allowing you to simply click to place a huge variety of ActiveX controls onto your form, and have the environment automatically add corresponding VB code to your program. If the aim with .NET is complete language interoperability however, (including the ability to step seamlessly between languages in the debugger, which is something that .NET does indeed make possible), then having separate developer environments is clearly unsatisfactory.

.NET comes with a new developer environment, Visual Studio.NET, which can cope equally well with C++, C#, and VB.NET, as well as with ASP.NET code. Visual Studio.NET integrates all the best features of the respective language specific environments of Visual Studio 6. It does mean that the first time you start coding with Visual Studio.NET you will have to get used to a different layout and different menu options, but the plus side is that you get a more powerful developer environment than ever before.

Just as with the languages, Microsoft have merged the environments not by finding the lowest common denominator of features, but rather by ensuring that, in general, any feature previously offered by Visual Studio to any one language is now available for all languages. Therefore, whatever your preferred language, you will notice new options. C++ users will see greater support for visually building forms, while VB developers will have new powerful debugging facilities and different build options. The biggest improvement, however, will almost certainly be noticed by writers of ASP pages currently confined to Visual Interdev.

We will cover how to use Visual Studio.NET in this book, but because it is a professional level book, we won't go into a huge amount of detail. We'll assume you're an experienced enough developer to figure out how to install it and to explore some of the menu options yourself. In Chapter 8 however, we will go over the main features of the developer environment – this is partly so that we can explain some of the new features that users of particular languages might not be familiar with, and partly so we can point out where some familiar tools or menu options have moved and are now in unexpected places.

What You Need to Write C# Code

.NET will run on Windows 98, 2000, or XP. In order to write code using .NET, you will need to install, the .NET SDK. Unless you are intending to write your C# code using a text editor or some other third party developer environment, you will almost certainly also want Visual Studio.NET. The full SDK isn't needed to run managed code, but the .NET runtime is needed. You may find you need to distribute the .NET runtime with your code for the benefit of those clients who do not have it already installed.

What This Book Covers

In this book, we start by reviewing the overall architecture of .NET in the next chapter in order to give us the background we need to be able to write managed code. After that the book is divided into a number of sections that cover both the C# language and its application in a variety of areas.

Section I – The C# Language

This section gives us a good grounding in the C# language itself. This section doesn't presume knowledge of any particular language, although it does assume you are an experienced programmer. We start from the basics – C# syntax and data types – and work through the principles of object-oriented programming to some of the more advanced topics in C#. At the end of this section, you will have a thorough grounding covering the entire language.

Section II – .NET Programming

In this section, we look at the principles of programming in the .NET environment. In particular, we look at Visual Studio.NET, Windows Forms (how to code up classic windows applications that display windows, or in more modern .NET parlance, forms), and we cover how to generate your own libraries as assemblies.

Section III – Data Access

We look at accessing databases with ADO.NET, and at interacting with directories and Active Directory. We also extensively cover support in .NET for XML and on the Windows operating system side, file and registry access.

Section IV – Internet Programming

In this section, we cover writing components that will run on web sites, serving up web pages. This covers both ASP.NET and the writing of web services.

Section V – Components

Backward compatibility with COM is an important part of .NET. Not only that, but COM+ is not strictly legacy – it will still be responsible for transactions, object pooling and message queuing. In this section we'll look at the support .NET offers for working with COM and COM+, as well as discussing how to write C# code that interacts with these technologies.

Section VI – Advanced .NET Programming

This section is the concluding part of the main body of the book and covers some miscellaneous advanced topics. These include advanced graphics with GDI+, Windows services (formerly known as NT services), remoting, and security.

Conventions

We have used a number of different styles of text and layout in the book to help differentiate between the different kinds of information. Here are examples of the styles we use and an explanation of what they mean:

Bullets appear indented, with each new bullet marked as follows:

❑ **Important Words** are in a bold type font

❑ Words that appear on the screen in menus like the File or Window are in a similar font to the one that you see on screen

❑ Keys that you press on the keyboard, like *Ctrl* and *Enter*, are in italics

Code has several fonts. If it's a word that we're talking about in the text, for example, when discussing the `if...else` loop, it's in `this` font. If it's a block of code that you can type in as a program and run, then it's also in a gray box:

```
public static void Main()
{
    AFunc(1,2,"abc");
}
```

Sometimes you'll see code in a mixture of styles, like this:

```
// If we haven't reached the end, return true, otherwise
// set the position to invalid, and return false.
pos++;
if (pos < 4)
    return true;
else {
    pos = -1;
    return false;
}
```

The code with a white background is code we've already looked at and that we don't wish to examine further.

Advice, hints, and background information come in an italicized, indented font like this.

> **Important pieces of information come in boxes like this.**

We demonstrate the syntactical usage of methods, properties (and so on) using the following format:

`Regsvcs BookDistributor.dll [COM+AppName] [TypeLibrary.tbl]`

Here, italicized parts indicate object references, variables, or parameter values to be inserted; the square braces indicate optional parameters.

Customer Support

We've tried to make this book as accurate and useful as possible, but what really matters is what the book actually does for you. Please let us know your views, either by returning the reply card at the back of the book, or by writing to us at feedback@wrox.com.

The source code for this book is available for download at http://www.wrox.com/.

We've made every effort to ensure there are no errors in this book. To err is human, however and we recognize the need to keep you informed of errors as they're spotted and corrected. **Errata sheets** are available for all our books, at http://www.wrox.com/. If you find an error that hasn't already been reported, please let us know.

Our web site acts as a focus for other information and support, including the code from all our books, sample chapters, and previews of forthcoming titles.

1

.NET Architecture

You'll find that we emphasize throughout this book that the C# language cannot be viewed in isolation, but must be considered in parallel with the .NET framework. The C# compiler specifically targets .NET, which means that all code written in C# will always run within the .NET framework. This has two important consequences for the C# language:

- ❑ The architecture and methodologies of C# reflect the underlying methodologies of .NET. For example, C# is based around single inheritance of classes, and has a type system that is based on the distinction between value and reference types, just as is the case for .NET.

- ❑ In many cases, specific language features of C# actually depend on features of .NET, or of the base classes. One obvious example of this is that all the basic data types in C# – int, float, string and so on are actually .NET base class types, which C# simply represents using a more convenient syntax.

Because of this dependence, it is important to gain some understanding of the architecture and methodology of .NET before we begin C# programming. That is the purpose of this chapter.

We will begin with an overview of the components of .NET so that we can get our bearings, and we will get an idea of how .NET works with your code by going over what typically happens when code that targets .NET is compiled and run. Once we have this broad overview, we will take a detailed look at the **Microsoft Intermediate Language** (**MSIL**, often abbreviated to **IL** – **Intermediate Language**), the language which all compiled code ends up in. In particular, we will see how IL, in common with the **Common Type System** (**CTS**) and **Common Language Specification** (**CLS**) works to give us interoperability between languages. Once we've done that, we will move on to examine some of the components of .NET in more detail, before concluding with a look at where the various languages, including C# and the existing languages of VB and C++, fit into this.

Overview of .NET

The easiest way to think about the .NET framework is that it is the environment seen by your code when it executes. This means that it is .NET that manages execution of your code – starting it up, granting the relevant permissions to it, giving it the memory in which to store its data, assisting with reclaiming certain memory and resources that are no longer needed, and so on. Besides carrying out these tasks, however, .NET also makes available a very comprehensive class library – the so-called **.NET base classes**, to perform a huge range of tasks on Windows. In this sense, .NET can be perceived as performing the dual roles of managing the execution of your code, and providing services to the code.

As mentioned earlier, .NET sits between your code and Windows, enabling it to provide the required services. Before we look at what normally happens when a .NET program is run, we'll quickly define some of the .NET components and other terms that we'll need. If you don't like reading lists of definitions, you might prefer to just skip this section for now and refer back to it as needed.

❑　The **.NET Runtime**, also known as the **Common Language Runtime** or **CLR**, is what actually manages your code. You can think of it as the code that handles loading your program, running it, and providing all the support services.

❑　**Managed Code**. Any code that is designed to run within the .NET environment is referred to as **managed code**. Other code, which simply runs on Windows, outside .NET, is **unmanaged code**.

❑　**Intermediate Language** (**IL**): When the .NET runtime loads and runs code, this is the language that it expects to find the code in. When you compile managed code, the compiler actually emits Intermediate Language, and the CLR handles the final stage of compilation just before the code is actually executed. IL is designed to be able to be very quickly compiled to native machine code, while at the same time supporting the features of .NET

❑　**Common Type System** (**CTS**): In order to permit language interoperability, it is imperative to have an agreed set of basic data types, so that all languages can be standardized. The CTS supplies this, and also supplies the rules for defining custom classes.

❑　**.NET Base Classes**: This is an extensive class library that contains pre-written code to perform a huge range of tasks on Windows, ranging through displaying windows and forms, accessing Windows base services, reading and writing to files, accessing networks and the Internet, and accessing data sources. Once we have covered the C# language itself, the bulk of this book will involve showing you how to use many of the .NET base classes.

❑　**Assemblies**: An assembly is the unit in which compiled managed code is stored. It has some similarities with a classic executable or DLL, but has the important feature of being completely self-describing. They contain so-called **metadata**, which gives details of the assembly and of all types, methods, and so on defined within it. An assembly can be private (only accessible to one application) or shared (accessible to any application on Windows).

❑　**Assembly Cache**: This is the area of disk in which shared assemblies are stored.

❑　**Common Language Specification** (**CLS**): This is a minimum set of standards that guarantees that code can be accessed from any language. All compilers that target .NET should support the CLS. The CLS forms a subset of the features available in .NET and IL, and it is fine for code to use features outside the CLS . If any non-CLS features are visible from outside the assembly in which the code is placed however, those features may not be useable from some languages.

- ❑ **Reflection**: Because assemblies are entirely self-describing, this opens the theoretical possibility of programmatic access to assembly metadata. There are in fact some base classes that are designed to achieve this. The technology is known as reflection (perhaps due to the intriguing fact that it means a program can actually use this facility to examine its own metadata).

- ❑ **Just-in-Time (JIT) Compilation**: This is the term for the process of performing the final stage of compilation from Intermediate Language into native machine code. It gets its name because portions of the code are compiled as required.

- ❑ **Manifest**: This is the area of an assembly that contains metadata.

- ❑ **Application Domain**: Application domains are a means by which the CLR allows different code to run in the same process space. Isolation between these code units is achieved by using the type safety of IL to verify prior to execution that each segment of code is well behaved.

- ❑ **Garbage Collection**: This is the means by which the CLR cleans up memory that is no longer needed, freeing applications from having to take responsibility for this.

What Happens When You Compile and Run a Program

We will first get a broad overview of how .NET works, and what services it provides by looking at what often happens when you run a program that has being targeted at the .NET runtime. The situation is summarized in the diagram below. We assume that you are coding an application which consists of the main part of the code, written in C#, and a library, written in VB.NET. The application also needs to call up a legacy COM component, and it goes without saying, that it will use at least some of the .NET base classes (it would be virtually impossible to write an application that does anything useful and which doesn't use the .NET base classes):

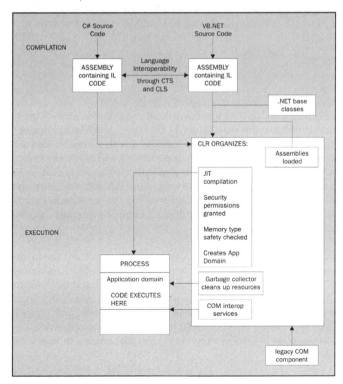

In the diagram, the boxes indicate the main components involved with compiling and running the program, while the arrows indicate the tasks being performed. The top part of the diagram shows the process of separately compiling each project into an assembly. The two assemblies are able to interact with each other, because of the language interoperability features of .NET. The lower half of the diagram shows the process of JIT-compiling from the IL in the assemblies to the actual code, which runs in an application domain inside a process…, and indicates some of the tasks that are performed by code within the CLR in order to accomplish this.

Compilation

Before your program can be run it must be compiled, and the compiled code presumably shipped. However, unlike with previous executable and DLL files, the compiled code does not contain native machine code instructions. Rather, it contains instructions in Microsoft Intermediate Language (MSIL, or IL). Intermediate Language has some similarities with the ideas of Java byte code. It is a fairly low level language that has been designed, so that it can be very rapidly converted (JIT-compiled) into native machine code.

The package that your compiled program will have been shipped in consists of a number of assemblies. Each assembly contains the Intermediate Language code, but it also contains metadata, to describe the data types and methods in the assembly. The metadata also includes a simple hash of the assembly contents, which can be used to verify that the assembly has not been tampered with, it also includes version information and details of which other assemblies this assembly will call, and possibly also information governing the permissions that the code will require in order to run.

In the past, a complete software package would consist of an executable that contains the main program starting entry point, and one or more libraries or COM components. With .NET, it contains a number of assemblies, one of which is designated as an executable and contains the main program entry point, with the others designated as libraries. In the case of our example, there will be two assemblies – an executable containing the compiled C# code, and a library containing the compiled VB.NET code.

Execution

When the program is run, the .NET runtime will load the first assembly – the one that contains the main program entry point. It will use the hash to verify that the assembly has not been tampered with, and it will use the metadata to check through the types defined with a view to insure that it will be able to run the assembly. Most well-designed commercial applications will explicitly indicate which .NET permissions they are going to need upfront (for example, will the application need to access the file system, or the registry, and so on). If this is the case, the CLR will check against the system's security policy and the account under which the program is to run, to see whether it can grant the requested permissions, and do so if possible. If the code doesn't explicitly request the permissions it needs, then they will be granted as required, if possible

Another thing the CLR will do at this stage is verify something called the **memory type safety** of the code. The code is memory type safe if it only ever accesses memory in a way that the CLR can control. The significance of this is that memory type safe code can be guaranteed not to attempt to read or write to any memory that does not belong to it. This is important because .NET has a mechanism (application domains) to allow multiple applications to run in the same process, and if this is happens, then we need to guarantee that any application won't attempt to access another application's memory. If the CLR is unable to verify that the code is memory type safe then, depending on the local security policy, it may refuse to run the code.

The CLR will then (at last) actually run the code. It creates a process for the code to run in, and also marks out an application domain, in which it places the program's main thread. In some cases, a program may request instead, to be placed in the same process as some other running code, in which case the CLR will only create a new application domain for it.

The CLR will next take the first portion of code that it needs to run and compile it from Intermediate Language into assembly language, and execute it from the appropriate program thread. Each time execution flow enters a new method that has not been executed before, that method will be compiled into executable code. This compilation, however, will only take place once. Once that method has been compiled, the address of the entry points to that method will be replaced by the address of the compiled executable code. In this way, performance is maintained, because only those portions of the code that are actually used will be compiled. This process is known as **just-in-time** (**JIT**) compiling. Note that the JIT compiler may, depending on the compilation settings specified in the assembly, optimize the code as it compiles, for example, by inlining some methods.

While the code is running, the CLR will monitor its memory usage. Based on this monitoring it will, at certain points, temporarily halt execution for short periods of time (typically milliseconds) and call up the garbage collector, which will examine the variables in the program in order to determine, which areas of memory are still actively being used by your code, so that it can free up any unused areas.

The CLR will also handle loading up assemblies as they are requested, including the COM component marked in the diagram via the .NET COM interop services.

Benefits of Running as Managed Code

From the description so far, we can already begin to see some of the benefits of running as managed code:

❑   There are obvious security benefits. Because of the fact that the assembly is written in Intermediate Language, the .NET runtime has the chance to check what sorts of things the code is going to do. The real advantage of this is that it makes it safer to run code that has been obtained, for example, from the Internet, and which you are not sure how much you trust. You simply set the .NET security policy to ensure that this code does not get permissions to do anything other than the tasks that you believe it should be doing. .NET supports both **role-based security** (based on the identity of the process running the code), and **code-based security** (based on how much the code itself is trusted).

❑   The presence of the garbage collector frees you from having to worry about writing explicit code to free up memory that you have been using. This also means that there is no risk of memory leaks for variables managed by the garbage collector.

❑   The new concept of application domains means that different applications which need to be isolated from each other, but also need to communicate with each other, may be placed in the same process, giving huge performance benefits.

Although our earlier example didn't really show this explicitly, it should be noted that we also gain the following benefits:

❑   In the above example, we've cited code segments for which the source is written in both C# and VB.NET. This means that we have language interoperability, which makes using code written in multiple languages simple.

❑   The self-describing structure of the assemblies makes it extremely unlikely that bugs will occur due to versioning problems or other applications overwriting shared assemblies, which saves both cost and time.

❑   We also haven't said anything about the role of the .NET base classes in all this. The .NET base classes offer a very intuitive, simple object model, which makes calling up most aspects of Windows functionality much easier (in terms of simplifying your source code) than in the past.

Set against this, it looks at first sight like there is a performance loss, because some compilation has to take place at runtime. Microsoft are arguing that in the long term this is unlikely to be the case however, and that just-in-time compiling will actually improve, rather than hinder, performance. We'll discuss this in more detail later in the chapter, when we cover JIT compilers, but in general terms this is because the JIT compiler knows which processor the code will run on. That information is not available to traditional compilers.

Intermediate Language

We have mentioned the Intermediate Language and drawn parallels with Java byte code. Intermediate Language shares with Java byte code the idea that it is a low-level language with a simple syntax (based on numeric codes rather than text), which can be very quickly translated into native machine code. Recall that the point of Java byte code was to provide platform independence. Having a well-defined universal syntax for the byte code would mean that the same file containing byte code instructions could be placed on any platform, for example UNIX, Linux, or Windows, and at runtime the final stage of compilation could then be easily accomplished so that the code would run on that particular platform.

This would mean that when writing the source code, you could simply compile it to Java byte code and be confident that it would run anywhere.

Intermediate language takes the same concept, but is much more ambitious. Significantly, Intermediate Language is just-in-time compiled whereas Java byte code was interpreted. This means that most of the performance loss associated with interpreting Java byte code does not apply to IL.

> **The Intermediate Language code gets compiled, not interpreted, to native machine code.**

The aim of Intermediate Language is not merely platform independence, but also language independence in an object-oriented environment. The idea is that you should be able to compile to intermediate code from any of a range of languages, and that the compiled code should be interoperable with code that has been compiled from other languages.

With .NET, that interoperability has been achieved, because you can write code that compiles to Intermediate language in C++, VB.NET or C#, and compilers for other languages including COBOL, Eiffel, and Perl are reported to be on the way from other vendors. The platform independence at present is only theoretical because, at time of writing, .NET is only available for Windows, although there is active talk of porting it to other platforms. Because of the requirements for language independence and interoperability, Intermediate Language is considerably more sophisticated than Java byte code.

Of course, language-independence does have some practical limits. In particular, Intermediate Language, however it is designed, is inevitably going to implement some particular programming methodology, which means that languages targeting it are going to have to be compatible with that methodology. The particular route that Microsoft have chosen to follow is that of classic object-oriented programming, with classes and inheritance. This means that classes and inheritance are defined within the Intermediate Language.

In the following sections, we will briefly review the characteristics of Intermediate Language.

Classic Object-Oriented Programming

In order to understand the principles of Intermediate Language, we need to understand classical object-oriented programming. This is something that Visual C++ and Java/J++ developers will be familiar with (because both of these languages are based around the concepts of OOP), but which will be new to Visual Basic developers.

> *Classic object-oriented programming represents a large subject, and is dealt with in detail in Chapters 4 and 5. In the next few paragraphs, we will summarize just enough information to get us through this chapter.*

The idea of classic object-oriented programming is that your code is divided into classes. VB developers can think of a class as something like a class module or a lightweight COM component or ActiveX control, but which in most cases does not have a user interface. Each class represents the definition of some identifiable unit that you might want to do things with. For example, in a Windows GUI environment, classes might include `ListBox`, `TextBox`, or `Form`.

The class can in one sense be viewed as something like a data type, just as, for example, an integer or a floating-point number. The difference is that a class is more complex, consisting of a number of primitive data types stored together, along with details of functions (**methods**) that can be called. The class is also a custom "data type" in the sense that it may be defined in your source code. Object-oriented programming works on the idea that your program will essentially work by creating instances of classes (**objects**), and then call various methods on these objects, so that the objects end up interacting with each other.

Classic object-oriented programming however, involves more than this. It is also heavily dependent on the concept of **implementation inheritance**.

Implementation inheritance is a technique that allows the features of a class to be reused in another class. The way it works is that when defining a class, you can declare that it is **inherited** from another class known as the **base** class. The class that you have defined, then automatically gets all of the data and methods, and so on that were defined in the base class. You can then add to these methods, or indicate that the implementations of some of them are to be replaced in the derived class. For example, in Appendix C, we write a sample involving a class, `Employee`, that stores information about company employees. This class can be used to calculate the amount each employee should be paid each month. For this example, we assume that the method for calculating the pay of managers is a slightly different, because they receive additional bonuses. To accommodate this, we write an additional class, `Manager`, which is derived from `Employee`, but in which we have replaced the method responsible for calculating the monthly payment. Programs that are written in classic object-oriented languages, such as C++ or Java, are usually designed around inheritance, and include definitions of whole hierarchies of classes that are inherited from each other.

Intermediate Language supports what is known as **single inheritance**, which means that a class can be directly derived from just one other class, but there is no limit to how many classes can be derived from a given class (and the class you derive from can in turn be derived from other classes). This means we end up with a tree-like structure of classes. In the case of Intermediate Language, all classes are ultimately derived from a class known as `Object`. This diagram illustrates the principle by showing some of the .NET base classes. Notice how as we move down the hierarchy, classes become increasingly more specialised.

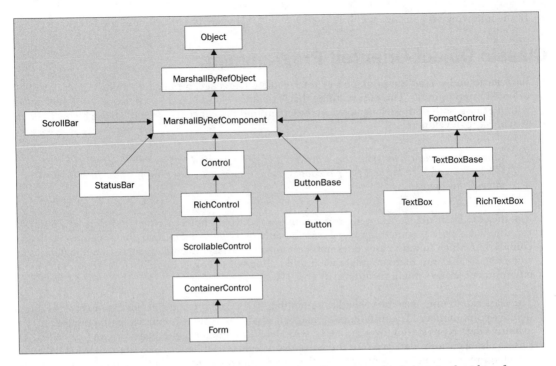

Besides classic object-oriented programming, Intermediate Language also brings in the idea of interfaces, which saw their first implementation under Windows with COM. .NET interfaces are not the same as COM interfaces; they do not need to support any of the COM infrastructure; for example, they are not derived from Iunknown, and they do not have associated GUIDs. However, they do share with COM interfaces the idea that they provide a contract, and classes that implement a given interface must provide implementations of the methods and properties specified by that interface.

Value and Reference Types

As with any programming language, Intermediate Language provides a number of predefined primitive data types. One characteristic of Intermediate Language however, is that it makes a strong distinction between **value** and **reference** types. Value types are those for which a variable directly stores its data, while reference types are those for which a variable simply stores the address at which the corresponding data can be found. This model very closely follows that used for value and reference types in Java.

In C++ terms, reference types can be considered to be similar to accessing a variable through a pointer, while for Visual Basic, the best analogy for reference types are Objects, which in VB are always accessed through references. Intermediate Language also lays down specifications about data storage: instances of reference types are always stored in an area of memory known as the **heap**, while value types are normally stored on the **stack**, although if value types are declared as fields within reference types, then they will be stored inline on the heap. (We will discuss the stack and the heap and how they work in Chapter 5).

Strong Typing

One crucial aspect of Intermediate Language is that it is based on exceptionally strong **typing**. What we mean by that is that all variables are clearly marked as being of a particular, specific data type (there is no room in Intermediate Language for, for example, the `Variant` datatype recognized by Visual Basic and scripting languages). In particular, Intermediate Language does not normally permit any operations that might leave any room for ambiguity concerning what data type a given reference is referring to.

C++ developers will be used to routinely casting pointers between different types. Being able to perform this kind of operation can be great for performance, but it breaks type safety. Hence, it is allowed only in very specific circumstances and supported only in very specific circumstances in some of the languages that compile to managed code. Indeed, pointers (as opposed to references) are only permitted in marked blocks of code in, for example C#, and not at all in VB. Using pointers in your code will immediately cause it to fail the memory type safety checks performed by the CLR. To some extent the thinking here is that although enforcing type safety might appear initially to hurt performance, this is in many cases far outweighed by the performance benefits gained from the services provided by .NET (such as application domains), which rely on that type safety.

Similarly, VB developers will be used to being able to pass variables around without worrying too much about their types, because VB will just automatically do whatever conversions are needed. If you pass an `Integer` in somewhere where a `String` is actually required, for example, VB will quietly convert the `Integer` to a `String`. The philosophy behind IL and .NET is that the convenience of this laxity is outweighed by the associated type safety problems, and in particular the potential for subtle runtime bugs associated with incorrect data types. Therefore, when writing source code that targets .NET, you will need to explicitly indicate these conversions yourself.

There are several important reasons why strong typing is important – indeed, several aspects of the .NET framework would not work without it.

❑ In the first place, the Common Language Runtime relies on being able to examine the code in order to determine what operations the code needs to perform before it actually runs the code. This is important both from the point of view of granting security permissions, and from the point of view of checking that the code cannot damage other code that is running in a different application domain, but in the same address space. Intermediate Language has been carefully designed to facilitate these checks, and clearly, if there were any doubts concerning data types in the code, this kind of checking would not be possible.

❑ In order to correctly identify memory that can be reclaimed, the garbage collector needs to be able to unambiguously identify the data type that is being stored at each memory location (if it cannot do this, then it will have no way of knowing how large an area of memory is being occupied by that variable). Again, any ambiguities in data types would cause problems and prevent the .NET runtime from functioning correctly.

❑ Language interoperability, one of the big selling points of the .NET framework, depends on there being a well-defined and consistent set of data types.

The type system used by Intermediate Language is known as the **Common Type System**, and we will examine it later in this chapter, when we look at language interoperability in more detail.

Summary of IL Features

The main characteristics of Intermediate Language can be summarised as follows:

❑   Object-oriented with single implementation inheritance of classes.

❑   Interfaces.

❑   Value and reference types.

❑   Error handling through exceptions.

❑   Very strong type system.

This broadly means, that in order for any language to target the .NET runtime it will need to support these same concepts. As far as the existing languages are concerned, it is not a problem for C++, but it does mean that the definition of Visual Basic has to be considerably enhanced in order to add support for these various concepts. The new version of Visual Basic, VB.NET, is very different from the previous version, VB6. C#, obviously, has been specifically designed with compilation to Intermediate Language in mind, and therefore includes full support for all these areas.

Language Interoperability

We have now seen that working with .NET means compiling to the Intermediate Language, and that in turn means that you will need to be programming using traditional object-oriented methodologies. That alone is not, however, sufficient to give us language interoperability. After all, C++ and Java both use the same object-oriented paradigms, but they are still not regarded as interoperable.

In this section, we will investigate in more detail how the .NET framework gives us the cross-language features. We will see that it depends crucially on the Common Type System as well as on the Common Language Specification.

To start with, we need to ask exactly what we mean by language interoperability. After all, COM allowed components written in different languages to work together in the sense of calling each other's methods. What was inadequate about that? COM, by virtue of being a binary standard, did allow components to instantiate other components and call methods or properties against them, without worrying about the language the respective components were written in. In order to achieve this however, each object had to be instantiated through the COM runtime, and accessed through an interface. Depending on the threading models of the relative components, there may have been large performance losses associated with marshalling data between apartments and/or running components on different threads. In the extreme case of components that are hosted in executable rather than DLL files, separate processes would need to be created in order to run them. The emphasis was very much that components could talk to each other, but only via the COM runtime. In no sense with COM did components written in different languages directly communicate with each other, or instantiate instances of each other – it was always done with COM as an intermediary. Not only that, but the COM architecture did not permit implementation inheritance, which meant that it lost many of the advantages of object-oriented programming.

An associated problem was that, when debugging, you would still have to independently debug components written in different languages. It was not possible to step between languages in the debugger. So what we really mean by language interoperability is that classes written in one language should be able to talk directly to classes written in another language. In particular:

❑ A class written in one language should be able to inherit from a class written in another language.

❑ The class should be able to contain an instance of another class, no matter what the languages are. An object should be able to directly call methods against another object written in another language.

❑ Objects (or references to objects) should be able to be passed around between methods.

❑ When calling methods between languages it should be possible to step between the method calls in the debugger, even where this means stepping between source code written in different languages.

This is all quite an ambitious aim, but amazingly, .NET and the Intermediate Language have achieved it. For the case of stepping between methods in the debugger, this facility is really offered by visual studio .NET rather from the .NET runtime itself, Therefore, we will not comment further on it here, beyond the fact that it is possible because Visual Studio .NET now supplies a single development environment for all the .NET languages as well as C++. The remaining aspects of language interoperability are achieved through the Common Type System, which we will examine next.

Common Type System (CTS)

What the Common Type Specification means, is that the Intermediate Language comes with a well defined and rich set of predefined data types. These data types are organized into a type hierarchy, typical of object-oriented programming environments.

Significance for Language Interoperability

The reason that the Common Type Specification is important is that, if a class is to derive from or contains instances of other classes, it needs to know about all the data types used by the other classes. Indeed, it is the absence of any agreed system in the past for specifying this information, which has always been the real barrier to inheritance across languages. This kind of information is simply not present in a standard executable file or DLL.

To some extent, the problem of getting access to type information is solved through the metadata in assemblies. Suppose, for example, that you are writing a class in C#, and you want it to derive from a class that is being written in VB.NET. In order to do so, you will instruct the compiler to reference the assembly in which the VB.NET class has been defined. The compiler can use the metadata in this assembly to find out about all the methods, properties, fields, and so on of the VB.NET class. Clearly, the compiler needs this information in order to compile your code. For C++ developers, this is analogous to including a header file. The real purpose of header files in C++ can, to some extent, be seen as one of making information about types available to source files.

However, the compiler needs slightly more information than what is provided by the metadata. Suppose, for example, that one of the methods in the VB.NET class is defined to return an Integer – one of the standard data types available in VB.NET. C# simply does not however, have any data type of that name. Clearly, we will only be able to derive from the class, and use this method and use the return type from C# code if the compiler knows how to map VB .NET's Integer type to some known type that is defined in C#.

This is possible because the Common Type Specification defines those predefined data types that are available in Intermediate Language, so that all languages that target the .NET framework will produce compiled code that is ultimately based on these types. For the example that we are considering, VB.NET's `Integer` is actually a 32-bit signed integer, which maps exactly to the Intermediate Language type known as `Int32`. This will therefore be the data type specified in the Intermediate Language code. Because the C# compiler is aware of this type, there is no problem. At source code level, C# refers to `Int32` with the keyword `int`, so the compiler will simply treat the VB.NET method as if it returned an `int`.

CTS Hierarchy

The Common Type System doesn't merely specify the primitive data types, but also defines a rich hierarchy of types, which includes well-defined locations, at which code is permitted to define its own types. The hierarchical structure of the Common Type System reflects the single-inheritance object-oriented methodology of Intermediate Language, and looks like this:

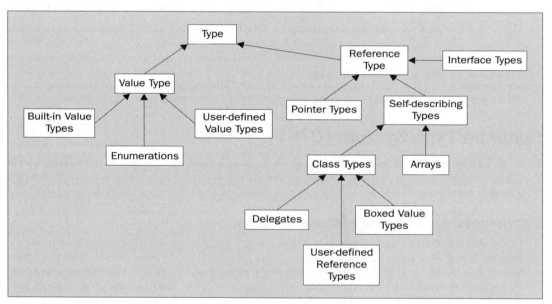

The types in this tree represent:

Type	Meaning
Arrays	Any type that contains an array of objects.
Boxed Value Types	A value type that is temporarily wrapped in a reference so that it can be stored on the heap.
Built-in Value Types	Includes most of the standard primitive types, which represent numbers, Boolean values or characters.
Class Types	Types that are self-describing but are not arrays.
Delegates	Types that are designed to hold references to methods.

Type	Meaning
Enumerations	Sets of enumerated values in which each value is represented by a label but stored as a numeric type, for example, if you wish to represent colors in this way, Enumerations let you write {Red, Green, Yellow} instead of {0, 1, 2}.
Interface Types	Interfaces
Pointer Types	Pointers.
Reference Types	Any data types that are accessed through a reference and stored on the heap.
Self-describing Types	Data types that provide information about themselves for the benefit of the garbage collector.
Type	Base class that represents any type.
User-defined Value Types	Types that have been defined in source code and are stored as value types. In C# terms, this means any struct.
User-defined Reference Types	Types that have been defined in source code and are stored as reference types. In C# terms, this means any class.
Value Type	Base class that represents any value type.

Note that we won't list the built-in value types here, because they are covered in detail in Chapter 3. In C#, each predefined type recognized by the compiler maps onto one of the IL built-in types. The same is true in VB.

One point worth commenting on is the existence of the boxed value types. When we start learning C#, we will discover that there are a number of circumstances in which value types may need to be temporarily converted to reference types and stored on the heap (this includes when they are passed by reference to a method, and when they are specifically cast to object). This process is known as **boxing**, and it requires that for each value type there is a corresponding reference type that represents a boxed heap version of that type. In general, whenever a value type is defined in your C# code, .NET quietly also defines a corresponding boxed type – a reference type used to represent variables of that type when they need to be treated as reference types.

Common Language Specification (CLS)

The Common Language Specification works with the Common Type System to ensure language interoperability. The CLS is a set of minimum standards laid down, which all compilers targeting .NET must support. The *raison d'être* of the CLS is that IL is a very rich language, and so it is possible that writers of some compilers may prefer to restrict the capabilities of a given compiler to only support a subset of the facilities offered by IL and the CTS. That is fine, as long as the compiler supports everything that is defined in the CLS.

As an example, the CTS defines two 32-bit integer data types – Int32 (a signed integer) and UInt32 (an unsigned integer). C# recognizes these types as int and uint. VB.NET on the other hand recognizes only Int32, for which it uses the keyword Integer.

Another example is provided by case sensitivity. IL is case-sensitive, and that allows case-sensitive languages such as C# and C++ to define names for variables that differ only by case, for example: `EmployeeName` and `employeeName`. Developers who work with these languages regularly take advantage of the flexibility this case sensitivity gives them when selecting variable names. VB.NET however, is not case sensitive. The CLS works round this by indicating that CLS-compliant code should not expose any two names that differ only in their case. Therefore, VB.NET code can work with CLS-compliant code.

This last example shows that the CLS works in two ways. First, it means that individual compilers do not have to be powerful enough to support the full features of .NET – this should encourage the development of compilers for other programming languages that target .NET. Second, it provides a guarantee that, if you restrict your classes to only exposing CLS-compliant features, then it is guaranteed that code written in any other language can use your classes. For example, if you want your code to be CLS-compliant, you will not have any methods return `UInt32`, because that type is not part of the CLS. You can of course return a `UInt32` if you wish, but then your code isn't guaranteed to work across all languages.

> **It is perfectly acceptable to write non-CLS-compliant code. However, if you do, the compiled IL code isn't guaranteed to be fully language-independent.**

The beauty of this idea is that the restriction to using CLS-compliant features only applies to items that may be visible outside a given assembly, in other words, to public and protected members of classes and public classes. Within the private implementations of your classes, you can write whatever non-CLS code you wish – this is not a problem because code in other assemblies cannot access this part of your code anyway.

We won't go into the details of the CLS specifications here. In general, the CLS won't affect your C# code very much, because there are very few non-CLS compliant features of C# anyway. Some examples however, will give you a flavour of CLS:

CLS requirement	Effect on C# Code
No global methods or variables are permitted	No effect – C# doesn't allow these anyway.
Certain data types are not permitted	If you want your code to be CLS-compliant, don't have public or protected members of type `sbyte`, `ushort`, `uint`, or `ulong`.
Names must be distinguishable to case-insensitive languages	If you want your code to be CLS-compliant, don't have public or protected members whose names differ only by case.
Exceptions (see later in the chapter) must be derived from the Exception base class	No effect – C# requires this anyway.
Pointer types are not permitted	If you want your code to be CLS-compliant, don't use unsafe code and pointers, except in private methods.
Variable parameter lists are not permitted	No effect – C# does allow variable parameter lists, but maps these to fixed size arrays (which are CLS-compliant) in the emitted IL code.

The .NET Base Class Library

Perhaps one of the biggest benefits of writing managed code, at least from the point of view of making it easier to write the code in the first place, is that you get to use the .NET base class library.

The .NET base classes are a massive collection of managed code classes that have been written by Microsoft, and which allow you to do almost any of the tasks that were previously available through the Windows API. These classes follow the same object model as used by Intermediate Language, based on single inheritance. This means that you can either instantiate objects of whichever .NET base class is appropriate, or you can derive your own classes from them.

The great thing about the .NET base classes is that they have been designed to be very easy to use and to be virtually self-documenting. For example, to start a thread, you call the `Start()` method of the `Thread` class. To open a file you call the `Open()` method of the `File` class. To disable a `TextBox`, you set the `Enabled` property of a `TextBox` object to `false`. Get the idea? This kind of self-documenting class will be familiar to Visual Basic and Java developers, whose respective libraries are similarly just as easy to use.

This will probably come as a great relief to C++ developers, who for years have had to cope with such API functions as `GetDIBits()`, `RegisterWndClassEx()`, and `IsEqualIID()`, as well as a whole plethora of functions that required Windows handles to be passed around. On the other hand, C++ developers always had easy access to the entire Windows API, whereas Visual Basic and Java developers were more restricted in terms of the basic operating system functionality that they have access to from their respective languages. What is new about the .NET base classes is that they combine the ease of use that was typical of the Visual Basic and Java libraries with the comprehensive coverage of the Windows API functions.

Once we have completed our coverage of the C# language, most of the rest of this book, while formally devoted to applications of C#, in practice will be showing you how to use various classes within the .NET bass class library. That is how comprehensive base classes are. As a rough guide, the areas covered by the .NET base classes include:

- Core features provided by IL, including, for example, the primitive data types in the Common Type System.
- Windows GUI support, controls and so on.
- Web Forms (ASP.NET).
- Data Access (ADO.NET).
- Directory Access.
- File System and registry access.
- Networking and web browsing.
- .NET attributes and reflection.
- Access to aspects of the Windows operating system, environment variables and so on.
- Access to source code and compilers in the different languages.
- COM interoperability.
- Graphics (GDI+).

Incidentally, according to Microsoft sources, a large proportion of the .NET base classes have actually been written in C#!

The Components of the .NET Framework

In this section we will examine the main components that make up the .NET framework.

Assemblies

We are not going to cover assemblies in great detail in this chapter, because they are covered in detail in Chapter 10, but we will summarize the main points here.

An **assembly** is the logical unit that contains compiled code targeted at .NET. To this extent, it is analogous to an old-style DLL or executable file, or a file that hosts COM components. An assembly is completely self-describing, and is a logical rather than a physical unit, which means that it can be stored across more than one file. If an assembly is stored in more than one file, then there will be one main file that contains the entry point, and which describes the other files in the assembly.

Note that the same assembly structure is used for both executable code and library code. The only real difference is that an executable assembly contains a main program entry point, whereas a library assembly doesn't.

Metadata and Manifests

We have already indicated that an important characteristic of assemblies is that they contain metadata that describes the types and methods defined in the corresponding code. An assembly however, also contains assembly metadata that describes the assembly itself. This assembly metadata, contained in an area known as the **manifest**, allows checks to be made on the version of the assembly, and on its integrity.

The fact that an assembly contains program metadata means that applications or other assemblies that call up code in a given assembly, do not need to refer to the registry, or to any other data source, in order to find out how to use that assembly. This is a significant break from the old COM way of doing things, in which the GUIDs of the components and interfaces had to be obtained from the registry, and in some cases, the details of the methods and properties exposed would need to be read from a type library.

Having data spread out in up to three different locations meant there was the obvious risk of something getting out of synchronization, which would prevent other software from being able to use the component successfully. With assemblies, there is no risk of this happening, because all the metadata is stored with the program executable instructions. Note that even though assemblies are stored across several files, there are still no problems with data going out of synchronization. This is because the file that contains the assembly entry point also stores details of, and a hash of, the contents of the other files, which means that if one of the files gets replaced, or in any way tampered with, this will almost certainly be detected and the assembly will refuse to load.

Shared and Private Assemblies

Assemblies come in two types: **shared** and **private** assemblies.

Private Assemblies

Private assemblies are the simplest type. They normally ship with software, and are intended only to be used with that software. The usual scenario in which you will ship private assemblies is the case in which you are supplying an application in the form of an executable and a number of libraries, where the libraries contain code that is only intended to be used with that application.

The system guarantees that private assemblies will not be used by other software, because an application may only load private assemblies that are located in the same folder that the main executable is loaded in, or in a subfolder thereof.

Because you would normally expect that commercial software would always be installed in its own directory, this means that there is no risk of one software package overwriting, modifying, or accidentally loading private assemblies intended for another package. As private assemblies can only be used by the software package that they are intended for, this means that you have much more control over what software uses them. There is, therefore, less need to take security precautions, since there is no risk, for example, of some other commercial software overwriting one of your assemblies with some new version of it (apart from the case where software is designed specifically to perform malicious damage). There are also no problems with name collisions. If classes in your private assembly happen to have the same name as classes in someone else's private assembly that doesn't matter, because any given application will only be able to see the one set of private assemblies.

Because a private assembly is entirely self-contained, the process of installing it is simple. You simply place the appropriate file(s) in the appropriate folder in the file system. There are no registry entries, etc. to be made. This process is known as **Zero Impact Installation**.

Shared Assemblies

Shared assemblies are those assemblies that are intended to be common libraries that any other application should be able to use.

Because any other software can access a shared assembly, more precautions need to be taken against the following risks:

- ❑   Name collisions, involving another company's shared assembly, implementing types that have the same names as those in your shared assembly. Because client code can theoretically have access to both assemblies simultaneously, this could be a serious problem.

- ❑   The risk of an assembly being overwritten by a different version of the same assembly – the new version being incompatible with some existing client code.

The solution to these problems involves placing shared assemblies in a special directory subtree in the file system, that is known as the **assembly cache**. Unlike the case with private assemblies, this cannot be done by simply copying the assembly into the appropriate folder – it needs to be specifically installed into the cache, a process that can be performed by a number of .NET utilities, and which involves carrying out certain checks on the assembly, as well as setting up a small folder hierarchy within the assembly cache that is used to ensure assembly integrity.

In order to avoid the risk of name collisions, shared assemblies are given a name that is based on private key cryptography (private assemblies are simply given the same name as their main file name). This name is known as a **strong name**, is guaranteed to be unique, and must be quoted by applications that wish to reference a shared assembly.

Problems associated with the risk of overwriting an assembly are addressed by specifying version information in the assembly manifest, and by allowing side-by-side installs.

Namespaces

Namespaces are the way that .NET avoids name clashes between classes. They are designed, for example, to avoid the situation in which you define a class to represent a customer, and call your class `Customer`, and someone else does the same thing. (Quite a likely scenario – the proportion of businesses that have customers seems to be quite high). A namespace is no more than a grouping of data types, but it has the effect that the names of all data types within a namespace automatically get prefixed with the name of the namespace. It is also possible to nest namespaces within each other. For example, most of the general-purpose .NET base classes are in a namespace called `System`. The base class, `Array`, is in this namespace, so its full name is `System.Array`.

.NET requires all types to be defined in a namespace, so for example you could place your `Customer` class in a namespace called `YourCompanyName`. This class would have the full name `YourCompanyName.Customer`.

> *If a namespace is not explicitly supplied, then the type will be added to a nameless global namespace.*

Microsoft recommend that for most purposes you supply at least two nested namespace names, the first one being the name of your company, the second being the name of the technology or software package that the class is a member of, such as `YourCompanyName.SalesServices.Customer`. Doing this will, in most situations, protect your class from possible name clashes with classes written by other organizations.

In most source languages, namespaces can be declared very simply in the source code. For example, in C# the syntax is:

```
namespace YourCompanyName.SalesServices
{
    class Customer

    // etc.

}
```

Application Domains

Application domains are an important innovation in .NET that are designed to ease the overhead involved with running applications that need to be isolated from each other, but also need to be able to communicate with each other. The classic example of this is a web server application, which may be simultaneously responding to a number of browser requests. It will, therefore, probably have a number of instances of the component responsible for servicing those requests running simultaneously.

In pre-.NET days, the choice would be between allowing those instances to share a process, with the resultant risk of a problem in one running instance bringing the whole web site down, and isolating those instances in separate processes, with the associated performance overhead.

Up until now, the only means of isolating code has been through processes. When you start a new application running, it runs within the context of a process. Windows isolates processes from each other through address spaces. The idea is that each process has available 4 gigabytes of virtual memory in which to store its data and executable code (the figure of 4GB is for 32-bit systems. 64-bit systems will have more). This memory is accessed by each application by quoting addresses, which are in the range of 0 to 4GB. This memory, however, is only virtual memory: Windows imposes an extra level of indirection by which this virtual memory maps into a particular area of actual physical memory or disk space. Each process will get a different mapping, with no overlap between the actual physical memories that the blocks of virtual address space map to. The situation is shown in the diagram:

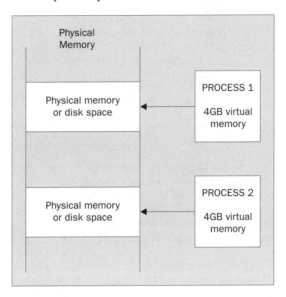

In general, any process is only able to access memory by specifying an address in virtual memory – processes do not have direct access to physical memory. Hence it is simply impossible for one process to access the memory allocated to another process. This provides an excellent guarantee that any badly behaved code will not be able to damage anything outside its own address space. (Note that on Windows 9x, these safeguards are not quite as thorough as they are on NT/2000, so the theoretical possibility exists of applications crashing Windows by writing to inappropriate memory).

Processes don't just serve as a means by which instances of running code can be isolated from each other. On Windows NT/2000 systems, they also form the unit to which a security privileges and permissions are assigned. Each process has its own security token, which indicates to Windows precisely what operations that process is permitted to do.

While processes are great for security in both senses (not overwriting other processes' memory and providing a boundary for security permissions), their big disadvantage is performance. Very often a number of processes will actually be working together, and therefore need to communicate with each other. The obvious example of this is where a process calls up a COM component, which is an executable, and therefore is required to run in its own process. The same thing happens in COM when surrogates are used. Since processes cannot share any memory, a complex marshalling process has to be used to copy data between the processes. This gives a very significant hit for performance. If you need components to work together and don't want that performance hit, then the only way up till now has been to use DLL-based components and have everything running in the same address space – with the associated risk that a badly behaved component will bring everything else down.

Application domains are designed as a way of separating components without resulting in the performance problems associated with passing data between processes. The idea is that any one process is divided into a number of application domains Each application domain roughly corresponds to a single application, and each thread of execution will be running in a particular application domain:

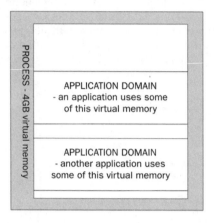

If different executables are running in the same process space, then they are clearly able to easily share data, because theoretically they can directly see each other's data. Although this is possible in principle, however the .NET runtime makes sure that this does not happen in practice by the technique of inspecting the code for each running application, to ensure that the code cannot stray outside its own data areas. This sounds at first sight like an almost impossible trick to pull off – after all how can you tell what the program is going to do without actually running it?

In fact, it is usually possible to do this because of the strong type safety of the Intermediate Language. In most cases, unless code is explicitly using unsafe features such as pointers, the data types it is using will ensure that memory is not accessed inappropriately. For example, .NET array types perform bounds checking to ensure that no out of bounds array operations are permitted. If a running application specifically does need to communicate or share data with other applications running in different application domains, then it must do so by calling on .NET's remoting services, which it can do through various .NET base classes under the System.Remoting namespace.

Code that has been verified to check that it cannot access data outside its application domain (other than through the explicit remoting mechanism) is said to be type safe (or memory type safe). Such code can safely be run alongside other type safe code in different application domains within the same process.

JIT Compilers

The JIT compiler (just-in-time compiler) is a crucial part of the .NET framework, and a vital part of Microsoft's effort to ensure that managed code actually gives a higher performance than unmanaged code.

The idea of performance actually going up as a result of compiling to intermediate language, may come as a surprise to some developers. After all, one of the disadvantages of Java was that the process of translating from Java byte code to native executable when an application was run, meant a loss of performance. There is, however, a big difference here in that Java byte code was interpreted whereas IL is compiled. Not only that, but, instead of compiling the entire application in one go (which could lead to a slow start-up time), the JIT compiler simply compiles each portion of code as it is called (just-in-time). When code has been compiled once, the resultant native executable is stored until the application exits, so that it does not need to be recompiled the next time that portion of code is run. Microsoft argue that this process is more efficient than compiling the entire assembly at the start, because of the likelihood that large portions of any assembly will not actually be executed in any given run. Using the JIT compiler, such code will never get compiled.

This explains why we can expect that execution of managed IL code will be almost as fast as executing native machine code. What it doesn't explain is why Microsoft expects that we will get a performance improvement. The reason for this is that, since the final stage of compilation takes place at runtime, the JIT compiler will know exactly what processor type the program will run on. This means that it can optimize the final executable code to take advantage of any features or particular machine code instructions offered by that particular processor.

Traditional compilers will optimize the code, but they can only perform optimizations that will be independent of the particular processor that the code will run on. This is because traditional compilers compile to native executable before the software is shipped. This means that the compiler doesn't know what type of processor the code will run on beyond basic generalities, such as that it will be an x86-compatible processor or an Alpha processor. Visual Studio 6, for example, optimizes for a generic Pentium machine, so the code that it generates cannot take advantages of hardware features of Pentium III processors. On the other hand, the JIT compiler can do all the optimizations that Visual Studio 6 can, and in addition to that it will optimize for the particular processor the code is running on.

.NET Tools

Besides the runtime services, .NET makes available a number of tools to assist in developing .NET applications. These include:

❑   Visual Studio.NET, the integrated developer environment with which you can write, compile, and debug code in all the .NET languages, C#, VB.NET, managed C++, as well as ASP.NET pages and unmanaged C++ code. Visual Studio.NET is the subject of Chapter 8.

❑   Command line compilers for C#, VB.NET and C++.

❑   ILDASM, a windows-based utility that can be used to inspect the contents of an assembly, including the manifest and metadata. We examine ILDASM in Chapter 10.

The Garbage Collector

The **garbage collector** is .NET's answer to memory management, and in particular to the question of what to do about reclaiming memory that running applications ask for. Up until now there have been two techniques used on Windows platform for deallocating memory that processes have dynamically requested from the system: having the application code do it all manually, and having objects maintain reference counts. In addition, Java uses a system of garbage collection similar to that used by .NET

Having the application code responsible for de-allocating memory is the technique used by lower-level, high-performance languages such as C++. It is efficient, and it has the advantage that (in general) resources are never occupied for longer than unnecessary. The big disadvantage however, is the frequency of bugs. Code that requests memory also has to explicitly inform the system when it no longer requires that memory. C++ has the `delete` keyword available for this purpose, and there are various Windows API functions that do the same thing. Programmers have to be very careful, however, to ensure that they delete all memory that they have requested. It is easy to forget to do so, resulting in memory leaks.

Although modern developer environments do provide tools to assist in detecting memory leaks, they remain difficult bugs to track down, because they have no effect until so much memory has been leaked, that Windows simply refuses to grant any more to the process. By this point, the entire computer may have appreciably slowed down due to the memory demands being made on it.

Maintaining reference counting is favored by COM objects. The idea is that each COM component maintains a count of how many clients are currently maintaining references to it. When this count falls to zero, the component can destroy itself and free up associated memory and resources. The problem with this is that it still relies on the good behavior of clients to notify the component that they have finished with it (which they do by calling the IUnknown.Release() method). It only takes one client to not do so, and the object sits in memory. In some ways, this is a potentially more serious problem than a simple C++-style memory leak, because the COM object may exist in its own process, which means that it will never be removed by the system (at least with C++ memory leaks, the system can reclaim all memory when the process terminates).

Now we have seen the alternatives, let's examine .NET's solution.

Then .NET runtime relies on the garbage collector, which is a program whose purpose is to clean up memory. The idea is that all dynamically requested memory is allocated on the heap (that is true for all languages). Every so often, when .NET detects that the heap for a given process is becoming full and therefore needs tidying up, it calls the garbage collector. The garbage collector runs through variables currently in scope in your code, examining references to objects stored on the heap to identify which ones are accessible from your code – that is to say which objects have references that refer them. Any objects that are not referred to by any, are deemed to be no longer accessible from your code and can therefore be removed.

To see how this works in practice, consider this C# code fragment:

```
{
    TextBox UserInputArea;
    UserInputArea = new TextBox();
    TextBox txtBoxCopy = UserInputArea;

    // assume garbage collector called here
    // more processing

}

// UserInputArea and txtBoxCopy are now out of scope
// assume garbage collector called again here
```

We haven't yet learnt the C# syntax involved with this code, but we can still understand roughly what is happening. The code starts by declaring a variable of type TextBox. This variable is called UserInputArea. As it happens, TextBox is a reference type. That means that UserInputArea simply contains an address, and we need to separately instantiate a TextBox objects on the heap, which is done in the new statement. We then set a new variable, txtBoxCopy, to UserInputArea, which means that txtBoxCopy will also refer to the TextBox.

At this point, let us suppose it just happens that the garbage collector gets called. Because it follows through the references in your code, the garbage collector will see that the TextBox is referred to by both variables. It can see that this TextBox instance is still in use and must remain on the heap. The garbage collector doesn't only delete objects – it may also tidy up the heap in order to optimize performance. It's possible, therefore, that it may move the location where the data for the TextBox instance is stored. If it does so, then it will quietly update the addresses held by UserInputArea and txtBoxCopy to reflect the change.

Later on, the variables UserInputArea and txtBoxCopy both go out of scope. We will assume here that no other variables have been set to refer to this TextBox. And we will assume that, at this time, the garbage collector gets called again. Now it will find that an area of the heap is being used to store the TextBox, but it will also find that there are no references amongst all the variables in use by your code that refer to it. The garbage collector will conclude that the TextBox is no longer required and delete it.

Notice that this mechanism is perfectly safe; if there are no references to the TextBox, then there is simply no legitimate way that your code can ever get access to that TextBox again. Intermediate Language simply does not provide any typesafe means of getting a reference to an object on the heap, other than by creating it or by copying an existing reference. If there are no references to copy, then it can't legitimately get a reference to an existing object.

> *I say "legitimately" above because theoretically you could write some unsafe code in either C++ or C# that used pointers and some fairly cunning pointer arithmetic and casting to retrieve a reference to the TextBox again. Other than for the sake of proving an academic point however, it's hard to see why anyone would want to do that – it certainly wouldn't be in the spirit of .NET methodologies. You could also get the reference much more easily by writing your code so it never loses it in the first place!*

Garbage collection works because Intermediate Language has been designed to facilitate the process. The principle requires, firstly, that you cannot get references to existing objects other than by copying existing references, and secondly, that Intermediate Language is type safe. In this context, what we mean is that if any reference to an object exists, then there is sufficient information in the reference to exactly determine the type of the object.

It would not be possible to use the garbage collection mechanism with a language such as unmanaged C++, for example, because C++ allows pointers to be freely cast between types. That means that no program that scoured your code looking at the values of pointers would be able to obtain enough information to determine what areas of the heap are actually in use. As remarked previously, IL also allows pointers inside unsafe code, and it also allows casts between pointers. With IL however, there are heavy restrictions on the way that you can use these pointers that are designed to ensure that any use of pointers in your code doesn't conflict with the requirements of the garbage collector. In particular, pointers are not permitted to be set up to point to reference objects.

One aspect of garbage collection that it is important to be aware of is that it is not deterministic. In other words, you cannot guarantee when the garbage collector will be called; it will be called when the .NET runtime decides that it is needed. Obviously, the more demanding your code is on memory, the more often the garbage collector will be called, but that is as much as it is possible to predict. It is possible to explicitly call up the garbage collector from your code using .NET base class System.GC – you might do this for example at a point at which your code has just finished using a large number of variables. In most situations, however, you will simply trust the .NET runtime to call up the garbage collector as appropriate.

Exceptions

.NET is designed to facilitate handling of error conditions using the same mechanism, based on exceptions, that is employed by Java and C++. C++ developers should note that, however, because of IL's stronger typing system, there is no performance penalty associated with the use of exceptions with IL in the way that there is in C++.

We will cover exceptions in detail in Chapter 6. Briefly, the idea is that certain areas of code are designated as exception handler routines, with each one able to deal with a particular error condition (for example, a file not being found, or being denied permission to perform some operation). These conditions can be defined as narrowly or as widely as you wish. For example, you might write a handler that deals with the situation in which some method in a library that you have written has been passed inappropriate parameters by the client code. You might also write another handler that deals more specifically with the situation in which one particular parameter contains an inappropriate value (for example, passing a temperature below absolute zero to a temperature conversion method). The exception architecture ensures that when an error condition occurs, execution can immediately jump to the exception handler routine that is most specifically geared to handle the error condition in question.

The architecture of exception handling also provides a convenient means by which an object that contains precise details of the error condition can be passed to the error handling routine. Information that this object might contain includes an appropriate message for the user and details of exactly where in the code the error was detected.

Most exception handling architecture, including the control of program flow when an exception occurs, is handled by the high level languages (C#, VB.NET, C++), and is not supported by any special Intermediate Language commands. C#, for example, handles this using `try{}`, `catch{}`, and `finally{}` blocks of code, as we'll see later in Chapter 6. What .NET does do however is provide the infrastructure to allow compilers that target .NET to support exception handling. In particular, it provides a set of .NET base classes that can represent the exceptions, and the language interoperability to allow the thrown exception objects to be interpreted by the error handling code, irrespective of what language the error handling code is written in. This language independence is absent from both the C++ and Java implementations of exception handling, although it is present to a limited extent in the COM mechanism for handling errors, which involves returning error codes from methods and passing error objects around. The fact that errors are handled consistently in different languages is a crucial aspect of facilitating multi-language development.

Security

Security is another area that we will mention only briefly here, because it is fully covered later in the book, in Chapter 25.

.NET brings benefits in the area of code security because it is able to do its own checking of what a given application should be allowed to do. However, where .NET security can really excel in terms of complementing the security mechanisms provided by Windows is that it can offer **code-based security**, whereas Windows only really offers **role-based security**.

Role-based security is based on the identity of the account under which the process is running. In other words, who owns and is running the process. Code-based security on the other hand is based on what the code actually does and on how much the code is trusted. Thanks to the strong type safety of Intermediate Language, the .NET runtime is able to inspect code before running it in order to determine required security permissions. .NET also offers a mechanism by which code can indicate in advance what security permissions it will require to run.

The importance of code-based security is that it reduces the risks associated with running code for which you are dubious about its origin (such as code that you've downloaded from the Internet). For example, even if code is running under the administrator account, it is possible use code-based security to indicate that that code should still not be permitted to perform certain types of operation that the administrator account would normally be allowed to do, such as read or write to environment variables, read or write to the event log, read or write to the registry, or to access the .NET reflection features.

Attributes

Attributes are a feature that have become common in Microsoft extensions to C++ in recent years, although they will not be familiar to Visual Basic or Java developers. The idea of an attribute was that it initially provided extra information concerning some item in the program, and that could be used by the compiler when compiling. Examples of using attributes in C# include indicating the threading model that the starting thread should run in:

```
[STAThread]
void Main()
{
```

Alternatively, an attribute can be used to mark the method as obsolete:

```
[Obsolete]
public int SomeObsoleteMethod()
{
```

An obsolete method will generate the compiler warning, or in some cases an error, if called by other code.

What is new about attributes in .NET, is that a mechanism exists whereby you can define your own attributes in source code. These user-defined attributes will be placed with the metadata for the corresponding data types or methods. This can be useful for documentation purposes, where they can be used in conjunction with reflection technology (described next) in order to perform programming tasks based on attributes. Also, in common with the .NET philosophy of language independence, attributes can be defined in source code in one language, and read by code that is written in another language.

Attributes are covered in Chapters 6 and 7 of this book.

Reflection

We indicated earlier that assemblies store metadata, including details of all the types and members of these types that are defined in the assembly. It is possible to access this metadata programmatically using .NET base classes in the `System.Reflection` namespace. Full details of this can be found in Chapter 7. Reflection raises interesting possibilities, since it means that managed code can actually examine other managed code, or can even examine itself, to determine information about that code. This will most commonly be used to obtain the details of attributes, although you can also use reflection, amongst other purposes, as an indirect way of instantiating classes or calling methods, given the names of those classes on methods as strings. In this way you can select classes to instantiate methods to call at runtime, rather than compile time, for example, based on user input.

Languages and Technologies

In this section we will look at how the main languages and some other existing technologies fit into the .NET framework.

C#

C# is a new object-oriented programming language, and is specifically targeted at the .NET runtime. The C# compiler will **only** produce managed code, and it is also aware of some of the .NET base classes.

C# is significant in two respects: first, it has been deliberately designed to be highly compatible with the .NET runtime. Second, it is a modern object-oriented language, and when designing it Microsoft have been able to learn from the experience of all the other similar languages that have been around over the 20 years or so since object-oriented principles came to prominence.

One important thing to make clear is that C# is a language in its own right. Although it is designed to generate code that targets the .NET, environment, it is not itself part of .NET. There are some features that are supported by .NET but not by C#, and you might be surprised to learn that there are actually features of the C# language that are not supported by .NET! We've already hinted that some of C#'s exception handling statements fall into this category. Obviously, if you use any of those C# features in your code, the compiler will translate them into things that are supported by .NET. One other example of this is provided by operator overloading. C# allows you to overload many of the operators such as plus, minus, and so on, so that, as demonstrated in one of the examples that we develop through Chapters 5-7, we could define a Vector class, then define versions of the addition operator, +, for it, enabling us to write:

```
Vector V1, V2, V3;

// initialize V2 and V3

V1 = V2 + V3;
```

Despite this being perfectly valid C# code, operator overloading is not defined in Intermediate Language. What happens is that if you overload an operator in your C# source code, then the C# compiler will internally generate some method in the compiled IL code that does the same thing as your operator overload, and will substitute this method whenever the corresponding operator overload is used in your code.

C++

C++ already has a large number of Microsoft specific extensions on Windows. More extensions will be added to support the .NET framework. This means that existing C++ source code will continue to compile to native executable without modification. This means however that it will run independently of the .NET runtime. If you want your C++ code to run within the .NET framework, then you can simply add the following line to the beginning of your code:

```
#using <mscorlib.dll>
```

You will also pass the flag /clr to the compiler, which will then assume you wish to compile to managed code, and will hence emit Intermediate Language instead of native machine code. This does mean that the compiler will raise an error if you attempt to use features that are not supported by .NET, for example, templates or multiple inheritance of classes. You will also find that you will need to use certain attributes and other new nonstandard C++ features in order to mark your classes.

Because of the freedom that C++ allows in terms of low-level pointer manipulation and so on, the C++ compiler is not able to generate code that will pass the CLR's memory type safety tests. If it's important that your code is recognized by the CLR as memory type safe, then you'll need to write your source code in some other language (such as C# or VB.NET).

J++

J++ will continue to be supported for backwards compatibility purposes only. It is not being upgraded for .NET, and it is not recommended that you write any new software in J++. As far as legacy J++ code is concerned, Microsoft are supplying a number of tools that go by the name **JUMP** (**Java User Migration Path**), and the slogan "JUMP to .NET". These tools will allow Visual Studio.NET to work with existing J++ code. If you prefer, a migration tool is available that will automatically convert J++ code into C# code. The similarities in syntax between J++ and C# are so great that this doesn't actually involve making many major changes to code structure – it's mostly a case of replacing J++ keywords with the corresponding C# keywords.

VB

Visual Basic is undergoing a complete revamp to bring it up to date with .NET. The way that Visual Basic has evolved over the last few years means that in its previous version, Visual Basic 6, it is not a suitable language for running .NET programs. For example, it is heavily integrated into COM, and works by exposing only event handlers as source code to the developer – most of the background code is not available as source code. Not only that, it does not support implementation inheritance, and the standard data types Visual Basic uses are not compatible with .NET.

Visual Basic is being upgraded to Visual Basic.NET, but in the light of the previous comments, you won't be surprised to learn that the changes being made to VB are extensive. Although we might talk about an upgrade, for all practical purposes you may as well regard Visual Basic.NET as a new language. Existing VB6 code will not compile as VB.NET code. Converting a VB6 program to VB.NET requires extensive changes to the code. However, most of the changes can be done automatically for you by Visual Studio.NET. If you attempt to read a VB6 project into Visual Studio.NET, Visual Studio.NET will upgrade the project for you, which means that it will rewrite the VB6 source code into VB.NET source code. Although this means that at the work involved for you is heavily cut down, you will need to check through the new VB.NET code to make sure that the project still works correctly.

One side effect of this is that it is no longer possible to compile VB.NET to native executable. VB.NET compiles only to Intermediate Language, just as C# does. If you need to continue coding in VB6, you may do so, but the executable code produced will completely ignore the .NET framework, and you'll need to keep Visual Studio 6 installed if you rely on Visual Studio as your developer environment.

ASP

ASP pages are regarded as obsolete within .NET. Instead, .NET upgrades IIS to support ASP.NET pages, in which code can be written directly in VB.NET, C#, or JScript.NET, and is compiled into classes that can respond to web requests by generating the appropriate HTML output. The performance gains associated with running compiled code in response to browser requests are obvious. In addition, Microsoft have written a number of classes that can simulate sophisticated "controls" in browsers by writing HTML output. The syntax for ASP.NET pages has also been redesigned to allow pages to be structured better, with greater separation of user interface logic and business logic.

ASP pages will continue to work alongside .NET, but in view of the improvements offered by ASP.NET, there is really no reason to use them other than as legacy pages.

Scripting Languages

Scripting languages are still around, although, in general, their importance is likely to decline. JScript, on the other hand, has been upgraded to JScript.NET. ASP.NET pages may be written in JScript.NET, and it is now possible to run JScript.NET as a compiled rather than an interpreted language, and it is also possible
to write strongly typed JScript.NET code. With ASP.NET there is no reason to use scripting languages in server-side web pages. VBA is, however, still used as a language for Microsoft Office and Visual Studio macros.

ADO/OLE DB

While it is possible to use ADO or OLE DB from managed code through the COM interoperability features, for communicating with data sources you will probably find it easier to use ADO.NET, a subset of the .NET base classes which is devoted to this purpose, and which is discussed in Chapter 11.

ADSI

The .NET base class, `System.DirectoryServices`, is intended to replace ADSI, and performs much the same features, although you can still use the old ADSI interfaces if you prefer.

COM and COM+

COM+ remains an important tool, since its features are not entirely duplicated in .NET. Also, COM components will still work – and .NET incorporates COM interoperability features that make it possible for managed code to call up COM components and vice versa (this is discussed in Chapter 19). In general, however, you will probably find it more convenient for most purposes to code new components as .NET components, so that you can take advantage of the .NET base classes as well as the other benefits of running as managed code.

Putting It All Together

We have now just about completed our tour of the .NET framework. Before we finish, we are going to have a look at a couple of examples of how the various features, in particular Intermediate Language, the CTS, the .NET base classes, and the C# language give you code that has good performance, combined with extremely good syntactical convenience for a couple of data types:

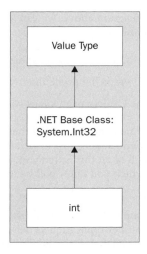

We will start off by examining what happens when you declare an int in C# code:

```
int X = 27;
```

As far as the developer is concerned, C# defines an int as a 32-bit signed integer data type which can contain values between -2,147,483,648 and 2,147,483,647 inclusive. In previous programming languages such as C++ and Visual Basic, the compiler would take such a type and map it directly to a corresponding type in native machine code. As we saw earlier, however the C# compiler will instead map int to one of the .NET base classes, System.Int32. According to the C# language specification, the keyword int is no more than a convenient predefined type name that represents this class. The fact that int is actually a class means that you get all the syntactical benefits of a class. Most notably, you can call methods on it. For example, you can write code like this:

```
string Text = X.ToString();
int Y = int.Parse("50");
int MaxValue = int.MaxValue;     // returns 2,147,483,647
```

The fact that int takes methods makes coding a lot easier. As illustrated above, it is easy to convert integers to or from strings, and to obtain their maximum and minimum values. As far as we are concerned, when writing code, the benefits of object-oriented programming have been extended to every data type, including types that were previously considered to be raw data types rather than objects. The amazing thing , is that this wrapping into objects has been achieved without any of the performance loss that you would usually associate with objects.

In the past, the reason that predefined data types were not wrapped up into objects was that with a struct or class, there is a level of indirection associated with retrieving members of it. This causes a performance loss, which is very slight, but nevertheless unacceptable when you're dealing with primitive data types that are used as often as for example ints and floats. In the case of .NET, however all this overhead simply doesn't happen. The reason is that Microsoft will have compiled and written the base classes so that, internally, System.Int32 maps to an Intermediate Language predefined type rather than to a user-defined value type. When we come to run the code, what gets instantiated when you write something like int X = 27; is a simple integer.

Looking down the hierarchy in the diagram above, we can identify the wrapper that gets put round the basic machine code data type as follows:

❑ Intermediate Language wraps the type as a recognized .NET predefined value type.

❑ The .NET base class library wraps the predefined value type as a fully qualified `struct`.

❑ C# wraps this struct with the C# language keyword, `int`.

Apart from the final step of just-in-time compiling, all of these wrappings get unraveled at compile time rather than runtime, so there is no performance loss associated with working through the wrappers when the code is executed. The result of all this is that you get the syntactical convenience of a keyword that you can call methods on, and which you know will be treated at runtime like a predefined type, not like a `struct`.

Of course, we have given these examples for `int`, but the same principles apply for all the other predefined data types, as well as for other types such as delegates, interfaces, and enumerations. An enumeration is a set of values that have labels attached. For example, if you want to represent types of user in your code, you might write:

```
enum UserType {Administrator, Customer, Staff}
```

Internally, these will be translated into the values 0, 1 and 2, and represented as such. The effect is that you get to write, for example, `UserType.Customer` instead of the value 1 in your code, making your code more self-documenting. Enumerations have been used in this way in a number of languages.

However, the syntactical convenience doesn't end there in C#. Like other predefined data types, C# considers enumerations to be fully qualified `structs` in their own right. This means that you can call methods against enumerations. One of the most useful aspects of this is that it is extremely easy to convert between enumerated values (any enumerated value that is, not just bitfield ones) and the corresponding strings:

```
UserType TheUser = UserType.Customer;
string User = TheUser.ToString();   // returns "Customer";
UserType AnotherUser = UserType.Parse("Staff");   // returns UserType.Staff;
```

This kind of thing is almost impossible to do in other programming languages, and is extremely useful if, for example, if you want to set up values of an enumeration by reading in text from a file.

In the past this kind of high-level syntax would only have been able to come at a cost of performance, in particular, the performance costs associated with turning an enumerated value into a class and having to access it as a member of a class. You may have guessed from the discussion up to now that .NET achieves this at no performance loss. For the particular case of bit field enumerations, it works like this.

First, C# takes the `enum` statement and internally defines a `struct` to represent it. This will be a `struct` that is derived from the .NET base class, `System.Enum`. The syntactical convenience the `enum` keyword is something that has been added by the C# language. Once C# has converted the definition into a `struct`, however the process works in the same way as for `int`. the `struct` the compiler has defined for us is in turn mapped on to the Intermediate Language enumerated type. As a result, what actually gets created at runtime is just a simple integer type. The result is the syntactical convenience of a `struct`, but no overhead.

A Historical Note

Throughout this chapter we've referred to the object-oriented methodology of .NET and IL as classic object-oriented programming. There have, in fact, been a number of approaches that claim to be OOP. The reason we've referred to the .NET (and C#) model as classic OOP is that in many ways it represents a return to the original OOP concepts of the early 1980s.

Object-oriented programming was initially based around defining classes in your code and deriving other classes from them. The idea of this was to facilitate easy code reuse by breaking up your program into more manageable segments. In this methodology, implementation inheritance was extremely important, both as a way of taking the code you needed from existing classes while being able to replace the code you didn't want, and as a way of modeling the kind of hierarchy of specializations of objects that tends to happen in real life. In practice, classic OOP didn't work as was expected, and even in C++, the most common method of code reuse arguably remained copying and pasting source code with an editor! The problem was partly due to the lack of language independence, and partly to do with the C++ model requiring a fairly messy inclusion of header files, which basically meant that inheritance was impossible unless you had access to at least part of the source code of the base classes.

One major deterrent to many developers adopting OOP principles was that the main language on Windows that was based around classic OOP methodology was C++. C++ is quite a low level language, and so features a number of fairly complex language constructs (including pointers and templates) that are not really necessary for object-oriented programming, but which served to put many developers off from learning the language because of the complexity involved.

In the early 1990s Microsoft responded to this by introducing COM, and with it the concepts of (a) separating the object from the interface, and (b) language independence via a binary standard. In terms of providing code reuse, COM was extremely successful, particularly when it came to user-interface ActiveX controls which could be used from any language. COM also meant that, in many cases, development effort shifted from writing programs to writing components. It became apparent, however, that COM was very difficult to learn. Mastering the details of interfaces and GUIDs involved a huge learning curve, requiring skills that were often only accessible to C++ programmers. VB got around this problem by presenting a user interface for coding that hid many of the details of COM, but at the expense of restricting the kinds of component that could be coded up in VB. More seriously, COM always suffered from the problem that it did not allow implementation inheritance, requiring the new objects to be defined instead.

With C# and .NET, object-oriented programming has in some ways returned to the concepts of C++ object-oriented programming. Once again, we have classes being defined in source code, without any need to invoke interfaces, and once again the standard way to reuse code is through implementation inheritance. The difference now is that Microsoft appears to have solved the main problems that hindered universal acceptance of object-oriented programming using C++. C# is much easier to learn than C++, since the language focuses more exclusively on the necessary OOP features. The language interoperability is there, and to a much greater extent than even COM allowed. The header files of C++ have been banished, replaced by self-describing assemblies. On the evidence so far, it looks like .NET will succeed in allowing code reuse through simple object-oriented programming methodologies to a greater extent than before.

Summary

In this chapter we have surveyed the relationship between C# and the .NET environment, focusing in particular on the various components of .NET, and on how .NET, in particular the Intermediate Language, works to give us cross-language compatibility.

We have also seen that how the self-describing assemblies of .NET assist with ensuring code is robust, and prevents versioning problems. We have also seen how .NET frees the developer from having to worry about freeing up memory, and provides a host of other useful services, including enhanced code-based security, application domains, the .NET base classes, and reflection.

Now we have this background, we will move on in the next few chapters to see how to actually write code in C#.

2

Introduction to C#

This chapter introduces the reader to C#, the premier language for .NET development. First, we'll trace C#'s evolutionary history. Then we'll compare C# to other popular programming languages in use today. Next, we'll examine the different kinds of projects that you can use C# to create. Finally, after an overview of some of C#'s most significant features, we'll conclude by briefly showing how to use the C# compiler.

The Development of C#

To understand the true significance of C#, you need to understand its historical context. In this section, we'll review the evolution of different kinds of programming languages, showing how C# is related to each one.

The Advent of Assembler

As you probably know, a **bit** (**binary digit**) is the smallest unit of information that can be represented inside a computer. Indeed, you can conceive of computer memory as a long, continuous line of bits with values of 1 or 0.

By feeding sequences of these bits to a digital computer's processor, you can instruct that processor to perform basic arithmetic and logical operations such as addition, subtraction, multiplication, and comparisons. By chaining millions of these simple instructions together, you can make a computer behave in complex and useful ways.

Initially, programming a digital computer's bits meant physically connecting and disconnecting wires inside the processor so that it would behave differently. With the advent of the von Neumann design, instructions could be stored in computer memory for later execution. Each processor instruction would be stored as a different set of 1s and 0s. 11110000, for example, might be the instruction for adding two different values together, while 11110001 might signal the processor to perform subtraction.

As you might imagine, storing such sequences of 1s and 0s in memory for later execution was a tedious, error-prone, and time consuming process. The introduction of assembly language expedited this process by allowing programmers to refer to processor operations by easier-to-remember mnemonics. For example, in assembly language, 11110000 could be replaced by the symbol ADD, or 11110001 could be symbolized by the assembly instruction SUB.

An assembly language programmer could write his program using these easy-to-remember mnemonics, and then run his program through an assembler program, which would translate the mnemonic instructions into their 1 and 0 equivalents (**op codes**).

As you've already read, .NET programs consist not of low-level machine code instructions ready for immediate execution by a microprocessor, but as sequences of intermediate language instructions that must be interpreted by a runtime program. These instructions are more abstract than assembly language instructions in that they do not directly correspond to op codes recognized by a microprocessor. There is, however, a close correspondence between these intermediate language instructions and the machine language commands into which they are translated. This partly accounts for the relative speed with which intermediate language programs perform.

Consequently, the "Intermediate Language Disassembler" program that comes with the .NET SDK, ILDASM.EXE, can translate a sequence of intermediate language commands into a series of commands that resemble assembly language mnemonics. In fact, when viewed in mnemonic form, an intermediate language program looks like an assembly language program with extra commands for dealing with objects thrown in.

.NET is not the only platform to employ an intermediate language format. Java does, too, and refers to its compiled format as Java **bytecode**. In the Microsoft world, the intermediate language format is variously known as **IL** (**Intermediate Language**), **MSIL** (**Microsoft Intermediate Language**), and occasionally **CIL** (**Common Intermediate Language**).

The First Compilers

Although writing assembly language was certainly easier than coding 1s and 0s, it still forced programmers to think of their programs in terms of individual instructions. It was still very difficult for a programmer to think of his or her code in higher degrees of abstraction.

Simple conventions that today's programmers take for granted, such as a loop, might require coding a dozen or more assembly language instructions. With assembly language, programmers wasted a lot of time writing the same patterns of mnemonics over and over again. Making a computer do something useful with assembly language required a lot of blood, sweat, and tears.

The time was right for the advent of "higher-level" languages. FORTRAN was the first. With FORTRAN, a programmer could write his or her code with fewer, more abstract instructions, and then submit these instructions to a **compiler program**, which would translate each high-level instruction into several dozen, hundred, or thousand machine language instructions.

Therefore, programmers could focus on *what* their programs did, rather than on the specific, mind-numbing details of the machine code instructions that accomplished them. Additionally, because higher-level languages, such as FORTRAN, were a step removed from the actual machine's hardware, programs written in a high-level language could be ported to any machine for which a suitable compiler had been derived.

To translate an abstract program written in high-level source code language to an executable one in machine language format, a compiler program made several passes at the source code file. The output of each pass was a representation of the program in a form more susceptible to further translation.

The output of the first pass, for example, might be a **parse tree** in memory, in which the hierarchical relationship between operators and operands was broken down. In the second pass, the program might walk each node of the parse tree, using something called **syntax directed translation** to crank out a version of the program in an intermediate language closely resembling assembler. In the third pass, the program could use the intermediate language to produce assembly language that could then be easily assembled into machine code.

Because compiler construction is a difficult and time-consuming discipline, compilers were often constructed with detachable back-ends and front-ends. The job of the front-end was to translate the source code into intermediate language; the job of the back-end was to translate intermediate language into machine code.

Because intermediate language served as a buffer between the compiler front-end and back-end, you could use the same back-end with different front-ends. In other words, you could develop different front-ends for translating FORTRAN or COBOL into intermediate language, and then re-use the same back-end to translate the intermediate language into executable code.

As you can see, .NET's approach to compilation and execution simply modifies the traditional approach developed long ago. In the past, source code programs were completely compiled to machine language instructions, and delivered to users in that format. With .NET, the IL code is what is delivered, and the final step of compilation occurs on the target machine at runtime in tandem with the program's execution. With this approach, software developers can leverage IL to great benefit because the programs that they distribute can theoretically be executed on any hardware platform equipped with a suitable .NET runtime. Because there are virtual machines for interpreting Java bytecode on multiple platforms, Java programs are already said to be portable, but we'll have to wait and see if ports of the .NET runtime will make .NET programs portable, too.

The development of compilers for high-level languages such as FORTRAN was a major breakthrough that required years of person-hours to accomplish. Although FORTRAN was (and continues to be) very useful in scientific applications, it achieved nowhere near the popularity of another higher-level language: **C**.

The C Programming Language

C was invented while Ken Thompson and Dennis Ritchie of Bell Labs were developing the UNIX operating system. First, they developed a partial C compiler, then used this compiler to compile the rest of the C compiler, and then used the completed compiler to compile UNIX. The Unix operating system was initially distributed as C source code to universities and laboratories that wanted it, and the recipient would compile that source code to machine code with a C compiler appropriate to his mainframe.

Being distributed in C source code was what made the UNIX operating system unique; the operating system could be modified by programmers, and the source code was portable from hardware system to hardware system. Today, the POSIX standard defines a standard set of UNIX system calls accessible from C that UNIX implementations seeking POSIX-compliant status must implement. C was the third language that Thompson and Ritchie developed in the UNIX effort; the first two were, of course, "A" and "B."

C improved upon an older language, BCPL, by adding data types of definite lengths. The int data type, for instance, could be used to create a variable with a certain number of bits (commonly 16), while the long data type could be used to create an integer variable with a greater number (commonly 32). Unlike other high-level languages, however, C could manipulate memory addresses directly, via pointers and references. Because C retained the ability to address computer hardware directly with a fine degree of control, it was sometimes referred to as a mid-level programming language, or jokingly as "portable assembly language."

In terms of grammar and syntax, C was a structured programming language. Whereas many of today's programmers think in terms of classes and objects, C programmers thought in terms of subroutines and functions. You could, however, define your own abstract data types using C's struct keyword. Similarly, you could define your own integer types (enumerations) and alias existing data types, with the typedef keyword. In this sense, C was a structured programming language with the seeds of an object-oriented language within it.

Bjarne Stroustrup unlocked C's latent OO potential by grafting Simula 67's class facilities onto C in what was first called "C with classes", and later popularized as C++. C++ first achieved popularity within AT&T Bell Labs before migrating to other industries and corporations. Today it is one of the most popular programming languages in the world. C++ inherits both C's good points and its bad ones.

C vs. C++

In the hands of an experienced programmer, C and C++ are elegant tools for writing powerful programs that run very efficiently. In the hands of a less experienced programmer (or even a good programmer having a bad day), the languages can be quite error prone. Some of the most common bugs are listed below.

It's easy to mistake C's assignment operator, "=", for its comparison operator, "==". Doing so can create a Boolean comparison statement that evaluates to true when you don't expect it to.

C/C++'s ability to directly allocate memory makes it easy to create memory leaks. These are caused by programs that don't release system resources as they finish with them and therefore slowly bring the execution environment to its knees.

C/C++'s preprocessor makes it easy to obfuscate your code. When you compile a C/C++ program, the preprocessor does initial scans through your program, linking in files prefaced with the #include pre-processor command, and "expanding" macro definitions (#define) by replacing them with equivalent values. It can be difficult to keep function declarations in one file in synch with function definitions in another, and next to impossible to detect errors caused by preprocessor macros that expand in unexpected ways (such as when used in the context of compound input arguments).

Null pointers are another C/C++ gotcha. A pointer is basically a memory address that holds the value of another memory address in which a data structure is stored. You can do fancy things with pointers, such as refer to the same data structure through several different variable names, or iterate through elements in a hierarchical data structure. In the midst of all this fanciness, it's all too easy to wind up with a "pointer to nowhere" – a pointer that does not contain the address of an expected data type. When you try to make an assignment to the structure that you think the pointer points to, you can generate a runtime error or **clobber** (overwrite) memory that is occupied by other data.

Despite their complexities, C and C++ give the programmer a lot of power. For platforms in which efficiency is of the essence (such as telephone switching networks and the Palm OS), C and C++ remain the development languages of choice. For many IT departments, however, C and C++ are not viable options for software development. In addition to a learning curve that is too steep for many real-world developers, the languages impose a development and debugging period that is too long to be practical in a world moving at Internet speed.

Programming Windows in C and C++

C was originally intended for the UNIX world of batch files, daemon processes, and redirectable input and output streams. The marriage of C and C++ to the Windows operating system was one fraught with complexity.

Unlike UNIX, Windows is an event driven operating system. The operating system constantly polls interrupts for information from the graphical user interface: mouse clicks, mouse moves, keystrokes, and so on. When a window receives such a message from the user, the Windows operating system has to route the message to that window through a message pump.

A window is by its very nature hierarchical. A typical Windows application might consist, for example, of a main window containing several document windows each of which contains a several buttons, each of which is also a window, and so on. Writing such an application in C requires nesting several functions together so that their `switch...case` constructions **bubble** operating system messages from the lowest level windows up to the higher level windows that can act upon them. As you might imagine, such C code can be messy, convoluted, and bug-prone.

In developing its products, Microsoft did its best to combat C's fussiness. First, Microsoft developed their own C compilers for in-house use and outfitted these compilers with state-of-the-art debuggers that could "step-through" code line by line. Second, they standardized defensive coding practices such as asserts, debugging prints, and Hungarian naming conventions. Third, they adopted a development regimen that kept the bugs at bay by emphasizing daily builds and close interaction between the programmers and testers.

Microsoft hoped that the move to C++ would make Windows programming less difficult for themselves and for other development companies. After all, wrapping functions into classes would seem a good way to organize an API that had swelled to literally thousands of calls. Unfortunately, Microsoft C++ failed to achieve popularity with the masses. The Microsoft Foundation Classes (the MFC) never achieved the popularity that they hoped that it would, and most MFC programs were strewn with cryptic constants and macros.

Enter VB

Although initially regarded as a toy, Microsoft's Visual Basic (VB) eventually took the programming world by storm. Its popularity is due to two things: its relative simplicity, and its productivity. While it's true that Visual Basic programs don't run quite as quickly as their C/C++ counterparts, they run quickly enough for most business situations and require a lot less time to develop.

Forms were the labor-saving abstraction that VB provided to Windows programmers. The VB IDE allowed you to design windows graphically, by dragging controls such as buttons and list boxes from a toolbox, and dropping them onto a form. When you were happy with the appearance of your form, you could flip over to its code aspect and write event-handling routines for each of the form's controls. Application development in VB thus consisted of the creation of several forms that talked to each other and perhaps queried a database for persisted information. In effect, a form was a wrapped window that exposed windows methods in a friendlier way.

VB also reduced bugs by eliminating some of the more esoteric elements of C/C++ syntax. Except in special cases, statements were restricted to single lines, and variables had to be declared and initialized in separate statements. The assignment and comparison operators used the same character, but VB's grammar dictated that these operators be used in a way that made their intent clear.

Perhaps most importantly, there were no pointers, a requirement that Bill Gates had made since the earliest versions of Microsoft BASIC. Although valuable because they allow programmers direct access to any address in memory, pointers are prone to bugs unless they are used very carefully. BASIC's emphasis on grammatical simplicity and clarity go back to the fact that BASIC was first designed as a learning language: "Beginner's All-purpose Symbolic Instructional Code."

By Version 6, VB had matured into a powerful language that you could use to create distributed applications using COM components and Microsoft Transaction Server. Microsoft touted the "three-tiered" approach to client-server architectures, in which "thin" user interfaces communicated with remote VB components to query data from a database on another machine.

With VBScript and VB for Applications, you could even script web browsers and automate Microsoft Office applications. Furthermore, you could use VB6 to create Active-X controls that would run inside Internet Explorer, although this was seldom done in practice because it required that the VB runtime DLL be installed on the web surfer's machine.

Although VB programs after VB5 did compile to machine code, they relied on this runtime DLL to provide them with commonly used routines and to implement VB's object facilities. Interestingly, VB's compiler took the multi-pass approach to translation, and relied on Microsoft's C++ compiler to output the final executable code once an intermediate representation was derived. In VB's reliance on a runtime and its sharing of the C++ back-end you can recognize the seeds of .NET.

Despite VB's power, it still had its drawbacks. Specifically, advanced programmers often encountered things that VB just wouldn't easily do, such as multithreading. Entire books were written on how to make VB do hardcore things that only C programmers would normally attempt, such as hooking into the stream of messages that the operating system delivered to VB forms. Because VB programs relied on a runtime component to provide much of their functionality, they were often slower than equivalent C programs and required the installation of the VB runtime component on the target machine.

Java

The needs of information technology were different in the mid-1990s than they had been in the mid-1970s when C was introduced. Specifically, the 90s saw a greater emphasis on distributed applications, in which various software components live on disparate platforms and negotiate with each other for information across local networks and the Internet. Java was an attempt by Sun Microsystems to meet these new demands. The Java language brought C++-style syntax into the Internet age.

Java's most remarkable feature is **platform independence**. Unlike C, C++, and Visual Basic, Java source code does not compile to machine code (1s and 0s), but to Java **bytecode**, in which each byte corresponds roughly to a type of machine code instruction typically supported by most microprocessors.

Because there's a layer of abstraction between a bytecode instruction and its machine code equivalent, the same bytecode program can be sent across the Internet for execution on different kinds of computers. A computer receiving the bytecode program is equipped with a **runtime program** that translates the bytecode into machine code instructions for execution. Because the correspondence between bytecode instructions and machine code instructions is roughly one-to-one, the translation process is fast, and bytecode programs execute quickly.

Although Java was originally intended for handheld consumer electronics devices such as television remote controls, Java became popular as a way to animate web pages. A Java **applet** is a bytecode program accessed from a web site. When a user with a Java-enabled browser surfs to a web page with an applet, his or her browser downloads the applet's bytecode and executes it. With the advent of streaming media and technologies such as Flash, however, Java applets are not quite as popular as they used to be.

Web sites use applets to collect order information and present information in entertaining ways. To prevent computer viruses, the capabilities of Java applets are restricted to a "sandbox" of features. It is impossible, for example, for a Java applet to write a file to a host computer's file system. As a Java applet executes, the runtime can dynamically request needed Java components from the Internet. As the bytecode is delivered, the runtime's bytecode verifier would frisk them to guard against malicious behavior.

As Java matured, it came to be used not only for applets, but for applications as well. Although there had always been Java applications, such as the web browser HotJava, Java applications became more feasible with the introduction of Java beans, Java's answer to COM components. Java beans could live on different machines in a network and communicate with each other remotely. In addition, Java beans could be endowed with transacting capabilities, a feature very important in client-server applications.

Java was attractive to application developers who were targeting multiple platforms. If, for example, you were developing a word processing program that had to run on Windows machines, Macintosh machines, and Unix machines, wouldn't it be great if you could write the program once, compile it once, and run it on all of these platforms without any modification? "Write once, run anywhere," was Java's alluring promise.

"Write once, debug everywhere" was the sarcastic retort of burned Java developers who found out the hard way that Java didn't always port. Sometimes, for example, a Java program's user interface would render correctly on a Macintosh computer, but incorrectly on a Windows machine.

Another attractive feature of Java is its availability; you can download the Java SDK from the Sun site (http://java.sun.com/) for free. To be truly productive, however, most Java development shops have to purchase commercial **Integrated Development Environments** (**IDEs**) in which to write their source code. Visual Café, Visual Age, and Jbuilder are IDEs that have proved popular with the Java crowd.

Syntactically, Java is much like C++, but there are some differences:

- ❑ Java does not support pointers because they are the source of so many hard-to-find errors in C++ programs. In Java, objects are always manipulated via references.

- ❑ Java does not support operator overloading because inappropriate operator overloading often causes a lot of confusion, particularly in large, multi-developer efforts.

- ❑ Java is completely object-oriented. That is, all functions have to be defined with in the scope of a class. Because it supported global functions, C++ enabled programmers to regress to their procedural roots.

- ❑ Java comes equipped with an extensive hierarchy of classes that can be used for windowing, networking, and other problem domains.

- ❑ Java encourages the practice of combining a class' declaration and implementation into the same file.

- ❑ The Java runtime provides a garbage collection mechanism that prevents memory leaks.

Microsoft hopped on the bandwagon by including J++ in its Visual Studio development suite. J++ extended Java with some neat features, such as the ability to automatically generate a COM interface for a Java class when you compile it.

Because many of these features were specific to the Windows platform, however, Sun claimed that J++ violated the spirit of Java with code that wasn't pure. They felt that users should be assured that any code bearing the Java name should be guaranteed to run on any Java runtime, and J++ couldn't do this with the platform-specific additions that Microsoft had made. As you're probably aware, this philosophical difference was the source of many legal woes for Redmond, and ultimately resulted in J++'s elimination.

Although Java is neat and useful, it can be expensive, and for a reason that is not always immediately recognizable to a developer. Specifically, Java development is more demanding than development in alternative languages like Delphi or VB, and therefore necessitates developers that are more experienced. Hiring such developers can be expensive, as can be re-training your existing development team to move into the Java world.

In terms of architecture, Java was one of the first languages to place the runtime at the heart of things. As previously mentioned, the Java runtime not only provided useful routines, but also interpreted code, managed memory, enforced security.

C#

C# is related to each of the programming languages that we've discussed so far. Like C, it's concise and powerful. Like C++, it is object-oriented. Like VB, it leverages the power of graphical design to make user interface creation easier. Like Java, C# compiles to a bytecode that relies on the housekeeping services of a runtime.

Now, let's take a moment for more detailed comparisons of C# and its programming languages. We'll restrict our comparisons to general-purpose languages, leaving out those designed for specific purpose like artificial intelligence, or teaching.

C# Compared to Other Languages

In this section, we'll be comparing C# to the other languages available for development. Let's start with VB6.

C# Compared to VB6

The most obvious difference between C# and VB6 is that C# compiles to MSIL, and VB6 compiles to native machine code. Programs written in either language require a runtime in order to execute. The advantages of the C# runtime are that it allows C# code to interoperate with code written in other programming languages, and that it allows C# code to leverage the wealth of functionality afforded by the .NET base classes.

In terms of features, C# is more object-oriented than VB6. VB6, for example, lacks parameterized constructors, operator overloading, and implementation inheritance. In terms of syntax, C# is more concise than VB6, and allows for variables to be simultaneously declared and initialized, and for statements to span an arbitrary number of lines.

Does C# mean that you should throw all your VB6 code away? No.

Many useful niche market applications have been developed in VB6 by people who understood the needs of those markets better than they understood programming. If you are such an entrepreneur/programmer, the great new features of C# and .NET will not rid your application of the bugs that are in it due to design flaws; if anything, the added complexities of C# syntax may make a flawed design even more susceptible to bugs. Also, the reliance of C# programs on the .NET runtime will necessitate deploying the runtime with all your installations.

Lastly, because VB6 is a mature product with a very wide customer base, Microsoft is likely to continue supporting it for a long time to come. If your skills have improved a whole lot since you first wrote your application in VB6, however, and if you feel confident that you can correct many design flaws by a complete re-write, then you might consider moving your application from VB6 to C#.

C# Compared to VB.NET

VB.NET can do almost everything that C# can do. The one thing that VB.NET can't do is allow for embedded blocks of pure C++ code with pointers and other unsafe C++ idioms. This is a feature that most people won't be interested in, anyway.

Just because VB.NET is powerful, however, it doesn't mean that it's easy to use. The addition of new features to VB has necessitated significant changes to VB's grammar and syntax. If you're a VB programmer who doesn't have a lot of object-oriented experience, learning VB.NET will not be a piece of cake.

In coding samples and press blurbs, Microsoft emphasizes C# over VB.NET. Also, Microsoft plans to rely heavily on C# for future development, and to publicize a C# standard so that other vendors can develop C# compilers that target other platforms. These facts imply that VB programmers might be marginalized in the future. On the other hand, name-recognition for VB is so strong that VB.NET might just marginalize C#!

In reality, it may make little difference whether you choose to use C# or VB.NET. Just don't choose VB.NET with the hopes of making an easy transition, because it won't be.

C# Compared to Visual C++

First of all, C# is simply a flavor of C++. This is implied by the fact that you can embed chunks of plain C++ in "unsafe" blocks in C# code. (We'll look at how to do this later in the book.) .

As C# is meant to be more productive than C++, C# prohibits bug-prone C++ idioms:

- ❑ C# prohibits pointers and pointer arithmetic (except in blocks of unsafe code).

- ❑ C# eliminates preprocessor macros (but retains conditional compilation and `#define-d` constants). Complex macros cause bugs when they expand in unexpected ways around compound input arguments.

- ❑ C# requires that a variable be explicitly initialized with a beginning value before that variable's value can be referenced.

- ❑ C# dispenses with fall-through `switch...case` statements. To guard against programmer oversight, every `case` clause inside a `switch` statement must be accompanied by a closing `break` command.

- ❑ C# forces you to embrace object-oriented programming by eliminating global functions. Every function in every program must be a member of a class, if only a static member. Even the opening `Main()` function is defined as a member of a class.

C# is meant to be easier than C++, too:

❑ When C# class libraries are compiled, the compiler automatically exposes them as components that can be re-used by client applications. You don't have to mess with GUIDs and ATL macros.

❑ C# supports the use of Windows Forms for the rapid development of graphical user interfaces. You don't have to write code to handle OnPaint events, and so on.

❑ C# standardizes the use of single files that contain both class definitions and class implementations. Combining a class definition and its implementation into a single file makes the class easier to maintain.

Because it is interpreted, C# code isn't quite as efficient as C++ code. C# is, however, fast enough to meet the needs of most IT departments, who will welcome the shortened development cycles that accompany C#'s emphasis on productivity and correctness. Because C# compiles only to IL and not to machine code, it's great stuff for web pages and business applications but less suitable for device drivers and operating system kernels. Programmers who code straight C++ will have job security for a long time to come.

One striking advantage of C# is the set of useful data types that it provides you through the System namespace. Without linking in any separate header files you have at your disposal dedicated types for financial values, string values, and Boolean values. Moreover, because these types are proper classes and not merely primitives, they are each equipped with useful static methods for conversions and formatting output.

To prevent errors, C# types are strongly **typed**. This means that conversions between certain data types must be requested explicitly. In C++, it was possible for an integer value to be implicitly interpreted as a Boolean value. This is not the case in C#. An integer value would have to be explicitly **cast** into a Boolean value in order to be interpreted in that way.

C# Compared to Managed C++

As you may know from Chapter 1, the .NET runtime component is said to manage client code, providing it with garbage collection, security checks, and other services. With VS.NET, Microsoft provides a collection of header files that C++ programmers can use to leverage these services. By referencing these header files and prefixing the definitions of existing C++ classes with attributes defined in them, programmers can avail legacy C++ code of the advantages of the .NET runtime.

If you're a C++ programmer targeting .NET, you probably want to do future development in C#. The extensions for marrying straight C++ code with the .NET runtime are most useful for upgrading existing code. Although managed C++ code does allow you to package managed and unmanaged classes together in the same physical component, you probably won't have an overwhelming need to do this very often.

C# Compared to C++ Builder

Borland's C++ development environment, C++ Builder, was most notable for combining the form approach of user interface design with the C++ language. As you'll learn later in this chapter, C# also supports forms. The advantage of C# over C++ Builder is that C# has the language interoperability provided by the .NET runtime. Because programs compiled with C++ Builder are rendered as machine code, they must rely on COM Services to interoperate with code written in other languages.

C# Compared to Delphi

Delphi, another Rapid Application Development (RAD) tool from Borland, combined forms with a proprietary, Pascal-like language. Delphi achieved its greatest popularity before VB6, when it was the only easy way for programmers who didn't know C++ to create COM objects and ActiveX controls.

With its reliance on BEGIN and END pairs to delimit statement blocks, Delphi syntax is clumsier and more obtuse than C# syntax. Like C++ Builder, Delphi compiles to machine code and must rely on COM Services for interoperability; you can't open a Delphi project alongside a VB.NET project and step through its code with the VS.NET debugger.

When comparing C# to machine-code languages like Delphi and C++ Builder, platform independence is another factor to consider. Although it's not yet a reality for C#, many people think that platform independence is coming soon. Because Delphi and C++ Builder don't utilize a bytecode, platform-independent versions of them are at least one release away, and would require intense effort on the part of Borland.

C# Compared to Java

There's no doubt that Java was a profound influence on C#. In fact, at least one cynic has dubbed C# "Cava." Anders Hejlsberg, the leader of the C# effort, also lead the development of J++, Microsoft's now-defunct Java compiler. The syntax of Java and C# are eerily similar. Even the structures of the Java library and the .NET base classes are close. Of course, both languages rely on bytecode.

At least at the present time, Java has one strong advantage over C#: platform independence. Because there are Java runtime implementations for all of the major computing platforms, the same Java code can theoretically execute on any of them. This is something that .NET programs can't do – at least not yet.

In contrast, C# has three smaller advantages over Java:

❑ C# syntax is a bit more powerful than Java's, because C# supports operator overloading and type safe enumerations. Also, if the need arises, you have the option of embedding pointers and other outlawed idioms in your C# programs as long as you enclose them within "unsafe" blocks.

❑ C# interoperates seamlessly with code written in other .NET languages. This means that an IT department needn't standardize C# in order to use it in its projects. For this reason, C# can be seen as a less expensive, less total alternative to Java.

❑ The .NET base classes provide C# with a unified, standardized source for commonly needed functionality like XML, networking, and graphics. To access the same kinds of functionality, Java programmers sometimes have to pull from a variety of disparate sources.

C# Compared to JavaScript

As you may know, JavaScript has nothing to do with Java. JavaScript is a client-side scripting language for animating web pages; dubbing it *Java*Script was a shameless marketing ploy designed to cash in on Java's hype. Back when Java was most often used to create web browser applets, JavaScript and Java sometimes served similar purposes.

C# is like JavaScript in that both languages inherit a C-like syntax. C#, however, is not strictly interpreted, but compiled to a bytecode that is cached, and cannot be used a scripting language inside a web browser (at least not yet). Whereas JavaScript focuses on responding to events that happen client-side, in a web browser, C# focuses on generating the HTML and retrieving the data that a web browser is first sent.

As you'll see when we discuss WebControls, JavaScript and C# can be used together for great effect. In an Internet application, C# code can basically determine what type of web browser that the requesting user has, and send them a portion of JavaScript that their browser can support. Of course, you can code ASP.NET pages in JavaScript (JScript) just like you could ASP pages.

C# Compared to VBScript

Until now, VBScript enjoyed the distinction of being the most widely used language for coding Active Server Pages. With ASP.NET, however, programmers will be able to use C#, VB.NET, or other .NET languages to code pages. This means that C# may displace VBScript on the server-side, though future releases of the Internet Explorer web browser are expected to continue to support client-side code in VBScript.

Using C#

In this section we'll be discussing some of the specifics of the use of C#, and where it can come in useful. Let's start with a look at ASP.NET Applications.

ASP.NET Applications

ASP was a Microsoft technology for creating web pages with dynamic content. An ASP page is basically an HTML file with embedded chunks of server-side VBScript or JavaScript. When a client browser requested an ASP page, the web server would deliver the HTML portions of the page, processing the server-side scripts as it came to them. Often these scripts would query a database for data, and mark up that data in HTML. ASP was an easy way for clients to build browser-based applications.

ASP was not, however, without its shortcomings. First, ASP pages sometimes rendered slowly because the server-side code was interpreted instead of compiled. Second, ASP files could be difficult to maintain because they were unstructured; the server-side ASP code and plain HTML were all jumbled up together. Third, ASP sometimes made development difficult because there was little support for error handling and type-checking. Specifically, if you wanted to implement error handling in your pages, you had to use the `On Error Resume Next` statement, and follow every component call with a check to `Err.Number` to make sure that the call had gone well.

ASP.NET, first known as ASP+, is a revision of ASP that fixes many of its problems. It does not replace ASP; rather, ASP.NET pages can live side by side on the same server with legacy ASP apps. Of course, you can also program ASP.NET with C#!

Although a subsequent chapter explores ASP.NET in greater detail, let's take a moment to explore some of its more significant features.

Features of ASP.NET

First, and perhaps most importantly, ASP.NET pages are **structured**. That is, each page is effectively a class that inherits from the .NET `WebPage` class, and can override a set of methods that are evoked during the `WebPage` class' lifetime. (You can think of these events as page-specific cousins of the `OnApp_Start` and `OnSession_Start` events that went in the `global.asa` files of plain old ASP.) Because you can factor a page's functionality into event handlers with explicit meanings, ASP.NET pages are easier to understand.

Another nice thing about ASP.NET pages is that you can create them in VS.NET, the same environment in which you create the business logic and data access components that those ASP pages use. A VS.NET project group, or solution, contains all of the files associated with an application. Moreover, you can debug your ASP pages in the editor as well. In the old days of Visual Interdev, it was often a vexing challenge to configure InterDev and the projects web server to turn debugging on. Those days are gone, as you'll see in a later chapter that explores ASP.NET's error handling and trace mechanisms.

For maximum clarity, ASP.NET's `code-behind` feature lets you take the structured approach even further. ASP.NET allows you to isolate the server-side functionality of a page to a class, compile that class into a DLL, and place that DLL into a directory below the HTML portion. A `code-behind` directive at the top of the page associates the file with its DLL. When a browser requests the page, the web server fires the events in the class in the page's `code-behind` DLL.

Last but not least, ASP.NET is remarkable for its increased performance. Whereas ASP pages are continually compiled and re-compiled with each page request, the web server caches ASP.NET pages after compilation. This means that subsequent requests of an ASP.NET page execute more quickly than the first.

The traditional wisdom is that form-based applications offer a richer user interface, but are harder to maintain because they run on so many different machines. For this reason, people have relied on form-based applications when rich user interfaces were a necessity and extensive support could be provided to the users.

With the advent of Internet Explorer 5 and the lackluster performance of Navigator 6, however, the advantages of form-based applications are clouded. IE5's consistent and robust support for DHTML allow the programmer to create web-based applications that are every bit as pretty as their fat client equivalents. Of course, such applications necessitate standardizing on IE and not supporting Navigator. In many industrial situations, this standardization is now an option.

Web Forms

To make web page construction even easier, Visual Studio.NET supplies **Web Forms**. They allow you to build ASP.NET pages graphically in the same way that VB6 or C++ Builder windows are created; in other words, by dragging controls from a toolbox onto a form, then flipping over to the code aspect of that form, and writing event handlers for the controls. When you use C# to create a Windows Form, you are creating a C# class that inherits from the `WebPage` base class, and an ASP page that designates that class as its code-behind. Of course, you don't have to use C# to create a Windows Form; you can use VB.NET or another .NET language just as well.

In the past, the difficulty of web development has discouraged some teams from attempting it. To succeed in web development, you had to know so many different technologies, such as VBScript, ASP, DHTML, JavaScript, and so on. By applying the Form concepts to web pages, Web Forms promise to make web development easier. Only time will tell, however, how successful Web Forms and **WebControls** (which we'll look at next) will be at insulating the developer from the complexities of web design .

WebControls

The controls with which you populate a web form, are not controls in the same sense as Active-X controls. Rather, they are XML tags in the ASP namespace that the web browser dynamically transforms into HTML, and client-side script when a page is requested. Amazingly, the web server is able to render the same server-side control in different ways, producing a transformation that is appropriate to the requestor's particular web browser.

You can use C# or VB.NET to expand the Windows Form toolbox. Creating a new server-side control is simply a matter of implementing .NET's web server class. (More on this in Chapter 7.)

Web Services

Today, HTML pages account for most of the traffic on the World Wide Web. With XML, however, computers have a device-independent format to use for communicating with each other on the Web. In the future, computers may use the Web and XML to communicate information rather than dedicated lines and proprietary formats such as **EDI** (**Electronic Data Interchange**). Web services are designed for a service-oriented web, in which remote computers provide each other with dynamic information that can be analyzed and re-formatted, before final presentation to a user. A Web Service is an easy way for a computer to expose information to other computers on the Web in the form of XML.

In technical terms, a Web Service is an ASP.NET page that returns XML instead of HTML to requesting clients. Such pages have a `code-behind` DLL containing a class that conforms to the `WebService` interface. The VS.NET IDE provides an engine that facilitates Web Service development.

There are two main reasons that an organization might choose to use Web Services. The first reason is that because they rely on HTTP, Web Services can use existing networks (the Web) as a medium for conveying information. The other is that because Web Services use XML, the data format is self-describing, non-proprietary, and platform independent.

Last and perhaps least, C# can be used to create console applications, text-only applications that run in a DOS window. These sorts of applications are best suited for creating daemon processes that will run in the background when periodically evoked by the scheduler, or for creating driver programs for unit testing components (class library projects).

Class Libraries

You can think of a component as a file of compiled classes that client applications can re-use. Therefore, Microsoft's approach to componentization was COM, a binary standard in which components could be implemented in any form as long as they supported an intricate interface (`IUnknown`). Because COM components were accessed only through this established interface, the same COM components could be used by applications coded in multiple languages.

In the new .NET approach, language interoperability is achieved by the fact that components all compile to a common format: Intermediate Language. This frees component developers from the intricacies of COM programming. You just create a component project, compile it, and let the compiler invisibly generate whatever IL plumbing is required in order to expose your classes to clients.

Another advantage of the .NET approach is registration. Simply put, you don't have to register .NET components; you just put a copy of the component into the client application's directory and the client is able to see it. In fact, the server component encapsulates its own metadata in a segment of the component known as the **manifest**.

When the client creates a .NET object from the server component, the .NET runtime retrieves interface information from the server's manifest through a process called probing. As discussed in Chapter 10, the localization of component metadata implies *side-by-side* versioning, the ability for different versions of the same component to peacefully co-exist on the same machine, thereby avoiding "DLL Hell."

To create a new .NET component, you simply open a new Class Library project from the VS.NET IDE, implement some classes, and compile the result. Typically, your VS.NET solutions will consist of a Windows Form (ASP.NET) project and several .NET Class Library projects that the ASP.NET pages use to manipulate data.

Microsoft makes it relatively easy to use .NET components together with legacy COM components. The .NET SDK provides a couple of utility programs for wrapping COM components in an IL interface and for wrapping .NET components in COM. These utilities crank out proxy components that delegate calls to the original COM components. Alternatively, you can .NET-enable existing C++ classes by prefixing them with x's, which are tags that instruct the C++ compiler to generate IL interfaces for them.

The x technique has other implications for components as well. By affixing x to .NET components, you can prepare them to leverage COM+ Services (formerly MTS). Besides support for transactions and method-based security, these services have increased to include events and message queuing.

Windows Applications

Although C# and .NET are particularly suited to web development, they still offer splendid support for so-called "fat client" apps, applications that have to be installed on the end-user's machine where most of the processing takes place. This support is in the form of **Windows Forms**.

A Windows Form is the .NET answer to a VB6 Form. To design a graphical window interface, you just drag controls from a toolbox onto a Windows Form. To determine the window's behavior, you write event-handling routines for the form's controls. A Windows Form project compiles to an EXE that must be installed alongside the .NET runtime on the end user's computer. Like other .NET project types, Windows Form projects are supported by both VB.NET and C#.

Windows Controls

Although Web Forms and Windows Forms are developed in much the same way, you use different kinds of controls to populate them. Web Forms use WebControls, and Windows Forms use **Windows Controls**.

A Windows Control is a lot like an ActiveX control. After a Window control is implemented, it compiles to a DLL that must be installed on the client's machine. In fact, the .NET SDK provides a utility that creates a wrapper for ActiveX controls, so that they can be placed on Windows Forms. Conversely, another utility wraps up Windows controls, so that they can be used as ActiveX controls. As is the case with WebControls, Windows Control creation involves implementing an interface defined by a particular class, `WindowControl`.

Console Applications

Last and perhaps least, C# can be used to create console applications, text-only applications that run in a DOS window. As mentioned earlier, you'll use console applications when unit testing class libraries, and for creating daemon processes.

C#'s Place in Enterprise Architectures

Because C# requires the presence of the .NET runtime, it's best suited for execution environments that can be closely monitored. Unless .NET achieves such popularity that retail software developers can be assured that the .NET runtime will exist on the vast majority of consumers' machines, retailers will probably want to leave C# and .NET to IT departments, ASPs (Application Service Providers), and other organizations that guarantee the presence of the .NET runtime in its correct version and can tweak it for optimum performance. This said, C# presents an outstanding opportunity for organizations that are interested in building robust, n-tiered client-server applications.

With ADO.NET, C# has the ability to quickly and generically access data stores like SQL Server and Oracle databases. The returned datasets can easily be manipulated via the ADO.NET object model, and automatically render as XML for transport across an office intranet.

Once a database schema has been established for a new project, C# presents an excellent medium for implementing a layer of data access objects, each of which could provide insertion, updates, and deletion access to a different database table. Enterprise developers, here's a word to the wise: create a program that will automatically generate a layer of data access objects for any SQL Server database.

Because it's the first component-based C language, C# is a great language for implementing a business object tier, too. It encapsulates the messy plumbing for inter-component communication, leaving the developer free to focus on gluing his data access objects together in methods that accurately enforce his organization's business rules. Moreover, with attributes, C# business objects can be outfitted for method-level security checks, object pooling, and JIT activation supplied by COM+ Services. Furthermore, .NET ships with utility programs that allow your new .NET business objects to interface with legacy COM components.

To create an enterprise application with C#, you'd probably create a Class Library project for the data access objects and another for the business objects. While developing, you could use Console projects to test the methods on your classes. Fans of extreme programming could build Console projects that could be automatically executed from batch files to unit test that working code has not been broken.

On a related note, C# and .NET will probably influence the way that you physically package your re-usable classes. In the past, many developers crammed a multitude of classes into a single physical component because this arrangement made deployment a lot easier; if there was a versioning problem, you knew just where to look. Because deploying .NET enterprise components simply involves copying files into directories, developers can now package their classes into more logical, discrete components without encountering "DLL Hell".

Last but not least, ASP.NET pages coded in C# constitute an excellent medium for user interfaces. Because ASP.NET pages compile, they execute quickly. Because they can be debugged in the VS.NET IDE, they are robust. Because they support full-scale language features like early binding, inheritance, and modularization, ASP.NET pages coded in C# are tidy and easily maintained.

Seasoned developers acquire a healthy skepticism about strongly hyped new technologies and languages, and are reluctant to utilize new platforms simply because they are urged to. If you're an enterprise developer in an IT department, though, or if you provide application services across the World Wide Web, let me assure you that C# and .NET offer at least three benefits, even if some of the more exotic features like Web Services and server-side controls don't pan out:

- ❏ Component conflicts will become infrequent and deployment will be easier, because different versions of the same component can run side by side on the same machine without conflicting.

- ❏ Your ASP code won't look like spaghetti anymore.

- ❏ You can leverage a lot of the functionality in the .NET base classes.

You may have noticed that I did not mention Windows Form applications in this section. This is because Windows Forms are not an option that I would choose for any user interface that I was developing right now. The ease-of-installation provided by browser-based apps and the richness of the IE5 simply make ASP.NET pages much more attractive. If you're a VB6 programmer who doesn't have a lot of web development experience however, a C# Windows Form project might be a good place for you to begin learning C#, since Windows Forms are so much like VB6 forms.

If you or your colleagues lack expertise in JavaScript, ASP, or related technologies however, Windows Forms are still a viable option for creating a user interface with speed and ease. Just remember to factor your code so that the user interface logic is separate from the business logic and the data access code. Doing so will allow you to migrate your application to the browser at some point in the future if you desire to do so.

An Overview of C#'s Features

The .NET Base Classes

In its early days, one of the biggest drawbacks of C++ was its dearth of useful data types. Sure, you could create a pointer to any data type that you wanted, and you could create any sort of class that you desired, but you had to expend a lot of energy just to create data types for string, Boolean, and financial values.

Flow-Control Statements

C# provides the normal flow-of-control statements that you would expect, such as `if...else` statements, `while` loops, `for` loops, and `do...while` loops. In addition C# supports the `for each` construction for iterating through items in collections, arrays, lists, and other containers. To save keystrokes, C# supports the ternary form of the `if...else` construction (`A?B:C`). To avoid mistakes, C# requires that each `case` clause in a `switch...case` block is supplied with a `break` statement.

Object-Oriented Facilities

C++ grafted classes onto C, and for this reason, there was always a certain awkwardness to object-oriented programming in C++. You could, for instance, backslide and adopt a more procedural approach, relying on global functions where you should have used objects. Or perhaps you just felt overwhelmed by the enormous number of options that you had when you wanted to express something, and never really felt that you were implementing a concept in the best way that was possible. How many ways were there, for example, to make a class abstract so that it could only provide an interface and not be instantiated?

By restricting the idioms to a crucial few, C# boasts an object-orientedness that is mature and productive. There is, for example, a keyword for designating classes as abstract. Similarly, to encourage you to build good class hierarchies, there are limitations placed upon inheritance. Specifically, a class can inherit interfaces from as many classes as needed, but can only inherit implementation from one base class.

As you'll see in later chapters that explore C# syntax in greater detail, the ambiguities regarding polymorphic functions have been resolved by a new, cleaner syntax for declaring virtual and "pure virtual" functions. Specifically, a class can forego providing a method implementation and force child classes to do so by prefixing that method with the `abstract` keyword. Furthermore, the `sealed` keyword allows you to create a class that cannot be inherited from. As in C++, a complete set of visibility keywords allow you to control who can see the data members and methods inside a class.

One of the nicest features of the C# class mechanism is its approach to properties. This approach centralizes the read and write aspects of a property into a single location so that you can control it more easily. The overall effect is objects that *feel* like objects, in that their properties seem syntactically more like characteristics, and less like disguised function calls. A specialized form of property called an **indexer** exposes arrays inside classes via a very intuitive syntax.

As mentioned earlier, C#, unlike Java, supports operator overloading, the ability to specify how instances of classes behave when language operators are applied to them. Operator overloading is one of those things that has to be used selectively; when applied indiscriminately, operator overloading can obfuscate code. To avoid such obfuscation, C# restricts the operators that can be overloaded to a sensible set. You can't, for instance, overload the assignment operator.

As you would expect, C# classes can sport multiple, parameterized constructors. They do not, however, implement destructors in the same way that normal C++ classes do. Instead of destructors, C# classes have `finalize` methods, which are supposed to be invoked not when objects go out of scope, but when the garbage collector in the runtime gets around to doing its work. For this reason, the finalize method is, at least at this point in time, an unreliable method for ensuring that objects release resources.

Furthermore, C# classes do not support templates for type-generic code. Microsoft has hinted that type-generic code will be possible in future iterations of C#, but that incarnation will rely on a mechanism other than templates.

In conclusion, remember that the first and most important rule for judging software is how well it performs its task. There are no rewards for buggy programs that use every idiom exposed by their language. I say this mostly for the benefit of VB6 programmers who will be new to implementation inheritance; just because you can do it, it doesn't mean that you should. Over-relying on implementation inheritance can result in class hierarchies that are bound tightly together, and can't be individually modified without affecting others in the hierarchy.

Reflection and Attributes

Although polymorphism and late binding are two of the means by which object-oriented programming realizes its greatest benefits, clients of late-bound objects often need to determine the subtypes of the objects that they are manipulating so that they can treat them in specific ways. Through reflection, a client can ascertain a server object's subclass and the methods that that subclass supports – all without weighing the server class down with hokey identifying code. Code can consider, or *reflect upon* itself.

Attributes are a way of associating metadata with classes, so that the metadata can be exposed by reflection. In .NET languages such as C# and VB.NET, you can create your own attributes to convey information via reflection, or you can use attributes created by other people. Certain attributes, for example, can determine how a class behaves in the context of COM+ Services (see Chapter 20). The C# compiler can interpret the attributes to provided compiled versions of the component with the "hooks" necessary to leverage those Services.

Other instances in which reflection is useful include code profiling applications and implementations of the "Visitor" design pattern (see *Design Patterns: Elements of Re-Usable Object-oriented Design* by Erich Gamma et al., ISBN: 0201633612).

Unsafe Code

One of the most misunderstood concepts in C#, **unsafe code** is *not* code that executes outside of the context of the .NET runtime, but rather code that uses C++ idioms deemed unsafe because they are often associated with bugs (such unsafe idioms would include pointers and pointer arithmetic).

In keeping with the spirit of liberty, C# does allow you to use such unsafe idioms, but only within special blocks of code prefixed with the `unsafe` keyword. Prefixing these blocks with the keyword signifies that you know the dangers to which you are exposing yourself, and serves as a flag to the C# compiler to lower the constraints on the unsafe code.

Using the C# Compiler

Overview

Freely distributed with the MS.NET SDK, the C# compiler, `csc.exe`, can be invoked from a DOS command line or from one of several graphical IDEs. These IDEs include the several shareware offerings that sprang up around the time that the PDC Tech Preview of C# was released as well as the VS.NET IDE that most readers will probably end up using.

The compiler's behavior is controlled by command line arguments. When you tell an IDE like VS.NET to compile a C# program, the IDE consults its settings to dynamically build the command string with the command line arguments and uses this string to shell out to a `csc.exe` process. Although using an IDE like VS.NET certainly saves you a lot of time and keystrokes, it's good to know the command line options for controlling the C# compiler in case you want to automate your organization's build process through scripts, batch files, and so on.

Again, the C# compiler does not output machine code. As has been mentioned previously, C# programs can only be compiled to MSIL. It's the job of the MS.NET runtime to translate that IL to machine code.

Input and Output Files

When invoking the C# compiler from the command line, you indicate your source file simply by listing its filename after the name of the compiler, `csc`. You indicate the name for the target file by using the output argument:

```
csc SourceFile.cs /out:TargetFile.exe
```

Compiling Different Project Types

As discussed earlier in this chapter, C# can be used to create different kinds of projects, such as console applications, Windows Form applications, components, and more. You use the `/target` command line option in order to tell the C# compiler what kind of project that it needs to build:

- ❑ The `/target:exe` argument tells the C# compiler to produce a console application.

- ❑ The `/target:winexe` argument tells the C# compiler to produce a Windows Form application.

- ❑ The `/target:library` argument tells the C# compiler to produce a stand-alone assembly containing a manifest.

- ❑ The `/target:module` arguments also tells the C# compiler to produce an assembly file, but without a manifest. Manifest-less assemblies produced with the `/target:module` argument can be subsumed into other assembly components that do contain manifests.

In all of these arguments, the `/target:` can be abbreviated as `/t:`.

Response Files

To make automating builds easier, the C# compiler supports **response files**. A response file contains a listing of command line options and can be linked in by a reference to the file when the compiler is invoked. You denote a response file on the command line by prefixing it with the "@" symbol:

```
csc /out:TargetFile.exe  @<responsefilename> SourceFile.cs
```

Summary

C# represents the next step in the evolution of programming languages. With its ability to create different types of projects, from class libraries to console apps to web interfaces, it presents the enterprise developer with a powerful tool for building client-server applications. It is a full-featured language with support for advanced facilities, such as attributes and reflection. The C# compiler, `csc.exe`, can be invoked from the VS.NET IDE or from the command line via command line arguments.

3

C# Basics

Now that you understand what C# can do, you'll probably want to learn how to use it. This chapter will give you a good start in that direction by providing you with a basic knowledge of the fundamentals of C# programming. If you're coming from a C++, Java, or VB6 background, we've included specific appendices to help you get started in C# quickly, and you might want to just skim over this chapter.

> **Note to VB Users: This chapter makes much of the similarities between C# and C/C++ in terms of keywords and general syntax. You are advised to read Appendix C, where C# and VB are directly compared, before reading this chapter.**

Getting Started

Let's start in the traditional way by looking at the simplest possible C# program – a simple console application that writes a message to the screen:

```
using System;

class MyFirstCSharpClass
{
    public static int Main()
    {
        Console.WriteLine("This isn't at all like Java!");
        return 0;
    }
}
```

You can compile this program simply by typing it into a text editor (such as Notepad), saving it with a .cs extension (for example, First.cs), and running the C# command line compiler (csc.exe) against the file:

```
csc First.cs
```

This will produce an executable file named First.exe, which we can run from the command line or from Windows Explorer like any other executable:

```
C:\WINNT\System32\cmd.exe

Microsoft Windows 2000 [Version 5.00.2195]
(C) Copyright 1985-2000 Microsoft Corp.

C:\>cd\ProCSharp

C:\ProCSharp>csc First.cs
Microsoft (R) Visual C# Compiler Version 7.00.9219 [CLR version v1.0.2901]
Copyright (C) Microsoft Corp 2000-2001. All rights reserved.


C:\ProCSharp>First
This isn't at all like Java!

C:\ProCSharp>
```

Well, maybe that message isn't quite true! There are some fairly fundamental similarities to Java here, although there are one or two points (such as the capitalized Main() function) to catch out the unwary Java or C++ émigré. Let's go through this program quickly to see the structure of a basic C# program.

First, let's make a few general comments. In C#, as in other C-style languages, every statement *must* end in a semi-colon, and statements can be joined into blocks using curly braces ({}). Statements can continue over multiple lines without needing a continuation character (such as the underscore in VB). Single-line comments begin with two forward slash characters (//), and multi-line comments begin with a slash and an asterisk (/*), and end with the same combination reversed (*/). As in Java, all code must be contained within a class (in our case, the MyFirstCSharpClass class) (or another type definition), and as we saw in Chapter 1, classes (and other types) in the .NET Framework are organized into **namespaces** (very similar to Java packages). In this case, we don't explicitly specify a namespace, so our class will be placed into the (nameless) global namespace.

The first line may be the most obscure to experienced Java and C++ developers. The using directive specifies the namespaces where the compiler should look to find any classes that aren't defined in the current namespace. This is very similar to the import statement in Java and to the using namespace statement in C++. C++ developers should be aware however, that it is very different from the #include directive, in that no code is physically included in the compiled file – the using directive simply tells the compiler where to look if it comes across any types which aren't in the current namespace and where the namespace isn't specified. In our case, we simply reference the standard System namespace, where the most commonly used .NET types reside. It's important to realize straight away that pretty well everything we do in C# depends on the .NET classes; in this case, we're using the Console class within the System namespace in order to write to the console window. C# has no built-in keywords of its own for input or output – it's completely reliant on the .NET classes.

Next, comes our class definition. At its simplest, this takes the form:

```
class classname
{
    // Class body
}
```

We'll look at classes in detail in Chapters 4 and 5, but for now it's enough to know that classes in C# are similar to classes in Java and C++, and very roughly comparable to class modules in VB6.

The actual code for the program is contained within the Main() method. Every C# executable (such as console applications, Windows applications, and Windows services) must have an entry point – a Main() method (note the capital M). This method is called when the program is started, similarly to the main() function in C++ or Java, or Sub Main() in a VB6 module. This method *must* return either nothing (void) or an integer (int). Method definitions in C# take the form:

```
[modifiers] return_type MethodName([parameters])
{
    // Method body
}
```

where the square brackets represent optional elements. Modifiers are used to specify certain features of the method we're defining, such as where the method can be called from. In our case, we have two modifiers: public and static. The public modifier means that the method can be accessed from anywhere, so it can be called from outside our class. The static modifier indicates that the method does not operate on a specific instance of our class, and therefore can be called without first instantiating the class. This is important, since we're creating an executable rather than a class library. We set the return type to int, and in this example, we don't include any parameters.

> **Note to VB Users:** The use of **static** in C# is not like the use of the **Static** keyword in VB.

Finally come the code statements themselves. In this case, we simply call the WriteLine() method of the System.Console class to write a line of text to the console window. WriteLine() is a static method, so we don't need to instantiate a Console object before calling it. We then call return to exit from the method (and, since this is the Main() method, the program). We specified int in our method header, therefore we must return an integer (in this case, zero).

C# Data Types

Now that we've seen just enough to get started, let's take a more systematic look at the main features of the language. We'll start by looking at the data types available in C#.

New, Specialized Types in the CTS

One of the nice things about VB (and one of the things that made it so productive) was the relatively rich set of data types that it provided to developers. It provided, for example, an intrinsic string type, a Boolean type, and a date/time type. This is in contrast to lower-level languages such as C and C++, which forced developers to construct their own data types by gluing primitives together into classes or structs, or to use messy templated code stored in header files (the STL) or complex proprietary libraries such as MFC.

Now C programmers have their own Rapid Application Development environment. Like the other .NET languages, C# supports the Common Type System (CTS), a collection of data types including not only the familiar primitives, such as int, char, float, etc., but also more complex types such as a native string type and a decimal type for monetary values. Furthermore, each of these data types is not merely a primitive, but an authentic class, with methods useful for formatting, serialization, type conversions, and more.

Type Safety

Several years ago, a space-bound rocket crashed just minutes after launch, costing the NASA millions of dollars. Upon investigation, it was discovered that the crash was the result of software failure. Specifically, the fault was traced to a buggy line of C code in which the programmer had mistakenly used a single "=" where a double "==" was needed, signifying an assignment statement instead of an equality test. Because C does not enforce type safety, the rocket's program had implicitly converted the result of the assignment statement into a Boolean value of true.

Although you may have not crashed a rocket, if you've spent any time programming in C/C++ you probably have made a similar error yourself. Such errors are hard to detect; you can spend hours poring over your source code looking for the implicit cast that's causing your problems. Spending hours seeking such miniscule errors is not acceptable in a corporate enterprise environment.

Consequently, C# is a strongly typed language. Among other things, this means that the dedicated Boolean type mentioned earlier does not automatically convert to an integer type. If you want such conversions, you have to ask for them explicitly, with an explicit cast. We look at casting between primitive types more thoroughly later on in this chapter.

Furthermore, C# allows you to specify how data types that you yourself create behave in the context of implicit and explicit casts. The syntax for specifying such typecasting behavior is covered in length in Chapter 6 (Advanced C# Topics).

Value Types and Reference Types

Data types in a C# program are stored in one or two places, depending on the specific type.

The first place is called the **stack**. This is used to store data of fixed length, such as ints (every int consists of four bytes). Every program in execution has its own separate stack that no other program can look into. When a function is called, all variables local to the calling function are **pushed** onto the program's stack, to be **popped** off later and retrieved when the thread of execution returns from the called function. If you've ever written a recursive program that generated an "out of stack space error", you've seen a situation in which a program pushed too many variables onto its stack and ran out of space.

The second place that a program can store data is called the **heap**. In older programming languages such as C and C++, the heap tended to be used partly to store data of variable length, such as strings, and partly to store data that needs to have a lifetime longer than the method in which it is first defined This is possible because when a function instantiates an object on the system's heap, that object will not be popped off and destroyed when the reference goes out of scope in the way that happens for stack-based objects, but instead can persist and be passed via a reference to other functions in the program. In C# the situation is slightly different as instead of the heap, we now have something called a **managed heap**. The managed heap is quite similar to the heap in its purpose, but operates internally in a more efficient way. Also, whereas in older languages, the developer would explicitly choose to use the heap for a given object, in C#, the choice is made by the compiler, based on the data type of the object.

C# divides its data types into two different categories based on which of these two locations that they are stored in. To put it simply, **value type** variables store their data on the stack, and **reference type** variables store their data on the heap. Accordingly, we will examine these two data areas in depth in Chapter 5.

The storage location of a data type implies how it will behave in the context of an assignment statement. Assigning one value variable to another value variable creates two distinct copies of the same data on the stack. In contrast, assigning one reference variable to another reference variable results in two references to the same location in memory.

In C#, basic data types like `bool` and `long` are value types. This means that if we declare a Boolean variable and assign it the value of another Boolean variable, we will have two separate Boolean values in memory. Later, if we change the value of the original Boolean variable, the value of the second Boolean variable does not change. These types are copied by value.

In contrast, most of the more complex C# data types, including classes that we ourselves declare, are reference types. They are allocated upon the heap, have lifetimes that can span multiple function calls, and can be accessed via one or several aliases. The CLR implements an elaborate algorithm to track which reference variables are still reachable, and which have been orphaned. Periodically, the CLR will "clean house", destroying orphaned objects and returning the memory that they once occupied back to the operating system.

We need to understand the difference between value data types and reference data types in order to understand how our variables behave in the context of assignment statements. Remember, although value types like `bool` and `long` are like classes in that they provide methods, they are like primitives in that they are created on the stack and result in copies in the context of assignment statements. Also, be aware that the `struct` type is a value type in C#.

Let's have a quick look at the difference between the behaviors of these two types. We'll create a class (reference type) named `RefTypeRectangle`, which has two fields named `Width` and `Height`. We'll instantiate this class, initializing it with values for these fields, create a copy of the object, and then change the values of the fields of the original object. We'll print out the values of the fields for the copy both before and after we change the fields of the original. We'll also define a struct named `ValTypeRectangle`, which is in all other respects identical to the class, and repeat the exercise (a struct in C# is very similar to a class, but a value type rather than a reference type). Here's the code to do that:

```
using System;

// Definition for the RefTypeRectangle class (Reference Type)
class RefTypeRectangle
{
   public int Width;
   public int Height;
}

// Definition for the ValTypeRectangle struct (Value Type)
// This is identical to the class, except that it's a value type
struct ValTypeRectangle
{
   public int Width;
   public int Height;
}

// Test client for the two types
class RefValTest
{
   public static int Main()
   {
      RefTypeRectangle rect1 = new RefTypeRectangle();
      rect1.Width = 10;
      rect1.Height = 15;
      RefTypeRectangle rect2 = rect1;
      Console.WriteLine("Dimensions of rect2 are " + rect2.Width +
                        " x " + rect2.Height);
      Console.WriteLine("Changing dimensions of rect1...");
      rect1.Width = 20;
      rect1.Height = 25;
      Console.WriteLine("Dimensions of rect2 now are " + rect2.Width +
                        " x " + rect2.Height);

      ValTypeRectangle rect3 = new ValTypeRectangle();
      //now set the width and height here
      ValTypeRectangle rect4 = rect3;
      Console.WriteLine("Dimensions of rect4 are " + rect4.Width +
                        " x " + rect4.Height);
      Console.WriteLine("Changing dimensions of rect3...");
      rect3.Width = 20;
      rect3.Height = 25;
      Console.WriteLine("Dimensions of rect4 now are " + rect4.Width +
                        " x " + rect4.Height);

      return 0;
   }
}
```

The output when we run this code is:

```
C:\WINNT\System32\cmd.exe                                              _□×

C:\ProCSharp>csc RefValTypes.cs
Microsoft <R> Visual C# Compiler Version 7.00.9219 [CLR version v1.0.2901]
Copyright <C> Microsoft Corp 2000-2001. All rights reserved.


C:\ProCSharp>RefValTypes
Dimensions of rect2 are 10 x 15
Changing dimensions of rect1...
Dimensions of rect2 now are 20 x 25
Dimensions of rect4 are 10 x 15
Changing dimensions of rect3...
Dimensions of rect4 now are 10 x 15

C:\ProCSharp>_
```

Notice how, when we change the fields of the original class, this also causes the fields of the copy to be changed. This is because classes are reference types; our two variables, rect1 and rect2, are merely references to the same location in memory where the object is stored. Therefore, changing the fields of one of them will also change the fields of the other. The behavior of the two structs, however, is quite different. Structs are value types, so when we declare a second struct and initialize it with the values of the first struct, this physically creates a second struct in memory. Therefore, changing the fields of the first struct, has no effect on the second.

This behavior gives us a clue as to why we need the two different groups of types. When copying primitives such as integers or passing them into methods, we probably want to copy the value, not the reference. More importantly, we don't want the overhead of creating an object on the heap every time we need an integer. When we're dealing with large objects however, it's far more efficient to copy a reference to the object than to copy the whole object. For example, if we pass a struct as a parameter into a method, all the data in the struct will need to be copied, and a new struct allocated on the stack. For this reason, we need to be careful about using structs, and should use them only as collections of simple data types. Using structs in this way can significantly improve performance, however, as they can reduce the overhead of instantiating objects.

C# Predefined Types

To facilitate working with the most common data types, the C# compiler recognizes a number of predefined types that map to types defined in the CTS. For example, we can declare an integer using the CTS type like this:

```
System.Int32 x;
```

This is somewhat alien to anyone coming from another language and used to types such as int and float. Fortunately, instead of having to reference the CTS System.Int32 type every time we want to declare an integer, we can use the C# alias int. Instead of the rather unwieldy declaration above, we can use the far more intuitive:

```
int x;
```

Apart from code readability, there is no difference between these two statements.

C# has fifteen of these predefined types, thirteen value types and two (`string` and `object`) reference types.

Value Types

The built-in value types represent primitives, such as integer and floating-point numbers, character, and Boolean types.

C# uses the same terse, flexible syntax for variable declaration as C and C++. To declare a value type, we simply give the name of the object's type followed by the name of the object itself. VB veterans will notice that there's no need for extra keywords like `Dim` or `As`:

```
int a;      // This declares an integer variable, a, on the stack.
a = 100;    // This assigns the value 100 to a.
```

Or, for convenience, we can declare a variable and initialize it with a value in one deft stroke:

```
int a = 100;
```

What's more, C# allows us to incorporate several variable declarations and instantiations on the same line, although this is generally considered bad form, because code written in this way is harder to understand and maintain:

```
int a = 100, b, c = 200, d;
```

VB6 programmers should be especially careful with the above syntax. A similar syntax in VB6 would create the first value as an integer type, and subsequent variables as variants. In multi-variable declarations in C-style languages, however, all subsequent variables are declared as being of the same data type of the first. In other words, in the example above, a is declared as an `int`, but b, c, and d are `int`s as well.

Value type declaration demonstrates another example of C#'s emphasis on safety. Briefly, the C# compiler requires that we explicitly initialize every value variable with a starting value before referring to that variable in an operation. Most modern compilers will flag violations of this as a warning, but the ever-vigilant C# compiler treats such violations as errors. This prevents us from unintentionally retrieving junk values from memory that is left over from other programs.

As an example, consider the following lines:

```
public static int Main()
{
   int d;
   Console.WriteLine(d);   // Can't do this! Need to initialize d
                           // before using it, e.g. int d = 2;
   return 0;
}
```

We try to use the variable d before we have initialized it with a value, so when we attempt to compile these lines, we will receive this message:

```
C:\My Documents\Visual Studio Projects\ConsoleApplication4\Class1.cs(21): Use of
unassigned local variable 'd'
```

Integer Types

C# supports eight predefined integer types:

Name	CTS Type	Description	Range
sbyte	System.SByte	8-bit signed integer	-128 to 127 (-2^7 to 2^7-1)
short	System.Int16	16-bit signed integer	-32768 to 32767 (-2^{15} to 2^{15}-1)
int	System.Int32	32-bit signed integer	-2147483648 to 2147483647 (-2^{31} to 2^{31}-1)
long	System.Int64	64-bit signed integer	-9223372036854775808 to 9223372036854775807 (-2^{63} to 2^{63}-1)
byte	System.Byte	8-bit unsigned integer	0 to 255 (0 to 2^8-1)
ushort	System.UInt16	16-bit unsigned integer	0 to 65535 (0 to 2^{16}-1)
uint	System.UInt32	32-bit unsigned integer	0 to 4294967295 (0 to 2^{32}-1)
ulong	System.UInt64	64-bit unsigned integer	0 to 18446744073709551615 (0 to 2^{64}-1)

Future versions of Windows will target 64-bit processors, which can move bits into and out of memory in larger chunks to achieve faster processing times. Consequently, C# supports provides a rich palette of signed and unsigned integer types ranging in size from 8 to 64 bits.

A byte is the standard 8-bit type for values in the range 0 to 255 inclusive. Be aware that, in keeping with its emphasis on type safety, C# regards the byte type and the char type as completely distinct, and any programmatic conversions between the two must be explicitly requested. Also be aware that unlike the other types in the integer family, a byte type is by default unsigned. Its signed version bears the special name sbyte. An sbyte can store values in the range -128 to 127 inclusive.

With .NET, a short is no longer quite so short. Specifically, a short is now 16 bits long and covers values in the range -32,768 to 32,767. Its unsigned version, ushort, covers values in the range 0 to 65535.

Even larger, the int type is 32 bits long, and can contain values in the range -2,147,483,648 to 2,147,483,647. Use uint for signed values in the range 0 to 4,294,967,295.

Now huge, the long type reserves 64 bits for values from -9,223,372,036,854,775,808 to 9,223,372,036,854,775,807. Its unsigned version ulong can hold values from zero to 18,446,744,073,709,551,615.

All integer-type variables can be assigned values in decimal or in hex notation. The latter require the `0x` prefix:

```
long x = 0x12ab;
```

If there is any ambiguity about whether an integer is `int`, `uint`, `long` or `ulong`, it will default to an `int`. In order to specify which of the other integer types the value is to take you can append one of the following characters to the number:

```
uint ui = 1234U;
long l = 1234L;
ulong ul = 1234UL;
```

We can also use lower case `u` and `l`, although the latter could be confused with the integer `1`.

Floating Point Numbers

Although C# provides a plethora of integer data types, it supports floating point types as well. They'll be familiar to C and C++ programmers:

Name	CTS Type	Description	Significant Figures	Range (approximate)
float	System. Single	32-bit single-precision floating point	7	$\pm 1.5 \times 10^{-45}$ to $\pm 3.4 \times 10^{38}$
double	System. Double	64-bit double-precision floating point	15/16	$\pm 5.0 \times 10^{-324}$ to $\pm 1.7 \times 10^{308}$

The `float` data type is for smaller floating-point values, for which less precision is required. Each float variable can have up to 7 digits. Therefore, the value of a `float` variable can range from 1.5×10^{-45} to 3.4×10^{38}, inclusive.

The `double` data type is bulkier than the `float` data type, but offers twice the precision (15 digits). Therefore, the value of a `float` variable can range from 5×10^{-324} to 1.7×10^{308}, inclusive.

If there is any ambiguity about whether the floating-point number is a `float` or a `double`, it will default to `double`. If we want to specify that the value is a `float`, we append the character F (or f) to it:

```
float f = 12.3F;
```

Decimal Type

In addition, there is a `decimal` type representing higher precision floating point numbers:

Name	CTS Type	Description	Significant Figures	Range (approximate)
decimal	System. Decimal	128-bit high precision decimal notation	28	$\pm 1.0 \times 10^{-28}$ to $\pm 7.9 \times 10^{28}$

One of the great things about the CTS and C# is the provision of a dedicated type for financial calculations. This is the `decimal` type, and it allows us to specify currency amounts in the range 1.0 x 10^{-28} to 7.9 x 10^{28}. How you use the 28 digits that the decimal type provides is up to you. In other words, you can track smaller dollar or pound amounts with greater accuracy for cents, or larger dollar or pound amounts with more rounding in the fractional area.

To specify that our number is of a `decimal` type rather than a `double`, `float` or an integer, we can append the M (or m) character to the value, like so:

```
decimal d = 12.30M;
```

Although `decimal` is designed to allow the high accuracy, you might need in financial calculations, you can use anywhere where you need a high precision number that may have a fractional part.

Boolean Type

The C# `bool` type is used to contain Boolean values of either `true` or `false`:

Name	CTS Type	Values
bool	System.Boolean	true and false

We cannot convert `bool` values to and from integer values. If a variable (or a function return type) is declared as a `bool`, then we can only use values of `true` and `false`. We will get an error if we try to use zero for `false` and a non-zero value for `true`.

Character Type

For storing the value of a single character, C# supports the `char` data type:

Name	CTS Type	Values
char	System.Char	Represents a single 16-bit (Unicode) character

Although this data type has a superficial resemblance to the `char` type provided by C and C++, there's a significant difference.

In our prior discussion on type safety, we mentioned that implicit conversions between the `char` type and the 8-bit `byte` type were not permitted. This is at least partly because the data types are different sizes – the `char` type is 16 bits long.

81

Although eight bits may be enough to encode every character in the English language and the digits 0-9, they aren't enough to encode every character in more expansive symbol systems (such as Chinese). In a gesture towards universality, the computer industry is moving away from the 8-bit character set and towards the 16-bit Unicode scheme, of which the ASCII encoding is a subset.

Keep in mind that char values are 16-bit Unicode values, particularly when manipulating them from pointers in embedded blocks of unsafe code. You'll learn more about unsafe code in Chapter 6.

Literals of type char are signified by being enclosed in single quotes, for example 'A'. If we try to enclose a character in double quotes, the compiler will treat this as a string, and throw an error.

As well as representing chars as character literals, we can represent them with four-digit hex Unicode values (for example '\u0041'), as integer values with a cast (for example, (char) 65), or as hexadecimal values ('\x0041'). They can also contain an escape sequence:

Escape Sequence	Character
\'	Single quote
\"	Double quote
\\	Backslash
\0	Null
\a	Alert
\b	Backspace
\f	Form feed
\n	Newline
\r	Carriage return
\t	Tab character
\v	Vertical tab

C++ developers should note that because C# has a native string type, we don't need to represent strings as arrays of chars.

Reference Types

We've said that C# allows the use of pointers only in very limited circumstances. How, then, does a C# programmer manipulate objects on the heap? Imagine we have a class called Something, and consider the following line of code:

```
Something objSomething;
```

In C++, the above line would create an instance of the Something class on the stack and point objSomething at it. In C#, this same line of code would only create a **reference** for a Something object, one which has not yet been instantiated. Any attempt to call a method or property through that null reference would result in an error.

Instantiating a reference object in C# requires use of the new keyword. In C#, we create a reference, and then point the reference at an object allocated on the heap with the new keyword:

```
Something objSomething;              // This reference isn't pointing
                                     // at anything yet.
objSomething = new Something();      // This initiates a Something on the heap.
```

We will look at object-oriented programming in C# in detail in Chapters 4 and 5.

C# supports two predefined reference types:

Name	CTS Type	Description
object	System.Object	The root type, from which all other types in the CTS derive (including value types).
string	System.String	Unicode character string.

The Object Type

Many programming languages and class hierarchies provide a root type, from which all other objects in the hierarchy derive. C# and .NET are no exception. In C#, the object type is the ultimate parent type from which all other intrinsic and user-defined types derive.

We can use an object reference to bind to an object of any particular sub-type. For example, later in this chapter we'll see how we can use the object type to box a value object on the stack to move it to the heap. Object references are also useful in reflection, when code must manipulate objects whose specific types are unknown.

Additionally, the object type implements a number of basic, general-purpose methods, which include Equals(), GetHashCode(), GetType(), and ToString(). Responsible user-defined classes that play well with others may need to provide replacement implementations of some of these methods using an object oriented technique known as overriding, which we will discuss in Chapter 4. When we override ToString(), for example, we equip our class with a method for intelligently providing a string representation of itself. If we don't provide our own implementations for these methods in our classes, the compiler will pick up the implementations in object, which may or may not be correct or sensible in the context of our classes.

The String Type

Veterans of C and C++ probably have battle scars from wrestling with C-style strings. A C or C++ string was nothing more than an array of characters, therefore the client programmer had to do a lot of work just to copy one string to another or to concatenate two strings. In fact, for a generation of C++ programmers, implementing a string class that wrapped up the messy details of these operations was a rite of passage requiring many hours of teeth gnashing and head scratching, while chasing memory leaks and faulty overloaded operators.

Fortunately, C# provides its own `string` type. With it, operations like string concatenation and string copying are a snap:

```
string str1 = "Hello ";
string str2 = "World";
string str3 = str1 + str2;
```

Despite this value type-style assignation, the CTS `System.String` type is a reference type. Behind the scenes, a `string` object is allocated on the heap, not the stack. Thus, when we assign one string variable to another string, we get two references to the same string in memory. Should we however then make changes to one of these strings, note that this will create an entirely new `string` object, leaving the other string unchanged. Consider the code:

```
using System;

class StringExample
{
    public static int Main()
    {
        string s1 = "A string";
        string s2 = s1;
        Console.WriteLine("s1 is " + s1);
        Console.WriteLine("s2 is " + s2);
        s1 = "Another string";
        Console.WriteLine("s1 is now " + s1);
        Console.WriteLine("s2 is now " + s2);
        return 0;
    }
}
```

(Note to VB users, the way to concatenate strings in C# uses + not &.)

The output from this is:

```
s1 is A string
s2 is A string
s1 is now Another string
s2 is now A string
```

In other words, changing the value of s1 had no effect on s2, contrary to what we'd expect with a reference type! What's happening here is that when s1 is initialized with the value "A string", a new string object is allocated on the heap. When s2 is initialized, the reference points to this same object, so s2 also has the value "A string". However, when we now change the value of s1, instead of replacing the original value, a new object will be allocated on the heap for the new value. Our s2 variable will still point to the original object, so its value is unchanged.

String literals are enclosed in double quotes (" ... "); if we attempt to enclose a string in single quotes, the compiler will take the value as a `char`, and throw an error. C# strings can contain the same Unicode and hexadecimal escape sequences as `chars`. Because these escape sequences start with a backslash therefore, we can't use this character unescaped in a string. Instead, we need to escape it with another backslash (`"\\"`):

```
string filepath = "C:\\ProfessionalCSharp\\First.cs";
```

Even if you're confident you can remember to do this all the time, it can prove annoying typing out all those double backslashes. Fortunately, C# gives us an alternative. We can prefix a string literal with the at character (@), and all the characters in it will be treated at face value – they won't be interpreted as escape characters:

```
string filepath = @"C:\ProfessionalCSharp\First.cs";
```

This even allows us to include line breaks in our string literals:

```
string Jabberwocky = @"'Twas brillig and the slithy toves
Did gyre and gimble in the wabe.";
```

Note that the formatting of the above string seems to have gone awry, in that the two lines of text are no longer aligned on the page. If we had aligned them as follows:

```
string Jabberwocky = @"'Twas brillig and the slithy toves
                        Did gyre and gimble in the wabe.";
```

Then the value of Jabberwocky would be this:

```
'Twas brillig and the slithy toves
                        Did gyre and gimble in the wabe.
```

with over 20 spaces between the two lines.

Complex Types

As well as the predefined types we've already met, C# and the .NET Framework allow us to define our own complex types based on these simple types. Most of these complex types will be covered in more detail in later chapters, but we will list all the forms here for completeness. As with primitives, the complex types can be divided into value and reference types.

Value Types

There are two sorts of value types we can define ourselves. We've already briefly met structs. In addition, we can define our own enumerations (sets of integers which represent specific predefined values).

Structs

As you may already know, stack-allocated types have at least three advantages over heap-allocated types. First, stack or value types can be allocated much more quickly than heap-allocated types. Second, values on the stack are instantly and automatically deallocated once they go out of scope. Third, and most importantly, it's easy to copy the value of one value type variable into another value type variable; you just use the equals sign:

```
int a = 100;
int b;
b = a;
```

Compared to value type variables, copying values between objects on the heap is hard. Usually you have to create a special method to handle that scenario.

In C#, a struct is special kind of class that is a value type rather than a reference type. Because a struct is on the stack, it can be created and copied slightly more efficiently than a class can. Consider the following struct for representing subscribers:

```
public struct Subscriber
{
    public long SubscriberID;
    public string FirstName;
    public string MiddleName;
    public string LastName;
    public decimal Balance;
}
```

If we want to copy the values from one struct to another, all we have to use is the equals sign. Below, we create one Subscriber object, objSubscriber1, and set its values. Only one line the last is required to copy all of those values from objSubscriber1 to objSubscriber2, another instance of the Subscriber struct:

```
Subscriber   Subscriber1;
Subscriber   Subscriber2;

Subscriber1 = new Subscriber();
Subscriber1.FirstName = "John";
Subscriber1.MiddleName = "Q";
Subscriber1.LastName = "Public";
Subscriber1.decBalance = 100;

Subscriber2 = Subscriber1;
```

Note that we're using the new operator to initialize a struct, even though structs are value types. However, the struct is actually available and its fields can be set even before we call new. The struct is initialized as soon as it is declared; all its fields will be set to default (zero) values. Note however, that the compiler won't allow us to copy the struct into another struct, or to read its field values before they are set if it hasn't first been initialized by using the new keyword or by setting all of its fields.

In addition to making copy code simpler, structs make function calls tidier, too. In fact, programmers often use structs to group together related data to be passed by value to another function; it's tidier to package all the related data into one variable and pass it than to pass 5 or 6 different arguments:

```
//We load the struct with information.
DataAccess.LoadSubscriber(out SubscriberID, Subscriber1);

//We modify the information.
Subscriber1.decBalance = Subscriber1.decBalance- 100;

//We update a database with the new information.
DataAccess.UpdateSubscriber(SubscriberID, Subscriber1);
```

If you're a C or C++ guru, you need to be careful with structs in C# – they've changed. In C and C++, the only big difference between a class and a struct was that a struct's data members were public rather than private by default. Structs in C# are a whole new ballgame. Not only are their data members private by default, but as we've seen, instances of structs are allocated in a different place in memory than instances of classes are.

In C#, a struct can do most things a class can do (although they don't support implementation inheritance), but you need to use them wisely. Because instances of structs take up stack space, they're best suited for representing relatively small objects. That's one reason that they were used to implement all of the other value data types in the .NET framework.

Enumerations

An enumeration is a user-defined integer type. When we declare an enumeration, we specify a set of acceptable values that instances of that enumeration can contain. Not only that, but we can give the values user-friendly names. If, somewhere in our code, we attempt to assign a value that is not in the acceptable set to an instance of that enumeration, the compiler will flag an error.

While programming, you've probably encountered a situation in which an enumeration would be useful. For instance, you've probably designed a class with a property that could be set to one of several pre-determined values. Or, you've created a function that can behave in one of several distinct ways based on a particular value of one of its input arguments (a function like SetWindowLong).

There are at least three benefits to using enumerations instead of plain integers:

❑ As mentioned, enumerations make your code easier to maintain by helping to ensure that your variables are assigned only legitimate, anticipated values.

❑ Enumerations make your code clearer by allowing you to refer to integer values by descriptive names rather than by obscure magic numbers.

❑ Enumerations make your code easier to type, too. When you go to assign a value to an instance of an enumerated type, the VS.NET IDE will, through Intellisense, pop up a list box of acceptable values in order to save you some keystrokes.

In programming, creating an enumeration is one of those little favors that you do yourself that ends up saving you lots of time and headaches in the long run. An intelligent and appropriate use of enumerations is one of the hallmarks of a professional developer.

We can define an enumeration as follows:

```
public enum TimeOfDay
{
   Morning = 0,
   Afternoon = 1,
   Evening = 2
}
```

In this case, we use an integer value to represent each period of the day in the enumeration. We can now access these values as members of the enumeration. For example, TimeOfDay.Morning will return the value 0. We will typically use this enumeration to pass an appropriate value into a method, and iterate through the possible values in a switch statement (we'll look at switch statements later in the chapter, but they're roughly equivalent to Select Case statements in VB):

```
class EnumExample
{
   public static int Main()
   {
      WriteGreeting(TimeOfDay.Morning);
      return 0;
   }

   static void WriteGreeting(TimeOfDay timeOfDay)
   {
      switch(timeOfDay)
      {
         case TimeOfDay.Morning:
            Console.WriteLine("Good morning!");
            break;
         case TimeOfDay.Afternoon:
            Console.WriteLine("Good afternoon!");
            break;
         case TimeOfDay.Evening:
            Console.WriteLine("Good evening!");
            break;
         default:
            Console.WriteLine("Hello!");
            break;
      }
   }
}
```

Reference Types

As well as classes, C# supports a number of other complex reference types: interfaces, delegates, and arrays.

Classes

Classes are the fundamental user-defined types in C# and the .NET Framework. Almost all C# executables have at least one class (it's theoretically possible to use a struct instead), which contains the `Main()` method – the entry point for the program. Classes are composite data types consisting of data members (fields, constants and events) and functions (chiefly methods and properties, but also operators, and so on); in other words, a class is the encapsulation of data and the functionality for accessing and working on that data. Classes can also contain nested data types.

We'll look at classes later in this chapter, and in much more detail in Chapters 4 and 5.

Interfaces

Interfaces are used to define functionality for classes which implement them. They can contain properties, methods, events, and indexers, but interfaces cannot be instantiated and do not define the implementation of these functions. For example, if an interface contains a method, it will define the return type and the arguments for the method, but it won't contain any of the code to implement it. Any classes implementing this interface will need to provide their own implementation of the method. We will look at interfaces in Chapter 5.

Delegates

Delegates are types which refer to methods. They are similar to function pointers in C++, but allow us to instantiate and call both the static methods of a class, and the methods of a specific instance of a class. Delegates allow us to determine at runtime which of a certain set of methods we want to call. We will look at delegates in Chapter 6.

Arrays

In C and C++, the name of an array is just a pointer to an address in memory, and the index to an array is simply an offset from that address. This is demonstrated by the fact that an element in a C or C++ array can be referenced using a pointer to the array element, calculated by adding the index of the element to the address of the first element:

```
// In C++, these assignments are both legal and equivalent.
a[100] = 1;
*(a + 100) = 1;
```

Although the C/C++ approach to arrays is flexible – you can do some fancy things with pointer arithmetic to move from element to element – it's also error prone. Because C and C++ do not track the size of the arrays therefore, there's nothing to stop a program from referencing an element outside the bounds of an array, possibly corrupting other, reserved data, and generating an error:

```
// In C++, this slips by the compiler.
char *pString = new char[50];
pString[100] = '\0';              // 100 is not within the allocated range
                                  // of the array.
```

To overcome the shortcomings of C and C++, C# supports the array as a definite, distinct type. By treating arrays as objects with methods and properties (including ranges), the CLR is able to catch these kinds of out-of-bounds errors. Moreover, if an index-out-of-bounds error occurs during the course of a C# program, the CLR will throw a special type of error object that error handling routines can specifically respond to.

C#'s Array Syntax

C# takes such a different approach to arrays, it enforces a unique syntax for them. As in other C-style languages, arrays are declared by fixing a set of square brackets to the end of the variable type of the individual elements (note that all the elements in an array must be of the same data type). For example, while int represents a single integer, int[] represents an array of integers:

```
int[] Integers;
```

To initialize the array with specific dimensions, we can use the new keyword, giving the size in the square brackets after the type name:

```
// Create a new array of 32 ints
int[] Integers = new int[32];
```

To access an individual element within the array, we use the normal syntax, placing the index of the element in square brackets after the name of the array. All C# arrays use zero-based indexing, so we can reference the first variable with the index zero:

```
Integer[0] = 35;
```

Accordingly, we reference the last, or thirty-second, value with an index value of 31:

```
aryInteger[31] = 432;
```

C#'s array syntax is flexible, too. In fact, C# allows us to declare arrays without initializing them, so that the array can be dynamically sized later in the program. With this technique, we're basically creating a null reference, and later pointing that reference at a dynamically allocated stretch of memory locations requested with the new keyword:

```
int[] Integers;
Integers = new int[32];
```

This syntax is certainly a lot easier than using `malloc` and `sizeof`. It's a lot less prone to memory leaks, too. In C or C++, a segment of memory referenced by an array could remain allocated on the heap unless specifically deallocated. In contrast, C# arrays, like other C# objects, are managed by the CLR and marked for automatic deallocation once they are no longer referenced.

One of the nice features of C and C++ arrays was the way that you could provide an array with a hard-coded list of initial values in curly braces. Thankfully, C# preserves this handy capability:

```
string[] String = {"first element", "second element", "third element"};
```

This is the equivalent of:

```
string[] String = new string[] { "first element", "second element",
                                  "third element"};
```

There are several pitfalls that you should avoid when initializing arrays with this syntax. For instance, you cannot use a variable to set how many elements the array will contain:

```
int len = 3;
// The following statement will not compile
string[] String = new string[len] { "first element", "second element",
                                     "third element"};
```

However declaring a constant for the length of the array is allowed:

```
const int len = 3;
// Allowed
string[] String = new string[len] { "first element", "second element",
                                     "third element"};
```

Using this syntax, you cannot determine at runtime how large an array will be. If you want an array whose length is determined dynamically or an array that can be extended at runtime, you have to create an instance of the `ArrayList` object, which is in the `System.Collections` namespace. This is covered in detail in Chapter 7.

Also, you cannot assign more values to an array as there are elements:

```
// The following statement will not compile
string[] String = new string[3] { "first element", "second element",
                                   "third element", "fourth element"};
```

> **Note to VB Users: arrays in C# use square brackets, not parentheses.**

Working with Arrays

Because arrays are represented by a specific type in C#, they have their own methods, for example to get the length of the array. This means that working with arrays in C# is very easy indeed.

For example, to find out the size of a one-dimensional array, we can use the `Length` property:

```
int ArrayLength = Integers.Length
```

If the array has more than one dimension, we can get the length of any specific dimension using the `GetLength` method:

```
// Get the length of the first dimension
int ArrayLength = Integers.GetLength(0);
```

If the array elements are of one of the predefined types, we can also sort the array into ascending order using the `Sort` method:

```
Array.Sort(String);
```

Notice, that we call this as a static method of the `Array` class, and not as a method of our array instance. We specify the array we want to sort by passing it in as a parameter to the method.

> *Sorting can alternatively be achieved using the `System.Array.Sort` method and the `IComparer` interface, but we'll demonstrate it this way as an example of delegates in Chapter 6.*

Finally, we can reverse the existing order of the elements in an array using the `Reverse()` method (again called as a static method, passing the array instance in as a parameter):

```
Array.Reverse(String);
```

The following short example stores a short list of famous artists' names in a string array, sorts the array into reverse alphabetical order, and then loops through the array to display each name in order in the console window:

```
// Define an array of artists' names
string[] Artists = {"Leonardo", "Monet", "Van Gogh", "Klee"};

// Sort the array elements alphabetically
Array.Sort(Artists);

// Reverse the array to sort it in descending order
Array.Reverse(Artists);

// Loop through each element and print out the name
for (int i = 0; i < Artists.Length; i++)
{
    Console.WriteLine(Artists[i]);
}
```

Multidimensional Arrays in C#

C# supports multidimensional arrays in two varieties. The first kind is the **rectangular** array. A two-dimensional rectangular array is one in which every row has the same number of columns. As demonstrated in the following example, rectangular arrays are relatively simple to declare and initialize. Here, we declare a two-dimensional rectangular array of four rows, each of which has exactly two columns:

```
string[,] BeatleName = { {"Lennon","John"},
                         {"McCartney","Paul"},
                         {"Harrison","George"},
                         {"Starkey","Richard"} };
```

Note that we use a comma to separate the dimensions in the array declaration, even though we don't actual specify the size of the dimensions. In order, to declare a three-dimensional string array, we would use:

```
string[,,] Strings;
```

An alternative way of initializing the array would be to use nested `for` loops:

```
double [,] Matrix = new double[10,10];
for (int I = 0 ; I < 10 ; I++)
{
    for (int J=0 ; J<10 ; J++)
        Matrix[I,J] = 4;
}
```

The second kind of multidimensional array that C# supports is the orthogonal, or so-called **jagged** array. A jagged two-dimensional array is one in which every row can have a different number of columns. Although obviously more flexible than rectangular arrays, jagged arrays are, as you might guess, more difficult to instantiate and initialize. In creating a jagged array, we're basically creating an array *of* arrays:

```
// This creates a jagged array
int[][] a = new int[3][];
a[0] = new int[4];
a[1] = new int[3];
a[2] = new int[1];
```

Here, instead of using commas to indicate the number of dimensions in the array, we use an extra set of square brackets for each dimension. Therefore, to declare a three-dimensional jagged array of ints, we would use:

```
int[][][] Ints;
```

Iterating through the elements in a jagged array requires more work than iterating through the elements in a rectangular array, too. As you loop through each row, you have to use the array's GetLength method to dynamically ascertain the number of columns that you should loop through:

```
// Declare a two-dimension jagged array of authors' names
string[][] Novelists = new string[3][];
Novelists[0] = new string[] { "Fyodor", "Mikhailovich", "Dostoyevsky" };
Novelists[1] = new string[] { "James", "Augustine", "Aloysius", "Joyce" };
Novelists[2] = new string[] { "Miguel", "de Cervantes", "Saavedra" };

// Loop through each novelist in the array
int i;
for (i = 0; i < Novelists.GetLength(0); i++)
{
    // Loop through each name for the novelist
    int j;
    for (j = 0; j < Novelists[i].GetLength(0); j++)
    {
        // Display current part of name
        Console.Write(Novelists[i][j] + " ");
    }
    // Start a new line for the next novelist
    Console.Write("\n");
}
```

Type Conversions

We often need to convert data from one type to another. Consider the code:

```
byte value1 = 10;
byte value2 = 23;
byte total;
total = value1 + value2;    // When two byte values are added, they are
                            // implicitly converted to int, so attempting
                            // to put the result back into a byte will
                            // cause an error
Console.WriteLine(total);
```

When we attempt to compile these lines, we get the error: Cannot implicitly convert type 'int' to 'byte'. The problem here is that when we add two bytes together, the result will be returned as an int, not as another byte. This is because a byte can only contain eight bits of data (up to 255), so adding two bytes together could very easily result in a value which can't be stored in a single byte. If we do want to store this result in a byte variable, then we're going to have to convert it back to a byte. There are two ways this can happen: implicitly, which means that the compiler will make the conversion for us, without us asking it to, or explicitly, which means that the we specifically ask the compiler to convert the value into another data type.

Implicit Conversions

Conversion between types can be achieved automatically, only if, by doing so, the value is not changed in any way. This means that the value of a short or int can be assigned to a long variable without any trouble. We can also assign an unsigned variable to a signed variable so long as the value fits between the limits of the signed variable, and certain conversions from integer to floating point types can be achieved.

This is why our previous code failed; by attempting a conversion from an int to a byte, we're potentially losing three bytes of data. The compiler isn't going to let us do that unless we explicitly tell it that that's what we want to do! If we store the result in a long instead of a byte however, we'll have no problems:

```
byte value1 = 10;
byte value2 = 23;
long total;
total = value1 + value2;
Console.WriteLine(total);
```

This is because a long holds more bytes of data than an int, so there's no risk of data being lost. In these circumstances, the compiler is happy to make the conversion for us, without us needing to ask for it explicitly.

The table below shows the implicit type conversions that are supported in C#:

From	To
sbyte	short, int, long, float, double, decimal
byte	short, ushort, int, uint, long, ulong, float, double, decimal
short	int, long, float, double, decimal
ushort	int, uint, long, ulong, float, double, decimal
int	long, float, double, decimal
uint	long, ulong, float, double, decimal
long, ulong	float, double, decimal
float	double
char	ushort, int, uint, long, ulong, float, double, decimal

Note that we can only perform implicit conversions from a smaller integer type to a larger one or from an unsigned integer to a signed integer of the same size. This means that we cannot convert from a uint to an int or vice versa as the two types do not cover the same range and so data could be lost in the conversion. However, we can convert from a uint to a long as the range of a uint is basically the upper (zero and above) range of the long. We can also convert between integers and floating point values. The rules are slightly different here. Though we can convert between types of the same size, such as int/uint to float and long/ulong to double, we can convert from long/ulong back to float. We might lose four bytes of data doing this, but this only means that the value of the float we receive will be less precise than if we had used a double; the magnitude of the value would not be affected at all. The float-to-double conversion follows the same pattern as for signed integers.

Explicit Conversions

However, there are still many conversions that cannot be implicitly made between types and the compiler will give an error if any are attempted. These are some of the transformations that cannot be made implicitly:

- ❑ `int` to `short` – may lose data
- ❑ `int` to `uint` – may lose data
- ❑ `uint` to `int` – may lose data
- ❑ `float` to `int` – will lose everything after the decimal point
- ❑ any numeric type to `char` – will lose data
- ❑ `decimal` to any numeric type – because the decimal type is internally structured differently to both integers and floating point numbers

However, we can explicitly carry out such transformations using **casts**. When we cast one type to another, we deliberately force the compiler to make the transformation. The general syntax for a cast is:

```
long val = 30000;
int i = (int)val;      // A valid cast. The maximum int is 2147483647
```

where the cast is denoted by the type to be cast to in parentheses before the value to be modified. For programmers familiar with C, this is the typical syntax for casts. For those familiar with the C++ special cast keywords such as `static_cast`, these do not exist in C# and you have to use the older C-type syntax.

This can be a dangerous operation to undertake, so you need to know what you are doing. Even a simple cast from a `long` to an `int` can land you in trouble if the value of the original `long` is greater than the maximum value of an `int`. If you run this code:

```
long val = 3000000000;
int i = (int)val;          // An invalid cast. The maximum int is 2147483647
```

In this case, you will not get an error, but you will not get the result you expect. If you run the code above and output the value stored in `i`, this is what you get:

```
-1294967296
```

You should never assume that the cast will give the results you expect. We'll see later on that C# provides a `checked` operator, which we can use to test whether an operation causes a stack overflow. We can use this operator to check that a cast is safe and to cause the runtime to throw an overflow exception if it isn't:

```
long val = 3000000000;
int i = checked((int)val);
```

Bearing in mind that all casts are potentially unsafe, you should take care to include code in your application to deal with possible failures of the casts. We will introduce structured exception handling using `try` and `catch` later on in the chapter, a useful and essential programmatic tool which will feature much in the remainder of this book.

Using casts we can convert most data types from one type to another, for example:

```
double price = 25.30;
int approximatePrice = (int)(price + 0.5);
```

This will give the price rounded to the nearest dollar. However, in this transformation, data is lost – namely everything after the decimal point. Therefore, such a transformation should never be used if you want to go on to do more calculations using this modified price value. However, it is useful if you want to output the approximate value of a completed or partially completed calculation – if you do not want to bother the user with lots of figures after the decimal point.

This example shows what happens if you convert an unsigned integer into a char:

```
ushort c = 43;
char symbol = (char)c;
Console.WriteLine(symbol);
```

The output is the character that has an ASCII number of 43, that is the + sign. You can try out any kind of transformation you want between the numeric types (including char), however ludicrous it appears, and it will work, such as converting a decimal into a char, or vice versa:

```
decimal d = 65m;
char symbol = (char)d;          // Gives you the letter A

char c = 'A';
decimal val = (decimal)c;       // Gives you the number 65
```

However, if the value that results from the cast operation cannot be fitted into the new data type, the cast seems to work but the result is not as you would expect. Take this example:

```
int i = -1;
char symbol = (char)i;
```

This cast should not work as the char type cannot take negative values. However, you do not get an error and instead the symbol variable is assigned the value of a question mark (?).

Converting between value types is not just restricted to isolated variables as we have shown. We can convert an array element of type double to a struct member variable of type int:

```
struct ItemDetails
{
    public string Description;
    public int ApproxPrice;
}

...

double[] Prices = { 25.30, 26.20, 27.40, 30.00 };

ItemDetails id;
id.Description = "Whatever";
id.ApproxPrice = (int)(Prices[0] + 0.5);
```

Using explicit casts and a bit of care and attention you can just about transform any instance of a simple value type to any other. However there are limitations on what we can do with explicit type conversions – as far as value types are concerned, we can only convert to and from the numeric and char types and enum types. We can't directly cast Booleans to any other type or vice versa.

If we do need to convert between numeric and string, for example, there are methods provided in the .NET class library. The object class has a ToString() method, which all classes should implement. This returns a string representation of the object, so we can retrieve a string representation of an int using the code:

```
int i = 10;
string s = i.ToString();
```

Similarly, if we need to parse a string to retrieve a numeric or Boolean value, we can use the Parse method supported by all the predefined value types:

```
string s = "100";
int i = int.Parse(s);
Console.WriteLine(i + 50);    // Add 50 to prove it's really an int
```

We'll see in Chapter 6 how we can define casts for our own classes and structs.

Boxing and Unboxing

We've seen that all types, both the simple predefined types such as int and char, and the complex types such as classes and structs, derive from the object type. This means that we can treat even literal values as though they were objects:

```
string s = 10.ToString();
```

However, we also saw that C# data types are divided into value types, which just contain a set amount of data and are allocated on the stack, and reference types, which are not of a predetermined size, and are allocated on the heap. How does this square with the ability to call methods on an int, if the int is nothing more than a four-byte value on the stack?

The way C# achieves this is through a bit of magic calling **boxing**. Boxing and unboxing allow us to convert value types to reference types and vice versa. This has been included in the section on casting as this is essentially what we are doing – we're casting our value to the object type. Boxing is the term used to describe the transformation of a value type to a reference type. Basically, the runtime creates a temporary reference-type "box" for the object on the heap.

This conversion can occur implicitly, as in the example above, but we can also perform it manually:

```
int i = 20;
object o = i;
```

Unboxing is the term used to describe the reverse process, where the value of a reference type is cast to a value type. We use the term "cast" here, as this has to be done explicitly. The syntax is similar to explicit type conversions already described:

```
int i = 20;
object o = i;     // Box the int
int j = (int)o;   // Unbox it back into an int
```

We can only unbox a variable that has previously been boxed.

One word of warning. When unboxing, we have to be careful that the receiving value variable has enough room to store all the bytes in the value being unboxed. C#'s ints, for example, are only 32 bits long, so unboxing a long value (64 bits) into an int will result in an error. Consider this code:

```
long a = 333333423;      // a is a local long stored on the stack.
object b = (object)a;    // b is a reference to a copy of a
                         // in a box the heap.
int c = (int)b;          // Error: a long variable is
                         // unboxed into an int.
```

Here, the value in a 64-bit long value in a is boxed onto the heap, then unboxed back into a 32-bit int. If this code is executed, c will simply not have enough bits to store a value of that size. Attempting to unbox a value from the heap into an inappropriate value type variable will result in a runtime error. When you box a value-type variable, it's up to you as the programmer to remember the variable's original type; attempts to unbox it to another type are likely to result in a runtime error.

Variables

As we've already seen, we declare variables in C# using the syntax:

```
[modifiers] datatype identifier;
```

For example:

```
public int i;  // A class field. Local variables cannot have access modifiers
```

This statement declares an int named i with an access level of public (that is, the variable can be accessed from anywhere). The compiler won't actually let us use this variable until we've initialized it with a value, but the declaration allocates four bytes on the stack to hold the value.

Once it's been declared, we can assign a value to the variable using the assignment operator (=):

```
i = 10;
```

If you're coming from VB6, remember that C# doesn't distinguish between objects and simple types, so there's no need for anything like the Set keyword, even if we want our variable to point to an object.

If we declare and initialize more than one variable in a single statement, all the variables will be of the same data type and declared with the same modifiers:

```
public static int x = 10, y =20; // x and y are both public static ints
```

We can't assign different modifiers or data types within a multiple variable declaration, so we can't do this:

```
public int x = 10, private byte y = 20; // Won't compile!
```

This is sensible, because we wouldn't save any typing, and it would be much less clear which types and modifiers applied to which variables.

A final point to note, is that variables with the same name can't be declared twice in the same scope, so we can't do this:

```
int x = 20;
// some more code
int x = 30;
```

We will look at the scoping of variables shortly.

Identifiers

Identifiers are the names we give to variables, to user-defined types such as classes and structs, and to members of these types. Identifiers are case sensitive, so `identifier` and `Identifier` would be different variables. There are a couple of rules determining what identifiers we can use in C#. First, they must begin with a letter or underscore, although they can contain numeric characters second, we can't use C# keywords as identifiers. C# has 76 of these reserved words:

abstract	do	implicit	params	switch
as	double	in	private	this
base	else	int	protected	throw
bool	enum	interface	public	true
break	event	internal	readonly	try
byte	explicit	is	ref	typeof
case	extern	lock	return	uint
catch	false	long	sbyte	ulong
char	finally	namespace	sealed	unchecked
checked	fixed	new	short	unsafe
class	float	null	sizeof	ushort
const	for	object	stackalloc	using
continue	foreach	operator	static	virtual
decimal	goto	out	string	void
default	if	override	struct	while
delegate				

If we do need to use one of these words as an identifier (for example, if we're accessing a class written in a different language), we can prefix the identifier with the "@" symbol to indicate to the compiler that what follows is to be treated as an identifier, not as a C# keyword (so abstract is not a valid identifier, but @abstract is).

Finally, identifiers can also contain Unicode characters, specified using the syntax \u*XXXX*, where *XXXX* is the four-digit hex code for the Unicode character. The following are some examples of valid identifiers:

- ❑ Name
- ❑ überfluß
- ❑ _Identifier
- ❑ \u005fIdentifier

These last two are identical and interchangeable (005f is the Unicode code for the underscore character), so couldn't be declared twice in the same scope. Note that although syntactically you are allowed to use the underscore character in identifiers, usually this isn't usually recommended in most situations because it doesn't follow the guidelines for naming variables that Microsoft have written in order to ensure that developers use the same conventions, making it easier to read each other's code. We discuss these naming conventions in Chapter 8.

Variable Scope

We noted earlier that variables with the same name can't be declared within the same scope. The scope of a variable is the region of code from which the variable can be accessed. Consider the following code:

```csharp
using System;

public class ScopeTest
{
   public static int Main()
   {
      for (int i = 0; i < 10; i++)
      {
         Console.WriteLine(i);
      }   // i goes out of scope here

      // We can declare a variable named i again, because
      // there's no other variable with that name in scope
      for (int i = 9; i >= 0; i--)
      {
         Console.WriteLine(i);
      }   // i goes out of scope here

      return 0;
   }
}
```

This code simply prints out the numbers from zero to nine, and then back again from nine to zero, using a for loop to iterate through the numbers. Don't worry about the syntax of the for loop at this stage – we'll look at that later in the chapter. The important thing to note is that we declare the variable i twice in this code, within the same method. The reason why we can do this is that in both cases i is declared within the loop, so the variables are local to the loop. As soon as their loop ends, the variables go out of scope, and are no longer accessible.

Let's have a look at another example:

```
using System;

public class ScopeTest
{
    public static int Main()
    {
        int j = 20;
        for (int i = 0; i < 10; i++)
        {
            int j = 30;    // Can't do this - j is still in scope
            Console.WriteLine(j + i);
        }
        return 0;
    }
}
```

If we try to compile this, we'll get an error:

```
ScopeTest.cs(10,14): error CS0136: A local variable named 'j' cannot be declared
        in this scope because it would give a different meaning to 'j', which is
        already used in a 'parent or current' scope to denote something else
```

The reason for this is that the variable j, which we defined before the start of the for loop, is still in scope within the for loop, and won't go out of scope until the Main() method has finished executing. Although, the second j (the illegal one) is in a different scope, that scope is nested within the Main() method's scope. The compiler has no way to distinguish between these two variables, so won't allow the second one to be declared.

Fields and Local Variables

In certain circumstances, however, we *can* distinguish between two identifiers with the same name, but with different scope, and in this case the compiler *will* allow us to declare the second variable. The reason is that C# makes a fundamental distinction between variables which are declared at the type level known as **fields**, and variables declared within methods known as **local variables**.

Consider this code:

```
using System;

public class ScopeTest
{
    static int j = 20;

    public static int Main()
    {
        int j = 30;
        Console.WriteLine(j);
        return 0;
    }
}
```

This code will compile, even though we have two variables named j in scope within the Main() method – the j which was defined at the class level, and doesn't go out of scope until the class is destroyed (in this case, when the Main() method terminates, and the program ends). In this case, the new variable named j, which we declare in the Main() method hides the class-level variable with the same name, so when we run this code, the number 30 will be displayed.

However, what if we want to refer to the class-level variable? We can actually refer to fields of a class or struct from outside the object, using the syntax *object.fieldname*. For example, if we define a class like this, with one field:

```
class SomeClass
{
    public int i = 20;
}
```

Then we can access the i field like this:

```
SomeClass objSomeClass = new SomeClass();
int x = objSomeClass.i;
```

Normally, we don't have to do this within a class, as the field is available within the current scope. If we've hidden the field by declaring a local variable with the same name within the current scope however, we can access the field with exactly the same syntax. In the example above, we're accessing a static field (we'll look at what this means in the next section) from a static method, so we don't need an instance of the class; we just use the name of the class itself:

```
Console.WriteLine(ScopeTest.j);
```

If we were accessing an instance field (a field which belongs to a specific instance of the class), we would need to use the this keyword instead. The this keyword is used within a class or struct to obtain a reference to the current instance; we'll look at this in more detail in the next chapter.

Variable Modifiers

We can include a number of modifiers in a variable declaration, which allow us to specify a number of features that we want to apply to our variable – such as whether it will be visible to code outside the current class, or whether its value can be modified.

These modifiers can include one or more of the following:

- internal
- new
- private
- protected
- public
- readonly
- static

These modifiers can only be applied to fields, and not to local variables.

The new modifier is used only in classes that inherit from another class, and hides an existing field in that class. We'll look at class inheritance in Chapter 4.

Accessibility Modifiers

The internal, private, protected, and public modifiers are all used to set the accessibility level of our variable. We can only use one of these modifiers in a variable declaration, except that we can use protected and internal together. There are therefore, five possible accessibility levels:

Accessibility	Description
public	The variable can be accessed from anywhere as a field of the type to which it belongs.
internal	The variable can only be accessed from the current program.
protected	The variable can only be accessed from within the type to which it belongs, or from types derived from that type.
protected internal	The variable can be accessed from the current program, or from types derived from the current type (that is, from anywhere that could access it if it were declared as protected or internal).
private	The variable can only be accessed from within the type to which it belongs.

Let's have a look at what this means in practice. Let's take a program with two classes. The first class, named AccessTest, has one variable (an int named x). In the other class, we will instantiate the AccessTest class, and try to access its x variable:

```
// AccessTest.cs
using System;

public class AccessTest
{
   public int x = 12;
}

public class AccessClient
{
   public static int Main()
   {
      AccessTest Test = new AccessTest();
      int x = Test.x;
      Console.WriteLine(x);
      return 0;
   }
}
```

Save this file as AccessTest.cs, and compile it using the command csc AccessTest.cs. In this case, the variable can be accessed, and the program compiles and runs fine, because we've declared x as public, so it could be accessed from anywhere. Similarly, there are no problems if we change the modifier to internal or protected internal, because the two classes form part of the same program, and are compiled together:

```
protected internal int x = 12;
```

However, if we change the modifier to `private` or `protected`, the variable won't be visible to our `AccessClient` class, and we'll get this error when we try to compile:

```
AccessTest.cs(14,15): error CS0122: 'AccessTest.x' is inaccessible due to its
            protection level
```

Now try compiling the two classes separately. First, save the `AccessTest` class on its own as `AccessTest.cs`:

```csharp
// AccessTest.cs
public class AccessTest
{
    public int x = 12;
}
```

Compile this into a class library using the command:

csc /t:library AccessTest.cs

Next, save the `AccessClient` class as `AccessClient.cs` (you'll need to add the `using System;` line to the top of this file):

```csharp
// AccessClient.cs
using System;
public class AccessClient
{
    public static int Main()
    {
        AccessTest objTest = new AccessTest();
        int x = objTest.x;
        Console.WriteLine(x);
        return 0;
    }
}
```

Now compile this into a console application, adding a reference to our newly compiled `AccessTest.dll` (we'll look at the compiler options later in the chapter):

csc /r:AccessTest.dll AccessClient.cs

This should compile and run without problems, so long as the accessibility of x was set to `public`. If we now change this to `protected` or `protected internal` and attempt to recompile the two files, we'll get an error when we try to compile `AccessClient.cs`. This is because the two files are no longer part of the same program from the C# compiler's point of view, as they are being compiled separately.

Static and Instance Variables

In our "C# isn't Java" example at the start of this chapter, we saw that we can define a method as static, and then call that method without first instantiating the class to which it belongs. We can do exactly the same thing with fields, again using the static modifier. By default, fields are **instance fields** – a separate copy of the variable is created for each instance of the class it belongs to. If we add the static keyword to our variable declaration, however, the field will be a **static field**. This means that there will only ever be one copy of the field, regardless of how many instances of the class are created.

In our example above, we first had to create an instance of our AccessTest class before we could access the x variable. If we add the static modifier to our variable declaration, we must now access the variable directly through the class, not through an instance of the class:

```
using System;

public class AccessTest
{
    public static int x = 12;
}

public class AccessClient
{
    public static int Main()
    {
        int x = AccessTest.x;
        Console.WriteLine(x);
        return 0;
    }
}
```

Read-Only Variables

The last modifier that we'll look at is readonly. Not surprisingly, this marks a variable as read-only – we can't modify the value once the variable has been initialized. The values of read-only fields can only be set when the variable is first declared, or in the constructor for the type to which it belongs; if it isn't set at that point, the field will always have its default value (zero for a numeric type, null for a reference type, and so on.) Note that static read-only fields can't be set in instance constructors, or instance read-only fields in static constructors.

The only exception to the rule that we can't re-set the value of a read-only field is that if a value is assigned to the variable when it is declared as a field of a class or struct, we can override that value in the constructor.

Read-only variables can't be passed as reference or output parameters to a method, except from within the constructor. We'll look at output and reference parameters later in this chapter.

For those readers who don't know what constructors are, they are introduced later in this chapter.

Constants

Constants are very similar to static read-only fields. Prefixing a variable with the `const` keyword when it is declared and initialized designates that variable as a constant. As the name implies, a constant is a variable whose value cannot be changed throughout its lifetime:

```
const int a = 100; // This value cannot be changed
```

Constants differ from read-only fields in four important respects:

❑   Local variables as well as fields can be declared as constants.

❑   Constants *must* be initialized when they are declared – they can't be declared at type level, and then assigned a value in a constructor. Once a value has been assigned, it can never be overwritten.

❑   The value of a constant must be computable at compile-time. Therefore, we can't initialize a constant with a value taken from a variable. If you need to do this, you will need to use a read-only field.

❑   Constants are always static. However, notice that we don't have to (and, in fact, aren't permitted to) include the `static` modifier in the constant declaration.

There are at least three advantages to using constants (or read-only variables) in your programs:

❑   Constants make your programs easier to read by replacing "magic numbers" and "magic strings" with readable names whose values are easy to understand.

❑   Constants make your programs easier to modify. Say, for instance, that you have a `SalesTax` constant in one of your C# programs, and that constant is assigned a value of 6%. If the sales tax rate changes at a later point in time, you can modify the behavior of all tax calculations simply by assigning a new value to the constant; you don't have to hunt throughout your code for the value `.06` and change each one, hoping that you've found all of them.

❑   Constants make it easier to avoid mistakes in your programs. If you attempt to assign another value to a constant somewhere in your program after you've already assigned it a value, the compiler will flag the error.

Like enumerations, constants are another convention to which professional developers discipline themselves in order to improve their accuracy.

Operators

Although most of C#'s operators should be familiar to C and C++ developers, we'll discuss the most important ones here for the benefit of new programmers and VB converts, and to shed some light on some of the changes introduced with C#.

C# supports the following operators, although four (`sizeof`, `*`, `->`, and `&`) are only available in unsafe code (code which bypasses C#'s type safety checking), which we will look at in Chapter 6:

Category	Operator
Arithmetic	+ - * / %
Logical	& | ^ ~ && || !
String concatenation	+
Increment and decrement	++ --
Bit shifting	<< >>
Comparison	== != < > <= >=
Assignment	= += -= *= /= %= &= |= ^= <<= >>=
Member Access (for objects)	.
Indexing (for arrays and indexers)	[]
Cast	()
Conditional (the Ternary Operator)	?:
Object Creation	new
Type information	sizeof (unsafe code only) is typeof
Overflow exception control	checked unchecked
Indirection and Address	* -> & (unsafe code only) []

One of the biggest pitfalls to watch out for when using C# operators is that, like other C-style languages, it uses different operators for assignment (=) and comparison (==). The statement

```
x = 3; // One equals sign for assignment
```

Means "let x equal three". Because we're assigning a value to the variable x therefore, we use the single equals sign (=). If we now want to compare x to a value, we need to use the double equals sign (==):

```
if (x == 3) // Two equals signs for comparison
```

Fortunately, C#'s very strict type safety rules prevent the very common C error we mentioned at the start of the chapter, where using an assignment operator instead of the comparison operator caused unpredictable behavior. In C or C++, the statement:

```
if (x = 3)
```

Would not generate an error. Instead, the value 3 would be assigned to x, and if the operation succeeded, this would be converted to a Boolean true. The effect of this is that it would *always* evaluate to true, whatever the value of x, and our program wouldn't behave as anticipated. Thankfully, C# doesn't allow these implicit conversions to bool, so this statement will generate an error in C#, and won't compile.

107

VB programmers who are used to using the ampersand (&) to concatenate strings will have to make an adjustment. In C#, the plus sign + is used to concatenate strings, while & denotes a bitwise AND between two different integer values. | allows you to perform a bitwise OR between two integers. VB programmers also might not recognize the % (modulus) operator. This returns the remainder after division, so for example x % 5 will return two if x is equal to seven.

You'll use few pointers in C#, and thus you'll use few indirection operators (->) too. Specifically, the only place you'll use them is within blocks of unsafe code, because that's the only place in C# where pointers are allowed.

Operator Shortcuts

One of C's hallmarks is the concise syntax, which allows the developer to signify complex operations. The increment and decrement operators (++ and --, respectively) are excellent examples of this concision. By applying these operators to a variable, we can increment or decrement the value of that variable while avoiding other languages' more cumbersome syntax.

These operators can occur both before and after the operand. The expressions x++ and ++x are both equivalent to x = x + 1, but there's a difference in the way they behave. The increment and decrement operators can act both as whole expressions and within expressions. In other words, x++ and ++x can stand as lines on their own, in which case they are identical and correspond to the statement x = x + 1.

They can also be used within expressions, however, and in this case there is a difference. The prefix operator (++x) will increment the value of x *before* the expression is evaluated; in other words, x is incremented and the new value is used in the expression. In contrast, the postfix operator increments the value of x *after* the expression is evaluated – the expression is evaluated using the original value. The following example shows the difference between the two operators:

```
int x = 5;
if (++x == 6)
{
    Console.WriteLine("This will execute");
}
if (x++ == 7)
{
    Console.WriteLine("This won't");
}
```

The first if condition evaluates to true, because x is incremented from 5 to 6 before the expression is evaluated. The condition in the second if statement is false, however, because x is only incremented to 7 after the entire expression has been evaluated.

The prefix and postfix operators --x and x-- behave in the same way, but decrement rather than increment the operand.

The other shortcut operators, such as += and -=, require two operands, and are used to modify the value of the first operand by performing an arithmetic, logical, or bitwise operation on it. For example:

```
x += 5;
```

Is exactly equivalent to:

```
x = x + 5;
```

The following table shows the full list of shortcut operators available in C#:

x++, ++x	x = x + 1 (The first form increments x after the expression has been evaluated; the second form increments x before the expression is carried out).
x--, --x	x = x - 1 (The first form decreases x after the expression has been evaluated; the second form decreases x before the expression is carried out).
x += y	x = x + y
x -= y	x = x - y
x *= y	x = x * y
x /= y	x = x / y
x %= y	x = x % y
x >>= y	x = x >> y
x <<= y	x = x << y
x &= y	x = x & y
x |= y	x = x | y
x ^= y	x = x ^ y

The Ternary Operator

The ternary operator "?:" is a shorthand form of the if...else construction. It gets its name from the fact that it involves three operands. It allows us to evaluate a condition, returning one value if that condition is true, or another value if it is false. The syntax is:

```
condition ? true_value : false_value
```

Where *condition* is the Boolean expression to be evaluated, *true_value* is the value that will be returned if *condition* is true, and *false_value* is the value that will be returned otherwise.

When used sparingly, the ternary operator can add a dash of terseness to your programs. It's especially handy for providing one of a couple of arguments to a function that is being invoked. You can use it to quickly convert a Boolean value to a string value of "true" or "false", for instance:

```
// X is an int
Console.WriteLine(X>= 0 ? "Positive" : "Negative");
```

It's also quite handy for displaying a correct singular or plural form, for example:

```
int x = 1;
string s = x.ToString() + " ";
s += (x == 1 ? "man" : "men");
Console.WriteLine(s);
```

This code will display 1 man if x is equal to one, but will display the correct plural form for any other number. Note however, that if your output needs to be localized to different languages then you will probably have to write more sophisticated routines to take account of the different grammatical rules of different languages.

checked and unchecked

The checked and unchecked operators allow us to specify how the CLR will handle stack overflows when we perform operations on integer types which causes their values to go outside the bounds of that data type. For example, consider the code:

```
byte b = 255;
b++;
Console.WriteLine(b.ToString());
```

The byte data type can only hold values in the range zero to 255, so incrementing the value of b causes an overflow. How the CLR handles this depends on a number of issues, including compiler options, so whenever there's a risk of an overflow, we really need some way of making sure that we get the result we want.

To do this, C# provides the checked and unchecked operators. If we mark a block of code as checked, the CLR will enforce overflow checking, and throw an exception if an overflow occurs. If we change our code to include the checked operator:

```
byte b = 255;
checked
{
    b++;
}
Console.WriteLine(b.ToString());
```

When we try to run this, we will get an error like this:

```
Unhandled Exception: System.OverflowException: Exception of type System.Overflow
Exception was thrown.
   at ConsoleApplication3.Class1.Main(String[] args)
```

We can enforce overflow checking for all unmarked code in our program by compiling with the /checked option.

If we want to suppress overflow checking, we can mark the code as unchecked:

```
byte b = 255;
unchecked
{
    b++;
}
Console.WriteLine(b.ToString());
```

In this case, no exception will be raised, but we will lose data – since the byte type can't hold a value of 256, the overflowing bits will be discarded, and our b variable will hold a value of zero.

is

The is operator allows us to check whether an object is compatible with a specific type. For example, to check whether a variable is compatible with the object type:

```
int i = 10;
if (i is object)
{
    // Everything's an object in C#!
    Console.WriteLine("i is an object");
}
```

int, like all other C# data types inherits from object, therefore the expression i is object will evaluate to true, and the message will be displayed.

sizeof

We can determine the size (in bytes) required by a value type on the stack using the sizeof operator:

```
string s = "A string";
unsafe
{
    Console.WriteLine(sizeof(int));
}
```

This will display the number 4, as ints are four bytes long.

Notice, that we can only use the sizeof operator in unsafe code. By default, the C# compiler will reject any code containing unsafe blocks, so we'll need to enable this either using the /unsafe option of the command-line compiler, or by setting the Allow unsafe code blocks option to true in Visual Studio.NET. This can be found on the property pages for the project, under Configuration Properties | Build. We'll look at unsafe code in more detail in Chapter 6.

typeof

The typeof operator returns a Type object representing a specified type. For example, typeof(string) will return a Type object representing the System.String type. This is useful when we want to use reflection to find out information about an object dynamically. We will look at reflection in Chapter 7.

Operator Precedence

The following table shows the order of precedence of the C# operators. The operators at the top of the table are those with the highest precedence (that is, the ones which are evaluated first in an expression containing multiple operators):

Group	Operators
	`() . [] x++ x-- new typeof sizeof checked unchecked`
Unary	`+ - ! ~ ++x --x` and casts.
Multiplication/Division	`* / %`
Addition/Subtraction	`+ -`
Bitwise shift operators	`<< >>`
Relational	`< > <= >= is`
Comparison	`== !=`
Bitwise AND	`&`
Bitwise XOR	`|`
Bitwise OR	`^`
Boolean AND	`&&`
Boolean OR	`||`
Ternary operator	`?:`
Assignment	`= += -= *= /= %=` etc.

Flow Control

In this section, we'll look at the real nuts and bolts of the language: the statements which allow us to control the flow of our program, rather than executing every line of code in the order it appears in the program. In fact, much of the rest of C#'s functionality apart from these keywords derives directly from the .NET Framework.

Conditional Statements

Conditional statements allow us to branch our code depending on whether certain conditions are met or on the value of an expression. C# has two constructs for branching code – the `if` statement, which allows us to test whether a specific condition is met, and the `switch` statement, which allows us to compare an expression with a number of different values.

The if Statement

For conditional branching, C# inherits C and C++'s `if...else` construct. The syntax should be fairly intuitive for anyone who has done any programming with a procedural language:

```
if (condition)
    statement(s)
else
    statement(s)
```

If more than one statement is to be executed as part of either condition, these statements will need to be joined together into a block using curly braces (`{ ... }`) (this also applies to other C# constructs where statements can be joined into a block, such as `for` and `while` loops):

```
bool Zero;
if (i == 0)
{
    Zero = true;
    Console.WriteLine("Zero");
}
else
{
    Zero = false;
    Console.WriteLine("Non-zero");
}
```

If we want to, we can use the `if` statement alone without an `else` statement:

```
if (Condition)
{
    // This executes if blnCondition == true.
}
```

We can also nest `if` statements within an `else` block to test for multiple conditions:

```
if (Condition1)
{
    // This executes if Condition1 == true.
}
else if (Condition2)
{
    // This executes if Condition1 == false and
    // Condition2 == true.
}
else
{
    // This executes if neither Condition1
    // nor Condition2 are true.
}
```

We don't need to use the braces if there's only one statement in the conditional branch:

```
if (i == 0)
    Console.WriteLine("Zero");      // This will only execute if i == 0
Console.WriteLine("Anything");      // This line will execute whatever the value
                                    // of i turns out to be
```

Like so many other programming shortcuts, however, this one may come back to haunt you. If, at a later time, you come back to associate *more* statements with the if and you forget to add the curly braces, you'll be puzzled at why the new statements always execute, regardless of whether the condition evaluates to true or false. Here, a stitch in time saves nine. For that reason, many programmers prefer to use curly braces whenever they use an if statement.

One crucial difference between if statements (and other flow control statements), in C# and in C/C++ lies in how C# handles the evaluation of an if statement's Boolean expression. As mentioned earlier, integer types do not implicitly convert to the bool type in C#. This means that we can't call a method that returns an integer value and use its output directly as an expression in an if statement. In C++, we could do this:

```
// this is C++, not C# code!
// objSomething->DoSomething() returns an int
if (objSomething->DoSomething())
{
    // Non-zero value returned
}
else
{
    // Returned zero
}
```

In C#, we have to convert the integer that is returned to a Boolean true or false, for example by comparing the value with zero or with null:

```
if (objSomething.DoSomething() != 0)
{
    // Non-zero value returned
}
else
{
    // Returned zero
}
```

We can't rely on the value of zero automatically converting to false any more; it doesn't. Although this arrangement requires a bit more discipline on the part of the programmer, it's bound to improve the accuracy of your code.

The switch Statement

The switch...case statement is good for selecting one branch of execution from a set of mutually exclusive ones. It takes the form of a switch argument followed by a series of case clauses. When the expression in the switch argument evaluates to one of the values beside a case clause, the code immediately following that case clause executes. This is one case where we don't need to use curly braces to join statements into blocks; instead, we mark the end of the code for each case using the break keyword. We can also include a default case in the switch statement, which will execute if the expression evaluates to none of the other cases:

```
switch (IntegerA)
{
   case 1:
      Console.WriteLine("IntegerA =1");
      break;
   case 2:
      Console.WriteLine("IntegerA =2");
      break;
   case 3:
      Console.WriteLine("IntegerA =3");
      break;
   default:
      Console.WriteLine("IntegerA is not 1,2, or 3");
      break;
}
```

Note that the case values *must* be constant expressions – variables are not permitted.

Though the switch...case statement should be familiar to C and C++ programmers, C#'s switch...case is a bit safer. Specifically, it prohibits fall-through conditions in almost all cases. This means that if a case clause is fired early on in the block, later clauses cannot be fired unless you use a goto statement to specifically mark that you want them fired too. The compiler enforces this restriction by flagging every case clause that is not equipped with a break statement as an error:

```
C:\My Documents\Visual Studio Projects\ConsoleApplication9\Class1.cs(24): Control
cannot fall through from one case label ('case 2:') to another
```

While it's true that fall-through behavior is desirable in a limited number of situations, in the vast majority of cases it is unintended and results in a logical error that's hard to spot. Isn't it better to code for the norm rather than for the exception?

By getting creative with goto statements (which C# does support) however, you can duplicate fall-through functionality in your switch...cases. However, if you find yourself really wanting to, you probably should re-consider your approach.

There is one exception to this however, in that we can fall through from one case to the next if that case is empty. This allows us to treat two or more cases in an identical way (without the need for goto statements):

```
switch(Country)
{
   case "au":
   case "uk":
   case "us":
      Language = "English";
      break;
   case "at":
   case "de":
      Language = "German";
      break;
}
```

One intriguing point about the `switch` statement in C# is that the order of the cases doesn't matter – we can even put the `default` case first! As a result, no two cases can be the same. This includes different constants which have the same value, so we can't, for example, do this:

```
const string ENGLAND = "uk";
const string BRITAIN = "uk";
switch(Country)
{
    case ENGLAND:
    case BRITAIN:   // This will cause the compiler to throw an error,
                    // because there's already a case for "uk"
        Language = "English";
        break;
}
```

Looping

C# provides four different looping mechanisms which allow us to execute a block of code repeatedly until a certain condition is met. The `for` loop is the first that we'll examine.

The for Loop

C# `for` loops provide a shorthand mechanism for iterating through a loop where we need to initialize some local variable, execute the statements in the loop while a given condition is true, performing some simple step before moving on to the next iteration.

The syntax is:

```
for (initializer; condition; iterator)
    statement(s)
```

Where the *initializer* is the expression evaluated before the loop is executed (usually initializing a local variable as a loop counter); the *condition* is the expression which is tested before every iteration of the loop (for example, checking that the loop counter is less than a certain value); and the *iterator* is an expression which will be evaluated after each iteration (for example, incrementing the loop counter).

The `for` loop is a so-called pre-test loop, because the loop condition is evaluated before the loop statements are executed, and these won't be executed at all if the loop condition is false. This condition is then re-evaluated before each iteration of the loop. The loop ends when the test condition evaluates to a Boolean `false`. The `for` loop is excellent for repeating a statement or a block of statements for a pre-determined number of times. The following example is typical of the use of a `for` loop:

```
for (int i = 0; i < 100; i++)
{
    // This loop will execute 100 times.
}
```

It's not unusual to nest `for` loops so that an inner loop executes once completely for each iteration of an outer loop. This scheme is typically employed to loop through every element in a rectangular multidimensional array. The outermost loop loops through every row, and the inner loop loops through every column in a particular row:

```
//This loop iterates through rows.
for (int i = 0; i < 100; i++)
{
    // This loop iterates through columns.
    for (int j = 0; j < 25; j++)
    {
        a[i,j] = 0;
    }
}
```

C programmers should take note of one particular feature of the example above. The counter variable in the innermost loop is effectively re-declared with each successive iteration of the outer loop. This syntax is legal not only in C#, but in C++ as well.

Although it's technically possible to evaluate something other than a counter variable in a for loop's test condition, it's certainly not typical. It's also possible to omit one (or even all) of the expressions in the for loop. In such situations however, perhaps consider using the next type of loop that we'll discuss.

The while Loop

Like the for loop, the while is a pre-test loop. This implies that if the value of its test condition evaluates to false, the while loop may not even execute a single time. The syntax is similar, but while loops take only one expression:

```
while(condition)
    statement(s);
```

Unlike the for loop, the while loop is most often used to repeat a statement or a block of a statements for a number of times that is not known before the loop begins. Usually, a statement inside the while loop's body will set a Boolean flag to false on a certain iteration, triggering the end of the loop:

```
bool Condition = false;
while (!Condition)
{
    // This loop spins until the Condition is true
    DoSomeWork();
    Condition = CheckCondition();
}
```

All of C#'s looping mechanisms, including the while loop, can forego the curly braces that follow them if they intend to repeat just a single statement and not a block of them. To avoid future errors if more statements are added to the loop, though, it's a good idea to use curly braces, even if only a single statement is being repeated at the current time.

The do...while Loop

The do...while loop is the post-test version of the while loop. This means that the loop's test condition is evaluated after the body of the loop has been executed. Consequently, do...while loops are useful for situations in which a block of statements must be executed at least one time:

```
bool Condition
do
{
    // this loop will at least execute once, even if Condition is false
    DoSomeWork();
    Condition = CheckCondition();
} while (Condition);
```

The foreach Loop

The foreach loop is the last C# looping mechanism that we'll discuss. While the other looping mechanisms were present in the earliest versions of C and C++, the foreach statement is a new addition (borrowed from VB), and a very welcome one at that.

The foreach loop allows us to iterate through each item in a container class that supports the IEnumerable interface. Such container classes include C#'s arrays, the collection classes in the System.Collection namespaces, and user-defined collection classes:

```
int[] Ints = {1,2,3};
foreach (int temp in Ints)
{
    Console.WriteLine(temp);
}
```

An important point to note is that we can't change the value of the item in the collection, so code such as the following will fail:

```
int[] Ints = {1,2,3};
foreach (int temp in Ints)
{
    temp++;    // This line will fail -
               // the items in a foreach loop are read-only!
    Console.WriteLine(temp);
}
```

If you need to iterate through the items in a collection and change their values, you'll need to use a for loop instead.

We'll learn how to implement our own collection classes later in this book, in Chapter 7. Interestingly, such classes can be iterated through with VB.NET's foreach statement, too.

Jump Statements

C# provides a number of statements which allow us to jump immediately to another line in the program. The first of these is, of course, the notorious goto statement.

The goto Statement

The goto statement allows us to jump directly to another line in the program, indicated by a label (this is just an identifier followed by a colon):

```
goto Label1;
   Console.WriteLine("This won't be executed");
Label1:
   Console.WriteLine("Continuing execution from here");
```

There are a couple of restrictions involved with `goto`. We can't jump into a block of code such as a `for` loop, we can't jump out of a class, and we can't exit a `finally` block after `try...catch` blocks (we'll look at exception handling with `try...catch...finally` shortly).

The reputation of the `goto` statement probably precedes it, and in most circumstances its use is sternly frowned upon. In general, it certainly doesn't conform to good object-oriented programming practice. However, there is one place where it's quite handy: jumping between cases in a `switch` statement, particularly since C#'s `switch` is so strict on fall-through.

As mentioned earlier, to facilitate jumping to other cases in a `switch` statement, C# doesn't require us to define separate labels – we can use the labels of the case statements, including the `default` label.

The break Statement

We've already met the `break` statement briefly – when we used it to exit from a case in a `switch` statement. In fact, `break` can also be used to exit from any `for`, `foreach`, `while`, or `do...while` loop. Control will switch to the statement immediately after the end of the loop:

```
for (int i = 0; i < 10; i++)
{
    Console.Write("Enter a word: ");
    string s = Console.ReadLine();
    if (s == "End")
    {
        // Exit the loop if the user types 'End'
        break;
    }
    Console.WriteLine("You entered: " + s);
}
// Execution will restart here after the user enters 'End'
```

If the statement occurs in a nested loop, control will switch to the end of the innermost loop. If the break occurs outside of a switch statement or a loop, a compile-time error will occur.

The continue Statement

The `continue` statement is similar to `break`, and must also be used within a `for`, `foreach`, `while`, or `do...while` loop. It exits only from the *current iteration* of the loop however, which means execution will restart at the beginning of the next iteration of the loop, rather than outside the loop altogether. Notice that (like other jump statements) `continue` can't be used to exit a `finally` block, and that if a `continue` statement would result in exiting a `try` block, any associated `finally` block will be executed before control passes to the next iteration of the loop.

The return Statement

The `return` statement is used to exit a method of a class, returning control to the caller of the method. If the method has a return type, `return` must return a value of this type; otherwise, it must be used without an expression. We will look at the syntax for writing and calling methods shortly.

119

The using Block Statement

The `using` statement (as opposed to the `using` directive, which we saw earlier and will examine in more detail at shortly) allows us to ensure that resource-intensive objects are disposed of as soon as we've finished with them. The syntax is:

```
using (object)
{
   // Code using object
}
```

Where *object* is an instance of a class which implements the `IDisposable` interface. All classes which implement `IDisposable` *must* implement a `Dispose` method, which can be used to free up any expensive resources used by the object. The `Dispose` method will be called as soon as the `using` block ends. We will look at this `using` statement and the `IDisposable` interface in more detail in Chapter 5.

Exception Handling

Structured error handling is a relatively recent addition to C++, and C# implements it as well. From the point of view of syntax, structured error handling consists of three different blocks of code. To add structured error handling to a method, you add each of these blocks to that method.

❑   The **try block** encapsulates the code that the program attempts to execute. If an error or exceptional condition arises during the execution of this code, an exception is said to be thrown.

❑   A **catch block** follows the `try` block, and encapsulates code that takes some sort of action to handle the error that has been generated in the `try` block code.

❑   The **finally block** occurs at the very end of the routine in which error handling is installed. Code within this block is always executed, whether the thread-of-execution is leaving the function in a normal state, or in an abnormal state due to an error that has been thrown. In addition, we cannot jump out of a `finally` block (for example, using `goto`), and if a jump statement causes control to pass out of a `try` block, any associated `finally` block will still be executed:

```
public void SomeRoutine()
{
   try
   {
      // Execution starts here.
      // This code may or may not throw an exception.
   }
   catch
   {
      // If an exception is thrown in the try block,
      // code in this catch block is activated.
   }
   finally
   {
      // Code in this block executes when the routine ends,
      // regardless of whether an exception was thrown.
   }
}
```

Errors are thrown automatically if a runtime anomaly such as division-by-zero, index-out-of-bounds, or checked integer overflow occurs. Furthermore, our code can explicitly raise exceptions when it determines that some exceptional condition has been met. (It could, for instance, throw an error if a crucial file cannot be found, or if it deems the value of an input argument is illogical).

When an exception is caught, the `catch` block that handles that error receives an object containing information about it. Specifically, the `catch` block receives a reference to an object that derives from the `System.Exception` class. There's a subclass of the `Exception` class for each of the most common types of runtime errors. We can implement our own `Exception` subclasses, too.

For robustness, we can equip a single method with several different `catch` blocks: one for each particular type of error that could occur. This arrangement allows our code to respond more intelligently to particular types of errors. For some errors, for example, the routine could attempt to do some repair work and re-execute. In the face of other, more serious errors, the routine could write a message to the log file and halt execution.

You should equip each method in your C# programs with an error handler.

We'll discuss structured error handling in more detail in Chapter 6.

Program Structure

So far, we've been introduced to most of the main "building blocks" which make up the C# language – the data types and program flow statements, but we haven't really seen however, how we can put these together to form a complete program. The key to this lies in working with classes.

Classes

As we've seen, classes play a huge role in C# programs, and we're going to dedicate the next two chapters entirely to object-oriented programming in C#. However, before we get there, we need to introduce the basics of working with classes in C#, because it really is pretty well impossible to write a C# program without them. Classes are essentially templates from which we can create objects. Each object contains data and has methods to manipulate and access that data. The class defines what data each object of that class can contain, but doesn't actually contain any data itself. For example, if we have a class which represents a customer, it might define fields such as `CustomerID`, `FirstName`, `LastName`, and `Address`, which we will use to hold information about a particular customer. We can then **instantiate** an object of this class to represent one specific customer, and set these fields for that object.

Class Members

The data and functions within a class are known as the class's **members**. Microsoft's official terminology distinguishes between data members and function members. As well as these members, classes can also contain nested types (such as other classes).

Data Members

Data members are those members which contain the data for the class – fields, constants, and events:

❏ Fields are any variables associated with the class. In fact, if we define any variable at the class level, that is in fact a field of the class. If fields are declared as `public`, they will be accessible from outside the class. For example, we can define a `PhoneCustomer` class with `CustomerID`, `FirstName` and `LastName` fields like this:

```
class PhoneCustomer
{
    public int CustomerID;
    public string FirstName;
    public string LastName;
}
```

Once we've instantiated a `PhoneCustomer` object, we can then access these fields using the *Object.FieldName* syntax:

```
PhoneCustomer Customer1 = new PhoneCustomer();
Customer1.CustomerID = 1000;
Customer1.FirstName = "Burton";
Customer1.LastName = "Harvey";
Console.WriteLine(Customer1.FirstName + " " + Customer1.LastName);
```

❏ Constants can be associated with classes in the same way as variables. Once again, if they are declared as public, they will be accessible from outside the class.

❏ Events are class members that allow an object to notify a caller whenever some particular programmatic occurrence happens, such as a field or property of the class changing, or some form of user interaction occurring. The client can contain code known as an error handler to react to the event. We won't look at events in this chapter, but we'll look at them in detail in Chapter 6.

Function Members

Function members are those members which provide some functionality for working on the data in the class. They include methods, properties, constructors and destructors, operators, and indexers:

❏ **Methods** are functions which are associated with a particular class. They can be either **instance methods**, which work on a particular instance of a class, or **static methods**, which provide more generic functionality that doesn't require us to instantiate a class (like the `Console.WriteLine()` method which we've already met). We'll look at methods in the next section.

❏ **Properties** are functions that can be accessed from the client in a similar way to the public fields of the class. C# provides a specific syntax for implementing read and write properties on our classes, so we don't have to jerry-rig methods whose names have the words `Get` or `Set` embedded in them. Because there's a dedicated syntax for properties that is distinct from that for normal functions, the illusion of objects as actual things is strengthened for client code. Even better, properties centralize the read/write aspects of a property, making property code easier to maintain for the developer of the class.

❏ **Constructors** are functions which are called when an object is instantiated. They must have the same name as the class to which they belong, and cannot have a return type. Constructors are useful for setting the values of fields when an object is instantiated.

❑ **Destructors** are similar to constructors, but are called when the object is destroyed. They have the name of the class, preceded by a tilde (~). Because the CLR handles garbage collection, it is impossible to predict when a destructor will be called, and destructors are used much less frequently in C# than in C++.

❑ Classes may also contain definitions for **operators**, so that we can define our own operators, or specify how existing operators will work with our class. We'll look at defining operators in Chapter 5.

❑ **Indexers** allow our objects to be indexed in the same way as an array or collection. We'll look at indexers in Chapter 5.

Methods

In VB and C, and even in C++, we could of course define global functions that were not associated with a particular class. This is not the case in C#. In C#, every function must be associated with a class or struct. Every function is, in other words, a method.

Note that official C# terminology does in fact make a distinction between functions and methods. In this terminology, the term "function" includes not only methods, but also other non-data members of a class or struct. This includes indexers, operators, constructors, destructors, and also – perhaps somewhat surprisingly – properties. These are contrasted with data members: fields, constants, and events.

Declaring Methods

The syntax for defining a method in C# is exactly what you'd expect from a C-style language: any method modifiers (such as the method's accessibility), the type of the return value, followed by the name of the method, followed by a list of input arguments enclosed in parentheses, followed by the body of the method enclosed in curly braces. Each parameter consists of the name of the type of the parameter, and the name by which it can be referenced in the body of the method:

```
public          // access modifier
bool            // return type
IsSquare        // function name
(Rectangle obj) // input args
{
    // body of method
    return (obj.Height == obj.Width);
}
```

If the method doesn't return anything, we specify a return type of void, as we can't omit the return type altogether, and if it takes no arguments, we still need to include an empty set of parentheses, "()", after the method name.

A method can take one or more of the following modifiers:

Modifier	Description
new	The method hides an inherited method with the same signature.
public	The method can accessed from anywhere, including outside the class.
protected	The method can be accessed from within the class to which it belongs, or a type derived from that class.
internal	The method can be accessed from within the same program.
private	The method can only be accessed from inside the class to which it belongs.
static	The method does not operate on a specific instance of the class.
virtual	The method can be overridden by a derived class.
abstract	A virtual method that defines the signature of the method, but doesn't provide an implementation.
override	The method overrides an inherited virtual or abstract method.
sealed	The method overrides an inherited virtual method, but cannot be overridden by any classes which inherit from this class. Must be used in conjunction with override.
extern	The method is implemented externally, in a different language.

Invoking Methods

To invoke (call or activate) a method, we simply give the name of the object on which you are calling the method, followed by the method name, followed by an argument list enclosed within parentheses. If the function delivers a return value, we can store that value in a variable, use it as an argument to another function, or just throw it away.

The following short example defines a class named MathTest with a single method, Square, which returns the square of a number passed in as a parameter. We'll also build a client class to test this method:

```
using System;

// Define a class named MathTest we'll call a method on
class MathTest
{
    // Define the Square method
    public int Square(int x)
    {
        return x * x;
    }
}

// Client class to test our MathTest class
class MathClient
{
    public static int Main()
```

```
    {
        // Instantiate the MathTest object
        MathTest Math = new MathTest();

        // Call the Square method
        int x = Math.Square(10);

        // Write the result
        Console.WriteLine(x);
        return 0;
    }
}
```

Of course, if we're invoking a static method, we must use the type name of the method's class, rather than the name of an instance of the class:

```
string[] Names = { "John", "Joe", "Jeff" };
Array.Sort(Names);   // Array.Sort is a static method,
                     // so we can't use Names.Sort();
```

You don't need to specify the object name if you're calling it from within the same class, but if that class is an executable, remember that you don't have an instance of your class, so you can only call static methods.

Input Arguments to Methods

Arguments can be passed into methods by reference, or by value. A variable that is passed by reference to a method is affected by any changes that the called method makes to it, while a variable that is passed by value to a method is not changed by any changes made within the body of the method. This is because methods refer to the original variables when those variables are passed by reference, but only to copies of those variables when they are passed by value.

In C#, all parameters are passed by value unless we specifically say otherwise. However, the data type of the parameter determines the effective behavior of any parameters passed to a method. Because reference types only hold a reference to an object, they will only pass this reference into the method. Value types, in contrast, hold the actual data, so a copy of the data itself will be passed into the method. An int, for instance, is passed by value to a method, and any changes that the method makes to the value of that int do not change the value of the original int object. Conversely, if an array or any other reference type, such as a class, is passed into a method, and the method changes a value in that array, the new value is reflected in the original array object:

```
using System;

class ParameterTest
{
    // This function takes an int array (a reference type)
    // and an int (a value type).
    static void SomeFunction(int[] Ints, int i)
    {
        Ints[0] = 100;
        i = 100;
    }

    public static int Main()
```

```
    {
        int i = 0;
        int[]Ints = { 0, 1, 2, 4, 8 };

        // Display the original values
        Console.WriteLine("i = " + i);
        Console.WriteLine("Ints[0] = " + Ints[0]);
        Console.WriteLine("Calling SomeFunction...");

        // After this method returns, Ints will be changed,
        // but i will not.
        SomeFunction(Ints, i);
        Console.WriteLine("i = " + i);
        Console.WriteLine("Ints[0] = " + Ints[0]);
        return 0;
    }
}
```

The output of this is:

```
i = 0
aryInts[0] = 0
Calling SomeFunction...
i = 0
aryInts[0] = 100
```

Notice how the value of i remains unchanged, but the value we changed in aryInts is also changed in the original array.

One point to remember is that strings are immutable (if we alter a string's value, we create an entirely new string), so strings don't display the typical reference-type behavior. Any changes made to a string within a method call won't affect the original string.

This is the default behavior. We can, however, force value parameters to be passed by reference. To do so, we use the ref keyword. If a parameter is passed to a method, and if the input argument for that method is prefixed with the ref keyword, then any changes that the method makes to the variable will affect the value of the original object:

```
// This function takes an array (a reference type)
// and an int (a value type). Because it modifies
// the second argument with "ref", that argument
// will be passed by reference.
```

```
static void SomeFunction(int[] Ints, ref int i)
{
    Ints[0] = 100;
    i = 100;
}
```

We will also need to add the ref keyword when we invoke the method:

```
SomeFunction(Ints, ref i);
```

The out Keyword

In C-style languages, it's common for functions to be able to output more than one value from a single routine. This is accomplished using **output parameters**, in other words, by assigning the output values to variables that have been passed to the method by reference.

Usually, the starting values of the variables that are passed by reference are unimportant. Those values will be overwritten by the function, which may never even look at them.

It would be convenient if we could use the same convention in C#, but if you'll remember, C# requires that variables be initialized with a starting value before they are referenced. Although we could initialize our input variables with meaningless values before passing them into a function that will fill them with real, meaningful ones, this practice seems at best needless, and at worst, confusing. However, there is a way to short-circuit the C# compiler's insistence on initial values for input arguments.

This is achieved with the out keyword. When a method's input argument is prefixed with the out keyword, that method can be passed a variable that has not been initialized with a starting value. The variable is passed by reference, so any changes that the method makes to the variable will persist when control returns from the called method. Again, we also need to use the out keyword when we call the method, as well as when we define it:

```
// This function can receive uninitialized int arguments,
// and they are passed by reference.
static void SomeFunction(out int i)
{
   i = 100;
}

public static int Main()
{
   //Here, "i" is declared but not initialized.
   int i;
   SomeFunction(out i);
   Console.WriteLine(i);
   return 0;
}
```

If the out parameter isn't assigned a value within the body of the function, the method won't compile.

Namespaces

Namespaces provide a way of organizing related classes and other types. Unlike a file or a component, a namespace is a logical, rather than a physical grouping. When we define a class in a C# file, we can include it within a namespace definition. Later, when we define another class that performs related work in another file, we can include it within the same namespace, creating a logical grouping that gives an indication to other developers using the classes how they are related and used:

```
// Here, a Customer struct is defined within the
// CustomerPhoneBookApp namespace
namespace CustomerPhoneBookApp
{
```

```
using System;

public struct Subscriber
{
    public long CustomerID;
    public String FirstName;
    public String MiddleName;
    public String LastName;
    public Decimal Balance;
}
}
```

Placing a type in a namespace effectively gives that type a long name, consisting of the type's namespace as a series of names separated with periods (.) (in the example above, the full name of the Subscriber struct is CustomerPhoneBookApp.Subscriber), and terminating with the name of the class. This allows distinct classes with the same short name to be used within the same program without ambiguity.

We can also nest namespaces within other namespaces, creating a hierarchical structure for our types:

```
namespace Wrox
{
    namespace ProfessionalCSharp
    {
        namespace Chapter03
        {
            class NamespaceExample
            {
                // Code for the class here...
            }
        }
    }
}
```

Each namespace name is composed of the names of the namespaces it resides within, separated with periods, starting with the outermost namespace and ending with its own short name. So the full name for the ProfessionalCSharp namespace is Wrox.ProfessionalCSharp, and the full name of our NamespaceExample class is:

```
Wrox.ProfessionalCSharp.Chapter03.NamespaceExample.
```

We can use this syntax to organize the namespaces in our namespace definitions, too, so the code above could also be written:

```
namespace Wrox.ProfessionalCSharp.Chapter03
{
    class NamespaceExample
    {
        // Code for the class here...
    }
}
```

Note that we're not permitted to declare a multi-part namespace nested within another namespace. Also, we're not allowed to have two types with the same name within the same namespace, so code like this can't be compiled, even though the classes are defined within different namespace definitions:

```
namespace Wrox.ProfessionalCSharp
{
    namespace Chapter03
    {
        class NamespaceExample
        {
            // Code for the class here...
        }
    }
}

namespace Wrox.ProfessionalCSharp.Chapter03
{
    class NamespaceExample   // This has the same full name as the class above,
                             // so this code won't compile
    {
        // Class code here
    }
}
```

The using Statement

Obviously, namespaces can grow rather long and tiresome to type, and the ability to indicate a
particular class with such specificity may not always be necessary. Fortunately, C# allows us to
abbreviate a class's full name. To do this, we list the class's namespace at the top of the file, prefixed
with the using keyword. Throughout the rest of the file, we can refer to the path by its shorter, relative
name, rather than its absolute one:

```
// FILE 1:
// Without "using", the full namespace must be invoked
System.Int32 a;

// FILE 2:
// With using, the relative namespace may be used
using System;
Int32 a;
```

If two namespaces referenced by a using directive contain a type of the same name, then we will have
to use the full (or at least, a longer) form of the name to ensure that the compiler knows which type is to
be accessed. For example, in the code below, because classes called NamespaceExample exist both in
the Wrox.ProfessionalCSharp.Chapter03 and Wrox.ProfessionalCSharp.Chapter04
namespaces, we need to specify which of these two namespaces we're talking about:

```
using Wrox.ProfessionalCSharp.Chapter03;
using Wrox.ProfessionalCSharp.Chapter04;

namespace Wrox.ProfessionalCSharp
{
    class Test
    {
        public static int Main()
        {
            // The line below won't compile, because the reference is ambiguous
```

```
            // NamespaceExample NSEx = new NamespaceExample();

            // Instead, we need to specify which namespace we mean:
            Chapter03.NamespaceExample NSEx =
                                        new Chapter03.NamespaceExample();
            return 0;
        }
    }

    namespace Chapter03
    {
        class NamespaceExample
        {
            // Class code here
        }
    }

    namespace Chapter04
    {
        class NamespaceExample
        {
            // Class code here
        }
    }
}
```

If you've taken time to glance through sample C# programs, you may have noticed the `using System;` statement at the start of many of them. The CTS types mentioned earlier are all contained within this namespace, so is much of .NET's core functionality, such as console I/O. Many programmers include this `using System;` statement in every file, because pretty much every C# program will make use of the `System` namespace.

Because `using` statements occur at the top of C# files, in the same place that C and C++ list `#include` statements, namespaces are often confused with header files. Don't make this mistake. The `using` statement does no physical linking between files.

Your organization will probably want to spend some time developing a namespace scheme, so that its developers can quickly locate functionality that they need and so that the names of the organization's homegrown classes won't conflict with those in off-the-shelf class libraries. You can refer to Microsoft's .NET SDK documentation for guidelines on establishing your own namespace scheme.

Namespace Aliases

Another use of the `using` keyword is to assign aliases to classes and namespaces. If we have a very long namespace name that we want to refer to several times in our code, but don't want to include in a `using` directive (for example, to avoid type name conflicts), we can assign an alias to the namespace. The syntax for this is:

```
using alias = NamespaceName;
```

The following example assigns the alias `Chapter03` to the `Wrox.ProfessionalCSharp.Chapter03` namespace, and uses this to instantiate a `NamespaceExample` object, which is defined in this namespace. This object has one method, `GetNamespace`, which uses the `GetType` method exposed by every class to access a `Type` object representing the class's type. We use this object to return a the name of the class's namespace:

```
using System;
using Chapter03 = Wrox.ProfessionalCSharp.Chapter03;

class Test
{
    public static int Main()
    {
        Chapter03.NamespaceExample NSEx = new Chapter03.NamespaceExample();
        Console.WriteLine(NSEx.GetNamespace());
        return 0;
    }
}

namespace Wrox.ProfessionalCSharp.Chapter03
{
    class NamespaceExample
    {
        public string GetNamespace()
        {
            return this.GetType().Namespace;
        }
    }
}
```

The Main() Method

We mentioned a while ago, at the start of this chapter, that C# programs start execution at a method named Main(). As we saw earlier, this must be a static method of a class (or struct), and must have a return type of either int or void:

```
public static int Main()
```

Or:

```
public static void Main()
```

Although it's common to specify the public modifier explicitly, because by definition the method must be called from outside the program, it doesn't actually matter what accessibility level we assign to the method; it will run even if we mark the method as private.

Multiple Main() Methods

When a C# console or Windows application is compiled, by default the compiler looks for exactly one Main() method in any class matching the signature listed above, and makes that class method the entry point for the program. If there's more than one Main() method, the compiler will return an error. For example, consider the code:

```
// MainExample.cs
using System;

namespace Wrox.ProfessionalCSharp.Chapter03
{
```

```
class Client
{
   public static int Main()
   {
      MathExample.Main();
      return 0;
   }
}

class MathExample
{
   static int Add(int x, int y)
   {
      return x + y;
   }

   public static int Main()
   {
      int i = Add(5,10);
      Console.WriteLine(i);
      return 0;
   }
}
```

This contains two classes, both of which have a Main() method. If we try to compile this in the usual way (using csc MainExample.cs), we will get the errors:

```
MainExample.cs(8,25): error CS0017: Program 'MainExample.exe' has more than one
       entry point defined: 'Wrox.ProfessionalCSharp.Chapter03.Client.Main()'
MainExample.cs(22,25): error CS0017: Program 'MainExample.exe' has more than one
       entry point defined:
'Wrox.ProfessionalCSharp.Chapter03.MathExample.Main()'
```

However, we can explicitly tell the compiler which of these methods to use as the entry point for the program using the /main switch, together with the full name (including namespace) of the class to which the Main() method belongs:

csc MainExample.cs /main:Wrox.ProfessionalCSharp.Chapter03.MathExample

Passing Arguments to Main()

In our examples so far, we've only shown the Main() method without any parameters. However, when the program is invoked, we can get the CLR to pass any command-line arguments to the program by including a parameter. This parameter is a string array, traditionally called args (although C# will accept any name). We can read this array to evaluate any options passed through the command line when the program is started.

The following sample loops through the string array passed in to the Main() method, and writes the value of each option to the console window:

```
// ArgsExample.cs
using System;

namespace Wrox.ProfessionalCSharp.Chapter03
{
   class ArgsExample
   {
      public static int Main(string[] args)
      {
         for (int i = 0; i < args.Length; i++)
         {
            Console.WriteLine(args[i]);
         }
         return 0;
      }
   }
}
```

We can compile this as usual using `csc ArgsExample.cs`. When we run the compiled executable, we can pass in arguments after the name of the program, for example:

ArgsExample /a /b /c

The result of running this command is as follows:

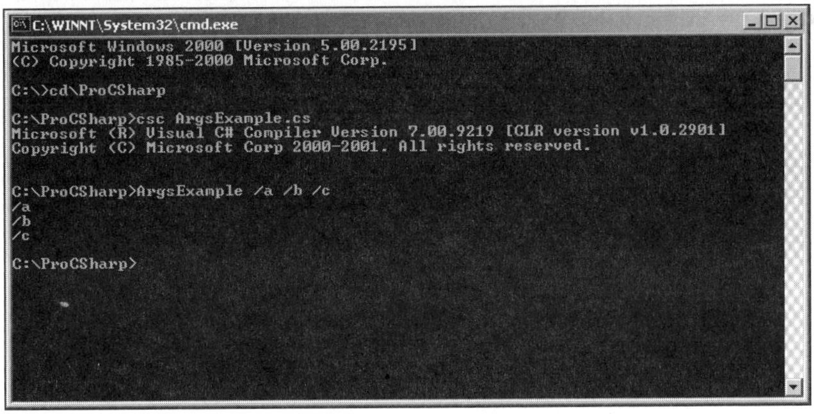

Compiling C# Files

So far, we've seen how to compile console applications using `csc.exe`, but what about other types of application? What if we want to reference a class library? We'll look at all the options for `csc.exe` in Appendix D, but for now we'll look at the most important options.

To answer the first question, we can specify what type of file we want to create using the `/target` option (this can also be abbreviated to `/t`). This can be one of the following:

Option	Output
`/t:exe`	A console application (the default).
`/t:library`	A class library with a manifest.
`/t:module`	A component without a manifest.
`/t:winexe`	A Windows application (without a console window).

If we want a non-executable file (such as a DLL) to be loadable by the .NET runtime, we must compile it as a library. If we compile a C# file as a module, no assembly will be created. Although modules cannot be loaded by the runtime, they can be compiled into another manifest using the `/addmodule` switch. As we'll see later in the book (in Chapter 19), this is particularly useful for including metadata held in `AssemblyInfo.cs` files in an assembly.

Another option we need to mention is `/out`. This allows us to specify the name of the output file produced by the compiler. If an `/out` option isn't specified, the compiler will base the name of the output file on the name of the input C# file, adding an extension according to the target type (for example, `.exe` for a Windows or console application, or `.dll` for a class library). Note that the `/out` and `/t` (or `/target`) options must precede the name of the file we want to compile.

If we want to reference types in assemblies which aren't referenced by default, we can use the `/reference` or `/r` switch, together with the path and filename of the assembly. The following example demonstrates how we can compile a class library, and then reference that library in another assembly. It consists of two files: the class library, and a console application, which will call a class in the library.

The first file is the code for our DLL. To keep things simple, it just contains one class, named `Math`, with a single method that adds two `int`s:

```csharp
// Math.cs
namespace Wrox.ProfessionalCSharp.Chatper03
{
   public class Math    // Notice that we make this class public,
                        // because we want to access it from another assembly
   {
      public int Add(int x, int y)
      {
         return x + y;
      }
   }
}
```

We can compile this C# file into a .NET DLL using the command:

```
csc /t:library Math.cs
```

The console application will simply instantiate this object, and call its `Add` method, displaying the result in the console window:

```
// Client.cs
using System;

namespace Wrox.ProfessionalCSharp.Chatper03
{
   class Client
   {
      public static int Main()
      {
         Math Math = new Math();
         Console.WriteLine(Math.Add(7,8));
         return 0;
      }
   }
}
```

We can compile this using the /r switch to point at our newly compiled DLL:

csc Client.cs /r:Math.dll

We can then run it as normal just by entering **Client** at the command prompt. This should display the number 15 – the result of our addition.

Console I/O

At this point, you should have a basic familiarity with C#'s data types, as well as some knowledge of how the thread-of-control moves through a program that manipulates those data types. So that you can start implementing simple programs that explore these concepts, we'll introduce you to some simple techniques for C# I/O. Subsequent chapters on Windows applications, ASP.NET applications, and web services will familiarize you with more advanced I/O strategies.

The Console Class

The methods for reading from and writing to the console window are actually provided by the .NET classes, rather than being integral to the C# language, but it's useful to cover them here. Specifically, they are provided by the System.Console class. This provides two methods for writing to the console window, and two methods for reading from it.

Console Input

To read a character of text from the console window, we use the Console.Read() method. This will read an input stream from the console window (for example, by allowing the user to enter some text) and return the next character in the stream as an int. For example, the following code lets the user input a line of text, and displays the first character:

```
int x = Console.Read();
Console.WriteLine((char)x);
```

The Console.ReadLine() method is similar, but returns the entire line of text as a string:

```
string s = Console.ReadLine();
Console.WriteLine(s);
```

135

Console Output

There are also two corresponding methods for writing to the console: Console.Write(), which writes the specified value to the console window, and Console.WriteLine(), which does the same, but adds a new line character at the end of the output. There are various forms (overloads) of these functions for all the predefined types (including object), so in most cases we don't have to convert values to strings before we display them.

Console.WriteLine() also allows us to display formatted output in a way comparable to C's printf function. To use WriteLine() in this way, we pass in a number of parameters. The first is a string containing markers in curly braces where the subsequent parameters will be inserted into the text. Each marker contains a zero-based index for the number of the parameter in the following list. For example, "{0}" represents the first parameter in the list, so the lines:

```
int i = 10;
int j = 20;
Console.WriteLine("{0} plus {1} equals {2}", i, j, i + j);
```

will display:

```
10 plus 20 equals 30
```

We can also specify a width for the value, and justify the text within that width, using positive values for right justification, and negative values for left justification. To do this, we use the format $\{n, w\}$, where n is the parameter index, and w is the width value:

```
int i = 940;
int j = 73;
Console.WriteLine(" {0,4}\n+{1,4}\n ----\n {2,4}", i, j, i + j);
```

The result of this is:

```
 940
+  73
 ----
1013
```

Finally, we can also add a one-character format string, together with an optional precision value. The possible format strings are:

String	Description
C	Local currency format.
D	Decimal format. Converts an integer to base 10, and pads with leading zeros if a precision specifier is given.
E	Scientific (exponential) format. The precision specifier sets the number of decimal places (6 by default). The case of the format string ("e" or "E") determines the case of the exponential symbol.
F	Fixed-point format; the precision specifier controls the number of decimal places. Zero is acceptable.

String	Description
G	General format. Uses E or F formatting, depending on which is the most compact.
N	Number format. Formats the number with commas as thousands separators, for example 32,767.44.
P	Percent format.
X	Hexadecimal format. The precision specifier can be used to pad with leading zeros.

Note that the format strings are case-insensitive.

For example, to format a `decimal` value as currency for the computer's locale, with precision to two decimal places, we would use C2:

```
decimal i = 940.23m;
decimal j = 73.7m;
Console.WriteLine(" {0,9:C2}\n+{1,9:C2}\n ---------\n {2,9:C2}", i, j, i + j);
```

The output of this in the United States is:

```
    $940.23
+    $73.70
  ---------
  $1,013.93
```

As a final trick, we can also use placeholder characters instead of these format strings to map out formatting. For example:

```
double d = 0.234;
Console.WriteLine("{0:#.00}", d);
```

This displays as .23, because the pound symbol (#) is ignored if there is no character in that place, and zeros will either be replaced by the character in that position if there is one, or else printed as a zero.

Comments

The last topic we'll look at in this chapter looks very simple on the surface – adding comments to our code. As we noted at the start of the chapter, C# uses the traditional C-type single-line (// ...) and multi-line (/* ... */) comments:

```
// This is a single-line comment
/* This comment
   spans multiple lines */
```

Everything in a single-line comment, from the // to the end of the line, will be ignored by the compiler, and everything from an opening /* to the next */ combination will be ignored. It's actually possible (although definitely not recommended) to put multi-line comments *within* a line of code:

```
Console.WriteLine(/* Please don't do this! */ "This will compile");
```

Although having said that, inline comments like this can be useful when debugging if, say, you temporarily want to try running the code with a different value somewhere:

```
DoSomething(Width, /*Height*/ 100);
```

If you do this, however, don't forget to change the code back again after you've finished debugging it!

Comment characters included in string literals are of course treated like normal characters:

```
string s = "/* This is just a normal string */";
```

The one point to be aware of is that we can't include the combination */ in any multi-line comments, as this will be treated as the end of the comment. Therefore, if we write something like this:

```
/* string s = "/* ... */"; */
```

Then it won't compile, since the compiler will treat the first */ as the end of the comment, and attempt to compile the remaining characters ("; */) as C# code.

XML Documentation

In addition to the C-type comments, illustrated above, C# has a very neat feature which we can't leave this chapter without discussing, namely: the ability to produce documentation in XML format automatically from special comments. These comments are single-line comments, but begin with three slashes (///), instead of the usual two. Within these comments, we can place XML tags containing documentation of the types and type members in our code.

The following tags are recognized by the compiler. For a few of these tags, the syntax will actually be validated by the compiler:

Tag	Description
<c>	Marks up text within a line as code, for example <c>int i = 10;</c>.
<code>	Marks multiple lines as code.
<example>	Marks up a code example.
<exception>	Documents an exception class. (Syntax verified by the compiler).
<include>	Includes comments from another documentation file. (Syntax verified by the compiler).
<list>	Inserts a list into the documentation.
<param>	Marks up a method parameter. (Syntax verified by the compiler).
<paramref>	Indicates that a word is a method parameter. (Syntax verified by the compiler).
<permission>	Documents access to a member. (Syntax verified by the compiler).

Tag	Description
<remarks>	Adds a description for a member.
<returns>	Documents the return value for a method.
<see>	Provides a cross-reference to another parameter. (Syntax verified by the compiler).
<seealso>	Provides a 'see also' section in a description. (Syntax verified by the compiler).
<summary>	Provides a short summary of a type or member.
<value>	Describes a property.

To see how this works, let's add some XML comments to the Math.cs file from the previous section. We'll add a <summary> element for the class and for its Add() method, and also a <returns> element and two <param> elements for the Add() method:

```
// Math.cs
namespace Wrox.ProfessionalCSharp.Chatper03
{

    ///<summary>
    ///   Wrox.ProfessionalCSharp.Chatper03.Math class.
    ///   Provides a method to add two integers.
    ///</summary>
    public class Math
    {
        ///<summary>
        ///   The Add method allows us to add two integers
        ///</summary>
        ///<returns>Result of the addition (int)</returns>
        ///<param name="x">First number to add</param>
        ///<param name="y">Second number to add</param>
        public int Add(int x, int y)
        {
            return x + y;
        }
    }
}
```

The C# compiler can extract the XML elements from the special comments and use them to generate an XML file. To get the compiler to generate the XML documentation for an assembly, we specify the /doc option when we compile, together with the name of the file we want to be created:

```
csc /t:library /doc:Math.xml math.cs
```

The compiler will throw an error if the XML comments don't result in a well-formed XML document.

This will generate an XML file named `Math.xml`, which looks like this:

```xml
<?xml version="1.0"?>
<doc>
    <assembly>
        <name>Math</name>
    </assembly>
    <members>
        <member name="T:Wrox.ProfessionalCSharp.Chatper03.Math">
            <summary>
                Wrox.ProfessionalCSharp.Chatper03.Math class.
                Provides a method to add two integers.
            </summary>
        </member>
        <member name=
"M:Wrox.ProfessionalCSharp.Chatper03.Math.Add(System.Int32,System.Int32)">
            <summary>
                The Add method allows us to add two integers
            </summary>
            <returns>Result of the addition (int)</returns>
            <param name="x">First number to add</param>
            <param name="y">Second number to add</param>
        </member>
    </members>
</doc>
```

Notice how the compiler has actually done some work for us; it's created an `<assembly>` element, and also added a `<member>` element for each type or member of a type in the file. Each `<member>` element has a `name` attribute with the full name of the member as its value, prefixed by a letter which indicates whether this is a type (`"T:"`), field (`"F:"`), or member (`"M:"`).

XML Documentation in Visual Studio.NET

We don't want to concentrate too much on VS.NET in this book, as most of the functionality it provides is quite straightforward. However, it is worth mentioning in this context that if you're using VS.NET, it can save you quite a lot of typing when compiling XML documentation.

Open up the `Math.cs` file in Visual Studio.NET, and add a blank line before the definition of the `Add` method. Now, type three forward slashes (`///`) at the start of the line. Visual Studio very kindly adds a whole lot of XML tags for us:

```csharp
/// <summary>
/// |
/// </summary>
/// <param name="x"></param>
/// <param name="y"></param>
/// <returns></returns>
public int Add(int x, int y)
{
    return x + y;
}
```

All we have to do is type in the actual descriptions. Notice how Visual Studio has even managed to put in the correct values for the parameter names in the <param> tags.

In order to generate the XML documentation when the project is compiled, specify an XML Documentation File on the Build menu under Configuration Properties on the project's property pages.

Visual Studio can also generate HTML-formatted documentation from these XML comments. To do this, select Tools | Build Comment Web Pages... from the menu. We are now asked whether we want to generate XML documentation for the entire solution, or just for selected projects. We're also asked where we want to save the generated HTML pages. When we select OK, Visual Studio will generate a whole set of HTML pages documenting our project, which we can browse through Visual Studio or any web browser:

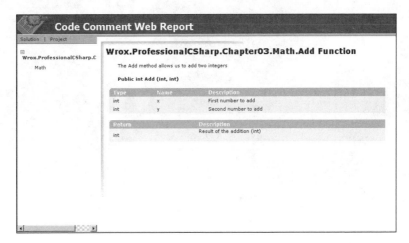

Summary

In this chapter, we've taken a brisk walk through the main features of C#'s syntax. We've covered a lot of ground, but much of it will be instantly recognizable to developers who are familiar with any C-style language (or even JavaScript). Some of the topics we've covered are:

- ❑ C#'s type system, particularly the difference between value types and reference types
- ❑ Converting data between different types
- ❑ Declaring and initializing variables in C#
- ❑ Variable scope and access levels
- ❑ C#'s operators
- ❑ Flow control statements
- ❑ Program structure and compilation
- ❑ Comments and XML auto-documentation

Now we've seen the basics of the C# language, we'll move on to an in-depth look at C#'s object-oriented programming features in the next two chapters.

4

Classes and Inheritance

Until now, we have concentrated on learning the basic syntax of C#: how to declare variables, how to control the flow of execution, and so on. C# is a fully object-oriented language however, which means that in order to write code that is not merely syntactically correct, but also good code (in the sense of being well designed) we are going to have to get to grips with its object-oriented features, and that means learning about **Object-Oriented Programming** (**OOP**). OOP is a generic term for a very powerful programming methodology that allows easily maintainable and reusable pieces of code to be written to perform even very complex tasks. In this chapter, we are going to introduce the principles of object-oriented programming and see how to use C# to write good, well-structured object-oriented code. This means that, while we'll be learning quite a bit of C# syntax in this chapter, the real emphasis is on understanding the concept of OOP itself.

OOP is an extremely powerful methodology. Once you've become used to writing your code using it, you will wonder how you ever got by without it. You'll find that it gives your code an intuitive, "natural" structure that is not possible with procedural languages, and is not really possible even in VB6, which does implement a few object-oriented features. Unfortunately, it is the sort of topic where there are an awful lot of new concepts to take in before you get to see how useful it really is. For this reason, you may find as you read this chapter that you're wondering what the point of it all is. Don't worry – you really are learning something that is important, not only for C#, but for writing good maintainable code in many languages.

We'll start by looking in some detail at the nature of an object before moving on to examine the concept of **inheritance**. Inheritance allows the code for classes to be re-used in a very convenient manner, and is at the heart of object-oriented programming. We'll look at both how to code up inheritance in C# and at how you would normally use inheritance in your programs in more conceptual terms.

Before We Begin

If you are coming to this chapter from a background of C++ or Java, you will of course already be familiar with the concepts of object-oriented programming and how to use OOP and inheritance to create well-designed modular programs. These concepts in are no way different in C# compared to C++ or Java, and apart from some minor syntactical differences, classes are used in C# in the same way as in those two languages. Because of this, you may prefer to quickly skim through this chapter, and concentrate instead on appendices B and C respectively, in which the differences between C# and C++/Java are highlighted.

If you are a skilled Visual Basic developer, but do not have experience of C++ or Java, then you will find many of the concepts in this chapter completely new. Visual Basic does allow you to code something that is often referred to as an object: the VB class module. Some texts even refer to this as involving object-oriented programming, although this actually bears little resemblance to the original concepts of OOP. It's more true to say that VB implements a few of the more basic features of OOP. A VB class module is essentially a COM component, but wrapped up in a way that hides much of what it does. In particular it does not support inheritance of its methods in the same way that inheritance is used in C# and conventional OOP.

When you start reading this chapter you'll probably think at first that we're just describing what you're used to in the class modules, but we're not. Because of the support for inheritance, C# classes are much more powerful than VB class modules, and are often used very differently. If you want to write good C#/.NET applications and assemblies, you will need to read this chapter carefully. Objects and inheritance are not just new language features. In a well-designed object-oriented program, the whole architecture of the program is often arranged around inheritance, so you'll find once you're comfortable with the concept, you'll be structuring your programs in a completely different way to how you would have done in VB, and your programs will be easier for others to maintain as a result.

A Closer Look at Objects and Classes

In this section, we're going to start with a recap of what a class is in very general terms. After this, we will look at how a class can be written in C#. To show you how universal objects are in our lives, we're actually going to start with examples that have nothing to do with computers before we see how to apply the concepts to programming.

Objects in Everyday Life

In everyday life, an object is anything that is identifiably a single material item. It could be a car, a house, a book, a document, or a pay check. For our purposes, we're going to extend that a bit and think of an object as anything whatsoever that is a single item that you might want to represent in a program. We'll therefore also include living "objects", such as a person, an employee, or a customer, as well as more abstract "objects", such as a company, a database, or a country.

The reason for thinking about objects in this way is partly so that we'll be able to write code that models the real world, to the extent that it contains objects, and partly to provide a way of breaking up a large program into smaller, more manageable, units. The idea really comes from the concept of a **black box**, that you may have encountered in school science.

The idea of a black box is that there are a lot of objects in life that you are able to use but you don't understand how they work. Look at your car radio, for example. Do you know exactly what's inside it? Unless you're an expert in that field, you probably don't. You do know however, that twiddling certain knobs will cause it to play CDs or tapes, or receive radio station broadcasts. Not only that, but you know you could take out your radio, plug in a different one and it'll do basically the same thing, even though the internal workings of it might be completely different. Black boxes formalize this idea that there's a difference between what something does, which you usually know, and how it works, which you usually don't need to know, and that two objects can do the same thing, but work differently inside.

Another example of "black boxes" would be light bulbs. My housemates, in an attempt to be environmentally friendly, recently replaced a couple of our traditional light bulbs with those low-energy fluorescent ones. Traditional light bulbs work by heating up a small wire of resisting material (the filament) until it is so hot that it glows strongly enough to light up a whole room. Fluorescent ones work by exciting molecules in a gas so that they radiate light because of electrons jumping between energy levels in the atoms, even though they actually stay roughly at room temperature. The internal design could hardly be more different, but that doesn't matter, because the result is the same (apart from the lower energy bills and the smug "hey-we're-being-eco-friendly" comments from the said housemates).

Just to prove objects don't have to come from electronics, I recently bought two new jumpers. One was made of a lovely soft furry material, while the other had a courser, grainier texture. They are obviously made out of very different fabrics and knitted together differently, but I don't care about that. All I know is they both do the same thing – they keep me warm! And that means I can interchange them without worrying about something going wrong.

In all these examples, replacing one object with another does have some subtle effects. Energy bills might be lower, one material might feel a bit different from another, but the basic function is unchanged. For example, it lights your room or keeps you warm. Another important point is that the basic user interface is unchanged; I plug in my fluorescent bulbs into the sockets in exactly the same way as I would plug in a tungsten filament one. Two jumpers might be made of a different material, but I still put them on in exactly the same way (roll them over my head, then locate where the arms are and thread my arms through, and so on.)

If you understand all that, then you basically understand object-oriented programming, because OOP is about applying these exact same concepts to computer programming. If, in other areas of our lives, we use things that have a well-designed interface, whose function we know, and we know how to use them, but don't care how they work, why not do the same thing in your programs? In other words, break each program into lots of units, each designed to perform a clearly specified purpose within the program. That's basically what an object is.

If you start thinking about your programs this way, you gain quite a few advantages. You'll find it becomes easier to design the programs. The architecture of the programs becomes more intuitive and easier to understand, because it more closely reflects whatever it is that the program is abstracting from real life. It becomes easier for multiple developers to work together, since they can work on different objects in the code, and only need to know what each other's objects do, without having to worry about the details of how each other's code works.

Objects in Programming

We've now established what an object is in general terms and seen a couple of examples from everyday life. We now need to see more specifically how to apply the concepts to programming.

If you've programmed on Windows before then you've almost certainly already been using objects extensively in your programs. For example, think about the various controls that you can place in windows – text boxes, list boxes, list views, and so on. Microsoft has written these controls for you, so that you don't need to know, for example, how a text box works internally. You just know that it does certain things. For example, you can set its Text property and the new text will appear on the screen, or you can set its Width property, and the text box will immediately resize itself for you.

You've also used objects in your C# programming in the last chapter. For example, in the Console.WriteLine() method that you use to write to the screen:

```
Console.WriteLine("Hello, World\n");
```

We mentioned in the last chapter that Console is an object and WriteLine is a method of this object. All the samples in the last chapter involved defining a **class**, usually called Class1, which contained the program's main entry point:

```
public class Class1
{
    public static int Main(string[] args)
    {
```

In programming, we need to distinguish between a **class** and an **object**. A class is the generic definition of what an object is – the template, if you like. For example, in everyday life, a class could be "house" – the abstract idea of a house. My house, on the other hand, is an object. Your house is a different object, but both objects are of the same class.

In the last chapter however, we simply used this class as a way of containing the main program entry point, in order to satisfy the C# requirement that all methods must be part of a class. We didn't use this class to perform any real object-oriented programming. In this chapter we'll start defining other classes in our code, and show how to design programs in a way that takes advantage of object-oriented features.

Class Members

In the everyday life examples above, I've continually emphasized that there are two sides to an object – what it does, which is usually publicly known, and how it works which is usually hidden. You don't need to know how it works in order to use the object. In programming, these two concepts remain. The "what it does" is normally represented in the first instance by **methods** that you can call. A method is just C#-parlance for a function. The "how it works" is represented both by methods, and by any data (variables) that the object stores. In Java and C++, this data is described as **member variables**, while in VB this data would be represented by any module-level variables in the class module. In C# the terminology is **fields**. In general, a class is completely defined by its fields and methods.

> *The above paragraph is something of a simplification. There are other things that make up a C# class, which we'll cover later in the chapter and in the next few chapters. These include indexers, properties, constructors, operators, delegates, and events. For the most part, these items are roughly the same as methods, but dressed up in a different syntax to make using the class more intuitive. It is also possible for fields to be publicly exposed as part of what the class does, though for reasons we'll explore later on, that is generally considered to be poor programming practice.*

We'll also use the term **member** by itself to denote anything that is part of a class, be it a field, method, or any of the other items just mentioned that can be defined within a class.

Example: The Authenticator Class

The easiest way to understand how to code up a class is by looking at an example. Therefore, over the next few sections, we're going to develop a simple class called Authenticator. We'll assume we're in the process of writing a large application, which at some point requires users to log in, supplying a password. Authenticator is the name of the class that will handle this aspect of the program. We won't worry about the rest of the application – we'll just concentrate on writing this class, but we will also write a small piece of test harness code to check that Authenticator works as intended.

Authenticator allows us to do two things: set a new password, and check whether a password is valid. The C# code we need to define the class looks like this:

```
public class Authenticator
{
    private string Password;

    public bool IsPasswordCorrect(string password)
    {
        return (password == Password) ? true : false;
    }
    public bool ChangePassword(string oldPassword, string newPassword)
    {
        if (oldPassword == Password)
        {
            Password = newPassword;
            return true;
        }
        else
            return false;
    }
}
```

In terms of the syntax used in this snippet, you'll probably be able to figure out yourself what's going on. The keyword class in C# indicates that we are going to define a new class (type of object). The word immediately following class is the name we're going to use for this class. Then the actual definition of the object follows in squiggly brackets – the definition consisting of a number of variables (the fields) and methods – in our case one field and two methods.

The ubiquity of classes is illustrated by the fact that we are already using another class in this example: string. string, which as we saw in the last chapter represents a Unicode character string, is defined as one of the base classes that has been supplied for us by Microsoft. Because Microsoft has already written this class, it is free for us to use in other parts of our code.

The only field in Authenticator, Password, stores the current password, and is marked by the keyword private. This means that it is not visible outside the class – the compiler and the .NET environment will not allow any code to access this field, apart from code that is part of the Authenticator class itself. Marking a field or method as private effectively ensures that that field or method will be part of the internal working of the class, as opposed to the external interface. The advantage of this is that if you decide to change the internal working (perhaps you later decide not to store Password as a string but to use some other more specialized data type), you can just make the change, and you know it won't break or affect any other code outside the Authenticator class definition. This is because any other code couldn't possibly have been accessing this field anyway.

Notice that we've taken advantage of C#'s case insensitivity here by using `Password` as the name of a member field and `password` as the name of a parameter to the `IsPasswordCorrect()` method.

Any code that uses the `Authenticator` class can only access the methods that have been marked with the keyword `public` – that is to say in this case the `IsPasswordCorrect()` and `ChangePassword()` methods. Both of these methods have been implemented in such a way that nothing will be done (other than returning `true` or `false`) unless the calling code supplies the current correct password, as you'd expect for software that implements security. The implementations of these functions both access the `Password` field, but that's okay because this code forms part of the `Authenticator` class itself. Notice that these public functions simultaneously give us the interface to the external world (in other words, any other code that uses the `Authenticator` class), and define what the `Authenticator` class does, as viewed by the rest of the world.

`private` and `public` are not the only access modifiers available to define what code is allowed to know about the existence of a member. Later in this chapter we'll encounter `protected`, which makes the member available to this class and certain related classes, and in Chapter 5 we'll meet `internal` and `protected internal`, which restrict access to other code within the same assembly.

Now we've defined the `Authenticator` class, how do we use it in our code? The easiest way to understand that is to think of the class as a new type of variable. You're used to the predefined variable types – in C# these are things like `int`, `float`, `double`, and so on. Well, by defining the `Authenticator` class, we've effectively told the compiler that there's a new type of variable called an `Authenticator`. By that I don't mean we're defining a new primitive data type, but that we're defining a new, more complex, type of variable that is made up by putting together some other variables (the member fields), and by telling the compiler what this new, complex, variable type can do (the methods).

The class definition contains everything the compiler needs to know to be able to process this variable type. Therefore, just as the compiler knows that a `double` contains a floating point number stored in a certain format, and you can do things with them such as adding them together, we've told the compiler that a variable of type `Authenticator` contains a `string` and allows you to call the `IsPasswordCorrect()` and `ChangePassword()` methods.

*Although we've described a class as a new type of variable, the more common terminology is **data type**, or simply **type**.*

If `Authenticator` is just another type of variable, we can use it with code that looks like this:

```
Authenticator Simon = new Authenticator();
bool Done;
Done = Simon.ChangePassword("", "MyNewPassword");
if (Done == true)
   Console.WriteLine("Password for Simon changed");
else
   Console.WriteLine("Failed to change password for Simon");
Done = Simon.ChangePassword("", "AnotherPassword");
if (Done == true)
   Console.WriteLine("Password for Simon changed");
else
```

```
      Console.WriteLine("Failed to change password for Simon");

   if (Simon.IsPasswordCorrect("WhatPassword"))
      Console.WriteLine("Verified Simon\'s password");
   else
      Console.WriteLine("Failed to verify Simon\'s password");
```

In other words, we define a variable of type `Authenticator`, and use it just like any other variable, with the dot (.) operator to indicate when we are calling member methods.

This code also demonstrates the difference between a class and an object. `Authenticator` is the class that we defined previously. When we declare the variable `Simon`, we are creating an object – an instance of the class `Authenticator`.

> **In most cases, you have to instantiate a class by creating an object of the type of that class before you can use the class.**

For the moment, don't worry too much about the `= new Authenticator()` bit of the line where we declare the variable. It's to do with allocating memory to store the `Authenticator`, and we'll explain more precisely what's going on later in the chapter. In C#, a variable whose type is a class that you have defined yourself actually contains only a reference to where the data for that variable is stored in memory. The memory itself has to be allocated separately, which is done with the `new` keyword.

C++ programmers can compare this to storing a pointer to an object. For Java programmers, it's the same as a Java reference. For VB programmers, you can compare this to ActiveX objects for which a reference is stored. The keyword new in this particular context in C# does pretty much the same thing as new does in C++, which in turn is somewhat similar to what New does in VB6.

As mentioned earlier, calling methods against a class is done using the period symbol (.) appended to the name of the variable. Again, this notation will be already familiar to C++, Java and VB programmers. Note, however, that we could not do this:

```
   string SimonsPassword = Simon.Password;
```

This code will actually cause a compilation error, the reason being that, as we've mentioned, the `Password` field was explicitly marked as `private`, so other code cannot explicitly access it. Also note that we could not do this:

```
   Authenticator Simon = new Authenticator();
   Authenticator Karli = new Authenticator();
   Authenticator Result = Simon + Karli;              // WRONG
```

The first two lines of code here are fine, but the third line will cause a compilation error, because we have not told the compiler how to add `Authenticator` objects together. The compiler simply won't know what to do with such a statement. This doesn't matter too much for an `Authenticator`, because for this class, addition doesn't really make much conceptual sense anyway. However, in your own code you might wish to define classes for which adding and multiplying are intuitive operations (for example, you might write a class that represents an amount of currency, or a mathematical matrix). In the next chapter we'll look at **operator overloading**, and we'll see how you can tell the compiler what the mathematical operators mean for a class that you've defined, so that you would be able to write code that adds, subtracts, multiplies, divides, or performs other operations with your classes.

Just to complete this example, we'll show you the code for the full program that uses the Authenticator class, so you can see how the code all fits together. This code is downloadable from the Wrox Press web site (http://www.wrox.com/) as the Authenticator sample:

```csharp
using System;
namespace Wrox.ProfessionalCSharp.Chapter4.Authenticator
{
    class ProgramEntryPoint
    {
        static void Main(string[] args)
        {
            Authenticator Simon = new Authenticator();
            bool Done;
            Done = Simon.ChangePassword("", "MyNewPassword");
            if (Done == true)
                Console.WriteLine("Password for Simon changed");
            else
                Console.WriteLine("Failed to change password for Simon");
            Done = Simon.ChangePassword("", "AnotherPassword");
            if (Done == true)
                Console.WriteLine("Password for Simon changed");
            else
                Console.WriteLine("Failed to change password for Simon");

            if (Simon.IsPasswordCorrect("WhatPassword"))
                Console.WriteLine("Verified Simon\'s password");
            else
                Console.WriteLine("Failed to verify Simon\'s password");
        }
    }
    public class Authenticator
    {
        private string Password;

        public bool IsPasswordCorrect(string password)
        {
            return (password == Password) ? true : false;
        }
        public bool ChangePassword(string oldPassword, string newPassword)
        {
            if (oldPassword == Password)
            {
                Password = newPassword;
                return true;
            }
            else
                return false;
        }
    }
}
```

Running this program gives this result, which if you follow through the logic of the code, you'll see is what we'd expect given that Simon starts with an empty string as the initial default password:

There are a couple of points to note from the code. First, you'll see in terms of what we've covered up to now in this book that there's actually nothing really new in this code sample. All the keywords have already been used in the code samples in the last chapter, and VB programmers will have seen essentially the same thing happening in VB class modules. The reason for going over this code here was to make sure we are clear about the concepts behind classes.

Secondly, the above example uses the Authenticator class directly in other code within the same source file. You'll often want to write classes that are used by other projects that you or others work on. In order to do this, you write the class in exactly the same way, but compile the code for the class into a library. How to do this is covered in Chapter 10.

Thirdly, there's a second class in this code, ProgramEntryPoint, which contains the main program entry point. This is a full-blown class in exactly the same way as is Authenticator – it can have its own members (that is, its own fields, methods and so on). We've chosen to use this class solely as a container for the program entry point however, the Main() function, and not to place any other members in ProgramEntryPoint. Doing it this way means that the Authenticator class can sit as a class in its own right, able to be used in other programs if we wish (either by cutting and pasting the code or by compiling it separately into an assembly), and so enables us to demonstrate object-oriented programming better. With this technique, ProgramEntryPoint only exists because of the syntactical requirement of C# that even the program's main entry point has to be defined within a class, rather than sitting as an independent function.

How Classes Are Implemented

In this section, we'll examine some aspects of the operation and internal implementation of classes that you need to understand in order to be able to use them effectively. In the process, we'll also develop our Authenticator example further.

Instance and Static Fields

In this section, we'll look at how fields are associated with classes, and see that this can be done in two different ways. First, let's discuss some terminology. Examine this code:

```
double Height=200.0 , Depth = 400.0;
```

In this case we declare two variables of type `double`. `double` is the **type** of data, and `Height` and `Depth` are each **instances** of a double. In the same way, if we write:

```
Authenticator Julian = new Authenticator();
Authenticator Karli = new Authenticator();
```

then `Julian` and `Karli` are two individual instances of the class `Authenticator`. Get the idea? In both cases, we declare the variables and initialize them, though the syntax is slightly different for doubles than it is for our own classes, for which we use the new keyword.

It's important to understand that each instance of a class (each object) has its own set of all the fields you've defined in the class by default. For example, if you write:

```
Karli.ChangePassword("OldKarliPassword", "NewKarliPassword")
Julian.ChangePassword("OldJulianPassword", "NewJulianPassword")
```

The variables `Karli` and `Julian` each contain their own string called `Password`. Changing the password in `Karli` has no effect on the password in `Julian`, and vice versa (unless the two references happen to be pointing to the same address in memory, which is something we'll come to later). The situation is a bit like this:

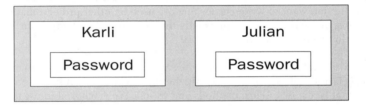

This is a crucial point to understand about classes, and one that I've seen confuse more than a few programmers trying to get to grips with object-oriented programming: Each time you declare a variable whose type is some class, that variable by default gets its own copy of all the fields in the class.

There are some cases in which this might not be the behaviour you want. For example, suppose in our `Authenticator` class we wished to define a minimum length for all passwords. Note that this is a universal minimum length that applies to all the passwords – in other words, to all the instances of the `Authenticator` class. We do not want each password to have its own minimum length. Therefore, we really want the minimum length to be stored only once in memory, no matter how many instances of `Authenticator` we create.

To indicate that a field should only be stored once, no matter how many instances of the class we create, we place keyword `static` in front of the field declaration in our code:

```
public class Authenticator
{
    private static uint minPasswordLength = 6;
    private string Password;
```

Storing a copy of `minPasswordLength` with each `Authenticator` instance would not only have wasted memory, but also caused problems if we wanted to be able to change its value! By declaring the field as `static`, we ensure that it will only be stored once. Note that in this code snippet we also set an initial value. Fields declared with the `static` keyword are referred to as **static fields** or **static data**, while fields that are not declared as static, are referred to as **instance fields** or **instance data**. Another way of looking at it is that an instance field belongs to an object, while a static field belongs to the class.

VB developers shouldn't confuse this with static variables in VB. VB static variables are something completely different – variables whose values remain between invocations of a method, but which are invisible outside the method. There is no corresponding concept in C# – it's not needed when you can define member fields instead.

> **`static` does not mean the same thing in C# as it does in VB**

If a field has been declared as `static`, then it exists when your program is running from the moment that the particular module or assembly containing the definition of the class is loaded. This will be as soon as your code tries to use something from that assembly, so you can always guarantee a static variable is there when you want to refer to it. This is independent of whether you actually declare any variables of that class. By contrast, instance fields only exist when there are variables of that class currently in scope – one set of instance fields for each variable. As we've just indicated, you can think of instance fields as being part of each individual variable (object) whereas static data is part of the class definition as a whole.

In some ways static fields perform the same functions as global variables performed for old procedural languages, such as C and FORTRAN. After you've had some experience with object-oriented programming you may well find that you are defining static fields in cases where you would have used global variables in other languages. VB doesn't have any equivalent to C# static fields.

The `static` keyword is independent of the accessibility of the member to which it applies. A class member can be `public static` or `private static`.

Just as for fields, by default a method such as `ChangePassword()` that has not been declared as `static` is called against a particular object (instance of a class), as indicated by the name of the variable in front of the `"."` operator. That method then implicitly has access to all the member fields (as well as methods, indexers, and so on) of that particular object.

Instance and Static Methods

Just as with fields, it is possible to declare methods as `static`, provided that they do not attempt to access any instance data or other instance methods. For example, we might wish to provide a method to allow users to view the minimum password length:

```
public class Authenticator
{
    private static uint minPasswordLength = 6;
    public static uint GetMinPasswordLength()
    {
        return minPasswordLength;
    }
```

The code for this is available on the Wrox Press website as the `Authenticator2` sample.

Note that while this example is correct C#, we'll see a better way of defining this particular method later on in the chapter when we examine properties.

If a method is not explicitly declared as `static`, then it is an instance method, and is associated with a particular variable – a particular instance of the class, just as for instance fields.

Accessing Static and Instance Members

The fact that static methods and fields are associated with a class rather than an object is reflected in how you access them: Instead of specifying the name of a variable before the "`.`" operator, you specify the name of the class, like this:

```
Console.WriteLine(Authenticator.GetMinPasswordLength());  // correct
Console.WriteLine(Julian.GetMinPasswordLength ());        // incorrect
```

By contrast:

```
bool bCorrect = Authenticator.IsPasswordCorrect("Hi");   // incorrect
bool bCorrect = Julian.IsPasswordCorrect("Hi");          // correct
```

> **The rule is that you always call static members by specifying the name of the class, and instance members by specifying the name of an instance.**

Note, that the syntax of C# differs from C++ and Java here. Those other languages will also allow you to call static members by specifying an object name. C# does not permit that syntax. Of course, if you are accessing member methods or fields from inside the class, you can just give the name of the member directly:

```
// this code is in a method inside the Authenticator class
string Passwd = Password;               // instance field in this object
int MinLen = minPasswordLength;         // static field in this class
```

How Instance and Static Methods are Implemented

We said earlier that each object stores its own copy of that class's instance fields. This is however, not the case for methods. If each object had its own copy of the code for a method, that would be incredibly wasteful of memory, since the code for the methods remains the same across all object instances. Therefore, instance methods, just like static methods, are stored only once, and associated with the class as a whole. Later on, we'll learn about other types of class member (constructors, properties, and so on) that contain code rather than data, and the same applies to these.

The full picture looks something like this:

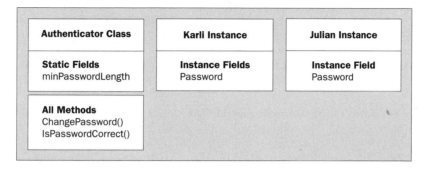

If instance methods are only stored once, how is a method able to access the correct copy of each field? In other words, when you write:

```
Karli.ChangePassword("OldKarliPassword", "NewKarliPassword")
Julian.ChangePassword("OldJulianPassword", "NewJulianPassword")
```

how is the compiler able to generate code that accesses Karli's password with the first method call and Julian's with the second? The answer is that instance methods actually take an extra implicit parameter, which is a reference to where in memory the relevant class instance is stored. You must never specify that extra parameter explicitly, but it is always there. You can almost think of it that the above code is the user-friendly version that you have to write, because it's how C# syntax works, but what's actually happening in your compiled code is:

```
// effectively, in the compiled code
ChangePassword(Karli, "OldKarliPassword", "NewKarliPassword")
ChangePassword(Julian "OldJulianPassword", "NewJulianPassword")
```

Declaring a method as `static` makes calling it slightly more efficient, because it will not be passed this extra parameter. On the other hand, if a method is declared as `static`, but attempts to access any instance data, the compiler will raise an error for the obvious reason that you can't access instance data, unless you have the address of a class instance!

> **You cannot access any instance fields from a method that has been declared as `static`.**

This means that in our `Authenticator` sample we could not declare either `ChangePassword()` or `IsPasswordCorrect()` as static, because both of these methods access the `Password` field, which is not `static`.

Interestingly, although the hidden parameter that comes with instance methods is never declared explicitly; you do actually have access to it in your code. You can get to it using the keyword `this`. As an example, we could rewrite the code for the `ChangePassword()` method as follows:

```
public bool ChangePassword(string oldPassword, string newPassword)
{
    if (oldPassword == this.Password)
    {
        this.Password = newPassword;
        return true;
    }
    else
        return false;
}
```

Generally, you wouldn't write your code like this – all you've achieved is to make the method longer and slightly harder to read. The compiler will automatically interpret any references to member fields that are not scoped with the name of a variable to mean `this.<the field>` anyway. The `this` reference is available if you do need to explicitly refer to it however, and we'll come across situations in which we do need to do so later in the chapter.

The `this` reference is very similar to the `this` keyword of C++ and Java, and the `Me` keyword of VB. The only real difference is that in C++ `this` represents a pointer rather than a reference.

One other point we should make is that the above discussion relates to when methods access fields and other members of the class. If a method, whether instance or static, defines its own local variables or takes parameters, then these are associated with the method, and so stored separately every time that method is called.

Reference and Value Types

It's important to understand the distinction in C# between **reference data types** and **value data types**.

When you declare a variable of any of the basic predefined types such as int, uint, double, float, bool, and so on, you are instantiating a **value type**. That means that each variable contains its own copy of the data it contains. For example, look at the following code:

```
int I=10;
int J, K;
J = I;
K=10;
```

After running this code, there are three variables, I, J, and K, all of which contain the value 10. Note that even though all the variables have the same value, this value is still stored three times in memory. If you add:

```
++J;
```

then J will be incremented to the value 11. Neither I nor K are changed, however – they still have the value 10.

This probably looks so obvious to you that you may be wondering why I'm even bothering to point it out in a professional level book. The reason is that when you create a variable of a type given by a class that you've defined (or, for that matter, string or any of the other base classes), it doesn't work the same way. Classes are all **reference types**, which means that each variable merely contains a reference to where the class instance is stored in memory – not the actual data that makes up that instance. As we've already mentioned that's one reason why you need to use the new operator when you instantiate a class:

```
Authenticator User1;      // doesn't actually create an authenticator. Just
                          // declares that the variable User1 can refer to
                          // an Authenticator

Authenticator User2 = new Authenticator();
                          // instantiates an Authenticator as well as
                          // declaring the variable that refers to it
```

The fact that classes are reference types can have some unexpected effects when it comes to comparing instances of classes for equality, and setting instances of classes equal to each other. For example, look at this:

```
Authenticator User1;
Authenticator User2 = new Authenticator();
Authenticator User3 = new Authenticator();
User1 = User2;
User2.SetPassword("", "Tardis")  // This sets password for User1 as well!
User3.SetPassword("", "Tardis")
if (User2 == User3)
{
    // contents of this if block will NOT be executed even though
    // objects referred to by User2 and User3 are now identical,
    // because the variables refer to different objects

}
if (User2 == User1)
{
    // any code here will be executed because User1 and User2 refer
    // to the same memory

}
```

In this code we declare three variables of type Authenticator: User1, User2, and User3. However, we only actually instantiate two objects of the Authenticator class, because we only use the new operator twice. Then we set the variable User1 equal to User2. Unlike with a value type, this does *not* copy any of the contents of User2. Rather, it means that User1 is set to refer to the same memory as User2 is referring to. What that means is that any changes we make to User2 also affect User1, because they are not separate objects; both variables refer to the same data. We can also say that they **point to** the same data, and the actual data referred to is sometimes described as the **referent**. So when we set the password of User2 to Tardis, we are implicitly also setting the password of User1 to Tardis. This is very different from how value types would behave. The situation after executing the above code looks like this.

The situation gets even less intuitive when we try to compare User2 and User3 in the next statement:

```
if (User2 == User3)
```

You might expect that this condition would return true, since User2 and User3 have both been set to the same password, so both instances contain identical data. The comparison operator for reference types however, doesn't compare the contents of the data by default – it simply tests to see whether the two references are referring to the same address in memory. Because they are not, this test will return false, which means anything inside this if block will not be executed. By contrast, comparing User2 with User1 will return true because these variables do point to the same address in memory.

Later in the chapter when we examine operator overloading, we'll see that it is possible to modify the behavior of the comparison operator (==) for a given class so that it compares contents instead of references. We should also note that for the very important class, string, Microsoft have already done this for us. Comparing two strings with "==" will always compare string content (any other behavior for strings would be extremely confusing!).

You'll need to be aware of this behavior since it can catch you out. Remember, it only applies to reference types, which essentially means to classes, not to any of the predefined value types. If you do think you will actually want to copy or compare the contents of class instances, then you'll need to define methods or operators in the class to allow client code to be able to do that; as mentioned, we'll see how to do this later in the chapter. Bear in mind, however, that many classes contain a lot of member fields, so copying or comparing the contents of a class instance often means processing a *lot* of data. The default behavior of just copying or comparing references is usually preferable: it gives far superior performance, because a reference is always just a single 32-bit number containing an address (or a 64-bit number on 64-bit machines).

Properties

So far we've shown you how to use methods and fields. I said earlier that there are some other types of class members – constructors, indexers, properties, delegates and events. For the most part these other items are used only in more advanced situations, and are not essential to understanding the principles of object-oriented design. For that reason we are not going to discuss them until Chapters 5 and 6. Properties are in extremely common use however, and can hugely simplify the external user interface exposed by classes. For this reason, we'll discuss them here.

VB programmers will find that C# properties correspond exactly to properties in VB class modules and are used in just the same way. For this reason VB programmers may wish to skim through this section.

Properties exist for the situation in which you wish to make a method call look like a field. We can see what a property is by looking again at the minimum password length in our Authenticator class. Let's extend the class so that users can read and modify the minimum password length. As a first attempt we might try something like this, in which we've defined two methods, SetMinPasswordLength() and GetMinPasswordLength():

```
// for example only. This is actually not a good way of doing this

public static uint GetMinPasswordLength()
{
   return minPasswordLength;
}
public static void SetMinPasswordLength(uint value)
{
   minPasswordLength = value;
}
```

If we were actually implementing this class, we would presumably want to set security permissions on the SetMinPasswordLength() *method so it could only be called by certain privileged users. We won't worry about that here, though. Security is covered in Chapter 25.*

The trouble with this approach is that it means the code that looks like this:

```
Authenticator.SetMinPasswordLength(7);
Console.WriteLine("Min password length is " +
                 Authenticator.GetMinPasswordLength());
```

That's okay as it goes, but not very user-friendly. As far as the outside world is concerned, SetMinPasswordLength() and GetMinPasswordLength() appear to be simply changing or accessing a number, and it would be a lot nicer to be able to do this:

```
Authenticator.MinPasswordLength = 7;
Console.WriteLine("Min password length is " +
                 Authenticator.MinPasswordLength);
```

That's where properties come in. A property is a method or pair of methods that are exposed to the outside world as if they are fields. To create a property for the minimum password length we modify the code for the authenticator class as follows:

```
public static uint MinPasswordLength
{
   get
   {
      return minPasswordLength;
   }
   set
   {
      minPasswordLength = value;
   }
}
```

As we can see from this, we define a property in much the same way as a field, except that after the name of the property, we have a code block enclosed by squiggly brackets. In the code block there may be two **accessor** methods called get and set. These are known as the **get accessor** and the **set accessor**. Note, that although no parameter is explicitly mentioned in the definition of the set accessor, there is an implicit parameter passed in, and referred to by the name value. Also, the get accessor always returns the same data type as the property was declared as (in this case a uint).

Now what happens is this: whenever the property is called in a situation in which the value is to be returned (generally on the right hand side of an expression), the `get` accessor will be implicitly called behind the scenes to return the appropriate value. Let's take a look at the following lines of code:

```
uint I;
I = Authenticator.MinPasswordLength;
```

What will actually happen here is that the `MinPasswordLength`'s `get` accessor is called. In this case, this method is implemented to simply return the value of the `minPasswordLength` field. Therefore, it will be set to this value.

On the other hand, if a property is called in a situation in which a value should be assigned to it (the most obvious example being on the left hand side of an assignment operator), the `set` accessor will be implicitly called:

```
Authenticator.MinPasswordLength = 7;
```

This code will cause the `MinPasswordLength`'s `set` accessor to be called, which is implemented to assign the required value to the `minPasswordLength` field. We said earlier that the `set` accessor has an implicit parameter, called `value`. The value passed in for this parameter is the quantity on the right hand side of the assignment operator – in this case 7. So running the above code will cause the `minPasswordLength` field to be assigned the value 7.

The simpler syntax allowed by properties is most evident when a property is modified in a single statement. For example, suppose we wanted to add two characters to the minimum password length. With `MinPasswordLength` implemented as a property, the statement to do this would be:

```
Authenticator.MinPasswordLength += 2;
```

Had `MinPasswordLength` been implemented as a pair of methods, the relevant statement would have been:

```
Authenticator.SetMinPasswordLength(Authenticator.GetMinPasswordLength()
    + 2);
```

I'll leave you to decide which of those is easier to read!

Note that in this particular example, the property in question happens to be static. In general that is not necessary. Just as for methods, you will normally declare properties as static only if they only refer to static data. In practice, most properties are not static, and are declared just as in the above code, but omitting the `static` keyword. We'll encounter instance properties in the examples later in this chapter.

Advantages of Properties

You may wonder what the point of all the above code is. Wouldn't it have been simpler to simply make the `minPasswordLength` field `public`, so that we could access it directly and not have to bother about any properties? The answer is that it would have been simpler, but doing it that way could be storing up a lot of trouble for us in the future.

The problem with making any field `public` is that doing so blurs the distinction between what an object does and how it works. Fields are really to do with how an object works in a very fundamental way: they represent the data that is stored internally by an object. It's important that they are not visible to external users, because then we have the option of modifying how a class works internally without this affecting any other code that uses the class. The principle of hiding fields from client code in this way is known as **data encapsulation**.

If that all sounds a bit abstract, suppose that in writing a later version of the `Authenticator` class, it is decided that all password information, including the minimum password length, must be stored in a relational database (The would for example, mean that multiple servers could access the same password information simultaneously, and so might be done for scalability reasons). If the `minPasswordLength` field were public, it would be very difficult to make this change.

If we use properties and keep the `minPasswordLength` field `private`, however, it becomes easy. We can remove the `minPasswordLength` field and rewrite the implementations of the `get` and `set` properties so they access the relational database instead. As the external interface to the `Authenticator` class (that is to say, the signatures of the public members) are unchanged, we can plug in the new version of the `Authenticator` and be confident that we will not break any client code.

Another aspect of properties is that we can use them to screen the values to which the corresponding fields are set, to automatically exclude silly data. For example, we might decide that it is silly for the minimum password length to ever be greater than 10. We can enforce this rule like this:

```
public static uint MinPasswordLength
{
    get
    {
        return minPasswordLength;
    }
    set
    {
        if (value <= 10)
            minPasswordLength = value;
        else

        // do something to indicate an error has occurred
        // this will normally be throwing an exception,
        // as discussed in Chapter 6

        Console.WriteLine("Error");
    }
}
```

Related to this, we can also use properties to provide read-only access to data. For example, in our `Authenticator` class, suppose we didn't want client code to be able to modify the minimum password length (or only wanted that to be possible by calling some other method, perhaps involving supplying special authentication information). With properties, we can achieve this by simply omitting the `set` accessor. As a result, we declare the property like this:

```
public static uint MinPasswordLength
{
    get
    {
        return minPasswordLength;
    }
}
```

Now client code that accesses the property value will work fine, but client code that attempts to set it will not compile, (because the compiler won't be able to find a `set` accessor that it can call):

```
uint I;
I = Authenticator.MinPasswordLength;        // correct
Authenticator.MinPasswordLength = 8;        // won't compile
++Authenticator.MinPasswordLength;          // won't compile
```

In principle, it is also possible to create write-only properties by supplying the `set` accessor and omitting the `get` accessor. One example might be a property that allows administrators to overwrite the values of users' passwords without having to supply the old password. Microsoft, however, advises against doing this. The suggestion is that ordinary methods should be used in this case instead of properties because write-only properties may be confusing to developers writing client code.

Finally, one other big benefit of using properties is the ability to place quite complex code in a `get` or `set` accessor. A good example of this is provided by most windows forms and controls. Take, for example, a basic dialog box. This is encapsulated by one of the base classes that Microsoft has written for us, a class called `Form`. Each dialog has an associated `Width` – the number of pixels that it occupies across the screen. In client code we are able to view and modify this value like this:

```
// MyForm is an instance of a class that represents a form (window)

int I = MyForm.Width;
MyForm.Width = 600;
```

Retrieving this value presumably involves little more than returning the appropriate number. The line here that sets the width to `600` actually involves quite a fair bit of processing, however, as the dialog box automatically resizes itself on the screen to match the new size. In other words, the setter function for this property will internally be doing a lot of work. This would be impossible if the `Width` was exposed as a field.

Defining it as a property gives us the convenience of field-like access while allowing this automatic resizing or whatever other processing is required. The same applies to the height and to a good many other properties of controls.

Note that you should only use properties where the purpose of the method is do something that appears to the client to just set or retrieve a value. That means that the `set` accessor must only take one parameter and return a void, while the `get` accessor cannot take any parameters. For example, it would not be possible to rewrite the `IsPasswordValid()` method in the `Authenticator` class as a property. The parameter types and return value for this method are not of the correct type.

The `Authenticator3` sample in the download illustrates the `Authenticator` with the minimum password length set. Note that for this sample, we use the minimum password length to check that new passwords are okay:

```
public bool ChangePassword(string oldPassword, string newPassword)
{
    if (oldPassword == Password && newPassword.Length >=
                                    minPasswordLength)
    {
        Password = newPassword;
```

```
        return true;
    }
    else
        return false;
}
```

Inheritance

Now we know how the basic object works, it's time to examine the topic that is the key factor in the power of object-oriented programming: **inheritance**.

Inheritance is about taking a class and creating more specialized versions of it, and is extremely useful when you have a number of objects that are different in some ways, but have a lot of functionality in common. It's a huge topic with a lot of subtleties – the section on inheritance is going to be the biggest section on this chapter, and if you've not encountered inheritance before you'll probably find it'll take you some effort to fully understand the topic, as well as a fair amount of practice writing C# programs before you are comfortable with it. The effort is worthwhile however, because it will ultimately allow you to write object-oriented programs that have a highly maintainable architecture that map in a very intuitive way to the whatever programming task they are concerned with.

We're going to look at inheritance in the same way that we looked at objects, by first understanding the concept in the context of everyday life, and then looking at how we can apply it to computers and computer programming.

Inheritance in Everyday Life

I'm going to examine inheritance by returning first to the earlier example of jumpers, except this time I'm going to think about my old Lancaster University Dance Society sweatshirt that I bought a couple of years ago. I don't wear it that often now, mostly because that sort of thing isn't really trendy these days (Yeah I know – us shallow, vain, author-types...). It's a bit like a jumper but has two extra features: A massive pocket across the front that you can put your hands in when it's cold, and a hood. The sweatshirt was designed by re-using much of the functionality of a jumper, and adding some extra features to it.

That's a characteristic of objects in everyday life in general: You don't get lots and lots of completely different types of object, but rather they tend to come in families of related things that share aspects of their design. My sofa is just like my armchairs, except that it can seat more than one person. An audio CD does the same sort of thing as a cassette tape, but with extra direct-access facilities.

Another example, which we're going to look at a bit more closely, is cars. My car at the moment is a 13-year-old Ford Escort. Back in the 1980s, Ford had three big-selling cars out that all had a very similar design – the Escort, the Orion, and the Fiesta. The reason I'm thinking about these cars in particular is that they shared a lot more than just being Ford cars. They had different shaped body shells, and the Fiesta was smaller, but internally their engines and other components were built in very much the same way, often using the same components.

What we're seeing in the Ford example is a slightly different type of inheritance. You see, referring back to the jumper/sweatshirt example, the main thing that the sweatshirt inherited from the jumper was the user interface; that you put the sweatshirt on and took it off the same way, and did the same things with it. It had the same overall design, but it was made of a different material and probably woven or knitted together differently. That's an example of **interface inheritance**, and the equivalent in computer programming would be of two classes, Sweatshirt and Jumper, which happen to expose methods that have the same names, purposes and signatures, but different implementations. By contrast, in our Ford example, the cars don't just have similar user interfaces, but how they work – what components they use inside – are the same too. That's an example of **implementation inheritance**, and the equivalent in object-oriented programming would be of some classes (EscortCar, OrionCar and FiestaCar, perhaps?), which not only expose methods with the same names, but these actually are the same methods, in the sense that when you call the methods you are running the same code.

Developers experienced in Java or in C++ and COM will recognize that implementation inheritance is the kind of inheritance that is supported by Java/C++ and other traditional object-oriented languages, while the more restricted interface inheritance was the only form of inheritance that was supported by COM and COM objects. VB on the other hand supports only interface inheritance, through the Implements *keyword.*

I should point out that these examples aren't exact – you could spend quite a while arguing about precisely how much of the internal design of a jumper is actually shared by a sweatshirt, but these examples have made their point. As far as C# programming is concerned, we're looking at the issue of how to define a new class, while re-using features from an existing class. The benefits are twofold – first, in that inheritance provides a convenient way to reuse existing, fully tested code in different contexts, thereby saving a lot of coding time, and second in that it can provide even more structure to your programs by giving a finer degree of granularity to your classes.

At this point we're going to move on to a coding example, based on a mobile phone company, which will demonstrate how implementation inheritance works in a C# program. Inheritance of classes in C# is always implementation inheritance. Interface inheritance does occur as well in C#, but we won't encounter it until Chapter 5 when we examine C# interfaces.

Inheritance in C#: The Mortimer Phones Sample

The example we'll use to demonstrate inheritance is going to be of a fictitious mobile phone company, which we'll call Mortimer Phones. We're going to develop a class that represents a customer account and is responsible for calculating that customer's phone bill. It's going to develop into a much longer, more complex sample than the Authenticator class, and as it develops we'll quickly find that one simple class is not adequate; rather, we are going to need a number of related classes, and in the next section inheritance will magically enter as the solution.

Mortimer is the name of the raven in one of my favourite series of books, the tales of Arabel's Raven, by Joan Aiken. He belongs to a little girl called Arabel Jones, can say "Nevermore!" and "Kaaaark!", and has an unfortunate tendency to eat anything, including gold bars and even complete staircases. He didn't actually eat any mobile phones in the books because they were mostly written before mobile phones were invented, but I'm sure he would have done.

We're going to write a class that works out the monthly bill for each customer of Mortimer Phones. The class is called `Customer`, and each instance of this class represents one customer's account. In terms of public interface, the class will contain two properties:

- `Name` representing the customer's name (read-write).

- `Balance`, representing the amount owed (read-only).

There will also be two methods:

- `RecordPayment()`, which is called to indicate that the customer has paid a certain amount of their bill.

- `RecordCall()`, which is called when the customer has made a phone call. It works out the cost of the call and adds it to that customer's balance.

The `RecordCall()` method is potentially quite a complex function, since in the real world it would involve figuring out what the type of call was from the number called, then applying the appropriate tariff, and keeping a history of the calls. To keep things simple here, we'll assume there are just two types of calls: calls to landlines, and calls to other mobiles, and that each of these are charged at a flat rate of 2 cents a minute for landlines and 30 cents a minute for other mobiles. Our `RecordCall` method will simply be passed the type of call as a parameter, and we won't worry about keeping a call history. In the real world, we'd also have to deal with WAP calls and distinguish calls to different mobile networks, as well as taking into account the time of the call and the existence of different tariffs for different customers.

With this simplification, we can look at the code for the project. The project was as usual created as a console application, and the first thing in it is an enumerated list for the types of call:

```
namespace Wrox.ProfessionalCSharp.Chapter4.MortimerPhones
{
    using System;
    public enum TypeOfCall
    {
        CallToMobile, CallToLandline
    }
```

Now, let's look at the definition of the `Customer` class:

```
    public class Customer
    {
        private string name;
        private decimal balance;
        public string Name
        {
            get
            {
                return name;
            }
            set
            {
                name = value;
            }
        }
```

```
        public decimal Balance
        {
           get
           {
              return balance;
           }
        }
        public void RecordPayment(decimal amountPaid)
        {
           balance -= amountPaid;
        }
        public void RecordCall(TypeOfCall callType, uint nMinutes)
        {
           switch (callType)
           {
              case TypeOfCall.CallToLandline:
                 balance += (0.02M * nMinutes);
                 break;
              case TypeOfCall.CallToMobile:
                 balance += (0.30M * nMinutes);
                 break;
              default:
                 break;
           }
        }
     }
```

This code should be reasonably self-explanatory. Note that for the call charges of 2c/minute and 30c/minute, we've hard coded these values into the program. In real life, they'd more likely to be read in from a relational database, or some file that allows the values to be changed easily.

Now let's add some code in the program's Main() method that displays the amounts of bills currently owing:

```
     public class MainEntryPoint
     {
        public static int Main(string[] args)
        {
           Customer Arabel = new Customer();
           Arabel.Name = "Arabel Jones";
           Customer MrJones = new Customer();
           MrJones.Name = "Ben Jones";
                  Arabel.RecordCall(TypeOfCall.CallToLandline, 20);
           Arabel.RecordCall(TypeOfCall.CallToMobile, 5);
           MrJones.RecordCall(TypeOfCall.CallToLandline, 10);
           Console.WriteLine("{0,-20} owes ${1:F2}", Arabel.Name,
                                                     Arabel.Balance);
           Console.WriteLine("{0,-20} owes ${1:F2}", MrJones.Name,
                                                     MrJones.Balance);

           return 0;
        }
     }
```

Running this code gives the following results:

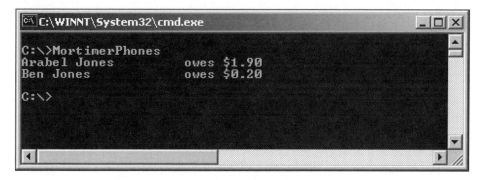

Adding Inheritance

Currently, the Mortimer Phones example is heavily simplified. In particular, it only has one tariff for all customers. The trouble is, that's not remotely realistic. I don't know if your mobile phone company is anything like the one I'm registered with, but mine has a myriad of different payment schemes. First there's the pay-as-you-go customers, who don't pay anything upfront, but then get charged at very high rates for each call they make. Then there's the subscription customers.

I'm registered under a tariff in which I pay a fixed rate each month, and for that I get 60 minutes of calls to landlines or mobiles on the same network for free, and then I pay a reduced rate for other calls. There's another scheme where you pay more per month and get more minutes of free calls. There's even another, more business-based scheme which offers higher charges at weekends in return for lower charges in the working day. Of course, you never know when the company is going to introduce another tariff.

The way we're working at the moment, if we try to take all that into account, our RecordCall() method is going to end up containing various nested switch statements and looking something like this:

```
// assume tariff is a member field of type Tariff that identifies tariff
// for this Customer instance. It's an enumerated type, values include
// Tariff1, Tariff2 etc.,

    public void RecordCall(TypeOfCall callType, uint nMinutes)
    {
        switch (tariff)
        case Tariff.Tariff1:
        {
            switch (callType)
            {
            case TypeOfCall.CallToLandline:

                // work out amount

            case TypeOfCall.CallToMobile:

                // work out amount
                // other cases
```

```
            // etc.

    }
    case Tariff.Tariff2:
    {
        switch (callType)
        {

// etc.

    }
```

That is not a satisfactory solution. Small `switch` statements are nice, but huge `switch` statements with large numbers of options – and in particular embedded `switch` statements – make for hard-to-understand code. This also means that whenever a new tariff is introduced the code for the method will need to be changed. This could accidentally introduce new bugs into the parts of the code responsible for processing existing tariffs.

The problem is really to do with the way the code for the different tariffs is mixed up in a `switch` statement. If we could cleanly separate the code for the different tariffs the problem would be solved. This is one of the issues that inheritance addresses. So, let's look at what we do.

We want to separate out the code for different types of customers. We'll start by defining a new class, which specifically represents customers on a new tariff, which we'll call the Nevermore60 tariff. Nevermore60 is designed for customers who use their mobiles a lot. Customers on this tariff pay a higher rate of 50 cents a minute for the first 60 minutes of calls to other mobiles, then a reduced rate of 20 cents a minute for all additional calls, so if they make a large enough number of calls they save money compared to the previous tariff.

We'll save actually implementing the new payment calculations for a little while longer, and we'll initially define `Nevermore60Customer` like this:

```
public class Nevermore60Customer : Customer
{

}
```

In other words, the class has no methods, no properties, nothing of its own. On the other hand, it's defined in a slightly different way from how we've defined any classes before. After the class name is a colon, followed by the name of our earlier class, `Customer`. This tells the compiler that `Nevermore60Customer` is **derived** from `Customer`. That means that every method, field and so on or property etc. in `Customer` also exists in `Nevermore60Customer`. Alternatively, to use the correct terminology, each member of `Customer` is **inherited** in `Nevermore60Customer`. Also, `Nevermore60Customer` is said to be a **derived class**, while `Customer` is said to be the **base class**. You'll also sometimes encounter derived classes referred to as **subclasses,** and base classes as **superclasses**.

Since we've not yet put anything else in the `Nevermore60Customer` class, it is effectively an exact copy of the definition of the `Customer` class. We can create instances of and call methods against the `Nevermore60Customer` class, just as we could with `Customer`. To see this, we'll modify one of the customers, Arabel, to be a Nevermore60 customer:

```
public static int Main(string[] args)
{
    Nevermore60Customer Arabel = new Nevermore60Customer();
    Arabel.Name = "Arabel Jones";
    Customer MrJones = new Customer();
    MrJones.Name = "Ben Jones";

    Arabel.RecordCall(TypeOfCall.CallToLandline, 20);
    Arabel.RecordCall(TypeOfCall.CallToMobile, 5);
    MrJones.RecordCall(TypeOfCall.CallToLandline, 10);
    Console.WriteLine("{0,-20} owes ${1:F2}", Arabel.Name,
                                              Arabel.Balance);
    Console.WriteLine("{0,-20} owes ${1:F2}", MrJones.Name,
                                              MrJones.Balance);
    Console.ReadLine();
    return 0;
}
```

In this code, we've changed just one line, the declaration of `Arabel`, to make this customer a `Nevermore60Customer` instance. All the method calls remain the same, and this code will produce exactly the same results as our earlier code. If you want to try this out, it's the `MortimerPhones2` sample.

By itself, having a copy of the definition of the `Customer` class might not look very useful. The power of this comes from the fact we can now make some modifications or additions to `Nevermore60Customer`. We can effectively say to the compiler, "Nevermore60Customer is almost the same as `Customer`, but with these differences." In particular, we're going to modify the way that `Nevermore60Customer` works out the charge for each phone call according to the new tariff.

The differences we can specify in principle are:

❏   We can add new members (of any type: fields, methods, properties, and so on) to the derived class, where these members are not defined in the base class.

❏   We can replace the implementation of existing methods or properties, and so on that are already present in the base class (but not fields, since these don't have an implementation!). There are two slightly different ways of doing this, which have different implications for how the method is called in some circumstances. The way we're going to do it here, the new implementation is said to **override** the previous implementation of the method.

Now we are in a position to see how we will solve the problem of the numerous different tariffs. We will override the `RecordCall()` method in `Customer` by a new `RecordCall()` method in `Nevermore60Customer`. Not only that, but whenever we need to add a new tariff, we can simply create another new class derived from `Customer`, with a new override of `RecordCall()`. In this way we can add code to cope with many different tariffs, while keeping the new code separate from all the existing code that is responsible for calculations using existing tariffs.

So let's modify the code for the `Nevermore60Customer` class, so that it implements the new tariff. To do this we need not only to override the `RecordCall()` method, but also to add a new field that indicates the number of free minutes that have been used:

```
public class Nevermore60Customer : Customer
{
    private uint highCostMinutesUsed;
    public override void RecordCall(TypeOfCall callType, uint nMinutes)
    {
        switch (callType)
        {
            case TypeOfCall.CallToLandline:
                balance += (0.02M * nMinutes);
                break;
            case TypeOfCall.CallToMobile:
                uint HighCostMinutes, LowCostMinutes;
                uint HighCostMinutesToGo =
                    (highCostMinutesUsed < 60) ? 60 - highCostMinutesUsed : 0;
                if (nMinutes > HighCostMinutesToGo)
                {
                    HighCostMinutes = HighCostMinutesToGo;
                    LowCostMinutes = nMinutes - HighCostMinutes;
                }
                else
                {
                    HighCostMinutes = nMinutes;
                    LowCostMinutes = 0;
                }
                highCostMinutesUsed += HighCostMinutes;
                balance += (0.50M * HighCostMinutes + 0.20M *
                                    LowCostMinutes);
                break;
            default:
                break;
        }
    }
}
```

As you can see, the algorithm to compute the call cost in this case is rather more complex, though if you follow through the logic you will see it does meet our definition for the Nevermore60 tariff. Notice that the extra keyword `override` has been added to the definition of the `RecordCall()` method. This informs the compiler that this method is actually an override of a method that is already present in the base class, and we must include this keyword.

Before this code will compile, we need to make a couple of modifications to the base class:

```
public class Customer
{
    private string name;
    protected decimal balance;

// etc.

    public virtual void RecordCall(TypeOfCall callType, uint nMinutes)
    {
        switch (callType)
```

The first change we've made is to the `balance` field. Previously it was defined as `private`, meaning that no code outside the `Customer` class could access it directly. Unfortunately this means that, even though `Nevermore60Customer` is derived from `Customer`, the code in the `Nevermore60Customer` class cannot directly access this field (even though a balance field is still present inside every `Nevermore60Customer` object). That would prevent `Nevermore60Customer` from being able to modify the balance when it records calls made, and so prevent the code we presented for the `Nevermore60Customer.RecordCall()` method from compiling.

The access modifier `protected` solves this problem. It indicates that any class that is derived from `Customer`, as well as `Customer` itself, should be allowed access to this member. The member is still invisible however, to code in any other class that is not derived from `Customer`. By marking a member as `protected`, we are essentially saying that this member is part of the internal working of the class, not part of its public interface, but that any derived classes are in some sense privileged and can get access to this member anyway. We're assuming that, because of the close relationship between a class and its derived class, it's okay for the derived class to know a bit about the internal workings of the base class, at least as far as protected members are concerned.

> *There is actually a controversial point here about good programming style here. Many developers would regard it as better practice to keep all fields private, and write a protected accessor method to allow derived classes to modify the balance. In this case, allowing the `balance` field to be `protected` rather than `private` prevents our example from becoming more complex than it already is.*

The second change we've made is to the declaration of the `RecordCall()` method in the base class. We've added the keyword `virtual`. We'll explain the precise effect of this keyword soon. For now, we'll just say that it slightly changes the manner in which the method is called when the program is run, in a manner that facilitates overriding it. C# will not allow derived classes to override a method unless that method has been declared as virtual in the base class.

One last point before we move on. It's important to understand that the new field we've added, `highCostMinutesUsed`, is only stored in instances of `Nevermore60Customer`. It is not stored in instances of the base class, `Customer`. The base class itself is never implicitly modified in any way by the existence of the derived class. The knowledge always goes one way: the derived class knows about its base class (though not about any members declared as private), but the base class knows nothing about any derived classes. This must always be the case because when you code up the base class, you don't necessarily know what other derived classes might be added in the future – and you wouldn't want your code to be broken when someone adds a derived class!

On the other hand, you do need to decide what methods are the ones that might sensibly be overridden, so that you can explicitly mark them as virtual. This sounds a bit like working in the dark if you don't know what derived classes are going to be added, but you'll find with practice that once you get used to coding in an object-oriented manner it's usually fairly easy to tell which methods need to be virtual.

Another point I should make is that there is no limit to how many derived classes you can write that are derived from one single base class. For example, suppose Mortimer Phones were to introduce another tariff, the Gold tariff, which offered reduced rates on phone calls for Mortimer Phones staff. You'd probably code up a class that looks like this:

```
public class GoldCustomer : Customer
   {
       public override void RecordCall(TypeOfCall callType, uint nMinutes)
       {

          // implementation of this for Staff customer

       }
   }
```

We can similarly define as many more classes as we wish. StaffCustomer knows nothing about Nevermore60Customer or any of its other sibling classes – it knows only about the base class.

On the other hand, each derived class can only inherit from one base class. The terminology to describe this is **single inheritance**. Some other languages, including C++, allow you to write classes that have more than one base class (**multiple inheritance**), but this is not permitted in C#.

The Object Class

Now that we've understood what inheritance involves, I can make a little confession about something I've not told you yet. The Customer class that we've used in our sample is itself derived from another class. Ditto for the Authenticator class in our previous sample. You see, the .NET framework defines a class known as System.Object (that is the class Object in the namespace System), and requires that all classes are ultimately derived from Object. In C#, if you don't specify that a class is derived from another class, the compiler will automatically assume that it derives from Object. The practical significance of this is that, besides the methods and properties and so on that you define, you also have access to a number of public and protected member methods that have been defined for the Object class, in all other classes that you define.

The methods available are:

Method	Access	Purpose
string ToString()	public virtual	Returns a string representation of the object.
int GetHashTable()	public virtual	Returns a hash of the object designed to allow you to efficiently look up instances of the object in certain tables.
bool Equals(object obj)	public virtual	Compares instances of the object for equality.
bool Equals(object objA, object objB)	public static	Compares instances of the object for equality.
bool ReferenceEquals(object objA, object objB)	public static	Compares whether two references refer to the same object.

Method	Access	Purpose
`Type GetType()`	`public`	Returns details of the type of the object.
`object MemberwiseClone()`	`protected`	Makes a copy of the object.
`void Finalize()`	`protected virtual`	May be used in some situations for cleaning up resources.

At this stage, you should consider this table as mostly for reference. We haven't yet covered enough of the C# language to be able to properly understand how to use all these methods, We're not going to examine these methods or how to use them in detail yet– we'll do that in Chapter 7 when we look at the .NET base classes more thoroughly. We will, however, modify our `MortimerPhones` sample to use the `ToString()` method –this will demonstrate more about the principles of overriding methods.

Before we do that, we'll make a couple of observations about the methods of `Object`:

1. First, notice how some of the methods are declared as `virtual`, because they are intended for you to override in your own classes if you wish, while others are not intended to ever be overridden and therefore are not declared as `virtual`. Also, notice that some of the methods are `protected`. These methods are intended for internal use within the class, and do not form part of the external interface.

2. There are also two different versions of the `Equals()` method. These have the same purpose, but allow the method to be called in different ways. It is a feature of C# that two methods can have the same name, provided that they can be distinguished by taking different parameters. This feature is known as **method overloading**, and we'll examine it Chapter 5.

3. There's a couple of return types here that will be unfamiliar to you. `GetType()` returns an instance of the class `System.Type` – this is another of the many base classes that Microsoft has written for us, and which we'll examine in Chapter 7.

4. `MemberwiseClone()` looks like it returns something a bit different – its return type is defined as `object`. This is actually just the class `System.Object`. C# makes it easy for you to refer to this class, because it defines the keyword `object`, which just maps to this class. Therefore, you can say `object` whenever you mean `System.Object`. Note the difference in case – C# is case sensitive, so that's important.

> The keyword **object** is also used in C# when we don't want to indicate explicitly what class we mean, for example when declaring variables or types of parameters.

The ToString() method

In this section we'll modify the `MortimerPhones` example to override the `ToString()` method. In `System.Object`, `ToString()` simply displays the name of the class, but that is not its intention; it is actually intended to provide an easy way for client code to get a string representation of the contents of an object, but you have to override it to do that for your classes.

In the process of developing this sample we'll also demonstrate the GetType() method. Both these methods are defined and implemented in System.Object, so we don't actually need to provide our own implementation. To see this, we'll start off by modifying the code that calls the Customer and Nevermore60Customer classes, by adding some extra lines that display the result of calling ToString() and GetType() against our Arabel and MrJones instances. This code is available in the download as the MortimerPhones4 sample:

```csharp
public static int Main(string[] args)
{
    Nevermore60Customer Arabel = new Nevermore60Customer();
    Arabel.Name = "Arabel Jones";
    Customer MrJones = new Customer();
    MrJones.Name = "Ben Jones";
    Arabel.RecordCall(TypeOfCall.CallToLandline, 20);
    Arabel.RecordCall(TypeOfCall.CallToMobile, 5);
    MrJones.RecordCall(TypeOfCall.CallToLandline, 10);
    Console.WriteLine("{0,-20} owes ${1:F2}", Arabel.Name,
                                              Arabel.Balance);
    Console.WriteLine("{0,-20} owes ${1:F2}", MrJones.Name,
                                              MrJones.Balance);
    Console.WriteLine("Arabel.ToString() is : "+ Arabel.ToString());
    Console.WriteLine("Arabel.GetType() is : "+ Arabel.GetType());
    Console.WriteLine("\nMrJones is : "+ MrJones);
    Console.WriteLine("MrJones.ToString() is : "+ MrJones.ToString());
    Console.WriteLine("MrJones.GetType() is : "+ MrJones.GetType());
    return 0;
}
```

Note that at this point we haven't made any changes to our classes, so what we'll pick up is the default implementations of ToString() and GetType() provided by Object. Running this code produces this result:

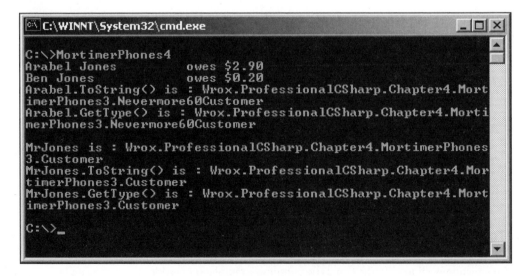

So what's going on? Let's look at the calls to GetType() first. Here GetType() is doing exactly what it is supposed to do: provide details of the nature of the class – in this case by giving the full name of each class, including the namespace in which the class is defined.

Our calls to ToString() have produced exactly the same output as our calls to GetType(). This isn't really the intention of ToString() – as mentioned earlier, ToString() is intended to supply a string representation of the contents of the class instance. We haven't yet provided an implementation of this method for our Customer or Nevermore60Customer classes however, so the .NET runtime just takes the base implementation from System.Object. If you call a method in a derived class, and that method has been defined in a base class and not overridden, then it will be the base class version that gets run. Microsoft have implemented System.Object.ToString() to simply return the name of the class – it's the best they can do since – rather obviously – the guys at Microsoft who wrote the Object class couldn't know any of the details of the classes that we were going to code up!

> *If you're being very observant, you might have noticed an apparent anomaly here. The implementations of ToString() and GetType() in System.Object have somehow managed to find out about the names of our derived classes, although I said earlier that in principle base classes know nothing about any derived classes. There's actually some clever technology here going on behind the scenes involving something called **reflection**, which allows classes to find out about other classes, and which we'll look at in Chapter 7.*

Now we've seen how ToString() works for System.Object, let's add our own override for our Customer class. This is very easy to do:

```
public class Customer
{
    private string name;
    protected decimal balance;
    public override string ToString()
    {
        string Result = "Customer: " + name;
        Result += ", owing: " + balance;
        return Result;
    }
}
```

Note that we use the override keyword to tell the compiler that we are overriding a function from the base class. Also notice that our override of ToString() returns a string, just like the Object version of ToString(). That's a general principle with method overrides – you have to match the return type and parameters of the method in the base class. Otherwise, you'll get a compilation error.

Our override of ToString() gives a quick summary of the state of the class instance – giving the name of the customer and the amount owed (although we aren't bothering to format the balance as a currency amount).

Now if we run our application (now the `MortimerPhones5` sample) again, we get this result:

```
C:\>MortimerPhones5
Arabel Jones              owes $2.90
Ben Jones                 owes $0.20
Arabel.ToString() is : Customer: Arabel Jones, owing: 2.9
Arabel.GetType() is : Wrox.ProfessionalCSharp.Chapter4.Morti
merPhones5.Nevermore60Customer

MrJones is : Customer: Ben Jones, owing: 0.2
MrJones.ToString() is : Customer: Ben Jones, owing: 0.2
MrJones.GetType() is : Wrox.ProfessionalCSharp.Chapter4.Mort
imerPhones5.Customer

C:\>
```

`GetType()` still returns the name of the class, but `ToString()` gives more useful details about the contents of the `Arabel` and `MrJones` variables. Notice that we haven't needed to supply a `ToString()` override for `Nevermore60Customer`. This is because `Nevermore60Customer` is derived directly from `Customer`, so it picks up the implementation of `ToString()` in `Customer` automatically. If we wanted to do something different in `Nevermore60Customer`, we could separately supply a different override of `ToString()` in that class.

Also note that because `System.Object.GetType()` has not been defined as virtual, the compiler would not let us override `GetType()` in the way we have for `ToString()`, even if we'd wanted to. `System.Object.GetType()` has not been defined as virtual, because its implementation in `System.Object` already does everything that `GetType()` is intended to do, so there should be no reason for any other class to ever need to override it.

Class Hierarchy Diagrams

When you're designing classes that are inherited from each other, it's normally easiest to use a diagram known as a class hierarchy diagram, which illustrates the relationships between the various base and derived classes in your program. Traditionally, class hierarchy diagrams are drawn with the base class at the top and arrows pointing from derived classes to their immediate base classes. For example, the hierarchy of our Mortimer Phones examples from `MortimerPhones3` onwards look like this:

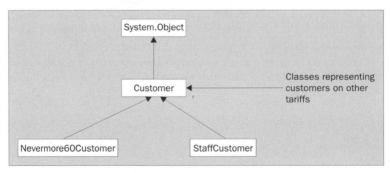

Consistent with the placing of classes on the diagram, we normally say that the ultimate base class, `System.Object` is at the top of the hierarchy, and we talk about moving up the hierarchy as we move from derived class to base class, and down the hierarchy when we move from base to derived class. Note that that terminology is the opposite way round from what you might have expected from the term *base class*.

Virtual and Non-Virtual Methods

In this section, we're going to take a closer look at the precise effect of defining a method as `virtual`. The difference between a virtual and a non-virtual method is to do with the way that the method is called at runtime and is quite subtle. It will however, lead us to a very powerful way of using inheritance.

The key to understanding virtual methods comes from the following fact about reference variables: if you declare a variable as referring to a particular class – call it A, then C# also allows that variable to store a reference to any derived class of A.

To make that more concrete, let's go back to our `MortimerPhones` sample. Earlier, we instantiated instances of customers with this code:

```
Nevermore60Customer Arabel = new Nevermore60Customer();
Arabel.Name = "Arabel Jones";
Customer MrJones = new Customer();
MrJones.Name = "Ben Jones";
```

In fact, we could have more simply declared the variables like this:

```
Customer Arabel = new Nevermore60Customer();
Arabel.Name = "Arabel Jones";
Customer MrJones = new Customer();
MrJones.Name = "Ben Jones";
```

Because `Nevermore60Customer` is derived from `Customer`, it's perfectly legitimate for a reference to a `Customer` to be set up to point to either a `Customer` or a `Nevermore60Customer`, or to an instance of any other class that is derived directly or indirectly from `Customer`. Notice that all we've changed here is the declaration of the reference variable. The actual object that gets instantiated with new is still a `Nevermore60Customer` object. If for example, you try to call `GetType()` against it, it'll tell you it's a `Nevermore60Customer`.

Being able to point to derived classes with a base reference may look like just a syntactical convenience but it's actually essential if we want to be able use derived classes easily. We can understand why if we think about how a real mobile phones company will want to store the various `Customer`-derived classes. You see in our example we only had two customers, so it was easy to define separate variables, but more realistically we'd have hundreds of thousands of customers and we'd probably want to be able to process them using an array, perhaps with code that looks like this:

```
Customer [] Customers = new Customer[NCustomers];

// do something to initialize customers

foreach (Customer NextCustomer in Customers)
```

```
    {
        Console.WriteLine("{0,-20} owes ${1:F2}", NextCustomer.Name,
                                            NextCustomer.Balance);
    }
```

We have an array of `Customer` references, each element can point to any type of customer, no matter what `Customer`-derived class is used to represent that customer. However, if variables could not store references to derived types we'd have to have lots of arrays – an array of `Customers`, an array of `Nevermore60Customers`, and another array for each type of class. That would have rendered our approach of using derived classes unworkable for any real problem.

Now we've ensured that we can mix different types of class in one array, but this will give the compiler a new problem. Suppose we have a snippet of code like this:

```
    Customer ACustomer;

    // Initialize ACustomer to some kind of customer, eg. perhaps based
    // on data read in from a file

    ACustomer.RecordCall(TypeOfCall.CallToLandline, 20);
```

What the compiler can see is a `Customer` reference, and we are to call the `RecordCall()` method on it. The trouble is that `ACustomer` might refer to a `Customer` instance or it might refer to a `Nevermore60Customer` instance or it might refer to an instance of some other class derived from `Customer`. Each of these classes might have its own implementation of `RecordCall()`. How will the compiler determine which method should be called? There are two answers to this, depending on whether the method is `virtual`:

❑   If the method is not `virtual`, then the compiler will simply use the type that the reference was declared to be. In this case, since `ACustomer` is of type `Customer`, it will arrange for the `Customer.RecordCall()` method to be called, no matter what `ACustomer` is actually referring to.

❑   If the method is `virtual`, then the compiler will generate code which at runtime checks up to see what the `ACustomer` reference is actually pointing to. It then identifies which class this instance is an instance of, and calls the appropriate `RecordCall()` override. For example, if it turns out that `ACustomer` actually refers to a `Nevermore60Customer()` instance, the `Nevermore60Customer.RecordCall()` method will be called. This runtime check will need to be made each time the statement is executed. For example, if the `virtual` method call occurs inside a `foreach` loop which executes 100 times, the program will need to check the instance type of the referent each of those 100 times. It has to, because each time through the loop the reference might be pointing to a different instance and therefore to a different class of object.

In most cases, the second behavior is the one we want. If we have a reference, for example, to a `Nevermore60Customer`, then it's highly unlikely that we'd want to call any override to any method other than the one that applies to `Nevermore60Customer` instances. In fact, you might wonder why you'd ever want the compiler to use the first, non-virtual, approach, since it looks like that means in many cases the "wrong" override will be called up. Why we don't just make `virtual` methods the normal behavior, and say that every method is automatically `virtual`? This is, incidentally, the approach taken by Java, which automatically makes all methods `virtual`. There are three good reasons, however, for not doing this:

1. **Performance**. When a virtual function is called, a runtime check needs to be made to identify which override needs to be called. For a non-virtual function, this information is available at compile-time (the compiler can identify the relevant override from the type that the reference is declared as!) Clearly, an extra check at runtime will hurt performance. The loss is very slight – the way that virtual functions are implemented internally means that it involves no more than an extra level of indirection – looking up an address in a table of methods that is known as a **vtable**. However, if we want our applications to perform well, we clearly don't want this to be happening every single time any method is called – that could easily be millions of times a second in a large processor-intensive application! For that reason, methods are only implemented as virtual if they are explicitly declared as such.

2. **Design**. It may be the case that when you design a class there are some methods that you do not want to ever be overridden. This actually happens very often, especially with methods that are primarily designed to be used internally within the class by other methods or whose implementations reflect the internal class design. When you design a class, you choose which features of its implementation are publicly available, which features you don't want to make public, but are prepared to make available to derived classes (protected methods), and which features you wish to keep strictly internal to the operation of that class. It's unlikely that you'll want methods that are primarily concerned with the internal operation of the class to be overrideable, so you typically won't declare these methods as virtual.

3. **Versioning**. Virtual methods can cause a particular problem connected with releasing new versions of base classes. We'll examine this problem soon, in the section on versioning.

This ability to call a class through a reference and have the class do whatever is appropriate for that class is known as **polymorphism**. You should note, however, that the method you are calling must exist on the class that the reference is defined through. For example, we added some other method, such as a property HighCostMinutesLeft, to Nevermore60Customer to allow outside code to find out this piece of information. Then the following would be legal code:

```
Nevermore60Customer MrLeggit = new Nevermore60Customer();

    // processing

int MinutesLeft = MrLeggit.HighCostMinutesLeft;
```

The following however, would not be legal code:

```
Customer MrLeggit = new Nevermore60Customer();

    // processing

int MinutesLeft = MrLeggit.HighCostMinutesLeft;
```

The reason is that, since MrLeggit has been defined as a Customer reference, it is possible that this variable might happen at any time to refer to a plain Customer, which doesn't implement HighCostMinutesLeft. Therefore, we cannot know for sure that the object referenced through MrLeggit does actually implement this method, the compiler will raise an error if we try to call this method through the MrLeggit reference.

Method Hiding

If a method has not been declared as `virtual` in a base class, then it is still possible to provide another method with the same signature in a derived class. The signature of a method is the set of all information needed to describe how to call that method: its name, return type, number of parameters, and parameter types. The new method will not, however, override the method in the base class. Rather, it is said to **hide** the base class method. As we've implied earlier, what this means is that the compiler will always examine the data type that the variable used to reference the instance is declared as when deciding which method to call. If a method hides a method in a base class, then you should normally add the keyword `new` to its definition. Not to doing so does not constitute an error, but it will cause the compiler to give you a warning.

Realistically, method hiding is not something you'll often deliberately want to do, but we'll demonstrate how it would work by adding a new method called `GetFunnyString()` to our `Customer` class, and hiding it in `Nevermore60Customer()`. `GetFunnyString()` just displays some information about the class, and is defined like this:

```
public class Customer
{
    public string GetFunnyString()
    {
        return "Plain ordinary customer. Kaark!";
    }

// etc.

public class Nevermore60Customer : Customer
{
    public new string GetFunnyString()
    {
        return "Nevermore60. Nevermore!";
    }

// etc.
```

`Nevermore60Customer`'s version of this function will be the one called up, but only if called using a variable that is declared as a reference to `Nevermore60Customer` (or some other class derived from `Nevermore60Customer`). We can demonstrate this with this client code:

```
public static int Main(string[] args)
{
    Customer Cust1;
    Nevermore60Customer Cust2;
    Cust1 = new Customer();
    Console.WriteLine("Customer referencing Customer: "
                                    + Cust1.GetFunnyString());
    Cust1 = new Nevermore60Customer();
    Console.WriteLine("Customer referencing Nevermore60Customer: "
                                    + Cust1.GetFunnyString());
    Cust2 = new Nevermore60Customer();
    Console.WriteLine("Nevermore60Customer referencing"
                                    + Cust2.GetFunnyString());
    return 0;
}
```

This code is downloadable as the `MortimerPhones5Funny` sample (not the `MortimerPhones6` sample, as it isn't part of the main development process of this sample). Running the sample gives this result:

```
C:\WINNT\System32\cmd.exe                                      _ □ ×

C:\>MortimerPhones5Funny
Customer referencing Customer: Plain ordinary customer. Kaar
k!
Customer referencing Nevermore60Customer: Plain ordinary cus
tomer. Kaark!
Nevermore60Customer referencingNevermore60. Nevermore!

C:\>_
```

Versioning

Hiding methods is something that looks at first sight like a quirky feature of C#. In most cases you would want to override methods rather than hide them, because hiding them gives a strong risk of the "wrong" method being called for a given class instance. It is relevant in a specific situation concerned with versioning however, which we'll investigate in this section. It is a rare and unusual situation, so if you're reading this chapter first time around and don't yet want to go into too much detail, you might prefer to skip this section. It's not going to affect any of the rest of the chapter, or subsequent chapters.

Imagine that someone has written a class. Let's call it `HisBaseClass`:

```
class HisBaseClass
{

    // various members

}
```

At some point in the future you write a derived class of your own, which adds some functionality to `HisBaseClass`. In particular, you add a method called `MyGroovyMethod()`, which is not present in the base class:

```
class MyDerivedClass
{
    int MyGroovyMethod()
    {

        // some groovy implementation

    }
}
```

That's all very well. One year later, the author of the base class decides to extend its functionality. By coincidence, he adds a method that is also called `MyGroovyMethod()`, which has the same name and signature as yours, but probably doesn't do the same thing. When you next compile your code using the new version of the base class, you have a potential clash about which method should be called. It's all perfectly legal C#, but since your `MyGroovyMethod()` is not intended to be related in any way to the base class `MyGroovyMethod()` the result of running this code probably won't be what you wanted. This sort of thing doesn't happen very often, but it does happen. Fortunately C# has been designed in such a way that it copes very well with the situation.

In the first place, you get warned about the problem. Your version of `MyGroovyMethod()` wasn't declared as `new`, so the compiler will pick up on the fact that it's hiding a base class method, but not declared explicitly to do so and generate a warning (this applies whether or not you declared `MyGroovyMethod()` as `virtual`). If you wish, you can react to the warning by renaming your version of the method, and if you can do so, that's probably the best course of action, since it'll save a lot of confusion. The great thing however, is that if you do decide that renaming your method isn't practical (for example, because you'd need to rewrite too much client code, or you've published your software as a library for other companies so you can't change any names of methods) and so you leave it, all your existing client code will still run correctly, picking up your version of `MyGroovyMethod()`. That's because any existing code that accesses this method must be doing so through a reference to `MyDerivedClass` (or a further derived class).

Any existing code cannot do so through a reference to `HisBaseClass`, because that would have generated a compilation error when compiled against the earlier version of `HisBaseClass`. The problem can only happen in any future client code that is written. C# arranges things so that you get a warning that a potential problem might occur in future code – and you will need to pay attention to this warning, and take care not to attempt to call your version of `MyGroovyMethod()` through any reference to `HisBaseClass` in any future code you add, but all your existing code will still work fine. It may be a subtle point, but it's quite an impressive example of how C# is able to cope with different versions of classes.

Abstract Functions and Base Classes

So far, every time we've defined a class we've actually created instances of that class, but that's not always the case. In many situations, you'll define a very generic class where you intend to derive other more specialized classes from it, but you don't intend to ever actually use the class. C# provides the keyword `abstract` for this purpose. If a class is declared as `abstract` it is not possible to instantiate it.

For example, suppose we have a class `MyBase`, declared like this:

```
abstract class MyBase
{

    // etc.
```

then the statement:

```
    MyBase MyBaseRef = new MyBase();
```

will not compile because `MyBase` has been declared as `abstract`. It's still perfectly legitimate to have `MyBase` references as long as they only point to derived classes. For example, you can derive a new class from `MyBase`:

```
class MyDerived : MyBase
{
    // etc.
```

then the following is all perfectly valid code:

```
MyBase MyBaseRef;
MyBaseRef = new MyDerived();
MyDerived MyDerivedRef;
```

It's also possible to define a method as `abstract`. This means that the method is treated as a `virtual` method, and that you are not actually implementing the method in that class, on the assumption that it will be overridden in derived classes. If you declare a method as `abstract` you do not need to supply a method body:

```
abstract class MyBase
{
    public abstract int MyAbstractMethod();    // look no body!

    // other methods etc.
```

If any method in a class is `abstract`, then that implies the class itself should be `abstract`, and the compiler will raise an error if the class is not so declared. Also, any non-abstract class that is derived from this class must override the `abstract` method. Those rules might take a bit of effort to get your head round, but they prevent you from ever actually instantiating a class that doesn't have implementations of all its methods.

At this stage, you're probably wondering what the use of abstract methods and classes is. They are actually extremely useful for two reasons. One is that they often allow a better design of class hierarchy, in which the hierarchy more closely reflects the situation you are trying to model. The other is that the use of abstract classes can shift certain potential bugs from hard-to-locate runtime errors into easy-to-locate compile time errors. It's a bit hard to see how that works in practice without looking at an example, so we'll work through an example next. We're going to improve the program architecture of `MortimerPhones` sample by rearranging the class hierarchy.

Redesigning Mortimer Phones: Adding an Abstract Class

Before we start, let me say that we're not redesigning the `MortimerPhones` sample just for the fun of it. There's actually a bit of a design flaw in the class hierarchy at the moment. Our class `Customer` represents pay-as-you-go customers as the base class for all the other customer types. We're treating that kind of tariff as if it's a special tariff from which all the others are derived. That's not really an accurate representation of the situation. In reality, the pay-as-you-go tariff is just one of a range of tariffs – there's nothing special about it – and a more carefully designed class hierarchy would reflect that. Therefore, in this section, we're going to rework the `MortimerPhones` sample to give it the class hierarchy shown in the diagram:

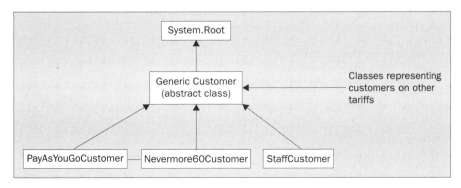

Our old `Customer` class is gone. In its place is a new base class, `GenericCustomer`. `GenericCustomer` implements all the stuff that is common to all types of customers, such as methods and properties that have the same implementation for all customers and so are not virtual. This will include such things as retrieving the balance or the customer's name or recording a payment.

`GenericCustomer` will not, however, provide any implementation of the `RecordCall()` method, which works out the cost of a given call and adds it to the customer's account. The implementation of this method is different for each tariff, so we require that every derived class supplies its own implementation of it. Instead, `RecordCall()` and the `GenericCustomer` class itself will be declared as `abstract`.

Having done that, we need to add a class that represents the pay-as-you-go customers. The `PayAsYouGo` class does this job, supplying the override to `RecordCall()` that with our previous hierarchy was defined in the base `Customer` class.

The diagram also shows the `GoldCustomer` class. As before, this is just to illustrate that in practice there may be many other classes derived from `GenericCustomer` – we won't actually code up this class in our sample.

You may wonder whether it is really worth the effort in redesigning the class hierarchy for the sample in this way. After all, the old hierarchy worked perfectly well didn't it? There is actually a practical reason for regarding the new hierarchy as a better designed architecture, in that it removes a possible subtle source of bugs. In a real application, `RecordCall()` probably wouldn't be the only virtual method that needed to be implemented separately for each tariff. Real applications tend to be a lot bigger than samples in books, so there would most likely be a fair number of such methods.

What happens if later on someone adds a new derived class, representing a new tariff, but forgets to add the overrides of some of these methods? Well, with the old class hierarchy, the compiler would have automatically substituted the corresponding method in the base class. With that hierarchy, the base class represented pay-as-you-go customers, so we would have ended up with subtle runtime bugs involving the wrong versions of methods being called. With our new hierarchy, however, we'll instantly get a compile-time error, with the compiler complaining that the relevant abstract methods haven't been overridden in the new class. Abstract classes aren't just a syntactical convenience – they ensure extra compile-time checking that all relevant overrides have been supplied in a program.

Anyway, on to the new code, and as you may by now have guessed, this is the `MortimerPhones6` sample. With the new hierarchy, the code for `GenericCustomer` looks like this. Most of the code is the same as for our old `Customer` class – in the following code we've highlighted the few lines that are different. Note the abstract declaration for the `RecordCall()` method:

```
public abstract class GenericCustomer
{
    private string name;
    protected decimal balance;
    public override string ToString()
    {
        string Result = "Customer: " + name;
        Result += ", owing: " + balance;
        return Result;
    }
    public string Name
    {
        get
```

```
        {
            return name;
        }
        set
        {
            name = value;
        }
    }
    public decimal Balance
    {
        get
        {
            return balance;
        }
    }
    public void RecordPayment(decimal amountPaid)
    {
        balance -= amountPaid;
    }
    public abstract void RecordCall(TypeOfCall callType, uint nMinutes);
}
```

Now for the implementation of pay-as-you-go customers. Again, notice that most of the code is taken directly from the former, obsolete, Customer, class. The only real difference is that RecordCall() is now an override rather than a virtual method:

```
public class PayAsYouGoCustomer : GenericCustomer
{
    public override void RecordCall(TypeOfCall callType, uint nMinutes)
    {
        switch (callType)
        {
            case TypeOfCall.CallToLandline:
                balance += (0.02M * nMinutes);
                break;
            case TypeOfCall.CallToMobile:
                balance += (0.30M * nMinutes);
                break;
            default:
                break;
        }
    }
}
```

We won't display the full code for Nevermore60Customer here as the RecordCall() override in this class is long and completely unchanged from the earlier version of the example. The only change we need to make to this class is to derive it from GenericCustomer instead of from the Customer class, which no longer exists:

```
public class Nevermore60Customer : GenericCustomer
{
    private uint highCostMinutesUsed;
    public override void RecordCall(TypeOfCall callType, uint nMinutes)
    {   // etc.
```

To finish off, we'll add some new client code to demonstrate the operation of the new class hierarchy. This time we've actually used an array to store the various customers, so this code shows how an array of references to the abstract base class can be used to reference instances of the various derived class, with the appropriate overrides of the methods being called:

```
public static void Main(string[] args)
{
    GenericCustomer Arabel = new Nevermore60Customer();
    Arabel.Name = "Arabel Jones";
    GenericCustomer MrJones = new PayAsYouGoCustomer();
    MrJones.Name = "Ben Jones";
    GenericCustomer [] Customers = new GenericCustomer[2];
    Customers[0] = Arabel;
    Customers[0].RecordCall(TypeOfCall.CallToLandline, 20);
    Customers[0].RecordCall(TypeOfCall.CallToMobile, 5);
    Customers[1] = MrJones;
    Customers[1].RecordCall(TypeOfCall.CallToLandline, 10);
    foreach (GenericCustomer NextCustomer in Customers)
    {
        Console.WriteLine("{0,-20} owes ${1:F2}", NextCustomer.Name,
                                                 NextCustomer.Balance);
    }
}
```

Running this code, once again, produces the correct results for the amounts owed:

Sealed Classes and Methods

In many ways you can think of a sealed class or method as the opposite of an abstract class or method. Whereas declaring something as abstract means that it must be overridden or inherited from, declaring it as sealed means that you cannot do so.

You can declare a class as sealed by placing the keyword `sealed` in front of its declaration. Doing this will cause a compilation error to be generated if any other class attempts to derive from the class:

```
sealed class FinalClass
{

    // etc.
```

```
class DerivedClass : FinalClass        // wrong. Will give compilation error
{

    // etc.
```

Marking a method of a class as sealed prevents it from being overridden further. In this sense, sealed does the same thing as the final keyword in Java:

```
class MyClass
{
    public sealed override FinalMethod()
    {

        // etc.
class DerivedClass
{
    public override NewMethod()         // wrong. Will give compilation error
    {
```

Note that it does not make sense to use the sealed keyword on a method unless that method is itself an override of another method in some base class. If you are defining a new method and you don't want anyone else to override it, then do not declare it as virtual in the first place. If, however, you have overridden a base class method then the sealed keyword provides a way of ensuring that the override you supply to a method is a "final" override in the sense that no-one else can override it again.

The most likely situation when you'll mark a class or method as sealed will be if it is very much internal to the operation of the library, class or other classes that you are writing, so you are fairly sure that any attempt to override some of its functionality will cause problems. You might also mark a class or method as sealed for commercial reasons, in order to prevent a third party from extending your classes in a manner that is contrary to the licensing agreements. In general, however, you should be careful about marking a class or member as sealed, since by doing so you are severely restricting how it can be used. Even if you don't think it would be useful to inherit from a class or override a particular member of it, it's still possible that at some point in the future someone will encounter a situation you hadn't anticipated in which it is useful to do so.

Calling Base Versions of Methods

So far, we've used method overriding and method hiding only in the context of wanting to replace the functionality of a method by something different. Sometimes, that won't be what you want to do. Rather, you'll want to override a method in order to extend what it does, in other words to do whatever the base class version of the method does, and something else as well. In this situation, you need some way of specifically telling the compiler to call the version of the method in the base class. The keyword that does this is base.

> *C++ does not have any equivalent to C#'s* base, *but Java has the keyword* super *which does roughly the same thing.*

To illustrate this, let's abandon Mortimer Phones for a while, and take a very similar example. We suppose we are running a car sales company and we have a base class, CustomerAccount, which represents a customer account. It contains a method, CalculatePrice(),which returns a decimal representing how much we will charge for a particular sale (we can't use MortimerPhones.RecordCall() for these particular examples, because they depend on the method returning something. ReturnCall() returns void):

```
class CustomerAccount
{
    public virtual decimal CalculatePrice()
    {

        // some other processing. For the sake of argument,
        // we'll say the result is $2000

        return 2000.0M;
    }
}
```

In any directly derived class, we can access this particular method by referring to it as `base.DoSomething()`. As far as what we do with this method is concerned, your imagination is your limit. A few examples of the sorts of things you might want an override of `CalculatePrice()` to do might be:

1. Return some multiple of the base method:

```
class GoldAccount : CustomerAccount
{
    public override decimal CalculatePrice()
    {
        return base.CalculatePrice()*0.9M;
    }
}
```

One example of this would be if in the `MortimerPhones` example, you wanted to implement the `GoldCustomer`'s `RecordCall()` method by discounting the cost calculated by another class.

2. Do something else, then do the base processing:

```
class GoldAccount : CustomerAccount
{
    public override decimal CalculatePrice()
    {
    InformPentagonOfSale();
        return base.CalculatePrice();
    }
}
```

3. Do the same as the base class, but only if some condition is met:

```
class QualifyingAccount : CustomerAccount
{
    public override decimal CalculatePrice()
    {
        if (IsOneMillionthSale())
        {
    InformCustomerHesWonAFreeCar();
            return 0.0M;
        }
        else
        {
    return base.CalculatePrice();
        }
}
```

It's even possible to explicitly call the base class version of a method from a *different* method in the derived class (although it's hard to find situations where you'd want to do this):

```
class MyDerived : MyBase
{
    public double DoSomethingElse()
    {
        base.DoSomething();

        // do some other processing

        return 12.0;
    }
```

For this example we've declared DoSomething() as virtual and the version in MyDerived as an override, but the same principles would have held if the base version was not virtual, and the version in MyDerived was declared as new, hiding the base version. Even with the base version of the method hidden, we can still call it using the base keyword.

Inheritance: Other Topics

We've now completed our discussion of the basic concepts involved in inheritance. We will come back to the subject in later chapters to show you some other aspects of the topic. The possible combinations of things you can do with inherited classes and overriding or hiding members is huge, and it is impossible to cover them all in one example. A couple of other points worth noting are that:

❑   It is not only methods that can be overridden or hidden. You can do the same thing with any other class member that has an implementation. That means you can declare properties as virtual and override them if you want. The same is true for indexers and operator overloads, which we cover in the next chapter.

❑   Fields cannot be declared as virtual or overridden. However, it is possible to hide a base version of a field by declaring another field of the same name in a derived class. In that case, if you wanted to access the base version from the derived class, you'd need to use the syntax base.<field_name>. You wouldn't do that anyway, because you'd have all your fields declared as private (wouldn't you?).

❑   Static methods and so on cannot be declared as virtual, but they can be hidden in the same way that instance methods etc. can be. It wouldn't make sense to declare a static member as virtual. virtual means that the compiler looks up the instance of a class when it calls that member, but static members are not associated with any class instance.

❑   Although a reference variable declared of type T can also refer to any instance of a class derived from T, you cannot use that reference to call any member unless that member is defined for T. In other words, if a method MyMethod is declared for the first time in a derived class D, you can only call MyMethod through a reference that points to D or class derived from D.

❑   Whenever we talk about a class Derived being derived from a class Base, the inheritance can be direct or indirect. For example, Derived might be derived from an intermediate class Inter2, which in turn might be derived from a class Inter1, which might be derived from Base. Suppose a certain method, MyMethod is defined in Base, overridden in Derived, but no version of the method is defined in Inter1 or Inter2. The compiler will always search in successive base classes when looking for a version of the method to use. For example, if `MyMethod` is called against an instance of `Inter2`, the compiler will use the version defined in Base, since neither `Inter2` nor `Inter1` contain versions of the method and `Base` is the next class working up the hierarchy:

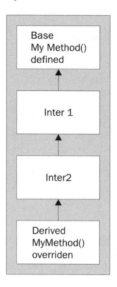

OOP Program Architecture

This chapter has been very intensive on concepts. The aim of it has been not only to introduce you to the relevant parts of the C# language, but also to get you used to the idea of object-oriented programming, and to familiarize you with the way that good object-oriented programs are structured. In a procedural language and even to some extent in a language like Visual Basic the emphasis is very much on functions, breaking the program down into what things you do and then writing a function to do each of those things. One way of looking at object-oriented programming is it shifts the emphasis from the verb to the noun, so that instead of thinking of what things the program does, you think about objects the program consists of, and then design classes to represent those objects. Once you've designed those classes, then you think about what the classes do and start writing the member methods.

Inheritance is also an extremely important feature of object-oriented programming, and a crucial stage in the design of your program is deciding on class hierarchies. In general, you will find that you have a number of specialized objects that are all particular types of more generic objects. As an example, if you're writing the traffic management or simulation program, you'll have many vehicles in your system. Some of those will be buses, some will be motor cars, some will be lorries, and so on. You may even want to fine-grade your vehicle types by separating road and other vehicles. That means that you'll probably choose a class hierarchy that looks like this:

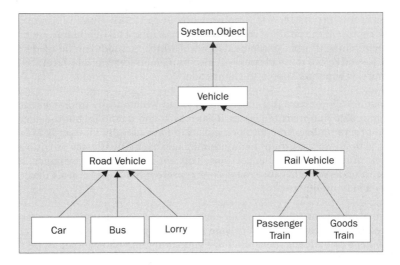

In this case `Vehicle` will be an abstract class, but it will implement some of the functions is common to all types of vehicles such as starting and stopping. `Bus` will probably add to this by implementing methods to do with picking up and setting down passengers as well as properties to do with the bus routes.

As another, more realistic example, we'll quickly look at one of the hierarchies from .NET base classes. Later on, in the chapter about Windows programming we will how to use the base classes that encapsulate windows (or to give them their more modern .NET terminology, forms). We won't discuss the classes here, but we will display part of the hierarchy, so you can get an idea of the structure. You may not have realized just how rich a hierarchy could be behind some of the controls that you can place on windows:

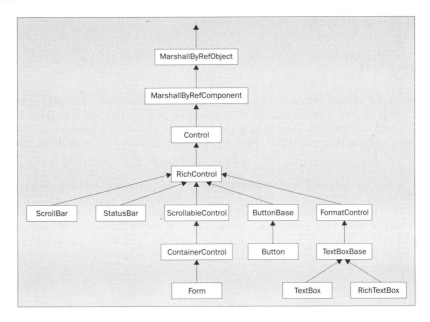

The `Form` class represents the generic window, while `ScrollBar`, `StatusBar`, `Button`, `TextBox`, and `RichTextBox` represent the familiar corresponding controls. The rich hierarchy behind these classes allows a very fine-tuning of what implementations of which methods can be made common to a number of different classes. Many of these classes will also implement certain interfaces, by which they can make their nature as windows known to client code.

A large application will not have just one hierarchy, but will typically implement a large number possibly stretching into hundreds of classes. That may sound daunting, but the alternative, before object-oriented programming came into being, was to have literally thousands of functions making up your program, with no way to group them into manageable units. Classes provide a very effective way of breaking your program into smaller sections. This not only helps maintenance, but also makes your program easier to understand because the classes represent the actual objects that your program is representing in a very intuitive way.

It's also important with your classes to think carefully about the separation between the public interface that is presented to client code, and the private internal implementation. In general the more of a class you are able to keep private, the more modular your program will become, in the sense that you can make modifications or improvements to the internal implementation of one class and be certain that it will not break or even have any effect on any other part of the program. That's the reason that we've emphasized that member fields in particular will almost invariably be private unless they are either constant, or they form part of a struct whose main purpose is to group together a small number of fields. We haven't always kept to that rule rigidly in this chapter, but that's largely so we can keep the samples as simple as possible.

In practice, there's always a balance between taking some extra time at the outset to make sure that your objects are properly designed in accordance with good object-oriented principles, and actually getting some code down and working quickly so you can satisfy your boss or your customer, and worrying about its maintainability and good design later. Good program and object architecture will, however, usually pay for itself very quickly when you start having to do further work to maintain or upgrade existing applications. C# helps considerably here because it has been designed with the benefit of the hindsight of 20 years of object-oriented programming.

Summary

This chapter has been very intensive on concepts. The aim of it has been not only to introduce you to the relevant parts of the C# language, but also to get you used to the idea of object-oriented programming and familiar with the way that good object-oriented programs are structured. We have seen an example of well-structured code with a good class hierarchy in the final version of `MortimerPhones`.

Inheritance and object-oriented programming is a topic that can take a while to become familiar with, but the effort is well worth it because it allows you to design your code in a much better, more well structured way. Throughout this book, we will be using classes that are inherited from other classes. As we learn to use the .NET base classes we will see time and time again that OOP and inheritance form a crucial aspect of how they have been designed. Microsoft has done this because with our current understanding of programming techniques, it simply is the most appropriate way of coding up any large library or application.

5
Object-Oriented C#

In the last chapter we introduced the ideas of object-oriented programming (OOP). We showed how classes can be defined that represent the different items in a program. We also saw how inheritance can be used to give a specialization to objects. We also started to show, through the `MortimerPhones` samples, how the principles of OOP can give a new and useful architecture to your code.

In this chapter, we will continue to focus on object-oriented programming. Whereas the last chapter focused on the concepts involved, here we will move on to examine some of the specific facilities that C# offers to make object-oriented programming particularly easy. In particular, we will cover:

❑ **Method Overloading** – C# allows you to define different versions of a method in a class, and the compiler will automatically select the most appropriate one based on the parameters supplied.

❑ **Construction and Destruction** – it is possible to specify how objects should be initialized as well as any action that needs to be automatically taken when they are destroyed.

❑ **Memory** – although C# frees you from having to take responsibility for memory management, understanding the memory management that C# handles for you automatically can help you to design efficient code. We examine this area.

❑ **Structs** – on occasions you need something that has the many of the features of a class without all the overhead involved in creating a class instance. Structs provide this facility.

❑ **Operator Overloading** – we examine how to define operators that allow you to for example add, subtract, multiply, or divide instances of your classes.

❑ **Indexers** – indexers allow a class to be treated syntactically as if it is an array, and can simplify the use of classes that contain sets of objects.

❑ **Interfaces** – C# supports interface inheritance as well as implementation inheritance. We examine this feature.

Method Overloading

We will introduce method overloading by means of an example from the .NET base classes, and an example that we have actually been using throughout the last chapters: If we want to display the value of an integer, we can write this:

```
int X = 10;
Console.WriteLine(X);
```

While to display a string we can write:

```
string Message = "Hello";
Console.WriteLine(Message);
```

How is this possible? What parameter type does `Console.WriteLine()` take? If it was expecting to take a string, then the first of these two examples would give a compilation error, because there is no implicit cast from `int` to `string`. If `Console.WriteLine()` was expecting to take any numeric data type however, then the second of these examples would give a compilation error because there is no implicit cast from `string` to any numeric type. Yet both of these lines will compile without error and run to give the expected results.

The reason is that there are two different `Console.WriteLine()` methods – one of them takes an `int` as a parameter, while the other one takes a `string`. There are many others, such as a 2-parameter one that takes a string and an object, and lets you write:

```
string Message = "Hello";
Console.WriteLine("The message is {0}", Message);
```

This works because any variable type can always be implicitly converted to an object, so there's no problem with passing a string as the second parameter.

Microsoft has provided all these `Console.WriteLine()` methods because they realized that there are many different data types that you might want to display the value of. This means, however, that there appear to be a number of methods in the `Console` class that have the same name. This is permitted in C#, and the different methods (or, if you like, the different versions of the `WriteLine()` method) are known as **overloads** of the method. Method overloading means that you can define several methods with the same name in a class, provided that these methods take different types or numbers of parameters.

> *Don't confuse method overloading with method overriding – the similarity in these names is unfortunate as they are completely different, unrelated, concepts. Method overloading has nothing to do with inheritance or virtual methods.*

Method overloading will be familiar to Java and C++ developers – it works in the same way in C# as in these languages. The concept will however, be new to VB developers. On the other hand, C# does not allow default values for parameters (optional parameters) as both VB and C++ do. As we'll see, one of the many benefits of method overloading is that it provides a more powerful (although syntactically more cumbersome) way of achieving the same thing.

Use method overloading in situations where you want a class to be able to do something, but there is more than one possibility for what information is supplied to the method that carries out the task, as demonstrated by the `Console.WriteLine()` method.

Defining Overloaded Methods

As an example that illustrates how to define method overloads, consider the `RecordCall()` method of the classes in the `Customer` class hierarchy from the `MortimerPhones` sample of the last chapter. The signature of this method is:

```
public virtual void RecordCall(TypeOfCall callType, uint nMinutes)
```

which means that the information passed to it is the type of call and the number of minutes the call lasted. Suppose you knew that in some cases the information available to the client code was the type of call, and the start and end times of the call. Then you might want to make another method available, with the following definition:

```
public virtual void RecordCall(TypeOfCall callType, DateTime startTime,
                                                    DateTime endTime)
```

In other words, we have another method with the same name, and which conceptually does the same thing, but using slightly different information.

Our new overload of `RecordCall()` uses one of the .NET base classes, a class called `System.DateTime`. The dependency of C# on the base classes is so close that we'll often have need to call on the services of one or two of these classes in our examples. How to use `DateTime` is fairly intuitive, so we're not going to devote a separate section to examining it. We'll just comment on those `DateTime` methods that we require as we come across them. The class is documented along with all the other base classes in the MSDN documentation.

There's no limit to how many overloads of a method you can have. You simply declare them in a class, just as if they were different methods that happened to have the same name. Continuing the `RecordCall()` example, you might also want a method that allows the class to work out the call charge given the number called, and the start and end times of the call. With this further override added in, the relevant part of the definition of `Customer` might look like this:

```
public virtual void RecordCall(TypeOfCall callType, uint nMinutes)
{
   // put implementation here
}
public virtual void RecordCall(TypeOfCall callType, DateTime startTime,
                                                    DateTime endTime)

{
   // put implementation here
}

public virtual void RecordCall(string numberCalled, DateTime startTime,
                                                     DateTime endTime)

{
   // put implementation here
}
```

Once you have overrides, how do you implement them? Well, that's basically up to you, but if you want people to be able to easily understand how to use your class, you'll want to implement the different overrides so that they all do the same kind of thing, so that once a developer has understood how to use one override of a method, it'll be pretty obvious to them how to use the other overrides. We'll demonstrate here one way that you might want to implement the second override of `RecordCall()`, and we will add this to the `MortimerPhones` sample, making the `MortimerPhones7` project which can be downloaded from the Wrox Press web site. This new overload of `RecordCall()` is placed in the `GenericCustomer` class.

```
public void RecordCall(TypeOfCall callType, DateTime startTime,
                                             DateTime endTime)
{
    // assume end Time is later than start time - in a real app we'd need
    // to check this explicitly.
    TimeSpan CallLength = endTime - startTime;
    uint nMinutes = (uint)CallLength.TotalMinutes;
    RecordCall(callType, nMinutes);
}
```

With this implementation we are treating our first `RecordCall()` override as the one that actually does the work, and our new override simply converts the parameters into the equivalent data, expressed as a call type and number of minutes before calling the original overload. It's very common to implement method overloads like this, because it's always a good idea to avoid duplicating the same code in different methods if you can avoid it.

In this implementation we've used an additional base class, TimeSpan, which represents an interval of time. You'd expect that one way of getting an interval of time is to work out the difference between two absolute times, and that's what we've done in the above code – subtracted the start time of a call from the end time of the call to work out how long the call lasted.

Notice as well that I've modified the definition of this new overload slightly by no longer declaring it as `virtual`. Why? Look at what this overload does. What is there in the implementation of this method that you could possibly want to override in a derived class? Internally, we simply do a data conversion (and how we do that is not going to depend on the type of customer) before transferring control to our original `RecordCall()` overload. The original overload is virtual, and the correct implementation of it for a given class instance will still automatically be picked out, without the new overload needing to be virtual.

As an extra bonus, the above code also gives us a good example to illustrate our point from the last chapter when we covered virtual methods, that there are some methods that, because of design considerations you will not want to ever be overridden, and which you will therefore not declare as virtual.

Calling Overloaded Methods

Once you have a couple of overloads, how do you call them? The answer is that it's not really any different to calling non-overloaded methods, except that the compiler has a bit more work to do in deciding which overload you intend to be called. For example, look at the code:

```
// Start and End have been declared of type DateTime and initialized
uint Mins = 30;
Arabel.RecordCall(TypeOfCall.CallToLandline, Mins);
Arabel.RecordCall(TypeOfCall.CallToLandline, Start, End);
```

Here the `RecordCall()` method is called twice. The first time we pass in a `TypeOfCall` and a `uint`. When it encounters this code, the compiler will look for the closest matching overload of `RecordCall()` – and in this case it's easy because there is an exact match. Recall that the overloads we have available are:

1. `public virtual void RecordCall(TypeOfCall callType, uint nMinutes)`

2. `public void RecordCall(TypeOfCall callType, DateTime startTime, DateTime endTime)`

3. `public void RecordCall(string numberCalled, DateTime startTime, DateTime endTime)`

We've also assumed that overload 3 will do some processing then call overload 1, and so does not need to be virtual.

Overload 1 requires a `TypeOfCall` and a `uint` – exactly the parameters that we are passing in. The compiler will generate code that calls this overload. Note that since this overload is declared as `virtual`, the generated code will also use a `vtable` to make sure the appropriate override is called for the particular object that it ends up getting called against.

The second call to `RecordCall()` attempts to pass in a `CallType` and two `DateTimes` in that order. Again, there is an exact match since we have supplied an overload to this method, which requires a `CallType` followed by two `DateTimes`. That's the overload that will be called – and since this overload is not virtual, no `vtable` will be used. The method is called against a reference to a `Customer`, the generated code will always pick up this method as defined in `Customer`.

Now look at this code:

```
ushort Mins = 12;
ulong LongMins = 16;
Arabel.RecordCall(TypeOfCall.CallToLandline, Mins);
Arabel.RecordCall(TypeOfCall.CallToLandline, LongMins);    // wrong
```

Now the compiler's task is harder since there is no exact match for either call. Let's take the first call. We have not declared any overload of `RecordCall()`, which takes a `CallType` and a `ushort` – the parameters we are attempting to pass in – so the compiler is going to have to try to identify the best matching overload. Since we are passing in two parameters, the compiler can immediately narrow it down to those overloads that take two parameters, so there's no way you can change the number of parameters! The only overload that takes two parameters is overload number 1 in our list, so the compiler will attempt to match the parameters supplied to this overload – a `TypeOfCall` enumerated value and a `uint`. Fortunately, implicitly converting a `ushort` to a `uint` is easy, so this will be the overload called.

The second call to `RecordCall()` also supplies two parameters, a `TypeOfCall` and a `ulong`. Again, overload number 1 in our list looks like the best match, however C# won't let you implicitly convert a `ulong` to a `uint` because of the risk of the number overflowing. This line of code will actually raise a compilation error because the compiler is unable to identify a best matching overload that it can call. Incidentally, if instead we had written:

```
Arabel.RecordCall(TypeOfCall.CallToLandline, (uint)LongMins);    // OK
```

then we'd have been OK, since the compiler will allow a `ulong` to be converted to a `uint` if we explicitly specify that's what we want to do. In fact, as far as the compiler is concerned, this method passes in a `TypeOfCall` and a `uint`, so there is an exact match to an overload. In general, it is usually better if you explicitly cast your parameters to exactly match one of the overloads since that leaves no room for any doubt about which overload will be called.

If there is no exact match, the compiler will always look for the closest match for the parameters passed in when deciding which overload to call. There are some precise rules about how this is done and what data conversions will be looked at first. As an example, it regards converting an `int` to a `long` as better than converting an `int` to a `double`, so if you have these methods defined:

```
public int GetNumb(long i) {return 1;}
public int GetNumb(double x) {return 2;}
```

Then attempt to call `GetNumb()` using:

```
int x = 5;
int y = GetNumb(x);
```

Then the first overload will be called and `y` will contain the value 1. However, we're not going to look at the details of the overload selection rules here, as they are fairly esoteric. If you need to use them they are detailed in Microsoft's documentation for the C# language definition. As a matter of good programming practice, though, you really should make sure that the parameters taken by your overloads are sufficiently different so that there can be no possible misunderstandings about what overload the compiler will use in any given circumstance, and you're not forcing other developers who use your code to refer to the detailed rules for type conversion. The overloads of `Customer.RecordCall()` from our earlier example are fine in this regard and would be regarded as good programming style. The above example of `GetNumb()` is potentially confusing and would be regarded as very poor programming practice, simply because it would be so easy for someone to write client code that calls the "wrong" overload.

Requirements for Method Overloads

If you do define overloads for a method, there are a couple of restrictions that the compiler imposes. The rule is that overloads must be different in their signature, which means the name and the number and type of their parameters. It's not sufficient for only the return type to be different. For example, the following code would produce a compilation error:

```
public void RecordCall(TypeOfCall callType, uint nMinutes)
{
    // implementation
}
public int RecordCall(TypeOfCall callType, uint nMinutes)
{
    // implementation
    return 1;
}
```

The reason this isn't permitted is that it would make it too easy to write ambiguous code in which it is not obvious to the developer which overload would be called.

However, you can add as many overloads as you want provided that they all differ in either the number of parameters or the type of at least one parameter; only after you have done this can you use different return types.

When to Use Overloading

Generally, you should consider overloading a method when you need a number of methods that take different parameters, but conceptually do the same thing. `Console.WriteLine()` is a good example. Another good example is a method, `Sign()` in the `System.Math` base class, which returns the sign of a number, and is overloaded to work out the sign of a `double`, a `decimal` and other signed types.

In general, you should not use overloads when two methods really do different things, otherwise you'll simply confuse the developers who have to use your classes.

The main situations in which you will normally use overloading are as follows.

Default Parameters

One common use of method overloads is to allow certain parameters to a method to have default values if the client code chooses not to specify their values explicitly. For example, consider this code:

```
public void DoSomething(int X, int Y)
{
    // do whatever
}

public void DoSomething(int X)
{
    DoSomething(X, 10);
}
```

These overloads allow client code to call `DoSomething()`, either supplying two integers as parameters, or just supplying one `int` as a parameter, in which we effectively assume the second `int` is `10`. For all practical purposes, it's as if Y has been given a default value of `10`.

Some languages, including VB and C++, allow default parameters to be specified explicitly in function declarations, with a syntax that looks like `public void DoSomething(int X, int Y=10)`. *C# does not allow this, so in C# you need to simulate default parameters by providing multiple overloads of methods as shown in the above example.*

Different Input Types

We have already seen a couple of examples of this very common reason for defining overloads. There may be different data types on which you want to perform the same operation, as in `Console.WriteLine()`, or there may be different combinations of information that allow you to perform the same processing, as shown in the `MortimerPhones` example.

Different Output Types

This situation is far less common, but you may occasionally have a method that calculates or obtains some quantity, and depending on the circumstances, you might wish this to be returned in more than one different way. For example, in an airline company, you might have a class that represents aircraft timetables, and you might wish to define a method that tells you where an aircraft should be at a particular time. Depending on the situation, you might want the method to return either a string description of the position ("over Atlantic Ocean en route to London") or the latitude and longitude of the position.

As just mentioned, we cannot distinguish overloads using the return type of a method. However, you can do so using `out` parameters. So you could define these:

```
void GetAircraftLocation(DateTime Time, out string Location) { // etc. }
void GetAircraftLocation(DateTime Time, out float Latitude,
                                        out float Longitude) { // etc. }
```

Note, however, that in most cases, using overloads to obtain different out parameters does not lead to an architecturally neat design. In the above example, for example, a neater design would perhaps involve defining a `Location` struct that contains the location string as well as the latitude and longitude, and returning this from the method call, hence avoiding the need for overloads.

Construction and Disposal

In this section we're going to look at the facilities C# offers to allow you to specify any particular actions that must always be taken when initializing or destroying a class instance. We'll start by looking at initialization.

Constructors

Looking for a moment at simple data types rather than classes, C# is normally quite fussy about variables being initialized before use, and with good reason. In general, in any language, if a variable for some reason doesn't get initialized by setting it to a particular value before its value gets used somewhere, then it will contain whatever random data happened to previously be in the memory locations it occupies. That random data will be the value used, which is a good way to generate hard-to-identify runtime errors.

For simple (value) data types, C# has two different ways of handling initialization in cases in which you have not specified any initial value for a variable:

❑   If a variable is local to a method, or is an `out` parameter to a method, the compiler will insist that your code explicitly sets the value of a variable before you attempt to use it.

❑   For all other situations (including instance and static member fields of classes), the compiler will arrange for variables to be initialized to default values when they are created. The default values are 0 for integer and floating point data types and `false` for `bool`. For strings, the default is an empty string, while all references will be initialized to the null reference. In all cases, the default value is the value you get from simply zeroing out the memory used to store the variable.

Obviously, if you indicate an initial value for a variable when you declare it (such as int X = 10), that value will always be used to initialize the variable.

C# is able to initialize simple data types to default values because those values have been specified in the definition of the C# language. For classes, however, no such default values exist for the rather obvious reason that when you write your own classes, only you know what the ideal default values are. That's what **constructors** are for.

VB developers will note that there are some similarities between constructors and the Initialize and Class_Load methods of VB class modules. Constructors however are far more flexible and powerful.

When you see a constructor definition, it looks much like a method definition, but the difference is that you don't usually call a constructor explicitly. It's like a method that is always called on your behalf whenever an instance of a class is created. In addition, because you never call the method explicitly, there is no way you can get access to any return value, which means that constructors never return anything. You can identify a constructor in a class definition because it always has the same name as the class itself. For example, if we have a class named MyClass, a skeleton constructor would be defined as follows:

```
public class MyClass
{

    public MyClass()
    {
    }
```

This constructor so far does nothing – we haven't added any code to it. Notice that no return type is specified, not even void. The compiler recognizes the constructor from the fact that it has the same name as the containing class. (This incidentally means that it is not possible to write a method that has that name, because if you try to do so the compiler will interpret it as a constructor).

> **A constructor is declared as a method that has the same name as its containing class. It must not have any return type.**

It's not necessary to provide a constructor for your class. We haven't supplied one for any of our examples so far. In general, if you don't explicitly supply any constructor, the compiler will just make a default one up for you behind the scenes. It'll be a very basic constructor that just initializes all the member fields to their normal default values (empty string for strings, zero for numeric data types, and false for bools, as we've already mentioned). Often, that will be adequate; otherwise, you'll need to write your own constructor.

Adding Constructors to the Authenticator

To illustrate constructors, we're going to go back to our Authenticator class from the last chapter, and improve it. Recall that whenever we declared a variable of type Authenticator in our earlier samples, the initial password would be set to an empty string (the default value for strings). For this class, that's probably not adequate. I'm not a security guru, but I have a strong suspicion that blank passwords are not in general good for security! Instead, let's arrange it so that whenever an Authenticator object is created, the password is initially set to the string ERRE34dj. Having every password set to the same string initially admittedly isn't much better for security than blank passwords, but it's a slight improvement, and we'll see how to make things a lot better soon.

To make the default password `ERRE34dj`, we modify the code for the `Authenticator` as follows:

```
// Authenticator 4

public class Authenticator
{
    public Authenticator()
    {
        Password = "ERRE34dj";
    }

    private static uint minPasswordLength = 6;
    private string Password;
```

Now, suppose we want to instantiate an `Authenticator` and give it the password `MyPassword45`. The code to do this would look like this:

```
Authenticator NewUser = new Authenticator();
NewUser.ChangePassword("ERRE34dj", "MyPassword45");
```

Constructors that Take Parameters

The code we've just presented will work, but as a way of setting up a password it's not very neat. What would really be nicer would be if we can specify the initial password when we first instantiate an `Authenticator`. It is possible to do this by supplying a constructor that takes parameters. In this regard, a constructor behaves like a method in that we can define whatever parameters we want for it and this is where constructors really score over VB's `Class_Load`. In addition, we can overload the constructor to a class in just the same way as we can for a method, by supplying different constructors that take different numbers or types of parameters.

For the `Authenticator`, we'd probably add a constructor that takes an initial password as a parameter:

```
// Authenticator 4

public class Authenticator
{
    public Authenticator()
    {
        Password = "ERRE34dj";
    }

    public Authenticator(string initialPassword)
    {
        Password = initialPassword;
    }

    private string Password;
    private static uint minPasswordLength = 6;
```

The advantage of using such a constructor is that it means an `Authenticator` object is guaranteed to be initialized the instant it is created. It is, therefore, not possible for other code to access the object before it has been initialized, as would be possible if we initialized it by calling a method after instantiating an object.

How do we ensure that this constructor is called when we instantiate the object? We just put the parameters in the brackets after the `new` operator, which is the point at which the class is instantiated. For example, if we want to instantiate two `Authenticator` objects, one with the default password and one with the password `MyPassword45`, we'd write this code:

```
Authenticator NewUser = new Authenticator();
Authenticator NewUser2 = new Authenticator("MyPassword45");
```

If you have overloaded constructors, the compiler treats them in the same way as overloaded methods. That is to say, when an object is instantiated, it looks at the parameter types in the brackets after the new operator and tries to find the best matching constructor. If it can't find a constructor that's suitable, it'll raise a compilation error.

The `Authenticator4` sample on the Wrox Press web site illustrates the use of these two constructors.

It is also possible to use constructors to force client code to supply parameters when instantiating a class. For example, in our `Authenticator` class, it's arguable that any default password is undesirable because of security considerations, and it would be best if the client code always indicated the initial password when a new `Authenticator` is instantiated. We can achieve this very simply by removing the no-parameter constructor to `Authenticator`, leaving only the constructor that takes a string as the parameter:

```
public class Authenticator
{
    public Authenticator(string initialPassword)
    {
        Password = initialPassword;
    }

    private string Password;
    private static uint minPasswordLength = 6;
```

Now if we reconsider the client code:

```
Authenticator NewUser = new Authenticator();          // wrong
Authenticator NewUser2 = new Authenticator("MyPassword45");
```

The first line of this code will no longer compile, because it does not supply any parameters, and the only constructor available requires one parameter. Hence, it is no longer possible to instantiate an `Authenticator` object without supplying the initial password. This code is downloadable as the `Authenticator5` sample.

Note that we mentioned earlier that if you do not define any constructors in a class, then the compiler will automatically supply a default one. This is only the case if you have not explicitly defined any constructors at all. In the above example, because we have explicitly defined a one-parameter constructor, the compiler will assume that this is the only constructor we wish to be available, and so will not implicitly supply any others.

We should mention that it is possible to achieve the same effect by keeping the no-parameter constructor, but declaring it as private or protected, so that it is invisible to code in unrelated classes:

```
public class Authenticator
{
    private Authenticator()
    {
        Password = "ERRE34dj";
    }

    public Authenticator(string initialPassword)
    {
        Password = initialPassword;
    }

    private string Password;
    private static uint minPasswordLength = 6;
```

Doing it this way means that it is possible to use such constructors within the class or (if declared as protected) any derived classes. This may be useful, for example in a Clone() or Copy() method, or some similar method within a class which needs to create further instances of that class.

Other Uses of Constructors

So far, the only thing we've done with constructors is to initialize the values of fields. In many cases that is all you will want to do. In many ways, however a constructor does act as a normal method so you can place any instructions you wish in a constructor – for example, you might perform some calculations to work out the initial values of the fields. If your class encapsulates access to a file or database, the constructor might attempt to open the file. The only thing to remember that you cannot do in a constructor is to return any value (such as indicating status) to the calling code.

Another novel use is to use a constructor to count how many instances of a class have been created while the program is running. If we wanted to do that for the Authenticator class, we could create a static field, nInstancesCreated, and amend the code for the constructor as follows:

```
public class Authenticator
{
    private static uint nInstancesCreated = 0;

    public Authenticator(string initialPassword)
    {
        ++nInstancesCreated;
        Password = initialPassword;
    }

    private string Password;
    private static uint minPasswordLength = 6;
```

This example is here more to demonstrate the kind of flexibility that being able to specify your own constructors gives you than because it's likely to have much practical benefit. Counting instances is, it should be said, something you're unlikely to want to do in release builds of code, but it's something that you might want to do for debugging purposes. In the next chapter, we'll see how to mark sections of code so that they are only compiled in debug builds.

Static Constructors

It's also possible to write a static no-parameter constructor for a class. Such a constructor will only ever be executed once, as opposed to the constructors we've written so far, which are instance constructors, and executed whenever an object of that class is created. One reason why you might want a static constructor is to initialize the values of any static variables.

As an example, so far we've specified a hard coded initial value of 6 for the (static) minimum password length in our `Authenticator` class. If, instead of hard coding this value, we'd wanted to read it in from a database, or do some other processing to calculate the value, we'd need to initialize it in a static constructor:

```
class Authenticator
{
    static Authenticator()
    {
        // do processing to work out min password length
        minPasswordLength = 6; // or whatever value we decide on
    }

    public Authenticator()
    {
        Password = "ERRE34dj";
    }

    public Authenticator(string initialPassword)
    {
        Password = initialPassword;
    }

    private string Password;
    private static uint minPasswordLength;
```

Notice that the static constructor does not have an access modifier defined. It's never called by any other C# code, but always by the .NET runtime when the class is loaded, so any access modifier like `public` or `private` would be meaningless. For this same reason, the static constructor cannot ever take any parameters, and there can only ever be one static constructor for a class. It should also be obvious that a static constructor can only access static members, not instance members, of the class.

Also notice that in the above code I've restored the other no-parameter constructor that we'd previously removed. I've done this to illustrate that a no-parameter constructor can happily sit in the class alongside the static constructor. This is the only case in which you can have two overloads of the same method that have the same parameter list. There is no conflict here because the static constructor is executed when the class is loaded, but the instance constructor is executed whenever an instance is created – so there won't be any confusion about which constructor gets executed when!

One thing to watch is that if you have more than one class that has a static constructor, which static constructor will be executed first is undefined. This means that you should not put any code in a static constructor that depends on other static constructors having been or not having been executed. It's also not guaranteed exactly when the static constructor will be executed, except that it will be before any instances of the class are created, or any static members of the class are accessed. On the other hand, if any static fields have been given default values, these will be allocated before the static constructor is called.

const and readonly Fields

While we're on the subject of constructors, it's a good opportunity to mention the facilities that C# offers to allow you to define member fields which cannot be changed. Depending on your requirements, there are two keywords you can use to indicate that a field should be treated as a constant that cannot have its value changed: const and readonly. We'll look at both of these cases in this section.

In the following examples we'll be using public fields extensively. That's OK, because const *and* readonly *fields are constant values rather than variables, so the argument that good programming practice requires fields to be private doesn't really apply as much to* const *and* readonly *fields.*

const Fields

If a field is declared as const, then it is not really a variable at all – it's treated as a fixed hard coded value in the program. To illustrate this, let's add a hard coded maximum password length to the Authenticator class:

```
public const uint MaxPasswordLength = 20;
```

MaxPasswordLength is a constant, so its value cannot be changed anywhere. Any attempt to assign a value to it will result in a compilation error. This also means that its value must be set when it is defined. Something like this:

```
public const uint MaxPasswordLength;    // wrong
```

will also cause a compilation error because the value of MaxPasswordLength is now undefined and can never be assigned.

Another peculiarity of const values is that they are implicitly static. The value is by definition constant, so there is no need to store copies of it with each class instance. That means that you must always refer to it with the syntax for a static member, using the class name rather than any variable name:

```
Authenticator Julian = new Authenticator()
uint Max1 = Authenticator.maxPasswordLength; // OK
uint Max2 = Julian.maxPasswordLength;        // wrong
                                             //will give compile-time error
```

Oddly enough, although const values are implicitly static, it is syntactically incorrect to explicitly declare them as such:

```
public const uint maxPasswordLength = 20;        // OK
public static const uint maxPasswordLength = 20; // wrong - will give
                                                 // compile-time error
```

readonly Fields

The readonly keyword gives a bit more flexibility than const, allowing for the case in which you might want a field to be constant, but need to carry out some calculations to determine its initial value. The rule is that you can assign values to a readonly field inside a constructor, but not anywhere else. It's also possible for a readonly field to be an instance rather than a static field, having a different value for each instance of a class which means that unlike a const field, if you want a readonly field to be static, you have to explicitly declare it as such.

If we want our `Authenticator` class to be able to read in the (fixed) value of the maximum password length from a database, then we'll need to declare this field as `readonly` instead of `const`. Since the same value applies to all accounts, it'll also be static and we'll want to set up its value in the static constructor. Indeed, the compiler will generate an error if we attempt to set the value of a static `readonly` field anywhere except in the static constructor. Here's how we'd code it up:

```
// Authenticator 6

public class Authenticator
{
    public static readonly uint MaxPasswordLength;

    static Authenticator()
    {
        // read in max password length from database. Assume result is 20
        MaxPasswordLength = 20;

        minPasswordLength = 6;
    }
```

For an example of a `readonly` field that is not static, suppose that each account has an associated creation date, which is also read in from the database. The creation date gives the date at which the account was initially set up, which is something that you wouldn't want to change, so this field should also be `readonly`. Here's what the relevant part of the definition of the `Authenticator` class looks like with the creation date added. Notice by the way that the creation date is represented by an instance of the base class `System.DateTime`, which we've already encountered briefly. In this code we use a `System.DateTime` constructor that takes three parameters (the year, month and day of the month):

```
//Authenticator 7

public class Authenticator
{
    private string Password;

    private static uint minPasswordLength;
    public readonly DateTime CreationDate;

    // note Pascal casing used because this field is public
    public static readonly uint MaxPasswordLength;

    static Authenticator()
    {
        // read in max password length from database. Assume result is 20
        maxPasswordLength = 20;

        minPasswordLength = 10;
    }

    public Authenticator()
    {
        // read in creation date from file. Assume result is 1 Jan 2001
        // but in general this can be different for different instances
        // of the class
        CreationDate = new DateTime(2000, 1, 1);

        // password will also be read in from database in real life.
        //Assume result is "ERRE34dj"
        Password = "ERRE34dj";
    }
```

```
public Authenticator(string initialPassword)
{
    // read in creation date from file. Assume result is 1 Jan 2001
    CreationDate = new DateTime(2000, 1, 1);

    Password = initialPassword;
}
```

Notice that we've separately initialized `CreationDate` in both of the instance constructors. That's important, since either constructor might be used to construct a given instance of `Authenticator`, and we don't want to leave `CreationDate` uninitialized for some instances. In the next section, we'll learn how achieve this more neatly, by calling one constructor from the other constructor. Beyond that, `CreationDate` is treated like any other instance field, except that because it is `readonly` – it cannot be assigned to outside of any of the instance constructors.

The above code for `readonly` fields is demonstrated in the `Authenticator7` sample from the code download.

It's also worth noting that you don't have to assign a value to a `readonly` field in a constructor. If you don't it'll be left with the default value for its particular data type or whatever value you initialized it to at its declaration. That applies to both static and instance `readonly` fields.

Incidentally, with the concept of reading things from a database, our Authenticator *class is starting to evolve out of all recognition, and it's beginning to look like a rather confused hotchpotch of fields. If we were going to develop it much further we'd need to start sorting out what this class is supposed to do. For example, we really should be passing in a username with the constructor, so the constructor knows which user's authentication information to read from the database! The one-parameter constructor that takes a password is looking a bit odd too – we probably don't need it anymore since the password should be read in from the database.*

Calling Constructors from Other Constructors

In this section, we're going to set aside for a short time our doubts about the `Authenticator` class, and make one more change to it. The state we've left our instance constructors in now doesn't look very satisfactory. We have two constructors that independently contain the same code (well, a comment saying "the code goes here", anyway) to read in a creation date from a file. That kind of code duplication is dangerous programming practice – it's asking for problems of one constructor gets upgraded, but the other one does not. We could of course get round this by encapsulating the common code in a method that's called from both constructors, but wouldn't it be neater if we could just get one constructor to call the other constructor? What we really have is a situation where the constructor takes one value, the password, which can have a default value. When we encountered the same situation for overloaded methods, we resolved it by having the overload with fewer parameters, set up the default parameter, then call the other overload of the method.

It is possible to do the same thing with constructors, but we need to use a special syntax to do so – that's because of the problem of not being able to call constructors explicitly. Here's how we do it (you can download this code as the `Authenticator8` sample):

```
public Authenticator()
    : this("ERRE34dj")
{
    // no other code here, but you could put some in if you wanted
}
```

```
public Authenticator(string initialPassword)
{
    // read in creation date from file. Assume result is 1 Jan 2001
    CreationDate = new DateTime(2000, 1, 1);

    Password = initialPassword;
}
```

Remember the `this` reference, which we introduced briefly earlier in the chapter, where we mentioned that `this` could be used in rare situations in which you need to refer to the containing object? This is one of those situations. What happens is that immediately after the constructor declaration, and before the opening curly brace that starts the implementation, you place a colon, followed by some indication that another constructor that should be executed first. The constructor is specified with the keyword `this`, followed by any parameters in brackets. Notice that there is no semi-colon here.

I should say this syntax doesn't give you as much flexibility as you get in overloaded methods, in which you can call another overload anywhere in the implementation. For a start, you can only specify one other constructor to be called up, and that other constructor will always be executed first. There's no way that you can do some initial processing, then call up another constructor, then do some more processing. Due to these restrictions, you'll need to think carefully about how to organize any inter-constructor calls for your particular class. Having said that, the above example does illustrate the standard way that you can arrange for constructors to take default parameters.

Constructors of Derived Classes

We've now seen how constructors work for simple classes, and we've also seen how classes can derive from other classes. An interesting question arises as to what happens when you start defining your own constructors for classes that are in a hierarchy, inherited from other classes that may also have custom constructors. This is something we didn't have to worry about when we developed our `MortimerPhones` sample to illustrate inheritance – that's because we didn't define any constructors at all in that sample, but left it to the compiler to supply default constructors everywhere. When the compiler supplies default constructors everywhere, it is able to arrange it so that things work out nicely all through the hierarchy and every field in every class gets initialized to whatever its default value is. From the moment that we add a constructor of our own however, we are effectively taking control of construction right through the hierarchy, and we will therefore need to make sure that we don't inadvertently do anything to prevent construction through the hierarchy from taking place smoothly.

You might be wondering why there is any special problem with derived classes. The reason is that when you create an instance of a derived class, there is actually more than one constructor at work. The constructor of the class you instantiate isn't by itself sufficient to initialize the class – the constructors of the base classes must also be called. That's why I've been talking about construction through the hierarchy.

To see why base class constructors must be called, let's go back to our `MortimerPhones` example. (You may prefer to remind yourself of the hierarchy of this sample, as was shown in chapter 4).

Let's look at what happens when you use the new operator to instantiate a `Nevermore60Customer` like this:

```
GenericCustomer Arabel = new Nevermore60Customer();
```

Clearly all of the member fields in a `Nevermore60Customer` must be initialized in the `Nevermore60Customer` constructor. If we refer back to the example earlier in the chapter, we'll see that there is one such field defined in `Nevermore60Customer`:

```
class Nevermore60Customer : GenericCustomer
{
    private uint highCostMinutesUsed;
```

That's no problem, the default `Nevermore60Customer` constructor supplied by the compiler will initialize this to the default value for a `uint`, zero.

That is not, however, the only field that needs to be initialized. There are also a couple that are defined in the base class `GenericCustomer`:

```
abstract class GenericCustomer
{
    private string name;
    protected decimal balance;
```

How are these initialized? Looking at the code, it's clear that the `Nevermore60Customer` can't initialize these values. The field `name` is declared as `private`, which means that derived classes don't have access to it. So the default `Nevermore60Customer` constructor simply won't even know that this field exists. The only things that have that knowledge are members of `GenericCustomer`, which means that name is going to have to be initialized by the default constructor of `GenericCustomer`. No matter how big your hierarchy is, this same reasoning applies right down to the ultimate base class, `System.Object`.

Now that we have an understanding of the issues involved, we can look at what actually happens whenever a derived class is instantiated. Assuming default constructors are used throughout, the compiler first grabs the constructor of the class it is trying to instantiate – in this case `Nevermore60Customer`. The first thing that the default `Nevermore60Customer` does is attempt to run the default constructor for the immediate base class, `GenericCustomer`, which is how default constructors always behave. The first thing the `GenericCustomer` constructor does is attempt to run the constructor for its immediate base, `System.Root`. `System.Root` doesn't have any base classes, so its constructor just executes and returns control to the `GenericCustomer` constructor. That constructor now executes, initializing name to an empty string and balance to zero, before returning control to the `Nevermore60Customer` constructor. That constructor in turn executes, initializing `highCostMinutesUsed` to zero, and exits. At this point, the `Nevermore60Customer` instance has been successfully constructed and initialized.

The net result of all this is that in effect the constructors are called in order of `System.Object` first, then progressing down the hierarchy until we reach the class being instantiated. Notice also that in this process, each constructor handles initialization of the fields in its own class. That's how it should normally work, and when you start adding your own constructors you should try to stick to that principle where possible.

Incidentally, working up the hierarchy is a sensible order because it means that if required, a constructor for the derived class can, in its implementation, call up base class methods, properties and any other members it is allowed to be aware of, confident that the base class has already been constructed and its fields initialized. It also means that if the derived class doesn't like the way that the base class has been initialized, it can change the initial values of the data, provided it has access to do so. However, good programming practice means you'll try to avoid that situation occurring, if you can, and trust the base class constructor to deal with its fields.

Anyway, now we've understood how the process of construction works, we can start fiddling with it by adding our own constructors.

Adding a No-Parameter Constructor in a Hierarchy

We'll take the simplest case first and see what happens if we simply replace the default constructor somewhere in the hierarchy with another constructor that takes no parameters. Suppose (to take a silly example) we decide that we want everyone's name to be initially set to <no name> instead of the empty string. We'd modify the code in GenericCustomer like this:

```
public abstract class GenericCustomer
{
    private string name;
    protected decimal balance;

    public GenericCustomer()
        : base()             // we could omit this line without any effect on
                             // the compiled code
    {
        name = "<no name>";
    }
}
```

Adding this code will work fine. Nevermore60Customer still has its default constructor, so the sequence of events described above will proceed as before, except that the compiler will use our custom GenericCustomer constructor instead of generating a default one, so the name field will be initialized to <no name> as required.

Notice that in our constructor, we've added an explicit call to the base class constructor before the GenericCustomer constructor is executed, using the same syntax as we were using earlier when we covered how to get different overloads of constructors to call each other. The only difference is that this time we use the base keyword instead of this, to indicate it's a constructor to the base class rather than a constructor to this class we want to call. There are no parameters in the brackets after the base keyword, so we are calling the no-parameter System.Object constructor, just as would happen by default.

In fact, we could have left that line out, and just written the following, as we've done for most of the constructors so far in the chapter:

```
public GenericCustomer()
{
    name = "<no name>";
}
```

If the compiler doesn't see any reference to another constructor before the opening curly brace, it assumes that we intended to call the base class constructor; this fits in with the way that we've just explained default constructors work.

> The **base** and **this** keywords are the only keywords allowed in the line which calls another constructor. Anything else will cause a compilation error. Also note that only one other constructor can be specified.

So far this code works fine. One good way to mess up the progression through the hierarchy of constructors, however, is to declare a constructor as `private`:

```
private GenericCustomer()
{
    name = "<no name>";
}
```

If you try this, you'll find you get an interesting compilation error, which could really throw you if you don't understand how construction down a hierarchy works. The precise error message for this example, if we'd included it in the next sample (we haven't) would be:

```
'Wrox.ProfessionalCSharp.Chapter5.MortimerPhones7.GenericCustomer.
GenericCustomer()' is inaccessible due to its protection level
```

The interesting thing is that the error occurs not in the `GenericCustomer` class, but in the derived classes, `Nevermore60Customer` and `PayAsYouGoCustomer`. Recall that in the sample both of these classes are directly derived from `GenericCustomer`. What's happened is that the compiler has tried to generate a default constructor for each of these classes, but not been able to because the default constructor calls the no-parameter `GenericCustomer` constructor. By declaring it as `private`, we've made this constructor inaccessible to the derived classes. A similar error will occur if we supply a constructor to `GenericCustomer`, which takes parameters, but no no-parameter constructor. In this case the compiler will not generate a default constructor for `GenericCustomer`, so when it tries to generate the default constructors for the derived classes, it'll again find that it can't because there is no no-parameter base class constructor for the derived classes to call. The way round this problem is to add your own constructors to the derived classes, even if you don't actually need to do anything in these constructors, so that the compiler doesn't try to generate any default constructor for them.

However, at this point I think we've had enough discussion of what can go wrong with constructors. We've got all the theoretical background we need and we're ready to move on to an example of how you should add constructors to a hierarchy of classes. In the next section we'll start adding constructors that take parameters to the `MortimerPhones` sample.

> *Incidentally, declaring a constructor as* `private` *is actually done in some cases. If for some reason you have a class that you never want to be instantiated, for example if the class only contains static members, then you can prevent instantiation by making all the constructors private. However, that will only work if you don't have any derived classes. This is one case in which you would almost certainly declare your class as* `sealed`*.*

Adding Constructors with Parameters to a Hierarchy

In this section, we're going to do some tidying up of the `MortimerPhones` sample from the last chapter, which will involve adding some constructors to the classes. In the process we'll create a sample, which is downloadable from the Wrox Press web site as `MortimerPhones8`. We're going to focus on the `Name` property of the `GenericCustomer` class, which stores the customer's name. Up until now this has been a read-write property, but that's not very sensible because customer's names shouldn't usually change (for this example we'll ignore the rare cases of customers getting married etc. and assume that their names really are immutable). We really want the customer's name to be something that is set when the class is instantiated, and is then fixed. Now that we understand how to write constructors that take parameters, we can do this. We'll remove the `set` accessor to the `Name` property, which effectively makes the name read-only, and we can even reinforce the point by declaring the corresponding name field as `readonly`. Then we require the name to be passed in to the constructor, by only having one constructor, which takes a parameter. The code that implements these changes looks like this:

```
abstract class GenericCustomer
{
    private readonly string name;
    protected decimal balance;

    public GenericCustomer(string name)
    {
        this.name = name;
    }

    public string Name
    {
        get
        {
            return name;
        }
    }
}
```

In this code, notice we have used the same name for the parameter to the constructor, name, as we have for the member field, and used the `this` reference to distinguish the two variables. This is common practice in C#, and fits in with the recommended guidelines for variable names. In general, names of parameters should begin with a small letter. We discuss the conventions for names at the end of Chapter 8.

So far so good, but as we've just said, this will cause a compilation error when the compiler tries to create a default constructor for the derived classes, since the default compiler-generated constructors for Nevermore60Customer and PayAsYouGoCustomer will both try to call a no-parameter GenericCustomer constructor, but GenericCustomer does not now possess such a constructor. Therefore, we'll need to supply our own constructors to the derived classes to avoid this. Let's look at PayAsYouGoCustomer first. Here's what we add to it:

```
class PayAsYouGoCustomer : GenericCustomer
{
    public PayAsYouGoCustomer(string name)
        : base(name)
    {
        // nothing here but you could add other code if you wanted
    }
```

Now instantiation of PayAsYouGoCustomer objects can only take place when a string containing the customer's name is supplied, which is what we want anyway. The interesting thing is what our PayAsYouGoCustomer constructor does with this string. Remember that it can't initialize the name field itself, because it has no access to a private field in a base class. Instead, it passes the name through to the base class for the GenericCustomer constructor to handle. It does this by specifying that the base class constructor to be executed first is the one that takes the name as a parameter. Clever, eh? Other than that, it doesn't take any action of its own.

In principle we could do the same thing with Nevermore60Customer, but to reinforce the point I'm going to complicate things a bit more here. We're going to investigate what happens if you have different overloads of the constructor as well as a class hierarchy to deal with.

To this end we're going to assume that `Nevermore60Customers` may have been referred to `MortimerPhones` by a friend, you know, one of these sign up a friend and get a discount offers. This means that when we construct a `Nevermore60Customer`, we may need to pass in the referrer's name as well. In real life the constructor would have to do something complicated with the name, like process the discount, but here we'll just store the referrer's name in another `readonly` field.

The `Nevermore60Customer` definition will look like this at this stage:

```
class Nevermore60Customer : GenericCustomer
{
    public Nevermore60Customer(string name, string referrerName)
        : base(name)
    {
        this.referrerName = referrerName;
    }

    private readonly string referrerName;
    private uint highCostMinutesUsed;
```

The constructor takes the name and passes it to the `GenericCustomer` constructor for processing. `ReferrerName` is the variable that is our responsibility here, so the constructor deals with that parameter in its main body.

However, not all `Nevermore60Customers` will have a referrer, so we also need a constructor that doesn't require this parameter (or, equivalently, a constructor that gives us a default value for it). Here's what the one-parameter constructor looks like:

```
public Nevermore60Customer(string name)
    : this(name, "<None>")
{
}
```

We've now got all our constructors set up correctly. It's rather instructive to examine the chain of events that occurs when we execute a line like our old favorite that we've encountered a few times before:

```
GenericCustomer Arabel = new Nevermore60Customer("Arabel Jones");
```

The compiler sees that it needs a one-parameter constructor that takes one string, so the constructor it'll identify is the last one that we've defined. This one:

```
public Nevermore60Customer(string Name)
    : this(Name, "<None>")
```

When we instantiate `Arabel`, this constructor will be called. It will immediately transfer control to the corresponding `Nevermore60Customer` 2-parameter constructor, passing it the values `Arabel Jones`, and `<None>`. Looking at the code for this constructor, we see that it in turn immediately passes control to the one-parameter `GenericCustomer` constructor, giving it the string `Arabel Jones`, and in turn that constructor passes control to the `System.Object` default constructor. Now the constructors will actually execute. First, the `System.Object` constructor executes. Since Microsoft have written that constructor and kept the code to themselves I can't tell you what it does precisely, but my guess is as little as possible, for obvious performance reasons. Next comes the `GenericCustomer` constructor; this will initialize the `name` field. Then the `Nevermore60Customer` 2-parameter constructor gets control back, and sorts out initializing the referrer name to `<None>`. Finally, the `Nevermore60Customer` one-parameter constructor gets to execute; this constructor doesn't do anything else.

All that might look complicated, but it's actually a very neat and well-designed process. Each constructor has handled initialization of the variables that are obviously its responsibility, and in the process our class has been correctly instantiated and prepared for use. If you follow the same principles when you write your own constructors for your classes, you should find that even the most complex classes get initialized smoothly and without any problems.

Before we finish the `MortimerPhones8` sample, we ought to add an override of `ToString()` to `Nevermore60Customer` so we can see the referrer name:

```
public override string ToString()        // in Nevermore60Customer
{
    return base.ToString() + ", referrer: " + referrerName;
}
```

Now we can test the sample. The test harness code in the `Main()` method looks like this:

```
static void Main(string[] args)
{
    GenericCustomer Arabel = new Nevermore60Customer("Arabel Jones");
    Arabel.RecordCall(TypeOfCall.CallToLandline, 30);

    // Start of call is 24 May 2001, 13:15:34
    DateTime Start = new DateTime(2001,5,24,13,15,34);
    // End of call is 24 May 2001, 13:18:47
    DateTime End = new DateTime(2001,5,24,13,18,47);
    Arabel.RecordCall(TypeOfCall.CallToLandline, Start, End);

    Console.WriteLine("Arabel's details: " + Arabel.ToString());

    GenericCustomer MrJones = new PayAsYouGoCustomer("Mr. Jones");
    Console.WriteLine(MrJones.ToString());

    GenericCustomer MrLeggit =
                    new Nevermore60Customer("Mr. Leggit", "Arabel");
    MrLeggit.RecordCall(TypeOfCall.CallToLandline, 30);
    Console.WriteLine(MrLeggit.ToString());
}
```

This code illustrates not only calling the new one-parameter constructors, but also the extra overload of `GenericCustomer.RecordCall()`. Running the code gives this screenshot:

Cleaning up: Destructors

We've seen that constructors allow you to specify certain actions or initializations that must take place whenever an instance of a class is created, so you might be wondering if it's possible to do the same thing whenever a class instance is destroyed. Indeed, if you're familiar with C++, you'll know that C++ allows you to do just that, by specifying a method known as a **destructor**. These are called whenever a class instance goes out of scope or, is otherwise removed from memory. Experienced C++ developers make extensive use of destructors, and sometimes not only to clean up resources, but also to provide debugging information or perform other tasks.

C# doesn't really support that programming style. Destructors do exist in C#, but because of the garbage collection system for cleaning up resources, it is not possible to predict when they will run, and in general their use is discouraged. Indeed, one of the results of the garbage collector in C# is that there simply isn't usually any need for destructors, because there is usually no need for the programmer to explicitly deal with freeing up memory, etc. In almost all cases, there is simply no point worrying about what happens when a class instance gets destroyed – you just leave the garbage collector to handle that behind the scenes.

However, having said that, there are a few cases for which you might wish to take some action when variables get destroyed (such as closing connections to files is one example), and C# provides two ways that you can do this: the `Dispose()` or `Close()` method and the `Finalize()` method. These methods are designed to work together. We'll examine how they work individually before working through a sample designed to illustrate the recommended way of using them.

Finalize()

Of the options for cleaning up resources, the `Finalize()` method comes closest in concept to that of a traditional destructor. If you supply a method named `Finalize()` in a class, this method will automatically be called when a class instance is destroyed. There are however, a couple of snags:

❑   `Finalize()` is not deterministic. This means that there's no way in general to predict when the instance will be destroyed, which means that you can't predict when `Finalize()` will be called. In general, instances will be destroyed when the garbage collector detects that they are no longer referenced, but to a large extent the garbage collector comes into action when the .NET runtime decides it's needed – and that's up to the .NET runtime, not your program. Hence, you should not place any code in the `Finalize()` method which relies on being run at a certain time, and you shouldn't even rely on `Finalize()` being called for different class instances in any particular order.

> *You force the garbage collector to run at a certain point in your code, if you want, by calling* `System.GC.Collect()`. `System.GC` *is a .NET base class that represents the garbage collector, and the* `Collect()` *method actually calls the garbage collector. However, this is intended for rare situations in which you know tha,t for example, it's a good time to call the garbage collector because a very large number of objects in your code have just stopped being referenced. You certainly wouldn't normally go to the trouble of calling up the entire garbage collection process just to get a* `Finalize()` *method called!*

❑ In general, you are advised not to implement a Finalize() method unless your class really does need it. Due to the way the garbage collector has been implemented, if an object implements Finalize(), then that puts a significant performance hit on garbage-collecting that object. It also delays the final removal of that object from memory. The way the garbage collector works, objects that need to have a Finalize() method called get placed in a special queue for finalizing. When the garbage collector runs, it does not destroy objects that are in this queue. Instead, they get their Finalize() methods called if appropriate and are then moved out of the queue – which means they won't actually get destroyed until the subsequent time the garbage collector is run.

In almost all cases, allowing the .NET runtime to handle resource cleanup will be adequate, and you will not need to implement a Finalize() method. The main situation in which you will need to implement Finalize() is if an object is maintaining resources that are not managed by .NET – for example file or database connections. In this case you will need to implement Finalize() to close those connections.

If you do want to define a Finalize() method, you need to use a special syntax, which corresponds to the way that C++ declares a destructor: you supply the name of the containing class, preceded by a tilde (~):

```
class MyClass
{
    ~MyClass()
    {
        // do whatever cleanup is needed
    }

    // etc.
```

Other than the tilde, this is a very similar syntax as for the static constructor. There are no parameters, no return type, and no access modifier.

Obviously, you should replace MyClass with whatever the name of your class happens to be. It is also worth noting that there is no need to explicitly call the base class's Finalize() method – the compiler will assume that and arrange for it to be called implicitly on your behalf.

Implementing a Finalize() method does guarantee that resources that need to be cleaned up at some point will be. However, by itself it's not very satisfactory because of the problems noted above – the lack of determinism and the effect on garbage collector performance. In particular, since the garbage collector will in all probability not be called until some time after you actually no longer need the object in question, the resources referenced by the object will be held onto for longer than necessary. If the resources include, for example, an exclusive lock on a file, then this could be a serious problem. This is where Dispose() and Close() come in.

Dispose() and Close()

These methods are to a large extent a convention rather than a part of the C# language, although there is some intrinsic support in C# for Dispose().The way that it works for the most part is that if you wish you can define one of these methods for your class, with the understanding that any client code should call this method explicitly in order to free up resources. The benefit of this is that the resource gets freed the moment it's no longer needed, which as we've just seen can be a huge advantage for something like an exclusive file lock. The disadvantage is that you're relying on the client to be well-behaved, and actually call the method; if it doesn't, you're stuck.

The usual solution is to use `Dispose()` and `Close()` in conjunction with `Finalize()`. Basically, you do something like this:

```
public void Dispose()
{
    // clean up resources
    GC.SuppressFinalize(this);
}

protected override void Finalize()
{
    // clean up resources
    base.Finalize();
}
```

By doing it this way, you have a backup. If the client code remembers to call `Dispose()`, then the resources get cleaned up in good time. If the client forgets, then all is not lost because `Finalize()` will be called eventually when the object is garbage collected. More interestingly, notice the call to `GC.SuppressFinalize()` in the `Dispose()` method. The `SuppressFinalize()` method in the `System.GC` class has the effect of informing the .NET runtime that the object passed in as a parameter no longer needs to be finalized. That means that the garbage collector will treat the object as if it didn't have a `Finalize()` method, so `Finalize()` won't get called when the object is garbage collected, and there won't be any of the associated performance disadvantages.

Close() vs. Dispose()

The difference between `Close()` and `Dispose()` is largely one of convention. `Close()` tends to suggest that it's a resource that might later be reopened, while `Dispose()` has more of an implication of finality – calling `Dispose()` means that the client has finished with this particular object for good. You can implement either one or both of these methods, but to avoid confusing other developers, you should implement them with those meanings in mind. You also might wish to implement `Close()` in situations in which a `Close()` method has been traditional programming practice or fits in with traditional terminology, such as closing a file or database connection. A case in which you might use `Dispose()` might be to release handles to various GDI or other Windows objects. You will also need to use `Dispose()` if you wish to take advantage of the `IDisposable` architecture, which we discuss next.

IDisposable

In the last section, we hinted that there was some support in C# for `Dispose()`. Basically, C# offers a syntax that you can use to guarantee that `Dispose()` (though not `Close()`) will automatically be called against an object when the reference goes out of scope. The syntax to do this involves the `using` keyword – though now in a very different context, which has nothing to do with namespaces. Suppose we have a class, let's call it `ResourceGobbler`, which relies on the use of some external resource, and we wish to instantiate an instance of this class. We could do it like this:

```
{
    ResourceGobbler TheInstance = new ResourceGobbler();

    // do your processing

    TheInstance.Dispose();
}
```

I've put braces around the above code. These aren't necessary, but I've put them there to emphasize that, after calling `TheInstance.Dispose()`, we have presumably finished with `TheInstance`, so there's presumably no more point the reference remaining in scope.

The above code is exactly equivalent to the following:

```
using (ResourceGobbler TheInstance = new ResourceGobbler())
{
    // do your processing
}
```

From this we see that the `using` statement, followed in brackets by a reference variable definition, will cause that variable to be scoped to the accompanying compound statement. In addition, when that variable goes out of scope, its `Dispose()` method will automatically be called.

The `using` syntax does have the disadvantage that it forces extra indentation of the code, and it doesn't save you very much coding. We will also see in Chapter 6, when we examine exceptions, that a similar effect can alternatively be achieved anyway by placing the call to `Dispose()` in a `finally` block. For these reasons, you may prefer to avoid the `using` construct.

In order to use the alternative using syntax, we do have to define the `ResourceGobbler` class in a certain way. In order to see what this involves, we're going to have to jump ahead of ourselves a bit, since it relies on use of interfaces. The restriction is that we have to derive `ResourceGobbler` from an interface called `IDisposable`, which is defined in the `System` namespace:

```
class ResourceGobbler : IDisposable
{
    // etc.

    public void Dispose()
    {
        // etc.
    }
}
```

Deriving from an interface is a bit different from deriving from a class. We'll examine the details later in the chapter. We'll just say here that deriving from `IDisposable` has the effect of forcing the derived class to implement a method called `Dispose()`; you'll actually get a compilation error if you derive from `IDisposable` and don't implement this method. The reason that we have to derive from `IDisposable` in order to use the `using` syntax is that it gives the compiler a way of checking that the object defined in the using statement does have a `Dispose()` method that it can automatically call. As we'll see later in the chapter, deriving from an interface is the usual way that a class can declare that it implements certain features.

Sample: DestructorDemo

In this section, we'll present a sample called `DestructorDemo`, which demonstrates how to code up a robust constructor.

The sample focuses on a class, `DataStoreConnection`, which we presume is used to perform some tasks involving a connection to some (unspecified) data store. Obviously, we won't actually connect to any data store, but we'll simulate the effect with a member field, `DataStoreHandle`, an `int` whose value is set to 1 when we are connected to a store and 0 otherwise. We also have a `bool` field, `CanOpen`, which is initially set to `true`, but is set to `false` after `Dispose()` has been called, indicating that we can no longer use this object to connect to a data store.

DataStoreConnection implements both `Close()` and `Dispose()`. The full class definition looks like this:

```
class DataStoreConnection :IDisposable
{
    private int DataStoreHandle = 0;
    private bool CanOpen = true;
    private readonly string name;

    public DataStoreConnection(string name)
    {
        this.name = name;
    }
    public void Open()
    {
        if (CanOpen == false)
            Console.WriteLine(name +
                        ": Error: Attempt to Open after calling Dispose()");
        if (DataStoreHandle == 0)
        {
            DataStoreHandle = 1;
            Console.WriteLine(name + ": Connected to DataStore");
        }
        else
            Console.WriteLine(name +
                        ": Error: Already connected to DataStore");
    }

    public void Close()
    {
        DataStoreHandle = 0;
    }

    public void Dispose()
    {
        Console.WriteLine("Disposing: " + name);
        CanOpen = false;
        Close();
        GC.SuppressFinalize(this);
    }

    ~DataStoreConnection()
    {
        Close();
    }

}
```

The constructor to this class takes one parameter, a string. This could, for instance, be the name of the data store we are connecting to. In our example, we just use it as a string to display that identifies the object instance when we are displaying messages.

`Open()` checks whether it is possible to open a connection, and does so if possible. In any event, it displays a message to indicate that it has been called. On the other hand, `Close()` simply simulates closing the connection by setting the `DataStoreHandle` field to zero. Notice that this means that no error occurs if it is accidentally called more than once; this is the recommended behavior. `Dispose()` does the same thing as `Close()`; in fact, it is implemented by calling `Close()`. However, it also suppresses finalization, since the presumption of calling `Dispose()` is that indicates we are finally finished with the object. `Dispose()` also sets the `CanOpen` field to indicate it is not now possible to open any more data store connections from this object. This is appropriate since we have suppressed finalization, and hence have lost the protective mechanism that guards against client code opening a data store connection then failing to explicitly close it.

Finally, the `Finalize()` method (the destructor) also closes the connection. Note that we have not used the `Close()` method to display any messages. This is because it can be called from `Finalize()`, and the .NET runtime will not allow you to write to the console from this method – you'll get a runtime error if you try it, because `Finalize()` is run under the control of the garbage collector, which does not have access to the console window.

We can test out our connection with this code:

```
static void Main(string[] args)
{
    DataStoreConnection Connection = new DataStoreConnection("FIRST");
    Connection.Open();
    Connection.Close();
    Connection.Dispose();

    Console.WriteLine();
    Connection = new DataStoreConnection("SECOND");
    Connection.Close();
    Connection.Open();
    Connection.Open();
    Connection.Dispose();
    Connection.Open();

    using (DataStoreConnection Connection2 = new DataStoreConnection("THIRD"))
    {
        Connection2.Open();
    }

    GC.Collect();
}
```

Notice, that in this code we've called the garbage collector towards the end of the code, just to demonstrate how to do it, although in practice you would not normally do this unless you know you have a large number of unused objects that can be removed from memory. It is certainly pointless calling the garbage collector just before your code exits, as we have done, since all managed resources associated with your code will be cleaned up when your program exits anyway.

Running this code produces this result:

```
Command Prompt                                              _ □ x
Microsoft Windows 2000 [Version 5.00.2195]
(C) Copyright 1985-2000 Microsoft Corp.

G:\>DestructorDemo
FIRST: Connected to DataStore
Disposing: FIRST

SECOND: Connected to DataStore
SECOND: Error: Already connected to DataStore
Disposing: SECOND
SECOND: Error: Attempt to Open after calling Dispose()
SECOND: Connected to DataStore
THIRD: Connected to DataStore
Disposing: THIRD

G:\>
```

What Happens in Memory: Reference and Value Variables

One of the declared advantages of C# programming is that the programmer doesn't need to worry about detailed memory management, in particular the garbage collector deals with all memory cleaning up on your behalf. The result is that you can get something close to the efficiency of languages like C++ without the complexity of the handling memory management yourself that you need to do in C++. However, although you don't have to manage the memory manually, if you are to write efficient code it still pays to understand what is going on behind the scenes. In this section we'll take a look at what happens in the computer's memory when you allocate variables. I should stress that the precise details of much of the content of this section is undocumented. You should interpret this section as a rather simplified guide to the general principles that are going on, rather than as a statement of exact implementation.

Value Data Types

We'll start off by looking at what happens when you create a variable of a value type. For this example, we'll take an integer. We'll examine what happens in memory when you execute these lines of code:

```
{
    int NRacingCars = 10;
    double EngineSize = 3000.0;
    // do calculations;
}
```

Recall that value data types include the predefined data types int, float, bool, *and so on, though not* string *or* object. *Later in the chapter, we'll examine* structs; *these are also value data types. All classes and all arrays are, by contrast, reference data types.*

In this code we've indicated to the compiler that we need space in memory to store an integer and a double and that these memory locations are to be referred to respectively as NRacingCars and EngineSize. The line that declares the each variable indicates the point at which we will start requiring access to this variable, and the closing curly brace indicates the point at which we will no longer require either variable. In programming parlance, we talk of the variables going **into scope** and coming **out of scope**.

Of course NRacingCars and EngineSize are names designed to be easily understandable by humans rather than by the computer itself. (Indeed, the names are so user-friendly that even by themselves they immediately give us a good idea of what the entire program is probably about!). Internally, the computer does not give its memory locations names like NRacingCars. Computers think only in terms of numbers, and as far as the computer is concerned, the memory available to your code looks like this:

Location 0x0
Location 0x1
Location 0x2
etc.
.
.
.
.
.
.
Location 0xffffffff

In other words, what we have is a large number of memory locations. For reasons to do with the way Windows manages its memory, we've put that number at 4 gigabytes. If you want to be exact, that's 0x100 000 000 = 4,294,967,296 bytes, where as usual 0x in front of a number indicates that the number is represented in hexadecimal notation. The final location is addressed at one less than this value because the locations start at address zero. Windows uses a system known as **virtual addressing**, in which the mapping from the memory address seen by your program to the actual location in hardware memory or on disk is entirely managed behind the scenes by Windows. The result of this is that each application on a 32-bit processor sees 4GB of available memory, irrespective of how much hardware memory you actually have in your computer. On 64-bit processors this number will be greater, but for simplicity we'll assume here that we're dealing with a 32-bit processor. This 4GB if memory is known as the **virtual address space**. This memory could also correctly be described as **virtual memory**, since it represents some Windows-controlled mapping onto physical memory, rather than the physical memory itself, but for convenience we'll continue referring to it simply as memory.

Each memory location from this 4GB is numbered starting from zero. If you want to indicate a value stored at a particular location in memory, you need to supply the number that represents that memory location. In any high level language, be it C#, VB, C++ or any other similar language, one of the things that the compiler does is convert the human-readable names that you've given your variables into the memory addresses that the processor understands. This 4GB of memory actually contains everything that is a part of the program, including the executable code and the contents of all variables used when the program runs. Any DLLs called up will all be loaded into this same address space; each item of code or data will have its own definite location.

Somewhere inside this memory is an area that is known as the **stack**. Remember that we introduced the stack and the heap in Chapter 3. The stack is where value data types are usually stored. When you call a method, the stack is also used to copy any parameters passed in. In order to understand how the stack works, we need to notice the following important fact about the scope of variables in C#. It is always the case that if a variable A goes into scope before variable B, then B will go out of scope first. Look at this code:

```
{
    int A;
    // do something
    {
        int B;
        // do something else
    }
}
```

First, A gets declared. Then inside the inner code block B gets declared. Then the inner code block terminates and B goes out of scope. Then A goes out of scope. So the lifetime of B is entirely contained within the lifetime of A. It's important to understand that that is how it *always* works. It is simply not possible to write a piece of C# code in which a variable B is declared after A but A goes out of scope first. (If you don't believe me, try and write some C# code that does that. You'll quickly find you just can't. The way that scope is controlled in C# by nested curly braces prevents it.)

Note that if the compiler hits a line like int I ,J, *the order of coming into scope looks indeterminate; both variables are declared at the same time and go out of scope at the same time. In this situation, it doesn't matter to us in what order the two variables are removed from memory. The compiler will internally always ensure that the one that was put in memory first is removed last, thus preserving our rule about no crossover of variable lifetimes.*

This idea that you always deallocate variables in the reverse order to how you allocate them might look a bit abstract, but it's crucial to the way that the stack works. Let's see what actually happens when we declare the variables NRacingCars and EngineSize from our earlier example.

Somewhere in the program is something called the **stack pointer**. This is simply a variable (or an address in memory) that contains the address of the next free location in the stack (though, because this variable is used so often, it's more likely to be stored in a special fast-access storage location known as a **register** inside the central processing unit). When the program first starts running, the stack pointer will point to the end (yes, the end) of the block of memory that is reserved for the stack. As data is put on the stack, the stack pointer will be adjusted accordingly, so it always points to the next free location. Now, I don't know exactly where in address space the stack is – that information is the sort of thing we don't need to know for C# development, but let us say for the sake of argument that immediately before the above code that allocates the variables is executed, the stack pointer contains the value 0x12FA78 (1243768 in decimal). This situation is illustrated in the diagram. In the diagram, bold text indicates the contents of memory locations; plain text indicates the address or a description of the location:

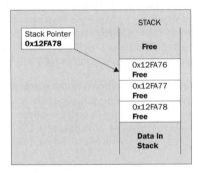

Incidentally, my suggested value for the stack pointer isn't a complete guess. I did some playing about with pointers using the unsafe code we develop in the next chapter to find out roughly whereabouts in address space the stack is. And just to confuse matters, the stack fills up downwards from a high address – so as data is stored in the stack, the stack pointer has to be decremented rather than incremented. That's why I emphasized that at the start, the stack pointer points to the end of the stack.

At this point the variable NRacingCars comes into scope, and the value 10 is placed in it. What happens is that the value 10 will be placed in location 0x12FA78, the location referred to by the stack pointer. Strictly speaking, since an int occupies 4 bytes, this value will be spread across the 4 bytes from 0x12FA75 to 0x12FA78, and 4 will be subtracted from to the stack pointer, so it now points to the next free location, 0x12FA74.

The next line declares the variable EngineSize, a double and initializes it to the value 3000.0. A double occupies 8 bytes, so the value 3000.0 will be placed in the next 8 bytes of the stack, in whatever format the processor uses for 8-byte floating point numbers, and the stack pointer will be decremented by 8, so that once again it tells the computer where the next free location in the stack is.

When EngineSize goes out of scope, the computer knows that it is no longer needed. Due to the way that variable lifetimes are always nested, we can guarantee that, whatever else has happened while EngineSize was in scope, the stack pointer will at this time happen to be pointing to the location just before where engine size was stored. The process of removing this variable from scope is simple. The stack pointer is incremented by 8, so that it now points to where EngineSize used to be. At this point we are at the closing curly brace, at which NRacingCars goes out of scope too, so the stack pointer gets incremented again, by 4 this time. If another variable were to come into scope at this point, it would just overwrite memory descending from location 0x12FA78, where NRacingCars used to be stored.

I've gone into a lot of detail about how variables are allocated, although even this discussion hasn't been exhaustive. For example, I've not touched on how the compiler is able to figure out the address of each variable. The thing I really want you to notice is just how fast and efficient the process of allocating variables on the stack is. There's little to be done other than increment the stack pointer – a simple arithmetic operation that will take just a few clock cycles.

Reference Data Types

While the stack gives very high performance, it's not really flexible enough to be used for all variables. The requirement that the lifetimes of variables must be nested is too restrictive for many purposes. Often you may want to use some method to allocate some memory to store some data, and be able to keep that data available long after that method exited. This possibility exists whenever storage space is requested with the new operator – as is the case for all reference types. That's where the **heap** comes in.

If you've done any coding that requires low level memory management in the past, you'll be familiar with the stack and the heap for pre-.NET programs. The managed heap is not the same as the heap for pre-.NET programs. The managed heap is not the same as the heap that pre-.NET code such as classic C++ uses. It works under the control of the garbage collector and carries significant performance benefits compared to traditional heaps.

The managed heap (or just heap for short) is just another area of memory from that available 4GB. To see how the heap works and how memory is allocated for reference data types, examine this bit of code:

```
void DoWork()
{
   Customer Arabel;
   Arabel = new Customer();
   Customer MrJones = new Nevermore60Customer();
}
```

In this code we've taken our Customer example for the sake of argument, but the same principles hold for any class (or any reference type).

We declare a Customer reference called Arabel. The space for this will be allocated on the stack, but remember that this is only a reference, not an actual Customer instance. The amount of space taken by the Arabel reference will be 4 bytes (the same number of bytes that an int or uint occupies). Why 4 bytes? It will need to store an address in memory therefore, the address at which an instance of a Customer is actually stored. In addition, we need 4 bytes to be able to store an integer value between 0 and 4GB. (Note that on a 64-bit processor, the address will occupy 8 bytes instead of 4 bytes).

Then we get to the next line:

```
Arabel = new Customer();
```

This line of code does several things. First, it allocates memory to store a Customer instance (a real instance, not just an address). Then it sets the variable Arabel to store the address of the memory it's allocated. It'll also call the appropriate Customer constructor to initialize the fields in the class instance, but we won't worry about that part here. The customer instance will not be placed in the stack. Rather it'll be placed in another area of memory known as the heap. Now, I don't know precisely how many bytes a Customer instance occupies, but let's say for the sake of argument it's 32. This 32 bytes contains the instance fields of Customer as well as some information that .NET uses to identify and manage its class instances, including the vtable.

The .NET runtime will look through the heap and grab the first continuous block of 32 bytes that is unused. For the sake of argument we'll say that this happens to be at address 0xC39E7C (12818556), and that the first free location in the stack immediately before executing this statement was as before, at location 0x12FA74 (this location won't change, since this line doesn't by itself put anything else on the stack, the Arabel reference already existed). This means that after executing this line, the contents of memory will look like this:

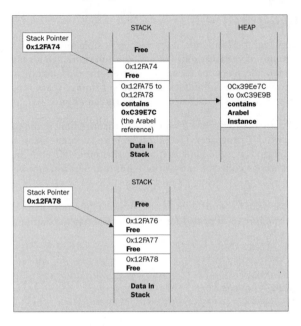

The next line of code that we execute does the same thing again, except that space on the stack for the MrJones reference needs to be allocated at the same time as the space for MrJones is allocated on the heap:

```
Customer MrJones = new Nevermore60Customer();
```

Also note that the data on the heap actually contains a Nevermore60Customer instance. After executing this line, our memory might look like this, where we've assumed for the sake of argument that the .NET runtime finds some free memory for MrJones at location 0Cx39644, and that Nevermore60Customer objects occupy a total of 36 bytes. At the time of writing it's not documented whether objects on the heap are stored going up or down addresses, so for the sake of argument we'll assume successive objects are placed at lower addresses, simply because that makes our diagrams simpler!

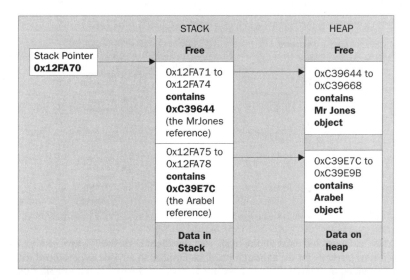

You can already see from this that the process of setting up a reference variable is more complex than it is for setting up a value variable, and inevitably there will be a performance hit. In fact we've somewhat oversimplified the process too, since the .NET runtime will need to maintain information about the state of the heap, and this information will also need to be updated whenever new data is added to the heap. However, we do now have a more flexible scheme for variable lifetime. To illustrate this, let's look at what happens when our method exits and the Arabel and MrJones references go out of scope. In accordance with the normal working of the stack, the stack pointer will be decremented so these variables no longer exist. However, these variables only stored addresses, not the actual class instances. The data for those class instances is still sitting there on the heap, where it will remain until either the program terminates, or the garbage collector is called. This is academic as far as we're concerned; the data might be sitting on the heap, but we have no way of accessing it any more because the variables that referred to it no longer exist, after all, that is what the garbage collector tests for when it determines what it can remove from the heap.

However, consider the situation if we modify the DoWork() method as follows:

```
Customer DoWork(out Customer myCustomer)
{
    Customer Arabel;
    Arabel = new Customer();
    Customer MrJones = new Customer();

    myCustomer = Arabel;
    return MrJones;
}
```

This code has been modified to return the value of the MrJones reference, while the Arabel reference is also passed back to the calling code, via an out parameter. In general, the return value and the method parameters are stored on the stack along with the local variables, and will have been placed on the stack immediately before the method is executed. This means that immediately after the method exits, our memory might look like this:

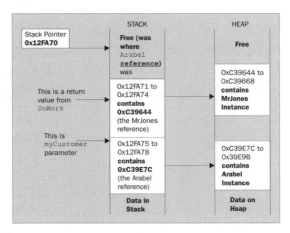

Now the two class instances still exist on the heap, and the client code that control returns to has access to their contents. This is new territory for us, although it will be familiar to anyone experienced with C++ or any other language that uses an equivalent of the new operator to perform dynamic memory allocation. A class instance has been created inside a method, but is still available when the method terminates. This circumvents the usual scope rules, which say that a variable ceases to exist at the closing curly brace that ends the block in which the variable was defined, and we've achieved that without making any copy of the data. That's the power of reference data types, and you'll see this feature used extensively in C# code. It means that we have a high degree of control over the lifetime of our data, since it is guaranteed to exist in the heap as long as we are maintaining some reference to it.

Of course, once we no longer need some data stored in a reference type we simply allow all the references to it to go out of scope. The data will then remain invisibly in memory, though if memory becomes short the garbage collector will come along and remove it.

The above discussion and diagrams show the managed heap working very much like the stack, to the extent that successive objects are placed next to each other in memory. This means that we can work out where to place the next object very simply, by using a heap pointer that indicates the next free memory location, and which gets adjusted as we add more objects to the heap. However, there appears to be a problem here. When we explained the operation of the stack, we emphasized that it was only possible for the stack to operate so efficiently because of the way that lifetimes of stack variables are nested. The lifetimes of reference have gone out of scope, yet the heap apparently works as if they did follow this rule. How is that possible? The answer is that it works thanks to the garbage collector. When the garbage collector runs, it will remove all those objects from the heap that are no longer referenced. Immediately after it has done this, the heap will have objects scattered on it, mixed up with memory that has just been freed, a bit like this:

If the managed heap stayed looking like that, allocating further objects on it would be an awkward process, with the computer having to search through it looking for a block of memory big enough to store each object. However, the garbage collector doesn't leave the heap in this state. As soon as it's freed up all the objects it can, it compacts all the others by moving them all back to the end of the heap to form one contiguous block again. This means that the heap can continue working just like the stack as far as locating where to store new objects is concerned. Of course, when the objects are moved about, all the references to those objects need to be updated with the correct new addresses, but the garbage collector handles that too.

This action of compacting by the garbage collector is where the managed heap really works differently from old unmanaged heaps. Unmanaged heaps really would contain data scattered about as in the last diagram. That meant that whenever you dynamically allocated a variable, e.g. in the C++, the runtime would have to trawl through a linked list of addresses to find somewhere to put the new data, whereas with the managed heap it's just a question of reading the value of the heap pointer. For this reason, instantiating reference types under .NET is much faster, because less page swapping is required. Microsoft believe that these performance gains will compensate, and possibly more than compensate, for the performance penalty that we get whenever the garbage collector needs to do some work.

We'll finish this section with a quick reminder of which data types, besides classes, will go on the managed heap.

Recall that reference types include all classes, as well as any arrays. For example, the line:

```
int [] X = {3,4,5,6,7};
```

is actually a shorthand for:

```
int [] X = new int [5] {3,4,5,6,7};
```

When either of these lines is executed, the contents of the array will be allocated on the heap, while the variable X, which simply contains the value of the relevant address in the heap, will sit on the stack, as is the case for class instances:

This example illustrates one of the simplifications we've made in this section. Earlier I simply stated that value types would be allocated on the stack. That's not always the case: If a value type is defined as part of a reference type (for example it's an element of an array or a member of a class) then it will sit inline on the heap, inside the data for the containing reference type.

Note that class instances may themselves contain references to other classes, just as array elements may actually be reference types. In this case, you'll find that the contents of the heap include the addresses of other locations in the heap – but we won't worry about that here. We've now covered enough detail of what happens in memory as far as writing C# code is concerned.

Structs

So far, we seen how classes can be great way of encapsulating objects in your program. We have also seen how they are stored on the heap in a way that gives you much more flexibility in data lifetime, but with a slight cost in performance. This performance cost is small thanks to the optimizations of managed heaps. However, there are some situations in which a class provides more functionality than you need, but in which for performance reasons you still want some of the functionality of a class while storing the data on the stack. The most obvious example is when we need to define an object whose only purpose is really to group a couple of related data items together. Look at this example:

```
class Dimensions
{
    public double Length;
    public double Width;
}
```

We've defined a class called `Dimensions`, which simply stores the length and width of some item. Perhaps we're writing a furniture-arranging program to let people experiment with rearranging their furniture on the computer and we want to store the dimensions of each item of furniture. It looks like we're breaking the rules of good program design by making the fields public, but the point is really that we don't really need all the facilities of a class for this at all. All we have is two numbers, which we find convenient to treat as a pair rather than individually. There is no need for lots of methods, nor for us to be able to inherit from the class, and we certainly don't want to have the .NET runtime go to the trouble of bringing in the heap with all the performance implications, just to store two `double`s.

Instead, we're better off defining `Dimensions` as something called a **struct**. To do this, the only thing we need to change in the code is replace the keyword `class` with `struct`:

```
struct Dimensions
{
    public double Length;
    public double Width;
}
```

You can think of structs in C# as being like scaled down classes. They are basically the same as classes, but designed more for cases where you simply want to group some data together. They differ from classes in the following ways:

❑ Structs are value types, not reference types. This means they are stored either in the stack or inline (if they are part of another object that is stored on the heap), and have the same lifetime restrictions as the simple data types. This has various performance implications.

❑ Structs do not support inheritance.

❑ There are some differences in the way constructors work for structs. In particular, the compiler *always* supplies a default no-parameter constructor, which you are not permitted to replace.

❑ With a struct, you can if you wish specify how the fields are to be laid out in memory.

Although we are presenting structs as simplified classes, historically, the concept of a struct as a device for grouping data together came first. Then the concepts of classes and OOP evolved as extensions of structs. For example, the C language defined something very much like a C# struct, but did not have classes.

Also, because structs like the `Dimensions` struct we've just demonstrated are really intended to group data items together, you'll sometimes find that most or all of their fields are declared as `public`. For simple structs, many developers would consider this acceptable programming practice, though if your structs become more complex and you start adding methods and constructors to them, it would be better to hide their internal implementation in the same way as you would for classes. In fact, in the .NET base classes, even for structs as simple as our `Dimensions` example, the fields are encapsulated by properties.

In the next subsections, we'll go through most of these differences in more detail. We won't however look at the facility to specify how the fields in a struct are laid out in memory. In C# this feature can be regarded as fairly esoteric; it is rarely needed, so we are treating it as beyond the scope of this book. If you do need to do this, you should look up the `StructLayout` attribute in the MSDN documentation.

Structs Are Value Types

Although structs are value types, you can often treat them syntactically in the same way as classes. For example, with our definition of Dimensions above, we could write:

```
Dimensions Pt = new Dimensions();
Pt.Length = 3;
Pt.Width = 6;
```

Note that because structs are value types, the new operator does not work in the same way as it does for classes and other reference types. Instead of allocating memory on the heap, the new operator simply calls the default constructor, initializing all fields to their default values on the stack (or inline on the heap). Indeed, for structs it is perfectly legal to write:

```
Dimensions Pt;
Pt.Length = 3;
Pt.Width = 6;
```

If Dimensions was a class, this would produce a compilation error, because Pt would contain an uninitialized reference – an address that points nowhere, so we could not start setting values to its fields. For a struct however, the variable declaration actually allocates space on the stack for the entire struct, so it's ready to assign values to. Note, however, that the above code will not initialize the struct, so something like:

```
Dimensions Pt;
Double D = Pt.Length;
```

Would cause a compilation error, with the compiler complaining about your using an uninitialized variable. A struct is considered fully initialized either when the new operator has been called against it, or when values have been individually assigned to all its fields.

The fact that structs are value types will affect performance, though depending on how you use your struct, this can be good or bad. On the positive side, allocating memory for structs is very fast because this takes place inline or on the stack. The same goes for removing structs when they go out of scope. On the other hand, whenever you pass a struct as a parameter or assign a struct to another struct (as in A=B, where A and B are structs), the full contents of the struct are copied, whereas for a class only the reference is copied. This will result in a performance loss that depends on the size of the struct, which should emphasize the fact that structs are really intended for *small* data structures. Note, however, that when passing a struct as a parameter to a method, you can avoid this performance loss by passing it as a ref parameter – in this case only the address in memory of the struct will be passed in, which is just as fast as passing in a class. On the other hand, if you do this, you'll have to be aware that it means the called method can in principle change the value of the struct.

> **Pass structs to methods as `ref` parameters in order to avoid the performance loss associated with copying data.**

Structs and Inheritance

Structs are not designed for inheritance. This means that it is not possible to inherit from a struct, and a struct cannot derive from any class. The only exception to this is that structs, in common with every other type in C#, derive from the class `System.Object`. Hence, structs also have access to the methods etc. of `System.Object`. It is even possible to override methods from `System.Object` in structs – an obvious example would be overriding the `ToString()` method.

> *Actually the inheritance is indirect: Structs derive from* `System.ValueType`, *which in turn derives from* `System.Object`. `ValueType` *adds no new methods of its own, but provides overrides of some of the* `Object` *methods that are more appropriate to value types.*

To see this, we'll extend the `Dimensions` struct to add a `ToString()` method for this struct.:

```
struct Dimensions
{
    public double Length;
    public double Width;

    Dimensions(double length, double width)
    { Length=length; Width=width; }

    public override string ToString()
    {
        return "( " + Length.ToString() + " , " + Width.ToString() + " )";
    }
```

We declare the method exactly as we would for a class. Note, however, that it is not possible to declare any member of a struct as `virtual`. To do so would imply that we were intending other classes to inherit from struct, but structs will not allow you to do that. Similarly, it is not permitted to declare a struct as `abstract`. Declaring a struct explicitly as `sealed` will also generate a compilation error. Structs are implicitly sealed anyway, so there's no need to declare them as such.

Constructors for Structs

You can define constructors for structs in exactly the same way that you can for classes, except that you are not permitted to define a constructor that takes no parameters. This may seem nonsensical, and the reason is buried in the implementation of the .NET runtime. There are some rare circumstances in which the .NET runtime would not be able to call a custom zero-parameter constructor that you have supplied. Microsoft have therefore taken the easy way out and banned zero-parameter constructors for structs in C#. This feature seems to be one of the few poor aspects of the design of .NET, and has caused some controversy in .NET related newsgroups.

Having said that, the default constructor, which initializes all fields to zero values, is always present implicitly, even if you supply other constructors that take parameters. It's also not possible to sneakily work round the default constructor by supplying initial values for fields. The following code will cause a compile-time error:

```
struct Dimensions
{
    public double Length = 1;       // error. Initial values not allowed
    public double Width = 2;        // error. Initial values not allowed
```

If `Dimensions` had been declared as a class, this code would have compiled without any problems.

On the subject of destruction, you can supply a `Close()` or `Dispose()` method for a struct in the same way you might choose to do so for a class, but the destructor, `Finalize()` is not supported, and the compiler will generate an error if you try to define a destructor. `Finalize()` is called by the garbage collector, but the garbage collector deals only with reference objects, not with structs, so a `Finalize()` method would not get called.

Operator Overloading

In this and the next section, we're going to look at two of the other types of members that you can define for a class or a struct: **operator overloads** and **indexers**. We start by discussing operator overloading in this section.

The point of operator overloading is that you don't always just want to call methods or properties on class instances. Often you need to do things like adding quantities together, multiplying them, or perform logical operations such as comparing objects. As an example, suppose you wrote a class that represented a currency value for a financial program. C# provides the decimal type that can represent currencies, but in a sophisticated program you might want a more powerful class, that contained methods to perform currency conversions as well as store values. You'd probably want to be able to use the class a bit like this:

```
Currency A, B, C, D;
// initialise A, B and D somehow
C = A + B;
D *= 2.5;
if (A==B && B>C)
{
    D = B + C;
}
```

Perhaps this snippet goes over the top in terms of mathematical operations, but you get the idea – you'd certainly want to be able to do some arithmetic, as well as comparing class instances for equality or to see which is greater.

The problem is that with what you've learnt so far, we couldn't do that. Up to now, operators like "+" and "*" have been strictly for the predefined data types, and for good reason: the compiler automatically knows what all the common operators mean for those data types. For example, it knows how to add two `long`s or how to divide one `double` by another `double`, and can generate the appropriate intermediate language code. When we define our own classes or structs, however, we have to tell the compiler everything: what methods are available to call, what fields to store with each instance, etc. Similarly, if we want to write something like `C=A+B;` for one of our own classes, we'll have to tell it what the relevant operator (in this case, "+") means in the context of that class. The way we do that is by defining overloads for the operator.

Why We Need Operator Overloading

At this point, I have to admit that operator overloading is in many ways purely a syntactical convenience. Whereas most of the topics we've covered so far are fundamental aspects of object-oriented programming and are necessary to be able to use classes properly, operator overloading doesn't actually give us anything that we couldn't have achieved with methods alone, except the easier syntax, which by itself is a huge bonus. Imagine, for example, that we wanted to write something like:

```
C = (A+B)*D;
```

for one of our classes. If we didn't have operator overloading, we'd have to define methods to perform those operations. The result would probably look a bit like:

```
A = D.Multiply (A.Add(B));
```

It should be obvious which of these lines of code is easier to understand and to maintain!

We should also say that there are many classes you could write for which operator overloading would not be relevant. After all, for something like our `Customer` or `Authenticator` classes that we used in our earlier examples, why would we want to add instances? Multiplying together two `MortimerPhones` customers just doesn't make any sense conceptually. It would be silly to try to define an overload for "+" or "*" for our `Customer` class.

There are, however, a large number of cases where you might want to write overloads for operators, including:

❑ From the world of mathematics, almost any mathematical object: coordinates, vectors, matrices, tensors, functions, and so on. If you are writing a program that does some mathematical or physical modeling, you will almost certainly use classes representing these objects.

❑ Graphics programs will also use mathematical or coordinate-related objects when calculating positions on screen.

❑ A class that represents an amount of money (for example, in a financial program).

❑ A word processing or text analysis program might have classes representing sentences, clauses and so on, and you might wish to use operators to combine sentences together. (This is really a more sophisticated version of concatenation for strings).

The other thing we should stress is that overloading isn't just concerned with arithmetic operators. We also need to consider the comparison operators, "==", "<", ">", "!=", ">=", and "<=". Take the statement if (a==b). For classes, this statement will, by default, compare the references a and b – it tests to see if the references point to the same location in memory, rather than checking to see if the instances actually contain the same data. For the `string` class, this behavior is overridden so that comparing strings really does compare the contents of each string. You might wish to do the same for your own classes. For structs, the "==" operator doesn't do anything at all by default. Trying to compare two structs to see if they are equal will produce a compilation error unless you explicitly overload "==" to tell the compiler how to perform the comparison.

There are a large number of situations in which being able to overload operators will help greatly to allow us to generate more readable, intuitive code.

Over the next few sections we're going to illustrate operator overloading by developing a new example, a struct called `Vector` that represents a 3D mathematical vector. In the world of mathematics, vectors can be added together or multiplied by other vectors or by numbers. Incidentally, in this context we'll use the term **scalar,** which is mathematical parlance for a simple number – in C# terms that's just a `double`. However, before we can understand how to overload operators, we need a bit of theoretical understanding about how operators work, which we cover next.

The fact that our example will be developed as a struct rather than a class is not significant. Operator overloading works in just the same way for both structs and classes.

How Operators Work

In order to understand how to overload operators, it's quite useful to think about what happens when the compiler encounters an operator – and for this we'll take the addition operator, "+", as an example. Suppose it meets the lines of code:

```
int a=3;
uint b=2;
double d=4.0;
long l = a+b;
double x = d+a;
```

Consider the line:

```
long l = a+b;
```

Saying a+b is really just a very intuitive, convenient syntax for saying that we are calling a method to add the numbers together. The method takes two parameters, a and b, and returns their sum. You can think of a+b as just an easier way of writing Add(a,b). For integers the compiler and the JIT compiler between them actually make sure this line is implemented internally as highly efficient inline code which does the addition using hardware; it doesn't start calling up software algorithms in the way that happens for most methods, but the principle as far as the C# code is concerned is the same.

The compiler will see it needs to add two integers and return a long, so it does the same thing as it does for any method call – it looks for the best matching overload of + given the parameter types. Adding two integers is fine – for modern processors there will be a specific machine code instruction to do this. The result will be an integer as well, so it will need to be cast to a long, which is allowed in C#, so there are no problems.

The next line:

```
double x = d+a;
```

is harder, and it is at this point that we realize that there are actually quite a few overloads of "+" kicking around already, even before we start defining our own classes. The thing is, we now need to add an integer a to a double. On most machines, that's probably not directly possible – rather, we'll need to implicitly convert the int to a double and add the two doubles together. In other words, we identify the best matching overload of "+" here as being a version of the operator that takes two doubles as its parameters. Adding together two doubles is a very different affair from adding two integers. Floating-point numbers are stored internally in modern processors as a mantissa and an exponent. Adding them involves bit-shifting the mantissa of one of the doubles so that the two exponents have the same value, adding the mantissas, then shifting the mantissa of the result and adjusting its exponent to maintain the highest possible accuracy in the answer. There will be hardware support for this in a modern Pentium processor, but it's still a completely different operation from adding two integers. Finally, the compiler needs to make sure it can cast the result to the required return type if necessary. In this case there's no problem – adding two doubles gives another double, which is what x is declared as.

Now, we're in a position to see what happens if the compiler finds something like this:

```
Vector Vect1, Vect2, Vect3;
// initialise Vect1 and Vect2
Vect3 = Vect1 + Vect2;
Vect1 = Vect1*2;
```

Where Vector is the struct we shall define shortly. The compiler will see that it needs to add two Vectors, Vect1, and Vect2 together. It'll look for an overload of the "+" operator which takes two Vectors as its parameters. This operator must also return either a Vector or something that can be implicitly converted to a Vector, so that we can set Vect3 equal to the return value. In other words, in order to compile this expression, it needs to be able to find a definition of an operator that has a signature something like this:

```
public static Vector operator + (Vector lhs, Vector rhs)
```

If it finds one, it'll call up the implementation of that operator. If it can't find one, it'll look to see if there is any other overload for "+" that it can use as a best match – perhaps something that has two parameters of other data types which can be implicitly converted to `Vector` instances. If it can't find anything suitable, it'll raise a compilation error, just as it would do if it couldn't find an appropriate overload for a method call.

Similarly, when the compiler gets to the line:

```
Vect1 = Vect1*2;
```

it sees that it needs to multiply a `Vector` by an integer and store the result in another `Vector`. It'll look for an overload of the "*" operator that takes a vector and an integer as its parameter. In fact in our example, we don't define one. Instead, we provide a "closest match" that takes a `Vector` and a `double` as its parameters. Since the compiler is happy to implicitly convert an `int` to a `double`, this isn't a problem.

Of course, arithmetic operators are not the only operators – there are also logical, comparison and assignment operators, and these still work on the same principles. Suppose the compiler sees something like this, where, as before, `Vector` is the struct that we will define in our next sample:

```
Vector Vect1, Vect2;
// initialize Vect1 and Vect2
if (Vect1 == Vect2)
{
```

The compiler will respond by looking for an overload of "==" which takes two `Vectors` as its parameters.

Addition Operator Overloading Example: The Vector Struct

Now that we've seen the theory of how operators work, it's time to introduce our example. We're going to write the struct `Vector`, which represents a 3-dimensional vector.

If you're worried that mathematics is not your strong point, don't worry. We'll keep things very simple. As far as we are concerned, a 3D-vector is just a set of three numbers (doubles) that tell you how far something is moving. The variables representing the numbers are called x, y and z; x tells you how far something moves East, y tells you how far it moves North and z tells you how far it moves upwards (in height). Combine the three numbers together and you get the total movement. For example, if x=3.0, y=3.0, and z=1.0, (which we'd normally write as (3.0, 3.0, 1.0) then you're moving 3 units East, 3 units North and rising upwards by 1 unit. If x=2.0, y=-4.0, and z=-4.0 (2.0, -4.0, -4.0), then you're moving 2 units East, 4 units South (negative number means in the opposite direction), and descending 4 units downwards.

The significance of addition should be clear here. If you move first by the vector (3.0, 3.0, 1.0) then you move by the vector (2.0, -4.0, -4.0), the total amount you have moved can be worked out by adding the two vectors. Adding vectors means adding each component individually, so you get (5.0, -1.0, -3.0). In this context, mathematicians will always write c=a+b, where a and b are the vectors and c is the result. We want to be able to use our `Vector` struct the same way.

We'll set the scene by coding up a basic outline for `Vector`, adding in a couple of constructors, and a `ToString()` method to display the value of the `Vector`. At this stage, we are just employing the principles we've already covered in this chapter:

```
struct Vector
{
    public double x, y, z;

    public Vector(double x, double y, double z)
    {
        this.x = x;
```

```
        this.y = y;
        this.z = z;
    }

    public Vector(Vector rhs)
    {
        x = rhs.x;
        y = rhs.y;
        z = rhs.z;
    }

    public override string ToString()
    {
        return "( " + x + " , " + y + " , " + z + " )";
    }
}
```

This code should be self-explanatory, since it does not use any concepts we have not already discussed. Note that in order to keep things simple I've left the fields as `public`. I could have made them `private` and written corresponding properties to access them, but it wouldn't have made any difference to the example, other than to make the code a lot more complicated. Besides, for a simple struct like this, which to a large extent is just a grouping of the x, y and z components, I think I can legitimately get away with keeping the fields `public`. Also, note that I've not supplied a default constructor, since this is not permitted for structs. Instead I've supplied two constructors that require the initial value of the vector to be specified, either by passing in the values of each component or by supplying another vector whose value can be copied.

Constructors like our second constructor, the one that runs `public Vector(Vector rhs)`, are often termed **copy constructors**, since they effectively allow you to initialize a class or struct instance by copying another instance.

With `Vector` defined as above, we can do things like:

```
Vector Vect1, Vect2, Vect3;
Vect1 = new Vector(1.0, 1.5, 2.0);
Vect2 = new Vector(Vect1);
```

We can't however, write something like:

```
Vect3 = Vect1 + Vect2;
```

Doing so will generate a compilation error because the compiler doesn't yet know what + means for a vector. We need to add code to the definition of `Vector` to tell it. Here's the code:

```
struct Vector
{
    public double x, y, z;

    // other members

    public static Vector operator + (Vector lhs, Vector rhs)
    {
        Vector Result = new Vector(lhs);
        Result.x += rhs.x;
        Result.y += rhs.y;
        Result.z += rhs.z;
    return Result;
    }
```

How does this work? The important syntax is in the declaration of the operator:

```
public static Vector operator + (Vector lhs, Vector rhs)
```

The operator is declared in much the same way as a method, except that we tell the compiler it's actually an operator we're defining by the `operator` keyword, followed by the actual symbol for the relevant operator. The return type is whatever type you get when you use this operator. In our case, adding two vectors gives us another vector, so the return type is `Vector`. For this particular override of "+", the return type is the same as the containing class, but that's not necessarily the case. Later on we'll add operators that return other types. The two parameters are the things you're operating on. For an operator that takes two parameters like "+", the first parameter is the object or value that goes on the left of the "+" sign, and the second is the object or value that goes to the right of it. In other words, if we write:

```
// a, b and c are declared of type Vector
c = a + b;
```

then the vector a is passed in to the body of our "+" overload as the first parameter, which we've called lhs; b is passed in as rhs, and c is set to equal the return value of the operator. By the way, lhs and rhs are common abbreviations for left-hand side and right-hand side.

Finally, note that the operator has been declared as `static`, which means that it is associated with the struct or class, not with any object, and so does not have access to a `this` pointer; C# requires that operator overloads are declared in this way. That's OK because the lhs and rhs parameters between them cover all the data the operator needs to know to perform its task.

Now we've dealt with the syntax for the operator "+" declaration, we can look at what happens inside the operator:

```
{
    Vector Result = new Vector(lhs);
    Result.x += rhs.x;
    Result.y += rhs.y;
    Result.z += rhs.z;
    return Result;
}
```

This part of the code is exactly the same as if we were declaring a method, and you should easily be able to convince yourself that this really will return a vector containing the sum of lhs and rhs as defined above. We simply add the individual doubles x, y, and z individually.

That one overload has illustrated all the concepts you need in order to overload arithmetic operators, but before we demonstrate the `Vector` class in action, we'll just reinforce the ideas involved by overloading a couple more arithmetic operators for `Vector`: multiplication by a scalar (or in C# terms, a double) and multiplication of two vectors.

Multiplying a vector by a scalar simply means multiplying each component by individually by the scalar. So, for example, `2 * (1.0, 2.5, 2.0)` gives `(2.0, 5.0, 4.0)`. The relevant operator overload looks like this:

```
public static Vector operator * (double lhs, Vector rhs)
{
    return new Vector(lhs*rhs.x, lhs*rhs.y, lhs*rhs.z);
}
```

This by itself however, is not sufficient. If a and b are declared as type Vector, it will allow us to write code like this:

```
b = 2*a;
```

The compiler will implicitly convert the integer 2 to a double in order to match the operator overload signature. Code like the following will however, still not compile:

```
b = a*2;
```

The thing is that compiler treats operator overloads exactly like method overloads. It examines all the available overloads of a given operator to find the best match. The above statement requires the first parameter to be a Vector and the second parameter to be an integer, or something that an integer can be implicitly converted to. We have not provided such an overload. The compiler can't start swapping the order of parameters so the fact that we've provided an overload that takes a double followed by a Vector is not sufficient. We need to explicitly define an overload that takes a Vector followed by a double as well. There are two possible ways of implementing this. The first way involves explicitly breaking down the vector multiplication operation in the same way that we've done for all operators so far:

```
public static Vector operator * (Vector lhs, double rhs)
{
    return new Vector(rhs*lhs.x, rhs*lhs.y, rhs*lhs.z);
}
```

Given that we've already written code to implement essentially the same operation, however, you might prefer to reuse that code by instead writing:

```
public static Vector operator * (Vector lhs, double rhs)
{
    return rhs*lhs;
}
```

This code works by effectively telling the compiler that if it sees a multiplication of a Vector by a double, it can simply reverse the parameters and call the other operator overload. Which you prefer is to some extent a matter of taste. In the actual sample code with this chapter we've gone for the second version, which looks neater and because we want to illustrate the idea in action. This version also makes for more maintainable code, since it saves duplicating the code to perform the multiplication in two separate overloads. Note however that the first version may give better performance, since it involves one less nested method call. On the other hand, there is quite a good chance that the JIT compiler will optimize out this extra method call anyway.

The next operator to be overloaded is vector multiplication. In mathematics there are a couple of ways of multiplying vectors together, but the one we are interested in here is known as the **dot product** or **inner product**, and it actually gives a scalar as a result. That's the reason we're introducing that example, so that we can demonstrate that arithmetic operators don't have to return the same type as the class in which they are defined. In mathematical terms, if you have two vectors (x, y, z) and (X, Y, Z), then the inner product is defined to be the value of $x*X + y*Y + z*Z$. That might look like a strange way to multiply two things together, but it's actually very useful, since it can be used to calculate various other quantities. Certainly, if you ever end up writing any code that displays any complex 3D graphics, for example using Direct3D or DirectDraw, you'll almost certainly find your code needs to work out inner products of vectors quite often as an intermediate step in calculating where to place objects on the screen. At any rate, what concerns us here is that we want people to be able to write double X = a*b where a and b are vectors and what they intend is for the dot product to be calculated. The relevant overload looks like this:

```
    public static double operator * (Vector lhs, Vector rhs)
    {
        return lhs.x*rhs.x + lhs.y+rhs.y + lhs.z*rhs.z;
    }
```

Now, we've defined the arithmetic operators, we can check that they work OK with a simple test harness routine:

```
static void Main(string[] args)
{
    // stuff to demonstrate arithmetic operations
    Vector Vect1, Vect2, Vect3;
    Vect1 = new Vector(1.0, 1.5, 2.0);
    Vect2 = new Vector(0.0, 0.0, -10.0);
    Vect3 = Vect1 + Vect2;
    Console.WriteLine("Vect1 = " + Vect1);
    Console.WriteLine("Vect2 = " + Vect2);
    Console.WriteLine("Vect3 = Vect1 + Vect2 = " + Vect3);

    Console.WriteLine("2*Vect3 = " + 2*Vect3);
    Vect3 += Vect2;
    Console.WriteLine("Vect3+=Vect2 gives " + Vect3);
    Vect3 = Vect1*2;
    Console.WriteLine("Setting Vect3=Vect1*2 gives " + Vect3);
    double dot = Vect1*Vect3;
    Console.WriteLine("Vect1*Vect3 = " + dot);
}
```

This code is available as the `VectorDemo` sample from the code download. Running this code produces this result:

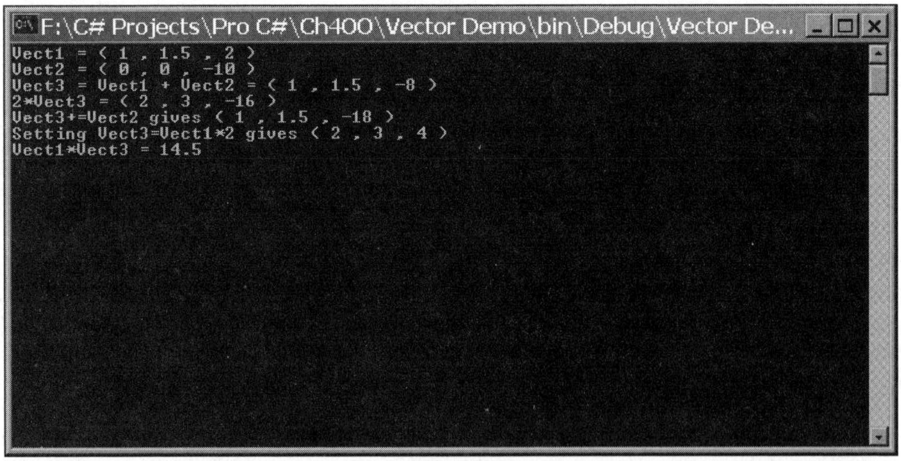

This screenshot shows that the operator overloads have given us the correct results, but if you look at the test harness code closely, you might be surprised to notice that we've actually sneakily used an operator that we hadn't overloaded – the addition assignment operator "+=":

```
    Vect3 += Vect2;
    Console.WriteLine("Vect3+=Vect2 gives " + Vect3);
```

Amazingly, it gave us the correct result! So what's going on? What's happened is that, although "+=" normally counts as a single operator, it really can be broken down into two steps – the addition and the assignment. Unlike C++, C# won't actually allow you to overload the "=" operator, but if you overload "+", the compiler will automatically use your overload of "+" to work out how to carry out a "+=" operation. The same principle works for the "++" operator, and for "-=", "--", "*=" and "/=" (though in order for these operators to work, you'll need to have respectively overloaded the "-", "*", and "/" operators). For a struct, C# always interprets assignment as meaning just copy the contents of the memory where the struct is stored, while for a class C# always copies just the reference.

Overloading the Comparison Operators

There are six comparison operators in C#, and they come in three pairs:

- ❑ == and !=
- ❑ > and >=
- ❑ < and <=

The significance of the pairing is twofold. First, within each pair, the second operator should always give exactly the opposite result to the first (whenever the first returns `true`, the second returns `false`, and vice versa), and second, C# always requires you to overload the operators in pairs. If you overload "==", then you must overload "!=" too, otherwise you get a compiler error.

In the case of overriding "==" and "!=", you should strictly also override the `Equals()` method which all classes and structs inherit from `System.Object`; you'll get a compiler warning if you don't. However, we'll ignore that for now, since we're not covering `System.Object` until Chapter 7.

One other restriction is that the comparison operators must return a `bool`. This is the fundamental difference between these operators and the arithmetic ones. The result of adding or subtracting two quantities, for example, might theoretically be any type depending on the quantities. We've already seen that multiplying two `Vectors` can be understood to give a scalar. Another example involves the .NET base class, `System.DateTime`, which we've briefly encountered. It's possible to subtract two `DateTimes`, but the result is not a `DateTime`, instead it is a a `System.TimeSpan` instance. By contrast, it doesn't really make much sense for a comparison to return anything other than a `bool`.

Apart from these differences, overloading the comparison operators follows the same principles as overloading the arithmetic operators. Comparing quantities isn't always as simple as you'd think however, as the example we use will illustrate. We're going to override the "==" and "!=" operators for our `Vector` class. Let's start off with "==". You might think a good way to do it would be like this:

```
public static bool operator == (Vector lhs, Vector rhs)   // wrong
{
   if (lhs.x == rhs.x && lhs.y == rhs.y && lhs.z == rhs.z)
      return true;
   else
      return false;
}
```

In fact, while this approach is syntactically fine, it's likely to give incorrect results a lot of the time. The problem is that it's not really satisfactory to compare floating point values for equality the way you compare integer values, because floating point values can differ by very small amounts. For an integer, it's pretty obvious that two integers containing the value 1 are equal whereas an integer that contains 1 is very different from one that contains 3. For floating point quantities, the issue is subtler. For example, if two doubles respectively contain the values 3.0000000 and 3.0000001, are they really different? The simple test that we've coded in above would say that they are not the same, but in all probability, a difference that small may well be due to rounding errors in some computations, and the two numbers really are the same. For `doubles` and `floats`, the comparison operator does actually check for exact equality, but in many cases you'll want an equality check to be more sophisticated than that.

For our `Vector` class, we are going to have to be more careful about what we mean by "equality". The solution we ultimately devise is going to depend on how we intend to use the class. What sorts of values will our `Vectors` contain? How willing are we to sacrifice performance in order to get a more sophisticated, more accurate, test of whether two `Vectors` should be regarded as identical? Would it perhaps be better to not define "==" and "!=" overloads at all and state in the documentation for the class that `Vector` does not support comparisons?

For the sake of argument, I'm going to propose the following "==" override as one possible solution. It's reasonable as far as performance is concerned, and will give results that accord well with our intuition provided the components of the vector are not too small. A more sophisticated solution would take into account the magnitude of the vector but hit performance more:

```
private const double Epsilon = 0.0000001;

public static bool operator == (Vector lhs, Vector rhs)
{
    if (System.Math.Abs(lhs.x - rhs.x) < Epsilon &&
        System.Math.Abs(lhs.y - rhs.y) < Epsilon &&
        System.Math.Abs(lhs.z - rhs.z) < Epsilon )
        return true;
    else
        return false;
}
```

This comparison operator defines a very small quantity, `Epsilon`, and regards `Vectors` as equal if none of their components differ by more than this quantity. It makes use of the static method `Abs` in the `System.Math` .NET base class. This method simply takes the absolute value of a number, removing the sign.

We also need to override the "!=" operator. The simple way to do it is like this:

```
public static bool operator != (Vector lhs, Vector rhs)
{
    return ! (lhs == rhs);
}
```

For performance reasons, however, we might prefer to expand out the implementation rather than simply call the "==" operator – that way we get one less method call at runtime.

As usual, we'll quickly check that our override works with a test harness. This time we'll define three `Vectors`, two of which are close enough that they should count as equal, and compare all the vectors:

```
Vector Vect1, Vect2, Vect3;
Vect1 = new Vector(3.0, 3.0, -10.0);
Vect2 = new Vector(3.0, 3.000000001, -10.0);
Vect3 = new Vector(2.0, 3.0, 6.0);
Console.WriteLine("Vect1==Vect2 returns   " + (Vect1==Vect2));
```

```
Console.WriteLine("Vect1==Vect3 returns  " + (Vect1==Vect3));
Console.WriteLine("Vect2==Vect3 returns  " + (Vect2==Vect3));
Console.WriteLine();
Console.WriteLine("Vect1!=Vect2 returns  " + (Vect1!=Vect2));
Console.WriteLine("Vect1!=Vect3 returns  " + (Vect1!=Vect3));
Console.WriteLine("Vect2!=Vect3 returns  " + (Vect2!=Vect3));
```

Running this code, (which is the `VectorDemo2` sample on the code download) produces this screenshot, which demonstrates the correct results:

Which Operators Can You Overload?

There are quite a number of operators in C#, some of which you can overload, and some of which you can't. Operators that you are allowed to overload include:

Category	Operators	Restrictions
Arithmetic binary	+, *, /, -, %	none
Arithmetic unary	+, -, ++, --	none
Bitwise binary	&, |, ^, <<, >>	none
Bitwise unary	!, ~, `true`, `false`	none
Comparison	==, !=, >=, <, <=, >	must be overloaded in pairs

This list leaves some gaps, but the gaps are there for logical reasons. A number of operators cannot be overloaded explicitly, but are evaluated in terms of other operators that can be overloaded. This includes the arithmetic and bitwise assignment operators "+=", "-=", "*=", "/=", ">>=", "<<=", "%=", "&=", "|=" and "^=", as well as the conditional logical operators "&&" and "||" (these last operators are evaluated using "&" and "|"). C++ developers will be surprised to learn that "[ ]" and "( )" cannot be overloaded. The reason is that C# achieves the same functionality by other means: using indexers in place of "[ ]" overloading, and user-defined casts in place of "( )" overloading; we cover user-defined casts in Chapter 6.

Indexers

Indexers share with properties the fact that they are not really an essential part of object-oriented programming. Rather, they represent a syntactical convenience that allows certain classes to be used in a more intuitive manner. In the case of indexers, the syntactical convenience they allow is for you to access an object as if it was an array.

Adding an Indexer to Vector

We're going to continue using our `Vector` struct as an example. As with operator overloads, indexers work in the same way for structs and classes, so the fact that we happen to be using a struct for our example is not significant.

Up to now we've referred to the components of our `Vector` struct with their names x, y, and z. The trouble is that that's not the only way that mathematicians like to refer to them. They also often find it useful to treat vectors as if they are arrays, with x being the first element, y the second, and z the third. In other words, in order to set the x-component they will tend to write:

```
MyVector[0] = 3.6;
```

If we can treat `Vector`s as arrays then we should also be able to do things like iterate through the components:

```
for(int i=0 ; i<3 ;i++)
{
    Vect2[i] = i;
}
```

With our current definition of `Vector`, these code snippets will produce a compile-time error, since the compiler won't understand what we mean by the first-element of a `Vector`. Indexers are a way of solving that. If you define an indexer for a class, you are telling the compiler what to do if it encounters code in which a class instance is being treated as if it were an array.

Indexers are defined in pretty much the same way as properties, with `get` and `set` functions. The main difference is that the name of the indexer is the keyword `this`. To define an indexer for the `Vector` class, we modify the class definition as follows:

```
struct Vector
{
public double x, y, z;

public double this [int i]
{
    get
    {
        switch (i)
        {
            case 0:
                return x;
            case 1:
                return y;
            case 2:
                return z;
```

```
                default:
                    throw new IndexOutOfRangeException(
                                "Attempt to retrieve Vector element " + i) ;
            }
        }
        set
        {
            switch (i)
            {
                case 0:
                    x = value;
                    break;
                case 1:
                    y = value;
                    break;
                case 2:
                    z = value;
                    break;
                default:
                    throw new IndexOutOfRangeException(
                                "Attempt to set Vector element " + i);
            }
        }
// etc.
```

There's a fair bit of new stuff in this code. To start with, let's look at the line that declares the indexer:

```
    public double this [int i]
```

This line basically says that we want to be able to treat each `Vector` instance as a one-dimensional array with an `int` as the index (or, equivalently in this case, the parameter), and that when we do so the return type is a `double`. Indexers actually give us quite a lot of freedom – we can use any data type as the index, though the types you'll most often want to use are the integer types `uint`, `int`, `ushort`, `short` etc., and `string`. Similarly, you can use whatever data type you think most appropriate for the return type.

Within the body of our indexer, we have the same `get` and `set` accessors that you see for properties. If we wanted to make our indexer read-only or write-only, we could do so by leaving out the appropriate accessor. The syntax for the accessors follows precisely that which is used when you define properties, except that we now have accessors to whatever variables we defined as the parameters to the indexer (recall that property `get` and `set` accessors never take any explicit parameters). The `get` accessor must return the type we have declared the indexer as returning, while the `set` accessor must not return anything, and has access to an additional implicit parameter, `value`, whose data type is the type we declared the indexer as (`double` in this case), and which is initialized as the value on the right hand side of the assignment operator we use the indexer expression in.

Beyond that, the code should be self-explanatory to the extent that we simply use the parameter passed in to determine which of the components of the `Vector` should be accessed, and either return or set the appropriate field. Notice, however, that the `switch` statements also each have a `default` case to handle the situation in which the indexer is called with an inappropriate value for the parameter. The action taken in this case is to throw an exception:

```
    throw new IndexOutOfRangeException(
                            "Attempt to retrieve Vector element " + i);
```

We haven't yet encountered exceptions – those will be covered in the next chapter. They are the way that you deal with unexpected error conditions in C#, and up to now in this chapter I've carefully avoided any error checking in any of the examples, precisely because we haven't yet covered exceptions. For an indexer however, you can't really get away without checking that the index passed in is within the appropriate bounds – for our `Vector` class, 0 to 2. So for the time being I'll just ask you to accept that the line above is the way you'd handle an index out of bounds. What it actually should do is cause execution to jump to a special area of code that you'll ideally have written and marked as responsible for handling this particular error situation. Since we haven't written any such code yet, this statement will instead cause program execution to terminate.

Now we've added our indexer, let's try it out. Here's the code to try it out:

```
Vector Vect1 = new Vector(1.0, -5.0, 4.6);
Vector Vect2 = new Vector();
Console.WriteLine("Vect1 = " + Vect1);
Console.WriteLine("Vect1[1] = " + Vect1[1]);

for(int i=0 ; i<3 ;i++)
{
    Vect2[i] = i;
}
Console.WriteLine("Vect2 = " + Vect2);
```

Note that in this example we are demonstrating using a `for` loop to index the components of the `Vector`.

> *Although we are able to use `for`, `do` and `while` loops with indexers, we cannot write a loop that uses `foreach`. The `foreach` statement works in a different way, treating the item as a collection rather than an array. It's possible to set up a class or struct so it acts as a collection, but that involves implementing certain interfaces rather than indexers. We'll show how to do this in Chapter 7.*

This is the result:

It is also possible to verify that our exception handling code does trap an out-of-bound index. If we try to access the `Vector` like this:

```
double TryThis = Vect1[6];
```

Then our console application immediately terminates and this dialog is displayed:

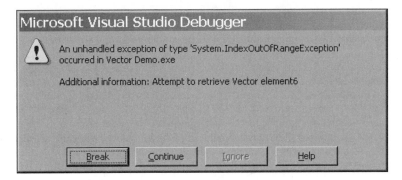

In the next chapter, we'll see how to handle exceptions so that you can determine what action your program takes, rather than simply terminating.

Other Indexer Examples

Indexers are extremely flexible. They are not, for example confined to one-dimensional arrays. We can treat classes and structs as multidimensional arrays as well, just by adding more than one parameter inside the square brackets. We can also overload indexers – a struct or class can have as many indexers as you want, provided they have different numbers or types of parameters.

One example to illustrate this would be that if we'd wanted to write a `Matrix` class, we'd probably want to be able to treat it as a 2D array of `doubles`. Not only that, but mathematicians would regard any individual row of the matrix as a vector. We won't actually work through the example, but in principle we could achieve this by defining two indexers like this:

```
// for struct Matrix
public double this [uint i, uint j]
public Vector this [uint i]
```

Another common use for indexers is to be able to access a part of a class or struct in a way that is described by a string. This means that you can have an array or some data structure that has named elements:

```
// for a class, ListOfCustomers
public Customer this[string Name]


// in client code
Customer NextCustomer = CustomerList["Simon Robinson"]
```

A useful variation of this is to access elements using an enumerated value.

Indeed, indexers are most commonly used for classes which represent some data structure, such as an array, a list, or a map, and are defined for the .NET base classes that represent these structures, which we'll examine in Chapter 7.

Interfaces

To understand interfaces in C#, it's worth revisiting the examples we gave of inheritance in the real world in the last chapter. We covered two main examples: Ford Cars, and jumpers and sweatshirts.

In the Ford Cars example, we demonstrated implementation inheritance – that is to say, the same implementation of certain functionality (describing the constituent components of the cars) was shared across different types of car. That's the kind of inheritance that we've essentially seen throughout the chapter up until now.

In the jumpers and sweatshirts example, the kind of inheritance described was a little different in that only the user interface – the "what-it-does" – was shared between different objects, while the actual implementation (that is the material in which the garment was made) was likely to be different for each object. Interfaces are the way that C# supports this latter type of inheritance.

In programming terms, an interface is similar to a class, except that none of its members are implemented. It's simply a grouping together of methods, properties, events, and indexers. You can't ever actually instantiate an interface; all it contains are the signatures for its members. Those four types of member are also the only ones an interface is allowed to contain. It does not have constructors (how can you construct something that you can't instantiate), or fields (because that would imply some internal implementation). An interface is not allowed to have operator overloads, though that's not because there is any problem in principle with declaring them – there isn't; it is because this would cause some incompatibility problems with other .NET languages, such as VB.NET, which do not support operator overloading.

You declare an interface in much the same way that you declare a class, except that the members don't have implementations (a little bit like abstract methods).

For a change, instead of creating our own interface, we'll show the syntax of an interface using one from the .NET base classes, IEnumerator, from the System.Collections namespace. The interface looks like this:

```
interface IEnumerator
{
    // Properties
    object Current {get; }

    // Methods
    bool MoveNext();
    void Reset();
}
```

The IEnumerator interface has two methods and one property. This interface is important in implementing collections, and is designed to encapsulate the functionality of moving through the items in a collection. MoveNext() moves to the next item, Reset() returns to the first item, while Current actually retrieves a reference to the current item.

Beyond the lack of implementations, the main point to note is the lack of any modifiers on the members. Interface members are always public, and cannot be declared as virtual or static. That's up to classes to do, not interfaces.

So why have interfaces? The main reason is that they effectively serve as a contract. Up to now we've treated classes as having certain members, and not bothered about grouping any members together – our classes have simply contained a list of various miscellaneous methods, fields, properties, etc. There are often situations in which in order to be able to use a class in a certain way, we need to know that the class implements certain features. The way we do that is by declaring that the class implements one or more interfaces. A class implements an interface by deriving from that interface, and providing implementations of all the members defined in that interface. This is similar to the use of the `Implements` keyword in VB6 to indicate an object implements an interface.

We have already seen one example of a class using an interface to declare that it implements certain features. Classes can derive from `IDisposable` to indicate that they support the `Dispose()` method. `IDisposable` is defined like this:

```
public interface IDisposable
{
   void Dispose();
}
```

Hence a class that implements `IDisposable` must implement the `Dispose()` method.

Another good example is provided by the `foreach` loop in C#. In principle, it is possible to use `foreach` to iterate through a class instance, provided that that class is able to act as if it is a collection. How can the .NET runtime tell whether a class instance represents a collection? It queries the instance to find out whether it implements the `System.Collections.IEnumerable` interface. If it does, then the runtime uses the methods on this interfaces to iterate through the members of the collection. If it doesn't, then `foreach` will raise an exception.

You might wonder why in this case we don't just see if the class implements the required methods and properties. The answer is that that wouldn't be a very reliable way of checking. For example, you can probably think of all sorts of different reasons why a class might happen to implement a method called `MoveNext()`, or one called `Reset()`, which don't have anything to do with collections. For example, the class might encapsulate access to a file, and `MoveNext()` moves to the next byte in the file. If the class declares that it implements the interfaces needed for collections, then you know that it really is a collection.

A second reason for having interfaces is for interoperability with COM. Before .NET came on the scene, COM, and its later versions DCOM and COM+ provided the main way that applications could communicate with each other on the Windows platform, and the particular object model that COM used was heavily dependent on interfaces. Indeed, it was through COM that the concept of an interface first became commonly known. We should stress, however, that C# interfaces are not the same as COM interfaces. COM interfaces have very strict requirements, such as that they must use GUIDs as identifiers, which are not necessarily present in C# interfaces. However, using attributes (a C# feature that we'll cover in the next chapter), it is possible to dress up a C# interface so it acts like a COM interface, and hence provide compatibility with COM. We'll discuss COM interoperability in Chapter 19.

Implementing Interfaces: The Jumper/Sweatshirt Example

We're going to finish our discussion of interfaces by developing a short sample that illustrates how we can use interfaces to develop an object that follows the interface inheritance paradigm. We're going to code up our jumper example!

To start with, we need an interface that encapsulates the features of jumpers. Here's what it looks like:

```
interface IJumper
{
   void PutOn(bool SleevesRolledUp);
   void TakeOff();

   int TemperatureIncrease
   {
      get;
   }
}
```

This interface allows us to take off or put on the jumper, and find out what temperature increase it is currently giving the owner – how effectively it's warming you up! The `PutOn()` method also takes a Boolean parameter that allows you to specify whether the sleeves are rolled up.

Notice the name, `IJumper`. It's a convention that interface names traditionally start with the letter `I`, so we know that it's an interface.

> *In most cases, .NET usage guidelines discourage the so-called "Hungarian" notation in which names are preceded by a letter that indicates the type of object being defined. Interfaces are one of the few cases in which Hungarian notation is recommended. We'll discuss the usage guidelines at the end of Chapter 8.*

The idea is that we can now write classes that represent jumpers. These classes don't have to be related to each other in any way, they can be completely different classes. They will however, all declare to the world that they represent jumpers by the fact that they implement the `IJumper` interface.

For our sample, we'll only code up one such class, which we'll call `PolyesterJumper`:

```
class PolyesterJumper : IJumper
{
  private int temperatureIncrease;
  public const string Manufacturer = "Wrox Press";
  public virtual void PutOn(bool SleevesRolledUp)
  {
      if (SleevesRolledUp)
         temperatureIncrease = 10;
      else
         temperatureIncrease = 15;
  }

  public void TakeOff()
  {
      temperatureIncrease = 0;
  }
```

```
public int TemperatureIncrease
{
    get
    {
        return temperatureIncrease;
    }
}

public override string ToString()
{
    switch (temperatureIncrease)
    {
    case 0:
        return "Jumper is off";
    case 10:
        return "Jumper is on but sleeves are rolled up";
    case 15:
        return "Jumper is on";
    default:
        return ""; // this can't ever happen
    }
}
}
```

It should be pretty obvious what the implementation of this class does. We assume that a polyester jumper is capable of warming you by 10°C if the sleeves are rolled up, and by 15°C if they are extended.

The only really interesting line in this code is the class declaration:

```
class PolyesterJumper : IJumper
```

We've declared that PolyesterJumper derives from one interface, IJumper, and we have not indicated any other classes. We've not indicated any base classes, so PolyesterJumper will also derive from System.Object. The rule is that a class must derive from one other class, System.Object being assumed if no class is specified, and can additionally derive from as many interfaces as you want.

We know what being derived from another class means: it means that PolyesterJumper automatically gets the all the members of the base class, which it can override or hide if it wishes. In this case we've supplied our own override of ToString() in order to be able to display the state of our class.

Being derived from IJumper means that PolyesterJumper gets all the members of IJumper too. But since an interface doesn't actually implement any of its methods, PolyesterJumper has to provide implementations of all of them. If any implementations are missing, you can rest assured that the compiler will complain. Recall also that the interface just indicates the presence of its members. It's up to the class to decide if it wants any of them to be virtual or abstract (though abstract is only allowed if the class itself is abstract and will be derived from). Here, we've decided that PutOn() is a suitable method for overriding, so we've declared that method as virtual.

As usual, any class doesn't just get the members it's inherited. It can also add any of its own. In this case, we've only added a private field to store the temperature increase, as well as a public constant that indicates the manufacturer of this particular class of jumpers.

Now we have our class, we can test it out:

```
static void Main(string[] args)
{
    PolyesterJumper MyJumper = new PolyesterJumper();
    MyJumper.PutOn(true);
    Console.WriteLine(MyJumper.ToString());
    MyJumper.TakeOff();
    Console.WriteLine(MyJumper.ToString());
    MyJumper.PutOn(false);
    Console.WriteLine(MyJumper.ToString());
    Console.WriteLine(" Made by: " + PolyesterJumper.Manufacturer);
    Console.ReadLine();
}
```

This code produces this output:

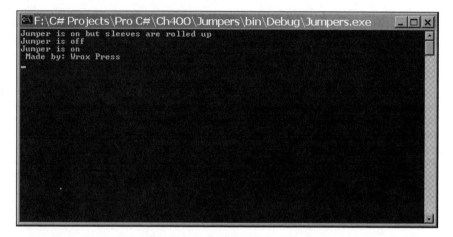

Testing out the `PolyesterJumper` in this way however, hasn't really demonstrated that it implements the `IJumper` interface. There's nothing in the client code above that relies on the fact that this interface is present. So if we did want to be sure that the jumper implements this interface and is therefore a jumper, adhering to the "contract" specifications for a jumper, how would we do it? The answer is that we can try to access it through a reference to the interface:

```
static void Main(string[] args)
{
    IJumper MyJumper = new PolyesterJumper();
    MyJumper.PutOn(true);
```

We can alternatively write:

```
static void Main(string[] args)
{
    PolyesterJumper TheJumper = new PolyesterJumper();
    IJumper MyJumper;
    MyJumper = TheJumper;
    MyJumper.PutOn(true);
```

Note that using an `IJumper` reference doesn't prevent us from accessing all the public members implemented by `PolyesterJumper`, whether or not those members are part of the interface, but it does confirm to the client code that our class is a *bona fide* jumper.

Interface Inheritance

It's possible for interfaces to inherit from each other in the same way that classes do. For example, suppose we want to define a contract for sweatshirts – a set of methods that anything claiming to be a sweatshirt must implement. Sweatshirts must be able to do anything a jumper can do, and also have hoods that can be put up. A suitable interface might look like this:

```
interface ISweatshirt : IJumper
{
    bool HoodUp
    {
        get;
        set;
    }
}
```

Now `ISweatshirt` contains the `HoodUp` property as well as all the members of `IJumper`. If we were to define a sweatshirt class like this:

```
class CottonSweatshirt : ISweatshirt
{
```

Then `CottonSweatshirt` would have to implement all the methods defined in `ISweatshirt` and all the methods defined in `IJumper`.

We leave the development of the `CottonSweatshirt` class to you as an exercise.

Summary

In this chapter we have examined some of the features that C# offers which make writing classes and objects easier and allows them to have a more intuitive syntax. We also looked at how C# handles its memory management internally. This information is useful if we are to write high performance code. We have examined how constructors and destructors allow you to specify how your objects should be initialized and what action, if any, should be taken to clean up resources when they are destroyed. We've considered how performance can sometimes be improved by defining structs instead of classes, and we've examined the syntactical convenience that is provided by operator overloads, indexers, and method overloads.

6

Advanced C# Topics

At this point we've covered all the basics of C# syntax as well as the principles of object-oriented programming, and how to carry out object-oriented programming in C#. We have learnt enough to be able to use C# to write well-designed object-oriented programs. However, we haven't yet completed our coverage of the C# language, because C# also offers a number of more advanced features that can be extremely useful in some circumstances. Those features are what we'll be looking at over the next two chapters.

The C# language tends to work in not isolation, but relies extensively on its interaction with the .NET framework and the base classes. In this chapter we'll focus on those advanced features that are predominantly part of the language itself. In Chapter 7, we will examine the topics for which support is provided mainly through the base classes, with minimal help from the C# language syntax. However, the distinction is blurred, so we will at various points find the base classes entering this chapter (just as they inevitably have in previous chapters). Conversely, although the topics in Chapter 7 involve more support from the base classes, we will find we are learning isolated new aspects of language syntax even in that chapter.

The topics that we cover in this chapter are:

❑ **Errors and exception handling** – C# provides a rich mechanism for handling error conditions, using a technique known as **exception handling**. This allows us to provide custom handling for each type of error condition, and also to cleanly separate the code that identifies errors from the code that handles them. This means, for example, that library code can take responsibility for identifying errors, while leaving it to the client code to decide how to handle them.

❑ **Casting** – we saw in Chapter 3 how it is possible to convert between data types by implicit or explicit casting. Here we will examine how to extend this process by defining casts between your own classes.

❑ **Delegates** – delegates are the means by which C# allows code to refer to a method, without specifying which method is being referred to until run-time. They are the similar to function pointers in C++, but are type safe and object-oriented.

❑ **Events** – it is often the case in programming that some code needs to be informed when an action takes place, for example when the user clicks a mouse button. C# provides inbuilt support for this scenario using events.

❑ **The C# preprocessor** – when your code is compiled, it is first put through a stage known as **preprocessing**. This allows certain textual substitutions to be made on your code, and can be useful for generating slightly different builds to match different situations.

❑ **Attributes** – attributes allow you to mark items in your code that are of interest in some way. This is useful for documentation and can also be used to control aspects of how your code is compiled.

❑ **Unsafe code** – although C# usually hides the details of memory access from the programmer in order simplify the coding process, there are some situations in which you need that direct memory access. C# allows this in blocks of code that you mark for the purpose, by declaring them as unsafe.

Errors and Exception Handling

No matter how good your coding is, your programs will always have to be able to handle possible errors. For example, in the middle of some calculation it might discover that it doesn't have permission to read a file it was expecting to read, or while it is sending network requests the network might go down. In such situations, it is usually not adequate for some method call to simply return an appropriate error code. We are talking about exceptional problems here. It might happen that when you encounter such a problem, you happen to be in the middle of some complex processing, perhaps with method calls nested to a level of 15 or 20 method calls, when your code suddenly discovers it simply can't complete the task at hand. Typically this means that you don't want to simply return from the method that you are currently executing, but what you really need the program to do is jump back up through all those 15 or 20 method calls in order to exit the task completely and sort out the mess. As you would expect from a modern object-oriented language, C# has very good facilities to handle this kind of situation, through the mechanism known as **exception handling**.

You can think of an exception as something that indicates that some exceptional error condition has occurred, and contains information about the problem. More formally, in terms of .NET classes, an exception is an instance of a class that has been derived directly or indirectly from the base class System.Exception.

This section is going to be of most use to Visual Basic developers. Error handling facilities in VB are very restricted, and essentially limited to the On Error GoTo *statement. If you're coming from a VB background, you'll find C# exceptions open up a whole new world of error handling in your programs. On the other hand, Java and C++ developers will be familiar with the principle of exceptions since these languages also handle errors in the same way as C#. C++ developers will note a couple of differences in C#. C# provides a* finally *block to clean up resources, which is absent in C++, and C# also requires exception classes to be derived from* System.Exception, *whereas in C++ anything can act as the exception.*

C++ developers should note that, due to the type safety of C#, using exceptions in C# does not carry the performance penalty from the need to carry extra type information that it does in C++.

Coding Up an Exception

In this section we will describe the basic idea behind an exception.

In order to deal with possible error conditions you will normally divide the relevant part of your program into a number of blocks of three different types:

❑   `try` blocks contain code that forms part of the normal operation of your program, but which might encounter some serious error conditions.

❑   `catch` blocks contain the code that deals with the various error conditions.

❑   `finally` blocks contain the code that cleans up any resources or takes any other action that you'll normally want done at the end of a try block.

It's easiest to understand the situation, if you think of the `try` block as conceptually containing its associated `catch` and `finally` blocks, as shown in the diagram (although when we come to actual coding, we'll find that syntactically the `catch` and `finally` blocks follow the `try` block, rather than being contained in it, and variables defined in the `try` block actually go out of scope when execution enters the `catch` or `finally` block). In this diagram the arrows indicate possible paths for the flow of execution:

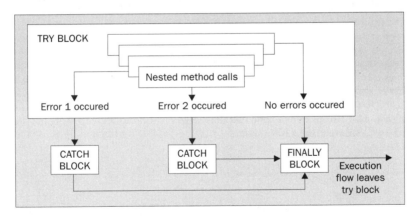

Execution flow enters a `try` block. This is simply a block of code marked with the keyword `try`, and delimited with braces. If no errors occur, execution proceeds normally. When program flow leaves the `try` block, even if nothing has happened, it will automatically enter the `finally` block, which should contain any instructions to clean up after the processing. If however, at any time in the `try` block, the program detects that an error condition has occurred, it leaves the `try` block immediately and enters the `catch` block that has been marked as handling that type of error. At the end of the `catch` block, execution automatically transfers to the `finally` block to take any final action.

That's the principle. The syntax used to bring all this about looks roughly like this (though it's not yet precise – we need to add some parameters to the `catch` block as shown in this code fragment):

```
try
{
    // code for normal execution
}
catch
{
    // error handling
}
finally
{
    // clean up
}
```

The above code isn't the only way of doing it – there are a couple of variations, but it should give an idea of the principle. If you prefer you can omit the `finally` block. You can also supply as many `catch` blocks as you want, to handle different types of error. You can even omit the `catch` blocks altogether, in which case the syntax serves not to identify exceptions, but as a way of guaranteeing that code in the `finally` block will be executed when execution leaves the `try` block, which can be useful if there are several exit points in the `try` block.

So far so good, but this leaves the question: if the code is running in the `try` block, how does it know to switch to the `catch` block if an error has occurred? This is where exceptions themselves come in. If an error is detected, the code does something that is known as **throwing an exception**. It instantiates an exception object, which is an instance of a class that is derived from the base class `System.Exception` (let's say for the sake of argument the name of the class is `MyException`), and throws it:

```
throw new MyException();
```

As soon as the computer encounters a `throw` statement inside a `try` block, it immediately looks for a corresponding `catch` block associated with the same `try` block, to which it can transfer control. You can actually define as many `catch` blocks as you want for a given `try` block, but the computer will identify the correct one using the `MyException` class. It looks for a `catch` block that indicates an instance of the same class (or of a base class). In the above code that illustrated `catch` blocks we simply left the `catch` statement empty, but we would more usually have written:

```
catch (MyException e)
{
```

which is the `catch` handler that responds to any `throw` statement that throws an instance of `MyException`.

With this extra information, we can expand out the `try` block we've just demonstrated. Let's assume, for the sake of argument, that there are two possible serious errors that can occur in it: an overflow (for example, converting a negative `long` value to a `ulong`), and an array out of bounds (perhaps you tried to access element `10` of an array of size `5`). Microsoft has already written exception classes for these conditions. They are known respectively as `OverflowException` and `IndexOutOfRangeException`, and both are defined in the `System` namespace.

Now our `try` block looks like this:

```
try
{
    // code for normal execution

    // assume two bool variables, Overflow and OutOfBounds, which are
    // set to true if relevant error has occurred
    if (Overflow == true)
        throw new OverflowException();

    // more processing

    if (OutOfBounds == true)
        throw new IndexOutOfRangeException ();

    // otherwise continue normal execution
}
catch (OverflowException e)
{
    // error handling for the overflow error condition
}
catch (IndexOutOfRangeException e)
{
    // error handling for the index out of range error condition
}
finally
{
    // clean up
}
```

So far this might not look like we've achieved much that you can't do with `On Error GoTo`, beyond the fact that we've more cleanly separated the different parts of the code. In fact, we have here a far more powerful and flexible mechanism for error handling. The key feature of this is that the `throw` statements don't have to be in the same method as the `try` block. Once program execution enters a `try` block, that `try` block continues to apply even as execution flow enters other methods that are called. If the computer encounters a `throw` statement, it immediately goes back up through all the method calls on the stack, looking for the end of the containing `try` block and the start of the appropriate `catch` block. As it does so, all the local variables in the intermediate method calls will correctly go out of scope. This makes the `try...catch` architecture beautifully suited to the situation we described at the beginning of this section, in which in the middle of some processing you are somewhere inside a method call that is perhaps nested by 15 to 20 calls since processing started when you encounter an error condition, and processing has to stop immediately.

> The **`throw` statement can be in any method called while executing the `try` block – it doesn't have to be in the same method that the `try` block was defined in.**

As you can probably gather from the above discussion, `try` blocks can play a very significant part of controlling the flow of execution of your code. However, it's important to understand that exceptions are intended for exceptional conditions, hence their name. It would be considered very bad programming style to, for example, use an exception as a way of controlling when to exit a `do...while` loop.

There's a lot to take in here, and the easiest way to see how this works in practice is with a couple of examples. We are going to start off with a simple example of a code sample that correctly handles a couple of possible error conditions. Then we'll discuss some more advanced features of exceptions, and finish with a more real-world example that illustrates some fairly sophisticated exception handling in a realistic scenario.

Example: SimpleExceptions

Our first sample is called SimpleExceptions. It repeatedly asks the user to type in a number and then does some processing on this number. For the sake of this example, the processing simply involves displaying the number. However, we'll imagine that for some reason the number needs to be between 0 and 5, and the program won't be able to do whatever it wanted to do with the number if it is outside this range. Hence we'll throw an exception if the user types in something anything bigger than 5 or anything negative.

The program continues to ask for more numbers to be processed until the user simply hits Return without entering anything.

> *You should note that this code does* not *provide a good example of when to use exception handling. As we've already indicated, the idea of exceptions is that they are provided for exceptional circumstances. Users are always typing in silly things, so this situation doesn't really count. Normally your program will handle incorrect user input by performing an instant check and asking the user to retype the input if there is a problem. However, generating exceptional situations is difficult in a small sample that you can read through in a few minutes! So we'll tolerate this bad practice for now in order to demonstrate how exceptions would work. The examples that follow will present more realistic situations.*

The code for SimpleExceptions looks like this:

```csharp
using System;

namespace Wrox.ProfessionalCSharp.Chapter6.SimpleExceptions
{
    public class MainEntryPoint
    {
        public static void Main(string[] args)
        {
            string userInput;
            while ( true )
            {
                try
                {
                    Console.Write("Input a number between 0 and 5 " +
                                            "(or just hit return to exit)> ");
                    userInput = Console.ReadLine();
                    if (userInput == "")
                        break;
                    int index = Convert.ToInt32(userInput);
                    if (index < 0 || index > 5)
                        throw new IndexOutOfRangeException("You typed in " +
                                                    userInput);
```

```
                    Console.WriteLine("Your number was " + index);
            }
            catch (IndexOutOfRangeException e)
            {
                Console.WriteLine("Exception: " +
                        "Number should be between 0 and 5. " + e.Message);
            }
            catch (Exception e)
            {
                Console.WriteLine("An exception was thrown. Message was: " +
                                                            e.Message);
            }
            catch
            {
                Console.WriteLine("Some other exception has occurred");
            }
            finally
            {
                Console.WriteLine("Thank you");
            }
        }
    }
}
```

The core of this code is a `while` loop, which continually uses `Console.ReadLine()` to ask for user input. `ReadLine()` takes in a string, so the first thing we do is convert it to an `int` using the `System.Convert.ToInt32()` method. The `System.Convert` class contains various useful methods to perform data conversions, and we should recall that the C# compiler resolves `int` to instances of the `System.Int32` base class. We also check for an empty string, since this is our condition for exiting the `while` loop. Notice how the `break` statement actually breaks right out of the enclosing `try` block as well as the `while` loop. As a way of controlling program flow, `try` works independently from all the other C# statements that can alter execution flow, so there's no problems about jumping out of a `try` block. Of course, as execution breaks out of the `try` block, the `Console.WriteLine()` statement in the `finally` block gets executed.

Next, we check for our exception condition:

```
if (index < 0 || index > 5)
    throw new IndexOutOfRangeException("You typed in " + UserInput);
```

When throwing an exception, we need to choose what type of exception to throw. Although the class `System.Exception` is available, it is really intended as a base class and it's considered bad programming practice actually to throw an instance of this class as an exception, because it conveys no information about the nature of the error condition. Instead, Microsoft has defined many other exception classes that are derived from `System.Exception`. Each of these matches a particular type of exception condition, and you are free to define your own ones too. The idea is that you give as much information as possible about the particular exception condition by throwing an instance of a class that matches the particular error condition. In this case we've picked `System.IndexOutOfRangeException` as the best choice in the circumstances. `IndexOutOfRangeException` has several constructor overloads. The one we've chosen takes a string, which describes the error.

Now let's look at what will happen when we run this sample. The program will start up and ask the user for some input. Assuming the user types in an appropriate value, the `if` clause will evaluate to `false` so the `throw` statement will not be executed. The computer will display a message saying what number was input, and at that point we hit the closing curly brace that marks the end of the `try` block. At this point the computer will look for the corresponding finally block to perform any final processing. We've implemented a `finally` block to display a "Thank you" message. More commonly you'll be doing tasks like closing file handles and calling the `Dispose()` method of various objects in order to perform any cleaning up. Once the computer leaves the `finally` block, it simply carries on execution at the next statement. In this case we iterate back to the start of the `while` loop, and enter the `try` block again.

Suppose the user then types in a number that is not between 0 and 5. This will be picked up by the `if` statement and an `IndexOutOfRangeException` object will be instantiated and thrown. At this point the computer will immediately exit the `try` block (so the statement `Console.WriteLine("Your number was " + index)` will not be executed). The computer will proceed to look for a `catch` block that handles `IndexOutOfRangeException` (actually that's not quite correct – the compiler will already have established which is the appropriate `catch` handler – but it's easier to understand the process if we think of the computer doing this at runtime).

The first `catch` block it comes to is this:

```
catch (IndexOutOfRangeException e)
{
    Console.WriteLine("Exception: Number should be between 0 and 5."
                                                    + e.Message);
}
```

Since this `catch` block takes a parameter of the appropriate class, this will be executed, and the error message displayed. The exception passed in, e, is the one that was thrown. This means we get access to any information contained in this exception instance. In this case we use the `Exception.Message` property, which returns the string we passed in to the constructor to this exception instance. After executing this `catch` block, control switches to the `finally` block, just as if no exception had occurred.

Notice that we've also provided another `catch` block:

```
catch (Exception e)
{
    Console.WriteLine("An exception was thrown. Message was: " + "
                                                    e.Message);
}
```

This `catch` block would also be capable of handling an `IndexOutOfRangeException` if it weren't for the fact that such exceptions will already have been caught by the previous catch block – recall from Chapter 4 that a reference to a class B can also refer to instances of any class derived from B. Since `IndexOutOfRangeException` is derived from `Exception`, the parameter e passed in here can quite happily be an `IndexOutOfRangeException` instance. So why doesn't this `catch` block get executed? The answer is that the computer executes only the first suitable `catch` block it finds. As soon as it finds a `catch` block that is capable of receiving the exception instance that has been thrown, it stops looking, and so ignores any remaining `catch` blocks. Of course, that being the case, you're probably wondering why we've coded up this second `catch` block, if it never gets executed. The answer is that it's there in case any other exception gets thrown. It's not only our code that is covered by the `try` block. Inside the block, we actually make three separate calls to functions in the `System` namespace – we call `Console.ReadLine()`, `Console.Write()`, and `Convert.ToInt32()`. What happens if one of these methods throws an exception?

In fact this situation can occur. If we type in something that's not a number – say "a" or "hello", then the `Convert.ToInt32()` method will throw an exception of the class `System.FormatException`, to indicate that the string passed into `ToInt32()` is not in a format that can be converted to an `int`. When this happens, the computer will trace back through the method calls, looking for a handler that can handle this exception. Our first `catch` block (the one that takes an `IndexOutOfRangeException`) won't do. The computer then looks at the second `catch` block. This one will do because `FormatException` is derived from `Exception`, so a `FormatException` instance can be passed in as a parameter here.

The structure here is fairly typical. We start off with `catch` blocks that are designed to trap very specific error conditions. Then we finish with more general blocks that will cover any errors for which we have not written specific error handlers. The order of the `catch` blocks is important. If we'd written these two blocks in the opposite order, the code would not have compiled:

```
// WRONG - WILL NOT COMPILE!
catch (Exception e)
{
    Console.WriteLine("An exception was thrown. Message was: " +
                                                    e.Message);
}
catch (IndexOutOfRangeException e)
{
    Console.WriteLine("Exception: " +
                "Number should be between 0 and 5. " + e.Message);
}
```

The reason is that here the code in the second `catch` block is unreachable. If an `IndexOutOfRangeException` is thrown, this will be picked up by the first `catch` block. The compiler will detect this and refuse to compile the code. The rule is that you always put the handlers for the most-derived exception class first.

This leaves the third `catch` block: We've actually finished up the code with this:

```
catch
{
    Console.WriteLine("Some other exception has occurred");
}
```

This is the most general `catch` block of all – it doesn't take any parameter. The reason this `catch` block is here is that exceptions might be thrown by other code that isn't written in C#, or isn't even managed code at all. It is a requirement of the C# language that only instances of classes that are derived from `System.Exception` can be thrown as exceptions. Other languages might not have this restriction – C++ for example allows any variable whatsoever to be thrown as an exception. If your code calls into libraries or assemblies that have been written in other languages, then it may find an exception has been thrown that is not derived from `System.Exception`. Our final `catch` block will pick up any such exceptions. However, there's not that much that it can do – because we have no idea what class the exception might represent, there isn't any parameter type we can use to represent it. Even `object` won't do, since the exception might have been thrown by pre-.NET code, and so not even be derived from `System.Object`. We simply have no access to the exception object to find out what has happened.

For our particular example, there's probably not much point adding this catch-all `catch` handler. Doing this is useful if you're directly calling into some other libraries that are not .NET-aware and which might throw exceptions. However, we've included it in our example to illustrate the principle.

Now we've analyzed the code for the example, we can try running it. The following screenshot illustrates what happens with different input, and demonstrates both the `IndexOutOfRangeException` and the `FormatException` being thrown:

Handling Exceptions From Other Code

In our example, we've demonstrated the handling of two exceptions. One of them, `IndexOutOfRangeException`, was thrown by our own code. The other, `FormatException`, was thrown from inside one of the base classes. This is actually a very common paradigm. It is very common for code in a library to throw an exception if it detects some problem has occurred, or one of the methods has been called inappropriately by being passed the wrong parameters. However, code in libraries rarely attempts to catch the exceptions so thrown. It is regarded as the responsibility of the client code to decide how to deal with any such problems.

Often you'll find that exceptions get thrown from the base class libraries while you are debugging, and occur because of bugs in your own code that result in the wrong parameters being passed to base class methods. The process of debugging to some extent involves determining why exceptions have been thrown and removing the causes. Your aim should be to ensure that by the time the code is actually shipped, exceptions really do only occur in very exceptional circumstances, and if possible are handled in some appropriate way in your code.

Other System.Exception Properties and Methods

In our example, we have only illustrated the use of one property of the exception object, `Message`. However, we will note that a number of other properties are available in `System.Exception`:

Property	Description
HelpLink	If appropriate, a link to a help file that provides more information about the exception.
Message	The text that was supplied, usually to the constructor of the exception, that describes the error condition.
Source	The name of the application or object that caused the exception.

Property	Description
StackTrace	Details of the method calls on the stack. This can help track down the method that threw the exception.
TargetSite	The name of the method that threw the exception.

Of these properties, `StackTrace` and `TargetSite` are supplied automatically by the .NET runtime. Depending on your compilation options, `TargetSite` may be unavailable, in which case it returns null. `Source`, `Message`, and `HelpLink` must be supplied by the code that threw the exception, by setting these properties immediately before throwing the exception. The code to do this might look something like this:

```
if (ErrorCondition == true)
{
    Exception MyException = new ClassMyException("Help!!!!");
    MyException.Source = "My Application Name";
    MyException.HelpLink = "MyHelpFile.txt";
    throw MyException;
}
```

Where `ClassMyException` is the name of the particular exception class you are throwing. Note that it is usual practice for the names of all exception classes to end with `Exception`. Also, because this class must have been derived from `System.Exception`, it's fine to use a `System.Exception` reference to refer to it.

What Happens If An Exception Isn't Handled

Sometimes an exception might be thrown, and there might not be a `try` block in your code that is able to handle that kind of exception. Our `SimpleExceptions` example can serve to illustrate this. Suppose, for example, we omitted the `FormatException` and catch-all `catch` blocks, and only supplied the block that traps an `IndexOutOfRangeException` (perhaps the developer writing the code simply didn't think about the possibility of base classes raising their own exceptions). In that event, what would happen if a `FormatException` got thrown?

The answer is that the .NET runtime would catch it. Later in this section we'll see how it is possible to nest `try` blocks, which is something that has already been done behind the scenes in the sample. You see, the `try` block in our code *isn't* the only one in the program. The .NET runtime has effectively placed our entire program inside another huge `try` block – it does this for every .NET program. This `try` block has a `catch` handler that can catch any type of exception. If an exception occurs that your code doesn't handle, then the execution flow will simply pass right out of your program and get trapped by this `catch` block in the .NET runtime. However, the results probably won't be what you wanted. It means execution of your code will be promptly terminated and the user will get presented with a dialog box that complains about your code having not handled an exception, as well as giving whatever details of the exception the .NET runtime was able to retrieve. But at least the exception will have been caught! This is what actually happened in Chapter 5 in the `Vector` sample when our program threw an exception.

In general, if you are writing an executable, you should try to catch as many exceptions as you reasonably can, and handle them in a sensible way. If you are writing a library, it's normally best not to catch exceptions (unless a particular exception represents something wrong in your code which you can handle), but to assume instead that the calling code will handle them.

Base Class Exceptions

In this section we'll do a quick survey of some of the exceptions that are available in the base classes. After that, we'll move on to present a more complex example that demonstrates how to nest `try` blocks, and how to define your own exception classes.

There are a large number of classes that Microsoft has defined, and it is not possible to provide anything like an exhaustive list here. This class hierarchy diagram shows a few of them, however, in order to give a flavor of the general pattern:

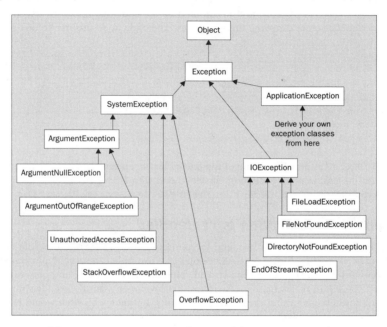

This table shows some of the `System` exceptions and some of the exceptions in the `System.IO` namespace. In this diagram, for reasons of clarity we have not given namespace names. Note, however, that all the classes in the diagram are in the `System` namespace, apart from `IOException` and the classes derived from `IOException`. These are in the namespace `System.IO`, which deals with reading and writing data to files. In general there is no specific namespace for exceptions; exception classes should be placed in whatever namespace is appropriate to the classes that they could be generated by – hence IO-related exceptions are in the `System.IO` namespace.

We're not going to explain in detail the various exception classes shown in diagram, since for the most part their purposes should be clear from their names, and our intention is in any case to give a general overview of the hierarchy. We will, however, note that:

❑ A `StackOverflowException` occurs if the area of memory allocated to the stack becomes completely full. Recall from Chapter 5 that we looked at how the stack is used to store method parameters and value data types. A stack overflow can occur if, for example, a method starts calling itself recursively. It is generally a fatal error since it prevents your application from doing anything else whatsoever, apart from terminating, and in this extreme case it's unlikely that even the `finally` block will execute. There is usually little point in your attempting to handle errors like this yourself.

❑ We'll cover streams in Chapter 14. A stream represents a flow of data between data sources. The usual cause of an EndOfStreamException is an attempt to read past the end of a file.

❑ An OverflowException is what will happen if for example you attempt to cast an int containing a value of –40 to a uint in a checked context.

We start off in the exception hierarchy with the generic exception object, System.Exception. As usual for any .NET class, this is derived from System.Object. In general you should not throw instances of this class your code. As already remarked, that is considered bad programming practice, because it gives no idea of the nature of the error condition.

There are two important classes in the hierarchy that are derived from System.Exception.

❑ System.SystemException – this is for exceptions that are usually thrown by the .NET runtime, or which are considered of a very generic nature and may be thrown by almost any application. As examples, StackOverflowException will be thrown by the .NET runtime if it detects the stack is full. On the other hand, you might choose to throw ArgumentException or its subclasses in your own code, if you detect that a method has been called with inappropriate arguments. Subclasses of System.SystemException include ones that represent both fatal and nonfatal errors.

❑ System.ApplicationException – this class is important, because it is the intended base for any class of exception defined by third parties (in other words, organizations other than Microsoft). Hence if you define any exceptions of your own which cover error conditions unique to your application, you should derive these directly or indirectly from System.ApplicationException.

These two exception classes and their subclasses together cover all those error conditions which are specific to third-party applications, or which are thrown by the .NET base classes or the .NET runtime and are generic to .NET. That leaves exceptions which are thrown by some of the base classes, but which are nevertheless specific to certain types of operation. In the diagram, we have drawn in the classes derived from System.IO.IOException as a good example of this. These exceptions represent some of the error conditions that can occur when attempting to read from files – an area which is covered by base classes in the System.IO namespace.

The class hierarchy for exceptions is somewhat unusual in that most of these classes do not add any functionality to their respective base classes. In most other situations when you derive a class from another class, you do so in order that you can override some methods (or properties etc.) or add new features through new methods. However, in the case of exception handling, the usual reason for adding inherited classes is simply to indicate more specific error conditions, and there is normally no need to override or add any methods. The idea of this hierarchy is that it enables you to use different catch blocks to narrow down the error condition your code handles as narrowly or as widely as you wish. For example you might have method for which you wish to trap any attempt to call it with inappropriate values passed in the method arguments. There might be some action that you take in general when this situation occurs, but there might be some different action that you wish to take in the particular case that an argument that should refer to an object instance actually contains null. You can handle this situation like this:

```
catch (ArgumentNullException e)
{
    // handle argument null error
}
catch (ArgumentException e)
{
    // handle all other argument-related problems
}
```

This ensures that if an `ArgumentNullException` is thrown, it will be trapped by the correct handling routine. If some other problem occurs with an argument which does not fall into this category however, for example, if your code detects an argument out of range and throws an `ArgumentOutOfRangeException`, then the runtime will ignore the first `catch` block, because it doesn't take the appropriate class of exception as an argument. The second `catch` block will, however, successfully catch and handle this exception.

Nested try Blocks

One nice feature of exceptions is that it is possible to nest `try` blocks inside each other. So you end up with code that looks a bit like this:

```
try
{
    // code for normal execution
    // Point A

    try
    {
        // code for normal execution
        // Point B
    }
    catch
    {
        // error handling
        // Point C
    }
    finally
    {
        // clean up
    }

    // more code for normal execution
    // Point D
}
catch
{
    // error handling
}
finally
{
    // clean up
}
```

For simplicity in this code, we've only placed one `catch` block with each of the two `try` blocks, and the following discussion talks about one `catch` block. But in each case we could string several `catch` blocks together.

The way nested `try` blocks work is like this: suppose an exception is thrown at either of the points marked A or D in the code snippet above. These points are completely outside the inner `try` block, and so will be handled in just the same way we already seen in this chapter – by the outer `catch` block, assuming that the outer `catch` block contains a handler for the appropriate exception type. This situation is handled just as if the inner `try` block wasn't there at all.

Suppose, however, that an exception is thrown at point B in the code. Now we are inside the inner try block, so the .NET runtime will look in the inner catch block for an appropriate handler. If it finds one, that handler will be executed, and then the inner finally block will be executed as usual, before execution continues at point D in the code. In other words, everything is dealt with by the inner try block and the outer try block does not enter the picture at all. Once again, it is as if there were only one try block in the program.

Now suppose an exception is thrown at point B, but that it is of a class for which no suitable handler exists in the inner catch block. Now the situation is a bit more interesting. The .NET runtime will have no choice but to leave the entire inner try block altogether in order to search for a handler. Since we are leaving the inner try block, any code in the inner finally block is executed as normal. (remember that code in a finally block is **always** executed when control leaves the associated try block, no matter what the reason for leaving the try block was). However, the code around point D will *not* be executed, because as soon as the inner finally block is completed the system will continue its search for a handler for the exception. The next obvious place to look is in the outer catch block. If the system finds one here then that handler will be executed and then the outer finally block. If there is no suitable handler here, then the search for one will go on. In this case it means the outer finally block will be executed, and then, since there are no more catch blocks, control will transfer to the .NET runtime which will terminate program execution and display the usual dialog box complaining about an unhandled exception. In this case, we see the two nested try blocks working together to find the best placed handler for the error condition.

An even more interesting thing happens if an exception is thrown at point C. If the program is at point C then it must be already processing an exception that was thrown at point B. It is in fact quite legitimate to throw another exception from inside a catch block (we'll see why you might do this soon). In this case the exception is treated as if it had been thrown by the outer try block, so flow of execution will immediately leave the inner catch block, execute the inner finally block, before the system searches the outer catch block for a handler. Similarly, if an exception is thrown in the inner finally block, control will immediately transfer to the best appropriate handler, with the search starting at the outer catch block.

Although we've shown the situation with just two try blocks, the same principles hold no matter how many try blocks you nest inside each other. At each stage the .NET runtime will smoothly transfer control up through the try blocks, looking for an appropriate handler. At each stage, as control leaves a catch block, any cleanup code in the corresponding finally block will be executed, but no code outside any finally block will be run until the correct catch handler has been found and run.

We've now shown how having nested try blocks can work. The obvious question is why would you want to do that? There are two reasons, which we will look at before we move on to our next example. This contains nested try loops and illustrates both of these motivations for using them. The two reasons for using nested try blocks are:

❑   To modify the type of exception thrown.

❑   To enable different types of exception to be handled in different places in your code.

Lets examine each of these reasons in a bit more detail.

Modifying the Type of Exception

Modifying the type of the exception can be useful when the original exception thrown does not adequately describe the problem. What typically happens is that something – possibly the .NET runtime – throws a fairly low-level exception that says something like an overflow occurred (OverflowException) or an argument passed to a method was incorrect (a class derived from ArgumentException). However, because of the context in which the exception occurred, you will know that this reveals some other underlying problem (for example, an overflow can only have happened because a file you've just read contained incorrect data). In that case, the most appropriate thing that your handler for the first exception can do is throw another exception that more accurately describes the problem, so that another catch block further along can deal with it more appropriately. In this case, it can also forward the original exception through a property implemented by System.Exception called InnerException. InnerException simply contains a reference to any other related exception that was thrown – in case the ultimate handler routine will need this extra information.

Of course we should also point out that an exception might genuinely occur inside a catch block. For example, you might normally read in some configuration file that contains detailed instructions for handling the error, and it might turn out that this file is not there.

Handling Different Exceptions in Different Places

The second reason for having nested try blocks is so that is different types of exception can be handled at different locations in your code. A good example of this might be if you have a loop. There may be various exception conditions that can occur inside the loop. Some of these might be serious enough that you need to abandon the entire loop, while others might be less serious and simply require that you abandon that iteration and move on to the next iteration around the loop. You could achieve this by having one try block inside the loop which handles the less serious error conditions, and an outer try block outside the loop, which handles the more serious error conditions. Again, we will see how this works in the exceptions example that we are going to unveil now.

Exceptions Example: MortimerColdCall

We are now ready to look at a second example that illustrates exceptions. This example, called MortimerColdCall, will contain two nested try blocks, and also illustrate the practice of defining our own custom exception classes, and throwing another exception from inside a try block.

For this example, we are going to return to the Mortimer Phones mobile phone company that we introduced in Chapter 4. We are going to assume that Mortimer Phones want some more customers. Their sales team is going to ring up a list of people to invite them to become customers, or to use sales jargon, they are going to "cold-call" some people. To this end we have a text file available that contains the names of the victims – sorry, clients – to be cold-called. The file should be in a well-defined format in which the first line contains the number of people in the file and each subsequent line contains the name of the next person. In other words a correctly formatted file of names might look like this:

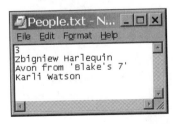

Since this is only an example, we are not really going to cold-call these people. Our version of cold-calling will be to display the name of the person on the screen (perhaps for the sales guy to read). That's why we've only put the names in the file. For the purposes of the example, we won't worry about reading in phone numbers.

Our program will ask the user for the name of the file, and will then simply read it in and display the names of people in it.

That sounds like a simple task, but even here there are a couple of things that can go wrong and require us to abandon the entire procedure:

1. The user might type in the name of a file that doesn't exist. This will be trapped as a `FileNotFound` exception.

2. The file might not be in the correct format. There are two possible problems here. Firstly, the first line of the file might not be an integer. Secondly, there might not be as many names in the file as the first line of the file indicates. In both cases we want to trap this as a custom exception that we've written specially for this purpose, `ColdCallFileFormatException`.

There is also something else that could go wrong which won't cause us to abandon the entire process, but which will mean we need to abandon that person and move on to the next person in the file (and hence this will need to be trapped by an inner `try` block). Some people are spies working for rival land-line telephone companies, and obviously we wouldn't want to let these people know what we are up to by accidentally phoning one of them. Our research has indicated that we can identify who the land-line spies are because their names begin with Z. Such people should have been screened out when the data file was first prepared, but just in case any have slipped through, we will need to check each name in the file, and throw a `LandLineSpyFoundException` if we detect a land-line spy. This, of course, is another custom exception object.

Finally, we will implement this sample by coding up a class, `ColdCallFileReader`, which maintains the connection to the cold-call file and retrieves data from it. We'll code up this class in a very safe way, which means its methods will all throw exceptions if they are called inappropriately – for example, if a method requiring a file read is called before the file has been opened. For this purpose, we will code up another exception class, `UnexpectedException`.

Defining Our Own Exception Classes

To start off with, we need to define the three exceptions of our own. Defining our own exception is quite easy, since there are rarely any extra methods to add. It's just a case of implementing a constructor to ensure that the base class constructor is called correctly. Here's the full implementation of `LandLineSpyFoundException`:

```
class LandLineSpyFoundException : ApplicationException
{
    public LandLineSpyFoundException(string spyName)
        :   base("LandLine spy found, with name " + spyName)
    {
    }

    public LandLineSpyFoundException(string spyName,
                                Exception innerException)
        :   base("LandLine spy found, with name " + spyName, innerException)
    {
    }
}
```

Notice we've derived it from `ApplicationException`, as you'd expect for a custom exception. In fact, if we'd been going about this even more formally, we'd probably have put in an intermediate class, something like `ColdCallFileException`, derived from `ApplicationException`, and derived both of our exception classes from this class, just to make sure that the handling code has that extra fine degree of control over which exception handlers handles which exception. But to keep the example simple, we won't do that.

We've done one bit of processing in `LandLineSpyFoundException`. We've assumed the "message" passed into its constructor is just the name of the spy found, and so turn this string into a more meaningful error message. We've also provided two constructors, one that simply takes a message, and one that also takes an inner exception as a parameter. When defining your own exception classes, it's best to include as a minimum at least these two constructors (although as it happens, we won't actually be using the second `LandLineSpyFoundException` constructor in this sample).

Now for the `ColdCallFileFormatException`. This follows the same principles, except that we don't do any processing on the message:

```
class ColdCallFileFormatException : ApplicationException
{
    public ColdCallFileFormatException(string Message)
        :   base(Message)
    {
    }

    public ColdCallFileFormatException(string Message,
                                       Exception InnerException)
        :   base(Message, InnerException)
    {
    }
}
```

And finally, `UnexpectedException`, which looks much the same as `ColdCallFileFormatException`:

```
class UnexpectedException : ApplicationException
{
    public UnexpectedException(string message)
        :   base(message)
    {
    }

    public UnexpectedException(string message, Exception innerException)
        :   base(message, innerException)
    {
    }
}
```

The Main() Method

Here's what the `Main()` method of the `MortimerColdCall` sample looks like. Notice that because we are going to be doing some file handling, we will be calling up stuff in the `System.IO` namespace as well as the `System` namespace.

We will cover how to read and write to files in in Chapter 14. But don't worry, the little bit of file processing we do here is very easy, and the code for it is quite intuitive.

```
using System;
using System.IO;

namespace Wrox.ProfessionalCSharp.Chapter6.MortimerColdCall
{
    class MainEntryPoint
    {
        static void Main(string[] args)
        {
            string fileName;
            Console.Write("Please type in the name of the file " +
                "\ncontaining the names of the people to be cold-called > ");
            fileName = Console.ReadLine();
            ColdCallFileReader peopleToRing = new ColdCallFileReader();

            try
            {
                peopleToRing.Open(fileName);
                for (int i=0 ; i<peopleToRing.NPeopleToRing; i++)
                {
                    peopleToRing.ProcessNextPerson();
                }
                Console.WriteLine("All callees processed correctly");
            }
            catch(FileNotFoundException e)
            {
                Console.WriteLine("The file {0} does not exist", fileName);
            }
            catch(ColdCallFileFormatException e)
            {
                Console.WriteLine("The file {0} appears to have been corrupted",
                                    fileName);
                Console.WriteLine("Details of problem are: {0}", e.Message);
                if (e.InnerException != null)
                    Console.WriteLine("Inner exception was: {0}",
                                        e.InnerException.Message);
            }
            catch(Exception e)
            {
                Console.WriteLine("Exception occurred:\n" + e.Message);
            }
            finally
            {
                peopleToRing.Dispose();
            }
        }
    }
```

This code is basically little more than a loop to process people from the file. We start off by asking the user for the name of the file. Then we instantiate an object of a class called `ColdCallFileReader`. This is the class that handles the reading in of data from the file. Notice that we do this outside the initial `try` block – that's because the variables that we instantiate here need to be available in the subsequent `catch` and `finally` blocks, and if we declared them inside the `try` block they'd go out of scope at the closing curly brace of the `try` block.

The `try` block basically opens the file (`ColdCallFileReader.Open()` method), and loops over all the people in it. The `ColdCallFileReader.ProcessNextPerson()` method that we will define just reads in and displays the name of the next person in the file, while the `ColdCallFileReader.NPeopleToRing` property tells us how many people should be in the file (as obtained by reading the first line of the file).

There are three `catch` blocks, one for each of the exceptions `FileNotFoundException` and `ColdCallFileFormatException`, and a third `catch` block that will trap any other .NET errors – which exists just in case anything else goes wrong. It would be this `catch` block that would handle, for example, any `UnexpectedExceptions`.

In the case of a `FileNotFound` exception, we display a message to that effect. Notice that in this `catch` block, we don't actually use the exception instance at all. The reason is that I decided to use this `catch` block to illustrate the user-friendliness of our application. Exception objects generally contain technical information that is useful for developers, but not the sort of stuff you want to show to your end users. So in this case we create a simpler message of our own.

For the `ColdCallFileFormatException` handler, we've done the opposite, and illustrated how to give fuller technical information, including details of the inner exception, if one is present.

Finally, we catch any other generic exception that is derived from `System.Exception`. This is just so we can display a user-friendly message, instead of letting any such exceptions fall through to the exception-not-handled dialog that the .NET runtime will give us if we don't handle an exception. However, we've chosen not to handle any other exceptions not derived from `System.Exception`. We are not calling directly into pre-.NET code here, so any such exceptions would certainly indicate something seriously, probably fatally wrong anyway.

The `finally` block is there to clean up resources. In this case, this means closing any open file. The `ColdCallFileReader.Dispose()` method does just that.

The ColdCallFileReader Class

Now let's have a look at the definition of the class that handles the file reading. Because this class maintains an external file connection, we will need to make sure it gets disposed of correctly in accordance with the principles we laid down for disposing objects in Chapter 5. Hence we derive this class from `IDisposable`.

First, we declare a couple of variables:

```
class ColdCallFileReader : IDisposable
{
    FileStream fs;
    StreamReader sr;
    uint nPeopleToRing;
    bool isDisposed = false;
    bool isOpen = false;
```

`FileStream` and `StreamReader`, both in the `System.IO` namespace, are the base classes that we will use to read the file. `FileStream` allows us to connect to the file in the first place, while `StreamReader` is specially geared up to reading text files, and implements a method, `StreamReader()`, which reads a line of text from a file.

The isDisposed field is concerned with the destruction (finalization) process. It indicates whether Dispose() has been called, while isOpen is also used for error checking – in this case, checking whether the StreamReader actually connects to an open file.

The process of opening the file and reading in that first line – the one that tells us how many people are in the file – is handled by the Open() method:

```csharp
public void Open(string fileName)
{
    fs = new FileStream(fileName, FileMode.Open);
    sr = new StreamReader(fs);
    if (isDisposed)
        throw new UnexpectedException(
            "Attempt to open cold-call file after Dispose() called.");
    try
    {
        string FirstLine = sr.ReadLine();
        nPeopleToRing = uint.Parse(FirstLine);
        isOpen = true;
    }
    catch (FormatException e)
    {
        throw new ColdCallFileFormatException(
                            "First line isn\'t an integer", e);
    }
}
```

This method contains the first of two inner try blocks. The purpose of this one is to catch any errors resulting from the first line of the file not containing an integer. If that problem arises, the .NET runtime will throw a FormatException, which we trap and convert to a more meaningful exception that indicates that there is actually a problem with the format of the cold-call file. Note that System.FormatException is there to indicate format problems with basic data types, not with files, and so is not a particularly useful exception to pass back to the calling routine in this case. The new exception thrown will be trapped by the outermost try block. Notice that since there is no cleanup needed here, there is no need for a finally block.

The Open() method also checks the isDisposed field to check whether Dispose() has already been called. Since calling Dispose() implies the caller has now finished with this object, we regard it as an error to attempt to open a new file connection if Dispose() has been called.

If everything goes OK, we set the isOpen field to true to indicate that there is now a valid file connection from which data can be read.

The ProcessNextPerson() method also contains an inner try block:

```csharp
public void ProcessNextPerson()
{
    if (!isOpen)
        throw new UnexpectedException(
                        "Attempt to access cold call file that is not open");
    try
    {
        string name;
        name = sr.ReadLine();
        if (name.Length == 0)
            throw new ColdCallFileFormatException("Not enough names");
```

```
        if (name[0] == 'Z')
        {
            throw new LandLineSpyFoundException(name);
        }
        Console.WriteLine(name);
    }
    catch(LandLineSpyFoundException e)
    {
        Console.WriteLine(e.Message);
    }
    finally
    {
    }
}
```

There are two possible problems with the file here (assuming there actually is an open file connection – the ProcessNextPerson() method checks this first). First, we might read in the next name and discover that it is a land-line spy. If that condition occurs, the exception is trapped by the first of the catch blocks in this method. Because that exception has been caught here, inside the loop, it means that execution can subsequently continue in the Main() method of the program, and the subsequent names in the file will continue to be processed.

A problem may also occur if we try to read the next name and discover we've already reached the end of the file. The way that the StreamReader's ReadLine() method works, if it's got past the end of the file it doesn't throw an exception, but simply returns an empty string. So if we find an empty string, we know that the format of the file was incorrect, in that the number in the first line of the file indicated a larger number of names than were actually present in the file. If that happens, we throw a ColdCallFileFormatException, which will be caught by the outer exception handler (which will cause execution to terminate).

Once again here, we don't need a finally block, since there's no cleanup to do, but this time we've put an empty one in, just to show that you can do that if you want.

We've nearly finished the example. We just have three more members of ColdCallFileReader to look at: the NPeopleToRing property, which returns the number of people supposed to be in the file, and the Dispose() method and destructor, which both close the file if one is open. Notice that the Dispose() method checks that there actually is a file stream to close and subsequently sets the file stream reference to null. This will ensure that there won't be any problems if for some reason a client attempts to call Dispose() more than once.

```
public uint NPeopleToRing
{
    get
    {
        if (!isOpen)
            throw new UnexpectedException(
                        "Attempt to access cold call file that is not open");
        return nPeopleToRing;
    }
}
```

```
public void Dispose()
{
    if (fs != null)
        fs.Close();
    fs = null;
    GC.SuppressFinalize(this);
    isDisposed = true;
    isOpen = false;
}

~ColdCallFileReader()
{
    if (fs != null)
        fs.Close();
}
```

Now we are ready to test the program. First, try the `people.txt` file whose contents we displayed earlier. This has three names (which matches the number given in the first line of the file). Then try the `people2.txt` file, which has an obvious formatting error:

Finally, try the example with `people3.txt`, which does not exist.

Running the program three times for the three filenames gives these results:

```
F:\>MortimerColdCall
Please type in the name of the file
containing the names of the people to be cold-called > people.txt
LandLine spy found, with name Zbigniew Harlequin
Avon from 'Blake's 7'
Karli Watson
All callees processed correctly

F:\>MortimerColdCall
Please type in the name of the file
containing the names of the people to be cold-called > people2.txt
LandLine spy found, with name Zbigniew Harlequin
Avon from 'Blake's 7'
Karli Watson
The file people2.txt appears to have been corrupted
Details of problem are: Not enough names

F:\>MortimerColdCall
Please type in the name of the file
containing the names of the people to be cold-called > people3.txt
The file people3.txt does not exist

F:\>
F:\>
```

User-Defined Casts

In Chapter 3, we examined how you can convert values between predefined data types. We saw that this is done through a process of casting. We also saw that C# allows two different types of casts: implicit and explicit. The difference is that for an explicit cast, you explicitly mark the cast in your code by writing the destination data type inside parentheses:

```
int I = 3;
long L = I;          // implicit
short S = (short)I   // explicit
```

For the predefined data types, explicit casts are required where there is a risk that the cast might fail or some data might be lost – for example if converting from an int to a short, as the short might not be large enough to hold the value. Other examples are that converting from signed to unsigned data types will return incorrect results if the signed variable holds a negative value, and when converting from floating point to integer data types, the fractional part of the number will be lost. The idea is that by making the cast explicit in your code, you are affirming to the compiler that you understand that there is a risk of data loss, and therefore presumably you have written your code to take this possibility into account.

Since C# allows you to define your own structs and classes, which in effect means that you are defining your own data types, you would expect that there would be some facility to allow casts between your data types too. C# does indeed allow this. The mechanism is that you can define a cast as a member operator of one of the relevant classes. Your cast must be marked as either implicit or explicit to indicate how you are intending it to be used. The expectation is that you follow the same guidelines as for the predefined casts. That is to say, if you know the cast is always safe, whatever the value held by the source variable, then you define it as implicit. If on the other hand you know there is a risk of something going wrong for certain values – perhaps some loss of data or an exception being thrown, then you should define the cast as explicit.

> **You should define any custom casts you write as explicit if there are any source data values for which the cast will fail, or if there is any risk of an exception being thrown.**

The syntax for defining a cast is a similar to that for overloading operators. This is not a coincidence, since in a way a cast can be regarded as an operator whose effect is to convert from the source type to the destination type. To illustrate the syntax, the following is taken from the sample that we will introduce later in this section:

```
public static implicit operator float (Currency value)
{
    // etc.
```

This code is part of a struct, Currency, which is used to store an amount of money. The cast defined here allows us to implicitly convert the value of a Currency into a float. Note that if a conversion has been declared as implicit, then the compiler will permit its use either implicitly or explicitly. If it has been declared as explicit, the compiler will only permit it to be used explicitly.

In this declaration, the cast has been declared as static. In common with operator overloads, C# requires casts to be static. This means that each cast also takes one parameter, which is of the data type of the source.

C++ developers will notice that this is the opposite of the situation in C++, in which casts are instance members of classes.

Example: The Currency Struct

In this section, we will illustrate the use of implicit and explicit user-defined casts in a sample called `SimpleCurrency` (which as usual is found in the code download). In this sample, we will define a struct, `Currency`, that holds a positive US$ monetary value. Normally, C# provides the `decimal` type for this purpose, but it's possible you might still want to write your own struct or class to represent monetary values if you want to perform sophisticated financial processing, and therefore want to implement specific methods on such a class.

The syntax for casting is the same for structs and classes. Our example happens to be for a struct, but would work just as well if we declared `Currency` *as a class.*

Initially, the definition of the currency structure is as follows:

```
struct Currency
{
   public uint Dollars;
   public ushort Cents;

   public Currency(uint Dollars, ushort Cents)
   {
      this.Dollars = Dollars;
      this.Cents = Cents;
   }

   public override string ToString()
   {
      return string.Format("${0}.{1,-2:00}", Dollars,Cents);
   }
}
```

The use of unsigned data types for the `Dollar` and `Cents` fields ensures that a `Currency` instance can only hold positive values. We're restricting it this way so that we can illustrate some points about explicit casts later on. The sort of situation in which you might wish to use a class like this might be, for example, to hold salary information for employees of a company (people's salaries tend not to be negative!). In order to keep the class simple, we are making our fields public, but usually you would make them private and define corresponding properties for the dollars and cents.

Let's start off by assuming that we want to be able to convert `Currency` instances to `float` values, where the integer part of the `float` represents the dollars. In other words we would like to be able to write code like this:

```
Currency Balance = new Currency(10,50);
float D = Balance; // We want D to be set to 10.5
```

To be able to do this, we need to define a cast. Hence we add the following to our `Currency` definition:

```
struct Currency
{
   // etc.

   public static implicit operator float (Currency value)
   {
      return value.Dollars + (value.Cents/100.0f);
   }
}
```

This cast is implicit. This is a sensible choice in this case, because, as should be clear from the definition of `Currency`, any value that can be stored in the currency can also be stored in a `float`. There's no way that anything should ever go wrong in this cast.

> *There is a slight cheat here – our definition of "nothing going wrong" is fairly broad; in fact, when converting a `uint` to a `float`, there can be a loss in precision, but Microsoft have deemed this error sufficiently marginal to count the `uint-to-float` cast as implicit anyway.*

What about converting back? In other words if we have a floating-point value, a `float`, which we would like to be converted to a currency. In this case the conversion is not guaranteed to work; `float`s can store negative values, which `Currency` instances can't, and they can store numbers of a far higher magnitude than can be stored in the (`uint`) `Dollar` field of `Currency`. So if a `float` contains an inappropriate value, converting it to a `Currency` could give unpredictable results. Because of this risk, the conversion from `float` to `Currency` should be defined as explicit. Here's our first attempt:

```
   public static explicit operator Currency (float value)
   {
      uint Dollars = (uint)value;
      ushort Cents = (ushort)((value-Dollars)*100);
      return new Currency(Dollars, Cents);
   }
```

In this code, we first work out the number of dollars as the integer part of the amount supplied. Suppose the value passed in is `45.63f`. Converting this to a `uint` gives `45` – which is the number of dollars. The difference between this and the original `float` is 0.63 – and multiplying that by 100 gives the number of cents.

The following code will now successfully compile:

```
   float Amount = 45.63f;
   Currency Amount2 = (Currency)Amount;
```

However, the following code will generate a compilation error, because you've attempted to use an explicit cast implicitly:

```
   float Amount = 45.63f;
   Currency Amount2 = Amount;   // wrong
```

Is this good enough? By making the cast explicit, you certainly warn the developer to be careful because data corruption might take place. But for the above example, this probably isn't what we really want. We will try writing a test harness and running the sample. Here's the `Main()` method, which instantiates a `Currency` struct and attempts a few conversions. At the start of this code, we write out the value of `balance` in two different ways (because I will want to use this to illustrate something else later on):

```
static void Main(string[] args)
{
   try
   {
      Currency balance = new Currency(50,35);
      Console.WriteLine("balance is " + balance);
      Console.WriteLine("balance is (using ToString()) " +
                        balance.ToString());
      float balance2= balance;
      Console.WriteLine("After converting to float, = " + balance2);
      balance = (Currency) balance2;
      Console.WriteLine("After converting back to Currency, = " + balance);

      Console.WriteLine("Now attempt to convert out of range value of " +
                        "-$100.00 to a Currency:");
      checked
      {
         balance = (Currency) (-50.5);
         Console.WriteLine("Result is " + balance.ToString());
      }
   }
   catch(Exception e)
   {
      Console.WriteLine("Exception occurred: " + e.Message);
   }
}
```

Notice that we've placed the entire code in a `try` block to catch any exceptions that occur during our casts. And we've placed the lines that test converting an out-of-range value to `Currency` in a `checked` block as well, so this looks like the negative value will be trapped. Or will it? Running this code gives this output:

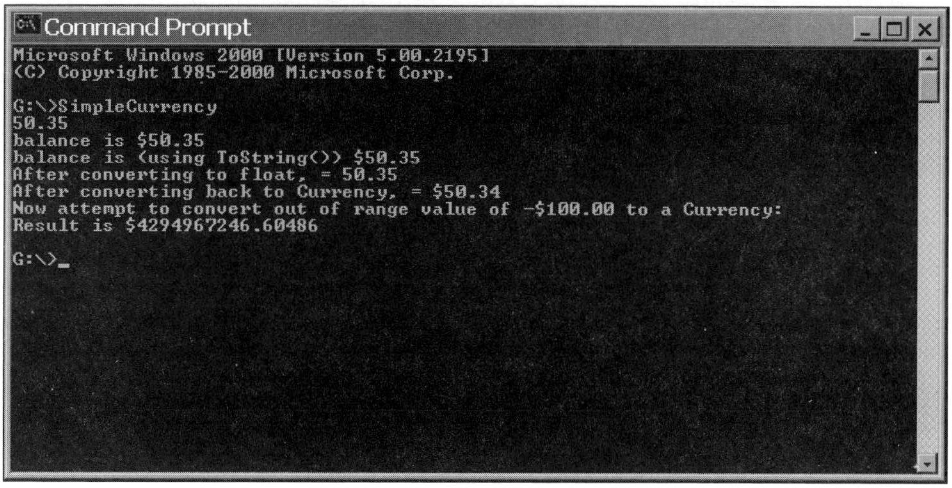

Most of the code worked fine, except that no exception was generated. The problem is not hard to identify, though. The place where the overflow really occurs isn't actually in the `Main()` routine at all – it's inside the code for the cast operator, which is called from the `Main()` method. And we didn't mark that code as `checked`.

One solution is to ensure that the cast itself is computed in a checked context too:

```
public static explicit operator Currency (float value)
{
    checked
    {
        uint Dollars = (uint)value;    // overflow happens here when
                                       // value is negative
        ushort Cents = (ushort)((value-Dollars)*100);
        return new Currency(Dollars, Cents);
    }
}
```

This will ensure that an exception is correctly generated as required (even if the calling code is not checked). Alternatively, you may prefer to throw your own exception from within the cast, which would take slightly more coding, but would allow you to supply a more specific error message. We won't show a new screenshot with this new checked cast just yet, because we have some more modifications to make to the SimpleCurrency example later in this section.

Of course, if you are defining a cast which will be used very often, and for which performance is at an absolute premium, you may prefer not to do any error checking. That's also a legitimate solution, provided the behavior of your cast and the lack of error checking are very clearly documented.

Although our example here involved converting to or from a float, the syntax is identical for other data types, and is also the same if you wish to define a cast between two classes or structs. A cast does not have to involve a predefined data type.

Casts Between Classes

Our Currency example involved only classes that converted to or from float – one of the predefined data types. However, it's not necessary to involve any of the simple data types. It's perfectly legitimate to defined casts to convert between instances of different structs or classes that you have defined. There are a couple of restrictions to be aware of, however. These are:

❑ You cannot cast between classes where one of them is inherited directly or indirectly from the other one.

❑ The cast must be defined inside the definition of either the source or destination data type.

To illustrate these requirements, suppose you have the following situation:

```
class A
{
    // implementation
}

class B : public A
{
    // implementation
}
```

```
class C : public B
{
    // implementation
}

class D : public B
{
    // implementation
}
```

In other words we have this class hierarchy:

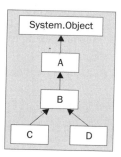

With this situation, it is quite legitimate to define casts to convert between classes C and D, because these classes are not derived from each other. The code to do so might look like this (if you want the casts to be implicit):

```
public static implicit operator D(C value)
{
    // etc.
}
public static implicit operator C(D value)
{
    // etc.
}
```

For each of these casts, you have a choice of where you place the definitions – inside the class definition of C, or inside the class definition of D, but not anywhere else. C# requires you to put the definition of a cast inside either the source class (or struct) or the destination class (or struct). A side effect of this is that you can't define a cast between two classes unless you have access to edit the source code for at least one of them. This is sensible because it prevents third parties from introducing casts into your classes.

Another point is that once you've defined a cast inside one of the classes, you can't define the same cast inside the other class. Obviously, there should only be one cast for each conversion – otherwise the compiler wouldn't know which one to pick.

However, with the above hierarchy, C-to-D and D-to-C are the only casts that you may define. Anything else (such as A-to-C or D-to-B) will cause a compilation error, because C# does not permit user-defined casts between derived classes. The reason for this is quite simple: such casts already exist. It is always possible to cast implicitly from derived class to base class, and explicitly from base class to derived class, as we'll explain next.

Casts Between Base and Derived Classes

To see how these casts work, let's start by considering the case where the source and destination are both reference types, and consider two classes, `MyBase` and `MyDerived`, where `MyDerived` is derived directly or indirectly from `MyBase`.

Firstly from `MyDerived` to `MyBase`: it is always possible (assuming the constructors are available) to write:

```
MyDerived DerivedObject = new MyDerived();
MyBase BaseCopy = DerivedObject;
```

In this case, we are casting implicitly from `MyDerived` to `MyBase`. This works because of the rule that any reference to a type `MyBase` is allowed to refer to objects of class `MyBase` or to objects of anything derived from `MyBase`. This is possible because – as remarked in the last chapter – instances of a derived class are in a real sense instances of the base class, plus something extra. All the functions and fields defined on the base class are defined in the derived class too.

Next the other way round. We can write:

```
MyBase DerivedObject = new MyDerived();
MyBase BaseObject = new MyBase();
MyDerived DerivedCopy1 = (MyDerived) DerivedObject;   // OK
MyDerived DerivedCopy2 = (MyDerived) BaseObject;      // throws exception
```

All the above code is perfectly legal C#, and illustrates casting from a base class to a derived class. However, the final statement will throw an exception when executed. What happens when we perform the cast is that the object being referred to is examined. Since a base class reference can in principle refer to a derived class instance, it is possible that this object is actually an instance of the derived class that we are attempting to cast to. If that's the case then the cast succeeds, and the derived reference is set to refer to the object. If, however, the object in question is not an instance of the derived class (or of any class derived from it) then the cast fails and an exception is thrown.

Notice that the casts that the compiler has supplied that convert between base and derived class do not actually do any data conversion on the object in question. All they do is set the new reference to refer to the object if it is legal for that conversion to occur. To that extent, these casts are different in nature to the ones that you will normally define yourself. For example, in our `SimpleCurrency` sample earlier, we defined casts that convert between a `Currency` struct and a `float`. In the `float`-to-`Currency` cast, we actually instantiated a new `Currency` struct and initialized it with the required values. Similarly, in our later example of a hierarchy, if we actually defined a cast from C-to-D, the implementation would probably look like this:

```
public static implicit operator D(C value)
{
    D Result = new D();
    // code to initialize D with appropriate values,
    // depending on contents of C
    return D;
}
```

Again, we're actually instantiating a new object here with values based on an old object. The predefined casts between base and derived classes do not do this. If you do want that sort of functionality – that is, you actually want to convert a `MyBase` instance into a real `MyDerived` object with values based on the contents of the `MyBase` instance, you would not be able to use the cast syntax to do this – you would instead have to write a method to do the conversion:

```
class Base
{
    public Derived ToDerived()
    {
        Derived Result = new Derived();
        // initialize Result with values based on this
        return Result;
    }
}
```

Boxing and Unboxing Casts

The above discussion focused on casting between base and derived classes where both were reference types. Similar principles apply when casting value types, although in this case it is not possible to simply copy references – some copying of data must take place.

It is not, of course, possible to derive from structs or primitive value types. So casting between base and derived structs invariably means casting between a primitive type or a struct and System.Object (theoretically, it is possible to cast between a struct and System.ValueType, though it's hard to see why you would want to do this).

The cast from any struct (or primitive type) to object is always available as an implicit cast – since it is a cast from derived to base type – and is just the familiar process of boxing that we have encountered briefly in Chapter 3. For example, with our Currency struct:

```
Currency Balance = new Currency(40,0);
object BaseCopy = Balance;
```

When the above implicit cast is executed, the contents of Balance are copied onto the heap, and the BaseCopy object reference set to refer to them. What actually happens behind the scenes is this: when we originally defined the Currency struct, the .NET framework implicitly supplied another (hidden) class, a boxed Currency class, which contains all the same fields as the Currency struct, but which is a reference type, stored on the heap. This happens whenever we define a value type – whether it is a struct or enum, and similar boxed reference types exist corresponding to all the primitive value types of int, double, uint, and so on. It is not possible to gain any direct programmatic access to any of these boxed classes in source code, but they are the objects that are working behind the scenes whenever a value type is cast to object. When we implicitly cast Currency to object, a boxed Currency instance gets instantiated, and initialized with all the data from the Currency struct. In the above code, it is this boxed Currency instance that BaseCopy will refer to. By this means it is possible for casting from derived to base type to work in syntactically the same way for value types as for reference types.

Casting the other way is known as **unboxing**. Just as for casting between a base reference type and a derived reference type, it is an explicit cast, since an exception will be thrown if the object being cast is not of the correct type:

```
object DerivedObject = new Currency(40,0);
object BaseObject = new object();
Currency DerivedCopy1 = (Currency)DerivedObject;   // OK
Currency DerivedCopy2 = (Currency)BaseObject;       // Exception thrown
```

The above code works analogously to the similar code presented earlier for reference types. Casting `DerivedObject` to `Currency` works fine, because `DerivedObject` actually refers to a boxed `Currency` instance – the cast will be performed by copying the fields out of the boxed `Currency` object into a new `Currency` struct. The second cast fails because `BaseObject` does not refer to a boxed `Currency` object.

Multiple Casting

One thing you will have to watch for when you're defining casts is that if the C# compiler is presented with a situation in which no direct cast is available to perform a requested conversion, it will attempt to find a way of combining casts to do the conversion. For example, with our `Currency` struct, suppose the compiler encounters a couple of lines of code like this:

```
Currency Balance = new Currency(10,50);
long Amount = (long)Balance;
double AmountD = Balance;
```

We first initialize a `Currency` instance, then we attempt to convert it to a `long`. The trouble is we haven't defined the cast that will do that. However, this code will still compile successfully. What will happen is that the compiler will realize that you have defined an implicit cast to get from `Currency` to `float`, and it knows how to explicitly cast a `float` to a `long`. Hence, it will compile that line of code into intermediate language code that converts balance first to a `float`, then converts that result to a `long`. The same thing happens in the final line of the above code, when we convert `Balance` to a `double`. However since the cast from `Currency` to `float` and the predefined cast from `float` to `double` are both implicit, we can write this conversion in our code as an implicit cast. If we'd preferred we could have specified the casting route explicitly:

```
Currency Balance = new Currency(10,50);
long Amount = (long)(float)Balance;
double AmountD = (double)(float)Balance;
```

However, in most cases this would be seen as needlessly complicating your code.

The following code by contrast would produce a compilation error:

```
Currency Balance = new Currency(10,50);
long Amount = Balance;
```

The reason is that best match for the conversion that the compiler can find is still to convert first to `float` then to `long`. But the conversion to from `float` to `long` needs to be specified explicitly. Even this code would generate an error:

```
Currency Balance = new Currency(10,50);
long Amount = (float) Balance;
```

since in this case we've (needlessly) made the first part of the conversion explicit, but not done so for the `float`-to-`long` conversion.

All this by itself shouldn't give you too much trouble. The rules are after all fairly intuitive and designed to prevent any data loss from occurring without the developer knowing about it. However, the problem is that if you're not careful when you define your casts, it's possible for the compiler to figure out a path that leads to unexpected results. For example, suppose it occurs to someone else in the group that's writing the Currency class that it would be useful to be able to convert a uint that contains the total number of cents in an amount into a Currency (cents not dollars because the idea is not to lose the fractions of a dollar). So this cast might be written to try to achieve this:

```
// DON'T DO THIS!
public static implicit operator Currency (uint value)
{
    return new Currency(value/100u, (ushort)(value%100));
}
```

Note the u after the first 100 in this code to ensure that value/100u is interpreted as a uint. If we'd written value/100 then the compiler would have interpreted this as an int, not a uint.

We've clearly commented "Don't do this" into this code, and here's why: look at the following code snippet; all we do in it is convert a uint containing 350 into a Currency and back again. What do you think Bal2 will contain after executing this?

```
uint Bal = 350;
Currency Balance = Bal;
uint Bal2 = (uint)Balance;
```

The answer is not 350, but 3! And it all follows logically. We covert 350 implicitly to a Currency, giving the result Balance.Dollars=3, Balance.Cents=50. Then the compiler does its usual figuring out of best path for the conversion back. Balance ends up getting implicitly converted to a float (value 3.5), and this gets converted explicitly to a uint – value 3.

Of course, other instances do exist in which converting to another data type and back again causes data loss. For example, converting a float containing 5.8 to an int and back to a float again will lose the fractional part, giving a result of 5. But there's a slight difference in principle between losing the fractional part of a number and "accidentally" dividing an integer by more than 100! Currency has suddenly become a rather dangerous class that does strange things to integers!

The problem is, of course, that there's a conflict between how our casts interpret integers. Our casts between Currency and float interpret an integer value of 1 as corresponding to one dollar, but our latest uint-to-Currency cast interprets this value as one cent. This is an example of very poor design. If you want your classes to be easy to use, then you should make sure all your casts behave in a way that is mutually compatible, in the sense that they intuitively give the same results. In this case, the solution is obviously to rewrite our uint-to-Balance cast so that it interprets an integer value of 1 as one dollar:

```
// OK!
public static implicit operator Currency (uint value)
{
    return new Currency(value, 0);
}
```

Incidentally, you might wonder whether this new cast is necessary at all. The answer is that it could be useful. Without this cast, the only way for the compiler to carry out a uint-to-Currency conversion would be via a float. Converting directly is a lot more efficient in this case, so having this extra cast gives performance benefits, but we need to make sure it gives the same result as we would get going via a float, which we've now done. In other situations, you may also find that separately defining casts for different predefined data types allows more conversions to be implicit rather than explicit, though that's not the case here.

A good test of whether your casts are compatible is to ask whether a conversion will give the same results (other than perhaps a loss of accuracy as in float-to-int conversions), irrespective of which path it takes. Our Currency class provides a good example of this. Look at this code:

```
Currency Balance = new Currency(50, 35);
ulong Bal = (ulong) Balance;
```

At present, there is only one way that the compiler can achieve this conversion: by converting the Currency to a float implicitly, then to a ulong explicitly. The float-to-ulong conversion requires an explicit conversion, but that's OK because we've provided one here.

Suppose, however, that we then added another cast, to convert implicitly from a Currency to a uint. We will actually do this by modifying the Currency struct by adding the casts both to and from uint. This code is available as the SimpleCurrency2 sample:

```
// OK!
public static implicit operator Currency (uint value)
{
    return new Currency(value, 0);
}
```

```
public static implicit operator uint (Currency value)
{
    return value.Dollars;
}
```

Now the compiler has another possible route to convert from Currency to ulong: to convert from Currency to uint implicitly then to ulong implicitly. Which of these two routes will it take? C# does have some precise rules (which we won't detail in this book, as they are in the MSDN documentation) to say how the compiler decides which is the best route if there are several possibilities. But the best answer is that you should design your casts so that all routes give the same answer (other than possible loss of precision), in which case it doesn't really matter which one the compiler picks. (As it happens in this case, the compiler picks the Currency-to-uint-to-ulong route in preference to Currency-to-float-to-ulong.)

To test the SimpleCurrency2 sample, we'll add this code to the test harness for simple currency:

```
try
{
    Currency balance = new Currency(50,35);
    Console.WriteLine(balance);
    Console.WriteLine("balance is " + balance);
    Console.WriteLine("balance is (using ToString()) " + balance.ToString());

    uint balance3 = (uint) balance;
    Console.WriteLine("Converting to uint gives " + balance3);
```

Running the sample now gives these results:

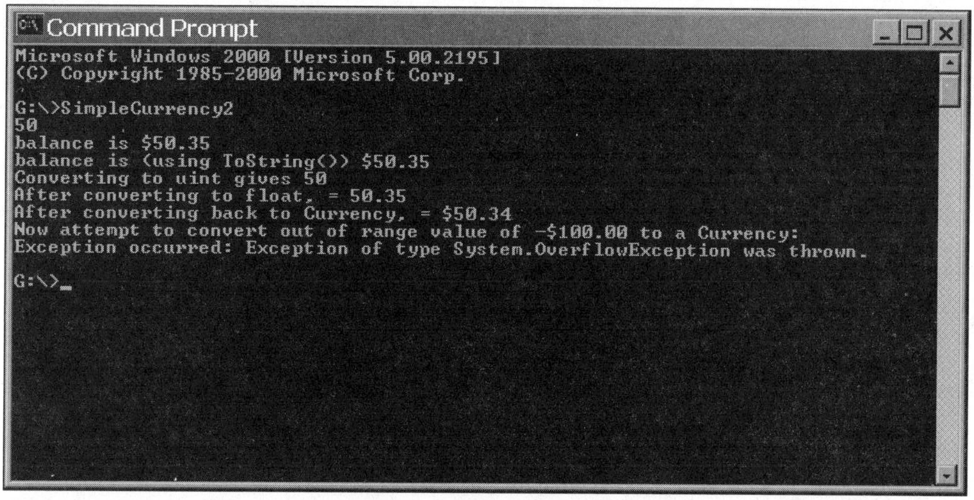

```
Command Prompt                                              _ □ x
Microsoft Windows 2000 [Version 5.00.2195]
(C) Copyright 1985-2000 Microsoft Corp.

G:\>SimpleCurrency2
50
balance is $50.35
balance is (using ToString()) $50.35
Converting to uint gives 50
After converting to float, = 50.35
After converting back to Currency, = $50.34
Now attempt to convert out of range value of -$100.00 to a Currency:
Exception occurred: Exception of type System.OverflowException was thrown.

G:\>_
```

The screenshot shows that the conversion to `uint` has been successful, though as expected we've lost the cents part of the `Currency` in making this conversion. Casting a negative `float` to `Currency` has also produced the expected overflow exception now that the `float`-to-`Currency` cast itself defines a `checked` context.

However, the output also demonstrates one last potential problem that you need to be aware of when working with casts. The very first line of output has not displayed the balance correctly, displaying `50` instead of £`50.35`. Of these lines:

```
    Console.WriteLine(balance);
    Console.WriteLine("balance is " + balance);
    Console.WriteLine("balance is (using ToString()) " + balance.ToString());
```

the last two lines correctly displayed the `Currency` as a string. So what's going on?

The problem here is that when you combine casts with method overloads, you get another source of unpredictability.

We'll look at these lines in reverse order. The third `Console.WriteLine()` statement explicitly calls the `Currency.ToString()` method ensuring the currency is displayed as a string. The second does not do so. However, the string literal `"balance is "` that is passed to `Console.WriteLine()` makes it clear to the compiler that the parameter is to be interpreted as a string. Hence the `Currency.ToString()` method will be called implicitly.

The very first `Console.WriteLine()` method, however, simply passes a raw `Currency` struct to `Console.WriteLine()`. Now `Console.WriteLine()` has many overloads, but none of them takes a `Currency` struct. So the compiler will start fishing around to see what it can cast the `Currency` to to make it match up with one of the overloads of `Console.WriteLine()`. As it happens, one of the `Console.WriteLine()` overloads is designed to display `uints` quickly and efficiently, and it takes a `uint` as a parameter. And we've now supplied a cast that converts `Currency` implicitly to `uint`. I'm sure you can guess the rest.

In fact, `Console.WriteLine()` has another overload that takes a `double` as a parameter and displays the value of that `double`. If you look closely at the output from the first `SimpleCurrency` example, you'll find the very first line of output displayed `Currency` as a `double`, using this overload. In that sample, there wasn't a direct cast from `Currency` to `uint`, so the compiler picked `Currency-to-float-to-double` as its preferred way of matching up the available casts to the available `Console.WriteLine()` overloads. But now there is a direct cast to `uint` available in `SimpleCurrency2`, the compiler has opted for this route.

The upshot of this is that if you have a method call that takes several overloads, and you attempt to pass it a parameter whose data type doesn't match any of the overloads exactly, then you are forcing the compiler to decide not only what casts to use to perform the data conversion, but which overload, and hence which data conversion, to pick. The compiler of course always works logically and according to strict rules. But the results may not be what you expected. If there is any doubt, you are probably better off specifying casts explicitly.

Delegates

Delegates can best be seen as a new type of object in C#, with some similarities to classes. They exist for situations in which you want to pass methods around to other methods. To see what we mean by that, consider this line of code:

```
int I = int.Parse("99");
```

Here we are calling the static method `Parse()` of the `System.Int32` class. This method takes one parameter – with this particular overload, a string. One way of looking at the situation is like this. The `Parse()` method does something, just as all methods do. In this particular case, what the method does is convert some data into an `int`. But in order to actually use the method you have to say what the relevant data is. We do this by passing in a parameter (or an argument). This is what arguments to methods are largely used for – the method takes the data passed to it via the argument and carries out some operation on it.

We are so used to passing data around as parameters that we don't consciously think about it, and for this reason the idea of passing methods around instead of data might sound a little strange. But there are cases in which you have a method that does something, and rather than operating on data, the method might need to do something with another method. To complicate things further, you do not know at compile time what this second method is. That information is only available at run-time, and hence will need to be passed in as a parameter to the first method. That might sound confusing, but should be clearer with a couple of examples:

❏   **Starting Threads** – In Chapter 7 we're going to examine threads. We will save the details for that chapter, but essentially a thread is a sequence of execution. When your application starts running, it starts with the static `Main()` method and follows the instructions in your code from then on. Now it is possible in C# to tell the computer to start some new sequence of execution in parallel with what it's currently doing. Such a sequence is known as a thread, and starting one up is done using a method, `Start()` on an instance of one of the base classes, `System.Treading.Thread`. Now when your application first starts running, it has to start somewhere, and as we've just commented, the place it starts is `Main()`. Similarly, if you're going to tell the computer to start a new sequence of execution, you've got to tell it were to start that sequence. You have to supply it with the details of a method in which execution can start, which means that the `Thread.Start()` method has to take a parameter, which consists of the details of a method.

❑ **Generic Library Classes** – This is the situation that our sample code later in this section is going to illustrate. There are of course many libraries around that contain code to perform various standard tasks. It is usually possible for these libraries to be self-contained, in the sense that you know when you write to the library exactly how the task must be performed. However, sometimes the task contains some sub-task, which only the individual client code that uses the library knows how to perform. The example that we are going to use in this chapter is concerned with sorting an array of objects. We're going to write a class that takes an array of objects and sorts them into ascending order. However, part of the process of doing the sort involves repeatedly taking two of the objects in the array, and comparing them in order to see which one should come first. Since the class we are going to write must be able to sort arrays of *any* object, there is no way that it can tell in advance how to do this comparison. The client code which hands our class the array of objects will also have to tell our class how to do this comparison for the particular objects it wants sorted. In other words, the client code will have to pass our class details of an appropriate method that can be called which does the comparison.

❑ **Events** – We will cover this topic later on in this chapter. Events play a hugely important part in Windows GUI programming. The generic idea is that often you have code that wants to be informed when some event takes place. GUI programming is full of situations like this. For example, at the moment I'm typing lots of characters into Word for Windows. Each time I hit a key on the keyboard, Word needs to be informed of the fact so that it can take the appropriate action (usually, this means adding the corresponding letter to the document and displaying it on the screen). The way that this works is that every time I hit a key, Windows calls up a particular method inside Word that takes the appropriate action – or, in the jargon, that **handles** the event. In order for Windows to be able to do this, Word must have at some point have informed Windows of which method should be called in response to a key press. So Word must have called a Windows API function, giving it the details of this method. Once again we see that details of a method must have been passed as a parameter. Obviously, in C# programming, we will be interacting with the .NET runtime rather than directly with Windows, but when we come to do GUI programming with Windows Forms in Chapter 9, the same principles will hold: our code will need to inform the .NET runtime of what methods handle what events. And to do so, it will need to start passing details of methods as parameters to other methods.

We have now established the principle that sometimes methods need to take details of other methods as parameters. Next we need to figure out how we can do that. The simplest way would have been just to pass in the name of a method as a parameter. To take our example from threading, suppose we are going to start a new thread, and we have a method called `EntryPoint`, which is where we want our thread to start running:

```
void EntryPoint()
{
    // do whatever the new thread needs to do
}
```

Could we perhaps start the new thread off with some code something like this?

```
Thread NewThread = new Thread();
Thread.Start(EntryPoint);                    // WRONG
```

In fact, this is a simple way of doing it, and it is what some languages such as C and C++ do in this kind of situation (in C and C++, the parameter `EntryPoint` is a function pointer). Incidentally, something like this is also going on behind the scenes in pre-.NET Visual Basic when you add event handlers, but the Visual Basic runtime is so good at shielding you from the details of what is happening that you would never realize that.

Unfortunately, this direct approach does cause some problems with type safety, and it also neglects the fact that when we are doing object-oriented programming, methods rarely exist in isolation, but usually need to be associated with a class instance before they can be called. Because of these problems, C# does not syntactically permit this direct approach. Instead, if you want to pass methods around, you have to wrap up the details of the method in a new kind of object, a **delegate**. Delegates quite simply are a special type of object – special in the sense that, whereas all the objects we've defined up to now contain data, a delegate just contains the details of a method.

Using Delegates in C#

When we want to use a class in C#, there are two stages. First, we need to define the class – that is, we need to tell the compiler what fields and methods make up the class. Then (unless we are using only static methods) we instantiate the class – we create an object of that class. With delegates it's the same thing. We have to start off by defining the delegates we want to use. In the case of delegates, defining it means telling the compiler what kind of method delegates of that type will represent. Then we have to create one or more instances of that delegate.

The syntax for defining delegates looks like this:

```
delegate void VoidOperation(uint X);
```

In this case we have defined a delegate called `VoidOperation`, and we have indicated that each instance of this delegate can hold details of a method that takes one `uint` parameter and returns `void`. The crucial point about delegates to understand is they are very type safe. When you define the delegate you have to give full details of the signature of the method that it is going to represent.

> One good way of understanding delegates is by thinking of a delegate as something that gives a name to a method signature.

Suppose we wanted to define a delegate called `TwoLongsOp` that will represent a function that takes two `longs` as its parameters and returns a `double`. We could do it like this:

```
delegate double TwoLongsOp(long L1, long L2);
```

Or, to define a delegate that will represent a method that takes no parameters and returns a `string`, we might write this:

```
delegate string GetAString();
```

The syntax is similar to that for a method definition, except that there is no method body, and the definition is prefixed with the keyword `delegate`. Since what we are doing here is basically defining a new class, we can define a delegate in any of the same places that we would define a class – that is to say either inside another class, or outside of any class and in a namespace as a top level object. Depending on how visible we want our definition to be we can apply any of the normal access modifiers to delegate definitions – `public`, `private`, `protected`, and so on:

```
public delegate string GetAString();
```

*We do literally mean what we say when we describe "defining a delegate" as "defining a new class".
Delegates are implemented as instances of classes derived from the base class, System.Delegate. The
C# compiler is aware of this class, and uses its delegate syntax to shield us from the details of the
operation of this class. This is another good example of how C# works in conjunction with the base
classes to make programming as easy as practicable.*

Once we've defined a delegate, we can create an instance of it so that we can use it to store details of a
particular method.

*There is an unfortunate problem with terminology here. With classes there are two distinct terms –
"class", which indicates the border definition, and "object", which means an instance of the class.
Unfortunately, with delegates there is only the one term. When you create an instance of delegates, what
you have created is also referred to as a delegate. You need to be aware of the context to know which
meaning we are using when we talk about delegates.*

The following code snippet demonstrates the use of a delegate. It is a rather long-winded way of calling the
ToString() method on an int:

```
private delegate string GetAString();

static void Main(string[] args)
{
    int X = 40;
    GetAString FirstStringMethod = new GetAString(X.ToString);
    Console.WriteLine("String is" + FirstStringMethod());

    // With FirstStringMethod initialized to X.ToString(),
    // the above statement is equivalent to saying
    // Console.WriteLine("String is" + X.ToString());
```

In this code, we instantiate a delegate of type GetAString, and we initialize it so that it refers to the
ToString() method of the integer variable X. Delegates in C# always syntactically take a one-parameter
constructor, the parameter being the method to which the delegate will refer. This method must match the
signature with which we originally defined the delegate. So in this case, we'd get a compilation error if we
tried to initialize FirstStringMethod with any method that did not take no parameters and return a
string. Notice that because int.ToString() is an instance method (as opposed to a static one) we need to
specify the instance (X) as well as the name of the method to initialize the delegate properly.

The next line actually uses the delegate to display the string. In any code, supplying the name of a delegate
instance, followed by brackets containing any parameters has exactly the same effect as calling the method
wrapped by the delegate. Hence in the above code snippet the Console.WriteLine() statement is
completely equivalent to the commented-out line.

One feature of delegates is that they are type safe to the extent that they ensure that the signature of the
method being called is correct. However, interestingly, they do not care what type of object the method is
being called against, or even whether the method is static or an instance method.

> **An instance of a given delegate can refer to any instance or static method on any object of any type, provided that the signature of the method matches the signature of the delegate.**

To see this, we will expand the above code snippet so that it uses the `FirstStringMethod` delegate to call a couple of other methods on another object – an instance method and a static method. For this, we'll reuse the `Currency` struct that we defined earlier in the chapter. Recall that the `Currency` struct already has its own overload of `ToString()`. In order to demonstrate using delegates with static methods, we'll also add a static method with the same signature to `Currency`:

```
struct Currency
{
    public static string GetCurrencyUnit()
    {
        return "Dollar";
    }
}
```

Now we can use our `GetAString` instance as follows.

```
private delegate string GetAString();

static void Main(string[] args)
{
    int X = 40;
    GetAString FirstStringMethod = new GetAString(X.ToString);
    Console.WriteLine("String is " + FirstStringMethod());

    Currency Balance = new Currency(34, 50);
    FirstStringMethod = new GetAString(Balance.ToString);
    Console.WriteLine("String is " + FirstStringMethod());
    FirstStringMethod = new GetAString(Currency.GetCurrencyUnit);
    Console.WriteLine("String is " + FirstStringMethod());
```

This code shows how you can call a method via a delegate, and subsequently reassign the delegate to refer to different methods on different instances of classes, even static methods or methods against instances of different types of class, provided that the signature of each method matches the delegate definition.

However, we still haven't demonstrated the process of actually passing a delegate to another method. Nor have we actually achieved anything particularly useful yet. It's possible to call the `ToString()` method of `int` and `Currency` objects in a much more straightforward way than using delegates! Unfortunately, it's in the nature of delegates that we need a fairly complex example before we can really appreciate their usefulness. We are now going to present two delegate samples. The first one simply uses delegates to call a couple of different operations. It illustrates how to pass delegates to methods, and how you can use arrays of delegates – although arguably it still doesn't do much that you couldn't do a lot more simply without delegates. Then we will present a second, much more complex example of a `BubbleSorter` class, which implements a method to sort out arrays of objects into increasing order. This class would be difficult to write without delegates.

Simple Delegate Example

For this example, we will define a `MathOperations` class that has a couple of static methods to perform two operations on doubles. Then we'll use delegates to call up these methods. The math class looks like this:

```
class MathOperations
{
   public static double MultiplyByTwo(double value)
   {
      return value*2;
   }

   public static double Square(double value)
   {
      return value*value;
   }
}
```

And we call up these methods like this:

```
using System;
namespace Wrox.ProfessionalCSharp.Chapter6.SimpleDelegate
{

   delegate double DoubleOp(double x);

   class MainEntryPoint
   {
      static void Main(string[] args)
      {
         DoubleOp [] operations =
         {
            new DoubleOp(MathOperations.MultiplyByTwo),
            new DoubleOp(MathOperations.Square)
         };

         for (int i=0 ; i<operations.Length ; i++)
         {
            Console.WriteLine("Using operations[{0}]:", i);
            ProcessAndDisplayNumber(operations[i], 2.0);
            ProcessAndDisplayNumber(operations[i], 7.94);
            ProcessAndDisplayNumber(operations[i], 1.414);
            Console.WriteLine();
         }
      }

      static void ProcessAndDisplayNumber(DoubleOp action, double value)
      {
         double result = action(value);
         Console.WriteLine("Value is {0}, result of operation is {1}",
                           value, result);
      }
```

In this code, we instantiate an array of `DoubleOp` delegates (remember that once we have defined a delegate class, we can basically instantiate instances just like we can with normal classes, so putting some into an array is no problem). Each element of the array gets initialized to refer to a different operation implemented by the `MathOperations` class. Then we loop through the array, applying each operation to three different values. This illustrates one way of using delegates – that you can group methods together into an array using them, so that you can call several methods in a loop.

The key lines in this code are the ones in which we actually pass the each delegate to the `ProcessAndDisplayNumber()` method, for example:

```
ProcessAndDisplayNumber(operations[i], 2.0);
```

Here we are passing in the name of a delegate, but without any parameters. Given that `operations[i]` is a delegate, syntactically:

- ❑ "`operations[i]`" means "the delegate", in other words the method represented by the delegate.

- ❑ "`operations[i](2.0)`" means "actually call this method, passing in the value in parentheses."

The `ProcessAndDisplayNumber()` method is defined to take a delegate as its first parameter:

```
static void ProcessAndDisplayNumber(DoubleOp action, double value)
```

Then, when in this method, we call:

```
double Result = action(value);
```

This actually causes the method that is wrapped up by the `action` delegate instance to be called, and its return result stored in `Result`.

Running this sample gives this result:

```
F:\C# Projects\Pro C# Code\Ch5AdvCSh\Testing\Simple Delegate...
Using Operations[0]:
Value is 2, result of operation is 4
Value is 7.94, result of operation is 15.88
Value is 1.414, result of operation is 2.828

Using Operations[1]:
Value is 2, result of operation is 4
Value is 7.94, result of operation is 63.0436
Value is 1.414, result of operation is 1.999396
```

Example: BubbleSorter

We are now ready for an example which will show delegates in action in a situation in which they are very useful. We are going to write a class, BubbleSorter. This class implements a static method, Sort(), which takes as its first parameter an array of objects, and rearranges this array into ascending order. In other words, suppose we were to pass it this array of ints: {0, 5, 6, 2, 1}. It would rearrange this array into {0, 1, 2, 5, 6}.

The bubble-sorting algorithm is a well-known and very simple (although very inefficient) way of sorting numbers. It works by repeatedly looping through the array, comparing each pair of number and swapping them, so that the largest numbers progressively move to the end of the array. For sorting ints, a method to do a bubble sort might look like this:

```
// NB. This isn't part of the sample
for (int i=0 ; i<sortArray.Length ; i++)
{
    for (int j=0 ; j<i ; j++)
    {
        if (j > i)    // problem with this test
        {
            int temp = sortArray[i];   // swap i and j
            sortArray[i] = sortArray[j];
            sortArray[j] = temp;
        }
    }
}
```

This is all very well for ints, but we want our Sort() method to be able to sort any object. In other words, if some client code hands us an array of Currency structs or any other class or struct that it may have defined, we need to be able to sort the array. This gives us a problem with the line if(j > i) in the above code, since that requires us to compare two objects on the array to see which one is greater. We can do that for ints, but how are we to do it for some new class that we have never encountered before? The answer is that the client code that knows about the class will have to pass us in a delegate that wraps a method that will do the comparison.

We define the delegate like this:

```
delegate bool CompareOp(object lhs, object rhs);
```

And give our Sort method this signature:

```
static public void Sort(object [] sortArray, CompareOp rhsIsGreater)
```

The documentation for this method will state that rhsIsGreater must refer to a static method that takes two arguments, and returns true if the value of the second argument is "greater than" (in other words should come later in the array than) the first one.

Now we are all set. Here is the definition for the BubbleSorter class:

```
class BubbleSorter
{
    static public void Sort(object [] sortArray, CompareOp rhsIsGreater)
    {
```

```
        for (int i=0 ; i<sortArray.Length ; i++)
        {
            for (int j=0 ; j<i ; j++)
            {
                if (rhsIsGreater(sortArray[i], sortArray[j]))
                {
                    object temp = sortArray[i];
                    sortArray[i] = sortArray[j];
                    sortArray[j] = temp;
                }
            }
        }
    }
}
```

In order to use this class, we need to define some other class, which we can set up an array that needs sorting. For this example, we will assume that our Mortimer Phones mobile phone company has a list of employees, and wants them sorted according to salary. The employees are each represented by an instance of a class, `Employee`, which looks like this:

```
class Employee
{
    private string name;
    private decimal salary;

    public Employee(string name, decimal salary)
    {
        this.name = name;
        this.salary = salary;
    }

    public override string ToString()
    {
        return string.Format(name + ", {0:C}", salary);
    }

    public static bool RhsIsGreater(object lhs, object rhs)
    {
        Employee Lhs = (Employee) lhs;
        Employee Rhs = (Employee) rhs;
        return (Rhs.Salary > Lhs.Salary) ? true : false;
    }
}
```

Notice that in order to match the signature of the `CompareOp` delegate, we've had to define `RhsIsGreater` in this class as taking two object references rather than `Employee` references as parameters. This means we've had to cast the parameters into `Employee` references in order to perform the comparison.

Now we are ready to write some client code to request a sort. Here it is:

```
using System;

namespace BubbleSorter
{
```

```
delegate bool CompareOp(object lhs, object rhs);

class Class1
{
    static void Main(string[] args)
    {
        Employee [] employees =
            { new Employee("Karli Watson", 20000),
            new Employee("Bill Gates", 10000),
            new Employee("Simon Robinson", 25000),
            new Employee("Mortimer", (decimal)1000000.38),
            new Employee("Arabel Jones", 23000),
            new Employee("Avon from 'Blake's 7'", 50000) };
        CompareOp EmployeeCompareOp = new CompareOp(Employee.RhsIsGreater);
        BubbleSorter.Sort(employees, EmployeeCompareOp);

        for (int i=0 ; i<employees.Length ; i++)
            Console.WriteLine(employees[i].ToString());

    }
}
```

Running this code shows that the `Employees` are correctly sorted according to salary:

Note that the above output shows salaries in £, because I'm in the UK, so my locale is set to UK, and this is picked up by the `decimal` struct when it formats each salary as a string. If you download and run this sample, £ will be replaced by the currency unit in your local currency. This might also make the salaries look a bit lower (10000 Italian lire aren't worth quite as much as GB£10000!).

Multicast Delegates

So far, each of the delegates we have used wraps just one single method call. Calling the delegate amounts to calling that method. If we want to call more than one method, we need to make an explicit call through a delegate more than once. However, it is possible for a delegate to wrap more than one method. Such a delegate is known as a **multicast delegate**. If a multicast delegate is called, it will successively call each method in order. Consider this code, which is adapted from the `SimpleDelegate` example:

```
    delegate void DoubleOp(double value);
//    delegate double DoubleOp(double value); // can't do this now

    class MainEntryPoint
    {
        static void Main(string[] args)
        {

            DoubleOp operations = new DoubleOp(MathOperations.MultiplyByTwo);
            operations += new DoubleOp(MathOperations.Square);
```

In this case, we have instantiated a delegate, `Operations`. In our earlier example, we wanted to store references to two methods so we instantiated an array of delegates. Here instead we simply add both operations into the same delegate. Delegates recognize the operators "+" and "+=". If we'd preferred, we could have expanded out the last two lines of the above code to this, which has the same effect:

```
    DoubleOp operation1 = new DoubleOp(MathOperations.MultiplyByTwo);
    DoubleOp operation2 = new DoubleOp(MathOperations.Square);
    DoubleOp operations = operation1 + operation2;
```

Delegates also recognize the operators "-" and "-=" to remove method calls from a delegate.

There is, however, one restriction. Notice that we've changed the definition of the `DoubleOp` delegate so now it refers to a method that returns a `void`. The compiler won't allow you to use "+" or "+=" to combine multiple methods into one delegate *unless* the method it refers to returns a `void` – and with good reason. Suppose that with the previous definition of `DoubleOp`, you had written:

```
    double result = operations(2.0);    // wrong
```

where `operations` contains more than one method. This would cause each method in `operations` to be called in turn, passing in the value of `2.0` as the parameter. What would happen to all the return results? The return value, `Result`, will only take one of them, so presumably the others would just get lost. To avoid this situation, the compiler will flag an error if you try to put more than one method into a delegate that returns anything other than `void`. For the same reason if you are using multicast delegates, then it's not a good idea to use `out` parameters in the method. In this case, the compiler will allow it, but you'll lose all the output values except for the last one.

> *Incidentally, what's going on behind the scenes is that if the compiler sees that the delegate you are defining represents a method that returns a `void`, it automatically assumes you want a multi-cast delegate, and instantiates a base class object, `System.MulticastDelegate`, which is derived from `System.Delegate`. `System.MulticastDelegate` has additional members to allow chaining of method calls together into a list.*

To illustrate the use of multicast delegates, we've recast the `SimpleDelegate` sample into a new sample, `MulticastDelegate`. Since we now need the delegate to refer to methods that return `void`, we've had to rewrite the methods in the `MathOperations` class, so they display their results instead of returning them:

```
class MathOperations
{
    public static void MultiplyByTwo(double value)
    {
        double result = value*2;
        Console.WriteLine("Multiplying by 2: {0} gives {1}", value, result);
    }

    public static void Square(double value)
    {
        double result = value*value;
        Console.WriteLine("Squaring: {0} gives {1}", value, result);
    }
}
```

To accommodate this change, we've rewritten `ProcessAndDisplayNumber`:

```
static void ProcessAndDisplayNumber(DoubleOp action, double value)
{
    Console.WriteLine("\nProcessAndDisplayNumber called with value = " +
                        value);
    action(value);
}
```

Now we can try out our multicast delegate like this:

```
static void Main(string[] args)
{

    DoubleOp operations = new DoubleOp(MathOperations.MultiplyByTwo);
    operations += new DoubleOp(MathOperations.Square);

    ProcessAndDisplayNumber(operations, 2.0);
    ProcessAndDisplayNumber(operations, 7.94);
    ProcessAndDisplayNumber(operations, 1.414);
    Console.WriteLine();
}
```

Now, each time that `ProcessAndDisplayNumber` is called, it will display a message to say that it has been called. Then the following statement:

```
action(value);
```

will cause each of the method calls in the `action` delegate instance to be called in succession. Running this code gives this result:

```
C:\Pro C#\Chapter06\Multicast Delegate\bin\Debug\Multicast Delegate.exe        _ □ X

ProcessAndDisplayNumber called with value = 2
Multiplying by 2: 2 gives 4
Squaring: 2 gives 4

ProcessAndDisplayNumber called with value = 7.94
Multiplying by 2: 7.94 gives 15.88
Squaring: 7.94 gives 63.0436

ProcessAndDisplayNumber called with value = 1.414
Multiplying by 2: 1.414 gives 2.828
Squaring: 1.414 gives 1.999396
```

Events

As we have indicated, **events** are the usual means by which a Windows application can receive notifications when something interesting happens. Whenever Windows is running, you can be pretty sure a lot of events are firing. For example, when you click the mouse button, the application in whose window you clicked will almost certainly been notified of this event. The same thing happens when you do almost anything with the mouse or keyboard. Similarly, when windows are minimized, restored, or maximized, the corresponding applications will be notified in case they wish to take any action in response.

*Actually we should point out that the above paragraph isn't completely accurate. Strictly, events aren't a part of the Windows operating system at all. Windows uses things called Windows **messages** in order to notify applications of interesting things that have happened. However, Windows messages are low-level C structures that are quite hard to work with, so high level languages such as VB have traditionally wrapped up the messages in a high level framework in which events are the main objects, to make things easier for the programmer. C# and the .NET runtime do this as well, which means we can work entirely in terms of events, even though it's the Windows messages that are actually doing the work behind the scenes.*

> **In C# terms, events are actually a special form of delegates.**

In the preceding section on delegates, believe it or not, we learnt just about everything we need to know to understand how events work. However, one of the great things about how Microsoft has designed C# events is that you don't actually need to understand anything about the underlying delegates in order to use them. So we are going to start off with a short discussion of events from the point of view of the client software. We will focus on what code you need to write in order to receive notifications of events, without worrying too much about what's happening behind the scenes – just so we can show how easy handling events really is. After we've done that we will write a sample that generates events, and as we do so we will see how the underlying delegates framework is working with us.

In this context we are using the term "event" in two different senses: as something interesting that happens, and as a precisely defined object in the C# language – the object that handles the notification process. When we mean the latter we'll usually refer to it either as a C# event, or, when the meaning is obvious from the context, simply as an event.

The Consumer's View of Events

The consumer here is any application wants to be notified when something happens. For the sake of argument we'll assume that the thing that happens is the mouse being clicked, but the event can be anything you like. There will also be some other software (often the Windows operating system or the .NET framework itself) that represents whatever it is that normally becomes aware that an event has occurred, and is responsible for notifying our application. We'll refer to this other software as the "event generator".

The pattern looks like this:

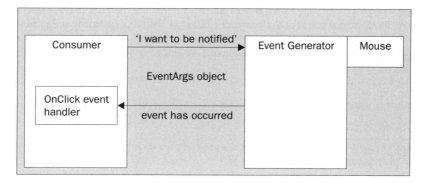

Now, somewhere inside the consumer, there will be a method, which is the one the consumer wants called when a `MouseClick` happens. This method is known as the **event handler** for the event, and a good name for it in this case is `OnClick` (this name isn't entirely random; in Chapter 21, we will see that the relevant Windows Forms base classes really do have a handler called `OnClick` for this purpose). At some point in the past, most likely when the consumer application started up, it will have informed the event generator of its interest in mouse clicks – and of the fact that it wants `OnClick()` to be called whenever a mouse click happens. You can see the delegates coming in here. In C# terms, in order to give the event generator this information, the consumer is going to have to somehow place a reference to `OnClick()` inside a delegate. Once the event generator has this information, whenever it detects that a mouse click happens, it can use this delegates to call the consumer's `OnClick()` method.

Let's look at the coding details now. The .NET Framework requires a very precise signature for any event handler. `OnClick()` and all other event handlers must look like this:

```
void OnClick(object sender, EventArgs e)     // e can also be derived from
                                             // EventArgs
{
    // code to handle event
}
```

Event handlers can't return anything other than `void`. There's no point in them returning any value – all the event generator wants to do is call the method. It doesn't want to know anything about what the consumer does in response; that's the consumer's business. Handlers must also take two parameters. The first parameter is a reference to the object that the generated the event. In other words, the event generator passes in a reference to itself. The second parameter must be a reference to either a .NET base class, `System.EventArgs`, or to a class derived from that. You can think of `EventArgs` as the generic base class for any notifications that events have occurred. In some cases the event generator will document that it will actually send in a reference to a derived class in response to certain specific events. A derived class might contain extra information pertaining to that event, such as the location of the mouse, or which key on the keyboard was pressed.

That's the event handler sorted out. All we need to do now is notify the event generator that we are interested in the event in the first place. For this to happen, we need the event generator to make some item available that is able to receive requests for notifications. This item will be a public member of the .NET class that represents the event generator, and is a member of type `event`. This member is the C# event itself, and is a specialist form of multicast delegate. Let us suppose here that the consumer has a reference to the event generator, via a reference variable called `Generator`, and that the member that represents the event is called `MouseClick`. In the code for the consumer class, we would presumably see something like this:

```
EventGenerator Generator = GetAReferenceToTheEventGeneratorSomehow();
```

where we assume that `EventGenerator` represents the event generator class.

The consumer can notify the event generator that it wants to receive notifications of mouse clicks with this line of code:

```
// Generator is a reference to the event generator
Generator. MouseClick += OnClick();
```

That is literally all the consumer needs to do.

Since we have already given away the fact that the event, `MouseClick`, is a kind of multicast delegate, you can probably guess what is really going on here. The event will contain references to all the event handlers that various consumers have registered to receive notifications, and this line of code simply adds our own event handler to the list. Another point of this is that if the consumer subsequently decides it's not interested in this particular event any more, it can inform the event generator like this:

```
Generator. MouseClick -= OnClick();
```

We might have had to learn a lot of concepts to get this far, but the amount of coding you need to do in the consumer is fairly trivial. And bear in mind that you will find yourself writing event consumers a lot more often than you write event generators. At least in the field of the Windows user interface, Microsoft has already written all the event generators you are likely to need (these are in the .NET base classes, in the `Windows.Forms` namespace, and we'll look at them in Chapter 9).

There is just one point you might notice in the above discussion. We were a bit vague about just how the consumer obtains a reference to the events generator in the first place. That is not part of the general events framework. You should find that the documentation for the particular event generator will tell you how to get this reference. In the case of Windows Forms, you can often just derive your consumer from a generator class. Very often, you will simply instantiate the event generator as one of the .NET base classes.

This architecture is actually extremely flexible. It means that your consumer can request notifications of as many events as it pleases; it can even request notifications from different sources. This is the reason for the first parameter passed to the event handler, the `sender` reference. Since the consumer has a reference to the object that generated the event, this means that if there is more than one possible source for the event, the event handler can easily work out which source is responsible. An example of this is that your application might be a Windows form that has several buttons on it. Any one of these buttons might have notified you that it has been clicked, and by examining the `sender` reference you can figure out which button is the correct one. Not only that, but also many different consumers can request to be notified of the same events. Each one simply adds its event handler to the events, and because of the way that multicast delegates work, when the event fires all the event handlers will be triggered in turn.

Events Sample: Console Notifications

We are now going to write a sample that generates events. The sample is called `UserInputNotify`. For this sample, we're going back to the Mortimer Phones mobile phone company. We are going to write a little console application for Mortimer Phones staff members, which displays a message to the user. The user gets a choice between seeing a personal message from Mortimer (the company president), and a general advertisement. The program keeps asking the user what message he wants to see until the user hits X to exit the program. However, we're going to structure the program so that it uses events. It will follow a classic event-notification architecture that has a general applicability and is also very similar to the architecture that Windows Forms uses.

There are two objects of interest in our code:

- ❑ The `UserInputMonitor` – This is the object that deals with use input. It is responsible for asking users which messages they want to see.
- ❑ The `MessageDisplayer` – This is the object that is responsible for displaying the appropriate message.

Because the message displayer is not concerned with user input, it has no direct means of knowing when to display a message or which message to display; it has to rely on the `UserInputMonitor` to tell it. The `UserInputMonitor` will do so by raising events. The `MessageDisplayer` will notify the `UserInputMonitor` that it wishes to be told whenever the user has asked to display a message. After that, whenever the user makes such a request, the `UserInputMonitor` will fire an appropriate event, resulting in the event handler in the `MessageDisplayer` getting called.

At this point, we have just designed a program that illustrates events nicely, but which doesn't actually do anything that we couldn't have done with a simple loop inside one method in one single class, with the knowledge of C# that we picked up in Chapter 3! But we are also now going to add something else that will demonstrate how flexible the events architecture is. You see, Mortimer quite likes to know when members of his staff have asked to see his personal message. It makes him feel popular and gives him a nice warm feeling inside. So he would like to be notified too whenever users request to see his personal messages.

To this end, we will code up another class, the `ManagersStaffMonitor`, which tells Mortimer when someone has asked to see his personal message. For the purposes of our sample, the `ManagersStaffMonitor` will simply display a dialog box that says "Kaark" (Mortimer likes saying "Kaark" when he's happy). Doing this, we can see the beauty of the events architecture, because all we have to do to let Mortimer know about the events is plug the `ManagersStaffMonitor`'s own event handler into the event as well. Then, when a customer asks to see a message, the resulting event will call both event handlers in succession. If some other software wanted to be notified of this event, it would do the same thing: write an event handler and add it to the event in the `UserInputMonitor`. In this way the event handlers can get effectively chained together.

The structure of our application looks like this:

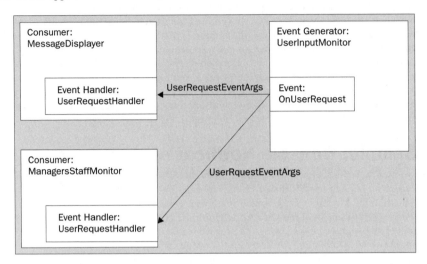

In this diagram we have marked in the event handlers for our two consumer classes, the MessageDisplayer and the ManagersStaffMonitor, as well as the event in our event generator class, the UserInputMonitor. In order to pass details of the event we're going to use a new class, UserRequestEventArgs, which we will derive from System.EventArgs, and which will implement one property, Request. This indicates which of the two possible requests the user has made.

To start off with, we need to write the UserRequestEventArgs class that will convey details of an event. For this we'll use an enumeration to list the possible events:

```
enum RequestType {AdRequest, PersonalMessageRequest};

class UserRequestEventArgs : EventArgs
{
    private RequestType request;

    public UserRequestEventArgs(RequestType request)
        :   base()
    {
        this.request = request;
    }

    public RequestType Request
    {
        get
        {
            return request;
        }
    }
}
```

This code should be fairly self-explanatory. We simply add a field and corresponding property that specifies which request the user has made. Our constructor takes a parameter that specifies this value, and then calls the base class constructor.

Now for the event generator, the `UserInputMonitor`:

```
class UserInputMonitor
{
    public delegate void UserRequest(object sender, UserRequestEventArgs e);

    public event UserRequest OnUserRequest;

    public void Run()
    {
        while (true)
        {
            Console.WriteLine("Select preferred option");
            Console.WriteLine("  Request advertisement - hit A then return");
            Console.WriteLine("  Request personal message from Mortimer - " +
                              "hit P then return");
            Console.WriteLine("  Exit - hit X then return");
            string response = Console.ReadLine();

            char responseChar = (response == "") ? ' ' :
                                 char.ToUpper(response[0]);
            switch(responseChar)
            {
                case 'A':
                    OnUserRequest(this,
                               new UserRequestEventArgs(RequestType.AdRequest));
                    break;
                case 'P':
                    OnUserRequest(this,
                      new UserRequestEventArgs(RequestType.PersonalMessageRequest));
                    break;
                case 'X':
                    return;
            }
        }
    }
}
```

This class contains the only line of code in which we actually use the `event` keyword to declare an event. The two lines of code of interest are these:

```
    public delegate void UserRequest(object sender, UserRequestEventArgs e);

    public event UserRequest OnUserRequest;
```

The pattern is much the same as when we were declaring delegates in the previous section of this chapter. We first define a delegate, and then declare an instance of one. Note that the definition of the delegate signature matches the signature that .NET requires all event handlers to have: it returns a `void`, and takes an `object` and something derived from `EventArgs` as parameters.

The next line is more interesting – here we tell the compiler that this class contains a member event, of a type given by the delegate. You can think of this line as meaning something like:

```
    // WRONG - just presented for comparison
    public UserRequest OnUserRequest = new UserRequest(// method);
```

Except that the event syntax allows the compiler to make sure the delegate has the correct signature. It also implies that we are instantiating the object, but not yet supplying any methods for it to refer to, something that we could not do with the alternative delegate syntax.

The rest of the `UserInputMonitor` class is given over to a method, `Run()`, which repeatedly loops, asking the user for input. Notice how the event actually gets fired:

```
switch(responseChar)
{
    case 'A':
        OnUserRequest(this, new UserRequestEventArgs(RequestType.AdRequest));
        break;
    case 'P':
        OnUserRequest(this,
                new UserRequestEventArgs(RequestType.PersonalMessageRequest));
        break;
    case 'X':
        return;
}
```

We simply call the event, which automatically invokes any methods that it currently references (these will be the event handlers that the consumers have notified it about). In each case, we instantiate a new `EventArgs`-derived class to pass to the event handler.

Now we can look at the consumer classes. First the `MessageDisplayer`:

```
class MessageDisplayer
{
    public MessageDisplayer(UserInputMonitor monitor)
    {
        monitor.OnUserRequest +=
            new UserInputMonitor.UserRequest(UserRequestHandler);
    }

    protected void UserRequestHandler(object sender, UserRequestEventArgs e)
    {
        switch (e.Request)
        {
            case RequestType.AdRequest:
                Console.WriteLine("Mortimer Phones is better than anyone else " +
                    "because \nall our software is written in C#!\n");
                break;
            case RequestType.PersonalMessageRequest:
                Console.WriteLine("Today Mortimer issued the following " +
                                "statement: \n  Nevermore!\n");
                break;
        }
    }
}
```

The constructor to the `MessageDisplayer` is where we actually tell the `UserInputMonitor` class that we want to receive event notifications. We do this by adding a reference to our event handler to the `UserRequest` event. The event handler is our `UserRequestHandler` method, and it simply checks the `EventArgs` parameter to see what type of message the user has requested, and displays the appropriate event. Note that, in line with common practice, we make the event handler `protected`. Generally, event handlers are intended to be called through events, in other words, through delegates. There's usually no reason for them to be called directly, so there's no reason for outside classes to be able to see them. (Notice that the fact that a method is invisible to outside classes does not prevent those classes from calling it through a delegate if that delegate has been supplied with a reference to that method).

Mortimer's personal `ManagersStaffMonitor` class does basically the same thing, except it displays a dialog box instead of writing to the console:

```
class ManagersStaffMonitor
{
   public ManagersStaffMonitor(UserInputMonitor monitor)
   {
      monitor.OnUserRequest +=
         new UserInputMonitor.UserRequest(UserRequestHandler);
   }

   protected void UserRequestHandler(object sender, UserRequestEventArgs e)
   {
      if (e.Request == RequestType.PersonalMessageRequest)
      {
         MessageBox.Show("Kaark!", "Mortimer says ...");
      }
   }
}
```

Finally we can see how the whole set of classes fit together. This is the code for the `Main` routine:

```
using System;
using System.Windows.Forms;

namespace Wrox.ProfessionalCSharp.Chapter6.UserInputNotify
{

   class MainProgramClass
   {
      static void Main(string[] args)
      {
      UserInputMonitor inputMonitor = new UserInputMonitor();
      MessageDisplayer inputProcessor = new MessageDisplayer(inputMonitor);
      ManagersStaffMonitor mortimer = new ManagersStaffMonitor(inputMonitor);
      inputMonitor.Run();
      }
   }

   // code for the other classes

}
```

Quite apart from the event architecture, this is actually a classic example of object-oriented programming. The main entry point does almost nothing itself. It simply instantiates the various objects that make up the application, and sets them off interacting with each other. In this sample, we create an instance of each of the three main classes, and initialize them appropriately. We then call the `InputMonitor`'s `Run()` method, which enters the main program loop, asking the user for input. When we cover Windows Forms in Chapter 9, we'll find that a Windows Forms application has a very similar structure to this. For this type of application, we instantiate our objects, then call a static method, `Run()` on a .NET base class, `Windows.Forms.Application`, which sets the whole events process going.

If we run our sample, we get this result:

The C# Preprocessor Directives

Besides the usual keywords, most of which we have now encountered, C# also includes a number of commands that are known as **preprocessor directives**. These commands never actually get translated to any commands in your executable code, but instead they affect aspects of the compilation process. For example, you can use preprocessor directives to prevent the compiler from compiling certain portions of your code. You might do this if you are planning to release two versions of the code, a basic version and an enterprise version, which will have more features. You could use preprocessor directives to prevent the compiler from compiling code related to the additional features when you are compiling the basic version of the software. Another scenario is that you might have written bits of code that are intended to provide you with debugging information. You probably don't want those portions of code compiled when you actually ship the software.

The preprocessor directives are all distinguished by beginning with the symbol "#".

C++ developers will recognize the preprocessor directives as something that plays an important part in C and C++. However, there aren't as many preprocessor directives in C#, and they are not used as often. C# provides other mechanisms that achieve the same effect as many of the C++ directives. Also note that C# doesn't actually have a separate preprocessor in the way that C++ does; the so-called preprocessor directives are actually handled by the compiler. Nevertheless, C# retains the name "preprocessor directive" because these commands give the impression of a preprocessor.

We'll briefly cover the purposes of the preprocessor directives here.

#define and #undef

`#define` is used like this:

```
#define DEBUG
```

What this does is tell the compiler that a symbol with the given name (in this case `DEBUG`) exists. It's a little bit like declaring a variable, except that this variable doesn't really have a value – it just exists. And this symbol isn't part of your actual code; it just exists while the compiler is compiling the code.

`#undef` does the opposite, and removes the definition of a symbol:

```
#undef DEBUG
```

If the symbol doesn't exist in the first place, then `#undef` has no effect. Similarly, `#define` has no effect if a symbol already exists.

You need to place any `#define` and `#undef` commands at the beginning of the C# source file, before any code that declares any objects to be compiled.

`#define` isn't much use on its own, but when combined with other preprocessor directives, especially `#if`, it becomes very powerful.

Incidentally, you might notice some changes from the usual C# syntax. Preprocessor directives are not terminated by semi-colons, and are normally the only command on a line. That's because for the preprocessor directives, C# abandons its usual practice of requiring commands to be separated by semicolons. If it sees a preprocessor directive, it assumes the next command is on the next line.

#if, #elif, #else and #endif

These directives inform the compiler whether or not to compile a block of code. Consider this method:

```
int DoSomeWork(double X)
{
    // do something
    #if DEBUG
        Console.WriteLine("X is " + X);
    #endif
}
```

This code will compile as normal, except for the `Console.WriteLine` command that is contained inside the `#if` clause. This line will only be executed if the symbol `DEBUG` has been defined by a previous `#define` command. When the compiler finds the `#if` statement, it checks to see if the symbol concerned exists, and only compiles the code inside the `#if` block if the symbol does exist. Otherwise, the compiler simply ignores all the code until it reaches the matching `#endif` directive. Typical practice is to define the symbol `DEBUG` while you are debugging, and have various bits of debugging related code inside `#if` clauses. Then, when you are close to shipping, you simply comment out the `#define` statement, and all the debugging code miraculously disappears, the size of the executable file gets smaller, and your end users don't get confused by being shown debugging information! (Obviously, you'd do a bit more testing to make sure your code still works without `DEBUG` defined). This technique is very common in C and C++ programming and is known as **conditional compilation**.

The #elif (=else if) and #else directives can be used in #if blocks and have the intuitively obvious meanings, and it is also possible to nest #if blocks:

```
#define ENTERPRISE
#define W2K

// further on in the file

#if ENTERPRISE
    // do something
    #if W2K
        // some code that is only relevant to enterprise edition running on W2K
    #endif
#elif PROFESSIONAL
    // do something else
#else
    // code for the learner version
#endif
```

Note that using #if is not the only way to conditionally compile code. C# provides an alternative mechanism via the Conditional attribute which we will explore in the next section.

#if and #elif support a limited range of logical operators too, using the operators "!", "==", "!=", and "||". A symbol is considered to be true if it exists and false if it doesn't exist. For example:

```
#if W2K && (ENTERPRISE==false) // if W2K is defined but ENTERPRISE isn't.
```

#warning and #error

Two other very useful preprocessor directives are #warning and #error. These will respectively cause a warning or an error to be raised when the compiler encounters them. If the compiler sees a #warning directive, then it will display whatever text appears after the #warning to the user, after which compilation continues. If it encounters a #error directive, it will display the subsequent text to the user as if it were a compilation error message, and then immediately abandon the compilation, so no IL code will be generated.

You can use these directives as checks that you haven't done anything silly with your #define statements, and you can also use the #warning statements to remind yourself to do something:

```
#if DEBUG && RELEASE
    #error "You've defined DEBUG and RELEASE simultaneously! "
#endif

#warning "Don't forget to remove this line before the boss tests the code! "
    Console.WriteLine("*I hate this job*")
```

#region and #endregion

The #region and #endregion directives are used to mark that a certain block of code is to be treated as a single block with a given name, like this:

```
#region Member Field Declarations
    int X;
    double D;
    Currency Balance;
#endregion
```

This doesn't look that useful by itself; it doesn't affect the compilation process in any way. However, the real advantage is that these directives are recognized by some editors, including the Visual Studio.NET editor. These editors can use these directives to lay out your code better on the screen. We will see how this works in Chapter 8, when we look at Visual Studio.NET.

#line

The #line directive can be used to alter the file name and line number information that is output by the compiler in warnings and error messages. You probably won't want to use this directive that often. Its main use occurs if you are coding in conjunction with some other package that alters the code you are typing in before sending it to the compiler, since this will mean line numbers, or perhaps the file names reported by the compiler, won't match up to the line numbers in the files or the file names you are editing. The #line directive can be used to restore the match. You can also use the syntax #line default to restore the line to the default line numbering:

```
#line 164 "Core.cs"    // we happen to know this is line 164 in the file
                       // Core.cs, before the intermediate
                       // package mangles it.

// later on

#line default          // restores default line numbering
```

Attributes

Attributes are in some ways similar to preprocessor directives, to the extent that for the most part they don't actually translate into statements in your compiled code, but rather serve as directives to the compiler. However, whereas preprocessor directives are specific to the C# compiler, attributes form part of the .NET Framework, and are even represented by .NET classes. And whereas there are a fixed number of preprocessor directives (we have just presented the full list in the last section), the number of attributes is theoretically unlimited, since the .NET Framework incorporates a mechanism for you to define your own custom attributes.

Essentially, an attribute is a marker that can be applied to an item in your code such as a method or class, or even an individual argument to a method, and which supplies extra information about that item. For example, the Conditional attribute can be used to mark a method as a debugging method like this:

```
[Conditional("DEBUG")]
public void DoSomeDebugStuff()
{
    // do something
}
```

From this example we can see that in order to apply an attribute to an item, you supply the name of the attribute in square brackets immediately before the definition of the item. Certain attributes take parameters – these are supplied inside round brackets immediately following the name of the attribute.

At its most basic level, applying an attribute to an item might simply mean that the extra information about that item is left in the compiled assembly where it can be used for additional documentation purposes (using the technique of reflection, which we will discuss in the next chapter, you can also access this information programmatically from C# code). This will be the case for any custom attributes that you define. However, a number of attributes that are defined in the base classes are explicitly recognized by the C# compiler. For these particular attributes, the compiler will take certain actions, which may affect the generated code. This is the case for the `Conditional` attribute illustrated above, which will cause the compiler to compile the code for the `Conditional` item only if the named symbol has been defined using an earlier `#define` statement.

With such a wide variety of attributes, it's not really possible to give a systematic statement of what they do. However, we will give a flavor of what can be achieved using attributes in this section by introducing three commonly used general-purpose attributes that are defined in the base classes, and which are recognized by the compiler. In Chapter 7, we will show you how to define your own custom attributes, and also provide examples of why you would want to do that. And in later chapters in the book, we will intermittently meet additional attributes from the .NET base classes.

Here will consider the following three attributes:

❑　`Conditional` – it is possible to mark any method with the `Conditional` attribute. This will prevent the compiler from compiling that method or any statements that refer to it unless a named symbol has been defined. This can be used to give conditional compilation (for example, for debug builds).

❑　`DllImport` – despite the extensive features of the .NET bass class library, there are occasions when you need to get access to the basic Windows API, or to other old-style functions that are implemented in DLLs. The `DllImport` attribute exists for this purpose. It is used to mark a method as being defined in an external DLL rather than in any assembly.

❑　`Obsolete` – this attribute is used to mark a method which is now regarded as obsolete. Depending on the settings you apply to this attribute, it will cause the compiler to generate either a warning or an error if it encounters any code that attempts to use this method.

Although the details are beyond the scope of this book, we'll also mention that it is possible to specify the exact layout of the fields in a struct in memory, using an attribute, `StructLayout`.

We will demonstrate the use of these attributes with a small sample program, the `attributes` sample. This sample displays a `MessageBox` using the Windows API function, `MessageBox`, and also displays two debug messages if we are doing a debug build. One of these debug messages is called via an obsolete method.

This is what the code for the attributes sample looks like:

```
#define DEBUG

using System;
using System.Runtime.InteropServices;
using System.Diagnostics;
```

```
namespace Wrox.ProfessionalCSharp.Chapter6.Attributes
{

    class MainProgramClass
    {
        [DllImport("User32.dll")]
        public static extern int MessageBox(int hParent, string Message,
                                            string Caption, int Type);

        static void Main(string[] args)
        {
            DisplayRunningMessage();
            DisplayDebugMessage();
            MessageBox(0, "Hello", "Message", 0);

            Console.ReadLine();
        }

        [Conditional("DEBUG")]
        private static void DisplayRunningMessage()
        {
            Console.WriteLine("Starting Main routine. Current time is " +
                              DateTime.Now);
        }

        [Conditional("DEBUG")]
        [Obsolete()]
        private static void DisplayDebugMessage()
        {
            Console.WriteLine("Starting Main routine");
        }
    }
}
```

We start off by indicating a number of additional namespaces to be used. This is because the `DllImport` attribute is defined in the `System.Runtime.InteropServices` namespace, while the `Conditional` attribute is defined in the `System.Diagnostics` namespace.

Inside the main entry class of the program, we define the method that we are going to call up from an external DLL. The `MessageBox()` API function is defined in the file `User32.dll`, so we pass the name of this file as a parameter to the `DllImport` attribute. Note that we also need to declare this method as `extern`. `MessageBox()` has been written in C, so the four parameters that it takes are strictly speaking defined in terms of data types available in C, but in C# terms these data types map to an `int` (used to store a Windows handle, which we can set to zero), two strings containing respectively the message to be displayed and the caption to be displayed in the title bar, and an integer that indicates what buttons should be displayed in the message box. Setting this final parameter to zero ensures there will be one button, entitled OK.

Looking further down at the debugging functions we have defined, `DisplayDebugMessage()` simply writes a line to the console saying we are starting to run the program. We only want this method run if we are doing a debug build, so we mark it as conditional upon the DEBUG symbol being present. We also regard this method as being obsolete, since we've written a better version, `DisplayRunningMessage()`, which additionally displays the current date and time. We are trying to discourage people from using `DisplayDebugMessage()` any more, so we mark it with the `Obsolete` attribute to make sure a compiler warning gets displayed if this method gets used. There are a couple of other overloads to this attribute:

```
[Obsolete("The DisplayDebugMessage is obsolete. Use " +
                   "DisplayRunningMessage instead.")]
```

will generate a compiler warning if this method is used, but it will be the specified custom error message instead of a default one, while:

```
[Obsolete("The DisplayDebugMessage is obsolete. Use " +
                    "DisplayRunningMessage instead."), true]
```

will actually cause a compilation error instead of a warning if this method is used. The second, optional parameter is a `bool` that indicates whether the compiler should treat it as an error instead of a warning if this `Obsolete` item is used in your code.

Before we run the code, a quick word about the `Conditional` attribute. This attribute is actually quite sophisticated, since if the condition is not met, the compiler will not only not compile the code for the method, but will also automatically ignore any lines of code anywhere else in the source file that call up this method. In order for the compiler to be able to do this, the method must return a `void`. This makes the `Conditional` attribute a much neater way of arranging for a conditional compilation than the preprocessor `#if...#endif` directives that we saw in the last section, since these directives must be applied separately to each section of code that needs to be conditionally compiled. On the other hand, the preprocessor directives are a little more flexible because of their capacity to evaluate some logical expressions, and because they can be applied to any arbitrary section of code. The `Conditional` attribute can only be applied to a complete method as a unit.

Compiling and running the `Attributes` sample with the `DEBUG` symbol defined gives these results:

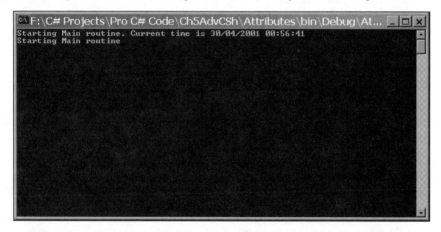

Unsafe Code

As we've seen in previous chapters, C# is very good at hiding much of the basic memory management from the developer, thanks to the garbage collector and the use of references. However, there are cases in which you will want direct access to memory. This is most commonly for performance reasons, or because you wish to access a function in an external (pre-.NET) DLL which requires a pointer to be passed as a parameter (as some Windows API functions do). Also, in some cases you may wish to inspect memory contents for debugging purposes, or you may be writing an application such as a debugger that analyses other processes, and where the user needs direct access to memory. In this section, we'll examine C#'s facilities which allow you to do this.

We should emphasize that although there are situations where you might need pointers, and we detail some of them below, they are really not that common. We'd also strongly advise against using pointers unnecessarily, because if you do, your code will not only be harder to debug, but will fail the memory type safety checks imposed by the Common Language Runtime, which we discussed in Chapter 1. If you believe you have a good reason in the particular application you are writing why you need pointers (the most likely reason is for backwards compatibility with some legacy code your application has to work with), then fine. Otherwise, you'll usually find that using pointers is unnecessary. This advice particularly applies to ex-C++ developers who will be used to using pointers in C++ in a wide variety of situations. Pointers in C# are available in case you need them, but they are not needed nearly as often as they are in C++.

Pointers

Although we are introducing pointers as if they are a new topic, in reality pointers are not new to us at all, because we've been using references freely in our code, and a reference is simply a dressed-up pointer. We've already seen how variables that represent classes and arrays actually store the address in memory of where the corresponding data (the referent) is actually stored. A pointer is simply a variable that stores the address of something else in the same way as a reference. The difference is that the C# syntax for reference does not allow you to access that address programmatically. With a reference, the variable is treated syntactically as if it stores the actual contents of the referent. If, say, the class instance referred to happened to be stored at memory location 0x334b38, then there is no way that you could gain access to that number 0x334b38 using a reference. C# references are designed that way to make the language simpler to use, and to prevent you from inadvertently doing something that corrupts the contents of memory, and possibly prevents the garbage collector from being able to do its job properly. With a pointer, on the other hand, the actual memory address is available to you. That gives you a lot of power to perform new kinds of operations. For example, you can add 4 bytes onto the address, so that you can examine or even modify whatever data happens to be stored 4 bytes further on.

There are three advantages to using pointers:

❑ Performance. Provided you know what you're doing, you can ensure that the data is accessed or manipulated in the most efficient way possible – that is the reason why languages such as C and C++ have always allowed pointers.

❑ Backwards compatibility. Remember that, despite all the facilities provided by the .NET runtime, it is still possible to call the old Windows API functions if you wish to – and for a small number of operations this may be the only way to accomplish your task. These API functions are all written in C, a language that uses pointers extensively, which means that many of these functions take pointers as parameters. Third parties may also in the past have supplied DLLs containing functions that take pointer parameters.

❑ You may need to make memory addresses available to the user (for example, if you are writing an application that provides some direct user interface to memory, such as a debugger).

However, this low-level memory access comes at a cost. In particular:

❑ The syntax required to get this functionality is more complex.

❑ Pointers are harder to use. You need very good programming skills and an excellent ability to think carefully and logically about what your code is doing in order to use them successfully. It's very easy to introduce subtle bugs to your program with pointers.

❑ In particular, if you're not careful, it's easy to overwrite other variables, cause stack overflows, access some area memory that doesn't store any variables as if it did, or even overwrite information about your code that is needed by the .NET runtime, thereby crashing your program.

Incidentally, not so many decades ago it was possible for careless use of pointers to crash not just your program, but also other programs running on the system – or in extreme cases, the entire operating system itself. These days, operating systems have much more security built in to prevent you from overwriting memory that belongs to other processes or to the operating system, and generally it is now only your own process that is at risk from careless use of pointers.

Despite these risks, pointers remain a very powerful and flexible tool in the writing of efficient code, and are worth learning about.

Because of the risks associated with pointer use, C# only allows the use of pointers in blocks of code which you have specifically marked for this purpose. The keyword to do this is unsafe (if the previous discussion wasn't enough to warn you of the potential dangers of pointers, Microsoft has even chosen a keyword that reinforces the point!). You can mark an individual method as being unsafe:

```
unsafe int GetSomeNumber()
{
    // code that can use pointers
}
```

Any method can be marked as unsafe, irrespective of what other modifiers may have been applied to it (for example, static methods, virtual methods).

Or you can mark an entire class or struct as unsafe:

```
unsafe class MyClass
{
    // any method in this class can now use pointers
}
```

If you mark a class or struct as unsafe, all of its members are assumed to be unsafe.

Similarly, you can mark a field as unsafe:

```
class MyClass
{
    unsafe int *pX;    // declaration of a pointer field in a class
```

Or you can mark a block of code within a method as unsafe:

```
unsafe
{
    // unsafe code here
}
```

Note, however, that you cannot mark a local variable by itself as `unsafe`:

```
int MyMethod()
{
    unsafe int *pX;     // WRONG.
```

If you want to use an unsafe local variable, you will need to declare and use it inside a method or block statement that is unsafe. There's one more step before you can use pointers. The C# compiler will reject unsafe code unless you tell it that your code includes unsafe blocks. The flag to do this is `unsafe`. Hence, to compile a file named `MySource.cs` which contains unsafe blocks (assuming no other compiler options), the command is:

```
csc /unsafe MySource.cs
```

Or:

```
csc -unsafe MySource.cs
```

Pointer Syntax

Once you've marked a block of code as unsafe, you can declare a pointer using this syntax:

```
int *pWidth, pHeight;
double *pResult;
```

> **C++ developers should beware that syntax is different in C#: the C# statement** `int *pX, pY;` **corresponds to the C++ statement** `int *pX, *pY;`.

This code declares three variables: `pWidth` and `pHeight` are pointers to integers, and `pResult` is a pointer to a `double`. When used in a variable declaration, the symbol "`*`" indicates that you are declaring a pointer, in other words, something that stores the address of a variable of the specified type.

It's common practice to use the prefix p in front of names of pointer variables to indicate that they are pointers.

Once you've declared variables of pointer types, you can use them in the same way as normal variables, but first we need to learn two more operators:

❑ "`&`" means "take the address of," and converts a value data type to a pointer, for example `int` to `*int`. This operator is known as the **address operator**.

❑ "`*`" means "get the contents of this address," and converts a pointer to a value data type (for example `*float` to `float`). This operator is known as the **indirection operator** (or sometimes as the **dereference operator**).

You'll see from these definitions that "&" and "*" have the opposite effect to one another.

You might be wondering how it's possible to use the symbols "&" and "" in this manner, since these symbols also refer to the operators of bitwise AND (&) and multiplication (*). The answer is that there is never any confusion in practice; it's always possible for both you and the compiler to know what is meant in each case, because with the new pointer meanings, these symbols always appear as unary operators – they only act on one variable and appear in front of that variable in your code. On the other hand, bitwise AND and multiplication are binary operators; they require two variables, so the "&" and "*" symbols must appear between two variable names when that is their meaning.*

As examples of how to use these operators, consider this code:

```
int X = 10;
int *pX, pY;
pX = &X;
pY = pX;
*pY = 20;
```

We start off by declaring an integer, X, followed by two pointers to integers, pX and pY. We then set pX to point to X (in other words, we set the contents of pX to be the address of X). Then we assign the value of pX to pY, so that pY also points to X. Finally, we change the contents of X to 20. This last part is probably the hardest to understand. Recall that the operator "*" means "get the contents of this address." Since pY happens to point to X, *pY will evaluate to X. So the statement *pY = 20; will result in the value of X being changed to 20. Note that in all this there is no particular connection between the variables pY and X. It's just that at the present time pY happens to point to the memory location that X is held at.

To understand what's going on further, let's suppose that X is stored at memory locations 0x12FA78 to 0x12FA7B in the stack (there are 4 locations because an int occupies 4 bytes). Since the stack allocates memory downwards, this means that the variables pX will be stored at locations 0x12FA74 to 0x12FA77, and pY will end up at locations 0x12FA70 to 0x12FA73. Note that pX and pY also occupy 4 bytes each. That is not because an int occupies 4 bytes. It's because on a 32-bit processor you need 4 bytes to store an address. If pX had been a pointer to, say, a double (8 bytes) or a byte (1 byte), it would still occupy 4 bytes. With these addresses, after executing the above code, the stack would look like this:

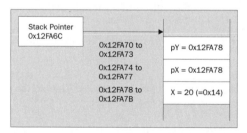

Although we have illustrated this process with ints, which will be stored consecutively on the stack on a 32-bit processor, this doesn't happen for all data types. The reason is that 32-bit processors work best retrieving data from memory in 4-byte chunks. Memory on such machines tends to be divided into 4-byte blocks, and each block is sometimes known under Windows as a DWORD because this was the name of a 32-bit unsigned int in pre-.NET days. It's most efficient to grab DWORDs from memory – storing data across DWORD boundaries normally gives a hardware performance hit. For this reason, the .NET runtime normally pads out data types so that the memory they occupy is a multiple of 4. For example, a short occupies 2 bytes, but if a short is placed on the stack, the stack pointer will still be decremented by 4, not 2, so that the next variable to go on the stack will still start at a DWORD boundary.

You can declare a pointer to any value type, in other words, any of the predefined types uint, int, byte, and so on, or to a struct. However, it is not possible to declare a pointer to a class or array; this is because doing so could cause problems for the garbage collector. In order to work properly, the garbage collector needs to know exactly what class instances have been created on the heap, and where they are. But if your code started manipulating classes using pointers, you could very easily corrupt the information on the heap concerning classes that the .NET runtime maintains for the garbage collector. In this context, any data type that the garbage collector can access is known as a **managed type**. Pointers can only be declared as **unmanaged types** since the garbage collector cannot deal with them.

Casting Pointers to Integer Types

Since a pointer really stores an integer that represents an address, you won't be surprised to know that the address in any pointer can be explicitly converted to or from any integer type. For example, it is perfectly legitimate to write the following:

```
int X=10;
int *pX, pY;
pX = &X;
pY = pX;
*pY = 20;
uint Y = uint(pX);
int *pD = (int*)Y;
```

Y will now be a uint which contains the value 1243768 (=0x12FA78). We've then converted this quantity back to an int*, stored in the new variable pD. Hence pD also points to the original value of X.

One reason for casting a pointer value to an integer type is in order to display it. The Console.Write() and Console.WriteLine() methods do not have any overloads that can take pointers, but will accept and display pointer values that have been cast to integer types:

```
Console.WriteLine("Address is" + pX);      // wrong - will give compilation error
Console.WriteLine("Address is" + (uint) pX);    // OK
```

Note that you can legally cast a pointer to any of the integer types. However, because an address occupies 4 bytes on 32-bit systems, casting a pointer to anything other than a uint, long or ulong is almost certain to lead to overflow errors, and is therefore probably not a good idea. (An int can also cause problems, because its range is from roughly –2 billion to 2 billion, whereas an address runs from zero to about 4 billion). When C# is released for 64-bit processors, an address will occupy 8 bytes. Hence, on such systems, casting a pointer to anything other than ulong is likely to lead to overflow errors. It's also important to be aware that the checked keyword does not apply to conversions involving pointers. For such conversions, exceptions will not be raised when overflows occur, even in a checked context. The .NET runtime assumes that if you're using pointers you probably know what you're doing and are happy about the overflows!

Pointer-to-integer-type conversions must be explicit. Implicit conversions are not available for these.

Casting Between Pointer Types

You can also explicitly convert between pointers pointing to different types. For example:

```
byte Byte = 8;
byte *pByte= &Byte;
double *pDouble = (double*)pByte;
```

This is perfectly legal code, though again if you try something like this, make sure you know what you are doing! With the above example, if we look up the double pointed to by pDouble, we'll actually be looking up some memory that contains a byte, and treating it as if it were a double, which won't give a meaningful value. However, you might want to convert between types in order to implement a union, or you might want to cast pointers to other types into pointers to sbyte in order to examine individual bytes of memory.

void Pointers

If you wish to maintain a pointer, but do not wish to specify what type of data it points to, you can declare it as a pointer to a void:

```
void *PointerToVoid;
PointerToVoid = (void*)PointerToInt;
```

The main use of this is if you need to call any API functions that require void* parameters. Within the C# language, there isn't a great deal that you can do using void pointers. In particular, the compiler will flag an error if you attempt to dereference a void pointer using the "*" operator.

The sizeof Operator

Throughout this section, we've been referring to the sizes of various data types. If you need to explicitly use the size of a type in your code, you can use the sizeof operator, which takes the name of a data type as a parameter, and returns the number of bytes occupied by that type. For example:

```
int X = sizeof(double);
```

This will set X to the value 8.

The advantage of using sizeof is that you don't have to remember the sizes of particular types, and you can be certain the value you are using in your program is correct. For the predefined data types, sizeof returns the following values:

sizeof(sbyte) = 1;	sizeof(byte) = 1;
sizeof(short) = 2;	sizeof(ushort) = 2;
sizeof(int) = 4;	sizeof(uint) = 4;
sizeof(long) = 8;	sizeof(ulong) = 8;
sizeof(char) = 2;	sizeof(float) = 4;
sizeof(double) = 8;	sizeof(bool) = 1;

You can also use sizeof for structs that you define yourself, though in that case the result will depend on what fields are in the struct. You cannot use sizeof for classes.

Sample: PointerPlayaround

We're now ready to present a sample that uses pointers. The following code is a sample that I've named PointerPlayaround. It does some simple pointer manipulation and displays the results, allowing us to see for ourselves what is happening in memory and where variables are stored:

```
static unsafe void Main(string[] args)
{
    int X=10;
    short Y = -1;
    double Z = 1.5;
    int *pX = &X;
    short *pY = &Y;
    double *pZ = &Z;

    Console.WriteLine("Address of X is {0}, size is {1}, value is {2}",
                        (uint)&X, sizeof(int), X);
    Console.WriteLine("Address of Y is {0}, size is {1}, value is {2}",
                        (uint)&Y, sizeof(short), Y);
    Console.WriteLine("Address of Z is {0}, size is {1}, value is {2}",
                        (uint)&Z, sizeof(double), Z);
    Console.WriteLine("Address of pX=&X is {0}, size is {1}, " +
                                                    "value is {2}",
                        (uint)&pX, sizeof(int*), (uint)pX);
    Console.WriteLine("Address of pY=&Y is {0}, size is {1}, " +
                                                    "value is {2}",
                        (uint)&pY, sizeof(short*), (uint)pY);
    Console.WriteLine("Address of pZ=&Z is {0}, size is {1}, " +
                                                    "value is {2}",
                        (uint)&pZ, sizeof(double*), (uint)pZ);

    *pX = 20;
    Console.WriteLine("After setting *pX, X = {0}", X);
    Console.WriteLine("*pX = {0}", *pX);

    pZ = (double*)pX;
    Console.WriteLine("X treated as a double = {0}", *pZ);
}
```

This code declares three value variables: an int X, a short Y, and a double Z, as well as pointers to these values. Then we display the values of all these variables as well as their sizes and addresses. Note that in taking the address of pX, pY, and pZ, we are effectively looking at a pointer *to* a pointer – an address of an address of a value!

Finally, we use the pointer pX to change the value of X to 20, and do some pointer casting to see what rubbish results if we try to treat the content of X as if it was a double!

Running this code results in this output:

```
F:\C# Projects\Pro C# Code\Ch6AdvCSh\PointerPlayaround\bin\D...
Address of X is 1243468, size is 4, value is 10
Address of Y is 1243464, size is 2, value is -1
Address of Y2 is 1243460, size is 1, value is 4
Address of Z is 1243452, size is 8, value is 1.5
Address of pX=&X is 1243448, size is 4, value is 1243468
Address of pY=&Y is 1243444, size is 4, value is 1243464
Address of pZ=&Z is 1243440, size is 4, value is 1243452
After setting *pX, X = 20
*pX = 20
X treated as a double = 3.57401619353244E-305
```

Checking through these results confirms our description of how the stack operates that we gave in Chapter 5. It allocates successive variables moving downwards in memory. Notice how it also confirms that blocks of memory on the stack are always allocated in multiples of 4 bytes. For example, Y is a short (size = 2), and has the address 1243464, indicating that the memory locations reserved for it are locations 1243764-1243467. If the .NET runtime had been strictly packing variables up next to each other, then Y would have occupied just the two locations 1243466-1243467.

Pointer Arithmetic

It is possible to add or subtract integers to pointers. However, the compiler is quite clever about how it arranges for this to be done. For example, suppose you have a pointer to an int, and you try to add 1 on to its value. The compiler will assume you actually mean you want to look at the memory location following the int, and so will actually increase the value by 4 bytes – the size of an int. If it's a pointer to a double, adding 1 will actually increase the value of the pointer by 8 bytes, the size of a double. Only if the pointer is a pointer to a byte or sbyte (1 byte each) will adding 1 to the value of the pointer actually change its value by 1.

You can use the operators "+", "-", "+=", "-=", "++", and "--" with pointers, with the variable on the right-hand side of these operators being a long or ulong.

> *Note that it is not permitted to carry out arithmetic operations on void pointers.*

For example, let us assume these definitions:

```
uint U = 3;
byte B = 8;
double D = 10.0;
uint *pUint= &U;       // size of a uint is 4
byte *pByte = &B;      // size of a byte is 1
double *pDouble = &D;  // size of a double is 8
```

And let us assume the addresses to which these pointers point are: pUint: 1243468, pByte: 1243464, pDouble: 1243456. After executing this code:

```
++pUint;               // adds 1= 4 bytes to pUint
pByte -= 3;            // subtracts 3=3bytes from pByte
double *pDouble2 = pDouble - 4; // pDouble2 = pDouble - 32 bytes (4*8bytes)
```

The pointers will contain: pUint: 1243472, pByte: 1243461, pDouble2: 1243424.

> **The general rule is that adding a number X to a pointer to type T with value P gives the result P + X*(sizeof(T)).**

> *You need to be careful of this rule. If successive values of a given type are stored in successive memory locations, then pointer addition works very well to allow you to move pointers between memory locations. But if you are dealing with types such as byte or char, whose sizes are not multiples of 4, successive values will not by default be stored in successive memory locations.*

You can also subtract one pointer from another pointer, provided both pointers point to the same data type. In this case, the result is a `long` whose value is given by the difference between the pointer values divided by the size of the type that they represent:

```
double *pD1 = (double*)1243424;    // note that it is perfectly valid to
                                   // initialize a pointer like this.
double *pD2 = (double*)1243400;    // note that it is perfectly valid to
                                   // initialize a pointer like this.
long L = pD1-pD2;                  // gives the result 3 (=24/sizeof(double))
```

Pointers to Structs. The Pointer Member Access Operator

We've not yet seen any examples of pointers that point to structs. In fact, pointers to structs work in exactly the same way as pointers to the predefined value types. There is, however, one condition – the struct must not contain any reference types. This is because of the restriction we mentioned earlier that pointers cannot point to any reference types. If a pointer pointed to a struct that had a reference type embedded in it, then you'd have circumvented the restriction! To avoid this, the compiler will flag an error if you create a pointer to any struct that contains any reference types.

Suppose we had a struct defined like this:

```
struct MyGroovyStruct
{
    public long X;
    public float F;
}
```

Then we could define a pointer to it like this:

```
MyGroovyStruct *pStruct;
```

And initialize it like this:

```
MyGroovyStruct Struct = new MyGroovyStruct();
pStruct = &Struct;
```

It is also possible to access member values of a struct through the pointer:

```
(*pStruct).X = 4;
(*pStruct).F = 3.4f;
```

However this syntax looks a bit complex. For that reason, C# defines another operator that allows you to access members of structs through pointers with a simpler syntax. It's known as the **pointer member access operator**, and the symbol is a dash followed by a greater than sign, so it looks like an arrow: "`->`".

Using the pointer member access operator, the above code can be rewritten:

```
pStruct->X = 4;
pStruct->F = 3.4f;
```

You can also directly set up pointers of the appropriate type to point to fields within a struct:

```
long *pL = &(Struct.X);
float *pF = &(Struct.F);
```

Or, equivalently:

```
long *pL = &(pStruct->X);
float *pF = &(pStruct->F);
```

Although these expressions also look syntactically rather complex, there is no equivalent of the "->" operator to help us out here.

Pointers to Class Members

We've indicated that it's not possible to create pointers to classes. That's because the garbage collector does not maintain any information about pointers, only about references, so creating pointers to classes could cause garbage collection not to work properly.

However, most classes do contain members that are themselves of value types, and you might wish to create pointers to them. This is possible, but requires a special syntax. For example, suppose we rewrite our struct from our previous example as a class:

```
class MyGroovyClass
{
    public long X;
    public float F;
}
```

Then you might wish to create pointers to its fields, X and F, in the same way as before. Unfortunately, doing so will produce a compilation error:

```
MyGroovyClass Class = new MyGroovyClass();
long *pL = &(Class.X);   // wrong
float *pF = &(Class.F);  // wrong
```

So what's the problem? We are, after all, declaring pointers of perfectly legitimate types here – long* and float*. What's wrong is that although X and F are themselves unmanaged types, they are embedded in a class, which sits on the heap. This means that they are still indirectly under the control of the garbage collector. In particular, the garbage collector may at any time kick in and decide to move MyGroovyClass to a new location in memory in order to tidy up the heap. If it does that, then the garbage collector will of course update all the references so that the variable Class will still point to the correct location. But the garbage collector doesn't know about what pointers might be around, so if it moves Class, pL and pF will still be unchanged and will end up pointing to the wrong memory locations. Because of the risk of this problem, the compiler will not let you assign addresses of members of managed types to pointers in this manner.

The way round this problem is to use a new fixed keyword, which tells the garbage collector that there may be pointers pointing to members of certain class instances, and so those instances must not be moved. The syntax for using fixed looks like this if we just want to declare one pointer:

```
MyGroovyClass Class = new MyGroovyClass();
// do whatever
fixed (long *pClass = &(Class.L))
{
    // do something
}
```

In other words, we mark out a block of code as `fixed`. The block of code is bounded by braces, while in round brackets we define and initialize the pointer that we want to point to a class member. This pointer variable (`pClass` in the example) will now be scoped to the `fixed` block, and the garbage collector will then know not to move the instance `Class` of `MyGroovyClass` while the code inside the `fixed` block is executing.

If you want to declare more than one such pointer, you can place multiple `fixed` statements before the same code block:

```
MyGroovyClass Class = new MyGroovyClass();
fixed (long *pL = &(Class.L))
fixed (float *pF = &(Class.F))
{
    // do something
}
```

You can nest entire `fixed` blocks if you wish to fix several pointers for different periods:

```
MyGroovyClass Class = new MyGroovyClass();
fixed (long *pL = &(Class.L))
{
    // do something with pL
    fixed (float *pF = &(Class.F))
    {
        // do something else with pF
    }
}
```

You can also initialize several variables within the same `fixed` statement, provided they are of the same type:

```
MyGroovyClass Class = new MyGroovyClass();
MyGroovyClass Class2 = new MyGroovyClass();
fixed (long *pL = &(Class.L), pL2 = &(Class2.L))
{
    // etc.
}
```

In all these cases, it is immaterial whether the various pointers you are declaring point to fields in the same or different instances of classes, or to static fields not associated with any class instance.

Adding Classes and Structs to our Example

In this section, we'll illustrate pointer arithmetic, as well as pointers to structs and classes, using a second example, which we'll imaginatively call `PointerPlayaround2`. To start off, we'll return to our earlier `Currency` struct that we introduced in the section of the chapter about casting, and define a class and a struct that each represent a `Currency`. These types are similar to the `Currency` struct that we defined earlier, but simpler and have slightly different fields:

```
struct CurrencyStruct
{
    public long Dollars;
    public byte Cents;

    public override string ToString()
    {
        return "$" + Dollars + "." + Cents;
    }
}

class CurrencyClass
{
    public long Dollars;
    public byte Cents;

    public override string ToString()
    {
        return "$" + Dollars + "." + Cents;
    }
}
```

There's nothing significant about our choice of Currency for the struct and class, except to make our example look a bit less abstract and more realistic. Note also that CurrencyStruct and CurrencyClass are identical, apart from CurrencyStruct being a struct and CurrencyClass being a class. This is just so we can demonstrate using pointers with both types of object.

Now we have our struct and class defined, we can apply some pointers to them. Here's the code for the new sample. Because the code is fairly long, we'll go through it in detail. We start off by displaying the size of the Currency struct, creating a couple of instances of it along with some pointers, and we use these pointers to initialize one of the currency structs, Amount1. Along the way we display the addresses of our variables:

```
public static unsafe void Main(string [] args)
{
    Console.WriteLine("Size of Currency struct is " +
                                        sizeof(CurrencyStruct));
    CurrencyStruct Amount1, Amount2;
    CurrencyStruct *pAmount = &Amount1;
    long *pDollars = &(pAmount->Dollars);
    byte *pCents = &(pAmount->Cents);

    Console.WriteLine("Address of Amount1 is " + (uint)&Amount1);
    Console.WriteLine("Address of Amount2 is " + (uint)&Amount2);
    Console.WriteLine("Address of pAmt is " + (uint)&pAmount);
    Console.WriteLine("Address of pDollars is " + (uint)&pDollars);
    Console.WriteLine("Address of pCents is " + (uint)&pCents);
    pAmount->Dollars = 20;
    *pCents = 50;
    Console.WriteLine("Amount1 contains " + Amount1);
```

Now we do some pointer manipulation that relies on our knowledge of how the stack works. Because of the order in which the variables were declared, we know that Amount2 will be stored at an address immediately below Amount1. sizeof(CurrencyStruc) returns 16 (as demonstrated in the screenshot coming up), so CurrencyStruct occupies a multiple of 4 bytes. Therefore, after we decrement our currency pointer, it will point to Amount2:

```
    --pAmount;   // this should get it to point to Amount2
    Console.WriteLine("Amount2 has address {0} and contains {1}",
                                    (uint)pAmount, *pAmount);
```

This `Console.WriteLine()` statement is interesting. We've displayed the contents of `Amount2`, but we haven't yet initialized it to anything! What gets displayed will be random garbage – whatever happened to be stored at that location in memory before execution of the sample. But there's an important point here. Normally, the C# compiler would prevent us from using an uninitialized value, but when you start using pointers, it's very easy to circumvent all the usual compilation checks. In this case we've done so because the compiler has no way of knowing that we're actually displaying the contents of `Amount2`. Only we know that, because our knowledge of the stack means we can tell what the effect of decrementing `pAmount` will be. Once you start doing pointer arithmetic, you find you can access all sorts of variables and memory locations that the compiler would usually stop you from accessing, hence the description of pointer arithmetic as unsafe.

Next in our sample, we do something else that's equally cheeky. We do some pointer arithmetic on our `pCents` pointer. `pCents` currently points to `Amount1.Cents`, but our aim here is to get it to point to `Amount2.Cents`, again using pointer operations instead of directly telling the compiler that's what we want to do. Since to do this we need to decrement the address it contains by `sizeof(Currency)`, we need to do some casting to get the arithmetic to work out:

```
// do some clever casting to get pCents to point to cents
// inside amount2
CurrencyStruct *pTempCurrency = (CurrencyStruct*)pCents;
pCents = (byte*) ( --pTempCurrency );
Console.WriteLine("Address of pCents is now " + (uint)&pCents);
```

Finally, we use the `fixed` keyword to create some pointers that point to the fields in a class instance, and use these pointers to set the value of this instance. Notice that this is also the first time that we've been able to look at the address of an item that's stored on the heap rather than the stack:

```
Console.WriteLine("\nNow with classes");
// now try it out with classes
CurrencyClass Amount3 = new CurrencyClass();

fixed(long *pDollars2 = &(Amount3.Dollars))
fixed(byte *pCents2 = &(Amount3.Cents))
{
   Console.WriteLine("Amount3.Dollars has address " + (uint)pDollars2);
   Console.WriteLine("Amount3.Cents has address " + (uint) pCents2);
   *pDollars2 = -100;
   Console.WriteLine("Amount3 contains " + Amount3);
}
```

Running this code gives this output:

Notice in this output the uninitialized value of `Amount2` that we display, and that the size of the currency struct is `16` – somewhat larger than we'd expect given the sizes of its fields (1 long=8 + 1 byte=1). Evidently, some more word alignment is going on here. We can also see from this code the typical value of addresses on the heap: `12819868 = 0xC39D9C`. The heap clearly exists in a very different area of the virtual address space to the stack.

Using Pointers to Optimize Performance

Up to now, we've spent a lot of time looking at the various things that you can do with pointers, but in all our examples so far we haven't really seen anything that would be very useful in many real applications. All we've done up to now essentially is to play around with memory in a way that is probably interesting to people who like to know what's happening under the hood, but doesn't really help us to write very good code. That's going to change in this section. Here we're going to apply our understanding of pointers and demonstrate an example in which judicious use of pointers will have a significant performance benefit.

Creating Stack-Based Arrays

In this section, we are going to look at the other main area in which pointers can be very useful: creating high-performance, low overhead arrays on the stack. We showed in Chapter 3 how C# includes rich support for handling arrays. While C# makes it very easy to use both one-dimensional and rectangular or jagged multidimensional arrays, it suffers from the disadvantage that these arrays are actually objects; they are instances of the `System.Array`. This means that the arrays are stored on the heap with all the overhead that involves. There may be occasions in which you just want to create an array for a short period of time and don't want the overhead of reference objects. It is possible to do this using pointers, although only for one-dimensional arrays.

In order to create a high-performance array we need another keyword: `stackalloc`. The `stackalloc` command instructs the .NET runtime to allocate a certain amount of memory on the stack. When you call it, you need to supply it with two pieces of information: the type of variable you want to store, and how many of these variables you need to store. As an example, to allocate enough memory to store 10 `decimals`, you would write this:

```
decimal *pDecimals = stackalloc decimal [10];
```

Note that this command simply allocates the memory. It doesn't attempt to initialize it to any value – it's up to you to do that. The idea is that this is an ultra-high performance array, and initializing values unnecessarily would hurt performance.

Similarly, to store 20 `doubles` you would write this:

```
double *pDoubles = stackalloc double [20];
```

Get the idea?

Although this line of code specifies the number of variables to store as a constant, this can equally be a quantity evaluated at runtime. So you could equally write the second example above like this:

```
int Size;
Size = 20;    // or some other value calculated at run-time
double *pDoubles = stackalloc double [Size];
```

You'll see from these code snippets that the syntax of stackalloc is slightly unusual. It is followed immediately by the name of the data type you want to store (and this must be a value type), and then by the number of variables you need space for in square brackets. The number of bytes allocated will be this number multiplied by sizeof(*data type*). The use of square brackets here suggests an array, which isn't too surprising, because if you've allocated space for, say, 20 doubles, then effectively what you have is an array of 20 doubles. The simplest, most basic type of array that it is possible to have: a block of memory that stores one element after another, like this:

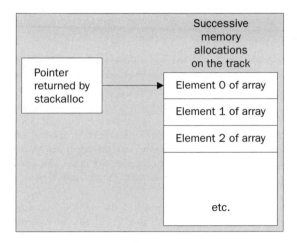

In this diagram, we've also shown the pointer returned by stackalloc, which always returns a pointer to the allocated data type, and sets this return value so that the pointer points to the start of the memory allocated.

The next question is how you use the memory you've just obtained. Carrying on our example, we've just said that the return value from stackalloc points to the start of the memory. It therefore follows that you can get to the first location of allocated memory by dereferencing that pointer. So, for example, to allocate our doubles and then set the first element (that is, element 0 of the array) to the value 3.0, you could write this:

```
double *pDoubles = stackalloc double [20];
*pDoubles = 3.0;
```

What about the next element? This is where the pointer arithmetic that we learnt earlier comes in. Recall that if you syntactically add 1 to a pointer, its value will actually be increased by the size of whatever data type it points to. In this case, this will be just enough to take us the next free memory location in the block that we've allocated. So we can set the second element of a block (that is to say, element number 1 of the array, since we always count arrays from zero) like this:

```
double *pDoubles = stackalloc double [20];
*pDoubles = 3.0;
*(pDoubles+1) = 8.4;
```

And by the same reasoning in general, we can obtain the element with index X of the array with the expression *(pDoubles+X).

That's good as far as it goes – we effectively have a means by which we can access elements of our array, but for general-purpose use, having to use that kind of syntax to get to array elements isn't going to win many friends. Fortunately, C# defines an alternative syntax. The way it works is that C# gives a very precise meaning to square brackets when they applied to pointers. In general, if the variable p is any pointer type and X is any numeric type, then in C# the expression p[X] is always interpreted by the compiler as meaning *(p+X). This is actually true in general – the pointer p doesn't need to have been initialized using stackalloc. And with this shorthand notation, we now have a very convenient syntax for accessing our array. In fact, it means that we have exactly the same syntax for accessing stack-based arrays as we do for accessing heap-based arrays that are represented by the System.Array class:

```
double *pDoubles = stackalloc double [20];
pDoubles[0] = 3.0;   // pDoubles[0] is the same as *pDoubles
pDoubles[1] = 8.4;   // pDoubles[1] is the same as *(pDoubles+1)
```

Incidentally, this idea of applying array syntax to pointers isn't new. It has been a fundamental part of both the C and the C++ languages ever since those languages were invented. Indeed, C++ developers will recognize the stack-based arrays we can obtain using stackalloc as being completely identical to classic stack-based C and C++ arrays. It is this syntax and the way it links pointers and arrays which was one of the reasons why the C language became popular back in the '70s, and the main reason why the use of pointers became such a popular programming technique in C and C++.

Although our high-performance array can be accessed in the same way as a normal C# array, we do need to point out one word of warning. The following code in C# will raise an exception:

```
double [] MyDoubleArray = new double [20];
MyDoubleArray[50] = 3.0;
```

The exception occurs for the obvious reason that we are trying to access an array using an index that is out of bounds (the index is 50, maximum allowed value is 19). However, if you declare the equivalent array using stackalloc, there is now no object wrapped around the array that can do any bounds checking. Hence the following code will *not* raise an exception:

```
double *pDoubles = stackalloc double [20];
pDoubles[50] = 3.0;
```

In this code, we allocate enough memory to hold 20 doubles. Then we set sizeof(double) memory locations starting at the location given by the start of this memory + 50*sizeof(double) to hold the double value 3.0. Unfortunately, that memory location is way outside the area of memory that we've allocated for the doubles. And who knows what data might be stored at that address? At best, we may have "merely" corrupted the value of another variable. But it's equally possible that we may have just overwritten some locations in the stack that were being used to store the return address from the method currently being executed – the address that tells the computer where to carry on from when the method returns. In this case the future execution path of our program is going to be, shall we say, novel! Once again, we see that the high performance to be gained from pointers comes at a cost: that you need to be certain you know what you're doing, or you'll get some very strange runtime bugs.

QuickArray Example

We will round off our discussion about pointers with a QuickArray example. In this example, the program simply asks the user how many elements they want to be allocated for an array. The code then uses stackalloc to allocate an array of longs that size. The elements of this array are populated with the squares of the integers starting from 0 and the results displayed on the console:

```
using System;

namespace Wrox.ProfessionalCSharp.Chapter6.QuickArray
{

   class MainEntryPoint
   {
      static unsafe void Main(string[] args)
      {
         Console.Write("How big an array do you want? \n> ");
         string userInput = Console.ReadLine();
         uint size = uint.Parse(userInput);

         long *pArray = stackalloc long [(int)size];
         for (int i=0 ; i<size ; i++)
            pArray[i] = i*i;

         for (int i=0 ; i<size ; i++)
            Console.WriteLine("Element {0} = {1}", i, *(pArray+i));
      }
   }
}
```

If we try out the sample we get this result:

Summary

This chapter has surveyed a number of separate topics in the C# language. We've covered the rich mechanism C# has for dealing with error conditions through exceptions, casting between different classes and structs, passing methods as parameters via delegates and the related area of notifying applications of interesting things that have happened, via events. We've looked at the two main ways that C# gives us to control how code is compiled, through preprocessor directives and attributes, before finishing up with the use of pointers to gain that extra level of performance when you really need it.

We've already seen from previous chapters that C# is a powerful, object-oriented language that allows you to write well-structured code that follows the latest object-oriented methodologies. In this chapter, we've seen how C# actually goes beyond that, to also provide facilities for handling a number of important programming paradigms that apply in specific circumstances on modern operating systems.

Although there are a couple of minor points of syntax that we are leaving until Chapter 7, we have at this point covered pretty much the entire C# language, as far as keywords and language syntax are concerned. In the next chapter we will move on to investigate how C# interacts with the base classes to give you access to powerful programming techniques in a number of other areas, including string handling, custom attributes and threading. We will see how, through the technique of reflection, it is even possible for a C# program to access the that describes its own objects, and those of other applications.

7

C# and the Base Classes

In this chapter, we are going to take a closer look at the base classes and how they interact with the C# language to give you support for writing code in a number of areas. In particular, we are going to examine the following topics:

❑   Strings and regular expressions

❑   Collections

❑   Custom Attributes

❑   Reflection

❑   Threading

We will also examine `System.Object`, the class from which everything else is derived, in more detail.

These look like a somewhat miscellaneous range of subjects to tackle in one chapter, but there's a good reason for it. You see, we've made it clear right from the start that it is not possible to view the C# language in isolation. The language interacts with both the .NET framework and the associated class library, the .NET base classes, in a very fundamental way. We've seen numerous examples of this as we've explored C# in the last few chapters. For example, all of the C# keywords that represent data types, such as `int`, `long` and `string`, are mapped by the compiler directly onto corresponding base classes (in these cases, `System.Int32`, `System.Int64` and `System.String`). Another example is that in the case of exceptions, the `throw` and `catch` statements depend on the exception object being inherited from `System.Exception` in order to work.

The interaction between C# and the base classes has made it impossible for us to introduce you to the C# language without covering a fair number of classes in the .NET base class library in the process. However, up to now the emphasis has largely been on features of C#, in which the language syntax is the predominant issue, and base classes have been seen as helpers. In this chapter, we will reverse that, and look at a number of features that are available in C# which are sufficiently fundamental to be considered as a part of the language, but which are explicitly implemented mainly through the use of certain base classes rather than through the C# language syntax. At the end of this, we'll have a sufficient grounding in C# that we'll be ready to look in detail at applications, and how the language is applied in a number of specific areas – the subject of the rest of the book.

System.Object

In the previous chapters, we've touched on System.Object and indicated that it is the universal base class from which everything else is inherited. In Chapter 4 we listed its main member methods. However, in that chapter we hadn't yet learnt sufficient C# to be able to understand the significance of all of the methods, and as a result the only System.Object methods that we were able to look at in any detail were ToString() and Finalize(). As we work through this chapter, we will need to work with many of the remaining System.Object methods. In this section, we'll provide a brief summary of them, and look in detail at the various ways of testing for equality.

To recap, below we reproduce the table from Chapter 4 that lists the methods available in System.Object:

Method	Access	Purpose
string ToString()	public virtual	Returns a string representation of the object.
int GetHashCode()	public virtual	Returns a hash of the object designed to allow you to efficiently look up instances of the object in dictionaries.
bool Equals(object obj)	public virtual	Compares this object with another instances of the class for equality.
bool Equals(object objA, object objB)	public static	Compares instances of the class for equality.
bool ReferenceEquals(object objA, object objB)	public static	Compares object references to see if they refer to the same object.
Type GetType()	public	Returns an object derived from System.Type that can give details of a data type.
object MemberwiseClone()	protected	Makes a shallow copy of the object (in other words, copies data in the object but not other objects any fields refer to).
void Finalize()	protected virtual	May be used in some situations for cleaning up resources.

Four of these methods are declared as `virtual` and are therefore available for you to override. In all cases, however, good programming practice places restrictions on how you should implement your overrides.

We will note the following about the `System.Object` members:

❑ `ToString()` – This is intended as a fairly basic quick and easy string representation, and is used for those situations when you just want a quick idea of the contents of an object, perhaps for debugging. You should implement it as such. If you need a more sophisticated string representation that, for example, takes account of the culture (the locale) and any requests that client code makes to have the object represented in a particular format, then you should implement the `IFormattable` interface, which we'll cover later in this chapter. For example, dates can be expressed in a huge variety of different formats – `DateTime.ToString()` does not offer you any choice about format.

❑ `GetHashCode()` – This is used if objects are placed in a data structure known as a **map** (also known as a **hashtable** or **dictionary**). It is used by classes that manipulate these structures in order to determine where to place an object in the structure. If you intend your class to be used as key for dictionary, then you will need to override `GetHashCode()`. There are some fairly strong requirements for how you implement your overload, and we deal with these later in this chapter in the section on dictionaries.

❑ `Equals()`, (both versions) and `ReferenceEquals()` – There are subtle differences between how these three methods, along with the comparison operator `"=="`, are intended to be used. There are also restrictions on how you should override the virtual, one-parameter version of `Equals()` if you choose to do so, because certain base classes in the `System.Collections` namespace call the method and expect it to behave in certain ways. We'll explore these issues in this chapter.

❑ `Finalize()` – We covered this method in Chapter 4. It is intended as the destructor, and is called when a reference object is garbage collected to clean up resources. You should override it only when necessary, for example if your object uses external resources such as file or database connections. If you do need to override it, then it's probably a good idea to provide a `Close()` or `Dispose()` method for clients to use too. Note that value types are not garbage collected so for these types there is no point overriding `Finalize()`.

❑ `GetType()` – This method returns an instance of a class derived from `System.Type`. This object can provide an extensive range of information about the class of which your object is a member, including base type, methods, properties, and so on. `System.Type` also provides the entry point into .NET's reflection technology. We'll examine this area in detail later in the chapter.

❑ `MemberwiseClone()` – This is the only member of `System.Object` that we don't examine in detail anywhere in the book. There is no need to, since it is fairly simple in concept. It simply makes a copy of the object and returns a reference (or in the case of a value type, a boxed reference) to the copy. Note that the copy made is a shallow copy – this means that it copies all the value types in the class. If the class contains any embedded references, then only the references will be copied, not the objects referred to.

Comparing Reference Objects for Equality

One aspect of `System.Object` that can look surprising at first sight is the fact that it defines three different ways of comparing objects for equality. Add to this the comparison operator, and we actually have four ways of comparing for equality. Why so many? There are in fact some subtle differences between the different methods, which we will now examine. We'll look first at the case where we are comparing reference types.

ReferenceEquals()

ReferenceEquals() is exactly what it says: it is there to test whether two references refer to the same instance of a class: whether the two references contain the same address in memory. As a static method, it is not possible to override it, so the System.Object implementation is what you always have. ReferenceEquals() will always return true if supplied with two references refer to the same object instance, and false otherwise. It does, however, consider null to be equal to null:

```
SomeClass X, Y;
X = new SomeClass();
Y = new SomeClass();
bool B1 = ReferenceEquals(null, null);     // returns true
bool B2 = ReferenceEquals(null,X);         // returns false
bool B3 = ReferenceEquals(X, Y);           // returns false because X and Y
                                           // point to different objects
```

Virtual Equals() Method

The virtual, instance version of Equals() can be seen pretty much as the opposite of ReferenceEquals(). While it is true that the System.Object implementation of Equals() works by comparing references, this method is provided in case you wish to override it to compare the values of object instances. In particular, if you intend your instances of your class to be used as keys in a dictionary, then you will need to override this method to compare values. Otherwise, depending on how you override GetHashCode(), the dictionary class that contains your objects will either not work at all, or will work very inefficiently. One point you should note when overriding Equals() is that your override should not ever throw exceptions. Once again, this is because doing so could cause problems for dictionary classes and possibly certain other .NET base classes that internally call this method.

We will show an example of how to override this method in the MortimerPhonesEmployees example later in this chapter, in the section on dictionaries (hash tables).

Static Equals() Method

The static version of Equals() actually does the same thing as the virtual, instance version. The difference is that the static version of this method is able to cope when either of the objects is null, and therefore, provides an extra safety guard against throwing exceptions if there is a risk that an object might be null. The static overload first checks whether the references it has been passed are null. If they are both null than it returns true (since null is considered to be equal to null). If just one of them is null than it returns false. If both references actually refer to something, then it calls the virtual instance version of Equals(). This means that when you override the instance version of Equals(), the effect is as if you were overriding the static version as well.

Comparison Operator (==)

The comparison operator can best be seen as an intermediate version between strict value comparison and strict reference comparison. In most cases, writing:

```
bool B = (X == Y);    // X, Y objects
```

should mean that you are comparing references. However, it is accepted that there are some classes whose meanings make more intuitive sense if they are treated as values. In those cases, it is better to override the comparison operator to perform a value comparison. The obvious example of this is for strings for which Microsoft has overridden this operator, because when developers think of performing string comparisons they are almost invariably thinking of comparing the contents of the strings rather than the references.

Given these interpretations for the various comparison methods, it should now be clear why the compiler raises a warning if you overload the comparison operator, but don't overload `Equals()`. Since `Equals()` is intended as a value comparison therefore, while "==" is more intended for reference comparison, it would look strange if we overloaded "==", but left `Equals()` performing a reference comparison.

By the way, don't be tempted to overload the comparison operator by calling the one-parameter version of `Equals()`. If you do that, and somewhere in your code, an attempt is made to evaluate (`objA == objB`) when `objA` happens to be null, you'll get an instant exception as the .NET runtime tries to evaluate `null.Equals(objB)`! Working the other way round (overriding `Equals()` to call the comparison operator)should be safe.

Comparing Value Types for Equality

When comparing value types for equality, the same principles hold as for reference types: `ReferenceEquals()` is used to compare references, `Equals()` is intended for value comparisons, and the comparison operator is viewed as an intermediate case. However the big difference here is that value types need to be boxed in order to convert them to references, and that Microsoft has in fact already overloaded the instance `Equals()` method in the `System.ValueType` class in order to provide meanings more appropriate to value types. If you call `sA.Equals(sB)` where `sA` and `sB` are instances of some struct, then the return value will be `true` or `false` according to whether `sA` and `sB` contain the same values in all their fields. On the other hand, no overload of "==" is available by default for your own structs. Writing (`sA == sB`) in any expression will result in a compilation error unless you have provided an overload of "==" in your code for the struct in question.

Another point is that `ReferenceEquals()` will always return `false` when applied to value types, because in order to call this method, the value types will need to be boxed into objects. Even if you write:

```
bool B = ReferenceEquals(V,V);    // V is a variable of some value type
```

you'll still get the answer of `false` because `V` will be boxed separately when converting each parameter, which will mean you get different references! Calling `ReferenceEquals()` to compare value types doesn't really make much sense.

Although the default override of `Equals()` supplied by `System.ValueType` will almost certainly be adequate for the vast majority of structs that you define, you may wish to override it again for your own structs in order to improve performance. Also, if a value type contains reference types as fields, you may wish to override `Equals()` to provide appropriate semantics for these fields, as the default override of `Equals()` will simply compare their addresses.

String Handling

Since Chapter 3, we have been almost constantly using strings, and have taken for granted the stated mapping that the `string` keyword in C# actually refers to the .NET base class `System.String`. `System.String` is a very powerful and versatile class, but it is not by any means the only string-related class in the .NET armory. In this section, we start off by reviewing the features of `System.String`, and then we will go on to have a look at some quite nifty things you can do with strings using some of the other .NET classes – in particular those in the `System.Text` and `System.Text.RegularExpressions` namespaces. We will cover the following areas:

- ❏ **Building Strings**. If you're performing repeated modifications on a string, for example in order to build up a lengthy string prior to displaying it or passing it to some other method or software, the string class can be very inefficient. For this kind of situation, another class, `System.Text.StringBuilder` is more suitable.

- ❏ **Formatting Expressions**. We will also take a closer look at those formatting expressions that we have been using in the `Console.WriteLine()` method throughout these last few chapters. These formatting expressions are processed using a couple of useful interfaces, `IFormatProvider` and `IFormattable`, and by implementing these interfaces on your own classes, you can actually define your own formatting sequences so that `Console.WriteLine()` and similar classes will display the values of your classes in whatever way you specify.

- ❏ **Regular Expressions**. .NET also offers some very sophisticated classes that deal with the situation in which you need to identify or extract substrings that satisfy certain fairly sophisticated criteria from a long string. By sophisticated, I mean situations such as needing to find all occurrences within string where a character or set of characters is repeated, or needing to find all words that begin with "s" and contained at least one "n". Although you can write methods to perform this kind of processing using the string class, such methods are cumbersome to write. Instead, you can use some classes from `System.Text.RegularExpressions`, which are designed specifically to perform this kind of processing.

System.String

Before we examine the other string classes, we will quickly review some of the available methods on the `String` class.

`System.String` is a class that is specifically designed to store a string, and allow a large number of operations on the string. Not only that, but because of the importance of this data type, C# has its own keyword and associated syntax to make it particularly easy to manipulate strings using this class. You can concatenate strings using operator overloads:

```
string Message = "Hello";
Message += ", There";
string Message2 = Message1 + "!";
```

C# also allows extraction of a particular character using an indexer-like syntax:

```
char ess = Message[2];
```

There are also a large number of methods to perform such common tasks as replacing characters, removing whitespace, and capitalizing. The available methods include:

Method	Purpose
Compare	Compares the contents of strings, taking into account the culture (locale) in assessing equivalence between certain characters
CompareOrdinal	As Compare, but doesn't take culture into account
Format	Formats a string containing various values and specifiers for how each value should be formatted

Method	Purpose
IndexOf	Locates first occurrence of a given substring or character in the string
IndexOfAny	Locates first occurrence of any one of a set of characters in the string
LastIndexOf	As for IndexOf, but finds last occurrence
LastIndexOfAny	As for IndexOfAny, but finds last occurrence
PadLeft	Pads out the string by adding a specified repeated character to the beginning of the string
PadRight	Pads out the string by adding a specified repeated character to the end of the string
Replace	Replaces occurrences of a given character or substring in the string with another character or substring
Split	Splits the string into an array of substrings, the breaks occurring wherever a given character occurs.
SubString	Retrieves the substring starting at a specified position in the string
ToLower	Converts string to lowercase
ToUpper	Converts string to uppercase
Trim	Removes leading and trailing whitespace

Note that this table is not comprehensive, but is intended to give you an idea of the features offered by strings.

Building Strings

As we have seen, String is an extremely powerful class, that implements a large number of very useful methods. However, String has a problem that makes it very inefficient for making repeated modifications to a given string: it is actually an immutable data type, which is to say that once you initialize a string object, that string object can never change. The methods and operators that appear to modify the contents of a string actually create new strings, copying the contents of the old string over if necessary. For example, look at the following code:

```
String GreetingText = "Hello from all the people at Wrox Press. ";
GreetingText += "We do hope you enjoy this book as much as we enjoyed writing it";
```

What happens when this code executes is this: first, an object of type System.String is created and initialized to hold the text "Hello from all the people at Wrox Press. " When this happens, the .NET runtime will allocate just enough memory in the string to hold this text (39 chars), and we set the variable GreetingText to refer to this string instance.

In the next line, syntactically it looks like we're adding some more text onto the string. We're not. Instead, we create a new string instance, with just enough memory allocated to store the combined text – that's 103 characters in total. The original text, "Hello from all the people at Wrox Press. ", is copied into this new string along with the extra text, "We do hope you enjoy this book as much as we enjoyed writing it." Then the address stored in the variable GreetingText is updated, so the variable correctly points to the new String object. The old String object is now unreferenced – there are no variables that refer to it – and so will be removed the next time the garbage collector comes along.

By itself, that doesn't look too bad, but suppose that we wanted to encode that string by replacing each letter (not the punctuation) with the character with an ASCII code of one further on in the alphabet as part of some extremely simple encryption scheme. This would turn the string to `"Ifmmp gspn bmm uif hvst bu Xspy Qsftt. Xf ep ipqf zpv fokpz uijt cppl bt nvdi bt xf fokpzfe xsjujoh ju."` There are several ways of doing this, but the simplest and (if you are restricting yourself to using the `String` class) almost certainly the most efficient way is to use the `String.Replace()` method, which replaces all occurrences of a given substring in a string with another substring. Using `Replace()`, the code to encode the text would look like this:

```
String GreetingText = "Hello from all the guys at Wrox Press. ";
GreetingText += "We do hope you enjoy this book as much as we enjoyed
                writing it";
for(int i = (int)'z'; i>=(int)'a' ; i-)
{
    char Old = (char)i;
    char New = (char)(i+1);
    GreetingText = GreetingText.Replace(Old, New);
}
for(int i = (int)'Z'; i>=(int)'A' ; i-)
{
    char Old = (char)i;
    char New = (char)(i+1);
    GreetingText = GreetingText.Replace(Old, New);
}
Console.WriteLine("Encoded:\n" + GreetingText);
```

For simplicity, this code doesn't wrap Z to A or z to a. These letters get respectively encoded to `"["` and `"{"`.

How much memory do you think we needed to allocate in total to perform this encoding? `Replace()` works in a fairly intelligent way, to the extent that it won't actually create a new string unless it does actually make some changes to the old string. Our original string contained 23 different lowercase characters and 2 different uppercase ones. `Replace()` will therefore have allocated a new string 25 times in total, each new string storing 103 characters. That means that as a result of our encryption process there will be string objects capable of storing a combined total of 2575 characters now sitting on the heap waiting to be garbage collected! Clearly if you use strings to do text processing extensively, your applications will run into severe performance problems.

It is in order to address this kind of issue that Microsoft has supplied the `System.Text.StringBuilder` class. `StringBuilder` isn't as powerful as `String` in terms of the number of methods it supports. The processing you can do on a `StringBuilder` is limited to substitutions and appending or removing text from strings. However, it works in a much more efficient way.

Whereas when you construct a string just enough memory gets allocated to hold the string, the `StringBuilder` will normally allocate more memory than needed. You have the option to explicitly indicate how much memory to allocate, but if you don't then the amount will default to some value that depends on the size of the string that `StringBuilder` is initialized with. It has two main properties: `Length`, which gives the length of the string that it actually contains, and `Capacity`, which is how long a string it has allocated enough memory to store. Any modifications to the string take place within this block of memory, which makes appending substrings and replacing individual characters within strings very efficient. Removing or inserting substrings is inevitably still inefficient, because it means that the following part of the string has to be moved. Only if you perform some operation that exceeds the capacity of the string will new memory need to be allocated and the contained string possibly moved. At the time of writing, Microsoft has not documented how much extra capacity will be added, but from experiments the `StringBuilder` appears to approximately double its capacity if it detects the capacity has been exceeded and no new value for the capacity has been explicitly set.

As an example, if we use a `StringBuilder` object to construct our original greeting string, we might write this code:

```
StringBuilder GreetingBuilder =
        new StringBuilder("Hello from all the people at Wrox Press. ", 150);
GreetingBuilder.Append("We do hope you enjoy this book as much as we enjoyed
                        writing it");
```

In this code, we have set an initial capacity of 150 for the `StringBuilder`. It's always a good idea to set some capacity that covers the likely maximum length of string, to ensure the `StringBuilder` doesn't need to relocate because its capacity was exceeded. Theoretically, you can set as large a number as it is possible to pass in an `int` for the capacity, though the system will probably complain that it doesn't have enough memory if you try to actually allocate the maximum of 2 billion characters!

When the above code is executed, we first create a `StringBuilder` object that initially looks like this:

Then on calling the `Append()` method, the remaining text is placed in the empty space, without needing to allocate any more memory. However, the real efficiency gain from using a `StringBuilder` comes when we are making repeated text substitutions. For example, if we try to encrypt the text in the same way as before, then we can perform the entire encryption without allocating any more memory whatsoever:

```
StringBuilder GreetingBuilder =
        new StringBuilder("Hello from all the guys at Wrox Press. ", 150);
GreetingBuilder.Append("We do hope you enjoy this book as much as we enjoyed
                        writing it");
for(int i = (int)'z'; i>=(int)'a' ; i-)
{
   char Old = (char)i;
   char New = (char)(i+1);
   GreetingBuilder = GreetingBuilder.Replace(Old, New);
}
for(int i = (int)'Z'; i>=(int)'A' ; i-)
{
   char Old = (char)i;
   char New = (char)(i+1);
   GreetingBuilder = GreetingBuilder.Replace(Old, New);
}
Console.WriteLine("Encoded:\n" + GreetingBuilder.ToString());
```

This code uses the `StringBuilder.Replace()` method, which does the same thing as `String.Replace()`, but without copying the string in the process. The total memory allocated to hold strings in the above code is 200 for the builder, as well as the memory allocated during the string operations performed internally in the final `Console.WriteLine()` statement.

Normally you will use `StringBuilder` to perform any manipulation of strings, and string to store or display the final result.

StringBuilder Members

We have demonstrated one constructor of `StringBuilder`, which takes an initial string and capacity as its parameters. There are also several others. Amongst them, you can supply only a string:

```
StringBuilder sb = new StringBuilder("Hello");
```

or create an empty `StringBuilder` with a given capacity:

```
StringBuilder sb = new StringBuilder(20);
```

Apart from the `Length` and `Capacity` properties we have mentioned, there is a read-only `MaxCapacity` property, which indicates the limit to which a given `StringBuilder` instance is allowed to grow. By default, this is given by `int.MaxValue` (roughly 2 billion), but you can set this value to something lower when you construct the `StringBuilder` object if you wish:

```
// these will both set initial capacity to 100, but the max will be 500.
// Hence these StringBuilders can never grow to more than 500 characters.
// Will raise exception if you try to do that.

StringBuilder sb = new StringBuilder("Hello", 100, 500);
StringBuilder sb = new StringBuilder(100, 500);
```

You can also freely explicitly set the capacity at any time, though an exception will be raised if you set it to a value less than the current length of the string or which exceeds the maximum capacity:

```
StringBuilder sb = new StringBuilder("Hello");
sb.Capacity = 100;
```

The main `StringBuilder` methods available include:

Method	Purpose
Append()	Appends a string to the current string
AppendFormat()	Appends a string that has been worked out from a format specifier
Insert()	Inserts a substring into the current string
Remove()	Removes characters from the current string
Replace()	Replaces all occurrences of a character by another character or a substring by another substring in the current string
ToString()	Returns the current string cast to a `System.String` object (overridden from `System.Object`)

There are several overloads of many of these methods available.

`AppendFormat()` is actually the method that is ultimately called when you call `Console.WriteLine()`, which has responsibility for working out what all the format expressions like `{0:D}` should be replaced with. We'll examine this method in the next section.

At the time of writing, there is no cast (either implicit or explicit) from `StringBuilder` to `String`. If you want to output the contents of a `StringBuilder` as a `String`, the only way to do so is through the `ToString()` method.

Formatting Strings

So far, up to now, we've written a large number of classes and structs for the samples we've presented in this book, and we've normally implemented a `ToString()` method for each of these in order to be able to quickly display the contents of a given variable. However, quite often there are a number of possible ways that users might want the contents of a variable to be displayed, and often these are culture (locale) specific. The .NET base class, `System.DateTime` provides the most obvious example of this. Ways that you might want to display the same date include 14 February 2001, 14 Feb 2001, 2/14/01 (in the USA, at least; in the UK this would be written 14/2/01), or of course in Germany you'd write 14. Februar 2001, and so on.

Similarly, for our `Vector` struct that we wrote in Chapter 5, we implemented the `Vector.ToString()` method to display the vector in the format `(4, 56, 8)`. There is however, another very common way of writing vectors, in which this vector would appear as `4i + 56j + 8k`. If we want the classes that we write to be user-friendly then they need to support the facility to display their string representations in any of the formats that users are likely to want to use. The .NET runtime defines a standard way that this should be done: using an interface, `IFormattable`, and showing how to add this important feature to your classes and structs is the subject of this section.

The most obvious time that you need to specify the format in which you want a variable displayed is when you call `Console.WriteLine()`. Therefore, we are going to use this method as an example, although most of our discussion applies for any situation in which you wish to format a string. If for example, you wish to display the value of a variable in a listbox or textbox, you'll normally use the `String.Format()` method to obtain the appropriate string representation of the variable, but the actual format specifiers you use to request a particular format are identical to those passed to `Console.WriteLine()`, and as we'll see in this section the same underlying mechanism is used. Hence, in this section, we'll focus on `Console.WriteLine()` as an example. We'll start by examining what actually happens when you supply a format string to a primitive type, and from this we will see how we can plug in format specifiers for our own classes and structs into the process.

Recall from Chapter 3 that we use format strings in `Console.Write()` and `Console.WriteLine()` like this:

```
double D = 13.45;
int I = 45;
Console.WriteLine("The double is {0,10:E} and the int contains {1}", D, I);
```

The format string itself consists mostly of the text to be displayed, but wherever there is a variable to be formatted, its index in the parameter list appears in braces. The may be other information inside the brackets concerning the format of that item:

❑ The number of characters to be occupied by the representation of the item can appear. This information will be prefixed by a comma. A negative number indicates that the item should be left justified, while a positive number indicates that it should be right justified. If the item actually occupies more characters than have been requested it will still appear in full.

❑ A format specifier can also appear. This will be preceded by a colon, and indicates how we wish the item to be formatted. For example, do we want a number to be formatted as a currency, or displayed in scientific notation?

The common format specifiers for the numeric types are these:

Specifier	Applies to	Meaning	Example
C	numeric types	locale-specific monetary value	$4834.50 (USA) £4834.50 (UK)
D	integer types only	general integer	4834
E	numeric types	scientific notation	4.834E+003
F	numeric types	fixed point decimal	4384.50
G	numeric types	general number	4384.5
N	numeric types	usual locale-specific format for numbers	4,384.50 (UK/USA) 4 384,50 (continental Europe)
P	numeric types	Percentage notation	432,000.00%
X	integer types only	hexadecimal format	1120 (NB. If you want to display 0x1120, you'd need to write out the 0x separately)

If you want an integer to be padded with zeros, you can use the format specifier 0 (zero) repeated the required number of times. For example, the format specifier 0000 will cause 3 to be displayed as 0003, and 99 to be displayed as 0099, etc.

It is not possible, to give a complete list because other data types can add their own specifiers. Showing how to define our own specifiers for our own classes is the aim of this section.

How the String Is Formatted

As an example of how formatting of strings works, we will see what happens when the statement:

```
Console.WriteLine("The double is {0,10:E} and the int contains {1}", D, I);
```

is executed.

In fact, Console.WriteLine() just hands the entire set of parameters straight over to the static method, String.Format() – the same method that you'd call if you wanted to format these values for use in a string to be used in some other way, such being displayed in a textbox. With the usual provisos about it being impossible to verify what the actual source code for this method really is, the implementation of the 3-parameter overload of WriteLine() basically does this:

```
// likely implementation of Console.WriteLine()

public void WriteLine(string format, object arg0, object arg1)
{
    WriteLine(string.Format(format, arg0, arg1));
}
```

The one-parameter overload of this method, that is in turn getting called above, simply writes out the contents of the string it has been passed, without doing any further formatting on it.

`String.Format()` now needs to construct the final string by replacing each format specifier by a suitable string representation of the corresponding object. However, as we saw earlier, this kind of process of building up a string is exactly the situation in which we really need a `StringBuilder` instance rather than a string instance, and that's exactly what happens. For the particular example we are using here, A `StringBuilder` instance will be created and initialized with the first known portion of the string, the text `"The double is "`. The `StringBuilder.AppendFormat()` method will then be called, passing in the first format specifier, `{0,10:E}`, and the associated object, the `double`, in order to add the string representation of this object to the string being constructed, and this process will continue with `StringBuilder.Append()` and `StringBuilder.AppendFormat()` being called repeatedly until the entire formatted string has been obtained.

Now comes the interesting part, because `StringBuilder.AppendFormat()` will need to figure out how to actually format the object. The first thing it will do is probe the object to find out whether it implements an interface in the `System` namespace called `IFormattable`. You can find this out quite simply by trying to cast an object to this interface and seeing whether the cast succeeds, or by using the C# `is` keyword. If this test fails, then `AppendFormat()` will simply call the object's `ToString()` method, which all objects either inherit from `System.Object` or override. In the cases of all the classes and structs we have written so far in the samples we have presented, this is what will happen, since so far none of the classes we have written have implemented this interface. That is why our overrides of `Object.ToString()` have been sufficient to allow our structs and classes from earlier chapters such as `Vector`, `Customer`, and `Nevermore60Customer` to get displayed in `Console.WriteLine()` statements.

However, all of the predefined primitive numeric types do implement this interface, which means that for those types, and in particular for the `double` and the `int` in our example, the basic `ToString()` method inherited from `System.Object` will not be called. To understand what happens instead, we need to examine the `IFormattable` interface.

`IFormattable` defines just one method, which is also called `ToString()`. However, this method takes two parameters as opposed to the `System.Object` version which takes no parameters. This is the definition of `IFormattable`:

```
interface IFormattable
{
    string ToString(string format, IFormatProvider formatProvider);
}
```

The first parameter that this overload of `ToString()` expects is a string that specifies the requested format. In other words, it is the specifier portion of the string that appears in the `"{}"` in the string originally passed to `Console.WriteLine()` or `String.Format()`. For example, in our example the original statement was:

```
Console.WriteLine("The double is {0,10:E} and the int contains {1}", D, I);
```

Hence, when evaluating the first specifier, `{0,10:E}`, this overload will be called against the double variable, `D`, and the first parameter passed to it will be `E`. What `StringBuilder.AppendFormat()` will pass in here is always whatever text appears after the colon in the appropriate format specifier from the original string.

We won't worry about the second parameter to `ToString()` in this book. It's a reference to an object that implements the interface `IFormatProvider`. This interface gives further information that `ToString()` may need to consider when formatting the object, most notably including details of a culture to be assumed (recall that a .NET culture is similar to a Windows locale; if you are formatting currencies or dates then you need this information). If you are calling this `ToString()` overload directly from your source code, you may wish to supply such an object. However, `StringBuilder.AppendFormat()` passes in `null` for this parameter. If `formatProvider` is `null`, then `ToString()` is expected to use the culture specified in the system settings.

Moving back to our example, the first item we wish to format is a double, for which we are requesting exponential notation, with the format specifier E. As just mentioned, `StringBuilder.AppendFormat()` method will establish that double does implement `IFormattable`, and will, therefore, call the two-parameter `ToString()` overload, passing it the string "E" for the first parameter and `null` for the second parameter. It is now up to the double's implementation of this method to return the string representation of the double in the appropriate format, taking into account the requested format and the current culture. `StringBuilder.AppendFormat()` will then sort out padding the returned string with spaces, if necessary, in order to fill the 10 characters the format string specified in this case.

The next object to be formatted is an int, for which we are not requesting any particular format (the format specifier was simply {1}). With no format requested, `StringBuilder.AppendFormat()` will pass in a null reference for the format string. Again the two-parameter overload of `int.ToString()` will be expected to respond appropriately. No format has been specifically requested therefore, it will most likely simply call the no-parameter `ToString()` method.

The whole process can be summarized in this diagram:

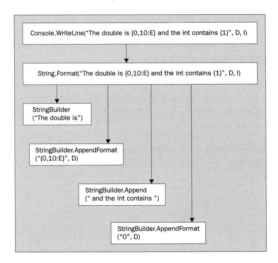

Sample: FormattableVector

Now that we have established how format strings are constructed, we are going to extend the `Vector` sample from Chapter 5, so that we can format vectors in a variety of ways. The sample code for this is downloadable as the `FormattableVector` sample. We'll find that, now that we have understood the principles involved, the actual coding is quite simple. All we need to do is implement `IFormattable`, and supply an implementation of the `ToString()` overload defined by that interface.

The format specifiers we are going to support are:

- ❑ N – should be interpreted as a request to supply a quantity known as the Norm of the Vector. This is just the sum of squares of its components, which for mathematics buffs happens to be equal to the square of the length of the Vector, and is usually displayed between double bars: ||34.5||.

- ❑ VE – should be interpreted as a request to display each component in scientific format, just as the specifier E applied to a double indicates (2.3E+01, 4.5E+02, 1.0E+00).

❑ IJK – should be interpreted as a request to display the vector in the form 23i + 450j + 1k.

❑ Anything else should simply return the default representation of the Vector (23, 450, 1.0).

To keep things simple, we're not going to implement any option to display the vector in combined IJK and scientific format. We will, however, allow make sure we test the specifier in a case-insensitive way, so that we allow ijk instead of IJK. Note that it's entirely up to us which strings we use to indicate the format specifiers.

To achieve this, we first modify the declaration of Vector so it implements IFormattable:

```
struct Vector : IFormattable
{
    public double x, y, z;
```

Now we add our implementation of the 2-parameter ToString() overload:

```
public string ToString(string format, IFormatProvider formatProvider)
{
    if (format == null)
        return ToString();
    string formatUpper = format.ToUpper();
    switch (formatUpper)
    {
        case "N":
            return "|| " + Norm().ToString() + " ||";
        case "VE":
            return String.Format("( {0:E}, {1:E}, {2:E} )", x, y, z);
        case "IJK":
            StringBuilder sb = new StringBuilder(x.ToString(), 30);
            sb.Append(" i + ");
            sb.Append(y.ToString());
            sb.Append(" j + ");
            sb.Append(z.ToString());
            sb.Append(" k");
            return sb.ToString();
        default:
            return ToString();
    }
}
```

That is all we have to do! Notice how we take the precaution of checking whether format is null before we call any methods against this parameter – we don't want any Exceptions occurring in this method. The format specifiers for all the primitive types are case-insensitive, so that's the behavior that other developers are going to expect from our class too. For the format specifier VE, we need each component to be formatted in scientific notation, so we just use String.Format() again to achieve this. The fields x, y, and z are all doubles. For the case of the IJK format, there are quite a few substrings to be added to the string, so we use a StringBuilder object to improve performance.

For completeness, we'll also reproduce the no-parameter ToString() overload that we developed in Chapter 5:

```
public override string ToString()
{
    return "( " + x + " , " + y + " , " + z + " )";
}
```

Finally, we need to add a `Norm()` method, since we hadn't actually supplied this method when we first developed the `Vector` struct in chapter 5:

```
public double Norm()
{
    return x*x + y*y + z*z;
}
```

Now we can try out our formattable vector with some suitable test code:

```
static void Main(string[] args)
{
    Vector V1 = new Vector(1,32,5);
    Vector V2 = new Vector(845.4, 54.3, -7.8);
    Console.WriteLine("\nIn IJK format,\nV1 is {0,30:IJK}\nV2 is {1,30:IJK}",
                      V1, V2);
    Console.WriteLine("\nIn default format,\nV1 is {0,30}\nV2 is {1,30}", V1,
                      V2);
    Console.WriteLine("\nIn VE format\nV1 is {0,30:VE}\nV2 is {1,30:VE}", V1,
                      V2);
    Console.WriteLine("\nNorms are:\nV1 is {0,20:N}\nV2 is {1,20:N}", V1,
                      V2);
}
```

The result of running this sample is this:

This shows that our custom specifiers are being picked up correctly.

Regular Expressions

Regular expressions form one of those little technology areas that is incredibly useful in a wide range of programs, but despite that isn't really that widely known amongst developers. It could almost be thought of as a mini programming language with one specific purpose: to locate substrings within a large string expression. It is not a new technology; it originated in the UNIX environment, and is commonly used with Perl. Microsoft ported it onto Windows, where it has up until now mostly been used with scripting languages. Regular expressions are, however, supported by a number of .NET classes in the namespace `System.Text.RegularExpressions`.

Many readers will not be familiar with the regular expressions language, so we will use this section as a very basic introduction to both regular expressions and to the related .NET classes. If you are already familiar with regular expressions then you'll probably want to just skim through this section to pick out the references to the .NET base classes. You might like to note that the .NET regular expression engine is designed to be mostly compatible with Perl 5 regular expressions, though it has a few extra features.

Introduction to Regular Expressions

These days just about all text editors have some kind of search facility. Usually, you bring up a dialog in which you type in the string you want to locate in one textbook box, and if you want to do a replacement operation of the same time you can type in a replacement string. In its simplest form, you might for example request to replace all instances of "MS" in a document with "Microsoft". This sort of problem can easily be tackled with the `string` class, using the `string.Replace()` method. What happens, however, if the situation is that you need to identify any repeated words in the document? Writing a routine that can pick repeated words out of a string class would be quite complicated. It's for this sort of situation that the regular expressions language is suited.

The regular expressions language is essentially a language in which you can write search expressions. In the language, text to be searched for in a document is combined with escape sequences and other characters that have a special meaning. For example, the sequence `\b` indicates the beginning or end of a word (a word boundary), so if we wanted to indicate we were looking for the characters `th` at the beginning of a word, we would search for the regular expression, `\bth`. (that is, the sequence word boundary – t – h). If we wanted to search for all occurrences of `th` at the end of a word, we would write `th\b` (the sequence t – h – word boundary). However, regular expressions are much more sophisticated than that, and include, for example, facilities to store portions of text that are found in a search operation. In this section, we'll merely scratch the surface of the power of regular expressions.

As another example, suppose your application needed to convert UK phone numbers from national to international format. In the UK, national format would be something like 0233 345532, which would sometimes be written (0233) 345532. International format would mean this number should always be written +44 233 345532, in other words the leading zero must be replaced by +44, and any brackets removed. As find-and-replace operations go, that's not too complicated, but would still require some coding effort if you were going to use the `String` class for this purpose (which would mean that you would have to write your code using the methods available on `System.String`); you would need to locate any zeros that occur at the beginning of a number or immediately following a left bracket. Again, the regular expressions language allows us to construct a short string that will be interpreted to have this meaning.

This section is intended only as a very simple example, so we will simply concentrate on finding strings, not on replacing them.

Sample: RegularExpressionsPlayaround

For the rest of this section, we will develop a short sample that simply illustrates some of the features of regular expressions and how to use the .NET regular expressions engine in C#, by performing and displaying the results of some searches. The text we are going to use as our sample "document" to search through is the introduction to another Wrox Press book on XML (*Professional XML 2nd Edition* by Jonathan Pinnock *et al.*, ISBN 1861005059):

```
string Text =
@"XML has made a major impact in almost every aspect of software development
Designed as an open, extensible, self-describing language,
it has become the standard for data and document delivery on the web.
The panoply of XML-related technologies continues to develop at breakneck
speed, to enable validation, navigation, transformation, linking, querying,
description, and messaging of data.";
```

Note that the above is valid C# code – it nicely illustrates the utility of verbatim strings that are prefixed by the "@" symbol.

We'll refer to this text as the **input string**. To get our bearings and get used to the regular expressions .NET classes, we'll start with a basic plain text search that doesn't feature any escape sequences or regular expression commands. Suppose that we want to find all occurrences of the string ion. We will refer to this search string as the **pattern**. Using regular expressions and the Text variable declared above, you could do it like this:

```
string Pattern = "ion";
MatchCollection Matches = Regex.Matches(Text, Pattern,
                              RegexOptions.IgnoreCase |
                              RegexOptions.ExplicitCapture);
foreach (Match NextMatch in Matches)
{
    Console.WriteLine(NextMatch.Index);
}
```

In this code, we have used the static method Matches() of the Regex class in the System.Text.RegularExpressions namespace. This method takes as parameters some input text, a pattern, and a set of optional flags taken from the RegexOptions enumeration. In this case we have specified that all searching should be case-insensitive. The other flag, ExplicitCapture, modifies the way that the match is collected in a way that, for our purposes, makes the search a bit more efficient (although it does have other uses that we won't explore here). Matches() returns a reference to a MatchCollections object. A **match** is the technical term for the results of finding an instance of the pattern in the expression. It is represented by the class System.Text.RegularExpressions.Match. Therefore, we return a MatchCollection that contains all the matches, each represented by a Match object. In the above code, we simply iterate over the collection, and use the Index property of the Match class, which returns the index in the input text of where the match was found. When I ran this code, it found four matches.

So far, there's not really anything new here apart from some new .NET base classes. However, the power of regular collections really comes from that pattern string. The reason is that the pattern string doesn't only have to contain plain text. As hinted at earlier, it can also contain what are known as **metacharacters**, which are special characters that give commands, as well as escape sequences, which work in much the same way as C# escape sequences. They are characters preceded by a backslash, "\", and also have special meanings.

For example, suppose we wanted to find words beginning with n. We could use the escape sequence \b, which indicates a word boundary (a word boundary is just a point where a an alphanumeric character precedes or follows a whitespace character or punctuation symbol). We would simply write this:

```
string Pattern = @"\bn";
MatchCollection Matches = Regex.Matches(Text, Pattern,
                              RegexOptions.IgnoreCase |
                              RegexOptions.ExplicitCapture);
```

Notice the "@" character in front of the string. We want the \b to be passed to the .NET regular expressions engine at runtime – we don't want the backslash intercepted by a well-meaning C# compiler that thinks it's an escape sequence intended for itself! If we want to find words ending with the sequence ion, then we could do this:

```
string Pattern = @"ion\b";
```

What if we want to find all words that begin with the letter n and end with the sequence ion? (This would pick out the one word "navigation" from the above text). That's a little more complicated. We clearly need a pattern that begins with \bn and ends with ion\b, but what goes in the middle? We need to somehow tell the computer that between that the n and the ion there can be any number of characters as long as none of them are whitespace. In fact, the correct pattern looks like this:

```
string Pattern = @"\bn\S*ion\b";
```

One thing you'll get used to with regular expressions is seeing weird sequences of characters like this, but it actually works quite logically. The escape sequence \S indicates any character that is not a whitespace character. The "*" is called a **quantifier**. It means that the preceding character can be repeated any number of times, including zero times. The sequence \S* means "any number of characters as long as they are not whitespace characters." The above pattern will, therefore, match any single word that begins with n and ends with ion.

The table shows some of the main special characters or escape sequences that you can use:

	Meaning	Example	Examples that this will match
^	Beginning of input text	^B	B, but only if first character in text
$	End of the input text	X$	X, but only if last character in text
.	Any single character except the newline character (\n)	i.ation	isation, ization,
*	Preceding character may be repeated 0 or more times	ra*t	rt, rat, raat, raaat, and so on
+	Preceding character may be repeated 1 or more times	ra+t	rat, raat, raaat and so on, (but not rt)
?	Preceding character may be repeated 0 or 1 times	ra?t	Will match rt and rat only.
\s	Any whitespace character	\sa	[space]a, \ta, \na (\t and \n have the same meanings as in C#)
\S	Any character that isn't a whitespace	\SF	aF, rF, cF, but not \tF
\b	Word boundary	ion\b	any word ending in ion
\B	Any position that isn't a word boundary	\BX\B	any X in the middle of a word

If you want actually search for one of the metacharacters, you can do so by escaping the corresponding character with a backslash. For example "." means any single character other than the newline character, while "\." means a dot.

You can request a match that contains alternative characters by enclosing them in square brackets. For example [1|c] means one character that can be either a 1 or a c. If you want to search for any occurrence of the words map or man, you would use the sequence ma[n|p]. Within the square brackets, you can also indicate a range, for example [a-z] to indicate any single lower case letter, [A-E] to indicate any uppercase letter between A and E, or [0-9] to represent a single digit. If you want to search for an integer (that is, a sequence that contains only the characters 0 through 9), you could write [0-9]+ (note the use of the + character to indicate there must be at least one such digit, but there may be more than one – so this would match 9, 83, 854, and so on).

Displaying Results

Now we've got a flavor for what regular expressions are about, we'll actually code up our RegularExpressionsPlayaround sample. This is not really intended as a serious example of a real situation; it lets you set up a few regular expressions and displays the results so you can get a feel for how the expressions work.

The core of the sample is a method called `WriteMatches()`, which writes out all the matches from a `MatchCollection` in a more detailed format. For each match, it displays the index of where the match was found in the input string, the string of the match, and a slightly longer string which consists of the match up to eight surrounding characters from the input text – up to 5 characters before the match and up to 5 afterwards (it's less than 4 characters if the match occurred within 5 characters of the beginning or end of the input text). In other words, a match on the word `messaging` that occurs near the end of the input text quoted earlier would display `" and messaging of d"` (five characters before and after the match), but a match on the final word `data` would display `"g of data."` (only one character after the match), because after that we hit the end of the string. This longer string lets you see more clearly where the regular expression located the match:

```
static void WriteMatches(string Text, MatchCollection Matches)
{
   Console.WriteLine("Original text was: \n\n" + Text + "\n");
   Console.WriteLine("No. of matches: " + Matches.Count);
   foreach (Match NextMatch in Matches)
   {
      int Index = NextMatch.Index;
      string Result = NextMatch.ToString();
      int CharsBefore = (Index < 5) ? Index : 5;
      int FromEnd = Text.Length- Index - Result.Length;
      int CharsAfter = (FromEnd < 5) ? FromEnd : 5;
      int CharsToDisplay = CharsBefore + CharsAfter + Result.Length;
      Console.WriteLine("Index: {0}, \tString: {1}, \t{2}",
                        Index, Result,
                        Text.Substring(Index-CharsBefore, CharsToDisplay));
   }
}
```

The bulk of the processing in this method is devoted to the logic of figuring out how many characters in the longer substring it can display without overrunning the beginning or end of the input text. Note that we use another property on the `Match` object, `Value`, which contains the string identified for the match. Other than that, `RegularExpressionsPlayaround` simply contains a number of methods with names like `Find1`, `Find2`, and so on, which perform some of the searches based on the examples in this section. For example, `Find2` looks for any string that contains n at the beginning of a word:

```
static void Find1()
{
   string Text = @"XML has made a major impact in almost every aspect of
      software development. Designed as an open, extensible, self-describing
      language, it has become the standard for data and document delivery on
      the web. The panoply of XML-related technologies continues to develop
      at breakneck speed, to enable validation, navigation, transformation,
      linking, querying, description, and messaging of data.";
   string Pattern = @"\bn\S*ion\b";
   MatchCollection Matches = Regex.Matches(Text, Pattern,
      RegexOptions.IgnoreCase | RegexOptions.IgnorePatternWhitespace |
      RegexOptions.ExplicitCapture);
   WriteMatches(Text, Matches);
}
```

Along with this is a simple `Main()` method that you can edit to select one of the `Find<n>()` methods:

```
static void Main(string[] args)
{
   Find1();
}
```

The code also makes use of the `RegularExpressions` namespace:

```
using System;
using System.Text.RegularExpressions;
```

For example, running the sample with the `Find1()` method as above gives these results:

```
C:\Documents and Settings\allanj.WROX_UK\Desktop\RegularExpressionPlayaround\bin\Debug...
Original text was:

XML has made a major impact in almost every aspect of software development
Designed as an open, extensible, self-describing language,
it has become the standard for data and document delivery on the web.
The panoply of XML-related technologies continues to develop at breakneck
speed, to enable validation, navigation, transformation, linking, querying,
description, and messaging of data.

No. of matches: 1
Index: 314,       String: navigation,       ion, navigation, tra
```

Matches, Groups, and Captures

One nice feature of regular expressions is that you can group characters together. It works the same way as compound statements in C#. Recall that in C# you can group any number of statements together by putting them in braces, and the result is treated as one compound statement. In regular expression patterns, you can group any characters (including metacharacters and escape sequences) together, and the result is treated as a single character. The only difference is you use parentheses instead of braces. The resultant sequence is known as a **group**.

For example, the pattern `(an)+` will locate any recurrences of the sequence an. The "+" quantifier applies only to the previous character, but because we have grouped the characters together, it now applies to repeats of ha treated as a unit. This means that `(an)+` applied to the input text, `"bananas came to Europe late in the annals of history"` will pick out the anan from bananas. On the other hand, if we'd written an+, that would pick out the ann from annals, as well as two separate sequences of "an" from "bananas".

> You might wonder why with the above example, `(an)+` picks out anan, but doesn't identify any of the individual an occurrences as a match. The rule is that matches must not overlap. If there are a couple of possibilities that would overlap, then by default the longest possible sequence will be matched.

However, groups are actually more powerful than that. By default, when you form part of the pattern into a group, you are also asking the regular expression engine to remember any matches against just that group, as well as any matches against the entire pattern. In other words you are treating that group as a pattern to be matched and returned in its own right. This can actually be extremely useful if you want to break up strings into component parts.

For example, URIs have the format: `<protocol>://<address>:<port>`, where the port is optional. An example of this is `http://www.wrox.com:4355`. Suppose you want to extract the protocol, the address, and the port from a URI, where you know that there may or may not be whitespace, (but no punctuation) immediately following the URI. You could do so using this expression:

```
\b(\S+)://(\S+)(?::(\S+))?\b
```

The way this expression works is this. First, the leading and trailing \b sequences ensure that we only consider portions of text that are entire words. Within that, the first group, (\S+):// will pick out one or more characters that don't count as whitespace, and which are followed by ://. This will pick out the http:// at the start of an HTTP URI. The brackets will cause the http to be stored as a group. The subsequent (\S+) will pick out expressions such as www.wrox.com in the above URI. This group will end either when it hits the end of the word (the closing \b) or when it hits a colon (:) as marked by the next group.

The next group is intended to pick out the port (:4355 in our case). The following "?" indicates that this group is optional in the match – if there is no :xxxx then this won't prevent a match from being marked.

That's very important as the port number isn't always specified in a URI – in fact it's absent most of the time. However, things are a bit more complicated than that. We want to indicate that the colon might or might not appear too, but we don't want to store this colon in the group. We've achieved this by having two nested groups. The inner (\S+) will pick out anything that follows the colon (for example the 4355 in our example). The outer group contains the inner group preceded by the colon, and that in turn is preceded by the sequence "?:". This sequence indicates that the group in question should not be saved (we only want to save the 4355; we don't need the :4355 as well!). Don't get confused by the two colons following each other – the first is part of the "?:" sequence that says "don't save this group," and the second is text to be searched for.

If you run this pattern on this string:

```
Hey I've just found this amazing URI at http:// what was it - oh yes
http://www.wrox.com
```

you'll get one match: http://www.wrox.com. Within this match, there are the three groups just mentioned as well as a fourth group which represents the match itself. Theoretically, it is possible that each group itself might pick none, one or more than one match. Each of these individual matches is known as a **capture**. So the first group, (\S+), has one capture, http. The second group has one capture too: www.wrox.com, but the third group has no captures, since there's no port number on this URI.

Notice that the string contained a second http:// on its own. Although this does match up to our first group, it will not be picked out by the search because the entire search expression will not match this part of the text.

We don't have space to show any examples of C# code that uses groups and captures, we will mention that the .NET RegularExpressions classes support groups and captures, through classes known as Group and Capture. There are also classes GroupCollection and CaptureCollection, which respectively represent collections of groups and captures. The Match class exposes a method, Groups(), which returns the corresponding GroupCollection object. The Group class correspondingly implements a method, Captures(), which returns a CaptureCollection. The relationship between the objects is as shown in the diagram:

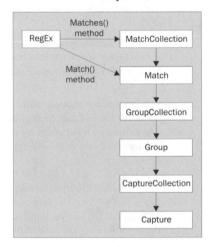

Returning a `Group` object every time you just want to group some characters together may not be what you want to do. There's a fair amount of overhead involved in instantiating the object, which is wasted if all you wanted was to group some characters together as part of your search pattern. You can disable this by starting the group with the character sequence "`?:`" for an individual group, as we did for our URI example, or for all groups by specifying the `RegExOptions.ExplicitCaptures` flag on the `RegEx.Matches()` method, as we did in the earlier examples.

Groups of Objects

We are now going to examine the support that the .NET base classes have for data structures in which a number of similar objects are grouped together. The simplest such data structure is the ordinary array, which we saw how to use in Chapter 3. The ordinary array is actually an instance of the class `System.Array`, but C# wraps its own syntax around this class. `System.Array` has the advantages of being relatively efficient for accessing an individual element given its index, and of having its own C# syntax, which obviously makes using it more intuitive. However, `Array` has the big disadvantage that you need to specify its size when you instantiate it. There is no facility for adding, inserting or removing elements later on. You also have to have a numeric index in order to be able to access an element. This is not particularly useful if, for example, you are dealing with a set of employee records and need to look up given record from the name of the employee.

.NET has quite extensive support for a number of other data structures that are useful in different circumstances. Not only that, but there are also a number of interfaces, which classes can implement in order to declare that they support all the functionality of a particular type of data structure. Here we are going to survey three of these structures: array lists, collections, and dictionaries (also sometimes known as maps).

Other than the basic `System.Array`, all the data structure classes are in the `System.Collections` namespace.

> The name `System.Collections` *reflects another of those terminology ambiguities that plague computing.* **Collection** *is often used informally to denote any data structure. However, it also has the more specific meaning of a class that implements* `IEnumerable` *or* `ICollection` *– a particular type of data structure which we will investigate later in the chapter. In this chapter, we will always use the term Collection to refer to the more specific meaning, except where .NET base class names force us to use it in the general sense.*

Array Lists

An **array list** is very similar to an array, except that it has the ability to grow. It is represented by the class `System.Collections.ArrayList`.

The `ArrayList` class also has some similarities with the `StringBuilder` class that we looked at earlier. Just as a `StringBuilder` allocated enough space in memory to store a certain number of characters, and allowed you to manipulate characters within the space, the `ArrayList` allocates enough memory to store a certain number of object references. You can then efficiently manipulate these object references, however you wish within that limit. If you try to add more objects to the `ArrayList` than the capacity allows, then it will automatically increase its capacity by allocating a new area of memory big enough to hold twice as many elements as the current capacity, and relocating to there.

You can instantiate an array list by indicating the initial capacity you want. For this example, we'll assume we are creating a list of `Vectors`:

```
ArrayList Vectors = new ArrayList(20);
```

If you don't specify the initial size, it defaults to `16`:

```
ArrayList Vectors = new ArrayList();    // capacity of 16
```

You can then add elements using the `Add()` method:

```
Vectors.Add(new Vector(2,2,2));
Vectors.Add(new Vector(3,5,6));
```

The `ArrayList` treats all its elements as object references. That means you can store whatever objects you like in an `ArrayList`, but when accessing the objects, you'll need to cast them back to the appropriate data type:

```
Vector Element2 = (Vector)Vectors[1];
```

This example also shows that `ArrayList` defines an indexer, so that you can access its elements with an array-like syntax. You can also insert elements into the `ArrayList`:

```
Vectors.Insert(1, new Vector(3,2,2));    // inserts at position 1
```

There is also a useful override of insert that allows you to insert all the elements of a collection into an `ArrayList`, given an `ICollection` interface references.

You may remove elements:

```
Vectors.RemoveAt(1);    // removes object at position 1
```

You can also supply an object reference to another method, `Remove()`. Doing this will take longer as it will cause the `ArrayList` to make a linear search through the array to find the object.

You can modify or read the capacity via the capacity property:

```
Vectors.Capacity = 30;
```

Note, however, that changing the capacity will cause the entire `ArrayList` to be reallocated to a new block of memory with the required capacity.

The number of elements actually in the `ArrayList` can be obtained via the `Count` property:

```
int nVectors = Vectors.Count;
```

An array list can be really useful if you need to build up an array of objects but you do not know in advance how big the array is going to end up. In that case you can construct the "array" in an `ArrayList`, and then convert the copy `ArrayList` back to an array when you've finished if you actually need the data as an array (this would be the case, for example, if the array is to be passed to a method that expects an array as a parameter). The relationship between `ArrayList` and `Array` is in many ways similar to that between `StringBuilder` and `String`.

Unfortunately, unlike the `StringBuilder` class, there is no single method to convert an array list to an array. You have to use a loop to manually copy references back. Note, however, that you are only copying the references not the objects, so this shouldn't give too much of a performance hit:

```
Vector [] VectorsArray = new Vector[Vectors.Count];
for (int i=0 ; i< Vectors.Count ; i++)
   VectorArray[i] = (Vector)Vectors [i];
```

Collections

The idea of a **collection** is that it represents a set of objects that you can access by stepping through each element in turn. In particular, it is the set of objects that you access using a `foreach` loop. In other words, when you write something like this:

```
foreach (string NextMessage in MessageSet)
{
   DoSomething(NextMessage);
}
```

you are assuming that the variable `MessageSet` is a collection. The ability to use a `foreach` loop is the main purpose of collections. They offer little in the way of additional features.

Over the next couple of pages, we're going to look in more detail at what a collection is and we're going to implement our own collection, by converting the `Vector` sample that we have been developing into a collection. The broad concepts behind collections are actually not new to .NET. Collections have been a part of COM for years, and have also been used in Visual Basic with the convenient `For...Each` syntax. Java also has a `foreach` loop, and in both cases the underlying architecture is very similar to that for .NET collections.

What is a Collection

Internally, an object is a collection if it is able to supply a reference to a related object, known as an **enumerator**, which is able to step through the items in the collection. More specifically a collection must implement the interface `System.Collections.IEnumerable`. `IEnumerable` defines just one method, and looks like this:

```
interface IEnumerable
{
   IEnumerator GetEnumerator();
}
```

The purpose of `GetEnumerator()` is to return the enumerator object. As you will gather from the above code, the enumerator object is expected to implement an interface `System.Collections.IEnumerator`.

There is an additional collections interface, `ICollection`, which is derived from `IEnumerable`. More sophisticated collections will implement this interface as well. Besides `GetEnumerator()`, it implements a property that directly returns the number of elements in the collection. It also features support for copying the collection to an array and can supply information indicating if it is thread safe. However, here we will only consider the simpler collection interface, `IEnumerable`.

`IEnumerator` looks like this:

```
interface IEnumerator
{
    object Current { get; }
    bool MoveNext();
    void Reset();
}
```

`IEnumerator` is intended to work like this: the object that implements it should be associated with one particular collection. When this object is first initialized, it does not yet refer to any elements in the collection, and you must call `MoveNext()`, which moves the enumerator so that it refers to the first element in the collection. You can then retrieve this element with the `Current` property. `Current` returns an object reference, so you will have to cast it to the type of object you are expecting to find in the collection. You can do whatever you want with that object then move to the next item in the collection by calling `MoveNext()` again. You repeat this process until there are no more items in the collection – you will know this has happened when the `Current` property returns `null`. If you wish, you can at any time return to the start of the collection by calling the `Reset()` method. Note that `Reset()` actually returns to just before start of the collection so if you call this method you will need to subsequently call `MoveNext()` again to get to the first element.

You can see from this that the point of the collection is simply to provide a way of stepping through all the elements when you don't want to supply an index, and you are happy to rely on the collection itself to choose the order in which the elements will be returned to you. This will usually mean that you are not bothered about the order in which the elements are retrieved, as long as you get to see all of them, although in some cases it may be that a particular collection is documented as returning the elements in a certain order. In one sense, a collection is a very basic type of group of objects, because it does not allow you to add or remove items from the group. All you can do is retrieve the items in an order determined by the collection, and examine them. It is not even possible to replace or modify items in the collection, because the `Current` property is read-only. The most frequent use of the collection is to give you the syntactical convenience of the `foreach` loop.

Arrays are also collections, as should be obvious because the `foreach` command works successfully with arrays. For the particular case of arrays the enumerator supplied by the `System.Array` class steps through the elements in increasing order of index from zero upwards.

From the above discussion we can see the above `foreach` loop in C# is just a syntactical shortcut for writing:

```
{
    Enumerator IEnumerator = MessageSet.GetEnumerator()
    string NextMessage;
    Enumerator.MoveNext();
    while ( (NextMessage = Enumerator.Current) != null)
    {
        DoSomething(NextMessage);    // NB. We only have read access to
                                     // NextMessage
        Enumerator.MoveNext();
    }
}
```

Note the enclosing curly braces around the above code snippet. We've supplied them in order to ensure that this code has exactly the same effect as the earlier `foreach` loop. If we hadn't included them then this code would have differed to the extent that the `NextMessage` and `Enumerator` variables would have remained in scope beyond the end of the loop.

One important aspect of collections is that the enumerator is returned as a separate object. It should not be the same object as the collection itself. The reason is to allow for the possibility that more than one enumerator might be applied simultaneously to the same collection.

Adding Collection Support to the Vector Struct

Our `Vector` struct that we started in Chapter 5, and to which we have already added formatting support earlier in this chapter, is about to get another extension, with collection support.

When we last left the `Vector` struct, a `Vector` instance contained three components, x, y, and z, and because we had defined an indexer in Chapter 5, it was possible to treat a `Vector` instance as an array, so that we could access the x-component by writing `SomeVector[0]`, the y-component by writing `SomeVector[1]` and the z-component by writing `SomeVector[2]`.

We will now extend the `Vector` struct into a new sample, the `VectorAsCollection` project, in which it is also possible to iterate through the components of a `Vector` by writing code like this:

```
foreach (double Component in SomeVector)
   Console.WriteLine("Component is " + Component);
```

Our first task is to mark `Vector` as a collection by having it implement the `IEnumerable` interface. We start by modifying the declaration of the `Vector` struct:

```
struct Vector : IFormattable, IEnumerable
{
   public double x, y, z;
```

Note that the `IFormattable` interface is present because we added support for string format specifiers earlier in this chapter. Now we need to implement the `IEnumerable` interface:

```
struct Vector : IFormattable, IEnumerable
{
   public IEnumerator GetEnumerator()
   {
      return new VectorEnumerator(this);
   }
```

The implementation of `GetEnumerator()` could hardly be simpler, but it depends on the existence of a new class, `VectorEnumerator`, which we need to define. Because `VectorEnumerator` is not a class that any outside code needs to be able to see directly, we declare it as a private class inside the `Vector` struct. Its definition looks like this:

```
private class VectorEnumerator : IEnumerator
{
   Vector theVector;        // Vector object that this enumerato refers to
   int location;            // which element of theVector the enumerator is
                            // currently referring to
   public VectorEnumerator(Vector theVector)
```

```
    {
        this.theVector = theVector;
        location = -1;
    }
    public bool MoveNext()
    {
        ++location;
        return (location > 2) ? false : true;
    }
    public object Current
    {
        get
        {
            if (location < 0 || location > 2)
                throw new InvalidOperationException(
                    "The enumerator is either before the first element or " +
                    "after the last element of the Vector");
            return theVector[(uint)location];
        }
    }
    public void Reset()
    {
        location = -1;
    }
}
```

As required for an enumerator, VectorEnumerator implements the IEnumerator interface. It also contains two member fields, theVector, which is a reference to the Vector (the collection) that this enumerator is to be associated with, and location, an int that indicates where in the collection the enumerator should reference – in other words whether the Current property should retrieve the x, y, or z component of the vector.

The way we will work in this case is by treating location as an index and internally implementing the enumerator to access the Vector as an array. When accessing the Vector as an array, the valid indices are 0, 1, and 2 – we'll extend this by using -1 as the value that indicates the enumerator is before the start of the collection, and 3 to indicate that it is beyond the end of the collection. Hence, the initialization of this field to -1 in the VectorEnumerator constructor:

```
public VectorEnumerator(Vector theVector)
{
    this.theVector = theVector;
    location = -1;
}
```

Notice the constructor also takes a reference to the Vector instance that we are to enumerate – this was supplied in the Vector.GetEnumerator() method:

```
public IEnumerator GetEnumerator()
{
    return new VectorEnumerator(this);
}
```

Dictionaries

Dictionaries represent a very sophisticated data structure that allows you to access an element based on some key, which can be of any data type you want. They are also known as **maps** or **hash tables**. Dictionaries are great for situations where you have wish to store objects as if they were an array, but where you want to use some other data type rather than a numeric type to index into the structure. They also allow you to freely add and remove items, a bit like an `ArrayList`.

We will illustrate the kinds of situations in which dictionaries can be useful using the sample that we will develop later in this section, the `MortimerPhonesEmployees` sample. This sample assumes that `MortimerPhones` (the mobile phone company that we first introduced in chapter 4) has some software that processes details of its employees. To that end we need a data structure – something like an array – that contains data for employees. We assume that each Mortimer Phones employee is identified by an employee ID, which is a set of characters such as B342 or W435, and is stored as an `EmployeeID` object. The employee's details are stored as an `EmployeeData` object; for our example, this just contains the employee's ID, name and salary.

Suppose we have this `EmployeeID`:

```
EmployeeID id = new EmployeeID("W435");
```

and we have a variable called `employees`, which we can treat syntactically as an array of `EmployeeData` objects. However, in actuality, it's not an array – it's a dictionary, and because it's a dictionary we can get the details of an employee with the ID declared above like this:

```
EmployeeData theEmployee = employees[id];
```

That's the power of dictionaries. They look like arrays (but more powerful than that; they are more like `ArrayLists` since you can dynamically set their capacity, and add and remove elements from them), but you don't have to use an integer to index into them; you can use any data type you want. For a dictionary, this is called a **key** rather than an index. Roughly speaking, what happens is that the dictionary takes the key supplied when you access an element (in the above example this is the ID object) and it does some processing on the value of this key. This processing returns an integer that depends on the value of the key, and is used to work out where in the "array" the entry should be stored or retrieved from. Other examples where you would use a dictionary to store objects include:

❑ You wish to store details of employees or other people, indexed by their social security numbers Although the social security number is basically an integer, you still couldn't use an array with social security numbers as the index since a US social security number can theoretically go up to the value 999999999. On a 32-bit system you'd never fit an array that big in a program's address space! Most of the array would be empty anyway. Using a dictionary, we can have a social security number to index an employee, but still keep the dictionary size small.

❑ If you want to store addresses, indexed by zip code. In the USA, zip codes are just numbers, but in Canada they have letters in too. In the UK, the equivalent (postal codes) are strings that contain both letters and numbers.

❑ Any data for objects or people that you wish to store, indexed by the name of the object or person.

Although the effect of a dictionary is that it looks to client code much like a dynamic array with a very flexible means of indexing into it, there's a lot of work that goes on behind the scenes to bring this about. Although in principle an object of any class can be used as the key to index into a dictionary, you do need to implement certain features on a class before it can be usefully used as a key. This also crucially involves the `GetHashCode()` method that all classes and structs inherit from `System.Object`. In this section we'll take a closer look under the hood at what a dictionary is, how it works and how `GetHashCode()` is involved. Then we'll move on to our `MortimerPhonesEmployees` example, which demonstrates both how to use a dictionary, and how to set up a class so that it can be used as a key.

Dictionaries in Real Life

The name "dictionary" is used because the structure is very similar to a real-life dictionary. In a real dictionary you will normally want to look up the meaning of a word (or in the case of a foreign dictionary, the details of how to translate a word); the couple of lines of text that give the meaning (or the translation) is the data that you are really interested in. The fact that a large dictionary will have tens of thousands of data items in it is no problem when you want to look a meaning up, because you just look for the word in alphabetical order. In a sense the word you are looking up is equivalent to the key that you use to get at the data you are really interested in. It's not really the word itself you are interested in so much as the data associated with it. The word just provides the means to locate the entry in the dictionary. This means that there are really three things here that you need to make a dictionary:

❑   The data you want to look up.

❑   The key.

❑   The algorithm that allows you to find where the data is in the dictionary.

The algorithm is a crucial part of the dictionary. Just knowing what the key is isn't sufficient – you also need a way that you can use the key to find out the location of the item in the data structure. In real-life dictionaries, this algorithm is provided by arranging words in alphabetical order.

Dictionaries in .NET

In .NET, the basic dictionary is represented by the class `Hashtable`, which works on the same principles of a real-life dictionary, except that it assumes that the key and item are both of type `Object`. This means that a `Hashtable` can store whatever data structure you want – whereas a real-life dictionary uses strings as the keys.

Although `Hashtable` represents the generic will-store-anything dictionary, it is permissible to define your own more specialized dictionary classes. Microsoft has provided an abstract base class, `DictionaryBase`, which provides basic dictionary functionality, and from which you can derive your classes. There is also a ready-made .NET base class, `System.Collections.Specialized.StringDictionary`, which you should use in place of `Hashtable` if your keys are strings.

When you create a `Hashtable` object, you can indicate its initial capacity, just as you do for `StringBuilder` and `ArrayList`:

```
Hashtable Employees = new Hashtable(53);
```

As usual there are many other constructors, but this is the one you'll probably most commonly be using. Notice the unusual size of the initial capacity that I've chosen: 53. There's a good reason for this. Due to the internal algorithms used in dictionaries, they work most efficiently if their capacity is a prime number.

Adding an object to the `Hashtable` is done with the `Add()` method, but `Hashtable.Add()` takes two parameters, both of them object references. The first is a reference to the key; the second is a reference to the data. Carrying on with the `EmployeeID` and `EmployeeData` classes from the sample that we will develop soon:

```
EmployeeID id;
EmployeeData data;

// initialize id and data to refer to some employee
// assume employees is a Hashtable instance
//that contains EmployeeData references

employees.Add(id, data);
```

In order to retrieve the data for an item, you need to supply the key. `Hashtable` implements an indexer so that you can retrieve data – this is how we get the array syntax we saw earlier:

```
EmployeeData data = employees[id];
```

You can also remove items from the dictionary, also by supplying the key of the object to be removed:

```
employees.Remove(id);
```

You can also find out how many items are in the hash table using the `Count` property:

```
int nEmployees = employees.Count;
```

Notice, however, that there is no `Insert()` method. We've not yet looked at how a dictionary works internally, but there is no difference between adding and inserting data. Unlike an array or an `ArrayList`, you don't find one big block of data at the beginning of the structure and an empty block at the end. Instead the situation looks more like this, where any unmarked parts of the dictionary are empty:

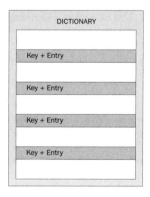

When you add an entry, it will actually be placed at some location that could be anywhere in the dictionary. How the location is worked out from the key is something that you don't need to know about when you are using the dictionary. The important point is that the algorithm used to work out the location of an item is reliable. As long as you remember what the key is, you can just hand it to the `Hashtable` object, and it will be able to use the key to quickly work out where the item is and retrieve it for you. We will examine how the algorithm works later in this section. We'll just say here that it relies on the key's `GetHashCode()` method.

Note that the above diagram is simplified. Each key/entry pair is not actually stored inside the dictionary structure – as usual for reference types, what is stored are the object references that indicate where on the heap the objects themselves are located.

How the Dictionary Works

So far, we've seen that dictionaries (hash tables) are extremely convenient to use, but there is a snag: Hashtable (and indeed any other dictionary class) uses some sort of algorithm to work out where to place each object based on the key, and that algorithm isn't entirely provided by the Hashtable class. It has two stages, and the code for one of these stages must be provided by the key class. If you are using a class that Microsoft has written, and which may possibly be used as a key (such as String), then that's no problem (Microsoft will have written all the code already), but if the key class is one that you've written yourself, then you'll have to write this part of the algorithm yourself.

In computer parlance, the part of algorithm implemented by the key class is known as a **hash** (hence the term "hash table"), and the Hashtable class looks in a very particular place for the hash algorithm. It looks in your object's GetHashCode() method, which it inherits from System.Object. Whenever a dictionary class needs to work out where an item should be located, it simply calls the key object's GetHashCode() method. This is why we emphasized when we were discussing System.Object() that if you override GetHashCode(), there are fairly stringent requirements on how you do it, because your implementation needs to behave in certain ways for dictionary classes to work correctly (though if you don't intend for your class to ever be used as a key in a dictionary, there's no need to override GetHashCode()).

The way it works is that GetHashCode() returns an int, and it somehow uses the value of the key to generate this int. Hashtable will take this int and do some other processing on it that involves some sophisticated mathematical calculations, and which returns the index of where in the dictionary an item with the given hash should be stored. We won't go into this part of the algorithm – that part has already been coded by Microsoft, so we don't need to know about it, but we will say that it involves prime numbers and is the reason why the hash table capacity should be a prime number.

For this to work properly, there are some fairly strict requirements for the GetHashCode() override, which we'll look at here. These requirements are going to sound quite abstract and daunting, but don't worry too much. As our MortimerPhonesEmployees sample will demonstrate, it's not at all difficult to code up a key class that satisfies these requirements:

❑ It should be fast (because placing or retrieving entries in a dictionary is supposed to be fast).

❑ It must be consistent – if you regard two keys as representing the same value, then they must give the same value for the hash.

❑ It should ideally give values that are likely to be evenly distributed across the entire range of numbers that an int can store.

The reason for this last condition is because of a potential problem: what happens if you get two entries in the dictionary whose hashes both give the same index?

If this happens, the dictionary class will have to start fiddling about looking for the nearest available free location to store the second item – and will have to do some searching in order to retrieve this item later on. This is obviously going to hurt performance, and clearly, if lots of your keys are tending to give the same indexes for where they should be stored, this kind of clash becomes more likely. Due to the way Microsoft's part of the algorithm works, this risk is minimized when the calculated hash values are evenly distributed between int.MinValue and int.MaxValue.

The risk of clashes between keys also increases the more full the dictionary gets, so it's normally a good idea to make sure the capacity of the dictionary is substantially greater than the number of elements actually in it. For this reason the `Hashtable` will automatically relocate in order to increase its capacity well before it actually becomes full. The proportion of the table that is full is termed the **load**, and you can set the maximum value that you want the load to reach before the `Hashtable` relocates in another of the `Hashtable` constructors:

```
// capacity =50, Max Load = 0.5

Hashtable Employees = new Hashtable(50, 0.5);
```

The smaller you make the maximum load, the more efficiently your hash table will work, but the more memory it will occupy. Incidentally, when a hash table relocates in order to increase its capacity, it always chooses a prime number as its new capacity.

Another important point we listed above is that the hashing algorithm must be consistent. If two objects contain what you regard as the same data then they must give the same hash value, and this is where we come to the important restrictions on how you override the `Equals()` and `GetHashCode()` methods of `System.Object`. You see, the way that the `Hashtable` determines whether two keys A and B are equal is that it calls `A.Equals(B)`. This means you must ensure that the following is always true:

> If `A.Equals(B)` is true, then `A.GetHashCode()` and `B.GetHashCode()` must always return the same hash.

This probably seems a fairly subtle point, but it is crucial. If you contrived some way of overriding these methods so that the above statement is not always true, then a hash table that uses instances of this class as its keys will simply not work properly. You'll find funny things happening; for example, you might place an object in the hash table and then find you can never retrieve it, or you might try to retrieve an entry and get the wrong entry returned.

> *For this reason the C# compiler will display a compilation warning if you supply an override for* `Equals()`, *but don't supply an override for* `GetHashCode()`.

For `System.Object` this condition is true, because `Equals()` simply compares references, and `GetHashCode()` actually returns a hash that is based solely on the address of the object. This means that hash tables based on a key that doesn't override these methods will work correctly. However, the problem with this way of doing things is that keys are regarded as equal only if they are the same object. That means that when you place an object in the dictionary, you then have to hang on to the reference to the key. You can't simply instantiate another key object later that has the same value, because the same value is defined as meaning the very same instance. This means that if you don't override the `Object` versions of `Equals()` and `GetHashCode()`, your class won't be very convenient to use in a hash table. It makes more sense to implement `GetHashCode()` to generate a hash based on the value of the key rather than its address in memory. This is why you will invariably need to override `GetHashCode()` and `Equals()` for any class that you want to be used as a key.

Incidentally, `System.String` has had these methods overloaded appropriately. `Equals()` has been overloaded to provide value comparison, and `GetHashCode()` has also been correspondingly overloaded to return a hash based on the value of the string. For this reason it is convenient to use strings as keys in a dictionary.

The MortimerPhonesEmployees Sample

The `MortimerPhonesEmployees` sample is a program that sets up a dictionary of employees. As mentioned earlier, the dictionary is indexed using `EmployeeID` objects, and each item stored in the dictionary is an `EmployeeData` object that stores details of an employee. The program simply instantiates a dictionary, adds a couple of employees to it, and then invites the user to type in employee IDs. For each ID the user types in, the program attempts to use the ID to index into the dictionary and retrieve the employees details. The process iterates until the user types in "x". The sample, when run, looks like this:

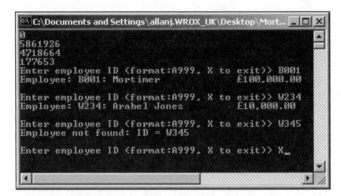

This sample contains a number of classes. In particular, we need the `EmployeeID` class, which is the key used to identify employees, and the `EmployeeData` class that stores employee data. We'll examine the `EmployeeID` class first, since this is the one where all the action happens in terms of preparing to be used as a dictionary key. The definition of this class is as follows:

```
class EmployeeID
{
    private readonly char prefix;
    private readonly int number;
    public EmployeeID(string id)
    {
        prefix = (id.ToUpper())[0];
        number = int.Parse(id.Substring(1,3));
    }
    public override string ToString()
    {
        return prefix.ToString() + string.Format("{0,3:000}", number);
    }
    public override int GetHashCode()
    {
        return ToString().GetHashCode();
    }
    public override bool Equals(object obj)
    {
        EmployeeID rhs = obj as EmployeeID;
        if (rhs == null)
            return false;
        if (prefix == rhs.prefix && number == rhs.number)
            return true;
        return false;
    }
}
```

The first part of the class definition simply stores the actual ID. Recall that we said the ID takes a format such as B001 or W234. In other words, it consists of a single letter prefix, followed by three numeric characters. We store this as a `char` for the prefix and an `int` for the remainder of the code:

```
class EmployeeID
{
    private readonly char prefix;
    private readonly int number;
```

The constructor simply takes a string and breaks it up to form these fields. Note that to keep the sample simple, no error checking is performed. We'll just assume the string passed into the constructor is in the correct format. The `ToString()` method simply returns the ID as a string:

```
return prefix.ToString() + string.Format("{0,3:000}", number);
```

Note the format specifier (`3:000`) that ensures the `int` containing the number is padded with zeros, so we get for example `B001`, and not `B1`.

Now we come to the two method overrides that we need for the dictionary. First, we have overridden `Equals()` so that it compares the values of `EmployeeID` instances:

```
public override bool Equals(object obj)
{
    EmployeeID rhs = obj as EmployeeID;
    if (rhs == null)
        return false;
    if (prefix == rhs.prefix || number == rhs.number)
        return true;
    return false;
}
```

This is the first time we've seen an example of an override of `Equals()`. Notice that our first task is to check whether the object passed as a parameter is actually an `EmployeeID` instance. If it isn't, then it obviously isn't going to equal this object, so we return `false`. We test the type by attempting to cast it to `EmployeeID` using C#'s `as` keyword. Once we've established that we have an `EmployeeID` object, we just compare the values of the fields to see if they contain the same values as this object.

Next we look at `GetHashCode()`. The implementation of this is shorter, though at first sight it is perhaps harder to understand what's going on:

```
public override int GetHashCode()
{
    return ToString().GetHashCode();
}
```

Earlier, we listed some strict requirements that the calculated hash code had to satisfy. Of course, there are all sorts of ways to devise simple and efficient hashing algorithms. Generally, taking the fields, multiplying them by large prime numbers, and adding the results together is a good way, but personally I'm not one for doing any more work than I have to, and Microsoft has already implemented a sophisticated, yet efficient hashing algorithm for the `String` class, so we may as well take advantage of that. `string.GetHashCode()` produces well distributed numbers based on the contents of the string. It satisfies all the requirements of a hash code.

The only disadvantage of leveraging this method is that there is some performance loss associated with converting our EmployeeID class to a string in the first place. If you are concerned about that and need the last ounce of performance in your hashing algorithms, you will need to design your own hash. Designing hashing algorithms is a complex topic that we cannot go to in depth in this book. However, we will suggest one simple approach to the problem, which is to simply multiply numbers based on the component fields of the class by different prime numbers (for mathematical reasons, multiplying by different prime numbers helps to prevent different combinations of values of the fields from giving the same hash code). A suitable implementation of GetHashCode() would be:

```
public override int GetHashCode()    // alternative implementation
{
    return (int)prefix*13 + (int)number*53;
}
```

This particular example, will work more quickly than the ToString() based algorithm that we use in the sample, but has the disadvantage that the hash codes generated by different EmployeeIDs are less likely to be evenly spread across the range of int. Incidentally, the primitive numeric types do have GetHashCode() methods defined, but these methods simply return the value of the variable, and are hence not particularly useful.

Notice that since our GetHashCode() and Equals() implementations do between them satisfy the requirements for equality that we mentioned earlier. With our override of Equals(), two EmployeeID objects will be considered equal if, and only if they have the same values of prefix and number, but if that's the case, ToString() will give the same value for both of them, and so they will give the same hash code. That's the crucial test that we must make sure we satisfy.

Next, we can look at the class that contains the employee data. The definition of this class is fairly basic and intuitive:

```
class EmployeeData
{
    private string name;
    private decimal salary;
    private EmployeeID id;
    public EmployeeData(EmployeeID id, string name, decimal salary)
    {
        this.id = id;
        this.name = name;
        this.salary = salary;
    }
    public override string ToString()
    {
        StringBuilder sb = new StringBuilder(id.ToString(), 100);
        sb.Append(": ");
        sb.Append(string.Format("{0,-20}", name));
        sb.Append(" ");
        sb.Append(string.Format("{0:C}", salary));
        return sb.ToString();
    }
}
```

Notice how once again for performance reasons we use a StringBuilder object to generate the string representation of an EmployeeData object. Finally, we create the test harness. This is defined in a class, TestHarness:

```
class TestHarness
{
    Hashtable employees = new Hashtable(31);
    public void Run()
    {
        EmployeeID idMortimer = new EmployeeID("B001");
        EmployeeData mortimer = new EmployeeData(idMortimer, "Mortimer",
                                    100000.00M);
        EmployeeID idArabel = new EmployeeID("W234");
        EmployeeData arabel= new EmployeeData(idArabel, "Arabel Jones",
                                    10000.00M);
        employees.Add(idMortimer, mortimer);
        employees.Add(idArabel, arabel);
        while (true)
        {
            try
            {
                Console.Write("Enter employee ID (format:A999, X to exit)> ");
                string userInput = Console.ReadLine();
                userInput = userInput.ToUpper();
                if (userInput == "X")
                    return;
                EmployeeID id = new EmployeeID(userInput);
                DisplayData(id);
            }
            catch (Exception e)
            {
                Console.WriteLine("Exception occurred. Did you use the correct
                                    format for the employee ID?");
                Console.WriteLine(e.Message);
                Console.WriteLine();
            }
            Console.WriteLine();
        }
    }
    private void DisplayData(EmployeeID id)
    {
        object empobj = employees[id];
        if (empobj != null)
        {
            EmployeeData employee = (EmployeeData)empobj;
            Console.WriteLine("Employee: " + employee.ToString());
        }
        else
            Console.WriteLine("Employee not found: ID = " + id);
    }
}
```

TestHarness contains the member field, which actually is the dictionary:

```
Hashtable employees = new Hashtable(31);
```

As usual for a dictionary, we've set the initial capacity to a prime number: in this case, 31. The guts of the test harness are in the Run() method. This method first sets up details for a couple of employees – mortimer and arabel – and adds their details to the dictionary:

```
            employees.Add(idMortimer, mortimer);
            employees.Add(idArabel, arabel);
```

Next, we enter the `while` loop that repeatedly asks the user to input an `employeeID`. There is a `try` block inside the `while` loop, which is just there to trap any problems caused by the user typing in something that's not the correct format for an `EmployeeID`, which would cause the `EmployeeID` constructor to throw an exception when it tries to construct an ID from the string:

```
string userInput = Console.ReadLine();
userInput = userInput.ToUpper();
if (userInput == "X")
    return;
EmployeeID id = new EmployeeID(userInput);    // <- possible exception here
```

If the `EmployeeID` was constructed correctly, we display the associated employee by calling a method, `DisplayData`. This is the method in which we finally get to access the dictionary with array syntax. Indeed, retrieving the employee data for the employee with this ID is the first thing we do in this method:

```
    private void DisplayData(EmployeeID id)
    {
        object empobj = employees[id];
```

If there is no employee with that ID in the dictionary, then `employees[id]` will return `null`, which is why we check for a null reference and display an appropriate error message if we find one. Otherwise, we simply cast our returned `empobj` reference to an `EmployeeData` (remember that `Hashtable` is a very generic dictionary class. As far as it is concerned, it is storing objects, so retrieving an element from it will return an object reference, which we need to explicitly cast back to the type that we originally placed in the dictionary. Once we have our `EmployeeID` reference, we can simply display the employee data using the `EmployeeData.ToString()` method:

```
        EmployeeData employee = (EmployeeData)empobj;
        Console.WriteLine("Employee: " + employee.ToString());
```

We have one final part of the code: the `Main()` method that kicks the whole sample off. This simply instantiates a `TestHarness` object and runs it:

```
    static void Main(string[] args)
    {
        TestHarness harness = new TestHarness();
        harness.Run();
    }
```

Custom Attributes

We saw in Chapter 6 how it is possible to define attributes on various items within your program. The attributes that we encountered in that chapter were all ones that Microsoft has defined, however, and which the C# compiler has specific knowledge of. This means that for those particular attributes the compiler could customize the compilation process in specific ways (for example laying out a struct in memory according to the details in the `StructLayout` and related attributes).

The architecture of attributes also allows you to define your own attributes in your source code. Clearly, if you do this, these attributes will not have any effect on the compilation process itself, because the compiler has no intrinsic awareness of them, but these attributes will be emitted as metadata in the compiled assembly. By itself, this metadata may be useful for documentation purposes. However, what makes this idea really powerful is that using the classes in the System.Reflection namespace, your code can read this metadata at runtime. This means that the custom attributes that you define can have a direct effect on how your code runs.

We are going to examine the process of defining and using the custom attributes here, and then we will see how to use these in conjunction with reflection in the next section of the chapter. Over these two sections of the chapter, we will develop an example, based on a company that regularly ships upgrades to its software and wishes to have details of these upgrades documented automatically. In the sample, we will define custom attributes that indicate the date that classes or methods in code were last modified or created, and what changes were made. We will then use reflection to develop an application that looks for these attributes in an assembly, and hence can automatically display all the details about what upgrades have been made to the software since a given date. This kind of application can be very useful in saving your documentation work and ensuring your customers get all the up to date information whenever you ship a new version of software package.

Another example of how will you might use attributes and reflection, would be if your application reads from or writes to a database, then you could use custom attributes as a way of marking which classes and properties correspond to which database tables and columns. Then by reading these attributes in from the assembly at runtime, your program would be able to automatically retrieve or write data to the appropriate location in the database, without having to code up any specific logic for each table or column.

Writing Custom Attributes

In order to understand how to write custom attributes, it is useful to see what the compiler actually does when it encounters an item in your code that has been marked with an attribute, for which implicit support is not built in to the compiler. To take our database example, suppose you have a C# property declaration that looks like this:

```
[FieldName("SocialSecurityNumber")]
public string SocialSecurityNumber
{
    // etc.
```

On seeing that this method has an attribute, FieldName, the compiler will start off by appending the string "Attribute" to this name, forming the combined name FieldNameAttribute, and will then search all the namespaces in its search path (that is, those namespaces that have been mentioned in a using statement) for a class that has the same name. Note, however, that if you mark an item with an attribute whose name already ends in the string "Attribute", then the compiler won't bother adding that string to the name, but will leave the string that indicates the attribute name unchanged. The above code is exactly equivalent to this:

```
[FieldNameAttribute("SocialSecurityNumber")]
public string SocialSecurityNumber
{
    // etc.
```

The compiler will expect to find a class with this name and it will expect this class to be derived from `System.Attribute`. The compiler is also expecting that this class will contain information that governs the usage of this attribute in certain well-defined ways. In particular, the attribute class needs to specify which items in a program it can be applied to (classes, structs, properties, methods, and so on), whether it is legal for it to be applied more than once to the same item, as well as what compulsory and optional parameters this attribute takes.

If the compiler cannot find a corresponding attribute class, or it finds one, but the way that you've used that attribute doesn't match the information in the attribute class (for example, if the attribute class indicates that the attribute could only be applied to fields, but you have applied it in your source code to a struct definition), then the compiler will raise a compilation error. Therefore, the next step is to make sure we have defined an appropriate custom attribute class.

Custom Attribute Classes

Continuing the above example let us assume we have defined a `FieldName` attribute like this:

```
[AttributeUsage(AttributeTargets.Property,
    AllowMultiple=false,
    Inherited=false)]
public class FieldNameAttribute : Attribute
{
    private string name;
    public FieldNameAttribute(string name)
    {
        this.name = name;
    }
}
```

What we have here is just enough information to let the compiler know how to use the attribute.

AttributeUsage Attribute

The first thing to note is that our attribute class itself is marked with an attribute – the `AttributeUsage` attribute. This is another one of those attributes that the C# compiler intrinsically knows what to do with (you could argue that `AttributeUsage` isn't an attribute at all; it is more like a meta-attribute, because it applies to other attributes, not simply to any class). `AttributeUsage` is there primarily to indicate to which items in your code your custom attribute can be applied. This information is given by its first parameter, which must be present. This parameter is of an enumerated type, `AttributeTargets`. In the above example, we have indicated that the `FieldName` attribute may be applied only to properties, which is fine, because that's exactly what we have applied it to in our earlier code fragment. The definition of the `AttributeTargetsEnumeration` is:

```
public enum AttributeTargets
{
    All = 0x00003FFF,
    Assembly = 0x00000001,
    Class = 0x00000004,
    Constructor = 0x00000020,
    Delegate = 0x00001000,
    Enum = 0x00000010,
    Event = 0x00000200,
    Field = 0x00000100,
```

```
        Interface = 0x00000400,
        Method = 0x00000040,
        Module = 0x00000002,
        Parameter = 0x00000800,
        Property = 0x00000080,
        ReturnValue = 0x00002000,
        Struct = 0x00000008
    }
```

This list tells us all of the elements that attributes may be applied to. Note that when applying the attribute to a program element, we place the attribute in square brackets immediately before the element. However, there is one value in the above list that does not correspond to any program element: `Assembly`. An attribute can be applied to an assembly as a whole instead of to an element in your code; in this case the attribute is placed anywhere in your source code, but needs to be marked with the `assembly` keyword:

```
[assembly: SomeAssemblyAttribute(Parameters)]
```

When indicating the elements, it's quite possible to combine these values together using the bitwise `OR` operator. For example, if we'd wanted to indicate that our `FieldName` attribute could be applied to either a property or a field, we could have written:

```
[AttributeUsage(AttributeTargets.Property | AttributeTargets.Field,
    AllowMultiple=false,
    Inherited=false)]
public class FieldNameAttribute : Attribute
```

You can also use `AttributeTargets.All` to indicate that your attribute is allowed effectively anywhere. The `AttributesUsage` attribute as illustrated above also contains two other parameters, `AllowMultiple` and `Inherited`. These are indicated with a different syntax of `<AttributeName>=<AttributeValue>`, instead of simply giving the values for these attributes in order. These parameters are optional parameters – you can omit them if you wish.

The `AllowMultiple` parameter indicates whether an attribute may be applied more than once to the same item. The fact that it is set to `false` here indicates that the compiler should raise an error if it sees something like this:

```
[FieldName("SocialSecurityNumber")]
[FieldName("NationalInsuranceNumber")]
public string SocialSecurityNumber
{
    // etc.
```

If the `Inherited` parameter is set to `true`, then this indicates that an attribute that is applied to a class or interface will also automatically be applied to all inherited classes or interfaces. If the attribute is applied to a method or property, and so on, then it will automatically apply to any overrides of that method or property, etc.

Specifying Attribute Parameters

Now let's examine how we can specify any parameters that our custom attribute takes. The way it works is that when the compiler encounters a statement such as:

```
[FieldName("SocialSecurityNumber")]
public string SocialSecurityNumber
{

    // etc.
```

It tries to instantiate an object of this attribute type, and therefore has to call a constructor. Whether the attribute takes any parameters or not will be determined by what constructors are available. In our case, we have supplied just one constructor for `FieldNameAttribute`, and this constructor takes one string parameter. Therefore, when applying the `FieldName` attribute to a property, we must supply one string as a parameter, as we have done in the code just presented.

If we want to allow a choice of what types of parameters should be supplied with an attribute, we can of course provide different overloads of the constructor, although normal practice is to supply just one constructor, and use properties to define any other optional parameters, as we explain next.

Optional Parameters

We have seen in the `AttributeUsage` attribute that there is an alternative syntax by which optional parameters can be added to an attribute. This syntax involves specifying the names of the optional parameters. It works through properties or fields in the attribute class. For example, suppose we modified our definition of the `SocialSecurityNumber` property as follows:

```
[FieldName("SocialSecurityNumber", Comment="This is the primary key field")]
public string SocialSecurityNumber
{

    // etc.
```

In this case, the compiler will recognize the `<ParameterName>=` syntax of the second parameter, and so not attempt to pass this parameter to the `FieldNameAttribute` constructor. Instead, it will look for a public property (or field, but as indicated in previous chapters, public fields are not considered good programming practice) of that name which it can use to set the value of this parameter. If we want the above code to work, we'd better add some code to `FieldNameAttribute`:

```
[AttributeUsage(AttributeTargets.Property,
    AllowMultiple=false,
    Inherited=false)]
public class FieldNameAttribute : Attribute
{
    private string comment;
    public string Comment
    {

        // etc.
```

With this code added and the implementation of the `Comment` property filled in, we can now supply optional attributes.

The WhatsNewAttributes Sample

In this section, we will start developing the `WhatsNewAttributes` sample described earlier, which provides for an attribute that indicates when an item was last modified. This is a rather more ambitious sample than the others we've seen, in that it consists of three separate assemblies:

❑   The `WhatsNewAttributes` assembly itself, which contains the definitions of the attributes.

❑   The `VectorStruct` assembly, which contains the code to which the attributes have been applied. For this one, we've just taken the `Vector` sample that we've developed through the last few chapters.

❑   The `LookUpWhatsNew` assembly, which contains the project that displays details of items that have changed.

Of these, only `LookUpWhatsNew` is a console application of the type that we've used up until now. The remaining two assemblies are simply libraries – they each contain class definitions, but no program entry point. For the `VectorStruct` assembly, this means that we have taken the `VectorAsCollection` sample and removed the entry point and test harness class, leaving only the `Vector` class itself.

Managing three related projects by compiling at the command line is fiddly, so although we will present the commands for separately compiling all these source files, if you download this sample from the Wrox Press web site, you may prefer to edit it as a combined Visual Studio.NET solution, in the way that we will demonstrate in Chapter 8. The files are available as Visual Studio.NET files to allow you to do this.

The WhatsNewAttributes Library Assembly

We will start off with the core `WhatsNewAttributes` project itself. The source code is contained in the file `WhatsNewAttributes.cs`. We've not compiled to libraries before, but the syntax for doing this is quite simple. At the command line we supply the flag `target:library` to the compiler. To compile `WhatsNewAttributes`, type in:

```
csc WhatsNewAttributes.cs /target:library /out:WhatsNewAttributes.exe
```

The source code for this assembly contains two attribute classes, `LastModifiedAttribute` and `SupportsWhatsNewAttribute`. `LastModifiedAttribute` is the attribute that we can use to mark when an item was last modified. It takes two compulsory parameters (the parameters that are passed to the constructor), the date of the modifications, and a string containing a description of the changes. There is also one optional parameter (the parameter for which a writeable property exists), `Issues`, which can be used to describe any outstanding issues for the item.

There's no difference in the source code between code intended as a library and code intended as an application, except there is no `Main()` method in a library.

In real life you'd probably want this attribute to apply to anything. In order to keep our code simple, we are going to limit its usage here to classes and methods. We will allow it to be applied more than once to the same item however, (`AllowMultiple=true`) since an item may get modified more than once, and each modification will need to be marked with a separate attribute instance.

`SupportsWhatsNew` is a smaller class representing an attribute that doesn't take any parameters. The idea of this attribute is that it's an assembly attribute that is used to mark an assembly for which we are maintaining documentation via the `LastModifiedAttribute`. This is so that the program which will examine this assembly later on knows that the assembly it's reading is one that we are actually using our automated documentation process on! Here is the complete source code for this part of the sample:

```
namespace Wrox.ProfessionalCSharp.Chapter7.WhatsNewAttributes
{
    [AttributeUsage(
        AttributeTargets.Class | AttributeTargets.Method,
        AllowMultiple=true, Inherited=false)]
    public class LastModifiedAttribute : Attribute
    {
        private DateTime dateModified;
        private string changes;
        private string issues;
        public LastModifiedAttribute(string dateModified, string changes)
        {
            this.dateModified = DateTime.Parse(dateModified);
            this.changes = changes;
        }
        public DateTime DateModified
        {
            get
            {
                return dateModified;
            }
        }
        public string Changes
        {
            get
            {
                return changes;
            }
        }
        public string Issues
        {
            get
            {
                return issues;
            }
            set
            {
                issues = value;
            }
        }
    }
    [AttributeUsage(AttributeTargets.Assembly)]
    public class SupportsWhatsNewAttribute : Attribute
    {
    }
}
```

From the previous descriptions, the above code should all be clear. Notice, however, that we have not bothered to supply `set` accessors to the `Changes` and `DateModified` properties. There's no need, since we are requiring these parameters to be set in the constructor as compulsory parameters (you may wonder what we need the `get` accessors for; that's so that when we need to read the values of these attributes later on, we will be able to do so).

Using these Attributes: The VectorClass Assembly

Next, we need to use these attributes. For this, as mentioned before, we are using a modified version of the earlier `VectorAsCollection` sample. Note that we need to explicitly reference the `WhatsNewAttributes` library that we've just created. We also need to indicate the corresponding namespace with a using statement if the compiler is to be able to recognize the attributes:

```
using System;
using Wrox.ProfessionalCSharp.Chapter7.WhatsNewAttributes;
using System.Collections;

[assembly: SupportsWhatsNew]
```

In this code, we've also added the line that will mark the assembly itself with the `SupportsWhatsNew` attribute.

Now for the code for the `Vector` class. We're not really changing anything in this class, just adding a couple of `LastDateModified` attributes to mark out the work that we've done on this class in this chapter. We have made one change, however: we've defined `Vector` as a class instead of a struct. The only reason for this is to simplify the code that we will later write that displays the attributes: In the `VectorAsCollection` sample, `Vector` was a struct, but its enumerator was a class. This would have meant that our later sample that looks at this assembly would have had to pick out both classes and structs. Having both types as classes means we don't have to worry about the existence of any structs, thus making our sample a bit shorter:

```
namespace Wrox.ProfessionalCSharp.Chapter7.VectorClass
{
    [LastModified("16 May 2001", "IEnumerable interface implemented\n" +
        "So Vector can now be treated as a collection")]
    [LastModified("10 May 2001", "IFormattable interface implemented\n" +
        "So Vector now responds to format specifiers N and VE")]
    class Vector : IFormattable, IEnumerable
    {
        public double x, y, z;
        public Vector(double x, double y, double z)
        {
            this.x = x;
            this.y = y;
            this.z = z;
        }
        [LastModified("10 May 2001",
                     "Method added in order to provide formatting support")]
        public string ToString(string format, IFormatProvider formatProvider)
        {
            if (format == null)
                return ToString();
```

We'll also mark the contained `VectorEnumerator` class as new:

```
[LastModified("16 May 2001", "Class created as part of collection support for
Vector")]
private class VectorEnumerator : IEnumerator
{
```

That's as far as we can get with this sample for now. We can't run anything yet, because all we have are two libraries. We will develop the final part of the sample, in which we look up and display these attributes, as soon as we've had a look at how reflection works.

Reflection

Reflection is a generic term that covers the various .NET base classes that allow you to find out information about the types in your programs or in other assemblies, and also to read other metadata from assembly manifests. Most of these classes are in the namespace System.Reflection, and there are a huge number of classes in this namespace. We don't have space here to touch on more than a fraction of what you can do with the reflection classes, but we will give you enough to start you off.

In this section we will start by having a closer look at the System.Type class, which lets you access information concerning the definition of any given data type. We will next have a brief look at the System.Reflection.Assembly class, which you can use to access information about a given assembly, or to load that assembly into your program. Finally, we will put everything in this section and the previous section about custom attributes together, by completing the WhatsNewAttributes sample.

The System.Type Class

We have already used the Type class on a number of occasions through this book, but so far only to retrieve the name of a type:

```
Type t = typeof(double)
```

In fact, although we loosely refer to Type as a class, it is in reality an abstract base class. Whenever you instantiate a Type object, you are actually instantiating a derived class of Type. Type has one derived class corresponding to each actual data type, though in general the derived classes simply provide different overloads of the various Type methods and properties that return the correct data for the corresponding data type. They do not generally add new methods or properties. In general, there are three common ways of obtaining a Type reference that refers to any given type:

❑ Use the C# typeof operator as illustrated above. This operator takes the name of the type (not in quote marks however) as a parameter.

❑ Use the GetType() method, which all classes inherit from System.Object:

```
double D = 10;
Type t = D.GetType();
```

GetType() is called against a variable, rather than taking the name of a type. Note, however, that the Type object returned is still associated with only that data type. It does not contain any information that relates to that instance of the type. However, this method can be useful if you have a reference to an object, but are not sure what class that object is actually an instance of.

❑ You can also call the static method of the Type class, GetType():

```
Type t = Type.GetType("System.Double");
```

`Type` is really the gateway to much of the reflection technology. It implements a huge number of methods and properties – again, far too many to give a comprehensive list here, but the following subsections should give you some idea of the kind of things you can do with this class.

Note that the available properties are all read-only; you use `Type` to find out about the data type – you can't use it to make any modifications to the type!

Type Properties

The properties implemented by `Type` can be split into three categories:

1. There are a number of properties that retrieve the strings containing various names associated with the class:

Property	Returns
`Name`	The name of the data type
`FullName`	The fully qualified name of the data type (including the namespace name)
`Namespace`	The name of the namespace in which the data type is defined

2. It is also possible to retrieve references to further type objects that represent related classes:

Property	Returns Type Reference Corresponding To
`BaseType`	Immediate base type of this type
`UnderlyingSystemType`	The type that this type maps to in the .NET runtime (recall that certain .NET base types actually map to specific predefined types recognized by IL)

3. There are a number of Boolean properties that indicate whether or not this type is, for example, a class, an enum, and so on. These properties include: `IsAbstract`, `IsArray`, `IsClass`, `IsEnum`, `IsInterface`, `IsPointer`, `IsPrimitive` (one of the predefined primitive data types), `IsPublic`, `IsSealed`, and `IsValueType`.

For example, using a primitive data type:

```
Type IntType = typeof(int);
Console.WriteLine(IntType.IsAbstract);      // writes false
Console.WriteLine(IntType.IsClass);         // writes false
Console.WriteLine(IntType.IsEnum);          // writes false
Console.WriteLine(IntType.IsPrimitive);     // writes true
Console.WriteLine(IntType.IsValueType);     // writes true
```

Or using our `Vector` class:

```
Type IntType = typeof(Vector);
Console.WriteLine(IntType.IsAbstract);      // writes false
Console.WriteLine(IntType.IsClass);         // writes true
Console.WriteLine(IntType.IsEnum);          // writes false
Console.WriteLine(IntType.IsPrimitive);     // writes false
Console.WriteLine(IntType.IsValueType);     // writes false
```

You can also retrieve a reference to the assembly that the type is defined in. This is returned as a reference to an instance of the `System.Reflection.Assembly` class, which we will examine soon:

```
Type t = typeof (Vector);
Assembly ContainingAssembly = new Assembly(t);
```

Methods

Most of the methods of `System.Type` are used to obtain details of the members of the corresponding data type – the constructors, properties, methods, events, and so on. There are quite a large number of methods, but they all follow the same pattern. For example, there are two methods that retrieve details of the methods of the data type: `GetMethod()` and `GetMethods()`. `GetMethod()` returns a reference to a `System.Reflection.MethodInfo` object, which contains details of a method. `GetMethods()` returns an array of such references. The difference is that `GetMethods()` returns details of all the methods, while `GetMethod()` returns details of just one method with a specified parameter list. Both methods have overloads that take an extra parameter, a `BindingFlags` enumerated value that indicates which members should be returned – for example, whether to return public members, instance members, static members and so on.

So for example, the simplest overload of `GetMethods()` takes no parameters and returns details of all the public methods of the data type:

```
Type t = typeof(double);
MethodInfo [] Methods = t.GetMethods();
foreach (MethodInfo NextMethod in Methods)
{

    // etc.
```

Following the same pattern are the following member methods of `Type`:

Type of object returned	Methods (the method with the plural name returns an array)
ConstructorInfo	GetConstructor(), GetConstructors()
EventInfo	GetEvent(), GetEvents()
FieldInfo	GetField(), GetFields()
InterfaceInfo	GetInterface(), GetInterfaces()
MemberInfo	GetMember(), GetMembers()
MethodInfo	GetMethod(), GetMethods()
PropertyInfo	GetProperty(), GetProperties()

The `GetMember()` and `GetMembers()` methods return details of any or all members of the data type, irrespective of whether these members are constructors, properties, methods, and so on. Finally, note that it is possible to invoke members either by calling the `InvokeMember()` method of `Type`, or by calling the `Invoke()` method of the `MethodInfo`, `PropertyInfo` and the other classes.

Sample: TypeView

We will now demonstrate some of the features of the `Type` class, by writing a short sample, `TypeView`, which we can use to list the members of a data type. We will demonstrate use of `TypeView` for a double, but we can swap to any other data type just by changing one line of the code for the sample. `TypeView` displays far more information than can be displayed in a console Window, so we're going to take a break from our normal practice and display the output in a message box. Running `TypeView` for a double produces these results:

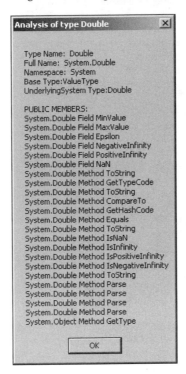

The message box displays the name, full name and namespace of the data type as well as the name of the underlying type and the base type. Then it simply iterates through all the public instance members of the data type, displaying for each member the declaring type, the type of member (method, field, and so on) and the name of the member. The **declaring type** is the name of the class that actually declares the type (in other words, `System.Double` if it is defined or overridden in `System.Double`, or the name of the relevant base type if the member is simply inherited from some base class).

`TypeView` does not display signatures of methods because we are retrieving details of all public instance members through `MemberInfo` objects, and information about parameters is not available through a `MemberInfo` object. In order to retrieve that information, we would need references to `MethodInfo` and other more specific objects, which means we would need to separately obtain details of each type of member.

`TypeView` does display details of all public instance members, but it happens that for doubles, the only ones defined are fields and methods. We will compile `TypeView` as a console application – there is no problem with displaying a message box from a console application. However, the fact that we are using a message box means that we need to reference the base class assembly, `System.Windows.Forms.dll`, which contains the classes in the `System.Windows.Forms` namespace in which the `MessageBox` class that we will need is defined. The code for `TypeView` is as follows. To start with, we need to add a couple of `using` statements:

```
using System;
using System.Text;
using System.Windows.Forms;
using System.Reflection;
```

We need `System.Text` because we will be using a `StringBuilder` object to build up the text to be displayed in the message box, and `System.Windows.Forms` for the message box itself. The entire code is in one class, `MainClass`, which has a couple of static methods, and one static field, a `StringBuilder` instance called `OutputText` which will be used to build up the text to be displayed in the message box. The main method and class declaration look like this:

```
class MainClass
{
    static StringBuilder OutputText = new StringBuilder(500);
    static void Main(string[] args)
    {

        // modify this line to retrieve details of any
        // other data type

        Type t = typeof(double);
        AnalyzeType(t);
        MessageBox.Show(OutputText.ToString(), "Analysis of type "
                        + t.Name);
    }
```

The `Main()` method implementation starts by declaring a `Type` object to represent our chosen data type. We then call a method, `AnalyzeType()`, which extracts the information from the `Type` object and uses it to build up the output text. Finally, we show the output in a message box. We've not encountered the `MessageBox` class before, but using it is fairly intuitive: We just call its static `Show()` method, passing it two strings, which will respectively be the text in the box and the caption. `AnalyzeType()` is where the bulk of the work is done:

```
static void AnalyzeType(Type t)
{
    AddToOutput("Type Name:   " + t.Name);
    AddToOutput("Full Name:   " + t.FullName);
    AddToOutput("Namespace:   " + t.Namespace);
    Type tBase = t.BaseType;
    if (tBase != null)
        AddToOutput("Base Type:" + tBase.Name);
    Type tUnderlyingSystem = t.UnderlyingSystemType;
    if (tUnderlyingSystem != null)
        AddToOutput("UnderlyingSystem Type:" + tUnderlyingSystem.Name);
    AddToOutput("\nPUBLIC MEMBERS:");
```

```
            MemberInfo [] Members = t.GetMembers();
            foreach (MemberInfo NextMember in Members)
            {
                AddToOutput(NextMember.DeclaringType + " " +
                        NextMember.MemberType + " " + NextMember.Name);
            }
        }
```

We implement this method by simply calling various properties of the Type object to get the information we need concerning the names, then call the GetMembers() method to get an array of MemberInfo objects that we can use to display the details of each method. Note that we use a helper method, AddToOutput(), to build up the text to be displayed in the message box:

```
        static void AddToOutput(string Text)
        {
            OutputText.Append("\n" + Text);
        }
    }
```

The Assembly Class

The Assembly class is defined in the System.Reflection namespace, and allows you access to the metadata for a given assembly. It also contains methods to allow you to execute an assembly, assuming the assembly is an executable. Like the Type class, it contains a very large number of methods and properties – too many for us to cover here. Instead, we will confine ourselves to covering those methods and properties that you need to get started and which we will use to complete the WhatsNewAttributes sample.

Before you can do anything with an Assembly instance, you need to load the corresponding assembly into the running process. You can do this with either of the static members Assembly.Load() and Assembly.LoadFrom(). The difference between these methods is that Load() takes the name of the assembly, which must be an assembly that is already referenced from the currently executing assembly (in other words, it must be an assembly that you referenced when you were first compiling the project), while LoadFrom() takes the pathname of an assembly, which can be any assembly that is present on your file system:

```
        Assembly Assembly1 = Assembly.Load("SomeAssembly");
        Assembly Assembly2 = Assembly.LoadFrom
            (@"C:\My Projects\GroovySoftware\SomeOtherAssembly");
```

There are a number of other overloads of both methods, which supply additional security information. Once you have loaded an assembly, you can use various properties on it to find out, for example, its full name:

```
        string Name = TheAssembly.FullName;
```

Finding out About Types Defined in an Assembly

One nice feature of the Assembly class is as it allows you to very conveniently obtain details of all the types that been defined in the corresponding assembly. You simply call the Assembly.GetTypes() method, which returns an array of System.Type references containing details of all the types. You can then manipulate these Type references just as you would with a Type object obtained from the C# typeof operator, or from Object.GetType():

```
Type[] Types = TheAssembly.GetTypes();
foreach(Type DefinedType in Types)
   DoSomethingWith(DefinedType);
```

Finding Out About Custom Attributes

The methods that you use to find out about what custom attributes are defined on an assembly or type depend on what type of object the type is attached to. If you want to find out what custom attributes are attached to an assembly as a whole, you need to call a static method of the `Attribute` class, `GetCustomAttributes()`, passing in a reference to the assembly:

```
Attribute [] DefinedAttributes =
          Attribute.GetCustomAttributes(TheAssembly);
```

This is actually quite significant. You may have wondered why, when we defined custom attributes, we had to go to all the trouble of actually writing classes for them, and why Microsoft hadn't come up with some simpler syntax. Well, the answer is here. The custom attributes do genuinely exist as objects, and once an assembly is loaded you can read these attribute objects in, examine their properties, and call their methods.

`GetCustomAttributes()`, as used to get assembly attributes, has a couple of overloads: if you call it without specifying any parameters other than a reference to the assembly then it will simply return all the custom attributes defined for that assembly. You can also call it by specifying a second parameter, which is a `Type` object that indicates the attribute class; in this case `GetCustomAttributes()` returns an array consisting of all the attributes present that are of that class. We will use this overload in the `WhatsNewAttributes` sample in order to find out whether the `SupportsWhatsNew` attribute is present in the assembly. To do this, we called `GetCustomAttributes()`, passing in a reference to the assembly, and the type of the `SupportWhatsNewAttribute` attribute. If this attribute is present, we get an array containing all instances of it. If there are no instances of it defined in the assembly, then we return `null`:

```
Attribute SupportsAttribute =
          Attribute.GetCustomAttributes(TheAssembly,
          typeof(SupportsWhatsNewAttribute));
```

Note that all attributes are retrieved as plain `Attribute` references. If you want to call any of the methods or properties you defined for your custom attributes, then you will need to cast these references explicitly to the relevant custom attribute classes. You can obtain details of custom attributes that are attached to a given data type by calling another overload of `Assembly.GetCustomAttributes()`, this time passing a `Type` reference that describes the type for which you want to retrieve any attached attributes. On the other hand, if you want to obtain attributes that are attached to methods, constructors, fields etc. then you will need to call a `GetCustomAttributes()` method that is a member of one of the classes `MethodInfo`, `ConstructorInfo`, `FieldInfo`, and so on. That is outside the scope of this chapter.

Completing the WhatsNewAttributes Sample

We now have enough information to complete the `WhatsNewAttributes` sample by writing the source code for the final assembly in the sample, the `LookUpWhatsNew` assembly. This part of the application is a console application. However, it needs to reference both of the other assemblies. Although this is going to be a command line application, we will follow the previous `TypeView` sample in actually displaying our results in a message box, since there is again going to be rather a lot of text output – far too much to show in a console window screenshot.

In the source code for this file, we first indicate the namespaces we wish to infer. `System.Text` is there because we need to use a `StringBuilder` object again:

```
using System;
using System.Reflection;
using System.Windows.Forms;
using System.Text;
using Wrox.ProfessionalCSharp.Chapter7.VectorClass;
using Wrox.ProfessionalCSharp.Chapter7.WhatsNewAttributes;
namespace Wrox.ProfessionalCSharp.Chapter7.LookUpWhatsNew
{
```

Next, the class that will contain the main program entry point as well as the other methods: `WhatsNewChecker`. All the methods we define will be in this class, which will also have two static fields. `outputText` contains the text as we build it up in preparation for writing it to the message box. `BackDateTo` stores the date we have selected – all modifications made since this date will be displayed. Normally, we would display a dialog box inviting the user to pick this date, but I don't want to get sidetracked into that kind of code (besides, we haven't reached the Windows Forms chapter yet, so we don't yet know how to display a dialog box other than a simple message box!). For this reason, I've initialized `BackDateTo` to a hard-coded date of 14 May 2001. You can easily change this date if you want when you download the code:

```
class WhatsNewChecker
{
    static StringBuilder outputText = new StringBuilder(1000);
    static DateTime BackDateTo = new DateTime(2001, 5, 14);

    static void Main(string[] args)
    {
        Assembly TheAssembly = Assembly.Load("VectorClass");
        Attribute SupportsAttribute =
            Attribute.GetCustomAttribute(TheAssembly,
                                    typeof(SupportsWhatsNewAttribute));
        string Name = TheAssembly.FullName;
        AddToMessage("Assembly: " + Name);
        if (SupportsAttribute == null)
        {
            AddToMessage(
                    "This assembly does not support WhatsNew attributes");
            return;
        }
        else
            AddToMessage("Defined Types:");
        Type[] Types = TheAssembly.GetTypes();
        foreach(Type DefinedType in Types)
            DisplayTypeInfo(TheAssembly, DefinedType);
        MessageBox.Show(outputText.ToString(),
            "What\'s New since " + BackDateTo.ToLongDateString());
        Console.ReadLine();
    }
```

The `Main()` method first loads the `VectorClass` assembly, and verifies that it is indeed marked with the `SupportsWhatsNew` attribute. It will do so, as we've only recently compiled that assembly with that attribute in, but this is a check that would be worth making if, more realistically, the user was given a choice of what assembly he wanted to check.

Assuming all is well, we use the `Assembly.GetTypes()` method to get an array of all the types defined in this assembly, then loop through them. For each one we call a method that we have written, `DisplayTypeInfo()`, which will add the relevant text, including details of any instances of `LastModifiedAttribute`, to the `outputText` field. Finally, we show the message box with the complete text. The `DisplayTypeInfo()` method looks like this:

```
static void DisplayTypeInfo(Assembly theAssembly, Type theType)
{

   // make sure we only pick out classes

   if (!(theType.IsClass))
      return;
   AddToMessage("\nclass " + theType.Name);
   Attribute [] Attribs = Attribute.GetCustomAttributes(theType);
   if (Attribs.Length == 0)
      AddToMessage("No changes to this class\n");
   else
      foreach (Attribute Attrib in Attribs)
         WriteAttributeInfo(Attrib);
   MethodInfo [] Methods = theType.GetMethods();
   AddToMessage("CHANGES TO METHODS OF THIS CLASS:");
   foreach (MethodInfo NextMethod in Methods)
   {
      object [] Attribs2 =
         NextMethod.GetCustomAttributes(typeof(LastModifiedAttribute),
                                        false);
      if (Attribs != null)
      {
         AddToMessage(NextMethod.ReturnType + " " +
                  NextMethod.Name + "()");
         foreach (Attribute NextAttrib in Attribs2)
            WriteAttributeInfo(NextAttrib);
      }
   }
}
```

Notice that the first thing we do in this method is check whether the Type reference we have been passed actually represents a struct. Since, in order to keep things simple, we've specified that the LastModified attribute can only be applied to classes or member methods, we'll be wasting our time doing any processing if the item is not a struct (it might in principle be a class, delegate or enum).

Next we use the Attribute.GetCustomAttributes() method to find out if this class does have any LastModifiedAttribute instances attached to it. If it does, we add their details to the output text, using a helper method, WriteAttributeInfo(), which we will consider next.

Finally, we use the Type.GetMethods() method to iterate through all the member methods of this data type, and then basically do the same thing with each method: check if it has any LastModifiedAttribute instances attached to it, and display them using WriteAttributeInfo() if it has.

The next bit of code shows the WriteAttributeInfo() method, which is responsible for working out what text to display for a given LastModifiedAttribute instance. Note that this method is passed an Attribute reference, so it needs to cast this to a LastModifiedAttribute reference first. Once it has done that, it uses the properties that we originally defined for this attribute to retrieve its parameters. It checks that the date of the attribute is sufficiently recent before actually adding it to the text to be displayed:

```
static void WriteAttributeInfo(Attribute Attrib)
{
   LastModifiedAttribute LastModifiedAttrib =
                           Attrib as LastModifiedAttribute;
   if (LastModifiedAttrib == null)
      return;

   // check that date is in range
```

```
                DateTime ModifiedDate = LastModifiedAttrib.DateModified;
                if (ModifiedDate < BackDateTo)
                    return;
                AddToMessage("  MODIFIED: " + ModifiedDate.ToLongDateString()
                                        + ":");
                AddToMessage("     " + LastModifiedAttrib.Changes);
                if (LastModifiedAttrib.Issues != null)
                    AddToMessage("     Outstanding issues:" +
                                            LastModifiedAttrib.Issues);
                AddToMessage("");
            }
```

Finally, here's the helper `AddToMessage()` method:

```
            static void AddToMessage(string message)
            {
                outputText.Append("\n" + message);
            }
```

Running this code produces these results:

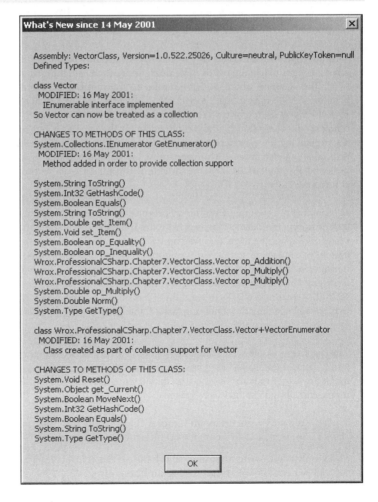

Notice that when we listed the types defined in the `VectorClass` assembly, we actually picked up two classes: `Vector`, and the embedded `VectorEnumerator` class that we added when we turned `Vector` into a collection earlier in the chapter. Also notice that, because we hard-coded a `BackDateTo` date of 14 May in this code, we've actually picked up the attributes that were dated 16 May (when we added the collection stuff), but not the ones dated 10 May (when we added the `IFormattable` interface).

Threading

In this section, we will look at the support that C# and the .NET base classes offer for developing applications that employ multiple threads. We will briefly examine the `Thread` class, through which much of the threading support takes place, and develop a couple of samples that illustrate threading principles. From there, we'll examine some of the issues that arise when we consider thread synchronization. Due to the complexity of the subject, the emphasis will be on understanding some of the basic principles involved – we won't really go on to develop any real applications.

A **thread** is a sequence of execution in a program. For all programs that we've written so far in C#, there has been one entry point: the `Main()` method. Execution has started with that the first statement in the `Main()` method and has continued until that method returns.

This program structure is all very well for programs in which there is one identifiable sequence of tasks, but often a program actually needs to be doing more than one thing at the same time. One familiar situation in which this occurs is when you have started up Internet Explorer and are sitting getting increasingly frustrated as some page takes ages to load. Eventually, you get so fed up (if you're like me, after about 2 seconds) that you click the Back button or type in some other URL to look at instead. For this to work, Internet Explorer must be doing at least three things: grabbing the data for the page as it gets returned from the Internet, along with any accompanying files, rendering the page, and watching for any user input that might indicate the user wants IE to do something else instead. More generally, the same situation applies to any case where a program is performing some task while at the same time displaying a dialog box that give you the chance to cancel the task at any time.

Let's look at the example with Internet Explorer in more detail. We'll simplify the problem a bit by ignoring the task of storing the data as it arrives from the Internet, and assume that Internet Explorer is simply faced with two tasks: displaying the page, and watching for user input. We'll assume for the sake of argument that this is a page that takes a long time to display; it might have some processor-intensive JavaScript in it, or it might contain a marquee element in it that needs to be continually updated. One way that you could approach the situation is to write a method that does a little bit of work in rendering the page. After a short time, let us say a twentieth of a second, the method checks to see if there has been any user input. If there has been, this is processed (which may mean canceling the rendering task). Otherwise, the method carries on rendering the page for another twentieth of the second.

This approach would work, but it's going to be a very complicated method to implement. More seriously, it totally ignores the event-based architecture of Windows. Recall from our coverage of events in the last chapter that if any user input arrives, the system will want to notify the application by raising an event. Let's modify our method to allow Windows to use events:

- ❑   We will write an event handler that responds to user input. The response may include setting some flag to indicate that rendering should stop.

- ❑   We will write a method that handles the rendering. This method is designed to be executed whenever we are not doing anything else.

This solution is better, because it works with the Windows event architecture, but personally I wouldn't like to be the person who has to write this rendering method. Look at what it has to do: for a start, it will have to time itself carefully. While this method is running, the computer cannot respond to any user input. That means that this method will have to make a note of the time that it gets called, continue monitoring the time as it works, and as soon as a fairly suitable period of time has elapsed (the absolute maximum to retain user responsiveness would be a bit less than a tenth of a second), should return. Not only that, but before this method returns, it will need to store the exact state of where it had got up to, so that the next time it is called it can carry on from there. It is certainly possible to write a method that would do that, and in the days of Windows 3.1, that's exactly what you would have to do to handle this sort of situation. Luckily, NT3.1 and then Windows 95 brought multithreaded processes, which are a far more convenient way of solving problems like this.

Applications with Multiple Threads

The above example illustrates the situation in which an application needs to do more than one thing, so the obvious solution is to give the application more than one thread of execution. As we said, a thread represents the sequence of instructions that the computer executes. There's no reason why an application should only have one such sequence. In fact, it can have as many as you want. All that is required is that each time you create a new thread of execution, you indicate a method at which execution should start. The first thread in an application always starts at the `Main()` method because the first thread is started by the .NET runtime, and `Main()` is the method that the .NET runtime picks. Subsequent threads will be started internally by your application, which means that your application gets to choose where those threads starts.

How Does This Work?

So far, we have rather loosely spoken about threads happening at the same time. In fact, one processor can only be doing one thing at a time. If you have a multiprocessor system then it is theoretically possible for more than one instruction to be executed simultaneously, one on each processor, but for the majority of us who work on single processor computers, things just don't happen simultaneously. What actually happens is that the Windows operating system gives the appearance of many things taking place at the same time by a procedure known as **pre-emptive multitasking**.

What pre-emptive multitasking means is that Windows picks a thread in some process and allows that thread to run for a short period of time. Microsoft hasn't documented how long this period is, because it is one of those internal operating system parameters that they want to be free to tweak as Windows evolves, in order to maintain optimum performance. In any case, it's not the kind of information you need to know to run the Windows applications. In human terms, this time is very short – certainly no more than milliseconds. It is known as the thread's **time slice**. When the time slice is finished, windows takes control back and picks another thread which will then be allocated a time slice. These time slices are so short that we get the illusion of lots of things happening simultaneously.

Even when your application only has one thread, this process of pre-emptive multitasking is going on because there are many other processes running on the system, and each process needs to be given time slices for each of its threads. That's how, when you have lots of windows on your screen, each one representing a different process, you can still click on any of them and have it appear to respond straight away. The response isn't instantaneous – it happens the next time that the thread in the relevant process that is responsible handling user input from that window gets a time slice. However, unless the system is very busy, the wait before that happens is so short that you don't notice it.

Manipulating Threads

Threads are manipulated using the class Thread, which can be found in the System.Threading namespace. A thread instance represents one thread – one sequence of execution. You can create another thread by simply instantiating a thread object.

Starting a Thread

To make the following code snippets more concrete, let's suppose you are writing a graphics image editor, and the user requests to change the color depth of the image. I've picked this example because for a large image this can take a while to perform. It's the sort of situation where you'd probably create a separate thread to do the processing so that you don't tie up the user interface while the color depth change is happening. You'd start by instantiating a thread object like this:

```
// EntryPoint has been declared previously as a delegate
// of type ThreadStart
Thread DepthChangeThread = new Thread(EntryPoint);
```

Here we've given the variable the name DepthChangeThread.

> *Additional threads that are created within an application in order to perform some task are often known as* **worker threads**.

The above code shows that the Thread constructor requires one parameter, which is used to indicate the entry point of the thread – that is, the method at which the thread starts executing. Since we are passing in the details of a method, this is a situation that calls for the use of delegates. In fact, a delegate has already been defined in the System.Threading class. It is called ThreadStart(), and its signature looks like this:

```
public delegate void ThreadStart();
```

The parameter we pass to the constructor must be delegate of this type.

After doing this, however, the new thread isn't actually doing anything so far. It is simply sitting there waiting to be started. We start a thread by calling the Thread.Start() method

With this information, we can start our new thread. Suppose we have a method, ChangeColorDepth(), which does this processing:

```
void ChangeColorDepth()
{
    // processing to change color depth of image
}
```

You would arrange for this processing to be performed with this code:

```
Thread DepthChangeThread = new Thread();
DepthChangeThread.Name = "Depth Change Thread";
ThreadStart EntryPoint = new ThreadStart(ChangeColorDepth);
DepthChangeThread.Start(EntryPoint);
```

After this point, both threads will be running simultaneously.

In this code, we have also assigned a user-friendly name to the thread using the `Thread.Name` property. It's not necessary to do this, but it can be useful.

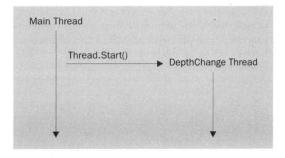

Note that because the thread entry point (`ChangeColorDepth()` in this example) cannot take any parameters, you'll have to find some other means of passing in any information that the method needs. The most obvious way would be to use member fields of whatever class this method is a member of. Also, the method cannot return anything. (Where would any return value be returned to? As soon as this method returns, the thread that is running it will terminate, so there's nothing around to receive any return value).

Once you have started another thread, you can also suspend, resume, or abort it. Suspending a thread means putting it to sleep – the thread will simply not run for a period, which means it will not take up any processor time. It can later be resumed, which means it will simply carry on from the point at which it was suspended. If a thread is aborted, then it will stop running for good. Windows will permanently destroy all data that it maintains relating to that thread, so the thread cannot subsequently be restarted.

Continuing the image editor example, we'll assume that for some reason the user interface thread displays a dialog gives the user a chance to temporarily suspend the conversion process (it's not usual for a user to want to do this, but it's only an example; a more realistic example might be the user pausing the playing of a sound or video file). We would code the response like this in the main thread:

```
DepthChangeThread.Suspend();
```

And if the user subsequently asked the processing to resume:

```
DepthChangeThread.Resume();
```

Finally, if the user (more realistically) decided that he or she didn't want to do the conversion after all, and chose to cancel it:

```
DepthChangeThread.Abort();
```

Note that the `Suspend()` and `Abort()` methods do not necessarily work instantly. In the case of `Suspend()`, .NET may allow the thread being suspended to execute a few more instructions in order to reach a point at which .NET regards the thread as safely suspendable. This is for technical reasons to do with ensuring the correct operation of the garbage collector, and full details are in the MSDN documentation. In the case of aborting a thread, the `Abort()` method actually works by throwing a `ThreadAbortException` in the affected thread. `ThreadAbortException` is a special exception class that is never handled. The point of doing it this way is that it means that if that thread is currently executing code inside `try` blocks, any associated `finally` blocks will be executed before the thread is actually killed. This ensures that any appropriate cleaning up of resources can be done, and also gives the thread a chance to make sure that any data it was manipulating (for example, fields of a class instance that will remain around after the thread dies) is left in a valid state.

> *Prior to .NET, aborting a thread in this way was not recommended except in extreme cases because the affected thread simply got killed immediately, which meant that any data it was manipulating could be left in an invalid state, and any resources the thread was using would be left open. The exception mechanism used by .NET in this situation means that aborting threads is safer and do is acceptable programming practice.*

Although this exception mechanism makes aborting a thread safe, it does mean that aborting a thread might actually take some time, since theoretically there is no limit on how long code in a finally block could take to execute. Due to this, after aborting a thread, you might want to wait until the thread has actually been killed before continuing any processing, if any of your subsequent processing relies on the other thread having been killed. You can wait for a thread to terminate by calling the `Join()` method:

```
DepthChangeThread.Abort();
DepthChangeThread.Join();
```

`Join()` also has other overloads that allow you to specify a time limit on how long you are prepared to wait. If the time limit is reached then execution will simply continue anyway. If no time limit is specified, then the thread that is waiting will wait for as long as it needs to.

The above coded snippets will show one thread performing actions on another thread (or at least in the case of `Join()`, waiting for another thread). However, what happens if the main thread wants to perform some actions on itself? In order to do this it needs a reference to a thread object which represents its own thread. It can get such a reference using the static property, `CurrentThread`, of the `Thread` class:

```
Thread MyOwnThread = Thread.CurrentThread;
```

`Thread` is actually a slightly unusual class to manipulate because there is always one thread present even before you instantiate any others: the thread that you are currently executing. This means that there are two different ways that you can manipulate the class:

❑ You can instantiate a thread object, which will then represent a running thread, and whose instance members apply to that running thread.

❑ You can call any of a number of static methods. These generally apply to the thread you are actually calling the method from.

One static method you may wish to call is `Sleep()`. This simply puts the running thread to sleep for a set period of time, after which it will continue.

The ThreadPlayaround Sample

We are going to start by illustrating how to use threads with a small sample, which we will call `ThreadPlayaround`. The aim of this sample is to give us a feel for how manipulating threads works, so it's not intended to illustrate any realistic programming situations. We are simply going to kick off a couple of threads and see what happens.

The core of the `ThreadPlayaround` sample is a short method, `DisplayNumbers()`, that counts up to a large number, displaying how far it's counted up to every so often. `DisplayNumbers()` also starts by displaying the name and culture of the thread that it is being run on:

```
static void DisplayNumbers()
{
    Thread ThisThread = Thread.CurrentThread;
    string Name = ThisThread.Name;
    Console.WriteLine("Starting thread: " + Name);
    Console.WriteLine(Name + ": Current Culture = " +
                      ThisThread.CurrentCulture);
```

```
        for (int i=1 ; i<= 8*Interval ; i++)
        {
            if (i%Interval == 0)
                Console.WriteLine(Name + ": count has reached " + i);
        }
    }
```

How far the count runs up to depends on `Interval`, which is a field whose value is typed in by the user. If the user types in 100, then we'll count up to 800, displaying the values 100, 200, 300, 400, 500, 600, 700, and 800. If the user types in 1000 then we'll count up to 8000, displaying the values 1000, 2000, 3000, 4000, 5000, 6000, 7000, and 8000 along the way, and so on. This might all seem like a pointless exercise, but the purpose of it is to tie up the processor for a period while allowing us to see how, far the processor is progressing with its task.

What `ThreadPlayaround` does is to start a second worker thread, which will run `DisplayNumbers()`, but immediately after starting the worker thread, the main thread begins executing the same method. This means that we should see both counts happening at the same time.

The `Main()` method for `ThreadPlayaround` and its containing class looks like this:

```
    class EntryPoint
    {
        static int Interval;
        static void Main(string[] args)
        {
            Console.Write("Interval to display results at?> ");
            Interval = int.Parse(Console.ReadLine());
            Thread ThisThread = Thread.CurrentThread;
            ThisThread.Name = "Main Thread";
            ThreadStart WorkerStart = new ThreadStart(StartMethod);
            Thread WorkerThread = new Thread(WorkerStart);
            WorkerThread.Name = "Worker";
            WorkerThread.Start();
            DisplayNumbers();
            Console.WriteLine("Main Thread Finished");
            Console.ReadLine();
        }
```

We've shown the start of the class declaration here so that we can see that `Interval` is a `static` field of this class. In the `Main()` method, we first ask the user for the interval. Then we retrieve a reference to the thread object that represents the main thread – this is done so that we can give this thread a name so that we can see what's going on in the output.

Next, we create the worker thread, set its name, and start it off, passing it a delegate that indicates that the method it must start in is a method called `WorkerStart`. Finally, we call the `DisplayNumbers()` method to start counting. The entry point for the worker thread is this:

```
        static void StartMethod()
        {
            DisplayNumbers();
            Console.WriteLine("Worker Thread Finished");
        }
```

Note that all these methods `Main()`, `StartMethod()`, and `DisplayNumbers()` are static methods in the same class, `EntryPoint`. Note also that the two counts will take place entirely separately, since the variable `i` in the `DisplayNumbers()` method used to do the counting is a local variable. Local variables are not only scoped only to the method they are defined in, but are also visible only to the thread that is executing that method. If another thread starts executing the same method, than that thread will get its own copy of the local variables. We'll start by running the code, and selecting a relatively small value of `100` for the interval:

```
C:\Documents and Settings\allanj.WROX_U...
Interval to display results at?> 100
Starting thread: Main Thread
Starting thread: Worker
Worker: Current Culture = en-GB
Worker: count has reached 100
Worker: count has reached 200
Worker: count has reached 300
Worker: count has reached 400
Worker: count has reached 500
Worker: count has reached 600
Worker: count has reached 700
Worker: count has reached 800
Worker Thread Finished
Main Thread: Current Culture = en-GB
Main Thread: count has reached 100
Main Thread: count has reached 200
Main Thread: count has reached 300
Main Thread: count has reached 400
Main Thread: count has reached 500
Main Thread: count has reached 600
Main Thread: count has reached 700
Main Thread: count has reached 800
Main Thread Finished
```

As far as threads working in parallel are concerned, this doesn't immediately look like it's working too well! We see that the main thread starts, counts up to 800, then claims to finish. The worker thread then starts and runs through separately.

The problem here is actually that starting a thread is quite a major process. After instantiating the new thread, the main thread hits this line of code:

```
WorkerThread.Start();
```

This call to `Thread.Start()` basically informs Windows that the new thread is to be started, then immediately returns. While we are counting up to 800, Windows is busily making the arrangements for the thread to be started. This internally means amongst other things, allocating various resources for the thread, and performing various security checks. By the time the new thread is actually starting up, the main thread has finished its work!

We can solve this problem by simply choosing a larger interval, so that both threads spend longer in the `DisplayNumbers()` method. We'll try `1000000` this time:

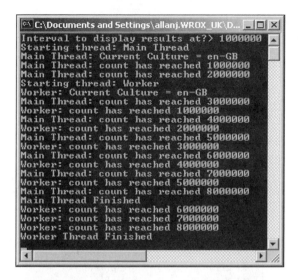

Now we can see the threads really working in parallel. The main thread starts and counts up to one million. At some point, while the main thread is counting the next million numbers, the worker thread starts off, and from then on, the two threads progress at the same rate until they both finish.

It is important to understand that unless you are running a multi-processor computer, using two threads in a CPU-intensive task will not have saved any time. On my single-processor machine, having both threads count up to 8 million will have taken just as long as having one thread count up to 16 million. Arguably, it will take slightly longer, since with the extra thread around, the operating system has to do a little bit more thread switching, but this difference will be negligible. The advantage of using more than one thread is twofold. First, you gain responsiveness, in that one of the threads could be dealing with user input while the other thread does some work behind the scenes. Second, you will save time if one or more threads is doing something that doesn't involve CPU time, such as waiting for data to be retrieved from the Internet, because the other threads can carry out their processing while the inactive thread(s) are waiting.

Thread Priorities

It is possible to assign different priorities to different threads within a process. In general, a thread will not be allocated any time slices if there are any higher priority threads working. The advantage of this is that you can guarantee user responsiveness by assigning a slightly higher priority to a thread that handles receiving user input. For most of the time, such a thread will have nothing to do, and the other threads can carry on their work. However, if the user does anything, this thread will immediately take priority over other threads in your application for the short time that it spends handling the event.

High priority threads can completely block threads of lower priority, so you should be careful about changing thread priorities. The thread priorities are defined as values of the ThreadPriorityEnumeration. The possible values are Highest, AboveNormal, Normal, BelowNormal, Lowest.

You should note each process has a base priority, and that these values are relative to the priority of your process. Giving a thread a higher priority may ensure that it gets priority over other threads in that process, but there may still be other processes running on the system whose threads get an even higher priority. Windows tends to give a higher priority to its own operating system threads.

We can see the effect of changing a thread priority by making the following change to the `Main()` method in the `ThreadPlayaround` sample:

```
ThreadStart WorkerStart = new ThreadStart(StartMethod);
Thread WorkerThread = new Thread(WorkerStart);
WorkerThread.Name = "Worker";
WorkerThread.Priority = ThreadPriority.AboveNormal;
WorkerThread.Start();
```

What we have done is indicate that the worker thread should have a slightly higher priority than the main thread. The result is dramatic:

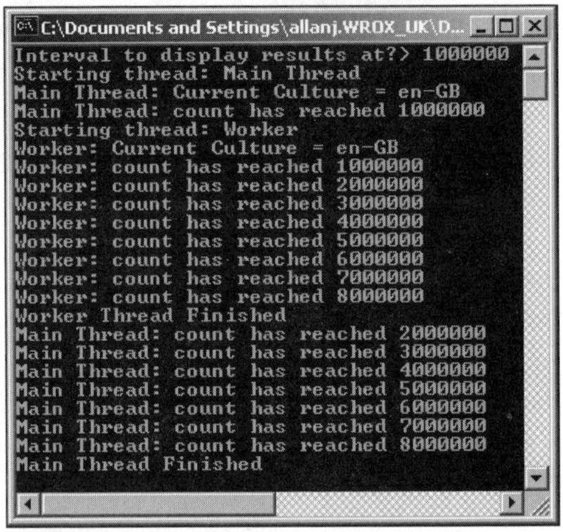

This screenshot shows that when the worker thread has an `AboveNormal` priority, the main thread scarcely gets a look-in once the worker thread has started.

Synchronization

One crucial aspect of working with threads is **synchronizing** access to any variables which more than one thread has access to. What we mean by synchronization is that only one thread should be able to access the variable at any one time. If we do not ensure that access to variables is synchronized, then subtle bugs can result. In this section, we'll briefly review some of the main issues involved.

What is Synchronization?

The issue of synchronization arises because what looks like a single statement in your C# source code in most cases will translate into many statements in the final compiled assembly language machine code. Take for example the statement:

```
message += ", there";   // message is a string that contains "Hello"
```

This statement looks syntactically in C# like one statement, but it actually involves a large number of operations when the code is being executed. Memory will need to be allocated to store the new longer string, the variable message will need to be set to refer to the new memory, the actual text will need to be copied, and so on.

Obviously, we've exaggerated the case here by picking a string – one of the more complex data types as our example, but even when performing arithmetic operations on primitive numeric types, there is quite often more going on behind the scenes than you would imagine from looking at the C# code. In particular, many operations cannot be carried out directly on variables stored in memory locations, and their values have to be separately copied into special locations in the processor known as **registers**.

In any situation where a single C# statement translates into more than one native machine code command, it is quite possible that the thread's time slice might end in the middle of executing that "statement" process. If this happens, then another thread in the same process may be given a time slice, and, if access to variables involved with that statement (message in the above example) are not synchronized, this other thread may attempt to read or write to the same variables. With our example, was the other thread intended to see the new value of message or the old value?

The problems can get worse than this, too. The statement we used in our example was relatively simple, but in a more complicated statement, some variable might have an undefined value for a brief period, while the statement is being executed. If another thread attempts to read that value in that instant, then it may simply read garbage. More seriously, if two threads simultaneously try to write data to the same variable, then it is almost certain that that variable will contain an incorrect value afterwards.

Synchronization is not an issue that affects the ThreadPlayAround sample, because in that sample both threads used mostly local variables. The only variable that both threads have access to was the Interval field, but this field was initialized by the main thread before any other thread started, and subsequently only ever read from either thread, so there was still not a problem. Synchronization issues only arise is at least one thread may be writing to a variable while other threads may be either reading or writing to it.

Fortunately, C# provides an extremely easy way of synchronizing access to variables, and unusually for this chapter, there's a C# language keyword that does it: lock. You use lock like this:

```
lock (X)
{
    DoSomething();
}
```

What the lock statements does is wrap an object known as a **mutual exclusion lock** (or **mutex**) around the variable in the round brackets. The mutex will remain in place while the compound statement attached to the lock keyword is executed. While the mutex is wrapped around a variable, no other thread is permitted access to that variable. We can see this with the above code; the compound statement will execute, and eventually this thread will lose its time slice. If the next thread to gain the time slice attempts to access the variable X, access to the variable will be denied. Instead, Windows will simply put the other thread to sleep until the mutex has been released.

The mutex is the simplest of a number of mechanisms that can be used to control access to variables. We don't have the space to go into the others here, but we'll mention that they are all controlled through the .NET bass class System.Threading.Monitor. In fact, the C# lock statement is simply a C# syntax wrapper around a couple of method calls to this class. We will see mutexes in action in the next sample.

In general, you should synchronize variables wherever there is a risk that any thread might try writing to a variable at the same time as other threads are trying to read or write from the variable. We don't have space here to cover the details of thread synchronization here in detail, but we will point out that it is a fairly big topic in its own right. Here, we will simply confine ourselves to pointing out a couple of the potential pitfalls.

Synchronization Issues

Synchronizing threads is vitally important in multithreaded applications. However, it's an area in which it is important to work carefully because a number of subtle and hard-to-detect bugs can easily arise, in particular **deadlocks** and **race conditions**.

Don't Overuse Synchronization

While thread synchronization is important, it's important to only use it where it is necessary, because it can hurt performance. This is for two reasons. First, there is some overhead associated with actually putting a lock on an object and taking it off, though this is admittedly minimal. Second, and more importantly, the more thread synchronization you have, the more threads can get held up waiting for objects to be released. Remember that if one thread holds a lock on any object, any other thread that needs to access that object will simply halt execution until the lock is released. It's important, therefore, that you place as little code inside `lock` blocks as you can without causing thread synchronization bugs. In one sense, you can think of `lock` statements as temporarily disabling the multithreading ability of an application, and therefore temporarily removing all the benefits of multithreading.

On the other hand, it has to be said that the dangers of using synchronization too much (performance and responsiveness go down) are not as great as the dangers associated with not using synchronization when you need it (subtle runtime bugs that are very hard to track down).

Deadlocks

A **deadlock** is a bug that can occur when two threads both need to access resources that are locked by each other. Suppose one thread is running the following code, where A and B are two object references that both threads have access to:

```
lock (A)
{

    // do something

    lock (B)
    {

        // do something

    }
}
```

At the same time another thread is running this code:

```
lock (B)
{

    // do something

    lock (A)
    {

        // do something

    }
}
```

Depending on the times that the threads hit the various statements, the following scenario is quite possible: the first thread acquires a lock on A, while at about the same time the second thread acquires a lock on B. A short time later, thread A hits the `lock(B)` statement, and immediately goes to sleep, waiting for the lock on B to be released. Soon afterwards, the second thread hits its `lock(A)` statement and also puts itself to sleep, ready for Windows to wake it up the instant the lock on A gets released. Unfortunately, the lock on A is never going to be released because the first thread, which owns this lock, is sleeping and won't wake up until the lock on B gets released, which won't happen until the second thread wakes up. The result is deadlock. Both threads just permanently sit doing nothing, each waiting for the other thread to release its lock. This kind of problem can cause an entire application to just hang, so that you can't do anything with it apart from use the Task Manager to just terminate the entire process.

> *In this situation, it's not possible for another thread to release the locks; a mutual exclusion lock can only be released by the thread that claimed the lock in the first place.*

Deadlocks can usually be avoided by having both threads claim locks on object in the same order. In the above example, if the second thread claimed the locks in the same order as the first thread: A first, then B, then whichever thread got the lock on A first would completely finish its task, then the other thread would start. This way, no deadlock can occur.

You might think that it's easy to avoid coding up deadlocks – after all, in the code shown above, it looks fairly obvious that a deadlock could occur so you probably wouldn't write that code in the first place, but remember that different locks can occur in different method calls. With this example, the first thread might actually be executing this code:

```
lock (A)
{

    // do bits of processing

    CallSomeMethod()
}
```

Here `CallSomeMethod()` might call other methods, and so on, and buried in there somewhere is a `lock(B)` statement. In this situation, it might not be nearly so obvious when you write your code that you are allowing for a possible deadlock.

Race Conditions

A **race condition** is somewhat subtler than a deadlock. It rarely halts execution of a process, but it can lead to data corruption. It is hard to give a precise definition of a race, but is generally occurs when several threads attempt to access the same data, and do not adequately take account of what the other threads are doing. Race conditions are best understood using an example.

Suppose we have an array of objects, where each element in the array needs to be processed somehow, and we have a number of threads that are between them doing this processing. We might have an object, let's call it `ArrayController`, which contains the array of objects as well as an `int` that indicates how many of them have been processed, and therefore, which one should be processed next. `ArrayController` might implement this method:

```
int GetObject(int index)
{

    // returns the object at the given index.

}
```

and this read-write property:

```
int ObjectsProcessed
{

    // indicates how many of the objects have been processed.

}
```

Now each thread that is helping to process the objects might execute some code that looks like this:

```
lock(ArrayController)
{
    int nextIndex = ArrayController.ObjectsProcessed;
    Console.WriteLine("object to be processed next is "  + index);
    ++ArrayController.ObjectsProcessed;
    object next = ArrayController.GetObject();
}
ProcessObject(next);
```

This by itself should work, but suppose that in an attempt to avoid tying up resources for longer than necessary, we decided not to hold the lock on `ArrayController` while we're displaying the user message. Therefore, we rewrite the above code like this:

```
lock(ArrayController)
{
    int nextIndex = ArrayController.ObjectsProcessed;
}
Console.WriteLine("object to be processed next is "  + index);
lock(ArrayController)
{
    ++ArrayController.ObjectsProcessed;
    object next = ArrayController.GetObject();
}
ProcessObject(next);
```

Here, we have a possible problem. What could happen is that one thread gets an object (say the 11th object in the array), and goes to display the message saying that it is about to process this object. Meanwhile, a second thread also starts executing the same code, calls `ObjectsProcessed`, and determines that the next object to be processed is the 11th object, because the first thread hasn't yet updated `ArrayController.ObjectsProcessed`. While the second thread is happily writing to the console that it will now process the 11th object, the first thread acquires another lock on the `ArrayController` and inside this lock increments `ObjectsProcessed`. Unfortunately, it's too late. Both threads are now committed to processing the same object, and that's the kind of situation that we refer to as a race condition.

For both deadlocks and race conditions, it's not often obvious when the condition can occur, and when it does, it is really obvious what the problem in the program is. In general, this is an area where you largely learn from experience. It is, however, important to consider very carefully all the parts of the code where you need synchronization when you are writing multithreaded applications to check whether there is any possibility of deadlocks or a race conditions arising, bearing in mind that it is not possible to predict the exact timing that different threads will hit different instructions.

Summary

In this chapter, we have examined some of the facilities provided by the .NET base classes. We have seen how to efficiently construct and process strings using the `StringBuilder` class, and also how to use the regular expressions engine to perform very sophisticated searches against strings. We then moved on and looked at the different collection objects available. The `System.Collections` and `System.Collections.Specialized` namespaces contain a huge number of classes that allow you to store different types of collections of objects. In particular, the `Hashtable` class enables code to store data in the dictionary with very efficient lookup based on any data type.

Custom attributes, used in conjunction with reflection, provide the very powerful ability for code to examine other code, or even to examine itself. This means that execution can depend on which user defined attributes have been applied to objects in your code. We saw one example of this with the `WhatsNewAttributes` sample, which was able to provide automatic reports on the new features that had been added to software. Finally, we examined some of the issues involved when we code up an application that uses multiple threads.

8

Programming in the .NET Environment

This is the first of three chapters in which we examine aspects of programming with .NET. At this point, we've familiarized ourselves with the C# language itself, and are almost ready to the move onto the applied sections of the book, in which we will look at how to use C# to program applications covering a variety of areas. Before we do that, however, we need to examine how we can use the tools and features provided by the .NET environment to get the best from our programs.

In this chapter, we will look at what programming in the .NET environment means in practice, covering some of the tools that are available to help you write and debug programs as well as the guidelines for writing good applications. In particular, we will examine:

❑   Visual Studio.NET – the main developer environment in which you will usually write, compile, debug, and optimize your C# programs.

❑   WinCV – a useful utility that allows you to examine the base classes.

❑   Usage guidelines and naming conventions – the guidelines that you should follow when writing C# code, so that your code can be easily understood by others and follows normal .NET practice.

This will be followed in the next two chapters by a look at Windows Forms and how to write user interface code in Chapter 9, and assemblies, including compiling to libraries in Chapter 10.

Visual Studio.NET

Visual Studio.NET is a fully integrated development environment. It is designed to make the process of writing your code, debugging it and compiling it to an assembly to be shipped, as easy as possible. What this means in practice is that Visual Studio.NET gives you a very sophisticated multiple-document-interface application in which you can do just about everything related to developing your code. It offers:

- ❑ **A text editor**, in which you can write your C# code (as well as VB.NET and C++ code). This text editor is quite sophisticated, and it is aware of the syntax of C#. This means that as you type, it can automatically lay out your code, for example by indenting lines, matching start and end brackets of code blocks, and color coding keywords. It will also perform some syntax checks as you type, and will underline code that it are likely to cause compilation errors. It also features **Intellisense**, a feature which automatically displays small list boxes as you start typing names of classes, fields or methods, detailing the possible ways to complete the names or parameter lists that are available from any classes accessible to your code. The screenshot shows this feature at work with one of the .NET base classes, ListBox.

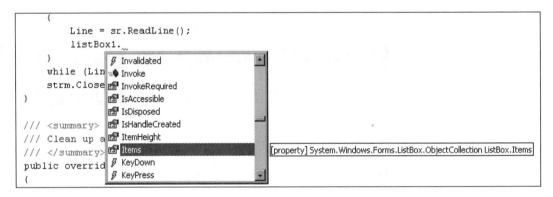

- ❑ **A design view** editor of your code, that allows you to visually place user-interface and data-access controls in your project. When you do this, Visual Studio.NET will automatically add the necessary C# code to your source files to instantiate these controls in your project (this is possible as under .NET, all the controls are actually just instances of particular base classes).

- ❑ **Supporting windows** that allow you to view and modify aspects of your project. For example, there are windows available that show you the classes in your source code and certain properties on Windows Forms and Web Forms classes. You can also use these windows to specify compilation options, such as which assemblies (particularly those containing the base classes) your code needs to reference.

- ❑ **Compilation from within the environment**. Instead of having to run the C# compiler from the command line, you can simply select a menu option to compile the project and Visual Studio.NET will call the compiler for you. It will pass all the relevant command line parameters to the compiler, detailing such things as which assemblies to reference, and what you want the project to be built as (executable or library, for example). If you so wish, it will even run the compiled executable for you straight away, so you can see whether it runs satisfactorily, and you can choose between different build configurations – for example, to do a release or debug build.

- ❏ **An integrated debugger**. It's in the nature of programming that you can virtually guarantee that your code won't run correctly the first time you try it. Or the second time. Or the third, and so on. Visual Studio.NET will seamlessly link up to a debugger for you, allowing you to set breakpoints and watches on variables all from within the environment. If, after hitting a breakpoint, you realize what the problem was, you can usually edit the code in the Visual Studio text editor to fix the bug, then get the code recompiled, and actually continue running with the revised code from where the program left off.

- ❏ **An integrated profiler**. Once your code is running and debugged, Visual Studio can hook up to a profiler, so that it can measure just how long your program is spending in each method. It can also give you other information which as informing you if any methods are ever being executed. You can use this information to fine-tune the performance. If you want your program to run faster, the data you get from profiling will tell you exactly which methods are eating up the time, and are therefore the ones you need to examine to try to optimize. The profiling facilities in Visual Studio.NET include higher level support than you would normally find in traditional profilers, allowing you to take a component-oriented view of a complete project, and analyze the performance of different components. This is done through a tool known as the **Visual Studio Analyzer**. We won't be covering profiling here, but details are in the MSDN documentation for Visual Studio Analyzer.

- ❏ **Integrated MSDN Help**. Visual Studio.NET can call up the MSDN documentation for you. For example, this means that if you're not sure of the meaning of a keyword in the text editor, you can select it, hit the F1 key, and Visual Studio.NET will then bring up MSDN to show you related topics. Similarly, if you're not sure what a certain compilation error means, you can bring up the documentation for that error.

- ❏ **Access to Other Programs**. If all that wasn't enough, Visual Studio.NET is also able to call on a number of other utilities that allow you to examine and modify aspects of your computer or network, without you having to leave the developer environment. Amongst the tools available, you can check running services, database connections, and there's even an Internet Explorer window that lets you browse the Web.

Assuming you are experienced in C++ or VB, you will already be familiar with the relevant Visual Studio 6 version of the developer environment for your particular language, so you will know that many of the features listed above are not new; you're probably already used to doing much the same thing in Visual Studio 6. However, what's new in Visual Studio.NET is that it combines all the features that were previously available across all VS6 developer environments. This means that whatever language you used in VS6, you'll find some new features in Visual Studio.NET. For example, in Visual Basic, you could not compile separate debug and release builds, nor could VB developers obtain access to a profiler through their VS6 developer environment. On the other hand, if you are coming to C# from a background of C++, much of the support for data access and the ability to drop controls into your application with a click of the mouse, which has long been part of the Visual Basic developers experience, will be new to you. The C++ developer environment did include some support for this, but it was very limited, and was restricted to the most common user-interface controls.

Whatever your background, you will find the overall look of the developer environment has changed to accommodate the new features, the single cross-language IDE and the integration with .NET. There are new menu options and toolbar options, and many of the existing ones from VS6 have been renamed. Therefore, you'll need to spend some time familiarizing yourself with the layout and commands available in Visual Studio.NET.

This is a professional level book, so we are not going to look in detail at every feature or menu option in Visual Studio.NET. We are assuming that you are a sufficiently competent programmer that you are capable of exploring the environment and seeing what's available for yourself. The real aim of our

Visual Studio.NET coverage is to ensure that you are sufficiently familiar with the all the concepts involved with building and debugging a C# application to be able to get the best out of Visual Studio.NET, and in particular to make sure that you are able to use particular features that might not have been available in the developer environment for whatever language you previously used.

To give you an idea of some of the features, the following screenshot shows what Visual Studio.NET might typically look like when you are coding (note that since the appearance of Visual Studio.NET is highly customizable, the windows might not be in the same locations or different windows might be visible when you launch the environment):

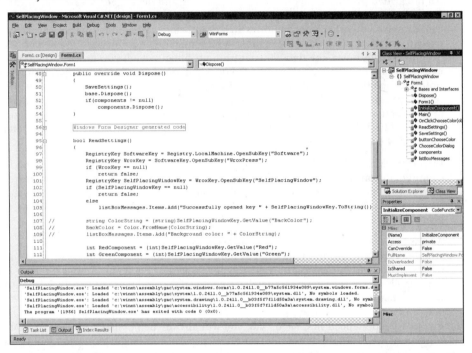

We shall now go through the process of creating, coding, debugging, and profiling a project, seeing what Visual Studio.NET can do to help you at each stage.

Creating A Project

Once you have installed Visual Studio.NET, you will want to start your first project. With Visual Studio.NET, you rarely start with a blank file that you type in C# code into from scratch, in the way that we've been doing in the previous chapters in this book. Instead, the idea is that you tell Visual Studio.NET roughly what type of project you are going to create, and Visual Studio.NET starts you off by automatically generating the C# code that gives you an outline framework for that type of project. You then work by adding your code to this outline. For example, if you are writing a Windows GUI-interface based application (or in .NET terminology, a Windows Form), Visual Studio.NET will start you off with a file containing C# source code that creates a basic form. This form is capable of talking to Windows and receiving events. It can be maximized, minimized, or resized, but it doesn't have any controls on it or any other functionality; that will be for you to add. If your application is intended to be a command line utility (a console application), then Studio.NET will give you a basic namespace, class and `Main()` method to start you off. Of course, the option is there to ask for an empty application if you really want to start writing your code from scratch.

Visual Studio.NET doesn't stop there in helping you start up your project. Remember we said earlier that Visual Studio.NET would call up the compiler for you when you need to compile your code. Well, when you create your project, it also sets up the compilation options that you are likely to need to supply to the C# compiler: whether it is to compile to a command line application, a library, or a Windows application. It also specifies which base class libraries you will need to reference (a Windows GUI application will need to reference many of the `Windows.Forms`-related libraries; a console application probably won't). You can of course modify all these settings as you are editing, if you need to.

The first time you start Visual Studio.NET, you will be presented with what is known as the **Start Page**. The Start Page is an HTML page that contains various links to take you to useful websites, lets you set the appearance and configuration of Visual Studio.NET (the My Profile link), open existing projects, or start a new project,

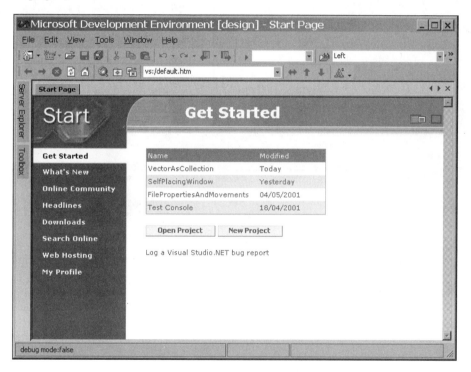

This screenshot shows the situation after I've used Visual Studio.NET a couple of times, and so features a list of the most recently edited projects. You can just click on one of these projects to open it again. Obviously, the first time you start up Visual Studio, this list will be empty.

Under the My Profile option, you can even change the appearance of Visual Studio.NET to match what you will have been used to in the previous developer environment for whatever your preferred language was, so that Visual Studio.NET looks a bit like the old VB or C++ IDEs. Note however, that this option only really changes where the various windows are positioned on the screen. You'll still find that most of the menu and toolbar options, as well as the detailed features of each window, are new.

Selecting A Project Type

You can create a new project either by clicking on the appropriate link on the Start Page, or by clicking on the File menu then choosing New, then Project. Either way, you will be presented with a dialog that gives you an idea of the variety of different projects you can create:

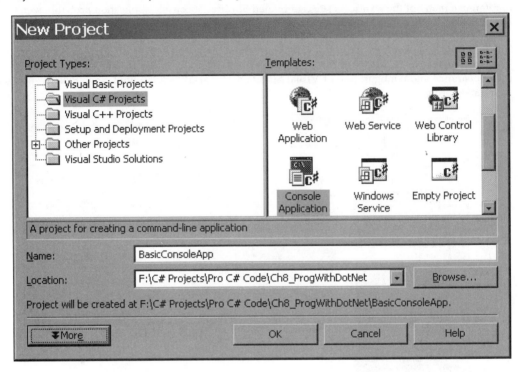

Effectively, what this dialog box is asking you is what kind of initial framework code you want Visual Studio.NET to generate for you, and what compilation options you want. It is also asking what compiler you want to compile your code – the C#, VB.NET, or C++ compiler. We can immediately see the language integration that Microsoft has promised for .NET at work here! For this particular example, we've opted for a C# console application, of the same type that we've been using up until now in the book.

We don't have space to cover all the various options for different types of project here. On the C++ side, all the old C++ project types are there – MFC application, ATL project etc. On the VB.NET side, the options have changed somewhat – for example, you can create a VB.NET command line application (Console Application), something that was impossible in VB6. You can also create a .NET component (Class Library) or .NET control (Windows Control Library), but you can't create an old-style COM-based control (the .NET control does the same thing).

This is a C# book; we will however, list all the options that are available to you for under Visual C# Projects. You should note that there are some other more specialized C# template projects available under the Other Projects option.

If You Choose...	You get the C# code and compilation options to generate...	Chapter
Windows Application	A basic empty form that responds to events.	9
Class Library	A .NET class that can be called up by other code.	10
Windows Control Library	A .NET class that can be called up by other code and which has a user interface. (Like an old-style ActiveX control).	9
Web Application	An ASP.NET-based web site: ASP.NET pages and C# classes that generate the HTML response sent to browsers from those pages.	16
Web Service	A C# class that acts as a fully operational Web Service.	17
Web Control Library	A control that can be called up by ASP.NET pages, to generate the HTML code that gives the appearance of a control when displayed on a browser.	18
Console Application	An application that runs at the command line prompt, or in a console window.	3
Windows Service	A service that runs in the background on Windows NT and Windows 2000.	24
Empty Project	Nothing. You have to write all your code from scratch but you still get the benefit of all the Visual Studio.NET facilities when you are writing.	
Empty Web Project	As for Empty Project, but the compilation settings are set to instruct the compiler to generate code for ASP.NET pages.	
New Project In Existing Folder	New project files for an empty project. Use this option if you have some straight C# source code (for example, typed in a text editor) and want to turn them into a Visual Studio.NET project.	

The final column of this table gives the number of the chapter(s) in this book in which we cover that type of application, for those types of project that represent concepts that are sufficiently complex to warrant their own chapters.

The Newly Created Console Project

Let's see what happens when we OK the above dialog to generate a C# console application. Visual Studio.NET gives us a number of files, including a source file, Class1.cs, which contains the initial framework code. We'll discuss the case for a console application here, but the same principles hold for all the other types of project.

This screenshot shows exactly what code Visual Studio.NET has written for us:

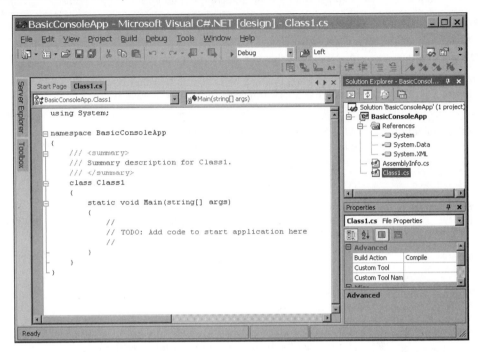

As you can see, we have here a C# program that doesn't yet actually do anything, but which contains the basic items required in any C# program: a namespace and a class that contains the Main() program entry point method. This code is all ready to compile and run, which you can do immediately by hitting the F5 key, or by selecting the Debug menu and choosing Start. Before we do that, however, we'll just add one line of code to make our application actually do something:

```
static void Main(string[] args)
{
    //
    // TODO: Add code to start application here
    //
    Console.WriteLine("Hello from all the editors at Wrox Press");
}
```

If you compile and run the project, you'll find a console window appears and disappears almost straight away, only just about giving you time to see the message. The reason this happens is that the Visual Studio.NET, remembering the settings you specified when you created the project, arranged for it to be compiled as a console application and then immediately run. Windows then realized that it needed to run a console application, but didn't have a console window to run it from. So Windows helpfully created a console window and ran the program. As soon as the program exited, Windows saw that it didn't need the console window any more and promptly destroyed it. That's all very logical, but doesn't help you very much if you actually want to look at the output from your project!

A good way to avoid this problem is to insert the following line just before the `Main()` method returns in your code:

```
static void Main(string[] args)
{
    //
    // TODO: Add code to start application here
    //
    Console.WriteLine("Hello from all the editors at Wrox Press");
    Console.ReadLine();
}
```

That way, your code will run, display its output, and then it will hit the `Console.ReadLine()` statement, at which point it will wait for you to hit the Return key before the program exits. This means that the console window will hang around until you hit Return.

Note that all this is only a problem for console applications that you test-run from Visual Studio.NET – if you are writing a Windows application, then the window displayed by the application will automatically stay on the screen until you explicitly exit it. Similarly, if you run a console application from the command line prompt, as we've been doing up till now, you won't have any problems about the window disappearing.

Other Files Created

The `class1.cs` source code file isn't the only file that Visual Studio.NET has created for you. If you have a look in the folder in where you asked Visual Studio.NET to create your project, you actually see not just the C# file, but a complete directory structure that looks like this:

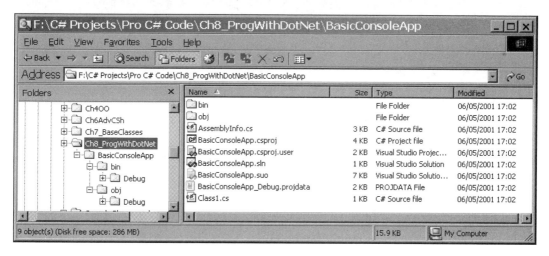

The two folders `bin` and `obj` are there for compiled and intermediate files. Subfolders of `obj` hold various temporary or intermediate files that may be generated, while subfolders of `bin` will hold the compiled assemblies.

This is something that may be unfamiliar to former VB developers. When running old VB6 and earlier applications, you would traditionally simply write the code then run it. In VB, as with all languages, the code would need to be compiled into something containing executable instructions before being shipped, but VB tended to hide the process when debugging. In C#, it's more explicit; to run the code, you have to compile (or build) it first, which means an assembly must be created somewhere.

The remaining files in the project's main folder, `BasicConsoleApp`, are there for Visual Studio.NET's benefit. They contain information about the project – what files are in it and so on, so that Visual Studio.NET knows how to have the project compiled, and also how to read it in the next time you open the project.

Solutions and Projects

One important distinction we need to understand is that between a project and a solution:

- ❑ A **project** is a set of all the source code files and resources that will compile into a single assembly (or in some cases, a single module). For example, a project might be a class library, or a windows GUI application.

- ❑ A **solution** is the set of all the projects that make up a particular software package (application).

To see the difference, we need to recall that when you ship an application it will probably consist of more than one assembly. For example, there might be a user interface; there may be certain custom controls and other components that ship as libraries of the parts of the application. There may even be a different user interface for administrators. Each of these parts of the application might be contained in a separate assembly, and therefore regarded by Visual Studio.NET as a separate project. It is quite likely however that you will be coding these projects in parallel and in conjunction with each other. Thus, it is quite useful to be able to edit them all as one single unit in Visual Studio.NET. Visual Studio.NET allows this by regarding all the projects as forming one solution, and treats the solution as the unit that it reads in and allows you to work on.

Up until now, we have been loosely talking about creating a console project. In fact, in the example we are working on, Visual Studio.NET has actually created a solution for us – this particular solution contains just one project. We can see the situation in a window in Visual Studio.NET known as the **Solution Explorer**, which contains a tree structure that defines your solution:

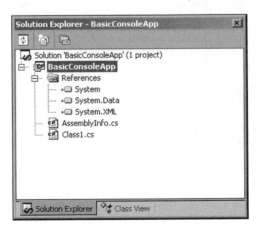

This screenshot shows that the project contains our source file, `Class1.cs`, as well as another C# source file, `AssemblyInfo.cs`, that contains information concerning the compilation of the project (we'll examine this file in chapter 10). The Solution Explorer also indicates the assemblies that our project references, by the namespace.

If you haven't changed any of the default settings in Visual Studio.NET, you will probably find the Solution Explorer in the top right corner of your screen. If you can't see it, just go to the View menu and click on Solution Explorer.

The solution is described by a file with the extension `.sln`, or in the case of our example, `BasicConsoleApp.sln`. The project is described by various other files in the project's main folder. If you attempt to edit these files using Notepad, you'll find that they are mostly plain text files, and in accordance with the principle that .NET and .NET tools rely on open standards wherever possible, they are mostly in XML format.

C++ developers will recognize that a Visual Studio.NET solution corresponds to an old C++ project workspace (stored in a `.dsw` file) and a Visual Studio project corresponds to an old C++ project (`.dsp` file). On the other hand, VB developers will recognize that a solution corresponds to an old VB project group (`.vbg` file) and the .NET project to an old VB project (`.vbp` file). Visual Studio.NET differs from the old VB IDE in that it always creates a solution for you automatically. In Visual Studio 6, VB developers would get a project initially, and a project group only if they explicitly asked the IDE for one.

Adding Another Project To The Solution

As we work through this chapter, we will want to demonstrate how Visual Studio.NET works with Windows applications as well as console applications. At this point, we are going to kill two birds with one stone, and simultaneously get ourselves a Windows project, while at the same time showing how to get a solution that contains more than one project. We are going to create a Windows project called `BasicWindow`, but instead of creating it as a new solution, we will ask Visual Studio.NET to add it to our current solution, `BasicConsoleApp`.

This means we'll end up with a solution containing a Windows application and a console application. That's not a very common scenario (you're more likely to have one application and a number of libraries), but it allows us to demonstrate more code! You can however, create a solution like our one if, for example, you are writing a utility that you want to be able to run either as a Windows application or as a command line utility.

There are a couple of ways of doing this. One way is to right-click on the name of the solution in the Solution Explorer. This will bring up a context menu in which one of the options is to add items to the solution. The other way is simply to go to the File menu and click on the New | Project option as we did before. Either way will bring up the same dialog box that we saw earlier, but this time it has two radio buttons at the bottom, which allow us to specify whether we want to create a new solution for this project or add it to the existing solution:

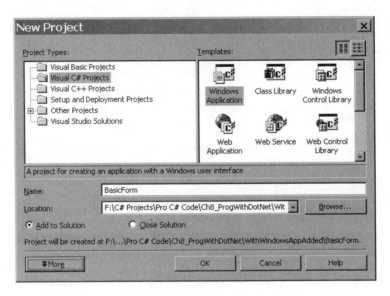

If we do this, and specify **Add to Solution**, will get a new project, and the solution now contains a console and a windows application.

In accordance with the language-independence of Visual Studio.NET, the new project doesn't have to be a C# project. It's perfectly acceptable to put a C# project, a VB.NET project, and a C++ project in the same solution.

Of course, this means that `BasicConsoleApp` isn't really an appropriate name for the solution any more! We can change this by right-clicking on the name of the solution and choosing **Rename** from the context menu. If we rename the solution to `DemoSolution`, the solution explorer will now look like this:

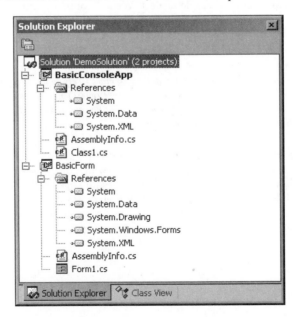

We can see from this that Visual Studio.NET has automatically had the windows project reference some of the extra base classes that are important for windows form functionality.

You'll notice if you look in Windows Explorer, that the name of the solution file has changed to `DemoSolution.sln`. In general, if you want to rename any files, the Solution Explorer is the best place to do so from, because Visual Studio.NET will then automatically be able to update any references to that file in the other project files. If you just rename files using Windows Explorer, you'll probably find you break the solution, because Visual Studio.NET won't be able to locate all the files it needs to read in, so you'll have to manually edit the project and solution files to update the file references.

Setting the Startup Project

One thing you'll need to bear in mind if you have multiple projects in a solution is that only one of them can be run at a time! When you compile the solution, all the projects in it will be compiled. But you have to specify which is the one you want Visual Studio.NET to start running when you want to debug your code. If you have one executable and several libraries that it calls, then this will clearly be the executable. In our case, where we have two independent executables in the project, we'd simply have to debug each in turn.

You can tell Visual Studio which project to run, by right-clicking on that project in the Solution Explorer and selecting **Set Startup Project** from the context menu. You can tell which is the current Startup project, because it is the one that appears in bold in the Solution Explorer; in the above screenshot it's `BasicConsoleApp`.

Windows Application Code

A Windows application contains a lot more code than a console application, because creating a window is an intrinsically more complex process. We're not going to discuss the code for a windows application in detail here – that's the subject of the next chapter, but for completeness, we'll present the code that Visual Studio.NET has given us for the `BasicForm` project. You'll notice it's given us a class called `Form1`, which will represent the main window:

```
using System;
using System.Drawing;
using System.Collections;
using System.ComponentModel;
using System.Windows.Forms;
using System.Data;

namespace BasicForm
{
    /// <summary>
    /// Summary description for Form1.
    /// </summary>
    public class Form1 : System.Windows.Forms.Form
    {
        /// <summary>
        /// Required designer variable.
        /// </summary>
        private System.ComponentModel.Container components;

        public Form1()
        {
            //
```

```
// Required for Windows Form Designer support
        //
        InitializeComponent();

        //
        // TODO: Add any constructor code after InitializeComponent call
        //
    }

    /// <summary>
    /// Clean up any resources being used.
    /// </summary>
    public override void Dispose()
    {
        base.Dispose();
        if(components != null)
            components.Dispose();
    }

    #region Windows Form Designer generated code
    /// <summary>
    /// Required method for Designer support - do not modify
    /// the contents of this method with the code editor.
    /// </summary>
    private void InitializeComponent()
    {
        this.components = new System.ComponentModel.Container();
        this.Size = new System.Drawing.Size(300,300);
        this.Text = "Form1";
    }
    #endregion

    /// <summary>
    /// The main entry point for the application.
    /// </summary>
    [STAThread]
    static void Main()
    {
        Application.Run(new Form1());
    }
}
}
```

Reading in Visual Studio 6 Projects

If you are coding in C#, then clearly you won't need to read in any old Visual Studio 6 projects, since C# doesn't exist in Visual Studio 6. However, language interoperability is a key part of the .NET framework, so it is possible that you will want your C# code to work alongside code written in VB.NET or in C++. In that situation, you may need to edit projects that were created with Visual Studio 6.

In fact, Visual Studio.NET is quite happy to read in Visual Studio 6 projects and workspaces, although as it does so it will upgrade them to Visual Studio.NET solutions. The situation is different for C++, VB, and J++ projects.

❏ In C++, no change to the source code is needed. All your old C++ code will still work fine with the new C++ compiler. Obviously it will not be managed code, but will still compile to code that runs outside the .NET runtime; if you want you code to integrate with the .NET framework then you will need to edit it. If you get Visual Studio.NET to read in an old C++ project, it will simply add a new solution file and updated project files. It will leave the old .dsw and .dsp files unchanged so that the project can still be edited by Visual Studio 6, if necessary.

❏ For Visual Basic we have more of a problem, since Visual Basic has been replaced by VB.NET. As we remarked in Chapter 1, although VB.NET has been designed very much around VB, and shares much of the same syntax, it is in many ways a new language. In Visual Basic, the source code largely consisted of the event handlers for the controls. The code that actually instantiated the main window and many of the controls on it, was not part of Visual Basic, but was instead hidden behind the scenes as part of the configuration of your project. By contrast, VB.NET works in the same way as C#, by putting the entire program out in the open as source code, so all the code that displays the main window and all the controls on it, needs to be in the source file. Like C#, VB.NET requires everything to be object-oriented and part of a class, whereas VB didn't even recognize the concept of classes in the .NET sense. If you try to read a Visual Basic project with Visual Studio.NET, it will have to upgrade the entire source code to Visual Basic.NET before it can handle it, and this involves making a lot of changes to the VB code. Visual Studio.NET can, to a large extent, make these changes automatically and will then create a new VB.NET solution for you. You will find that the source code it gives you looks very different to the corresponding VB code that it was converted from, and you will still need to carefully check through the generated code to make sure the project still works correctly. You may even find areas of code where Visual Studio.NET has left comments to the effect that it can't figure out exactly what you wanted the code to do, and you will have to edit the code manually.

❏ As far as Microsoft is concerned, J++ is now an obsolete language and is not directly supported in .NET. However, in order that existing J++ code can continue to operate, separate tools will be available to allow J++ code to work with .NET. There will also be a tool that will automatically convert J++ code to C# code, similar to the VB6 to VB.NET upgrade facility. These tools are grouped under the name **JUMP** (**Java User Migration Path**), and details are available at http://msdn.microsoft.com/visualj/jump/default.asp. JUMP also converts Java code written outside the VS environment to C#.

Exploring and Coding a Project

In this section, we will look at the features that Visual Studio.NET makes available you to help as you add code to project.

The Folding Editor

One exciting innovation with Visual Studio.NET is its use of a folding editor as its default code editor. Have a look at this screenshot:

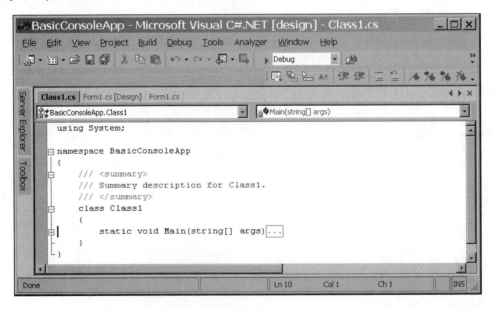

This shows the code for the console application that we generated earlier. Notice however, those little minus signs down the left-hand side of the window. Those marked the points where the editor thinks a new block of code starts. You can click on these icons to close up the view of the corresponding block of code, just as you would close a node in a tree control:

This means that while you are editing, you can focus on just the areas of code you want to look at, and you can close up the bits of code you're not interested in. Not only that, but if you don't like the way the editor has chosen to block off your code, you can specify a different way using the C# preprocessor directives, #region and #endregion, which we examined in Chapter 6. For example, suppose we decide we'd like to be able to collapse just the code inside the Main() method. We'd add this code:

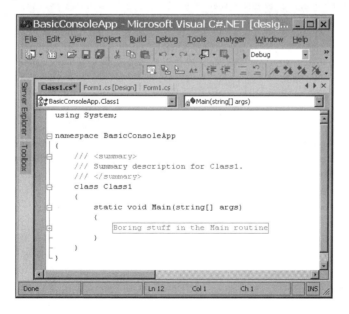

The code editor will automatically detect the #region block, and place a new minus sign by the #region directive as shown above, allowing you to close the region. Enclosing this code in a region it means that we can get the editor to close up the block of code, marking the area with the comment we specified in the #region directive:

*Incidentally, a folding editor is not really a new idea. I first encountered one about ten years ago when I was doing my PhD. The department had just invested a lot of money in a revolutionary machine known as the **transputer**. The idea was that instead of just one processor, it had many processors running in parallel, so your programs would run faster. (Oddly, although the idea has become commonplace since then, the name transputer never quite caught on). What impressed me most wasn't the speed – it was the fact that the transputer came with a folding editor for the program that divided processes between processors. Ever since then, a folding editor has been at the top of my wish list for developer environment features.*

Besides the folding editor feature, Visual Studio.NET's code editor brings across all the familiar abilities from Visual Studio 6. In particular, it features Intellisense. For example, if you type the name of the class instance followed by a dot, it will bring up a list box inviting you to pick a member of the class to be inserted in your code (you can also bring the list box back up by typing Ctrl+Space if you ever lose it). On typing the opening left bracket of a method call, you'll get a list of the parameters. This not only saves you typing, but also helps make sure that you get the parameters correct. C++ developers will notice that the Visual Studio.NET Intellisense feature is a bit more robust than the Visual Studio 6 version (which often missed items out of the lis tbox), and works more quickly.

The code editor will also perform some syntax checking on your code, and will underline most syntax errors with a short wavy line, even before you compile the code. Hovering the mouse over the underlined text will bring up a small box telling you what the error is. This feature is something that VB developers have been used to for years, but which will be new to developers coming to C# from C++.

Other Windows

Besides the code editor, Visual Studio.NET provides a number of other windows that allow you to view your project from different points of view.

For the rest of this section we'll be describing a number of other windows. If you find that one of these windows doesn't seem to be visible in your Visual Studio.NET setup, then you should just go to the View menu and click on the name of the appropriate window. The only exception to this is the design view and code editor, since these are regarded as two tabs of the same window. You display these by either right clicking on the file name in the Solution explorer and selecting View Design or View Code from the context menu, or from the toolbar at the top of the Solution Explorer.

The Design View Window

If you are designing a Windows application (or an ASP.NET application), one window that you will use most frequently is Design View, which presents a visual overview of what your application will look like. You normally use the Design View in conjunction with a window known as the toolbox. The toolbox contains a large number of .NET components that you can drag onto your program:

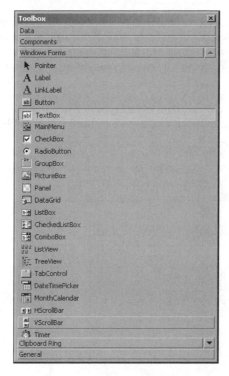

The principle of the toolbox was applied in all developer environments in Visual Studio 6, but with .NET the number of components available from the toolbox has vastly increased. The categories of component available through the toolbox depends, to some extent, on the type of project you are editing. You'll find, for example, that you get a far wider range when you are editing the BasicForm project in the DemoSolution solution than you do when you are editing the BasicConsoleApp project. The most important ranges of items available includes:

❑   **Data Access Components**. Classes that allow you to connect to data sources.

❑   **Windows Forms Components**. Classes that represent visual controls such as text boxes, list boxes, tree views and so on.

❑   **Web Forms Components**. Classes that basically do the same thing as windows controls, but which work in the context of web browsers, and which work by sending HTML output to simulate the controls to the browser.

❑   **Components**. Miscellaneous .NET classes that perform various useful tasks on your machine, such as connecting to directory services or to the event log.

As you can see from the screenshot above, this list is not exhaustive.

You can also add your own custom categories of item to the toolbox if you wish, by right-clicking on any category and selecting Add Tab from the context menu. You can place other tools in the toolbox by selecting Customize Toolbox from the same context menu; this is particularly useful for adding your favorite COM components and ActiveX controls, which are not present in the toolbox by default. If you add a COM control, you can still click to place it in your project just as you would with a .NET control. Visual Studio.NET will automatically add all the required COM interoperability code to allow your project to call up the control.

C++ developers will recognize the toolbox as Visual Studio.NET's (much enhanced) version of the resource editor. VB developers will probably think at first sight that there is not much new about the toolbox, since they have one in Visual Studio 6, but should beware because this toolbox has a dramatically different effect on your source code than the one in the VB6 IDE did.

We'll see how the toolbox works by using it to place a textbox in our basic form project. We simply click on the textbox in the toolbox, then click again to place it in the form in the Design View. Now the Design View looks like this, showing roughly what BasicForm will look like if we compile and run it:

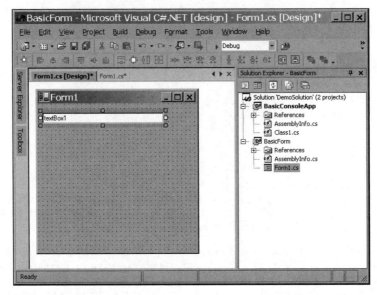

What is more interesting, however, is that if we look at the code we see the developer environment has added the code that instantiates a textbox object to go on the form. There's a new member variable in the Form1 class:

```
public class Form1 : System.Windows.Forms.Form
{
    private System.Windows.Forms.TextBox textBox1;
```

Also, some code to initialize it, has been placed in the method, InitializeComponent(), which is called from the Form1 constructor:

```
/// <summary>
/// Required method for Designer support - do not modify
/// the contents of this method with the code editor.
/// </summary>
private void InitializeComponent()
{
    this.textBox1 = new System.Windows.Forms.TextBox();
    this.SuspendLayout();
    //
    // textBox1
    //
```

```
        this.textBox1.Location = new System.Drawing.Point(8, 16);
        this.textBox1.Name = "textBox1";
        this.textBox1.Size = new System.Drawing.Size(224, 20);
        this.textBox1.TabIndex = 0;
        this.textBox1.Text = "textBox1";
```

The code editor and the Design View really present different views of the same code. When we click to place the text box on the form, what happens is that the toolbox (or strictly, Visual Studio.NET responding to our mouse clicks in the toolbox) places this extra code in our C# source file. The Design View simply reflects this change, because Visual Studio.NET is able to read our source code and determine from it what controls should be around when the application starts up, and show these controls in the Design View. This is a fundamental shift from the old VB way of looking at things, in which everything was based around the visual design. Now, your C# source code is the fundamental thing that controls your application, and the design view is just a different way of viewing the source code and if you do write any VB.NET code with Visual Studio.NET, you'll find the same principles apply.

If we'd wanted to, we could have worked the other way round. If we manually added the same code as above to our C# source files, then Visual Studio.NET would have detected from the code that our application contained a textbox, and would have shown it in the Design View at the designated position. It is best to add these controls visually, and let Visual Studio handle the initial code generation; it's a lot quicker to click the mouse button twice than to type quite a few lines of code!

Another reason for adding these controls visually is that in order to recognize that they are there, Visual Studio.NET does need the relevant code to conform to certain criteria, and code that you write by hand might not conform. In particular, you'll notice that the `InitializeComponent()` method that contains the code to initialize the textbox is commented to warn you against modifying it. That's because this is the method that Visual Studio.NET looks at in order to determine what controls are around that it should be aware of. If you create and define a control somewhere else in your code, Visual Studio.NET won't be aware of it, and you won't be able to edit it in the design view or certain other useful windows.

Despite these warnings, you can modify the code in `InitializeComponent()` provided you are careful. For example, there's generally no harm in changing the values of some of the properties so that a control displays different text, or so that it is a different size. And in practice, the developer studio is pretty robust when it comes to working around any other code you place in this method. Just be aware, however, that if you make too many changes to `InitializeComponent()`, you do run the risk that you will prevent Visual Studio.NET from recognizing some of your controls. We should stress that this won't affect your application at all when it is compiled, but it may disable some of the editing features of Visual Studio.NET for those controls. Therefore, if you want to any other substantial initialization, it's probably better to do so in the `Form1` constructor or in some other method.

The Properties Window

This is another window that has its origins in the old VB IDE. We know from Chapter 4 that classes can implement properties. In fact, as we'll discover in the next chapter, the .NET base classes that represent forms and controls have many properties that define their action or appearance – properties such as `Width`, `Height`, `Enabled` (whether the user can type input to the control), `Text` (the text displayed by the control), and Visual Studio.NET knows about many of these properties. The Properties window displays and allows you to edit the initial values of many of these properties, for the controls that Visual Studio.NET has been able to detect by reading your source code:

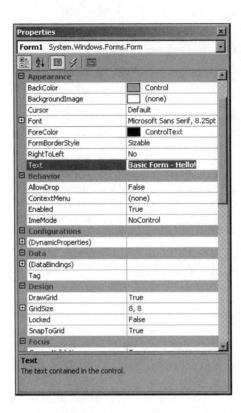

The *Properties* window can also show events. You can view events by clicking on the icon that looks like a flash of lightning at the top of the window.

At the top of the **Properties** Window is a list box that allows you to select which control you want to view. We've selected `Form1`, the main form class for our `BasicForm` project and have edited the text to "`Basic Form - Hello!`" If we now check the source code, we can see that what we have actually done is edit the source code, via a more friendly user interface:

```
this.AutoScaleBaseSize = new System.Drawing.Size(5, 13);
this.ClientSize = new System.Drawing.Size(292, 269);
this.Controls.AddRange(new System.Windows.Forms.Control[]
                                          {this.textBox1});
this.Name = "Form1";
this.Text = "Basic Form - Hello!";
```

Not all the properties shown in the **Properties** window are explicitly mentioned in our source code. For the ones that aren't, Visual Studio.NET will be displaying the default values that were set when the form was created and which are set when the form is actually initialized. Obviously, if you change a value for one of these properties in the **Properties** window, a statement explicitly setting that property will appear in your source code, and vice versa.

The **Properties** window provides a convenient way to get a broad overview of the appearance and properties of a particular control or window.

The Class View

Unlike the Properties window, the Class View is a window that owes its origins to the C++ (and J++) developer environments. It will be new to VB developers, since VB6 did not even support the concept of the class, other than in the sense of a COM component. The class view is not actually treated by Visual Studio.NET as a window in its own right; rather, it is an additional tab to the Solution Explorer window. The class view shows the hierarchy of the namespaces and classes in your code. It gives you a tree view that you can expand out to see what namespaces contain what classes and what classes contain what members:

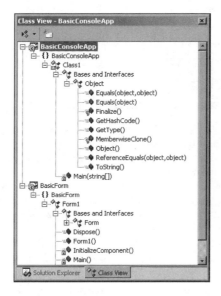

A nice feature of the Class View is that if you right-click on the name of any item for which you have access to the source code, the context menu features an option, Go To Definition, which immediately takes you to the definition of the item in the code editor. You can alternatively do this by double-clicking on the item in Class View. The context menu also gives you the option to add a field, method, property, or indexer to a class. This means that you specify the details of the relevant member in a dialog box, and the code is added for you. This is possibly not so useful for fields or methods, for which the effort to type in the definition manually into your code is small, but you may find it helpful for properties and indexers, where it can save you quite a bit of typing.

The Object Browser

One important aspect of programming in the .NET environment is being able to find out what methods etc. are available in the base classes and any other libraries that you are referencing from your assembly. This feature is available through a window called the Object Browser.

The object browser is quite similar to the Class View window in that it displays a tree view that gives the class structure of your application, allowing you to inspect the members of each class. The user interface is slightly different in that it displays class members in a separate pane rather than in the tree view itself. The real difference, however, is that it lets you look at not just the namespaces and classes in your project, but also at the ones in all the assemblies that are referenced by the project. The screenshot shows the object browser viewing the ArgumentException class from the .NET base classes:

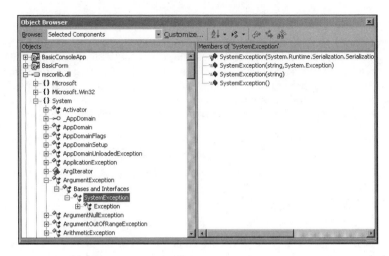

The only point you have to watch with the Object Browser is that it groups classes by the library in which they are located first, and by namespace second. Unfortunately, since namespaces for the base classes are often spread across several libraries, this means you might have trouble locating a particular class unless you know what library it is in.

The Object Browser is there to view .NET objects. If for any reason you want to investigate installed COM objects, you'll find that the OLEView tool previously used in the C++ IDE is still available; it's under the Tools menu, along with several other similar utilities.

> *VB developers should not confuse the .NET Object Browser with the Object Browser of the VB6 IDE – they are different. The .NET object viewer is there to view .NET classes, whereas the tool of that name in VB6 was there to view COM components. If you want the functionality of the old object browser, you should now use the OLEView tool.*

The Server Explorer

The Server Explorer is a useful window that you can use to find out about aspects of the computer while coding:

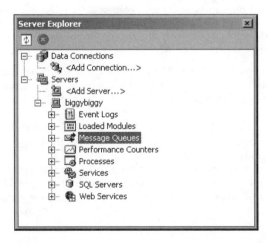

As you can see from the screenshot, amongst the things you can access through the Server Explorer are database connections, information about services, web services, and running processes.

The Server Explorer is linked to the Properties window so that, for example, if you open the Services node and click on a particular service, the properties of that service will be displayed in the Properties window.

Pin Buttons

While exploring Visual Studio.NET you may have noticed that many of the "windows" we are describing have some interesting functionality more reminiscent of toolbars. In particular, apart from the code editor, they can all be docked. Another, very new, feature of them is that when they are docked, they have an extra icon that looks like a pin next to the minimize button in the top right corner of each window. This icon really does act like a pin – it can be used to pin the windows open. When they are pinned (the pin is displayed vertically), they behave just like all the "normal" windows that you are used to. When they are unpinned however (the pin is displayed horizontally), they only remain open as long as they have the focus. As soon as they lose the focus (because you clicked somewhere else) they smoothly retreat into the main border around the entire Visual Studio.NET application. So, for example, the top of the Toolbox looks like this when it is pinned:

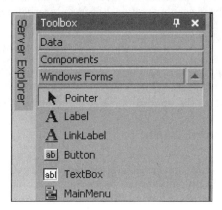

If you unpin it, but leave the cursor over it, it looks like this,

While subsequently moving the mouse away and clicking elsewhere will cause the toolbox to retract:

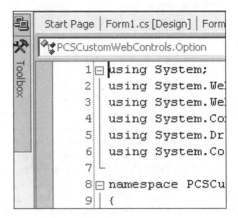

Pinning and unpinning windows provides another way of making the best used of the limited space on your screen. It's not really been seen a great deal on Windows before, though a few third party applications such as Paint Shop Pro have used similar concepts. Pinned windows have, however, been around on many Unix-based systems for quite a while.

Building a Project

In this section, we will examine the options that Visual Studio.NET gives you for building your project.

Building, Compiling, and Making

Before we examine the various build options, we will just clarify one point of terminology. You'll often see three different terms used in connection with the process of getting from your source code to some sort of executable code: **compiling**, **building**, and **making**. The origin of these various terms lies with the fact that until recently, the process of getting from source code to executable code involved more than one step (and this is still the case in C++). This was largely because, typically, a program would contain many source files. In C++, for example, each source file needs to be compiled individually. This leads to what are known as **object files**, each of which contains something like executable code, but where each object file relates to only one source file. In order to generate executable code, these object files need to be linked together, a process that is officially known as **linking**. The combined process was usually referred to (at least on the Windows platform) as **building** your code. However, in C# terms the compiler is more sophisticated and is able to read in and treat all your source files as one block. Therefore, there isn't really a separate linking stage, and so in the context of C# the terms **compile** and **build** are used interchangeably.

The term **make** basically means the same as build, though it's not really used in the context of C#. The term originated on old mainframe systems on which, when a project was composed of many source files, a separate file would be written that contained instructions to the compiler on how to build a project: which files to include, and what libraries to link in, and so on. This file was generally known as a **make file**, and is still quite standard on Unix and Linux etc. Make files are not normally needed on Windows, though you can still write them (or get Visual Studio.NET to generate them) if you need to.

Debug and Release Builds

The idea of having separate builds is something that will be well known to developers with a C++ background, and less so to those with VB background. The point here is that when you are debugging, you tend to want a rather different behavior from your executable than you do when you actually ship the software. When you ship, what you are mostly concerned with, besides the fact that your code works, is that the size of the executable should be as small as possible, and that it should run as fast as possible. Unfortunately, these requirements aren't really compatible with your needs when you are debugging code, for the following reasons.

Optimization

High-performance is achieved partly by the compiler doing a lot of optimizations on the code. This means that the compiler actively looks at your source code as it's compiling in order to identify places where it can modify the precise details of what you're doing in a way that doesn't change the overall effect, but which makes things more efficient. As one example, if the compiler encountered the following source code:

```
double InchesToCm(double Ins)
{
    return Ins*2.54;
}

// later on in the code

Y = InchesToCm(X);
```

It might replace it with this:

```
Y = X * 2.54;
```

Or it might replace this code:

```
{
    string Message = "Hi";
    Console.WriteLine(Message);
}
```

with this:

```
Console.WriteLine("Hi");
```

thereby saving having to declare an unnecessary object reference in the process.

It's not possible to say what optimizations the C# compiler does, or whether the above two examples actually would occur with any particular example, because those kinds of details are not documented. For obvious commercial reasons, companies that write compilers are usually quite reluctant to give too many details about the tricks that their compilers use. We should also stress that optimizations do not affect your source code – they affect only the contents of the executable code. However, the above examples should give you a good idea of what to expect from optimizations.

435

The problem is that while optimizations like the ones above help a great deal for making your code run faster, they aren't so good for debugging. Suppose with the first example, that you want to set a breakpoint inside the `InchesToCm()` method to see what's going on in there. How can you possibly do that if the executable code doesn't actually have an `InchesToCm()` method, because the compiler has removed it? How can you set a watch on the `Message` variable when that doesn't now exist in the compiled code either?

Debugger Symbols

When you're debugging, you often need to look at values of variables, and you will specify them by their source code names. The trouble is that executable code generally doesn't contain those names – the compiler replaces the names with memory addresses. .NET has modified this situation somewhat, to the extent that certain items in assemblies are stored with their names, but this is only true of a small minority of items, such as public classes and methods. Asking the debugger to tell you what the value is in the variable called `HeightInInches` isn't going to get you very far if, when the debugger examines the executable code, it sees only addresses and no reference to `HeightInInches` anywhere. Therefore, in order to debug properly, you need to have extra debugging information made available in the executable. This information will include, amongst other things, names of variable and line information that allows the debugger to match up which executable machine assembly language instructions correspond to which of your original source code instructions. You won't want that information in a release build, however, both for commercial reasons (debugging information makes it a lot easier for other people to disassemble your code), and because it increases the size of the executable.

Extra Source-Code Debugging Commands

A related issue is that quite often, while you are debugging, there will be extra lines in your code to display crucial debugging-related information. Obviously, you want the relevant commands removed entirely from the executable before you ship the software. You could do this manually, but it would be so much easier if you could simply mark those statements in some way so that the compiler ignores them when it is compiling your code is to be shipped. We've already seen in Chapter 6 how this can be done in C# by defining a suitable processor symbol, and possibly using this in conjunction with the `Conditional` attribute, giving you what is known as **conditional compilation**.

What all these factors add up to is that you need to compile almost all commercial software in a slightly different way when debugging, compared to the final product that is shipped. Visual Studio.NET is able to take this into account because, as we have already seen, it stores details of all the options that it is supposed to pass to the compiler when it has your code compiled. All that Visual Studio needs to do in order to support different types of build is to store more than one set of such details. The different sets of build information are referred to as **configurations**. When you create a project Visual Studio.NET will automatically give you two configurations, called **Debug** and **Release**:

❑ The **Debug** configuration will usually specify that no optimizations are to take place, extra debugging information is to be present in the executable, and the compiler is to assume that the debug preprocessor symbol `DEBUG` is present unless it is explicitly `#undefined` in the source code.

❑ The **Release** configuration will usually specify that the compiler should optimize, that there should be no extra debugging information in the executable, and that the compiler should not assume that any particular preprocessor symbol is present.

You can define your own configurations as well. You might do this if, for example, you wish to set up professional level builds and an enterprise level builds so you can ship two versions of the software. In the past, for C++ projects, because of issues concerning the Unicode character encodings supported on Windows NT but not on Windows 95, it was common for C++ projects to feature both a Unicode configuration and an ASCII configuration.

Selecting a Configuration

Since Visual Studio.NET is storing details of more than one configuration, how does it determine which one to use when arranging for a project to be built? The answer is that there is always an active configuration, which is the configuration that will be used when you ask Visual Studio.NET to build a project. (Note that configurations are set for each project rather than for each solution).

By default, when you create a project, the debug configuration will be the active configuration. You can change which configuration is the active one by clicking on the Debug menu option and selecting Set Active Configuration.

Editing Configurations

Besides choosing the active configuration, you can also examine and edit the configurations. To do this, you need to click on the Project menu, while the relevant project is selected in the Solution Explorer, and then select the Properties menu item. This brings up a very sophisticated dialog box. (You can alternatively reach the same dialog box by right clicking on the name of the project in the Solution Explorer, and then selecting Properties from the context menu).

This dialog contains a tree view, which allows you to select quite a lot of different general areas to examine or edit. We don't have space to show all of these areas, but we will show a couple of the most important ones.

The screenshot below shows that the tree view has two top-level nodes, Common Properties, and Configuration Properties. Common properties are those properties that are common across all the configurations while configuration properties are specific to a particular configuration:

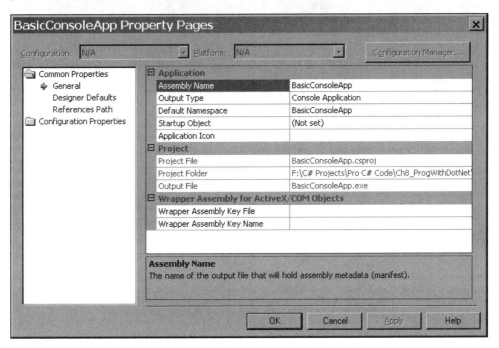

For this screenshot, we are showing the general cross-configuration compiler options for the `BasicConsoleApp` project that we created earlier in the chapter. Note that we can select the name of the assembly as well as the type of assembly to be generated. The options here are **Console Application**, **Windows Application**, and **Class Library**. You can, of course, change the assembly type if you want.

The next screenshot shows the build configuration properties. You'll notice that a list box near the top of the dialog allows you to specify which configuration you wish to look at. In this case we can see – for the **Debug** configuration – that the `DEBUG` and `TRACE` preprocessor symbols are to be assumed, as defined by the compiler. Also, the code is not optimized and extra debugging information is generated, which as we mentioned above is typical for **Debug** configurations:

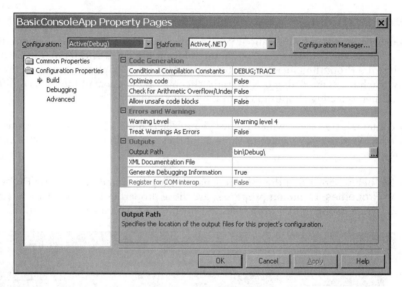

In general, although we've gone into some detail about configurations, it's not that often that you'll need to adjust them. However, you will need to be able to select the appropriate configuration depending on why you are building your project, and it is useful to know what the effect of the different configurations is.

Debugging

After the long discussion about building and build configurations, you might be surprised to learn that we're not going to spend a great deal of time discussing debugging itself. The reason for this is that the principles and the process of debugging – setting breakpoints and examining the values of variables – isn't really significantly different in Visual Studio.NET than in any of the various Visual Studio 6 IDEs. Instead, we will briefly review the features offered by Visual Studio.NET, focusing on those areas that may be new to some developers. We will also discuss in more detail how to deal with exceptions, since these can cause problems for debugging.

In C#, as in pre-.NET languages, the main technique involved in debugging is simply setting breakpoints, and using them to examine what is going on in your code at a certain point in the execution of your code.

Breakpoints

You can set breakpoints from Visual Studio.NET on any line your code that actually is executed. The simplest way is simply to click on the line in the code editor, in the shaded area towards the far left of the window (or hit the **F9** key when the appropriate line is selected). This will set up a breakpoint on that line, which will cause execution to break and control to be transferred to the debugger as soon as that line is reached. As in previous versions of Visual Studio, a breakpoint is indicated by a large circle to the left of the line in the code editor. Visual Studio.NET also highlights the line by displaying the text in a different color. Clicking on the line again removes the breakpoint.

If breaking every time a particular line is hit isn't adequate for your particular problem, you can also set conditional breakpoints. To do this, click on the **Debug** menu and select the **Breakpoints** menu option. This brings up the dialog box asking you for details of the breakpoint you wish to set. From the available options you can:

- ❑ Specify that execution should break only after the breakpoint has been hit a certain number of times.

- ❑ Specify for the breakpoints to come into effect every so-many times that the line is reached, for example every twentieth time that a line is executed (useful when debugging large loops).

- ❑ Set the breakpoints relative to a variable rather than to an instruction. In this case, the value of the variable will be monitored and the breakpoints will be triggered whenever the value of this variable changes. You may find however, that using this option slows your code down very considerably. Checking whether the value of a variable has changed after every instruction adds a lot of processor time.

Watches

Once a breakpoint has been hit, you will usually want to investigate the values of variables. The simplest way to do this is to simply hover the mouse cursor over the name of the variable in the code editor. This will cause a little box to appear that gives the value of that variable. However, you may also prefer to use the **Watch** window to examine the contents of variables. The **Watch** window is a tabbed window that appears only when the program is running under the debugger. It looks like this:

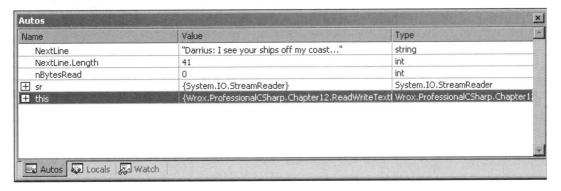

This screenshot is taken from running the `ReadWriteText` sample in Chapter 14. Variables that are classes or structs are shown with a "+" icon next to them, which you can click on to expand the variable and see the values of its fields.

The three tabs to this window are each designed to monitor different variables:

❏ **Autos** monitors the last few variables that have been accessed as the program was executing.

❏ **Locals** monitors variables that are accessible in the method currently being executed.

❏ **Watch** monitors any variables that you have explicitly specified by typing their names into the **Watch** window.

Exceptions

Exceptions are great when you ship your application for making sure that error conditions are handled in an appropriate way within your application. Used well, they can ensure that your application copes well and the user never gets presented with some technical dialog box. Unfortunately, exceptions are not so great when you're trying to debug. The problem is twofold:

❏ If an exception occurs, then when you're debugging you quite often don't want it to be automatically handled by your program, especially if handling it means retiring gracefully and terminating execution! Rather, you want the debugger to come in so that you can investigate and find out why the exception has occurred, with a view to removing the cause before the program ships. The trouble is that if you have written good, robust, defensive, code, then your program will automatically handle almost anything – including the bugs that you want to detect!

❏ If an exception occurs that you haven't written a handler for, the .NET run-time will still go off looking for handler. By the time it discovers that there isn't one however, it will have terminated your program. There won't be a call stack left, and you won't be able to look at the values of any of your variables because they will all have got out of scope.

Of course, you can set breakpoints in your `catch` blocks, but that often doesn't help very much because when the `catch` block is reached, flow of execution will, by definition, have exited the corresponding `try` block. That means that the variables you probably wanted to examine the values of in order to find out what's gone wrong, will have gone out of scope. You won't even be able to look at the stack trace to find out what method was being executed when the `throw` statement occurred, because control will have left that method. Setting the breakpoints at the `throw` statement will of course solve this, except that if you are coding defensively there will be a lot of `throw` statements in your code. How can you tell which one is the one that threw the exception?

In fact, Visual Studio has a very neat answer to all this. If you look at the main **Debug** menu, you'll find a menu item in it called **Exceptions**. This brings up a dialog box that allows you to specify what happens when an exception is thrown. You can choose to continue execution or to automatically stop, and start debugging, in which case execution stops and the debugger steps in at the `throw` statement itself:

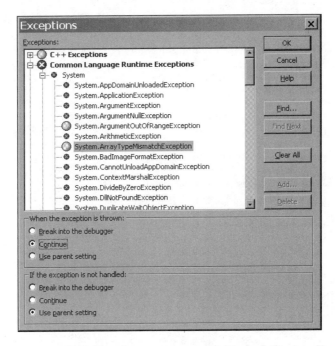

What makes this a really powerful tool is that you can customize the behavior according to which class of exception is thrown. For example, in the above screenshot, we've told Visual Studio.NET to break into the debugger whenever it encounters any exception thrown by a .NET base class (shown by the circled "X" next to the category of exception), but not to break into the debugger if the exception in `ArgumentOutOfRangeException` or an `ArrayTypeMismatchException`.

Visual Studio.NET knows about all the exceptions classes available in the .NET base classes, and about quite a few exceptions that can be thrown outside the .NET environment. Visual Studio.NET isn't automatically aware of your own custom exception classes that you write, but you can manually add your exception classes to the list, and thereby specify which of your exceptions should cause execution to stop immediately. To do this you just click on the Add button above (which is enabled when you have selected a top-level node from the tree) and type in the name of your exception class.

Other .NET Tools

We've spent a lot of time exploring Visual Studio.NET, because that is the tool that you will almost certainly be spending most of your development time using. However, there are a number of other tools available to assist with your programming, which we will cover as we go through the book. Here we will mention one general-purpose utility, WinCV, which you can use to browse the base classes.

WinCV

WinCV is a utility that Microsoft has provided for you to explore the base classes and see what methods are available. It is very similar to the Visual Studio.NET object browser, except that is an independent application, and it will show you *all* the base classes, whereas the object browser shows only those in the assemblies that are referenced by your project:

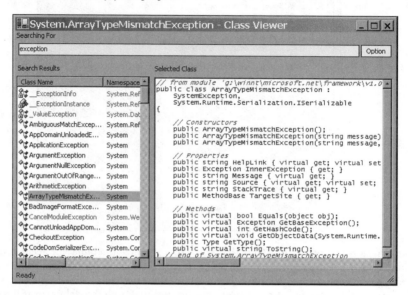

WinCV is quite simple to use. You run it from the command line prompt or run dialog by typing in **wincv**. Then when it is running, you simply type in some text in the list box near the top of the WinCV window. As you type, WinCV will search through the base classes and pick out all the classes whose name includes the word you have typed in. These classes are displayed in the left hand list box. If you click on a particular class, its members are displayed, roughly in a format that corresponds to C# syntax, on the right.

.NET Usage Guidelines

In this final section of the .NET Programming chapter, we're going to look at the guidelines Microsoft has written for .NET programming.

In any development language, there usually arise certain traditional programming styles. The styles are not part of the language itself, but are conventions concerning, for example, how variables are named or how certain classes, methods, or functions are used. If most developers using that language follow the same conventions, it makes it easier for different developers to understand each other's code, which in turn generally helps program maintainability. For example, a common (though not universal) convention in Visual Basic 6 was that variables that represented strings had names beginning with lowercase s or lowercase `str`, as in `String sResult` or `String strMessage`. Conventions do, however, depend on the language and the environment. For example, C++ developers programming on the Windows platform have traditionally used the prefixes `psz` or `lpsz` to indicate strings, for example: `char *pszResult; char *lpszMessage;`, but on Unix machines it's more common not to use any such prefixes: `char *Result; char *Message;`.

You'll have gathered from the sample code in this book, that the convention in C# is to name variables without prefixes: `string Result; string Message;`.

> *Incidentally, the convention by which variable names are prefixed with letters that represent the data type, is known as* **Hungarian notation**. *It means that other developers reading the code can immediately tell from the variable name what data type of the variable represents.*

Whereas with many languages usage conventions simply evolved as the language was used, with C# and the whole of the .NET framework Microsoft has written very comprehensive usage guidelines, which are detailed in the .NET/C# MSDN documentation. This should mean that right from the start, .NET programs will have a high degree of interoperability, in terms of developers being able to understand code. The guidelines have also been developed with the benefit of some twenty years hindsight in object-oriented programming, and as a result have been carefully thought out and appear to have been well received in the developer community to judge by the relevant newsgroups. Therefore, the guidelines are well worth following.

It should be noted, however, that guidelines are not the same as language specifications. You should try to follow the guidelines when you can. However, if you do have a good reason for not doing so then that's no problem. The general rule is that if you don't follow the usage guidelines you must have a convincing reason. Departing from the guidelines should be a positive decision rather than about simply not bothering. As you read the guidelines, you'll notice that in numerous examples in this book, we have chosen not to follow the conventions, usually because the conventions are designed for much larger programs than our samples, and while they are great if you are writing a complete software package, they are not really so suitable for small 20-line standalone programs. In many cases, following the conventions would have made our samples harder rather than easier to follow.

The full guidelines for good programming style are quite extensive. Here, we will confine ourselves to describing some of the more important ones, as well as the ones most likely to catch you out. If you want to make certain your code follows the usage guidelines completely, then you will need to refer to the MSDN documentation.

Naming Conventions

One important aspect to making your programs understandable is how you choose to name your items, and that includes the names of variables, methods, classes, enumerations and namespaces.

It is intuitively obvious that your names should reflect the purpose of the item, and should be designed not to clash with other names. The general philosophy in the .NET framework is also that the name of a variable should reflect the purpose of that variable instance and not the data type. For example, `Height` is a good name for a variable, while `IntegerValue` isn't. However, you will probably feel that the principle is an ideal that is hard to achieve. Particularly when you are dealing with controls, in most cases, you'll probably feel happier sticking with variable names like `ConfirmationDialog` and `ChooseEmployeeListBox`.

Particular recommendations for names include the following sections:

Casing of Names

In almost all cases, you should use **Pascal casing** for names. Pascal casing means that the first letter of each word in a name is capitalized: `EmployeeSalary`, `ConfirmationDialog`, `PlainTextEncoding`. You will notice that essentially all of the names of namespaces, classes, and members in the base classes follow Pascal casing. In particular, the convention of joining words using the underscore character is discouraged. Therefore, you should try not to write names like `employee_salary`. It has also been common in other languages to use all capitals for names of constants. This is not advised in C#, since such names are harder to read; the convention is to use Pascal casing throughout:

```
const int MaximumLength;
```

The only other casing scheme that you are advised to use is **camel casing**. Camel casing is similar to Pascal casing, except that the first letter of the first word in the name is not capitalized: `employeeSalary`, `confirmationDialog`, `plainTextEncoding`. There are two situations in which you are advised to use camel casing.

Names of all parameters passed to methods should be camel-cased:

```
public void RecordSale(string salesmanName, int quantity);
```

You can also use camel casing is in order to distinguish between two items that would otherwise have the same name – a common case is when a property wraps around a field:

```
private string employeeName;

public string EmployeeName
{
   get
   {
      return employeeName;
   }
}
```

The above code is regarded by the guidelines as perfectly acceptable. Note however, that if you are doing this, you should always use camel casing for the private member and Pascal casing for the public or protected member, so that other classes that use your code see only Pascal-cased names (except for parameter names).

In almost all cases, you should use Pascal casing. Camel casing however, is recommended for private variables that are not seen outside the class where two variables to items have a similar purpose. For example, if you have a `public` property that simply encapsulates a `private` field of the same name, you can use camel casing for the field and Pascal casing for the property – as in the `EmployeeName` example above

You should also be wary about case-sensitivity. C# is case sensitive, so it is quite legal syntactically for names in C# to differ only by the case, as in the above example. However, you should bear in mind that your assemblies might at some point be called from VB.NET applications – and VB.NET is not case sensitive. Hence, if you do use names that differ only by case, it is important to do so only in situations in which both names will never be seen outside your assembly (the above example qualifies because the camel-cased name is attached to a `private` variable). Otherwise, you may prevent other code written in VB.NET from being able to use your assembly correctly.

Name Styles

You should try to be consistent about your style of names. For example, if one of the methods in a class is called `ShowConfirmationDialog()`, then you should not give another method a name like `ShowDialogWarning()`, or `WarningDialogShow()`. The other method should be called `ShowWarningDialog()`.

Namespace Names

Namespace names are particularly important to design carefully, in order to the avoid risk of ending up with the same name for one of your namespaces as someone else uses. Remember, namespace names are the *only* way that .NET distinguishes names of objects in shared assemblies. If you use the same namespace name for your software package as another package, and both packages get installed on the same computer, there are going to be problems. Due to this, it's almost always a good idea to create a top-level namespaces with the name of your company, and then nest successive namespaces that narrow down the technology, group or department you are working in or the name of the package your classes are intended for. Microsoft recommend namespace names that begin `<CompanyName>.<TechnologyName>`, for example: `WeaponsOfDestructionCorp.RayGunControllers`, or `WeaponsOfDestructionCorp.Viruses`. The samples in this book generally follow this idea. You'll notice that most of the samples are in namespaces with names that run something like `Wrox.ProfessionalCSharp.Chapter<X>.<SampleName>`. These namespace names ought to be safe – it is extremely unlikely that anyone else is going to write namespaces with the same names as these.

Names and Keywords

It is important the names should not clash with any keywords. In fact, if you attempt to name an item in your code with a word that happens to be a C# keyword, you'll almost certainly get a syntax error, because the compiler will assume the name refers to a statement. However, because of the possibility that your classes will be accessed by code written in other languages, it is important that you don't use names that are keywords in other .NET languages. Generally speaking, C++ keywords are similar to C# keywords, so confusion with C++ is unlikely and those commonly encountered keywords that are unique to Visual C++ tend to start with two underscore characters. Like C#, C++ keywords are spelled in lowercase, so if you hold to the convention of naming your public classes and members with Pascal-style names, then they will always have at least one uppercase letter in their names, and there will be no risk of clashes with C++ keywords. On the other hand, you are more likely to have problems with VB.NET, which has many more keywords than C# does, and being non-case sensitive means you cannot rely on Pascal-style names for your classes and methods.

The following table lists the keywords and standard function calls in VB.NET that should not be used in your code if you wish to call it from VB.NET.

Abs	Do	Loc	RGB
Add	Double	Local	Right
AddHandler	Each	Lock	RmDir
AddressOf	Else	LOF	Rnd
Alias	ElseIf	Log	RTrim
And	Empty	Long	SaveSettings
Ansi	End	Loop	Second
AppActivate	Enum	LTrim	Seek
Append	EOF	Me	Select
As	Erase	Mid	SetAttr
Asc	Err	Minute	SetException
Assembly	Error	MIRR	Shared
Atan	Event	MkDir	Shell
Auto	Exit	Module	Short
Beep	Exp	Month	Sign

Binary	Explicit	MustInherit	Sin
BitAnd	ExternalSource	MustOverride	Single
BitNot	False	MyBase	SLN
BitOr	FileAttr	MyClass	Space
BitXor	FileCopy	Namespace	Spc
Boolean	FileDateTime	New	Split
ByRef	FileLen	Next	Sqrt
Byte	Filter	Not	Static
ByVal	Finally	Nothing	Step
Call	Fix	NotInheritable	Stop
Case	For	NotOverridable	Str
Catch	Format	Now	StrComp
CBool	FreeFile	NPer	StrConv
CByte	Friend	NPV	Strict
CDate	Function	Null	String
CDbl	FV	Object	Structure
CDec	Get	Oct	Sub
ChDir	GetAllSettings	Off	Switch
ChDrive	GetAttr	On	SYD
Choose	GetException	Open	SyncLock
Chr	GetObject	Option	Tab
CInt	GetSetting	Optional	Tan
Class	GetType	Or	Text
Clear	GoTo	Overloads	Then
CLng	Handles	Overridable	Throw
Close	Hex	Overrides	TimeOfDay
Collection	Hour	ParamArray	Timer
Command	If	Pmt	TimeSerial
Compare	IIf	PPmt	TimeValue
Const	Implements	Preserve	To
Cos	Imports	Print	Today
CreateObject	In	Private	Trim
CShort	Inherits	Property	Try
CSng	Input	Public	TypeName
CStr	InStr	Put	TypeOf
CurDir	Int	PV	UBound
Date	Integer	QBColor	UCase
DateAdd	Interface	Raise	Unicode
DateDiff	IPmt	RaiseEvent	Unlock
DatePart	IRR	Randomize	Until
DateSerial	Is	Rate	Val
DateValue	IsArray	Read	Weekday
Day	IsDate	ReadOnly	While
DDB	IsDbNull	ReDim	Width
Decimal	IsNumeric	Remove	With
Declare	Item	RemoveHandler	WithEvents
Default	Kill	Rename	Write
Delegate	LCase	Replace	WriteOnly
DeleteSetting	Left	Reset	Xor
Dim	Lib	Resume	Year
Dir	Line	Return	

Use of Properties and Methods

One area that can cause confusion in a class is whether a particular quantity should be represented by a property or a method. The rules here are not hard and fast, but in general, you should use a property if something really should look and feel like a variable. This means, amongst other things that:

❑ Client code should be able to read its value. Write-only properties are not recommended, so use a SetPassword() method not a Password property.

❑ Reading the value should not take too long. The fact that something is a property usually suggests that reading it will be relatively quick.

❑ Reading the value will not have any observable side effect. For example, setting the value of a property will not have any side effect that is not directly related to the property. Setting the width of a dialog box has the obvious effect of changing the appearance of the dialog box on the screen. That's fine, as that's obviously related to the property in question.

❑ It should be possible to set properties in any order. It is not good practice for setting a property to throw an exception because another related property has not yet been set. For example, if in order to use a class that accesses a database, you need to set `ConnectionString`, `UserName`, and `Password`, make sure the class is implemented, so the user really can set them in any order.

❑ Successive reads of a property should give the same result. If the value of a "property" is likely to change unpredictably, then you should code it up as a method instead. `Speed`, in a class that monitors the motion of an automobile, is not a good candidate for a property. Use a `GetSpeed()` method here; on the other hand, `Weight` and `EngineSize` are good candidates for properties as they will not change for a given object.

If the item you are coding up satisfies all of the above criteria, then it is probably a good candidate for a property. Otherwise, you should use a method.

Use of Fields

The guidelines are pretty simple here. Fields should usually be private, except in some cases where it may be acceptable for constant or read-only fields to be public. The reason is that if you make a field public, you may hinder your ability to extend or modify the class in the future.

The above guidelines should give you an idea of good practices, and you should use them in conjunction with good object-oriented programming style.

It's also worth bearing in mind that Microsoft has been careful about being consistent, and has followed its own guidelines when writing the .NET base classes. So a very good way to get an intuitive feel for the conventions to follow when writing .NET code is to simply look at the base classes; see how classes, members, and namespaces are named, and how the class hierarchy works. If you try to write your code in the same style as the base classes, then you shouldn't go too far wrong.

Summary

In this chapter we've looked at two sides of programming in the .NET environment. We spent the bulk of the chapter examining the tools that Microsoft has supplied to make your work writing C# (and C++ and VB.NET) code as easy as possible, particularly Visual Studio.NET. Then we finished off by examining some of the conventions you should try to follow when writing C# code. I quite like to think of the situation in terms of rights and responsibilities (by analogy with certain political debates). With .NET, you get the benefit of some really great tools that will have a huge impact on the speed with which you can get software written and debugged. On the other hand you have the responsibility to use these tools carefully by writing code that will be easy for others to use or maintain, and you can best show that responsibility by following the guidelines for writing good code.

Windows Applications

There have always been some difficulties with building and deploying Windows applications. In the very beginning, C programmers used the Win32 API directly to create Windows applications. Almost all programmers in this category own a copy of Charles Petzold's book *Programming Windows* (Microsoft Press, ISBN 157231995X). Visual Basic came along and simplified building Windows applications by introducing a graphical design programming environment. Visual Basic programmers would create a form, add controls, and implement event handlers.

The Visual Basic and Visual C++ environments have always been quite different in the way that they support developers who build applications. Visual C++ programmers rely heavily on the Microsoft Foundation Classes (MFC) for building applications. The Visual C++ programmer uses a wizard describing the functionality they want, and then MFC code is generated to implement that functionality. Both Visual Basic and Visual C++ use resource editors to create and modify user interface items, but they still each have their own resource editor. Both languages also have a different model for describing the user interface.

Visual Studio.NET combines the best of both worlds into a versatile environment for creating Windows applications. Developers still get the ease of use of building applications through a form designer. Now though, the user interface components are represented by a common set of classes. Therefore, whether your language of choice is Visual Basic or C#, both the programming model and the resource editor are the same. That programming model is **Windows Forms** (also called **WinForms**).

In this chapter we will look at:

- ❑ Creating a Windows application
- ❑ Using controls in a Windows application
- ❑ Creating a custom control
- ❑ Using menu items in an application

While the .NET Framework provides the classes for building Windows application, Visual Studio.NET is the Integrated Development Environment (IDE) used to design the Windows application visually, and to automatically generate the code. Visual Studio.NET provides a way to create much of the code behind Windows applications. If you are familiar with the resource editor in either Visual C++ or Visual Basic, you will be familiar with the way the IDE works with Visual Studio.NET. You drag controls from a toolbox and drop them onto a form. You can set properties on the form and controls using the IDE. The IDE is covered in detail in Chapter 8.

The main difference is that the IDE is purely a code generator. All of the information required by the IDE to create the form is stored in the source code. In addition, the look and feel of the IDE is the same no matter which programming language you use. The features supported in the IDE are dependent on the features supported in the language. An example of this is the two drop-down lists in the text editors (object and event drop-downs), which are available when working in Visual Basic, but not in C#.

You do not need Visual Studio.NET to create Windows applications; you just need a text editor and a compiler. The IDE certainly makes it much easier, however, to design the application. Since Windows applications are based on a graphical user interface, it makes sense that designing the application visually would be easier.

In this chapter, we are going to create a sample application for creating a Bezier curve. With the application you will be able to change x and y coordinates with different user interface controls and view the change of the curve.

Architecture

Most of the functionality for building Windows Forms applications is in the `System.Windows.Forms` namespace. It contains all the classes for building desktop applications that use the user interface features of the Microsoft Windows operating system. If you are a C++ programmer the types of user interface classes formally in Microsoft Foundation Classes are now in `System.Windows.Forms`.

Of course, all the other .NET classes are available for use in your Windows application. In particular, you might use `System.Drawing` to perform graphics operations. This namespace contains classes for creating brushes, fonts, icons, and other graphics objects. It also has functionality for drawing objects and writing text to a drawing surface. The example later in this chapter uses this namespace to draw a Bezier curve. If your Windows application is built to view and manipulate data, you will be using the `System.Data` namespace to encapsulate data that can be bound to controls from `System.Windows.Forms`.

Ok, let's start with the basics of building a Windows application with Windows Forms.

Every Windows Forms application is a class that derives from `System.Windows.Forms.Form`. Therefore, the most basic Windows Forms application is the following:

```
using System;
using System.Windows.Forms;

public class MyForm : Form
{
    public MyForm()
    {
    }
```

```
    public static void Main(string[] args)
    {
        MyForm aForm = new MyForm();
    }
}
```

Use the following command to compile the program:

csc form.cs

Every WinForms application has to have an entry point from which the program starts and ends. This entry point is defined by implementing the public static Main() method. This method may return either void or int. If you want to pass a return value back to the calling application, you have a return type of int.

Main() is also where command line arguments are passed to your Windows application. You may wish to implement command line arguments to your application to control such things as configuration settings or files to load.

This program won't do much more than create a MyForm object and then immediately exit. We need to have the application participate in the message loop from the operating system.

Windows applications are event-driven. They don't make explicit function calls – they wait for the system to pass input to them as messages. The message loop is the part of the Windows application that checks for Windows messages. To process messages in a form, call the Run() method of the Application class:

```
using System;
using System.Windows.Forms;

public class MyForm : Form
{
    public MyForm()
    {
    }

    public static void Main(string[] args)
    {
        MyForm aForm = new MyForm();

        Application.Run(aForm);
    }
}
```

The Application class belongs in the System.Windows.Forms namespace. It provides static methods and properties for idle processing, message filters, managing an application, and processing Windows messages. Messages are generated by both the system and applications. The system generates messages for each input event such as key presses and mouse clicks. An application can generate messages to direct its own windows to perform tasks or to communicate with windows in other applications.

The `Application.Run()` method processes messages from the operating system to the application. A `Form` object is displayed by providing it as a parameter to the `Run()` method. Now the application will sit and wait to do something interesting. It is now up to developer to provide the interesting aspects of the application.

Later in the chapter we'll see how to retrieve application properties from the `Application` class and display them in a dialog box.

Let's see how to create the same thing with the IDE. From Visual Studio create a new Visual C# project. Use the Windows Application template:

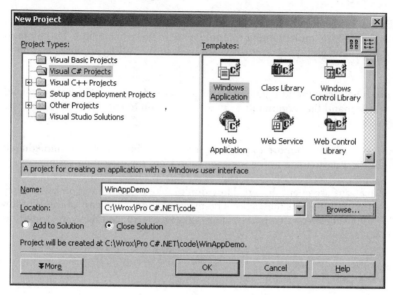

After selecting OK, Visual Studio will create for you all the files required for the basics of a Windows application. The generated file that you will work with most is the form file, which we will look at next.

Forms

Any window displayed in an application is created as a form. Standard windows, tool windows, borderless windows, and floating windows can all be created using the `Form` class. You can also use the `Form` class to create a modal window such as a dialog box.

A special kind of form, the **Multiple Documentation Interface** (**MDI**) form can contain other forms called **MDI child forms**. Setting the IsMDIContainer property to true creates an MDI form. Setting the MDIParent property to the MDI parent form that will contain the child form creates MDI child forms.

Using the properties available in the `Form` class, you can determine the appearance, size, color, and window management features of the window or dialog box you are creating. The Text property allows you to specify the caption of the window in the title bar. The Size and DesktopLocation properties allow you to define the size and position of the window when it is displayed. You can use the ForeColor color property to change the default foreground color of all controls placed on the form. The BorderStyle, MinimizeBox, and MaximizeBox properties allow you to control whether the form can be minimized, maximized, or resized at runtime.

The properties of the form can be set using the Properties Window in Visual Studio. For example, you can see in the following Properties window that the Text property has been changed to WinAppDemo:

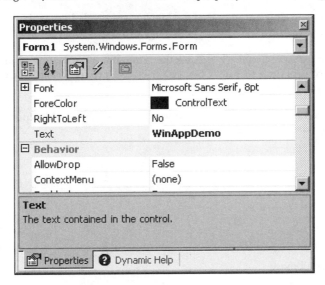

Code is generated for each property you change in the Properties window. By selecting View and then Code from the Visual Studio menu, you will see the code for the form. Specifically, there is a section titled Windows Form Designer generated code. You can expand it to reveal the generated code that will look something like the following:

```
#region Windows Form Designer generated code

/// <summary>
///     Required method for Designer support - do not modify
///     the contents of this method with the code editor.
/// </summary>

private void InitializeComponent()
{
    this.AutoScaleBaseSize = new System.Drawing.Size(5, 13);
    this.ClientSize = new System.Drawing.Size(292, 373);
    this.Text = "WinAppDemo";
}
#endregion
```

Here you can see that the Size and Text for the form are being set. If you change additional properties in the properties window, it will be reflected here as well.

In addition to properties, you can use the methods of the class to manipulate a form. For example, you can use the ShowDialog() method to show a form as a modal dialog box. You can use the SetDesktopLocation() method to position the form on the desktop.

The events of the Form class allow you to respond to actions performed on the form. You can use the Activate event to perform operations such as updating the data displayed in the controls of the form when the form is activated.

Controls

Obviously, a form by itself is not very useful. Controls are needed to display and manipulate data and interact with the user interface. Windows Forms has two base classes for controls:

`System.Windows.Forms.Control` defines the minimum set of features and code to be a Windows Forms control. A control derived from `Control` has basic properties, and only the most basic events, such as keyboard and mouse events.

Controls in Windows Forms are the typical controls a developer would expect from a class library for graphical user interfaces including:

- ❑ labels
- ❑ buttons
- ❑ checkboxes
- ❑ menus
- ❑ radio buttons
- ❑ combination boxes
- ❑ listboxes
- ❑ textboxes
- ❑ tab controls
- ❑ toolbars
- ❑ tree views

and so on. Some of the more specific controls include:

- ❑ `DataTimePicker`
- ❑ `FontDialog`
- ❑ `FileDialog`
- ❑ `LinkLabel`
- ❑ `MonthCalendar`
- ❑ `NumericUpDown`
- ❑ `PrintDialog`
- ❑ `ProgressBar`

Note that a form is derived from the `Control` class, so it is itself a control. This means that all properties and events of a control are also available to a form. The general procedure for adding controls is:

1. Declare a private variable of the type of control required

2. Create a control and assign in to the variable in the constructor of the form

3. Set the properties of the control

4. Add the control to the control collection of the form

5. Implement events handlers for the control

Visual Studio will do this work for you if you use it to add controls to a form. To add a control to a form from Visual Studio, you drag it from the toolbox and drop it on the form. The code for adding the control is automatically placed in the form source code. You can see the toolbox on the left in the following screen shot:

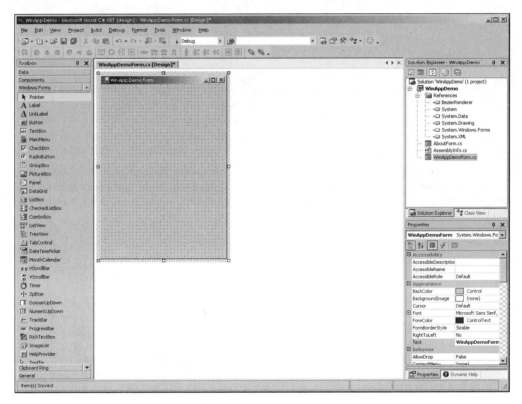

Let's add a `TextBox` to the form. Drag and drop it from the toolbox onto the form. Then in the Properties window set the following properties:

Name: xTextBox
Size: (40,20)
Location: (64,366)

Also, change the size of the form to 300, 410.

When you view the Windows Form Designer generated code you will see the changes made for the text box. It might look something like this:

```
private void InitializeComponent()
{
        //
        // xTextBox
        //
        this.xTextBox.Location = new System.Drawing.Point(136, 376);
        this.xTextBox.Name = "xTextBox";
        this.xTextBox.Size = new System.Drawing.Size(40, 20);
        this.xTextBox.TabIndex = 3;
        this.xTextBox.Text = "0";

        //
        // WinAppDemoForm
        //
        this.AutoScaleBaseSize = new System.Drawing.Size(5, 13);
        this.ClientSize = new System.Drawing.Size(288, 403);
        this.Controls.AddRange(new System.Windows.Forms.Control[]
                        {this.xTextBox});
        this.Text = "WinAppDemo";
}
```

In addition to creating the TextBox object the Location, Text, TabIndex, and Size are also set. Finally, the control is added to the Controls collection of the form. Note that because this is a collection, you can enumerate through the child controls of another control at any point in a program. You can also add and remove them.

Note that a private member variable is also added to the form for the text box:

```
private System.Windows.Forms.TextBox xTextBox;
```

> By declaring a namespace with **using**, you can use the types within the namespace without qualifying the use of a type in that namespace. For instance, instead of referring to a textbox class as **System.WinForms.TextBox**, you could just use **TextBox**. Note that **using** does not give you access to the namespaces that may be nested in the namespace you specify. It's up to you which one you use. Just adhere to the number one programming rule – be consistent. If you decide to omit namespaces, do so with all of the namespaces declared with **using**.

Next, we are going to add a trackbar control and hook it together with the textbox. A trackbar is a scrollable control similar to a scrollbar but has a different look to it. The user scrolls the trackbar to manipulate a data value. The intent is that the textbox will show the value represented by the trackbar. Therefore, a change in the trackbar will have to be reflected in the text box and vice versa.

Drag and drop a **TrackBar** from the toolbox to the form. In the **Properties** windows for the trackbar set the following properties:

Name: xTrackBar
Maximum: 200
Size: (200,42)
Location: (64,288)
TickFrequency: 10
TickStyle: TopLeft

When you view the generated code, you should see the following changes:

```
private void InitializeComponent()
{
private void InitializeComponent()
{

        //
        // xTextBox
        //

        this.xTextBox.Location = new System.Drawing.Point(136, 376);
        this.xTextBox.Name = "xTextBox";
        this.xTextBox.Size = new System.Drawing.Size(40, 20);
        this.xTextBox.TabIndex = 3;
        this.xTextBox.Text = "0";


        //
        // WinAppDemoForm
        //

        this.AutoScaleBaseSize = new System.Drawing.Size(5, 13);
        this.ClientSize = new System.Drawing.Size(288, 403);
        this.Controls.AddRange(new System.Windows.Forms.Control[]
                    {this.xTextBox, this.xTrackBar});
        this.Text = "WinAppDemo";
}

        ((System.ComponentModel.ISupportInitialize)
                    (this.xTrackBar)).EndInit();
}
```

The form should look something like the following:

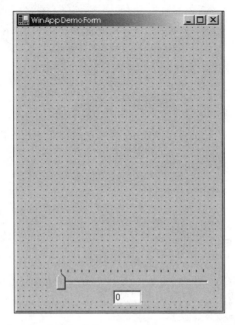

For the controls to know what each other is doing we need to use event handling.

Events and Delegates

Many programming languages have artificial plumbing for handling events. For instance, event handling and notification in C++ is often built with notification classes that use function pointers. With C#, event handling capability is built into the language with events and delegates.

A delegate in C# is similar to a function pointer in C or C++. A delegate allows a programmer to encapsulate a reference to a method inside a delegate object. The method can be either a static or an instance method. A delegate object can then be passed to code, which can call the referenced method without having to know at compile time which method will be invoked. A difference between delegates in C# and function pointers in C or C++ is that delegates are object-oriented, type-safe, and secure.

An interesting and useful property of a delegate is that it does not know or care about the class of the object that it references. Any object will do; all that matters is that the method's argument types and return type match those of the delegate. This makes delegates perfectly suited for "anonymous" invocation.

The following is an example of declaring, assigning, and invoking a delegate:

```
delegate int MyDelegate();

MyDelegate aDelegate = new MyDelegate(myClass.InstanceMethod);

// Call the instance method:

aDelegate()
```

Closely tied with delegates are events. An event in C# is a way for a class to provide notifications to clients of that class when some thing interesting happens to an object.

So, what do events and delegates have to do with Windows applications? Programs based on graphical user interfaces are strongly event driven. The user manipulates the user interface and the program must respond to those events. Typically, the classes that represent controls in the user interface are notified by events. For example, a class representing a textbox would receive an event that a key has been pressed. Events provide a useful way for objects to signal state changes that may be useful to clients of that object.

In C#, events are declared using delegates. An event is a way for a class to allow clients to give it delegates to methods that should be called when the event occurs. When the event occurs, the delegate(s) given to it by its clients are invoked. The `event` keyword lets you specify a delegate that will be called upon the occurrence of some event in your code.

Although the C# language allows events to use any delegate type, the .NET Framework has some stricter guidelines on the delegate types that should be used for events. If you intend your component to be used with the .NET Framework, you will probably want to follow these guidelines.

The .NET Framework guidelines indicate that the delegate type used for an event should take two parameters, an "object source" parameter indicating the source of the event, and an "e" parameter that encapsulates any additional information about the event. The type of the "e" parameter should derive from the `EventArgs` class. For events that do not use any additional information, the .NET Framework has already defined an appropriate delegate type: `EventHandler`.

Event Handlers

Event handlers typically capture user input to a control and inform the program that something has happened. You would want to implement event handlers for such things as updating display, or validating user input.

In Visual Basic, event handlers were magically hooked up by following a certain naming convention, such as `Button_Click`. Visual C++ developers usually used macros in MFC to create artificial maps (called message maps) that mapped Windows events to function pointers.

Windows Forms makes event-handling part of the Framework by utilizing delegates. In addition to methods and properties, all controls have event collections. More specifically, controls have event handler collections. If you want to capture an event, you simply write a method and add it to the collection of the event you want to handle.

Visual Studio .NET provides the same ease of adding event handlers that is present in Visual Basic 6. By double-clicking on a control, the event handler code is automatically generated for the default event.

In our examples, event handlers have to be implemented so that we can have the textbox and trackbar communicating with one another. An event handler must have the same parameters as the `EventHandler` delegate declaration, which looks like the following:

```
public delegate void EventHandler(object sender, EventArgs e);
```

When you create an `eventhandler` delegate, you identify the method that will respond to the specified event. To associate the event with your event-handling method, add an instance of the delegate to the event. The event-handling method is called whenever the event occurs.

Lets go back to hooking together the textbox and trackbar control. By double-clicking controls in the designer, the default event is implemented for you, which is `TextChanged`. We're going to use the `Leave` event however, which will mean that we'll have to click somewhere else after entering our value to cause the form to update. The `Leave` event belongs to the `Control` classes and is raised whenever the control is left. Looking at the declaration of `Leave` we see that it is an event:

```
public event EventHandler Leave;
```

So to add a notification method in the `InitializeComponent` function, you insert the following line of code after the call to the `InitializeComponent` function:

```
xTextBox.Leave += new System.EventHandler (this.xTextBox_Leave );
```

Now we want to implement the method that is to be notified. Note that the name of the method can be anything you want. Visual Studio generates the name of the method as *objectName_Event*:

```
protected void xTextBox_Leave (object sender, System.EventArgs e)
{
        TextBox theTextBox;
        theTextBox = (TextBox)sender;

        // Make sure the maximum is not exceeded.

        if ( Convert.ToInt32(theTextBox.Text) > 200 )
        {
            xTrackBar.Value = 200;
            theTextBox.Text = "200";
        }
        xTrackBar.Value = Convert.ToInt32(theTextBox.Text);
}
```

Notice that the method parameters correspond to those defined by the `EventHandler` delegate. The code knows who sent the notification by the `sender` object. We are interested in events raised by the textbox. In order to access the textbox methods, the `sender` object is casted to the `TextBox` type.

Then we will implement the same type of code for the trackbar. This time you can use the designer by double-clicking the control, and it will automatically generate the shell code for the default event. You then need to add the highlighted code:

```
protected void xTrackBar_Scroll (object sender, System.EventArgs e)
{
        TrackBar theTrackBar;
        theTrackBar = (TrackBar)sender;
        xTrackBar.Value = theTrackBar.Value;
        xTextBox.Text = xTrackBar.Value.ToString();
}
```

The method receives the trackbar as an object. By casting it to a `TrackBar` class, we then have access to the `TrackBar` methods. The value of the text box is then set to the value of the trackbar after being converted to a string value. At this point, when either the text box or trackbar changes, the other one is updated to have the same value.

Events that are available for all controls are:

Event	Description
ChangeUICues	Occurs when focus, keyboard, or both cues have changed.
Click	Occurs when a control in clicked.
ControlAdded	Occurs when a new control is added to the current control.
ControlRemoved	Occurs when a control is removed from the current control.
DoubleClick	Occurs when the control is double-clicked.
Enter	Occurs when the control is entered.
GotFocus	Occurs when the control receives focus.
HandleCreated	Occurs when a handle is created from the control.
HandleDestroyed	Occurs when the control's handle is destroyed.
KeyDown	Occurs when a key is pressed down.
KeyPress	Occurs when a key is pressed.
KeyUp	Occurs when a key is released.
Layout	Occurs when a control's layout properties have changed.
Leave	Occurs when the control is left.
LostFocus	Occurs when the control loses focus.
MouseDown	Occurs when the mouse button is pressed, while the mouse pointer is over the control.
MouseEnter	Occurs when the mouse pointer enters the control.
MouseHover	Occurs when the mouse pointer hovers over the control.
MouseLeave	Occurs when the mouse pointer leaves the control.
MouseMove	Occurs when the mouse pointer is moved over the control.
MouseUp	Occurs when the mouse button is released, while the mouse pointer is over the control.
MouseWheel	Occurs when the mouse wheel moves, while the control has focus.
Move	Occurs when the control is moved.
PropertyChanged	Occurs when a property of the control has changed.
Resize	Occurs when the control is resized.
Validated	Occurs when the control is done validating.
Validating	Occurs when the control is validating.

Individual controls will have additional events that they generate. For example, we saw how the TrackBar control generates a Scroll event.

An alternative to trapping events using event handlers is to subclass the control and override the event method. For instance, instead of adding an event handler to the `GotFocus` event, you can override the `OnGotFocus()` method. If you do this be sure to call `base.OnGotFocus()` so that the event is also sent to any registered event listeners. The section later on this chapter demonstrates how to override the `OnPaint()` method.

Typically, you would override the event method if you want to change the behavior of a control. For instance, it makes sense to override `OnPaint()` because you want to render the control differently. Trapping events is usually used to extend current functionality. You would want to keep the existing behavior the same, but add some new behavior.

At this point, we have two ways of entering an X co-ordinate: a textbox and a trackbar. After we repeat the above process to create a version for the Y co-ordinate, the result should look something like the following:

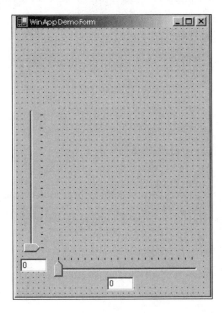

Grouping Controls

There are four control points that have to be manipulated using the controls. We will enable this by implementing four radio buttons and a group box.

Use a GroupBox if you have a set of controls on a form that you want to be grouped so that they're visually distinct from others. The GroupBox displays a frame around a group of controls with or without a caption. A GroupBox is often used to define groups of RadioButton controls. By using a GroupBox with radio buttons, you can have more than one set of radio buttons, each of which maintain their own set of values.

Drag a GroupBox control and four radio buttons from the Toolbox and place them as in the following screenshot. Use the Properties window to set the text for each of the controls. Also, set the Checked property to True for Point 1:

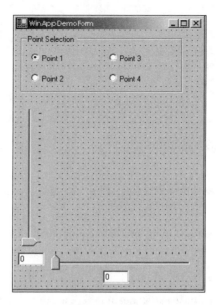

Next, we need to add event handlers for the radio buttons. By double clicking the control, the default event handler will be implemented, which is for the CheckedChanged event. We will implement the code for the event handler later in the chapter.

The next step in our Windows Forms application is to create a control that can draw a Bezier curve. Before we do that, however we will cover some background on drawing with Windows Forms.

Drawing Classes

This chapter does not go into detail of the drawing classes but it is important to know how they relate to Windows applications. Chapter 21 goes into the details of the drawing classes.

If you want to change the rendering of a control, or are creating a custom control, you will probably be using the drawing classes. You would do this if the standard Windows controls did not support the functionality you wanted, or provide the desired look and feel.

The System.Drawing namespace provides access to GDI+ basic graphics functionality. More advanced functionality is provided in the System.Drawing.Drawing2D, System.Drawing.Imaging, and System.Drawing.Text namespaces.

Dimensions

You have seen some of the types in the System.Drawing namespace already. All dimension types are in this namespace such as Point, Size, and Rectangle. The great thing for developers is that these built in dimension types know how to display themselves as strings, as in the following code:

```
using System;
using System.Drawing;

class MainApp
public static void Main()
    {
```

```
        Point myPoint = new Point( 34, 23 );
        Rectangle myRect = new Rectangle( 20, 10, 25, 15 );
        Size mySize = new Size( 14, 16 );
        Console.WriteLine( myPoint.ToString());
        Console.WriteLine( myRect.ToString() );
        Console.WriteLine( mySize.ToString() );
    }
}
```

This code yields the following output:

```
{X=34,Y=23}
{X=20,Y=10,Width=25,Height=15}
{Width=14, Height=16}
```

As you can imagine, it makes developing and debugging much easier since you don't need to write code to display dimension values.

Brushes

The `Brush` class is an **abstract base class**, meaning that it cannot be instantiated itself; only classes derived from `Brush` can be implemented. The derived classes are used to define objects used to fill the interiors of graphical shapes such as rectangles, ellipses, pies, polygons, and paths. Derived classes include `SolidBrush`, `TextureBrush`, and `RectangleGradientBrush`.

As an example, the following code creates a linear gradient brush. Linear gradient brushes start with one color and blend to another color:

```
Rectangle endPoints = new Rectangle(0, 0, 200, 200);
LinearGradientBrush lb = new LinearGradientBrush(endPoints,
            Color.Red, Color.Yellow, LinearGradientMode.BackwardDiagonal);
```

The rectangle specifies the endpoints of the linear gradient. The starting point is the upper left corner of the rectangle, and the ending point is the upper right corner of the rectangle. The `LinearGradientMode` specifies how the blend will occur. In this case, `BackwardDiagonal` specifies a gradient from upper-right to lower-left. Linear gradients create nice effects for form backgrounds or as separation areas.

This class is in the `System.Drawing.Drawing2D` namespace.

Pens

A `Pen` is an object used to draw lines and curves of a specific width, color, and style. Use the `DashStyle` property to draw several varieties of dashed lines. The line drawn by a `Pen` can be filled in a variety of fill styles including solid colors and textures. The fill style depends on brush or texture that is used as the fill object.

There are many constructors available for creating `Pens`. The following shows a simple blue pen:

```
Pen bluePen = new Pen( Color.Blue );
```

You can create more complex `Pens` by specifying other properties such as a brush, width, and dash style:

```
Pen myPen = new Pen( new SolidBrush( ) );
myPen.Width = 5;
myPen.DashStyle = DashStyle.DashDotDot
```

Fonts

Fonts are also part of the `System.Drawing` namespace. To create a font, first define the font family you are working with. A font family is a group of typefaces that have similar basic design, but certain variation in styles. The three `GenericFontFamilies` that you can choose from are `Monospace`, `SansSerif`, and `Serif`.

The `Font` class defines a particular format for text, including font face, size, and style attributes. The following code creates a Serif 16pt font:

```
FontFamily theFamily = new FontFamily( GenericFontFamilies.Serif );
Font theFont = new Font( theFamily, 16 );
```

After creating the font, you can then write text to a drawing surface, which we will try next.

Graphics

The most fun class is `System.Drawing.Graphics`. This class encapsulates a GDI+ drawing surface. It has methods to draw lines, curves, and strings.

You may be eager to start drawing pictures on a drawing surface, but the first problem you will run into is finding a constructor for a `Graphics` class. The trick is that there isn't a public constructor – the class uses a **factory design pattern** for creating `Graphics` objects (where one object is responsible for creating another object). A drawing surface must be associated with an existing resource such as a bitmap or Windows handle. There are static methods available on the `Graphics` class that accept a resource as a parameter and return a `Graphics` object. The advantage of this is the drawing operations can be abstracted from a specific drawing surface. For example, if you are drawing a line from point A to point B, it doesn't matter whether the final result is a JPEG file or a Windows window.

The following code demonstrates many of the concepts of the `System.Drawing` namespace:

```
using System;
using System.Drawing;
using System.Drawing.Text;

class MainApp
{
   public static void Main()
   {
       Bitmap image = new Bitmap( 200, 150 );
       Graphics graphic = Graphics.FromImage( image ) ;

       FontFamily theFamily = new FontFamily(GenericFontFamilies.Serif );
       Font theFont = new Font( theFamily, 16 );
       SolidBrush theBrush = new SolidBrush( Color.AliceBlue );

       graphic.DrawString( "Rock'n'roll", theFont, theBrush,
          new Point( 10, 10) );

       image.Save( "myImage.jpg", System.Drawing.Imaging.ImageFormat.PNG );
   }
}
```

First, a bitmap is created and a graphics class is created based on that bitmap. The tools for drawing text are created to include a font and a brush. The text is drawn on the drawing surface. Finally, the bitmap is written to a file as a PNG file. You can view this file in Internet Explorer.

The reason the `System.Drawing` classes are important to creating Windows Applications is that custom controls rely on you overriding the `OnPaint()` method and do the rendering yourself. Let's have a look at how to do this.

Custom Controls

The Windows Forms framework provides a large variety of controls to use in your application. There may be times, however, when you need to create your own controls. Examples of situations when you would want to create your own control ares:

❑   You have a data model that is not represented well by the standard controls

❑   You want to provide a specific interaction method with the user

❑   You want a control to render differently than the standard controls

Keep in mind that users will be unfamiliar with how to use a custom control first time they see it. A custom control should be designed so that it is both easy to learn to use, and to operate.

For our sample application, we need a custom control to render the Bezier curve.

To create a custom control, perform the following steps:

1. Define a class that derives from `System.Windows.Forms.UserControl`

2. Define properties for the control. The properties determine how the control will look and operate.

3. Override the `OnPaint()` method to provide the rendering logic of the control.

4. Provide attributes for the control. The attributes will determine what the control looks in Visual Studio.

5. Optionally provide resources for the control (such as bitmaps).

Example: Bezier Renderer

To demonstrate the steps for creating a custom control, we are going to create a Bezier renderer. It will be a control that displays a Bezier curve. As the properties of the control are manipulated, the curve will change.

First, a quick background on Bezier curves. Bezier curves are often used in graphic design applications because of their ability to provide a smooth bending curve between two fixed points. The curves are aesthetically pleasing. Four points define a cubic Bezier curve. The first point defines the start of the curve and the fourth point defines the end of the curve. The first and fourth point lie on the curve. The second and third points are the **control points**. Control points determine how "sharp" the curve is leaving the first point and entering the last point. The control points don't actually lie on the curve.

Step 1

Create a new Windows Control Library project in Visual Studio:

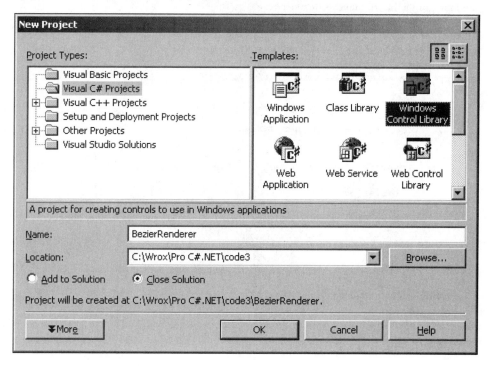

This will create a form similar to when you create a Windows application, but this time it is derived from `UserControl`:

```
namespace BezierRenderer
{
    using System;
    using System.Collections;
    using System.ComponentModel;
    using System.Drawing;
    using System.Drawing.Drawing2D;
    using System.Data;
    using System.Windows.Forms;

    /// <summary>
    ///        Summary description for Control1.
    /// </summary>

    public class BezierControl : System.Windows.Forms.UserControl
    {
```

Step 2

Next, some properties are declared for the `BezierControl` class. Specifically, a blue pen is created and the four points that define the Bezier curve:

```csharp
private Pen curvePen = new Pen( Color.Blue);
private Point pt1 = new Point( 0, 0);
private Point pt2 = new Point( 10, 30);
private Point pt3 = new Point( 50, 20);
private Point pt4 = new Point( 100, 40);

/// <summary>
///       Required designer variable.
/// </summary>

private System.ComponentModel.Container components;

public BezierControl()
{
    // This call is required by the Windows.Forms Form Designer.

    InitializeComponent();

    // TODO: Add any initialization after the InitForm call

}

/// <summary>
///       Clean up any resources being used.
/// </summary>

public override void Dispose()
{
    base.Dispose();
    components.Dispose();
}

/// <summary>
///       Required method for Designer support - do not modify
///       the contents of this method with the code editor.
/// </summary>

private void InitializeComponent()
{
    components = new System.ComponentModel.Container();
}
```

In order to modify the Bezier curve, the control points are exposed as properties, as shown in the code below:

```csharp
public Point Pt1
{
    get
    {
        return pt1;
```

```
                    }
                set
                {
                    pt1 = value;
                    Invalidate();
                }
            }
```

This is repeated for the other points as follows:

```
        public Point Pt2
        {
            get
            {
                return pt2;
            }
            set
            {
                pt2 = value;
                Invalidate();
            }
        }

        public Point Pt3
        {
            get
            {
                return pt3;
            }
            set
            {
                pt3 = value;
                Invalidate();
            }
        }

        public Point Pt4
        {
            get
            {
                return pt4;
            }
            set
            {
                pt4 = value;
                Invalidate();
            }
        }
```

This code highlights the importance of being able to perform operations when a property is set. When the control point is changed, the Bezier curve needs to be redrawn. Calling `Invalidate()` causes an `OnPaint()` messages to be sent to the control which will then force a redraw.

Step 3

Now the fun begins. First, the `OnPaintBackground()` method is overridden to demonstrate the drawing of a custom background. This message is sent when the operating system generates an erase background request. In this case, the background is painted using the `LinearGradientBrush` that was illustrated earlier in the chapter:

```
protected override void OnPaintBackground( PaintEventArgs e )
{
    Rectangle r = new Rectangle(0, 0, this.Size.Width,
                                this.Size.Height);
    LinearGradientBrush lb = new LinearGradientBrush(r,
                            Color.Red, Color.Yellow,
                            LinearGradientMode.BackwardDiagonal);
    e.Graphics.FillRectangle( lb, r );
}
```

In the `OnPaint()` method, the `Graphics` class is used to draw the Bezier curve and also small circles to represent the control points. The blue pen that was declared as a member variable is used to do the drawing:

```
protected override void OnPaint( PaintEventArgs e )
{
    base.OnPaint( e );

    // Draw the bezier curve.

    e.Graphics.DrawBezier( curvePen, pt1, pt2, pt3, pt4 );

    // Draw the points.

    e.Graphics.DrawEllipse( curvePen, pt1.X - 1, pt1.Y - 1, 3, 3 );
    e.Graphics.DrawEllipse( curvePen, pt2.X - 1, pt2.Y - 1, 3, 3 );
    e.Graphics.DrawEllipse( curvePen, pt3.X - 1, pt3.Y - 1, 3, 3 );
    e.Graphics.DrawEllipse( curvePen, pt4.X - 1, pt4.Y - 1, 3, 3 );
    }
    }
}
```

Step 4

C# has the ability to provide attributes to class members. Attributes provide meta data about the class member. For custom controls, providing attributes on properties allows Visual Studio to integrate the properties into the design environment. For example, a category and description can be provided for the first control point. This information will then be used in the Visual Studio design environment:

```
[
    Category("Appearance"),
    Description("Start point of the curve.")
]
public Point Pt1
```

No resources are used for this control, so we don't need to worry about. Add the necessary references using the **Solution Explorer** window, and compile the code to create the DLL. The custom control is now ready to be used in a Windows Forms application.

Deployment and Use

Once you have the custom control compiled to a DLL, you can use it within your project. You can declare it within a form just as you do with any other control:

```
private BezierControl bezierControl1;
```

Note that if the control were created in a different namespace to the form, the class would have to be scoped with the custom control's namespace.

Creating the control is just the same as any other control:

```
// Create the custom control.

this.bezierControl1 = new BezierControl();
this.bezierControl1.Location = new Point( 60, 100 );
this.bezierControl1.Size = new Size( 200, 200 );
```

Finally it is added to the `Controls` collection of the form:

```
this.Controls.Add (this.bezierControl1);
```

Any custom control you create can be added to the toolbox in Visual Studio. This allows you to drag and drop custom controls onto a form. The properties identified within the custom control using attributes can be manipulated from within Visual Studio.

To add a custom control to the toolbox, right click in the ToolBox area, and select Customize Toolbox. Select the .NET Framework Components tab, then Browse for the DLL that you just created:

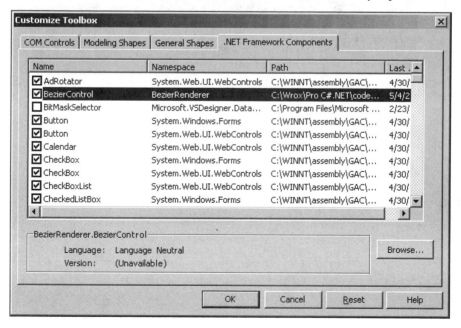

After adding it, you can drag and drop it from the toolbox just like any other control:

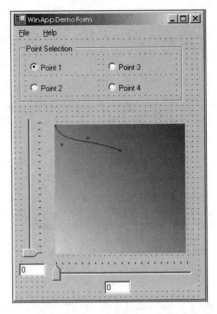

The next step is to hook up the custom control to the controls within the user interface. For example, the xTrackBar_Scroll event handler would change to the following code. The current radio button selection determines which control point is updated. When the control point property changes, the custom control receives an Invalidate() message and will redraw itself:

```
private void xTrackBar_Scroll(object sender, System.EventArgs e)
{
    TrackBar theTrackBar;
    theTrackBar = (TrackBar)sender;
    xTrackBar.Value = theTrackBar.Value;
    xTextBox.Text = xTrackBar.Value.ToString();
    if ( radioButtonPoint1.Checked == true )
    {
        bezierControl1.Pt1 = new Point( xTrackBar.Value,
                                         bezierControl1.Pt1.Y );
    }
    else if ( radioButtonPoint2.Checked == true )
    {
        bezierControl1.Pt2 = new Point( xTrackBar.Value,
                                         bezierControl1.Pt2.Y );
    }
    else if ( radioButtonPoint3.Checked == true )
    {
        bezierControl1.Pt3 = new Point( xTrackBar.Value,
                                         bezierControl1.Pt3.Y );
    }
    else if ( radioButtonPoint4.Checked == true )
    {
        bezierControl1.Pt4 = new Point( xTrackBar.Value,
                                         bezierControl1.Pt4.Y );
    }
}
```

The textbox and Bezier control are updated with the new value. Updating the Bezier control causes an invalidate message to be sent, and the control redraws with the new point:

```
private void yTrackBar_Scroll(object sender, System.EventArgs e)
{
    TrackBar theTrackBar;
    theTrackBar = (TrackBar)sender;
    yTrackBar.Value = theTrackBar.Value;
    yTextBox.Text = (200- yTrackBar.Value).ToString();
    if ( radioButtonPoint1.Checked == true )
    {
        bezierControl1.Pt1 = new Point( bezierControl1.Pt1.X, 200
                                        - yTrackBar.Value );
    }
    else if ( radioButtonPoint2.Checked == true )
    {
        bezierControl1.Pt2 = new Point( bezierControl1.Pt2.X, 200
                                        - yTrackBar.Value );
    }
    else if ( radioButtonPoint3.Checked == true )
    {
        bezierControl1.Pt3 = new Point( bezierControl1.Pt3.X, 200
                                        - yTrackBar.Value );
    }
    else if ( radioButtonPoint4.Checked == true )
    {
        bezierControl1.Pt4 = new Point( bezierControl1.Pt4.X, 200
                                        - yTrackBar.Value );
    }
}
private void xTextBox_Leave(object sender, System.EventArgs e)
{
    TextBox theTextBox;
    theTextBox = (TextBox)sender;

    // Make sure the maximum is not exceeded.

    if ( Convert.ToInt32(theTextBox.Text) > 200 )
    {
        xTrackBar.Value = 200;
        theTextBox.Text = "200";
    }
    xTrackBar.Value = Convert.ToInt32(theTextBox.Text);

    // Make appropriate changes depending upon the point currently
    // selected

    if ( radioButtonPoint1.Checked == true )
    {
        bezierControl1.Pt1 = new Point( xTrackBar.Value,
                                        bezierControl1.Pt1.Y );
    }
    else if ( radioButtonPoint2.Checked == true )
    {
        bezierControl1.Pt2 = new Point( xTrackBar.Value,
                                        bezierControl1.Pt2.Y );
    }
}
```

```
            else if ( radioButtonPoint3.Checked == true )
            {
                bezierControl1.Pt3 = new Point( xTrackBar.Value,
                                            bezierControl1.Pt3.Y );
            }
            else if ( radioButtonPoint4.Checked == true )
            {
                bezierControl1.Pt4 = new Point( xTrackBar.Value,
                                            bezierControl1.Pt4.Y );
            }
    }
    private void yTextBox_Leave(object sender, System.EventArgs e)
    {
        TextBox theTextBox;
        theTextBox = (TextBox)sender;

        if ( Convert.ToInt32(theTextBox.Text) > 200 )
        {
            yTrackBar.Value = 200;
            theTextBox.Text = "200";
        }
        yTrackBar.Value = 200 - (Convert.ToInt32(theTextBox.Text));

        // Make appropriate changes depending upon the point currently
        // selected

        if ( radioButtonPoint1.Checked == true )
        {
            bezierControl1.Pt1 = new Point( bezierControl1.Pt1.X, 200
                                        - yTrackBar.Value );
        }
        else if ( radioButtonPoint2.Checked == true )
        {
            bezierControl1.Pt2 = new Point( bezierControl1.Pt2.X, 200
                                        - yTrackBar.Value );
        }
        else if ( radioButtonPoint3.Checked == true )
        {
            bezierControl1.Pt3 = new Point( bezierControl1.Pt3.X, 200
                                        - yTrackBar.Value );
        }
        else if ( radioButtonPoint4.Checked == true )
        {
            bezierControl1.Pt4 = new Point( bezierControl1.Pt4.X, 200
                                        - yTrackBar.Value );
        }
    }
```

Now we add the event handling code for the radio buttons. The highlighted portions of the code below show the additions that we need to make to the existing code:

```
    private void radioButtonPoint1_CheckedChanged(object sender,
                                            System.EventArgs e)
    {
        xTrackBar.Value = bezierControl1.Pt1.X;
        yTrackBar.Value = 200 - bezierControl1.Pt1.Y;
```

```
        xTextBox.Text = bezierControl1.Pt1.X.ToString();
        yTextBox.Text = bezierControl1.Pt1.Y.ToString();
    }
    private void radioButtonPoint2_CheckedChanged(object sender,
                                                  System.EventArgs e)
    {
        xTrackBar.Value = bezierControl1.Pt2.X;
        yTrackBar.Value = 200 - bezierControl1.Pt2.Y;
        xTextBox.Text = bezierControl1.Pt2.X.ToString();
        yTextBox.Text = bezierControl1.Pt2.Y.ToString();
    }
    private void radioButtonPoint3_CheckedChanged(object sender,
                                                  System.EventArgs e)
    {
        xTrackBar.Value = bezierControl1.Pt3.X;
        yTrackBar.Value = 200 - bezierControl1.Pt3.Y;
        xTextBox.Text = bezierControl1.Pt3.X.ToString();
        yTextBox.Text = bezierControl1.Pt3.Y.ToString();
    }
    private void radioButtonPoint4_CheckedChanged(object sender,
                                                  System.EventArgs e)
    {
        xTrackBar.Value = bezierControl1.Pt4.X;
        yTrackBar.Value = 200 - bezierControl1.Pt4.Y;
        xTextBox.Text = bezierControl1.Pt4.X.ToString();
        yTextBox.Text = bezierControl1.Pt4.Y.ToString();
    }
```

The code is similar for the other radio buttons – it is just for different points of the Bezier control.

While the functionality for the radio buttons is automatically generated, you'll still need to add in the functionality for the remaining textboxes and scrollbars:

```
        //
        // Required for Windows Form Designer support
        //

        InitializeComponent();
        xTextBox.Leave += new System.EventHandler (this.xTextBox_Leave );
        yTextBox.Leave += new System.EventHandler (this.yTextBox_Leave );
        xTrackBar.Scroll += new System.EventHandler
                                        (this.xTrackBar_Scroll);
        yTrackBar.Scroll += new System.EventHandler
                                        (this.yTrackBar_Scroll);
```

The sample application is now functional. You can change the control points using the controls and the control is updated. However, the application is missing one of the most important controls of software programs – menus!

Menus

Menus are the most familiar part of a graphical user interface. The .NET framework provides the following classes for menu support:

- ❑ System.Windows.Forms.MainMenu
- ❑ System.Windows.Forms.MenuItem
- ❑ System.Windows.Forms.ContextMenu

The System.Windows.Forms.MainMenu class contains the menu structure of a form. A menu is composed of many MenuItem objects that represent the individual menu items in the menu structure. A MenuItem object either represents a command in an application or is the parent menu for other menu items.

Building menus is easy with the Designer. Start by dragging and dropping a MainMenu control from the toolbox to the form. Then type the name of the menu in the boxes titled Type Here. To provide a shortcut key, prefix the relevant letter with an ampersand. For example, E&xit would produce Exit. If you want a separator in the menu, type a dash and it will produce a line.

For our example, we'll need a &File menu containing &Save, a separator (–), and E&xit, as well as an &Help menu containing an &About option:

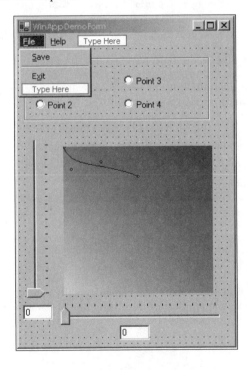

The next step is to provide code for the menu item so it actually does something. Double-click the About menu item to create the shell of an event handler for the menu item, and add the following code:

```csharp
private void menuItemAboutHelp_Click(object sender,
                                     System.EventArgs e)
{
    AboutForm aboutForm = new AboutForm();
    aboutForm.ShowDialog();
}
```

This code creates a new form that is displayed as a dialog box, which we will look at in the next section.

Dialog Boxes

A dialog box is characterized by a modal style of interaction with the user. **Modal** means that the user is not able to use the rest of the software application while the modal dialog box is present. Dialog boxes are often used to provide or collect information from the user.

To create a dialog box, you start by adding a form to your project. Then you set the following properties on the form:

FormBorderStyle: FixedDialog
MaximizeBox: false
MinimizeBox: false
ControlBox: false
StartPosition: CenterParent

To create an About box, drag a label control and a button to the form. You can then change the text as indicated in the following form:

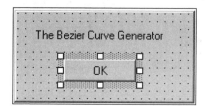

The other key point is that the ShowDialog() method is used to invoke the form – as we say in the event handler for the About menu item. By using ShowDialog() the form is run as modal dialog box.

The ShowDialog() method returns a DialogResult that can be checked to see what the user selected if there are multiple buttons on the form. For example, the event handler for the button listed above could be changed to return an OK value. The event handler can be created by double-clicking the button in the designer:

```csharp
private void OKbutton_Click(object sender, System.EventArgs e)
{
    ((Button)sender).DialogResult = DialogResult.OK;
    this.Close();
}
```

There are some ready-made dialog boxes within the WinForms classes. For example, if you want to save the data in a document you will want to use the `SaveFileDialog()` class.

For our example, we will create a file that creates a Bezier curve that can be rendered in Internet Explorer. The following code is an event handler for a **Save** menu item. The `SaveFileDialog()` is created and initialized. If the user selects a file name a stream is returned where data representing the current document can be written. In this case, a **Vector Markup Language** (**VML**) representation is written to the file. Note that you have to add the `System.IO` namespace to the class in order to have access to these methods:

```
private void menuItemFileSave_Click(object sender, System.EventArgs e)
{
    Stream myStream;
    SaveFileDialog saveFileDialog1 = new SaveFileDialog();
    String outText;
    saveFileDialog1.Filter = "htm files (*.htm)|*.htm|All files
                                                 (*.*)|*.*"  ;
    if(saveFileDialog1.ShowDialog() == DialogResult.OK)
    {
        if((myStream = saveFileDialog1.OpenFile()) != null)
        {

            // Code to write the file

            StreamWriter myWriter = new StreamWriter( myStream );
            outText = "<html xmlns:v=\"urn:schemas-microsoft-com:vml\">";
            outText += "<head><style>v\\:*
                                    { behavior: url(#default#VML); }
                                    </style></head>";
            outText += "<body><v:shape style='width: 200; height: 200'
                                    strokecolor='blue'
                                    coordorigin='0 0'
                                    coordsize='200 200'>";
            outText += "<v:path v='m ";
            outText += bezierControl1.Pt1.X.ToString() + ','
                            + bezierControl1.Pt1.Y.ToString();
            outText += " c " + bezierControl1.Pt2.X.ToString() + ','
                            + bezierControl1.Pt2.Y.ToString() + ',';
            outText += bezierControl1.Pt3.X.ToString() + ','
                            + bezierControl1.Pt3.Y.ToString() + ',';
            outText += bezierControl1.Pt4.X.ToString() + ','
                            + bezierControl1.Pt4.Y.ToString();
            outText += "' />";
            outText += "</v:shape></body></html>";
            myWriter.Write( outText );
            myWriter.Close();
            myStream.Close();
        }
    }
}
```

After the file is saved, you can double-click it and the Bezier curve will appear in Internet Explorer.

The final control that we'll need to add is the action upon clicking File | Exit in the menu system which looks like this:

```
private void menuItemFileExit_Click(object sender, System.EventArgs e)
{
        this.Close();
}
```

All that now remains is to build the application, and run the resulting file.

Summary

No matter how rich browser-based application become with Dynamic HTML, they do not take full advantage of the processing power available on a desktop computer. This includes both calculation power and graphics display power.

The chief benefit of writing Windows-based applications the Windows Forms way is that Windows Forms homogenize the programming model and eliminate many of the bugs, quirks, and inconsistencies that plague the Windows API.

Desktop applications also have full access to the system resources of the computer including local files and the Windows Registry. Windows Forms applications can also use the .NET classes to take advantage of GDI+.

The .NET platform makes it easy to build desktop applications. The System.WinForms and System.Drawing namespace have rich classes for building desktop applications.

There are many other controls that were not explored in the chapter. The graphics classes are also much more extensive than was discussed in this chapter. I encourage you to explore the System.Windows.Forms classes and try those that are of interest to you.

10

Assemblies

In this chapter we'll be discussing **assemblies**. We'll discuss what they are, how they can be used, and why they're such a useful feature. In particular, we'll cover:

❑ The innovations with assemblies compared to previous technologies.

❑ How to create and view assemblies.

❑ What the Common Language Specification means, and how cross-language support is made possible.

❑ How to create resource-only assemblies and use them for localization.

❑ How to share assemblies. (For this we have to create unique names and look at versioning).

Let's begin this chapter by taking an overview of what assemblies are.

What are Assemblies?

Before the .NET Platform was introduced we had to deal with the predecessors of assemblies: normal DLLs exporting global functions, and COM DLLs exporting COM classes. Microsoft itself introduced the phrase "DLL-Hell" to describe traditional problems with DLLs – problems that we know all too well.

Often applications break because a newly installed application overwrites a DLL that was also used by another application. Sometimes it happens that the installation replaces a new DLL with an old one, because the installation program doesn't correctly check the versions, or the versions are not correctly set. More often, an old DLL is replaced by a new version. Normally, this shouldn't be a problem, but the reality is different. Although the new DLL should be backwardly compatible with the old version, sometimes it isn't. This situation arises far too often.

Windows 2000 introduced the **side-by-side** feature that allows the installation of DLLs in the application's directory. With side-by-side, a different version of an already-installed, shared DLL may be installed to the directory of the application. The LoadLibrary() Win32 API call was rewritten so that it first checks for a .local file in the application directory. If it's found, the API first checks if a DLL was in the same directory of the application, before the other mechanisms are used to find a shared DLL. This also overwrites the fixed path that is in the registry for COM DLLs. Side-by-side is an afterthought, and doesn't solve all of the issues, and also introduces some new problems with COM DLLs. Another feature of Windows 2000 that deals with DLL-Hell is file protection: system-DLLs are protected from being overwritten by unauthorized parties. All of these Windows 2000 features treat the symptoms and not the causes.

The versioning problems of DLLs exist because it's not clear which version of a specific DLL each application needs. Dependencies are not tracked or enforced with the traditional DLL architecture. **COM DLLs** seem to solve a lot of the DLL problems because of a better separation of the implementation and the interface. The interface is a contract between the client and the component, which, according to COM rules, may never be changed, and thus can't break. However, even with COM, changes of implementations break existing applications.

Side-by-side also supports COM DLLs. If you're ever tried side-by-side with COM DLLs, you have seen it's just a hack. New problems arise when using side-by-side COM DLLs. Also, if we're not uninstalling, rather we're installing the new DLL over the old one, what happens when two versions of the same component use different threading configurations? The settings are taken from the last installed version. This problem exists because the configuration of a COM component is not stored in the component DLL itself.

The Answer to DLL-Hell

The .NET platform's answer to all these problems is **assemblies**. Assemblies are self-describing installation units, consisting of one or more files. One assembly could be a single DLL or EXE that includes meta data, or it can be made of different files, for example, resource files, meta data, DLLs, and an EXE. Installation of an assembly can be as simple as copying all of its files. An xcopy installation can be done. Another big feature of assemblies is that they can be private or shared. If you search for a COM component in the registry or using OleView, you have to walk through hundreds and hundreds of components. Just a very few of these components were ever meant to be used from more than one application, but every component must have a global unique identifier (GUID).

There's a big difference between private and shared assemblies. Many developers will be happy with just private assemblies. No special management, registration, versioning, and so on must be done with private assemblies. The only application that could have version problems with private assemblies is your own application. The private components you use within your application are installed at the same time as the application itself. Local application directories are used for the assemblies of the components, so you shouldn't have any versioning problem. No other application will ever overwrite your private assemblies.

Of course, with private assemblies you can still have versioning problems during development time. Let's see an example: if a component you use in your application references version 1 of assembly X, and you use version 2 of assembly X in your application, which version of the assembly is copied to your application directory?

This depends on what you referenced first. This versioning problem must be solved during development time. On the installed system to a application, a hot fix can be easily applied by simply replacing a private assembly with a new version. The only application that could have problems with the new version is the one where this fix is applied, as no other applications can be influenced.

When using shared assemblies, several applications can use this assembly and have a dependency on it. With shared assemblies, many rules must be fulfilled. A shared assembly must have a special version number, a unique name, and usually it's installed in the **global assembly cache**.

Features of Assemblies

The features of assemblies can be summarized as follows:

❑ Assemblies are **self-describing**. It's no longer necessary to pay attention to registry keys for apartments, to get the type library from some other place, and so on Assemblies include meta data that describe the assembly. The meta data includes the types exported from the assembly and a manifest. In the next section we will look at what a manifest is exactly.

❑ **Version dependencies** are recorded inside an assembly manifest. The version of a referenced assembly is stored in the manifest of the assembly. This way we know exactly what the version is number is of the assembly that was used during development. The version of the referenced assembly that will be used can be configured by the developer and the system administrator. In a later section of this chapter, we will look at which version policies are available, and how they work.

❑ Assemblies can be loaded **side-by-side**. Using Windows 2000 we already have a side-by-side feature where different versions of the same DLL can be used on a system. .NET extends the functionality of Windows 2000; now different versions of the same assembly can be used inside a single process! Maybe you're asking where this could be useful? If assembly A references version 1 of the shared assembly Shared, and assembly B uses version 2 of the shared assembly Shared, and you are using both assembly A and B, guess which versions of the shared assembly Shared are needed in your application!

❑ Application isolation is assured using **application domains**. With application domains a number of applications can run independently inside a single process. Faults in one application cannot affect other applications inside the same process.

❑ Installation can be as easy as copying the files that belong to an assembly. An xcopy can be enough. This feature is named **zero-impact installation**.

Why the Microsoft Windows Installer (MSI) is Still Important

I'm often asked why is the Microsoft Windows Installer still needed when xcopy is enough to install .NET applications? The simple answer is that copying files is not really all that's needed from Windows applications.

Usually, you want to access the application from the Start menu, install it in a subdirectory of Program Files, let the user choose some options, show copyright screens, and so on. The Windows Installer supports a lot of additional features that can't be solved using assemblies. Applications can use their own registry settings, **group policies** for easier management where specific users can access specific features, **advertisement** where parts of the application are installed later when requested by the user, and the **repair** feature to easily do repairs when files are corrupted.

Application Domains and Assemblies

Before .NET processes were used as isolation boundaries, every process had its private virtual memory; an application running in a process cannot write to the memory of another application and thereby crash the other application. The process is used as an isolation and security boundary between applications. With the .NET architecture we have a new boundary for applications: application domains. With managed IL code the runtime can assure that access to the memory of another application inside a single process can't happen. Multiple applications can run in a single process within multiple application domains:

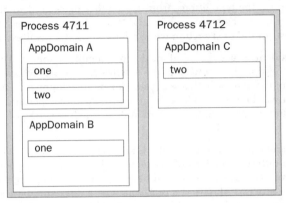

An assembly is loaded into an application domain. In the above picture you see process 4711 with two application domains. In application domain A, the objects one and two are instantiated, one probably in assembly One, and two in assembly Two. The second application domain in process 4711 has an instance one. To minimize memory consumption, the code of assemblies is only loaded once into an application domain. Instance and static members are not shared between application domains. It's not possible to directly access objects within another application domain. A proxy is needed instead. You can read more about proxies and communications across application domains in chapter 23.

The AppDomain class is used to create and terminate application domains, load and unload assemblies and types, and to enumerate assemblies and threads in a domain. Let's do a small example to see application domains in action.

First I'm creating a C# Console Application AssemblyA. I'm just doing a Console.WriteLine() in the Main() method so that we can see when this method gets called. In addition, I've added a constructor with two int values as arguments, so that we can also see how to create instances with the AppDomain class. The AssemblyA.exe assembly will be loaded from the second application that we're creating:

```
namespace AssemblyA
{
    class Class1
    {
        public Class1(int val1, int val2)
        {
            Console.WriteLine("Constructor with the values {0}, {1}" +
                        " in domain {2} called", val1, val2,
                        AppDomain.CurrentDomain.FriendlyName);
        }
}
```

```
        static void Main(string[] args)
        {
            Console.WriteLine("Main in domain {0} called",
                             AppDomain.CurrentDomain.FriendlyName);
        }
    }
}
```

The second project created is again a C# Console Application: `DomainTest`. First, I'm displaying the name of the current domain. With the `CreateDomain()` method, a new application domain with the friendly name `New AppDomain` is created. Then we are loading the assembly `AssemblyA` into the new domain and calling the `Main()` method by calling `ExecuteAssembly()`:

```
using System;

namespace DomainTest
{
    class Class1
    {
        static void Main(string[] args)
        {
            AppDomain currentDomain = AppDomain.CurrentDomain;

            Console.WriteLine(currentDomain.FriendlyName);

            AppDomain secondDomain =
                    currentDomain.CreateDomain("New AppDomain");
            secondDomain.ExecuteAssembly("AssemblyA.exe");
        }
    }
}
```

Before starting the program `DomainTest.exe`, we have to copy the assembly `AssemblyA.exe` to the directory of `DomainTest.exe` so that the assembly can be found. It's not possible to add a reference to the `AssemblyA.exe` assembly, because only references to assemblies in DLLs can be done within Visual Studio.NET. If the assembly cannot be found, we would get a `System.IO.FileNotFoundException` exception.

When it is run, we see this console output:

`DomainTest.exe` is the friendly name of the first application domain. The second line is the output of the newly loaded assembly in the `New AppDomain`. If you add a `Thread.Sleep()` method in the `AssemblyA.Class1.Main()` method, you will have no chance to see the process `Assembly1.exe` in the process viewer. There's no new process created. `AssemblyA` is loaded into the process `DomainTest.exe`.

Instead of calling the `Main()` method in the newly loaded assembly, you can also create a new instance. In the following example I'm replacing the `ExecuteAssembly()` method with a `CreateInstance()`. The first argument is the name of the assembly, `AssemblyA`. The second argument defines the type that should be instantiated: `AssemblyA.Class1`. The third argument, `true`, means that case is ignored. `System.Reflection.BindingFlags.CreateInstance` is a binding flag enumeration value to specify that the constructor should be called:

```
AppDomain secondDomain =
                    currentDomain.CreateDomain("New AppDomain");

// secondDomain.ExecuteAssembly("AssemblyA.exe");

secondDomain.CreateInstance("AssemblyA",
                "AssemblyA.Class1", true,
                System.Reflection.BindingFlags.CreateInstance,
                null, new object[] {7, 3}, null, null, null);
```

With a successful run we get this console output:

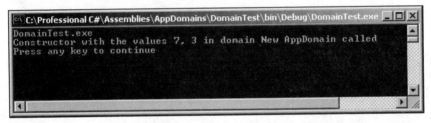

```
DomainTest.exe
Constructor with the values 7, 3 in domain New AppDomain called
Press any key to continue
```

We have seen how to create and call application domains. In runtime hosts application domains are created automatically. ASP.NET creates an application domain for each Web application that runs on a web server. Internet Explorer creates application domains in which managed controls will run. For applications it can be useful to create application domains if you want to unload an assembly. Unloading assemblies can only be done by terminating an application domain.

Assembly Structure

An assembly consists of assembly metadata describing the complete assembly, type metadata describing the exported types and methods, MSIL code, and resources. All these parts can be inside one file or spread across several files.

In this example the assembly metadata, type metadata, MSIL Code, and resources are all in one file – `Component.dll`. The assembly consists of a single file.

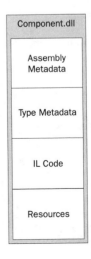

The second example shows a single assembly spread across three files. Component.dll has assembly meta data, type metadata, and MSIL code, but no resources. The assembly uses a picture from picture.jpeg, that is not embedded inside Component.dll, but is referenced from within the assembly metadata. The assembly metadata also references a module called util.netmodule, which itself includes only type metadata and MSIL code for a class. A module has no assembly metadata. So the module has no version information; it also cannot be installed separately. All three files in this second example make up a single assembly. The assembly is the installation unit. It would also be possible to put the manifest in a different file:

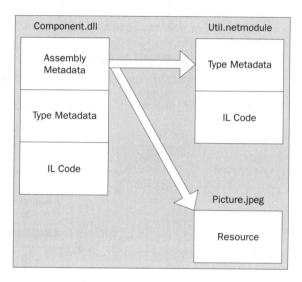

Assembly Manifests

An important part of an assembly is a **manifest**, which is part of the meta data. It describes the assembly with all the information that's needed to reference it. The parts of the manifest are:

❑   **Identity** (name, version, culture, and public key).

❑   A **list of files** belonging to this assembly. A single assembly must have at least one file, but may contain a number of files.

❑   A list of **referenced assemblies**. All assemblies that are used from the assembly including the version number, and the public key, are documented inside the manifest.

❑   A set of **permission requests** – permissions needed to run this assembly. We will not talk about permissions in this chapter. More information can be found in Chapter 25, .NET Security.

❑   **Exported types** are not part of the manifest, unless the types are included from a module. A module is a unit of reuse. The type description is stored as meta data inside the assembly. We can get the structures and classes with the properties and methods from the meta data. This replaces the type library that was used with COM to describe the types. For the use of COM clients it's easy to generate a type-library out of the manifest. The reflection mechanism uses the information about the exported types for late binding to classes. See Chapter 7 for more about reflection.

Namespaces, Assemblies, and Components

Maybe you're now confused by the meanings of namespaces, types, assemblies, and components. How does a namespace fit into the assembly concept? The namespace is completely independent of an assembly. You can have different namespaces in a single assembly, but the same namespace can be spread across assemblies. The namespace is just an extension of the type name - it belongs to the name of the type.

The following diagram should help to make this concept clearer. It shows three assemblies being built later in this chapter. (an assembly written with Managed C++, one with VB.NET, and one with C#). All these assemblies have classes in the same namespace: Wrox.ProCSharp. The assembly HelloCSharp in addition, has a class Math that's in the namespace Wrox.Utils.

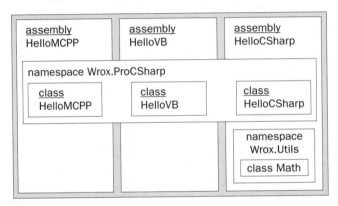

Now another question often arises: what is a component in the .NET language? Is an assembly a component? The answer to that is "no". A component is the binary form of a class. A single assembly can have a lot of components.

Private and Shared Assemblies

Assemblies can be **shared** or **private**. A private assembly is found either in the same directory as the application, or within one of its subdirectories. With a private assembly, it's not necessary to think about naming conflicts with other classes or versioning problems. The assemblies that are referenced during the build process are copied to the application directory. Private assemblies are the normal way to build assemblies, especially when applications and components are built within the same company.

When sharing assemblies, we have to be aware of some rules. The assembly must be unique, and therefore have a unique name (called a **strong name**). Part of the strong name is a mandatory version number. Shared assemblies will be mostly used when the component is built by a different vendor than the application or where a large application is split into sub-projects.

Viewing Assemblies

Assemblies can be viewed using the command line utility **ILDASM**, the MSIL disassembler. An assembly can be opened by starting ildasm from the command line, with the assembly as argument or by selecting the File | Open menu.

The picture below shows `ildasm` opening a sample program, `HelloCSharp.exe`, that we are going to build. `ildasm` shows the manifest, and the `HelloCSharp` type in the `Wrox.ProfessionalCSharp` namespace. Opening the manifest, we can see the version number, and the assembly attributes as well as the referenced assemblies and their versions. Opening the methods of the class, we can see the MSIL code:

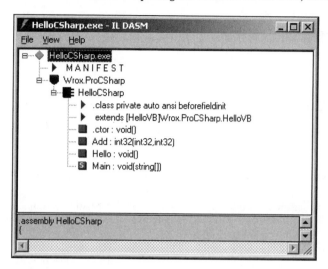

Building Assemblies

Now we have learned what assemblies are, we are going to build some. Of course, we already built an assembly in Chapter 3, because a .NET executable is an assembly anyway, but now we will have a look at special options for assemblies.

Creating Modules and Assemblies

All C# project types in Visual Studio.NET create an assembly. Whether you choose a DLL or EXE project type, an assembly is always created. With the command line C# compiler `csc`, it's also possible to create modules. A module is a DLL without assembly attributes (so it's not an assembly, but it can be added to assemblies at a later time). The command `csc /target:module hello.cs` creates a module `hello.netmodule`. It's possible to view this module using `ildasm`.

A module also has a manifest, but there is no `.assembly` entry inside the manifest. A module clearly has no assembly attributes. It's not possible to configure versions or permissions with modules; that's only possible at the assembly scope. In the manifest of the module, references to assemblies can be found. With the `/addmodule` option of `csc`, it's possible to add modules to existing assemblies.

To compare modules to assemblies, I'm generating a simple class `A` and compiling it using:

```
csc /target:module A.cs
```

The compiler generates the file `A.netmodule`, which doesn't include assembly information (as we can see using `ildasm` looking at the manifest information). The manifest of the module shows the referenced assembly `mscorlib` and the `.module` entry:

```
MANIFEST                                                    _|□|X
.assembly extern mscorlib
{
  .publickeytoken = (B7 7A 5C 56 19 34 E0 89 )
  .hash = (8B BB 5A BD 8D A3 12 7D 08 A2 25 D0 48 17 28 4F    //
           20 57 EA 07 )                                      //
  .ver 1:0:2411:0
}
.module A.netmodule
// MVID: {F53B087D-18DB-4302-A860-0338B91FD548}
.subsystem 0x00000003
.file alignment 512
.corflags 0x00000001
// Image base: 0x030e0000
```

Next, I'm generating an assembly B that includes the module A.netmodule. It's not necessary to have a source file to generate this assembly. The command to build the assembly is:

```
csc /target:library /addmodule:A.netmodule /out:B.dll
```

When looking at the assembly using ildasm, only a manifest can be found. In the manifest, the assembly mscorlib is referenced. Next we see the assembly section with a hash algorithm and the version. Part of the manifest is a list of all modules belonging to the assembly. Here we see .module A.netmodule that belongs to the assembly. This module exports the class Wrox.ProfessionalCSharp.A. Classes exported from modules are part of the assembly manifest; classes exported from the assembly itself are not:

```
MANIFEST                                                    _|□|X
.assembly extern mscorlib
{
  .publickeytoken = (B7 7A 5C 56 19 34 E0 89 )               //
  .hash = (8B BB 5A BD 8D A3 12 7D 08 A2 25 D0 48 17 28 4F    // ..Z....}..%
           20 57 EA 07 )                                      // W..
  .ver 1:0:2411:0
}
.assembly B
{
  // --- The following custom attribute is added automatically, do not uncc
  //   .custom instance void [mscorlib]System.Diagnostics.DebuggableAttribut
  //
  .hash algorithm 0x00008004
  .ver 0:0:0:0
}
.file A.netmodule
    .hash = (7E 25 E2 1A CC 2E 9E 31 E0 72 8F B3 35 99 20 BE   // ~%.....1.
             05 58 6C 0D )                                     // .X1.
.class extern public Wrox.ProfessionalCSharp.A
{
  .file A.netmodule
  .class 0x02000002
}
.module B.dll
// MVID: {946A91B2-96E3-4555-817D-158C8EF6023F}
.subsystem 0x00000003
.file alignment 512
.corflags 0x00000001
// Image base: 0x030e0000
```

What's the purpose of modules? Modules can be used for faster startup of assemblies because not all types are inside a single file. The modules are only loaded when needed. Another reason to use modules is if you want to create an assembly with more than one programming language; one module could be written using VB.NET, another module using C#, and these two modules can be included in a single assembly.

Creating Assemblies Using Visual Studio.NET

As already mentioned, all project types in Visual Studio.NET create assemblies. With the first version of Visual Studio.NET there's no support for creating modules. When creating a Visual Studio.NET project, the source file `AssemblyInfo.cs` is generated where we can configure the assembly attributes using the normal source code editor. This is the file generated from the wizard:

```
using System.Reflection;
using System.Runtime.CompilerServices;

//
// General Information about an assembly is controlled through the following
// set of attributes. Change these attribute values to modify the
// information associated with an assembly.
//

[assembly: AssemblyTitle("")]
[assembly: AssemblyDescription("")]
[assembly: AssemblyConfiguration("")]
[assembly: AssemblyCompany("")]
[assembly: AssemblyProduct("")]
[assembly: AssemblyCopyright("")]
[assembly: AssemblyTrademark("")]
[assembly: AssemblyCulture("")]

//
// Version information for an assembly consists of the following four
// values:
//
//      Major Version
//      Minor Version
//      Revision
//      Build Number
//
// You can specify all the values or you can default the Revision and Build //
Numbers by using the '*' as shown below:

[assembly: AssemblyVersion("1.0.*")]

//
// In order to sign your assembly you must specify a key to use. Refer to
// the Microsoft .NET Framework documentation for more information on
// assembly signing.
//
// Use the attributes below to control which key is used for signing.
//
// Notes:
//   (*) If no key is specified - the assembly cannot be signed.
//   (*) KeyName refers to a key that has been installed in the Crypto
//       Service Provider (CSP) on your machine.
//   (*) If the key file and a key name attributes are both specified, the
//       following processing occurs:
//       (1) If the KeyName can be found in the CSP - that key is used.
//       (2) If the KeyName does not exist and the KeyFile does exist, the
//           key in the file is installed into the CSP and used.
//   (*) Delay Signing is an advanced option - see the Microsoft .NET
//       Framework documentation for more information on this.
//

[assembly: AssemblyDelaySign(false)]
[assembly: AssemblyKeyFile("")]
[assembly: AssemblyKeyName("")]
```

This file is used for configuration of the assembly manifest. The compiler reads the assembly attributes to inject the specific information into the manifest.

`[assembly]` and `[module]`, are global attributes. Global attributes are, in contrast to the other attributes, not attached to a specific language element. The arguments that can be used for the assembly attribute are classes of the namespaces `System.Reflection`, `System.Runtime.CompilerServices`, and `System.Runtime.InteropServices`.

You can read more about attributes and how to create custom attributes in Chapter 5.

Here's a list of all assembly attributes from the `System.Reflection` namespace:

❑ `AssemblyCompany` specifies the company name.

❑ `AssemblyConfiguration` has build information such as retail or debugging information.

❑ `AssemblyCopyright` and `AssemblyTrademark` hold the copyright and trademark information.

❑ `AssemblyDefaultAlias` can be used if the assembly name is not easily readable (as with a GUID). With this attribute an alias name can be specified.

❑ `AssemblyDescription` is a description about the assembly or the product.

❑ `AssemblyInformationalVersion` is a version for information only. This attribute isn't used for version checking when assemblies are referenced.

❑ `AssemblyProduct` names the product name where the assembly belongs.

❑ `AssemblyTitle` is a friendly name of the assembly. The friendly name can include spaces.

Here's an example of how these attributes might be configured:

```
[assembly: AssemblyTitle("Professional C#")]
[assembly: AssemblyDescription("")]
[assembly: AssemblyConfiguration("Retail version")]
[assembly: AssemblyCompany("Wrox Press")]
[assembly: AssemblyProduct("Wrox Professional Series")]
[assembly: AssemblyCopyright("Copyright (C) Wrox Press 2001")]
[assembly: AssemblyTrademark("Wrox is a registered trademark of Wrox Press
                                                             Ltd")]

[assembly: AssemblyCulture("en-US")]
```

These attributes are from the `System.Runtime.CompilerServices` namespace:

❑ `AssemblyCulture` tells about the culture of the assembly. We will talk about the culture when doing localization.

❑ `AssemblyDelaySign`, `AssemblyKeyFile`, `AssemblyKeyName` are used to create strong names for shared assemblies.

❑ `AssemblyVersion` specifies the version number of the assembly. Versioning plays an important part for shared assemblies.

Additional COM Interoperability attributes within the `System.Runtime.InteropServices` *namespace can be used to make .NET types visible to COM, to specify application-id's etc. You can read about these attributes in Chapter 19.*

Cross Language Support

One of the best features of COM was its support for multiple languages. It's possible to create a COM component with Visual Basic and make use of it from within a scripting client such as JavaScript. On the other hand, it's also possible to create a COM component using C++ that a Visual Basic program can't make use of. A scripting client has different requirements to a VB client. A C++ client is able to use many more COM features than any other client's languages.

When writing COM components it's always necessary to have the client in mind. The server must be developed for a specific client language, or for a group of client languages. If designing a COM component for a scripting client, this component can also be used from within C++, but the C++ client then has some disadvantages. Many rules must be followed when different clients should be supported, and the compiler can't help with COM; the COM developer has to know the requirements of the client language, and has to create the interfaces accordingly.

How does this compare with the .NET platform? .NET exactly defines how a component can be written to be used by multiple languages. This definition is called the **Common Language Specification** (**CLS**). The compiler can check for valid code according to the CLS specification with .NET. However, we are not restricted to using only the types that all languages support. With C# we can create components using data types that are not available to all .NET consumer languages. It's still possible to create components that aren't available to all .NET consumer languages using .NET.

All types are declared in the **Common Type System** (**CTS**), but not all types are available to all languages. To build components that should be accessible from all .NET languages the CLS should be used. The Common Language Specification is a subset of the Common Type System. The CTS defines rules that language compilers must follow to define, reference, use, and store types. Therefore, objects written in different languages can interact with each other. With .NET the features of these languages are not reduced to the common subset. With .NET it's still possible to create components that can't be used from different languages. That said, supporting all languages is much easier with .NET than it was with COM. If you restrict yourself to the CLS, it's guaranteed that this component can be used from all languages.

The .NET framework was designed from the ground up to support multiple languages. During the design phase of .NET, Microsoft invited many compiler vendors to build their own .NET languages. Microsoft itself delivers VB.NET, Managed C++, C#, and JScript. In addition, more than twenty languages from different vendors, such as Cobol, Smalltalk, Perl, and Eiffel are available. Each of these languages has its specific advantages, and many different features. The compilers of all these languages have been extended to support .NET.

> **The CLS is the minimum specification of requirements that a language must support. This means that if we restrict our public methods to the CLS, all languages supporting .NET can use our classes!**

Most, but not all, of the classes in the .NET framework are CLS compliant. The non-compliant classes and methods are specially marked as not compliant in the MSDN documentation. One example is the `UInt32` structure in the `System` namespace. `UInt32` represents a 32-bit unsigned integer. Not all languages (e.g. Visual Basic.NET) support unsigned data types; such data types are not CLS compliant.

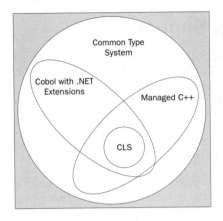

Language Independence in Action

Let's see CLS in action. The first assembly we create will include a base class with Managed C++. The second assembly has a VB.NET class that inherits from the C++ class. The third assembly is a C# console application with a class deriving from the VB.NET code, and a `Main` function that's using the C# class. The implementation should just show how the languages make use of .NET classes, and how they handle numbers. So all these classes have a simple `Hello()` method where the `System.Console` class is used, and a `Add()` method where two numbers are added:

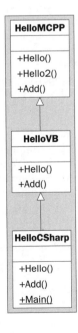

Writing a Class using Managed C++

The first project type to create is a Managed C++ Class Library, which is created using Visual Studio, and given the name HelloMCPP:

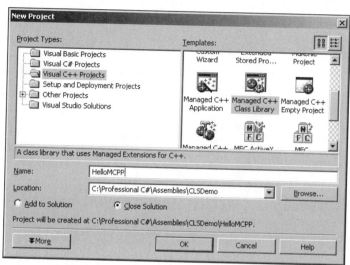

The application wizard generates a class HelloMCPP that is marked using the Managed C++ attribute _gc to make the class a managed type. Without a special attribute, the class would be a normal unmanaged C++ class generating native code.

In the generated header file stdafx.h, you'll see a #using <mscorlib.dll> statement. In C++, other assemblies can be referenced with the #using preprocessor statement. The code for the .NET class can be found in the file HelloMCPP.h:

```
// HelloMCPP.h

#pragma once

using namespace System;
public __gc class HelloMCPP
{

    // TODO: Add your methods for this class here.

};
```

For demonstration purposes, I'm adding three methods. The virtual method Hello2() is using a C runtime function printf() that demonstrates the use of native code within a managed class. Within the Hello() method we are using the Console managed class from the System namespace. The C++ using namespace statement is similar to the C# using statement. using namespace System opens the System namespace, so we needn't write System::Console::WriteLine(). The Hello() method is also marked virtual, so that it can be overridden. We will override Hello() in the VB and C# classes. C++ member functions are not virtual by default. A third method which returns the sum of two int arguments is added to the class so that we can compare the generated MSIL to the different languages to see how they handle numbers. All three examples use the same namespace Wrox.ProCSharp. To create a namespace in C++ I'm using the C++ namespace statement.

```
// HelloMCPP.h

#pragma once
#include <stdio.h>

using namespace System;
namespace Wrox
{
    namespace ProCSharp
    {
        public __gc class HelloMCPP
        {
        public:
            virtual void Hello()
            {
                Console::WriteLine("Hello, Managed C++");
            }
            virtual void Hello2()
            {
                printf("Hello, calling native code\n");
            }
            int Add(int val1, int val2)
            {
                return val1 + val2;
            }
        };
    }
}
```

To compare the programs with running code we are using the release build instead of the debug configuration. Looking at the generated DLL using ILDASM, we see two static methods used, `printf()` and `DllMainCrtStartup()`. Both of these methods are native unmanaged functions using `pinvoke`. `DllMainCrtStartup()` is used within every Managed C++ program. It is the entry point in the DLL, and is called when the DLL is loaded. `printf()` is used within our `Hello()` method. The private fields `$ArrayType$0xec5a014e`, and `$ArrayType$0xf7078e56` hold our strings `"Hello, Managed C++"` and `"Hello, calling native code\n"`:

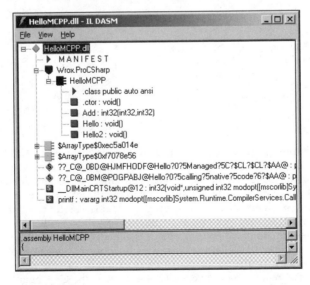

```
HelloMCPP::Hello2 : void()                                          _□×
.method public newslot virtual instance void
        Hello2() cil managed
{
  // Code size       12 (0xc)
  .maxstack  1
  IL_0000:  ldsflda     valuetype $ArrayType$0xec5a014e ??_C@_0BM@POGPABJ@Hello?0?
  IL_0005:  call        vararg int32 modopt([mscorlib]System.Runtime.CompilerServ:
  IL_000a:  pop
  IL_000b:  ret
} // end of method HelloMCPP::Hello2
```

The `Hello2()` method pushes the address of the field `$ArrayType$0xec5a014e`, that keeps the string on the stack. In line `IL_0005` a call to the static `printf()` method can be seen where a pointer to the string "Hello, calling native code" is passed.

`printf()` itself is called via the **platform invoke** mechanism (as shown below). With the platform invoke, we can call all native functions like the C runtime and Win32 API calls. In Chapter 19 you will get more information about platform invoke when we call COM components from managed code:

```
Global Functions::printf : vararg int32 modopt([mscorlib]System.Runtime.CompilerServices.CallConvC... _□×
.method public static pinvokeimpl(/* No map */)
        vararg int32 modopt([mscorlib]System.Runtime.CompilerServices.CallConvC
        printf(int8 modopt([Microsoft.VisualC]Microsoft.VisualC.NoSignSpecified:
{
  .custom instance void [mscorlib]System.Security.SuppressUnmanagedCodeSecurity.
  // Embedded native code
  //  Disassembly of native methods is not supported.
  //  Managed TargetRVA = 0xa22c
} // end of method 'Global Functions'::printf
```

The `Hello()` method is completely made up of MSIL code; there's no native code. Again, a pointer to the string is pushed on the stack. Line `IL_0005` creates a new instance of a `String` object; in line `IL_000a` we are calling the `WriteLine()` method of the `System.Console` class passing the string object:

```
HelloMCPP::Hello : void()                                           _□×
.method public newslot virtual instance void
        Hello() cil managed
{
  // Code size       16 (0x10)
  .maxstack  1
  IL_0000:  ldsflda     valuetype $ArrayType$0xf7078e56 ??_C@_0BD@HJMFHODF@Hello?0?
  IL_0005:  newobj      instance void [mscorlib]System.String::.ctor(int8*)
  IL_000a:  call        void [mscorlib]System.Console::WriteLine(string)
  IL_000f:  ret
} // end of method HelloMCPP::Hello
```

```
HelloMCPP::Add : int32(int32,int32)                                 _□×
.method public instance int32  Add(int32 val1,
                                   int32 val2) cil managed
{
  // Code size       4 (0x4)
  .maxstack  2
  IL_0000:  ldarg.1
  IL_0001:  ldarg.2
  IL_0002:  add
  IL_0003:  ret
} // end of method HelloMCPP::Add
```

To demonstrate how numbers are used within Managed C++, we're now going to take a look at the MSIL code of the Add() method. With ldarg.1, and ldarg.2, the passed arguments are put on the stack, add adds the stack values, and puts the result on the stack, in line IL_0003 the result is returned.

What's the advantage of using Managed C++ compared to C# and other languages of the .NET framework? Managed C++ makes it easy to make traditional C++ code available to .NET. MSIL code and native code can be mixed easily.

Be aware however that it's not possible to create a Managed C++ application without native code. With the current implementation, there's always native start-up code.

Writing a Class using VB.NET

Now we're going to use VB.NET to create a class. Again, we are using the **Class Library** wizard; the project will be called HelloVB:

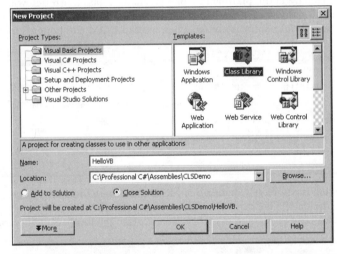

The namespace of the class should be changed to Wrox.ProCSharp. In a VB.NET project this can be done by changing the root namespace of the project in the project properties:

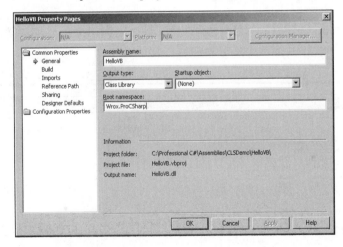

To make it possible to derive the class from `HelloMCPP` a reference to `HelloMCPP.dll` is needed. The reference is done using **Project | Add Reference**, or can also be done from inside the **Solution Explorer**. When building the assembly the reference can be seen inside the manifest: `.assembly extern HelloMCPP`. The referenced assembly is also copied to the output directory of the $\bar{V}$B.NET project, so that we are independent of later changes made to the original referenced assembly:

```
 MANIFEST                                                          _ □ ×
  .ver 1:0:2411:0
}
.assembly extern HelloMCPP
{
  .ver 1:0:476:28327
}
.assembly HelloVB
{
  .custom instance void [mscorlib]System.CLSCompliantAttribute::.ctor(
  .custom instance void [mscorlib]System.Reflection.AssemblyTrademarkA
  .custom instance void [mscorlib]System.Reflection.AssemblyCopyrightA
  .custom instance void [mscorlib]System.Reflection.AssemblyProductAtt
  .custom instance void [mscorlib]System.Reflection.AssemblyCompanyAtt
  .custom instance void [mscorlib]System.Reflection.AssemblyDescriptio
  .custom instance void [mscorlib]System.Reflection.AssemblyTitleAttri
  .hash algorithm 0x00008004
  .ver 1:0:476:31917
}
.module HelloVB.dll
// MVID: {7AF2294B-B2C3-4D88-9ACC-3D09A301FCA5}
.subsystem 0x00000002
.file alignment 512
.corflags 0x00000001
// Image base: 0x030e0000
```

The class `HelloVB` inherits from `HelloMCPP`. VB.NET has the keyword `Inherits` to derive from a base class. `Inherits` must be in the same line as, and follow the `Class` statement. The `Hello()` method in the base class is overridden. The VB.NET `Overrides` keyword does the same thing as the C# `override` keyword. In the implementation of the `Hello()` method, the `Hello()` method of the base class is called using the VB.NET keyword `MyBase`. The `MyBase` keyword is the same as `base` in C#. The method `Add()` is implemented so that we can examine the generated MSIL code to see how VB.NET works with numbers. The `Add()` method from the base class is not virtual, so it can't be overridden. VB.NET has the keyword `Shadows` to hide a method of a base class. `Shadows` is similar to C#'s `new`:

```
Public Class HelloVB
   Inherits HelloMCPP

   Public Overrides Sub Hello()
      MyBase.Hello()
      System.Console.WriteLine("Hello, VB.NET")
   End Sub

   Public Shadows Function Add(ByVal val1 As Integer,
                           ByVal val2 As Integer) As Integer
      Return val1 + val2
   End Function

End Class
```

Let's look at the MSIL code that is generated from the VB.NET compiler.

The `HelloVB.Hello()` method first calls the `Hello()` method of the base class `HelloMCPP`. In line `IL_0006`, a string stored in the meta data is pushed on the stack using `ldstr`. In comparison, Managed C++ used a `System.String` object and initialized it using a static string.

```
HelloVB::Hello : void()                                          _ □ X
.method public virtual instance void  Hello() cil managed
{
  // Code size       17 (0x11)
  .maxstack  8
  IL_0000:  ldarg.0
  IL_0001:  call         instance void [HelloMCPP]Wrox.ProCSharp.Hello
  IL_0006:  ldstr        "Hello, VB.NET"
  IL_000b:  call         void [mscorlib]System.Console::WriteLine(stri
  IL_0010:  ret
} // end of method HelloVB::Hello
```

The other method we are looking at is Add(). VB.NET uses add.ovf instead of the add() method which was used in the MC++ generated MSIL code. This is just a single MSIL statement that's different between MC++ and VB.NET, but the statement add.ovf generates more lines of native code, as add.ovf performs overflow checking. If the result of the addition of the two arguments is too large to be represented in the target type, add.ovf generates an exception of type OverflowException. In contrast, add() just performs an addition of the two values, whether or not the target fits. In the case where the target is not big enough, the true value of the summation is lost, and the result is a wrong number. So, add() is faster, but add.ovf is safer:

```
HelloVB::Add : int32(int32,int32)                               _ □ X
.method public instance int32  Add(int32 val1,
                                   int32 val2) cil managed
{
  // Code size       7 (0x7)
  .maxstack  2
  .locals init (int32 V_0)
  IL_0000:  ldarg.1
  IL_0001:  ldarg.2
  IL_0002:  add.ovf
  IL_0003:  br.s        IL_0006
  IL_0005:  ldloc.0
  IL_0006:  ret
} // end of method HelloVB::Add
```

Writing a Class using C#

The third class is created using the language we know best: C#. For this project, we will create a C# Console Application. The HelloVB assembly is referenced to make a derivation of the class HelloVB:

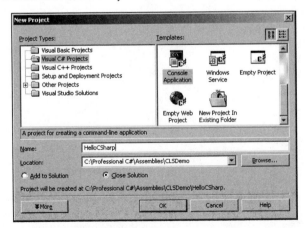

The methods implemented in the C# class are similar to the MC++ and the VB.NET classes. `Hello()` is an overridden method of the base class; `Add()` is a new method:

```
namespace Wrox.ProCSharp
{
    using System;

    /// <summary>
    ///     Summary description for HelloCSharp.
    /// </summary>

    public class HelloCSharp : HelloVB
    {
        public HelloCSharp()
        {

            // TODO: Add Constructor Logic here

        }

        public override void Hello()
        {
            base.Hello();
            Console.WriteLine("Hello, C#");
        }

        public new int Add(int val1, int val2)
        {
            return val1 + val2;
        }

        public static void Main()
        {
            HelloCSharp hello = new HelloCSharp();
            hello.Hello();
        }
    }
}
```

As you can see, the generated MSIL code for the `Hello()` method is the same as the MSIL code from the VB.NET compiler:

```
HelloCSharp::Hello : void()                                              _|□|×|
.method public hidebysig virtual instance void
        Hello() cil managed
{
  // Code size       17 (0x11)
  .maxstack  8
  IL_0000:  ldarg.0
  IL_0001:  call       instance void [HelloVB]Wrox.ProCSharp.HelloVB::Hello
  IL_0006:  ldstr      "Hello, C#"
  IL_000b:  call       void [mscorlib]System.Console::WriteLine(string)
  IL_0010:  ret
} // end of method HelloCSharp::Hello
```

The `Add()` method differs, and yet is similar to the MC++ code. When doing calculations, the C# compiler doesn't use the methods with overflow; checking with the default compiler settings in a Visual Studio.NET project. The faster MSIL method `add()` is used instead of `add.ovf`; but it's possible to change this option using the configuration properties of the project both with C# and VB.NET. When `Check for overflow underflow` is set to `true` in a C# project, the same MSIL code that VB.NET generates is done by the C# compiler. With C# it's also possible to choose this option on an expression by expression basis with the `checked` and `unchecked` operators:

```
HelloCSharp::Add : int32(int32,int32)                    _ □ ×
.method public hidebysig instance int32   Add(int32 val1,
                                              int32 val2)
{
  // Code size        4 (0x4)
  .maxstack  8
  IL_0000:   ldarg.1
  IL_0001:   ldarg.2
  IL_0002:   add
  IL_0003:   ret
} // end of method HelloCSharp::Add
```

Because all the .NET languages generate MSIL code and all the languages make use of the classes in the .NET framework, it's often said that there is no difference in regard to performance. As you can see, however, small differences are still there. First, depending on the language, some languages support other date types than others. Second, the generated MSIL code can still be different. One example that we've seen is that the number calculations are implemented differently: with the default configuration VB.NET is on the safe side, the default for C# is the fast version. C# is also more flexible.

CLS Requirements

We saw the CLS in action when we looked at cross-language inheritance between MC++, VB.NET, and C#. Until now we didn't pay any attention to the CLS requirements when building our project. We were lucky – the methods we defined in the base classes were callable from the derived classes. If a method had the `System.UInt32` data type as one of its arguments, we wouldn't be able to use it from VB.NET. Unsigned data types are not CLS compliant; for a .NET language, it's not necessary to support this data type.

The Common Language Specification exactly defines the requirements to make a component CLS compliant, which enables it to be used with different .NET languages. With COM we had to pay attention to language specific requirements when designing a component. JScript had other requirements than VB6, and the requirements of VJ++ were different again. That's no longer the case with .NET. When designing a component that should be used from other languages, we just have to make it CLS compliant; it's guaranteed that this component can be used from all .NET languages. If we mark a class as CLS compliant, the compiler can warn us about non-compliant methods.

All .NET languages must support the CLS. When talking about .NET languages we have to differentiate between **.NET consumer** and **.NET extender** tools. A .NET consumer tool just uses classes from the .NET framework – it can't create .NET classes that can be used from other languages. A consumer tool can use any CLS compliant class. A .NET extender tool has the requirements of a consumer, and can in addition inherit any CLS compliant .NET class, and define new CLS compliant classes that can be used by consumers. C++, VB.NET, and C# all are extender tools. With these languages, it's possible to create CLS compliant classes. The Cobol that's available for .NET currently is just a consumer tool. With Cobol, we can use all CLS compliant classes, but not extend it.

CLSCompliant Attribute

With the CLSCompliant attribute, we can mark our assembly to be CLS compliant. Doing this guarantees that our classes in this assembly can be used from all .NET consumer tools. The compiler gives us warnings when we are using non-CLS compliant data types in public and protected methods. The data types we use in the private implementation don't matter – when using other languages outside of the class, we don't have access to private and protected methods anyway.

To get compiler warnings when a type is not compliant in public methods, we can set the attribute CLSCompliant in the assembly. We can add this attribute in the file AssemblyInfo.cs:

```
[assembly: System.CLSCompliant(true)]
```

This way, all the defined types and public methods inside the assembly are compliant. Using a non-compliant uint type as argument type, we get this error from the compiler:

```
error CS3001: Argument type uint is not CLS-compliant
```

When we mark an assembly as compliant, it's still possible to define methods that are not compliant. This can be useful if you want to override some methods to make it available with both compliant and not compliant argument data types.The methods that are not compliant must be marked with the CLSCompliant attribute with a value of false. The CLSCompliant attribute can be applied to types, methods, properties, fields, and events:

```
[CLSCompliant(false)]
void Method(uint i) {
   //...
```

CLS Rules

What are the requirements to be CLS compliant?

❑ All types appearing in a method prototype must be CLS compliant.

❑ Array elements must have a CLS compliant element type. Arrays must also be 0-indexed.

❑ A CLS compliant class must inherit from a CLS compliant class. System.Object is CLS compliant.

❑ Although method names in CLS-compliant classes are not case-sensitive, no two method names can be different only in the case of the letters in their name.

❑ Enumerations must be of type Int16, Int32, or Int64. Enumerations of other types are not compliant.

All the listed requirements only apply to public and protected members. The private implementation itself doesn't matter – non-compliant types can be used there, and the assembly is still compliant.

Besides these requirements, there are some more rules that should be followed. These rules are not a strict requirement of being CLS compliant, but it makes life much easier. The classes in the .NET framework follow these guidelines:

❑ **Classes** should be named with nouns or noun phrases; the classes should not be prefixed with "C" as was usually done with VC++, and no underscores should be used inside the name.

❑ **Methods** should be named with verbs or verb phrases.

❑ **Properties** should be named with noun or noun phrases.

❑ **Pascal casing** should be used for classes, enumerations, events, methods, namespaces, and properties. With Pascal casing the first letter is uppercase (as in BackColor). If the name is made of a compound word, the second word should start with an uppercase letter again.

❑ **Camel casing** should be used for parameters. With camel casing (for example, backColor), the first letter is lowercase. If the name is made of a compound word, the second word should start with an uppercase letter.

❑ **Interfaces** should be prefixed with the letter I, exception classes should be named with the "Exception" suffix, and event handlers should be named with the "EventHandler" suffix.

❑ Hungarian type notations should not be used. There is a controversial ongoing discussion because most C++ developers used the Hungarian type notation regurlarly. Remember that CLS is here to make components available to multiple languages. Not all programmers are used to the Hungarian type notation because it's not used in many languages, so avoid it. You'll also have a bigger advantage if a good self-describing variable name is used.

Data type names are language specific, for example, the C# int, long, and float types are equivalent to the VB.NET Integer, Long, and Single types. When a data type name is used in a name of a method, the universal type names, and not the language specific type names should be used, in other words Int32, Int64, and Single:

```
int ReadInt32();
long ReadInt64();
float ReadSingle();
```

As you can see when complying with the CLS specs and guidelines, it's easy to create components that can be used from multiple languages. It's not necessary to test the component using all .NET consumer languages.

Adding Resources to Assemblies

As you have seen earlier, assemblies can consist of a single file, or a number of files. To make it easy to change strings and pictures in a program, it would be useful to put the strings in a different file. This way, translators in different countries just need to edit the files with the resources, and don't need to get their hands dirty going through the C# code. The .NET architecture has great support for resource files. Using Visual Studio.NET, it's easy to embed resources like pictures in the main assembly. Just add the file to the project and set the BuildAction property of the file to Embedded Resource.

Creating Resource Files

Pictures, string tables, and so on can be part of resource files. To create resource files, either a normal text file can be used, or a .resX file that utilizes XML. We will start with a simple text file.

A resource that embeds a string table can be created using a normal text file. The text file just assigns strings to keys. The key is a name that can be used from a program to get the value. Spaces are allowed in both keys and values.

This example shows a simple string table in the file `strings.txt`:

```
Title = Professional C#
Chapter = Assemblies
Author = Christian Nagel
Publisher = WROX Press
```

ResGen

The `resgen.exe` utility can be used to create a resource file out of `strings.txt`. Typing:

```
resgen strings.txt
```

will create the file `strings.resources`. This resulting resource file can be added to an assembly either as an external file or embedded into the DLL or EXE. ResGen also supports the creation of resource files with XML-based `.resX` files. One easy way to build an XML file is by using ResGen itself: `resgen strings.resources strings.resX` creates the XML resource file `strings.resX`. We will look at how to work with XML resource files soon when we look at localization later in this chapter.

The `resgen` utility doesn't support adding pictures. With the .NET Framework SDK Samples, you'll get a ResXGen sample. With ResXGen it's possible to add pictures to a `.resX` file. Adding pictures to resources can also be easily done using the `ResourceWriter` class.

ResourceWriter

Instead of using the `resgen` utility to build resource files, a simple program can be written. `ResourceWriter` is a class in the `System.Resources` namespace that also supports picture and other resource types.

Here we're creating a `ResourceWriter` object rw using a constructor with the filename `Demo.resources`. After creating an instance, a number of resources of up to 2GB in total size can be added using the `AddResource()` method of the `ResourceWriter` class. The first argument of `AddResource()` specifies the key, and the second argument specifies the value. A picture resource can be added using an instance of the `Image` class. To use the `Image` class, the `System.Drawing` assembly must be referenced. We are also opening the namespace `System.Drawing` with the `using` directive.

Here I'm creating an `Image` object by opening the file `logo.gif`. You'll have to copy the picture to the directory of the executable, or specify the full path to the picture in the method argument of `Image.FromFile()`. The `using` statement specifies that the image resource should automatically be disposed of at the end of the using block. You have to pay attention to the fact that the `Image` object gets disposed earliest after the resource is written. Additional simple string resources are added to the `ResourceWriter` object. The `Close()` method of the `ResourceWriter` class automatically calls `ResourceWriter.Generate()` to write the resources finally to the file `Demo.resources`:

```
using System;
using System.Resources;
using System.Drawing;
public class rs
{
```

```
public static void Main()
{
    ResourceWriter rw = new ResourceWriter("Demo.resources");
    using (Image image = Image.FromFile("logo.gif"))
    {
        rw.AddResource("WroxLogo", image);
        rw.AddResource("Title", "Professional C#");
        rw.AddResource("Chapter", "Assemblies");
        rw.AddResource("Author", "Christian Nagel");
        rw.AddResource("Publisher", "Wrox Press");
        rw.Close();
    }
}
```

Starting this small program creates the resource file Demo.resources. The resources will be used in a Windows application.

Using Resource Files

Resource files can be added to assemblies using the Assembly Generation Tool Al.exe using the /embed option, or directly with Visual Studio.NET. For a demonstration on how to use resource files with Visual Studio.NET, I'm creating a C# **Windows Application** and calling it ResourceDemo:

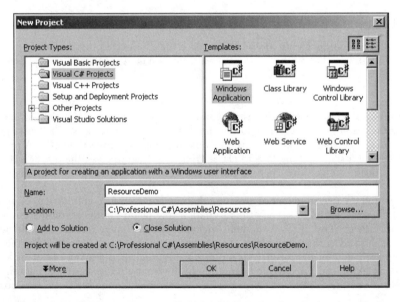

In the context menu of the **Solution Explorer** (**Add** | **Add Existing Item**), the previously created resource file Demo.resources can be added to this project. Selecting the properties of this resource file, we can now change the BuildAction from None to Embedded Resource, so that the resource gets embedded into the output assembly:

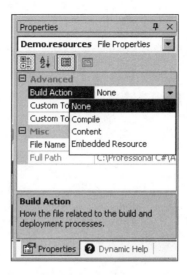

When building the project and viewing the assembly using `ildasm`, `.mresource` can be seen in the manifest. `.mresource` declares the name for the resources in the assembly. If `.mresource` is declared `public` (as in our example), the resource is exported from the assembly and can be used from classes in other assemblies. `.mresource private` means the resource is not exported and only available within the assembly.

When adding the resource to the assembly using Visual Studio.NET, the resource is always public. If the assembly generation tool is used to create assemblies, we can use command line options to differentiate between adding public and private resources. The `al` option `/embed:demo.resources,Y` adds the resource as `public`, while `/embed:demo.resources,N` adds the resource as `private`.

If the assembly was created using Visual Studio.NET it's possible to change the visibility of the resources later. Opening the assembly using `ildasm` with File | Dump generates an MSIL source file. The MSIL code can then be changed using a text editor such as Notepad. Using the text editor, we can change `.mresource public` to `.mresource private`. Using the tool `ildasm`, it's then possible to regenerate the assembly with the MSIL source code:

```
   .custom instance void [mscorlib]System.Reflection.Assembly
   .hash algorithm 0x00008004
   .ver 1:0:477:25338
}
.mresource public ResourceDemo.Form1.resources
{
}
.mresource public ResourceDemo.Demo.resources
{
}
.module ResourceDemo.exe
// MVID: {68E5720C-D646-49CB-A2A7-CE9BD2C56A53}
.subsystem 0x00000002
.file alignment 512
.corflags 0x00000001
// Image base: 0x030e0000
```

I'm adding some text boxes and a picture by dropping **Windows Forms** elements from the **Toolbox** to the designer where we will display the values from the resources. I'm changing the Text and Name properties of the textboxes and the labels to the values that you see below. The Name property of the PictureBox is changed to logo. The final form opened in the **Forms Designer** looks like this:

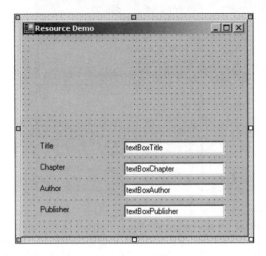

The rectangle in the upper left corner is a WinForms PictureBox.

To use that embedded resource, the ResourceManager class from the System.Resources namespace can be used. We can pass the assembly where the resources are embedded in the constructor. In our case we have the resources embedded in the executing assembly, so we pass the result of Assembly.GetExecutingAssembly() as the second argument. The first argument is the root name of the resources. The root name is made of the namespace, with the name of the resource file, without the resources extension. As you've seen earlier, ildasm shows the name. It's just necessary to remove the file extension resources. We can also get the name programmatically using the GetManifestResourceNames() method of the System.Reflection.Assembly class.

Using the ResourceManager instance rm we can get all the resources by specifying the key:

```
using System.Reflection;
using System.Resources;

// ...

private System.Resources.ResourceManager rm;

    public Form1()
    {
        //
        // Required for Windows Form Designer support
        //

        InitializeComponent();
        Assembly assembly = Assembly.GetExecutingAssembly();

        rm = new ResourceManager("ResourceDemo.Demo", assembly);
```

```
            logo.Image = (Image)rm.GetObject("WroxLogo");
            textBoxTitle.Text = rm.GetString("Title");
            textBoxChapter.Text = rm.GetString("Chapter");
            textBoxAuthor.Text = rm.GetString("Author");
            textBoxPublisher.Text = rm.GetString("Publisher");
    }
```

When we run the code, this is what we see:

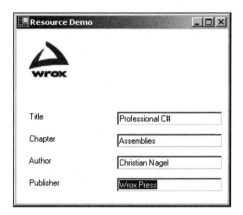

The picture and the string resources are loaded. But what is the advantage of using resources instead of storing these data items directly in the program code? The answer is that the resource files can be easily changed by non-programmers, although it may take a programmer, or at least a few batch files to recompile them into new resource files. It's not necessary to search in the source code for strings when using resource files, as the strings all are in one place. It is advantageous to have strings in resource files when programs are localized to different languages. Satellite assemblies can be used for localization. They hold resources, but no program code. We will create satellite assemblies next.

Internationalization and Resources

NASA's Mars Climate Orbiter was lost on September 23rd 1999 at a cost of $125 million because one engineering team used metric units, while another used imperial units for a key spacecraft operation.

When writing applications for international distribution, different **cultures** and **regions** must be kept in mind. Culture defines *who* you are, whereas region defines *where* you are. Together, the culture and the region are called the **locale**. One example of the challenges with internationalization is the decimal divider: for the US, the decimal divider is ".", but for Germany it's a ",".

Here are some examples of different number formats:

US English	123,456,789.23
German	123.456.789,23
Swiss German	123'456'789.23
French	123 456 789,23

And of examples of different date formats:

US English	6/15/2001	Friday, June 15, 2001
UK English	15/06/2001	15 June 2001
German	15.06.2001	Freitag, 15. Juni 2001
French	15/06/2001	Vendredi 15 juin 2001

Culture

Culture is a set of preferences based on a user's language and cultural conventions. The class `CultureInfo` is used to format dates, times, and numbers, to sort strings, and to determine the language choice for text. The user selects the culture during system installation and can configure it using the **Regional Options** in the Windows Control Panel.

The culture name defines a 2-letter language and a 2-letter country/region code that follow RFC1766 conventions. Some examples of the culture names are listed here:

Culture name	Culture
En	English
en-GB	English (United Kingdom)
en-US	English (United States)
Fr	French
fr-FR	French (France)
De	German

Using the `System.Globalization.CultureInfo` class it's possible to get the name of the culture and supported cultures, create a new culture using a culture name string, and so on. Particular things to note are some of the static properties of `CultureInfo`. We have to differentiate between these culture types:

❑ `CurrentCulture` is the culture of the current thread. The default is set to the user settings, but the culture of the thread can be changed. This culture is used for locale-dependent formatting like numbers and dates.

❑ `CurrentUICulture` is the culture that is used for resource lookups. It is also dependent on the current thread. This culture can be used to get strings or pictures from resources.

❑ `InstalledUICulture` is the system default culture for resource lookups.

❑ `InvariantCulture` is a neutral culture. This culture does not map any real culture, and so is not linguistically correct (no real existing culture does apply). If you've ever had the problem where a date appears differently on an Active Server Page depending on who is logged on, you know the reason for this is culture. This language-independent culture is useful for services.

Region

The **region** is different from the culture. The region does not represent the user's preferences, but defines the location. Switzerland is a multi-language country where the cultures de-ch, fr-ch, and it-ch are specified for Swiss people using their own versions of the German, French, and Italian languages. Be assured that the Swiss German language is different from German in Germany. In contrast to three cultures for Swiss people, only a single region, CH, is defined for Switzerland. When the language is defined by the culture, the region defines the currency and the unit of measurement. The currency used in a region is independent of the language. There's even one bigger aspect of culture vs. region: a Swiss person can go to a different country where he can still use his "home-culture", but of course has to change the region.

The location can also be set using the Regional Options in Control Panel. The System.Globalization.RegionInfo class has methods to get to these values. RegionInfo has a static property CurrentRegion to get the configured region. It's also possible to create a RegionInfo object by passing a 2- or 3-letter ISO3166 name as a string to the constructor. Examples of this string are AT or AUT for Austria, DE or DEU for Germany, FR or FRA for France, GB or GBR for the United Kingdom, and US or USA for the United States of America.

System.Globalization Namespace

The System.Globalization namespace holds all the culture and region classes to support different date formats, different number formats, and even different calendars like GregorianCalendar, HebrewCalendar, JapaneseCalendar, and so on. By using these classes, it's possible to use different representations depending on the locale.

Numbers

The number structures Int16, Int32, Int64, and so on in the System namespace all have an overloaded ToString() method. This method can be used to create a different representation of the number depending on the locale. For the Int32 structure, ToString() is overloaded with these four versions:

```
public string ToString();
public string ToString(IFormatProvider);
public string ToString(string);
public string ToString(string, IFormatProvider);
```

ToString() without arguments returns a string without formatting options. We can also pass a string and a class that implements IFormatProvider. The string specifies the format of the representation. The format can be a standard numeric formatting string, or a picture numeric formatting string. For standard numeric formatting, strings are predefined where C specifies a currency notation, D creates a decimal output, E scientific output, F fixed-point output, G general output, N number output, and X hexadecimal output. With a picture numeric format string, it's possible to specify the number of digits, section and group separators, percent notations, and so on. The picture numeric format string ###,### is meant for two 3-digit blocks separated by a group separator.

With the default constructor of NumberFormatInfo, a culture-independent or invariant object is created. Using the properties of this class it's possible to change all the formatting options like a positive sign, percent symbol, number group separator, currency symbol, and a lot more. A read-only culture-independent NumberFormatInfo object is returned from the static property InvariantInfo. A NumberFormatInfo object, where the format values are based on the CultureInfo of the current thread, is returned from the static property CurrentInfo.

`IFormatProvider` is an interface that is implemented from some different service objects. This interface defines a single method `GetFormat()` to return a format object for a specified type. `IFormatProvider` is implemented from `NumberFormatInfo`, `DateTimeFormatInfo`, and `CultureInfo`.

In the next examples I'm using a simple **Console Project**. In this code, the first example shows a number displayed in the format of the culture of the current thread. On my operating system, the setting is en-us. That's the default for the thread. The second example uses the `ToString()` method with the `IFormatProvider` argument. `CultureInfo` implements `IFormatProvider`, so I'm creating a `CultureInfo` object with the French culture. The third example changes the culture of the current thread. Using the property `CurrentCulture` of the `Thread` instance the culture is changed to German:

```
using System;
using System.Globalization;
using System.Threading;

namespace Numbers
{

    class Class1
    {
        static void Main(string[] args)
        {
            int val = 1234567890;

            // culture of the current thread

            Console.WriteLine(val.ToString("N"));

            // use IFormatProvider

            Console.WriteLine(val.ToString("N",
                        new CultureInfo("fr-fr")));

            // change the culture of the thread

            Thread.CurrentThread.CurrentCulture =
                        new CultureInfo("de-de");
            Console.WriteLine(val.ToString("N"));
        }
    }
}
```

The expected resulting output is here. You can compare the outputs with the previously listed differences for US English, French, and German:

```
C:\Professional C#\Assemblies\Localization\Numbers\bin\D...
1,234,567,890.00
1 234 567 890,00
1.234.567.890,00
Press any key to continue_
```

Date

The same support as for numbers is here for dates. The DateTime struct has some methods for date-to-string conversions. The public instance methods ToLongDateString(), ToLongTimeString(), ToShortDateString(), ToShortTimeString() all create string representations using the current culture. Using the ToString() method a different culture can be assigned:

```
public string ToString();
public string ToString(IFormatProvider);
public string ToString(string);
public string ToString(string, IFormatProvider);
```

With the string argument of the ToString() method, a predefined format character or a custom format string can be specified for converting the date to a string. The class DateTimeFormatInfo specifies the possible values. With the IFormatProvider argument the culture can be specified. Using an overloaded method without the IFormatProvider argument means that the culture of the current thread is used:

```
DateTime d = new DateTime(2001, 6, 15);

// current culture

System.Console.WriteLine(d.ToLongDateString());

// use IFormatProvider

System.Console.WriteLine(d.ToString("D",
                              new CultureInfo("fr-fr")));

// use culture of thread

CultureInfo ci = Thread.CurrentThread.CurrentCulture;
Console.WriteLine(ci.ToString() + ": " + d.ToString("D"));
ci = new CultureInfo("de-de");
Thread.CurrentThread.CurrentCulture = ci;
Console.WriteLine(ci.ToString() + ": " + d.ToString("D"));
```

The output of our sample program shows ToLongDateString() with the current culture of the thread, a French version where a CultureInfo instance is passed to the ToString() method, and a German version where the CurrentCulture of the thread where the culture is changed to de-de is used:

Resources for Localization

Besides having a different formatting and measurement system depending on the locale, the strings should have different texts; perhaps some pictures should also be replaced depending on the locale. This is where satellite assemblies are used.

Satellite Assemblies

Satellite assemblies are used in applications to support language dependent strings. Satellite assemblies are assemblies that hold only resources and no code. A string table, pictures, videos, and so on can be included. Of course, the AssemblyCulture attribute must be set. A satellite assembly for the de culture must be placed into the de subdirectory of the program. The satellite assembly supporting Austria's version of German is placed into the de-at subdirectory.

de and de-at have many translations in common. There are only a few differences. With the .NET architecture of satellite assemblies, it's not necessary to store all resources in the de-at assembly, just the differences. We just have to create a resource file with the different strings. If the user has a system where the region de-at is configured, and resources cannot be found there, the parent assembly is used; de is the parent assembly for de-at. If a resource can't be found there, then the resources of the neutral assembly are used. The neutral assembly is the assembly where no assembly culture is set. That's the reason why you shouldn't set a culture for the main assembly.

System.Resources Namespace

In the System.Resources namespace we have these classes to deal with resources:

❑   The ResourceManager can be used to get resources for the current culture from satellite assemblies. Using the ResourceManager it's also possible to get a ResourceSet for a particular culture.

❑   A ResourceSet represents the resources for a particular culture. When a ResourceSet instance is created it enumerates over a class implementing the interface IresourceReader, and stores all resources in a Hashtable.

❑   The interface IResourceReader is used from the ResourceSet to enumerate resources. The class ResourceReader implements this interface.

❑   We already used the ResourceWriter class to create a resource file. ResourceWriter implements the interface IResourceWriter.

❑   Additionally there are some classes: ResXResourceSet, ResXResourceReader, and ResXResourceWriter. These files are similar to ResourceSet, ResourceReader, and ResourceWriter; but create a XML-based resource file .resX instead of a binary file . ResXFileRef can be used to make a link to a resource instead of embedding it inside a XML file.

Localization Example using Visual Studio.NET

We are going to create a simple WinForms application to demonstrate localization using Visual Studio.NET. This application doesn't use complex Windows Forms, and doesn't have any real inner functionality because the main feature that is being demonstrated here is localization. In the source code I'm changing the namespace to Wrox.ProCSharp, and the class name to BookOfTheDayForm. The namespace is not only changed in the source file BookOfTheDayForm.cs, but also in the project settings, so that all generated resource files will get this namespace, too. This is done within the Common Properties of Project I Properties.

To show some issues with localization, this program has a picture, some text, a date, and a number. The picture will also be localized so that the French version is different.

This form is created using the Windows Forms Designer:

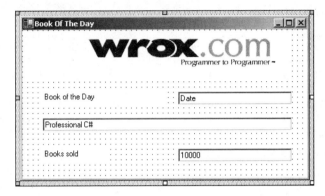

The values for the Name and Text properties I'm using for the Windows Forms elements are listed in this table:

Name	Text
labelBookOfTheDay	Book of the day
labelItemsSold	Books sold
textBoxDate	Date
textBoxTitle	Professional C#
textBoxItemsSold	10000

In addition to this form, we want to display a message box with a greeting where the greeting message is different depending on the current time. This should demonstrate that the localization for dynamically created dialogs must be done differently. In the method WelcomeMessage(), we display a message box using MessageBox.Show(). We call the method WelcomeMessage() in the constructor of the form class BookOfTheDayForm, before the call to InitializeComponent(). Here's the code for the WelcomeMessage method:

```
public void WelcomeMessage()
{
    DateTime time = DateTime.Now;
    string message;
    if (time.Hour <= 12)
    {
        message = "Good Morning";
    }
    else if (time.Hour <= 19)
    {
        message = "Good Afternoon";
    }
```

```
        else
        {
           message = "Good Evening";
        }
        MessageBox.Show(message + " \nThis is a localization sample.");
    }
```

The number and date in the form should be set using formatting options. That can't be done using properties, so we add a new method SetDateAndNumber() to set the values. In a real application these values could be received from a Web Service or a database, but in this example we want to concentrate on localization. Again, we call this method before the call to InitializeComponent(). The date is formatted using the D option (to display the long date name). The number is displayed using the picture number format string ###,###,### where "#" represents a digit and "," is the group separator:

```
public void SetDateAndNumber()
{
   DateTime date = DateTime.Today;
   textBoxDate.Text = date.ToString("D");
   Int32 itemsSold = 327444;
   textBoxItemsSold.Text = itemsSold.ToString("###,###,###");
}
```

A magic feature of the Windows Forms designer is started when we set the Localizable property of the form from false to true. This results in the creation of an XML based resource file for the dialog box that stores all resource strings, properties (including the location of WinForms elements), embedded pictures, and so on. In addition, the implementation of the method InitializeComponent() is changed: an instance of the class System.Resources.ResourceManager is created, and to get to the values and positions of the text fields and pictures, the GetObject() method is used instead of writing the values directly in the code. GetObject() uses the CurrentUICulture property of the current thread for finding the correct resources.

Here is part of InitializeComponent() before the Localizable property is set to true, where all properties of the textBoxTitle are set:

```
private void InitializeComponent()
{
   //...

   this.textBoxDate = new System.Windows.Forms.TextBox();

   //...

   this.textBoxTitle.Location =
               new System.Drawing.Point(32, 136);
   this.textBoxTitle.Name = "textBoxTitle";
   this.textBoxTitle.Size = new System.Drawing.Size(432, 20);
   this.textBoxTitle.TabIndex = 3;
   this.textBoxTitle.Text = "Professional C#";
```

This is the automatically changed code for `InitalizeComponent()` with the `Localizable` property set to `true`:

```csharp
private void InitializeComponent()
{
    System.Resources.ResourceManager resources =
        new System.Resources.ResourceManager(
            typeof(BookOfTheDayForm));

    //...

    this.textBoxDate = new System.Windows.Forms.TextBox();

    //...

    this.textBoxTitle.AccessibleDescription = ((string)
        (resources.GetObject("textBoxTitle.AccessibleDescription")));
    this.textBoxTitle.AccessibleName = ((string)
        (resources.GetObject("textBoxTitle.AccessibleName")));
    this.textBoxTitle.Anchor = ((System.Windows.Forms.AnchorStyles)
        (resources.GetObject("textBoxTitle.Anchor")));
    this.textBoxTitle.AutoSize = ((bool)
        (resources.GetObject("textBoxTitle.AutoSize")));
    this.textBoxTitle.BackgroundImage = ((System.Drawing.Image)
        (resources.GetObject("textBoxTitle.BackgroundImage")));
    this.textBoxTitle.Cursor = ((System.Windows.Forms.Cursor)
        (resources.GetObject("textBoxTitle.Cursor")));
    this.textBoxTitle.Dock = ((System.Windows.Forms.DockStyle)
        (resources.GetObject("textBoxTitle.Dock")));
    this.textBoxTitle.Enabled = ((bool)
        (resources.GetObject("textBoxTitle.Enabled")));
    this.textBoxTitle.Font = ((System.Drawing.Font)
        (resources.GetObject("textBoxTitle.Font")));
    this.textBoxTitle.ImeMode = ((System.Windows.Forms.ImeMode)
        (resources.GetObject("textBoxTitle.ImeMode")));
    this.textBoxTitle.Location = ((System.Drawing.Point)
        (resources.GetObject("textBoxTitle.Location")));
    this.textBoxTitle.MaxLength = ((int)
        (resources.GetObject("textBoxTitle.MaxLength")));
    this.textBoxTitle.Name = "textBoxTitle";
    this.textBoxTitle.PasswordChar = ((char)
        (resources.GetObject("textBoxTitle.PasswordChar")));
    this.textBoxTitle.RightToLeft = ((System.Windows.Forms.RightToLeft)
        (resources.GetObject("textBoxTitle.RightToLeft")));
    this.textBoxTitle.ScrollBars = ((System.Windows.Forms.ScrollBars)
        (resources.GetObject("textBoxTitle.ScrollBars")));
    this.textBoxTitle.Size = ((System.Drawing.Size)
        (resources.GetObject("textBoxTitle.Size")));
    this.textBoxTitle.TabIndex = ((int)
        (resources.GetObject("textBoxTitle.TabIndex")));
    this.textBoxTitle.Text = resources.GetString("textBoxTitle.Text");
    this.textBoxTitle.TextAlign =
        ((System.Windows.Forms.HorizontalAlignment)
        (resources.GetObject("textBoxTitle.TextAlign")));
    this.textBoxTitle.Visible = ((bool)
        (resources.GetObject("textBoxTitle.Visible")));
    this.textBoxTitle.WordWrap = ((bool)
        (resources.GetObject("textBoxTitle.WordWrap")));
```

How does it work – where does the resource manager get the data? At the same time that we set the `Localizable` property to `true`, a resource file, `BookOfTheDay.resX`, was generated. In this file, the scheme of the XML resource can be found first, followed by all elements in the form: `Type`, `Text`, `Location`, `TabIndex`, and so on.

The following example shows that the `Name` of `textBoxTitle` has a value of `textBoxTitle`, the `Type` is `System.WinForms.TextBox`, the `Parent` is `this` which means that the `Location` is of type `System.Drawing.Point` with a value of `32, 136`, and so on.

Why are the locations and sizes also stored in this XML file? With translations, many strings will have completely different sizes and don't any longer fit in to the original positions. When the locations and sizes all are stored inside the resource file all that's needed for localizations is in these files, separated from the C# code:

```
<data name="textBoxTitle.Location" type="System.Drawing.Point,
                                        System.Drawing">
   <value>32, 136</value>
</data>
<data name="textBoxTitle.MaxLength" type="System.Int32, mscorlib">
   <value>32767</value>
</data>
<data name="textBoxTitle.RightToLeft"
         type="System.Windows.Forms.RightToLeft, System.Windows.Forms">
   <value>Inherit</value>
</data>
<data name="textBoxTitle.ScrollBars"
           type="System.Windows.Forms.ScrollBars, System.Windows.Forms">
   <value>None</value>
</data>
<data name="textBoxTitle.Size" type="System.Drawing.Size,
                                  System.Drawing">
   <value>432, 20</value>
</data>
<data name="textBoxTitle.TabIndex" type="System.Int32, mscorlib">
   <value>3</value>
</data>
<data name="textBoxTitle.Text">
   <value>Professional C#</value>
</data>
<data name="textBoxTitle.Visible" type="System.Boolean, mscorlib">
   <value>True</value>
</data>
<data name="textBoxTitle.WordWrap" type="System.Boolean, mscorlib">
   <value>True</value>
</data>
<data name="&gt;&gt;textBoxTitle.Name">
   <value>textBoxTitle</value>
</data>
<data name="&gt;&gt;textBoxTitle.Type">
   <value>System.Windows.Forms.TextBox, System.Windows.Forms</value>
</data>
<data name="&gt;&gt;textBoxTitle.Parent">
   <value>$this</value>
</data>
<data name="&gt;&gt;textBoxTitle.ZOrder">
   <value>2</value>
</data>
```

When changing some of these resource values, it's not necessary to work directly with the XML code. We can change these resources directly in the Visual Studio Designer. Whenever we change the `Language` property of the form and the properties of some form elements, a new resource file is generated for the specified language. We create a German version of the form by setting the `Language` property to German, and a French version by setting the `Language` property to French. For every language we get a resource file with the changed properties: `BookOfTheDayForm.de.resx` and `BookOfTheDayForm.fr.resx`. Here are the changes needed for the German version of the form:

German – Name	Value
`$this.Text` (title of the form)	Buch des Tages
`labelItemsSold.Text`	Bücher verkauft:
`labelBookOfTheDay.Text`	Buch des Tages

These are the changes for the French version. For the French version of the form we also change the picture, because Wrox Press has an office in France with a localized logo:

French – Name	Value
`$this.Text` (title of the form)	Le livre du jour
`labelItemsSold.Text`	Des livres vendus
`labelBookOfTheDay.Text`	Le livre du jour

Compiling the project now creates a **satellite assembly** for each language. Inside the `debug` directory (or `release`, depending on your active configuration), language subdirectories like `de` and `fr` are created. In such a subdirectory you'll find the file `BookOfTheDay.resources.dll`. These files are satellite assemblies that only include our localized resources. Opening this assembly using `ildasm`, we see this manifest with the embedded resources, and a defined locale. This assembly has the locale `de` in the assembly attributes, and so it can be found in the `de` subdirectory. You can also see the name of the resource with `.mresource`; it's prefixed with the namespace name `Wrox.ProfessionalCSharp`, followed by the class name `BookOfTheDayForm` and the language code `de`:

```
MANIFEST
.assembly LocalizationDemo.resources as "LocalizationDemo.resources"
{
  .hash algorithm 0x00008004
  .ver 0:0:0:0
  .locale = (64 00 65 00 00 00 )                          // d.e...
}
.manifestres public Wrox.ProfessionalCSharp.BookOfTheDayForm.de.resources
{
}
.module LocalizationDemo.resources.mcl
// MVID: {D42B702F-3E84-4D84-850D-D73E176901F3}
```

Changing the Culture Programmatically

After translating the resources and building the satellite assemblies we will get the correct translations depending on the configured culture for the user. The welcome message isn't translated at this time. This has been done in a different way, as we'll see shortly.

In addition to the system configuration, it should be possible to send the language code as command line arguments to our application for testing purposes. The `Main()` method and the `BookOfTheDayForm` constructor are changed to support command line arguments. In the `Main()` method we pass the culture string to the `BookOfTheDayForm` constructor. In the constructor we have to change something more: a `CultureInfo` instance is created to pass it to the `CurrentCulture` and `CurrentUICulture` properties of the current thread. Remember that the `CurrentCulture` is used for formatting, while the `CurrentUICulture` is used for loading of resources.

To use the class `CultureInfo` without writing the namespace, we have to open the namespace `System.Globalization`. For the `Thread` class the namespace `System.Threading` must be specified:

```
[STAThread]
public static void Main(string[] args)
{
    string culture = "";
    if (args.Length == 1)
    {
        culture = args[0];
    }
    Application.Run(new BookOfTheDayForm(culture));
}

public BookOfTheDayForm(string culture)
{
    if (culture != "")
    {
        CultureInfo cultureInfo = new CultureInfo(culture);

        // set culture for formatting

        Thread.CurrentThread.CurrentCulture = cultureInfo;

        // set culture for resources
        Thread.CurrentThread.CurrentUICulture = cultureInfo;
    }
    WelcomeMessage();

    //
    // Required for Windows Form Designer support
    //

    InitializeComponent();
    SetDateAndNumber();
}
```

Now it's possible to start the application using command line options. The formatting options and the resources that were generated from the Windows Forms Designer are used. Here are two screenshots where the application is started using the `fr` and the `de` cultures:

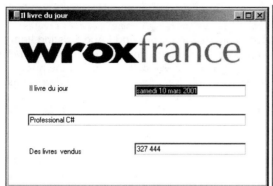

Using Binary Resource Files

There's still a problem with our welcome message box. These strings are hard-coded inside the program. Since these strings are not properties of elements inside the form, the Forms Designer doesn't extract XML resources like it does from the properties inside the `InitializeComponent()` method by changing the `Localizable` property of the form. We have to create resources ourselves.
The English text with a translation into German and French is listed in this table:

English	German	French
Good Morning	Guten Morgen	Bonjour
Good Afternoon	Guten Tag	Bonjour
Good Evening	Guten Abend	Bonsoir
This is a localization sample.	Das ist ein Beispiel mit Lokalisation.	C'est un exemple avec la localisation

To support this I'm creating a simple text file (`Welcome.txt`), representing the default as well as German and French versions:

Welcome.txt:

```
GoodMorning=Good Morning
GoodAfternoon=Good Afternoon
GoodEvening=Good Evening
Description=This is a localization sample.
```

Welcome.de.txt:

```
GoodMorning=Guten Morgen
GoodAfternoon=Guten Tag
GoodEvening=Guten Abend
Descpription=Das ist ein Beispiel mit Lokalisierung.
```

Welcome.fr.txt:

```
GoodMorning=Bonjour
GoodAfternoon=Bonjour
GoodEvening=Bonsoir
Description=C'est un exemple avec la localisation.
```

With `resgen` we can create the binary resource files `Welcome.resources`,
`Welcome.de.resources`, and `Welcome.fr.resources`. `resgen welcome.de.txt` creates
`welcome.de.resources`. These files can be added to the solution using **Add | Add Existing Item** in
Solution Explorer. In all these resource files the property `BuildAction` must be changed from `None` to
`Embedded Resource`, otherwise the satellite assembly won't be created. The name of the resources
can be found using `ildasm`, as usual. The resources from the file `Welcome.de.resources` are named
`Wrox.ProfessionalCSharp.Welcome.de` (the name of the namespace followed by the filename).
Instead of using binary resource files, we can also add XML-based resource files to Visual Studio.NET
projects, as we see next.

Using XML Resource Files

With the `resgen` command, we create XML resources out of the text based resource files:

- ❏ `resgen welcome.txt welcome.resx`
- ❏ `resgen welcome.de.txt welcome.de.resx`
- ❏ `resgen welcome.fr.txt welcome.fr.resx`

These generated XML based resource files are then added to the project using **Add | Add Existing Item**
in the **Solution Explorer**. It's not necessary to change the `BuildAction` for `.resx` files because the
default is already `Embedded Resource`. When building the project, the resources are added to the
satellite assemblies.

Now there are two `.mresource` entries in a satellite assembly – the resource
`Wrox.ProfessionalCSharp.BookOfTheDayForm.de` is the resource that was originally created
from the Windows Forms Designer, and `Wrox.ProfessionalCSharp.Welcome.de` is the resource
from the new `Welcome.de.resx` resource file:

```
/ MANIFEST                                              _|□|×|
.assembly BookOfTheDay.resources
{
    .hash algorithm 0x00008004
    .ver 1:0:483:31652
    .locale = (64 00 65 00 00 00 )
}
.mresource public BookOfTheDay.welcome.de.resources
{
}
.module BookOfTheDay.resources.dll
// MVID: {C73F1B4D-515C-47AF-9A6D-9ABD46A01384}
.subsystem 0x00000003
.file alignment 512
.corflags 0x00000001|
// Image base: 0x030e0000
```

Of course, the source code of the `WelcomeMessage()` must also be changed to use the resources. A
`ResourceManager` instance is created to get the resource named
`Wrox.ProfessionalCSharp.Welcome` from the current assembly. With this resource manager we get
the resources we created previously in the resource files using `GetString()` methods.
For the `ResourceManager` class, we have to declare the use of the `System.Resources` namespace;
the `Assembly` class is in the `System.Reflection` namespace:

```csharp
public void WelcomeMessage()
{
    ResourceManager resource =
                    new ResourceManager("Wrox.ProfessionalCSharp.Welcome",
                    Assembly.GetExecutingAssembly());
    DateTime time = DateTime.Now;
    string message;

    if (time.Hour <= 12)
    {
        message = resource.GetString("GoodMorning");
    }
    else if (time.Hour <= 19)
    {
        message = resource.GetString("GoodAfternoon");
    }
    else
    {
        message = resource.GetString("GoodEvening");
    }
    MessageBox.Show(message + "\n\n" + resource.GetString("Description"));
}
```

When the program is started using English, German, and French we get these message boxes:

Changing Resources for Sub-Languages

For the French and German versions, we've included all resources inside the satellite assemblies. If not all values are changing, that's not necessary. It's possible just to have the changed values in the satellite assembly when the other values are in the parent assembly. For example, for de-at (Austria) we could change the value for the GoodAfternoon resource to Grüß Gott, but no other values should be different. During runtime, when looking for the value of the resource GoodMorning that aren't in the de-at satellite assembly, the parent assembly would be searched. The parent for de-at is de. In cases where the de assembly doesn't have this resource too, the value would be searched in the parent assembly of de. That's the neutral assembly. The neutral assembly doesn't have a culture code.

> **Remember: the culture code of the main assembly should be blank!**

Global Assembly Cache

The Global Assembly Cache is, as the name implies, a cache for assemblies. Most shared assemblies are installed inside this cache, but some private assemblies can also be found here. If a private assembly is compiled to native code using the native image generator, the compiled native code goes into this cache, too! Another way to store assemblies in this cache is when .NET components within HTML pages are downloaded to the client.

Native Image Generator

With the native image generator Ngen.exe we can compile the IL code to native code at installation time. This way the program can start faster because the compilation during runtime is no longer necessary. The ngen utility installs the native image in the **native image cache,** which is part of the global assembly cache.

With ngen myassembly, we can compile the MSIL code to native code, and install it into the native image cache. This should be done from an installation program if we would like to put the assembly in the native image cache.

> **After compiling the assembly to native code you cannot delete the original assembly with the MSIL code because the meta data is still needed, and, if the security changes on the system, the native code will be rebuilt.**

With ngen we can also display all assemblies from the native image cache with the option /show. If we add an assembly name to the /show option we get the information about all installed versions of this assembly:

```
C:\WINNT\System32\cmd.exe

C:\WINNT\Microsoft.NET\Framework\v1.0.2728>ngen /show System.Windows.Forms
NGen - CLR Native Image Generator - Version 1.0.2728.0
Copyright (C) Microsoft Corp. 2001. All rights reserved.
System.Windows.Forms, Version=1.0.2411.0, Culture=neutral, PublicKeyToken=b77a5
561934e089

C:\WINNT\Microsoft.NET\Framework\v1.0.2728>
```

Global Assembly Cache Viewer

The global assembly cache can be displayed using shfusion.dll that is a Windows shell extension to view and manipulate the contents of the cache. A Windows shell extension is a COM DLL that integrates with the Windows explorer. You just have to start the explorer and go to the <windir>/assembly directory.

> *If the shell extension doesn't work on your machine, you can register the COM DLL manually using* regsvr32 shfusion.dll.

> *If you want to create a custom shell extension, Wrox has a great book in this area too: Dino Esposito's* Visual C++ Windows Shell Programming *(ISBN 1861001843).*

The picture below shows the assembly cache viewer:

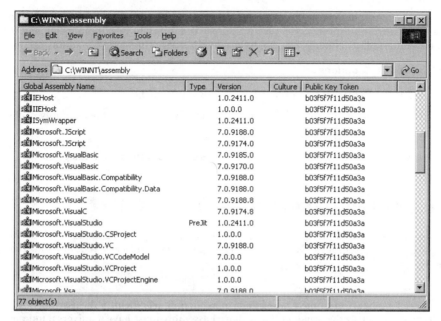

With the Assembly Viewer, the **Global Assembly Name, Type, Version, Culture,** and the **Public Key Token** can be seen. With the type we can see if the assembly was installed using the native image generator. Using the context menu when selecting an assembly, it's possible to delete an assembly, and to view the properties:

The real files and directories behind the assembly cache can be seen using the command line. Inside the c:\winnt\assembly directory there's a GAC, downloaded, and NativeImages_v1.0.2728 directory. downloaded, as the name says, keeps assemblies that are downloaded from a Web server or a shared directory. GAC is the directory for shared assemblies, and in NativeImages_v1.0.2728 we can find the assemblies compiled to native code. If you go deeper in the directory structure you find directories names that are similar to the assembly name, and below that a version directory and the assemblies itself. This makes it possible that different versions of the same assembly can be installed.

Global Assembly Cache Utility (gacutil.exe)

The assembly viewer can be used to view and delete assemblies using the Windows explorer, but it's not possible to use it from scripting code. `gacutil.exe` is a utility to install, uninstall, and list assemblies using the command line. Naturally, it can be used within scripting code for administration purposes.

Some of the `gacutil` options are:

❑   `gacutil /l` lists all assemblies from the assembly cache.

❑   `gacutil /i mydll` installs the shared assembly `mydll` into the assembly cache.

❑   `gacutil /u mydll` uninstalls the assembly `mydll`.

❑   `gacutil /upre mydll` uninstalls the assembly from the native image cache.

Create Shared Assemblies

Assemblies can be isolated for use by a single application – not sharing an assembly is the default. When using private assemblies it's not necessary to pay attention to any requirements that are necessary for sharing.

> A shared assembly must have a **strong name** to uniquely identify the assembly. A strong name solves the problem that a shared assembly must have a universal unique name.

A strong name already exists for these items:

❑   The **name** of the assembly itself.

❑   A **version number**. This makes it possible to use different versions of the same assembly at the same time. Different versions can also work side-by-side, and can be loaded concurrently inside the same process.

❑   A **public key** guarantees that the strong name is unique. It also guarantees that a referenced assembly can't be replaced from a different source.

❑   A **culture**. We already talked about cultures when doing localization. Cultures are useful for private assemblies too.

Let's look at these requirements in more detail.

Shared Assembly Names

The goal of a shared assembly name is that it must be globally unique, and it must be possible to protect the name. At no time may another person create an assembly using the same name.

COM solved only the first problem by using a globally unique identifier (GUID). The second problem, however, still existed as everyone could steal the GUID and create a different object with the same identifier. Both problems are solved with the strong names of .NET assemblies. A strong (shared) name is a simple text name accompanied by a public key and a digital signature. You wouldn't create a new public key with every assembly, but you'd have one in the company, so the key uniquely identifies your company's assemblies.

This cannot be used as a trust key. Assemblies can carry Authenticode signatures to build up a trust. The key for the Authenticode signature can be a different one from the key used for the strong name. You can read more about Authenticode in Chapter 25.

For development purposes a different public key can be used, and later exchanged easily with the real key.

To uniquely identify the assemblies in your companies, a useful namespace hierarchy should be used to name your classes. Here is a simple example showing how to organize namespaces: Wrox Press can use the major namespace `Wrox` for its classes and namespaces. In the hierarchy below the namespace, the namespaces must be organized so that all classes are unique. The classes from the book *Professional C#* can be placed into the namespace `Wrox.ProCSharp`, so that classes created for a different book can be differentiated even if they have the same name; utility classes that are used across different books go into the namespace `Wrox.Utilities`.

A company name is not necessarily unique, so something more must be used to build a strong name. For this the public key is used. Because of the public/private key principle in strong names, no one without access to your private key can destructively create an assembly that could be unintentionally called by the client.

Public Key Cryptography

If you already known about public key cryptography, you can skip this section. There'll be a discussion of .NET security in Chapter 25. For the rest of you, this is a simple introduction to keys. For encryption, we have to differentiate between **symmetric** encryption and **public/private key** encryption.

With a symmetric key, the same key can be used for encryption and decryption, but this is not the case with a public/private key. If something is encrypted using a public key, it can be decrypted using the corresponding private key, but not with the public key. This also works the other way around: if something is encrypted using a private key, it can be decrypted using the corresponding public key, but not the private key.

Public and private keys are always created as a pair. The public key can be made available to everybody, and it can even be put on a web site, but the private key must be safely locked away. Let's look at some examples where these public and private keys are used.

If Sarah sends a mail to Julian, and Sarah wants to make sure that no one else but Julian can read the mail, she uses Julian's public key. The message is encrypted using Julian's public key. Julian opens the mail and can decrypt it using his secretly stored private key. This way guarantees that no one else, other than Julian can read Sarah's mail.

There's one problem left: Julian can't be sure that the mail is from Sarah. Anyone could use Julian's public key to encrypt mails sent to Julian. We can extend this principle. Let's start again with Sarah sending a mail to Julian. Before Sarah encrypts the mail using Julian's public key, she adds her signature and encrypts the signature using her own private key. Then she encrypts the mail using Julian's public key. Therefore, it is guaranteed that no one else but Julian can read the mail. When Julian decrypts the mail, he detects an encrypted signature. The signature can be decrypted using Sarah's public key. For Julian it's no problem to access Sarah's public key, because this key is public. After decrypting the signature, Julian can be sure that Sarah sent the mail.

Next we will look at how this public/private key principle is used with assemblies.

Integrity Using Strong Names

When creating a shared component, a public/private key pair must be used. The compiler writes the public key to the manifest, creates a hash of all files belonging to the assembly, and signs the hash with the private key. The private key is not stored within the assembly. This way it is guaranteed that no one can change your assembly. The signature can be verified with the public key.

During development, the client assembly must reference the shared assembly. The compiler writes the public key of the referenced assembly to the manifest of the client assembly. To reduce storage, it is not the public key that is written to the manifest of the client assembly, but a public key token. The public key token is the last eight bytes of a hash of the public key, and that is unique.

At runtime, during loading of the shared assembly (or at install-time if the client is installed using the native image generator), the hash of the shared component assembly can be verified using the public key stored inside the client assembly. Only the owner of the private key can change the shared component assembly. There is no way a component Math that was created by vendor A, and referenced from a client can be replaced by a component from a hacker. Only the owner of the private key can replace the shared component with a new version. Integrity is guaranteed in so far that the shared assembly is from the expected publisher:

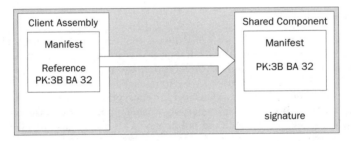

Replacing the Key for delivery

The private key of a company should be safely stored. Most companies don't give access to the private key for all the developers; just a few security people have access to it. That's why the key inside an assembly can be replaced at a later time. When the global assembly attribute AssemblyDelaySign is set to true, no key is stored in the assembly, but enough free space is reserved so that this key can be added later. However, without using a key, we can't test the assembly and install it in the global assembly cache. We can also use a temporary key for testing purposes, and replace this key with the real company key later.

Creating a Shared Assembly

In our example, we will create a shared assembly and a client that uses it.
Before we create the shared assembl,y we start with a simple Visual C# Class Library project. I'm changing the namespace to Wrox.ProCSharp, and the class name to SimpleShared. This class just reads all the lines of a file that's passed inside the constructor in a StringCollection at creation time, and returns in the method GetQuoteOfTheDay() a random string of this collection:

```
using System;
using System.Collections.Specialized;
using System.IO;
```

```
namespace Wrox.ProCSharp
{
   public class SimpleShared
   {
      private StringCollection quotes;
      private Random random;
      public SimpleShared(string filename)
      {
         quotes = new StringCollection();
         Stream stream = File.OpenRead(filename);
         StreamReader streamReader = new StreamReader(stream);
         string quote;
         while ((quote = streamReader.ReadLine()) != null)
         {
            quotes.Add(quote);
         }
         streamReader.Close();
         stream.Close();
         random = new Random();
      }
      public string GetQuoteOfTheDay()
      {
         int index = random.Next(1, quotes.Count);
         return quotes[index];
      }
   }
}
```

Create a Strong Name

To share this component we first need to create a strong name. To create such a name we can use the **strong name utility** (sn):

```
sn -k mykey.snk
```

The strong name utility generates a public/private key pair. Now we can set the `AssemblyKeyFile` attribute in the wizard-generated file `Assemblyinfo.cs`. The attribute must be either set to an absolute path to the key file, or the key file must be addressed relative from the `%ProjectDirectory%\obj\<configuration>` directory, so `../../mykey.snk` references a key in the project directory. When starting a build of the project the key is installed in the **Crypto Service Provider** (**CSP**). If the key is already installed in the CSP, it's possible to use the `AssemblyKeyName` attribute instead.

Here are our changes to `AssemblyInfo.cs`. The attribute `AssemblyKeyFile` is set to the file `mykey.snk`:

```
[assembly: AssemblyDelaySign(false)]
[assembly: AssemblyKeyFile("../../mykey.snk")]
[assembly: AssemblyKeyName("")]
```

After rebuilding, the public key can be found inside the manifest when looking at the assembly using ildasm:

```
 MANIFEST                                                              _□×
.assembly SimpleShared
{
  .custom instance void [mscorlib]System.Reflection.AssemblyKeyNameAttribute
  .custom instance void [mscorlib]System.Reflection.AssemblyKeyFileAttribute

  .custom instance void [mscorlib]System.Reflection.AssemblyDelaySignAttribu
  .custom instance void [mscorlib]System.Reflection.AssemblyTrademarkAttribu
  .custom instance void [mscorlib]System.Reflection.AssemblyCopyrightAttribu
  .custom instance void [mscorlib]System.Reflection.AssemblyProductAttribute
  .custom instance void [mscorlib]System.Reflection.AssemblyCompanyAttribute
  .custom instance void [mscorlib]System.Reflection.AssemblyConfigurationAtt:
  .custom instance void [mscorlib]System.Reflection.AssemblyDescriptionAttri
  .custom instance void [mscorlib]System.Reflection.AssemblyTitleAttribute::
  // --- The following custom attribute is added automatically, do not uncom:
  //   .custom instance void [mscorlib]System.Diagnostics.DebuggableAttribute
  //
  .publickey = (00 24 00 00 04 80 00 00 94 00 00 00 06 02 00 00   // .$.....
                00 24 00 00 52 53 41 31 00 04 00 00 01 00 01 00   // .$..RSA
                01 3D D5 DE A1 CD 91 8A F1 FB 1B 67 71 64 6C 1D   // .=.....
                D6 6F 09 D2 80 0E 60 3F 20 22 7A 7A 40 8A 82 B4   // .o.....
                F2 DB EF 43 14 54 C4 37 C3 62 9B 1C B8 29 99 E6   // ...C.T.
                37 8A 9F 74 D8 5D FA 9A 35 79 67 26 DE 1E 5A 44   // 7..t.].
                99 FD 60 F9 59 A0 82 D6 D6 02 75 58 E2 BB FC 70   // ..`.Y..
                3B 74 1A E4 F6 9E 32 D2 C2 9D 72 2F 56 80 F7 06   // ;t....2
                87 E1 19 2D CD 80 2E 9B 05 CC F2 EA 89 7C B5 8E   // ...-...
                8E D5 94 70 E9 BA 9E 65 8D DE 16 31 6A 68 9A C0 ) // ...p...
  .hash algorithm 0x00008004
  .ver 1:1:484:31355
}
```

Install the Shared Assembly

With a public key in the assembly, it's now possible to install it in the global assembly store using the Global Assembly Cache tool gacutil with the /i option:

```
gacutil /i SimpleShared.dll
```

We can use the Global Assembly Cache Viewer to check the version of the shared assembly, and check if it is successfully installed.

Using the Shared Assembly

To use the shared assembly we will now create a C# Console Application called Client. Instead of adding the new project to the previous solution, you should create a new solution so that the shared assembly doesn't get rebuilt when rebuilding the client. I'm changing the name of the namespace to Wrox.ProCSharp, and the name of the class to Client.

We reference the assembly SimpleShared.dll in the same way we are referencing private assemblies: use the menu Project | Add Reference, or use the context menu in Solution Explorer. Then select the Browse button to find the assembly SimpleShared.dll. Because the SimpleShared assembly is shared, the CopyLocal property of the reference is automatically set to false, so that the shared assembly is not copied to the client directory; the assembly installed into the global assembly store will be used.

Here's the code for the client application:

```
using System;

namespace Wrox.Samples.ProfessionalCSharp.Assemblies.Client
{
    class Client
    {
        public static void Main(string[] args)
        {
            SimpleShared quotes = new SimpleShared(@"C:\Wrox\Quotes.txt");
            for (int i=0; i < 3; i++)
            {
                Console.WriteLine(quotes.GetQuoteOfTheDay());
                Console.WriteLine();
            }
        }
    }
}
```

When viewing the manifest in the client assembly using ILDASM we can see the reference to the shared assembly SimpleShared: .assembly extern SimpleShared. Part of this referenced information is the version number we will talk about next, and the token of the public key.

The token of the public key can also be seen within the shared assembly using the strong name utility: sn -T shows the token of the public key in the assembly, sn -Tp shows the token, and the public key. Pay attention to use the uppercase T!

The result of our program with a sample quotes file could now look like this:

Configuration

COM components used the registry to configure components. Configuration of .NET applications is done using configuration files. With registry configurations, an xcopy-deployment is not possible. The configuration files use XML syntax to specify startup and runtime settings for applications. We can group the configuration into these categories:

- ❑ With **startup settings,** the version of the required runtime can be specified. It's possible that different versions of the runtime could be installed on the same system. With the `<startup>` element, the version of the runtime can be specified.

- ❑ With the **runtime settings** we can specify how garbage collection is performed by the runtime, and how the binding to assemblies works. We can also specify the version policy and the code base with these settings. We will look more detailed into the runtime settings later in this chapter.

- ❑ **Remoting settings** are used to configure applications using .NET Remoting. We will look into these configurations in Chapter 23.

- ❑ **Security settings** are introduced in Chapter 25. Configuration for Crypto and permissions is done here.

These settings can be given in two types of configuration files:

- ❑ **Application Configuration Files** include specific settings for an application, such as binding information to assemblies, configuration for remote objects, and so on. Such a configuration file is placed into the same directory as the executable; it has the same name as the executable with a `.config` appended. ASP.NET configuration files are named `web.config`. The configuration for ASP.NET applications will be done in Chapter 16.

- ❑ **Machine Configuration Files** are used for system-wide configurations. We can also specify assembly binding and remoting configurations here. During a binding process, the machine configuration file is consulted before the application configuration file. The application configuration can override settings from the machine configuration. The application configuration file should be the preferred place for application-specific settings so that the machine configuration file stays smaller and manageable. A machine configuration file is located in `%runtime_install_path%\config\Machine.config`.

How are these configuration files used? How a client finds an assembly (also called **binding**) depends upon whether the assembly is private or shared. Private assemblies must be in the directory of the application or a subdirectory thereof. A process called **probing** is used to find such an assembly. Versioning does not apply to private assemblies, but the culture is an important aspect as we've seen in our localization example.

Shared assemblies can be installed in the global assembly cache, placed in a directory, a network share, or on a web Site. The **codeBase** mechanism is used here. The public key, version, and culture are all important aspects when the binding to a shared assembly. The reference of the required assembly is recorded in the manifest of the client assembly, including the name, the version, and the public key token. All configuration files are checked to apply the correct version policy. The global assembly cache and codebases specified in the configuration files are checked, followed by the application directories, and probing rules are then applied.

Versioning

For private assemblies, versioning is not important because the referenced assemblies are copied with the client. The client uses the assembly it has in its private directories.

This is, however, different for shared assemblies. Let's look at the traditional problems that can occur with sharing. Using shared components, more than one client application can use the same component. The new version can break existing clients when updating a shared component with a newer version. We can't stop shipping new versions because new features are requested and introduced with new versions of existing components. We can try to program carefully to be backwards compatible, but that's not always going to be possible.

A solution to this dilemma could be an architecture that allows installation of different versions of shared components, with clients using the version that they referenced during the build process. This solves a lot of problems, but not all of them. What happens if we detect a bug in a component that's referenced from the client? We would like to update this component and make sure that the client uses the new version instead of the version that was referenced during the build process.

Therefore, depending on the type in the fix of the new version, sometimes we want to use a newer version, and sometimes we want to use the older referenced version. All this is possible with the .NET architecture.

In .NET, the original referenced assembly is used by default. We can redirect the reference to a different version using configuration files. Versioning plays a key role in the binding architecture – how the client gets the right assembly where his components live.

Version Number

Assemblies have a 4-part version number, e.g. `1.0.479.36320`. The parts are:

```
<Major>.<Minor>.<Build>.<Revision>
```

How these numbers are used depends on your application configuration. A good policy would be that you change the major or minor number on incompatible changes with the previous version.

We specify the version number in the assembly with the assembly attribute `AssemblyVersion`. In Visual Studio.NET projects we find this attribute in `AssemblyInfo.cs`:

```
[assembly: AssemblyVersion("1.0.*")]
```

The first two numbers specify the major and minor version, and the "`*`" means that the build and revision numbers are auto-generated. The build number is the number of days since January 1st, 2000, and the revision is the number of seconds since midnight local time. Of course, you can also specify four values, but be sure to change the numbers when rebuilding the assembly.

This version is stored in the `.assembly` section of the manifest.

Referencing the assembly in the client application stores the version of the referenced assembly in the manifest of the client application.

Get the Version Programmatically

To make it possible to check the version of the assembly that is used from our client application, we are adding the method `GetAssemblyFullName()` to the `SimpleShared` class to return the strong name of the assembly. For easy use of the `Assembly` class, we have to add the `System.Reflection` namespace:

```
public string GetAssemblyFullName()
{
    Assembly assembly = Assembly.GetExecutingAssembly();
    return assembly.FullName;
}
```

`FullName` is a property of the `Assembly` class. This property holds the name of the class, the version, the locality, and the public key token as you see here in our output when calling `GetAssemblyFullName()` in our client application.

In the client application, we just add a call to `GetAssemblyFullName()` in the `Main()` method after creating the shared component:

```
static void Main(string[] args)
{
    SimpleShared quotes = new SimpleShared(@"c:\wrox\quotes.txt");
    Console.WriteLine(quotes.GetAssemblyFullName());
```

Be sure to register the new version of the shared assembly `SimpleShared` again in the global assembly cache using `gacutil`. If the referenced version cannot be found, you will get a `System.IO.FileLoadException`, because the binding to the correct assembly failed.

With a successful run, we can see the full name of the referenced assembly:

Using this client program, we can now try different configurations of this shared component.

Application Configuration Files

With a configuration file we can specify that the binding should happen to a different version of a shared assembly. Let's say we create a new version of the shared assembly `SimpleShared` with major and minor versions 1.1. We don't want to rebuild the client – we just want to use the new version of the assembly with the existing client. This is useful in cases where either a bug is fixed with the shared assembly, or we just want to get rid of the old version because the new version is compatible.

With the global assembly cache viewer, we can see that the versions `1.0.479.36320`, `1.0.484.29127`, and `1.1.484.31355` are installed for the `SimpleShared` assembly:

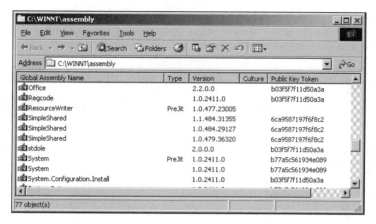

The manifest of the client application says that the client references version `1.0.484.29127` of the assembly `SimpleShared`:

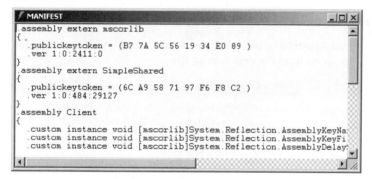

Now we need an application configuration file. It's not necessary to work directly with XML; the .NET Admin tool can create application and machine configuration files. The .NET Admin Tool is a MMC Snap-in that can be started with:

mmc mscorcfg.msc.

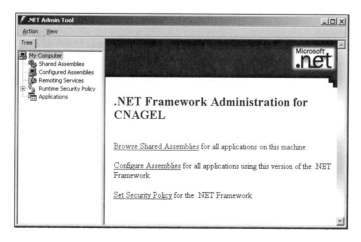

Selecting **Applications** on the left side, and the menu **Action | Add...** we can create an application configuration file for our client application. After adding our client application to the .NET Admin Tool, we can view the assembly dependencies:

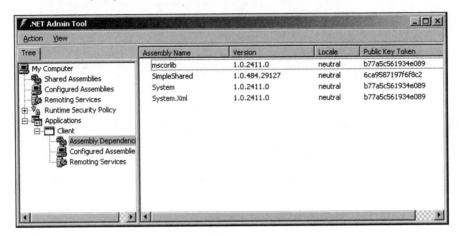

Selecting **Configured Assemblies** and the menu **Action | Add...** we can configure the dependency of the assembly `SimpleShared` from the dependency list:

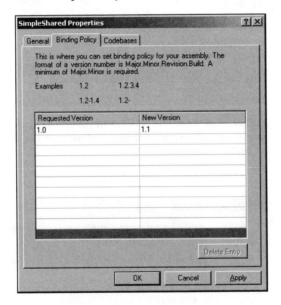

For the **Requested Version**, we specify the version that's referenced in the manifest of the client assembly. **New Version** specifies the new version of the shared assembly. `Major.Minor` is the minimum requirement to specify a version, but `Build.Revision` can be added optionally. We can also define a version range; 1.2-1.4 means that the minor version can be 2, 3, or 4.

Now we can find an application configuration file `Client.exe.config` in the directory of the `Client.exe` application that includes this XML code:

```
<?xml version="1.0"?>
<configuration>
   <runtime>
      <assemblyBinding xmlns="urn:schemas-microsoft-com:asm.v1">
         <dependentAssembly xmlns="">
            <assemblyIdentity name="SimpleShared"
                              publicKeyToken="6ca9587197f6f8c2" />
            <bindingRedirect oldVersion="1.0" newVersion="1.1" />
         </dependentAssembly>
      </assemblyBinding>
   </runtime>
</configuration>
```

With the `<runtime>` element, runtime settings can be configured. The sub-element of `<runtime>` is `<assemblyBinding>`, which in turn has a sub-element `<dependentAssembly>`. `<dependentAssembly>` has a required sub-element `<assemblyIdentity>`. We specify the name of the referenced assembly with `<assemblyIdentity>` . name is the only mandatory attribute for `<assemblyIdentity>`. The optional attributes are `publicKeyToken` and `culture`. The other sub-element of `<dependentAssembly>` that's needed for version redirection is `<bindingRedirect>`. With this element the old and the new version of the dependent assembly is specified.

Starting the client with this configuration file, we get the redirected version 1.1.

Runtime Version

In an application configuration file, it's not only possible to redirect versions of referenced assemblies; we can also define the required version of the runtime. Different .NET runtime versions can be installed on a single machine. We can specify the version that's required for the application in an application configuration file:

```
<?xml version="1.0"?>
<configuration>
   <startup>
      <requiredRuntime version="v1.0.2728" safeMode="true" />
   </startup>
</configuration>
```

The `version` attribute of the `<requiredRuntime>` element specifies the version number of the runtime. The version number must be the same name as the directory of the runtime. The runtime I'm using is in the directory `c:\winnt\Microsoft.NET\Framework\v1.0.2728`, so the version I have to specify is `v1.0.2728`.

Configuring Directories

We've already seen how to redirect referenced assemblies to a different version so that we can locate our assemblies, but there are more options to configure! For example, it's not necessary to install a shared assembly in the global assembly cache. It's also possible that shared assemblies can be found with the help of specific directory settings in configuration files. This feature can be used if you want to make the shared components available on a server. Another possible scenario is if you want to share an assembly between your applications, but you don't want to make it publicly available in the global assembly cache, so you put it into a shared directory instead.

There are two ways to find the correct directory for an assembly: the `codeBase` element in an XML configuration file, or through probing. The `codeBase` configuration is only available for shared assemblies, and probing is done for private and shared assemblies.

<codeBase>

The `<codeBase>` can also be configured using the .NET Admin Tool. Codebases can be configured by selecting the properties of the configured application, `SimpleShared`, inside the **Configured Assemblies** in the **Applications** tree. Similar to the **Binding Policy**, we can configure lists of versions with the `Codebases` tab. In the following screen we have configured that the version 1.0 should be loaded from the Web server http://CNagel/WroxUtils:

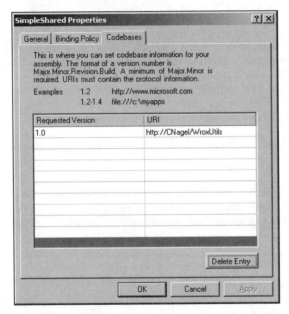

The .NET Admin tool creates this application configuration file:

```xml
<?xml version="1.0"?>
<configuration>
    <runtime>
        <assemblyBinding xmlns="urn:schemas-microsoft-com:asm.v1">
            <dependentAssembly xmlns="">
                <assemblyIdentity name="SimpleShared"
                                  publicKeyToken="6ca9587197f6f8c2" />
                <codeBase version="1.0" href="http://CNagel/WroxUtils" />
            </dependentAssembly>
        </assemblyBinding>
    </runtime>
</configuration>
```

The `<dependentAssembly>` element is the same used previously for the version redirection. The `<codeBase>` element has the attributes `version` and `href`. With `version`, the original referenced version of the assembly must be specified. With `href`, we can define the directory from where the assembly should be loaded. In our example, a path using the HTTP protocol is used. A directory on a local system or a share is specified using `href="file:C:/WroxUtils"`.

When using that assembly loaded from the network a System.Security.Permissions exception occurs. You must configure the required permissions for assemblies loaded from the network. In Chapter 23 we show how to configure security for assemblies.

<probing>

When the <codeBase> is not configured and the assembly is not stored in the global assembly cache, the runtime tries to find an assembly with **probing**. The .NET runtime tries to find an assembly with either a .dll or a .exe file extension in the application directory. If the assembly is not found here, the search continues. You can configure search directories with the <probing> element in the <runtime> section of application configuration files. This XML configuration can also be done easily by selecting the properties of the application with the .NET Admin Tool. We can configure the directories where the probing should occur by using the search path:

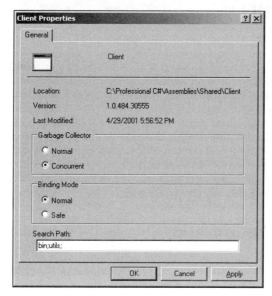

The resultant XML file has these entries:

```xml
<?xml version="1.0"?>
<configuration>
   <runtime>
      <gcConcurrent enabled="enabled" />
      <assemblyBinding xmlns="urn:schemas-microsoft-com:asm.v1">
         <probing privatePath="bin;utils;" xmlns="" />
      </assemblyBinding>
   </runtime>
</configuration>
```

The <probing> element has just a single required attribute: privatePath. This application configuration file tells the runtime that assemblies should be searched for in the base directory of the application, followed by the bin and the util directory. Both directories are subdirectories of the application base directory. It's not possible to reference a private assembly outside the application base directory or a subdirectory thereof. An assembly outside of the application base directory must have a shared name and can be referenced using the <codeBase> element as we've done before.

Deployment

How the assemblies should be packaged and distributed depends on the application type. WinForms applications should be packaged in a Windows Installer Package and distributed using the Windows Installer. Controls inside web pages should be packaged in a `.cab` file or just the DLL. Distribution be via a code download. See Chapter 18 for more information about controls.

ASP.NET applications should be distributed using `xcopy` or `ftp`. In Chapter 16 you will find more information about deployment of ASP.NET applications.

Now we will talk a little more about the deployment of simple DLLs.

Deployment of DLLs

The packaging of DLLs could be useful in different ways. DLLs can be packaged as built; if the assembly exists as just a single DLL, a single DLL can be enough for packaging. It's also possible to package DLLs and all dependent files into a cabinet file. With a cabinet file, it's possible to put more DLLs and configuration files inside a compressed single file. Downloading can be faster and easier this way, but you have to watch that the cabinet file doesn't get too large because of too many assemblies.

Another useful format for packaging is a Windows Installer Package. It is to be expected that a DLL will be installed with other applications that need this DLL. Building a **merge module** would be useful in most cases. A merge module allows the creation of reusable setup modules. A merge module file (`.msm`) is a single package that contains DLLs, registry entries, resource files, and setup logic to install the component. When a Windows Installer Package is built for a Windows application, the merge module can be easily included with this installer package.

Creating a Merge Module

A merge module can be easily created within Visual Studio.NET. Of course, InstallShield or Wise for Windows do have a lot more features than the Merge Module Project in Visual Studio, but the Merge Module Project is included within Visual Studio.NET and will solve a lot of installation issues where the "bigger brothers" are not needed.

When selecting Build | Deploy Solution with the opened class library project, a message box appears saying that a deployment project must be created. Merge Module Project should be selected. A File System View is opened in Visual Studio.NET; the left pane shows directories where the files can be configured for installation. Three folders are created automatically:

- The **Common Files Folder** is used for common files that are shared between applications. With default installations, it points to `C:\Program Files\Common Files`. This folder can be used for shared assemblies that are not installed in the global assembly cache.

- Assemblies put into the **Global Assembly Cache Folder** will be installed in the global assembly cache during installation.

- The **Module Retargetable Folder** is mostly used for merge modules. The merge module will be used from an MSI Package. The MSI package can then define in which directories the files of the retargetable folder should be installed.

We can also add special folders like the program files folder, the users desktop folder, etc.

Selecting the **Module Retargetable Folder** using the context menu **Add | Project Output** we see this dialog:

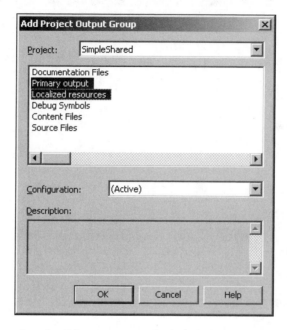

Now it's just necessary to select the **Primary output** which includes DLL and EXE files, and (if available) **Localized resources** that include the satellite assemblies. All the referenced assemblies are automatically included in the merge module. This merge module can now be used within Windows Installer packages for other applications.

Summary

Assemblies are the new installation unit for the .NET platform. Microsoft learned from problems with previous architectures and did a complete redesign to avoid the old problems. Assemblies can be DLL or EXE files that are self-describing, and no additional registry configuration or type library is needed. We differentiate between private and shared assemblies. Private assemblies are easy to build and use, and it is not necessary to think about the version or a public key. Using shared assemblies, we no longer have the problems with the sharing of simple DLLs because the version is a required attribute that's also recorded in the manifest of the client assembly. The default policy always uses the same shared assembly that was used during development time.

If a different policy is needed, we can use application or machine configuration files to override the settings. Satellite assemblies used for localization may not be forgotten. Easy-to-do localization is built into the architecture of assemblies.

11

Data Access with .NET

In this chapter, we'll be discussing how to get at your data in .NET using ADO.NET. Over the course of this chapter, we'll be covering the following areas:

❑ Connections
❑ Executing Commands
❑ Calling Stored Procedures
❑ Data Sets
❑ Using XML and XML Schemas

We'll also present a guide to the naming conventions that preside in the world of ADO.NET and explain some of the reasoning behind them. First, though, let's take a brief tour of ADO.NET and see what's on offer.

ADO.NET Overview

Like most of the .NET framework, ADO.NET is more than just a thin veneer over some existing API. The similarity to ADO is in name only – the classes and method of accessing data are completely different. The one thing that you can use from the "old" world are your OleDB drivers. The main classes in ADO.NET are as follows:

Shared Classes

❑ DataSet – This object may contain a set of DataTables, can include relationships between these tables, and is designed for disconnected use.

- ❑ DataTable – A container of data. A DataTable consists of one or more DataColumns, and when populated will have one or more DataRows containing data.

- ❑ DataRow – A number of values, akin to a row from a database table, or a row from a spreadsheet.

- ❑ DataColumn – Contains the definition of a column, such as the name and data type.

- ❑ DataRelation – A link between two DataTables within a DataSet. Used for foreign key and master/detail relationships.

- ❑ Constraint – Defines a rule for a DataColumn (or set of data columns), such as unique values.

- ❑ DataColumnMapping – Maps the name of a column from the database with the name of a column within a DataTable.

- ❑ DataTableMapping – Map a table name from the database to a DataTable within a DataSet.

Database Specific Classes

- ❑ SqlCommand, OleDbCommand – A wrapper for SQL statements or stored procedure calls.

- ❑ SqlCommandBuilder, OleDbCommandBuilder – A class used to generate SQL commands (such as insert, update and delete statements) from a select clause.

- ❑ SqlConnection, OleDbConnection – The connection to the database. Similar to an ADO Connection.

- ❑ SqlDataAdapter, OleDbDataAdapter – A class used to hold select, insert, update and delete commands, which are then used to populate a DataSet and update the Database.

- ❑ SqlDataReader, OleDbDataReader – A forward only, connected data reader.

- ❑ SqlParameter, OleDbParameter – Defines a parameter to a stored procedure.

- ❑ SqlTransaction, OleDbTransaction – A database transaction, wrapped in an object.

The most important new feature of the ADO.NET classes is that they are designed to work in a disconnected manner. ADO 2.1 introduced the disconnected recordset, but this was often cumbersome to use, as disconnected behavior hadn't been designed in from the start. The ADO.NET classes are different – in all but one case (the Sql/OleDb DataReader) they are designed for use offline from the database.

Namespaces

All of the examples in this chapter access data in one way or another. The following namespaces expose the classes and interfaces used in .NET data access:

- ❑ System.Data – All generic data access classes

- ❑ System.Data.Common – Classes shared (or overridden) by individual data providers

- ❑ System.Data.OleDb – OleDb provider classes

- ❑ System.Data.SqlClient – SqlServer provider classes

- ❑ System.Data.SqlTypes – SqlServer data types

The classes and interfaces within these namespaces will be introduced as the chapter continues. I shall mainly concentrate on the `Sql` classes when connecting to the database, as the Framework SDK samples install an MSDE database (SQL Server). The `OleDb` classes in most cases mimic exactly the `Sql` code.

Connections

In order to access the database, you need to provide some sort of connection arguments, such as the machine that the database is running on, and possibly your login credentials. Anyone who has worked with ADO will be immediately familiar with the .NET connection classes, `OleDbConnection` and `SqlConnection`:

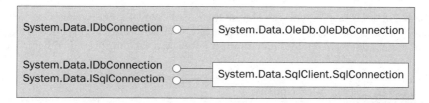

To open a connection, you need to provide some form of connection parameters. The following example shows how to create and open a connection to the `Northwind` database. In the examples within this chapter I use the `Northwind` database, which is installed with the .NET Framework SDK samples:

```
string source = "server=(local)\\NetSDK;" +
                "uid=QSUser;pwd=QSPassword;" +
                "database=Northwind";
SqlConnection  conn = new SqlConnection(source);
conn.Open();

// Do something useful

conn.Close();
```

As you'll notice if you have ever used ADO or OLE DB before, the connection string is very similar to before – indeed, you should be able to cut and paste from your old code if you use the `OleDb` provider.

Once the connection has been opened, you can then issue commands against the data source, and when complete the connection can be closed.

Transactions

Often when there is more than one update to be made to the database, these updates must be performed within the scope of a transaction. A transaction in ADO.NET is begun by calling one of the `BeginTransaction()` methods on the database connection object. These methods return an object that implements the `IDbTransaction` interface, defined within `System.Data`.

The following sequence of code initiates a transaction on a SQL Server connection:

```
string source = "server=(local)\\NetSDK;" +
                "uid=QSUser;pwd=QSPassword;" +
                "database=Northwind";
SqlConnection  conn = new SqlConnection(source);
conn.Open();
SqlTransaction tx = conn . BeginTransaction();

// Execute some commands, then commit the transaction

tx.Commit();
conn.Close();
```

When you begin a transaction, you can choose the isolation level for commands executed within that transaction. The level determines how isolated your transaction is from others occurring on the database server, and certain database engines may support fewer than the four presented here. The options are as follows:

Isolation Level	Description
ReadCommitted	The default for SQL Server. This level ensures that data written by one transaction will only be accessible in a second transaction after the first commits.
ReadUncommitted	This permits your transaction to read data within the database, even data that has not yet been committed by another transaction. As an example, if two users were accessing the same database, and the first inserted some data without concluding their transaction (by means of a Commit or Rollback), then the second user with their isolation level set to ReadUncommitted could read the data.
RepeatableRead	This level, which extends the ReadCommitted level, ensures that if the same statement is issued within the transaction, regardless of other potential updates made to the database, the same data will always be returned. This level does require extra locks to be held on the data, which could adversely affect performance.
	This level guarantees that, for each row in the initial query, no changes can be made to that data. It does however permit "phantom" rows to show up – these are completely new rows that another transaction may have inserted whilst your transaction is running.
Serializable	This is the most "exclusive" transaction level, which in effect serializes access to data within the database. With this isolation level, phantom rows can never show up, so a SQL statement issued within a serializable transaction will always retrieve the same data.
	The performance impact of a serializable transaction should not be underestimated.

The SQL Server default isolation level, ReadCommitted, is a good compromise between data coherence and data availability, as fewer locks are required on data than in RepeatableRead or Serializable modes. However, there are situations where the isolation level should be increased, and so within .NET you can simply begin a transaction with a different level than the default. There are no hard and fast rules as to which levels to pick – that comes with experience.

Commands

I briefly touched on database commands in the previous section on `Connections`. A command is, in it's simplest form, a string of SQL text that is to be issued to the database. A command could also be a stored procedure, or the name of a table that will return all columns and all rows from that table (in other words, a `SELECT *`-style clause).

A command can be constructed by passing the SQL clause as a parameter to the constructor as shown below:

```
string source = "server=(local)\\NetSDK;" +
                "uid=QSUser;pwd=QSPassword;" +
                "database=Northwind";
string select = "SELECT ContactName,CompanyName FROM Customers";
SqlConnection conn = new SqlConnection(source);
conn.Open();
SqlCommand cmd = new SqlCommand(select, conn);
```

The `SqlCommand` and `OleDbCommand` classes have a property called `CommandType`, which is used to define whether the command is a SQL clause, call to a stored procedure, or a full table statement. The following table summarizes each of these types:

CommandType	Example

Text
 	
(default)
	`String select = "SELECT ContactName FROM Customers";`
	
	`SqlCommand cmd = new SqlCommand(select , conn);`

StoredProcedure	`SqlCommand cmd = new SqlCommand("CustOrderHist" ,`
	`                                conn);`
	
	`cmd.CommandType = CommandType.StoredProcedure;`
	
	`cmd.Parameters.Add("@CustomerID" , "QUICK");`

TableDirect	`OleDbCommand cmd =`
	`          new OleDbCommand("Categories" , conn);`
	
	`cmd.CommandType = CommandType.TableDirect;`

When executing a stored procedure, it may be necessary to pass parameters to that procedure. The example above sets the `@CustomerID` parameter directly, although there are other ways of setting the parameter value, which we will look at later in the chapter.

> **Note: The `TableDirect` command type is only valid for the `OleDb` provider – an exception is thrown by the `SqlProvider` if you attempt to use this command type with it.**

Executing Commands

Once you have the command defined, you need to execute it. There are a number of ways to issue the statement, depending on what you expect to be returned (if anything) from that command. The `SqlCommand` and `OleDbCommand` classes provide the following execute methods:

❏   ExecuteNonQuery() – Execute the command but do not return any output

❏   ExecuteReader() – Execute the command and return a typed IDataReader

❏   ExecuteScalar() – Execute the command and return a single value

The SqlCommand class also provides the following two methods:

❏   ExecuteResultset() – "Reserved for future use"

❏   ExecuteXmlReader() – Execute the command and return an XmlReader

The example code in this section can be found in the 01_ExecutingCommands subdirectory of the code download.

ExecuteNonQuery ( )

This method is commonly used for UPDATE, INSERT, or DELETE statements, where the only returned value is the number of records affected. This method can, however, return results if you call a stored procedure that has output parameters:

```
string source = "server=(local)\\NetSDK;" +
                "uid=QSUser;pwd=QSPassword;" +
                "database=Northwind";
string select = "UPDATE CUSTOMER " +
                " SET NAME = 'Bob' " +
                " WHERE NAME = 'Bill'";
SqlConnection  conn = new SqlConnection(source);
conn.Open();
SqlCommand cmd = new SqlCommand(select, conn);
cmd.ExecuteNonQuery();
conn.Close();
```

ExecuteNonQuery() returns the number of rows affected by the command as an int.

ExecuteReader ( )

This method executes the command and returns a SqlDataReader or OleDbDataReader object, depending on the provider in use. The object returned can be used to iterate through the record(s) returned, as shown in the following code:

```
string source = "server=(local)\\NetSDK;" +
                "uid=QSUser;pwd=QSPassword;" +
                "database=Northwind";
string select = "SELECT ContactName,CompanyName FROM Customers";
SqlConnection conn = new SqlConnection(source);
conn.Open();
SqlCommand cmd = new SqlCommand(select, conn);
SqlDataReader reader = cmd.ExecuteReader();
while(reader.Read())
{
    Console.WriteLine("{0,-30} {1}" , reader[0] , reader[1]);
}
```

The DataReader object is discussed later in this chapter.

ExecuteScalar ( )

On many occasions it is necessary to return a single result from a SQL statement, such as the count of records in a given table, or the current date/time on the server. The `ExecuteScalar` method can be used in these situations:

```
string source = "server=(local)\\NetSDK;" +
                "uid=QSUser;pwd=QSPassword;" +
                "database=Northwind";
string select = "SELECT COUNT(*) FROM Customers";
SqlConnection conn = new SqlConnection(source);
conn.Open();
SqlCommand cmd = new SqlCommand(select, conn);
Object o = cmd.ExecuteScalar();
```

The method returns an object, which you can cast into the appropriate type if required.

ExecuteResultSet ( ) (Sql Provider Only)

This method is marked as "Reserved for future use," and if you inadvertently call it, you will be rewarded with a `System.NotSupportedException`.

ExecuteXmlReader ( ) (Sql Provider Only)

As its name implies, this method will execute the command and return an `XmlReader` object to the caller. SQL Server permits a SQL clause to be extended with a `FOR XML` clause. This clause can take one of three options:

❑   FOR XML AUTO

❑   FOR XML RAW

❑   FOR XML EXPLICIT

The SQL Server online books include complete descriptions of these options. For this example I shall use AUTO:

```
string select = "SELECT ContactName,CompanyName " +
                "  FROM Customers FOR XML AUTO";
SqlConnection conn = new SqlConnection(source);
conn.Open();
SqlCommand cmd = new SqlCommand(select , conn);
XmlReader xr = cmd.ExecuteXmlReader();
while(xr.Read() )
{
    Console.WriteLine(xr.ReadOuterXml());
}
conn.Close();
```

Here I include the `FOR XML AUTO` clause in the SQL statement, then call the `ExecuteXmlReader()` method. A screenshot of the output from this code is shown below:

```
C:\WINNT\System32\cmd.exe
*** SqlProvider ***
Use ExecuteXmlReader with a FOR XML AUTO SQL clause

<Customers ContactName="Maria Anders" CompanyName="Alfreds Futterkiste"/>
<Customers ContactName="Antonio Moreno" CompanyName="Antonio Moreno Taquería"/>
<Customers ContactName="Christina Berglund" CompanyName="Berglunds snabbköp"/>
<Customers ContactName="Frédérique Citeaux" CompanyName="Blondesddsl père et fils"/>
<Customers ContactName="Laurence Lebihan" CompanyName="Bon app&apos;"/>
<Customers ContactName="Victoria Ashworth" CompanyName="B&apos;s Beverages"/>
<Customers ContactName="Francisco Chang" CompanyName="Centro comercial Moctezuma"/>
<Customers ContactName="Pedro Afonso" CompanyName="Comércio Mineiro"/>
<Customers ContactName="Sven Ottlieb" CompanyName="Drachenblut Delikatessen"/>
<Customers ContactName="Ann Devon" CompanyName="Eastern Connection"/>
<Customers ContactName="Aria Cruz" CompanyName="Familia Arquibaldo"/>
<Customers ContactName="Martine Rancé" CompanyName="Folies gourmandes"/>
<Customers ContactName="Peter Franken" CompanyName="Frankenversand"/>
<Customers ContactName="Paolo Accorti" CompanyName="Franchi S.p.A."/>
<Customers ContactName="Eduardo Saavedra" CompanyName="Galería del gastrónomo"/>
<Customers ContactName="André Fonseca" CompanyName="Gourmet Lanchonetes"/>
```

Calling Stored Procedures

Calling a stored procedure with a command object is just a matter of defining the name of the stored procedure, adding a parameters definition for each parameter of the procedure, then calling one of the Execute functions presented in the previous section.

In order to make the examples in this section more useful, I have defined a set of stored procedures that can be used to insert, update, and delete records from the Region table in the Northwind example database. I have chosen this table despite its small size, as it can be used to define examples for each of the types of stored procedures you will commonly write.

Calling a Stored Procedure that Returns Nothing

The simplest example of calling a stored procedure is one that returns nothing to the caller. There are two such procedures defined below, one for updating a pre-existing Region record, and the other for deleting a given Region record.

Record Update

Updating a Region record is fairly trivial, as there is only one column that can be modified (assuming primary keys cannot be updated). You can type these examples directly into the SQL query analyzer, or run the StoredProcs.sql file in the 02_StoredProcs subdirectory, which will install each of the stored procedures in this section:

```
CREATE PROCEDURE RegionUpdate(@RegionID INTEGER,
                              @RegionDescription NCHAR(50))AS
    SET NOCOUNT OFF;
    UPDATE Region
        SET RegionDescription = @RegionDescription
        WHERE RegionID = @RegionID;
GO
```

An update command on a more real-world table might need to re-select and return the updated record in its entirety. To run this stored procedure from within .NET code, you need to define an SQL command and execute it:

```
SqlCommand aCommand = new SqlCommand("RegionUpdate" , conn);

aCommand.CommandType = CommandType.StoredProcedure;
aCommand.Parameters.Add(new SqlParameter ("@RegionID" ,
                                          SqlDbType.Int ,
                                          0 ,
                                          "RegionID"));
aCommand.Parameters.Add(new SqlParameter("@RegionDescription" ,
                                          SqlDbType.NChar ,
                                          50 ,
                                          "RegionDescription"));
aCommand.UpdatedRowSource = UpdateRowSource.None;
```

This code creates a new `SqlCommand` object named `RegionDelete`, and defines it as a stored procedure. We then add each parameter in turn, and finally set the expected output from the stored procedure to one of the values in the `UpdateRowSource` enumeration, which is discussed later in this section.

The stored procedure takes two parameters: the unique primary key of the region record being updated, and the new description to be given to this record.

Once the command has been created, it can be executed by issuing the following commands:

```
aCommand.Parameters[0].Value = 999;
aCommand.Parameters[1].Value = "South Western England";
aCommand.ExecuteNonQuery();
```

Here we are setting the value of the parameters, then executing the stored procedure. As the procedure returns nothing, `ExecuteNonQuery()` will suffice.

Command parameters may be set by ordinal as shown above, or set by name.

Record Deletion

The next stored procedure required is one that can be used to delete a region record from the database:

```
CREATE PROCEDURE RegionDelete (@RegionID INTEGER) AS
    SET NOCOUNT OFF;
    DELETE FROM Region
        WHERE RegionID = @RegionID;
GO
```

This procedure only requires the primary key value of the record. The `SqlCommand` to call this stored procedure is as follows:

```
SqlCommand aCommand = new SqlCommand("RegionDelete" , conn);
aCommand.CommandType = CommandType.StoredProcedure;
aCommand.Parameters.Add(new SqlParameter("@RegionID" , SqlDbType.Int , 0 ,
                                         "RegionID"));
aCommand.UpdatedRowSource = UpdateRowSource.None;
```

This command only accepts a single parameter as shown in the following code, which will execute the `RegionDelete` stored procedure:

```
aCommand.Parameters["@RegionID"].Value= 999;
aCommand.ExecuteNonQuery();
```

Calling a Stored Procedure that Returns Output Parameters

Both of the previous examples execute stored procedures that return nothing. If a stored procedure includes output parameters, then these need to be defined within the .NET client so that they can be filled when the procedure returns.

The following example shows how to insert a record into the database, and return the primary key of that record to the caller.

Record Insertion

The region table only consists of a primary key (`RegionID`) and description field (`RegionDescription`). To insert a record, this numeric primary key needs to be generated, then a new row inserted into the database. I have chosen to simplify the primary key generation in this example by creating one within the stored procedure. The method used is exceedingly crude, which is why I have devoted a section to key generation later in the chapter. For now this primitive example will suffice:

```
CREATE PROCEDURE RegionInsert(@RegionDescription NCHAR(50),
                              @RegionID INTEGER OUTPUT)AS
   SET NOCOUNT OFF;
   SELECT @RegionID = MAX(RegionID)+ 1
                   FROM Region;
   INSERT INTO Region(RegionID, RegionDescription)
      VALUES(@RegionID, @RegionDescription);
GO
```

The insert procedure creates a new `Region` record. As the primary key value is generated by the database itself, this value is returned as an output parameter from the procedure. This is sufficient for this simple example, but for a more complex table (especially one with default values), it is more common not to utilize output parameters, and instead select the entire inserted row and return this to the caller. The .NET classes can cope with either scenario.

```
SqlCommand  aCommand = new SqlCommand("RegionInsert" , conn);
aCommand.CommandType = CommandType.StoredProcedure;
aCommand.Parameters.Add(new SqlParameter("@RegionDescription" ,
                                         SqlDbType.NChar ,
                                         50 ,
                                         "RegionDescription"));
aCommand.Parameters.Add(new SqlParameter("@RegionID" ,
                                         SqlDbType.Int,
                                         0 ,
                                         ParameterDirection.Output ,
                                         false ,
                                         0 ,
                                         0 ,
                                         "RegionID" ,
                                         DataRowVersion.Default ,
                                         null));
aCommand.UpdatedRowSource = UpdateRowSource.OutputParameters;
```

Here, the definition of the parameters is much more complex. The second parameter, @RegionID, is defined to include its parameter direction, which in this example is Output. In addition to this flag, we utilize the UpdateRowSource parameter to describe that we expect to return data from this stored procedure via OutputParameters. This flag is mainly used when issuing stored procedure calls from a DataTable (which is covered later in the chapter).

Calling this stored procedure is similar to the previous examples, except in this instance we need to read the output parameter after executing the procedure:

```
aCommand.Parameters["@RegionDescription"].Value = "South West";
aCommand.ExecuteNonQuery();
int newRegionID = (int) aCommand.Parameters["@RegionID"].Value;
```

After executing the command, we read the value of the @RegionID parameter and cast this to an integer.

You may be wondering what to do if the stored procedure you call returns output parameters and a set of rows. In this instance, define the parameters as appropriate, and rather than calling ExecuteNonQuery(), call one of the other methods (such as ExecuteReader()) that will permit you to traverse over any record(s) returned.

Data Readers

A DataReader is the simplest way of selecting some data from a data source, but also the least capable. You cannot directly instantiate a data reader – an instance is returned from a SqlCommand or OleDbCommand object having called the ExecuteReader() method.

The following code demonstrates how to select data from the Customer table in the Northwind database. The example connects to the database, selects a number of records, loops through these selected records and outputs them to the console.

This example utilizes the OLE DB provider as a brief respite from the SQL provider. In most cases the classes have a one-to-one correspondence with their SqlClient cousins, so for instance there is the OleDbConnection object, which is similar to the SqlConnection object used in the previous examples.

To execute commands against an OLE DB data source, the OleDbCommand class is used. The following code shows an example of executing a simple SQL statement and reading the records by returning an OleDbDataReader object.

The code for this example can be found in the 03_DataReader directory.

The using clause below imports the OleDb classes into the namespace:

```
using System;
```

All the data providers currently available are shipped within the same DLL, so it is only necessary to reference the System.Data.dll assembly to import all classes used in this section:

```csharp
using System.Data.OleDb;

public class DataReader
{
    public static void Main(string[] args)
    {
        string source = "Provider=SQLOLEDB;" +
                        "server=(local)\\NetSDK;" +
                        "uid=QSUser;pwd=QSPassword;" +
                        "database=northwind";
        string select = "SELECT ContactName,CompanyName FROM Customers";
        OleDbConnection conn = new OleDbConnection(source);
        conn.Open();
        OleDbCommand cmd = new OleDbCommand(select , conn);
        OleDbDataReader aReader = cmd.ExecuteReader();
        while(aReader.Read())
            Console.WriteLine("'{0}' from {1}" , aReader.GetString(0) ,
                              aReader.GetString(1));
        aReader.Close();
        conn.Close();
    }
}
```

The preceding code includes many familiar aspects of C# covered in other chapters. To compile the example, issue the following command:

csc /t:exe /debug+ DataReader.cs /r:System.Data.dll

The following code creates a new `OleDb.NET` database connection, based on the source connection string:

```csharp
OleDbConnection con = new OleDbConnection(source);
con.Open();
OleDbCommand cmd = new OleDbCommand(select, con);
```

The third line creates a new `OleDbCommand` object, based on a particular select statement, and the database connection to be used when the command is executed. When you have a valid command, you then need to execute it, which returns an initialized `OleDbDataReader`:

```csharp
OleDbDataReader aReader = cmd.ExecuteReader();
```

An `OleDbDataReader` is a forward-only "connected" cursor, in other words, you can only traverse through the records returned in one direction, and the database connection used is kept open until the `DataReader` has been closed.

> **An `OleDbDataReader` keeps the database connection open until explicitly closed.**

The `OleDbDataReader` class cannot be directly instantiated – it is always returned by a call to the `OleDbCommand` class's `ExecuteReader()` method. Once you have an open data reader, there are various ways to access the data contained within the reader.

When the `OleDbDataReader` object is closed (via an explicit call to `Close()`, or the object being garbage collected), the underlying connection may also be closed, depending on which of the `ExecuteReader()` methods is called. If you call `ExecuteReader()` and pass a `CommandBehavior.CloseConnection`, you can force the connection to be closed when the reader is closed. More on this in the section below on SQL Server.

The `OleDbDataReader` class has an indexer that permits access (although not type safe access) to any field using the familiar array style syntax:

```
object o = aReader[0];
object o = aReader["CategoryID"];
```

Assuming that the `CategoryID` field was the first in the select statement used to populate the reader, these two lines are functionally equivalent, although the second is slower than the first.

I wrote a simple test application that performed a million iterations of accessing the same column from an open data reader, just to get some numbers that were big enough to read. I know – you probably don't read the same column a million times in a tight loop, but every (micro) second counts, and you might as well write code that is as close to optimal as possible.

Just for interest, the numeric indexer took on average 0.67 seconds for the million accesses, and the textual one 3.9 seconds. The reason for this difference is that the textual method looks up the column number internally from the schema and then accesses it using its ordinal. If you know this information beforehand you can do a better job of accessing the data.

So should you use the numeric indexer? Maybe, but there is a better way.

In addition to the indexers presented above, the `OleDbDataReader` has a set of type safe methods that can be used to read columns. These are fairly self explanatory, and all begin with `Get`. There are methods to read most types of data, such as `GetInt32`, `GetFloat`, `GetGuid` and so on.

My million iterations using `GetInt32` took 0.57 seconds. The overhead in the numeric indexer is incurred while getting the data type, calling the same code as `GetInt32`, then boxing (and in this instance unboxing) an integer. So, if you know the schema beforehand, and are willing to use cryptic numbers instead of column names, and you can be bothered to use a type safe function for each and every column access, you stand to gain somewhere in the region of a sixfold speed increase over using a textual column name (when selecting those million copies of the same column).

Needless to say, there is a trade-off between maintainability and speed. If you must use numeric indexers, define constants within class scope for each of the columns that you will be accessing.

The code above can be used to select data from any OLE DB database; however, there are a number of SQL Server-specific classes that can be used to improve performance (with the obvious portability trade-off).

The following example is the same as the above, except in this instance I have replaced the OLE DB provider and all references to OLE DB classes with their SQL counterparts. The changes in the code from the previous example have been highlighted. The example is in the `04_DataReaderSql` directory:

```
using System;
using System.Data.SqlClient;

public class DataReaderSql
{
    public static int Main(string[] args)
    {
        string source = "server=(local)\\NetSDK;" +
                        "uid=QSUser;pwd=QSPassword;" +
                        "database=northwind";
        string select = "SELECT ContactName,CompanyName FROM Customers";
        SqlConnection conn = new SqlConnection(source);
        conn.Open();
        SqlCommand cmd = new SqlCommand(select , conn);
        SqlDataReader aReader = cmd.ExecuteReader();
        while(aReader.Read())
            Console.WriteLine("'{0}' from {1}" ,
                              aReader.GetString(0) ,
                              aReader.GetString(1));
        aReader.Close();
        conn.Close();
        return 0;
    }
}
```

Notice the difference? If you're typing this in then do a global replace on OleDb with Sql, change the data source string and recompile. It's that easy!

I ran the same performance tests on the indexers for the SQL provider, and this time the numeric indexers were both exactly the same at 0.23 seconds for the million accesses, and the string-based indexer ran at about 3.12 seconds. You would expect the native SQL provider to be faster than going through OleDb, which it obviously is.

If you are interested in running the code on your own computer to see what performance is like, see the 05_IndexerTestingOleDb and 06_IndexerTestingSql examples included in the code download.

Note that when calling ExecuteReader() on the SqlClient provider, the passed connection is closed automatically when the reader is closed, which is the opposite behavior to the OleDb provider when calling ExecuteReader() with no parameter. This must be a "feature" – I'm writing this code on Build 9188 (April 2001), so hopefully one of these methods will be changed – preferably the SqlClient's. To overcome this particular quirk, call ExecuteReader(CommandBehavior.KeyInfo) and it will no longer close the connection.

Data Sets

The DataSet class has been designed as an offline container of data. It has no notion of database connections. In fact, the data held within a DataSet doesn't necessarily need to have come from a database – it could just as easily be records from a CSV file, or points read from a measuring device.

A data set consists of a set of data tables, each of which will have a set of data columns and data rows. In addition to defining the data, you can also define links between tables within the DataSet. One common scenario would be when defining a parent/child relationship (commonly known as master/detail). One record in a table (say Order) links to many records in another table (say Order_Details). This relationship can be defined and navigated within the DataSet.

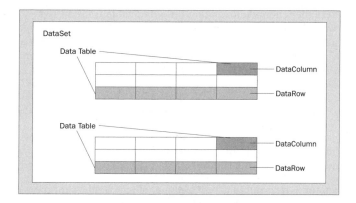

The following sections describe the classes that are used with a `DataSet`.

Data Tables

A data table is very similar to a physical database table – it consists of a set of columns with particular properties, and may contain zero or more rows of data. A data table may also define a primary key, which can be one or more columns, and may also contain constraints on columns. The generic term for this information used throughout the rest of the chapter is **schema**.

There are several ways to define the schema for a particular data table (and indeed the data set as a whole). These are discussed after the data columns and data rows have been introduced.

The following diagram shows some of the objects that are accessible through the data table:

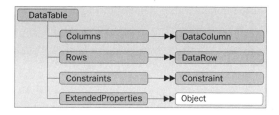

A `DataTable` object (and also a `DataColumn`) can have an arbitrary number of extended properties associated with it. This collection can be populated with any user-defined information pertaining to the object. As an example, a given column might have an input mask used to validate the contents of that column – the canonical example would be the US social security number. Extended properties are especially useful when the data is constructed within a middle tier and returned to the client for some processing. You could for example store validation criteria (such as `min` and `max`) for numeric columns.

When a data table has been populated, either by selecting data from a database, reading data from a file, or manually populating within code, the `Rows` collection will contain this retrieved data.

The `Columns` collection contains `DataColumn` instances that have been added to this table. These define the schema of the data, such as the data type, nullability, default values etc. The `Constraints` collection can be populated with either unique or primary key constraints.

One example of where the schema information for a data table is used is when displaying that data in a `DataGrid` (which we'll discuss at length in the next chapter). The `DataGrid` control uses properties such as the data type of the column to decide on what control to use for that column. A bit field within the database will be displayed as a check box within the `DataGrid`. If a column is defined within the database schema as NOT NULL, then this fact will be stored within the `DataColumn` so that it can be tested when the user attempts to move off a row.

Data Columns

A `DataColumn` object defines properties of a column within the data table such as the data type of that column, whether the column is read only, and various other facts. A column can be created in code, or can be automatically generated by the runtime.

When creating a column, it is useful to give it a name, otherwise the runtime will generate a name for you in the form `Columnn` where n is an incrementing number. This is not too useful.

The data type of the column can be set either by supplying it in the constructor, or by setting the `DataType` property. Once you have loaded data into a data table you cannot alter the type of a column – you'll just receive an `ArgumentException`.

Data columns can be created to hold the following data types:

Boolean	Decimal	Int64	TimeSpan
Byte	Double	Sbyte	UInt16
Char	Int16	Single	UInt32
DateTime	Int32	String	UInt64

Once created, the next thing to do with a `DataColumn` object is to set up other properties, such as the nullability of the column or the default value. The following code fragment shows a few of the more common options to set on a `DataColumn`:

```
DataColumn customerID = new DataColumn("CustomerID" , typeof(int));
customerID.AllowDBNull = false;
customerID.ReadOnly = false;
customerID.AutoIncrement = true;
customerID.AutoIncrementSeed = 1000;
DataColumn name = new DataColumn("Name" , typeof(string));
name.AllowDBNull = false;
name.Unique = true;
```

The following properties can be set on a `DataColumn`:

Property	Description
AllowDbNull	If true, permit the column to be set to DBNull.
AutoIncrement	Defines that this column value is automatically generated as an incrementing number.
AutoIncrementSeed	The initial seed value for an AutoIncrement column.
AutoIncrementStep	Defines the step between automatically generated column values, with a default of one.

Property	Description
Caption	Can be used for displaying the name of the column on screen.
ColumnMapping	Defines how a column is mapped into XML when a DataSet is saved by calling DataSet.WriteXml.
ColumnName	The name of the column. This is auto-generated by the runtime if not set in the constructor.
DataType	The System.Type value of the column.
DefaultValue	Can define a default value for a column.
Expression	A column may be defined as a computed column by utilising this property.

Data Rows

This class makes up the other part of the DataTable class. The columns within a data table are defined in terms of the DataColumn class. The actual data within the table is accessed using the DataRow object. The following example shows how to access rows within a data table. The code for this example is available in the 07_SimpleDatasetSql directory:

```
string source = "server=(local)\\NetSDK;" +
                "uid=QSUser;pwd=QSPassword;" +
                "database=northwind";
string select = "SELECT ContactName,CompanyName FROM Customers";
SqlConnection  conn = new SqlConnection(source);
```

The following code presents the SqlDataAdapter class, which is used to select data into a data set. The SqlDataAdapter will issue the SQL clause, and fill a table in the dataset called Customers with the output of this following query. We'll be discussing the DataAdapter class further in the *Populating a DataSet* section:

```
SqlDataAdapter da = new SqlDataAdapter(select , conn);
DataSet ds = new DataSet();
da.Fill(ds , "Customers");
```

Here you may notice the use of the DataRow indexer to access values from within that row. The value for a given column can be retrieved using one of the several overloaded indexers. These permit you to retrieve a value knowing the column number, name or DataColumn:

```
foreach(DataRow row in ds.Tables["Customers"].Rows)
   Console.WriteLine("'{0}' from {1}" ,
                     row[0] ,
                     row[1]);
```

One of the most appealing aspects to a DataRow is that it is versioned. This permits you to receive various values for a given column. The versions are described in the following table:

DataRowVersion enum	Description
Current	The value existing at present within the column. If no edit has occurred, this will be the same as the original value. If an edit (or edits) have occurred, the value will be the last valid value entered.
Default	The default value (in other words, any default setup for the column).
Original	The value of the column when originally selected from the database. If the DataRow's AcceptChanges method is called, then this value will update to be the current value.
Proposed	When changes are in progress for a column, it is possible to retrieve this changed (i.e. proposed) value. If you call BeginEdit() on the row and make changes, each column will have a proposed value until either EndEdit() or CancelEdit() are called.

The version of a given column could be used in many ways. One example is when updating rows within the database, in which instance it is common to issue an SQL statement such as the following:

```
UPDATE Products
    SET Name = Column.Current
    WHERE ProductID = xxx
        AND Name = Column.Original;
```

Obviously this code would never compile, but it shows one use for original and current values of a column.

To retrieve a versioned value from the DataRow, use one of the indexer methods that accepts a DataRowVersion value as a parameter.

It's not only the column that has state information. The whole row has a state flag called RowState, which can be used to determine what operation is needed on the row when it is persisted back to the database. The RowState flag is set to keep track of all the changes made to the DataTable, such as adding new rows, deleting existing rows, and changing columns within the table. When the data is reconciled with the database, the row state flag is used to determine what SQL operations should occur. These flags are defined by the DataRowState enumeration:

DataRowState enum	Description
Added	The row has been newly added to a DataTable's Rows collection. All rows created on the client are set to this value, and will ultimately issue SQL Insert statements when reconciled with the database.
Deleted	This indicates that the row has been marked as deleted from the DataTable by means of the DataRow.Delete() method. The row still exists within the DataTable, but will not normally be viewable on screen (unless a DataView has been explicitly setup). DataViews will be discussed in the next chapter. Rows marked as deleted in the DataTable will be deleted from the database when reconciled.

DataRowState enum	Description
Detached	A row is in this state immediately after it is created, and can also be returned to this state by calling `DataRow.Remove()`. A detached row is not considered to be part of any data table, and as such no SQL for rows in this state will be issued.
Modified	A row will be modified if any column has been changed.
Unchanged	The row has not been changed since the last call to `AcceptChanges`.

The state of the row depends also on what methods have been called on the row. The `AcceptChanges()` method is generally called after successfully updating the data source (that is, after persisting changes to the database).

The most common way to alter data in a `DataRow` is to use the indexer, however if you have a number of changes to make you also need to consider the `BeginEdit()` and `EndEdit()` methods.

When an alteration is made to a column within a `DataRow`, the `ColumnChanging` event is raised on the row's `DataTable`. This permits you to override the `ProposedValue`, and change it as required. This is one way of performing some data validation on column values. If you call `BeginEdit()` before making changes, the `ColumnChanging` event will not be raised. This permits you to make multiple changes and then call `EndEdit()` to persist these changes. If you wish to revert to the original values, call `CancelEdit()`.

A `DataRow` can be linked in some way to other rows of data. This permits the creation of navigable links between rows, which is common in master/detail scenarios. The `DataRow` contains a `GetChildRows()` method which will return an array of associated rows from another table in the same `DataSet` as the current row. These are discussed in the section on data relationships later in this chapter.

Schema Generation

There are three ways to create the schema for a `DataTable`. These are:

- ❏ Let the runtime do it for you
- ❏ Write code to create the table(s)
- ❏ Use the XML schema generator. This will be shown later in the chapter.

Runtime Schema Generation

The `DataRow` example shown earlier presented the following code for selecting data from a database and populating a `DataSet`:

```
SqlDataAdapter da = new SqlDataAdapter(select , conn);
DataSet ds = new DataSet();
da.Fill(ds , "Customers");
```

This is obviously easy to use, but it has a few drawbacks too. One example is that you have to make do with the column names selected from the database, which may be OK, but in certain instances you might want to rename a physical database column (say `PKID`) to something more user friendly.

You could naturally rename columns within your SQL clause, as in `SELECT PID AS PersonID FROM PersonTable`, but SQL doesn't tend to like column names with spaces, whereas users often do. I would always recommend not renaming columns within SQL, as the only place a column really needs to have a "pretty" name is on screen.

Another potential problem with automated `DataTable`/`DataColumn` generation is that you have no control over the column types that the runtime chooses for your data. It does a fairly good job of deciding the correct data type for you, but as usual there are instances where you need more control. You might for example have defined an enumerated type for a given column, so as to simplify user code written against your class. If you accept the default column types that the runtime generates, the column will likely be an integer with a 32-bit range, as opposed to an `enum` with five options.

Lastly, and probably most problematic, is that when using automated table generation, you have no type safe access to the data within the `DataTable` – you are at the mercy of indexers which return instances of `object` rather than derived data types. If you like sprinkling your code with typecast expressions then skip the following sections.

Hand-Coded Schema

Generating the code to create a `DataTable`, replete with associated `DataColumns` is fairly easy. The examples within this section will access the `Product` table from the `Northwind` database shown below. The code for this section is available in the `08_ManufacturedDataSet` example.

Products			
Column Name	Data Type	Length	Allow Nulls
🔑 ProductID	int	4	
ProductName	nvarchar	40	
SupplierID	int	4	✓
CategoryID	int	4	✓
QuantityPerUnit	nvarchar	20	✓
UnitPrice	money	8	✓
UnitsInStock	smallint	2	✓
UnitsOnOrder	smallint	2	✓
ReorderLevel	smallint	2	✓
Discontinued	bit	1	

The following code manufactures a `DataTable`, which corresponds to the above schema.

```
public static void ManufactureProductDataTable(DataSet ds)
{
    DataTable  products = new DataTable("Products");
    products.Columns.Add(new DataColumn("ProductID",
                                      typeof(int)));
    products.Columns.Add(new DataColumn("ProductName",
                                      typeof(string)));
    products.Columns.Add(new DataColumn("SupplierID",
                                      typeof(int)));
    products.Columns.Add(new DataColumn("CategoryID",
                                      typeof(int)));
    products.Columns.Add(new DataColumn("QuantityPerUnit",
                                      typeof(string)));
    products.Columns.Add(new DataColumn("UnitPrice",
                                      typeof(decimal)));
```

```
       products.Columns.Add(new DataColumn("UnitsInStock",
                                            typeof(short)));
       products.Columns.Add(new DataColumn("UnitsOnOrder",
                                            typeof(short)));
       products.Columns.Add(new DataColumn("ReorderLevel",
                                            typeof(short)));
       products.Columns.Add(new DataColumn("Discontinued",
                                            typeof(bool)));
       ds.Tables.Add(products);
}
```

You can alter the code in the `DataRow` example to utilize this newly generated table definition as follows:

```
string source = "server=localhost;" +
                "integrated security=sspi;" +
                "database=Northwind";
string select = "SELECT * FROM Products";
SqlConnection con = new SqlConnection(source);
SqlDataAdapter cmd = new SqlDataAdapter(select, con);
DataSet ds = new DataSet();
ManufactureProductDataTable(ds);
cmd.Fill(ds, "Products");
foreach(DataRow row in ds.Tables["Products"].Rows)
    Console.WriteLine("'{0}' from {1}", row[0], row[1]);
```

The `ManufactureProductDataTable()` method creates a new `DataTable`, adds each column in turn, and finally appends this to the list of tables within the `DataSet`. The `DataSet` has an indexer which takes the name of the table and returns that `DataTable` to the caller.

The above example is still not really type safe, as I'm using indexers on columns to retrieve the data. What would be better is a class (or set of classes) derived from `DataSet`, `DataTable` and `DataRow`, that defined type safe accessors for tables, rows and columns. You can generate this code yourself – it's not particularly tedious and you end up with truly type safe data access classes.

If you don't like the sound of generating these type safe classes yourself then help is at hand. The .NET framework includes support for using XML schemas to define a `DataSet`, `DataTables` and the other classes that I have touched on in this section. Skip forward to the section on XML schema generation for full details.

Data Relationships

When writing an application, it is often necessary to obtain and cache various tables of information. The `DataSet` is the container for this information. With regular `OleDb` it was necessary to provide a strange SQL dialect to enforce hierarchical data relationships, and the provider itself was not without its own subtle quirks.

The `DataSet` class on the other hand has been designed from the start to accomplish relationships between data tables with aplomb. For the code in this section I decided to hand-generate and populate two tables with data. So, if you haven't got SQL Server or the `NorthWind` database to hand, you can run this example anyway. The code is available in the `09_DataRelationships` directory:

```
DataSet ds = new DataSet("Relationships");
ds.Tables.Add(CreateBuildingTable());
ds.Tables.Add(CreateRoomTable());
ds.Relations.Add("Rooms",
                ds.Tables["Building"].Columns["BuildingID"],
                ds.Tables["Room"].Columns["BuildingID"]);
```

The tables simply contain a primary key and name field, with the rooms table having `BuildingID` as a foreign key.

These tables were kept deliberately simple, as my fingers were wearing out at this point so I didn't want to add too many columns to either one.

I then added some default data to each table. Once that was done, I could then iterate through the `Buildings` and `Rooms` using the code below.

```
foreach(DataRow theBuilding in ds.Tables["Building"].Rows)
{
    DataRow[] children = theBuilding.GetChildRows("Rooms");
    int roomCount = children.Length;

    Console.WriteLine("Building {0} contains {1} room{2}",
                    theBuilding["Name"],
                    roomCount,
                    roomCount > 1 ? "s" : "");

    // Loop through the rooms

    foreach(DataRow theRoom in children)
        Console.WriteLine("Room: {0}", theRoom["Name"]);
}
```

The big difference between the `DataSet` and the older style hierarchical `recordset` is in the way the relationship is presented. In a hierarchical `recordset`, the relationship was presented as a pseudo column within the row. This column itself was a `recordset` that could be iterated through.

```
DataRow[] children = theBuilding.GetChildRows("Rooms");
```

Under ADO.NET, however, a relationship is traversed simply by calling the `GetChildRows()` method. This method has a number of overrides, but the simple example shown above just uses the name of the relationship to traverse between parent and child rows. It returns an array of rows that can be updated as appropriate by using the indexers as shown in earlier examples.

What's more interesting with data relationships is that they can be traversed both ways. Not only can you go from a parent to the child rows, but you can also find a parent row (or rows) from a child record simply by using the `ParentRelations` property on the data table:

```
foreach(DataRow theRoom in ds.Tables["Room"].Rows)
{
    DataRow[] parents = theRoom.GetParentRows("Rooms");

    foreach(DataRow theBuilding in parents)
        Console.WriteLine("Room {0} is contained in building {1}",
                          theRoom["Name"],
                          theBuilding["Name"]);
}
```

There are two methods with various overrides available for retrieving the parent row(s) –
GetParentRows() (which returns an array of zero or more rows), or GetParentRow() (which
retrieves a single parent row given a relationship).

Data Constraints

Changing the data type of columns created on the client is not the only thing a DataTable is good for.
ADO.NET permits you to create a set of constraints on a column (or columns), which are then used to
enforce rules within the data.

The runtime currently supports the following constraint types.

Constraint	Description
ForeignKeyConstraint	Enforce a link between two DataTables within a DataSet
UniqueConstraint	Ensure that a given column is unique within the DataTable

As is common for a table in a relational database, you can supply a primary key, which can be based on
one or more columns from the DataTable.

The code below creates a primary key for the Product table. The example code is available in the
08_ManufactureDataSet example:

```
public static void ManufacturePrimaryKey(DataTable dt)
{
    DataColumn[] pk = new DataColumn[1];
    pk[0] = dt.Columns["ProductID"];
    dt.PrimaryKey = pk;
}
```

As a primary key may contain several columns, it is typed as an array of DataColumns. A table's
primary key can be set to those columns simply by assigning an array of columns to the property.

A primary key on a table is just one form of constraint. When a primary key is added to a DataTable, the
runtime also generates a unique constraint over the key column(s). This is because there isn't actually a
constraint type of PrimaryKey – a primary key is simply a unique constraint over one or more
columns.

To check the constraints for a table, you can iterate through the `ConstraintsCollection`. For the auto-generated constraint produced by the above code, the name of the constraint is `Constraint1`. That's less than useful, so to avoid this problem it is always best to create the constraint in code first, then define which column(s) make up the primary key.

As a long time database programmer, I find named constraints much simpler to understand, as most databases produce a cryptic name for constraints, rather than something simple and legible. The code below names the constraint before creating the primary key:

```
DataColumn[] pk = new DataColumn[1];
pk[0] = dt.Columns["ProductID"];
dt.Constraints.Add(new UniqueConstraint("PK_Products", pk[0]));
dt.PrimaryKey = pk;
```

Unique constraints can be applied to as many columns as you wish.

In addition to unique constraints, a `DataTable` may also contain `Foreign Key` constraints. These are primarily used to enforce master/detail relationships, but can also be used to replicate columns between tables if you set the constraint up correctly. A master/detail relationship is one where there is commonly one parent record (say an order) and many child records (order lines), linked by the primary key of the parent record.

A foreign key constraint can only operate over tables within the same `DataSet`, so the following example utilizes the `Categories` table from the `Northwind` database, and assigns a constraint between it and the `Products` table.

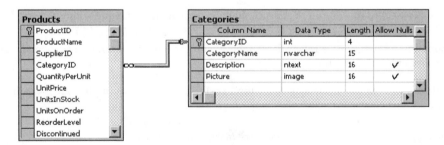

The first step is to generate a new data table for the category table. The `08_ManufactureDataSet` example shown above includes this code:

```
DataTable categories = new DataTable("Categories");
categories.Columns.Add(new DataColumn("CategoryID", typeof(int)));
categories.Columns.Add(new DataColumn("CategoryName", typeof(string)));
categories.Columns.Add(new DataColumn("Description", typeof(string)));
categories.Constraints.Add(new UniqueConstraint("PK_Categories",
                          categories.Columns["CategoryID"]));
categories.PrimaryKey = new DataColumn[1]
                       {categories.Columns["CategoryID"]};
```

The last line of the above code creates the primary key for the categories table. The primary key in this instance is a single column, however it is possible to generate a key over multiple columns using the array syntax shown.

Then I need to create the constraint between the two tables:

```
DataColumn parent = ds.Tables["Categories"].Columns["CategoryID"];
DataColumn child = ds.Tables["Products"].Columns["CategoryID"];
ForeignKeyConstraint fk =
    new ForeignKeyConstraint("FK_Product_CategoryID", parent, child);
fk.UpdateRule = Rule.Cascade;
fk.DeleteRule = Rule.SetNull;
ds.Tables["Products"].Constraints.Add(fk);
```

This constraint applies to the link between `Categories.CategoryID` and `Products.CategoryID`. There are four different constructors for `ForeignKeyConstraint`, but again I would suggest using those that permit you to name the constraint.

In addition to defining the fact that there is some type of constraint between parent and child tables, you can define what should happen when a column in the constraint is updated.

The above example sets the update rule and the delete rule. These rules are used when an action occurs to a column (or row) within the parent table, and the rule is used to decide what should happen to row(s) within the child table that could be affected.

The most obvious example is what occurs to child records when the parent record is deleted. There are four different rules that can be applied.

❑ `Cascade` – If the parent key was updated then copy the new key value to all child records. If the parent record was deleted, delete the child records also. This is the default option

❑ `None` – No action whatsoever. This option will leave orphaned rows within the child data table.

❑ `SetDefault` – Each child record affected has the foreign key column(s) set to their default value, if one has been defined.

❑ `SetNull` – All child rows have the key column(s) set to `DBNull`. (Following on from the naming convention that Microsoft uses, this should really be `SetDBNull`, but hey, who's checking).

> **Constraints are only enforced within a `DataSet` if the `EnforceConstraints` property is `true`.**

I have covered the main classes that make up the constituent parts of the `DataSet`, and shown how to manually generate each of these classes in code. There is another way to define `DataTables`, `DataRows`, `DataColumns`, `DataRelations` and `Constraints` – the use of XML schema file(s) and the XSD tool that now ships with .NET. The following section describes how to set up a simple schema and generate type safe classes to access your data.

XML Schema

XML is firmly entrenched into ADO.NET – indeed, the remoting format for passing data between objects is now XML. With the .NET runtime, it is now possible to describe a `DataTable` within an XML schema definition file (XSD). What's more, you can define an entire `DataSet`, with a number of `DataTables`, a set of relationships between these tables, and include various other details to fully describe the data.

When you have defined an XSD file, there is a new tool in the runtime which will convert this schema to the corresponding data access class(es), such as the type safe product `DataTable` class shown above. In this section we'll start with a simple XSD file that describes the same information as the products sample previously shown, and then extend this to include some extra functionality:

```xml
<?xml version="1.0" encoding="utf-8"?>
<xsd:schema
    id="Products"
    targetNamespace="http://tempuri.org/product.xsd"
    xmlns="http://tempuri.org/XMLSchema1.xsd"
    xmlns:xsd="http://www.w3.org/2001/XMLSchema" >
    <xsd:element name="Product">
        <xsd:complexType>
            <xsd:sequence>
                <xsd:element name="ProductID" type="xsd:int" />
                <xsd:element name="ProductName" type="xsd:string" />
                <xsd:element name="SupplierID" type="xsd:int" />
                <xsd:element name="CategoryID" type="xsd:int" />
                <xsd:element name="QuantityPerUnit" type="xsd:string" />
                <xsd:element name="UnitPrice" type="xsd:number" />
                <xsd:element name="UnitsInStock" type="xsd:short" />
                <xsd:element name="UnitsOnOrder" type="xsd:short" />
                <xsd:element name="ReorderLevel" type="xsd:short" />
                <xsd:element name="Discontinued" type="xsd:boolean" />
            </xsd:sequence>
        </xsd:complexType>
    </xsd:element>
</xsd:schema>
```

We won't give a full account of the options within this file, as that's the subject of another book. In basic terms, this file defines a schema with the `id` attribute set to `Products`. A complex type called `Product` is defined, which contains a number of elements, one for each of the fields within the products table.

These items map onto data classes as follows. The `Products` schema maps to a class derived from `DataSet`. The `Product` complex type maps to a class derived from `DataTable`. Each sub-element maps to a class derived from `DataColumn`. The collection of all columns maps onto a class derived from `DataRow`.

Thankfully there is a tool within the .NET framework that will produce all of the code for these classes given only the input XSD file. Because it's sole job in life is to perform various functions on XSD files, the tool itself is `XSD.EXE`.

Generating Code with XSD

Assuming you save the above file as `Product.xsd`, you would convert the file into code by issuing the following command in a command prompt:

There are various switches that can be used with XSD to alter the output generated. Some of the more commonly used are shown in the table below.

Switch	Description
/dataset (/d)	Generate classes derived from DataSet, DataTable and DataRow.
/language:<language>	Permits you to choose which language the output file will be written in. C# is the default, but you can choose from VB for a Visual Basic file or JS for JavaScript output.
/namespace:<namespace>	Define the namespace that the generated code should reside within. The default is no namespace.

An abridged version of the output from XSD for the products schema is shown below. I've removed some of the less necessary code to concentrate on the most important aspects, and done some reformatting so that it will fit within the confines of a couple of pages. To see the complete output, run XSD on the products schema (or one of your own making) and take a look at the .cs file generated. The example includes the entire source code plus the Products.XSD file, and can be found in the 10_XSD_DataSet directory:

```
//---------------------------------------------------------------------------
// <autogenerated>
//     This code was generated by a tool.
//     Runtime Version: 1.0.2728.2
//
//     Changes to this file may cause incorrect behavior and will be lost if
//     the code is regenerated.
// </autogenerated>
//---------------------------------------------------------------------------

using System;
using System.Data;
using System.Runtime.Serialization;

public class Products : System.Data.DataSet
{
    private ProductDataTable tableProduct;

    public Products()
    {
        this.InitClass();
    }
    public ProductDataTable Product
    {
        get { return this.tableProduct; }
    }
    private void InitClass()
    {
        this.DataSetName = "Products";
        this.Namespace = "http://tempuri.org/product.xsd";
        this.tableProduct = new ProductDataTable();
        this.Tables.Add(this.tableProduct);
    }
/*   public class ProductDataTable : DataTable,
                                  System.Collections.IEnumerable
    public class ProductRow : DataRow */
```

You'll notice I have taken some liberties with this source code, as I have actually split it into three sections. The emboldened and commented out `ProductDataTable` and `ProductRow` definitions show are the positions of two nested classes, which we're going to implement next. We'll look at the code for these after a brief explanation of the `DataSet` derived class.

The `Products` constructor calls a private method, `InitClass`, which constructs an instance of the `DataTable` derived class `ProductDataTable`, and adds the table to the `Tables` collection of the `DataSet`. The product data table can be accessed by the following code:

```
DataSet ds = new Products();
DataTable products = ds.Tables["Products"];
```

Or, more simply by using the property `Product`, available on the derived data set object:

```
DataTable products = ds.Product;
```

As the `Product` property is strongly typed, you could naturally use `ProductDataTable` rather than the `DataTable` reference I showed above.

The `ProductDataTable` class includes far more code:

```
public delegate void ProductRowChangeEventHandler(object sender,
                       ProductRowChangeEvent e);
public class ProductDataTable : DataTable, System.Collections.IEnumerable
{
    private DataColumn columnProductID;

    // Other private DataColumns removed for clarity

    private DataColumn columnProductName;
    private DataColumn columnSupplierID;
    private DataColumn columnCategoryID;
    private DataColumn columnQuantityPerUnit;
    private DataColumn columnUnitPrice;
    private DataColumn columnUnitsInStock;
    private DataColumn columnUnitsOnOrder;
    private DataColumn columnReorderLevel;
    private DataColumn columnDiscontinued;
    internal ProductDataTable() : base("Product")
    {
        this.InitClass();
    }
    public int Count
    {
        get
        {
            return this.Rows.Count;
        }
    }
    internal DataColumn ProductIDColumn
    {
        get
        {
            return this.columnProductID;
        }
    }
}
```

```
    // Other row accessors removed for clarity
    // Other internal field accessors deleted for clarity

    internal DataColumn ProductNameColumn
    {
        get
        {
            return this.columnProductName;
        }
    }
    internal DataColumn SupplierIDColumn
    {
        get
        {
            return this.columnSupplierID;
        }
    }
    internal DataColumn CategoryIDColumn
    {
        get
        {
            return this.columnCategoryID;
        }
    }
    internal DataColumn QuantityPerUnitColumn
    {
        get
        {
            return this.columnQuantityPerUnit;
        }
    }
    internal DataColumn UnitPriceColumn
    {
        get
        {
            return this.columnUnitPrice;
        }
    }
    internal DataColumn UnitsInStockColumn
    {
        get
        {
            return this.columnUnitsInStock;
        }
    }
    internal DataColumn UnitsOnOrderColumn
    {
        get
        {
            return this.columnUnitsOnOrder;
        }
    }
    internal DataColumn ReorderLevelColumn
    {
        get
        {
            return this.columnReorderLevel;
        }
    }
    internal DataColumn DiscontinuedColumn
    {
```

```
       get
       {
          return this.columnDiscontinued;
       }
    }
    public ProductRow this[int index]
    {
       get
       {
          return ((ProductRow)(this.Rows[index]));
       }
    }
    public event ProductRowChangeEventHandler ProductRowChanged;
    public event ProductRowChangeEventHandler ProductRowChanging;
    public event ProductRowChangeEventHandler ProductRowDeleted;
    public event ProductRowChangeEventHandler ProductRowDeleting;
    public void AddProductRow(ProductRow row)
    {
       this.Rows.Add(row);
    }
    public ProductRow AddProductRow(int ProductID, string ProductName,
                                    int SupplierID, int CategoryID,
                                    string QuantityPerUnit,
                                    System.Decimal UnitPrice,
                                    short UnitsInStock,
                                    short UnitsOnOrder,
                                    short ReorderLevel,
                                    bool Discontinued )
    {
       ProductRow rowProductRow = ((ProductRow)(this.NewRow()));
       rowProductRow.ItemArray = new Object[]
       {
          ProductID, ProductName, SupplierID, CategoryID,
          QuantityPerUnit, UnitPrice, UnitsInStock, UnitsOnOrder,
          ReorderLevel, Discontinued};
       this.Rows.Add(rowProductRow);
       return rowProductRow;
    }
    public System.Collections.IEnumerator GetEnumerator()
    {
       return this.Rows.GetEnumerator();
    }
    private void InitClass()
    {
       this.columnProductID = new DataColumn("ProductID" ,
                                  typeof(int), "",
                                  System.Data.MappingType.Element);
       this.columnProductID.AllowDBNull = false;
       this.Columns.Add(this.columnProductID);

       // Other columns removed for clarity

       this.columnProductName = new DataColumn("ProductName",
                   typeof(string), "", System.Data.MappingType.Element);
       this.columnProductName.AllowDBNull = false;
       this.Columns.Add(this.columnProductName);
       this.columnSupplierID = new DataColumn("SupplierID", typeof(int),
                   "", System.Data.MappingType.Element);
       this.columnSupplierID.AllowDBNull = false;
       this.Columns.Add(this.columnSupplierID);
       this.columnCategoryID = new DataColumn("CategoryID", typeof(int),
                   "", System.Data.MappingType.Element);
```

```
        this.columnCategoryID.AllowDBNull = false;
        this.Columns.Add(this.columnCategoryID);
        this.columnQuantityPerUnit = new DataColumn("QuantityPerUnit",
                  typeof(string), "", System.Data.MappingType.Element);
        this.columnQuantityPerUnit.AllowDBNull = false;
        this.Columns.Add(this.columnQuantityPerUnit);
        this.columnUnitPrice = new DataColumn("UnitPrice",
            typeof(System.Decimal), "", System.Data.MappingType.Element);
        this.columnUnitPrice.AllowDBNull = false;
        this.Columns.Add(this.columnUnitPrice);
        this.columnUnitsInStock = new DataColumn("UnitsInStock",
            typeof(short), "", System.Data.MappingType.Element);
        this.columnUnitsInStock.AllowDBNull = false;
        this.Columns.Add(this.columnUnitsInStock);
        this.columnUnitsOnOrder = new DataColumn("UnitsOnOrder",
            typeof(short), "", System.Data.MappingType.Element);
        this.columnUnitsOnOrder.AllowDBNull = false;
        this.Columns.Add(this.columnUnitsOnOrder);
        this.columnReorderLevel = new DataColumn("ReorderLevel",
            typeof(short), "", System.Data.MappingType.Element);
        this.columnReorderLevel.AllowDBNull = false;
        this.Columns.Add(this.columnReorderLevel);
        this.columnDiscontinued = new DataColumn("Discontinued",
            typeof(bool), "", System.Data.MappingType.Element);
        this.columnDiscontinued.AllowDBNull = false;
        this.Columns.Add(this.columnDiscontinued);
    }
    public ProductRow NewProductRow()
    {
        return((ProductRow)(this.NewRow()));
    }
    protected override DataRow NewRowFromBuilder(DataRowBuilder builder)
    {
        return new ProductRow(builder);
    }
    protected override System.Type GetRowType()
    {
        return typeof(ProductRow);
    }
    protected override void OnRowChanged(DataRowChangeEventArgs e)
    {
        base.OnRowChanged(e);
        if ((this.ProductRowChanged != null))
        {
            this.ProductRowChanged(this, new
                ProductRowChangeEvent(((ProductRow)(e.Row)), e.Action));
        }
    }
    protected override void OnRowChanging(DataRowChangeEventArgs e)
    {
        base.OnRowChanging(e);
        if ((this.ProductRowChanging != null))
        {
            this.ProductRowChanging(this, new
                ProductRowChangeEvent(((ProductRow)(e.Row)), e.Action));
        }
    }
    protected override void OnRowDeleted(DataRowChangeEventArgs e)
    {
        base.OnRowDeleted(e);
```

```
              if ((this.ProductRowDeleted != null))
              {
                  this.ProductRowDeleted(this, new
                      ProductRowChangeEvent(((ProductRow)(e.Row)), e.Action));
              }
          }
          protected override void OnRowDeleting(DataRowChangeEventArgs e)
          {
              base.OnRowDeleting(e);
              if ((this.ProductRowDeleting != null))
              {
                  this.ProductRowDeleting(this, new
                      ProductRowChangeEvent(((ProductRow)(e.Row)), e.Action));
              }
          }
          public void RemoveProductRow(ProductRow row)
          {
              this.Rows.Remove(row);
          }
      }
```

The `ProductDataTable` class, derived from `DataTable` and including the `IEnumerable` interface, defines a private `DataColumn` instance for each of the columns within the table. These are initialized again from the constructor by calling the private `InitClass` member. Each column is given an internal accessor, which the `DataRow` class described later uses.

Adding rows to the table is taken care of by the overloaded (and significantly different, except unfortunately by name) `AddProductRow()` methods. One takes an already constructed `DataRow` and returns a void. The latter takes a set of values, one for each of the columns in the `DataTable`, constructs a new row, sets the values within this new row, adds the row to the `DataTable` and returns the row to the caller. Such widely different functions shouldn't really have the same name, in my opinion.

Just like the `InitClass` member in the `DataSet` derived class, which added the table into the `DataSet`, the `InitClass` member in `ProductDataTable` adds in columns to the `DataTable`. Each columns properties are set as appropriate, and the column is then appended to the columns collection. We'll describe the options for a `DataColumn` later in the chapter.

The last method I want to show, `NewRowFromBuilder`, is called internally from the `DataTable`'s `NewRow()` method. Here it creates a new strongly typed row. The `DataRowBuilder` instance is created by the `DataTable`, and its members are only accessible within the `System.Data` assembly.

The last class to discuss is the `ProductRow` class, derived from `DataRow`:

```
public class ProductRow : DataRow
{
    private ProductDataTable tableProduct;
    internal ProductRow(DataRowBuilder rb) : base(rb)
    {
        this.tableProduct = ((ProductDataTable)(this.Table));
    }
    public int ProductID
    {
```

```csharp
    get
    {
        return ((int)(this[this.tableProduct.ProductIDColumn]));
    }
    set
    {
        this[this.tableProduct.ProductIDColumn] = value;
    }
}

// Other column properties removed for clarity

public string ProductName
{
    get
    {
        return ((string)(this[this.tableProduct.ProductNameColumn]));
    }
    set
    {
        this[this.tableProduct.ProductNameColumn] = value;
    }
}
public int SupplierID
{
    get
    {
        return ((int)(this[this.tableProduct.SupplierIDColumn]));
    }
    set
    {
        this[this.tableProduct.SupplierIDColumn] = value;
    }
}
public int CategoryID
{
    get
    {
        return ((int)(this[this.tableProduct.CategoryIDColumn]));
    }
    set
    {
        this[this.tableProduct.CategoryIDColumn] = value;
    }
}
public string QuantityPerUnit
{
    get
    {
        return((string)(this[this.tableProduct.QuantityPerUnitColumn]));
    }
    set
    {
        this[this.tableProduct.QuantityPerUnitColumn] = value;
    }
}
public System.Decimal UnitPrice
{
    get
    {
        return((System.Decimal)
            (this[this.tableProduct.UnitPriceColumn]));
    }
    set
```

```
            {
                this[this.tableProduct.UnitPriceColumn] = value;
            }
        }
        public short UnitsInStock
        {
            get
            {
                return ((short)(this[this.tableProduct.UnitsInStockColumn]));
            }
            set
            {
                this[this.tableProduct.UnitsInStockColumn] = value;
            }
        }
        public short UnitsOnOrder
        {
            get
            {
                return ((short)(this[this.tableProduct.UnitsOnOrderColumn]));
            }
            set
            {
                this[this.tableProduct.UnitsOnOrderColumn] = value;
            }
        }
        public short ReorderLevel
        {
            get
            {
                return ((short)(this[this.tableProduct.ReorderLevelColumn]));
            }
            set
            {
                this[this.tableProduct.ReorderLevelColumn] = value;
            }
        }
        public bool Discontinued
        {
            get
            {
                return ((bool)(this[this.tableProduct.DiscontinuedColumn]));
            }
            set
            {
                this[this.tableProduct.DiscontinuedColumn] = value;
            }
        }
    }
    public class ProductRowChangeEvent : EventArgs
    {
        private ProductRow eventRow;
        private System.Data.DataRowAction eventAction;
        public ProductRowChangeEvent(ProductRow row, DataRowAction action)
        {
            this.eventRow = row;
            this.eventAction = action;
        }
        public ProductRow Row
        {
```

```
            get
            {
                return this.eventRow;
            }
        }
        public DataRowAction Action
        {
            get
            {
                return this.eventAction;
            }
        }
    }
}
```

Now that the source code for these data access classes has been generated by XSD.EXE, I can incorporate the classes into code. The following code utilizes these classes to retrieve data from the products table and display that data to the console:

```
using System;
using System.Data;
using System.Data.SqlClient;

public class XSD_DataSet
{
    public static void Main()
    {
        string source = "server=(local)\\NetSDK;" +
                        "uid=QSUser;pwd=QSPassword;" +
                        "database=northwind";
        string select = "SELECT * FROM Products";
        SqlConnection conn = new SqlConnection(source);
        SqlDataAdapter da = new SqlDataAdapter(select , conn);
        Products ds = new Products();
        da.Fill(ds , "Product");
        foreach(Products.ProductRow row in ds.Product )
        Console.WriteLine("'{0}' from {1}" ,
                        row.ProductID ,
                        row.ProductName);
    }
}
```

The main areas of interest are highlighted. The output of the XSD file contains a class derived from DataSet (Products), which is created and then filled by the use of the data adapter. The foreach statement utilizes the strongly typed ProductRow and also the Product property, which returns the product data table.

To compile this example, issue the following two commands:

xsd product.xsd /d

and:

csc /t:exe /debug+ /r:System.dll /r:System.Data.dll /recurse:*.cs

The first generates the .cs file from the product XSD, and then the csc command utilizes the /recurse:*.cs parameter to go through all files with the extension .cs and add these to the resulting assembly.

577

Populating a Data Set

Once you have fully defined the schema of your data set, replete with `DataTables`, `DataColumns`, constraints, and whatever else was necessary, you need to be able to populate the `DataSet` with some information. There are two main ways to read data from an external source and insert it into the `DataSet`:

❑ Use a data adapter

❑ Read XML into the data set

Populating a DataSet with a Data Adapter

The section on data rows briefly introduced the `SqlDataAdapter` class, as shown in the following code:

```
string select = "SELECT ContactName,CompanyName FROM Customers";
SqlConnection conn = new SqlConnection(source);
SqlDataAdapter da = new SqlDataAdapter(select , conn);
DataSet ds = new DataSet();
da.Fill(ds , "Customers");
```

The two highlighted lines show the `SqlDataAdapter` in use – the `OleDbDataAdapter` is again virtually identical in functionality to the `Sql` equivalent.

The `SqlDataAdapter` and `OleDbDataAdapter` are two of the classes that are derived from a common base class rather than a set of interfaces, as are most of the other `SqlClient` or `OleDb` specific classes. The inheritance hierarchy is shown below:

```
System.Data.Common.DataAdapter
    System.Data.Common.DBDataAdapter
        System.Data.OleDb.OleDbDataAdapter
        System.Data.SqlClient.SqlDataAdapter
```

In order to retrieve data into a `DataSet`, it is necessary to have some form of command that is executed to select that data. The command in question could be a SQL `SELECT` statement, a call to a stored procedure, or for the `OleDb` provider, a `TableDirect` command. The example above utilizes one of the constructors available on `SqlDataAdapter` that converts the passed SQL `SELECT` clause into a `SqlCommand`, and issues this when the `Fill` method is called on the adapter.

Going back to the example on stored procedures earlier in the chapter, I defined insert, update, and delete commands but didn't at that point present a select procedure. We'll fill that gap in this section, and show how you can call a stored procedure from an `SqlDataAdapter` to populate data in a `DataSet`.

Using a Stored Procedure in a Data Adapter

First off we need to define a stored procedure and install it into the database. The code for this example is available in the `11_DataAdapter` directory. The select stored procedure is as follows:

```
CREATE PROCEDURE RegionSelect AS
    SET NOCOUNT OFF;

    SELECT * FROM Region;
GO
```

Again this example is fairly trivial, and not really worthy of a stored procedure, as a direct SQL statement would normally suffice. This stored procedure can be typed directly into SQL query analyser, or you can run the `StoredProc.sql` file that is provided for use by this example.

Next, we need to define a `SqlCommand` that will execute this stored procedure. Again the code is very simple, and most of it was already presented in the earlier section on issuing commands:

```
private static SqlCommand GenerateSelectCommand(SqlConnection conn )
{
    SqlCommand  aCommand = new SqlCommand("RegionSelect" , conn);
    aCommand.CommandType = CommandType.StoredProcedure;
    aCommand.UpdatedRowSource = UpdateRowSource.None;
    return aCommand;
}
```

This method generates the `SqlCommand` that will call the `RegionSelect` procedure when executed. All that remains is to hook this command up to a `SqlDataAdapter`, and call the `Fill()` method:

```
DataSet ds = new DataSet();

// Create a data adapter to fill the DataSet

SqlDataAdapter da = new SqlDataAdapter();

// Set the data adapters select co

da.SelectCommand = GenerateSelectCommand (conn);
da.Fill(ds , "Region");
```

Here I create a new `SqlDataAdapter`, assign the generated `SqlCommand` to the `SelectCommand` parameter of the data adapter, and then call fill which will execute the stored procedure and insert all rows returned into the `Region DataTable` (which in this instance is generated by the runtime).

There's more to a data adapter than just selecting data by issuing some form of command. In the section on persisting data set changes I shall explore the rest of the facilities of the data adapter.

Populating a Data Set from XML

In addition to generating the schema for a given `DataSet` and associated tables and so on, a `DataSet` can read and write data in native XML, such as a file on disk, a stream, or a text reader.

To load XML into a `DataSet`, simply call one of the `ReadXML()` methods, such as that shown below which will read data from a disk file:

```
DataSet ds = new DataSet();
ds.ReadXml(".\\MyData.xml");
```

The `ReadXml()` method attempts to load any inline schema information from the input XML, and if found, uses this schema in the validation of any data loaded from that file. If no inline schema is used then the `DataSet` will extend its internal structure as data is loaded. This is similar to the behavior of `Fill()` in the previous example, which retrieves the data and constructs a `DataTable` based on the data selected.

Further details of XML are available in the chapter devoted to the subject.

Persisting Data Set Changes

After editing data within a DataSet, it is probably necessary to persist these changes. The most common example would be selecting data from a database, displaying it to the user, and returning those updates back to the database.

In a less "connected" application, changes might be persisted to an XML file, transported to a middle-tier application server, and then processed to update several data sources.

A DataSet can be used for either of these examples, and what's more it's really easy to do.

Updating Via Data Adapters

In addition to the SelectCommand that a SqlDataAdapter most likely includes, you can also define an InsertCommand, UpdateCommand and DeleteCommand. As these names imply, these objects are instances of SqlCommand or OleDbCommand for the OleDbDataAdapter, so any of these commands could be straight SQL or a stored procedure.

With this level of flexibility, you are free to tune the application by judicious use of stored procedures for frequently used commands (say SELECT and INSERT), and use straight SQL for less commonly used commands such as DELETE.

For the example in this section I have resurrected the stored procedure code for inserting, updating and deleting Region records, coupled these with the RegionSelect procedure written above, and produced an example which utilizes each of these commands to retrieve and update data in a DataSet. The main body of code is shown below; the full source code is available in the 12_DataAdapter2 directory.

Inserting a New Row

There are two ways to add a new row to a DataTable. The first method is to call the NewRow() function, which returns a blank row which you then populate and add to the Rows collection, as follows:

```
DataRow r = ds.Tables["Region"].NewRow();
r["RegionID"]=999;
r["RegionDescription"]="North West";
ds.Tables["Region"].Rows.Add(r);
```

The second method would be to pass an array of data to the Rows.Add() method as shown in the following code snippet:

```
DataRow r = ds.Tables["Region"].Rows.Add
            (new Object [] { 999 , "North West" });
```

Each new row within the DataTable will have its RowState set to Added. The example dumps out the records before each change is made to the database, so after adding the following row (in either way) to the DataTable, the rows will look something like the following.

```
New row pending inserting into database
    1   Eastern                              Unchanged
    2   Western                              Unchanged
    3   Northern                             Unchanged
    4   Southern                             Unchanged
  999 North West                             Added
```

To update the database from the `DataAdapter`, call one of the `Update` methods as shown below:

```
da.Update(ds , "Region");
```

For the new row within the `DataTable`, this will execute the stored procedure (in this instance `RegionInsert`), and subsequently I dump the records in the `DataTable` again.

```
New row updated and new RegionID assigned by database
   1    Eastern                                         Unchanged
   2    Western                                         Unchanged
   3    Northern                                        Unchanged
   4    Southern                                        Unchanged
   5    North West                                      Unchanged
```

Look at the last row in the `DataTable`. I had set the `RegionID` in code to 999, but after executing the `RegionInsert` stored procedure the value has been changed to 5. This is intentional – the database will often generate primary keys for you, and the updated data in the `DataTable` is due to the fact that the `Command` definition within our source code has the `UpdatedRowSource` parameter set to `UpdateRowSource.OutputParameters`:

```
SqlCommand aCommand = new SqlCommand("RegionInsert" , conn);

aCommand.CommandType = CommandType.StoredProcedure;
aCommand.Parameters.Add(new SqlParameter("@RegionDescription" ,
                        SqlDbType.NChar ,
                        50 ,
                        "RegionDescription"));
aCommand.Parameters.Add(new SqlParameter("@RegionID" ,
                        SqlDbType.Int,
                        0 ,
                        ParameterDirection.Output ,
                        false ,
                        0 ,
                        0 ,
                        "RegionID" ,    // Defines the SOURCE column
                        DataRowVersion.Default ,
                        null));
aCommand.UpdatedRowSource = UpdateRowSource.OutputParameters;
```

What this means is that whenever a `DataAdapter` issues this command, the output parameters should be mapped back to the source of the row, which in this instance was a row in a `DataTable`. The flag states what data should be updated – the stored procedure has an output parameter that is mapped back into the `DataRow`. The column it applies to is `RegionID`, as this is defined within the command definition.

The values for `UpdateRowSource` are as follows:

UpdateRowSource Enum	Description
Both	Any output parameters plus the first returned record are applied to the source row.
FirstReturnedRecord	This infers that the command returns a record, and that the contents of that record should be merged into the original source `DataRow`. This is useful where a given table has a number of default (or computed) columns, as after an insert statement these need to be synchronized with the `DataRow` on the client.

Table continued on following page

UpdateRowSource Enum	Description
None	All data returned from the command is discarded.
OutputParameters	Any output parameters from the command are mapped onto the appropriate column(s) in the DataRow.

Updating an Existing Row

Updating a row that already exists within the DataTable is just a case of utilizing the DataRow's indexer with either a column name or column number, as show in the following code:

```
r["RegionDescription"]="North West England";
r[1] = "North East England";
```

Both of these statements are equivalent (in this example):

```
Changed RegionID 5 description
    1    Eastern                          Unchanged
    2    Western                          Unchanged
    3    Northern                         Unchanged
    4    Southern                         Unchanged
    5    North West England               Modified
```

Prior to updating the database, the row updated has its state set to Modified as shown above.

Deleting a Row

Deleting a row is a matter of calling the Delete() method:

```
r.Delete();
```

A deleted row has its row state set to Deleted, however you cannot read columns from the deleted DataRow as these are no longer valid. When the adaptors Update() method is called, all deleted rows will utilise the DeleteCommand, which in this instance executes the RegionDelete stored procedure.

Writing XML Output

As you have seen already, the DataSet has great support for defining its schema in XML, and as you can read data from an XML document, you can also write data to an XML document.

The DataSet.WriteXml method and overrides permits you to output various parts of the data stored within the DataSet. You can elect to output just the data, or the data and the schema. The following code shows an example of both for the Region example shown above:

```
ds.WriteXml(".\\WithoutSchema.xml");
ds.WriteXml(".\\WithSchema.xml" , XmlWriteMode.WriteSchema);
```

The first file, WithoutSchema.xml is shown below:

```
<?xml version="1.0" standalone="yes"?>
<NewDataSet>
   <Region>
      <RegionID>1</RegionID>
      <RegionDescription>Eastern                              </RegionDescription>
   </Region>
   <Region>
      <RegionID>2</RegionID>
      <RegionDescription>Western                              </RegionDescription>
   </Region>
   <Region>
      <RegionID>3</RegionID>
      <RegionDescription>Northern                             </RegionDescription>
   </Region>
   <Region>
      <RegionID>4</RegionID>
      <RegionDescription>Southern                             </RegionDescription>
   </Region>
</NewDataSet>
```

The closing tag on `RegionDescription` is over to the right of the page as the database column is defined as `NCHAR(50)`, which is a 50 character string padded with spaces.

The output produced as the `WithSchema.xml` file includes, not surprisingly, the XML schema for the `DataSet` as well as the data itself:

```
<?xml version="1.0" standalone="yes"?>
<NewDataSet>
   <xsd:schema id="NewDataSet" targetNamespace="" xmlns=""
      xmlns:xsd="http://www.w3.org/2001/XMLSchema"
      xmlns:msdata="urn:schemas-microsoft-com:xml-msdata">
      <xsd:element name="NewDataSet" msdata:IsDataSet="true"
         msdata:Locale="en-GB">
         <xsd:complexType>
            <xsd:choice maxOccurs="unbounded">
               <xsd:element name="Region" msdata:Locale="en-GB">
                  <xsd:complexType>
                     <xsd:sequence>
                        <xsd:element name="RegionID"
                           msdata:AutoIncrement="true"
                           msdata:AutoIncrementSeed="1" type="xsd:int"
                           msdata:Ordinal="0" />
                        <xsd:element name="RegionDescription"
                           type="xsd:string"
                           msdata:Ordinal="1" />
                     </xsd:sequence>
                  </xsd:complexType>
               </xsd:element>
            </xsd:choice>
         </xsd:complexType>
      </xsd:element>
   </xsd:schema>
   <Region>
      <RegionID>1</RegionID>
      <RegionDescription>Eastern                              </RegionDescription>
   </Region>
   <Region>
      <RegionID>2</RegionID>
      <RegionDescription>Western                              </RegionDescription>
   </Region>
```

```
<Region>
   <RegionID>3</RegionID>
   <RegionDescription>Northern                    </RegionDescription>
</Region>
<Region>
   <RegionID>4</RegionID>
   <RegionDescription>Southern                    </RegionDescription>
</Region>
</NewDataSet>
```

Note the usage within this file of the `msdata` schema, which defines extra attributes for columns within a `DataSet`, such as `AutoIncrement` and `AutoIncrementSeed` – these attributes correspond directly with the properties definable on a `DataColumn`.

For more information about XML in .NET, please refer to the XML chapter.

Working with ADO.NET

This last section will attempt to address some common scenarios when developing data access applications with ADO.NET.

Tiered Development

Producing an application that interacts with data is often done by splitting the application up into tiers. A common model is to have an application tier (the front end), a data services tier and the database itself.

One of the difficulties with this model is deciding what data to transport between tiers, and the format that it should be transported in. With ADO.NET you'll be pleased to hear that these wrinkles have been ironed out, and support for this style of architecture has been designed in from the start.

Copying and Merging Data

Ever tried copying an entire `OleDb` recordset? In .NET it's easy:

```
DataSet source = {some dataset};
DataSet dest = source.Copy();
```

This will create an exact copy of the source `DataSet` – all `DataTables`, `DataColumns`, `DataRows`, and `Relations` will be copied across verbatim, and all data will be in exactly the same state as it was in the source. If all you want to copy is the schema of the `DataSet`, you can try the following:

```
DataSet source = {some dataset};
DataSet dest = source.Clone();
```

This will again copy all tables, relations, etc. However, each copied `DataTable` will be empty. It really couldn't be more straightforward.

A common requirement when writing a tiered system, whether based on Win32 or the web, is to be able to ship as little data as possible between tiers. This reduces the amount of resources consumed.

To cope with this requirement, the `DataSet` has the `GetChanges()` method. This simple method performs a huge deal of work, and returns a `DataSet` with only the changed rows from the source dataset. This is ideal for passing between tiers, as only a minimal set of data has to be passed across the wire.

The following example shows how to generate a changes `DataSet`:

```
DataSet source = {some dataset};
DataSet dest = source.GetChanges();
```

Again, this is trivial. Under the covers things are a little more interesting. There are two `GetChanges` methods – the latter takes a value of the `DataRowState` enum, and returns only rows that correspond to that state (or states). `GetChanges()` simply calls `GetChanges(Deleted | Modified | Added)`. The method first checks to ensure that there are some changes by calling `HasChanges()`. If no changes have been made then a null is returned to the caller immediately.

The next operation is to clone the current data set. Once done, the new data set is set up to ignore constraint violations (`EnforceConstraints = false`), and then each changed row for every table is copied into the new `DataSet`.

Once you have a `DataSet` that just contains changes, you can then move these off to another tier for processing. Once written to the database, the changes dataset can be returned to the caller (as there may, for example, be some output parameters from the stored procedures that have updated values in the columns). These changes can then be merged into the original `DataSet` using the `Merge()` method. This sequence of operations is depicted below:

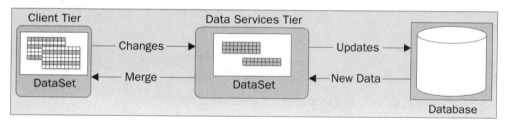

The client prepares the data by calling `GetChanges()`. This is passed to the data services tier, which updates the database. Any changed columns are returned back to the client where the changes are merged into the existing data set.

SQL Server Key Generation

The `RegionInsert` stored procedure presented earlier in the chapter was one example of generating a primary key value on insertion into the database. The method for generating the key was fairly crude and wouldn't scale well, so for a real application you should look at utilizing some other strategy for generating keys.

Your first instinct might be simply to define an identity column, and return the `@@IDENTITY` value from the stored procedure. The following stored procedure shows how this might be defined for the `Categories` table in the `Northwind` example database. Type this stored procedure into SQL Query Analyzer, or run the `StoredProcs.sql` file in the `13_SQLServerKeys` directory:

```
CREATE PROCEDURE CategoryInsert(@CategoryName NVARCHAR(15),
                                @Description NTEXT,
                                @CategoryID INTEGER OUTPUT)AS
    SET NOCOUNT OFF;
    INSERT INTO Categories (CategoryName,Description)
        VALUES(@CategoryName, @Description);
    SELECT @CategoryID = @@IDENTITY;
GO
```

This inserts a new row into the `Category` table, and returns the generated primary key to the caller. You can test the procedure by typing in the following SQL in Query Analyzer:

```
DECLARE @CatID int;
EXECUTE CategoryInsert 'Pasties' , 'Heaven Sent Food' , @CatID OUTPUT;
PRINT @CatID;
```

When executed as a batch of commands, this will insert a new row into the `Categories` table, and return the identity of the new record, which is then displayed to the user.

Let's say that some months down the line, someone decides to add in a simple audit trail, which will record all insertions and modifications made to the category name. You define a table such as that shown below which will record the old and new value of the category:

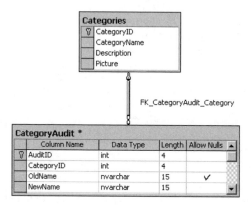

The creation script for this table is included in the `StoredProcs.sql` file. The `AuditID` column is defined as an `IDENTITY` column. You then construct a couple of database triggers that will record changes to the `CategoryName` field:

```
CREATE TRIGGER CategoryInsertTrigger
    ON Categories
    AFTER UPDATE
AS
    INSERT INTO CategoryAudit(CategoryID , OldName , NewName )
        SELECT old.CategoryID, old.CategoryName, new.CategoryName
        FROM Deleted AS old,
             Categories AS new
        WHERE old.CategoryID = new.CategoryID;
GO
```

For those of you used to Oracle stored procedures, SQL Server doesn't exactly have the concept of OLD and NEW rows, instead for an insert trigger there is an in memory table called Inserted, and for deletes and updates the old rows are available within the Deleted table.

This trigger retrieves the CategoryID of the record(s) affected, and stores this together with the old and new value of the CategoryName column.

Now, when you call your original stored procedure to insert a new CategoryID, you receive an identity value, however this is no longer the identity value from the row inserted into the Categories table, it is now the new value generated for the row in the CategoryAudit table. Ouch!

To view the problem first hand, open up a copy of SQL Server Enterprise manager, and view the contents of the Categories table.

CategoryID	CategoryName	Description
1	Beverages	Soft drinks, coffees, teas, beers, and ales
2	Condiments	Sweet and savory sauces, relishes, spreads, and seasonings
3	Confections	Desserts, candies, and sweet breads
4	Dairy Products	Cheeses
5	Grains/Cereals	Breads, crackers, pasta, and cereal
6	Meat/Poultry	Prepared meats
7	Produce	Dried fruit and bean curd
8	Seafood	Seaweed and fish
20	Pasties	Heaven Sent Grub

This lists all the categories I have in my instance of the database.

The next identity value for the Categories table should be 21, so we'll insert a new row by executing the code shown below, and see what ID is returned as follows:

```
DECLARE @CatID int;
EXECUTE CategoryInsert 'Pasties' , 'Heaven Sent Food' , @CatID OUTPUT;
PRINT @CatID;
```

The output value of this on my PC was 17. If I look into the CategoryAudit table, I find that this is the identity of the newly inserted audit record, not that of the category record created.

AuditID	CategoryID	OldName	NewName
17	30	<NULL>	Vegetables

The problem lies in the way that @@IDENTITY actually works. It returns the LAST identity value created by your session, so as shown above it isn't 100% reliable.

There are two other identity functions that you can utilize instead of @@IDENTITY, but neither are free from possible problems. The first, SCOPE_IDENTITY(), will return the last identity value created within the current "scope". SQL Server defines scope as a stored procedure, trigger, or function. This may work most of the time, but if for some reason someone adds another INSERT statement into the stored procedure, then you will receive this value rather than the one you expected.

The other, IDENT_CURRENT() will return the last identity value generated for a given table in any scope, so for instance, if two users were accessing SQL Server at exactly the same time, it might be possible to receive the other user's generated identity value.

As you might imagine, tracking down a problem of this nature isn't easy. The moral of the story is to beware when utilizing Identity columns in SQL Server.

Naming Conventions

Having worked in database applications all my working life, I've picked up a few recommendations for naming entities, which are worth sharing. I know, this isn't really .NET related, but the conventions are useful especially when naming constraints as above. Feel free to skip this section if you already have your own views on the subject.

Database Tables

❑ Always use singular names – `Product` rather than `Products`. This one is largely due to having to explain to customers a database schema – it's much better grammatically to say "The `Product` table contains products" than "The `Products` table contains products". Have a look at the `Northwind` database as an example of how not to do this.

❑ Adopt some form of naming convention for the fields that go into a table – ours is `<Table>_ID` for the primary key of a table (assuming that the primary key is a single column), `Name` for the field considered to be the user friendly name of the record, and `Description` for any textual information about the record itself. Having a good table convention means you can look at virtually any table in the database and instinctively know what the fields are used for.

Database Columns

❑ Use singular rather than plural names again.

❑ Any columns that link to another table should be named the same as the primary key of that table. So, a link to the `Product` table would be `Product_ID`, and to the sample table `Sample_ID`. This isn't always possible, especially if one table has multiple references to another. In that case use your own judgment.

❑ Date fields should have a suffix of _On, as in `Modified_On`, `Created_On`. It's easy to read some SQL output and infer what a column means just by its name.

❑ Fields that record the user should be suffixed with _By, as in `Modified_By` and `Created_By`. Again, this aids legibility.

Constraints

❑ If possible, include in the name of the constraint the table and column name, as in `CK_<Table>_<Field>`. Examples would be `CK_PERSON_SEX` for a check constraint on the sex column of the person table. A foreign key example would be `FK_Product_Supplier_ID`, for the foreign key relationship between product and supplier.

❑ Show the type of constraint with a prefix, such as `CK` for a check constraint and `FK` for a foreign key constraint. Feel free to be more specific, as in `CK_PERSON_AGE_GT0` for a constraint on the age column indicating that the age should be greater than zero.

❑ If you have to trim the length of the constraint, do it on the table name part rather than the column name. When you get a constraint violation, it's usually easy to infer which table was in error, but sometimes not so easy to check which column caused the problem. Oracle has a 30-character limit on names, which you can easily hit.

Above all, when naming entities whether within the database or within code, *be consistent.*

Performance

The current set of managed providers available for .NET are somewhat limited – you can choose OleDb or SqlClient; OleDb permits connection to any data source exposed with an OLE DB driver (such as Oracle), and the SqlClient provider is tailored for SqlServer.

The SqlClient provider has been written completely in managed code, and uses as few layers as possible in order to connect to the database. This provider writes **TDS** (**Tabular Data Stream**) packets direct to SQL Server, which should be substantially faster than the OleDb provider, which naturally has to go through a number of layers before actually hitting the database.

To test the theory, the following code was run against the same database on the same machine, the only difference being the use of the SqlClient managed provider over the ADO provider:

```
SqlCommand cmd = new SqlCommand(insert, con);
long timeInitial, timeElapsed;
timeInitial = System.Diagnostics.Counter.Value;
for(int i = 0; i < iterations; i++)
    cmd.ExecuteNonQuery();
timeElapsed = System.Diagnostics.Counter.Value - timeInitial;
```

Naturally the OleDb version utilizes OleDbCommand rather than SqlCommand. I created a simple database table with two columns as shown below, and manually added a single row:

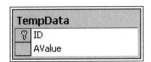

The SQL clause used was a simple UPDATE command:

```
UPDATE TempData SET AValue = 1 WHERE ID = 1.
```

The SQL was kept deliberately simple to attempt to highlight the differences in the providers. The results (in seconds) achieved for various combinations of iterations were as follows :

Provider	100	1000	10000	50000
OleDb	0.2586	1.726	16.586	95.925
Sql	0.1185	0.787	8.384	39.954

If you are only targeting SQL Server then the obvious choice is the Sql provider. Back in the real world, if you target anything other than SQL Server you naturally have to use the OleDb provider. Or do you?

As Microsoft have done an excellent job of making database access generic with the System.Data.Common classes, it would be better to write code against those classes, and use the appropriate managed provider at runtime. It's fairly simple to swap between OleDb and Sql now, and if other database vendors write managed providers for their products, you will be able to swap out ADO for a native provider with little (or no) code changes.

Summary

Over the course of this chapter, we've seen how we can access and manipulate our data using ADO.NET. We've discussed several important concepts, such as populating `DataSets`, and using XML Schemas in conjunction with `XSD.EXE` to provide alternative access solutions to our data, and using stored procedures in our code. We've also discussed performance issues, and given you some guidelines on the conventions used when working with ADO.NET. Armed with this knowledge, we're now in a good position to move onto the next chapter, where we'll explore the use of Visual Studio and .NET's Windows Forms data controls.

12

Viewing .NET Data

The last chapter was devoted to various ways of selecting and changing data. This chapter will carry on from where the last chapter left off, and show how you can display that data to the user by binding to various Windows controls.

The data binding capabilities of .NET are similar to ADO and the Visual Basic controls. All .NET languages are now capable of using the same controls and methods however, which can make life a good deal easier. The most revolutionary aspect of the .NET data access model is the new `DataGrid`. I'll spend quite a large part of this chapter describing its features.

The chapter will also cover the use of the XSD schema editor within Visual Studio.NET, giving an example of the code generated by the editor.

I'll conclude with an example of how to utilize hit testing and reflection on rows in the `DataGrid`. This example brings together some aspects discussed elsewhere in the book, such as responding to events, reflection, custom attributes, and there's some data access thrown in too!

The DataGrid Control

The `DataGrid` is a completely new control, written specifically for .NET, which permits various views of data to be displayed. In its simplest guise, you can display data (as in a `DataSet`) by calling the `SetDataBinding()` method. More complex capabilities are also built into the control, which I'll come onto throughout the course of this chapter.

Displaying Tabular Data

The last chapter showed numerous ways of selecting data and getting it into a data table, although the data was displayed somewhat simply, as all I covered was using `Console.WriteLine()`.

The first example will show how to retrieve some data and display it in a `DataGrid` control. The following is a screenshot from the application we're about to build. The source code for this application is available in the `01_DisplayTabularData` subdirectory:

The application (simple as it is), selects every record from the customer table within the `Northwind` database, and displays these to the user in the `DataGrid`. The code is fairly short and is shown in its entirety here:

```
using System;
using System.Windows.Forms;
using System.Data;
using System.Data.SqlClient;

public class DisplayTabularData : System.Windows.Forms.Form
{
    private System.Windows.Forms.Button retrieveButton;
    private System.Windows.Forms.DataGrid dataGrid;
    public DisplayTabularData()
    {
        this.AutoScaleBaseSize = new System.Drawing.Size(5, 13);
        this.ClientSize = new System.Drawing.Size(464, 253);
        this.Text = "01_DisplayTabularData";
```

Below we create the grid control, and set up its properties. The second line: `dataGrid.BeginInit();` disables firing of events on the grid, which is useful when making many modifications to the control. If events are not inhibited, each change to the grid could force a redraw on screen. We then set the location and size of the control, define the tab index, and anchor the control to both the top left and bottom right corners of the window, so that it will resize nicely:

```
        this.dataGrid = new System.Windows.Forms.DataGrid();
        dataGrid.BeginInit();
        dataGrid.Location = new System.Drawing.Point(8, 8);
        dataGrid.Size = new System.Drawing.Size(448, 208);
        dataGrid.TabIndex = 0;
        dataGrid.Anchor = AnchorStyles.Bottom | AnchorStyles.Top |
```

```
                        AnchorStyles.Left | AnchorStyles.Right;
        this.Controls.Add(this.dataGrid);
        dataGrid.EndInit();
```

Now we create the button. The same basic steps are followed in initializing the button:

```
        this.retrieveButton = new System.Windows.Forms.Button();
        retrieveButton.Location = new System.Drawing.Point(384, 224);
        retrieveButton.Size = new System.Drawing.Size(75, 23);
        retrieveButton.TabIndex = 1;
        retrieveButton.Anchor = AnchorStyles.Bottom | AnchorStyles.Right;
        retrieveButton.Text = "Retrieve";
        retrieveButton.Click += new System.EventHandler
                                (this.retrieveButton_Click);
        this.Controls.Add(this.retrieveButton);
    }
```

We also have a `Click` event, which calls the `retrieveButton_Click` event handler:

```
    protected void retrieveButton_Click(object sender, System.EventArgs e)
    {
        retrieveButton.Enabled = false;
        string source = "server=(local)\\NetSDK;" +
                        "uid=QSUser;pwd=QSPassword;" +
                        "database=northwind";
```

After selecting the data from the `Customers` table and filling the data set, I call `SetDataBinding` to bind the data set to the grid. To this method I pass the data set and the name of the table within the dataset that I wish to display. A grid can only display the data from one `DataTable` at a time, even if the `DataSet` contains multiple tables. Further on in the chapter, I will show an example of displaying data from a `DataSet` with multiple `DataTables`. The data could naturally come from many actual database tables (or a view over many tables):

```
        string select = "SELECT * FROM Customers" ;
        SqlConnection conn = new SqlConnection(source);
        SqlDataAdapter da = new SqlDataAdapter( select , conn);
        DataSet ds = new DataSet();
        da.Fill(ds , "Customers");
        dataGrid.SetDataBinding(ds , "Customers");
    }
    static void Main()
    {
        Application.Run(new DisplayTabularData());
    }
}
```

To compile this example, type the following at a command prompt:

```
csc /t:winexe /debug+ /r:System.dll /r:System.Data.dll /r:system.windows.forms.dll
/recurse:*.cs
```

The `/recurse:*.cs` parameter will compile all `.cs` files in your current directory and all subdirectories – I use it as shorthand, so I don't have to remember what the name of the file(s) in the application are called, and I ensure that I've only got the files I expect in a given directory.

Data Sources

The `DataGrid` is a very flexible way to display data – in addition to calling `SetDataBinding` with a dataset and the name of the table to display, the method can be called with any of the following data sources:

- ❏ An array – The grid can bind to any one dimensional array
- ❏ `DataTable`
- ❏ `DataView`
- ❏ `DataSet` or `DataViewManager`
- ❏ `IListSource`
- ❏ `IList`

The following sections will give an example of each of these data sources.

Array

At first glance this seems to be easy. Create an array, fill it with some data, and call `SetDataSource(array, null)` on the data grid. Here's some example code:

```
string[] stuff = new string[] {"One", "Two", "Three"};
dataGrid1.SetDataBinding(stuff, null);
```

As you may have noticed, `SetDataBinding` accepts two parameters. The first is the data source, which is the array in this instance. The second parameter should be `null` unless the data source is a `DataSet` or `DataViewManager`, in which case it should be the name of the table that you wish to display.

You could replace the code in the previous example's `retrieveButton_Click` event handler with the array code above. The problem with this code is the resulting display:

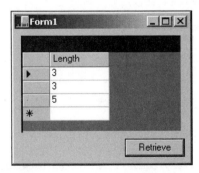

As you can see, rather than displaying the strings defined within the array, the grid is actually displaying the length of those strings. The reason for this is that when using an array as the source of data for a `DataGrid`, the grid looks for the first public property of the object within the array, and displays this value rather than the string you were expecting. The first (and only) public property of a string is its length, so that is what is displayed.

One way to rectify this is to create a wrapper class for strings, such as that shown below:

```
protected class Item
{
    public Item(string text)
    {
        m_text = text;
    }
    public string Text
    {
        get{return m_text;}
    }
    private string m_text;
}
```

When adding an array of this `Item` class (which could as well be a `struct` for all the processing that it does), you will receive the expected output. The source code for this example is available in the `02_DataSourceArray` directory:

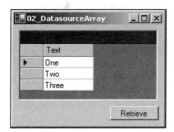

DataTable

There are two main ways to display a `DataTable` within a `DataGrid`:

❏ If your `DataTable` is standalone, call `SetDataBinding(DataTable, null)`.

❏ If your `DataTable` is contained within a `DataSet`, call `SetDataBinding(DataTable, "Table")`.

The example screenshot, taken from the code available in `03_DatasourceDataTable`, shows some of the column:

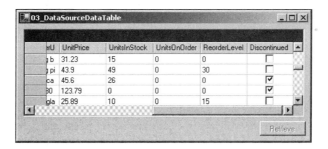

Note the display of the last column; it shows a check box instead of the more common edit control. The `DataGrid`, in the absence of any other information, will read the schema from the data source (which in this case is the `Products` table), and infer from the column types what control is to be displayed.

Don't get too excited, though – the only two types that are currently supported are textboxes and checkboxes – any other sort of mapping has to be done manually. I'll return to the subject of changing column types later in this chapter.

DataView

A `DataView` provides a means to filter and sort data within a `DataTable`. When you have selected data from the database, it is common to permit the user to sort that data, by means of clicking on column headings, etc. In addition, you may want to filter the data to only show certain rows, such as all those that have been changed by the user. A `DataView` allows you to limit the rows shown to the user, however it does not limit the columns from the `DataTable`.

> **A `DataView` does not allow you to change which columns are displayed, just which rows.**

An example of how to limit the columns shown is provided later in the chapter.

The code to create a `DataView` based on an existing `DataTable` is shown below. The example code for this section is available in the `04_DataSourceDataView` directory:

```
DataView  dv = new DataView(dataTable);
```

Once created, you can then alter settings on the view, which affect the data and operations permitted on that data when the view is displayed within the data grid. Some examples are:

- ❑ Setting `AllowEdit = false` disables all column edit functionality for rows.
- ❑ Setting `AllowNew = false` will disable the new row functionality.
- ❑ Setting `AllowDelete = false` will disable the delete row capability.
- ❑ Set the `RowStateFilter` to display only rows of a given state.
- ❑ Set the `RowFilter` to filter rows.
- ❑ Sort by certain columns.

Filtering Rows by Data

Once you have created a `DataView`, you can alter the data displayed by that view by setting the `RowFilter` property. This property, typed as a string, is used as a means of filtering based on certain criteria – the value of the string is used as the filter criteria. It is similar to a `WHERE` clause in regular SQL, but it is issued against data already selected from the database.

Some examples of filter clauses are shown in the following table:

Clause	Description
UnitsInStock > 50	Show only those rows where the UnitsInStock column is greater than 50.
Client = 'Smith'	Return only those records for a given client.
County LIKE 'C*'	Returns all records where the County field begins with a C – so for example this would return rows for Cornwall, Cumbria, Cheshire, and Cambridgeshire. You can use "%" as a single character wildcard.

The runtime will do its best to coerce the data types used within the filter expression into the appropriate types for the source columns. As an example, it is perfectly legal to write "UnitsInStock > '50'" in the earlier example, even though the column is an integer.

Filtering Rows on State

Each row within a DataView has a defined row state, which will be one of the following values:

DataViewRowState	Description
Added	All rows which have been newly created.
CurrentRows	All rows except those that have been deleted.
Deleted	All rows that were originally selected and have been deleted – does not show newly created rows that have been deleted.
ModifiedCurrent	List the current value of all rows that have been modified.
ModifiedOriginal	List the original values of all rows that have been modified.
OriginalRows	All rows which were originally selected from a data source. Does not include new rows. Shows the original values of the columns (that is, not the current values if changes have been made).
Unchanged	All rows that have not changed in any way.

To view the effect of these states on a grid, I've written an example which displays two grids – one being data selected from the database that you can interact with, the other showing rows in one of the above states:

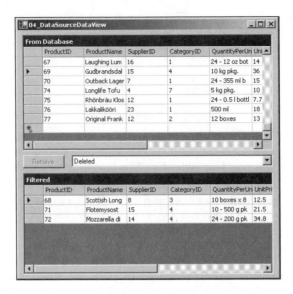

The filter not only applies to the rows that are visible, but also the state of the columns within those rows. This is evident when choosing the `ModifiedOriginal` or `ModifiedCurrent` selections. These states were described in the previous chapter, and are based on the `DataRowVersion` enumeration. If, for example, you have updated a row in some form, then the row will show up when you choose either `ModifiedOriginal` or `ModifiedCurrent`, however the actual value will either be the `Original` value selected from the database (if you choose `ModifiedOriginal`), or the current value in the `DataColumn` if you choose `ModifiedCurrent`.

Sorting Rows

As well as filtering data, it is sometimes necessary to sort the data within a `DataView`. You can click on a column header within the `DataGrid` control, and this will sort a column in either ascending or descending order. The only trouble is that the control can only sort by one column, whereas the underlying `DataView` can sort by many columns:

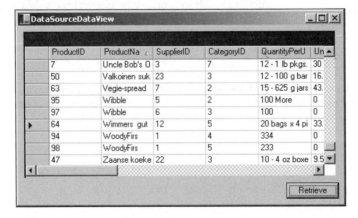

When a column is sorted, either by clicking on the header or within code, the `DataGrid` displays an arrow bitmap to indicate which column the sort has been applied to.

To programmatically set the sort order on a column, use the `Sort` property:

```
dataView.Sort = "ProductName";
dataView.Sort = "ProductName ASC, ProductID DESC";
```

The `DataView` supports both ascending and descending sort orders on columns – the default being ascending. If you do choose to sort on more than one column within the `DataView`, the `DataGrid` will cease to display any sort arrows.

If you have done any Win32 programming with `ListView` controls, you'll appreciate the work that the .NET team have gone through for sorting within the grid. As each column within the grid can be strongly typed, its sort order is not based upon the string representation of the column. Instead, it is based on the actual data.

The upshot is that if you have a date column within the `DataGrid`, and you try to sort it, the grid will do date comparisons to sort rather than string comparisons.

DataSet

The `DataGrid` comes in to its own when displaying data from a `DataSet`. As with the preceding examples, the `DataGrid` can only display a single `DataTable` at a time. However, as you'll see in this example, it is possible to navigate relationships within the `DataSet` on screen. The following code can be used to generate such a `DataSet` based on the `Customers` and `Orders` tables within the `Northwind` database. The code is available in the `05_DataSourceDataSet` directory. The example adds in these two `DataTables`, and then creates a relationship between these tables called `CustomerOrders`:

```
string source = "server=(local)\\NetSDK;" +
                "uid=QSUser;pwd=QSPassword;" +
                "database=northwind";
string orders = "SELECT * FROM Orders";
string customers = "SELECT * FROM Customers";
SqlConnection con = new SqlConnection(source);
SqlDataAdapter da = new SqlDataAdapter(orders , con);
DataSet ds = new DataSet();
da.Fill(ds , "Orders");
da = new SqlDataAdapter(customers , con);
da.Fill(ds , "Customers");
ds.Relations.Add("CustomerOrders",
                ds.Tables["Customers"].Columns["CustomerID"],
                ds.Tables["Orders"].Columns["CustomerID"]);
```

Once created, you can bind the `DataSet` to the `DataGrid` simply by calling `SetDataBinding`:

```
dataGrid1.SetDataBinding(ds, "Customers");
```

This will produce a view something like the following screenshot:

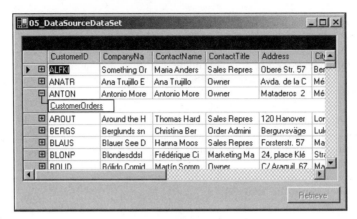

You may immediately notice that unlike the other data grids that have been shown in this chapter, there is a "+" to the left of each record. This reflects the fact that we created a `DataSet` with a navigable relationship, between customers and orders. You can naturally have a number of such relationships defined in code.

When you click on the "+" sign, the list of relationships is shown (or hidden if already visible). Clicking on the name of the relationship will navigate the grid to the linked records, in this case listing all orders placed by the selected customer:

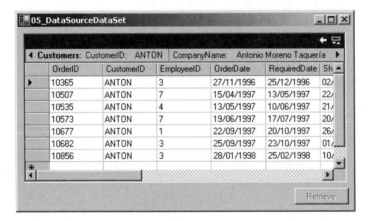

The grid control also includes a couple of new icons in the top right corner. The arrow permits you to navigate back to the parent row, and will change the display to that on the previous page. The header row showing details of the parent record can be shown or hidden by clicking on the other button.

The display of data in a `DataViewManager` is the same as that for the `DataSet` just shown. However, when a `DataViewManager` is created for a `DataSet`, an individual `DataView` is created for each `DataTable`, which then permits you to alter the rows shown based on a filter or the row state as shown in the `DataView` sample. Even if you don't expect to want to filter data, I would suggest always wrapping a `DataSet` in a `DataViewManager` for display, as it gives you more options when revising your code.

The following creates a `DataViewManager` based on the `DataSet` from the previous example, and then alters the `DataView` for the `Customers` table to only show customers from the UK:

```
DataViewManager dvm = new DataViewManager(ds);
dvm.DataViewSettings["Customers"].RowFilter = "Country='UK'";
dataGrid.SetDataBinding(dvm , "Customers");
```

This code creates a new `DataViewManager` object, and then sets the data view for the `Customers` table to list only those customers within the UK.

The output of this code is shown below:

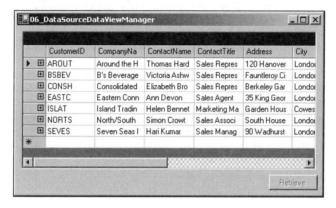

IListSource and IList

The `DataGrid` also supports any object that exposes one of the above interfaces. `IListSource` has only one member, `GetList()` which returns an `IList` interface. `IList` on the other hand is somewhat more interesting, and is implemented by a large number of classes in the runtime. Some of the classes that implement this interface are `Array`, `ArrayList` and `StringCollection`.

When using `IList`, the same caveat for the object within the collection holds true as for the `Array` implementation shown earlier – if you use a `StringCollection` as the data source for the `DataGrid`, the length of the strings is what is displayed within the grid, not the text of the item as you would hope.

DataGrid Class Hierarchy

The class hierarchy for the main parts of the `DataGrid` is shown below:

The DataGrid consists of zero or more DataGridTableStyles. These styles consist of zero or more DataGridColumnStyles. A given cell in the grid can be accessed by means of the DataGridCell struct.

We touched briefly on DataGridTableStyles and DataGridColumnStyles in the above section. However, there's more to DataGridTables and DataGridColumns than simply letting the runtime create them for you. The following sections will describe these and the other main classes shown in the above figure. The following sections will discuss these in detail, and show howS you can alter many facets of the on-screen display of data using these classes.

DataGridTableStyle and DataGridColumnStyle

A DataGridTableStyle contains the visual representation of a DataTable. The DataGrid contains a collection of these styles, accessible by the TableStyles property. When a DataTable is displayed, a check is made through all DataGridTableStyle objects to find one with its MappingName equal to the TableName of the DataTable. On finding a match, that style will be used in the display of the table.

The DataGridTableStyle permits you to define visual parameters for the DataGrid, such as the background and foreground color, the font used in the column header, and various other properties. The DataGridColumnStyle allows you to refine the display options on a column-by-column basis, such as setting the alignment for the data in the column, the text that is displayed for a null value, and the width of the column on screen.

When the DataGrid displays a DataTable with a defined DataGridTableStyle, you can define which columns of data are actually displayed by adding (or not adding) DataGridColumnStyles. Only columns that have a defined style will be displayed, which can be useful for "hiding" columns such as primary key values that are not normally displayed. You may also define a column style as ReadOnly.

The code below shows an example of creating a DataGridTableStyle. The code creates a DataGridTableStyle object, adds in two DataColumnStyle objects, and then displays all of the data within the Customers table. We'll show the code in its entirety, as this will be the basis for several examples in this section. The first part of the code should be familiar from our earlier example:

```
using System;
using System.Windows.Forms;
using System.Data;
using System.Data.SqlClient;
public class CustomDataGridTableStyle : System.Windows.Forms.Form
{
    private System.Windows.Forms.Button retrieveButton;
    private System.Windows.Forms.DataGrid dataGrid;
    public CustomDataGridTableStyle()
    {
        this.AutoScaleBaseSize = new System.Drawing.Size(5, 13);
        this.ClientSize = new System.Drawing.Size(464, 253);
        this.Text = "07_CustomDataGridTableStyle";
        this.dataGrid = new System.Windows.Forms.DataGrid();
        dataGrid.BeginInit();
        dataGrid.Location = new System.Drawing.Point(8, 8);
        dataGrid.Size = new System.Drawing.Size(448, 208);
        dataGrid.TabIndex = 0;
```

```
        dataGrid.Anchor = AnchorStyles.Bottom | AnchorStyles.Top |
                        AnchorStyles.Left | AnchorStyles.Right;
        this.Controls.Add(this.dataGrid);
        dataGrid.EndInit();
        this.retrieveButton = new System.Windows.Forms.Button();
        retrieveButton.Location = new System.Drawing.Point(384, 224);
        retrieveButton.Size = new System.Drawing.Size(75, 23);
        retrieveButton.TabIndex = 1;
        retrieveButton.Anchor = AnchorStyles.Bottom | AnchorStyles.Right;
        retrieveButton.Text = "Retrieve";
        retrieveButton.Click += new
                        System.EventHandler(this.retrieveButton_Click);
        this.Controls.Add(this.retrieveButton);
    }
    protected void retrieveButton_Click(object sender, System.EventArgs e)
    {
        retrieveButton.Enabled = false;
```

These generate the dataset that will be used, then create the DataGridTableStyle(s) for use in the example, and finally bind the DataGrid to the DataSet. The CreateDataSet function is nothing particularly new – I just select all rows from the Customers table:

```
        DataSet ds = CreateDataSet();
        CreateStyles(dataGrid);
        dataGrid.SetDataBinding(ds , "Customers");
    }
```

The CreateStyles function is, however, more interesting. The first few lines create the new DataGridTableStyle object, and define its MappingName. This property is used when the DataGrid displays a given DataTable. The DataGrid can display rows in alternating colors. The code here also defines the color for every second row, and the output is displayed in the screenshot later in this section:

```
    private void CreateStyles(DataGrid dg)
    {
        DataGridTableStyle style = new DataGridTableStyle();
        style.MappingName = "Customers";
        style.AlternatingBackColor = System.Drawing.Color.Bisque;
        DataGridTextBoxColumn customerID = new DataGridTextBoxColumn();
        customerID.HeaderText = "Customer ID";
        customerID.MappingName = "CustomerID";
        customerID.Width = 200;
        DataGridTextBoxColumn name = new DataGridTextBoxColumn();
        name.HeaderText = "Name";
        name.MappingName = "CompanyName";
        name.Width = 300;
```

When the columns have been defined, they are added to the GridColumnStyles collection of the DataGridTableStyle object, which itself is then added to the TableStyles property of the DataGrid:

```
        style.GridColumnStyles.AddRange
            ( new DataGridColumnStyle[]{customerID , name});
        dg.TableStyles.Add(style);
```

```
    }
    private DataSet CreateDataSet()
    {
        string source = "server=(local)\\NetSDK;" +
                        "uid=QSUser;pwd=QSPassword;" +
                        "database=northwind";
        string customers = "SELECT * FROM Customers";
        SqlConnection con = new SqlConnection(source);
        SqlDataAdapter da = new SqlDataAdapter(customers , con);
        DataSet ds = new DataSet();
        da.Fill(ds , "Customers");
        return ds;
    }
    static void Main()
    {
        Application.Run(new CustomDataGridTableStyle());
    }
}
```

After creating the `DataGridTableStyle` object, we created two objects derived from `DataGridColumnStyle` – in this instance these were textboxes. Each column has a number of properties defined. All of these properties are displayed in the following table:

Property	Description
Alignment	One of the `HorizontalAlignment` enumerated values – `Left`, `Center` or `Right`. This indicates how data in the column is justified.
FontHeight	The size of the font in pixels. This will default to that of the `DataGrid` if no value is set.
HeaderText	The text displayed in the column heading.
MappingName	The column from the `DataTable` that this on screen column displays.
NullText	The text displayed within the column if the underlying data value is `DBNull`.
PropertyDescriptor	This will be discussed later in the chapter.
ReadOnly	Flag indicating whether the column is read write or read only.
Width	The width of the column in pixels.

The resulting display from this code is shown below:

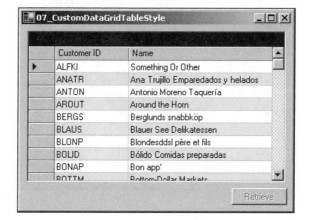

Data Binding

The previous examples have all used the `DataGrid` control, which is only one of the controls within the .NET runtime that can be used to display data. The process of linking a control to a data source is termed **data binding**.

If you have any experience with programming Windows applications in MFC, you'll probably at one time or another utilised the **Dynamic Data Exchange** (**DDX**) capabilities, to hook member variables of one class to a Win32 control. You'll probably be pleased to know that you can close the door on DDX as it's considerably easier to hook data to controls in .NET. You can bind data not only to windows controls, but also to web pages using ASP.NET. That subject will be covered elsewhere in the book.

Simple Binding

A control that supports single binding typically displays only a single value at once, such as a textbox or radio button. The following example shows how to bind a column from a `DataTable` to a `TextBox`:

```
DataSet ds = CreateDataSet();
textbox.DataBindings.Add("Text" , ds , "Products.ProductName");
```

After retrieving some data from the products table and storing this in the returned `DataSet`, the second line binds the `Text` property of the control (`textBox1`) to the `Products.ProductName` column. If you were to write this code and retrieve data from the `Northwind` database, you would see something like the following on screen:

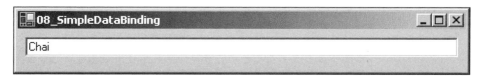

The text box is indeed displaying something from the database. To check that it is the right column and value, you could use the SQL Server Query Analyzer tool to verify the contents of the product table:

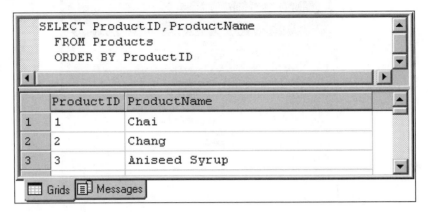

Having a single text box on screen with no way to scroll to next/previous records and no way to update the database is not very useful, so the next section will show a more realistic example, and introduce the other objects that are necessary in order for data binding to work. I'll begin with an overview of some of the classes used.

Data Binding Objects

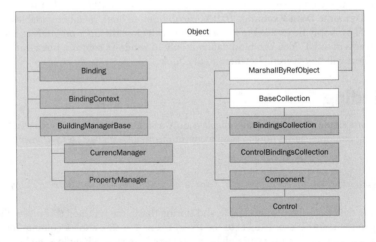

In the previous example, we used the `DataBindings` property of the `TextBox` control to bind a column from a data set to the `Text` property of the control. The `DataBindings` property is an instance of the `ControlsBindingsCollection` shown above:

```
textbox.DataBindings.Add("Text" , ds , "Products.ProductName");
```

This line added a `Binding` object to the `ControlBindingsCollection`.

Binding Context

Each Windows form has a `BindingContext` property. Incidentally, `Form` is derived from `Control`, which is where this property is actually defined, so most controls have this property. This class maintains a collection of `BindingManagerBase` instances. These instances are created and added to the binding manager object when a control is data bound:

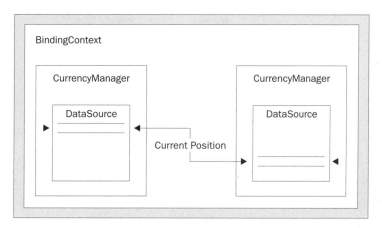

The `BindingContext` may contain several data sources, wrapped in either a `CurrencyManager` or a `PropertyManager`. The decision on which class is used is based on the data source itself.

If the data source contains a list of items, such as a `DataTable`, `DataView`, or any object that implements `IList`, then a `CurrencyManager` will be used as this can maintain the current position within that datasource. If the data source is a single value then a `PropertyManager` will be stored within the `BindingContext`.

A `CurrencyManager` or `PropertyManager` is only created once for a given data source. If you bind two textboxes to a row from a `DataTable`, only one `CurrencyManager` would be created within the binding context.

Each control added to a form is linked to the forms binding manager, so all controls share the same instance. When a control is initially created, its `BindingContext` property is null. When the control is added to the `Controls` collection of the form, this sets the `BindingContext` to that of the form.

To bind a control to a column, you need to add an entry to its `DataBindings` property, which is an instance of `ControlBindingsCollection`. The code shown below creates a new binding:

```
textBox1.DataBindings.Add("Text", ds, "Products.ProductName");
```

Internally, the `Add` method of `ControlBindingsCollection` creates a new instance of a `Binding` object from the parameters passed to this method, and adds this to the bindings collection:

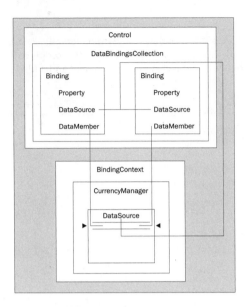

The image above shows roughly what is going on when you add a `Binding` to a `Control`. The binding links the control to a data source, which is maintained within the `BindingContext` of the `Form` (or control itself). Changes within the data source are reflected into the control, as are changes in the control.

Binding

This class links a property of the control to a member of the data source. When that member changes, the control's property is updated to reflect this change. The opposite is also true – if the text within the textbox is updated, this change is reflected in the data source.

Bindings can be set up from any column to any property of the control, so, for instance, you would bind a column to a textbox and could also bind another column to the textbox color (or length).

You could bind properties of a control to completely different data sources – maybe the color of the cell is defined in a colors table, and the actual data is defined within another table.

CurrencyManager and PropertyManager

When a `Binding` object is created, a corresponding `CurrencyManager` or `PropertyManager` object will also be created if this is the first time that data from the given source has been bound. The purpose of this class is to define the position of the "current" record within the data source, and to coordinate all `ListBindings` when this current record is changed.

The following example displays two fields from the products table, and includes a way to move between records by means of a trackbar control:

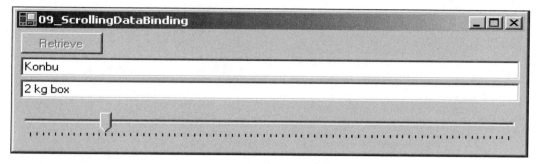

The example code for this application is shown in its entirety. The code is available in the `09_ScrollingDataBinding` directory:

```
using System;
using System.Windows.Forms;
using System.Data;
using System.Data.SqlClient;

public class ScrollingDataBinding : System.Windows.Forms.Form
{
    private Button retrieveButton;
    private TextBox textName;
    private TextBox textQuan;
    private TrackBar trackBar;
    private DataSet ds;
```

The application creates the window, and all controls for that window, within the `ScrollingDataBinding` constructor:

```
public ScrollingDataBinding()
{
    this.AutoScaleBaseSize = new System.Drawing.Size(5, 13);
    this.ClientSize = new System.Drawing.Size(464, 253);
    this.Text = "09_ScrollingDataBinding";
    this.retrieveButton = new Button();
    retrieveButton.Location = new System.Drawing.Point(4, 4);
    retrieveButton.Size = new System.Drawing.Size(75, 23);
    retrieveButton.TabIndex = 1;
    retrieveButton.Anchor = AnchorStyles.Top | AnchorStyles.Left;
    retrieveButton.Text = "Retrieve";
    retrieveButton.Click += new System.EventHandler
                        (this.retrieveButton_Click);
    this.Controls.Add(this.retrieveButton);
    this.textName = new TextBox();
    textName.Location = new System.Drawing.Point(4, 31);
    textName.Text = "Please click retrieve...";
    textName.TabIndex = 2;
    textName.Anchor = AnchorStyles.Top | AnchorStyles.Left |
                    AnchorStyles.Right ;
    textName.Size = new System.Drawing.Size(456, 20);
    textName.Enabled = false;
    this.Controls.Add(this.textName);
    this.textQuan = new TextBox();
```

611

```
        textQuan.Location = new System.Drawing.Point(4, 55);
        textQuan.Text = "";
        textQuan.TabIndex = 3;
        textQuan.Anchor = AnchorStyles.Top | AnchorStyles.Left |
                          AnchorStyles.Top;
        textQuan.Size = new System.Drawing.Size(456, 20);
        textQuan.Enabled = false;
        this.Controls.Add(this.textQuan);
        this.trackBar = new TrackBar();
        trackBar.BeginInit();
        trackBar.Dock = DockStyle.Bottom ;
        trackBar.Location = new System.Drawing.Point(0, 275);
        trackBar.TabIndex = 4;
        trackBar.Size = new System.Drawing.Size(504, 42);
        trackBar.Scroll += new System.EventHandler(this.trackBar_Scroll);
        trackBar.Enabled = false;
        this.Controls.Add(this.trackBar);
    }
```

When the Retrieve button is clicked on the UI, the event handler selects all records from the Products table, and stores this data within the private dataset ds:

```
    protected void retrieveButton_Click(object sender, System.EventArgs e)
    {
        retrieveButton.Enabled = false ;
        ds = CreateDataSet();
```

Next, the two text controls are bound:

```
        textName.DataBindings.Add("Text" , ds ,
                                  "Products.ProductName");
        textQuan.DataBindings.Add("Text" , ds ,
                                  "Products.QuantityPerUnit");
        trackBar.Minimum = 0 ;
        trackBar.Maximum = this.BindingContext[ds,"Products"].Count - 1;
        textName.Enabled = true;
        textQuan.Enabled = true;
        trackBar.Enabled = true;
    }
```

Here we have a trivial record scrolling mechanism, which responds to movements of the TrackBar thumb:

```
    protected void trackBar_Scroll(object sender , System.EventArgs e)
    {
        this.BindingContext[ds,"Products"].Position = trackBar.Value;
    }
    private DataSet CreateDataSet()
    {
        string source = "server=(local)\\NetSDK;" +
                        "uid=QSUser;pwd=QSPassword;" +
                        "database=northwind";
        string customers = "SELECT * FROM Products";
        SqlConnection con = new SqlConnection(source);
        SqlDataAdapter da = new SqlDataAdapter(customers , con);
        DataSet ds = new DataSet();
        da.Fill(ds , "Products");
        return ds;
    }
```

```
static void Main()
{
    Application.Run(new ScrollingDataBinding());
}
}
```

When the data is originally retrieved, the maximum position on the track bar is set to be the number of records. Then, in the scroll method above, we set the position of the `BindingContext` for the products `DataTable` to the position of the scroll bar thumb. This effectively changes the current record from the `DataTable`, so all controls bound to the current row (in this example the two text boxes) are updated.

Visual Studio and Data Access

With the new version of Visual Studio comes some new ways to bolt data access into your applications. This section will discuss some of the ways that Visual Studio.NET allows data to be integrated into the GUI, so that you can interact with data just as you would with regular controls.

The tools available allow you to create a database connection, using either the `OleDbConnection` or `SqlConnection` classes. The class used is based on which database you connect to. Once you have defined a connection, you can then create a `DataSet` and populate it within the Visual Studio GUI. This generates an XSD file for the `DataSet`, just as we did manually within the previous chapter, and auto generates the `.cs` code for you. This results in the creation of a type safe dataset.

Within this section I'll show you how to create a connection, select some data, generate a data set, and use all of the generated objects to produce a simple application.

Creating a Connection

To begin this section, create a new Windows application. Once created, you'll most probably see a blank form. The first task is to create a new database connection. Bring up the **Server Explorer** – either type **Ctrl + Alt + S**, or select **Server Explorer** item from the **View** menu. This will display a window similar to that shown below:

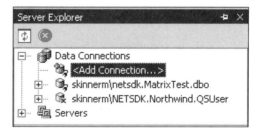

Within this window you can manage various aspects of data access. For this example, you need to create a connection to the `Northwind` database. Double-clicking <Add Connection...> will bring up a wizard where you can select which OLE DB provider to use – choose **Microsoft OLE DB Provider for SQL Server** if you will be connecting to the `Northwind` database installed as part of the Framework SDK samples. The second page of the **Data Link** dialog is shown here:

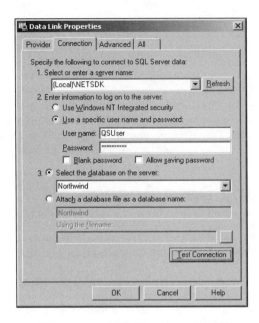

Type (Local)\NETSDK for the name of the server, and click on Use a specific user name and password as shown in the dialog. The user name will be QSUser and the password QSPassword. You can also use your Windows NT authentication if you have SQL Server set up appropriately.

Select the Northwind database from the dropdown list of databases, and to ensure you have everything setup correctly click on the Test Connection button. This will attempt to connect to the database and should display a message box when complete. Of course, if you'll have to set the server up appropriately for your machine's configuration, so the user name, password, and server name may all be different.

To create a connection object, click and drag the newly added server onto the main application window. This will create a member variable of type System.Data.SqlClient.SqlConnection, or System.Data.OleDb.OleDbConnection if you chose a different provider, and add the following code into the InitializeComponent method of the main form:

```
this.sqlConnection1 = new System.Data.SqlClient.SqlConnection();

//
// sqlConnection1
//

this.sqlConnection1.ConnectionString = "data source=skinnerm\\NETSDK;" +
                                "initial catalog=Northwind;" +
                                "user id=QSUser;password=QSPassword;" +
                                "persist security info=True;" +
                                "workstation id=SKINNERM;" +
                                "packet size=4096";
```

As you can see, the connection string information is persisted directly in code.

When you have added this object to the project, you will notice that the sqlConnection1 object appears in the tray area at the bottom of the Visual Studio window:

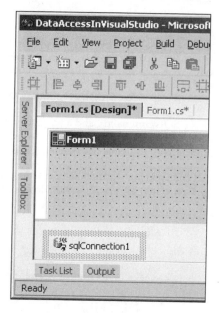

You can alter properties of this object by selecting it and showing the Properties dialog (F4).

Selecting Data

When you have defined a data connection, you can then select a table (or view) from the available list, and drag that table into an active form from your project:

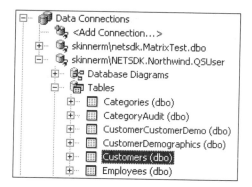

For this example, I have chosen the Customers table. When you drag this object into your project (you can drop this on the form or the server controls palette), it will add an object to your form derived from `SqlDataAdapter`, or `OleDbDataAdaptor` if you're not using `SqlServer`.

The data adapter generated contains commands for SELECT, INSERT, UPDATE, and DELETE. Needless to say, these may (and probably should), be tailored to call stored procedures rather than using straight SQL. The wizard-generated code will do for now, however.

The IDE adds the following code to your `.cs` file:

```
private System.Data.SqlClient.SqlCommand sqlSelectCommand1;
private System.Data.SqlClient.SqlCommand sqlInsertCommand1;
private System.Data.SqlClient.SqlCommand sqlUpdateCommand1;
private System.Data.SqlClient.SqlCommand sqlDeleteCommand1;
private System.Data.SqlClient.SqlDataAdapter sqlDataAdapter1;
```

There is an object defined for each of the SQL commands, and an `SqlDataAdapter`. Further down the file, in the `InitializeComponent()` method, the wizard has generated code to create each one of these commands and the data adapter too. The code is fairly verbose, so I have only included excerpts here.

There are two aspects of the generated code that are worth looking at – the `UpdateCommand()` and `InsertCommand()` methods that are generated by Visual Studio. Here is an abridged version showing the pertinent information:

```
//
// sqlInsertCommand1
//

this.sqlInsertCommand1.CommandText = @"INSERT INTO dbo.Customers
                            (CustomerID, CompanyName, ContactName,
                            ContactTitle, Address, City, Region,
                            PostalCode, Country, Phone, Fax)
        VALUES(@CustomerID, @CompanyName, @ContactName, @ContactTitle,
                @Address, @City, @Region, @PostalCode, @Country, @Phone, @Fax);
        SELECT CustomerID, CompanyName, ContactName, ContactTitle, Address,
                City, Region, PostalCode, Country, Phone, Fax
        FROM dbo.Customers WHERE (CustomerID = @Select2_CustomerID)";
this.sqlInsertCommand1.Connection = this.sqlConnection1;


//
// sqlUpdateCommand1
//

this.sqlUpdateCommand1.CommandText = @"UPDATE dbo.Customers
            SET CustomerID = @CustomerID, CompanyName = @CompanyName,
                ContactName = @ContactName, ContactTitle = @ContactTitle,
                Address = @Address, City = @City, Region = @Region,
                PostalCode = @PostalCode, Country = @Country,
                Phone = @Phone, Fax = @Fax
            WHERE (CustomerID = @Original_CustomerID)
            AND (Address = @Original_Address) AND (City = @Original_City)
            AND (CompanyName = @Original_CompanyName)
            AND (ContactName = @Original_ContactName)
            AND (ContactTitle = @Original_ContactTitle)
            AND (Country = @Original_Country)
            AND (Fax = @Original_Fax)
            AND (Phone = @Original_Phone)
            AND (PostalCode = @Original_PostalCode)
            AND (Region = @Original_Region);
            SELECT CustomerID, CompanyName, ContactName, ContactTitle,
                Address, City, Region, PostalCode, Country, Phone, Fax
            FROM dbo.Customers
            WHERE (CustomerID = @Select2_CustomerID)";
this.sqlUpdateCommand1.Connection = this.sqlConnection1;
```

The main area of interest in these commands is the SQL that has been generated. For both the INSERT and UPDATE commands there are actually two SQL statements: one to do the insert or update, and the other to reselect the row from the database.

These seemingly redundant clauses are used as a way to re-synchronize the data on the client machine with that on the server. There may be defaults applied to columns when inserted, or database triggers that fire to update some of the columns in the inserted/updated record, so re-syncing the data has some benefit. The @Select2_CustomerID parameter used to reselect the data is the same value passed into the INSERT/UPDATE statement for the primary key; the name is just something auto-generated by the wizard.

For tables that include an IDENTITY column, the SQL generated utilizes the @@IDENTITY value after the INSERT statement. As I described within the previous chapter, relying on @@IDENTITY to produce primary keys can cause some interesting bugs, so that's one area of the SQL you may want to change. Similarly, if you have no calculated columns it seems a little wasteful to re-select all columns from the original table just incase something has been updated.

The wizard-generated code may work, but is less than optimal. For a production system, you would probably want to replace some, if not all of these SQL clauses with calls to stored procedures. If your INSERT or UPDATE clauses didn't need to re-sync the data then the removal of the redundant SQL clause could speed up the application a little.

Generating a DataSet

Now you have defined the DataAdapter, you can create a DataSet from that DataAdapter. To generate the dataset, click on the DataAdapter and display the properties for the object (F4). Towards the bottom of the property sheet you'll notice the following three options:

Clicking on **Generate DataSet…** will permit you to choose a name for the new DataSet object, and to choose which table(s) to add into that data set – if you have dragged several tables from the server explorer onto the form, you can link them together within a single DataSet if you wish.

What is actually created is an XSD schema, that defines the data set and each table that you have included within the data set. This is similar to the hand crafted example in the previous chapter, but in this instance the XSD file has been created for you:

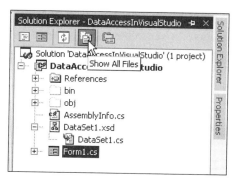

In addition to the XSD file there is a (hidden) `.cs` file that defines a number of type safe classes. To view this generated file, click on the **Show All Files** toolbar button as shown above, and then expand the XSD file. You'll notice a `.cs` file with the same name as the XSD file. The classes defined are as follows:

- ❑ A class derived from `DataSet`
- ❑ A class derived from `DataTable` for the `DataAdapter` you chose
- ❑ A class derived from `DataRow`, defining the columns accessible within the `DataTable`
- ❑ A class derived from `EventArgs`, used when a row changes

You may have guessed what tool is used to generate this file and these classes – it's `XSD.EXE`, which I discussed within the last chapter.

You can naturally choose to update the XSD file once the wizards have done their thing, but don't be tempted to edit the `.cs` file to tweak it in some way, as it will be regenerated when you recompile the project, and all those changes will be lost.

Building a Schema

I spent a few pages in the previous chapter defining an XSD schema in text, which isn't the only way to do it. Visual studio includes an editor for creating XSD schemas – from the **Project** menu, choose **Add Class**, then select the XML schema item:

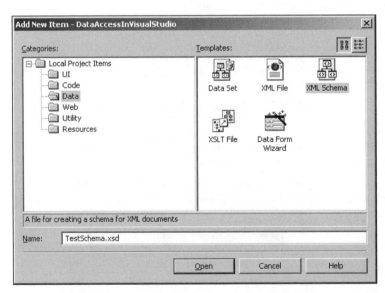

This will add two new files to your project – the .XSD file and a corresponding `.cs` file. Even though the XSD schema is currently empty, the C# source code includes a class derived from `DataSet`:

If you click from **Schema** view to **XML** view, you will see the raw schema template:

```
<?xml version="1.0" encoding="utf-8" ?>
<xsd:schema id="TestSchema"
            targetNamespace="http://tempuri.org/TestSchema.xsd"
            elementFormDefault="qualified"
            xmlns="http://tempuri.org/TestSchema.xsd"
            xmlns:xsd="http://www.w3.org/2001/XMLSchema">
</xsd:schema>
```

This XSD script generates the following C#:

```csharp
namespace DataAccessInVisualStudio
{
    using System;
    using System.Data;
    using System.Runtime.Serialization;
    [System.ComponentModel.DesignerCategoryAttribute("code")]
    public class TestSchema : System.Data.DataSet
    {
        public TestSchema()
        {
            this.InitClass();
        }
        private TestSchema(SerializationInfo info, StreamingContext context)
        {
            this.InitClass();
            this.GetSerializationData(info, context);
        }
        protected override bool ShouldSerializeTables()
        {
            return false;
        }
        protected override bool ShouldSerializeRelations()
        {
            return false;
        }
        private void InitClass()
        {
            this.DataSetName = "TestSchema";
            this.Namespace = "http://tempuri.org/TestSchema.xsd";
        }
    }
}
```

I'll use this as the starting point for this section, so that you can see what code changes are made as items are added into the XSD schema.

Adding an Element

The first thing to do is add a new top-level element. Right-click on the workspace and choose Add | New Element:

This will create a new, unnamed element on screen. You should type in a name for the element; in this example we'll use Product:

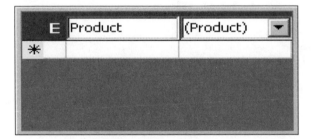

When you save the XSD file, the C# file will be modified and a number of new classes generated. The diagram below lists the main classes that are generated, and shows the derivation of these classes:

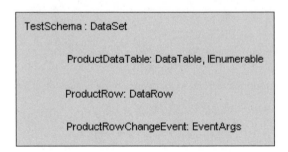

I'll discuss the most pertinent aspects of the code generated:

```
public class TestSchema : System.Data.DataSet
{
    private ProductDataTable tableProduct;
    [System.ComponentModel.DesignerSerializationVisibilityAttribute
            (System.ComponentModel.DesignerSerializationVisibility.Content)]
    public ProductDataTable Product
    {
        get
        {
            return this.tableProduct;
        }
    }
}
```

A new member variable of the class `ProductTable` (described in a moment) is created. This object is returned by the `Product` property, and is constructed within the updated `InitClass` function. From this small section of code, it's evident that the user of these classes can now construct a `DataSet` from the class in this file, and use `DataSet.Products` to return the products `DataTable`.

Generated DataTable

The code below is generated for the `DataTable` (`Product`) that was added to the schema template:

```
public delegate void ProductRowChangeEventHandler
                    (object sender, ProductRowChangeEvent e);
public class ProductDataTable : DataTable, System.Collections.IEnumerable
{
    internal ProductDataTable() : base("Product")
    {
        this.InitClass();
    }
    [System.ComponentModel.Browsable(false)]
    public int Count
    {
        get { return this.Rows.Count;}
    }
    public ProductRow this[int index]
    {
        get { return ((ProductRow)(this.Rows[index]));}
    }
    public event ProductRowChangeEventHandler ProductRowChanged;
    public event ProductRowChangeEventHandler ProductRowChanging;
    public event ProductRowChangeEventHandler ProductRowDeleted;
    public event ProductRowChangeEventHandler ProductRowDeleting;
```

The generated `ProductTable` class is derived from `DataTable`, and includes an implementation of `IEnumerable`. Four events are defined that use the delegate defined above the class when raised. This delegate is passed an instance of the `ProductRowChangeEvent` class, again defined by Visual Studio.

The generated code includes a class derived from `DataRow`, which permits type safe access to columns within the table. You can create a new row in one of two ways:

- ❏ Call the `NewRow()` (or generated `NewProductRow()`) function to return a new instance of the row class. Pass this new row to the `AddRow()` function (or the type safe `AddProductRow()`).

- ❏ Call the `AddRow()` (or generated `AddProductRow()`) function and pass an array of objects, one for each column in the table.

The `AddProductRow()` functions are shown below:

```
public void AddProductRow(ProductRow row)
{
    this.Rows.Add(row);
}
public ProductRow AddProductRow()
{
    ProductRow rowProductRow = ((ProductRow)(this.NewRow()));
    rowProductRow.ItemArray = new Object[0];
    this.Rows.Add(rowProductRow);
    return rowProductRow;
}
```

As can be seen from the code, this second function not only creates a new row, it then inserts that row into the `Rows` collection of the `DataTable`, and then returns this object to the caller. The bulk of the other methods on the `DataTable` are mainly for raising events, which I won't discuss here.

Generated DataRow

The `ProductRow` class generated is shown below:

```
public class ProductRow : DataRow
{
    private ProductDataTable tableProduct;
    internal ProductRow(DataRowBuilder rb) : base(rb)
    {
        this.tableProduct = ((ProductDataTable)(this.Table));
    }
}
```

As yet there are no "columns" defined within the XSD file, so the `ProductRow` class is fairly empty. To add an element to the XSD template that can become a column in the `ProductRow` class, click on screen and define the type as **Element**, then type in the name of the column and the data type:

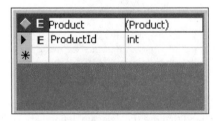

When you save the XSD template, the `.cs` file is automatically rebuilt. When adding the above `ProductID` element, several changes are made to the `.cs` file.

At first the `ProductDataTable` class (derived from `DataTable`) has a private member added, which is the new `DataColumn`:

```
private DataColumn columnProductId;
```

This is joined by a property named `ProductIDColumn` as shown below. This property is defined as `internal`:

```
internal DataColumn ProductIdColumn
{
    get { return this.columnProductId; }
}
```

The `AddProductRow()` function shown above is also modified. The function now takes an integer `ProductID`, and stores the value entered in the newly created column:

```
public ProductRow AddProductRow(int ProductId)
{
    ProductRow rowProductRow = ((ProductRow)(this.NewRow()));
    rowProductRow.ItemArray = new Object[] {ProductId};
    this.Rows.Add(rowProductRow);
    return rowProductRow;
}
```

Finally in the `ProductDataTable` is a modification to the `InitClass()` method:

```
private void InitClass()
{
    this.columnProductId =
        new DataColumn ( "ProductId",
                        typeof(int),
                        "",
                        System.Data.MappingType.Element);
    this.columnProductId.AllowDBNull = false;
    this.Columns.Add(this.columnProductId);
}
```

This creates the new `DataColumn` and adds it to the `DataTable`'s `Columns` collection. The final parameter to the `DataColumn` constructor defines how this column is mapped back into XML, when for instance the `DataSet` is saved to an XML file.

The `ProductRow` class is updated to add in an accessor for this column:

```
public int ProductId
{
    get { return ((int)(this[this.tableProduct.ProductIdColumn])); }
    set { this[this.tableProduct.ProductIdColumn] = value; }
}
```

Generated EventArgs

The final class added into the source code is a derivation of `EventArgs`, which provides methods for directly accessing the row that has changed (or is changing), and the action being applied to that row.

Other Common Requirements

A common requirement when displaying data is to provide a popup menu for a given row. There are numerous ways of doing this, but I'll concentrate on one that can simplify the code required, especially if the display context is a `DataGrid`, where a dataset with some relations is displayed. The problem here is that the context menu is dependent on the row being selected, and that row could come from any of a number of source data tables within the dataset.

As the context menu functionality is likely to be fairly general purpose, the implementation here utilizes a base class (`ContextDataRow`) which supports the menu building code, and each class wishing to support a popup menu derives from this base class.

When the user right clicks on any part of a row in the `DataGrid`, we'll lookup the row and check if it derives from `ContextDataRow`, and if so the `PopupMenu()` function can be called. You could implement this by using an interface, however in this instance a base class is probably simpler.

This example will show how to generate `DataRow` and `DataTable` classes, which can be used to provide type safe access to data, in much the same way as the previous XSD sample. However, this time the code will be hand crafted. It also shows one use for custom attributes and reflection.

The following illustration shows the class hierarchy for this example:

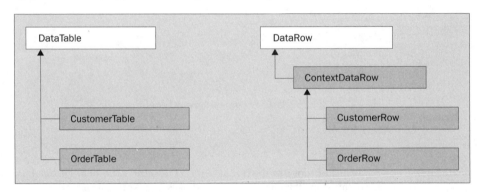

The full code for this example: is available in the `11_Miscellaneous` directory:

```
using System;
using System.Windows.Forms;
using System.Data;
using System.Data.SqlClient;
using System.Reflection;
public class ContextDataRow : DataRow
{
    public ContextDataRow(DataRowBuilder builder) : base(builder)
    {
    }
    public void PopupMenu(System.Windows.Forms.Control parent, int x, int y)
    {

        // Use reflection to get the list of popup menu commands
```

```
            MemberInfo[] members = this.GetType()FindMembers(MemberTypes.Method,
                            BindingFlags.Public | BindingFlags.Instance ,
                            new System.Reflection.MemberFilter(Filter),
                            null);
        if (members.Length > 0)
        {

            // Create a context menu

            ContextMenu menu = new ContextMenu();

            // Now loop through those members and generate the popup menu
            // Note the cast to MethodInfo in the foreach

            foreach(MethodInfo meth in members)
            {

                // Get the caption for the operation from the
                // ContextMenuAttribute

                ContextMenuAttribute[] ctx = (ContextMenuAttribute[])
                    meth.GetCustomAttributes(typeof(ContextMenuAttribute), true);
                MenuCommand callback = new MenuCommand(this , meth);
                MenuItem item = new MenuItem(ctx[0].Caption, new
                                EventHandler(callback.Execute));
                item.DefaultItem = ctx[0].Default;
                menu.MenuItems.Add(item);
            }
            System.Drawing.Point pt = new System.Drawing.Point(x,y);
            menu.Show(parent,pt);
        }
    }
    private bool Filter(MemberInfo member , object criteria)
    {
        bool  bInclude = false;

        // Cast MemberInfo to MethodInfo

        MethodInfo  meth = member as MethodInfo;
        if(meth != null)
            if(meth.ReturnType == typeof(void))
            {
                ParameterInfo[] parms = meth.GetParameters();
                if ( parms.Length == 0 )
                {

                    // Lastly check if there is a ContextMenuAttribute on the
                    // method...

                    object[] atts = meth.GetCustomAttributes
                            ( typeof(ContextMenuAttribute), true);
                    bInclude =(atts.Length == 1);
                }
            }
        return bInclude;
    }
}
```

The context data row class is derived from `DataRow`, and contains just two member functions. The first, `PopupMenu`, uses reflection to look for methods that correspond to a particular signature, and it displays a popup menu of these options to the user. The `Filter()` function is used as a delegate by `PopupMenu` when enumerating methods. It simply returns `true` if the member function does correspond to the appropriate calling convention:

```
MemberInfo[] members = t.FindMembers(MemberTypes.Method,
        BindingFlags.Public | BindingFlags.Instance,
        new System.Reflection.MemberFilter(Filter),
        null);
```

This single statement is used to filter all methods on the current object, and return only those that match the following criteria:

- ❏   The member must be a method
- ❏   The member must be a public instance method
- ❏   The member must return `void`
- ❏   The member must accept zero parameters
- ❏   The member must include the `ContextMenuAttribute`

The last of these is a custom attribute, written specifically for this example. I'll discuss this after completing the dissection of the `PopupMenu` method:

```
ContextMenu menu = new ContextMenu();
foreach(MethodInfo meth in members)
{

    // ... Add the menu item

}
System.Drawing.Point pt = new System.Drawing.Point(x,y);
menu.Show(parent,pt);
```

A context menu instance is created, and we loop through each method that match the above criteria, and add the item to the menu. The menu is subsequently displayed as shown in the following image:

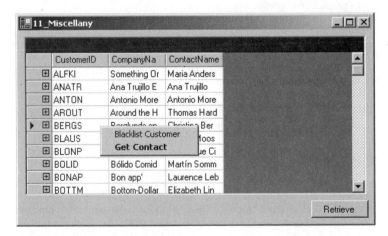

The main area of difficulty within this example, is the following section of code, repeated once for each member function that is to be displayed on the popup menu:

```
System.Type ctxtype = typeof(ContextMenuAttribute);
ContextMenuAttribute[] ctx = (ContextMenuAttribute[])
                            meth.GetCustomAttributes(ctxtype);
MenuCommand callback = new MenuCommand(this, meth);
MenuItem item = new MenuItem(ctx[0].Caption,
               new EventHandler(callback.Execute));
item.DefaultItem = ctx[0].Default;
menu.MenuItems.Add(item);
```

Each method is attributed with the `ContextMenuAttribute`. This defines a user friendly name for the menu option, as the method name cannot include spaces. The attribute is retrieved from the method, and a new menu item created and added to the menu items collection of the popup menu.

Menus within .NET call delegates, rather than sending windows messages. As the signature for a menu item, delegate is not the same as the signature I have decided upon. For the methods that should show up on the context menu, I have implemented a simple command class called `MenuCommand`. This wraps the object to be called and the method to be called into a simple object that can be triggered by the menu choice.

Manufactured Tables and Rows

The XSD sample earlier in the chapter showed the code that was generated when using the Visual Studio editor to generate a set of data access classes, and you may be wondering what the minimal set of code for these classes looks like. The following class shows the required methods for a `DataTable`, which are fairly minimal:

```
public class CustomerTable : DataTable
{
    public CustomerTable() : base("Customers")
    {
        this.Columns.Add("CustomerID", typeof(string));
        this.Columns.Add("CompanyName", typeof(string));
        this.Columns.Add("ContactName", typeof(string));
    }
    protected override System.Type GetRowType()
    {
        return typeof(CustomerRow);
    }
    protected override DataRow NewRowFromBuilder(DataRowBuilder builder)
    {
        return(DataRow) new CustomerRow(builder);
    }
}
```

The first prerequisite of a `DataTable` is that you override the `GetRowType()` function. This is used by the .NET internals when generating new rows for the table. You should return the type of the class used to represent each row.

The next prerequisite is that you implement `NewRowFromBuilder()`, again called by the runtime when creating new rows for the table. That's enough for a minimal implementation. Ours includes adding columns to the `DataTable`, as in this example we know beforehand what the columns are, so we can add them accordingly. The corresponding `CustomerRow` class is fairly simple. It implements properties for each of the columns within the row, and then implements the functions that ultimately are displayed on the context menu:

```
public class CustomerRow : ContextDataRow
{
    public CustomerRow(DataRowBuilder builder) : base(builder)
    {
    }
    public string CustomerID
    {
        get { return (string)this["CustomerID"];}
        set { this["CustomerID"] = value;}
    }

    // Other properties omitted for clarity

    [ContextMenu("Blacklist Customer")]
    public void Blacklist()
    {

        // Do something

    }
    [ContextMenu("Get Contact",Default=true)]
    public void GetContact()
    {

        // Do something else

    }
}
```

The class simply derives from `ContextDataRow`, including the appropriate getter/setter methods on properties named the same as each field, and then a set of methods may be added which are used when reflecting on the class:

```
[ContextMenu("Blacklist Customer")]
public void Blacklist()
{

    // Do something

}
```

Each method that you wish to have displayed on the context menu has the same signature, and includes the custom `ContextMenu` attribute.

Using an Attribute

The idea behind writing the `ContextMenu` attribute was to be able to supply a free text name for a given menu option. I have also implemented a `Default` flag, which is used to indicate the default menu choice. The entire attribute class is presented here:

```
[AttributeUsage(AttributeTargets.Method,AllowMultiple=false,Inherited=true)]
public class ContextMenuAttribute : System.Attribute
{
    public ContextMenuAttribute(string caption)
```

```
    {
        Caption = caption;
        Default = false;
    }
    public readonly string Caption;
    public bool Default;
}
```

The `AttributeUsage` attribute on the class marks the `ContextMenuAttribute` as only being usable on a `Method`. It also defines that there may be only one instance of this object on any given method. The `Inherited=true` clause defines whether the attribute can be placed on a superclass method, and still reflected upon by a subclass.

You can probably think of a number of other members to add to this attribute. Some examples are:

- ❑ The hotkey for the menu option
- ❑ The image to be displayed
- ❑ Text to be displayed in the toolbar as the mouse rolls over the menu option
- ❑ The help context ID

Dispatching Methods

When a menu is displayed within .NET, each menu option is linked to the processing code for that option by means of a delegate. In implementing the mechanism for hooking menu choices to code, you have basically two choices.

The first is to implement a method with the same signature as the `System.EventHandler`. This is defined as shown below:

```
public delegate void EventHandler(object sender, EventArgs e);
```

The second choice is to define a proxy class, which implements the above delegate, and forwards calls onto the received class. This is known as the `Command` pattern, and is what I have chosen for this example.

The command pattern separates the sender and the receiver of the call by means of a simple intermediate class. You may think this is overkill for such an example, however it makes the methods on each `DataRow` simpler (as they don't need the parameters passed to the delegate), and it is more extensible:

```
public class MenuCommand
{
    public MenuCommand(object receiver, MethodInfo method)
    {
        Receiver = receiver;
        Method = method;
    }
    public void Execute(object sender, EventArgs e)
    {
        Method.Invoke(Receiver, new object[] {} );
    }
    public readonly object Receiver;
    public readonly MethodInfo Method;
}
```

The class simply provides an `EventHandler` delegate (the `Execute` method), which invokes the desired method on the receiver object. The example shows two different types of `Row`: rows from the `Customers` table and rows from the `Orders` table. Naturally, the processing options for each of these types of data are likely to differ. The previous image showed the operations available for a `Customer` row. The image below shows the options for an `Order` row:

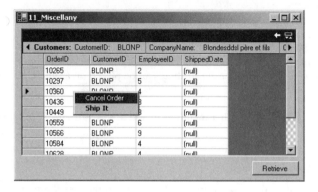

Getting the Selected Row

The last piece of the puzzle for this example is how to work out which row within the `DataSet` the user has clicked upon. Your first thought might be "it must be a property on the `DataGrid`", however try as you like you won't find it there. You might look at the hit test information that you can obtain from within the `MouseUp()` event handler, but that only helps if you are displaying data from a single `DataTable`.

Going back to how the grid is filled for a moment, the line of code is:

```
dataGrid.SetDataBinding(ds, "Customers");
```

Remember the section on `DataBinding`? This method adds a new `CurrencyManager` into the `BindingContext`, which represents the current data table and the dataset. Now, the `DataGrid` has two members, `DataSource` and `DataMember`, which are set when you call `SetDataBinding`. `DataSource` in this instance will be a `DataSet`, and `DataMember` will be `Customers`.

We have a data source, a data member, and know that this information is stored within the `BindingContext` of the form. All we need to do is look up the information:

```
protected void dataGrid_MouseUp(object sender, MouseEventArgs e)
{
    // Perform a hit test
    if(e.Button == MouseButtons.Right)
    {
        // Find which row the user clicked on, if any
        DataGrid.HitTestInfo hti = dataGrid.HitTest(e.X, e.Y);

        // Check if the user hit a cell
        if(hti.Type == DataGrid.HitTestType.Cell)
        {
            // Find the DataRow that corresponds to the cell
            //the user has clicked upon
```

After calling `dataGrid.HitTest()` to calculate where the user has clicked the mouse, we then retrieve the `BindingManagerBase` instance for the data grid:

```
BindingManagerBase bmb =
                 this.BindingContext[dataGrid.DataSource,
                 dataGrid.DataMember];
```

This uses the data grid's `DataSource` and `DataMember` to name the object we want to be returned. All we want to do now is find the row the user clicked on, and display the context menu. With a right mouse click on a row, the current row indicator doesn't normally move, but that's not good enough for us. We want to move the row indicator and then pop up the menu. From the `HitTestInfo` object we have the row number, so all I need to do is move the `BindindManagerBase` objects current position:

```
bmb.Position = hti.Row;
```

This changes the cell indicator, and at the same time means that when I call into the class to get the `Row`, I end up with the current row and not the last one selected:

```
DataRowView drv = bmb.Current as DataRowView;
if(drv != null)
{
    ContextDataRow ctx = drv.Row as ContextDataRow;
    if(ctx != null) ctx.PopupMenu(dataGrid,e.X,e.Y);
}
    }
  }
}
```

As the `DataGrid` is displaying items from a `DataSet`, the `Current` object within the `BindingManagerBase` collection is a `DataRowView`. I can then retrieve the actual row that the `DataRowView` wraps, check if it is indeed a `ContextDataRow`, and finally pop up a menu.

In the example, you'll notice that I have created two data tables: `Customers` and `Orders`, and defined a relationship between these records so that when you click on `CustomerOrders` you see a filtered list of orders. When you do this, the `DataGrid` changes the `DataMember` from `Customers` to `Customers.CustomerOrders`, which just so happens to be the correct thing that the `BindingContext` indexer uses to retrieve the data being shown.

Summary

This chapter has introduced some of the methods of displaying data under .NET. There are a large number of classes to be explored in `System.Windows.Forms`, and we've attempted to touch on some of the commonly used classes. We've explored the `DataGrid` and shown many of its features, but there is more to it than the examples shown here.

The integration of Visual Studio and XML schemas was explored in detail with the section on XSD and the code generated, and we provided a hand crafted example to show a minimal implementation. Hopefully, this has given you an appetite for the other XML facilities of .NET, which are tackled further in the next chapter.

13

XML

XML plays a very large role in the .NET framework. Not only does the framework allow you to make use of XML in your application; the framework itself uses XML for such things as configuration files and source code documentation. To accommodate the extensive use of XML, the .NET framework includes the System.Xml namespace. This namespace is loaded with classes to use for the processing of XML.

In this chapter will look at how to use the DOM implementation and what .NET offers as a replacement for SAX. We'll see how XML and ADO.NET work together and how easy it is to transform one to the other. We will also look at how you can serialize your objects to XML and create an object from (deserialize) an XML document. More to the point, we will look at how you can incorporate XML into your C# applications. Some of the classes that we will be looking at in detail are:

- ❑ XmlReader and XmlTextReader
- ❑ XmlWriter and XmlTextWriter
- ❑ XmlDocument and the DOM
- ❑ XPath and XslTransform
- ❑ ADO.NET and XmlDataDocument
- ❑ XMLSerialization

Let's begin this chapter by taking a look at the current state of XML standards.

W3C Standards

The World Wide Web Consortium (W3C) has developed a set of standards that give XML its power and potential. Without these standards, XML would not have the impact on the development world that it does. This book is not going to teach you the finer points of XML; for that you should look to other sources. Books include Wrox's *Beginning XML* (ISBN 1861003412), *Professional XML* (ISBN 1861003110), and *The XML Handbook* (ISBN 013055068). Of course, the W3C website (http://www.w3.org/) is a valuable source of all things XML.

As of May 2001, the .NET framework supports the following standards:

❑ XML 1.0 (http://www.w3.org/TR/REC-xml), including DTD support (XmlTextReader).

❑ XML Namespaces (http://www.w3.org/TR/REC-xml-names), both stream-level and DOM.

❑ XML Schemas (http://www.w3.org/TR/xmlschema-1). Supported for schema mapping and serialization, but not yet for validation.

❑ XPath expressions (http://www.w3.org/TR/xpath).

❑ XSL/T transformations (http://www.w3.org/TR/xslt).

❑ DOM Level 2 Core (http://www.w3.org/TR/DOM-Level-2-Core/).

❑ Soap 1.1 (http://msdn.microsoft.com/xml/general/soapspec.asp).

The level of standards support will be changing as the framework matures, and as the W3C continues to update the recommended standards. Because of this, you will always need to make sure you stay current with both the standards and the level of support that Microsoft is providing.

The System.Xml Namespace

Let's take a look (in no particular order) at some of the classes that the System.Xml namespace has for us to use. This is by no means a complete list, but a sample of some of the more important classes:

Class Name	Description
XmlReader	Abstract. A reader that provides fast, un-cached XML data. XmlReader is forward only, similar to the SAX parser.
XmlWriter	Abstract. A writer that provides fast, un-cached XML data in stream or file format.
XmlTextReader	Implements XmlReader. Provides fast forward-only stream access to XML data.
XmlTextWriter	Implements XmlWriter. Fast forward-only generation of XML streams.
XmlNode	Abstract. A class that represents a single node in an XML document. Base class for several classes in the XML namespace.
XmlDocument	Implements XmlNode. The W3C Document Object Model (DOM). Gives a tree representation in memory of an XML document, enabling navigation and editing.

Class Name	Description
XmlDataDocument	Implements XmlDocument. That is, a document that can be loaded from XML data or from relational data from an ADO.NET DataSet. Allows the mixing of XML and relational data in the same view.
XmlResolver	Abstract. Resolves external XML based resources such as DTD and schema references. Also used to process `<xsl:include>` and `<xsl:import>` elements.
XmlUrlResolver	Implements XmlResolver. Resolves external resources named by a URI (Uniform Resource Identifier).

XML is also part of the System.Data namespace in the DataSet class:

Class Name	Description
ReadXml	Reads XML data and schema into a DataSet
ReadXmlSchema	Reads XML schema into a DataSet
WriteXml	Writes XML and schema from a DataSet into an XML document
WriteXmlSchema	Writes the schema from a DataSet to an XML document.

> It should be noted that this is a book on the C# language, so all of the examples will be written in C#. However, the XML namespace is available to any language that is part of the .NET family. This means that all of the examples that you will see could also be written in VB.NET, Managed C++, and so on.

XML 3.0 (MSXML3.DLL) in C#

What if you have a ton of code developed using Microsoft's latest parser (currently XML 3.0)? Do you have to toss it away and start over? On the other hand, what if you are comfortable using the XML 3.0 DOM object model? Do you have to switch to .NET right away?

The answer is "no". XML 3.0 can be used directly in your applications. Once you add a reference to msxml3.DLL to your solution, we can start writing some code.

The next few examples will use books.xml as the source of data. This can be downloaded from the Wrox web site (http://www.wrox.com/), but it is also included in several examples in the .NET SDK. The books.xml file is a book catalog for an imaginary bookstore. It includes information such as genre, author name, price, and ISBN number. All of the code examples in this chapter are also available on the Wrox web site. In order to run the examples, the XML data files will need to be in a path structure that looks something like this:

```
/XMLChapter/Sample1
/XMLChapter/Sample2
/XMLChapter/Sample3
```

and so on. The XML files should be in the `XMLChapter` subdirectory, and the code for the examples should be in the `Sample1`, `Sample2`, etc. subdirectories. You can call the directories anything you wish, but the relative position is important. You can also modify the examples to point to anywhere you wish. The example code will be commented to show which line(s) to change.

This is what the `books.xml` file looks like:

```xml
<?xml version='1.0'?>
<!-- This file represents a fragment of a book store inventory database -->
<bookstore>
    <book genre="autobiography" publicationdate="1981" ISBN="1-861003-11-0">
        <title>The Autobiography of Benjamin Franklin</title>
        <author>
            <first-name>Benjamin</first-name>
            <last-name>Franklin</last-name>
        </author>
        <price>8.99</price>
    </book>
    <book genre="novel" publicationdate="1967" ISBN="0-201-63361-2">
        <title>The Confidence Man</title>
        <author>
            <first-name>Herman</first-name>
            <last-name>Melville</last-name>
        </author>
        <price>11.99</price>
    </book>
    <book genre="philosophy" publicationdate="1991" ISBN="1-861001-57-6">
        <title>The Gorgias</title>
        <author>
            <name>Plato</name>
        </author>
        <price>9.99</price>
    </book>
</bookstore>
```

Let's look at some code that uses MSXML 3.0 to load a listbox with the ISBN numbers from `books.xml`. Here is the code, which you'll find in the `SampleBase1` folder of the download. You can copy this into the Visual Studio IDE or create a new Windows Form from scratch. This form contains a listbox and a button. Both use the default names of `listBox1` and `button1`:

```csharp
namespace SampleBase
{
    using System;
    using System.Drawing;
    using System.Collections;
    using System.ComponentModel;
    using System.Windows.Forms;
    using System.Data;
```

Now we'll include the namespace for the `msxml3.dll` reference. Remember that you'll need to include a reference to this in your project (this can be found under the **COM** tab of the **Add Reference** dialog box):

```
using MSXML2;

/// <summary>
/// Summary description for Form1.
/// </summary>

public class Form1 : System.Windows.Forms.Form
{
    private System.Windows.Forms.ListBox listBox1;
    private System.Windows.Forms.Button button1;

    /// <summary>
    ///  Required designer variable.
    /// </summary>

    private System.ComponentModel.Container components;
```

Now we'll declare the DOM document at the module level:

```
    private DOMDocument30 doc;

    public Form1()
    {

      //
      // Required for Windows Form Designer support
      //

      InitializeComponent();

      //
      // TODO: Add any constructor code after InitializeComponent call
      //

    }

    /// <summary>
    ///  Clean up any resources being used.
    /// </summary>

    public override void Dispose()
    {
      base.Dispose();
      if(components != null)
        components.Dispose();
    }

    #region Windows Form Designer generated code

    /// <summary>
    ///  Required method for Designer support - do not modify
    ///  the contents of this method with the code editor.
    /// </summary>
```

```
private void InitializeComponent()
{
    this.listBox1 = new System.Windows.Forms.ListBox();
    this.button1 = new System.Windows.Forms.Button();
    this.listBox1.Anchor = ((System.Windows.Forms.AnchorStyles.Top |
                             System.Windows.Forms.AnchorStyles.Left) |
                             System.Windows.Forms.AnchorStyles.Right);
    this.listBox1.Size = new System.Drawing.Size(336, 238);
    this.listBox1.TabIndex = 0;
    this.listBox1.SelectedIndexChanged += new System.EventHandler
                             (this.listBox1_SelectedIndexChanged);
    this.button1.Anchor = System.Windows.Forms.AnchorStyles.Bottom;
    this.button1.Location = new System.Drawing.Point(136, 264);
    this.button1.TabIndex = 1;
    this.button1.Text = "button1";
    this.button1.Click += new System.EventHandler(this.button1_Click);
    this.AutoScaleBaseSize = new System.Drawing.Size(5, 13);
    this.ClientSize = new System.Drawing.Size(339, 320);
    this.Controls.AddRange(new System.Windows.Forms.Control[]
                             {this.button1, this.listBox1});
    this.Text = "Form1";

}
#endregion

/// <summary>
///   The main entry point for the application.
/// </summary>

[STAThread]
static void Main()
{
    Application.Run(new Form1());
}
```

We want to take the ISBN number from the listbox, and, using a simple XPath search, we'll find the
book node that it matches and display the node text (book title and book price) in a MessageBox. XML
Path Language (XPath) is an XML notation that can be used for querying and filtering text in an XML
document. We will look at XPath in .NET later in the chapter. Here is the event handler code for
selecting an entry in the listbox:

```
protected void listBox1_SelectedIndexChanged (
                        object sender, System.EventArgs e)
{
    string srch=listBox1.SelectedItem.ToString();

    IXMLDOMNode nd=doc.selectSingleNode(
                        "bookstore/book[@ISBN='" + srch + "']");
    MessageBox.Show(nd.text);

}
```

Now we'll look at the event handler for clicking the button. First, we load the books.xml file – note
that if you're running the executable from somewhere that isn't the bin/debug or bin/release
folder, you'll need to adjust the path appropriately:

```
            protected void button1_Click (object sender, System.EventArgs e)
            {
                doc=new DOMDocument30();
                doc.load("..\\..\\..\\books.xml");
```

The next lines declare that `nodes` is a `NodeList` of book nodes. In this case there are three nodes:

```
                IXMLDOMNodeList nodes;
                nodes = doc.selectNodes("bookstore/book");
                IXMLDOMNode node=nodes.nextNode();
```

We loop through the nodes, and add the text value of the ISBN attribute to `listBox1`:

```
                while(node!=null)  {
                    listBox1.Items.Add(node.attributes.getNamedItem("ISBN").text);
                    node=nodes.nextNode ();
                }
            }
        }
    }
```

Here is a screenshot of what the sample looks like when it's executing:

This is right after `button1` has been pressed, and `listBox1` has been loaded with the ISBN numbers of the books. After selecting an ISBN number, this is what you'll see:

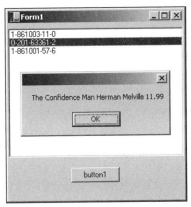

System.Xml

If you have done any work with MSXML 3.0, this will look very familiar. So why would you want to do this if the .NET framework is supposed to have all of these wonderful XML classes to use?

While the `System.Xml` namespace is powerful and relatively easy to use, it is different to using the MSXML 3.0 model. If you are comfortable using MSXML 3.0, then use it until you become familiar with the `System.Xml` namespace. However, you will find that the `System.Xml` namespace offers greater flexibility and is easier to extend.

This XML file will be used for several samples in the chapter. The code sample we just looked at will be the basis for several examples in the chapter. In most of the other examples, we'll show only the pertinent code and not repeat what we have already seen.

Reading and Writing XML

Now that we have seen how things can be done today, let's take a look at what .NET will allow us to do. If you have ever used SAX, then the `XmlReader` and `XmlWriter` classes will feel familiar. `XmlReader`-based classes provide a very fast, forward-only, read-only cursor that streams the XML data for processing. Since it is a streaming model, the memory requirements are not very demanding. However, you don't have the navigation flexibility and the read/write capabilities of using the DOM model. `XmlWriter` based classes will produce an XML document that conforms to the W3C's XML 1.0 Namespace Recommendations.

`XmlReader` and `XmlWriter` are both abstract classes. The graphic below shows what classes are derived from `XmlReader` and `XmlWriter`:

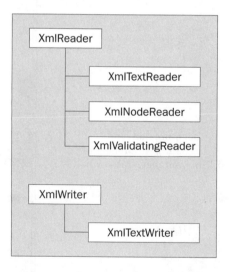

`XmlTextReader` and `XmlTextWriter` work with either a stream-based object or a `TextReader` or `TextWriter` based object. `XmlNodeReader` uses an `XmlNode` as its source instead of a stream. The `XmlValidatingReader` adds DTD and schema validating and therefore offers data validation. We'll look at these in a little more detail later in the chapter.

XmlTextReader

Again, `XmlTextReader` is a lot like SAX. One of the biggest differences, however, is that while SAX is a **push** type of model (that is, it pushes data out to the application, and the developer has to be ready to accept it), the `XmlTextReader` has a **pull** model, where data is pulled in to the application requesting it. This gives an easier and more intuitive programming model. Another advantage to this is that a pull model can be selective about what data is sent to the application. If not all of the data is desired, then you don't need to process it. In a push model, all of the XML data has to be processed by the application whether it is needed or not.

Let's take a look at a very simple example of reading XML data, and then we can take a closer look at the `XmlTextReader` class. You'll find the code in the `XmlReaderSample1` folder. You can replace the `button1_Click` method in the previous example with the following code. This version of the code can be found in the `SampleBase2` folder of the code download. Don't forget to change:

```
using MSXML2;
```

to:

```
using System.Xml;
```

We need to do this because we are no longer using MSXML 3.0 and are using the `System.Xml` namespace instead. We also need to remove the method for `listBox1_SelectedIndexChanged` because this method includes some unsupported methods, as well as the line:

```
private DOMDocument30 doc;
```

This is what our button click event from the previous sample looks like with these changes:

```
protected void button1_Click (object sender, System.EventArgs e)
{
    //Modify this path to find books.xml

    string fileName = "..\\..\\..\\books.xml";

    //Create the new TextReader Object

    XmlTextReader tr = new XmlTextReader(fileName);

    //Read in node at a time

    while(tr.Read())  {
      if(tr.NodeType == XmlNodeType.Text)
        listBox1.Items.Add(tr.Value);
    }
}
```

This is `XmlTextReader` at its simplest. First we create a `string` object with the name of the XML file. We then create a new `XmlTextReader` passing in the `fileName` string. `XmlTextReader` currently has thirteen different constructor overloads, passing in various combinations of strings (file names and URLs), streams and name tables. After an `XmlTextReader` object has been initialized, no node is selected. This is the only time that a node isn't current. When we go into the `tr.Read()` loop, the first `Read()` will move us to the first node in the document. This would typically be the XML Declaration node. In this sample, as we move to each node we compare `tr.NodeType` against the `XmlNodeType` enumeration, and when we find a text node, we add the text value to the listbox. Here is a screenshot after the listbox is loaded:

There are several ways to move through the document. As we just saw, Read() takes us to the next node. We can then check to see if the node has a value (HasValue) or, as you will see shortly, if the node has any attributes (HasAttributes). There is ReadStartElement which will check to see if the current node is the start element, and then position you on to the next node. If you are not on the start element, an XmlException is raised. This method is the same as calling IsStartElement followed by a Read().

The ReadString() and ReadChars() methods both read in the text data from an element. ReadString() returns a string object containing the data, while ReadChars() reads the data in an array of chars that you set up.

ReadElementString() is similar to ReadString(), except that you can optionally pass in the names of an element. If the next content node is not a start tag, or if the Name parameter does not match the current node Name, then an exception is raised. Here is an example of how it can be used (you'll find the code in the XmlReaderSample2 folder):

```
protected void button1_Click (object sender, System.EventArgs e) {

    //use a filestream to get the data

    FileStream fs = new FileStream("..\\..\\..\\books.xml",FileMode.Open);
    XmlTextReader tr = new XmlTextReader(fs);

    while(!tr.EOF)  {

        //if we hit an element type, try and load it in the listbox

        if(tr.MoveToContent()== XmlNodeType.Element && tr.Name=="title") {
            listBox1.Items.Add(tr.ReadElementString());
        }
        else

            //otherwise move on

            tr.Read();
    }
}
```

In the `while` loop we use `MoveToContent()` to find each node of type `XmlNodeType.Element` and the name `title`. If the node is not of type `Element` or not named `title`, the `else` clause will issue a `Read()` method to move to the next node. When we find a node that matches the criteria, we add the result of a `ReadElementString` to the `listbox`. This should leave us with just the book titles in the listbox. Notice that we don't have to issue a `Read()` call after a successful `ReadElementString()`. This is because `ReadElementString()` consumes the entire `Element`, and positions you on the next node.

If we remove `&& tr.Name=="title"` from the `if` clause, you will now have to catch the `XmlException` exception when it is thrown. If you look at the data file, you will see that the first element that `MoveToContent()` will find is the `<bookstore>` element. Since it is an element, it will pass the check in the `if` statement. However since it does not contain a simple text type, it will cause `ReadElementString()` to raise an `XmlException`. One way to work around this is to put the `ReadElementString()` call in a function of its own. We'll call it `LoadList()`. Pass in the `XmlTextReader` as a parameter. Now, if the call to `ReadElementStrin()g` fails inside this function, we can deal with the error and return back to the calling function. This is what the sample looks like with these changes (you'll find the code in the `XmlReaderSample3` folder):

```
protected void button1_Click (object sender, System.EventArgs e) {

  //use a filestream to get the data

  FileStream fs = new FileStream("..\\..\\..\\books.xml",FileMode.Open);
  XmlTextReader tr = new XmlTextReader(fs);

  while(!tr.EOF)  {

    //if we hit an element type, try and load it in the listbox

    if(tr.MoveToContent() == XmlNodeType.Element) {
      LoadList(tr);
    }
    else

      //otherwise move on

      tr.Read();
  }
}
private void LoadList(XmlReader reader) {
  try {
    listBox1.Items.Add(reader.ReadElementString());
  }

  // if an XmlException is raised, ignore it.

  catch(XmlException er){}
}
```

This is what you should see when you run this code:

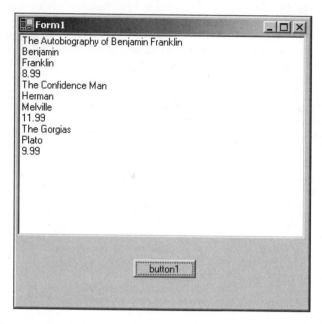

Looks familiar? It's the same result that we had before. What we are seeing is that there is more then one way to accomplish the same goal. This is where the flexibility of the `System.Xml` namespace starts to become apparent.

As you are reading nodes, you will notice that you won't see any attributes. This is because attributes are not considered part of a document's structure. When you are on an element node, you can check for the existence of attributes, and move sideways in the element to get the attribute values. `HasAttributes()` will return `true` if there are any attributes, otherwise `false` is returned. The `AttributeCount` property will tell you how many attributes there are. The `GetAttribute()` method will get an attribute by name or by index. If you want to iterate through the attributes one at a time, there is a `MoveToFirstAttribute()` and a `MoveToNextAttribute()` method. Here is an example of iterating through the attributes from `XmlReaderSample4`:

```
protected void button1_Click (object sender, System.EventArgs e)
{
    //set this path to match your data path structure

    string fileName = "..\\..\\..\\books.xml";

    //Create the new TextReader Object

    XmlTextReader tr = new XmlTextReader(fileName);

    //Read in node at a time

    while(tr.Read()) {

        //check to see if it's a NodeType element
```

```
        if(tr.NodeType == XmlNodeType.Element)  {

          //if it's an element, then let's look at the attributes.

          for(int i=0;i<tr.AttributeCount;i++)  {
            listBox1.Items.Add(tr.GetAttribute(i));
          }
        }
      }
   }
```

This time we are looking for element nodes. When we find one, we loop through all of the attributes, and using the `GetAttribute()` method, we load the value of the attribute into the listbox.

Validation

If you want to validate the XML document, you'll need to use `XmlValidatingReader`. It contains all of the same functionality of `XmlTextReader` (both implement `XmlReader`, but `XmlValidatingReader` adds a `ValidationType` property, a `Schemas` property and a `SchemaType` property). You set the `ValidationType` property to the type of validation that you want to do. The valid values for this property are:

Property Value	Description
Auto	If a DTD is declared in a `<!DOCTYPE...>` declaration, the DTD will be loaded and processed. Default attributes and general entities defined in the DTD will be made available.
	If an XSD `schemalocation` attribute is found, the XSD is loaded and processed and will return any default attributes defined in the schema.
	If a namespace with the MSXML `x-schema:` prefix is found, it will load and process the XDR schema and return any default attributes defined.
DTD	Validate according to DTD rules.
Schema	Validate according to XSD schema.
XDR	Validate according to XDR schema.
None	No validation is performed.

Once the property is set, a `ValidationEventHandler` will need to be assigned. This is an event that gets raised on every validation error that happens. You can then react to the error in any way you see fit. Let's look at an example of how this works. First we will add an XDR (XML Data Reduced) schema namespace to our `books.xml` file and name this file `booksVal.xml`. It now looks like this (the added schema namespace is in the shaded area):

```
<?xml version='1.0'?>
<!-- This file represents a fragment of a book store inventory database -->
<bookstore xmlns="x-schema:books.xdr">
    <book genre="autobiography" publicationdate="1981" ISBN="1-861003-11-0">
        <title>The Autobiography of Benjamin Franklin</title>
```

```
        <author>
            <first-name>Benjamin</first-name>
            <list-name>Franklin</list-name>
        </author>
        <price>8.99</price>
    </book>
    <book genre="novel" publicationdate="1967" ISBN="0-201-63361-2">
        <title>The Confidence Man</title>
        <author>
            <first-name>Herman</first-name>
            <last-name>Melville</last-name>
        </author>
        <price>11.99</price>
    </book>
    <book genre="philosophy" publicationdate="1991" ISBN="1-861001-57-6">
        <title>The Gorgias</title>
        <author>
            <name>Plato</name>
        </author>
        <price>9.99</price>
    </book>
</bookstore>
```

Notice that the bookstore element now has the attribute `xmlns="x-schema:books.xdr"`. This will point to the following XDR schema:

```
<?xml version="1.0"?>
<Schema xmlns="urn:schemas-microsoft-com:xml-data"
                        xmlns:dt="urn:schemas-microsoft-com:datatypes">
    <ElementType name="first-name" content="textOnly"/>
    <ElementType name="last-name" content="textOnly"/>
    <ElementType name="name" content="textOnly"/>
    <ElementType name="price" content="textOnly" dt:type="fixed.14.4"/>
    <ElementType name="author" content="eltOnly" order="one">
        <group order="seq">
            <element type="name"/>
        </group>
        <group order="seq">
            <element type="first-name"/>
            <element type="last-name"/>
        </group>
    </ElementType>
    <ElementType name="title" content="textOnly"/>
    <AttributeType name="genre" dt:type="string"/>
    <ElementType name="book" content="eltOnly">
        <attribute type="genre" required="yes"/>
        <element type="title"/>
        <element type="author"/>
        <element type="price"/>
    </ElementType>
    <ElementType name="bookstore" content="eltOnly">
        <element type="book"/>
    </ElementType>
</Schema>
```

Now everything looks good except for the fact that we have a couple of attributes in the XML file that are not defined in the schema. If you look closely, you will see that the attributes `publicationdate` and `ISBN` from the `book` element are not in the schema. We will do this to show that validation is really taking place. We can use the following code to verify this. You will need to add `using System.Xml.Schema` to your class. The complete code is available in `XMLReaderSample5`:

```
protected void button1_Click (object sender, System.EventArgs e)
{
    //change this to match your path structure.

    string fileName = "..\\..\\..\\booksVal.xml";
    XmlTextReader tr=new XmlTextReader(fileName);
    XmlValidatingReader trv = new XmlValidatingReader(tr);

    //Set validation type

    trv.ValidationType=ValidationType.xdr;

    //Add in the Validation eventhandler

    trv.ValidationEventHandler +=
                  new ValidationEventHandler(this.ValidationEvent);

    //Read in node at a time

    while(trv.Read())  {
        if(trv.NodeType == XmlNodeType.Text)
        listBox1.Items.Add(trv.Value);
    }
}

public void ValidationEvent (object sender, ValidationEventArgs args)
{
    MessageBox.Show(args.Message);
}
```

We create an `XmlTextReader` to pass to the `XmlValidatingReader`. Once the `XmlValidatingReader` trv is created, we can use it in much the same way that we used `XmlTextReader` in the previous examples. The differences are that we specified the `ValidationType`, and added a `ValidationEventHandler`. Every time a validation error occurs, the `ValidationEvent` is raised. You can then handle the validation error any way that you see fit. In this example we are showing a `MessageBox` with the error. This is what the `MessageBox` looks like when the `ValidationEvent` is raised:

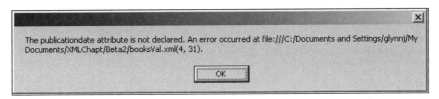

Unlike some parsers, once a validation error occurs, things don't stop. The `XmlValidatingReader` keeps on reading; you have the choice in determining the seriousness of the validation error. If you feel it is a critical error, then it will be up to you to stop reading and deal with the errors accordingly.

The `Schemas` property of `XmlValidatingReader` holds an `XmlSchemaCollection`, which is found in the `System.Xml.Schema` namespace. This collection holds pre-loaded XSD and XDR schemas. This allows for very fast validation, especially if you need to validate several documents, since the schema will not have to be reloaded on each validation. In order to utilize this performance gain, you create an `XmlSchemaCollection` object. The `Add()` method has four overloads. You can pass in an `XmlSchema` based object, an `XmlSchemaCollection` based object, a `string` with the `namespace` along with a `string` with the URI of the schema file, and finally a string with the `namespace` and an `XmlReader`-based object that contains the schema.

Writing XML

The `XmlTextWriter` class allows you write out XML to a stream, file, or `TextWriter` object. Like `XmlTextReader`, it does it in a forward-only, non-cached manner. `XmlTextWriter` is highly configurable, allowing you to specify such things as whether or not to indent, amount to indent, what quote character to use in attribute values, and whether namespaces are supported. The `DataTypeNamespace` property determines how strongly-typed values are converted to XML text. The values allowed for this property are `urn:schemas-microsoft-com:datatypes`, which supports XDR data types, and the other value is `http://www.w3.org/1999/XMLSchema-datatypes` which is for the W3C schema XSD data types. To use the `TimeSpan` data type, for example, you would need to set this property to support the XSD data types.

We can look at a simple example to see how the `XmlTextWriter` class can be used. This can be found in the `XMLWriterSample1` folder:

```
private void button1_Click(object sender, System.EventArgs e)
{
    // change to match your path structure

    string fileName="..\\..\\..\\booknew.xml";

    // create the XmlTextWriter

    XmlTextWriter tw=new XmlTextWriter(fileName,null);

    // set the formatting to indented

    tw.Formatting=Formatting.Indented;
    tw.WriteStartDocument();

    // Start creating elements and attributes

    tw.WriteStartElement("book");
    tw.WriteAttributeString("genre","Mystery");
    tw.WriteAttributeString("publicationdate","2001");
    tw.WriteAttributeString("ISBN","123456789");
    tw.WriteElementString("title","Case of the Missing Cookie");
    tw.WriteStartElement("author");
    tw.WriteElementString("name","Cookie Monster");
    tw.WriteEndElement();
    tw.WriteElementString("price","9.99");
    tw.WriteEndElement();
    tw.WriteEndDocument();

    //clean up

    tw.Flush();
    tw.Close();
}
```

Here we are going to create a new booknew.xml file, and add a new book. XmlTextWriter will overwrite an existing file with a new one. We will look at inserting a new element or node into an existing document later in the chapter. We are instantiating the XmlTextWriter object using a FileStream object as a parameter. You can also pass in a string with a file name and path, or a TextWriter-based object. The next thing that we do is set the Indenting property. Once this is set, child nodes are automatically indented from the parent. From here on, we are writing data. WriteStartDocument() will put in the document declaration. Now we start writing data. First comes the book element. Add the genre, publicationdate, and ISBN attributes. Now we write the title, author, and price elements. Notice that the author element has a child element name.

When we click on the button, we'll produce the booknew.xml file, which looks like this:

```
<?xml version="1.0"?>
<book genre="Mystery" publicationdate="2001" ISBN="123456789">
  <title>Case of the Missing Cookie</title>
  <author>
    <name>Cookie Monster</name>
  </author>
  <price>9.99</price>
</book>
```

As you can see, just as in an XML document, there is a start method and an end method (WriteStartElement and WriteEndElement). Nesting is controlled by paying attention to when you start and finish writing elements and attributes. You can see this when we add the name child element to the authors element. Note how the WriteStartElement and WriteEndElement method calls are arranged and how that relates to the outputted XML document.

To go along with the WriteElementString() and WriteAttributeString() methods there are several other specialized write methods. WriteCData() will output a CData section (<!CDATA[...]]>), taking the text to write out as a parameter. WriteComment writes out a comment in proper XML format. WriteChars() writes out the contents of a char buffer. This works similar to ReadChars that we looked at earlier. They both use the same type of parameters. WriteChar() needs a buffer (an array of characters), the starting position for writing (an integer) and the number of characters to write (an integer).

Reading and writing XML using the XmlReader and XmlWriter-based classes is surprisingly flexible and simple to use. Next, we will look at using the DOM implementation of the System.Xml namespace. These are the XmlDocument and XmlNode-based classes.

Document Object Model in .NET

The Document Object Model (DOM) implementation in .NET supports the W3C DOM Level 1 and Core DOM Level 2 specifications. The DOM is implemented through the XmlNode class. XmlNode is an abstract class that represents a node of an XML document. XmlNodeList is an ordered list of nodes. This is a live list of nodes, and any changes to any node are immediately reflected in the list. XmlNodeList supports indexed access or iterative access. These two classes make up the core of the DOM implementation in the .NET framework. Here is a list of some of the classes that are based on XmlNode.

Class Name	Description
XmlLinkedNode	Extends XmlNode. Returns the node immediately before or after the current node. Adds NextSibling and PreviousSibling property to XmlNode.
XmlDocument	Extends XmlNode. Represents the entire document. Implements the DOM Level 1 and Level 2 specifications.
XmlAttribute	Extends XmlNode. An attribute object of an XmlElement object.
XmlCDataSection	Extends XmlCharacterData. An object that represents a CData section of a document.
XmlCharacterData	Abstract class that provides text manipulation methods for other classes. Extends XmlLinkedNode.
XmlComment	Extends XmlCharacterData. Represents an XML comment object.
XmlDeclaration	Extends XmlLinkedNode. Represents the declaration node (<?xml version='1.0'...>).
XmlDocumentFragment	Extends XmlNode. Represents a fragment of the document tree.
XmlDocumentType	Extends XmlLinkedNode. Data relating to the document type declaration.
XmlElement	Extends XmlLinkedNode. An XML element object.
XmlEntity	Extends XmlNode. A parsed or unparsed entity node.
XmlEntityReferenceNode	Extends XmlLinkedNode. Represents an entity reference node.
XmlNotation	Extends XmlNode. Contains a notation declared in a DTD or schema.
XmlProcessingInstruction	Extends XmlLinkedNode. Contains an XML processing instruction.
XmlSignificantWhitespace	Extends XmlCharacterData. Represents a node with whitespace. Nodes created only if the PreserveWhiteSpace flag is true.
XmlWhitespace	Extends XmlCharacterData. Represents whitespace in element content. Nodes are created only if the PreserveWhiteSpace flag is true.
XmlText	Extends XmlCharacterData. The textual content of an element or attribute.

As you can see, .NET makes available a class to fit just about any XML type that you may encounter. Because of this, you end up with a very flexible and powerful toolset. We won't look at every class in detail, but we will look at several examples to give you an idea of what you might be able to accomplish. This is what the inheritance diagram looks like:

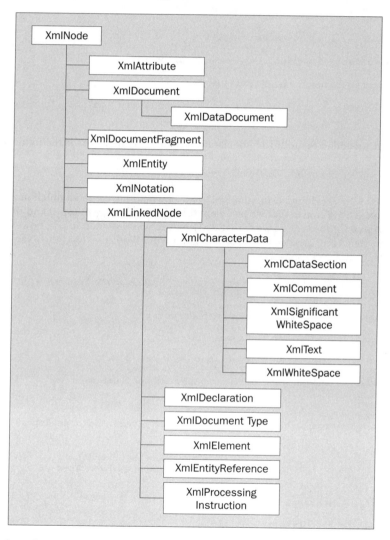

The first example will be to create an `XmlDocument` object, load a document from disk, and load the listbox with data from the title elements. This is similar to one of the examples that we did in the `XmlReader` section. This difference here is that we will be selecting what nodes we want to work with instead of going through the entire document like the `XmlReader` based example does. Here is the code for doing it in the `XmlNode` world. Look at how simple it looks in comparison (the file can be found in the `DOMSample1` folder of the download):

```
private void button1_Click(object sender, System.EventArgs e)
{
    // doc is declared at the module level
    // change path to match your path structure

    doc.Load("..\\..\\..\\books.xml");

    // get only the nodes that we want

    XmlNodeList nodeLst=doc.GetElementsByTagName("title");

    // iterate through the XmlNodeList

    foreach(XmlNode node in nodeLst) listBox1.Items.Add(node.InnerText);
}
```

Take note that we added the following declaration at the module level for the following examples:

```
private XmlDocument doc=new XmlDocument();
```

If this is all that we were doing, using the XmlReader would have been a much more efficient way to load the listbox. The reason is that we just went through the document once, and then were finished with it. This is exactly the type of work that XmlReader was designed for. If, however, we wanted to revisit a node, then using XmlDocument is the better way. We can extend the example a little so we can see the difference in DOMSample2:

```
private void button1_Click(object sender, System.EventArgs e) {

    // doc is declared at the module level
    // change path to match your path structure

    doc.Load("..\\..\\..\\books.xml");

    // get only the nodes that we want

    XmlNodeList nodeLst=doc.GetElementsByTagName("title");

    // iterate through the XmlNodeList

    foreach(XmlNode node in nodeLst) listBox1.Items.Add(node.InnerText);
}
```

```
private void listBox1_SelectedIndexChanged(object sender,
                                           System.EventArgs e)
{

    //create XPath search string

    string srch="bookstore/book[title='" + listBox1.SelectedItem.ToString()
                                       + "']";

    //look for the extra data

    XmlNode foundNode=doc.SelectSingleNode(srch);
    if(foundNode!=null)
        MessageBox.Show(foundNode.InnerText);
    else
        MessageBox.Show("Not found");
}
```

In this example, we load the listbox with the titles from the `books.xml` document. When we click on the listbox, causing the `SelectedIndexChange` event to fire (don't forget to add the code to hook up the event handler in the `InitializeComponent()` function), we take the text of the selected item in the listbox, in this case the book title, create an XPath statement and pass it to the `SelectSingleNode()` method of the `doc` object. This returns the `book` element that the `title` is part of (foundNode). We display the `InnerText` of the node in a message box to see this. We can keep clicking on items in the listbox as many times as we want, since the document is loaded and stays loaded until we release it.

A quick comment regarding the `SelectSingleNode()` method. This is the XPath implementation in the `XmlDocument` class. There is `SelectSingleNode` and `SelectNodes`. Both are defined in `XmlNode`, which `XmlDocument` in based on. `SelectSingleNode()` returns an `XmlNode` and `SelectNodes()` returns an `XmlNodeList`. The `System.Xml.XPath` namespace contains a richer XPath implementation, and we will be looking at that in a later section.

Earlier we looked at an example using `XmlTextWriter` that created a new document. The limitation was that it would not insert a node into a current document. With `XmlDocument` class we can do just that. If we change the `button1_Click` event from the last example to look like this (in `DOMSample3`):

```
private void button1_Click(object sender, System.EventArgs e)
{
    //change path to match your structure

    doc.Load("..\\..\\..\\books.xml");

    //create a new 'book' element

    XmlElement newBook=doc.CreateElement("book");

    //set some attributes

    newBook.SetAttribute("genre","Mystery");
    newBook.SetAttribute("publicationdate","2001");
    newBook.SetAttribute("ISBN","123456789");

    //create a new 'title' element

    XmlElement newTitle=doc.CreateElement("title");
    newTitle.InnerText="Case of the Missing Cookie";
    newBook.AppendChild(newTitle);

    //create new author element

    XmlElement newAuthor=doc.CreateElement("author");
    newBook.AppendChild(newAuthor);

    //create new name element

    XmlElement newName=doc.CreateElement("name");
    newName.InnerText="C. Monster";
    newAuthor.AppendChild(newName);
```

```
        //create new price element

        XmlElement newPrice=doc.CreateElement("price");
        newPrice.InnerText="9.95";
        newBook.AppendChild(newPrice);

        //add to the current document

        doc.DocumentElement.AppendChild(newBook);

        //write out the doc to disk

        XmlTextWriter tr=new XmlTextWriter("..\\..\\..\\booksEdit.xml",null);
        tr.Formatting=Formatting.Indented;
        doc.WriteContentTo(tr);

        tr.Close();

        //load listBox1 with all of the titles, including new one

        XmlNodeList nodeLst=doc.GetElementsByTagName("title");
        foreach(XmlNode node in nodeLst)
            listBox1.Items.Add(node.InnerText);
    }

    private void listBox1_SelectedIndexChanged(object sender,
                                               System.EventArgs e)
    {
        string srch="bookstore/book[title='" + listBox1.SelectedItem.ToString()
                                              + "']";
        XmlNode foundNode=doc.SelectSingleNode(srch);
        if(foundNode!=null)
            MessageBox.Show(foundNode.InnerText);
        else
            MessageBox.Show("Not found");
    }
```

After executing this code, you end up with the same functionality of the previous example, however there is one additional book, *The Case of the Missing Cookie* (a soon-to-be classic) in the listbox. Clicking on the cookie caper title will show all of the same info as the other titles. Breaking the code down a little, we can see that this is actually a fairly simple process. The first thing that we do is create a new book element:

```
    XmlElement newBook=doc.CreateElement("book");
```

`CreateElement()` has three overloads that allow you to specify:

- ❏   The element name
- ❏   The name and namespace URI
- ❏   The `prefix`, `localname` and `namespace`

Once the element is created we need to add attributes:

```
    newBook.SetAttribute("genre","Mystery");
    newBook.SetAttribute("publicationdate","2001");
    newBook.SetAttribute("ISBN","123456789");
```

Remember that the XmlAttribute class extends the XmlNode class, so you have all of the properties and methods of XmlNode available to you. If you have a complex structure, you should not have a problem accommodating it.

Now that we have the attributes created, we need to add the other elements of a book:

```
XmlElement newTitle=doc.CreateElement("title");
newTitle.InnerText="Case of the Missing Cookie";
newBook.AppendChild(newTitle);
```

Once again we create a new XmlElement-based object (newTitle). Set the InnerText property to the title of our new classic, and append the element as a child to the book element. We repeat this for the rest of the elements in the book element. Note that we add the name element as a child to the author element. This will give us the proper nesting relationship as in the other book elements.

Finally we append the newBook element to the doc.DocumentElement node. This is the same level as all of the other book elements. We now have updated an existing document with a new element, whereas with the XmlWriter all we could do was create a new document. The last thing to do is to write out a new XML document to disk. In this example we create a new XmlTextWriter, and pass it in to the WriteContentTo() method. Make sure to call the Close() method on XmlTextWriter to flush the internal buffers and close the file. WriteContentTo() and WriteTo() both take an XmlTextWriter as a parameter. WriteContentTo() saves the current node and all of the children to the XmlTextWriter, whereas WriteTo() saves the current node. Because doc is an XmlDocument based object, it represents the entire document and so that is what is saved. We could also use the Save() method. It will always save the entire document. Save() has four overloads. You can specify a string with the file name and path, a Stream-based object, a TextWriter-based object, or an XmlWriter-based object. This is what we get when we run this example. Notice the new entry at the bottom of the list:

If we wanted to create a document from scratch, we could use the `XmlTextWriter`, which we saw in action earlier in the chapter. We can also use `XmlDocument`. Why would you use one in preference to the other? If the data that you want streamed to XML is available and ready to write, then the `XmlTextWriter` class would be the best choice. However, if you need to build the XML document a little at a time, inserting nodes into various places, then creating the document with `XmlDocument` may be the better choice. Here is the same example that we just looked at, but instead of editing a current document, we will create a new one (DOMSample4):

```csharp
private void button1_Click(object sender, System.EventArgs e)
{
    //create the declaration section

    XmlDeclaration newDec=doc.CreateXmlDeclaration("1.0",null,null);
    doc.AppendChild(newDec);

    //create the new root element

    XmlElement newRoot=doc.CreateElement("newBookstore");
    doc.AppendChild(newRoot);

    //create the new 'book' element

    XmlElement newBook=doc.CreateElement("book");

    //create and set the attributes on the 'book' element

    newBook.SetAttribute("genre","Mystery");
    newBook.SetAttribute("publicationdate","2001");
    newBook.SetAttribute("ISBN","123456789");

    //create the 'title' element

    XmlElement newTitle=doc.CreateElement("title");
    newTitle.InnerText="Case of the Missing Cookie";
    newBook.AppendChild(newTitle);

    //create an author element

    XmlElement newAuthor=doc.CreateElement("author");
    newBook.AppendChild(newAuthor);

    //create the name element

    XmlElement newName=doc.CreateElement("name");
    newName.InnerText="C. Monster";
    newAuthor.AppendChild(newName);

    //create the price element

    XmlElement newPrice=doc.CreateElement("price");
    newPrice.InnerText="9.95";
    newBook.AppendChild(newPrice);

    //append the 'book' element to the doc

    doc.DocumentElement.AppendChild(newBook);

    //write to disk Note new filename booksEdit.xml
```

```
    XmlTextWriter tr=new XmlTextWriter("..\\..\\..\\booksEdit.xml",null);
    tr.Formatting=Formatting.Indented;
    doc.WriteContentTo(tr);

    tr.Close();

    //load the title in the listbox

    XmlNodeList nodeLst=doc.GetElementsByTagName("title");

    foreach(XmlNode node in nodeLst)
      listBox1.Items.Add(node.InnerText);
}

private void listBox1_SelectedIndexChanged(object sender,
                                           System.EventArgs e)
{
    string srch="newBookstore/book[title='"
                        + listBox1.SelectedItem.ToString() + "']";
    XmlNode foundNode=doc.SelectSingleNode(srch);
    if(foundNode!=null)
        MessageBox.Show(foundNode.InnerText);
    else
        MessageBox.Show("Not found");
}
```

If you look carefully, you will see that the only thing that has changed is the first couple of lines. Before we had a doc.Load(), whereas now we create a couple of new elements:

```
XmlDeclaration newDec=doc.CreateXmlDeclaration("1.0",null,null);
doc.AppendChild(newDec);
XmlElement newRoot=doc.CreateElement("newBookstore");
doc.AppendChild(newRoot);
```

First, we create a new XmlDeclaration. The parameters are version (always 1.0 for now), encoding (null defaults to UTF-8), and finally the standalone flag. This can be yes or no, but if a null or empty string is entered, as is the case here, the attribute will not be added when the document is saved. The encoding parameter should be set to a string that is part of the System.Text.Encoding class if null isn't used.

The next element that is created will become the DocumentElement. In this case, we called it newBookstore so that you can see the difference. The rest of the code is the same as the previous example, and works in the same way. This is booksEdit.xml, which is generated from this code:

```xml
<?xml version="1.0"?>
<newBookstore>
    <book genre="Mystery" publicationdate="2001" ISBN="123456789">
        <title>Case of the Missing Cookie</title>
        <author>
            <name>C. Monster</name>
        </author>
        <price>9.95</price>
    </book>
</newBookstore>
```

We have not looked at every nook and cranny of the `XmlDocument` class, or of the other classes that help to create the DOM model in .NET. However, we have seen the power and flexibility that the DOM implementation in .NET offers. You will want to use the `XmlDocument` class when you want to have random access to the document. Use the `XmlReader` based classes when you want a streaming type model. Remember that the flexibility of the `XmlNode`-based `XmlDocument` is that memory requirements are higher, so think carefully about which method is best for the situation.

XPath and XslTransform

We are going to look at `XPath` and `XslTransform` together, even though they are separate namespaces in the framework. `XPath` lives in `System.Xml.XPath`, and `Xsl` is found in `System.Xml.Xsl`. The reason that we are looking at them together is that `XPath`, specifically the `XPathNavigator` class, provides a very performance-oriented way of performing XSL Transforms in .NET. We will first look at `XPath` and then how it is used to feed the `System.Xsl` classes.

XPath

The `XPath` namespace is built for speed. It provides a read-only view of your XML documents, so no editing capabilities here. `XPath` is built to do fast iteration and selections on the XML document in a cursory fashion. The `XPath` functionality is exposed via the `XPathNavigator` class. This class can be used instead of `XmlDocument`, `XmlDataDocument` and `XPathDocument`. If you need editing capabilities, then `XmlDocument` is the choice to go for; if you're utilizing ADO.NET, then `XmlDataDocument` (we will see this later in the chapter) is what you'll use. If speed is of concern, then use `XPathDocument` as your store. You can extend `XPathNavigator` to use such things as the file system or registry as the store. Here is a table that lists the `XPath` classes and gives a short description of the purpose of each class:

Class Name	Description
XPathDocument	A view of the entire XML document. Read-only.
XPathNavigator	Provides the navigation capabilities to an `XPathDocument`.
XPathNodeIterator	Provides iteration capabilities to a node set. `XPath` equivalent to a nodeset in `Xpath`.
XPathExpression	A compiled `XPath` expression. Used by `SelectNodes`, `SelectSingleNodes`, `Evaluate` and `Matches`.
XPathException	XPath exception class.

`XPathDocument` doesn't offer any of the functionality of the `XmlDocument` class. It has four overloads allowing you to open an XML document from a file and path string, a `TextReader` object, an `XmlReader` object, or a `Stream`-based object.

The best way to see how this fits in is to look at some code. Let's load up the `books.xml` document and move around in it so that you can see how the navigation works. In order to use these examples, you will need to add a reference to the `System.Xml.Xsl` and `System.Xml.XPath` namespaces like this:

```
using System.Xml.XPath;
using System.Xml.Xsl;
```

For this example we are using `booksxpath.xml`. It is similar to the `books.xml` that we have been using, except there are a couple of extra books added. Here's the form code, which can be found in the `XPathXSLSample1` folder:

```
private void button1_Click(object sender, System.EventArgs e)
{

    //modify to match your path structure

    XPathDocument doc=new XPathDocument("..\\..\\..\\booksxpath.xml");

    //create the XPath navigator

    XPathNavigator nav=((IXPathNavigable)doc).CreateNavigator();

    //create the XPathNodeIterator of book nodes
    // that have genre attribute value of novel

    XPathNodeIterator iter=nav.Select("/bookstore/book[@genre='novel']");

    while(iter.MoveNext()) {
        LoadBook(iter.Current);
    }
}

private void LoadBook(XPathNavigator lstNav)
{

    //We are passed an XPathNavigator of a particular book node
    //we will select all of the descendents and
    //load the list box with the names and values

    XPathNodeIterator iterBook=lstNav.SelectDescendants
                            (XPathNodeType.Element,false);
    while(iterBook.MoveNext())
        listBox1.Items.Add(iterBook.Current.Name + ": "
                                    + iterBook.Current.Value);
}
```

The first thing we do is to create the `XPathDocument`, passing in the file and path string of the document we want opened. The next line is where the `XPathNavigator` is created:

```
XPathNavigator nav=((IXPathNavigable)doc).CreateNavigator();
```

Notice that we do a cast of the `IXPathNavigable` interface to the `XPathDocument` we just created. This will give us the `CreateNavigator` method call. Once the `XPathNavigator` is created, we can start navigating the document.

In the example you can see that we use the `Select` methods to get a set of nodes that all have novel as the value of the genre attribute. We then use the `MoveNext()` loop to iterate through all of the novels in the book list.

To load the data into the listbox, we use the `XPathNodeIterator.Current` property. This will create a new `XPathNavigator` object based on just the node that the `XPathNodeIterator` is pointing at. In this case, we are creating an `XPathNavigator` for one book node in the document. `LoadBook()` creates another `XPathNodeIterator` by issuing another type of select method, the `SelectDescendants` method. This will give us an `XPathNodeIterator` of all of the child nodes and children of the child nodes of the book node that we sent to the `LoadBook` method. We do another `MoveNext()` loop on this `XPathNodeIterator` and load the listbox with the element names and element values.

`XPathNavigator` contains all of the methods for moving and selecting elements that you need. Some of the move methods are:

Method Name	Description
MoveTo()	Takes an `XPathNavigator` as a parameter. Move the current position to be the same as that passed in to `XPathNavigator`.
MoveToAttribute()	Move to the named attribute. Takes the attribute name and namespace as parameters.
MoveToFirstAttribute()	Move to the first attribute in the current element. Returns `true` if successful.
MoveToNextAttribute()	Move to the next attribute in the current element. Returns `true` if successful.
MoveToFirst()	Move to the first sibling in the current node. Returns `true` if successful, otherwise returns `false`.
MoveToLast()	Move to the last sibling in the current node. Returns `true` if successful.
MoveToNext()	Move to the next sibling in the current node. Returns `true` if successful.
MoveToPrevious()	Move to the previous sibling in the current node. Returns `true` if successful.
MoveToFirstChild()	Move to the first child of the current element. Returns `true` if successful.
MoveToId()	Move to the element with the ID supplied as a parameter. There needs to be a schema for the document, and the data type for the element must be of type ID.
MoveToParent()	Move to the parent of the current node. Returns `true` if successful.
MoveToRoot()	Move to the root node of the document.

There are also several `Select` methods for selecting out a subset of nodes to work with. All of the `Select` methods return an `XPathNodeIterator` object. `XPathNodeIterator` can be thought of as the equivalent of a `NodeList` or a `NodeSet` in XPath. This object has three properties and two methods:

- ❑ `Clone` – Creates a new copy of itself.
- ❑ `Count` – Number of nodes in the `XPathNodeIterator` object.
- ❑ `Current` – Returns an `XPathNavigator` pointing to the current node.
- ❑ `CurrentPosition()` – Returns an integer with the current position.
- ❑ `MoveNext()` – Moves to the next node that matches the `Xpath` expression that created the `XPathNodeIterator`.

There is also a `SelectAncestors()` and a `SelectChildren()` method that can be used. All return an `XPathNodeIterator`. While `Select()` takes an `XPath` expression as a parameter, the other select methods take an `XPathNodeType` as a parameter. In our example, we chose all of the `XPathNodeType.Element` nodes.

This is what the screen looks like after running the code. Notice that the only books listed are the novels:

Now what if we wanted to add up the cost of these books? `XPathNavigator` has included the `Evaluate()` method for just this reason. `Evaluate()` has three overloads. The first one contains a string that is the `XPath` function call. The second overload uses the `XPathExpression` object as a parameter, and the third uses `XPathExpression` and an `XPathNodeIterator` as parameters. The changes are highlighted below (this version of the code can be found in `XPathXSLSample2`):

```
private void button1_Click(object sender, System.EventArgs e) {

    //modify to match your path structure

    XPathDocument doc=new XPathDocument("..\\..\\..\\booksxpath.XML");

    //create the XPath navigator

    XPathNavigator nav=((IXPathNavigable)doc).CreateNavigator();

    //create the XPathNodeIterator of book nodes
    // that have genre attribute value of novel

    XPathNodeIterator iter=nav.Select("/bookstore/book[@genre='novel']");

    while(iter.MoveNext())
    {
        LoadBook(iter.Current.Clone());
    }
```

661

```
        //add a break line and calculate the sum

    listBox1.Items.Add("=========================");
    listBox1.Items.Add("Total Cost = "
            + nav.Evaluate("sum(/bookstore/book[@genre='novel']/price)"));
}
```

The output will change to the following:

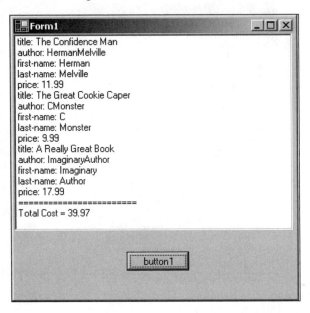

XslTransform

The `System.Xml.Xsl` namespace contains the XSL classes used by .NET. `XslTransform` can be used with any store that implements the `IXPathNavigable` interface. In the .NET Framework, that would currently include `XmlDocument`, `XmlDataDocument`, and `XPathDocument`. Again, just as in XPath, use the store that makes the most sense. If you plan on creating a custom store, such as the file system, and you want to be able to do transforms, be sure to implement the `IXPathNavigable` interface in your class.

`XslTransform` is based on a streaming pull model. Because of this, you can chain several transforms together. You could even apply a custom reader between transforms if needed. This allows a great deal of flexibility in design.

The first example we will look at takes the `books.xml` document and transforms it into a simple HTML document for display. (This code can be found in the `XPathXSLSample3` folder.) We will need to add the following `using` statements:

```
using System.IO;
using System.Xml.Xsl;
using System.Xml.XPath;
```

Here is the code to do the transform:

```
private void button1_Click(object sender, System.EventArgs e)
{

    //create the new XPathDocument

    XPathDocument doc=new XPathDocument("..\\..\\..\\booksxpath.XML");

    //create a new XslTransForm

    XslTransform transForm=new XslTransform();
    transForm.Load("..\\..\\..\\books.xsl");

    //this FileStream will be our output

    FileStream fs=new FileStream("..\\..\\..\\booklist.html",
                            FileMode.Create);

    //Create the navigator

    XPathNavigator nav=((IXPathNavigable)doc).CreateNavigator();

    //Do the transform. The outut file is created here

    transForm.Transform(nav,null,fs);
}
```

This is about as simple a transform as can be. We create an XPathDocument-based object and an XslTransform-based object. We load the booksxpath.xml file into doc, and books.xsl into transForm. In this example, we are creating a FileStream object to write the new HTML document to disk.

If this were an ASP.NET application, we would have used a TextWriter object and passed it into the HttpResponse object. If we were transforming to another XML document we would have used an XmlWriter based object. After the XPathDocument and XslTransform objects are ready, we create the XPathNavigator on doc, and pass nav and the stream into the Transform() method of transForm. XslTransform has several overloads, passing in combinations of navigators, XsltArgumentList (more on this later) and IO streams. The navigator parameter can be XPathNavigator, or anything that implements the IXPathNavigable interface. The IO streams can be a TextWriter, Stream, or XmlWriter-based object.

The books.xsl document is a fairly straightforward stylesheet. The document looks like this:

```
<xsl:stylesheet version="1.0"
                    xmlns:xsl="http://www.w3.org/1999/XSL/Transform">

<xsl:template match="/">
    <html>
        <head>
            <title>Price List</title>
        </head>
        <body>
```

```
            <table>
               <xsl:apply-templates/>
            </table>
         </body>
      </html>

   </xsl:template>

   <xsl:template match="bookstore">
      <xsl:apply-templates select="book"/>
   </xsl:template>

   <xsl:template match="book">
      <tr><td>
         <xsl:value-of select="title"/>
      </td><td>
         <xsl:value-of select="price"/>
      </td></tr>
   </xsl:template>

</xsl:stylesheet>
```

Earlier we mentioned `XsltArgumentList`. This is a way that you can bind an object with methods to a namespace. Once this is done, you can invoke the methods during the transform. Let's look at an example to see how this works (found in `XPathXSLSample4`):

```
private void button1_Click(object sender, System.EventArgs e)
{
   //new XPathDocument

   XPathDocument doc=new XPathDocument("..\\..\\..\\booksxpath.xml");

   //new XslTransform

   XslTransform transForm=new XslTransform();
   transForm.Load("..\\..\\..\\booksarg.xsl");

   //new XmlTextWriter since we are creating a new XML document

   XmlWriter xw=new XmlTextWriter("..\\..\\..\\argSample.xml",null);

   //create the XsltArgumentList and new BookUtils object

   XsltArgumentList argBook=new XsltArgumentList();
   BookUtils bu=new BookUtils();

   //this tells the argumentlist about BookUtils

   argBook.AddExtensionObject("urn:ProCSharp",bu);

   //new XPathNavigator

   XPathNavigator nav=((IXPathNavigable)doc).CreateNavigator();

   //do the transform
```

```
        transForm.Transform(nav,argBook,xw);
        xw.Close();
}

//simple test class

public class BookUtils
{
    public BookUtils(){}

    public string ShowText()
    {
        return "This came from the ShowText method!";
    }
}
```

This is what the output of the transform looks like (`argSample.xml`):

```xml
<?xml version="1.0"?>
<books>
   <discbook>
       <booktitle>The Autobiography of Benjamin Franklin</booktitle>
       <showtext>This came from the ShowText method!</showtext>
   </discbook>
   <discbook>
       <booktitle>The Confidence Man</booktitle>
       <showtext>This came from the ShowText method!</showtext>
   </discbook>
   <discbook>
       <booktitle>The Gorgias</booktitle>
       <showtext>This came from the ShowText method!</showtext>
   </discbook>
   <discbook>
       <booktitle>The Great Cookie Caper</booktitle>
       <showtext>This came from the ShowText method!</showtext>
   </discbook>
   <discbook>
       <booktitle>A Really Great Book</booktitle>
       <showtext>This came from the ShowText method!</showtext>
   </discbook>
</books>
```

We define a new class, `BookUtils`. In this class we have one rather useless method that returns the string "`This came from the ShowText method!`". In the `button1_Click` event, we create the `XPathDocument` and `XslTransform` just as we did before, with a couple of exceptions. This time we are going to create an XML document, so we use the `XMLWriter` instead of the `FileStream` from before. The next change is here:

```
XsltArgumentList argBook=new XsltArgumentList();
BookUtils bu=new BookUtils();
argBook.AddExtensionObject("urn:ProCSharp",bu);
```

This is where we create the `XsltArgumentList`. We create an instance of our `BookUtils` object, and when we call the `AddExtensionObject()` method, we pass in a namespace for our extension, and the object that we want to be able to call methods from. When we make the `Transform` call, we pass in the `XsltArgumentList` (argBook) along with the `XPathNavigator` and the `XmlWriter` object we made. Here is the `booksarg.xsl` document:

```
<xsl:stylesheet version="1.0" xmlns:xsl="http://www.w3.org/1999/XSL/Transform"
                                    xmlns:bookUtil="urn:ProCSharp">
    <xsl:output method="xml" indent="yes"/>

    <xsl:template match="/">
       <xsl:element name="books">
          <xsl:apply-templates/>
       </xsl:element>
    </xsl:template>

    <xsl:template match="bookstore">
       <xsl:apply-templates select="book"/>
    </xsl:template>

    <xsl:template match="book">
       <xsl:element name="discbook">
          <xsl:element name="booktitle">
             <xsl:value-of select="title"/>
          </xsl:element>
          <xsl:element name="showtext">
             <xsl:value-of select="bookUtil:ShowText()"/>
          </xsl:element>
       </xsl:element>
    </xsl:template>

</xsl:stylesheet>
```

The two important lines are highlighted in gray. First we add the namespace that we created when we added the object to the `XsltArgumentList`. Then when we want to make the method call, we use standard XSLT namespace prefixing syntax and make the method call.

Another way we could have accomplished this is with XSLT scripting. You can include C#, VB, and JavaScript code in the stylesheet. The great thing about this is that unlike current implementations, the script is compiled at the `Transform.Load` call; this way you are executing already compiled scripts, much the same way that ASP.NET works. Let's do the previous example in this way. First we add the script to the stylesheet. You can see these changes in `booksscript.xsl`:

```
<xsl:stylesheet version="1.0" xmlns:xsl="http://www.w3.org/1999/XSL/Transform"
                                    xmlns:msxsl="urn:schemas-microsoft-com:xslt"
                                    xmlns:user="http://wrox.com">

    <msxsl:script language="C#" implements-prefix="user">

       string ShowText()
         {

             return "This came from the ShowText method!";

         }
```

```
            </msxsl:script>

        <xsl:output method="xml" indent="yes"/>
            <xsl:template match="/">
        <xsl:element name="books">
            <xsl:apply-templates/>
        </xsl:element>
            </xsl:template>

        <xsl:template match="bookstore">
            <xsl:apply-templates select="book"/>
        </xsl:template>

            <xsl:template match="book">
            <xsl:element name="discbook">
            <xsl:element name="booktitle">
                <xsl:value-of select="title"/>
            </xsl:element>
            <xsl:element name="showtext">
              <xsl:value-of select="user:ShowText()"/>
            </xsl:element>
         </xsl:element>
        </xsl:template>

    </xsl:stylesheet>
```

Once again the changes are highlighted in gray. Set the scripting namespace, add the code (which was copied and pasted in from the VS.NET IDE), and make the call in the stylesheet. The output looks the same as that of the previous example.

The key thing to keep in mind when doing transforms is to remember to use the proper store; use XPathDocument if you don't need edit capabilities, XmlDataDocument if you're getting your data from ADO.NET, and XmlDocument if you need to be able to edit the data. The process is the same regardless.

XML and ADO.NET

XML is the glue that binds ADO.NET to the rest of the world. ADO.NET was designed from the ground up to work within the XML environment. XML is used to transfer the data to and from the data store and the application or web page. Since ADO.NET uses XML as the transport, data can be exchanged with applications and systems that are not even aware of ADO.NET. As long as XML can be processed, they can share the data. ADO.NET can read the XML returned from these same applications. Because of the importance of XML in ADO.NET, there are some powerful features in ADO.NET that allow the reading and writing of XML documents. The XML namespace also contains classes that can consume or utilize ADO.NET relational data.

ADO.NET Data to XML Document

The first example that we are going to look at uses ADO.NET, streams, and XML to pull some data from the Northwind database into a DataSet, load an XmlDocument object with the XML from the DataSet, and load the XML into a listbox. In order to run the next few samples, you need to add the following using statements:

```
using System.Data;
using System.Xml;
using System.Data.SqlClient;
using System.IO;
```

Also, for the ADO samples we have added a `DataGrid` to the forms. This will allow us to see the data in the ADO.NET `DataSet` since it is bound to the grid, as well as the data from the generated XML documents that we load in the listbox. Here is the code for the first example, which can be found in the `ADOSample1` folder:

```
private void button1_Click(object sender, System.EventArgs e)
{
    //create a dataset

    DataSet ds=new DataSet("XMLProducts");

    //connect to the northwind database and
    //select all of the rows from products table
    //make sure your login matches your version of SqlServer

    SqlConnection conn=new SqlConnection
                (@"server=GLYNNJ_CS\NetSDK;uid=sa;pwd=;database=northwind");
    SqlDataAdapter da=new SqlDataAdapter("select * from products",conn);
```

After we create the `SqlDataAdapter`, da, and the `DataSet`, ds, we instantiate a `MemoryStream` object, a `StreamReader` object, and a `StreamWriter` object. The `StreamReader` and `StreamWriter` objects will use the `MemoryStream` to move the XML around:

```
MemoryStream memStrm=new MemoryStream();
StreamReader strmRead=new StreamReader(memStrm);
StreamWriter strmWrite=new StreamWriter(memStrm);
```

We will use a `MemoryStream` so we don't have to write anything to disk, however, we could have used any object that was based on the `Stream` class such as `FileStream`. Next, we fill the `DataSet` and bind it to the `DataGrid`. The data in the `DataSet` will now be displayed in the `DataGrid`:

```
da.Fill(ds,"products");

//load data into DataGrid

dataGrid1.DataSource=ds;
dataGrid1.DataMember="products";
```

This next step is where the XML is generated. We call the `WriteXml()` method from the `DataSet` class. This method generates an XML document. There are two overloads to `WriteXml()`: one takes a string with the file path and name, and the other adds a mode parameter. This mode is an `XmlWriteMode` enumeration. The possible values are `DiffGram`, `IgnoreSchema` and `WriteSchema`. We will look at `DiffGram` later in the section. `IgnoreSchema` is used if you don't want `WriteXml()` to write an inline schema in your XML file; use the `WriteSchema` parameter if you do want one. In order to get just the schema, we call `WriteXmlSchema()`. This method has four overloads. One takes a string, which is the path and file name of where to write the XML document. The second overload uses an object that is based on the `XmlWriter` class. The third overload uses an object that is based on the `TextWriter` class. The fourth overload is the one that we used in the example and is derived from the `Stream` class:

```
        ds.WriteXml(strmWrite,XmlWriteMode.IgnoreSchema);
        memStrm.Seek(0,SeekOrigin.Begin);

        //read from the memory stream to an XmlDocument object

        doc.Load(strmRead);

        //get all of the products elements

        XmlNodeList nodeLst=doc.GetElementsByTagName("ProductName");

        //load them into the list box

        foreach(XmlNode nd in nodeLst)
          listBox1.Items.Add(nd.InnerText);
    }

    private void listBox1_SelectedIndexChanged(object sender,
                                        System.EventArgs e)
    {
        //when you click on the listbox,
        //a message box appears with unit price

        string srch="XmlProducts/products[ProductName=
                        " + '"' + listBox1.SelectedItem.ToString() + '"'
                        + "]";
        XmlNode foundNode=doc.SelectSingleNode(srch);
        if(foundNode!=null)
            MessageBox.Show(foundNode.SelectSingleNode("UnitPrice").InnerText);
        else
            MessageBox.Show("Not found");
    }
```

Here is a screenshot so you can see the data in the list as well as the bound data grid:

If we wanted to persist the XML document to disk, we would have done something like this:

```
string file="c:\\test\\product.xml");
ds.WriteXml(file);
```

This would give us a well-formed XML document on disk that could be read in by another stream, by `DataSet`, or used by another application or web site. Since no `XmlMode` parameter is specified, this `XmlDocument` would have the schema included. In our example, we use the stream as a parameter to the `XmlDocument.Load()` method.

Once the `XmlDocument` is prepared, we load the listbox using the same `XPath` that we used before. If you look closely, you'll see that we changed the `listBox1_SelectedIndexChanged` event slightly. Instead of showing the `InnerText` of the element, we do another `XPath` search using `SelectSingleNode()` to get the `UnitPrice` element. So every time you click on a product in the listbox, a `MessageBox` appears with the `UnitPrice`. We now have two views of the data, but more importantly, we can manipulate the data using two different models. We can use the `Data` namespace to use the data or we can use the XML namespace on the data. This can lead to some very flexible designs in your applications, because now you are not tied to just one object model to program with. This is the real power to the ADO.NET and `System.Xml` combination. You have multiple views of the same data, and multiple ways to access the data.

The next example will simplify the process by eliminating the three streams and by using some of the ADO capabilities built into the XML namespace. We will need to change the module-level line of code:

```
private XmlDocument doc=new XmlDocument();
```

to:

```
private XmlDataDocument doc;
```

We need this because we are now going to be using the `XmlDataDocument`. Here is the code, which can be found in the `ADOSample2` folder:

```
private void button1_Click(object sender, System.EventArgs e)
{
    //create a dataset

    DataSet ds=new DataSet("XMLProducts");

    //connect to the northwind database and
    //select all of the rows from products table
    //make changes to connect string to match your login and server name

    SqlConnection conn=new SqlConnection
                (@"server=GLYNNJ_CS\NetSDK;uid=sa;pwd=;database=northwind");
    SqlDataAdapter da=new SqlDataAdapter("select * from products",conn);

    //fill the dataset

    da.Fill(ds,"products");
```

```
      //load data into grid
      dataGrid1.DataSource=ds;
      dataGrid1.DataMember="products";
      doc=new XmlDataDocument(ds);


      //get all of the products elements

      XmlNodeList nodeLst=doc.GetElementsByTagName("ProductName");

      //load them into the list box
      //we'll use a for loop this time

      for(int ctr=0;ctr<nodeLst.Count;ctr++)
          listBox1.Items.Add(nodeLst[ctr].InnerText);
  }
```

As you can see, the code to load the `DataSet` into the XML document has been simplified. Instead of using the `XmlDocument` class, we are using the `XmlDataDocument` class. This class was built specifically for using data with a `DataSet` object.

The `XmlDataDocument` is based on the `XmlDocument` class, so it has all of the functionality that the `XmlDocument` class has. One of the main differences is the overloaded constructor that the `XmlDataDocument` has. Note the line of code that instantiates the `XmlDataDocument`:

```
  XmlDataDocument doc=new XmlDataDocument(ds);
```

It passes in the `DataSet` that we created, `ds`, as a parameter. This creates the XML document from the data set, and we don't have to use the `Load` method. There is also a `DataSet` property that can be set with a current `DataSet`. In fact, if you instantiate a new `XmlDataDocument` object without passing in a `DataSet` as the parameter, it contains a `DataSet` with the name `NewDataSet` that has no `DataTables` in the tables collection. There is also a `DataSet` property that you can set after an `XmlDataDocument` based object is created.

If the following line of code is added after the `DataSet.Fill()` call:

```
  ds.WriteXml("c:\\test\\sample.xml", XmlWriteMode.WriteSchema);
```

the following XML is produced. Notice that we include the XSD schema in the document. If you do not want the schema included in the file, you can pass in the `XmlWriteMode.IgnoreSchema` enum member:

```
  <?xml version="1.0" standalone="yes"?>
  <XMLProducts>
    <xsd:schema id="XMLProducts" targetNamespace="" xmlns=""
                xmlns:xsd="http://www.w3.org/2001/XMLSchema"
                xmlns:msdata="urn:schemas-microsoft-com:xml-msdata">
      <xsd:element name="XMLProducts" msdata:IsDataSet="true">
        <xsd:complexType>
          <xsd:choice maxOccurs="unbounded">
            <xsd:element name="products">
              <xsd:complexType>
                <xsd:sequence>
```

```
                    <xsd:element name="ProductID" type="xsd:int" minOccurs="0" />
                    <xsd:element name="ProductName" type="xsd:string"
                           minOccurs="0" />
                    <xsd:element name="SupplierID" type="xsd:int" minOccurs="0" />
                    <xsd:element name="CategoryID" type="xsd:int" minOccurs="0" />
                    <xsd:element name="QuantityPerUnit" type="xsd:string"
                           minOccurs="0" />
                    <xsd:element name="UnitPrice" type="xsd:decimal"
                           minOccurs="0" />
                    <xsd:element name="UnitsInStock" type="xsd:short"
                           minOccurs="0" />
                    <xsd:element name="UnitsOnOrder" type="xsd:short"
                           minOccurs="0" />
                    <xsd:element name="ReorderLevel" type="xsd:short"
                           minOccurs="0" />
                    <xsd:element name="Discontinued" type="xsd:boolean"
                           minOccurs="0" />
                  </xsd:sequence>
               </xsd:complexType>
             </xsd:element>
          </xsd:choice>
       </xsd:complexType>
    </xsd:element>
  </xsd:schema>
  <products>
    <ProductID>1</ProductID>
    <ProductName>Chai</ProductName>
    <SupplierID>1</SupplierID>
    <CategoryID>1</CategoryID>
    <QuantityPerUnit>10 boxes x 20 bags</QuantityPerUnit>
    <UnitPrice>18</UnitPrice>
    <UnitsInStock>39</UnitsInStock>
    <UnitsOnOrder>0</UnitsOnOrder>
    <ReorderLevel>10</ReorderLevel>
    <Discontinued>false</Discontinued>
  </products>
  <products>
    <ProductID>2</ProductID>
    <ProductName>Chang</ProductName>
    <SupplierID>1</SupplierID>
    <CategoryID>1</CategoryID>
    <QuantityPerUnit>24 - 12 oz bottles</QuantityPerUnit>
    <UnitPrice>19</UnitPrice>
    <UnitsInStock>17</UnitsInStock>
    <UnitsOnOrder>40</UnitsOnOrder>
    <ReorderLevel>25</ReorderLevel>
    <Discontinued>false</Discontinued>
  </products>
</XMLProducts>
```

Only the first two products are shown. The actual XML file would contain all of the products in the Products table of Northwind database.

This looks simple enough for a single table, but what about relational data, such as multiple DataTables and Relations in the DataSet? It all still works the same way. Let's make the following changes to the code that we've been using (this version can be found in ADOSample3):

```csharp
private void button1_Click(object sender, System.EventArgs e)
{
    //create a dataset

    DataSet ds=new DataSet("XMLProducts");

    //connect to the northwind database and
    //select all of the rows from products table and from suppliers table
    //make sure your connect string matches your server configuration

    SqlConnection conn=new SqlConnection
                (@"server=GLYNNJ_CS\NetSDK;uid=sa;pwd=;database=northwind");
    SqlDataAdapter daProd=new SqlDataAdapter("select * from products",conn);
    SqlDataAdapter daSup=new SqlDataAdapter("select * from suppliers",conn);

    //Fill DataSet from both SqlAdapters

    daProd.Fill(ds,"products");
    daSup.Fill(ds,"suppliers");

    //Add the relation

    ds.Relations.Add(ds.Tables["suppliers"].Columns["SupplierId"],
                    ds.Tables["products"].Columns["SupplierId"]);

    //Write the XML to a file so we can look at it later

    ds.WriteXml("..\\..\\..\\SuppProd.xml",XmlWriteMode.WriteSchema);

    //load data into grid

    dataGrid1.DataSource=ds;
    dataGrid1.DataMember="suppliers";

    //create the XmlDataDocument

    doc=new XmlDataDocument(ds);

    //Select the productname elements and load them in the grid

    XmlNodeList nodeLst=doc.SelectNodes("//ProductName");
    foreach(XmlNode nd in nodeLst)
        listBox1.Items.Add(nd.InnerXml);
}
```

In this sample we are creating two DataTables in the XMLProducts DataSet: Products and Suppliers. The relation is that Suppliers supply Products. We create a new relation on the column SupplierId in both tables. This is what the DataSet looks like:

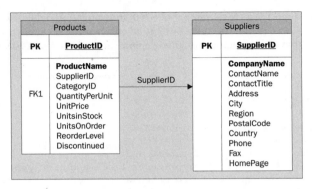

By making the same `WriteXml()` method call that we did on the previous example, we will get the following XML file (`SuppProd.xml`):

```
<?xml version="1.0" standalone="yes"?>
<XMLProducts>
  <xsd:schema id="XMLProducts" targetNamespace="" xmlns=""
         xmlns:xsd="http://www.w3.org/2001/XMLSchema"
         xmlns:msdata="urn:schemas-microsoft-com:xml-msdata">
    <xsd:element name="XMLProducts" msdata:IsDataSet="true">
      <xsd:complexType>
        <xsd:choice maxOccurs="unbounded">
          <xsd:element name="products">
            <xsd:complexType>
              <xsd:sequence>
                <xsd:element name="ProductID" type="xsd:int"
                        minOccurs="0" />
                <xsd:element name="ProductName" type="xsd:string"
                        minOccurs="0" />
                <xsd:element name="SupplierID" type="xsd:int"
                        minOccurs="0" />
                <xsd:element name="CategoryID" type="xsd:int"
                        minOccurs="0" />
                <xsd:element name="QuantityPerUnit" type="xsd:string"
                        minOccurs="0" />
                <xsd:element name="UnitPrice" type="xsd:decimal"
                        minOccurs="0" />
                <xsd:element name="UnitsInStock" type="xsd:short"
                        minOccurs="0" />
                <xsd:element name="UnitsOnOrder" type="xsd:short"
                        minOccurs="0" />
                <xsd:element name="ReorderLevel" type="xsd:short"
                        minOccurs="0" />
                <xsd:element name="Discontinued" type="xsd:boolean"
                        minOccurs="0" />
              </xsd:sequence>
            </xsd:complexType>
          </xsd:element>
          <xsd:element name="suppliers">
            <xsd:complexType>
              <xsd:sequence>
                <xsd:element name="SupplierID" type="xsd:int"
                        minOccurs="0" />
```

```xml
                <xsd:element name="CompanyName" type="xsd:string"
                            minOccurs="0" />
                <xsd:element name="ContactName" type="xsd:string"
                            minOccurs="0" />
                <xsd:element name="ContactTitle" type="xsd:string"
                            minOccurs="0" />
                <xsd:element name="Address" type="xsd:string"
                            minOccurs="0" />
                <xsd:element name="City" type="xsd:string"
                            minOccurs="0" />
                <xsd:element name="Region" type="xsd:string"
                            minOccurs="0" />
                <xsd:element name="PostalCode" type="xsd:string"
                            minOccurs="0" />
                <xsd:element name="Country" type="xsd:string"
                            minOccurs="0" />
                <xsd:element name="Phone" type="xsd:string"
                            minOccurs="0" />
                <xsd:element name="Fax" type="xsd:string"
                            minOccurs="0" />
                <xsd:element name="HomePage" type="xsd:string"
                            minOccurs="0" />
              </xsd:sequence>
            </xsd:complexType>
          </xsd:element>
        </xsd:choice>
      </xsd:complexType>
      <xsd:unique name="Constraint1">
        <xsd:selector xpath=".//suppliers" />
        <xsd:field xpath="SupplierID" />
      </xsd:unique>
      <xsd:keyref name="Relation1" refer="Constraint1">
        <xsd:selector xpath=".//products" />
        <xsd:field xpath="SupplierID" />
      </xsd:keyref>
    </xsd:element>
</xsd:schema>
<products>
  <ProductID>1</ProductID>
  <ProductName>Chai</ProductName>
  <SupplierID>1</SupplierID>
  <CategoryID>1</CategoryID>
  <QuantityPerUnit>10 boxes x 20 bags</QuantityPerUnit>
  <UnitPrice>18</UnitPrice>
  <UnitsInStock>39</UnitsInStock>
  <UnitsOnOrder>0</UnitsOnOrder>
  <ReorderLevel>10</ReorderLevel>
  <Discontinued>false</Discontinued>
</products>
<products>
  <ProductID>2</ProductID>
  <ProductName>Chang</ProductName>
  <SupplierID>1</SupplierID>
  <CategoryID>1</CategoryID>
  <QuantityPerUnit>24 - 12 oz bottles</QuantityPerUnit>
  <UnitPrice>19</UnitPrice>
```

```
    <UnitsInStock>17</UnitsInStock>
    <UnitsOnOrder>40</UnitsOnOrder>
    <ReorderLevel>25</ReorderLevel>
    <Discontinued>false</Discontinued>
  </products>
  <suppliers>
    <SupplierID>1</SupplierID>
    <CompanyName>Exotic Liquids</CompanyName>
    <ContactName>Charlotte Cooper</ContactName>
    <ContactTitle>Purchasing Manager</ContactTitle>
    <Address>49 Gilbert St.</Address>
    <City>London</City>
    <PostalCode>EC1 4SD</PostalCode>
    <Country>UK</Country>
    <Phone>(171) 555-2222</Phone>
  </suppliers>
  <suppliers>
    <SupplierID>2</SupplierID>
    <CompanyName>New Orleans Cajun Delights</CompanyName>
    <ContactName>Shelley Burke</ContactName>
    <ContactTitle>Order Administrator</ContactTitle>
    <Address>P.O. Box 78934</Address>
    <City>New Orleans</City>
    <Region>LA</Region>
    <PostalCode>70117</PostalCode>
    <Country>USA</Country>
    <Phone>(100) 555-4822</Phone>
    <HomePage>#CAJUN.HTM#</HomePage>
  </suppliers>
</XMLProducts>
```

The schema includes both `DataTables` that were in the `DataSet`. In addition, the data includes all of the data from both tables. Several products and suppliers were deleted from the final file to save space. As before we could have saved just the schema or just the data by passing in the correct `XmlWriteMode` parameter.

XML Document to ADO.NET Data

So let's say that you have an XML document that you would like to get into an ADO.NET `DataSet`. You would want to do this so you could load the XML into a database, or perhaps bind the data to a .NET data control such as `DataGrid`. This way you could actually use the XML document as your data store, and could eliminate the overhead of the database altogether. Here is some code to get you started (`ADOSample4`):

```
private void button1_Click(object sender, System.EventArgs e)
{

    //create a new DataSet

    DataSet ds=new DataSet("XMLProducts");

    //read in the XML documnet to the Dataset

    ds.ReadXml("..\\..\\..\\prod.xml");
    //load data into grid
```

```
        dataGrid1.DataSource=ds;
        dataGrid1.DataMember="products";

        //create the new XmlDataDocument

        doc=new XmlDataDocument(ds);

        //load the product names into the listbox

        XmlNodeList nodeLst=doc.SelectNodes("//ProductName");

        foreach(XmlNode nd in nodeLst)
            listBox1.Items.Add(nd.InnerXml);
    }
```

It is that easy. Instantiate a new `DataSet` object. Call the `ReadXml()` method, and you now have XML in a `DataTable` in your `DataSet`. As with the `WriteXml()` methods, `ReadXml()` has an `XmlReadMode` parameter. `ReadXml()` has a couple more options in the `XmlReadMode`. This table describes them:

Enumeration Name	Description
Auto	Sets the `XmlReadMode` to the most appropriate setting.
	If data is in `DiffGram` format, `DiffGram` is selected.
	If a schema has already been read, or an inline schema is detected, then `ReadSchema` is selected.
	If no schema has been assigned to the `DataSet`, and none is detected inline, then `IgnoreSchema` is selected.
DiffGram	Reads in the `DiffGram` and applies the changes to the `DataSet`. `DiffGrams` are described later in the chapter.
Fragment	Reads documents that contain XDR schema fragments, such as the type created by SQL Server.
IgnoreSchema	Ignores any inline schema that may be found. Reads data into the current `DataSet` schema. If data does not match `DataSet` schema it is discarded.
InferSchema	Ignores any inline schema. Creates the schema based on data in the XML document. If a schema exists in the `DataSet`, that schema is used, and extended with additional columns and tables if needed. An exception is thrown if a column exists, but is of a different data type.
ReadSchema	Reads the inline schema and loads the data. Will not overwrite a schema in the `DataSet`, but will throw an exception if a table in the inline schema already exists in the `DataSet`.

There is also the ReadSchema() method. This will read in a standalone schema and create the tables, columns and relations accordingly. You would use this if your schema is not inline with your data. ReadSchema() has the same four overloads: string with file and path name, Stream-based object, TextReader-based object and an XmlReader-based object.

To show that the data tables are getting created properly, let's load the XML document that contains the Products and Suppliers tables that we used in an earlier example. This time however, let's load the listbox with the DataTable names and the DataColumn names and data type. We can look at this and compare it back to the original Northwind database to see that all is still well. Here is the code that we will use, which can be found in ADOSample5:

```
private void button1_Click(object sender, System.EventArgs e)
{

    //create the DataSet

    DataSet ds=new DataSet("XMLProducts");

    //read in the XML document

    ds.ReadXml("..\\..\\..\\SuppProd.xml");

    //load data into grid

    dataGrid1.DataSource=ds;
    dataGrid1.DataMember="products";

    //load the listbox with table, column and datatype info

    foreach(DataTable dt in ds.Tables)  {
       listBox1.Items.Add(dt.TableName);
       foreach(DataColumn col in dt.Columns) {
          listBox1.Items.Add
                  ('\t' + col.ColumnName + " - " + col.DataType.FullName);
       }
    }
}
```

Note the addition of the two foreach loops. The first loop is getting the table name from each table in the tables collection of the DataSet. Inside the foreach loop we get the name and data type of each column in the DataTable. We load this data into the listbox to allow us to display it. Here is a screenshot of what that looks like:

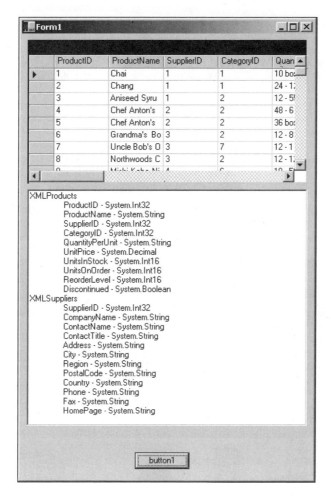

Looking at the listbox you can see that the `DataTables` were created with the columns all having the correct names and data types.

Something else you may want to note is that since the last two examples didn't transfer any data to or from a database; there were no `SqlDataAdapters` or `SqlConnections` defined. This starts to show the real flexibility of both the `System.Xml` namespace and ADO.NET. You can look at the same data in multiple formats. If you need to do a transform and show the data in HTML format, or if you need to bind to a grid, you can take the same data, and with just a method call, have it in the required format.

Writing and Reading a DiffGram

A `DiffGram` is an XML document that contains the before and after data of an edit session. This can include any combination of data changes, additions and deletions. A `DiffGram` can be used as an audit trail or for a commit/rollback process. Most DBMS systems today have this built in, but sometimes it is nice to be able to take things into your own hands. If you happen to be working with a DBMS that does not have these features or if XML is your data store and you do not have a DBMS, you can implement commit/rollback features yourself.

Here is some code that shows how a `DiffGram` is created and how a `DataSet` can be created from a `DiffGram:pwd` (this can be found in the `ADOSample6` folder). The beginning part of this code should look familiar. We are defining and setting up a new `DataSet`, ds, a new `SqlConnection`, conn, and a new `SqlDataAdapter`, da. We connect to the database, select all of the rows from the `Products` table, creating a new `DataTable`, named `products`, and load the data from the database into the `DataSet`:

```
private void button1_Click(object sender, System.EventArgs e)
{

    //new DataSet

    DataSet ds=new DataSet("XMLProducts");

    //Make connection and load products rows

    SqlConnection conn=new SqlConnection
            (@"server=GLYNNJ_CS\NetSDK;uid=sa;pwd=;database=northwind");
    SqlDataAdapter da=new SqlDataAdapter("select * from products",conn);

    //fill the DataSet

    da.Fill(ds,"products");

    //edit first row

    ds.Tables["products"].Rows[0]["ProductName"]="NewProdName";
```

In this next section we are doing two things. First, we are modifying the `ProductName` column in the first row to `NewProdName`. Second, we are creating a new row in the `DataTable`, setting the column values, and finally adding the new data row to the `DataTable`.

```
    //add new row

    DataRow dr=ds.Tables["products"].NewRow();;
    dr["ProductId"]=100;
    dr["CategoryId"]=2;
    dr["Discontinued"]=false;
    dr["ProductName"]="This is the new product";
    dr["QuantityPerUnit"]=12;
    dr["ReorderLevel"]=1;
    dr["SupplierId"]=12;
    dr["UnitPrice"]=23;
    dr["UnitsInStock"]=5;
    dr["UnitsOnOrder"]=0;
    ds.Tables["products"].Rows.Add(dr);
```

This is the interesting part of the code. First we write out the schema with `WriteXmlSchema()`. This is important because you cannot read back in a `DiffGram` without the schema. `WriteXml()` with the `XmlWriteMode.DiffGram` parameter passed to it actually creates the `DiffGram`. The next line accepts the changes that we made. It is important that the `DiffGram` is created before calling `AcceptChanges()`, otherwise there would not be anything different between the before and after.

```
    //Write the Schema

    ds.WriteXMLSchema("..\\..\\..\\diffgram.xsd");

    //generate the DiffGram

    ds.WriteXml("..\\..\\..\\diffgram.xml",XmlWriteMode.DiffGram);
    ds.AcceptChanges();

    //load data into grid

    dataGrid1.DataSource=ds;
    dataGrid1.DataMember="products";

    //new XmlDataDocument

    doc=new XmlDataDocument(ds);

    //load the productnames in the list

    XmlNodeList nodeLst=doc.SelectNodes("//ProductName");
    foreach(XmlNode nd in nodeLst)
        listBox1.Items.Add(nd.InnerXml);
}
```

In order to get the data back into a `DataSet`, we can do the following:

```
        DataSet dsNew=new DataSet();
        dsNew.ReadXmlSchema("..\\..\\..\\diffgram.xsd");
        dsNew.XmlRead("..\\..\\..\\diffgram.xml",XmlReadMode.DiffGram);
```

In this example, we are creating a new `DataSet`, `dsNew`. The call to the `ReadXmlSchema()` method creates a new `DataTable` based on the schema information. In this case it would be a clone of the products `DataTable`. Now we can read in the `DiffGram`. The `DiffGram` does not contain schema information, so it is important that the `DataTable` be created and ready before you call the `ReadXml()` method.

Here is a sample of what the `DiffGram` (`diffgram.xml`) looks like:

```
<?xml version="1.0" standalone="yes"?>
<diffgr:diffgram xmlns:msdata="urn:schemas-microsoft-com:xml-msdata"
                 xmlns:diffgr="urn:schemas-microsoft-com:xml-diffgram-v1">
  <XMLProducts>
    <products diffgr:id="products1" msdata:rowOrder="0"
              diffgr:hasChanges="modified">
      <ProductID>1</ProductID>
      <ProductName>NewProdName</ProductName>
      <SupplierID>1</SupplierID>
      <CategoryID>1</CategoryID>
      <QuantityPerUnit>10 boxes x 20 bags</QuantityPerUnit>
      <UnitPrice>18</UnitPrice>
      <UnitsInStock>39</UnitsInStock>
      <UnitsOnOrder>0</UnitsOnOrder>
      <ReorderLevel>10</ReorderLevel>
      <Discontinued>false</Discontinued>
    </products>
    <products diffgr:id="products2" msdata:rowOrder="1">
      <ProductID>2</ProductID>
      <ProductName>Chang</ProductName>
```

```
        <SupplierID>1</SupplierID>
        <CategoryID>1</CategoryID>
        <QuantityPerUnit>24 - 12 oz bottles</QuantityPerUnit>
        <UnitPrice>19</UnitPrice>
        <UnitsInStock>17</UnitsInStock>
        <UnitsOnOrder>40</UnitsOnOrder>
        <ReorderLevel>25</ReorderLevel>
        <Discontinued>false</Discontinued>
      </products>
  ...
      <products diffgr:id="products78" msdata:rowOrder="77"
              diffgr:hasChanges="inserted">
        <ProductID>100</ProductID>
        <ProductName>This is the new product</ProductName>
        <SupplierID>12</SupplierID>
        <CategoryID>2</CategoryID>
        <QuantityPerUnit>12</QuantityPerUnit>
        <UnitPrice>23</UnitPrice>
        <UnitsInStock>5</UnitsInStock>
        <UnitsOnOrder>0</UnitsOnOrder>
        <ReorderLevel>1</ReorderLevel>
        <Discontinued>false</Discontinued>
      </products>
    </XMLProducts>
    <diffgr:before>
      <products diffgr:id="products1" msdata:rowOrder="0">
        <ProductID>1</ProductID>
        <ProductName>Chai</ProductName>
        <SupplierID>1</SupplierID>
        <CategoryID>1</CategoryID>
        <QuantityPerUnit>10 boxes x 20 bags</QuantityPerUnit>
        <UnitPrice>18</UnitPrice>
        <UnitsInStock>39</UnitsInStock>
        <UnitsOnOrder>0</UnitsOnOrder>
        <ReorderLevel>10</ReorderLevel>
        <Discontinued>false</Discontinued>
      </products>
    </diffgr:before>
  </diffgr:diffgram>
```

Notice how each `DataTable` row is repeated, and that there is a `diffgr:id` attribute for each `<products>` element. `diffgr` is the namespace prefix for `urn:schemas-microsoft-com:xml-diffgram-v1`. For the row that we modified and the row that we inserted, ADO.NET has added a `diffgr:hasChanges` attribute. There's also a `<diffgr:before>` element after the `<XMLProducts>` element, which contains a `<products>` element indicating the previous contents of any modified rows. For the row we added, there is no "before", so this doesn't have an element in `<diffgr:before>`; however, there is one for the modified row.

After the `DiffGram` has been read into the `DataTable`, it is in the state that it would be in after changes were made to the data but before `AcceptChanges()` is called. At this point you can actually roll back changes by calling the `RejectChanges()` method. By looking at the `DataRow.Item` property and passing in either `DataRowVersion.Original` or `DataRowVersion.Current`, we can look and see the before and after values in the `DataTable`.

Serializing Objects in XML

Serializing is the process of taking an object and persisting the object to disk. Another part of your application, or even another application can de-serialize the object and it will be in the same state it was prior to serialization. The .NET framework includes a couple of ways to do this. We are going to take a look at the `System.Xml.Serialization` namespace.

As the name implies, serialization is done in an XML format. This is done by converting an object's public properties and public fields into elements and/or attributes. The XML serializer cannot convert private data, only public data. Think of it as a way to save the state of your object. If you need to save private data, then take a look at the `BinaryFormatter` in the `System.Runtime.Serialization.Formatters.Binary` namespace. Some of the things that you can do are:

❑ Determine if the data should be an attribute or element.

❑ Specify the namespace.

❑ Change the attribute or element name.

Along with only being able to serialize public data, you are not able to serialize object graphs (objects that are reachable from the object you are serializing). This should not be a serious limitation. By carefully designing your classes, this should be easily avoided. If you need to be able to serialize public and private data as well as an object graph containing many nested objects, then you will want to use the `System.Runtime.Serialization.Formatters.Binary` namespace.

Data that can be serialized can be primitive types, fields, arrays, and embedded XML in the form of `XmlElement` and `XmlAttribute` objects. The link between your object and the XML document is the custom attributes that annotate your classes. These attributes are what are used to inform the serializer how to write out the data.

There is a tool that is included with the .NET framework that can help you create the attributes for you if you wish; `xsd.exe` can do the following:

❑ Generate an XML schema from an XDR schema file.

❑ Generate an XML schema from an XML file.

❑ Generate `DataSet` classes from an XSD schema file.

❑ Generate runtime classes that have the custom attributes for `XmlSerialization`.

❑ Generate an XSD from classes that you have already developed.

❑ Limit which elements are created in code.

❑ Determine which programming language the generated code should be in (C#, VB.Net, or JScript.NET).

❑ Create schemas from types in compiled assemblies.

See the framework documentation for details of command line options.

Despite the capabilities, you don't have to use `xsd.exe` to create the classes for serialization. The process is quite simple. Let's take a look at a simple application that serializes a class that reads in the products data we saved earlier in the chapter. This can be found in the `SerialSample1` folder. The start of the example is very simple code that creates a new `Product` object, `pd`, and fills it with some data:

```
private void button1_Click(object sender, System.EventArgs e)
{

    //new products object

    Products pd=new Products();

    //set some properties

    pd.ProductID=200;
    pd.CategoryID=100;
    pd.Discontinued=false;
    pd.ProductName="Serialize Objects";
    pd.QuantityPerUnit="6";
    pd.ReorderLevel=1;
    pd.SupplierID=1;
    pd.UnitPrice=1000;
    pd.UnitsInStock=10;
    pd.UnitsOnOrder=0;
```

The `Serialize()` method of the `XmlSerializer` class has six overloads. One of the parameters that is required is a stream to write the data out to. It can be a `Stream`, `TextWriter`, or an `XmlWriter`. In this case we have created a `TextWriter` based object, `tr`. The next thing to do is to create the `XmlSerializer`-based object `sr`. The `XmlSerializer` needs to know type information for the object that it is serializing, so you use the `typeof` keyword with the type that is to be serialized. After the `sr` object is created, you call the `Serialize()` method passing in the `tr` (`Stream`-based object) and the object that you want serialized, in this case `pd`. Be sure to close the stream when you are finished with it.

```
    //new TextWriter and XmlSerializer

    TextWriter tr=new StreamWriter("..\\..\\..\\serialprod.xml");
    XmlSerializer sr=new XmlSerializer(typeof(Products));

    //serialize object

    sr.Serialize(tr,pd);
    tr.Close();
}
```

Here we add another button event to create a new `Products` based object `newPd`. This time we will be using a `FileStream` object to read in the XML:

```
private void button2_Click(object sender, System.EventArgs e)
{

    //create a reference to products type

    Products newPd;

    //new filestream to open serialized object

    FileStream f=new FileStream("..\\..\\..\\serialprod.xml",FileMode.Open);
```

Once again, we create a new `XmlSerializer`, passing in the type information of `Product`. We can then make the call to the `Deserialize()` method. Note that we still need to do an explicit cast when we create the `newPd` object. At this point `newPd` is in the exact same state as `pd` was:

```
//new serializer

XmlSerializer newSr=new XmlSerializer(typeof(Products));

//deserialize the object

newPd=(Products)newSr.Deserialize(f);

//load it in the list box.

listBox1.Items.Add(newPd.ProductName);
f.Close();
}
```

Now we're going to examine the `Products` class. The only difference between this and any other class that you may write is the attributes that have been added. Don't confuse these attributes with the attributes in your XML document. These attributes extend the `SystemAttribute` class. An attribute is simply some declarative information that can be retrieved at runtime by the CLR (see Chapter 6 for more details). In this case, we are adding attributes that will describe how the object should be serialized:

```
//class that will be serialized.
//attributes determine how object is serialized

[System.Xml.Serialization.XmlRootAttribute(Namespace="", IsNullable=false)]
public class Products {
    [System.Xml.Serialization.XmlElementAttribute(IsNullable=false)]
    public int ProductID;
    [System.Xml.Serialization.XmlElementAttribute(IsNullable=false)]
    public string ProductName;
    [System.Xml.Serialization.XmlElementAttribute()]
    public int SupplierID;
    [System.Xml.Serialization.XmlElementAttribute()]
    public int CategoryID;
    [System.Xml.Serialization.XmlElementAttribute()]
    public string QuantityPerUnit;
    [System.Xml.Serialization.XmlElementAttribute()]
    public System.Decimal UnitPrice;
    [System.Xml.Serialization.XmlElementAttribute()]
    public short UnitsInStock;
    [System.Xml.Serialization.XmlElementAttribute()]
    public short UnitsOnOrder;
    [System.Xml.Serialization.XmlElementAttribute()]
    public short ReorderLevel;
    [System.Xml.Serialization.XmlElementAttribute()]
    public bool Discontinued;
}
```

If we take a look at the XML document that was created, you can see that it looks like any other XML document that we may have created, which would be the point of the exercise. Let's take a look at the document:

```xml
<?xml version="1.0"?>
<Products xmlns:xsi="http://www.w3.org/2001/XMLSchema-instance"
          xmlns:xsd="http://www.w3.org/2001/XMLSchema">
  <ProductID>200</ProductID>
  <ProductName>Serialize Objects</ProductName>
  <SupplierID>1</SupplierID>
  <CategoryID>100</CategoryID>
  <QuantityPerUnit>6</QuantityPerUnit>
  <UnitPrice>1000</UnitPrice>
  <UnitsInStock>10</UnitsInStock>
  <UnitsOnOrder>0</UnitsOnOrder>
  <ReorderLevel>1</ReorderLevel>
  <Discontinued>false</Discontinued>
</Products>
```

Nothing out of the ordinary here. We could use this any way that you would use an XML document. We could do a transform on it and display it as HTML, load into a `DataSet` using ADO.NET, load an `XmlDocument` with it, or, as you can see in the example, de-serialize it and create an object in the same state that pd was in prior to serializing it (which is exactly what we're doing with our second button).

The example that we just looked at is very simple. Normally you would have a series of property `get` and `set` methods to deal with the data in your object. But what if your object is composed of a couple of different objects, or is derived from a base class that other types are derived from as well?

These situations can be handled by the `XmlSerializer` class. Let's look at a slightly more complex example. First let's make this a more realistic example (found in `SerialSample2`) by making each property accessible via `get` and `set` methods:

```csharp
private void button1_Click(object sender, System.EventArgs e)
{

    //new products object

    Products pd=new Products();

    //set some properties

    pd.ProductID=200;
    pd.CategoryID=100;
    pd.Discontinued=false;
    pd.ProductName="Serialize Objects";
    pd.QuantityPerUnit="6";
    pd.ReorderLevel=1;
    pd.SupplierID=1;
    pd.UnitPrice=1000;
    pd.UnitsInStock=10;
    pd.UnitsOnOrder=0;
    pd.Discount=2;

    //new TextWriter and XmlSerializer

    TextWriter tr=new StreamWriter("..\\..\\..\\serialprod1.xml");
    XmlSerializer sr=new XmlSerializer(typeof(Products));
```

```
   //serialize object

   sr.Serialize(tr,pd);
   tr.Close();
}

private void button2_Click(object sender, System.EventArgs e)
{

   //create a reference to products type

   Products newPd;

   //new filestream to open serialized object

   FileStream f=new FileStream("..\\..\\..\\serialprod1.XML",FileMode.Open);

   //new serializer

   XmlSerializer newSr=new XmlSerializer(typeof(Products));

   //deserialize the object

   newPd=(Products)newSr.Deserialize(f);

   //load it in the list box.

   listBox1.Items.Add(newPd.ProductName);
   f.Close();
}

//class that will be serialized.
//attributes determine how object is serialized

[System.Xml.Serialization.XmlRootAttribute()]
public class Products {
   private int prodId;
   private string prodName;
   private int suppId;
   private int catId;
   private string qtyPerUnit;
   private Decimal unitPrice;
   private short unitsInStock;
   private short unitsOnOrder;
   private short reorderLvl;
   private bool discont;
   private int disc;

   //added the Discount attribute

   [XmlAttributeAttribute(AttributeName="Discount")]
   public int Discount {
      get {return disc;}
      set {disc=value;}
   }
```

```csharp
    [XmlElementAttribute()]
    public int  ProductID {
       get {return prodId;}
       set {prodId=value;}
    }
    [XmlElementAttribute()]
    public string ProductName {
       get {return prodName;}
       set {prodName=value;}
    }
    [XmlElementAttribute()]
    public int SupplierID {
       get {return suppId;}
       set {suppId=value;}
    }

    [XmlElementAttribute()]
    public int CategoryID {
       get {return catId;}
       set {catId=value;}
    }

    [XmlElementAttribute()]
    public string QuantityPerUnit {
       get {return qtyPerUnit;}
       set {qtyPerUnit=value;}
    }

[XmlElementAttribute()]
public Decimal UnitPrice {
  get {return unitPrice;}
  set {unitPrice=value;}
}

    [XmlElementAttribute()]
    public short UnitsInStock {
       get {return unitsInStock;}
       set {unitsInStock=value;}
    }

    [XmlElementAttribute()]
    public short UnitsOnOrder {
       get {return unitsOnOrder;}
       set {unitsOnOrder=value;}
    }

    [XmlElementAttribute()]
    public short ReorderLevel {
       get {return reorderLvl;}
       set {reorderLvl=value;}
    }

    [XmlElementAttribute()]
    public bool Discontinued {
       get {return discont;}
       set {discont=value;}
    }
}
```

Running this code in place of the `Products` class in the earlier example will give the exact same results with one exception. We added the `Discount` attribute so you can see that attributes can also be serialized. The output for this appears as follows (`serialprod1.xml`):

```xml
<?xml version="1.0" encoding="utf-8"?>
<Products xmlns:xsi=http://www.w3.org/2001/XMLSchema-instance
          xmlns:xsd=http://www.w3.org/2001/XMLSchema
          Discount="2">
    <ProductID>200</ProductID>
    <ProductName>Serialize Objects</ProductName>
    <SupplierID>1</SupplierID>
    <CategoryID>100</CategoryID>
    <QuantityPerUnit>6</QuantityPerUnit>
    <UnitPrice>1000</UnitPrice>
    <UnitsInStock>10</UnitsInStock>
    <UnitsOnOrder>0</UnitsOnOrder>
    <ReorderLevel>1</ReorderLevel>
    <Discontinued>false</Discontinued>
</Products>
```

Notice the `Discount` attribute on the `Products` element. So, now that you have property `gets` and `sets` defined, you can add more complex validation code in the properties.

What about situations where you will have derived classes, and possibly properties that return an array? `XmlSerializer` has that covered as well. Let's look at a slightly more complex situation.

In the `button1_Click` event, we create a new `Product`-based object and a new `BookProduct` based object (`newProd` and `newBook`). We add data to the various properties of each object, and add the objects to a `Product` based array. We create a new `Inventory`-based object and pass in the array as a parameter. We can then serialize the `Inventory` object to recreate it at a later time:

```csharp
private void button1_Click(object sender, System.EventArgs e)
{

    //create new book and bookproducts objects

    Product newProd=new Product();
    BookProduct newBook=new BookProduct();

    //set some properties

    newProd.ProductID=100;
    newProd.ProductName="Product Thing";
    newProd.SupplierID=10;

    newBook.ProductID=101;
    newBook.ProductName="How to Use Your New Product Thing";
    newBook.SupplierID=10;
    newBook.ISBN="123456789";

    //add the items to an array

    Product[] addProd={newProd,newBook};
```

```
//new inventory object using the addProd array

Inventory inv=new Inventory();
inv.InventoryItems=addProd;

//serialize the Inventory object

TextWriter tr=new StreamWriter("..\\..\\..\\order.xml");
XmlSerializer sr=new XmlSerializer(typeof(Inventory));

sr.Serialize(tr,inv);
tr.Close();
}
```

Notice in the `button2_Click` event that we iterate through the array in the newly created `newInv` object to show that it is the same data:

```
private void button2_Click(object sender, System.EventArgs e)
{
    Inventory newInv;
    FileStream f=new FileStream("..\\..\\..\\order.xml",FileMode.Open);
    XmlSerializer newSr=new XmlSerializer(typeof(Inventory));
    newInv=(Inventory)newSr.Deserialize(f);
    foreach(Product prod in newInv.InventoryItems)
        listBox1.Items.Add(prod.ProductName);
    f.Close();
}

public class Inventory
{

    private Product[] stuff;
    public Inventory() {}
```

We have an `XmlArrayItem` for each type that can be added to the array. The first parameter is what we would like the element name to be in the XML document that is created. If you leave off the `ElementName` parameter, the elements have the same name as the object type (`Product` and `BookProduct` in this case). There is also an `XmlArrayAttribute` class that you would use if the property were returning an array of objects or primitive type. Since we are returning different types in the array, we use `XmlArrayItemAttribute`, which allows the higher level of control:

```
//need to have an attribute entry for each data type

[XmlArrayItem("Prod",typeof(Product)),
XmlArrayItem("Book",typeof(BookProduct))]

//public Inventory(Product[] InventoryItems)  {
//   stuff=InventoryItems;
//}

public Product[] InventoryItems {
    get {return stuff;}
    set {stuff=value;}
}
}
```

```
//product class

public class Product {

    private int prodId;
    private string prodName;
    private  int suppId;
    public Product() {}
    public int  ProductID {
        get {return prodId;}
        set {prodId=value;}
    }
    public string ProductName {
        get {return prodName;}
        set {prodName=value;}
    }
    public int SupplierID  {
        get {return suppId;}
        set {suppId=value;}
    }
}

//Bookproduct class

public class BookProduct:Product
{
    private string isbnNum;

    public BookProduct() {}
    public string ISBN  {
        get {return isbnNum;}
        set {isbnNum=value;}
    }
}
```

We have added couple of new classes to the sample. The `Inventory` class is what will keep track of what is being added to our inventory. We can add stuff based on `Product` or on `BookProduct`, which extends `Product`. We could add others, but this will show what we need to see. In `Inventory` we keep an array of what we have added so far, and it can contain both `BookProducts` and `Products`. This is what the XML document looks like:

```
<?xml version="1.0"?>
<Inventory xmlns:xsi="http://www.w3.org/2001/XMLSchema-instance"
           xmlns:xsd="http://www.w3.org/2001/XMLSchema">
    <InventoryItems>
        <Prod>
            <ProductID>100</ProductID>
            <ProductName>Product Thing</ProductName>
            <SupplierID>10</SupplierID>
        </Prod>
        <Book>
            <ProductID>101</ProductID>
            <ProductName>How to Use Your New Product Thing</ProductName>
            <SupplierID>10</SupplierID>
            <ISBN>123456789</ISBN>
        </Book>
    </InventoryItems>
</Inventory>
```

Well this all works great, but what if you don't have access to the source code for the types that are being serialized? You can't add the attribute if you don't have the source. There is another way. You would use the `XmlAttributes` class and the `XmlAttributeOverrides` class. Together these classes will allow you to accomplish exactly what we have just done, but without adding the attributes. Here is an example of how this works, taken from the `SerialSample4` folder:

```
private void button1_Click(object sender, System.EventArgs e)
{
    //create the XmlAttributes object

    XmlAttributes attrs=new XmlAttributes();

    //add the types of the objects that will be serialized

    attrs.XmlElements.Add(new
                    XmlElementAttribute("Book",typeof(BookProduct)));
    attrs.XmlElements.Add(new
                    XmlElementAttribute("Product",typeof(Product)));
    XmlAttributeOverrides attrOver=new XmlAttributeOverrides();

    //add to the attributes collection

    attrOver.Add(typeof(Inventory),"InventoryItems",attrs);

    //create the Product and Book objects

    Product newProd=new Product();
    BookProduct newBook=new BookProduct();
    newProd.ProductID=100;
    newProd.ProductName="Product Thing";
    newProd.SupplierID=10;
    newBook.ProductID=101;
    newBook.ProductName="How to Use Your New Product Thing";
    newBook.SupplierID=10;
    newBook.ISBN="123456789";
    Product[] addProd={newProd,newBook};
    //Product[] addProd={newBook};

    Inventory inv=new Inventory();
    inv.InventoryItems=addProd;
    TextWriter tr=new StreamWriter("..\\..\\..\\inventory.xml");
    XmlSerializer sr=new XmlSerializer(typeof(Inventory),attrOver);
    sr.Serialize(tr,inv);
    tr.Close();
}

private void button2_Click(object sender, System.EventArgs e)
{

    //we need to do the same process to deserialize
    //create the new XmlAttributes collection

    XmlAttributes attrs=new XmlAttributes();

    //add the type information to the elements collection
```

```csharp
        attrs.XmlElements.Add(new
                     XmlElementAttribute("Book",typeof(BookProduct)));
        attrs.XmlElements.Add(new
                     XmlElementAttribute("Product",typeof(Product)));
        XmlAttributeOverrides attrOver=new XmlAttributeOverrides();

        //add to the Attributes collection

        attrOver.Add(typeof(Inventory),"InventoryItems",attrs);

        //need a new Inventory object to deserialize to

        Inventory newInv;

        //deserialize and load data into the listbox from deserialized object

        FileStream f=new FileStream("..\\..\\..\\inventory.xml",FileMode.Open);

        XmlSerializer newSr=new XmlSerializer(typeof(Inventory),attrOver);
        newInv=(Inventory)newSr.Deserialize(f);
        if(newInv!=null) {
           foreach(Product prod in newInv.InventoryItems)
               listBox1.Items.Add(prod.ProductName);
        }
        f.Close();
    }

// these classes are the same as previous example
// with the exception tha the attributes are removed
// from the Inventory InventoryItems property

public class Inventory
{
    private Product[] stuff;

    public Inventory() {}

    public Product[] InventoryItems {
        get {return stuff;}
        set {stuff=value;}
    }
}

public class Product {

    private int prodId;
    private string prodName;
    private  int suppId;
    public Product() {}
    public int  ProductID {
        get {return prodId;}
        set {prodId=value;}
    }
    public string ProductName {
        get {return prodName;}
        set {prodName=value;}
    }
    public int SupplierID  {
        get {return suppId;}
        set {suppId=value;}
    }
}
```

```
public class BookProduct:Product
{
    private string isbnNum;
    public BookProduct() {}
    public string ISBN  {
        get {return isbnNum;}
        set {isbnNum=value;}
    }
}
```

Same example as before, but the first thing you should notice is that there are no attributes added to the `Inventory` class. So for this example, imagine that the `Inventory`, `Product`, and the derived `BookProduct` classes are in a separate DLL, and that we don't have the source.

The first step in the process is to create an `XmlAttributes`-based object, and an `XmlElementAttribute` object for each data type that you will be overriding:

```
XmlAttributes attrs=new XmlAttributes();
attrs.XmlElements.Add(new XmlElementAttribute("Book",typeof(BookProduct)));
attrs.XmlElements.Add(new XmlElementAttribute("Product",typeof(Product)));
```

Here you can see that we are adding a new `XmlElementAttribute` to the `XmlElements` collection of the `XmlAttributes` class. The `XmlAttributes` class has properties that correspond to the attributes that can be applied; `XmlArray` and `XmlArrayItems`, which we looked at in the previous example, are just a couple. We now have an `XmlAttributes` object with two `XmlElementAttribute`-based objects added to the `XmlElements` collection.

The next thing we have to do is create an `XmlAttributeOverrides` object:

```
XmlAttributeOverrides attrOver=new XmlAttributeOverrides();

attrOver.Add(typeof(Inventory),"InventoryItems",attrs);
```

The `Add()` method has two overloads. The first one takes the type information of the object to override and the `XmlAttributes` object that we created earlier. The other overload, which is the one we are using, also takes a string value that is the member in the overridden object. In our case we want to override the `InventoryItems` member in the `Inventory` class.

Now we create the `XmlSerializer` object, adding the `XmlAttributeOverrides` object as a parameter. Now the `XmlSerializer` knows which types we want to override and what we need to return for those types. If we execute the `Serialize()` method we will end up with this XML output:

```
<?xml version="1.0"?>
<Inventory xmlns:xsi=http://www.w3.org/2001/XMLSchema-instance
           xmlns:xsd="http://www.w3.org/2001/XMLSchema">
    <Product>
        <ProductID>100</ProductID>
        <ProductName>Product Thing</ProductName>
        <SupplierID>10</SupplierID>
    </Product>
    <Book>
        <ProductID>101</ProductID>
        <ProductName>How to Use Your New Product Thing</ProductName>
        <SupplierID>10</SupplierID>
        <ISBN>123456789</ISBN>
    </Book>
</Inventory>
```

As you can see, we get the very same XML as we did with the earlier example. In order to de-serialize this object and recreate the `Inventory`-based object that we started out with, we need to create all of the same `XmlAttributes`, `XmlElementAttribute` and `XmlAttributeOverrides` objects that we created when we serialized the object. Once we do that we can read in the XML and recreate the `Inventory` object just as we did before. Here is the code to deserialize the `Inventory` object:

```
private void button2_Click(object sender, System.EventArgs e)
{
    XmlAttributes attrs=new XmlAttributes();
    attrs.XmlElements.Add(new
                    XmlElementAttribute("Book",typeof(BookProduct)));
    attrs.XmlElements.Add(new
                    XmlElementAttribute("Product",typeof(Product)));
    XmlAttributeOverrides attrOver=new XmlAttributeOverrides();
    attrOver.Add(typeof(Inventory),"InventoryItems",attrs);
    Inventory newInv;
    FileStream f=new FileStream("..\\..\\..\\inventory.xml",FileMode.Open);
    XmlSerializer newSr=new XmlSerializer(typeof(Inventory),attrOver);
    newInv=(Inventory)newSr.Deserialize(f);
    foreach(Product prod in newInv.InventoryItems)
        listBox1.Items.Add(prod.ProductName);
    f.Close();
}
```

Notice that the first few lines of code are identical to the code we used to serialize the object.

The `XmlSerialize` namespace provides a very powerful toolset for serializing objects to XML. By serializing and de-serializing objects to XML instead of serializing to binary format, you are given the option of doing something else with the XML. This can really add to the flexibility of your designs.

Summary

In this chapter we explored many of the corners of the `System.Xml` namespace of the .NET framework. We looked at how to read and write XML documents using the very fast `XMLReader` and `XmlWriter`-based classes. We looked at how the DOM is implemented in .NET, and how to use the power of DOM. We saw that XML and ADO.NET are indeed very closely related. A `DataSet` and an XML document are just two different views of the same underlying architecture. We serialized objects out to XML, and were able to bring them back to life with just a couple of method calls. The combination of `Reflection` and `XMLSerialization` will lead to some very unique and powerful designs. And, of course, `XPath` and `XslTransform` were explored. XML is going to be, if it isn't already, an important part of your application development over the next several years. The .NET Framework has made a very rich and powerful toolset available to work with XML.

File and Registry Operations

In this chapter, we will examine how to perform tasks involving reading from and writing to files and the system registry in C#. In particular, we are going to cover:

❑   Exploring the directory structure, finding out what files and folders are present and checking their properties

❑   Moving, copying, and deleting files and folders

❑   Reading and writing text in files

❑   Reading and writing in the registry

Microsoft has provided very intuitive object models covering these areas, and during this chapter we will show you how to use .NET base classes to perform the tasks mentioned above. For the case of file system operations, the relevant classes are almost all found in the `System.IO` namespace, while registry operations are dealt with by a couple of classes in the `System.Win32` namespace.

> *The .NET base classes also include a number of classes and interfaces in the*
> `System.Runtime.Serialization` *namespace that are concerned with serialization – that is*
> *the process of converting some data (for example, the contents of a document) into a stream of bytes*
> *for storage somewhere. We won't be focusing with these classes in this chapter, since we are focusing*
> *on the classes that are available to give you direct access to files.*

Note that although security affects all areas, security is particularly important when modifying files or registry entries. The whole area of security is covered separately in Chapter 25. In this chapter, however, we will simply assume that you have sufficient access rights to run all the examples that modify files or registry entries, which should be the case if you are running from an account with administrator privileges.

Managing the File System

The classes that are used to browse around the file system and perform operations, such as moving, copying, and deleting files, are shown in the following diagram. The namespace of each class is shown in brackets beneath the class name in the diagram:

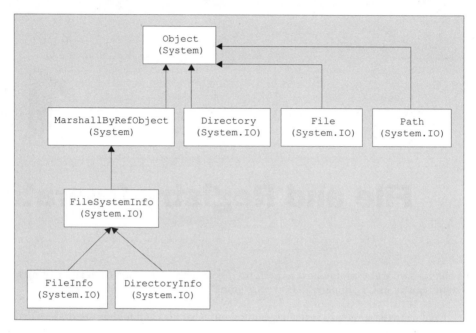

The purposes of these classes are:

❑ `System.MarshalByRefObject` – Base object class for .NET classes that are remotable; permits marshaling of data between application domains

❑ `FileSystemInfo` – Base class that represents any file system object

❑ `FileInfo` and `File` – These classes represent a file on the file system

❑ `DirectoryInfo` and `Directory` – These classes represent a folder on the file system

❑ `Path` – This class contains static members that you can use to manipulate pathnames

> *Notice that on Windows, the objects that contain files and are used to organize the file system are termed **folders**. For example, in the path C:\My Documents\ReadMe.txt, ReadMe.txt is a file and My Documents is a folder. Folder is a very Windows-specific term: On virtually every other operating system the term **directory** is used in place of folder, and in accordance with the Microsoft's desire for .NET to ultimately be platform-independent, the corresponding .NET base classes are called Directory and DirectoryInfo. However, due to the potential for confusion with LDAP directories (as discussed in Chapter 15), and because this is a Windows book, we'll stick to the term **folder** in this discussion.*

NET Classes that Represent Files and Folders

You will notice from the above list that there are two classes used to represent a folder and two classes for a file. Which one of these classes you use will depend largely on how many times you need to access that folder or file:

❑   `Directory` and `File` contain only static methods and are never instantiated. You use these classes by supplying the path to the appropriate file system object whenever you call a member method. If you only want to do one operation on a folder or file then using these classes is more efficient, because it saves the overhead of instantiating a .NET class.

❑   `DirectoryInfo` and `FileInfo` implement roughly the same public methods as `Directory` and `File`, as well as some public properties and constructors, but they are stateful and the members of these classes are not static. You need to actually instantiate these classes and then each instance is associated with a particular folder or file. This means that these classes are more efficient if you're performing multiple operations using the same object, because they will read in the authentication and other information for the appropriate file system object on construction, and then will not need to read that information again, no matter how many methods and so on you call against each object (class instance). In comparison, the corresponding stateless classes will need to check the details of the file or folder again with every method you call.

In this section, we will be mostly using the `FileInfo` and `DirectoryInfo` classes, but it happens that many (though not all) of the methods we call are also implemented by `File` and `Directory` (although in those cases these methods require an extra parameter – the pathname of the file system object, and a couple of the methods have slightly different names). For example:

```
FileInfo MyFile = new FileInfo(@"C:\Program Files\My Program\ReadMe.txt");
MyFile.CopyTo(@"D:\Copies\ReadMe.txt");
```

Has the same effect as:

```
File.Copy(@"C:\Program Files\My Program\ReadMe.txt" ,
                          @"D:\Copies\ReadMe.txt");
```

The first code snippet above will take slightly longer to execute, because of the need to instantiate a `FileInfo` object, `MyFile`, but it leaves `MyFile` ready for you to perform further actions on the same file.

You instantiate a `FileInfo` or `DirectoryInfo` class by passing a string containing the path to the corresponding file system to the constructor. We've just illustrated the process for a file. For a folder the code looks similar:

```
DirectoryInfo MyFolder = new DirectoryInfo(@"C:\Program Files");
```

If the path represents an object that does not exist, then an exception will not be thrown at construction, but will instead be thrown the first time that you call a method that actually requires the corresponding file system object to be there. You can find out whether the object exists and is of the appropriate type by checking the `Exists` property, which is implemented by both of these classes:

```
FileInfo Test = new FileInfo(@"C:\Windows");
Console.WriteLine(Test.Exists.ToString());
Console.WriteLine(Test.CreationTime.ToString());
```

Note that for this property to return `true`, the corresponding file system object must be of the appropriate type. In other words, if you instantiate a `FileInfo` object supplying the path of a folder, or you instantiate a `DirectoryInfo` object, giving it the path of a file, `Exists` will have the value `false`. On the other hand, most of the properties and methods of these objects will return a value if at all possible – they won't necessarily throw an exception just because the wrong type of object has been called, unless they are asked to do something that really is impossible. For example, the above code snippet will first display `false` (because `C:\Windows` is a folder – at least on my computer!), but will still then correctly display the time the folder was created – because a folder still has that information. On the other hand if we then tried to open the folder as if it was a file, using the `FileInfo.Open()` method, we'd then get an exception.

After you have established whether the corresponding file system object exists, you can (if you are using the `FileInfo` or `DirectoryInfo` class) find out information about it using a number of properties, including:

Name	Purpose
`CreationTime`	Time file or folder was created
`DirectoryName (FileInfo)`, `Parent (DirectoryInfo)`	Full pathname of the containing folder
`Exists`	Whether file or folder exists
`Extension`	Extension of the file; returns blank for folders
`FullName`	Full pathname of the file or folder
`LastAccessTime`	Time file or folder was last accessed
`LastWriteTime`	Time file or folder was last modified
`Name`	Name of the file or folder
`Root`	The root portion of the path (`DirectoryInfo` only)
`Length`	The size of the file in bytes (`FileInfo` only)

You can also perform actions on the file system object using these methods:

Name	Purpose
`Create()`	Creates a folder or empty file of the given name. For a `FileInfo` this also returns a stream object to let you write to the file. *We cover streams later in the chapter.*
`Delete()`	Deletes the file or folder. For folders there is an option for the `Delete` to be recursive.
`MoveTo()`	Moves and/or renames the file or folder.
`CopyTo()`	(`FileInfo` only) Copies the file. Note that there is no copy method for folders. If copying complete directory trees you'll need to individually copy each file and create new folders corresponding to the old folders.
`GetDirectories()`	(`DirectoryInfo` only) Returns an array of `DirectoryInfo` objects representing all folders contained in this folder.

Name	Purpose
GetFiles()	(DirectoryInfo only) Returns an array of FileInfo objects representing all files contained in this folder.
GetFileSystemObjects()	(DirectoryInfo only) Returns FileInfo and DirectoryInfo objects representing all objects contained in this folder, as an array of FileSystemInfo references.

Note that the above tables give the main properties and methods, and are not intended to be exhaustive.

In the above tables we've not listed most of the properties or methods that allow you to write to or read the data in files. This is actually done using stream objects, which we'll cover later in the chapter. FileInfo also implements a number of methods (Open(), OpenRead(), OpenText(), OpenWrite(), Create(), and CreateText() that return stream objects for this purpose).

Interestingly, the creation time, last access time, and last write time, are all write-able:

```
// Test is a FileInfo or DirectoryInfo. Set creation time to
// 1 Jan 2001, 7.30 am

Test.CreationTime = new DateTime(2001, 1, 1, 7, 30, 0);
```

This might seem strange, but it can be quite useful. For example, if you have a program that effectively modifies a file by simply reading it in, then deleting it and creating new file with the new contents, then you'd probably want to modify the creation date to match the original creation date of the old file.

The Path Class

The Path class is not a class that you would instantiate. Rather, it exposes some static methods that make operations on pathnames easier. For example, suppose you want to display the full pathname for a file, ReadMe.txt in the folder C:\My Documents. You could find the path to the file with the following:

```
Console.WriteLine(Path.Combine(@"C:\My Documents", "ReadMe.txt"));
```

Using the Path class is a lot easier than trying to fiddle about with separation symbols manually, especially because the Path class is aware of different formats for pathnames on different operating systems. At the time of writing, Windows is the only operating system supported by .NET, but if, for example, .NET was later ported to Unix, Path would be able to cope with Unix paths, in which /, rather than \, is used as a separator in pathnames. Path.Combine is the method of this class that you are likely to use most often, but Path also implements other methods that supply information about the path or the required format for it.

In the following section we present a example that illustrates how to browse directories and view the properties of files.

Example: A File Browser

In this section we'll present a sample C# application called `FileProperties`. `FileProperties` presents a simple user interface that allows you to browse around the file system, and view the creation time, last access time, last write time, and size of files.

The `FileProperties` application looks like this. You type in the name of a folder or file in the main textbox at the top of the window and click the Display button. If you type in the path to a folder, its contents are listed in the listboxes. If you type in the path to a file, its details are displayed in the textboxes at the bottom of the form and the contents of its parent folder are displayed in the listboxes. The screenshot shows `FileProperties` being used to examine a folder:

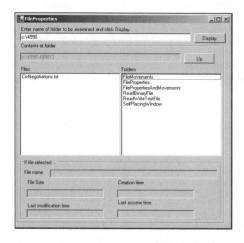

The user can very easily navigate around the file system by clicking on any of the folders in the right-hand listbox to move down to that folder, or by clicking the Up button to move up to the parent folder. In the above screenshot I typed in `C:\4990` into the main textbox to get the contents of that partition then used the listbox to navigate down. The user can also select a file by clicking on its name in the listbox – in which case its properties are displayed in the textboxes. The next screenshot shows this:

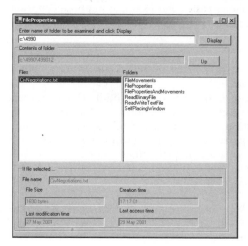

Note that if we'd wanted, we could also display the creation time, last access time and last modification time for folders too – `DirectoryInfo` does implement the appropriate properties. We are going to display these properties only for a selected file to keep things simple.

We create the project as a standard C# Windows application in Visual Studio.NET, and add the various textboxes and the listbox from the Windows Forms area of the toolbox. We've also renamed the controls with the more intuitive names of `txtBoxInput`, `txtBoxFolder`, `buttonDisplay`, `buttonUp`, `listBoxFiles`, `listBoxFolders`, `textBoxFileName`, `textBoxCreationTime`, `txtBoxLastAccessTime`, `txtBoxLastWriteTime`, and `textBoxFileSize`.

Then we add the following code:

Firstly, we need to indicate that we will be using the `System.IO` namespace:

```
using System;
using System.Drawing;
using System.Collections;
using System.ComponentModel;
using System.Windows.Forms;
using System.Data;
using System.IO;
```

We need to do this for all the file system-related examples in this chapter, but we won't explicitly show this part of the code in the remaining examples. We then add a member field to the main form:

```
public class Form1 : System.Windows.Forms.Form
{

    #region Member Fields
    private string currentFolderPath;
```

`currentFolderPath` will store the path of the folder whose contents are currently being shown in the listboxes.

Now we need to add event handlers for the user-generated events. The possible user inputs are:

❑ User clicks the Display button: In this case we need to figure out whether what the user has typed in the main textbox is the path to a file or folder. If it's a folder we list the files and subfolders of this folders in the listbox. If it is a file, we still do this for the folder containing that file, but we also display the file properties in the lower textboxes.

❑ User clicks on a file name in the Files listbox: In this case we display the properties of this file in the lower textboxes.

❑ User clicks on a folder name in the Folders listbox: In this case we clear all the controls and then display the contents of this subfolder in the listboxes.

❑ User clicks on the Up button: In this case we clear all the controls and then display the contents of the parent of the folder being displayed in the listboxes.

Before we show the code for the event handlers, we'll list the code for a the methods that will actually do all the work. First, we need to clear the contents of all the controls. This method is fairly self-explanatory:

```
protected void ClearAllFields()
{
    listBoxFolders.Items.Clear();
    listBoxFiles.Items.Clear();
    txtBoxFolder.Text = "";
    txtBoxFileName.Text = "";
    txtBoxCreationTime.Text = "";
    txtBoxLastAccessTime.Text = "";
    txtBoxLastWriteTime.Text = "";
    txtBoxFileSize.Text = "";
}
```

Secondly, we define a method, `DisplayFileInfo()`, which handles the process of displaying the information for a given file in the textboxes. This method takes one parameter, the full pathname of the file, and it works by creating a `FileInfo` object based on this path:

```
protected void DisplayFileInfo(string fileFullName)
{
    FileInfo TheFile = new FileInfo(fileFullName);
    if (!TheFile.Exists)
        throw new FileNotFoundException("File not found: " + fileFullName);
    txtBoxFileName.Text = TheFile.Name;
    txtBoxCreationTime.Text = TheFile.CreationTime.ToLongTimeString();
    txtBoxLastAccessTime.Text = TheFile.LastAccessTime.ToLongDateString();
    txtBoxLastWriteTime.Text = TheFile.LastWriteTime.ToLongDateString();
    txtBoxFileSize.Text = TheFile.Length.ToString() + " bytes";
}
```

Note that we take the precaution of throwing an exception if there are any problems locating a file here. The exception will be handled in the calling routine (one of the event handlers). Finally, we define a method, `DisplayFolderList()`, which displays the contents of a given folder in the two listboxes. The full pathname of the folder is passed in as a parameter to this method:

```
protected void DisplayFolderList(string folderFullName)
{
    DirectoryInfo TheFolder = new DirectoryInfo(folderFullName);
    if (!TheFolder.Exists)
        throw new DirectoryNotFoundException("Folder not found: "
                                             + folderFullName);
    ClearAllFields();
    txtBoxFolder.Text = TheFolder.FullName;
    currentFolderPath = TheFolder.FullName;

    // list all subfolders in folder

    foreach(DirectoryInfo NextFolder in TheFolder.GetDirectories())
        listBoxFolders.Items.Add(NextFolder.Name);

    // list all files in folder

    foreach(FileInfo NextFile in TheFolder.GetFiles())
        listBoxFiles.Items.Add(NextFile.Name);
}
```

Now we will examine the event handlers. The handler for the event of the user clicking the Display button is the most complex, since it needs to handle three different possibilities for the text the user typed in; it could be the pathname of a folder, the pathname of a file, or neither.

```
protected void OnDisplayButtonClick(object sender, EventArgs e)
{
    try
    {
        string FolderPath = txtBoxInput.Text;
        DirectoryInfo TheFolder = new DirectoryInfo(FolderPath);
        if (TheFolder.Exists)
        {
            DisplayFolderList(TheFolder.FullName);
            return;
        }
        FileInfo TheFile = new FileInfo(FolderPath);
        if (TheFile.Exists)
        {
            DisplayFolderList(TheFile.Directory.FullName);
            int Index = listBoxFiles.Items.IndexOf(TheFile.Name);
            listBoxFiles.SetSelected(Index, true);
            return;
        }
        throw new FileNotFoundException("There is no file or folder with "
                                + "this name: " + txtBoxInput.Text);
    }
    catch(Exception ex)
    {
        MessageBox.Show(ex.Message);
    }
}
```

In the above code, we establish if the supplied text represents a folder or file by in turn instantiating `DirectoryInfo` and `FileInfo` instances and examining the `Exists` property of each object. If neither exists, then we throw an exception. If it's a folder, we call `DisplayFolderList` to populate the listboxes. If it's a file, we need to populate the listboxes and sort out the textboxes that display the file properties. We handle this case by first populating the listboxes. We then programmatically select the appropriate file name in the files listbox. This has exactly the same effect as if the user had selected that item – it'll raise the item selected event. We can then simply exit the current event handler, knowing that the selected item event handler will immediately be called to display the file properties.

The following code is the event handler that gets called when an item in the files listbox is selected, either by the user or, as indicated above, programmatically. It simply constructs the full pathname of the selected file, and passes this to the `DisplayFileInfo()` method that we presented earlier:

```
protected void OnListBoxFilesSelected(object sender, EventArgs e)
{
    try
    {
        string SelectedString = listBoxFiles.SelectedItem.ToString();
        string FullFileName = Path.Combine(currentFolderPath, SelectedString);
        DisplayFileInfo(FullFileName);
    }
    catch(Exception ex)
    {
        MessageBox.Show(ex.Message);
    }
}
```

The event handler for the event of a folder in the folders listbox being selected is implemented in a very similar way, except that in this case we call `DisplayFolderList()` to update the contents of the listboxes:

```
protected void OnListBoxFoldersSelected(object sender, EventArgs e)
{
    try
    {
        string SelectedString = listBoxFolders.SelectedItem.ToString();
        string FullPathName = Path.Combine(currentFolderPath, SelectedString);
        DisplayFolderList(FullPathName);
    }
    catch(Exception ex)
    {
        MessageBox.Show(ex.Message);
    }
}
```

Finally, when the Up button is clicked, `DisplayFolderList()` must also be called, except that this time we need to obtain the path of the parent of the folder currently being displayed. This is obtained through the `FileInfo.DirectoryName` property, which returns the parent folder path:

```
protected void OnUpButtonClick(object sender, EventArgs e)
{
    try
    {
        string FolderPath = new FileInfo(currentFolderPath).DirectoryName;
        DisplayFolderList(FolderPath);
    }
    catch(Exception ex)
    {
        MessageBox.Show(ex.Message);
    }
}
```

Note that for this project, we have not displayed the code that adds the event handlers to the relevant events for the controls. We do not need to add this code manually, since, as noted in Chapter 9, we can use the Properties window in Visual Studio to associate each event handler with the event.

Moving, Copying, and Deleting Files

We have already mentioned that moving and deleting files or folders is done by the `MoveTo()` and `Delete()` methods of the `FileInfo` and `DirectoryInfo` classes. The equivalent methods on the `File` and `Directory` classes are `Move()` and `Delete()`. The `FileInfo` and `File` classes also respectively implement methods, `CopyTo()` and `Copy()`. No methods exist to copy complete folders, however – you need to do that by copying each file in the folder.

Use of all these methods is quite intuitive – and you can find full details in MSDN. In this section we are going to illustrate their use for the particular cases of calling the static `Move()`, `Copy()`, and `Delete()` methods on the `File` class. To do this we will develop our previous `FileProperties` example into a new example, `FilePropetiesAndMovement`. This example will have the extra feature that whenever the properties of a file are displayed, the application gives us the option of deleting that file, or moving or copying it to another location.

The FilePropertiesAndMovement Example

The new example looks like this:

From this screenshot, we can see that it is very similar in appearance to the FileProperties example, except that there is an additional group of three buttons and a textbox at the bottom of the window. These controls are only enabled when the example is actually displaying the properties of a file – at other times, they are disabled. We've also squashed the existing controls up a bit to stop the main form from getting too big. When the properties of a file are displayed, FilePropertiesAndMovement automatically places the full pathname of that file in the bottom textbox for the user to edit. The user can then click on any of the buttons to perform the appropriate operation. When they do, an appropriate message box is displayed that confirms the action. In the above case, if the user clicks on Copy To we will see this message:

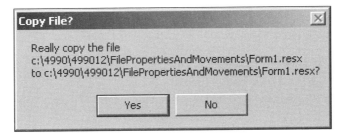

Assuming the user confirms the action, it will go ahead. In the case of moving or deleting a file, we obviously can't carry on displaying the contents of that file in the same location. As well as this, if we copy a file to another filename in the same folder, our display will also be out of date. In all of these cases, the example resets its controls to display only the containing folder after the file operation.

To code this up, we need to add the relevant controls, as well as their event handlers to the code for the FileProperties example. We have given the new controls the names buttonDelete, buttonCopyTo, buttonMoveTo, and txtBoxNewPath.

We'll look first at the event handler that gets called when the user hits the **Delete** button;

```
protected void OnDeleteButtonClick(object sender, EventArgs e)
{
    try
    {
        string FilePath = Path.Combine(currentFolderPath,
                                    txtBoxFileName.Text);
        string Query = "Really delete the file\n" + FilePath + "?";
        if (MessageBox.Show(Query,
            "Delete File?", MessageBoxButtons.YesNo) == DialogResult.Yes)
        {
            File.Delete(FilePath);
            DisplayFolderList(currentFolderPath);
        }
    }
    catch(Exception ex)
    {
        MessageBox.Show("Unable to delete file. The following exception"
                        + " occurred:\n" + ex.Message, "Failed");
    }
}
```

The code for this method is contained in a `try` block because of the obvious risk of an exception being thrown if, for example, we don't have permission to delete the file, or the file got moved by another process in the time between our example displaying it, and the user hitting the delete button. We construct the path of the file to be deleted from the `CurrentParentPath` field, which will contain the path of the parent folder, and the text in the `textBoxFileName` textbox, which will contain the name of the file.

The methods to move and copy the file are structured in a very similar manner:

```
protected void OnMoveButtonClick(object sender, EventArgs e)
{
    try
    {
        string FilePath = Path.Combine(currentFolderPath,
                                    txtBoxFileName.Text);
        string Query = "Really move the file\n" + FilePath + "\nto "
                        + txtBoxNewPath.Text + "?";
        if (MessageBox.Show(Query,
            "Move File?", MessageBoxButtons.YesNo) == DialogResult.Yes)
        {
            File.Move(FilePath, txtBoxNewPath.Text);
            DisplayFolderList(currentFolderPath);
        }
    }
    catch(Exception ex)
    {
        MessageBox.Show("Unable to move file. The following exception"
                        + " occurred:\n" + ex.Message, "Failed");
    }
}
protected void OnCopyButtonClick(object sender, EventArgs e)
{
```

```
    try
    {
        string FilePath = Path.Combine(currentFolderPath,
                                  txtBoxFileName.Text);
        string Query = "Really copy the file\n" + FilePath + "\nto "
                       + txtBoxNewPath.Text + "?";
        if (MessageBox.Show(Query,
            "Copy File?", MessageBoxButtons.YesNo) == DialogResult.Yes)
        {
            File.Copy(FilePath, txtBoxNewPath.Text);
            DisplayFolderList(currentFolderPath);
        }
    }
    catch(Exception ex)
    {
        MessageBox.Show("Unable to copy file. The following exception"
                       + " occurred:\n" + ex.Message, "Failed");
    }
}
```

We're not quite done yet. We also need to make sure the new buttons and textbox are enabled and disabled at the appropriate times. To enable them when we are displaying the contents of a file, we add the following code to `DisplayFileInfo()`:

```
protected void DisplayFileInfo(string fileFullName)
{
    FileInfo TheFile = new FileInfo(fileFullName);
    if (!TheFile.Exists)
        throw new FileNotFoundException("File not found: " + fileFullName);

    txtBoxFileName.Text = TheFile.Name;
    txtBoxCreationTime.Text = TheFile.CreationTime.ToLongTimeString();
    txtBoxLastAccessTime.Text = TheFile.LastAccessTime.ToLongDateString();
    txtBoxLastWriteTime.Text = TheFile.LastWriteTime.ToLongDateString();
    txtBoxFileSize.Text = TheFile.Length.ToString() + " bytes";

    // enable move, copy, delete buttons

    txtBoxNewPath.Text = TheFile.FullName;
    txtBoxNewPath.Enabled = true;
    buttonCopyTo.Enabled = true;
    buttonDelete.Enabled = true;
    buttonMoveTo.Enabled = true;
}
```

We also need to make one change to `DisplayFolderInfo`:

```
protected void DisplayFolderList(string folderFullName)
{
    DirectoryInfo TheFolder = new DirectoryInfo(folderFullName);
    if (!TheFolder.Exists)
        throw new DirectoryNotFoundException("Folder not found: " + folderFullName);

    ClearAllFields();
    DisableMoveFeatures();
    txtBoxFolder.Text = TheFolder.FullName;
    currentFolderPath = TheFolder.FullName;

    // list all subfolders in folder

    foreach(DirectoryInfo NextFolder in TheFolder.GetDirectories())
        listBoxFolders.Items.Add(NextFolder.Name);
```

```
  // list all files in folder
    foreach(FileInfo NextFile in TheFolder.GetFiles())
        listBoxFiles.Items.Add(NextFile.Name);
}
```

`DisableMoveFeatures` is a small utility function that disables the new controls:

```
        void DisableMoveFeatures()
        {
           txtBoxNewPath.Text = "";
           txtBoxNewPath.Enabled = false;
           buttonCopyTo.Enabled = false;
           buttonDelete.Enabled = false;
           buttonMoveTo.Enabled = false;
        }
```

We also need to add extra code to `ClearAllFields()` to clear the extra textbox:

```
        protected void ClearAllFields()
        {
           listBoxFolders.Items.Clear();
           listBoxFiles.Items.Clear();
           txtBoxFolder.Text = "";
           txtBoxFileName.Text = "";
           txtBoxCreationTime.Text = "";
           txtBoxLastAccessTime.Text = "";
           txtBoxLastWriteTime.Text = "";
           txtBoxFileSize.Text = "";
           txtBoxNewPath.Text = "";
        }
```

With that, the code is complete.

Reading and Writing to Files

Reading and writing to files is in principle very simple; however, it is not done through the `DirectoryInfo` or `FileInfo` objects that we've just been examining. Instead, it is done through a number of classes that represent a generic concept called a **stream**, which we will examine next.

Streams

The idea of a stream has been around for a very long time. A stream is an object used to transfer data. The data can be transferred in one of two directions:

❑   If the data is being transferred from some outside source into your program then we talk about **reading** from the stream

❑   If the data is being transferred from your program to some outside source then we talk about **writing** to the stream

Very often, the outside source will be a file, but that is not necessarily the case. Other possibilities include:

❏ Reading or writing data on the network using some network protocol, where the intention is for this data to be picked up by or sent from another computer

❏ Reading or writing to a named pipe

❏ Reading or writing to an area of memory

Of these examples, Microsoft has supplied a .NET base class for writing to or reading from memory, `System.IO.MemoryStream`, while `System.Net.Sockets.NetworkStream` handles network data. There are no base stream classes for writing to or reading from pipes, but there is a generic stream class, `System.IO.Stream`, from which you would inherit if you wished to write such a class. Stream does not make any assumptions about the nature of the external data source.

The outside source might even be a variable within your own code. This might sound paradoxical, but the technique of using streams to transmit data between variables can be a useful trick for converting data between data types. The C language used something like this to convert between integer data types and strings or to format strings using a function, `sprintf()`, while in C# two .NET base classes, `StringReader` and `StringWriter`, can be used in this context.

The advantage of having a separate object for the transfer of data, rather than using the `FileInfo` or `DirectoryInfo` classes to do this, is that by separating the concept of transferring data from the particular data source, it makes it easier to swap data sources. Stream objects themselves contain a lot of generic code that concerns the movement of data between outside sources and variables in your code, and by keeping this code separate from any concept of a particular data source, we make it easier for this code to be reused (through inheritance) in different circumstances. As an example of this, the `StringReader` and `StringWriter` classes mentioned above are part of the same inheritance tree as two classes that we will be using later on to read and write text files, `StreamReader` and `StreamWriter`. The classes will almost certainly share a substantial amount of code behind the scenes.

The actual hierarchy of stream-related classes in the `System.IO` namespace looks like this:

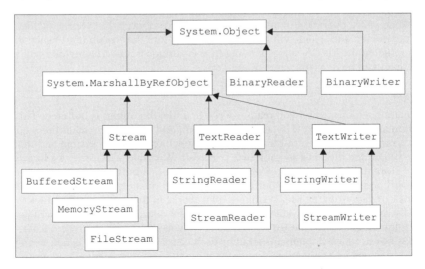

As far as reading and writing files is concerned, the classes that we are going to be most concerned with are:

❑   `FileStream`. This class is intended for reading and writing binary data in a binary file – though if you wish you can use it to read from or write to any file

❑   `StreamReader` and `StreamWriter`. These classes are designed specifically for reading from and writing to text files

Although we won't be using them in our examples, we'll also mention a couple of other classes that you may find useful, `BinaryReader` and `BinaryWriter`. If you wish to use these classes, you should refer to the MSDN documentation for details of their operation.

These classes do not actually implement streams themselves, but they are able to provide wrappers around other stream objects. `BinaryReader` and `BinaryWriter` provide extra formatting of binary data, which allows you to directly read or write the contents of C# variables to the relevant stream. The easiest way to think about it is that the `BinaryReader` and `BinaryWriter` sit between the stream and your code, providing extra formatting:

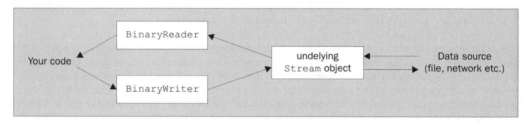

The difference between using these classes and directly using the underlying stream objects is that a basic stream works in bytes. For example, suppose as part of the process of saving some document you want to write the contents of a variable of type `long` to a binary file. Each `long` occupies 8 bytes, and if you used a plain ordinary binary stream you would have to explicitly write each of those 8 bytes of memory. In C# code that would mean you'd have to explicitly perform some bitwise operations to extract each of those 8 bytes from the `long` value. Using a `BinaryWriter` instance, you can encapsulate the entire operation in an overload of the `BinaryWriter.Write()` method that takes a `long` as a parameter, and which will place those 8 bytes into the stream (and hence if the stream is directed to a file, in the file). A corresponding `BinaryReader.Read()` method will extract 8 bytes from the stream and recover the value of the `long`.

BufferedStream

For performance reasons, when you read or write to a file, the output is buffered. This means that if your program asks for the next 2 bytes of a file stream, and the stream passes the request on to Windows, Windows will not go to the trouble of connecting to the file system and then locating and reading the file off the disk, just to get 2 bytes. Instead, Windows will retrieve a large block of the file in one go, and store this block in an area of memory known as a **buffer**. Subsequent requests for data from the stream will be satisfied from the buffer until the buffer runs out, at which point Windows will grab another block of data from the file. Writing to files works in the same way. For files this is done automatically by the operating system, but it may be the case that you need to write a stream class to read from some other device that isn't buffered. If so, you can derive your class from `BufferedStream`, which implements a buffer itself. (`BufferedStream` is not, however, designed for the situation in which an application frequently alternates between reading and writing data.)

Reading and Writing to Binary Files

Reading and writing to binary files is usually done using the `FileStream` class.

The FileStream Class

A `FileStream` instance is used to read or write data to or from a file. In order to construct a `FileStream`, you need four pieces of information:

- ❑ The **file** you want to access.

- ❑ The **mode**, which indicates how you want to open the file. For example, are you intending to create a new file or open an existing file, and if opening an existing file should any write operations be interpreted as overwriting the contents of the file or appending to the file?

- ❑ The **access**, indicating how you want access to file – are you intending to read or write to the file or do both?

- ❑ The **share** access – in other words do you want exclusive access to the file, or are you willing for other streams to be able to access this file simultaneously? If so, should other streams have access to read the file, to write to it, or to do both?

The first of these pieces of information is usually represented by a string that contains the full pathname of the file, and in this chapter we will only consider those constructors that require a string here. Besides those constructors, however, there are some additional ones that take an old Windows-API style Windows handle to a file instead. The remaining three pieces of information are represented by three .NET enumerations respectively called `FileMode`, `FileAccess`, and `FileShare`. The values of these enumerations should be self-explanatory, and they are:

Enumeration	Values
FileMode	Append, Create, CreateNew, Open, OpenOrCreate, or Truncate
FileAccess	Read, ReadWrite, or Write
FileShare	None, Read, ReadWrite, or Write

Note that in the case of `FileMode`, exceptions can be thrown if you request a mode that is inconsistent with the existing status of the file. `Append`, `Open`, and `Truncate` will throw an exception if the file does not already exist, and `CreateNew` will throw an exception if it does. `Create` and `OpenOrCreate` will cope with either scenario, but `Create` will delete any existing file to replace it with a new, initially empty, one.

There are a large number of constructors for the `FileStream`. The three simplest ones work as follows:

```
// creates file with read-write access and allows other streams read
// access

FileStream fs = new FileStream(@"C:\C# Projects\Projects.doc",
                  FileMode.Create);

// as above, but we only get write access to the file

FileStream fs2 = new FileStream(@"C:\C# Projects\Projects2.doc",
                  FileMode.Create, FileAccess.Write);

// as above but other streams don't get any access to the file while
```

```
// fs3 is open

FileStream fs3 = new FileStream(@"C:\C# Projects\Projects3.doc",
                        FileMode.Create, FileAccess.Read, FileShare.None);
```

From this code we can see that these overloads of the constructors have the effect of providing default values of `FileAccess.ReadWrite` and `FileShare.Read` to the third and fourth parameters. It is also possible to create a file stream from a `FileInfo` instance:

```
FileInfo MyFile4 = new FileInfo(@"C:\C# Projects\Projects4.doc");
FileStream fs4 = MyFile4.OpenRead();
FileInfo MyFile5= new FileInfo(@"C:\C# Projects\Projects5doc");
FileStream fs5 = MyFile5.OpenWrite();
FileInfo MyFile6= new FileInfo(@"C:\C# Projects\Projects6doc");
FileStream fs6 = MyFile6.Open(FileMode.Append, FileAccess.Read,
                    FileShare.None);
FileInfo MyNewFile = new FileInfo(@"C:\C# Projects\ProjectsNew.doc");
FileStream fs7 = MyNewFile.Create();
```

`FileInfo.OpenRead()` supplies a stream that gives you read-only access to an existing file, while `FileInfo.OpenWrite()` gives you read-write access. `FileInfo.Open()` allows you to specify the mode, access, and file share parameters explicitly.

You won't be surprised to learn that once you've finished with a stream, you should close it:

```
fs.Close();
```

Closing the stream frees up the resources associated with it, and allows other applications to set up streams to the same file. In between opening and closing the stream, you'll want to read data from it and/or write data to it. `FileStream` implements a number of methods to do this.

`ReadByte()` is the simplest way of reading data. It grabs one byte from the stream, and casts the result to an `int` having a value between 0 and 255. If we have reached the end of the stream, it returns –1:

```
int NextByte = fs.ReadByte();
```

If you prefer to read a number of bytes at a time, you can call the `Read()` method, which reads a specified number of bytes into an array. `Read()` returns the number of bytes actually read – if this value is zero then you know you're at the end of the stream:

```
// to read 100 bytes in.

int nBytes = 100;
byte [] ByteArray = new byte[nBytes];
int nBytesRead = fs.Read(ByteArray, 0, nBytes);
```

The second parameter to `Read()` is an offset, which you can use to request that the `Read` operation starts populating the array at some element other than the first.

If you wish to write data to a file, then there are two parallel methods available, WriteByte() and Write(). WriteByte() writes a single byte to the stream:

```
byte NextByte = 100;
fs.WriteByte(NextByte);
```

Write(), on the other hand, writes out an array of bytes:

```
// to write out 100 bytes.

int nBytes = 100;
byte [] ByteArray = new byte[nBytes];

// obviously, do something here to initialize the array with the values
// you want written out

fs.Write(ByteArray, 0, nBytes);
```

As with Read(), the second parameter allows you to start writing from some point other than the beginning of the array. Both WriteByte() and Write() return void.

Besides these methods, FileStream implements various other methods and properties to do with bookkeeping tasks like determining how many bytes are in the stream, locking the stream or flushing the buffer. These other methods aren't usually required for basic reading and writing, and if you need them, full details are in the MSDN documentation.

Example: Binary File Reader

We'll illustrate the use of the FileStream class by writing an example, BinaryFileReader, which reads in and displays any file. The example is as usual created in Visual Studio.NET as a windows application. We've added one menu item, which brings up a standard OpenFileDialog asking what file to read in, then displays the file. As we are reading in binary files, we need to be able to display non-printable characters. The way we will do this is by displaying each byte of the file individually, with 16 bytes on each line of a multiline textbox. If the byte represents a printable ASCII character, we'll display that character, otherwise we'll display the value of the byte in hexadecimal format. In either case, we pad out the displayed text with spaces so that each 'byte' displayed occupies four columns so the bytes line up nicely under each other.

This is what the BinaryFileReader looks like when viewing a text file, (since the BinaryFileReader can view any file, it's quite possible to use it on text files as well as binary ones). In this case, the example has read in a file that contains some negotiations that went on in a recent game of Civ:

If you're wondering, Civ is Sid Meier's well-known computer game, Civilization, in which players start of with a couple of settlers, and have to go and explore a computer-generated world, build cities, and try to make their civilization bigger and more powerful than anyone else's. The author of this chapter has occasionally been spotted playing Civ against various opponents on the Internet. His excuse is that he claims it assists logical thinking.

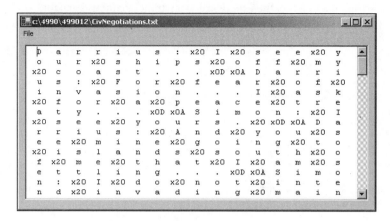

Clearly this format is more suited to looking at the values of individual bytes rather than to displaying text! Later in the chapter, we'll develop an example that is specifically designed to read text files – then we will be able to see what this file really says. On the other hand, the advantage of this example is that we can look at the contents of any file.

For this example, we won't demonstrate writing to files. That's because we don't want to get bogged down in the complexities of trying to translate the contents of a textbox like the one above into a binary stream! We will demonstrate writing to files later on when we develop an example that can read or write to text files.

Let's look at the code used to get these results. First, we need an extra `using` statement, since besides `System.IO`, this example is going to use the `StringBuilder` class from the `System.Text` namespace to construct the strings in the textbox:

```
using System.IO;
using System.Text;
```

Next, we add a couple of fields to the main form class – one representing the file dialog, and a string that gives the path of the file currently being viewed:

```
public class Form1 : System.Windows.Forms.Form
{
    OpenFileDialog ChooseOpenFileDialog = new OpenFileDialog();
    string ChosenFile;
```

We also need to add some standard Windows Forms `stuff` to deal with the handlers for the menu and the file dialog:

```
public Form1()
{
    InitializeComponent();

    menuFileOpen.Click += new EventHandler(OnFileOpen);
    ChooseOpenFileDialog.FileOk += new
                        CancelEventHandler(OnOpenFileDialogOK);
}
void OnFileOpen(object Sender, EventArgs e)
```

```
    {
ChooseOpenFileDialog.ShowDialog();
    }
      void OnOpenFileDialogOK(object Sender, CancelEventArgs e)
      {
         ChosenFile = ChooseOpenFileDialog.FileName;
         this.Text = ChosenFile;
         DisplayFile();
      }
```

From this we see that once the user clicks OK to select a file in the file dialog, we call a method, `DisplayFile()`, which actually does the work of reading in the file:

```
      void DisplayFile()
      {
         int nCols = 16;
         FileStream InStream = new FileStream(ChosenFile, FileMode.Open,
                                                   FileAccess.Read);
         long nBytesToRead = InStream.Length;
         if (nBytesToRead > 65536/4)
            nBytesToRead = 65536/4;
         int nLines = (int)(nBytesToRead/nCols) + 1;
         string [] Lines = new string[nLines];
         int nBytesRead = 0;
         for (int i=0 ; i<nLines ; i++)
         {
            StringBuilder NextLine = new StringBuilder();
            NextLine.Capacity = 4*nCols;
            for (int j = 0 ; j<nCols ; j++)
            {
               int NextByte = InStream.ReadByte();
               nBytesRead++;
               if (NextByte < 0 || nBytesRead > 65536)
                  break;
               char NextChar = (char)NextByte;
               if (NextChar < 16)
                  NextLine.Append(" x0" + string.Format("{0,1:X}",
                                                   (int)NextChar));
               else if
                  (char.IsLetterOrDigit(NextChar) ||
                                    char.IsPunctuation(NextChar))
                  NextLine.Append("  " + NextChar + " ");
               else
                  NextLine.Append(" x" + string.Format("{0,2:X}",
                                             (int)NextChar));
            }
            Lines[i] = NextLine.ToString();
         }
         InStream.Close();
         this.textBoxContents.Lines = Lines;
      }
```

There's quite a lot going on in this method, so we'll break it down. We instantiate a `FileStream` for the selected file, specifying that we wish to open an existing file for reading. We then work out how many bytes there are to read in and how many lines should be displayed. The number of bytes will normally be the number of bytes in the file. Textboxes can only display a maximum of 65,536 characters, however, and with our chosen format, we are displaying 4 characters for every byte in the file, so we will need to cap the number of bytes shown if the file is longer than $65,536/4 = 16,384$.

If you want to display longer files in this sort of environment, you might want to look up the
RichTextBox *class in the* System.Windows.Forms *namespace.* RichTextBox *is similar*
to a textbox, but has many more advanced formatting facilities and does not have a limit on how
much text it can display. We are using TextBox *here to keep the example simple and focussed on*
the process of reading in files.

The bulk of the method is given over to two nested for loops that construct each line of text to be
displayed. We use a StringBuilder class to construct each line for performance reasons: We will be
appending suitable text for each byte to the string that represents each line 16 times. If on each occasion
we allocate a new string and take a copy of the half-constructed line, we are not only going to be
spending a lot of time allocating strings, but will be wasting a lot of memory on the heap. Notice that
our definition of "printable" characters is anything that is a letter, digit, or punctuation, as indicated by
the relevant static System.Char methods. We've excluded any character with a value less than 16 from
the printable list, however, which means we'll trap the carriage return (13) and line feed (10) as binary
characters (a multilane textbox isn't able to display these characters properly if they occur individually
within a line).

Finally, we close the stream and set the contents of the textbox to the array of strings that we've built up.

Reading and Writing to Text Files

Theoretically, it's perfectly possible to use the FileStream class to read in and display text files. We
have, after all, already demonstrated doing that. The format in which we displayed the
CivNegotiations.txt file above wasn't particularly user-friendly, but that wasn't due to any intrinsic
problem with the FileStream class – that was just because of the way we'd chosen to display the
results in the textbox.

Having said that, if you know that a particular file contains text, you will usually find it more convenient
to read and write it using the StreamReader and StreamWriter classes. That's because these classes
work at a slightly higher level, and are specifically geared to reading text. The methods that they
implement are able to automatically detect where convenient points to stop reading text are, based upon
the contents of the stream. In particular:

❑   These classes implement methods to read or write one line of text at a time,
    StreamReader.ReadLine() and StreamWriter.WriteLine(). In the case of reading,
    this means that is the stream will automatically figure out for you where the next carriage
    return is, and stop reading at that point. In the case of writing, it means that the stream will
    automatically append the carriage return-line feed combination to the text that it writes out.

❑   By using the StreamReader and StreamWriter classes you don't need to worry about the
    encoding used in the file. What the encoding means is the format that the text in the file has
    been stored in. Possible encodings include ASCII (1 byte for each character), or any or the
    Unicode-based formats, UNICODE, UTF7, and UTF8. Text files on Windows 9x systems are
    always in ASCII, because Windows 9x doesn't support Unicode, but Windows NT, 2000 and
    XP all do support Unicode, and so text files might theoretically contain Unicode, UTF7, or
    UTF8 data instead of ASCII data. The convention is that if the file is in ASCII format, it will
    simply contain the text. If is in any Unicode format, this will be indicated by the first two or
    three bytes of the file, which are set to particular combinations of values to indicate the format.

These bytes are known as the **byte code markers**. When you open a file using any of the standard windows applications, such as Notepad or WordPad, you don't need to worry about this because these applications are aware of the different encoding methods and will automatically read the file correctly. This is also the case for the StreamReader class, which will correctly read in a file in any of these formats, while the StreamWriter class is capable of formatting the text it writes out using whatever encoding technique you request. On the other hand, if you wanted to read in and display a text file using the FileStream class, you would have to handle all this yourself.

The StreamReader Class

StreamReader is used to read text files. Constructing a StreamReader is in some ways simpler than constructing a FileStream instance, because some of the FileStream options are not required. In particular, the mode and access types are not relevant, because the only thing you can do with a StreamReader is read! As well as this, there is no direct option to specify the sharing permissions. However, there are a couple of new options:

❑   We need to specify what to do about the different encoding methods. We can instruct the StreamReader to examine the byte order marks in the file to determine the encoding method, or we can simply tell the StreamReader to assume that the file uses a specified encoding method.

❑   Instead of supplying a file name to be read from, we can supply a reference to another stream.

This last option deserves a bit more discussion, because it illustrates another advantage of basing our model for reading and writing data around the concept of streams. Because the StreamReader works at a relatively high level, you might find it useful if you are in the situation in which you have another stream that is there to read data from some other source, but you would like to use the facilities provided by StreamReader to process that other stream as if it contained text. You can do so by simply passing the output from this stream to a StreamReader. In this way, StreamReader can be used to read and process data from any data source – not only files. This is essentially the situation we discussed earlier with regard to the BinaryReader class. However, in this book we will only use StreamReader to connect directly to files.

The result of these possibilities is that StreamReader has a large number of constructors. Not only that, but there are a couple of FileInfo methods that return StreamReader references too: OpenText() and CreateText(). Here we will just illustrate some of the constructors.

The simplest constructor takes just a file name. This StreamReader will examine the byte order marks to determine the encoding:

```
StreamReader sr = new StreamReader(@"C:\My Documents\ReadMe.txt");
```

Alternatively, if you prefer to specify that UTF8 encoding should be assumed:

```
StreamReader sr = new StreamReader(@"C:\My Documents\ReadMe.txt",
                            Encoding.UTF8Encoding);
```

We specify the encoding by using one of several properties on a class, System.Text.Encoding. This class is an abstract base class, from which a number of classes are defined, which implement methods that actually perform the text encoding. Each property returns an instance of the appropriate class, and the possible properties we can use here are:

❑   ASCII

❑   Unicode

- ❏   UTF7

- ❏   UTF8

- ❏   BigEndianUnicode

The following example demonstrates hooking a `StreamReader` up to a `FileStream`. The advantage of this is that we can explicitly specify whether to create the file and the share permissions, which we cannot do if we directly attach a `StreamReader` to the file:

```
FileStream fs = new FileStream(@"C:\My Documents\ReadMe.txt",
                    FileMode.Open, FileAccess.Read, FileShare.None);
StreamReader sr = new StreamReader(fs);
```

For this example, we specify that the `StreamReader` will look for byte order marks to determine the encoding method used, as it will do in the following examples, in which the `StreamReader` is obtained from a `FileInfo` instance:

```
FileInfo MyFile = new FileInfo(@"C:\My Documents\ReadMe.txt");
StreamReader sr = MyFile.OpenText();
```

Just as with a `FileStream`, you should always close a `StreamReader` after use. Failure to do so will result in the file remaining locked to other processes (unless you used a `FileStream` to construct the `StreamReader` and specified `FileShare.ShareReadWrite`):

```
sr.Close();
```

Now we've gone to the trouble of instantiating a `StreamReader`, we can do something with it. As with the `FileStream`, we'll simply point out the various ways there are to read data, and leave the other, less commonly used, `StreamReader` methods to the MSDN documentation.

Possibly the easiest method to use is `ReadLine()`, which keeps reading until it gets to the end of a line. It does not include the carriage return-line feed combination that marks the end of the line in the returned string:

```
string NextLine = sr.ReadLine();
```

Alternatively, you can grab the entire remainder of the file (or strictly, the remainder of the stream) in one string:

```
string RestOfStream = sr.ReadToEnd();
```

You can read a single character:

```
int NextChar = sr.Read();
```

This overload of `Read()` casts the returned character to an `int`. This is so that it has the option of returning
−1 if the end of the stream has been reached.

Finally, you can read a given number of characters into an array, with an offset:

```
// to read 100 characters in.

int nChars = 100;
char [] CharArray = new char[nChars];
int nCharsRead = sr.Read(CharArray, 0, nChars);
```

`nCharsRead` will be less than `nChars` if we have requested to read more characters than are left in the file.

The StreamWriter Class

This works in basically the same way as the `StreamReader`, except that you can only use `StreamWriter` to write to a file (or to another stream). Possibilities for constructing a `StreamWriter` include:

```
StreamWriter sw = new StreamWriter(@"C:\My Documents\ReadMe.txt");
```

The above code will use UTF8 Encoding, which is regarded by .NET as the default encoding method. If you want to specify an alternative encoding:

```
StreamWriter sw = new StreamWriter(@"C:\My Documents\ReadMe.txt", true
    Encoding.ASCII);
```

In this constructor, the second parameter is a `Boolean` that indicates whether the file should be opened for appending. There is, oddly, no constructor that takes only a file name and an encoding class.

Of course, you may want to hook a `StreamWriter` up to a file stream to give you more control over the options for opening the file:

```
FileStream fs = new FileStream(@"C:\My Documents\ReadMe.txt",
    FileMode.CreateNew, FileAccess.Write, FileShare.ShareRead);
StreamWriter sw = new StreamWriter(fs);
```

`FileInfo` does not implement any methods that return a `StreamWriter`.

Alternatively, if you want to create a new file and start writing data to it, you'll find this sequence useful:

```
FileInfo MyFile = new FileInfo(@"C:\My Documents\NewFile.txt");
StreamWriter sw = MyFile.CreateText();
```

Just as with all other stream classes it is important to close a `StreamWriter` when you have finished with it:

```
sw.Close();
```

Writing to the stream is done using any of four overloads of `StreamWriter.Write()`. The simplest writes out a string, and appends it with a carriage return-line feed combination:

```
string NextLine = "Groovy Line";
sw.Write(NextLine);
```

It is also possible to write out a single character:

```
char NextChar = 'a';
sw.Write(NextChar);
```

An array of characters is also possible:

```
char [] CharArray = new char[100];

// initialize these characters

sw.Write(CharArray);
```

It is even possible to write out a portion of an array of characters:

```
int nCharsToWrite = 50;
int StartAtLocation = 25;
char [] CharArray = new char[100];

// initialize these characters

sw.Write(CharArray, StartAtLocation, nCharsToWrite);
```

Example: ReadWriteText

The `ReadWriteText` example displays the use of the `StreamReader` and `StreamWriter` classes. It is similar to the earlier `ReadBinaryFile` example, but it assumes the file to be read in is a text file and displays it as such. It is also capable of saving the file (with any modifications you've made to the text in the textbox). It will save any file in Unicode format.

The screenshot shows `ReadWriteText` being used to display the same `CivNegotiations` file that we saw earlier. This time, however, we are able to read the contents a bit more easily!

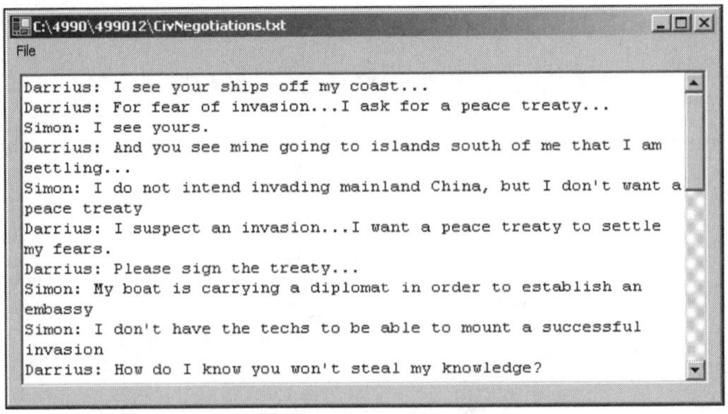

...milar treeview/listview style user interface to Windows explorer, which matches the ...ure of the Registry itself. As we'll soon see, however, there are some differences.

...he topmost level nodes can be thought of as being the partitions on your disks, C:\, ...n the registry, the equivalent to a partition is the **registry hive**. It is not possible to ...es are there – they are fixed, and there are seven of them (although only five are ...hrough regedit):

...CLASSES_ROOT (HKCR) contains details of types of files on the system (.txt, .doc ...n), and which applications are able to open files of each type. It also contains ...tion information for all COM components (this latter area is usually the largest single ...the Registry, since Windows these days comes with a huge number of COM ...nents).

..._CURRENT_USER (HKCU) contains details of user preferences for the user currently ...on to the machine.

..._LOCAL_MACHINE (HKLM) is a huge hive that contains details of all software and ...ware installed on the machine. It also includes the HKCR hive: HKCR is actually not ...' an independent hive in its own right, but is simply a convenient mapping onto the ...ry key HKLM/SOFTWARE/Classes.

...Y_USERS (HKUSR) contains details of user preferences for all users. As you might ...s, it also contains the HKCU hive, which is simply a mapping onto one of the keys in ...Y_USERS.

...Y_CURRENT_CONFIG (HKCF) contains details of hardware on the machine.

...ng two keys contain information that is of a temporary nature, and which changes

...EY_DYN_DATA is a general container for any volatile data that needs to be stored ...newhere in the Registry

...KEY_PERFORMANCE_DATA contains information concerning the performance of running ...plications

...e hives is a tree structure of registry **keys**. Each key is in many ways analogous to a folder or ...e file system. However, there is one very important difference. The file system distinguishes ...iles (which are there to contain data), and folders (which are primarily there to contain other ...lders), but in the registry there are only keys. A key may contain both data and other keys.

...contains data, then this will be present as a series of values (you could argue that it is these ...at are roughly equivalent to files on the file system). Each value will have a name, a data type ...lue. In addition, a key may have a default value, which is unnamed.

...see this structure by using regedit to examine registry keys. The screenshot shows the ...s of the key HKCU/Control Panel/Appearance, which contains the details of the chosen color ...of the currently logged in user. regedit shows which key is being examined by displaying it ...open folder icon in the tree view:

We won't go over the details of adding the event handlers for the open file dialog, because they are basically the same as with the BinaryFileReader example. As with that example, opening a new file causes the DisplayFile() method to be called. The only real differences between this example and the previous one are the implementation of DisplayFile, and also that we now have the option to save a file. This is represented by another menu option, save. The handler for this option calls another method we've added to the code, SaveFile(). (Note that new file always overwrites the original file – this example does not have an option to write to a different file.)

We'll look at SaveFile first, since that is the simplest function. We simply write each line of the textbox, in turn, to a StreamWriter stream, relying on the StreamReader.WriteLine() method to append the trailing carriage return and line feed at the end of each line:

```
void SaveFile()
{
    StreamWriter sw = new StreamWriter(ChosenFile, false,
                           Encoding.Unicode);
    foreach (string Line in textBoxContents.Lines)
        sw.WriteLine(Line);
    sw.Close();
}
```

ChosenFile is a string field of the main form, which contains the name of the file we have read in (just as for the previous example). Notice that we specify Unicode encoding when we open the stream. If we'd wanted to write files in some other format then we'd simply need to change the value of this parameter. The second parameter to this constructor would be set to true if we wanted to append to a file, but we don't in this case. The encoding must be set at construction time for a stream writer. It is subsequently available as a read-only property, Encoding.

Now we'll examine how files are read in. The process of reading in is complicated by the fact that we don't know until we've read in the file how many lines it is going to contain (in other words, how many (char)13(char)10 sequences are in the file). We solve this problem by initially reading the file into an instance of the StringCollection class, which is in the System.Collections.Specialized namespace. This class is designed to hold a set of strings that can be dynamically expanded. It implements two methods that we will be interested in: Add(), which adds a string to the collection, and CopyTo(), which copies the string collection into a normal array (a System.Array instance). Each element of the StringCollection object will hold one line of the file.

The DisplayFile() method calls another method, ReadFileIntoStringCollection(), which actually reads in the file. After doing this, we now know how many lines there are, so we are in a position to copy the StringCollection into a normal, fixed size array and feed this array into the textbox. Since when we make the copy it is only the references to the strings that get copied, not the strings themselves, the process is reasonably efficient:

```
void DisplayFile()
{
    StringCollection LinesCollection = ReadFileIntoStringCollection();
    string [] LinesArray = new string[LinesCollection.Count];
    LinesCollection.CopyTo(LinesArray, 0);
    this.textBoxContents.Lines = LinesArray;
}
```

The second parameter of StringCollection.CopyTo() indicates the index within the destination array of where we want the collection to start at.

Now we will examine the `ReadFileIntoStringCollection()` method. We use a `StreamReader` to read in each line. The main complication here is the need to count the characters read in to make sure we don't exceed the capacity of the textbox:

```
ArrayList ReadFileIntoStringCollection()
{
    const int MaxBytes = 65536;
    StreamReader sr = new StreamReader(ChosenFile);
    StringCollection Result = new StringCollection();
    int nBytesRead = 0;
    string NextLine;
    while ( (NextLine = sr.ReadLine()) != null)
    {
        nBytesRead += NextLine.Length;
        if (nBytesRead > MaxBytes)
            break;
        Result.Add(NextLine);
    }
    sr.Close();
    return Result;
}
```

That completes the code for the example.

If we run `ReadWriteText`, read in the `CivNegotiations` file, and then save it, the file will now be in Unicode format. We wouldn't be able to tell this from any of the usual windows applications: Notepad, Wordpad, and even our own `ReadWriteText` example, will still read the file in and display it correctly under Windows NT/2000/XP, although because Windows 9x doesn't support Unicode, applications like Notepad won't be able to understand the Unicode file on those platforms. (If you download the example from the Wrox Press web site, you can try this!) However, if we try to display the file again using our earlier `ReadBinaryFile` example, we can see the difference immediately, as shown in the following screenshot. The two initial bytes that indicate the file is in Unicode format are visible, and thereafter we see that every character is represented by two bytes. This last fact is very obvious, because the high-order byte of every character in this particular file is zero, so every second byte in this file now displays `x00`:

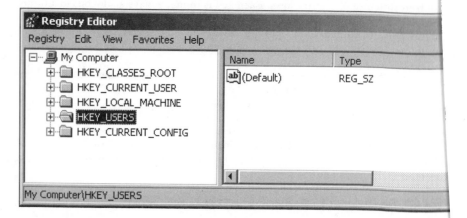

Reading and Writing to the Regi...

In all versions of Windows since Windows 95, the Registry has configuration information relating to Windows setup, user prefe... devices. Almost all commercial software these days uses the Reg... and COM components must place information about themselves clients. The .NET framework and its accompanying concept of ze... the significance of the Registry for applications in the sense that a... so no information about particular assemblies needs to be placed in assemblies.

The fact that applications can now be installed using the Windows In... some of the direct manipulation of the Registry that used to be involve... However, despite this, it is likely that if you distribute any complete ap... use the Registry to store information about its configuration. If you wan... the **Add/Remove Programs** dialog under the control panel, then this wil... entries being made.

As you'd expect from a library as comprehensive as the .NET library, it in... access to the Registry. There are two classes concerned with the Registry, a... `Microsoft.Win32` namespace. The classes are `Registry` and `RegistryK`... these classes, we will briefly review the structure of the Registry itself.

The Registry

The Registry has a hierarchical structure much like that of the file system. The... modify the contents of the Registry is with one of two utilities – `regedit` or re... `regedit` comes with all versions of Windows, since Windows 95 as standard. F... Windows NT and Windows 2000 – it is less user-friendly than `regedit`, but all... information that `regedit` is unable to view. For our discussion here, we'll use r... launch by typing in `regedit` at the **Run...** dialog or command prompt.

When you first launch `regedit` up you'll see something like this:

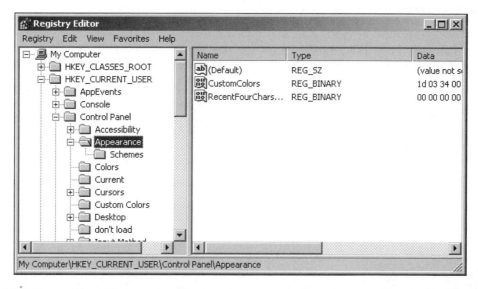

The HKCU/Control Panel/Appearance key has three named values set, although the default value does not contain any data. The column in the screenshot marked **Type** details the data type of each value. Registry entries may be formatted as one of three data types. The types are **REG_SZ** (which roughly corresponds to a .NET string instance – the matching is not exact because the registry data types are not .NET data types), **REG_DWORD** (corresponds roughly to uint), and **REG_BINARY** (array of byte).

An application that wishes to store data in the registry will do so by creating a number of registry keys, usually under the key HKLM/Software/<CompanyName>. Note that it is not necessary for these keys to contain any data. Sometimes the very fact of whether a key exists, provides enough information for an application.

The .NET Registry Classes

Access to the Registry is via two classes in the Microsoft.Win32 namespace, Registry and RegistryKey. A RegistryKey instance represents a registry key. This class implements methods to browse down into child keys, to create new keys or to read or modify the values in the key. In other words, to do everything you would normally wish to do with a registry key (except set security levels for the key). RegistryKey will be the class you use for almost all your work with the Registry. Registry, by contrast, is a class that you will never instantiate. Its role is simply to provide you with RegistryKey instances that represent the top-level keys – the different hives – in order to start you off navigating through the Registry. Registry provides these instances through static properties, and there are seven of them, called respectively ClassesRoot, CurrentConfig, CurrentUser, DynData, LocalMachine, PerformanceData, and Users. I bet you can't guess which of these properties corresponds to which hive!

So, for example, to obtain a RegistryKey instance that represents the HKLM key, you would write:

```
RegistryKey Hklm = Registry.LocalMachine;
```

The process of obtaining a reference to a RegistryKey object is known as opening the key.

Although you might expect that the methods exposed by `RegistryKey` would be similar to those implemented by `DirectoryInfo`, given that the Registry has a similar hierarchical structure to the file system, this actually isn't the case. Often, the way that you access the registry is different from the way that you would use files and folders, and `RegistryKey` implements methods that reflect this.

The most obvious difference is in how you open a registry key at a given location in the Registry. The `Registry` class does not have any public constructor that you can use, nor does it have any methods that let you go directly to a key, given its name. Instead, you are expected to browse down to that key from the top of the relevant hive. If you want to instantiate a `RegistryKey` object, the only way is to start off with the appropriate static property of `Registry`, and work down from there. So, for example, if you want to read some data in the `HKLM/Software/Microsoft` key, you'd get a reference to it like this:

```
RegistryKey Hklm = Registry.LocalMachine;
RegistryKey HkSoftware = Hklm.OpenSubKey("Software");
RegistryKey HkMicrosoft = HkSoftware.OpenSubKey("Microsoft");
```

A registry key accessed in this way will give you read-only access. If you want to be able to write to the key (that includes writing to its values or creating or deleting direct children of it), you need to use another override to `OpenSubKey`, which takes a second parameter, of type `bool`, that indicates whether you want read-write access to the key. So for example, if you want to be able to modify the `Microsoft` key (and assuming you are a systems administrator with permission to do this) you would write this:

```
RegistryKey Hklm = Registry.LocalMachine;
RegistryKey HkSoftware = Hklm.OpenSubKey("Software");
RegistryKey HkMicrosoft = HkSoftware.OpenSubKey("Microsoft", true);
```

Incidentally, since this key contains information used by Microsoft's applications, in most cases you probably shouldn't be modifying this particular key.

The `OpenSubKey()` method is the one you will call if you are expecting the key to already be present. If the key isn't there, it will return a `null` reference. If you wish to create a key, then you should use the `CreateSubKey()` method (which automatically gives you read-write access to the key through the reference returned):

```
RegistryKey Hklm = Registry.LocalMachine;
RegistryKey HkSoftware = Hklm.OpenSubKey("Software");
RegistryKey HkMine = HkSoftware.CreateSubKey("MyOwnSoftware");
```

The way that `CreateSubKey()` works is quite interesting. It will create the key if it doesn't already exist, but if it does already exist, then it will quietly return a `RegistryKey` instance that represents the existing key. The reason for the method behaving in this manner is to do with how you will normally use the registry. The registry, on the whole, contains long-term data such as configuration information for Windows and for various applications. It's not very common, therefore, that you find yourself in a situation where you need to explicitly create a key.

What is much more common is that your application needs to make sure that some data is present in the Registry – in other words create the relevant keys if they don't already exist, but do nothing if they do. `CreateSubKey()` fills that need perfectly. Unlike the situation with `FileInfo.Open()`, for example, there is no chance with `CreateSubKey()` of accidentally removing any data. If deleting registry keys is your intention, then you'll need to explicitly call the `RegistryKey.Delete()` method. This makes sense given the importance of the Registry to Windows. The last thing you want is to accidentally completely break Windows by deleting a couple of important keys, while you're debugging your C# registry calls!

Once you've located the registry key you want to read or modify, you can use the `SetValue()` or `GetValue()` methods to set or get at the data in it. Both of these methods take a string giving the name of the value as a parameter, and `SetValue()` requires an additionally object reference containing details of the value. Since the parameter is defined as an object reference, it can actually be a reference to any class you want. `SetValue()` will decide from the type of class actually supplied whether to set the value as a REG_SZ, REG_DWORD, or REG_BINARY value. For example:

```
RegistryKey HkMine = HkSoftware.CreateSubKey("MyOwnSoftware");
HkMine.SetValue("MyStringValue", "Hello World");
HkMine.SetValue("MyIntValue", 20);
```

This code will set the key to have two values: MyStringValue will be of type REG_SZ, while MyIntValue will be of type REG_DWORD. These are the only two types we will consider here, and use in the example that we present later.

`RegistryKey.GetValue()` works in much the same way. It is defined to return an object reference, which means it is free to actually return a string reference if it detects the value is of type REG_SZ, and an int if that value is of type REG_DWORD:

```
string StringValue = (string)HkMine.GetValue("MyStringValue");
int IntValue = (int)HkMine.GetValue("MyIntValue");
```

Finally, once you've finished reading or modifying the data, you should close the key:

```
HkMine.Close();
```

Besides these methods, `RegistryKey` implements a large number of other methods and properties. The tables give a selection of the most useful ones:

Properties

Property Name	Purpose
Name	Name of the key (read-only)
SubKeyCount	The number of children of this key
ValueCount	How many values the key contains

Methods

Name	Purpose
Close()	Closes the key
CreateSubKey()	Creates a subkey of a given name (or opens it if it already exists)
DeleteSubKey()	Deletes a given subkey
DeleteSubKeyTree()	Recursively deletes a subkey and all its children
DeleteValue()	Removes a named value from a key
GetSubKeyNames()	Returns an array of strings containing the names of the subkeys
GetValue()	Returns a named value
GetValueNames()	Returns an array of strings containing the names of all the values of the key
OpenSubKey()	Returns a reference to a RegistryKey instance that represents a given subkey
SetValue()	Sets a named value

Example: SelfPlacingWindow

We will illustrate the use of the registry classes with an application, which we will call the SelfPlacingWindow. This example is a simple C# Windows application, which actually has almost no features. The only thing you can do with it is click on a button, which brings up a standard Windows color dialog box (represented by the System.Windows.Forms.ColorDialog class), to let you choose a color, which will become the background color of the form.

The self-placing window scores over just about every other application that we developed in this book in one important and very user-friendly way. If you drag the window around the screen, change its size, or maximize or minimize it before you exit the application, it will remember the new position, as well as the background color, so that the next time it is launched it can automatically resume the way you chose last time. It remembers this information, because it writes it to the Registry whenever it shuts down. In this way, we get to demonstrate not only the .NET registry classes themselves, but also a very typical use for them, which you'll almost certainly want to replicate in any serious commercial Windows Forms application you write.

The location that SelfPlacingWindow stores its information in the Registry is a key, HKLM/Software/WroxPress/SelfPlacingWindow. HKLM is the usual place for application configuration information, but note that it is not user-specific. If you wanted to be more sophisticated in a real application, you'd probably want to replicate the information inside the HK_Users hive as well, so that each user can have their own profile.

The very first time that you run the example, it will look for this key and not find it, obviously! It, therefore is forced to use a default size, color, and position that we set in the developer environment. The example also features a listbox in which it displays any information read in from the Registry. On its first run it will look like this:

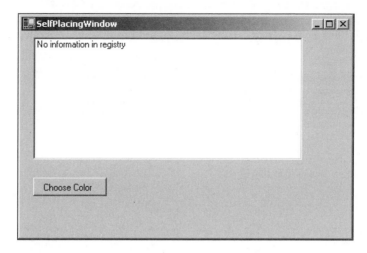

If we now modify the background color and move or resize the SelfPlacingWindow around on the screen a bit before exiting, it will, just before it exits, create the HKLM/Software/WroxPress/SelfPlacingWindow key and write its new configuration information into it. We can examine the information using regedit:

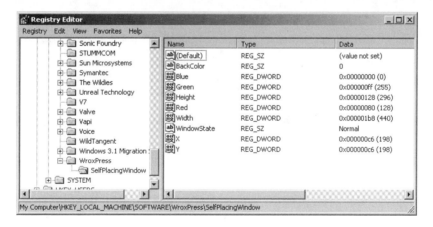

We can see from this screenshot that SelfPlacingWindow has placed a number of values in the registry key.

The values, Red, Green, and Blue give the color components that make up the selected background color. If you're not familiar with color components, don't worry, as we will explain these in the GDI+ chapter. For now, just take it that any color display on the system can be completely described by these three components, which are each represented by a number between 0 and 255 (or 0x00 and 0xff in hexadecimal). The values given here make up a bright green color. There are also four more REG_DWORD values, which represent the position and size of the window: X and Y are the coordinates of top left of the window on the desktop – that is to say the numbers of pixels across from the top left of the screen and the numbers of pixels down. Width and Height give the size of the window. WindowsState is the only value for which we have used a string data type (REG_SZ), and it can contain one of the strings normal, maximised, or minimised, depending on the final state of the window when we exited the application.

If we now launch SelfPlacingWindow again it will read this registry key, and automatically position itself accordingly (I know it's a black and white book, but I can promise you that background color really is bright green):

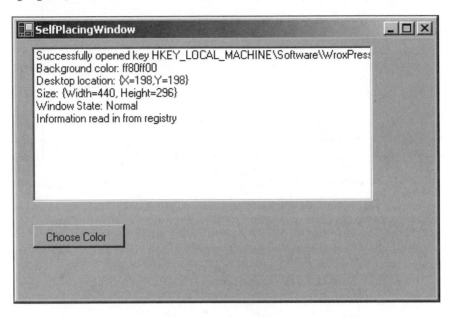

This time when we exit SelfPlacingWindow, it will overwrite the previous registry settings with whatever new values are relevant at the time that we exit it. To code up the example, we create the usual Windows Forms project in Visual Studio.NET, and add the listbox and button, using the developer environment's toolbox. We will change the names of these controls respectively to listBoxMessages and buttonChooseColor. We also need to ensure that we use the Microsoft.Win32 namespace:

```
using System;
using System.Drawing;
using System.Collections;
using System.ComponentModel;
using System.Windows.Forms;
using System.Data;
using Microsoft.Win32;
```

We need to add one field to the main Form1 class, which will represent the color dialog box:

```
public class Form1 : System.Windows.Forms.Form
{

    /// <summary>
    /// Required designer variable.
    /// </summary>
    private System.ComponentModel.Container components;
    private System.Windows.Forms.ListBox listBoxMessages;
    private System.Windows.Forms.Button buttonChooseColor;
    ColorDialog ChooseColorDialog = new ColorDialog();
```

We won't go over the details of adding the event handlers for the open file dialog, because they are basically the same as with the `BinaryFileReader` example. As with that example, opening a new file causes the `DisplayFile()` method to be called. The only real differences between this example and the previous one are the implementation of `DisplayFile`, and also that we now have the option to save a file. This is represented by another menu option, save. The handler for this option calls another method we've added to the code, `SaveFile()`. (Note that new file always overwrites the original file – this example does not have an option to write to a different file.)

We'll look at `SaveFile` first, since that is the simplest function. We simply write each line of the textbox, in turn, to a `StreamWriter` stream, relying on the `StreamReader.WriteLine()` method to append the trailing carriage return and line feed at the end of each line:

```
void SaveFile()
{
    StreamWriter sw = new StreamWriter(ChosenFile, false,
                        Encoding.Unicode);
    foreach (string Line in textBoxContents.Lines)
        sw.WriteLine(Line);
    sw.Close();
}
```

`ChosenFile` is a string field of the main form, which contains the name of the file we have read in (just as for the previous example). Notice that we specify Unicode encoding when we open the stream. If we'd wanted to write files in some other format then we'd simply need to change the value of this parameter. The second parameter to this constructor would be set to `true` if we wanted to append to a file, but we don't in this case. The encoding must be set at construction time for a stream writer. It is subsequently available as a read-only property, `Encoding`.

Now we'll examine how files are read in. The process of reading in is complicated by the fact that we don't know until we've read in the file how many lines it is going to contain (in other words, how many `(char)13(char)10` sequences are in the file). We solve this problem by initially reading the file into an instance of the `StringCollection` class, which is in the `System.Collections.Specialized` namespace. This class is designed to hold a set of strings that can be dynamically expanded. It implements two methods that we will be interested in: `Add()`, which adds a string to the collection, and `CopyTo()`, which copies the string collection into a normal array (a `System.Array` instance). Each element of the `StringCollection` object will hold one line of the file.

The `DisplayFile()` method calls another method, `ReadFileIntoStringCollection()`, which actually reads in the file. After doing this, we now know how many lines there are, so we are in a position to copy the `StringCollection` into a normal, fixed size array and feed this array into the textbox. Since when we make the copy it is only the references to the strings that get copied, not the strings themselves, the process is reasonably efficient:

```
void DisplayFile()
{
    StringCollection LinesCollection = ReadFileIntoStringCollection();
    string [] LinesArray = new string[LinesCollection.Count];
    LinesCollection.CopyTo(LinesArray, 0);
    this.textBoxContents.Lines = LinesArray;
}
```

The second parameter of `StringCollection.CopyTo()` indicates the index within the destination array of where we want the collection to start at.

Now we will examine the `ReadFileIntoStringCollection()` method. We use a `StreamReader` to read in each line. The main complication here is the need to count the characters read in to make sure we don't exceed the capacity of the textbox:

```
ArrayList ReadFileIntoStringCollection()
{
    const int MaxBytes = 65536;
    StreamReader sr = new StreamReader(ChosenFile);
    StringCollection Result = new StringCollection();
    int nBytesRead = 0;
    string NextLine;
    while ( (NextLine = sr.ReadLine()) != null)
    {
        nBytesRead += NextLine.Length;
        if (nBytesRead > MaxBytes)
            break;
        Result.Add(NextLine);
    }
    sr.Close();
    return Result;
}
```

That completes the code for the example.

If we run `ReadWriteText`, read in the `CivNegotiations` file, and then save it, the file will now be in Unicode format. We wouldn't be able to tell this from any of the usual windows applications: Notepad, Wordpad, and even our own `ReadWriteText` example, will still read the file in and display it correctly under Windows NT/2000/XP, although because Windows 9x doesn't support Unicode, applications like Notepad won't be able to understand the Unicode file on those platforms. (If you download the example from the Wrox Press web site, you can try this!) However, if we try to display the file again using our earlier `ReadBinaryFile` example, we can see the difference immediately, as shown in the following screenshot. The two initial bytes that indicate the file is in Unicode format are visible, and thereafter we see that every character is represented by two bytes. This last fact is very obvious, because the high-order byte of every character in this particular file is zero, so every second byte in this file now displays x00:

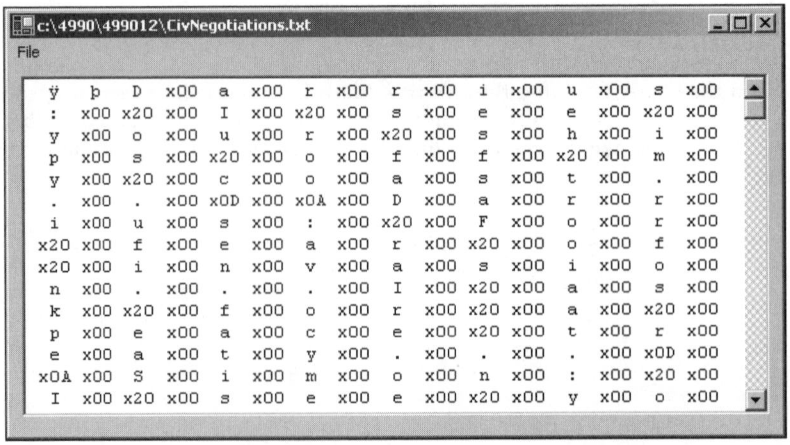

Reading and Writing to the Registry

In all versions of Windows since Windows 95, the Registry has been the central repository for all configuration information relating to Windows setup, user preferences, and installed software and devices. Almost all commercial software these days uses the Registry to store information about itself, and COM components must place information about themselves in the Registry in order to be called by clients. The .NET framework and its accompanying concept of zero-impact-installs has slightly reduced the significance of the Registry for applications in the sense that assemblies are entirely self-contained, so no information about particular assemblies needs to be placed in the Registry – even for shared assemblies.

The fact that applications can now be installed using the Windows Installer also frees developers from some of the direct manipulation of the Registry that used to be involved in installing applications. However, despite this, it is likely that if you distribute any complete application, your application will use the Registry to store information about its configuration. If you want your application to show up in the **Add/Remove Programs** dialog under the control panel, then this will involve appropriate registry entries being made.

As you'd expect from a library as comprehensive as the .NET library, it includes classes that give you access to the Registry. There are two classes concerned with the Registry, and both are in the `Microsoft.Win32` namespace. The classes are `Registry` and `RegistryKey`. Before we examine these classes, we will briefly review the structure of the Registry itself.

The Registry

The Registry has a hierarchical structure much like that of the file system. The usual way to view or modify the contents of the Registry is with one of two utilities – `regedit` or `regedt32`. Of these, `regedit` comes with all versions of Windows, since Windows 95 as standard. `Regedt32` comes with Windows NT and Windows 2000 – it is less user-friendly than `regedit`, but allows access to security information that `regedit` is unable to view. For our discussion here, we'll use `regedit`, which you can launch by typing in `regedit` at the **Run...** dialog or command prompt.

When you first launch `regedit` up you'll see something like this:

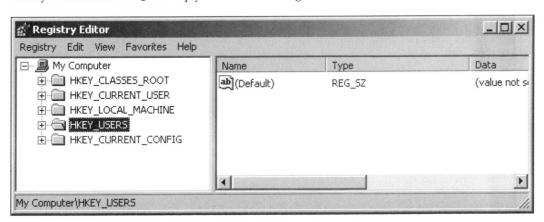

`Regedit` has a similar treeview/listview style user interface to Windows explorer, which matches the hierarchical structure of the Registry itself. As we'll soon see, however, there are some differences.

In a file system, the topmost level nodes can be thought of as being the partitions on your disks, `C:\`, `D:\`, and so on. In the registry, the equivalent to a partition is the **registry hive**. It is not possible to change which hives are there – they are fixed, and there are seven of them (although only five are actually visible through `regedit`):

❑ HKEY_CLASSES_ROOT (HKCR) contains details of types of files on the system (`.txt`, `.doc` and so on), and which applications are able to open files of each type. It also contains registration information for all COM components (this latter area is usually the largest single area of the Registry, since Windows these days comes with a huge number of COM components).

❑ HKEY_CURRENT_USER (HKCU) contains details of user preferences for the user currently logged on to the machine.

❑ HKEY_LOCAL_MACHINE (HKLM) is a huge hive that contains details of all software and hardware installed on the machine. It also includes the HKCR hive: HKCR is actually not really an independent hive in its own right, but is simply a convenient mapping onto the registry key HKLM/SOFTWARE/Classes.

❑ HKEY_USERS (HKUSR) contains details of user preferences for all users. As you might guess, it also contains the HKCU hive, which is simply a mapping onto one of the keys in HKEY_USERS.

❑ HKEY_CURRENT_CONFIG (HKCF) contains details of hardware on the machine.

The remaining two keys contain information that is of a temporary nature, and which changes frequently:

❑ HKEY_DYN_DATA is a general container for any volatile data that needs to be stored somewhere in the Registry

❑ HKEY_PERFORMANCE_DATA contains information concerning the performance of running applications

Within the hives is a tree structure of registry **keys**. Each key is in many ways analogous to a folder or file on the file system. However, there is one very important difference. The file system distinguishes between files (which are there to contain data), and folders (which are primarily there to contain other files or folders), but in the registry there are only keys. A key may contain both data and other keys.

If a key contains data, then this will be present as a series of values (you could argue that it is these values that are roughly equivalent to files on the file system). Each value will have a name, a data type and a value. In addition, a key may have a default value, which is unnamed.

We can see this structure by using `regedit` to examine registry keys. The screenshot shows the contents of the key HKCU/Control Panel/Appearance, which contains the details of the chosen color scheme of the currently logged in user. `regedit` shows which key is being examined by displaying it with an open folder icon in the tree view:

Quite a lot of action takes place in the `Form1` constructor:

```
public Form1()
{
    InitializeComponent();
    buttonChooseColor.Click += new EventHandler(OnClickChooseColor);
    try
    {
        if (ReadSettings() == false)
            listBoxMessages.Items.Add("No information in registry");
        else
            listBoxMessages.Items.Add("Information read in from
                                        registry");
        StartPosition = FormStartPosition.Manual;
    }
    catch (Exception e)
    {
        listBoxMessages.Items.Add("A problem occurred reading in data
                                    from registry:");
        listBoxMessages.Items.Add(e.Message);
    }
}
```

In this constructor, we start off by setting up the event handler for when the user clicks on the button. The handler is a method called `OnClickChooseColor`, which we will cover soon. Reading in the configuration information is done using another method that we will write, `ReadSettings()`. `ReadSettings()` returns `true` if it finds the information in the registry, and `false` if it doesn't, (which will presumably be because this is the first time we have run the application). We place this part of the constructor in a try block, just in case any exceptions are generated while reading in the registry values (this might happen if some user has come in and played around with the registry using `regedit`).

The `StartPosition = FormStartPosition.Manual;` statement tells the form to take its initial starting position from the `DeskTopLocation` property instead of using the Windows default location (the default behavior). Possible values are taken from the `FormStartPosition` enumeration.

`SelfPlacingWindow` is also the one of the few applications in this book in which we have a serious use for adding code to the `Dispose()` method. Remember that `Dispose()` is called whenever the application terminates normally, so this is the ideal place from which to save the configuration information to the Registry. This is done using another method that we will write, `SaveSettings()`:

```
/// <summary>
/// Clean up any resources being used.
/// </summary>

public override void Dispose()
{
    SaveSettings();
    base.Dispose();
    if(components != null)
        components.Dispose();
}
```

The `SaveSettings()` and `ReadSettings()` methods are the ones that contain the registry code we are interested in, but before we examine them we have one more piece of housekeeping: to handle the event of the user clicking that button. This involves displaying the color dialog and setting the background color to whatever color the user chose:

```
void OnClickChooseColor(object Sender, EventArgs e)
{
    if(ChooseColorDialog.ShowDialog() == DialogResult.OK)
        BackColor = ChooseColorDialog.Color;
}
```

Now let's have look at how we save the settings:

```
void SaveSettings()
{
    RegistryKey SoftwareKey =
                Registry.LocalMachine.OpenSubKey("Software", true);
    RegistryKey WroxKey = SoftwareKey.CreateSubKey("WroxPress");
    RegistryKey SelfPlacingWindowKey =
                WroxKey.CreateSubKey("SelfPlacingWindow");
    SelfPlacingWindowKey.SetValue("BackColor",
                (object)BackColor.ToKnownColor());
    SelfPlacingWindowKey.SetValue("Red", (object)(int)BackColor.R);
    SelfPlacingWindowKey.SetValue("Green", (object)(int)BackColor.G);
    SelfPlacingWindowKey.SetValue("Blue", (object)(int)BackColor.B);
    SelfPlacingWindowKey.SetValue("Width", (object)Width);
    SelfPlacingWindowKey.SetValue("Height", (object)Height);
    SelfPlacingWindowKey.SetValue("X", (object)DesktopLocation.X);
    SelfPlacingWindowKey.SetValue("Y", (object)DesktopLocation.Y);
    SelfPlacingWindowKey.SetValue("WindowState",
                (object)WindowState.ToString());
}
```

There's quite a lot going on here. We start off by navigating through the Registry to get to the `HKLM/Software/WroxPress/SelfPlacingWindow` registry key using the technique we demonstrated earlier, starting with the `Registry.LocalMachine` static property that represents the HKLM hive:

```
RegistryKey SoftwareKey =
            Registry.LocalMachine.OpenSubKey("Software", true);
RegistryKey WroxKey = SoftwareKey.CreateSubKey("WroxPress");
RegistryKey SelfPlacingWindowKey =
                    WroxKey.CreateSubKey("SelfPlacingWindow");
```

We use the `RegistryKey.OpenSubKey()` method, rather than `RegistryKey.CreateSubKey()` to get to the `HKLM/Software` key. That's because we can be very confident this key already exists – if it doesn't then there's something very seriously wrong with our computer, as this key contains settings for a lot of system software! We also indicate that we need write access to this key. That's because if the `WroxPress` key doesn't already exist we will need to create it – which involves writing to the parent key.

The next key to navigate to is `HKLM/Software/WroxPress` – and here we are not certain whether the key already exists, so we use `CreateSubKey()` to automatically create it if it doesn't. Note that `CreateSubKey()` automatically gives us write access to the key in question. Once we have reached `HKLM/Software/WroxPress/SelfPlacingWindow`, it is simply a matter of calling the `RegistryKey.SetValue()` method a number of times to either create or set the appropriate values. There are, however, a couple of complications.

Firstly, you might notice that we are using a couple of classes that we've not encountered before. The `DeskTopPosition` property of the `Form` class indicates the position of the top left corner of the screen, and is of type `Point`. We'll cover the `Point` struct in the GDI+ chapter. What we need to know here is that it contains two `ints`, `X` and `Y`, which represent the horizontal and vertical position on the screen. We also look up three member properties of the `Color` class: `R`, `G`, and `B`: `Color` you'll guess represents a color, and these properties on it give the red, green, and blue components that make up the color and are all of type `byte`. We also use the `Form.WindowState` property – this contains an enumeration that gives the current state of the window – minimized, maximized, or restored.

The other complication here is that we need to be a little careful about our casts: `SetValue()` takes two parameters – a `string` that gives the name of the key, and a `System.Object` instance, which contains the value. `SetValue` has a choice of format for storing the value – it can store it as `REG_SZ`, `REG_BINARY` or `REG_DWORD` – and it is actually pretty intelligent about making a sensible choice depending on the data type that has been given. Hence for the `WindowState`, we pass it a `string`, and `SetValue()` sensibly determines that this should be translated to `REG_SZ`. Similarly, for the various positions and dimensions we supply `ints`, which will be converted into `REG_DWORD`. However, the color components are more complicated as we want these to be stored as `REG_DWORD` too because they are numeric types. However, if `SetValue()` sees that the data is of type `byte`, it will store it as a string – as `REG_SZ` in the registry. In order to prevent this, we cast the color components to `ints`.

We've also explicitly cast all the values to the type `object`. We don't really need to do this as the cast from any other data type to object is implicit, but we are doing so in order to make it clear what's going on and remind ourselves that `SetsValue` is defined to take just an object reference as its second parameter.

The `ReadSettings()` method is a little longer because for each value read in, we also need to interpret it, display the value in the listbox, and make the appropriate adjustments to the relevant property of the main form. `ReadSettings()` looks like this:

```
bool ReadSettings()
{
   RegistryKey SoftwareKey =
               Registry.LocalMachine.OpenSubKey("Software");
   RegistryKey WroxKey = SoftwareKey.OpenSubKey("WroxPress");
   if (WroxKey == null)
      return false;
   RegistryKey SelfPlacingWindowKey =
               WroxKey.OpenSubKey("SelfPlacingWindow");
   if (SelfPlacingWindowKey == null)
      return false;
   else
      listBoxMessages.Items.Add("Successfully opened key " +
               SelfPlacingWindowKey.ToString());
   int RedComponent = (int)SelfPlacingWindowKey.GetValue("Red");
   int GreenComponent = (int)SelfPlacingWindowKey.GetValue("Green");
   int BlueComponent = (int)SelfPlacingWindowKey.GetValue("Blue");
   BackColor = Color.FromArgb(RedComponent, GreenComponent,
               BlueComponent);
   listBoxMessages.Items.Add("Background color: " + BackColor.Name);
   int X = (int)SelfPlacingWindowKey.GetValue("X");
   int Y = (int)SelfPlacingWindowKey.GetValue("Y");
   DesktopLocation = new Point(X, Y);
   listBoxMessages.Items.Add("Desktop location: " +
               DesktopLocation.ToString());
```

```
        Height = (int)SelfPlacingWindowKey.GetValue("Height");
        Width = (int)SelfPlacingWindowKey.GetValue("Width");
        listBoxMessages.Items.Add("Size: " + new
                    Size(Width,Height).ToString());
        string InitialWindowState =
                    (string)SelfPlacingWindowKey.GetValue("WindowState");
        listBoxMessages.Items.Add("Window State: " + InitialWindowState);
        WindowState = (FormWindowState)FormWindowState.Parse
                    (WindowState.GetType(), InitialWindowState);
        return true;
    }
```

In `ReadSettings()` we first have to navigate to the
`HKLM/Software/WroxPress/SelfPlacingWindow` registry key. In this case, however, we are
hoping to find the key there so that we can read it. If it's not there, then it's probably the first time we
have run the example. In this case, we just want to abort reading the keys, and we certainly don't want
to create any keys. Now we use the `RegistryKey.OpenSubkey()` method all the way down. If at any
stage `OpenSubkey()` returns a `null` reference then we know that the registry key isn't there and we
can simply return the value `false` back to the calling code.

When it comes to actually reading the keys, we use the `RegistryKey.GetValue()` method, which is
defined as returning an object reference – which means this method can actually return an instance of
literally any class it chooses. Like `SetValue()`, it will return a class of object appropriate to the type of
data it found in the key – so we can usually assume that the `REG_SZ` keys will give us a string and the
other keys will give us an `int`. We also cast the return reference from `SetValue()` accordingly. If
there is an exception, say someone has fiddled with the Registry and mangled the value types, then our
cast will cause an exception to be thrown – which will be caught by the handler in the `Form1`
constructor.

The rest of this code uses one more data type that you might not be familiar with – again because we
don't cover it until the GDI+ chapter – the `Size` struct. This is similar to a `Point` struct, but is
used to represent sizes rather than coordinates. It has two member properties, `Width` and `Height`, and
we use the `Size` struct here simply as a convenient way of packaging up the size of the form for
displaying in the listbox.

Summary

In this chapter, we have examined how to use the .NET base classes to access the Registry and the file
system from your C# code. We've seen that in both cases, the base classes expose simple, but powerful,
object models that make it very simple to perform almost any kind of action in these areas. In the case
of the Registry, these are creating, modifying, or reading keys, and in the case of the file system,
copying files, moving, creating and deleting files and folders, and reading and writing both binary and
text files.

In this chapter we have assumed that you are running your code from an account that has sufficient
access rights to do whatever the code needs to do. Obviously, the question of security is an important
one where file access is concerned, and we will examine that area in Chapter 25.

15

Working with the Active Directory

As part of Windows 2000 Server we get the **Active Directory**. The Active Directory is a **directory service** where user information, printers, services, and custom data can be stored. Microsoft's Exchange Server 2000 uses the Active Directory intensively to store public folders and other items. We can also store data we define in the Active Directory. In a file system the directory stores files; a telephone directory stores phone numbers and names. A directory service makes the information in the directory available. With Windows Explorer we can find files, for example.

Before the Active Directory Services, the Exchange Server could use the Active Directory to store its objects. It was necessary for a system administrator to configure two user IDs for a single person: a user account in the Windows NT domain so that a logon was possible, and a user in the Exchange Directory. This was necessary because additional information for users was needed (such as e-mail addresses, phone numbers, and so on), and the user information for the NT domain was not extensible to let us put the required information in there. Now the system administrator only needs to configure a single user for a person in the Active Directory; the information for a user object can be extended so that it fits the requirements of the Exchange Server. We can also extend this information.

Consider a project manager in a big company who is searching, using the Active Directory, for a developer who has skills developing C# applications. How great would it be if they could do a simple query to get a list of all developers fulfilling the requirements? That's possible with the Active Directory; we can extend the user object with a list of skills.

Consider another example where the Active Directory can play a useful role: a user who has configured a default printer (a black and white laser printer) that they normally use, but now needs a color printout. They know that there's a color printer two rooms away on the same floor that fits the requirements, but what's the name of the printer? In the print dialog a printer can be selected from a list of hundred funny names like Pikachu, Poliwag, Cloyster, Jynx, or Staryu that a system administrator once selected. How to choose the correct printer? Let's create a solution where the user can enter the requirements like the location, double-sided, and color to find a printer. This additional printer information can be stored in the Active Directory, too.

With the .NET Framework we can easily access and manipulate the data in a directory service using classes from the `System.DirectoryServices` namespace.

> *To use the examples in this chapter you need a Windows 2000 Server with the Active Directory installed and configured. The classes of the `System.DirectoryServices` namespace can also be used for Novell Directory Services and Windows NT 4. With small adaptations to the programs you can use these classes there, too.*

In this chapter we will look at:

- ❑ The Architecture of the Active Directory
- ❑ How to read and modify data in the Active Directory
- ❑ Searching for objects in the Active Directory

Architecture of the Active Directory

Before we start programming we have to know how the Active Directory works, what it is used for, and what data we can store there.

Features

The features of the Active Directory can be grouped into this list:

- ❑ The data in the Active Directory is grouped **hierarchically**. Objects can be stored inside other container objects. Instead of having a single, large list of users, the users can be grouped inside organizational units. An organizational unit can embed other organizational units, and we can build a tree that way.

- ❑ The Active Directory uses a **multi-master replication**. Contrary to Windows NT 4 domains, where the primary domain controller was the master, with the Active Directory all servers are masters. If the primary domain controller in a Windows NT 4 domain is down, no user can change the password; the system administrator can only update users when the primary domain controller is up and running. With the Active Directory, updates can be applied to every server. This model is much more scalable, as updates can happen to different servers concurrently. The disadvantage of this model is that replication is more complex. We will talk about the replication issues later in this chapter.

- ❑ The **replication topology** is flexible, to support replications across slow links in WANs. How often data should be replicated is configurable by the domain administrators.

- ❑ The Active Directory supports **open standards**. LDAP, the Lightweight Directory Access Protocol, is one of the standards that can be used to access the data in the Active Directory. LDAP is an Internet standard that can be used to access a lot of different directory services. With LDAP a programming interface, LDAP API, is also defined. The LDAP API can be used to access the Active Directory with the C language. Microsoft's preferred programming interface to directory services is ADSI, the Active Directory Service Interface. This, of course, is not an open standard. In contrast to the LDAP API, ADSI makes it possible to access all features of the Active Directory. Another standard that's used within the Active Directory is **Kerberos**. Kerberos is used for authentication. The Windows 2000 Kerberos service can also

❑ be used to authenticate Unix clients. It doesn't work the other way around; Unix Kerberos servers can't authenticate Windows 2000 clients because Microsoft extended the Kerberos protocol for its own use.

❑ With the Active Directory we have a **fine-grained security**. Every object stored in the Active Directory can have an associated access control list that defines who can do what with the object.

The objects in the directory are **strongly typed**, which means that the type of the objects is exactly defined; no attributes may be added to an object that are not specified. In the **Schema**, the object types as well as the parts of an object (attributes) are defined. Attributes can be mandatory or optional.

Active Directory Concepts

Before programming the Active Directory we have to know about some concepts. There are many new terms we have to be aware of when talking about the Active Directory.

Objects

We store objects in the Active Directory. An object refers to something concrete such as a user, a printer, or a network share. Objects have mandatory and optional attributes that describe the object. Some examples of the attributes of a user object are the first name, last name, e-mail address, phone number, and so on.

The following figure shows some objects: a container object, Wrox Press, some user objects, a contact, a printer, and a user group object:

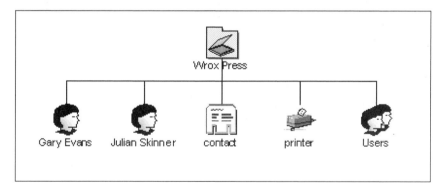

Schema

Every object is an instance of a class that is defined in the **schema**. The schema **defines the types**, and is itself stored within objects in the Active Directory. We have to differentiate between classSchema and attributeSchema. The type of objects are defined in the classSchema, as well as detailing what mandatory and optional attributes an object has. The attributeSchema defines what an attribute looks like, and what the allowed syntax for a specific attribute is.

We can define custom types and attributes, and add these to the schema. Be aware however, that a new schema type can never be removed from the Active Directory. It's possible to mark it as inactive so that new objects cannot be created any more, but there can be existing objects of that type, so it's not possible to remove classes or attributes that are defined in the schema. The Windows 2000 Administrator doesn't have enough rights to create new schema entries; the Windows 2000 Domain Enterprise Administrator is needed here.

Configuration

Not only objects are stored in the Active Directory. We can also find the class-definitions (in the schema) and the configuration. The configuration of the Active Directory stores the information about all sites, the replication intervals, etc. that is set up by the system administrator. The configuration itself is stored in the Active Directory, so we can access the configuration information like all other objects in the Active Directory.

Active Directory Domain

A domain is a security boundary of a Windows network. In the Active Directory domain, the objects are stored in a hierarchical order. The Active Directory itself is made up of one or more domains. The hierarchical order of objects within a domain is presented in the figure below, in which we see a domain represented by a triangle. Container objects such as Users, Computers, and Books can store other objects. Each oval in the picture represents an object; with the lines between the objects we can see a parent-child relationship. Books is the parent of .NET; and Java. Pro C#, Beg C#, and ASP.NET are child objects of the .NET object.

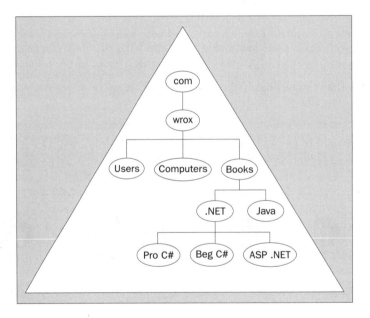

Domain Controller

A single domain can have multiple servers, each of which stores all of the objects within the domain. There is no master server, and all servers are treated equally; we have a multi-master model. The objects are replicated across the servers inside the domain.

In the next picture the domain, wrox.com is represented by the triangle. DC1 and DC2 are two domain controllers of this domain:

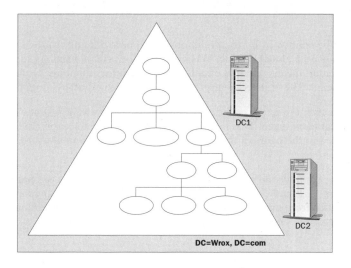

Site

A **site** is a location in the network holding Active Directory servers (domain controllers). If we have multiple locations in the enterprise, which are connected with slow network links, we can use multiple sites for a single domain. For backup or scalability reasons, each site has one or more domain controllers running. Replication between servers in a site can happen at shorter intervals dueto the faster network connection. Replication is configured to occur at larger time intervals between servers across sites, depending on the speed of the network. Of course, the domain administrator can configure this.

In the following picture we can see a single domain, wrox.com, which has multiple sites: Seattle, New York and Chicago. In each of these sites two domain controllers are running:

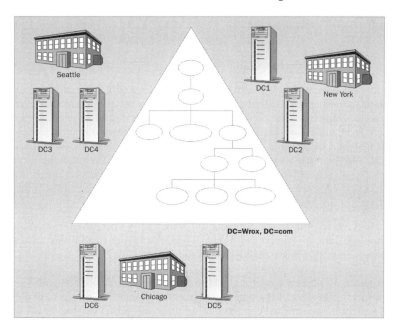

Domain Tree

Multiple domains can be connected by trust relationships. These domains share a **common schema**, a **common configuration**, and a **global catalog**. We will talk about global catalogs soon. A common schema and common configuration means that this data is replicated across domains. Domain trees share the same class and attribute schema. The objects themselves are not replicated across domains.

Domains connected in such a way are called a Domain Tree. Domains in a Domain Tree have a **contiguous, hierarchical namespace**. This means that the domain name of the child domain is the name of that child domain added to the name of the parent domain. Between domains, trusts that use the Kerberos protocol are established.

In the following picture we have the root domain `wrox.com`, which is also the **parent domain** of the **child domains** `france.wrox.com` and `uk.wrox.com`. A trust is set up between the parent and the child domains, so that accounts from one domain can be authenticated by another domain:

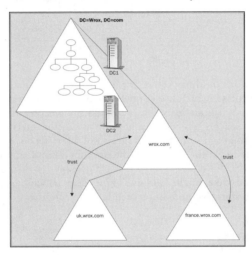

Forest

Multiple domain trees connected using a common schema, a common configuration, and a global catalog without a contiguous namespace are called a forest. A forest is a set of domain trees. A forest can be used if the company has a sub-company where a different domain name should be used. Let's say, `asptoday.com` should be relatively independent of the domain `wrox.com`, but it should be possible to have a common management, and it should be possible for users from `asptoday.com` to access resources from the `wrox.com` domain, and the other way around. With a forest we can have trusts between multiple domain trees.

Global Catalog

A search for an object can span multiple domains. If we look for a specific user object with some attributes we have to search every domain. Starting with `wrox.com`, the search continues to `uk.wrox.com` and `france.wrox.com`; across slow links such a search can take a while.

To make searches faster, all objects are copied to the global catalog. The global catalog is replicated in every domain of a forest. There's at least one server in every domain holding a global catalog. For performance and scalability reasons we can have more than one global catalog server in a domain. Using a global catalog, a search through all the objects can happen on a single server.

In the following picture we see three domains in a domain tree. Each of these domains has a global catalog (GC). By default, the global catalog is installed on the first domain controller of a domain, but more catalogs can be added:

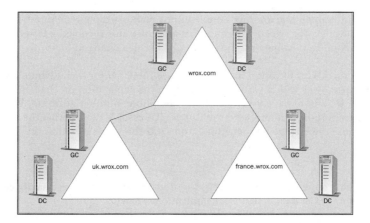

The global catalog is a **read-only cache** of all the objects. The catalog can only be used for searches; the domain controllers must be used to do updates.

Not all attributes of an object are stored in the global catalog. You can define whether or not an attribute should be stored with an object. The decision whether to store an attribute in the global catalog depends on the frequency of its use in searches. A picture of a user isn't useful in the global catalog, because you would never search for a picture. Instead, the phone number would be a useful addition to the store. You can also define that an attribute should be indexed so that a query for it is faster.

Replication

As programmers we will not configure replication, but because it's an important aspect about the data we store in the Active Directory we have to know how it works. The Active Directory uses a **multi-master** server architecture. Updates can and will happen to every domain controller in the domain. The **replication latency** defines how long it takes until an update happens.

❑ The configurable **change notification** happens, by default, every 5 minutes inside a site if some attributes change. The server where a change occurred informs one server after the other with 30-second intervals, so the fourth server can get the change notification after 7 minutes. The default change notification across sites is set to 180 minutes. Intra- and Inter-site replication can each be configured to other values.

❑ If no changes occurred, the **scheduled replication** occurs every 60 minutes inside a site. This is to ensure that a change notification wasn't missed.

❑ For security-sensitive information such as account lockout **immediate notification** can occur.

With a replication, only the changes are copied to the domain controllers. With every change of an attribute a version number (USN, update sequence number) and a time stamp are recorded. These are used to resolve conflicts if updates happened to the same attribute on different servers.

Let's look at one example. The mobile phone attribute of the user John Doe has the USN number 47. This value is already replicated to all domain controllers. One system administrator changes the phone number. The change occurs on the server DC1; the new USN of this attribute on the server DC1 is now 48, whereas the other domain controllers still have the USN 47. If someone is still reading the attribute the old value can be read until the replication to all domain controllers has occurred.

Now the rare case can happen that another administrator changes the phone number attribute, and here a different domain controller was selected because this administrator received a faster response from the server DC2. The USN of this attribute on the server DC2 is also changed to 48.

At the notification intervals, notification happens because the USN for the attribute changed, and the last time replication occurred was with a USN value 47. With the replication mechanism it is now detected that the servers DC1 and DC2 both have a USN of 48 for the phone number attribute. What server is the winner is not really important, but one server must win. To resolve this conflict the time stamp of the change is used. Because the change happened later on DC2 the value stored in the DC2 domain controller gets replicated.

> **When reading objects, we have to be aware that the data is not necessarily current. The currency of the data depends on replication latencies.**

> **When updating objects, another user can still read some old values after the update. It's also possible that different updates can happen at the same time.**

Characteristics of Active Directory Data

The Active Directory doesn't replace a relational database or the Registry. What data can we store there?

- ❑ We have **hierarchical data** within the Active Directory. We can have containers that store further containers, and also objects. Containers themselves are objects, too.

- ❑ The data should be used for **read-mostly**. Because we have replication that happens at some configured time-intervals, we cannot be sure that we will read up-to-date data. In applications we must be aware that the information we read is possibly not the current up-to-date information.

- ❑ Data is **globally of interest** for the enterprise. Adding a new data type to the schema replicates it to the servers in the enterprise. If the data types were only interesting for a small number of users, the Domain Enterprise Administrator wouldn't install new schema types.

- ❑ The data should be of **reasonable size** because of replication. The term reasonable size is used because of replication issues. If the data size is 100K, it is OK to store it in the directory if the data changes only once per week. Data of this size is too large, however, if it changes once per hour. Always think about replication: where the data gets transferred to, and at what intervals. If you have larger data it's possible to put a link into the Active Directory, and store the data itself in a different place.

To summarize, the data we store in the Active Directory should be hierarchically organized, of reasonable size, and important for the enterprise.

Schema

Active Directory objects are strongly typed. The schema defines the types of the objects, mandatory and optional attributes, and the syntaxes and constraints of attributes. The schema itself is stored as objects in the Active Directory data store. In the schema we can differentiate class-schema and attribute-schema objects. A class is a collection of attributes. With the classes, single inheritance is supported. As can be seen in the following class diagram, the user class derives from the organizationalPerson class, organizationalPerson is a subclass of person, and the base class is top. The classSchema that defines a class describes the attributes with the systemMayContain attribute.

In the following diagram only a few of all the systemMayContain values are listed. You can easily see all the values with ADSIEdit. In the root class top we can see that every object can have common name (cn), displayName, objectGUID, whenChanged, and whenCreated attributes. The person class derives from top. A person object also has a password and a telephoneNumber. organizationalPerson derives from person. In addition to the attributes of person it has a manager, department, and company; and a user has extra attributes needed to log on to a system:

Administration of the Active Directory

We will not really talk about the administration of the Active Directory. Administration is the responsibility of the Windows 2000 system administrators, and we want to talk about programming the Active Directory. However, looking into some of the administration tools can help to give us an idea of the Active Directory, what data is in there, and what can be done programmatically.

The system administrator has a lot of tools to enter new data, update data, and configure the Active Directory. With the **Active Directory Users and Computers** tool we can update user data, and enter new users. The **Active Directory Sites and Services** tool is used to configure sites in a domain and replication between these sites. **Active Directory Domains and Trusts** can be used to build up a trust relationship between domains in a tree. The registry editor for the Active Directory, where every object can be viewed and edited, is **ADSI Edit**. In addition to the tools for the system administrator we get a tool with the Microsoft Platform SDK: **ADSI Viewer**.

Active Directory Users and Computers

The Active Directory Users and Computers tool is the tool that's mainly used by System Administrators to manage users. Select Start | Programs | Administrative Tools | Active Directory Users and Computers:

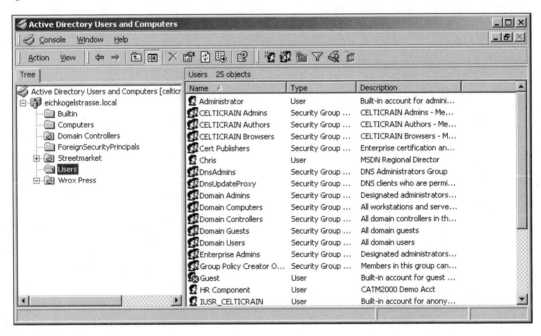

With this tool we can add new users, groups, contacts, organizational units, printers, shared folders, or computers, and modify existing ones. In the next screenshot you can see the attributes that can be entered for a user object: office, phone numbers, e-mails, web pages, organization information, addresses, groups, and so on. Much more information than was ever possible with an NT 4 domain:

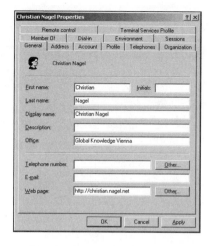

Active Directory Users and Computers can also be used in big enterprises with maybe millions of objects. It's not necessary to look through a list with a thousand objects, because we can select a custom filter so that only some of the objects are displayed. We can also do an LDAP query to search for the objects in the enterprise.

ADSI Edit

ADSI Edit is the registry editor of the Active Directory. This tool is not installed automatically. On the Windows 2000 Server CD you can find a directory named Supporting Tools. When the supporting tools are installed you'll find the ADSI Edit from the start menu: Start | Programs | Windows 2000 Support Tools | Tools | ADSI Edit.

With the easy-to-use tool Active Directory Users and Computers, the user interface to change the attributes of a user object is fixed. We will not see attributes we add to the schema in the mouse-click user interface of this tool. With ADSI Edit everything can be configured, and we can also look at the schema and the configuration. This tool is not that easy to use, however, and it is very easy to enter wrong data:

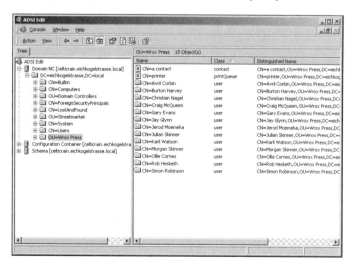

By opening the Properties window of an object, we can view and change every attribute of an object in the Active Directory. We see mandatory and optional attributes, with their types and values:

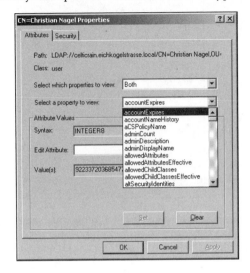

ADSI Viewer

You should also install the Active Directory Browser that's part of the Microsoft Platform SDK. The Microsoft Platform SDK is not part of the Visual Studio.NET distribution. You get a CD with the MSDN subscription, or you can download it from the MSDN Web. After installing the Platform SDK you can start the tool by selecting Start | Programs | Microsoft Platform SDK | Tools | ADSI Viewer.

The ADSI Viewer has two modes. With File | New we can start a query or use the Object Viewer to display and modify attributes of objects. After starting the Object Viewer we can specify an LDAP path, as well as username and password to open the object. Soon, when we start doing this programmatically, you will see what form the LDAP path can take. Here I'm specifying LDAP://OU=Wrox Press, DC=eichkogelstrasse, DC=local to access a organizational unit object:

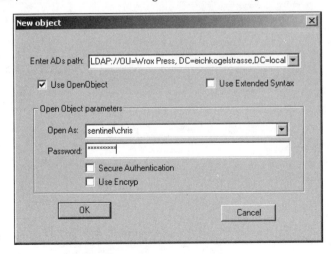

If the object we specify with the path and the username and password are valid, we get the Object Viewer screen, where we can view and modify the properties of the object and its child objects:

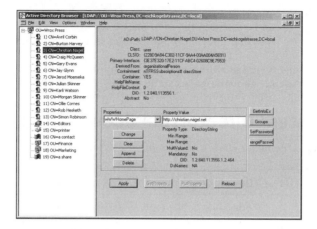

Active Directory Service Interfaces (ADSI)

The **Active Directory Service Interfaces** (ADSI) is a programmatic interface to directory services. ADSI defines some COM interfaces that are implemented by ADSI providers. This means that the client can use different directory services with the same programmatic interfaces. The .NET Framework classes in the System.DirectoryServices namespace make use of the ADSI interfaces.

In the following picture we can see some ADSI Providers (LDAP, WinNT, NDS) that implement COM interfaces like IADs and IUnknown. The assembly System.DirectoryServices makes use of the ADSI providers:

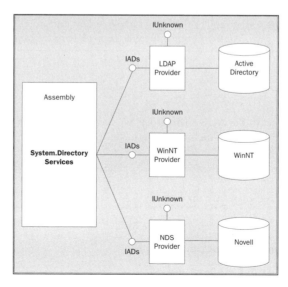

Programming the Active Directory

To develop programs for the Active Directory, we use classes from the `System.DirectoryServices` namespace. All these classes can be found in the `System.DirectoryServices` namespace. With these classes we can query objects, view and update properties, and search for objects.

In the following code segments we use a simple C# console application to demonstrate how the classes in the `System.DirectoryServices` namespace can be used.

Classes in System.DirectoryServices

The following table shows the major classes in the `System.DirectoryServices` namespace:

Class	Description
DirectoryEntry	This class is the main class used in the `System.DirectoryServices` namespace. An object of this class represents an object in the Active Directory store. We use this class to bind to an object, and to view and update properties. The properties of the object are represented in a `PropertyCollection`. Every item in the `PropertyCollection` again has a `PropertyValueCollection`.
DirectoryEntries	`DirectoryEntries` is a collection of `DirectoryEntry` objects. The `Children` property of a `DirectoryEntry` object returns a list of objects in a `DirectoryEntries` collection.
DirectorySearcher	This class is the main class used for searching objects with specific attributes. To define the search the `SortOption` class and the enumerations `SearchScope`, `SortDirection`, and `ReferalChasingOption` can be used. The search results in a `SearchResult` or a `SearchResultCollection`. We also get `ResultPropertyCollection` and `ResultPropertyValueCollection` objects.

Binding

To get the values of an object in the Active Directory, we have to connect to the Active Directory. The connecting process is called **binding**. The binding path can look like this:

```
LDAP://dc01.globalknowledge.net/OU=Marketing, DC=GlobalKnowledge, DC=Com
```

With the binding process we can specify these items:

- ❏ The **Protocol** specifies the provider to be used
- ❏ The **Server Name** of the domain controller
- ❏ The **Port Number** of the server process
- ❏ The **Distinguished Name** of the object to identify the object we want to access

❑ The **Username** and **Password** if a different user is needed for accessing the Active Directory

❑ An **Authentication** type can also be specified if encryption is needed

Let's have a more detailed look into these options:

Protocol

The first part of a binding path specifies the ADSI provider. The provider is implemented as a COM server; for identification a progID can be found in the registry directly under HKEY_CLASSES_ROOT. The providers we get with Windows 2000 are listed in this table:

Protocol	Description
LDAP	LDAP Server, such as the Exchange directory and the Windows 2000 Active Directory Server.
GC	GC is used to access the global catalog in the Active Directory. It can be used for fast queries.
IIS	With the ADSI provider for IIS it's possible to create new web sites in the IIS catalog.
WinNT	To access the user database of old Windows NT 4 domains we can use the ADSI provider for WinNT. The fact that NT 4 users only have a few attributes remains unchanged.
NDS	This progID is used to communicate with Novell Directory Services.
NWCOMPAT	With NWCOMPAT we can access old Novell directories: Novell Netware 3.x.

Server Name

The **server name** follows after the protocol in the binding string. The server name is optional if you are logged on to an Active Directory domain. Without a server name **serverless binding** occurs; this means that Windows 2000 tries to get the "best" domain controller in the domain that's associated with the user doing the bind. If there's no server inside a site, the first domain controller that can be found will be used.

A serverless binding can look like LDAP://OU=Sales, DC=GlobalKnowledge, DC=Com.

Port Number

After the server name we can specify the **port number** of the server process, by using the syntax :xxx. The default port number for the LDAP server is port 389: LDAP://dc01.globalknowledge.net:389. The Exchange server uses the same port number as the LDAP server. If the Exchange server is installed on the same system – for example, as a domain controller of the Active Directory – a different port can be configured.

Distinguished Name

The fourth part that we can specify in the path is the **distinguished name (DN).** The distinguished name is a guaranteed unique name that identifies the object we want to access. With the Active Directory we can use LDAP syntax that is based on X.500 to specify the name of the object:

The distinguished name

```
CN=Christian Nagel, OU=Trainer, DC=GlobalKnowledge, DC=com
```

specifies the Common Name (CN) Christian Nagel in the Organizational Unit (OU) Trainer in the Domain Component (DC) GlobalKnowledge of domain GlobalKnowledge.com. The part that is specified rightmost is the root object of the domain. The name has to follow the hierarchy in the object tree.

The LDAP specification for the string representation of distinguished names can be found in RFC 2253: http://www.ietf.org/rfc/rfc2253.txt.

Relative Distinguished Name

A relative distinguished name (RDN) is used to reference objects within a container object. With an RDN the specification of OU and DC is not needed, a common name would be enough. CN=Christian Nagel is the relative distinguished name inside the organizational unit. A relative distinguished name can be used if we already have a reference to a container object and we want to access child objects.

Default Naming Context

If a distinguished name is not specified in the path, the binding process will be made to the default naming context. We can read the default naming context with the help of rootDSE. LDAP 3.0 defines rootDSE as the root of a directory tree on a directory server. For example:

```
LDAP://rootDSE
```

or:

```
LDAP://servername/rootDSE
```

By enumerating all properties of the rootDSE we can get the information about the defaultNamingContext that will be used when no name is specified. schemaNamingContext and configurationNamingContext specify the required names to be used to access the schema and the configuration in the Active Directory store.

The following code is used to get all properties of the rootDSE. We will talk about the binding using the DirectoryEntry class:

```csharp
using (DirectoryEntry de = new DirectoryEntry())
{
    de.Path = "LDAP://celticrain/rootDSE";
    de.Username = @"sentinel\chris";
    de.Password = "mausemaus3";

    PropertyCollection props = de.Properties;

    foreach (string prop in props.PropertyNames)
    {
        PropertyValueCollection values = props[prop];
        foreach (string val in values)
        {
            Console.Write(prop + ": ");
            Console.WriteLine(val);
        }
    }
}
```

Beside other properties the resulting output of this program shows the defaultNamingContext DC=eichkogelstrasse, DC=local, the context that can be used to access the schema: CN=Schema, CN=Configuration, DC=eichkogelstrasse, DC=local, and the naming context of the configuration: CN=Configuration, DC=eichkogelstrasse, DC=local:

```
C:\Professional C#\Directory\DirectoryTest\bin\Debug\DirectoryTest.exe       _ □ X

currentTime: 20010531211107.0Z
subschemaSubentry: CN=Aggregate,CN=Schema,CN=Configuration,DC=eichkogelstrasse
C=local
dsServiceName: CN=NTDS Settings,CN=CELTICRAIN,CN=Servers,CN=Default-First-Site
ame,CN=Sites,CN=Configuration,DC=eichkogelstrasse,DC=local
namingContexts: CN=Schema,CN=Configuration,DC=eichkogelstrasse,DC=local
namingContexts: CN=Configuration,DC=eichkogelstrasse,DC=local
namingContexts: DC=eichkogelstrasse,DC=local
defaultNamingContext: DC=eichkogelstrasse,DC=local
schemaNamingContext: CN=Schema,CN=Configuration,DC=eichkogelstrasse,DC=local
configurationNamingContext: CN=Configuration,DC=eichkogelstrasse,DC=local
rootDomainNamingContext: DC=eichkogelstrasse,DC=local
supportedControl: 1.2.840.113556.1.4.319
supportedControl: 1.2.840.113556.1.4.801
supportedControl: 1.2.840.113556.1.4.473
supportedControl: 1.2.840.113556.1.4.528
supportedControl: 1.2.840.113556.1.4.417
supportedControl: 1.2.840.113556.1.4.619
```

Object Identifier

Every object has a unique identifier, a GUID. A GUID is a unique 128-bit number as you may already know from COM development. We can bind to an object using the GUID. This way we always get to the same object no matter if the object was moved in a different container. The GUID is generated at object creation and always remains the same.

We can get to a GUID string representation with DirectoryEntry.NativeGuid. This string representation then can be used to bind to the object. If the object is moved to a different container, we always get the same object.

This example shows the path name for a serverless binding to bind to a specific object represented by a GUID:

```
LDAP://<GUID=14abbd652aae1a47abc60782dcfc78ea>
```

Object Names in Windows NT Domains

The WinNT provider doesn't allow LDAP syntax in the name part of the binding string. With this provider the object is specified using ObjectName, ClassName. Valid binding strings for a Windows NT domain are:

```
WinNT:
WinNT://DomainName
WinNT://DomainName/UserName, user
WinNT://DomainName/dc01/MyGroup, group
```

Username

If a user other than the one logged on must be used for accessing the directory, because the logged on user doesn't have the required permissions to access the Active Directory, explicit **user credentials** must be specified for the binding process. With Active Directory we have a number of ways to set the username.

Downlevel Logon

With a downlevel logon the username can be specified with the pre-Windows 2000 domain name:

```
domain\username
```

Distinguished Name

The user can also be specified by a distinguished name of a user object, for example:

```
CN=Administrator, CN=Users, DC=eichkogelstrasse, DC=local
```

User Principal Name (UPN)

The UPN of an object is defined with the attribute `userPrincipalName`. The system administrator specifies this with the logon information in the **Account** tab of the **User** properties with the Active Directory Users and Computers tool. This is not the e-mail address of the user.

This information also uniquely identifies a user, and can be used for a logon:

```
Nagel@eichkogelstrasse.local
```

Authentication

For secure encrypted authentication the **authentication** type can also be specified. The authentication can be set with the `AuthenticationType` property of the `DirectoryEntry` class. The value that can be assigned is one of the `AuthenticationTypes` enumerations.

Binding with the DirectoryEntry Class

The `System.DirectoryServices.DirectoryEntry` class can be used to specify all the binding information. We can use the default constructor and define the binding information with the properties `Path`, `Username`, `Password`, and `AuthenticationType`, or pass all the information in the constructor:

```
using (DirectoryEntry de = new DirectoryEntry())
{
    de.Path = "LDAP://celticrain/DC=eichkogelstrasse, DC=local";
    de.Username = "nagel@eichkogelstrasse.local";
    de.Password = "someSecret";


    // use the current user credentials
    DirectoryEntry de2 =
        new DirectoryEntry("LDAP://DC=eichkogelstrasse, DC=local");
```

Even if constructing the `DirectoryEntry` object is successful, this doesn't mean that the binding was a success. Binding will happen the first time a property is read to avoid unnecessary network traffic. Whether the object exists, and the specified user credentials are correct, can be seen at the first access of the object.

Getting Directory Entries

Now that we know how to specify the binding attributes to an object in the Active Directory, let's read the attributes of an object.

Properties of User Objects

The `DirectoryEntry` class has some properties to get information about the object: the `Name`, `Guid`, and `SchemaClassName` properties. The first time we access a property of the `DirectoryEntry` object, the binding occurs and the cache is filled. When we access the other properties, we're reading them just from the cache, and communication with the server isn't necessary for data from the same object.

In this example we are accessing a user object with the common name Christian Nagel in the organization unit Wrox Press.

```
DirectoryEntry de = new DirectoryEntry();
de.Path = "LDAP://celticrain/CN=Christian Nagel, " +
    "OU=Wrox Press, DC=eichkogelstrasse, DC=local";

Console.WriteLine("Name: " + de.Name);
Console.WriteLine("GUID: " + de.Guid);
Console.WriteLine("Type: " + de.SchemaClassName);
Console.WriteLine();
```

An Active Directory object holds much more information. The information available depends on the type of the object. To get all the information about an object, the property `Properties` returns a `PropertyCollection`. Each property is itself a collection, because a single property can have multiple values, for example, the user object can have multiple phone numbers. We go through the values with an inner `foreach` loop. The collection that is returned from `properties[name]` is an `object` array. The attribute values can be strings, numbers, or other types. We are just using the `ToString()` method to display the values.

```
Console.WriteLine("Attributes: ");
PropertyCollection properties = de.Properties;
foreach (string name in properties.PropertyNames)
{
    foreach (object o in properties[name])
    {
        Console.WriteLine(name + ": " + o.ToString());
    }
}
```

In the resulting output we see all attributes of the user object Christian Nagel. We can see that `otherTelephone` is a multivalue property that has many phone numbers. Some of the property values just display the type of the object, `System.__ComObject`. To get the values of these attributes we have to use the ADSI COM interfaces directly from the classes in the `System.DirectoryServices` namespace.

In Chapter 19 you can read about how to work with COM objects and interfaces.

To get more information about ADSI you can read Simon Robinson's Professional ADSI Programming, *Wrox Press, ISBN 1-861002-26-2.*

Access a Property Directly by its Name

With `DirectoryEntry.Properties` we can access all properties. If a property name is known we can access the values directly:

```
foreach (string homePage in de.Properties["wWWHomePage"])
    Console.WriteLine("Home page: " + homePage);
```

Object Collections

Objects are stored hierarchically in the Active Directory. Container objects contain children. We can enumerate child objects in a container with the `Children` property of the class `DirectoryEntry`. In the other direction we can get the container of an object with the `Parent` property.

A user object doesn't have children, so now I'm using an organizational unit instead. Let's get all user objects from the organizational unit Wrox Press in the domain `eichkogelstrasse.local`. The `Children` property returns a `DirectoryEntries` collection that collects `DirectoryEntry` objects. We iterate through all `DirectoryEntry` objects to display the name of the child objects:

```
DirectoryEntry de = new DirectoryEntry();
de.Path = "LDAP://celticrain/OU=Wrox Press, " +
    "DC=eichkogelstrasse, DC=local";

Console.WriteLine("Children of " + de.Name);
foreach (DirectoryEntry obj in de.Children)
{
    Console.WriteLine(obj.Name);
}
```

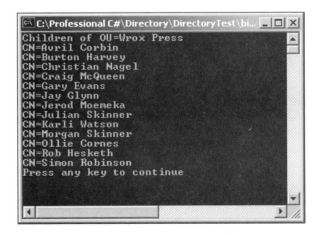

In this example we've seen all the objects in the organizational unit: users, contacts, printers, shares, and others. If we want to see only some object types we can use the SchemaFilter property of the DirectoryEntries class:

```
DirectoryEntry de = new DirectoryEntry();
  de.Path = "LDAP://celticrain/OU=Wrox Press, " +
     "DC=eichkogelstrasse, DC=local";

  Console.WriteLine("Children of " + de.Name);
  de.Children.SchemaFilter.Add("user");
  foreach (DirectoryEntry obj in de.Children)
  {
      Console.WriteLine(obj.Name);
  }
```

As a result we only see the user objects in the organizational unit:

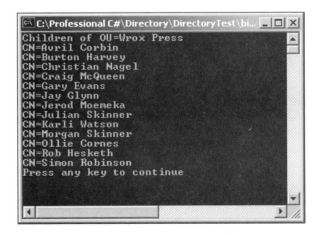

Cache

To reduce the network transfers, ADSI uses a cache for the object properties. As we've seen earlier, the server isn't accessed when we create a `DirectoryEntry` object; instead when we first read a value from the directory store all the properties are written into the cache, so that a round trip to the server isn't necessary when we read the next property. This property cache can be turned off by setting the property `DirectoryEntry.UsePropertyCache` to `false`. It's better not to do this because this would generate a lot of unnecessary round trips to the server.

Writing changes to objects also does this only in the cache. Setting a lot of properties doesn't generate network traffic. `DirectoryEntry.CommitChanges()` is required to flush the cache and transfer all changed data to the server. To get the newly written data from the directory store again we can use `DirectoryEntry.RefreshCache()` to read to properties. `UsePropertyCache` set to `false` can be very useful for debugging to see what property change goes wrong.

Updating Directory Entries

Objects in the Active Directory can be updated as easily as they can be read. We can change the values after reading the object. To remove all values of a single property the method `PropertyValueCollection.Clear()` can be called. With `Add()` new values can be added to a property. `Remove()` and `RemoveAt()` remove specific values from a property collection:

```
using (DirectoryEntry de = new DirectoryEntry())
{
    de.Path = "LDAP://celticrain/CN=Christian Nagel, " +
        OU=Wrox Press, DC=eichkogelstrasse, DC=local";

    if (de.Properties.Contains("mobile"))
    {
        de.Properties["mobile"][0] = "+43(664)3434343434";
    }

    de.CommitChanges();
}
```

We can change a value simply by setting it to the specified value. With the following code line the mobile phone number is set to a new value by using an indexer for the `PropertyValueCollection`. With the indexer a value can only be changed if it exists. Therefore, we should always check with `DirectoryEntry.Properties.Contains()` if the attribute is available.

```
de.Properties["mobile"][0] = "+43(664)3434343434";
```

> Remember to call **`DirectoryEntry.CommitChanges()`** after creating or updating new directory objects. Otherwise only the cache gets updated, and the changes are not sent to the directory service.

Creating New Objects

When we want to create new Active Directory objects like users, computers, printers, contacts, and so on, we can do this programmatically with the `DirectoryEntries` class.

To add new objects to the directory we first have to bind to a container object like an organizational unit where new objects can be inserted. Objects that can't contain other objects can't be used. Here I'm using the container object with the distinguished name CN=Users, DC=eichkogelstrasse, DC=local:

```
DirectoryEntry de = new DirectoryEntry();
de.Path = "LDAP://celticrain/CN=Users, " +
    "DC=eichkogelstrasse, DC=local";
```

We can get to the DirectoryEntries object with the Children property of a DirectoryEntry:

```
DirectoryEntries users = de.Children;
```

With DirectoryEntries we have methods to add, remove, and find objects in the collection. Here I'm creating a new user object. With the Add() method we need a name of the object and a type name. We can get to the type names easily using ADSI Edit.

```
DirectoryEntry user = users.Add("John Doe", "user");
```

The object now has the default property values. To assign specific property values we can add properties with the Add() method of the Properties property. Of course, all of the properties must exist in the schema for the user object. If a specified property doesn't exist you'll get a COMException "**The specified directory service attribute or value doesn't exist**". If the attribute names are OK, but the server refuses the entry because of an illegal password or a missing property, the COMException has the message "**The server is unwilling to process the request**":

```
user.Properties["company"].Add("Some Company");
user.Properties["department"].Add("Sales");
user.Properties["employeeID"].Add("4711");
user.Properties["samAccountName"].Add("John Doe");
user.Properties["userPassword"].Add("someSecret");
```

All the data isn't written to the Active Directory at this point. We have to flush the cache:

```
user.CommitChanges();
```

Searching in the Active Directory

Most of the time we will use the Active Directory to search for some values. It's a data store that's optimized for **read-mostly**, so we will mostly read data.

To search in the Active Directory, the .NET Framework has the class DirectorySearcher.

We can use the search only with the LDAP provider. DirectorySearcher doesn't work with NDS or IIS providers.

In the constructor of the class DirectorySearcher we can define four important parts for the search. We can also use a default constructor and define the search options with properties.

SearchRoot

The search root specifies where the search should start. The default of the SearchRoot is the root of the domain you're currently using. The SearchRoot is specified with the Path of a DirectoryEntry object.

Filter

The filter defines the values where we want to get hits. The filter is a string that must be enclosed in parentheses.

Relational operators such as <=, =, >= are allowed in expressions. (objectClass=contact) will search all objects of type contact; (lastName>=Nagel) searches all objects where the lastName property is equal or larger than Nagel, which means that it follows in the alphabet.

Expressions can be combined with the & and | prefix operators. (&(objectClass=user)(description=Auth*)) searches all objects of type user where the property description starts with the string Auth. Because the & and | operators are at the beginning of the expressions it's possible to combine more than two expressions with a single prefix operator.

The default filter is (objectClass=*) so all objects are valid.

The filter syntax is defined in RFC 2254, "*The String Representation of LDAP Search Filters*". This RFC can be found at http://www.ietf.org/rfc/rfc2254.txt.

PropertiesToLoad

With PropertiesToLoad we define a StringCollection of all the properties that we are interested in. As you've already seen, objects can have a lot of properties. Most of them will not be important for our search request. We define the properties that should be loaded into the cache. The default properties we get if nothing is specified are the Path and the Name of the object.

SearchScope

SearchScope is an enumeration that defines how deep the search should extend:

- ❑ SearchScope.Base only searches the attributes in the object where the search started, so we get at most one object.
- ❑ With SearchScope.OneLevel the search continues in the child collection of the base object. The base object itself is not searched for a hit.
- ❑ SearchScope.Subtree defines that the search should go down the complete tree.

The default SearchScope is Subtree.

Search Limits

Such a search can span multiple domains. To limit the search to the number of objects or the time taken we have some additional properties to define.

DirectorySearcher properties	Description
ClientTimeout	The maximum time the client waits for the server to return a result. If the server does not respond no records are returned.
PageSize	With a **paged search** the server returns a number of objects defined with the PageSize instead of the complete result. This reduces the time for the client to get a first answer and the memory needed. The server sends a cookie to the client, which is sent back to the server with the next search request, so that the search can continue at the point where it finished.
ServerPageTimeLimit	For paged searches this value defines the time a search should continue to return a number of objects that's defined with the PageSize value. If the time is reached before the PageSize value, the objects that were found up to that point are returned to the client. The default value is –1, which means infinite.
ServerTimeLimit	Defines the maximum time the server will search for objects. When this time is reached all objects that are found up to this point are returned to the client. The default is 120 seconds, and you cannot set the search to a higher value.
ReferalChasing	A search can cross multiple domains. If the root that's specified with SearchRoot is a parent domain or no root was specified, the search can continue to child domains. With this property we can specify if the search should continue on different servers. ReferalChasingOption.None means that the search does not continue to other servers. With the value ReferalChasingOption.Subordinate it's specified that the search should go on to child domains. When the search starts at DC=Wrox, DC=COM the server can return a result set and the referral to DC=France, DC=Wrox, DC=COM. The client can continue the search in the subdomain. ReferalChasingOption.External means that the server can refer the client to an independent server that is not in the subdomain. This is the default option. With ReferalChasingOption.All both external and subordinate referrals are returned.

In our search example we want to search for all `user` objects in the organizational unit Wrox Press, where the property `description` has a value of `Author`.

First, we bind to the organizational unit `Wrox Press`. This is where the search should start. We are creating a `DirectorySearcher` object where the `SearchRoot` is set. The filter is defined as `(&(objectClass=user)(description=Auth*))`, so that we find all objects of type `user` with a description of `Auth` following by something else. The scope of the search should be a sub-tree, so that child organizational units within `Wrox Press` are searched, too:

```
DirectoryEntry de = new DirectoryEntry();
de.Path = "LDAP://OU=Wrox Press, " +
    "DC=eichkogelstrasse, DC=local";

DirectorySearcher searcher = new DirectorySearcher())

searcher.SearchRoot = de;
searcher.Filter = "(&(objectClass=user)(description=Auth*))";
searcher.SearchScope = SearchScope.Subtree;
```

The properties we want to have in the result of the search are name, `description`, `givenName`, and `wWWHomePage`.

```
searcher.PropertiesToLoad.Add("name");
searcher.PropertiesToLoad.Add("description");
searcher.PropertiesToLoad.Add("givenName");
searcher.PropertiesToLoad.Add("wWWHomePage");
```

We are ready to do the search. However, the result should also be sorted. `DirectorySearcher` has a property `Sort`, where we can set a `SortOption`. The first argument in the constructor of the `SortOption` defines the property that will be sorted; the second argument defines the direction of the sort. The `SortDirection` enumeration has values `Ascending` and `Descending`.

To start the search we can use the method `FindOne()` to find the first object, or `FindAll()`. `FindOne()` returns a simple `SearchResult`; `FindAll()` returns a `SearchResultCollection`. We want to get all the authors, so `FindAll()` is used here:

```
searcher.Sort = new SortOption("givenName",
    SortDirection.Ascending);

SearchResultCollection results = searcher.FindAll();
```

With a `foreach` we are accessing every `SearchResult` in the `SearchResultCollection`. A `SearchResult` represents a single object in the search cache. The `Properties` property returns a `ResultPropertyCollection`, where we access all properties and values with the property name and the indexer:

```
SearchResultCollection results = searcher.FindAll();

foreach (SearchResult result in results)
{
    ResultPropertyCollection props = result.Properties;
    foreach (string propName in props.PropertyNames)
    {
```

```
            Console.Write(propName + ": ");
            Console.WriteLine(props[propName][0]);
        }
        Console.WriteLine();
        }
    }
}
```

If you would like to get to the complete object after a search that's also possible: SearchResult has a method GetDirectoryEntry() that returns the corresponding DirectoryEntry of the found object.

The resulting output shows the beginning of the list of all authors of Professional C# with the properties we've chosen:

```
C:\Professional C#\Directory\GetUser\bin\Debug\GetUser.exe                    _ |□| x|
givenname: Burton
description: Author
name: Burton Harvey
adspath: LDAP://celticrain/CN=Burton Harvey,OU=Wrox Press,DC=eichkogelstrasse,DC
=local

givenname: Christian
description: Author
adspath: LDAP://celticrain/CN=Christian Nagel,OU=Wrox Press,DC=eichkogelstrasse,
DC=local
name: Christian Nagel
wwwhomepage: http://christian.nagel.net

givenname: Craig
description: Author
name: Craig McQueen
adspath: LDAP://celticrain/CN=Craig McQueen,OU=Wrox Press,DC=eichkogelstrasse,DC
=local

givenname: Jay
description: Author
name: Jay Glynn
adspath: LDAP://celticrain/CN=Jay Glynn,OU=Wrox Press,DC=eichkogelstrasse,DC=loc
al
```

Searching for User Objects

The final application we will create in this chapter is a Windows Forms application. With this application it's possible to search all user objects of a domain with a dynamically defined filter string. It's also possible to set the properties of the user objects that should be displayed.

User Interface

The user interface shows numbered steps to indicate how to use the application:

1. In the first step Username, Password, and the Domain Controller can be entered. All this information is optional. If no domain controller is entered the connection works with serverless binding. If the username is missing the security context of the current user is taken.

2. A button allows all the property names of the user object to be loaded dynamically in the listBoxProperties listbox.

3. After the property names are loaded, the properties that should be displayed can be selected. The `SelectionMode` of the listbox is set to `MultiSimple`.

4. The filter to limit the search can be entered. The default value that's set in this dialog box searches for all user objects: `(objectClass=user)`.

5. Now the search can start:

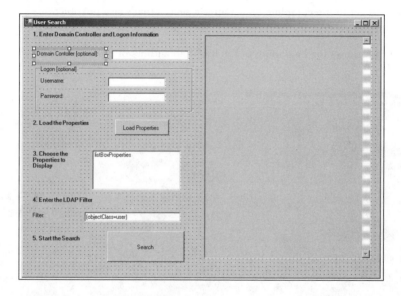

Get the Schema Naming Context

This application just has two handler methods: the first handler method for the button to load the properties, and the second to start the search in the domain. In the first part we read the properties of the `user` class dynamically from the schema to display it in the user interface.

In the handler method `buttonLoadProperties_Click()` `SetLogonInformation()` reads the username, password, and hostname from the dialog and stores them in members of the class. Next the method `SetNamingContext()` sets the LDAP name of the schema and the LDAP name of the default context. This schema LDAP name is used in the call to set the properties in the listbox: `SetUserProperties()`.

```
        private void buttonLoadProperties_Click(object sender,
          System.EventArgs e)
        {
          try
          {
            SetLogonInformation();
            SetNamingContext();

            SetUserProperties(schemaNamingContext);
          }
```

```
        catch (Exception ex)
        {
            MessageBox.Show("Check your inputs! " + ex.Message);
        }
    }


    protected void SetLogonInformation()
    {
        username = (textBoxUsername.Text == "" ? null :
            textBoxUsername.Text);
        password = (textBoxPassword.Text == "" ? null :
            textBoxPassword.Text);
        hostname = textBoxHostname.Text;
        if (hostname != "") hostname += "/";
    }
```

In the helper method `SetNamingContext()`, we are using the root of the directory tree to get the properties of the server. We are just interested in the value of two properties: `schemaNamingContext` and `defaultNamingContext`.

```
    protected string SetNamingContext()
    {
        using (DirectoryEntry de = new DirectoryEntry())
        {
            string path = "LDAP://" + hostname + "/rootDSE";
            de.Username = username;
            de.Password = password;
            de.Path = path;

            schemaNamingContext =
                de.Properties["schemaNamingContext"][0].ToString();
            defaultNamingContext =
                de.Properties["defaultNamingContext"][0].ToString();
        }
    }
```

Get the Property Names of the user Class

We have the LDAP name to access the schema. We can use this to access the directory and read the properties. We are not only interested in the properties of the `user` class, but also of the base classes of user: `Organizational-Person`, `Person`, and `Top`. In this program, the names of the base classes are hard-coded. It would be also possible to read the base class dynamically with the `subClassOf` attribute. `GetSchemaProperties()` returns a string array with all property names of the specific object type. All the property names are collected in the `StringCollection` properties:

```
    protected void SetUserProperties(string schemaNamingContext)
    {
        StringCollection properties = new StringCollection();
        string[] data = GetSchemaProperties(schemaNamingContext, "User");
        properties.AddRange(GetSchemaProperties(schemaNamingContext,
            "Organizational-Person"));
        properties.AddRange(GetSchemaProperties(schemaNamingContext,
            "Person"));
```

```
        properties.AddRange(GetSchemaProperties(schemaNamingContext,
            "Top"));

        listBoxProperties.Items.Clear();
        foreach (string s in properties)
        {
            listBoxProperties.Items.Add(s);
        }
    }
```

In `GetSchemaProperties()` we are accessing the Active Directory again. This time `rootDSE` is not used, rather the LDAP name to the schema that we discovered earlier. The property `systemMayContain` holds a collection of all attributes that are allowed in the class `objectType`:

```
    protected string[] GetSchemaProperties(string schemaNamingContext,
        string objectType)
    {
        string[] data;
        using (DirectoryEntry de = new DirectoryEntry())
        {
            de.Username = username;
            de.Password = password;

            de.Path = "LDAP://" + hostname + "/CN=" + objectType + "," +
                schemaNamingContext;

            DS.PropertyCollection properties = de.Properties;
            DS.PropertyValueCollection values =
                properties["systemMayContain"];

            data = new String[values.Count];
            values.CopyTo(data, 0);
        }
        return data;
    }
```

One interesting side-note to this code is that in a Windows Forms application the `PropertyCollection` class of the `System.DirectoryServices` namespace has a naming conflict with `System.Data.PropertyCollection`. Because I don't want to write such long names as `System.DirectoryServices.PropertyCollection` to resolve the conflict I've shortened the namespace name using:

```
    namespace DS = System.DirectoryServices;
```

That's where `DS.PropertyCollection` comes from.

Step 2 in the application is completed. The `listbox` has all the property names of the user objects.

Search User Objects

The handler for the search button just calls the helper method `FillResult()`:

```
private void buttonSearch_Click(object sender, System.EventArgs e)
{
   try
   {
      FillResult();
   }
   catch (Exception ex)
   {
      MessageBox.Show("Check your input: " + ex.Message);
   }
}
```

In `FillResult()` we are doing a normal search in the complete Active Directory Domain as we've seen earlier. `SearchScope` is set to `Subtree`, the `Filter` to the string we get from a `TextBox`, and the properties that should be loaded into the cache are set by the values the user selected in the listbox:

```
protected void FillResult()
{
   using (DirectoryEntry root = new DirectoryEntry())
   {
      root.Username = username;
      root.Password = password;
      root.Path = "LDAP://" + hostname + defaultNamingContext;

      using (DirectorySearcher searcher = new DirectorySearcher())
      {
         searcher.SearchRoot = root;
         searcher.SearchScope = SearchScope.Subtree;
         searcher.Filter = textBoxFilter.Text;
         searcher.PropertiesToLoad.AddRange(GetProperties());

         SearchResultCollection results = searcher.FindAll();
         StringBuilder summary = new StringBuilder();
         foreach (SearchResult result in results)
         {
            foreach (string propName in
               result.Properties.PropertyNames)
            {
               foreach (string s in result.Properties[propName])
               {
                  summary.Append(" " + propName + ": " + s + "\r\n");
               }
            }
            summary.Append("\r\n");
         }
         textBoxResults.Text = summary.ToString();
      }
   }
}
```

Starting the application we get a list of all objects where the filter is valid:

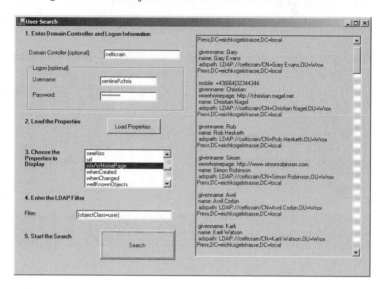

Summary

In this chapter we've seen the architecture of the Active Directory: the important concepts of domains, trees, and forests. We can access information in the complete enterprise. Writing applications that access the Active Directory we have to be aware that the data we read may not be up-to-date because of the replication latency.

With the classes in the `System.DirectoryServices` namespaces we have easy ways to access the Active Directory in a thin layer to the ADSI providers. The `DirectoryEntry` class makes it possible to read and write objects directly in the data store.

With the `DirectorySearcher` class we can do complex searches and define filters, timeouts, properties to load, and a scope. Using the Global Catalog we can speed up the search for objects in the complete enterprise, because it stores a read-only version of all objects in the forest.

16

ASP.NET Pages

If you are new to the world of C# and .NET in general you may wonder why a chapter on ASP.NET has been included in this book. It's a whole new language, right? Well, not really. In fact, as we will see, it is possible to use C# to create ASP.NET pages. But we're getting ahead of ourselves here – first off we should discuss exactly what ASP.NET is.

ASP.NET, or Active Server Pages.NET, ships as part of the .NET framework and is a technology that allows dynamic creation of documents on a web server when they are requested via HTTP. This mostly means HTML documents, although it is equally possible to create, say, WML documents for consumption on WAP browsers, or indeed anything else with a MIME type.

In some ways ASP.NET is similar to many other technologies, such as PHP, ColdFusion, and so on – but there is one important difference. ASP.NET, as its name suggests, has been designed to be fully integrated with the .NET framework, part of which includes support for C#.

It is quite possible that you have had experience of the last Microsoft technology for achieving dynamic content generation – ASP. If this is the case then you will probably know that programming in this technology used scripting languages such as VBScript or JScript. This worked, but did mean that some things were awkward for those of us used to 'proper' programming languages, and certainly resulted in a loss of performance.

One major difference, related to the use of more advanced programming languages, is the provision of a complete server-side object model for use at run time. ASP.NET gives access to all controls on a page as objects, in a rich environment. Also on the server side we have access to any other .NET classes required, allowing integration of many useful services. Controls used on a page expose a lot of functionality, in fact we can do almost as much as with windows forms classes, which gives plenty of flexibility. For this reason, ASP.NET pages generating HTML content are often called **web forms**.

In this chapter we will take a more detailed look at ASP.NET, including how it works, what we can do with it, and where C# fits in.

ASP.NET Introduction

ASP.NET works with Internet Information Server (IIS) to deliver content in response to HTTP requests. ASP.NET pages are found in .aspx files, and the basic architecture looks like this:

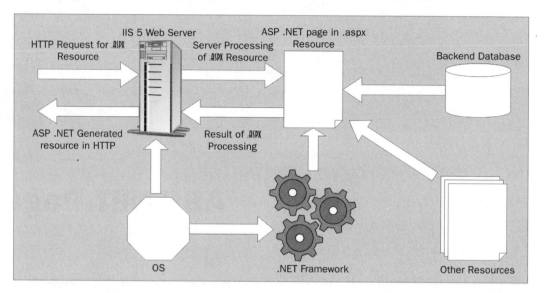

During ASP.NET processing we have access to all .NET classes, custom components created in C# or other languages, databases, etc. In fact, we have as much power as we would have running a C# application – using C# in ASP.NET is in effect running a C# application.

An ASP.NET file may contain any of the following:

- ❑ Processing instructions for the server
- ❑ Code in C#, VB.NET, JScript.NET, or any other language that the .NET framework supports now or might support in the future
- ❑ Content in whatever form is appropriate for the generated resource, such as HTML
- ❑ Embedded ASP.NET server controls

So, in fact we could have an ASP.NET file as simple as:

```
Hello!
```

with no additional code or instructions at all. This would simply result in an HTML page being returned (as HTML is the default output of ASP.NET pages) containing just this text.

As we will see later in this chapter, it is also possible to split certain portions of the code into other files, which can provide a more logical structure.

State Management in ASP.NET

One of the key properties of ASP.NET pages is that they are effectively stateless. By default no information is stored on the server between user requests (although there are methods for doing this should you wish, as we'll see later). At first glance this seems a little strange, as state management is something that seems essential for user-friendly interactive sessions. However, ASP.NET provides a rather nice way around this problem, in such a way as to make session management almost completely transparent. It just happens.

Basically, information about (for example) the state of controls on a web form (data entered in text boxes, selections from drop-down lists etc.) is stored in a hidden **viewstate** field that is part of the page generated by the server and passed to the user. Subsequent actions, such as triggering events that require server-side processing like submitting form data, result in this information being sent back to the server, known as **postback**. On the server this information is used to repopulate the page object model allowing us to operate on it as if the changes had been made locally.

We'll see this in action shortly and point out the details.

ASP.NET Web Forms

As mentioned earlier, much of the functionality in ASP.NET is achieved using Web Forms. Before long we'll dive in and create a simple web form to give us a starting point to explore this technology. First, though, we should look at a couple of quick points pertinent to web form design. It should be noted that many ASP.NET developers simply use a text editor such as Notepad to create files. This is made easier by the fact that it is possible, as noted earlier, to combine all code in one file. This is achieved by enclosing code in <script> tags, using two attributes on the opening <script> tag as follows:

```
<script language="c#" runat="server">

   // Server-side code goes here.

</script>
```

The runat="server" attribute here is crucial (and we'll see it time and again in this chapter), as it instructs IIS to execute this code on the server rather than sending it to the client, thus giving us access to the rich environment discussed earlier. We can place our functions, event handlers etc. in server-side script blocks.

If we omit the runat="server" attribute we are effectively providing client-side code, which will fail if it uses any of the server-side style coding we will see in this chapter. However, there might be times when we want to provide client-side code (indeed, ASP.NET generates some itself sometimes, depending on browser capabilities and what web form code is used). Unfortunately we can't use C# here, as this would require the .NET framework on the client which might not always be the case, so JScript is probably the next best option (as it is supported on the widest variety of client browsers). To change the language we simply change the value of the language attribute as follows:

```
<script language="jscript">

   // Client-side code goes here, can also use vbscript.

</script>
```

775

It is equally possible to create ASP.NET files in Visual Studio, which is great for us as we are already familiar with this environment for C# programming. However, the default project setup for web applications in this environment provides a slightly more complex structure than a single .aspx file. This isn't a problem for us though, and does make things a bit more logical (read: more programmer-like and less web developer-like). Based on this we'll use Visual Studio.NET throughout this chapter for our ASP.NET programming.

Now it's time for an example. Create a new project of type C# Web Application as shown below:

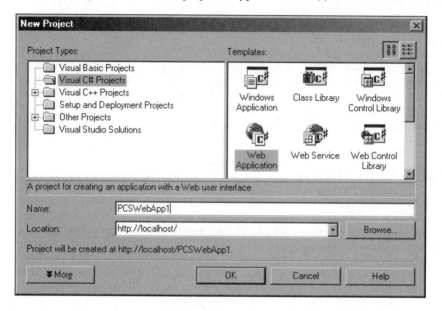

By default, VS will use FrontPage extensions to set up a web application at the required location, which may be remote if your web server is on a different machine. However, it also provides an alternative (and slightly faster) method for doing this, using the file system over a LAN (which is of course impossible if your remote web server isn't on the same LAN as your development server). If the first method fails then VS will try the second.

Regardless of which method is used, VS keeps a local cache of all project files, and keeps these in sync with the files on the web server.

After a few moments Visual Studio should have set up the following:

- ❏ A new solution, PCSWebApp1, containing the C# Web Application PCSWebApp1
- ❏ AssemblyInfo.cs – the standard code for assembly description
- ❏ Global.asax – application global information and events (see later in this chapter)
- ❏ PCSWebApp1.disco – a file describing any web services in the project, enabling dynamic discovery (see next chapter for details)
- ❏ Web.config – configuration information for the application (see later in this chapter)
- ❏ WebForm1.aspx – the first ASP.NET page in the web application

We'll cover all of the generated files over the course of this and the next two chapters; for now we should concentrate on the meat of the application, which is the `.aspx` file generated.

We can view `.aspx` files in two ways – in design or code view. This is exactly the same as for WinForms, as we saw earlier in the book. The initial view in VS is the design view:

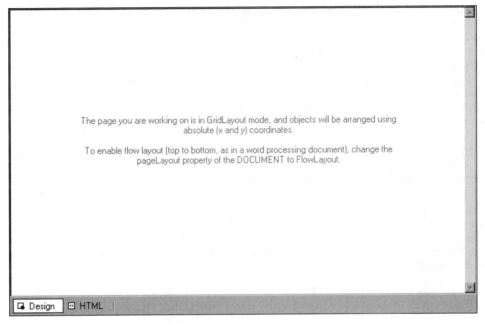

The text shown in this view by default isn't text that we'll see in our application, it's just a note from VS to say what layout mode is in use. Here we are using *GridLayout* mode, which allows extra flexibility in control positioning, but we can change this to *FlowLayout* if we require a more traditional HTML-type positioning scheme. We'll look at this a little later.

If we select the HTML view from the buttons below the layout display we'll see the code generated inside the `.aspx` file:

```
<%@ Page language="c#" Codebehind="WebForm1.aspx.cs" AutoEventWireup="false"
        Inherits="PCSWebApp1.WebForm1" %>

<html>
    <head>
        <meta name=vs_targetSchema content="Internet Explorer 5.0">
        <meta name="GENERATOR" Content="Microsoft Visual Studio 7.0">
        <meta name="CODE_LANGUAGE" Content="C#">
    </head>
    <body MS_POSITIONING="GridLayout">
        <form method="post" runat="server">
        </form>
    </body>
</html>
```

The <html> element here has been populated with a little metadata that doesn't really concern us, and a <form> element to contain ASP.NET code. The most important thing about this element is the runat attribute. Just like with the server-side code blocks we saw at the start of this section this is set to server, meaning that the processing of the form will take place on the server. If we don't include this then no server-side processing will be performed and the form won't do anything.

The other interesting thing about this code is the <@% Page %> tag at the top. This tag defines page characteristics that are important to us as C# web application developers. Firstly there is a language attribute that specifies that we will use C# throughout our page, as we saw earlier with <script> blocks (the default for web application is VB.NET, although this can be changed through IIS configuration). The next three attributes are necessary, as the code driving the page has been set up by VS to reside in a separate file, WebForm1.aspx.cs. This file, which we'll look at in a moment, contains a class definition that is used as the base class for the web forms page. (Now we start to see how ASP.NET ties in with a rich object model!) This base class will be used in conjunction with code in this file to generate the HTML that reaches the user.

> *Note that not all .aspx files require this multi-layer model, it is possible just to use the base .NET web form class as the base class for the page, which is the default. In this case the .aspx file would include all of our C# code in <script> blocks as mentioned earlier.*

Since we are providing a customized base class for the page we might also have customized events. To ensure that IIS is aware of this we use the AutoEventWireup attribute, which signifies whether the Page_Load() event handler (called, surprisingly enough, on loading the page) is automatically wired up to the OnPageLoad event. By setting this attribute to false we must provide our own code to do this if required, but this does allow us a bit more freedom in what we do.

Next we'll look at the "code-behind" code generated for this file. To do this right-click on **WebForm1.aspx** in the solution explorer and select **View Code**. This should load the code in WebForm1.aspx.cs into the text editor. First off, we see a namespace declaration for our web application followed by the default set of references required for basic usage:

```
namespace PCSWebApp1
{
    using System;
    using System.Collections;
    using System.ComponentModel;
    using System.Data;
    using System.Drawing;
    using System.Web;
    using System.Web.SessionState;
    using System.Web.UI;
    using System.Web.UI.WebControls;
    using System.Web.UI.HtmlControls;
```

Moving on we see the definition of WebForm1, the base class used for the .aspx page. This class inherits from System.Web.UI.Page, the base class for web forms:

```
    /// <summary>
    ///     Summary description for WebForm1.
    /// </summary>

    public class WebForm1 : System.Web.UI.Page
    {
```

The rest of the code in this form performs various initialization tasks, and includes the code required to design web forms in VS. The constructor registers an event handler for Page_Init(), called during page activation and used by VS for code related to design-time additions to the form (stored in InitializeComponent(), which is called by this handler). There is also the Page_Load() event handler mentioned earlier:

```csharp
public WebForm1()
{
    Page.Init += new System.EventHandler(Page_Init);
}

protected void Page_Load(object sender, System.EventArgs e)
{

    // Put user code to initialize the page here

}

protected void Page_Init(object sender, EventArgs e)
{
    //
    // CODEGEN: This call is required by the ASP.NET Windows
    // Form Designer.
    //

    InitializeComponent();
}
```

InitializeComponent() itself is contained in a #region block such that we can use the outline view in VS to hide it, as it will quickly become full with VS-generated code, much like its analogous method in WinForms code:

```csharp
#region Web Form Designer generated code

/// <summary>
///     Required method for Designer support - do not modify
///     the contents of this method with the code editor.
/// </summary>

private void InitializeComponent()
{
    this.Load += new System.EventHandler(this.Page_Load);
}
#endregion
    }
}
```

Since AutoEventWireup was set to false, InitializeComponent() has to register Page_Load() with the Load event.

Strictly speaking, this is more code than is required for a simple ASP.NET web form page, which might be much simpler as we've already seen (albeit as a trivial example). However, the structure created does lend itself to reusability and expansion using C# techniques, without causing a noticeable amount of overhead, so we'll run with it.

779

ASP.NET Server Controls

Our generated code doesn't do very much as yet, so next we need to add some content. We can do this in VS using the web form designer, which supports drag-and-drop and adding via code in just the same way as the WinForms designer.

There are four types of control that we can add to our ASP.NET pages:

❑ **HTML server controls** – controls that mimic HTML elements, which will be familiar to HTML developers.

❑ **Web-server controls** – a new set of controls, some of which have the same functionality as HTML controls but with a common naming scheme for properties etc. to ease development, and provide consistency with analogous WinForms controls. There are also some completely new and very powerful controls as we will see later.

❑ **Validation controls** – a set of controls capable of performing validation of user input in a simple way.

❑ **Custom and user controls** – controls defined by the developer, which are possible to define in a number of ways as we will see in Chapter 18.

> *We'll see a complete list of web-server and validation controls in the next section, along with usage notes. HTML controls will not be covered in this chapter. These controls don't supply anything that web-server controls don't, and the web-server controls provide a richer environment for those more used to programming than HTML design (which I'm assuming applies to the majority of the audience of this book). Learning how to use the web-server controls will provide enough knowledge to use HTML server controls without much difficulty, should you be interested.*

Let's add a couple of web-server controls to our project. All web-server and validation controls are used in the following XML element-type form:

```
<asp:X runat="server" attribute="value">Contents</asp:X>
```

Where X is the name of the ASP.NET server control, `attribute="value"` is one or more attribute specifications, and `Contents` specifies the control content, if any. Some controls allow properties to be set using attributes and control-element content, such as `Label` (used for simple text display) where `Text` can be specified in either way. Other controls may use an element containment scheme to define their hierarchy, for example `Table` (which, spookily enough, defines a table), which can contain `TableRow` elements in order to specify table rows declaratively.

Note that, as the syntax for controls is based on XML (although they may be used embedded in non-XML code such as HTML), it is an error to omit the closing tags, omit the `/>` for empty elements, or overlap controls.

Finally, we once again see the `runat="server"` attribute on web-server controls. It is just as essential here as it is elsewhere, and it is a common mistake to miss this attribute off (trust me, you'll do it occasionally), resulting is dead web forms.

We'll keep things simple for this first example. Change the HTML design view for `WebForm1.aspx` as follows:

```
<%@ Page language="c#" Codebehind="WebForm1.aspx.cs" AutoEventWireup="false"
    Inherits="PCSWebApp1.WebForm1" %>

<html>
  <head>
    <meta name=vs_targetSchema content="Internet Explorer 5.0">
    <meta name="GENERATOR" Content="Microsoft Visual Studio 7.0">
    <meta name="CODE_LANGUAGE" Content="C#">
  </head>
  <body MS_POSITIONING="GridLayout">
    <form method="post" runat="server">
      <asp:Label Runat="server" ID="resultLabel"/><br>
      <asp:Button Runat="server" ID="triggerButton" Text="Click Me"/>
    </form>
  </body>
</html>
```

Note that as you do this that VS IntelliSense predicts our code entry just like in C# design.

Here we have added two web-form controls, a label and a button.

Going back to the design screen we can see that our controls have been added, named using their ID attributes. As with WinForms we have full access to properties, events, etc. through the Properties window, and can see instant feedback in code or design whenever we make changes.

Next, have another look at `WebForm1.aspx.cs`. The following two members have been added to our `WebForm1` class:

```
protected System.Web.UI.WebControls.Button triggerButton;
protected System.Web.UI.WebControls.Label resultLabel;
```

Any server controls we add will automatically become part of the object model for our form that we are building in this code-behind file. This is an instant bonus for WinForms developers – the similarities are beginning to make themselves known!

To make this application actually do something, let's add an event handler for clicking on the button. Here we can either enter a method name in the Properties window for the button or just double-click on the button to get the default event handler. If we double-click on the button we'll automatically add an event handling method as follows:

```
protected void triggerButton_Click(object sender, System.EventArgs e)
{
}
```

This is hooked up to the button by some code added to `InitializeComponent()`:

```
private void InitializeComponent()
{
  this.triggerButton.Click +=
    new System.EventHandler(this.triggerButton_Click);
  this.Load += new System.EventHandler(this.Page_Load);
}
```

Modify the code in `triggerButton_Click()` as follows:

```
protected void triggerButton_Click(object sender, System.EventArgs e)
{
    resultLabel.Text = "Button clicked!";
}
```

Now we're ready to make it go. Build the application from VS in the normal way and all files will be compiled and/or placed on the web server ready for use. To test the web application out we can either run the application (which will give us full use of VS debugging facilities), or just point a browser at http://localhost/PCSWebApp1/WebForm1.aspx. Either way you should see the Click Me button on a web page. Before pressing the button, take a quick look at the code received by the browser using View | Source (in IE). The `<form>` section should look something like the following:

```
<form name="ctrl1" method="post" action="webform1.aspx" id="ctrl1">
    <input type="hidden" name="__VIEWSTATE"
           value="dDwtMzQ3NzI5OTM4Ozs+0RD39htoKLKMO7Yf4lcFXM2GjQU=" />
    <span  id="resultLabel"></span><br>
    <input type="submit" name="triggerButton" value="Click Me"
           id="triggerButton" />
</form>
```

The web-server controls have generated straight HTML, `<span>` and `<input>` for `<asp:Label>` and `<asp:Button>`, respectively. There is also a `<input type="hidden">` field with the name `__VIEWSTATE`. This encapsulates the state of the form as mentioned earlier. This information is used when the form is posted back to the server to recreate the UI, keeping track of changes etc. Note that the `<form>` element has been configured for this; it will post data back to `WebForm1.aspx` (specified in `action`) via an HTTP POST operation (specified in `method`). It has also been assigned the name `ctrl1` – when you look at the HTML generated by more complex web forms you'll see that this is a common type of assignment and is just down to the way ASP.NET works.

After clicking the button and seeing the text appear, check out the source HTML again (spacing added for clarity below):

```
<form name="ctrl1" method="post" action="WebForm1.aspx" id="ctrl1">
    <input type="hidden" name="__VIEWSTATE"
           value="dDwtMzQ3NzI5OTM4O3Q8O2w8MTwxPjs+O2w8dDw7bDwxPDE+Oz47bDx0
PHA8cDxsPFRleHQ7PjtsPEJ1dHRvbiBjbGlja2VkITs+Pjs+Ozs+Oz4+
Oz4+Oz6TChBE9Ywrgb7dL38o2VsGzc/RgA==" />
    <span  id="resultLabel">Button clicked!</span><br>
    <input type="submit" name="triggerButton" value="Click Me"
           id="triggerButton" />
</form>
```

This time the value of the viewstate contains more information, as the HTML result relies on more than the default output from the ASP.NET page. In complex forms this may be a very long string indeed, but we shouldn't complain, as so much is done for us behind the scenes, and we can almost forget about state management, keeping field values between posts, etc.

The Control Palette

In this section we'll take a quick look at the available controls before we put more of them together into a full, and more interesting, application. I'll divide this section up into web-server controls and validation controls. Note that I refer to 'properties' in the control descriptions – in all cases the corresponding attribute for use in ASP.NET code is identically named. I haven't attempted to provide a complete reference here, so I've missed out many properties etc. and only included the most frequently used ones.

Web-Server Controls

Web-server controls all inherit from System.Web.UI.WebControls.WebControl, which in turn inherits from System.Web.UI.Control. As such they have many common properties and events that we can use if required. There are quite a lot of these, so I won't attempt to cover them all here, just as with the properties and events of the web-server controls themselves.

Many of the frequently used inherited properties are those that deal with display style. This can be controlled simply, using properties such as ForeColor, BackColor, Font, and so on, but can also be controlled using CSS (Cascading Style Sheet) classes. This is achieved by setting the string property CssClass to the name of a CSS class in a separate file. Other notable properties include Width and Height to size a control, AccessKey and TabIndex to ease user interaction, and Enabled to set whether the control's functionality is activated in the web form.

Of the events, we are likely to use the inherited Load event most often, to perform initialization on a control, and PreRender, to perform last-minute modifications before HTML is output by the control.

There are plenty more events and properties for us to make use of, and we'll see many of these in more detail in our later chapter concerning *Custom Controls*.

The list of web-server controls is as follows:

Control	Description
Label	Simple text display, use the Text property to set and programmatically modify displayed text.
TextBox	Provides a textbox that users can edit. Use the Text property to access the entered data, and the TextChanged event to act on selection changes on postback. If automatic postback is required (as opposed to using a button etc.) set the AutoPostBack property to true.
DropDownList	Allows the user to select one of a list of choices, either by choosing it directly from a list or typing the first letter or two. Use the Items property to set the item list (this is a ListItemCollection class containing ListItem objects) and the SelectedItem and SelectedIndex properties to determine what is selected. The SelectedIndexChanged event can be used to determine whether the selection has changed, and this control also has an AutoPostBack property so that this selection change will trigger a postback operation.

Table continued on following page

Control	Description
ListBox	Allows the user to make one or more selections from a list. Set SelectionMode to Multiple or Single to set how many items may be selected at once and Rows to determine how many items to display. Other properties and events as for DropDownList.
Image	Displays an image. Use ImageUrl for the image reference, and AlternateText to provide text if the image fails to load.
AdRotator	Displays several images in succession, with a different one displayed after each server round trip. Use the AdvertisementFile property to specify the XML file describing the possible images (see MSDN for details) and the AdCreated event to perform processing before each image is sent back. Can also use the Target property to name a window to open when an image is clicked.
CheckBox	Displays a box that can be checked or unchecked. The state is stored in the Boolean property Checked, and the text associated with the checkbox in Text. The AutoPostBack property can be used to initiate automatic postback and the CheckedChanged event to act on changes.
CheckBoxList	Creates a group of checkboxes. Properties and events are identical to other list controls, such as DropDownList.
RadioButton	Displays a button that can be turned on or off. Generally these are grouped such that only one in the group can be active. Use the GroupName property to link RadioButton controls into a group. Other properties and events are as per CheckBox.
RadioButtonList	Creates a group of radio buttons where only one button in the group can be selected at a time. Properties and events are as other list controls.
Calendar	Allows the user to select a date from a graphical calendar display. This control has many style-related properties, but essential functionality can be achieved using the SelectedDate and VisibleDate properties (of type System.DateTime) to get access to the date selected by the user and the month to display (which will always contain VisibleDate). The key event to hook up to is SelectionChanged. Postback from this control is automatic.

Control	Description
Button	A standard button for the user to click. Use the Text property for text on the button, and the Click event to respond to clicks (server postback is automatic). Can also use the Command event to respond to ticks, which gives access to additional CommandName and CommandArgument properties on receipt.
LinkButton	Identical to Button, but displays button as a hyperlink.
ImageButton	Displays an image that doubles as a clickable button. Properties and events are inherited from Button and Image.
HyperLink	HTML hyperlink. Set the destination with NavigateUrl and the text to display with Text. You can also use ImageUrl to specify an image to display for the link and Target to specify the browser window to use. This control has no non-standard events, so use a LinkButton instead if additional processing is required when the link is followed.
Table	Specifies a table. Use this in conjunction with TableRow and TableCell at design time or programmatically assign rows using the Rows property, of type TableRowCollection. You can also use this property for run-time modifications. This control has several styling properties unique to tables, as do TableRow and TableCell.
TableRow	Specifies a row within a Table. The key property is Cells, which is a TableCellCollection class containing TableCell objects.
TableCell	Specifies an individual cell within a TableRow. Use Text to set the text to display, Wrap to determine whether to wrap text, and RowSpan and ColumnSpan to set how much of the table is covered by the cell.
Panel	A container for other controls. You can use HorizontalAlign and Wrap to specify how the contents are arranged.
Repeater	Used to output data from a data query, allowing great flexibility using templates. We'll look at this control in detail later in the chapter.
DataList	Similar to the Repeater control, but has more flexibility when it comes to arranging data and formatting. Can automatically render a table, which may be editable, for example. Again, this is a subject for later in the chapter.
DataGrid	Similar to Repeater and DataList with a few extra facilities, such as sorting. See later.

Validation Controls

Validation controls provide a method of validating user input without (in most cases) writing any code at all. Whenever postback is initiated each control checks the control it is validating and changes its `IsValid` property accordingly. If this property is `false` then the user input for the validated control has failed validation. The page containing all controls also has an `IsValid` property – if any of the validation controls has its version of this property set to `false` then this will be `false` also. We can check this property from our server-side code and act on it.

However, validation controls have a second function. Not only do they validate controls at run time, they can also output helpful hints to the user automatically. Simply setting the `ErrorMessage` property to the text you want means the user will see it when they attempt to post back invalid data.

The text stored in `ErrorMessage` may be output at the point where the validation control is located, or at a separate point, along with the messages from all other validation controls on a page. This latter behavior is achieved using the `ValidationSummary` control, which displays all error messages along with additional text as required.

On browsers that support it, these controls even generate client-side JavaScript functions to streamline their validation behavior. This means that in some cases postback won't even occur – as the validation controls can prevent this in certain circumstances and output error messages without needing to involve the server.

All validation controls inherit from `BaseValidator`, and so share several important properties. Perhaps the most important is the `ErrorMessage` property discussed above, in which case the `ControlToValidate` property must come a close second. This property specifies the ID of the control that is being validated. Another important property is `Display`, which determines whether to place text at the validation summary position (if set to `none`), or at the validator position. We also have the choice to make space for the error message even when it's not being displayed (set `Display` to `Static`) or to dynamically allocate space when required, which might shift page contents around slightly (set `Display` to `Dynamic`).

We'll look at an example shortly; first let's briefly describe the various validation controls.

Control	Description
RequiredFieldValidator	Used to check if the user has entered data in a control such as a `TextBox`.
CompareValidator	Used to check that data entered fulfils simple requirements, by use of an operator set using the `Operator` property and a `ValueToCompare` property to validate against. `Operator` may be one of `Equal`, `GreaterThan`, `GreaterThanEqual`, `LessThan`, `LessThanEqual`, `NotEqual`, and `DataTypeCheck`. The last of these simply compares the data type of `ValueToCompare` with the data in the control to be validated. `ValueToCompare` is a string property, but is interpreted as different data types based on its contents.

Control	Description
RangeValidator	Validates that data in the control to validate falls between MaximumValue and MinimumValue property values.
RegularExpressionValidator	Validates the contents of a field based on a regular expression stored in ValidationExpression. This can be useful for known sequences such as zip codes, phone numbers, IP numbers, etc.
CustomValidator	Used to validate data in a control using a custom function. ClientValidationFunction is used to specify a *client-side* function used to validate a control (which means, unfortunately, that we can't use C#). This function should return a Boolean value indicating whether validation was successful. Alternatively, we can use the ServerValidate event to specify a server-side function to use for validation. This function is a bool type event handler that receives a string containing the data to validate instead of an EventArgs parameter. We return true if validation succeeds, otherwise false.

Server Control Example

Now we've seen what's available to us, and played with a simple example, it's time to look at a more involved scenario. Here we will create the framework for a web application, a meeting room booking tool. For now this will just include the front end and simple event processing; later we will extend this with ADO.NET and data binding to include server-side business logic.

The web form we are going to create will contain fields for user name, event name, meeting room, and attendees, along with a calendar to select a date (I'm assuming for the purposes of this example that the events last for entire days). We will include validation controls for all fields except the calendar, which we will validate on the server side, and provide a default date in case none has been entered.

For UI testing we will also have a Label control on the form that we can use to display submission results.

To kick things off, create a new web application project in Visual Studio, named **PCSWebApp2**. Next we design the form, which is generated using the following code in WebForm1.aspx (with auto-generated code not highlighted):

```
<%@ Page language="c#" Codebehind="WebForm1.aspx.cs" AutoEventWireup="false"
        Inherits="PCSWebApp2.WebForm1" %>

<html>
    <head>
        <meta content=False name=vs_showGrid>
        <meta content="Internet Explorer 5.0" name=vs_targetSchema>
        <meta content="Microsoft Visual Studio 7.0" name=GENERATOR>
        <meta content=C# name=CODE_LANGUAGE>
    </head>
```

```
<body>
    <form method="post" runat="server">
        <h1 align="center">
            Enter details and set a day to initiate an event.
        </h1>
        <br>
        <table borderColor="#000000" cellSpacing="0" cellPadding="8"
                rules="none" align="center" bgColor="#fff99e" border="2"
                width="540">
        <tr>
            <td vAlign="top">Your Name:</td>
            <td vAlign="top">
                <asp:textbox id="nameBox" runat="server" width="160px"/>
                <asp:requiredfieldvalidator id=validateName
                        Runat="server"
                        errormessage="You must enter a name."
                        ControlToValidate="nameBox" display="None"/>
            </td>
            <td vAlign="center" rowSpan="4">
                <asp:calendar id="calendar" runat="server"
                        BackColor="White"/>
            </td>
        </tr>
        <tr>
            <td vAlign="top">Event Name:</td>
            <td vAlign="top">
                <asp:textbox id="eventBox" runat="server" width="160px"/>
                <asp:requiredfieldvalidator id="validateEvent"
                        Runat="server"
                        errormessage="You must enter an event name."
                        ControlToValidate="eventBox" display="None"/>
            </td>
        </tr>
        <tr>
            <td vAlign="top">Meeting Room:</td>
            <td vAlign="top">
                <asp:dropdownlist id="roomList" runat="server" width="160px">
                    <asp:ListItem Value="1">The Happy Room</asp:ListItem>
                    <asp:ListItem Value="2">The Angry Room</asp:ListItem>
                    <asp:ListItem Value="3">The Depressing Room</asp:ListItem>
                    <asp:ListItem Value="4">The Funked Out Room</asp:ListItem>
                </asp:dropdownlist>
                <asp:requiredfieldvalidator id="validateRoom" Runat="server"
                        errormessage="You must select a room."
                        ControlToValidate="roomList" display="None"/>
            </td>
        </tr>
        <tr>
            <td vAlign="top">Attendees:</td>
            <td vAlign="top">
                <asp:listbox id="attendeeList" runat="server"
                        width="160px"
                        selectionmode="Multiple" rows="6">
                    <asp:ListItem Value="1">Bill Gates</asp:ListItem>
                    <asp:ListItem Value="2">Monika Lewinsky</asp:ListItem>
```

```
                            <asp:ListItem Value="3">Vincent Price</asp:ListItem>
                            <asp:ListItem Value="4">Vlad the Impaler</asp:ListItem>
                            <asp:ListItem Value="5">Iggy Pop</asp:ListItem>
                            <asp:ListItem Value="6">William
                                              Shakespeare</asp:ListItem>
                        </asp:listbox>
                        <asp:requiredfieldvalidator id="validateAttendees"
                                Runat="server"
                                errormessage="You must have at least one attendee."
                                ControlToValidate="attendeeList" display="None"/>
                    </td>
                </tr>
                <tr>
                    <td align="middle" colSpan="3">
                        <asp:button id="submitButton" runat="server" width="100%"
                                    Text="Submit meeting room request"/>
                    </td>
                </tr>
                <tr>
                    <td align="middle" colSpan="3">
                        <asp:validationsummary id="validationSummary"
                                Runat="server"
                                headertext="Before submitting your request:"/>
                    </td>
                </tr>
            </table>
            <br>
            Results:
            <asp:Label Runat="server" ID="resultLabel" Text="None."/>
        </form>
    </body>
</html>
```

After the title of the page, which is written out enclosed in HTML <h1> tags to get large, title-style text, the main body of the form is enclosed in an HTML <table>. We could use a web server control table, but this introduces unnecessary complexity as we are using a table purely for formatting the display, not to be a dynamic UI element. The table is divided up into three columns, the first holding simple text labels, the second holding UI fields corresponding to the text labels (along with validation controls for these), and the third containing a calendar control for date selection, which spans four rows. The fifth row contains a submission button spanning all columns, and the sixth row contains a ValidationSummary control to display error messages when required (all the other validation controls have display="none" as they will use this summary for display). Beneath the table is a simple label that we can use to display results for now, before we add database access later.

Most of the ASP.NET code in this file is remarkably simple, and much can be learned simply by reading through it. Of particular note in the code is the way in which list items are attached to the controls for selecting a meeting room and multiple attendees for the event:

```
        <asp:dropdownlist id="roomList" runat="server"
                        width="160px">
            <asp:ListItem Value="1">The Happy Room</asp:ListItem>
            <asp:ListItem Value="2">The Angry Room</asp:ListItem>
            <asp:ListItem Value="3">The Depressing
                            Room</asp:ListItem>
```

```
                    <asp:ListItem Value="4">The Funked Out
                                        Room</asp:ListItem>
        </asp:dropdownlist>

        ...

        <asp:listbox id="attendeeList" runat="server"
                    width="160px"
                    selectionmode="Multiple" rows="6">
            <asp:ListItem Value="1">Bill Gates</asp:ListItem>
            <asp:ListItem Value="2">Monika Lewinsky</asp:ListItem>
            <asp:ListItem Value="3">Vincent Price</asp:ListItem>
            <asp:ListItem Value="4">Vlad the Impaler</asp:ListItem>
            <asp:ListItem Value="5">Iggy Pop</asp:ListItem>
            <asp:ListItem Value="6">William
                                Shakespeare</asp:ListItem>
        </asp:listbox>
```

Here we are associating `ListItem` objects with the two web-server controls. These objects are not web-server controls in their own right, which is why we don't need to use `runat="server"` on them. When the page is processed the `<asp:ListItem>` entries are used to create `ListItem` objects, which are added to the `Items` collection of their parent list control. This makes it easier for us to initialize lists than having to write code for this ourselves (we'd have to create a `ListItemCollection` object, add `ListItem` objects, and then pass the collection to the list control). Of course, we can still do all of this programmatically if preferred.

In design view the form we have created looks like this:

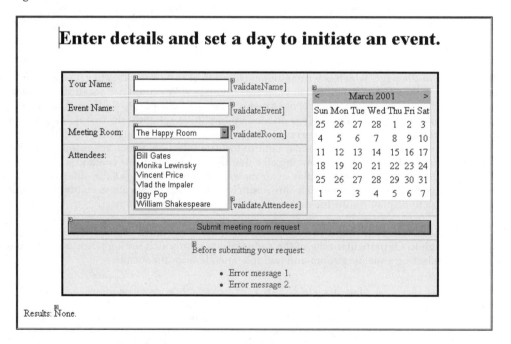

790

This is a fully functioning UI, which maintains its own state between server requests, and validates user input. Considering the brevity of the above code this is quite something. In fact, it leaves us very little to do, at least for this example; we just have to wire up the button click event for the submission button.

Actually, that's not quite true. So far we have no validation for the calendar control. Still, this is simple as it is impossible to clear the selection in this control, so all we have to do is give it an initial value. We can do this in the `Page_Load()` event handler for our page:

```
private void Page_Load(object sender, System.EventArgs e)
{
    if (!this.IsPostBack)
    {
        calendar.SelectedDate = System.DateTime.Now;
    }
}
```

Here we just select today's date as a starting point. Note that we first check to see if `Page_Load()` is being called as the result of a postback operation by checking the `IsPostBack` property of the page. If a postback is in progress this property will be `true` and we leave the selected date alone (we don't want to lose the user's selection, after all).

To add the button click handler simply double-click on the button and add the following code:

```
protected void submitButton_Click(object sender, System.EventArgs e)
{
    if (this.IsValid)
    {
        resultLabel.Text = roomList.SelectedItem.Text +
                           " has been booked on " +
                           calendar.SelectedDate.ToLongDateString() +
                           " by " + nameBox.Text + " for "
                           + eventBox.Text + " event. ";
        foreach (ListItem attendee in attendeeList.Items)
        {
            if (attendee.Selected)
            {
                resultLabel.Text += attendee.Text + ", ";
            }
        }
        resultLabel.Text += " and " + nameBox.Text
                          + " will be attending.";
    }
}
```

Here we just set the `resultLabel` control `Text` property to a result string, which will then appear below the main table. In IE the result of such a submission might look something like the following:

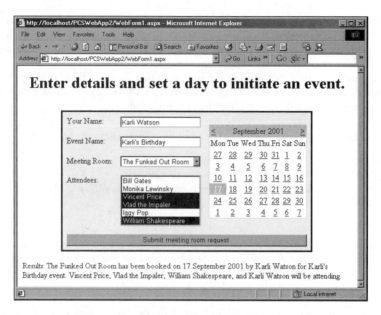

unless there are errors, in which case the ValidationSummary will activate instead:

Enabling Non-Validating Postback

If you play around with this example for a while you may notice that the validation summary appears if you change the date before entering any other data. This is an example of something that is likely to annoy the user, who will immediately think: "I will enter that data if you give me a chance!" To get round this we can disable the validation summary (using its Enabled property) unless the submission button is pressed. However, this leads to another problem. Validation controls are capable of preventing postback occurring, for example when the submit button is clicked, and dynamically filling the

validation summary on the client without a server round trip. If we disable the summary in
Page_Load() and enable it in the event handler for the button click then the validation summary will
never be displayed on browsers that support client-side validation (such as IE), as only enabled
summaries will intercept postback requests.

What we have to do, then, is disable all validation controls by default, then re-enable these controls in
the button click handler and force them to validate before we check the form IsValid property.

The required code changes to do all this are as follows. In Page_Load() we disable *all* validation
controls. We can use the Validators collection of the form to help us here; it contains all validators
on the page, so we can iterate through them:

```
private void Page_Load(object sender, System.EventArgs e)
{
    validationSummary.Enabled = false;
    foreach (System.Web.UI.WebControls.WebControl validator in
            this.Validators)
    {
        validator.Enabled = false;
    }
    ...
}
```

In submitButton_Click() we enable all validation controls except the summary straight away, cause
them to validate their allotted controls by calling the form Validate() method, and then check the
IsValid property as before. We also add an else clause to this check, which re-enables the validation
summary if IsValid is found to be false. This will give feedback to the user if and only if controls
have invalid data and the submit button is clicked.

```
protected void submitButton_Click(object sender, System.EventArgs e)
{
    foreach (System.Web.UI.WebControls.WebControl validator in
            this.Validators)
    {
        validator.Enabled = true;
    }
    this.Validate();
    if (this.IsValid)
    {
        ...
    }
    else
    {
        validationSummary.Enabled = true;
    }
}
```

This does effectively disable client-side validation, but is definitely worth doing due to the additional
usability it provides.

ADO.NET and Data Binding

The web form application we created in the last section is perfectly functional, but only contains static data. In addition, the event booking process does not include persisting event data. In order to solve both of these problems we can make use of ADO.NET to access data stored in a database, such that we can store and retrieve event data along with the lists of rooms and attendees.

Data binding makes the process of retrieving data even easier. Controls such as listboxes (and some of the more specialized controls we'll look at a bit later) come enabled for this technique. They can be bound to any object that exposes an `IEnumerable`, `ICollection`, or `IListSource` interface, which includes `DataTable` objects.

In this section we will start by updating our event booking application to be data-aware, and then move on to take a look at some of the other things we can do with data binding, using some of the other data-aware web controls.

Updating the Event Booking Application

To keep things separate from the last example, create a new web application called `PCSWebApp3` and copy the code across from the `PCSWebApp2` application created earlier. Before we start on our new code, let's look at the database we will be accessing.

The Database

For the purposes of this example I will use a Microsoft Access database called `PCSWebApp3 .mdb`, which may be found along with the downloadable code for this book. For an enterprise-scale application it would make more sense to use a SQL Server database, but the techniques involved are practically identical and Access makes life a bit easier for testing. I will point out the differences in code as they occur.

The database provided contains three tables:

❑   `Attendees`, containing a list of possible event attendees

❑   `Rooms`, containing a list of possible rooms for events

❑   `Events`, containing a list of booked events

Attendees

The `Attendees` table contains the following columns:

Column	Type	Notes
ID	AutoNumber, primary key	Attendee identification number
Name	Text, required, 50 chars	Name of attendee
Email	Text, optional, 50 chars	E-mail address of attendee

The supplied database includes entries for 20 attendees, all of whom have (made up) e-mail addresses. It is envisioned that in a more developed application e-mails could automatically be sent to attendees when a booking is made, but this is left to the reader as an optional exercise using techniques found elsewhere in this book.

Rooms

The `Rooms` table contains the following columns:

Column	Type	Notes
ID	AutoNumber, primary key	Room identification number
Room	Text, required, 50 chars	Name of room

20 records are supplied in the database.

Events

The `Events` table contains the following columns:

Column	Type	Notes
ID	AutoNumber, primary key	Event identification number
Name	Text, required, 255 chars	Name of event
Room	Number, required	ID of room for event
AttendeeList	Memo, required	List of attendee names
EventData	Date/Time, require	Date of event

A few events are supplied in the downloadable database.

Binding to the Database

The two controls we'd like to bind to data are `attendeeList` and `roomList`. To do this we have to set the `DataSource` properties of these controls to tables containing our data. Our code must load data into these tables and perform this binding at run time. Both of these controls also have `DataTextField` and `DataValueField` properties that specify what columns to use for displaying list items and setting `value` properties, respectively. In both cases we can set these properties at design time, to `Name` and `ID`, which will be used as soon as the `DataSource` property is set to populate the list items in the control.

We can do this now in the web form designer. Also, remove the existing entries from the ASP.NET code for these controls such that the declarations read as follows:

```
...
<asp:dropdownlist id="roomList" runat="server" width="160px"
                  datatextfield="Room" datavaluefield="ID" />
...
<asp:listbox id="attendeeList" runat="server" width="160px"
             selectionmode="Multiple" rows="6"
             datatextfield="Name"
             datavaluefield="ID" />
...
```

The next task is to create a connection to the database. There are several ways to do this, as we saw in the *Data Access with .NET* chapter earlier, I used the **Server Explorer** window to create a new connection. As we are using Access the provider type for this connection is **Microsoft Jet 4.0 OLE DB**

Provider. Once this is set up in the server window we can drag the connection onto our web form, which will add a `Data.OleDb.OleDbConnection` object to our form called `oleDbConnection1`:

```
public class WebForm1 : System.Web.UI.Page
    {
    ...
        protected System.Data.OleDb.OleDbConnection oleDbConnection1;
```

For a SQL Server connection the object added would be a `SqlClient.SqlConnection` object.

Code will also be added to `InitializeComponent()` to set the `ConnectionString` property of `oleDbConnection1` so it is all ready for us to use in our code.

We want to perform our data binding in the `Page_Load()` event handler, such that the controls are fully populated when we want to use them in other parts of our code. We will read data from the database regardless of whether a postback operation is in progress (even though the list controls will persist their contents via the viewstate) to ensure that we have access to all the data we might need, although we don't need to perform the data binding itself in a postback. This might seem slightly wasteful, but I will again leave it as an exercise to the reader to add additional logic to the code to optimize this behavior. Here we are concentrating on how to get things working, without going into practical details like this.

All of our code will be placed in between calling the `Open()` and `Close()` methods of our connection object:

```
private void Page_Load(object sender, System.EventArgs e)
{
    validationSummary.Enabled = false;
    foreach (System.Web.UI.WebControls.WebControl validator in
            this.Validators)
    {
        validator.Enabled = false;
    }
    oleDbConnection1.Open();
    if (!this.IsPostBack)
    {
        calendar.SelectedDate = System.DateTime.Now;
    }
    oleDbConnection1.Close();
}
```

We'll see why the calendar date setting is left inside this postback-checking code shortly.

For our data exchange we need to use several objects to store our data in. We can declare these at the class level such that we have access to them from other functions. We need a `DataSet` object to store the database information, three `OleDb.OleDbDataAdapter` objects to execute queries on the dataset, and a `DataTable` object to store our events for later access. These are declared as folows:

```
public class WebForm1 : System.Web.UI.Page
    {
```

```
        ...
        protected System.Data.DataSet ds;
        protected System.Data.DataTable eventTable;
        protected System.Data.OleDb.OleDbDataAdapter daAttendees;
        protected System.Data.OleDb.OleDbDataAdapter daRooms;
        protected System.Data.OleDb.OleDbDataAdapter daEvents;
```

SQL Server versions of all the OLE DB objects exist, and their usage is identical.

`Page_Load()` now needs to create the `DataSet` object:

```
        private void Page_Load(object sender, System.EventArgs e)
        {
            ...
            oleDbConnection1.Open();
            ds = new DataSet();
```

Then we must assign the `OleDbDataAdapter` objects with queries and a link to the connection object:

```
        ds = new DataSet();
        daAttendees = new System.Data.OleDb.OleDbDataAdapter(
                    "SELECT * FROM Attendees", oleDbConnection1);
        daRooms = new System.Data.OleDb.OleDbDataAdapter(
                    "SELECT * FROM Rooms", oleDbConnection1);
        daEvents = new System.Data.OleDb.OleDbDataAdapter(
                    "SELECT * FROM Events", oleDbConnection1);
```

Next we execute the queries using calls to `Fill()`:

```
        daEvents = new System.Data.OleDb.OleDbDataAdapter(
                    "SELECT * FROM Events", oleDbConnection1);
        daAttendees.Fill(ds, "Attendees");
        daRooms.Fill(ds, "Rooms");
        daEvents.Fill(ds, "Events");
```

Now we come to the data binding itself. As mentioned earlier, this simply involves setting the `DataSource` property on our bound controls to the tables we want to bind to:

```
        daEvents.Fill(ds, "Events");
        attendeeList.DataSource = ds.Tables["Attendees"];
        roomList.DataSource = ds.Tables["Rooms"];
```

This sets the properties, but data binding itself won't occur until we call the `DataBind()` method of the form, which we'll do in a moment. Before we do this we'll populate the `DataTable` object with the event table data:

```
        roomList.DataSource = ds.Tables["Rooms"];
        eventTable = ds.Tables["Events"];
```

We will only data bind if a postback is not in progress; otherwise, we will simply be refreshing data (which we're assuming is static in the database for the duration of an event booking request). Data binding in a postback would also wipe the selections in the `roomList` and `attendeeList` controls. We could make a note of these before binding and then renew them, but it is simpler to call `DataBind()` in our existing `if` statement (the reason why this statement was kept in the region of code where the data connection was open):

```
eventTable = ds.Tables["Events"];
if (!this.IsPostBack)
{
    calendar.SelectedDate = System.DateTime.Now;
    this.DataBind();
}
oleDbConnection1.Close();
}
```

Running the application now will result in the full attendee and room data being available from our data bound controls.

Customizing the Calendar Control

Before we discuss adding events to the database let's make a modification to our calendar display. It would be nice to display any day where a booking has previously been made in a different color, and prevent such days from being selectable. This requires modifications to the way we set dates in the calendar, and the way day cells are displayed.

We'll start with date selection. There are three places where we need to check for dates where events are booked and modify selection accordingly: when we set the initial date in `Page_Load()`, when the user attempts to select a date from the calendar, and when an event is booked and we wish to set a new date to prevent the user booking two events on the same day in succession before selecting a new date. As this is going to be a common feature we may as well create a private method to perform this calculation. This method should accept a trial date as a parameter and return the date to use, which will either be the same date as the trial date, or the next available day after the trial date.

The code to do this, `getFreeDate()`, is shown below:

```
private System.DateTime getFreeDate(System.DateTime trialDate)
{
    if (eventTable.Rows.Count > 0)
    {
        System.DateTime testDate;
        bool trialDateOK = false;
        while (!trialDateOK)
        {
            trialDateOK = true;
            foreach (System.Data.DataRow testRow in eventTable.Rows)
            {
                testDate = (System.DateTime)testRow["EventDate"];
                if (testDate.Date == trialDate.Date)
                {
                    trialDateOK = false;
                    trialDate = trialDate.AddDays(1);
                }
            }
        }
```

```
            }
        }
        return trialDate;
    }
```

This simple code uses the `eventTable` object that we populated in `Page_Load()` to extract event data. First we check for the trivial case where no events have been booked, in which case we can just confirm the trial date by returning it. Next we iterate through the dates in the `Event` table comparing them with the trial date. If we find a match we add one day to the trial date and perform another search.

Extracting the date from the `DataTable` is remarkably simple:

```
            testDate = (System.DateTime)testRow["EventDate"];
```

Casting the column data into `Sytem.DateTime` works fine.

The first place we will use `getFreeDate()`, then, is back in `Page_Load()`. This simply means making a minor modification to the code that sets the calendar `SeletedDate` property:

```
            if (!this.IsPostBack)
            {
                System.DateTime trialDate = System.DateTime.Now;
                calendar.SelectedDate = getFreeDate(trialDate);
                this.DataBind();
            }
```

Next we need to respond to date selection on the calendar. To do this we simply need to add an event handler for the `SelectionChanged` event of the calendar, and force the date to be checked against those of existing events:

```
            protected void calendar_SelectionChanged(object sender,
                                                     System.EventArgs e)
            {
                System.DateTime trialDate = calendar.SelectedDate;
                calendar.SelectedDate = getFreeDate(trialDate);
            }
```

The code here is identical to that in `Page_Load()`.

The third place that we must perform this check is in response to the booking button being pressed. We'll come back to this in a little while, as we have many changes to make there.

Next we want to color the day cells of the calendar to signify existing events. To do this we need to add an event handler for the `DayRender` event of the calendar object. This event is raised each time an individual day is being rendered, and gives us access to the cell object being displayed and the date of this cell through the `Cell` and `Date` properties of the `DayRenderEventArgs` parameter we receive in the handler function. We simply need to compare the date of the cell being rendered to the dates in our `eventTable` object, and color the cell using the `Cell.BackColor` property if there is a match:

```
                protected void calendar_DayRender(object sender,
                        System.Web.UI.WebControls.DayRenderEventArgs e)
        {
            if (eventTable.Rows.Count > 0)
            {
            System.DateTime testDate;
            foreach (System.Data.DataRow testRow in eventTable.Rows)
                {
                    testDate = (System.DateTime)testRow["EventDate"];
                    if (testDate.Date == e.Day.Date)
                    {
                        e.Cell.BackColor = Color.Red;
                    }
                }
            }
        }
```

Here we are using red, which will give us a display along the lines of:

Here the 15th, 27th, 28th, 29th, and 30th of March all contain events, and the user has selected the 17th. With the addition of the date-selection logic it is now impossible to select a day that is shown in red; if an attempt is made then a later date is selected instead. For example, clicking on the 28th of March on the calendar shown above will result in the 31st being selected.

Adding Events to the Database

The submitButton_Click() event handler currently assembles a string from the event characteristics and displays it in the reulstLabel control. To add an event to the database we simply need to reformat the string created into a SQL INSERT query and execute it.

Much of the following code will therefore look familiar:

```
        protected void submitButton_Click(object sender, System.EventArgs e)
        {
            foreach (System.Web.UI.WebControls.WebControl validator in
                    this.Validators)
            {
                validator.Enabled = true;
```

```
    }
    this.Validate();
    if (this.IsValid)
    {
        String attendees = "";
        foreach (ListItem attendee in attendeeList.Items)
        {
            if (attendee.Selected)
            {
                attendees += attendee.Text + " (" + attendee.Value + "), ";
            }
        }
        attendees += " and " + nameBox.Text;
        String dateString =
                calendar.SelectedDate.Date.Date.ToShortDateString();
        String oleDbCommand = "INSERT INTO Events (Name, Room, " +
                        "AttendeeList, EventDate) VALUES ('" +
                        eventBox.Text + "', '" +
                        roomList.SelectedItem.Value + "', '" +
                        attendees + "', '" + dateString + "')";
```

Once we have created our SQL query string we can use it to build an `OleDb.OleDbCommand` object:

```
System.Data.OleDb.OleDbCommand insertCommand =
    new System.Data.OleDb.OleDbCommand(oleDbCommand,
                                       oleDbConnection1);
```

Next we reopen the connection that was closed in `Page_Load()` (again, this is perhaps not the most efficient way of doing things, but it works fine for demonstration purposes) and execute the query:

```
oleDbConnection1.Open();
int queryResult = insertCommand.ExecuteNonQuery();
```

`ExecuteNonQuery()` returns an integer representing how many table rows were affected by the query. If this is equal to 1 then we know that our insertion was successful. If so then we put a success message in `resultLabel`, execute a new query to repopulate `eventTable` and our dataset with our new list of events (we clear the dataset first, otherwise events will be duplicated), and change the calendar selection to a new, free, date:

```
if (queryResult == 1)
{
    resultLabel.Text = "Event Added.";
    daEvents = new System.Data.OleDb.OleDbDataAdapter(
                "SELECT * FROM Events", oleDbConnection1);
    ds.Clear();
    daEvents.Fill(ds, "Events");
    eventTable = ds.Tables["Events"];
    calendar.SelectedDate =
                getFreeDate(calendar.SelectedDate.AddDays(1));
}
```

If `ExecuteNonQuery()` returns a number other than 1 we know that there has been a problem. For this example we won't worry about this, and simply display a failure notification in `resultLabel`:

```
        else
        {
            resultLabel.Text = "Event not added due to DB access "
                                + "problem.";
        }
```

Finally, we close the connection again:

```
            oleDbConnection1.Close();
        }
        else
        {
            validationSummary.Enabled = true;
        }
    }
```

and our data-aware version of the event booking application is complete.

> *Note that due to the syntax of the SQL INSERT query we must avoid using certain characters in the event name, such as apostrophes "'", as they will cause an error. It would be relatively easy to enforce a custom validation rule that prevented the user from using such characters, or to perform some type of character escaping before inserting data and after reading data, but the code for this will not be covered here.*

More on Data Binding

When we looked at the available Server Controls earlier in this chapter we saw three that dealt with data display: `DataGrid`, `Repeater`, and `DataList`. These are all extremely useful when it comes to outputting data to a web page, as they perform many tasks automatically that would otherwise require a fair amount of coding.

To start with, let's look at the simplest of these to use, `DataGrid`. As a simple example of this control let's add an event-detail display to the bottom of the display of `PCSWebApp3`. This enables us to ignore database connections as this is already set up for this application.

Add the following to the bottom of `PCSWebApp3.aspx`:

```
            <br>Results:
            <asp:label id=resultLabel Runat="server"
                        Text="None.">None.</asp:label>
            <br>
            <br>
            <asp:DataGrid Runat="server" ID="eventDetails1" />
            </form>
        </body>
    </HTML>
```

And the following to `Page_Load()` in `PCSWebApp3.aspx.cs`:

```
        attendeeList.DataSource = ds.Tables["Attendees"];
        roomList.DataSource = ds.Tables["Rooms"];
        eventTable = ds.Tables["Events"];
        eventDetails1.DataSource = eventTable;
        if (!this.IsPostBack)
        {
            calendar.SelectedDate = System.DateTime.Now;
            this.DataBind();
        }
        else
        {
            eventDetails1.DataBind();
        }
        oleDbConnection1.Close();
    }
```

Note that the event list may have changed between requests if another user has added an event, so we need to call DataBind() on the DataGrid to reflect these changes. Remember that calling DataBind() on the whole form will result in room and attendee selections being lost, so this is a fair compromise.

If you load the application in your web browser again you should see a list underneath the booking details section containing the full list of events:

ID	Name	Room	AttendeeList	EventDate
1	My Birthday	4	Iggy Pop (5), Sean Connery (7), Albert Einstein (10), George Clooney (14), Jules Verne (18), Robin Hood (20), and Karli Watson	17.09.2001 00:00:00
2	Dinner	1	Bill Gates (1), Monika Lewinsky (2), and Bruce Lee	05.08.2001 00:00:00
5	Discussion of darkness	6	Vlad the Impaler (4), Darth Vader and Beelzebub	29.10.2001 00:00:00
6	Christmas with Pals	9	Dr Frank N Furter (11), Bobby Davro (15), John F Kennedy (16), Stephen King (19), and Karli Watson	25.12.2001 00:00:00
7	Escape	17	Monika Lewinsky (2), Stephen King (19), and Spartacus	10.05.2001 00:00:00
8	Planetary Conquest	14	Bill Gates (1), Albert Einstein (10), Dr Frank N Furter (11), Bobby Davro (15), and Darth Vader	15.06.2001 00:00:00
9	Homecoming Celebration	7	William Shakespeare (6), Christopher Columbus (12), Robin Hood (20), and Ulysses	22.06.2001 00:00:00
10	Dalek Reunion Ball	12	Roger Moore (8), George Clooney (14), Bobby Davro (15), and Davros	12.06.2001 00:00:00
11	Romantic meal for two	13	George Clooney (14), and Donna Watson	29.03.2001 00:00:00

We can also make one further modification in `submitButton_Click()` to ensure that this data is updated when new records are added:

```
if (queryResult == 1)
{
    resultLabel.Text = "Event Added.";
    daEvents = new System.Data.OleDb.OleDbDataAdapter(
                    "SELECT * FROM Events", oleDbConnection1);
    ds.Clear();
    daEvents.Fill(ds, "Events");
    eventTable = ds.Tables["Events"];
    calendar.SelectedDate =
                    getFreeDate(calendar.SelectedDate.AddDays(1));
    eventDetails1.DataBind();
}
```

Note that we call `DataBind()` on the `DataGrid`, not on this. This prevents all data bound controls from being refreshed, which would be unnecessary. All data-bindble controls support this method, which is normally called by the form if we call the top-level (this) `DataBind()` method.

As you might expect, the `DataGrid` control contains many properties that we can use to format the displayed data in a more user-friendly way, but I'll leave these for you to discover.

Data Display with Templates

The other two data displaying controls, `Repeater` and `DataList`, require you to use templates to format data for display. Templates, in an ASP.NET sense, are parameterized sections of HTML that are used as elements of output in certain controls. They enable us to customize exactly how data is output to the browser, and can result in professional-looking displays without too much effort.

There are several templates available to customize various aspects of list behavior, but the one template that is essential for both `Repeater` and `DataList` is `<ItemTemplate>`, which is used in the display of each data item. We declare this template (and all the others) inside the control declaration, for example:

```
<asp:DataList Runat="server" ... >
    <ItemTemplate>
        ...
    </ItemTemplate>
</asp:DataList>
```

Within template declarations we will normally want to output sections of HTML along with parameters from the data bound to the control. There is a special syntax that we can use to output such parameters:

```
<%# expression %>
```

`expression` might be simply an expression binding the parameter to a page or control property, but is more likely to consist of a `DataBinder.Eval()` expression. This useful function can be used to output data from a table bound to a control simply by specifying the column, using the following syntax:

```
<%# DataBinder.Eval(Container.DataItem, "ColumnName") %>
```

There is also an optional third parameter that allows us to format the data returned, which has identical syntax to string formatting expressions used elsewhere.

The full list of available templates and when they are used is shown below:

Template	Description
`<ItemTemplate>`	Template to use for list items
`<HeaderTemplate>`	Template to use for output before the list
`<FooterTemplate>`	Template to use for output after the list
`<SeparatorTemplate>`	Template for use between items in list
`<AlternatingItemTemplate>`	Template for alternate items; can aid visibility
`<SelectedItemTemplate>`	(DataList only) Template to use for selected items in the list
`<EditItemTemplate>`	(DataList only) Template to use for items in a list that are being edited

Again, the easiest way to look at this is with an example, and we can use our existing data query in PCSWebApp3 to achieve this.

Example

We'll extend the table at the top of the page to contain a `DataList` displaying each of the events stored in the database. We'll make these events selectable such that details of any event can be displayed by clicking on its name.

The changes to the code in PCSWebApp3 are shown below:

```
<tr>
   <td align=middle colSpan=3>
      <asp:validationsummary id=validationSummary Runat="server"
                headertext="Before submitting your request:"/>
   </td>
</tr>
<tr>
   <td align=left colSpan=3 width="100%">
      <table cellspacing=4>
         <tr>
            <td width="40%" bgcolor="#ccffcc" >
               <asp:DataList Runat="server" ID="eventDetails2"
                       OnSelectedIndexChanged=
                       "eventDetails2_SelectedIndexChanged">
                  <ItemTemplate>
                     <asp:LinkButton Runat="server"
                                CommandName="Select"
                                forecolor="#0000ff"
                                ID="Linkbutton1">
                        <%# DataBinder.Eval(Container.DataItem,
                                   "Name")%>
                     </asp:LinkButton>
```

```
                              <br>
                          </ItemTemplate>
                          <SelectedItemTemplate>
                              <b><%# DataBinder.Eval(Container.DataItem,
                                                "Name") %></b>
                              <br>
                          </SelectedItemTemplate>
                      </asp:DataList>
                  </td>
                  <td valign="top">
                      <asp:Label Runat="server" ID="edName"
                                  Font-Name="Arial" Font-Bold="True"
                                  Font-Italic="True" Font-Size="14">
                          Select an event to view details.
                      </asp:Label>
                      <br>
                      <asp:Label Runat="server" ID="edDate"/>
                      <br>
                      <asp:Label Runat="server" ID="edRoom"/>
                      <br>
                      <asp:Label Runat="server" ID="edAttendees"/>
                  </td>
              </tr>
          </table>
      </td>
  </tr>
</table>
```

Here we have added a new table row containing a table with a `DataList` in one column and a detail view in the other. The detail view is simply four labels for event properties, one of which contains the text "Select an event to view details." when no event is selected (the situation when the form is first loaded).

The `DataList` uses `<ItemTemplate>` and `<SelectedItemTemplate>` to display event details. To facilitate selection we raise a `Select` command from the event name link rendered in `<ItemTemplate>`, which automatically changes the selection. We also use the `OnSelectedIndexChanged` event, triggered when the `Select` command changes the selection, to populate the event detail labels. The event handler for this is shown below. (Note that we need to `DataBind()` first to update the selection.)

```
protected void eventDetails2_SelectedIndexChanged(object sender,
                                              System.EventArgs e)
{
    eventDetails2.DataBind();
    DataRow selectedEventRow =
            eventTable.Rows[eventDetails2.SelectedIndex];
    edName.Text = (string)selectedEventRow["Name"];
    edDate.Text = "<b>Date:</b> " +
        ((DateTime)selectedEventRow["EventDate"]).ToLongDateString();
    edAttendees.Text = "<b>Attendees:</b> " +
        (string)selectedEventRow["AttendeeList"];
    DataRow selectedEventRoomRow =
        ds.Tables["Rooms"].Rows[(int)selectedEventRow["Room"] - 1];
    edRoom.Text = "<b>Room:</b> " + selectedEventRoomRow["Room"];
}
```

This uses data in `ds` and `eventTable` to populate the details.

As with the `DataGrid` we used earlier, we need to set the data for `eventDetails2` and bind in `Page_Load()`:

```
eventDetails1.DataSource = eventTable;
eventDetails2.DataSource = eventTable;
...
    eventDetails1.DataBind();
    eventDetails2.DataBind();
```

and re-bind in `submitButton_Click()`:

```
eventDetails1.DataBind();
eventDetails2.DataBind();
```

Now event details are available in the table:

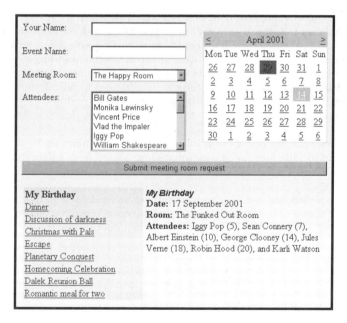

There is *much* more that we can do with templates and data bound controls in general, enough in fact to fill a whole book. However, this should be enough to get you started with your experimentation.

Application Configuration

One thing that has been alluded to throughout this chapter, but without any details being supplied, is the existence of a conceptual application containing web pages and configuration settings. This is an important concept to grasp, especially when configuring your web sites for multiple concurrent users.

A few notes on terminology and application lifetime are necessary here.

An **application** is defined as all files in your project configured by web.config files. An Application object is created when an application is started for the first time, which will be when the first HTTP request arrives. Also at this time the Application_Start event is triggered, the event handler for which can be detailed in global.asax (along with handlers for all other events discussed here), and a pool of HttpApplication instances is created. Each incoming request receives one of these instances, which performs request processing. Note that this means HttpApplication objects do not need to cope with concurrent access, unlike the global Application object. When all HttpApplication instances finish their work the Application_End event fires and the application terminates, destroying the Application object.

When an individual user uses the web application a **session** is started. Similar to the application, this involves the creation of a user-specific Session object, along with the triggering of a Session_Start event. Within a session individual **requests** trigger Application_BeginRequest and Application_EndRequest events. These may occur several times over the scope of a session as different resources within the application are accessed. Individual sessions may be terminated manually, or will time out if no further requests are received. Session termination triggers a Session_End event and the destruction of the Session object.

With this process in mind, then, how does this help us? Well, there are several things we can do to streamline our application. Consider the example application we have been developing in this chapter. Every time our .aspx page is accessed a recordset is populated with the contents of PCSWebApp3.mdb. This recordset is only ever used for reading data, as the method of inserting events into the database is different. In cases like this we could populate the recordset in the Application_Start event handler and make it available to all users. The only time we would need to refresh the recordset would be if an event were added. This will drastically improve performace with multiple users, as in most requests no DB access will be required.

Another technique we can use is to store session-level information for use by individual users across requests. This might include user-specific information extracted from a data store when the user firsts connects, and available until the user ceases to submit requests, or explicitly logs out.

I won't detail these techniques here, as this is something better dealt with in specialized ASP.NET books, but it helps to have a broad understanding of the processes nevertheless. In the next chapter, dealing with web services, we will see some of these techniques in action.

Summary

This chapter has provided an overview of web application creation with ASP.NET. We have seen how we can use every bit as much C# as we have looked at in this book, combined with web-server controls to provide a truly rich development environment. We have developed a meeting room booking application to illustrate many of the techniques available, such as the variety of server controls that exist, and data binding with ADO.NET.

In the next two chapters we will see two more important web subjects: web services and custom controls. We will continue to develop the example from this chapter in these chapters, taking it in radically different directions to illustrate the tools at our disposal.

In conclusion, ASP.NET is a powerful new weapon in the web developer's arsenal. The server-side processing is second to none, and being able to use the full power of C# and the .NET framework is an attractive proposition.

17

Web Services

Web services are a new way of performing remote method calls over HTTP that can make use of the **SOAP** (**Simple Object Access Protocol**). In the past this issue has been fraught with difficulty, as anyone who has any DCOM (Distributed COM) experience will bear witness to. The act of instantiating an object on a remote server, calling a method, and obtaining the result was far from simple – and the necessary configuration was even trickier.

SOAP simplifies matters immensely. This technology is an XML-based standard that details how method calls may be made over HTTP in a reproducible manner. A remote SOAP server is capable of understanding these calls and performing all the hard work for us, such as instantiating the required object, making the call, and returning a SOAP-formatted response to the client.

The .NET framework makes it very easy for us to make use of all this. As with ASP.NET, we are able to use the full array of C# and .NET techniques on the server, but (perhaps more importantly) the simple consumption of web services can be achieved from any platform with HTTP access to the server. In other words, it is conceivable that Linux code could, for example, use .NET services, or even Internet-enabled fridges.

In addition, web services may be completely described using **WSDL** (**Web Service Description Language**), allowing dynamic discovery of web services at run time. WSDL provides descriptions of all methods (along with the types required to call them) using XML with XML schemas. There are a wide variety of types available to web services, which range from simple primitive types to full `DataSet` objects, such that full in-memory databases can be marshaled to a client, which can result in a dramatic reduction in load on a database server.

In this chapter we will start by looking at the syntax of SOAP and WSDL, then move on to see how they are used by web services. We will discuss how to expose and consume web services, and work through a complete example building on the meeting room booker from the last chapter to illustrate their use.

SOAP

As mentioned above, one method used to exchange data with web services is SOAP. This technology has had a lot of press, especially since Microsoft decided to adopt it for use in the .NET framework. Now, though, the excitement seems to be dying down a bit as the SOAP specification is finalized. When you think about it, finding out exactly how SOAP works is a bit like finding out about how HTTP works – interesting, but not essential. Most of the time we never have to worry about the format of the exchanges made with web services, they just happen, we get the results we want, and everyone is happy.

For this reason I won't go into a huge amount of depth in this section, but I will show some simple SOAP requests and responses so you can get a feel for what is going on under the hood should you so desire.

Let's imagine that we want to call a method in a web service with the following signature:

```
int DoSomething(string stringParam, int intParam)
```

The SOAP headers and body required for this are shown below, with the address of the web service (more on this later) at the top:

```
POST /SomeLocation/myWebService.asmx HTTP/1.1
Host: karlivaio
Content-Type: text/xml; charset=utf-8
Content-Length: length
SOAPAction: "http://tempuri.org/DoSomething"

<?xml version="1.0"?>
<soap:Envelope xmlns:xsi="http://www.w3.org/2000/10/XMLSchema-instance"
               xmlns:xsd="http://www.w3.org/2000/10/XMLSchema"
               xmlns:soap="http://schemas.xmlsoap.org/soap/envelope">
  <soap:Body>
    <DoSomething xmlns="http://tempuri.org/">
      <stringParam>string</stringParam>
      <intParam>int</intParam>
    </DoSomething>
  </soap:Body>
</soap:Envelope>
```

The *length* parameter here specifies the total byte size of the content, and will vary depending on the values sent in the *string* and *int* parameters.

The soap namespace referenced here defines various elements that we use to build up our message. When we send this over HTTP the actual data sent will be slightly different (but related). For example, we could call the above method using the simple GET method:

```
GET /PCSWebSrv1/Service1.asmx/AddEvent?stringParam=string&intParam=int HTTP/1.1
Host: hostname
```

The SOAP response of this method will be as follows:

```
HTTP/1.1 200 OK
Content-Type: text/xml; charset=utf-8
Content-Length: length

<?xml version="1.0"?>
<soap:Envelope xmlns:xsi="http://www.w3.org/2000/10/XMLSchema-instance"
               xmlns:xsd="http://www.w3.org/2000/10/XMLSchema"
               xmlns:soap="http://schemas.xmlsoap.org/soap/envelope">
  <soap:Body>
    <DoSomethingResponse xmlns="http://tempuri.org/">
      <DoSomethingResult>int</DoSomethingResult>
    </DoSomethingResponse>
  </soap:Body>
</soap:Envelope>
```

where *length* is again varied according to the contents, in this case *int*.

Again, the actual response over HTTP may be far simpler, for example:

```
HTTP/1.1 200 OK
Content-Type: text/xml; charset=utf-8
Content-Length: length

<?xml version="1.0"?>
<int xmlns="http://tempuri.org/">int</int>
```

This is a far simpler XML format.

As discussed at the start of this section, the beauty of all this is that we can ignore it completely. It is only if we want to do something really odd that the exact syntax becomes important, and I can assure you that it won't in this book!

WSDL

WSDL completely describes web services, the methods available, and the various ways of calling these methods. Again, the exact details of this won't really benefit us that much, but a general understanding is useful.

WSDL is another fully XML-compliant syntax, and specifies web services by the methods available, the types used by these methods, the formats of request and response messages sent to and from methods via various protocols (pure SOAP, HTTP GET, etc.), and various bindings between the above.

Perhaps the most important part of a WSDL file is the type-definition section. This uses XML schemas to describe the format for data exchange via the XML elements that may be used and their relationships.

For example, the web service method used as an example in the last section:

```
int DoSomething(string stringParam, int intParam)
```

would have types declared for the request as follows:

```xml
<?xml version="1.0" ?>
<definitions xmlns:s="http://www.w3.org/2000/10/XMLSchema"
             xmlns="http://schemas.xmlsoap.org/wsdl/"
             ...other namespaces...>
   <types>
      <s:schema attributeFormDefault="qualified" elementFormDefault="qualified"
                targetNamespace="http://tempuri.org/">
         <s:import namespace="http://www.w3.org/2000/10/XMLSchema" />
         <s:element name="DoSomething">
            <s:complexType>
               <s:sequence>
                  <s:element name="stringParam" nullable="true"
                             type="s:string" />
                  <s:element name="intParam" nullable="true"
                             type="s:int" />
               </s:sequence>
            </s:complexType>
         </s:element>
         <s:element name="DoSomethingResponse">
            <s:complexType>
               <s:sequence>
                  <s:element name="DoSomethingResult" type="s:int" />
               </s:sequence>
            </s:complexType>
         </s:element>
         <s:element name="int" type="s:int" />
      </s:schema>
   </types>
   ...other definitions...
</definitions>
```

These types are all that are required for the SOAP and HTTP requests and responses we saw earlier, and are bound to these operations later in the file. All the types are specified using standard XML schema syntax, for example:

```xml
<s:element name="DoSomethingResponse">
   <s:complexType>
      <s:sequence>
         <s:element name="DoSomethingResult" type="s:int" />
      </s:sequence>
   </s:complexType>
</s:element>
```

This specifies that an element called <DoSomethingResponse> has a child element called <DoSomethingResult> that contains an integer.

If we have access to the WSDL for a web service then we can use it. As we will see shortly, this isn't that difficult to do.

Now we've had a brief look as SOAP and WSDL it's time to move on to look at how we create and consume web services.

Web Services

The discussion of web services falls into two categories:

❏ Exposing web services, which concerns writing web services and placing them on web servers

❏ Consuming web services, which concerns using the services you design on a client

We will look at these subjects in the two sections that follow.

Exposing Web Services

Web services are exposed by placing code either directly into `.asmx` files or by referencing web service classes from these files. As with ASP.NET pages, creating a web service in VS.NET uses the latter method, and we will too for demonstration purposes.

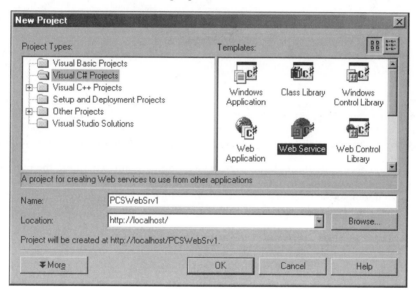

Creating a web service project called `PCSWebSrv1` as shown above results in a similar set of files being generated to those for a web application project. In fact, the only difference is that instead of a file called `WebForm1.aspx` being generated, a file called `Service1.asmx` is created. The `.vsdisco` file generated is responsible for identifying the web service such that Visual Studio.NET can add a web reference to it, as we will see shortly.

The code in `Service1.asmx` isn't directly accessible through VS.NET, but inspection with Notepad reveals the following single line of code:

```
<%@ WebService Language="c#" Codebehind="Service1.asmx.cs"
    Class="PCSWebSrv1.Service1" %>
```

This references the code file that we can see in VS.NET, `Service1.asmx.cs`, accessible by right-clicking on `Service1.asmx` in the Solution Explorer and selecting View Code. The generated code, with comments removed for brevity, is shown below:

```
namespace PCSWebSrv1
{
    using System;
    using System.Collections;
    using System.ComponentModel;
    using System.Data;
    using System.Diagnostics;
    using System.Web;
    using System.Web.Services;

    public class Service1 : System.Web.Services.WebService
    {
        public Service1 ()
        {
            InitializeComponent();
        }

        private void InitializeComponent()
        {
        }

        public override void Dispose()
        {
        }
    }
}
```

This code defines the PCSWebSrv1 namespace, with several standard namespace references, and a web service class called Service1 (which we saw referenced above in Service1.asmx), descended from System.Web.Services.WebService. It is up to us to provide methods on this web service class.

Adding a method accessible through the web service simply requires defining the method as public and giving it the WebMethod attribute. This attribute simply labels the methods we want to be accessible. We'll look at the types we can use for the return type and parameters shortly, but for now add the following method:

```
[WebMethod]
public String CanWeFixIt()
{
    return "Yes we can!";
}
```

and compile the project.

We can check things are working by pointing our web browser at Service1.asmx:

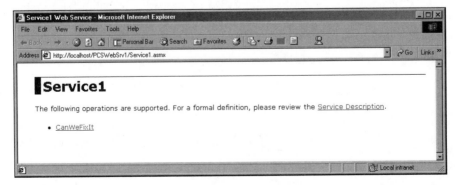

Clicking on the method name gives us information about the SOAP request and response, as well as examples of how the request and response will look via HTTP GET and HTTP POST methods. We can also test the method by clicking on the Invoke button provided. If the method requires simple parameters we can enter these on this form as well. If we do this we will see the XML returned by the method call:

```
<?xml version="1.0" ?>
<string xmlns="http://tempuri.org/">Yes we can!</string>
```

This demonstrates that our method is working perfectly.

Following the Service Description link from the browser screen shown above allows us to view the WSDL description of the web service. The most important part as far as we are concerned is the description of the element types for requests and responses:

```
<types>
    <s:schema attributeFormDefault="qualified" elementFormDefault="qualified"
            targetNamespace="http://tempuri.org/">
        <s:element name="CanWeFixIt">
            <s:complexType />
        </s:element>
        <s:element name="CanWeFixItResponse">
            <s:complexType>
                <s:sequence>
                    <s:element name="CanWeFixItResult" nullable="true"
                            type="s:string" />
                </s:sequence>
            </s:complexType>
        </s:element>
        <s:element name="string" nullable="true" type="s:string" />
    </s:schema>
</types>
```

The description also contains descriptions of the types required for requests and responses, as well as various bindings for the service, making it quite a long file.

Types Available for Web Services

Web services can be used to exchange any of the following types:

String	Char	Byte
Boolean	Int16	Int32
Int64	UInt16	UInt32
UInt64	Single	Double
Guid	Decimal	DateTime
XmlQualifiedName	class	struct
XmlNode	DataSet	

Arrays of all the above types are also allowed. Note also that only public properties and fields of class and struct types are marshaled.

817

Consuming Web Services

Now we know how to create web services it's time to look at how we use them. To do this we need to generate a proxy class in our code that knows how to communicate with a given web service. Any calls from our code to the web service will go through this proxy, which looks identical to the web service, giving our code the illusion that we have a local copy of it. In actual fact there is a lot of HTTP communication going on, but we are shielded from the details. There are two ways of doing this. We can either use the `WSDL.exe` command-line tool or the **Add Web Reference** menu option in VS.NET.

Using `WSDL.exe` generates a `.cs` file containing a proxy class, based on the WSDL description of the web service. We specify this using the URL, for example:

```
WSDL http://localhost/PCSWebSrv1/Service1.asmx?WSDL
```

This will generate a proxy class for the example from the last section in a file called `Service1.cs`. The class will be named after the web service, in this case `Service1`, and contain methods that call identically named methods of the service. To use this class we simply add the `.cs` file generated to a project and use code along the lines of:

```
Service1 myService = new Service1();
String result = myService.CanWeFixIt();
```

By default the class generated will be placed in the root namespace, so no `using` statement is necessary, but we can specify a different namespace to use with the **/n: <namespace>** `WSDL.exe` command-line option.

This technique works fine but can be a pain to continually redo if the service is being developed and changing continuously. Of course, it could be executed in the build options for a project in order to automatically update the generated proxy before each compile, but there is a better way.

We'll illustrate this better way by creating a client for the example in the last section, in a new web application called `PCSWebClient1`. The body of the form in the `.aspx` page generated needs the following code to replace the existing `form` declaration:

```
<form method="post" runat="server">
    <asp:Label Runat="server" ID="resultLabel"/><br>
    <asp:Button Runat="server" ID="triggerButton"
                Text="Invoke CanWeFixIt()"/>
</form>
```

In a moment we'll bind the button-click event handler to the web service. First we need to add a reference to the web service to our project. To do this, right-click on the application in the Solution Explorer and select the **Add Web Reference...** option. In the window that appears type in the URL of the web service `.vsdisco` file:

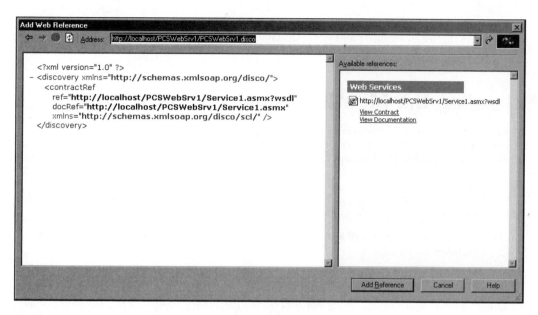

From here we can follow the links on the right to get the same web page descriptions of a service as we saw in the last section, and add a reference with the **Add Reference** button. Pressing this button now will result in the following being added to the Solution Explorer:

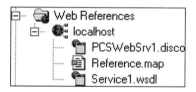

The folder containing our web reference is named after the server where the service is located, which is `localhost` here. This is also the namespace we need to reference to use the proxy class, so it makes sense to rename this, which we can do by right-clicking on the folder. If we rename this folder as `myWebService` and add the `using` statement to our code:

```
using PCSWebClient1.myWebService;
```

then we can use the service in our class.

Add an event handler to the button on the form with the following code:

```
protected void triggerButton_Click(object sender, System.EventArgs e)
{
    Service1 myService = new Service1();
    resultLabel.Text = myService.CanWeFixIt();
}
```

Running the application and clicking the button will now result in the result of `CanWeFixIt()` being displayed in the browser window.

This web service might change later, but with this method we can simply right-click on the web reference in the server explorer and select **Update Web Reference**. This will generate a new proxy class for us to use.

Extending the Meeting Room Booker Example

Now we know the basics of creating and consuming web services, let's apply our knowledge to extending the meeting room booker application from the last chapter. Specifically, we will extract the database access aspects from the application and place them into a web service. This web service will have two methods:

❑ GetData(), which will return a DataSet containing all three tables in the PCSWebApp3.mdb database

❑ AddEvent(), which will add an event and return an updated version of DataSet that includes the change

In addition, we'll design the web service with some of the load-reducing techniques from the last chapter in mind. Specifically, we will store the DataSet at the application level in the web service application. This means that multiple requests for the data won't require additional database requests to work. The data in this application-level DataSet will only be refreshed when new data is added to the database. This means that changes made to the database by other means, such as manual editing, will *not* be reflected in this DataSet. Still, as long as we know that our web service is the only thing with direct access to the data we have nothing to worry about.

The Meeting Room Booking Web Service

Create a new web service project in VS.NET called PCSWebSrv2. The first thing we'll add to this project is some code in the Application_Start() handler in global.asax. We want to load all the data in PCSWebApp3.mdb into a dataset and store it. This will mostly involve code that we've already seen, as getting the database into a DataSet is something we've already done. In fact, we can copy all the code we need from WebForm1.aspx.cs in PCSWebApp3 from the last chapter – including the database connection string (which I won't show here because yours is likely to be different):

```
protected void Application_Start(Object sender, EventArgs e)
{
    System.Data.DataSet ds;
    System.Data.OleDb.OleDbConnection oleDbConnection1;
    System.Data.OleDb.OleDbDataAdapter daAttendees;
    System.Data.OleDb.OleDbDataAdapter daRooms;
    System.Data.OleDb.OleDbDataAdapter daEvents;

    oleDbConnection1 = new System.Data.OleDb.OleDbConnection();
    oleDbConnection1.ConnectionString = @" ... ";
    oleDbConnection1.Open();
    ds = new DataSet();
    daAttendees = new System.Data.OleDb.OleDbDataAdapter(
                "SELECT * FROM Attendees", oleDbConnection1);
    daRooms = new System.Data.OleDb.OleDbDataAdapter(
                "SELECT * FROM Rooms", oleDbConnection1);
```

```
        daEvents = new System.Data.OleDb.OleDbDataAdapter(
                "SELECT * FROM Events", oleDbConnection1);
        daAttendees.Fill(ds, "Attendees");
        daRooms.Fill(ds, "Rooms");
        daEvents.Fill(ds, "Events");
        oleDbConnection1.Close();

        Application["ds"] = ds;
    }
```

The important code to note here is in the last line. Application (and Session) objects have a collection of name-value pairs that we can use to store data in. Here we are creating a name in the Application store called ds, which takes the serialized value of the ds DataSet containing the Attendees, Rooms, and Events tables from our database. This value will be accessible to all instances of the web service at any time.

In order for the above code to work we also need to add a reference to the System.Data namespace to the PCSWebSrv2 namespace in global.asax:

```
namespace PCSWebSrv2
{
    ...

    using System.Data;
```

This technique is very useful for read-only data as multiple threads will be able to access it, reducing the load on our database. Note, though, that the Events table is likely to change, and we'll have to update the application-level DataSet when this happens. We'll look at this shortly.

Next we need to add the GetData() method to our service in Service1.asmx.cs:

```
    [WebMethod]
    public DataSet GetData()
    {
        return (DataSet)Application["ds"];
    }
```

This uses the same syntax as Application_Load() to access the DataSet, which we simply cast to the correct type and return.

The AddEvent() method is slightly more complicated. Conceptually, we need to do the following:

❑   Accept event data from the client

❑   Create a SQL INSERT statement using this data

❑   Connect to the database and execute the SQL statement

❑   If the addition is successful then refresh the data in Application["ds"]

❑   Return a success or failure notification to the client (we'll leave it up to the client to refresh their DataSet if required)

821

Starting from the top, we'll accept all fields as strings:

```
[WebMethod]
public int AddEvent(String eventName, String eventRoom,
                    String eventAttendees, String eventDate)
{
}
```

Next we declare the objects we'll need for database access, connect to the database, and execute our query, all using similar code to that in PCSWebApp3 (again, we need the connection string here, but I won't show it):

```
[WebMethod]
public int AddEvent(String eventName, String eventRoom,
                    String eventAttendees, String eventDate)
{
    System.Data.OleDb.OleDbConnection oleDbConnection1;
    System.Data.OleDb.OleDbDataAdapter daEvents;
    DataSet ds;

    oleDbConnection1 = new System.Data.OleDb.OleDbConnection();
    oleDbConnection1.ConnectionString = @" ... ";
    String oleDbCommand = "INSERT INTO Events (Name, Room, AttendeeList," +
                          " EventDate) VALUES ('" + eventName + "', '" +
                          eventRoom + "', '" + eventAttendees + "', '" +
                          eventDate + "')";
    System.Data.OleDb.OleDbCommand insertCommand =
        new System.Data.OleDb.OleDbCommand(oleDbCommand,
                                           oleDbConnection1);

    oleDbConnection1.Open();

    int queryResult = insertCommand.ExecuteNonQuery();
}
```

We use queryResult to store the number of rows affected by the query as before. We can check this to see if it is 1 to gauge our success. If we are successful then we execute a new query on the database to refresh the Events table in our DataSet. It is vital to lock the application data while we perform our updates, to ensure that no other threads can access Application["ds"] while we update it. We can do this using the Lock() and UnLock() methods of the Application object:

```
[WebMethod]
public int AddEvent(String eventName, String eventRoom,
                    String eventAttendees, String eventDate)
{
    ...
    int queryResult = insertCommand.ExecuteNonQuery();

    if (queryResult == 1)
    {
        daEvents = new System.Data.OleDb.OleDbDataAdapter(
                       "SELECT * FROM Events", oleDbConnection1);
        Application.Lock();
        ds = (DataSet)Application["ds"];
        ds.Tables["Events"].Clear();
        daEvents.Fill(ds, "Events");
        Application["ds"] = ds;
        Application.UnLock();
        oleDbConnection1.Close();
    }
}
```

Finally, we return queryResult, allowing the client to know if the query was successful:

```
[WebMethod]
public int AddEvent(String eventName, String eventRoom,
                    String eventAttendees, String eventDate)
{
    ...
    return queryResult;
}
```

And with that, we have completed our web service. As before, we can test this service out simply by pointing a web browser at the .asmx file, so we can add records and look at the XML representation of the DataSet returned by GetData() without writing any client code.

The Meeting Room Booker Client

The client we'll use will be a development of the PCSWebApp3 web application from the last chapter. We'll call this application, unsurprisingly enough, PCSWebApp4, and use the code from PCSWebApp3 as a starting point.

We'll make two major modifications to the project. Firstly, we'll remove all direct database access from this application and use the web service instead. Secondly, we'll introduce an application-level store of the DataSet returned from the web service that is only updated when necessary, meaning that even less of a load is placed on the database.

The first thing to do to our new web application is to add a web reference to the PCSWebSrv2/Service1.asmx service. We can do this exactly the way we saw earlier in the chapter, by locating the .vsdisco file, and calling it eventDataService.

The first thing we'll do, then, is to add code to Global.asax in much the same way as we did for our web service. This code, though, is a lot simpler. First we reference the web service and System.Data namespace:

```
namespace PCSWebApp4
{
    ...
    using System.Data;
    using eventDataService;
```

Next we fill a DataSet and place it into an application-level data store called ds:

```
    protected void Application_Start(Object sender, EventArgs e)
    {
        Service1 dataService = new Service1();
        DataSet ds = dataService.GetData();
        Application["ds"] = ds;
    }
```

This DataSet is now available to all instances of PCSWebApp4, meaning that multiple users can read data without any calls to the web service, or indeed to the database.

Now we have this DataSet we need to modify WebForm1.aspx.cs to use it. The first thing that we can do is remove the declarations of oleDbConnection1, daAttendees, daRooms, and daEvents, as we won't be performing any database access. Next we need to change Page_Load() as follows:

```
private void Page_Load(object sender, System.EventArgs e)
{
    validationSummary.Enabled = false;
    foreach (System.Web.UI.WebControls.WebControl validator in
            this.Validators)
    {
        validator.Enabled = false;
    }
    ds = (DataSet)Application["ds"];

    attendeeList.DataSource = ds.Tables["Attendees"];
    roomList.DataSource = ds.Tables["Rooms"];
    eventTable = ds.Tables["Events"];
    eventDetails1.DataSource = eventTable;
    eventDetails2.DataSource = eventTable;
    if (!this.IsPostBack)
    {
        System.DateTime trialDate = System.DateTime.Now;
        calendar.SelectedDate = getFreeDate(trialDate);
        this.DataBind();
    }
    else
    {
        eventDetails1.DataBind();
        eventDetails2.DataBind();
    }
}
```

Most of the code remains the same, all we need to do is to use `Application["ds"]` instead of getting the `DataSet` ourselves.

We also need to change `submitButton_Click()` to use the web service `AddData()` method. Again, much of the code remains unchanged:

```
protected void submitButton_Click(object sender, System.EventArgs e)
{
    foreach (System.Web.UI.WebControls.WebControl validator in
            this.Validators)
    {
        validator.Enabled = true;
    }
    this.Validate();
    if (this.IsValid)
    {
        String attendees = "";
        foreach (ListItem attendee in attendeeList.Items)
        {
            if (attendee.Selected)
            {
                attendees += attendee.Text + " (" + attendee.Value + "), ";
            }
        }
        attendees += " and " + nameBox.Text;
        String dateString =
                calendar.SelectedDate.Date.Date.ToShortDateString();
        Service1 dataService = new Service1();
        int queryResult = dataService.AddEvent(eventBox.Text,
                                        roomList.SelectedItem.Value,
                                        attendees,
                                        dateString);
        if (queryResult == 1)
        {
            resultLabel.Text = "Event Added.";

            ds = dataService.GetData();
            Application.Lock();
            Application["ds"] = ds;
            Application.UnLock();
```

```
        eventTable = ds.Tables["Events"];
        calendar.SelectedDate =
                    getFreeDate(calendar.SelectedDate.AddDays(1));
        eventDetails1.DataSource = eventTable;
        eventDetails1.DataBind();
        eventDetails2.DataSource = eventTable;
        eventDetails2.DataBind();
    }
    else
    {
        resultLabel.Text = "Event not added due to DB access problem.";
    }
}
else
{
    validationSummary.Enabled = true;
}
}
```

In fact, all we've really done is simplify things a great deal. This is often the case when using well designed web services – we can forget about much of the workings and instead concentrate on the user experience.

There isn't a huge amount to comment on in this code. Continuing to make use of `queryResult` is a bonus, and locking the application is essential as already noted.

The `PCSWebApp4` web application should look and function exactly like `PCSWebApp3`, but perform substantially better. We can also use the same web service for other applications very easily – simply displaying events on a page, for example, or even editing events, attendee names, and rooms if we add some more methods. Doing this won't break `PCSWebApp4` as it will simply ignore any new methods created.

Summary

In this chapter we have seen how to create and consume web services using C# and the VS.NET development platform. Doing this is perhaps surprisingly simple, but is instantly recognizable as something that could prove to be incredibly useful. Already we are seeing many announcements about new web services, and I suspect that they will be everywhere before long.

It has also been pointed out, and I'll reiterate it here to push the point home, that web services may be accessed from any platform. This is due to the simple SOAP protocol, which doesn't limit us to .NET.

The example developed in this chapter illustrates how we can create .NET distributed applications with ease. I have assumed here that you are using a single server to test things out, but there is no reason why the web service shouldn't be completely separate from the client. It may even be on a separate server to the database if an additional data tier is required.

The use of data caching throughout is another important technique to master for use in large-scale applications, which may have thousands of users connecting simultaneously. Of course, in such a situation using Microsoft Access as a data source might not necessarily be the best idea!

Finally, it is worth bearing in mind that web service consumers don't necessarily have to be web applications. There is no reason why we can't use web services from WinForm applications – which certainly seems like an attractive option for a corporate intranet.

All in all, the potential of web services certainly astounds me, and I hope you're impressed too!

18

Custom Controls

It has often been the case with web development that the tools available, however powerful, don't quite match up with your requirements for a specific project. Perhaps a given control doesn't quite work as you'd like it to, or perhaps one section of code, intended for reuse on several pages, would be unworkably complex in the hands of multiple developers. In cases such as these there is a strong argument for **custom controls**. Custom controls can, at their simplest, wrap multiple existing controls together, perhaps with additional properties specifying layout, or can be completely different from any existing control. Using a custom control can be as simple as using any other control in ASP.NET, which can certainly ease web site coding.

In the past it has been tricky to implement such custom-built controls, especially on large-scale systems, where complex registration procedures may be required in order to use them. Even on simple systems, the coding required to create a custom control could become a very involved process. The scripting capabilities of older web languages also suffered from not giving perfect access to your cunningly crafted object models, and resulted in poor performance all round.

The .NET framework provides an ideal setting for the creation of custom controls. The dynamic discovery of assemblies that is inherent in a .NET system makes installation on a new web server as simple as copying the directory structure containing your code, along with any DLLs used. In addition, care has been taken to make it really quite easy to create your own controls, using simple programming techniques.

In this chapter we will look at two different kinds of controls:

❑ **User controls** – converting existing ASP.NET pages into controls

❑ **Custom controls** – grouping the functionality of several controls, extending existing controls, and creating new controls from scratch

We'll illustrate user controls by converting the meeting room booker application from the last chapter into a user control, so that we can embed it in other ASP.NET pages with ease. In the case of custom controls, we'll create a straw poll control allowing the user to vote for an option in a list and see how the vote is progressing.

User Controls

User controls are controls that you create using ASP.NET code, just as you would in standard ASP.NET web pages. The difference is that once you have created a user control you can reuse it in multiple ASP.NET pages with a minimum of difficulty.

For example, let's say that you have created a page that displays some information from a database, perhaps information about an order. Instead of creating a fixed page that does this, it is possible to place the relevant code into a user control, and then insert that control into as many different web pages as you wish.

In addition, it is possible to define properties and methods for user controls; for instance, you could specify the background color for displaying your database table in a web page, or re-run a database query to check for changes.

Let's dive in and create a simple user control, discussing the relevant points as they come up, then build on it to see how we can add methods and properties.

A Simple User Control

In VS.NET, create a new web application called `PCSUserCWebApp1`, by opening VS.NET, clicking on **Getting Started**, and then selecting **New Project** and clicking on the **Web Application** icon. A dialog box should open allowing you to save this project.

Once the standard files have been generated, select the **Project | Add New Item...** menu option, and add a **Web User Control** called `PCSUserC1.ascx` as shown below:

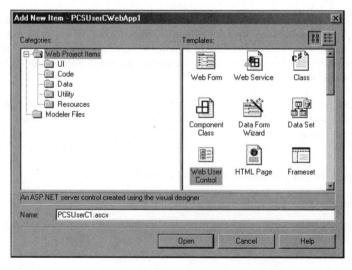

The files added to our project, with the extensions `.ascx` and `.ascx.cs`, work in a very similar way to the `.aspx` files we've seen already. The `.ascx` file will contain our ASP.NET code and look very similar to a normal `.aspx` file. The `.ascx.cs` file is our code-behind file, which defines the user control, much in the same way that forms are defined in `.aspx.cs` files.

`.ascx` files can be viewed in designer or HTML view just like `.aspx` files. Looking at the file in HTML view reveals an important difference – there is no `<form>` element in the `<body>` element. This is because user controls will be inserted inside ASP.NET forms in other files, and so don't need a form tag of their own.

Looking at the generated boilerplate code here reveals another important difference: the class generated inherits from `System.Web.UI.UserControl`. Again, this is because the control will be used inside a form.

Our simple control will be one that displays a graphic corresponding to one of the four standard suits in cards (clubs, diamonds, hearts, spades). The graphics required for this are shipped as part of double clicking Visual Studio.NET; you can find them in: `C:\Program Files\Microsoft Visual Studio.NET\Common7\Graphics\bitmaps\assorted`, with the filenames CLUB.BMP, DIAMOND.BMP, HEART.BMP, and SPADE.BMP. Copy these into your project directory, so we can use them in a moment.

Let's add some code to our new control. In the HTML view of `PCSUserC1.ascx` add the following:

```
<HTML>
    <HEAD>
    </HEAD>
    <BODY>
        <TABLE cellSpacing=4>
            <TR vAlign=middle>
                <TD>
                    <asp:Image Runat="server" ID="suitPic" ImageURL="club.bmp"/>
                </TD>
                <TD height=20>
                    <asp:Label Runat="server" ID="suitLabel">Club</asp:Label>
                </TD>
            </TR>
        </TABLE>
    </BODY>
</HTML>
```

This defines a default state for our control, which will be a picture of a club along with a label. Before we add any additional functionality, we'll test this default by adding this control to our project web page `WebForm1.aspx`.

In order to use a custom control in a `.aspx` file, we first need to specify how we will refer to it, that is, the name of the tag that will represent the control in our HTML. To do this we use the `<%@ Register %>` directive at the top of the code as follows:

```
<%@ Register TagPrefix="PCS" TagName="UserC1" Src="PCSUserC1.ascx" %>
```

We use the `Src` attribute to point to the file containing our user control, and the `TagPrefix` and `TagName` attributes to specify the tag name to use (in the form `TagPrefix:TagName`). Now we can use our control by adding the following element:

```
<%@ Page language="c#" Codebehind="WebForm1.aspx.cs" AutoEventWireup="false"
    Inherits="PCSUserCWebApp1.WebForm1" %>
<%@ Register TagPrefix="PCS" TagName="UserC1" Src="PCSUserC1.ascx" %>

<HTML>
    <HEAD>
        <meta name=vs_targetSchema content="Internet Explorer 5.0">
        <meta name="GENERATOR" Content="Microsoft Visual Studio 7.0">
        <meta name="CODE_LANGUAGE" Content="C#">
    </HEAD>
    <BODY MS_POSITIONING="GridLayout">
        <form method="post" runat="server">
            <PCS:UserC1 Runat="server" id="myUserControl"/>
        </form>
    </BODY>
</HTML>
```

User controls may not be declared by default in the code behind our form, so we may also need to add the following declaration to WebForm1.aspx.cs:

```
public class WebForm1 : System.Web.UI.Page
{
    protected PCSUserC1 myUserControl;
    ...
```

This is all we need to do to test our user control, and running the project results in the following:

 club

As it stands this control groups two existing controls together, an image and a label in a table layout. As such it falls into the category of a **composite** control.

To gain control over the suit being displayed, we can use an attribute on the <PCS:UserC1> element. Attributes on user control elements are automatically mapped to properties on user controls, so all we have to do to make this work is add a property to the code behind our control, PCSUserC1.ascx.cs. We'll call this property Suit, and let it take any suit value. To make it easier for us to represent the state of the control, we'll define an enumeration to hold the four suit names, inside the PCSUserCWebApp1 namespace:

```
namespace PCSUserCWebApp1
{
    ...
    public enum suit
    {
        club, diamond, heart, spade
    }
    ...
}
```

The `PCSUserC1` class needs a member variable to hold the suit type, `currentSuit`:

```
public class PCSUserC1 : System.Web.UI.UserControl
{
    protected System.Web.UI.WebControls.Image suitPic;
    protected System.Web.UI.WebControls.Label suitLabel;
    protected suit currentSuit;
```

As well as a property to access this member variable, `Suit`:

```
public suit Suit
{
    get
    {
        return currentSuit;
    }
    set
    {
        currentSuit = value;
        suitPic.ImageUrl = currentSuit.ToString() + ".bmp";
        suitLabel.Text = currentSuit.ToString();
    }
}
```

The `set()` accessor here sets the URL of the image to one of the files we copied earlier, and the text displayed to the suit name.

Now the control is finished, we need to add code to `WebForm1.aspx` to access this new property. We'll use a radio button list to select a suit:

```
<BODY MS_POSITIONING="GridLayout">
    <form method="post" runat="server">
        <PCS:UserC1 Runat="server" id="myUserControl"/>
        <asp:RadioButtonList Runat="server" ID="suitList"
                        autopostback="True">
            <asp:ListItem Value="club" Selected="True">Club</asp:ListItem>
            <asp:ListItem Value="diamond">Diamond</asp:ListItem>
            <asp:ListItem Value="heart">Heart</asp:ListItem>
            <asp:ListItem Value="spade">Spade</asp:ListItem>
        </asp:RadioButtonList>
    </form>
</BODY>
```

We also need to add an event handler for the `SelectedIndexChanged` event of the list, which we can do simply by double-clicking on the control in design view.

> Note that we need to set the `autopostback` property of this list to `true`, as the
> `suitList_SelectedIndexChanged()` event handler won't be executed on the server unless a
> postback is in operation, and this control doesn't trigger a postback by default.

The `suitList_SelectedIndexChanged()` method needs the following code in `WebForm1.aspx.cs`:

```
protected void suitList_SelectedIndexChanged(object sender,
                                           System.EventArgs e)
{
    myUserControl.Suit = (suit)Enum.Parse(typeof(suit),
                              suitList.SelectedItem.Value);
}
```

We know that the `value` attributes on the `<ListItem>` elements represent valid values for the `suit` enumeration we defined earlier, so we simply parse these as enumeration types (we are using the same namespace here so we don't have to redefine the type), and use them as values of the `Suit` property of our user control. We cast the returned `object` type to `suit` using simple casing syntax, as this can't be achieved implicitly.

Note that we don't have to get this complicated; we can simply specify a single value using the `Suit` attribute in a web form, for example:

```
<PCS:UserC1 Runat="server" id="myUserControl" Suit="diamond"/>
```

The ASP.NET processor is intelligent enough to get the correct enumeration item from the string provided.

Now we can change the suit when we run our web application:

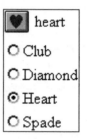

Next we'll give our control some methods. Again, this is very simple; we just need to add methods to our `PCSUserC1` class:

```
public void Club()
{
    Suit = suit.club;
}

public void Diamond()
{
    Suit = suit.diamond;
}

public void Heart()
{
    Suit = suit.heart;
}

public void Spade()
{
    Suit = suit.spade;
}
```

These four methods, `Club()`, `Diamond()`, `Heart()`, and `Spade()`, change the suit displayed on the screen to the respective suit clicked.

We'll call these functions from four `ImageButton` controls in our `.aspx` page:

```
<asp:ImageButton Runat="server" ID="clubButton"
                 ImageUrl="CLUB.BMP"
                 OnClick="clubButton_OnClick"/>
<asp:ImageButton Runat="server" ID="diamondButton"
                 ImageUrl="DIAMOND.BMP"
                 OnClick="diamondButton_OnClick"/>
<asp:ImageButton Runat="server" ID="heartButton"
                 ImageUrl="HEART.BMP"
                 OnClick="heartButton_OnClick"/>
<asp:ImageButton Runat="server" ID="spadeButton"
                 ImageUrl="SPADE.BMP"
                 OnClick="spadeButton_OnClick"/>
</form>
```

With the following event handlers:

```
protected void clubButton_OnClick(object sender,
                            System.Web.UI.ImageClickEventArgs e)
{
   myUserControl.Club();
}

protected void diamondButton_OnClick(object sender,
                            System.Web.UI.ImageClickEventArgs e)
{
   myUserControl.Diamond();
}

protected void heartButton_OnClick(object sender,
                            System.Web.UI.ImageClickEventArgs e)
{
   myUserControl.Heart();
}

protected void spadeButton_OnClick(object sender,
                            System.Web.UI.ImageClickEventArgs e)
{
   myUserControl.Spade();
}
```

Now we have four new buttons we can use to change the suit:

Note that these buttons don't change the selected radio button, although this would be trivial to implement.

Now we've created our user control, we can use it in any other web page simply by using the <%@ Register %> directive and the two source code files (PCSUserC1.ascx and PCSUserC1.ascx.cs) we have created for the control.

Converting the Event Booker to a User Control

In most cases, converting an ASP.NET page into a user control is easy, as we can simply copy the required code into empty .ascx and .ascx.cs files. We can even get away with simply changing the file name to .ascx in some cases, if we have placed all the C# code in this file rather than using the "code behind" option.

However, this is not possible in some cases, and there are certain hurdles that we need to address to get the web application from the last chapter into a user control.

For a start, this application makes use of an application-level variable – the DataSet that holds the event details, attendees, and room name tables. If we want to use this variable in the same way we will need to place the DataSet retrieval code in the global.asax file for this project. This also means that we need to add a web reference to the required web service to the project.

There are other changes that need to be made, in order to account for the fact that the control has a base class of UserControl, not Form. For example, UserControl has no Validators collection, so we can't cycle through the Validator objects in this collection using code as we did before:

```
protected void submitButton_Click(object sender, System.EventArgs e)
{
    foreach (System.Web.UI.WebControls.WebControl validator
            in this.Validators)
    {
        validator.Enabled = true;
    }
    this.Validate();
    if (this.IsValid)
    {
        ...
```

Instead we have to use the long-winded approach:

```
protected void submitButton_Click(object sender, System.EventArgs e)
{
    validateEvent.Enabled = true;
    validateRoom.Enabled = true;
    validateName.Enabled = true;
    validateAttendees.Enabled = true;
    validateEvent.Validate();
    validateRoom.Validate();
    validateName.Validate();
    validateAttendees.Validate();
    if (validateAttendees.IsValid && validateEvent.IsValid &&
        validateRoom.IsValid && validateName.IsValid)
    {
        . . .
```

There is also the problem that the control uses a validation summary. This means that other regions in the page using this control will require additional work to validate. This is because the validation summary works for the whole page, including all validation controls regardless of where they are situated, which could make things confusing. Perhaps the simplest solution here is to create our own validation handler that only uses the validation controls in the user control, such as a label control to which we output the required text manually. I won't, however, cover this here.

In general, we should make any user controls we create completely independent of any page that might use them, which effectively means that this application is not an ideal example. However, it has brought to light some of the limitations of user controls.

In the next section we will see how we can customize controls to a much greater degree, using the full custom control syntax.

Custom controls

Custom controls go a step beyond user controls in that they are entirely self contained in C# assemblies, requiring no separate ASP.NET code. This means that we don't need to go through the process of assembling a UI in a .ascx file. Instead, we have complete control over what is written to the output stream, that is, the exact HTML generated by our control.

In general, it will take longer to develop custom controls than user controls, as the syntax is more complex, and we often have to write significantly more code to get results. A user control may be as simple as a few other controls grouped together as we've seen, whereas a custom control can do just about anything short of making you a cup of coffee.

To get the most customizable behavior for our custom controls, we can derive a class from System.Web.UI.WebControls.WebControl. If we do this then we are creating a **full** custom control. Alternatively, we can extend the functionality of an existing control, creating a **derived** custom control. Finally, we can group existing controls together, much as we did in the last section, but with a more logical structure, to create a **composite** custom control.

Whatever we create can be used in ASP.NET pages in pretty much the same way. All we need to do is to place the generated assembly in the `bin` directory of the web application that will use it, and register the element names to use with the `<%@ Register %>` directive. This directive takes a slightly different syntax for custom controls:

```
<%@ Register TagPrefix="PCS" Namespace="PCSCustomWebControls"
             Assembly="PCSCustomWebControls"%>
```

We use the `TagPrefix` option in the same way as before, but we don't use the `TagName` or `Src` attributes. This is because the custom control assembly we use may contain several custom controls, and each of these will be named by its class, so `TagName` is redundant. In addition, since we are using an assembly in the `bin` directory, we can use the dynamic discovery capabilities of the .NET framework to find our assembly simply by naming it and the namespace in it that contains our controls.

In the example line of code above, we are saying that we want to use an assembly called `PCSCustomWebControls.dll` with controls in the `PCSCustomWebControls` namespace, and use the tag prefix `PCS`. If we have a control called `Control1` in this namespace we could use it with the ASP.NET code:

```
<PCS:Control1 Runat="server" ID="MyControl1"/>
```

With custom controls it is also possible to reproduce some of the control nesting behavior, such as we see in list controls:

```
<asp:dropdownlist id="roomList" runat="server" width="160px">
    <asp:ListItem Value="1">The Happy Room</asp:ListItem>
    <asp:ListItem Value="2">The Angry Room</asp:ListItem>
    <asp:ListItem Value="3">The Depressing Room</asp:ListItem>
    <asp:ListItem Value="4">The Funked Out Room</asp:ListItem>
</asp:dropdownlist>
```

We can create controls that should be interpreted as being children of other controls in a very similar way. We'll see how to do this later in this section.

Custom Control Project Configuration

Let's start putting some of this theory in practice. We'll use a single assembly to hold all the example custom controls in this chapter for simplicity, which we can create in Visual Studio.NET by choosing a new project of type **Web Control Library**. We'll call our library `PCSCustomWebControls`:

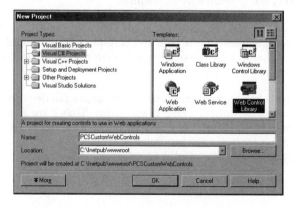

Here I have created the project in my wwwroot directory, although this isn't necessary. We can create web control libraries anywhere, as long as we remember to copy the generated assembly into the bin directory of the web application that uses it.

One technique we can use to facilitate testing in a single solution, is to add a web application project to the same solution:

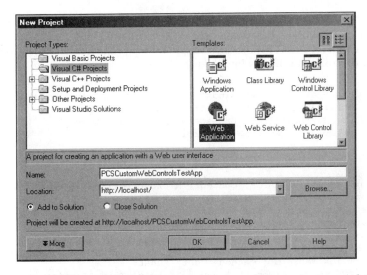

For now, this is the only application that will use our custom control library, so to speed things up a little we can make the output assembly for our library be created in the correct bin directory (this means that we don't have to copy the file across every time we recompile). We can do this through the property pages for the PCSCustomWebControls project:

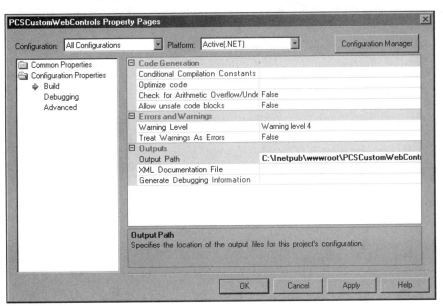

Note that I have changed the Configuration drop down to All Configurations, so debug and release build will be created in the same place. The Output Path has been changed to C:\Inetpub\wwwroot\PCSCustomWebControlsTestApp\bin. To make debugging easier we can also change the Start URL option on the Debugging property page to http://localhost/PCSCustomWebControlsTestApp/WebForm1.aspx, and the Debug Mode to URL, so we can just execute our project in debug mode to see our results.

We can make sure that this is all working by testing out the control that is supplied by default in the .cs file for our custom control library, called WebCustomControl1. We just need to make the following changes to the code in WebForm1.aspx, which simply reference the newly created control library and embed the default control in this library into the page body:

```
<%@ Page language="c#" Codebehind="WebForm1.aspx.cs" AutoEventWireup="false"
        Inherits="PCSCustomWebControlsTestApp.WebForm1" %>
<%@ Register TagPrefix="PCS" Namespace="PCSCustomWebControls"
        Assembly="PCSCustomWebControls"%>

<html>
    <head>
        <meta name="GENERATOR" Content="Microsoft Visual Studio 7.0">
        <meta name="CODE_LANGUAGE" Content="C#">
        <meta name=vs_defaultClientScript content="JScript">
        <meta name=vs_targetSchema content="Internet Explorer 5.0">
    </head>
    <body MS_POSITIONING="GridLayout">
        <form id="WebForm1" method="post" runat="server">
            <PCS:WebCustomControl1 Runat="server" Text="Testing again..."/>
        </form>
    </body>
</html>
```

Now, as long as we have the PCSCustomWebControls library configured as our startup application, we can hit the Debug button to see our results:

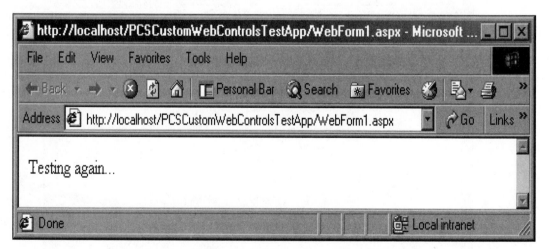

Also, add a project reference to `PCSCustomWebControls` in the test application:

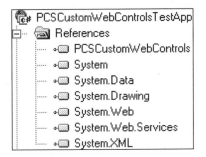

Then add a `using` statement to our `PCSCustomWebControlsTestApp` namespace in `WebForm1.aspx.cs`:

```
using PCSCustomWebControls;
```

This will enable us to use our custom controls from the code behind the form.

Basic Custom Controls

As can be inferred from the results in the last section, the sample control generated by default is simply a version of the standard `<asp:Label>` control. The code generated in the `.cs` file for the project, `WebCustomControl1.cs`, is as follows:

```
namespace PCSCustomWebControls
{
    using System;
    using System.Web.UI;
    using System.Web.UI.WebControls;
    using System.ComponentModel;

    /// <summary>
    ///    Summary description for WebCustomControl1.
    /// </summary>
    [DefaultProperty("Text"),
     ToolboxData("<{0}:WebCustomControl1 runat=server></{0}:WebCustomControl1>")]
    public class WebCustomControl1 : System.Web.UI.WebControls.WebControl
    {
        private string text;

        [Bindable(true),
         Category("Appearance"),
         DefaultValue("")]
        public string Text
        {
            get
            {
                return text;
            }

            set
            {
```

```
                text = value;
            }
        }

        /// <summary>
        ///     Render this control to the output parameter specified.
        /// </summary>
        /// <param name="output"> The HTML writer to write out to </param>
        protected override void Render(HtmlTextWriter output)
        {
            output.Write(Text);
        }
    }
}
```

The initial namespace using statements are fairly standard, as is the XML commenting throughout.

The single class defined here is the WebCustomControl1 class (note how the class name mapped straight onto an ASP.NET element in the simple example we just saw), which is descended from the WebControl class as discussed earlier. Two attributes are provided for this class: DefaultProperty and ToolboxData. The DefaultProperty attribute specifies what the default property for the control will be if used in languages that support this functionality. The ToolboxData attribute specifies exactly what HTML will be added to an .aspx page if this control is added using the Visual Studio toolbox, (once the project is compiled we can add the control to the toolbox by configuring the toolbox to use the assembly created).

The class contains one property: Text. This is a very simple text property much like those we've seen before. The only point to note here is the three attributes:

❑   Bindable – whether the property can be bound to data

❑   Category – where the property will be displayed in the property pages

❑   DefaultValue – the default value for the property

Exposing properties in this way works in exactly the same way as it did for custom controls, and is definitely preferable to exposing public fields.

The remainder of the class consists of the Render() method. This is the single most important method to implement when designing custom controls, as it is where we have access to the output stream to display our control content. There are only two cases where we don't need to implement this method:

❑   Where we are designing a control that has no visual representation (usually known as a **component**)

❑   Where we are deriving from an existing control and don't need to change its display characteristics

Custom controls may also expose custom methods, raise custom events, and respond to child controls (if any exist). We'll look at all of this in the remainder of this chapter, where we'll see:

❑   Creating a derived control

❑   Creating a composite control

❑   Creating a more advanced control

The final example will be a straw poll control, capable of allowing the user to vote for one of several options, and displaying voting progress graphically. Options will be defined using nested child controls, in the manner described earlier.

We'll start simply, though, and create a simple derived control.

The RainbowLabel Derived Control

For this first example, we'll derive a control from a `Label` control and override its `Render()` method to output multicolored text. To keep the example controls in this chapter separate we'll create new source files as necessary, so for this control add a new `.cs` file called `RainbowLabel.cs` and add the following code:

```
namespace PCSCustomWebControls
{
    using System;
    using System.Web.UI;
    using System.Web.UI.WebControls;
    using System.ComponentModel;
    using System.Drawing;

    public class RainbowLabel : System.Web.UI.WebControls.Label
    {
        private Color[] colors = new Color[] {Color.Red, Color.Orange,
                                     Color.Yellow, Color.GreenYellow,
                                     Color.Blue, Color.Indigo,
                                     Color.Violet};

        protected override void Render(HtmlTextWriter output)
        {
            string text = Text;

            for (int pos=0; pos < text.Length; pos++)
            {
                int rgb = colors[pos % 7].ToArgb() & 0xFFFFFF;
                output.Write("<font color='#" + rgb.ToString("X6") + "'>"
                        + text[pos] + "</font>");
            }
        }
    }
}
```

This class derives from the existing `Label` control (`System.Web.UI.WebControls.Label`) and doesn't require any additional properties as the inherited `Text` one will do fine. We have added a new private field, `colors[]`, which contains an array of colors that we'll cycle through when we output text.

The main functionality of the control is in `Render()`, which we have overridden as we want to change the HTML output. Here we get the string to display from the `Text` property and display each character in a color from the `colors[]` array.

To test this control, we need to add it to the form in `PCSCustomWebControlsTestApp`:

```
<form method="post" runat="server" ID="Form1">
    <PCS:RainbowLabel Runat="server" Text="Multicolored label!"
                      ID="rainbowLabel1"/>
</form>
```

We also need to add the relevant declaration in the code behind the form (if this is not added automatically):

```
public class WebForm1 : System.Web.UI.Page
{
    protected RainbowLabel rainbowLabel1;
    ...
```

This gives us:

Multicolored label!

Maintaining State in Custom Controls

Each time a control is created on the server in response to a server request it is created from scratch. This means that any simple field of the control will be reinitialized. In order for controls to maintain state between requests they must use the ViewState maintained on the client, which means we need to write controls with this in mind.

To illustrate this, we'll add an additional capability to the RainbowLabel control. We'll add a method called Cycle() that cycles through the colors available, which will make use of a stored offset field to determine which color should be used for the first letter in the string displayed.

This field will need to make use of the ViewState of the control in order to be persisted between requests. If we don't do this and initialize it in the control then things won't work properly.

I'll show the code for both cases to see the trap that is all too easy to fall into. First we'll look at code that fails to make use of the ViewState:

```
public class RainbowLabel : System.Web.UI.WebControls.Label
{
    private Color[] colors = new Color[] {Color.Red, Color.Orange,
                                          Color.Yellow, Color.GreenYellow,
                                          Color.Blue, Color.Indigo,
                                          Color.Violet};
    private int offset = 0;

    protected override void Render(HtmlTextWriter writer)
    {
        string text = Text;
        for (int pos=0; pos < text.Length; pos++)
        {
            int rgb  = colors[(pos + offset) % 7].ToArgb() & 0xFFFFFF;
            output.Write("<font color='#" + rgb.ToString("X6") + "'>"
```

```
                                    + text[pos] + "</font>");
        }
    }

    public void Cycle()
    {
        offset = ++offset % 7;
    }
}
```

Here we initialize the `offset` field to zero, then allow the `Cycle()` method to increment it, using the `%` operator to ensure that it wraps round to 0 if it reaches 7.

To test this we need a way of calling `cycle()`, and the simplest way to do that is to add a button to our form:

```
<form method="post" runat="server" ID="Form1">
    <PCS:RainbowLabel Runat="server" Text="Multicolored label!"
                      ID="rainbowLabel1"/>
    <asp:Button Runat="server" ID="cycleButton" Text="Cycle colors"
                OnClick="cycleButton_Click"/>
</form>
```

with the following event handler:

```
protected void cycleButton_Click(object sender, System.EventArgs e)
{
    this.rainbowLabel1.Cycle();
}
```

If you run this code you'll find that the colors change the first time we click the button, but further clicks will leave the colors as they are.

If this control persisted itself on the server between requests then it would work adequately, as the `offset` field would maintain its state without us having to worry about it. However, this technique wouldn't make sense for a web application, with thousands of users potentially using it at the same time. Creating a separate instance for each user would be counterproductive.

In any case, the solution is quite simple. We have to use the `ViewState` property bag of our control to store and retrieve data. We don't have to worry about how this is serialized, recreated, or anything else, we just put things in and take things out, safe in the knowledge that state will be maintained between requests in the standard ASP.NET way.

To place the `offset` field into the `ViewState` we simply use:

```
ViewState["_offset"] = offset;
```

`ViewState` consists of name-value pairs, and here we are using one called `_offset`. We don't have to declare this anywhere; it will be created the first time this code is used.

Similarly, to retrieve state we use:

```
offset = (int)ViewState["_offset"];
```

If we do this when nothing is stored in the ViewState under that name we will get a null value. The simplest way to deal with this case is to make this call in a try block.

Putting all of this together, we need the following code changes:

```
public class RainbowLabel : System.Web.UI.WebControls.Label
{
    private Color[] colors = new Color[] {Color.Red, Color.Orange,
                                          Color.Yellow, Color.GreenYellow,
                                          Color.Blue, Color.Indigo,
                                          Color.Violet};
    private int offset;

    protected override void Render(HtmlTextWriter writer)
    {
        string text = Text;
        GetOffset();
        for (int pos=0; pos < text.Length; pos++)
        {
            int rgb  = colors[(pos + offset) % 7].ToArgb() & 0xFFFFFF;
            writer.Write("<font color=#" + rgb.ToString("X6") + "'>"
                        + text[pos] + "</font>");
        }
    }

    private void GetOffset()
    {
        try
        {
            offset = (int)ViewState["_offset"];
        }
        catch
        {
            offset = 0;
        }
    }

    public void Cycle()
    {
        GetOffset();
        offset = ++offset % 7;
        ViewState["_offset"] = offset;
    }
}
```

This time, the control allows the Cycle() method to work each time.

In general, we might see ViewState being used for simple properties, such as string properties:

```
public string Name
{
   get
   {
      return (string)ViewState["_name"];
   }
   set
   {
      ViewState["_name"] = value;
   }
}
```

One further point about using the ViewState concerns child controls. If our control has children and is used more than once on a page, then we have the problem that the children will share their ViewState by default. In almost every case this isn't the behavior we'd like to see, and luckily we have a simple solution. By deriving our parent control from INamingContainer we force child controls to use qualified storage in the ViewState, such that child controls will not share their ViewState with similar child controls with a different parent.

Using this interface doesn't require any additional implementation, we just need to say that we are using it, as if it were simply a marker for interpretation by the ASP.NET server. We'll need to do this in the next section.

Creating a Composite Custom Control

As a simple example of a composite custom control, we can combine the control from the last section with the cycle button we had in the test form.

We'll call this composite control RainbowControl2, and place it in a new file, RainbowControl2.cs. This control needs to:

❑   Descend from WebControl (not Label this time)

❑   Support INamingContainer

❑   Possess two fields to hold its child controls

```
public class RainbowLabel2 : System.Web.UI.WebControls.WebControl,
                             INamingContainer
{
   private RainbowLabel rainbowLabel = new RainbowLabel();
   private Button cycleButton = new Button();
```

In order to configure a composite control we need to ensure that any child controls are added to the Controls collection and properly initialized. We do this by overriding the CreateChildControls() method and placing the required code there:

```
protected override void CreateChildControls()
{
   cycleButton.Text = "Cycle colors.";
   cycleButton.Click += new System.EventHandler(cycleButton_Click);
   Controls.Add(cycleButton);
   Controls.Add(rainbowLabel);
}
```

Here we just use the Add() method of Controls to get things set up correctly. We've also added an event handler for the button so that we can make it cycle colors, which is achieved in exactly the same way as for other events. The handler is the now familiar:

```
protected void cycleButton_Click(object sender, System.EventArgs e)
{
   rainbowLabel.Cycle();
}
```

This call simply makes the label colors cycle.

To give users of our composite control access to the text in the rainbowLabel child we can add a property that maps to the Text property of the child:

```
public string Text
{
   get
   {
      return rainbowLabel.Text;
   }
   set
   {
      rainbowLabel.Text = value;
   }
}
```

The last thing to do is to implement Render(). By default, if we don't override this method, each child control Render() method is called. However, to get more control over this we can call these methods, or rather the public instance RenderControl() methods, ourselves:

```
protected override void Render(HtmlTextWriter writer)
{
   rainbowLabel.RenderControl(writer);
   cycleButton.RenderControl(writer);
}
```

Here we aren't outputting any other HTML, although we could easily do so. We just need to pass the HtmlTextWriter instance we receive to the RenderControl() method for a child, and the HTML normally generated by that child will be inserted.

We can use this control in much the same way as RainbowLabel:

```
<form method="post" runat="server" ID="Form1">
   <PCS:RainbowLabel2 Runat="server" Text="Multicolored label composite"
                     ID="rainbowLabel2"/>
</form>
```

along with the associated declaration in the code behind the form.

A Straw Poll Control

Next we'll use and build on the techniques we've covered so far to make a more involved custom control. The end result of this will enable the following ASP.NET code:

```
<form method="post" runat="server" ID="Form1">
    <PCS:StrawPoll Runat="server" ID="strawPoll1" PollStyle="voteonly"
                   Title="Who is your favorite James Bond?">
        <PCS:Option Name="Sean Connery" Votes="101"/>
        <PCS:Option Name="Roger Moore" Votes="83"/>
        <PCS:Option Name="George Lazenby" Votes="32"/>
        <PCS:Option Name="Timothy Dalton" Votes="28"/>
        <PCS:Option Name="Pierce Brosnan" Votes="95"/>
    </PCS:StrawPoll>
</form>
```

to give us:

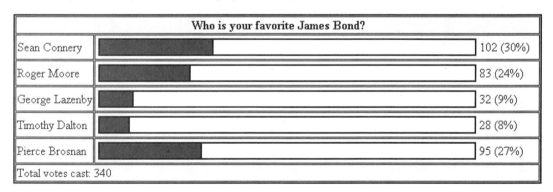

And when we click on a vote button the display will change to:

Alternatively, we can view results and voting buttons at the same time, and allow multiple votes, mainly for testing purposes.

The ASP.NET code is involved explicitly in setting the Name and Votes property for each Option. This is fine for this example, although it is foreseeable that a more advanced version of this control might be data-bindable to get these results. However, I won't cover this in this chapter, as that could get quite involved.

When the ASP.NET code is parsed, structures such as this one are interpreted in a consistent way: each child element is interpreted in the way that we specify in a **control builder** class associated with the parent control. This control builder, the code for which we'll see shortly, handles anything nested inside the control it is associated with, including literal text.

The two controls we need to create are Option, to hold individual options, and StrawPoll, which will contain and render the straw poll control. Both of these will be placed in a new source file: StrawPoll.cs.

The Option Controls

To start with, we'll create our Option controls, each of which will store an option name and amount of votes cast for that option. In addition, these controls will maintain a voting button, and handle any clicks made using this button.

Therefore, we need:

❑   Code for the Name and Votes properties (stored in the ViewState)

❑   Initialization code in CreateChildControls()

❑   Code for our button-click handler

We'll also include a utility method, Increment(), which will add a vote to the current count. The button-click handler will call this utility method.

We'll also need to support INamingContainer, as we'll have multiple instances of these controls with their own children.

The code for the Option class will go in StrawPoll.cs, which we should add to our project along with the standard namespace and using statements as per the RainbowLabel controls we saw earlier. The code is as follows:

```
public class Option : System.Web.UI.WebControls.WebControl, INamingContainer
{
   public string Name
   {
      get
      {
        return (string)ViewState ["_name"];
      }
      set
      {
         ViewState["_name"] = value;
      }
   }

   public long Votes
   {
      get
      {
         return (long)ViewState["_votes"];
      }
      set
```

```
      {
         ViewState["_votes"] = value;
      }
   }

   public void Increment()
   {
      ViewState["_votes"] = (long)ViewState["_votes"] + 1;
   }

   public void Reset()
   {
      ViewState["_votes"] = 0;
   }

   protected override void CreateChildControls()
   {
      Button btnVote = new Button();
      btnVote.Text = "Vote";
      btnVote.Click += new System.EventHandler(btnVote_Click);
      Controls.Add(btnVote);
   }

   protected void btnVote_Click(object sender, System.EventArgs e)
   {
      Increment();
   }
}
```

Note that `Render()` hasn't been overridden here. This is because this control has a single child, the voting button, and no other information to display. Therefore, we can just go with the default, which will simply be a rendering of the button.

The StrawPoll Control Builder

Next we'll look at how we can translate the ASP.NET code for each option into a control that is a child of our `StrawPoll` control. To do this we need to associate a control builder with the `StrawPoll` class, using the `ControlBuilderAttribute` attribute. We also need to specify that child controls should not be parsed in any other way using the `ParseChildren` attribute:

```
[ ControlBuilderAttribute(typeof(StrawPollControlBuilder)) ]
[ ParseChildren(false) ]
public class StrawPoll : System.Web.UI.WebControls.WebControl,
                         INamingContainer
{
}
```

Here we are using a class called `StrawPollControlBuilder`, defined as follows:

```
internal class StrawPollControlBuilder : ControlBuilder
{
   public override Type GetChildControlType(string tagName,
                                            IDictionary attribs)
```

```
        {
            if (tagName.ToLower().EndsWith("option"))
                return typeof(Option);

            return null;
        }

        public override void AppendLiteralString(string s)
        {
            // Do nothing to avoid embedded text being added to control
        }
    }
```

Here we override the `GetChildControlType()` method of the base `ControlBuilder` class to return the type of our `Option` class in response to a tag named `<Option>`. In fact, to make sure things work smoothly in as many situations as possible, we just look for any tag name that ends with the string `"option"`, with letters in upper or lower case.

We also override the `AppendLiteralString()` method so that any intervening text, including whitespace, is ignored and won't cause us any problems.

Once this is set up, and assuming we don't contain any other controls in `StrawPoll`, we will have all of our `Option` controls contained in the `Controls` collection of `StrawPoll`. This collection won't contain any other controls.

Note that the control builder makes use of a collection of attributes. In order to support this we need to add the following using statement to our namespace:

```
using System.Collections;
```

Straw Poll Style

Before we look at the `StrawPoll` class itself, there is one more design consideration. The straw poll should be able to display itself in three forms:

- Voting buttons only
- Results only
- Voting buttons and results

We can define an enumeration for this that we can use as a property of our `StrawPoll` control:

```
public enum pollStyle
{
    voteonly,
    valuesonly,
    voteandvalues
}
```

As we saw earlier, properties that are enumerations are easy to use – we can simply use the text names as attribute values in ASP.NET.

The Straw Poll Control

Now we can start putting things together. To start with we'll define two properties, `Title` for the title to display for the control, and `PollStyle` to hold the enumerated display type. Both of these will use the `ViewState` for persistence:

```
[ ControlBuilderAttribute(typeof(StrawPollControlBuilder)) ]
[ ParseChildren(false) ]
public class StrawPoll : System.Web.UI.WebControls.WebControl,
                         INamingContainer
{
    private string title = "Straw Poll";
    private pollStyle currentPollStyle = pollStyle.voteandvalues;

    public string Title
    {
        get
        {
            return title;
        }
        set
        {
            title = value;
        }
    }

    public pollStyle PollStyle
    {
        get
        {
            return currentPollStyle;
        }
        set
        {
            currentPollStyle = value;
        }
    }
}
```

The remainder of this class is taken up with the `Render()` method. This will display the whole straw poll control along with any options, taking into account the poll style to use. We'll display voting buttons simply by calling the `RenderControl()` method of child `Option` controls, and display the votes cast graphically and numerically using the `Votes` properties of child `Option` controls to generate simple HTML.

The code is as follows, commented for clarity:

```
protected override void Render(HtmlTextWriter writer)
{
    Option currentOption;
    long iTotalVotes = 0;
    long iPercentage = 0;
    int iColumns = 2;

    // Start table, display title
```

```
            if (currentPollStyle == pollStyle.voteandvalues)
            {
                iColumns = 3;
            }
            writer.Write("<TABLE border='1' bordercolor='black' bgcolor='#DDDDBB'"
                        + " width='90%' cellpadding='1' cellspacing='1'"
                        + " align='center'>");
            writer.Write("<TR><TD colspan='" + iColumns + "' align='center'"
                        + " bgcolor='#FFFFDD'>");
            writer.Write("<B>" + title + "</B></TD></TR>");

            if (Controls.Count == 0)
            {
                // Default text when no options contained
                writer.Write("<TR><TD bgcolor='#FFFFDD'>No options to"
                            + " display.</TR></TD>");
            }
            else
            {
                // Get total votes
                for (int iLoop = 0; iLoop < Controls.Count; iLoop++)
                {
                    // Get option
                    currentOption = (Option)Controls[iLoop];
                    // Sum votes cast
                    iTotalVotes += currentOption.Votes;
                }

                // Render each option
                for (int iLoop = 0; iLoop < Controls.Count; iLoop++)
                {
                    // Get option
                    currentOption = (Option)Controls[iLoop];
                    // Place option name in first column
                    writer.Write("<TR><TD bgcolor='#FFFFDD' width='15%'> "
                                + currentOption.Name + " </TD>");
                    // Add voting option to second column if required
                    if (currentPollStyle != pollStyle.valuesonly)
                    {
                        writer.Write("<TD width='1%' bgcolor='#FFFFDD'>"
                                    + "<FONT color='#FFFFDD'>.</FONT>");
                        currentOption.RenderControl(writer);
                        writer.Write("<FONT color='#FFFFDD'>.</FONT></TD>");
                    }

                    // Place graph, value, and percentage in third column if required
                    if (currentPollStyle != pollStyle.voteonly)
                    {
                        if (iTotalVotes > 0)
                        {
                            iPercentage = (currentOption.Votes * 100) / iTotalVotes;
                        }
                        else
                        {
                            iPercentage = 0;
                        }
```

```
            writer.Write("<TD bgcolor='#FFFFDD'><TABLE width='100%'>"
                      + "<TR><TD><TABLE border='1' bordercolor='black'"
                      + " width='100%' cellpadding='0'"
                      + " cellspacing='0'>");
            writer.Write("<TR><TD bgcolor='red' width='" + iPercentage
                      + "%'><FONT color='red'>.</FONT></TD>");
            writer.Write("<TD bgcolor='white' width='" + (100-iPercentage)
                      + "%'><FONT color='white'>."
                      + "</FONT></TD></TR></TABLE></TD>");
            writer.Write("<TD width='75'>" + currentOption.Votes + " ("
                      + iPercentage + "%)</TD></TR></TABLE></TD>");
        }
        // End row
        writer.Write("</TR>");
    }
    // Show total votes cast if values displayed
    if (currentPollStyle != pollStyle.voteonly)
    {
        writer.Write("<TR><TD bgcolor='#FFFFDD' colspan='" + iColumns
                  + "'>Total votes cast: " + iTotalVotes
                  + "</TD></TR>");
    }
}
// Finish table
writer.Write("</TABLE>");
}
```

There is one more thing to do. If the straw poll is being displayed in `voteonly` mode then voting should trigger a change of display to `valuesonly` mode. To do this we need a minor modification in the voting button handler in our `Option` class:

```
protected void btnVote_Click(object sender, System.EventArgs e)
{
    Increment();
    StrawPoll parent = (StrawPoll)Parent;
    if (parent. PollStyle == pollStyle.voteonly)
    {
        parent.PollStyle = pollStyle.valuesonly;
    }
}
```

Now you are free to vote for you favorite James Bond to your heart's content!

Adding an Event Handler

It is often the case with custom controls that you want to raise custom events, and allow users of the control to act on them. In the case of the straw poll control it would be nice to have a `Voted` event, which will notify the form that a vote has been made, and supply it with all the information needed to act on this.

To register a custom event we have to add code such as the following to a control:

```
public event EventHandler Voted;

protected void OnVoted(EventArgs e)
```

```
        {
            Voted(this, e);
        }
```

Then, whenever we want to raise the event we simply call `OnVoted()`, passing the event arguments.

Whenever we call `OnVoted()` an event is raised that the user of the control can act on. To do this the user needs to register an event handler for this event:

```
        strawPoll1.Voted += new EventHandler(this.strawPoll1_OnVoted);
```

The user also needs to provide the handler code, `strawPoll1_OnVoted()` here.

We'll extend this slightly by having custom arguments for our event, in order to make the `Option` control that triggers the event available. We'll call our custom argument object `OptionEventArgs`, defined in `StrawPoll.cs` as follows:

```
        public class OptionEventArgs : EventArgs
        {
            public Option originatingOption;
        }
```

We've simply added an additional public field to the existing `EventArgs` class. As we've changed the arguments we're using, we also need a specialized version of the `EventHandler` delegate that can be declared in the `PCSCustomWebControls` namespace as follows:

```
        public delegate void OptionEventHandler(object sender, OptionEventArgs e);
```

We can use these examples in `StrawPoll` as follows:

```
        public class StrawPoll : System.Web.UI.WebControls.WebControl,
                                 INamingContainer
        {
            private string title = "Straw Poll";
            private pollStyle currentPollStyle = pollStyle.voteandvalues;
            public event OptionEventHandler Voted;

            protected void OnVoted(OptionEventArgs e)
            {
                Voted(this, e);
            }
            ...
```

We'll also have a method to raise the event, called from child `Option` controls when voting buttons are clicked:

```
        public void ChildVote(OptionEventArgs e)
        {
            OnVoted(e);
        }
```

Finally we need to make a further modification to the voting button click handler in Option to call this method, supplying it with the correct parameters:

```
protected void btnVote_Click(object sender, System.EventArgs e)
{
    Increment();
    StrawPoll parent = (StrawPoll)Parent;
    if (parent.PollStyle == pollStyle.voteonly)
    {
        parent.PollStyle = pollStyle.valuesonly;
    }
    OptionEventArgs eOption = new OptionEventArgs();
    eOption.originatingOption = this;
    parent.ChildVote(eOption);
}
```

Now we're ready to implement the handler on the page using the control. We simply have to specify it in our ASP.NET page, adding a label to use in the handler:

```
<form id=Form1 method=post runat="server">
    <PCS:StrawPoll id=strawPoll1 title="Who is your favorite James Bond?"
                    Runat="server" OnVoted="strawPoll1_OnVoted"
                    PollStyle="voteonly">
        <PCS:Option Name="Sean Connery" Votes="101"/>
        <PCS:Option Name="Roger Moore" Votes="83"/>
        <PCS:Option Name="George Lazenby" Votes="32"/>
        <PCS:Option Name="Timothy Dalton" Votes="28"/>
        <PCS:Option Name="Pierce Brosnan" Votes="95"/>
    </PCS:StrawPoll>
    <br>
    <br>
    <asp:Label Runat="server" ID="resultLabel" Text="No vote cast."/>
</form>
```

along with the associated declaration in the code behind the form, if it is not added automatically:

```
public class WebForm1 : System.Web.UI.Page
{
    protected StrawPoll strawPoll1;
```

Then do something in the event handler itself:

```
protected void strawPoll1_OnVoted(object sender, OptionEventArgs e)
{
    resultLabel.Text = "You voted for " + e.originatingOption.Name + ".";
}
```

Now when we vote, we will get feedback on our vote:

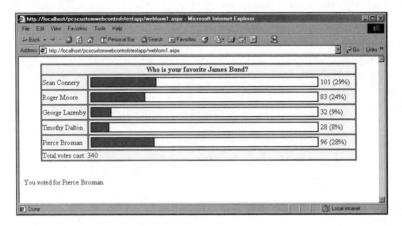

Summary

In this chapter we have looked at the various way we can create reusable ASP.NET server controls using C#. We have seen how to create simple user controls from existing ASP.NET pages, and also how to create custom controls from scratch.

There is a lot we can do with custom controls, and unfortunately it would have been impossible to cover all of it in a single chapter. However, hopefully there is enough information here to get you started. In particular it would have been interesting to have looked at data-binding, and how we can create our controls with this in mind, and to have looked in more depth at many areas (particularly an extended coverage of properties and control builders) would also have been fruitful. Unfortunately, topics such as these are really better suited to more specialized books.

This chapter completes the three web chapters in this book. Next we will move on to look at how COM and .NET interoperate.

19

COM Interoperability

COM components and .NET components are not innately compatible because they rely on different internal architectures. Fortunately, however, Microsoft provides tools in the .NET SDK for generating COM proxies for .NET components and .NET proxies for COM components. Using these proxies, along with a couple of other techniques, organizations can use legacy COM components in their .NET projects and can also use .NET components in their non-.NET applications.

In this chapter, we'll show you how to achieve interoperability between COM and .NET, and help you to understand why COM and .NET will play separate but vital roles in the Windows applications of the future.

COM and .NET Compared

COM stands for Component Object Model. For newcomers to the Windows platform, understanding what COM does can be difficult, and understanding how it operates can seem almost impossible. If you're such a newcomer and aren't interested in building device drivers or working at Microsoft, the advent of .NET and .NET components may allow you to avoid the complexities of COM programming. However, because COM has been such an essential part of Windows programming to date, you'll probably want to be familiar with how it came about and what benefits it provides.

Code reuse is one of the holy grails of software development, and early developers achieved this by maintaining files of utility functions. When a developer wanted to use utility functions in one of their programs, they used an #include statement to join the library file and the main program file together. After compilation, the utility functions and the program that called them were statically linked together into a single executable file.

There were at least two drawbacks to static linking: it wasted storage space by placing redundant copies of identical functions in multiple executables, and if you found a bug in one of the utility functions you had to re-compile and re-distribute every executable that called that function. To avoid these problems, developers found a way to compile function libraries into standalone binary files that could be *dynamically linked* to from separate executable files. With this scheme, several executable programs could share the same binary library file, the **Dynamic Link Library** (DLL). If you wanted to fix a utility function, you could just re-distribute the DLL that that function was in, without re-compiling or re-distributing all the executables that referenced it.

Despite their convenience and efficiency, DLLs had one serious shortcoming: they were language-specific. In other words, a DLL that was compiled from C source code could only be referenced from a client program that was also written in C. (OK, there were exceptions to this, but such exceptions required special effort from the programmer.)

COM was the next step in the evolution of code reuse. With it, a programmer could write a class library in a language such as C++, compile that library, and use the classes in that library from another COM-compatible language like Delphi or Visual Basic. COM was the technology underlying other technologies such as OLE (Object Linking and Embedding) and ActiveX controls.

COM+ Services, the latest version of the COM technology, originally known as Microsoft Transaction Server, are a part of the Windows 2000 operating system that COM components can leverage for commonly needed component functionality such as transaction support, security enforcement, and events, saving COM developers valuable programming time. They're discussed in greater detail in the next chapter.

How COM Works

To understand why COM components and .NET components aren't innately compatible, it helps to have a general understanding of how COM works. A grossly simplified explanation follows. For more detailed information, see "*Professional COM Applications with ATL*" from Wrox Press (ISBN 1-861001-70-3).

COM imposes a standard for the interfaces through which client code talks to component classes. Because client code communicates with component classes only through these standardized interfaces, it can remain blissfully ignorant of the language-specific details of how those component classes are implemented. For example, using COM interfaces as an intermediary, a VB client can reference COM components originally coded in C++.

COM interfaces provide other benefits in addition to cross-language communication. COM's IUnknown interface, for example, allows a COM object to count the number of clients that are referencing it, and to automatically deallocate itself from memory when this count falls to zero. Furthermore, by implementing interfaces recognized by COM+ Services, a COM class can make use of prewritten functionality for security, object pooling, and resource conservation.

Each COM class and each interface it supports has a 128-bit identifier that is guaranteed to be unique across all time and space. These globally unique identifiers, or GUIDs, are centrally stored in a machine's registry, and COM-compliant languages have facilities for getting the value of a COM component's GUID and using it to call the component's functionality.

The Drawbacks of COM

Although COM provides considerable benefits, it has a couple of drawbacks as well. First, COM components can be difficult to code. In C++, developing a COM component involves implementing the standard COM interfaces and using GUIDGEN.EXE to generate GUIDs for each class and each interface. (Although technologies like VB and the ATL Object Wizard simplify the process of COM creation, they only expose a subset of COM's features.)

Second, COM components can be difficult to deploy. Developers of COM server components supposed to ensure that new versions of their components are compatible with older versions, but they sometimes fail at this, and the installation of a new application that references a new version of a COM component can suddenly cause existing applications to fail. Problems of this variety are known as DLL Hell, and are the cause of a lot of head-scratching and wasted time.

For more information about how .NET addresses DLL Hell, see http://msdn.microsoft.com/library/techart/dplywithnet.htm.

How .NET Components Work

.NET's approach to componentization promises to deliver many of COM's benefits while eliminating a couple of its drawbacks. Components have to have some way to describe the classes that they support to clients. Instead of using GUIDs and the registry to do this, each .NET component file encapsulates its own description in an internal segment known as the **manifest**.

This means that component deployment is simple; all you have to do is copy a .NET component into the folder of the executable that references it. When the executable needs to create the component, it probes the component's file for the information that it needs from the component's manifest. Different versions of the same component can live side-by-side on the same machine, as long as they are stored in different folders. (There's a central folder for storing components that you want to make available to multiple applications; this is sometimes called the Global Assembly Cache. (For more information about the Global Assembly Cache, see Chapter 10.)

.NET components are easy to create, too. In both C# and VB.NET, the developer is shielded from the process of generating the manifest. The developer simply creates a class library project, fills it with classes, and lets the compiler do the dirty work of exposing these classes to clients.

COM or .NET?

.NET will not eliminate COM. Many organizations, including Microsoft, have invested considerable development resources in COM. Also, because .NET components are interpreted and rely on the .NET runtime, they are not as well suited as COM components for execution environments in which speed and efficiency are the primary concerns.

However, if you're an enterprise developer, you may find that .NET components prove more practical than COM components. In organizations that move at the speed of the Internet, good-enough software that meets deadlines is preferable to optimized software that falls six months behind. If your software runs from your web server, then you can ensure that the .NET runtime is properly configured, and you will gain from the development and deployment time that .NET will save you.

This is not to say that COM components are better than .NET assemblies, or that .NET assemblies are better than COM components. Although they require more run-time support, .NET assemblies simply make componentized architecture more accessible to everyday programmers.

Using COM Components in .NET

If your organization is typical, it is probably unable (or at least unwilling) to throw out the COM components that it has developed simply because .NET components are neat. Consequently, you can expect to reference legacy COM components from new .NET code, at least in your first .NET enterprise projects. Specifically, if you're building a new .NET application on top of an existing database, you will probably want to use existing COM data access objects as your project's data access layer. While accessing data through the legacy components, your .NET components will enforce business rules and deliver data to an ASP.NET or Windows Forms user interface.

COM interoperability uses "wrapper" classes and "proxy" components, conventions common in the programming world in general. A wrapper class surrounds a class that adheres to another architecture, providing a familiar interface to it for clients that would not recognize the wrapped class's native interface. Similarly, a client can use a proxy component to access a component that adheres to a different architecture or is geographically remote.

The References Dialog

Before we get into the intricacies of how interoperability with legacy COM objects works, let's take a quick look at what you need to do in order to achieve it. Our explanation is from the perspective of the VS.NET IDE because most readers will be using it to write their C# programs, but alternative editors may provide their own equivalent methods.

You need to use the References Dialog, which is available from the **Add Reference...** option on the **Project** menu of the Visual Studio.NET IDE. This dialog has three tabs, the first of which simply lists DLLs which are both crucial and ancillary to the .NET run-time environment:

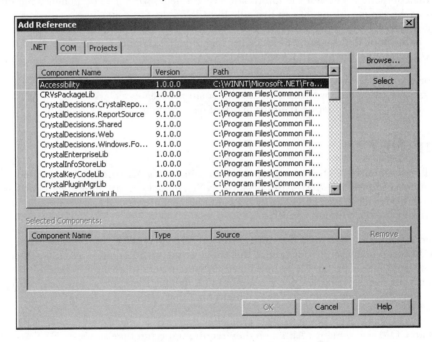

The rightmost, or **Projects**, tab lists all of the .NET projects that are referenced in the current solution. In the following screenshot, for example, a C# client application for online ordering relies on several C# class library projects that enforce business rules. (Of course, these wouldn't have to be C# projects in order to be referenced by the C# client; they could just as easily be VB.NET projects. In fact, one .NET client could simultaneously reference component projects in several different .NET languages.)

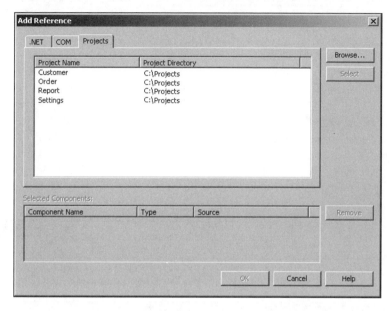

The middle, or **COM**, tab is the one that we need to use in order to import COM components for use in a .NET project.

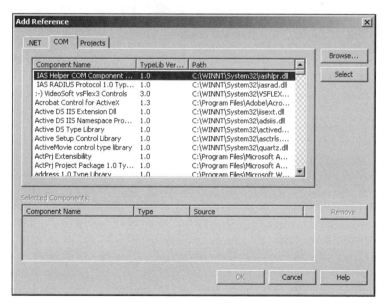

As you can see, there's a Browse... button in the upper right-hand corner of the dialog. When you click on this button, you're presented with another dialog that allows you to search the file system for the COM DLL that your .NET project needs:

When you locate that file, selecting it adds it to the list of components on the COM tab of the form:

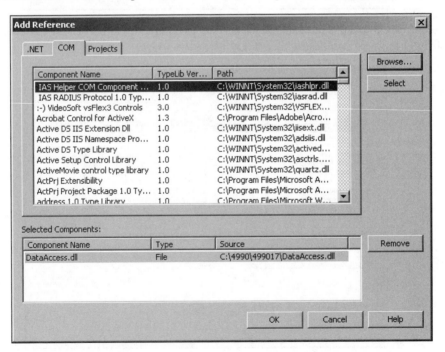

Once you've used the references dialog to locate a COM DLL and add it to the list of COM references, you can use that COM component in your .NET code. VS.NET creates a namespace bearing the same name as the original COM component, and classes provided by that COM component are placed within that namespace. You create a reference, instantiate, and invoke COM object wrappers with the same syntax that you reference, instantiate, and invoke objects native to C#.

Take a look at this code sample. In it, we define a method for adding a new customer to the database. As an input argument, this method receives a reference to a `CustomerInfo` object, whose fields contain a particular customer's name, social security number, etc. We create an instance of a `CustomerTable` data access class from a COM component, and use this instance to insert the customer's information into the database. What's significant about this example is that the code associated with the COM object is ordinary C# object code. We're creating an instance of the .NET wrapper, and allowing it to delegate its work to the real COM object behind the scenes:

```
/// <summary>
/// THIS ADDS A NEW CUSTOMER TO THE DATABASE, ENFORCING
/// BUSINESS RULES AS IT DOES SO.
/// </summary>

public long AddNewCustomer(CustomerInfo objCustomerInfo)
{
        long lngNewCustomerID;
        DataAccess.CustomerTable objCustomerTable;

        //ADD A RECORD TO THE CUSTOMER TABLE.

        objCustomerTable=new DataAccess.CustomerTable();
        lngNewCustomerID=objCustomerTable.InsertRecord(
                            objCustomerInfo.LastName,
                            objCustomerInfo.FirstName,
                            objCustomerInfo.MiddleName,
                            objCustomerInfo.SocialSecurityNumber);
```

Of course, if you tire of typing a COM component's namespace, a `using` statement at the top of each file will allow you to refer to classes in the COM component wrapper by abbreviated, relative names:

```
//PLACING THIS NEAR THE TOP OF A FILE…

using DataAccess;

//ALLOWS YOU TO REFER TO DataAccess CLASSES BY THEIR RELATIVE NAMES.

CustomerTable objCustomerTable;
objCustomerTable=new CustomerTable();
```

The VS.NET IDE will even use IntelliSense to help you remember the component's class members:

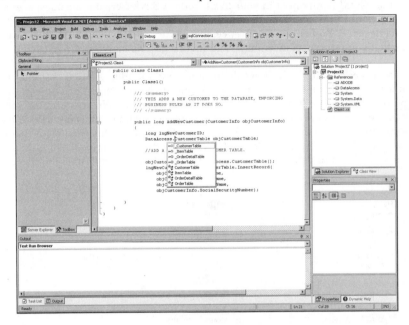

It will also help with data members, and the argument lists. Seems like magic doesn't it? There's more going on than meets the eye, however, as we'll see in the next section.

Runtime Callable Wrappers

When you use the References dialog to add a reference to a COM DLL, the VS.NET IDE does some work behind the scenes. Specifically, it generates a .NET proxy component for the COM DLL, and places a copy of the COM DLL in the .NET project's directory.

Remember how we said that .NET components describe themselves, while COM components store their descriptions in the registry? Well, the proxy that the VS.NET IDE generates describes the COM DLL and serves as a delegate for it, forwarding calls from the .NET client through COM Services to the COM DLL that it wraps. The .NET client has no knowledge that it's invoking a COM component; it only talks to the proxy, and receives data that the proxy relays back from the COM DLL.

In .NET-speak, the term for such a proxy is a **Runtime Callable Wrapper**, or **RCW**. The IDE creates a DLL that bears the same name as the original COM component, but is in reality a .NET RCW that simply wraps the original component, exposing it to .NET clients through a .NET interface that they can understand. An interesting side note is that the VS.NET IDE creates a wrapper not only for every COM DLL that you import, *but for every COM DLL that the imported COM DLL references in its public interface*, so in that folder you will also find the ADODB.dll file that is referenced by DataAccess.dll.

Our sample COM DLL, DataAccess.dll, provides methods for inserting, retrieving, updating, and deleting records in several database tables. Because the insert methods return ADO recordsets, clients of the COM component need a reference to the ADO type library. When I imported DataAccess.dll, the IDE was intelligent enough to recognize this necessity, and automatically created a RCW for the ADO COM component, too.

TlbImp.exe

It's dangerous for an RCW generated by the VS.NET IDE to bear the same name as the original COM DLL, isn't it? After all, if you were migrating an application from one machine to another, it would be very easy to confuse the RCW with the COM DLL that it wraps and accidentally overwrite the COM DLL file. Or, you could mistakenly attempt to register the RCW with COM Services, wondering all the while why the COM registration program (`regsvr32.exe`) doesn't work.

To avoid such problems, you might consider using `TlbImp.exe` directly. Provided with the .NET SDK, this executable program specializes in creating .NET proxies for COM DLLs. Because it is invoked from the command line, you can provide `TlbImp.exe` with an `out` command-line argument so that the resulting RCW will have a different name from the COM DLL:

`TlbImp` is shorthand for **Type Library Importer**. When you execute this program against a COM DLL, it interrogates the COM DLL's type library and translates the information therein into a .NET format, converting COM standard data types into those recognized by .NET. Once you've run `TlbImp.exe` against a COM DLL, you simply place its output file (an RCW) into the folder of the client executable that will use it. (That's the extra step that you have to go through when using `TlbImp.exe` explicitly rather than using the references dialog in the IDE.) In the sample above, I've run `TlbImp.exe` against a COM DLL that is in the same folder as `TlbImp.exe`, but `TlbImp.exe` works like any other command-line utility in that you can specify a file in another folder using an absolute or relative path.

In closing, let me give you a couple of warnings about `TlbImp.exe` and RCWs. First, don't forget to provide an `out` argument if you use `TlbImp.exe`! If you forget to provide one, the `TlbImp.exe` program will complain that it cannot overwrite the original file:

```
C:\WINNT\System32\cmd.exe                                        _ □ ×
C:\4990\499017>TlbImp DataAccess.dll
TlbImp - Type Library to .NET Assembly Converter Version 1.0.2728.0
Copyright (C) Microsoft Corp. 2001.  All rights reserved.

TlbImp error: Output file would overwrite input file
```

Second, remember that even though the RCW serves as an intermediary between the COM component and the .NET client that invokes it, the COM component is still doing the actual work. This means that you have to take the same deployment care with the COM component that you would if you were referencing it directly. In a word, this means that the wrapped COM component still has to be registered with COM Services! If you attempt to reference an unregistered COM component, the VS.NET IDE will flag an error:

To correct this problem, you will need, of course, to use the COM registration program, `regsvr32.exe`. You can invoke this program from the Windows Run dialog, which is available from the Desktop's Start button:

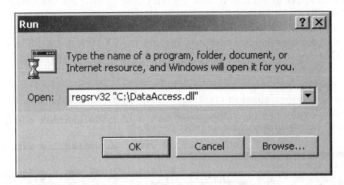

So don't forget to register your COM components!

Late Binding to COM Components

Before a client executable can invoke a component object's methods and properties, it needs to know the memory addresses of those methods and properties. There are two different techniques that client programs can use to determine those addresses.

Early-bound programs learn the addresses early on in the compilation/execution process, at compile time. When an early-bound program is compiled, the compiler uses the component's type library to include the addresses of the component's methods and properties into the client executable so that the addresses can be very quickly and unambiguously accessed. The COM interoperability techniques that we have examined thus far rely on early binding.

On the other hand, late-bound programs learn the addresses of properties and methods later in the compilation/execution process, *at very the moment that those properties and methods are invoked*. Late-bound code typically refers to client objects through generic data types, such as `object`, and relies on the runtime to dynamically ascertain the method addresses. Although late-bound code permits some sophisticated programming techniques, like polymorphism, it exacts some associated penalties too, which we'll look at shortly.

But first, let's examine how late binding is accomplished via reflection in C#. (Reflection is a way for code to determine information about server classes' interfaces at run time. For more information read the section *Reflection* in Chapter 7, where you'll find more information about the `Type` class that we discuss below and about reflection in general.)

When you late-bind to a COM object in a C# program, you don't need to create a RCW for the COM component. Instead, you call the `GetTypeFromProgID` class method on the `Type` class to instantiate an object representing the COM object's type. The `Type` class is a member of the `System.Runtime.InteropServices` namespace, and in the code below, we configure a `Type` object for the same data access COM component that we've seen in our previous examples:

```
using System.Runtime.InteropServices;
Type objCustomerTableType;
objCustomerTableType=Type.GetTypeFromProgID("DataAccess.CustomerTable");
```

Once you have a `Type` object encapsulating the COM object's type information, you use it to create an instance of the COM object itself. This is accomplished by passing the `Type` object to the `CreateInstance` class method on the `Activator` class. `CreateInstance` instantiates the COM object and returns a late-bound instance to it, which you can store in an `object` reference.

```
object objCustomerTable;
objCustomerTable=Activator.CreateInstance(objCustomerTableType);
```

At this point, your C# code has a late-bound reference to a full-fledged instance of the COM class!

Unfortunately, you can't invoke methods directly on the `object` reference. Instead, to talk to the COM object, you have to rely on the `InvokeMember` method of the `Type` object that you first created. When you call `InvokeMember`, you pass it a reference to the COM object, along with the name of the COM method that you are invoking and an `object` array of any input arguments to that method.

```
objCustomerTableType.InvokeMember("Delete",
                                  BindingFlags.InvokeMethod,
                                  null,
                                  objCustomerTable,
                                  aryInputArgs);
```

In case you've gotten lost along the way, you:

1. Create a `Type` object for the COM object's type with the class method `Type.GetTypeFromProgID()`

2. Use that `Type` object to create the COM object with `Activator.CreateInstance()`

3. Call methods on the COM object by firing `InvokeMember` on the `Type` object, passing in the `object` reference as an input argument

For your convenience, here are the sample code snippets combined together into one block:

```
using System.Runtime.InteropServices;
Type objCustomerTableType;
object objCustomerTable;
objCustomerTableType=Type.GetTypeFromProgID("DataAccess.CustomerTable");
objCustomerTable=Activator.CreateInstance(objCustomerTableType);
objCustomerTableType.InvokeMember("Delete",
                                  BindingFlags.InvokeMethod,
                                  null,
                                  objCustomerTable,
                                  aryInputArgs);
objCustomerTableType=Type.GetTypeFromProgID("DataAccess.CustomerTable");
```

Although C#'s late-binding facilities allow you to avoid the hassle of RCWs, you need to be aware of some of its associated drawbacks.

First, late binding can be dangerous. When you use early binding, the compiler is able to consult the COM component's type library to make sure that all of the methods that you call on the COM objects actually exist. In late binding, however, there's nothing to stop a typo in an `InvokeMember()` call from generating a run-time error.

Second, late binding can be slow. Each time you use `InvokeMember()` on an `object` reference, the runtime has to look up the desired member in the COM class's function library. This exacts a performance hit on your program.

Third, writing late-bound code can be difficult and time-consuming. Since you don't have a reference to the COM component's type library, the VS.NET IDE can't use IntelliSense to help you with member names and argument lists, so you can add errors to your code and they will not be found until run time.

Using ActiveX Controls in .NET

As you may already know, an ActiveX control is a particular type of COM component that supports a special set of interfaces to provide graphical aspect. Just as you can import standard COM components for use in .NET projects, you can import ActiveX controls, too. `AxImp.exe` is the utility program that allows you to do this.

AxImp.exe

To import an ActiveX component into .NET with `AxImp.exe`, you invoke `AxImp.exe` from the command line. Your there are two parts to the command:

1. The name `AxImp` (of course)

2. An absolute or relative path to the ActiveX (`*.ocx`) file that is to be imported

For an example, consider the screenshot below. Here, we're importing the Win32 MAPI ActiveX control and specifying the location of the `.ocx` file (`C:\windows\system\msmapi32.ocx`):

As you can see, the `AxImp.exe` program outputs two files. Here's why.

The first output file, `MSMAPI.dll`, is the assembly proxy. It allows you to reference the ActiveX component as if it were a non-graphical object, using its methods and properties in the same way that you'd use the methods and properties of any non-graphical class.

The second file, `AxMSMAPI.dll`, is the Windows control. It allows you to use the graphical aspect of the imported Active-X control as a Windows control in .NET Windows Forms projects.

When you use `AxImp.exe`, you'll want to make sure to provide explicit and unique names for these two output files, because, at least in the beta version of the .NET SDK, `AxImp.exe` has the potential to overwrite input files without warning!

Referencing an ActiveX's Proxy Assembly

As stated above, the proxy assembly output by AxImp.exe allows you to reference an ActiveX component programmatically without accessing its graphical aspects. To accomplish this, you just add a reference to the assembly proxy with the VS.NET IDE's **Reference** tab after AxImp.exe has done its work:

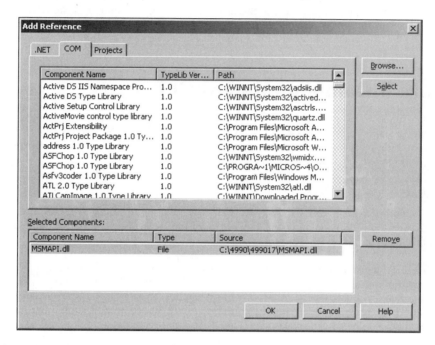

Once you've referenced the proxy assembly, you're ready to use the ActiveX component in your code. In the sample below, we use the MSMAPI32.ocx's proxy to send a mail message:

```
public static int Main()
{
    MAPISession objSession=new MAPISession();
    MAPIMessages objMessage=new MAPIMessages();
    objSession.Password="password";
    objSession.UserName="me@mydomain.com";
    objSession.SignOn();
    objMessage.SessionID=objSession.SessionID;
    objMessage.Compose();
    objMessage.MsgSubject="MAPI Control Test";
    objMessage.MsgNoteText="The message body.";
    objMessage.RecipAddress="you@yourdomain.com";
    objMessage.ResolveName();
    objMessage.Send(null);
    objSession.SignOff();
    return 0;
}
```

Hosting an ActiveX Control on a Windows Form

It's also quite simple to host an ActiveX control on a Windows Form. To do so, you must first launch the VS.NET IDE's Customize Toolbox dialog by right-clicking on the IDE's toolbox and selecting the appropriate option from the context menu that pops up. Once the dialog is shown, navigate to the .NET Framework Components tab and browse to the Windows control file that AxImp.exe generated. After you close the Customize Toolbox dialog, the imported control will appear in the IDE's toolbox, and you'll be able to add it to a Windows Form in the same way that you would add any other Windows control.

Using .NET Components in COM

Just as you can use COM components and ActiveX controls in .NET code, you can use .NET components in standard Windows code, too. Only a few features of .NET assemblies are not accessible via COM, including parameterized constructors, static methods, and constant fields. Additionally, accessing overloaded .NET methods from COM requires a little work.

RegAsm.exe

Using COM components in .NET code requires the use of another utility program that comes with the .NET SDK, one that is the analog of the Type Library Importer program that we looked at earlier. The name of this utility program is RegAsm.exe.

RegAsm's name (Register Assembly) denotes its function; it's in charge of entering a .NET component's type information into the system registry so that COM Services can access it. Once you've registered a .NET component, with RegAsm, standard Windows clients can late-bind to the classes in the component. The process of registering the component only has to be done one time. After it is registered, all COM clients can access it.

As an example, consider the following code. It's from a class in a .NET class library. The function simply accepts a number as an input argument and returns the factorial of that number:

```
namespace Factorial
{
    using System;
    public class Factorial
    {

        //THIS METHOD COMPUTES THE FACTORIAL FOR A NUMBER.

        public int ComputeFactorial(int n)
        {
            int intFactorial=n;
            for (int i=1;i<n;i++)
            {
                intFactorial*=i;
            }
            return intFactorial;
        }
    }
}
```

After we compile our sample class into a .NET assembly, we can register that assembly with COM services via RegAsm.exe:

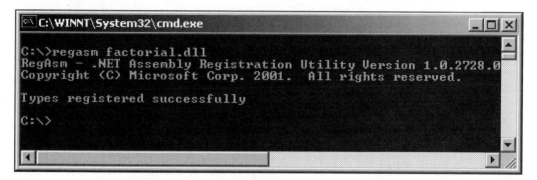

Now that the assembly has been registered with COM Services via RegAsm, we're free to late-bind to the .NET assembly through COM Services. For demonstration purposes, we'll create a simple VB Script that does so (You can create a VB script with a text editor such as Notepad; just type in the following code, and save the file with a .vbs extension. Assuming that you have Windows Script Host installed, the file will run as a script when invoked. Remember that VB Script employs late binding for COM components.)

```
Option Explicit

Dim objFactorial
Dim lngResult
Dim lngInputValue

Set objFactorial=CreateObject("Factorial.Factorial")
lngInputValue=InputBox("Number?")
lngResult=objFactorial.ComputeFactorial(CLng(lngInputValue))
Call MsgBox(lngResult)
```

Before we can use this, however, we have to install the assembly into the global cache. To do this, we first must create a strong name for the assembly using this command:

sn -k Factorial.snk

We then need to create an AssemblyInfo.cs file with the following contents:

```
using System.Reflection;
[assembly: AssemblyKeyFile("factorial.snk")]
```

This must then be compiled with the following line to turn it into a module:

csc /t:module /out:AssemblyInfo.dll AssemblyInfo.cs

After this, we compile the Factorial.cs file, and install the resulting DLL into the global cache with gacutil as follows:

```
csc /t:library /addmodule:assemblyinfo.dll Factorial.cs
gacutil /i Factorial.dll
```

When you execute the VB script, it uses COM Services to instantiate the .NET object, calls a method on that object, and displays the value returned from the .NET object in a message box:

An interesting technique, yes? But unfortunately, this technique does not solve any of the aforementioned dangers associated with late binding. Luckily, another member of the .NET SDK toolbox can help us out: TlbExp.exe.

Before we say goodbye to TlbImp.exe, though, there's one thing that you need to remember: COM Services has to be able to locate the .NET assembly component when it's invoked. That means that the assembly should be located in the client's working folder, or in the global assembly code for the system.

TlbExp.exe

TlbExp stands for Type Library Exporter. When run against a .NET assembly file, TlbExp can interrogate that assembly's internal manifest and output a corresponding COM type library file (*.tlb). Once TlbExp has created a type library file for a .NET component, non-.NET development languages such as VB 6 can reference it, using it to effectively achieve early binding to the .NET components:

```
C:\WINNT\System32\cmd.exe                                    _ □ ×

C:\>TlbExp Factorial.dll
TlbExp - .NET Assembly to Typelib Converter Version 1.0.2204.21
Copyright (C) Microsoft Corp. 2000.  All Rights Reserved
Assembly exported succesfully to C:\Factorial.tlb

C:\>
```

As you have probably inferred, TlbExp and RegAsm are designed to work hand-in-hand. You use RegAsm to register a .NET component with COM Services. Then you use TlbExp to export a COM type library for the client and reference it from your non-.NET languages.

Platform Invocation Services

We've talked about interoperability between COM components and .NET. While we're on the subject of interoperability, let's talk about another kind: that which is between .NET code and so-called unmanaged code. The technology for achieving this is called Platform Invocation Services, or **PInvoke** for short.

Unmanaged Code and Unsafe Code

The first thing that you need to be aware of is that the terms **unmanaged** and **unsafe** are not synonymous.

Unsafe C# code is that which is embedded in a block prefixed with the unsafe keyword. Code in such a block is free to use the entire range of C++ idioms, such as pointers and stack-based arrays. It's considered unsafe because such idioms are frequently associated with bugs, but *such code is still managed by the .NET runtime*.

On the other hand, unmanaged code is not managed by the .NET runtime. When a .NET application's thread-of-execution enters a segment of unmanaged code, the .NET runtime no longer has control over what that code does, and is unable to enforce garbage collection or security rules on it. (For this reason, applications that use unmanaged code must be endowed with a trust by the system administrator.)

Platform Invocation Services allow .NET code to interoperate with code that is not only unsafe, but also authentically unmanaged.

Accessing Unmanaged Code

Although .NET can interoperate with unmanaged code in any DLL, it most often interoperates with code in the DLLs that constitute the core functionality of the Windows API. These include user32.dll, gdi32.dll, and kernel32.dll. The process of exposing functions in these DLLs to .NET code should seem familiar to anyone who used the Declare keyword to exposed Win32 API calls to VB 6 code:

```
[sysimport(dll="user32.dll")]
public static extern int MessageBoxA(int Modal,
                string Message,
                string Caption,
                int Options);
```

In the example above, we've exposed the Windows API call that displays a message box to .NET by providing a .NET wrapper for the call. In an attribute above the wrapper function, we specified the DLL to which the wrappered function should delegate its work. Now, client .NET code can invoke the wrapper function to call the API functions:

```
MessageBoxA(0,"PInvoke worked!","PInvoke Example",0);
```

Although we chose to give the wrapper function the same name as the Windows API call to which it maps, we could give it a different name as well, as we do in the example below. Here, we change the name `MessageBox` to one that more accurately specifies how the API call will be used. We do this by specifying an extra value in the `sysimport` attribute:

```
[sysimport(dll="user32.dll",name="MessageBoxA")]
public static extern int ErrorMessage(int Modal,
                string Message,
                string Caption,
                int Options);
```

With the Windows API call renamed in this way, clients can invoke the function with the new name:

```
ErrorMessage(0,"PInvoke worked!","PInvoke Example",0);
```

The Drawback to Pinvoke

As you've seen, it's pretty easy to reference and invoke an unmanaged function from .NET code. Unfortunately, there is a potential drawback to using unmanaged code in this fashion.

Although Microsoft has consistently sidestepped the issue of platform interoperability, many people suspect that it is on the horizon for .NET. With platform interoperability in place, you could run a .NET program on any platform from Macintosh to Unix, provided that the platform was equipped with a .NET runtime. However, when you use `PInvoke`, you couple your .NET code to the Windows operating system.

When you consider using `PInvoke`, first check to see that the functionality you need isn't exposed somewhere by the .NET base classes; the most useful stuff is in there. If the .NET runtime were ever ported to a different platform, the .NET base classes would be ported, too, and your code would have a good chance of running correctly on the new platform with a few (if any) changes.

Conclusion

As this chapter has demonstrated, COM and .NET are distinct technologies that can work together if you apply the proper techniques. Using interoperability tools such as `TlbImp.exe`, `RegAsm.exe`, and `TlbExp.exe`, developers can use legacy COM components as building blocks for new .NET applications.

Compared to COM components, assemblies are easier to build, deploy, and maintain. It is unlikely that .NET will ever completely displace COM for developers for whom execution speed is the primary concern. However, it *is* likely that developers of web applications and programs to be used by organizations internally will find .NET assemblies to be a welcome respite from DLL Hell.

20

COM+ Services

Introduction

This is an ambitious chapter, because it attempts to explain two large subjects: what COM+ Services are, how they have developed, and how they work; and how COM+ Services can be leveraged from .NET in general, and from C# in particular.

We'll tackle the first subject in the first part of this chapter. Even if you're an old hand with COM+ Service's forerunner, MTS, you'll benefit from the coverage of new services like message queuing and events. As you'll see, COM+ Services provide much more than transaction support; they are a wealth of prefabricated functionality from which every professional C# programmer can benefit.

The last part of the chapter will address the second subject: how COM+ Services can be used in .NET. There, we'll take a look at the classes, interfaces, and attributes that are in the `EnterpriseServices` namespace. We'll also take a look at the `RegSvcs.exe` tool. It's at this point that we'll drill down into code samples.

Although COM+ Services may seem intimidating at first – particularly when you have to jump the interoperability hurdles – you'll be pleasantly surprised at how much time they can save you, and how robust applications built upon them can be.

Let's begin by taking a look at how COM+ Services came about.

COM+ Services in Perspective

In the bad old days of programming, the application developer had to build everything from scratch. If the developer wanted database functionality, for example, then they would have to implement it, devising a mechanism for maintaining indexes and searching for records through flat files. In those freewheeling frontier days of software engineering, people wasted a lot of time re-inventing the wheel.

As the programming techniques evolved, vendors packed useful functionality into reusable server components. (Now, for example, if a developer wants database functionality they can utilize Oracle or SQL Server.) As time went on, more and more useful functionality was pressed downward out of application programs and into the level of server programs, and even the operating system.

You can view COM+ Services as a manifestation of this trend.

COM+ Services make life easier for the enterprise developer by providing valuable functionality that the user's components can easily employ. When a component needs a capability such as transaction enforcement, the developer can rely on COM+ Services to provide a robust solution.

What COM+ Services Include

COM+ Services began life as a Windows NT add-on called Microsoft Transaction Server, MTS. Now, Windows 2000 has subsumed MTS as an integral part of the operating system, renaming it in the process. In addition to all of the original features of MTS, COM+ Services boast exciting new ones that further reduce the amount of code that the component developer has to write.

The COM+ Services that were present even in MTS include:

- ❏ Transaction enforcement
- ❏ Object pooling
- ❏ Just-In-Time (JIT) object activation
- ❏ Security

The new services introduced with COM+ Services include:

- ❏ Event support
- ❏ Component message queuing
- ❏ Component Load Balancing

Later in this chapter, we'll take a look at each of the COM+ Services, both those that you may remember from MTS, and the new ones with which you may not yet be familiar. First let's take a quick look at the COM+ programmer's best friend: the Component Services "snap-in." (A snap-in is a special type of program, like SQL Server or IIS, that runs inside the Microsoft Management Console (MMC) interface.)

The Component Services Snap-In

Seasoned developers may recall that the MTS administrator was accessed from the Windows NT Option Pack option on the Start menu. In keeping with its new status as an integral part of the operating system, COM+ Services is listed more prominently on the Administrative Tools menu in Windows 2000, under the title Component Services.

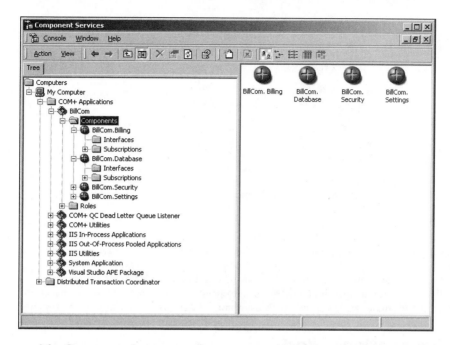

The left pane of the Component Services window contains a hierarchical tree with computer, COM+ application, and component nodes. (In the parlance of Component Services, an application is a group of COM+ components that are administered as a whole; this was called a package in MTS.) Each component class in an application is represented by a golden ball with a plus sign in the middle, which spins when the component is being accessed.

There are two methods for importing .NET assemblies into Component Services. The first method relies on functionality provided by the Component Services snap-in, while the second relies on the CLR.

We'll look at both import methods later on. Right now, let's begin our overview of the different services that COM+ provides.

COM+ Transactions

How Transactions Help

A transaction is a set of operations that succeed or fail as a unit, that is, if one operation in the set fails, all the other previously completed operations in the transaction must be rolled back to the original state before the transaction was started. A practical example follows.

Consider a web site that features credit card processing for orders. If a user orders a product from the site, it is essential that not only is the user's account charged, but that an order record is placed in the order database as well. If there's a problem entering an order record into the database, the charging of the credit card must be undone, and the order also needs to be canceled, otherwise a user will be charged for an item that they will never receive.

```
public void PlaceOrder(OrderInfo objOrderInfo, UserInfo objUserInfo)
{
    CreditCard objCreditCard=new CreditCard();
    OrderTable objOrderTable=new OrderTable();

    //Step 1: Charge the credit card.
    objCreditCard.PlaceCharge(objOrderInfo,objUserInfo);

    //If an error occurs here, between steps one and two,
    //the customer will not receive the product for which
    //he has been charged.

    //Step 2: Record the order.
    objOrderTable.RecordOrder(objOrderInfo,objUserInfo);
}
```

In the old days, developers had to cook up their own transaction enforcement schemes in order to get the sort of functionality mentioned above. These schemes usually involved lots of Boolean variables and elaborate error-handling strategies, and were bug-prone. More recently, the ADODB.Connection object offered support for transactions in a form that was quite elegant. Now, by means of the ContextUtil object that we'll look at shortly, COM+ Services presents developers with a transaction mechanism that is robust, ready-made, and even easier to use than the ADODB.Connection approach.

How Transactions Work

Let's take a quick peek "under the hood" to see how COM+ transactions work.

The Distributed Transaction Coordinator (DTC), a component of the Windows operating system, is in charge of administering transactions. Components that can enlist and participate in transactions must match an interface that the DTC understands, and must provide a resource manager that is capable of rolling back or committing units of work when told to do so by the DTC. This high degree of abstraction allows components as diverse as database engines and credit card processors to work together.

The DTC enforces transactions through a process called the two-phase commit. When enforcing a transaction, the DTC first asks every resource manager participating in the transaction whether it will be able to complete its work; this is the first phase. If and only if the DTC receives an OK from every participant, it tells each participant to go ahead and commit the changes; this is the second phase. If one of the participants experiences problems in the first phase, the DTC will tell every participant to undo its work.

Context is an abstraction important to transaction processing. Every transaction operation – such as a credit card charge and the subsequent insertion of an order record – has a context with which it is associated. To say that an operation occurs in the context of a transaction is to say that the operation is a part of the transaction, and can suggest to the DTC that the transaction be rolled back or committed. Such an operation effectively has the power to "veto" the committal of all the operations in its context.

Although a bit detailed, you may find this explanation of the inner working of transactions to be helpful a bit later, when we tackle coding transaction support into a .NET assembly.

Transactions in n-Tier Architectures

Architecturally, the typical client-server application that makes use of COM+ transactions consists of a layer of data access objects that perform the grunt work of adding, deleting, retrieving, and updating records in the database, wrapped with a layer of business objects that enforce the business rules, topped by a Windows Form-based or browser-based user interface.

It's common for a single business object method to call several different methods on several different data access objects. If one of the data access methods fails to execute properly, the business object method can use the COM+ transaction mechanism to ask the DTC to roll the operation back.

COM+ Services and Object Lifetime

The name Microsoft Transaction Server was something of a misnomer, because MTS provided more than just transaction support. In this section, we'll look at two COM+ Services that were first mentioned back in MTS: JIT activation and object pooling. Both of these services are techniques for ensuring that server machines use their resources effectively when manipulating server objects.

In order to understand how JIT activation and object pooling work, you need to be aware that there are two different types of COM+ applications.

❑ A **library application** is a collection of component classes, that, when instantiated, are created within the calling client's process

❑ A **server application** is a collection of component classes that are instantiated in a dedicated, surrogate process separate from the processes of all calling clients

Most ASP-based applications use components stored in server applications. Because the components are hosted in a dedicated, surrogate process, the failure of a server component doesn't crash the web server. For standard (non-.NET COM applications), you set the Activation type property on the Activation tab of the application's Properties window:

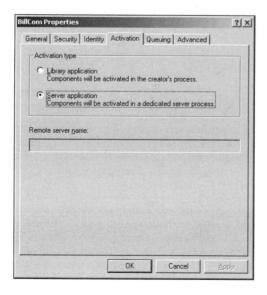

As you'll see later, there's a different procedure for specifying a .NET assembly's activation type. You'll learn how to do it programmatically, with attributes.

Only COM+ applications with an activation type of **Server application** can take advantage of object pooling, which is the COM+ service that we'll discuss next.

Object Pooling

In terms of processor cycles and bytes, it's expensive to instantiate and initialize an object. This expense is compounded for a web server that must serve tens of thousands of users simultaneously. So that users don't experience delays while the web server struggles to create component objects, COM+ Services provides object pooling.

As you might infer, this COM+ service allows the maintenance of a pool of objects that are created and waiting for use even before they are needed. When a server session needs a particular component object, it just requests one from the pool of available ones, getting one immediately if one is ready, or waiting in a queue until a new one becomes available. When the object is released by the client, COM+ Services does not destroy it, but instead allows it to persist in the pool, ready in the event that another client needs it. Because you can determine the minimum and maximum number of objects in the pool, you can discretely control how much of the server's resources are dedicated to the component class.

By its very nature, object pooling can share the same object instance between several different client processes. This means that if one of the sharing processes changes the state of the shared object just before it relinquishes it, the new state will be visible to the next process that gets the object – *even if that state is not one that the inheriting process expected*. There are a couple of ways to get around this problem.

First, you can design your component classes to be stateless. This means that you don't outfit them with properties that have to be set before methods are called. Instead, you persist these property values outside the objects, in the user interface itself, and pass them in as input arguments to the objects when their methods are called. Because the objects are no longer associated with any persistent data, this scheme effectively reduces your classes to glorified function libraries.

Second, you can endow your components with the intelligence necessary to serialize and restore their state themselves.

Object state is not only a concern when making use of object pooling, but when leveraging JIT activation tools. That's the next COM+ Service that we'll address.

Just-In-Time Activation (JIT)

Because object instantiation consumes server resources, developers have traditionally had to be careful about when in the program they performed it. Specifically, they had to be sure that heavily used, multi-user programs with a lot of traffic only created objects when required, and deallocated them immediately that they were no longer needed. Fortunately for us, COM+ Services provides another approach that frees the developer from this concern.

With just-in-time activation, a developer can instantiate objects once at the beginning of the program, and then use them whenever needed, without worrying about the resources that they consume while they are dormant. Invisibly, COM+ Services deallocates the space occupied by the objects when they're unused, and resurrects them at the moment that the client code invokes their methods. Thus, the client code can hold references to many objects for as long as it wants, confident that COM+ Services will provide the objects as necessary, and deallocate their memory whenever possible.

Like pooled classes, JIT-activated classes must manage state wisely. If COM+ Services deallocates the space occupied by your object between subsequent calls to it, there's no guarantee that the same property values will persist between the first and second call.

We've all used server objects that require some initialization before their methods can be invoked. The `ADODB.Connection` object is one example; you need to initialize its `ConnectionString` property before you can tell it to `Execute()` a SQL query. Because a pooled object can't persist state between calls, you can't initialize it and invoke its methods in separate steps. Instead, a call to a pooled object must pass to that object all the values that it needs to perform its work.

Security

There are two aspects to the security model that COM+ Services provide.

The first aspect is authentication. Briefly, COM+ Services allows you to place restrictions on who has access to serviced components and the methods that they provide. Using the Component Services snap-in, you can set an application's authentication level to determine when authentication is performed: upon the client's connection to the server object, with each network packet of communication to the object, as each method is invoked, etc.

The second aspect to the COM+ Services security model is a component's impersonation level. Since a server object performs work on behalf of a client, it can sometimes be useful for a server object to assume the access privileges and identity of the client that it serves. The impersonation level allows you to determine this.

Role-based security is the convention typically associated with client-server applications that utilize COM+ Services. In this approach, a server object first checks that its client belongs to a certain Windows security role before performing work on its behalf.

We'll implement role-based security for a .NET assembly later in this chapter.

New COM+ Services

So far, we've talked about COM+ Services that you may already be familiar with from MTS. Now, let's move on to talk about services introduced with COM+.

Events

One of the new services that COM+ offers is an event mechanism, whose architecture differs from the traditional mechanism of using connection points.

This new event service has often been termed the "publisher-subscriber" model. In this approach, you develop an event interface and register it with COM+ Services. Next, you register classes that want to be able to raise events defined in the interface as publishers. Last, you register classes that want to be able to handle events defined in the event interface as subscribers. When a publisher/server object raises an event, COM+ Services is in charge of notifying all of the subscribers. Because the subscriber classes are not directly coupled to the publisher classes, but instead rely on COM+ Services to serve as an intermediary, this architecture is often described as "loosely-coupled" events.

To implement this scheme, you must follow these steps:

1. Create an event class DLL that implements the event interface

2. Register the event class DLL with COM+ Services

3. Create a server component that internally instantiates the event class and invokes methods on the instance in order to raise events

4. Register the server component as a publisher with COM+ Services

5. Create client components that implement the event interface in order to catch events

6. Register the client components as subscribers with COM+ Services

When these steps are completed, a publisher class can raise an event simply by creating an instance of the event class and invoking one of its methods. As noted above, COM+ services will tell each subscriber class that the event has been raised. However, despite the robustness of this approach, there are at least two drawbacks to the way that COM+ Services implements this event model.

❑ First, because subscriber objects are notified of raised events one at a time, each subscriber object has the potential to make the others wait if its event handler is slow

❑ Second, at least at the time of writing, COM+ Services does not have the ability to raise events from publisher objects to subscriber objects on different machines

Again, the principal advantage of the publisher-subscriber event architecture is that the publisher and subscriber classes remain loosely coupled, able to communicate without maintaining direct references to each other.

Message Queuing

Special conditions may arise during the course of a program's execution. The database server may crash, or the user may attempt, purposefully or accidentally, to submit work from a disconnected terminal. Traditionally, developers have had to make special provisions in their application code to deal with these anomalies.

Now, the COM+ message queuing service will allow developers to avoid coding for disconnected situations. Briefly, the queuing service will record method calls from a client object to a server object that is unavailable, so that they can be played back to the server object when it once again comes online. The client code remains blissfully unaware that anything out of the ordinary has happened, and that COM+ Services is acting as an intermediary.

As you might imagine, message queuing comes in handy when you're designing applications that must run from both disconnected and connected machines. Also, message queuing is an integral part of Microsoft's new BizTalk Server, a new server program that can orchestrates how data moves through and between organizations. When you install Windows 2000 Server, message queuing is an option that you can install or leave out.

Despite its advantages, message queuing has a serious limitation, too. Obviously, when COM+ Services queues a message to an unavailable server object and returns control to the client, it's unable to return a complex response. For this reason, you have to take into account the possibility of unacknowledged errors occurring when you're designing components that make use of message queuing. Furthermore, you can't use values returned from queued components to do processing; if the components are offline, they can't return values.

Component Load Balancing

Even with the benefits that object pooling and just-in-time activation provide for maximizing server resources, there may be times when one server machine just isn't strong enough to serve all of an application's clients. In such situations, developers can make use of COM+'s Component Load Balancing Service. This service distributes application objects out across a farm of cooperating web servers, so that no one server is overwhelmed by object requests and so that end users continue to enjoy smooth, consistent performance.

The crux of the Component Load Balancing strategy is the Component Load Balancing server, or the CLB. The CLB is a Windows Advanced Server or Windows Data Server machine that serves as a manager to the other servers in the farm. The CLB is in charge of distributing the object requests between the available servers.

The algorithm that the CLB server uses for picking object hosts is a sophisticated one. It proceeds in order down a list of available servers, handing creation requests to the first server that is available. Because this list is sorted from most robust to least robust server, stronger servers are more likely to host requests.

Once a connection is established between the client application and the server machine that the CLB has assigned to the client, communication proceeds between them without subsequent intervention by the CLB. Because there's no guarantee that the client's server object will continue to be hosted on the same server machine, components must be stateless, and object pooling is not available.

Using COM+ Services with .NET Assemblies

Now that we understand what the various COM+ Services are, let's look at how the services can be used with .NET assemblies. We'll present an overview of the general technique here, and drill down into the details of using specific services in later sections. By the end of the chapter, you should feel comfortable implementing transactions, role-based security, object pooling, and JIT activation from .NET components.

Interoperability with COM+ Services from .NET assemblies is made possible largely through attributes. By prefixing class definitions with attributes defined in the System.EnterpriseServices namespace, you're able to specify how COM+ Services treat those classes. The C# compiler knows how to translate the attributes into the necessary code "hooks" that COM+ Services expect from components.

The attributes defined in the `EnterpriseServices` namespace include:

❑   `Transaction`

❑   `ObjectPooling`

❑   `JustInTimeActivation`

❑   `EventClass`

❑   `ApplicationActivation`

In addition to these attributes, the `System.EnterpriseServices` namespace defines various classes and enumerations as well, several of which we'll examine in detail shortly. If you'd like to see everything that the namespace exposes, use the `WinCV` tool. To see the classes in the `System.EnterpriseServices` namespace, you need to add this line to `WinCV.exe.config`:

```
<assembly name = "System.EnterpriseServices" />
```

within the `<wincv>` element.

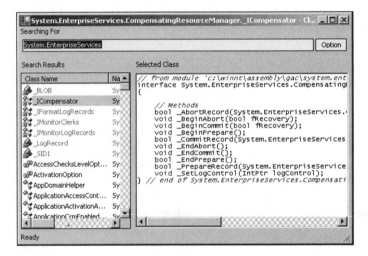

Preparing .NET Assemblies for COM+ Services

You'll probably agree that attributes are a tidy, non-invasive approach to making .NET classes available as COM+ Services. You just paste them onto the front of the applicable classes, right? Unfortunately, things are not quite as easy as that. Let's begin with the preliminary steps that you have to take to ready your classes for COM+ Services.

Providing Assembly Attributes

First, Microsoft suggests a standardized set of "assembly attributes" that should be included inside every .NET assembly that uses COM+ Services. The following code sample lists them:

```
[assembly:ApplicationActivation(ActivationOption.Server)]
[assembly:ApplicationID("448934a3-324f-34d3-2343-129ab3c43b2c")]
[assembly:ApplicationName("SomeApplicationName")]
[assembly:Description("Description of your assembly here.")]
```

Let's examine each of these attributes in turn.

Remember earlier when we mentioned that there are two kinds of COM+ applications, server applications and library applications? The first attribute in the code sample, the `ApplicationActivation` attribute, allows you to specify which of these two kinds of applications a particular assembly is. (Handily, the acceptable values for this attribute are defined in the `ActivationOption` enumeration, which you may have noticed inside the attribute's parentheses.) By specifying the application's type programmatically, with this attribute, you avoid having to open up the Component Services manager and do so manually. This enumeration has two values, `ActivationOption.Library` and `ActivationOption.Server`.

The second attribute, `ApplicationID`, associates a 128-bit globally unique identifier (GUID) with the assembly. (GUIDs are identifying numbers that are guaranteed to be unique across a very long stretch of time. COM+ Services expects such an ID from every application.) There's nothing significant about the random GUID in our code sample; it's just there for demonstration purposes. You'll need to create your own for each assembly that you create. To do so, you can use Microsoft's `GuidGen.exe` utility program, which is distributed with Visual Studio.

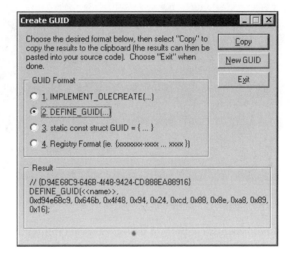

The third attribute in our code sample, `ApplicationName`, allows you to specify the name of the COM+ Services application that will be created to host the .NET assembly when the assembly is imported into COM+ Services. In our example, we've used the value `SomeApplicationName`.

The fourth and final attribute, `ApplicationDescription`, allows you to associate a description with the assembly to give developers who inherit your work some idea of what the assembly does.

Again, the Microsoft documentation specifies that any .NET assembly that is to be used in conjunction with COM+ Services should utilize all four of these attributes.

Deploying an Assembly for COM+ Services

Deploying an assembly that is to be used with COM+ Services is only a little harder than deploying any other .NET assembly.

First, you have to provide the assembly with a strong name. This is done by using the .NET SDK's sn.exe utility, which is discussed in the Chapter 10. sn.exe will output a strong name file, which you can reference from the command line when the assembly is compiled, to embed the strong name into the compiled assembly.

Second, you have to register the assembly in the global assembly cache. (This topic was also discussed in Chapter 10.)

If only managed clients (that is, .NET clients) will be using the assembly, no further deployment efforts are needed. When a managed client creates an instance of a serviced class in the assembly, the CLR will use the attributes in the assembly to automatically register the component with COM+ Services.

However, if classes in the assembly will be used by non-managed code, you have to explicitly register the assembly with COM+ Services yourself, prior to any client program's execution. The program for doing this registration, RegSvcs.exe, is provided by Microsoft as part of the .NET SDK. When you run RegSvcs against a .NET component, it will create a COM+ application with the name specified by the ApplicationName attribute in the assembly and import the assembly into it.

```
C:\WINNT\System32\cmd.exe                                          _ |□| x|
Microsoft Windows 2000 [Version 5.00.2195]
(C) Copyright 1985-2000 Microsoft Corp.

C:\>regsvcs DataAccess.dll DataAccess
RegSvcs - .NET Services Installation Utility Version 1.0.2901.4
Copyright (C) Microsoft Corp. 2000-2001. All rights reserved.

Installed Assembly:
        Assembly: C:\DataAccess.dll
        Application: DataAccess
        TypeLib: c:/DataAccess.tlb

C:\>
```

You may be wondering why RegSvcs.exe is necessary.

As you may recall from the previous chapter on COM interoperability, .NET assemblies adhere to a different architecture from COM components. It's the job of RegSvcs.exe to resolve these discrepancies, so that .NET assemblies meet the interface expected by COM+ Services. To fulfill its job, RegSvcs.exe does four things:

1. *It loads and registers the .NET assembly*

2. It creates a type library for the .NET assembly

3. It imports the type library into a COM+ Services application

4. It uses metadata inside the DLL to properly configure the type library inside the COM+ Services application

Not only does RegSvcs take care of all the messy details for importing your assembly into COM+ Services, but it also grants you a pretty fine degree of control of how it does so. You're granted that control in the form of optional command-line parameters. Here's the syntax of the command:

```
Regsvcs .NetComponentName [COM+AppName] [Typelibrary.tlb]
```

With the second argument (COM+AppName), you can specify a different name for the COM+ application that will be created, by providing a second command-line argument when calling RegSvcs. For even more flexibility, you can determine the name of the type library file that will be generated by providing a third argument (TypeLibrary.tlb). It's a good idea to always provide these arguments when invoking RegSvcs, because early versions of the program would silently overwrite any existing files that happened to have the same names as the new ones that they created.

Summary of Topics Covered up to This Point

Now you know how to prepare a .NET assembly for use with COM+ Services. This preparation includes:

❑ Outfitting the assembly with recommended assembly attributes

❑ Relating proxy classes to the internal "worker" classes with the ComEmulate attribute

❑ Deploying the assemblies, using sn.exe, al.exe, and possibly RegSvcs.exe

With this information under our belts, let's move on to the good stuff: the down-and-dirty details of utilizing specific COM+ Services from .NET assemblies.

Let's start with transactions.

Using Transactions with .NET Assemblies

There are two things that you have to do in order to equip a .NET class for transactions. First, you have to modify the class's proxy with an attribute to indicate its level of transactional support. Second, you have to add code to the class to control its behavior when it participates in transactions.

Remember the concept of transaction context that we covered earlier in the chapter? It's important here, so you may want to return to that section (*How Transactions Work*) for a quick review.

Specifying Transactional Support

If you've used transactions from COM+ Services before, you may have seen the Transaction support setting on a class's Property window in the Component Services snap-in. This setting allows you to set the level of transactional support that COM+ Services will grant to a standard COM component.

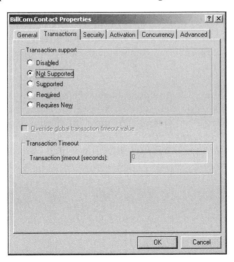

In .NET, you determine an assembly's level of transactional support differently, not by means of a graphical window in the Component Services snap-in, but programmatically, by means of the `Transaction` attribute defined in the `EnterpriseServices` namespace. For example, in the sample below, we've specified that the following proxy class should support transactions. Given this attribute value, our component will be configured to support transactions when it is imported into COM+ Services by `RegSvcs.exe`.

```
[Transaction(TransactionOption.Supported)]
public class ProxyClass:ServicedComponent
{
}
```

`Supported` is only one of several values that you can assign to a component's `Transaction` attribute. In fact, there are five, and they are listed in the `TransactionOption` enumeration, which is part of the `System.EnterpriseServices` namespace.

❑ When a class's `Transaction` attribute is set to `Disabled`, COM+ Services provides no transactional support for the class, even if such support is specified elsewhere in code. (In other words, calls that the class makes to `ContextUtil` to commit or roll back transactions are ignored. We'll see learn about `ContextUtil` in the next section.)

❑ When a class's `Transaction` attribute is set to `NotSupported`, that class does not enlist in transactions started by its clients; in other words, it's not placed in their context. When so configured, the objects of that class do not vote on whether the calling transaction is committed or rolled back.

❑ When a class's `Transaction` attribute is set to `Supported`, objects of that class *can* enlist in the transactional context of its calling clients, *if those calling clients did indeed begin a transaction.* Such an object cannot instigate a transaction by itself.

❑ When a class's `Transaction` attribute is set to `Required`, COM+ Services knows that objects of the class can only execute within the context of a transaction. If such an object is invoked by a client that has a transaction context, the object inherits the client's transaction context. If, however, the object is invoked by a client that does *not* have a transaction context, COM+ Services creates a context for the object.

❑ When a class's `Transaction` attribute is set to `RequiresNew`, COM+ Services creates a brand new transaction for the class every time that it is invoked. Even if the object's client already has a transaction, COM+ Services creates a new one for the server object. As you might infer, classes configured in this way can only roll back their own transactions, and not the work of their clients.

If you're feeling confused, relax. In practice, most developers only use one or two of these settings. The `Supported` value is great for a class like a `Settings` class that will need to serve both transactional and non-transactional classes. For most other transactional classes in most situations, you can usually get away with designating the `Required` value. However, this is not to say that you will sometimes encounter situations in which one of the more complex values is needed; for further information, consult *Professional Windows DNA Programming*, ISBN 1-861004-45-1, from Wrox Press.

Coding Transactions with ContextUtil

Modifying a class with the `Transaction` attribute is only part of what you have to do in order to enable it for transactions. You also have to specify how each *method* in that class will behave when invoked as part of a transaction. This is accomplished by means of the `System.EnterpriseServices` namespace's `ContextUtil` class.

To put it simply, the `ContextUtil` class exposes a transaction's context. Once you have a reference to the transaction's context, you can explicitly cause that context to be committed or rolled back. The methods that you need to call for committing and rolling back transactions are exposed as *class* methods on the `ContextUtil` class, so you don't have to create an instance of the `ContextUtil` class in order to invoke them.

As an example, take a quick glance through the code snippet below. (An explanation follows it.)

```
public bool PlaceOrder(bool CommitTrans)
{
    //Attempt the work.
    try
    {
        if(CommitTrans)
        {
            // This transaction should commit

            // step 1 -  Increase units of Product ID=2 by 10 items
            .IncreaseUnits(2, 10);

            // step 2 - Reduce stock of ProductID=2 by 10 items
            ReduceStock(2, 10);

        }
        else
        {
            // This transaction should roll back

            // step 1 - Increase units of Product ID=5 by 5 items
            IncreaseUnits(5, 5);

            // step 2 - Reduce stock of ProductID=5 by 5 items
            ReduceStock(5, 5);
        }

        //If all has gone well, complete the transaction.
        ContextUtil.SetComplete();

        return true;
    }
    //This code executes if an error was encountered.
    catch (Exception e)
    {
        //Roll back the work that this function has performed.
        ContextUtil.SetAbort();
        return false;
    }
}
```

What's happening here?

There are two transactions that may be processed, depending on the value of CommitTrans. In either transaction, PlaceOrder() calls two methods, both which connect to the Northwind database to make changes to the Products table. The ReduceStock() method reduces the amount of stock in the UnitsInStock column, the IncreaseUnits() method increases the value of the UnitsOnOrder() column. For both methods, the first parameter is the ProductID for the row we wish to change, the second parameter is the amount by which we wish to change the relevant column.

The transaction that will run is controlled by the CommitTrans Boolean variable passed into PlaceOrder(). The first transaction should commit, as the stock level for ProductID=2 is 17, so we can remove ten items and still have stock remaining. However, the second transaction is doomed to failure, as ProductID=5 has no stock items, and there is a constraint on the UnitsInStock column that doesn't let its value fall below zero. This means that we can check whether the transaction has rolled back or not; there should have been no problem with the call to IncreaseStock(), so we can see if the transaction has been rolled back by checking the value of the UnitsOnOrder column for ProductID=5.

In the try block, if all goes well, in other words, if the thread of execution is to leave PlaceOrder() normally through the return true; statement, PlaceOrder() invokes ContextUtil's SetComplete() method, effectively telling the DTC through the resource manager that, as far as it's concerned, the transaction needs to be committed.

On the other hand, if an error occurs somewhere in PlaceOrder() and an exception is thrown, program control will transfer to the catch() clause. In this clause, PlaceOrder() will invoke the ContextUtil's SetAbort() method. This method casts PlaceOrder()'s vote for the cancellation of the transaction in which it is involved, and the DTC, after receiving this vote from the resource manager, will ask every participant in the transaction to roll its work back.

Remember, you don't have to create an instance of the ContextUtil object in order to invoke its SetComplete() and SetAbort() methods. These are class methods, so you can call them on the class directly.

Most transaction-enabled code resembles that in the example. It invokes SetComplete() just before its exit point to commit all the work that has successfully been performed, or it invokes the ContextUtil's SetAbort() method in its error handler to roll everything back because of the error. Pretty easy, eh? There's another way that's even easier.

Microsoft provides a .NET attribute called AutoComplete. Methods modified with this attribute automatically apply the approach described above. Even though such methods never explicitly reference the ContextUtil class, they implicitly complete their transactions if they exit normally, or roll back all work if they exit due to an error (when an exception is thrown). We still have to call SetAbort() to get our transaction to roll back if an exception is thrown.

```
[AutoComplete]
public bool PlaceOrder(bool CommitTrans)
{
    try
    {
        if(CommitTrans)
        {
            // This transaction should commit
```

```
                // step 1 -  Increase units of Product ID=2 by 10 items
                IncreaseUnits(2, 10);

                // step 2 - Reduce stock of ProductID=2 by 10 items
                ReduceStock(2, 10);
            }
            else
            {
                // This transaction should roll back

                // step 1 - Increase units of Product ID=5 by 5 items
                IncreaseUnits(5, 5);

                // step 2 - Reduce stock of ProductID=5 by 5 items
                ReduceStock(5, 5);
            }
            return true;
        }
        catch (Exception e)
        {
            ContextUtil.SetAbort();
            return false;
        }
    }
```

This is the complete code for the complete transaction example, so you can see how you would fit the pieces together. The following is just built into a class library, given a strong name, and registered in the global assembly cache.

```
using System;
using System.EnterpriseServices;
using System.Data.SqlClient;

namespace OrderTransaction
{
    [Transaction(TransactionOption.Required)]
    public class Purchase : ServicedComponent
    {
        public Purchase()
        {
        }
        public bool PlaceOrder(bool CommitTrans)
        {
            //Attempt the work.
            try
            {
                if(CommitTrans)
                {
                    // This transaction should commit

                    // step 1 -  Increase units of Product ID=2 by 10 items
                    IncreaseUnits(2, 10);

                    // step 2 - Reduce stock of ProductID=2 by 10 items
                    ReduceStock(2, 10);
                }
```

```
            else
            {
                // This transaction should roll back

                // step 1 - Increase units of Product ID=5 by 5 items
                IncreaseUnits(5, 5);

                // step 2 - Reduce stock of ProductID=5 by 5 items
                ReduceStock(5, 5);
            }

            //If all has gone well, complete the transaction.
            ContextUtil.SetComplete();

            return true;
        }
        //This code executes if an error was encountered.
        catch (Exception e)
        {
            //Roll back the work that this function has performed.
            ContextUtil.SetAbort();
            return false;
        }
    }

    public void ReduceStock(int ProductID, int amount)
    {
        string source = "server=ephemeral;uid=sa;pwd=garysql;database=Northwind";
        SqlConnection conn = new SqlConnection(source);

        string command = "UPDATE Products SET UnitsInStock = UnitsInStock - " +
                amount.ToString() + " WHERE ProductID = " + ProductID.ToString();

        conn.Open();

        SqlCommand cmd = new SqlCommand(command, conn);
        cmd.ExecuteNonQuery();

        conn.Close();
    }

    public void IncreaseUnits(int ProductID, int amount)
    {
        string source = "server=ephemeral;uid=sa;pwd=garysql;database=Northwind";
        SqlConnection conn = new SqlConnection(source);
        string command = "UPDATE Products SET UnitsOnOrder = UnitsOnOrder + " +
                amount.ToString() + " WHERE ProductID = " + ProductID.ToString();

        conn.Open();

        SqlCommand cmd = new SqlCommand(command, conn);
        cmd.ExecuteNonQuery();

        conn.Close();
    }
```

```
        public void Restore()
        {
           //Restore stock for ProductID=2
           ReduceStock(2, -10);

           //Restore units for ProductID=2
           IncreaseUnits(2, -10);

           // Don't need to restore stock or units for ProductID=5
           // as transaction should have rolled back

        }
    }
}
```

We can build a client to test this class library; here the client is built so that it waits for the user to check out the contents of the database before restoring the database back to its original values. This allows you to see what the results of the transactions are for yourself.

```
        static void Main(string[] args)
        {
           Purchase Order = new Purchase();

           Console.WriteLine("\nThis transaction should commit");
           Console.WriteLine("ProductID = 2, ordering 10 items");
           if (Order.PlaceOrder(true))
              Console.WriteLine("Transaction Successful");
           else
              Console.WriteLine("Transaction Unsuccessful");

           Console.WriteLine("\nThis transaction should roll back");
           Console.WriteLine("ProductID = 5, ordering 5 items");
           if (Order.PlaceOrder(false))
              Console.WriteLine("Transaction Successful");
           else
              Console.WriteLine("Transaction Unsuccessful");

           Console.WriteLine("\nTake a look at the database then hit enter to " +
                                           "return database to original state");
           Console.ReadLine();

           Order.Restore();
        }
```

Other Useful ContextUtil Methods

While we're on the subject of the ContextUtil class, let's look at a couple of other methods that may prove useful to you in C# programming.

First, the IsCallerInRole() method provides for role-based security. As an input variable, this method accepts a string variable containing the name of a particular Windows 2000 security role. It returns a Boolean value indicating whether or not the user who is currently invoking the object is a member of the specified role.

In the code sample below, we've added a check to make sure that the user attempting to invoke `PlaceOrder()` is an authorized member of `Administrators` role. If the user isn't in the role, `PlaceOrder()` throws an exception.

```
[AutoComplete]
public bool PlaceOrder(bool CommitTrans)
{

    if (!ContextUtil.IsCallerInRole("Administrators"){
    {
        throw new AccessViolationException("User is not authorized to place " +
                                                              "orders.");
    }

    // Put transaction code here
}
```

The second useful `ContextUtil` method that we'll look at is `IsInTransaction()`. This method returns a Boolean value indicating whether the object is currently participating in a transaction.

As a professional C# programmer, you'll probably develop transactional components for use on a remote machine at remote installation that you do not control. To make sure that assemblies requiring transactional support are properly configured for it, you can call `ContextUtil` class's `IsInTransaction` property, and throw an error if this property is set to `false`.

In the code sample below, we use `IsInTransaction` to ensure that the assembly is properly configured before allowing it to start any work. It throws an exception if `IsInTransaction` has a value of `false`. You can test this out by changing the class's attribute to `TransactionalOptionDisabled`.

```
[AutoComplete]
public bool PlaceOrder(bool CommitTrans)
{

    if (!ContextUtil.IsInTransaction){
    {
        throw new ConfigurationException("This assembly needs to be configured for "
                                                      + "transactions.");
    }

    // Perform transaction
}
```

This completes our discussion of COM+ transactions and the `ContextUtil` class. Let's move on to object pooling.

Using Object Pooling with .NET Assemblies

It's not difficult to configure a .NET component for object pooling. Doing so entails modifying the class with an attribute, and implementing an interface in that class.

The ObjectPooling Attribute

The attribute with which you should modify the class is `ObjectPooling`. This attribute receives four arguments.

1. *The `Enabled` argument is first. It should be assigned a value of `true`*

2. The `MinPoolSize` argument specifies the minimum number of object instances that COM+ Services should maintain in the class's object pool

3. The `MaxPoolSize` argument specifies the maximum number of object instances that COM+ Services should maintain in the class's object pool

4. The `CreationTimeOut` argument specifies the length of time that COM+ Services should attempt to get an object from the pool before returning a failure

Here's an example of an `ObjectPooling` attribute with all four arguments applied to a class. We'll combine this snippet into a larger code sample near the end of this section.

```
[ObjectPooling (Enabled=True, MinPoolSize=1, MaxPoolSize=100, CreationTimeout=30)]
public class CreditCard:ServicedComponent
{
```

The ServicedComponent Interface

As you may have noticed, the class in the example above inherits the `ServicedComponent` interface. All .NET classes that utilize object pooling must implement this interface. `ServiceComponent` contains three methods to override.

1. *The `CanBePooled()` method is used by clients to ascertain whether the class can be pooled. This method should return a Boolean value of `true`.*

2. The `Activate()` method is invoked by COM+ Services on a pooled object just before that object is handed to a new client. Endow this method with code for any initialization that the object should do between uses.

3. The `Deactivate()` method, `Activate()`'s counterpart, is fired by COM+ Services when the object is released by a client to return to the available pool.

The following code snippet shows a sample class configured for object pooling.

```
[ObjectPooling (Enabled=true, MinPoolSize=1, MaxPoolSize=100, CreationTimeout=30)]
public class CreditCard:ServicedComponent
{
    //THIS METHOD WOULD BE INVOKED BY COM SERVICES TO DETERMINE IF THE
    //OBJECT IS POOLED.
    public override bool CanBePooled()
    {
        return true;          //YOU SHOULD RETURN A BOOLEAN "TRUE."
    }

    //THIS METHOD WOULD BE INVOKED BY COM SERVICES WHEN THE OBJECT
```

```
    //IS BEING GIVEN TO A CLIENT.
    public override void Activate()
      {
            //INITIALIZATION CODE WOULD GO HERE.
      }


      //THIS METHOD WOULD BE INVOKED BY COM SERVICES WHEN THE OBJECT IS     //BEING
    RETURNED TO THE POOL.
    public override void Deactivate()
      {
            //TERMINATION CODE WOULD GO HERE.
      }


      //THIS METHOD WOULD BE INVOKED BY THE CLIENT.
    public void PlaceCharge(int OrderInfo, int UserInfo)
      {
        //CODE FOR PLACING A CHARGE AGAINST A CREDIT CARD WOULD GO HERE.
      }
    }
```

As the example demonstrates, both the `ObjectPooling` attribute and the `ServicedComponent` interface are required in order for a .NET class to implement object pooling. You'll also note that, unlike the `Transaction` attribute, the `ObjectPooling` attribute is applied directly to the "worker" .NET assembly, and not to the proxy class established with the `ComEmulate` attribute that was discussed earlier in this chapter.

Using JIT Activation with .NET Assemblies

To configure a .NET class for JIT activation, you merely modify the class with the `JustInTimeActivation` attribute, providing a Boolean value of `true`. Here, we take the `CreditCard` class from our previous example, and outfit it for JIT activation.

```
[JustInTimeActivation(true)]
public class CreditCard:ServicedComponent
{
    //THIS METHOD WOULD BE INVOKED BY THE CLIENT.
    public void PlaceCharge(OrderInfo objOrderInfo, UserInfo objUserInfo)
      {
        //CODE FOR PLACING A CHARGE AGAINST A CREDIT CARD WOULD GO HERE.
      }
    }
```

Summary

Before you embark on your next enterprise development project, familiarize yourself with COM+ Services. The *Professional Windows DNA* book from Wrox Press, mentioned earlier, is a good start. When correctly utilized, COM+ Services offer a wealth of functionality that would take a long time to replicate, and even longer to completely debug. What's more, the approaches that COM+ Services take to transaction support, resource conservation, and inter-process communication are quite generic: once you've learned them, you can apply them to a wide variety of problem domains.

21

Graphics with GDI+

This is the second of the two chapters in this book that cover the elements of interacting directly with the user, that is displaying information on the screen and accepting user input via the mouse or keyboard. In Chapter 9 we focused on Windows Forms, where we learned how to display a dialog box or SDI or MDI window, and how to place various controls on it such as buttons, textboxes, and listboxes. In that chapter, the emphasis was very much on using the familiar, predefined controls at a high level and relying on the fact that these controls are able to take full responsibility for getting themselves drawn on the display device. Basically, all you need to do is set the controls' properties and add event handlers for those user input events that are relevant to your application. The standard controls are powerful, and you can achieve a very sophisticated user interface entirely by using them. Indeed, they are by themselves quite adequate for the complete user interface for many applications, most notably dialog-type applications, and those with Explorer style user interfaces.

However there are situations in which simply using controls doesn't give you the flexibility you need in your user interface. For example, you may want to draw text in a given font in a precise position in a window, or you may want to display images without using a picture box control, simple shapes or other graphics. A good example, is the Word for Windows program that I am using to write this chapter. At the top of the screen are various menus and toolbars that I can use to access different features of Word. Some of these menus and buttons bring up dialog boxes or even property sheets. That part of the user interface is what we covered in Chapter 9. However, the main part of the screen in Word for Windows is very different. It's an SDI window, which displays a representation of the document. It has text carefully laid out in the right place and displayed with a variety of sizes and fonts. Any diagrams in the document must be displayed, and if you're looking at the document in Print Layout view, the borders of the actual pages need to be drawn in too. None of this can be done with the controls from Chapter 9. To display that kind of output, Word for Windows must take direct responsibility for telling the operating system precisely what needs to be displayed where in its SDI window. How to do this kind of thing is subject matter for this chapter.

We're going to show you how to draw a variety of items including:

- ❑ Lines and simple shapes
- ❑ Images from bitmap and other image files
- ❑ Text

In all cases, the items can be drawn wherever you like within the area of the screen occupied by your application, and your code directly controls the drawing – for example when and how to update the items, what font to display text in, and so on.

In the process, we'll also need to use a variety of helper objects including pens (used to define the characteristics of lines), brushes (used to define how areas are filled in – for example, what color the area is and whether it is solid, hatched, or filled according to some other pattern), and fonts (used to define the shape of the characters of text). We'll also go into some detail on how devices interpret and display different colors.

The code needed to actually draw to the screen is often quite simple, and it relies on a technology called **GDI+**. GDI+ consists of the set of .NET base classes that are available for the purpose of carrying out custom drawing on the screen. These classes are able to arrange for the appropriate instructions to be sent to the graphics device drivers to ensure the correct output is placed on the monitor screen (or printed to a hard copy). Just as for the rest of the .NET base classes, the GDI+ classes are based on a very intuitive and easy-to-use object model.

Although the GDI+ object model is conceptually fairly simple we still need a good understanding of the underlying principles behind how Windows arranges for items to be drawn on the screen in order to draw effectively and efficiently using GDI+.

This chapter is broadly divided into two main sections. In the first two-thirds of the chapter we will explore the concepts behind GDI+ and examine how drawing takes place, which means that this part of the chapter will be quite theoretical, with the emphasis on understanding the concepts. There will be quite a few samples, almost all of them very small applications that display specific hard-coded items (mostly simple shapes such as rectangles and ellipses). Then for the last third of the chapter we change tack and concentrate on working through a much longer sample, called `CapsEditor`, which displays the contents of a text file and allows the user to make some modifications to the displayed data. The purpose of this sample is to show how the principles of drawing should be put into practice in a real application. The actual drawing itself usually requires little code – the GDI+ classes work at quite a high level, so in most cases only a couple of lines of code are required to draw a single item (for example, an image or a piece of text). However, a well designed application that uses GDI+ will need to do a lot of additional work behind the scenes, that is it must ensure that the drawing takes place efficiently, and that the screen is updated when required, without any unnecessary drawing taking place. (This is important because most drawing work carries a very big performance hit for applications.) The `CapsEditor` sample shows how you'll typically need to do much of this background management.

The GDI+ base class library is huge, and we will scarcely scratch the surface of its features in this chapter. That's a deliberate decision, because trying to cover more than a tiny fraction of the classes, methods, and properties available would have effectively turned this chapter into a reference guide that simply listed classes and so on. We believe it's more important to understand the fundamental principles involved in drawing; then you will be in a good position to explore the classes available yourself. (Full lists of all the classes and methods available in GDI+ are of course available in the MSDN documentation.) Developers coming from a VB background, in particular, are likely to find the concepts involved in drawing quite unfamiliar, since VB's focus lies so strongly in controls that handle their own painting. Those coming from a C++/MFC background are likely to be in more comfortable territory since MFC does require developers to take control of more of the drawing process, using GDI, the predecessor of GDI+. However, even if you have a good background in GDI, you'll find a lot of the material is new. GDI+ does actually sit as a wrapper around GDI, but nevertheless GDI+ has an object model that hides many of the workings of GDI very effectively. In particular, GDI+ replaces GDI's largely stateful model, in which items were selected into a device context, with a more stateless one, in which each drawing operation takes place independently. A `Graphics` object (representing the device context) is the only object that persists between drawing operations.

By the way, in this chapter we'll use the terms drawing and painting interchangeably to describe the process of displaying some item on the screen or other display device.

Before we get started we will quickly list the main namespaces you'll find in the GDI+ base classes. They are:

Namespace	Contains
System.Drawing	Most of the classes, structs, enums, and delegates concerned with the basic functionality of drawing
System.Drawing.Drawing2D	More specialized classes, and so on, that give more advanced effects in drawing to the screen
System.Drawing.Imaging	Various classes that assist in the manipulation of images (bitmaps, GIF files, and so on)
System.Drawing.Printing	Classes to assist when specifically targeting a printer or print preview window as the "output device"
System.Drawing.Design	Some predefined dialog boxes, property sheets, and other user interface elements concerned with extending the design-time user interface
System.Drawing.Text	Classes to perform more advanced manipulation of fonts and font families

Almost all the classes, structs, etc. that we use in this chapter will be taken from the System.Drawing namespace.

Understanding Drawing Principles

In this section, we'll examine the basic principles that we need to understand in order to start drawing to the screen. We'll start by giving an overview of GDI, the underlying technology on which GDI+ is based, and see how it and GDI+ are related. Then we'll move on to a couple of simple examples.

GDI and GDI+

In general, one of the strengths of Windows – and indeed of modern operating systems in general – lies in their ability to abstract the details of particular devices away from the developer. For example, you don't need to understand anything about your hard drive device driver in order to programmatically read and write files to disk; you simply call the appropriate methods in the relevant .NET classes (or in pre-.NET days, the equivalent Windows API functions). This principle is also very true when it comes to drawing. When the computer draws anything to the screen, it does so by sending instructions to the video card telling it what to draw and where. The trouble is that there are many hundreds of different video cards on the market, many of them made by different manufacturers, and most of which have different instruction sets and capabilities. The way you tell one video card to draw, for example a simple line or a character string may involve different instructions from how you would tell a different video card to draw exactly the same thing. If you had to take that into account, and write specific code for each video driver in an application that drew something to the screen, writing the application would be an almost impossible task. Which is why the Windows **Graphical Device Interface** (**GDI**) has always been around since the earliest versions of Windows.

GDI hides the differences between the different video cards, so that you simply call the Windows API function to do the specific task, and internally the GDI figures out how to get your particular video card to do whatever it is you want drawn. However, GDI also does something else. You see, most computers have more than one device that output can be sent to. These days you will typically have a monitor, which you access through the video card and you will also have a printer. Some machines may have more than one video card installed, or you may have more than one printer. GDI achieves the remarkable feat of making your printer seem the same as your screen as far as your application is concerned. If you want to print something instead of displaying it, you simply inform the system that the device the output is being sent to is the printer and then call the same API functions in exactly the same way. That's the whole purpose of GDI – to abstract the features of the hardware into a relatively high-level API.

Although GDI exposes a relatively high-level API to developers, it is still an API that is based on the old Windows API, with C-style functions, and so is not as simple to use as it could be. GDI+ to a large extent sits as a layer between GDI and your application, providing a more intuitive, inheritance-based object model. Although GDI+ is basically a wrapper around GDI, Microsoft has been able through GDI+ to provide new features and claims to have made some performance improvements:

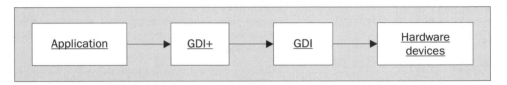

Device Contexts and the Graphics Object

In GDI, the way that you identify which device you want your output to go to is through an object known as the **device context (DC)**. The device context stores information about a particular device and is able to translate calls to the GDI API functions into whatever instructions need to be sent to that device. You an also query the device context to find out what the capabilities of the corresponding device are (for example, whether a printer prints in color or only black and white), so you can adjust your output accordingly. If you ask the device to do something it's not capable of, the device context will normally detect this, and take appropriate action (which depending on the situation might mean throwing an error or modifying the request to get the closest match that the device is actually capable of).

However, the device context doesn't only deal with the hardware device. It acts as a bridge to Windows, and is, therefore, able to take account of any requirements or restrictions placed on the drawing by Windows. For example, if Windows knows that only a portion of your application's window needs to be redrawn (perhaps because you've minimized another window that had been hiding part of your application), the device context can trap and nullify attempts to draw outside that area. Due to the device context's relationship with Windows, working through the device context can simplify your code in other ways. For example, hardware devices need to be told where to draw objects, and they usually want coordinates relative to the top left corner of the screen (or output device). Usually, however, your application will be thinking of drawing something at a certain position within the client area of its own window. (The **client area** of a Window is the part of the window that's normally used for drawing – which normally means the window with the borders excluded; on many applications the client area will be the area that has a white background.) However, since the window might be positioned anywhere on the screen, and a user might move it at any time, translating between the two coordinates is potentially a difficult task. However, the device context always knows where your window is and is able to perform this translation automatically. This means that you can just ask the device context to get an item drawn at a certain position within your window, without needing to worry about where on the screen your application's window is currently located.

As you can see, the device context is a very powerful object and you won't be surprised to learn that under GDI *all* drawing had to be done through a device context. You even sometimes use the device context for operations that don't involve drawing to the screen or to any hardware device. For example, if you have an image such as a bitmap to which you are making some modifications (perhaps resizing it), it's more efficient to do so via a device context because the device context may be able to take advantage of certain hardware features of your machine in order to carry out such operations more quickly. Although modifying images is beyond the scope of this chapter, we'll note that device contexts can be used to prepare images in memory very efficiently, before the final result is sent to the screen.

With GDI+, the device context is still there, although it's now been given a more friendly name. It is wrapped up in the .NET base class, `Graphics`. You'll find that, as we work through the chapter, most drawing is done by calling methods on an instance of `Graphics`. In fact, since the `System.Drawing.Graphics` class is the class that is responsible for actually handling most drawing operations, very little gets done in GDI+ that doesn't involve a `Graphics` instance somewhere. Understanding how to manipulate this object is the key to understanding how to draw to display devices with GDI+.

Example: Drawing Shapes

We're going to start off with a short example to illustrate drawing to an application's main window. The examples in this chapter are all created in Visual Studio.NET as C# Windows applications. Recall that for this type of project the code wizard gives us a class called `Form1`, derived from `System.Windows.Form`, which represents the application's main window. Unless otherwise stated, in all samples, new or modified code means code that we've added to this class.

> *In .NET usage, when we are talking about applications that display various controls, the terminology* form *has largely replaced* window *to represent the rectangular object that occupies an area of the screen on behalf of an application. In this chapter, we've tended to stick to the term window, since in the context of manually drawing items it's rather more meaningful. We write Windows (capital W) when we are referring to the operating system, and windows (small w) to refer to windows on the screen. We'll also talk about the Form when we're referring to the .NET class used to instantiate the form/window.*

The first example will simply create a form and draw to it in the `InitializeComponent()` method. I should say at the start that this is not actually the best way to draw to the screen – we'll quickly find that this example has a problem in that it is unable to redraw anything when it needs to after starting up. However the sample will illustrate quite a few points about drawing without our having to do very much work.

For this sample, we start Visual Studio.NET, create a Windows application, and modify the code in the `InitializeComponent()` method as follows:

```
private void InitializeComponent()
{
    this.components = new System.ComponentModel.Container();
    this.Size = new System.Drawing.Size(300,300);
    this.Text = "Display At Startup";

    this.BackColor = Color.White;
```

and we add the following code to the `Form1` constructor:

```
public Form1()
{
    InitializeComponent();

    Graphics dc = this.CreateGraphics();
    this.Show();
    Pen BluePen = new Pen(Color.Blue, 3);
    dc.DrawRectangle(BluePen, 0,0,50,50);
    Pen RedPen = new Pen(Color.Red, 2);
    dc.DrawEllipse(RedPen, 0, 50, 80, 60);
}
```

Those are the only changes we make. This sample is the `DisplayAtStartup` sample from the code download.

We set the background color of the form to white – so it looks like a 'proper' window that we're going to display graphics in! We've put this line in the `InitializeComponent()` method, so that Visual Studio.NET recognizes the line and is able to alter the design view appearance of the form. Alternatively, we could have used the design view to set the background color, which would have resulted in the same statement appearing in `InitializeComponent()`. Recall that this method is the one used by Visual Studio.NET to establish the appearance of the form. If we don't set the background color explicitly, it will remain as the default color for dialog boxes – whatever color is specified in your Windows settings.

Next, we create a `Graphics` object using the Form's `CreateGraphics()` method. This `Graphics` object contains the Windows device context we need to draw with. The device context created is associated with the display device, and also with this window. Notice, that we've used the variable name `dc` for the `Graphics` object instance, reflecting the fact that it really represents a device context behind the scenes.

We then call the `Show()` method to display the window. This is really a fudge to force the window to display immediately, because we can't actually do any drawing until the window has been displayed – there's nothing to draw onto.

Finally, we display a rectangle, at coordinates (0,0), and with width and height 50, and an ellipse with coordinates (0, 50) and with width 80 and height 50. Note that coordinates (x, y) means x pixels to the right and y pixels down from the top left corner of the client area of the window – and these are the coordinates of the top left corner of the shape being displayed:

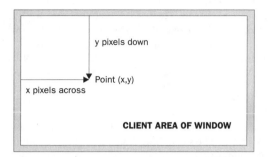

The notation (x,y) is standard mathematical notation and is very convenient for describing coordinates. The overloads that we are using of the DrawRectangle() and DrawEllipse() methods each take five parameters. The first parameter of each is an instance of the class System.Drawing.Pen. A Pen is one of a number of supporting objects to help with drawing – it contains information about how lines are to be drawn. Our first pen says that lines should be blue and with a width of 3 pixels, the second says that lines should be red and have a width of 2 pixels. The final four parameters are coordinates and size. For the rectangle, they represent the (x,y) coordinates of the top left hand corner of the rectangle, and its width and height, all expressed in terms of numbers of pixels. For the ellipse these numbers represent the same thing, except that we are talking about a hypothetical rectangle that the ellipse just fits into, rather than the ellipse itself.

We'll go into more detail about these new structs and the methods of the Graphics object later in the chapter. For now, we'll just worry about getting something drawn!

Running this code gives this result:

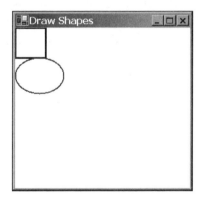

I know – the book's printed in grayscale. As with all the screenshots in this chapter, you'll just have to take my word for it that the colors are correct. Or you can always try running the samples yourself!

This screenshot demonstrates a couple of points. First, you can see clearly what the client area of the window means. It's the white area – the area that has been affected by our setting the BackColor property. And notice that the rectangle nestles up in the corner of this area, as you'd expect when we specified coordinates of (0,0) for it. Second, notice how the top of the ellipse overlaps the rectangle slightly, which you wouldn't expect from the coordinates we gave in the code. That results from where Windows places the lines that border the rectangle and ellipse. By default, Windows will try to center the line on where the border of the shape is – that's not always possible to do exactly, because the line has to be drawn on pixels (obviously), but the border of each shape theoretically lies between two pixels. The result is that lines that are 1 pixel thick will get drawn just *inside* the top and left sides of a shape, but just *outside* the bottom and right sides – which means that shapes that strictly speaking are next to each other will have their borders overlap by one pixel. We've specified wider lines; therefore the overlap is greater. It is possible to change the default behavior by setting the `Pen.Alignment` property, as detailed in the MSDN documentation, but for our purposes the default behavior is adequate.

The screenshot also looks like our code has worked fine. Seems like drawing couldn't be simpler! Unfortunately, if you actually run the sample you'll notice the form behaves a bit strangely. It's fine if you just leave it there, and it's fine if you drag it around the screen with the mouse. Try minimizing it then restoring it however and our carefully drawn shapes just vanish! The same thing happens if you drag another window across the sample. Even more interestingly, if you drag another window across it so that it only obscures a portion of our shapes, then drag the other window away again, you'll find the temporarily obscured portion has disappeared and you're left with half an ellipse or half a rectangle!

So what's going on? Well the problem arises because if a window or part of a window gets hidden for any reason (for example, it is minimized or hidden by another window), Windows usually immediately discards all the information concerning exactly what was being displayed there. It has to – otherwise the memory usage for storing screen data would be astronomical. Think about it. A typical computer might be running with the video card set to display 1024 x 768 pixels, perhaps with 24-bit color mode. We'll cover what 24-bit color means later in the chapter, but for now I'll say that implies that each pixel on the screen occupies 3 bytes. That means 2.25MB to display the screen. However, it's not uncommon for a user to sit there working, with 10 or 20 minimized windows in the taskbar. Let's do a worst-case scenario: 20 windows, each of which would occupy the whole screen if it wasn't minimized. If Windows actually stored the visual information those windows contained, ready for when the user restored them, you'd be talking about 45MB! These days, a good graphics card might have 64MB of memory and be able to cope with that, but it's only a couple of years ago that 4MB was considered generous in a graphics card – and the excess would need to be stored in the computer's main memory. A lot of people still have old machines – I still use a spare computer that has a 2 MB graphics card. Clearly it wouldn't be practical for Windows to manage its user interface like that.

The moment any part of a window gets hidden, those pixels get lost. What happens is that Windows just makes a note that the window (or some portion of the window) is hidden, and when it detects that that area is no longer hidden, it asks the application that owns the window to redraw its contents. There are a couple of exceptions to this rule – generally for cases in which a small portion of a window is hidden very temporarily (a good example is when you select an item from the main menu and that menu item drops down, temporarily obscuring part of the window below). In general however, you can expect that if part of your window gets hidden, your application will need to redraw it later.

That's a problem for our sample application. We placed our drawing code in the `Form1` constructor, which is called just once when the application starts up, and you can't call the constructor again to redraw the shapes when required later on.

In Chapter 9, when we covered controls, we didn't need to know about any of that. This is because the standard controls are pretty sophisticated and they are able to redraw themselves correctly whenever Windows asks them to. That's one reason why when programming controls you don't need to worry about the actual drawing process at all. If we are taking responsibility for drawing to the screen in our application then we also need to make sure our application will respond correctly whenever Windows asks it to redraw all or part of its window. In the next section, we will modify our sample to do just that.

Painting Shapes using OnPaint()

If the above explanation has made you worried that drawing your own user interface is going to be terribly complicated, don't worry. It isn't. I went into a lot of detail about the process, because it's important to understand what the issues you will face are, but getting your application to redraw itself when necessary is actually quite easy.

What happens, is that Windows notifies an application that some repainting needs to be done by raising a Paint event. Interestingly, the Form class has already implemented a handler for this event so you don't need to add one yourself. You can feed into this architecture by using the fact that the Form1 handler for the Paint event will at some point in its processing call up a virtual method, OnPaint(), passing to it a single PaintEventArgs parameter. This means that all we need to do is override OnPaint() to perform our painting. We'll create a new example, called DrawShapes to do this. As before, DrawShapes is a Visual Studio.NET-generated Windows application, and we add the following code to the Form1 class:

```
protected override void OnPaint( PaintEventArgs e )
{
   Graphics dc = e.Graphics;
   Pen BluePen = new Pen(Color.Blue, 3);
   dc.DrawRectangle(BluePen, 0,0,50,50);
   Pen RedPen = new Pen(Color.Red, 2);
   dc.DrawEllipse(RedPen, 0, 50, 80, 60);
   base.OnPaint( e );
}
```

Notice that OnPaint() is declared as protected. OnPaint() is normally used internally within the class, so there's no reason for any other code outside the class to know about its existence.

PaintEventArgs is a class that is derived from the EventArgs class normally used to pass in information about events. PaintEventArgs has two additional properties, of which the more important is a Graphics instance, already primed and optimized to paint the required portion of the window. This means that you don't have to call CreateGraphics() to get a device context in the OnPaint() method – you've already been provided with one. We'll look at the other additional property soon – it contains more detailed information about which area of the window actually needs repainting.

In our implementation of OnPaint(), we first get a reference to the Graphics object from PaintEventArgs, then we draw our shapes exactly as we did before. At the end we call the base class's OnPaint() method. This step is important. We've overridden OnPaint() to do our own painting, but it's possible that Windows may have some additional work of its own to do in the painting process – any such work will be dealt with in an OnPaint() method in one of the .NET base classes.

For this example, you'll find that removing the call to base.OnPaint() doesn't seem to have any effect, but don't ever by tempted to leave this call out. You might be stopping Windows from doing its work properly and the results could be unpredictable.

OnPaint() will also be called when the application first starts up and our window is displayed for the first time, so there is no need to duplicate the drawing code in the constructor, though we still need to set the background color there along with any other properties of the form. Again we can do this either by adding the command explicitly or by setting the color in the Visual Studio.NET properties window:

```
private void InitializeComponent()
{
    this.components = new System.ComponentModel.Container();
    this.Size = new System.Drawing.Size(300,300);
    this.Text = "Draw Shapes";
    this.BackColor = Color.White;
}
```

Running this code gives the same results initially as for our previous example – except that now our application behaves itself properly when you minimize it or hide parts of the window.

Using the Clipping Region

Our DrawShapes sample from the last section illustrates the main principles involved with drawing to a window, however it's not very efficient. The reason is that it attempts to draw everything in the window, irrespective of how much needs to be drawn. Consider the situation shown in this figure. I ran the DrawShapes example, but while it was on the screen I opened another window and moved it over the DrawShapes form, so it hid part of it. The other window here happens to be the Windows 2000 Task Manager but it doesn't matter what the other window is; the principle is the same:

So far, so good. What will happen, however, when I move the overlapping window (in this case the Task Manager) so that the DrawShapes window is fully visible again? Well, Windows will as usual send a Paint event to the form, asking it to repaint itself. The rectangle and ellipse both lie in the top left corner of the client area, and so were visible all the time; therefore, there's actually nothing that needs to be done in this case apart from repaint the white background area. However, Windows doesn't know that. As far as Windows is concerned, part of the window needs to be redrawn, and that means we need to raise the Paint event, resulting in our OnPaint() implementation being called. OnPaint() will then unnecessarily attempt to redraw the rectangle and ellipse.

In this case, the shapes will not get repainted. The reason is to do with the device context. Remember that I said that the device context inside the Graphics object passed to OnPaint() will have been optimized by Windows to the particular task at hand? What this means, is that Windows has pre-initialized the device context with information concerning what area actually needed repainting. This is the rectangle that was covered with the Task Manager window in the screenshot above. In the days of GDI, the region that is marked for repainting used to be known as the **invalidated region**, but with GDI+ the terminology has largely changed to **clipping region**. The device context knows what this region is; therefore, it will intercept any attempts to draw outside this region, and not pass the relevant drawing commands on to the graphics card. That sounds good, but there's still a potential performance hit here. We don't know how much processing the device context had to do before it figured out that the drawing was outside the invalidated region. In some cases it might be quite a lot, since calculating which pixels need to be changed to what color can be very processor-intensive (although a good graphics card will provide hardware acceleration to help with some of this). A rectangle is quite easy. An ellipse is harder because the position of the curve needs to be calculated. Displaying text takes a *lot* of work – the information in the font needs to be processed to figure out the shape of each letter, and each letter will be composed of a number of lines and curves which need to be drawn individually. If, like most common fonts, it's a variable width font, that is, each letter doesn't take up a fixed size, but takes up however much space it needs, then you can't even work out how much space the text will occupy without doing quite a few calculations first.

The bottom line to this is that asking the `Graphics` instance to do some drawing outside the invalidated region is almost certainly wasting processor time and slowing your application down. In a well designed application, your code will actively help the device context out by carrying out a few simple checks, to see if the usual drawing work is actually needed, before it calls the relevant `Graphics` instance methods. In this section we're going to code up a new example – `DrawShapesWithClipping` – by modifying the `DisplayShapes` example to do just that. In our `OnPaint()` code, we'll do a simple test to see whether the invalidated region intersects the area we need to draw in, and only call the drawing methods if it does.

First, we need to obtain the details of the clipping region. This is where an extra property on the `PaintEventArgs` comes in. The property is called `ClipRectangle`, and it contains the coordinates of the region to be repainted, wrapped up in an instance of a struct, `System.Drawing.Rectangle`. `Rectangle` is quite a simple struct – it contains four properties of interest: `Top`, `Bottom`, `Left`, and `Right`. These respectively contain the vertical coordinates of the top and bottom of the rectangle, and the horizontal coordinates of the left and right edges.

Next, we need to decide what test we'll use to determine whether drawing should take place. We'll go for a simple test here. Notice, that in our drawing, the rectangle and ellipse are both entirely contained within the rectangle that stretches from point (0,0) to point (80,130) of the client area; actually, point (82,132) to be on the safe side, since we know that the lines may stray a pixel or so outside this area. So we'll check whether the top left corner of the clipping region is inside this rectangle. If it is, we'll go ahead and redraw. If it isn't, we won't bother.

Here is the code to do this:

```
protected override void OnPaint( PaintEventArgs e )
{
    Graphics dc = e.Graphics;

    if (e.ClipRectangle.Top < 132 && e.ClipRectangle.Left < 82)
    {
        Pen BluePen = new Pen(Color.Blue, 3);
        dc.DrawRectangle(BluePen, 0,0,50,50);
        Pen RedPen = new Pen(Color.Red, 2);
        dc.DrawEllipse(RedPen, 0, 50, 80, 60);
    }
    base.OnPaint(e);
}
```

Note that what gets displayed is exactly the same as before – but performance is improved now by the early detection of some cases in which nothing needs to be drawn. Notice, also that we've chosen a fairly crude test of whether to proceed with the drawing. A more refined test might be to check separately, whether the rectangle needs to be drawn, or whether the ellipse needs to be redrawn, or both. There's a balance here. You can make your tests in OnPaint() more sophisticated – as you do, you'll improve performance, but you'll also make your own OnPaint() code more complex and create more work for yourself. How far you go is up to you. It's almost always worth putting some test in, however, simply because you've got the benefit of understanding the broad picture of what it is you are drawing (for example, in our example we have the advance knowledge that nothing we draw will ever go outside the rectangle (0,0) to (82,132)). The Graphics instance doesn't have that understanding – it blindly follows drawing commands. That extra knowledge means you may be able to code up more useful or efficient tests than the Graphics instance could possibly do.

Measuring Coordinates and Areas

In our last example, we encountered the base struct, Rectangle, which is used to represent the coordinates of a rectangle. GDI+ actually uses several similar structures to represent coordinates or areas, and we're at a convenient point in the chapter to go over the main ones. We'll look at the following structs, which are all defined in the System.Drawing namespace:

Struct	Main Public Properties
struct Point struct PointF	X, Y
struct Size struct SizeF	Width, Height
struct Rectangle struct RectangleF	Left, Right, Top, Bottom, Width, Height, X, Y, Location, Size

Note that many of these objects have a number of other properties, methods, or operator overloads not listed here. In this section we'll just discuss the most important ones.

Point and PointF

We'll look at Point first. Point is conceptually the simplest of these structs. Mathematically, it's completely equivalent to a 2D vector. It contains two public integer properties, which represent how far you move horizontally and vertically from a particular location (perhaps on the screen). In other words, look at this diagram:

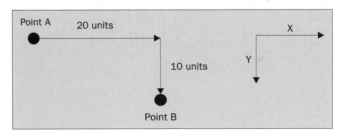

In order to get from point A to point B, you move 20 units across and 10 units down, marked as x and y on the diagram as this is how they are commonly referred to. We could create a `Point` struct that represents that as follows:

```
Point AB = new Point(20, 10);
Console.WriteLine("Moved {0} across, {1} down", AB.X, AB.Y);
```

X and Y are read-write properties, which means you can also set the values in a `Point` like this:

```
Point AB = new Point();
AB.X = 20;
AB.Y = 10;
Console.WriteLine("Moved {0} across, {1} down", AB.X, AB.Y);
```

Note that although conventionally horizontal and vertical coordinates are referred to as x and y coordinates (lowercase), the corresponding `Point` properties are X and Y (uppercase) because the usual convention in C# is for public properties to have names that start with an uppercase letter.

`PointF` is essentially identical to `Point`, except that X and Y are of type `float` instead of `int`. `PointF` is used when the coordinates are not necessarily integer values. Casts have been defined for these structs, so that you can implicitly convert from `Point` to `PointF` and explicitly from `PointF` to `Point` – this last one is explicit, because of the risk of rounding errors:

```
PointF ABFloat = new PointF(20.5F, 10.9F);
Point AB = (Point)ABFloat;
PointF ABFloat2 = AB;
```

One last point about the coordinates. In this discussion of `Point` and `PointF`, I've deliberately been a bit vague about the units. Am I talking 20 pixels across, 10 pixels down, or do I mean 20 inches or 20 miles? The answer is that how you interpret the coordinates is up to you.

By default, GDI+ will interpret units as pixels along the screen (or printer, whatever the graphics device is) – so that's how the `Graphics` object methods will view any coordinates that they get passed as parameters. For example, the point `new Point(20,10)` represents 20 pixels across the screen and 10 pixels down. Usually these pixels will be measured from the top left corner of the client area of the window, as has been the case in our examples up to now. However, that won't always be the case – for example, on some occasions you may wish to draw relative to the top left corner of the whole window (including its border), or even to the top left corner of the screen. In most cases, however, unless the documentation tells you otherwise, you can assume you're talking pixels relative to the top left corner of the client area.

We'll have more to say on this subject later on, after we've examined scrolling, when we mention the three different coordinate systems in use, world, page, and device coordinates.

Size and SizeF

Like `Point` and `PointF`, sizes come in two varieties. The `Size` struct is for when you are using `int`s; `SizeF` is available if you need to use `float`s. Otherwise `Size` and `SizeF` are identical. We'll focus on the `Size` struct here.

In many ways the `Size` struct is identical to the `Point` struct. It has two integer properties that represent a distance horizontally and a distance vertically – the main difference is that instead of X and Y, these properties are named `Width` and `Height`. We can represent our earlier diagram by:

```
Size AB = new Size(20,10);
Console.WriteLine("Moved {0} across, {1} down", AB.Width, AB.Height);
```

Although strictly speaking, a `Size` mathematically represents exactly the same thing as a `Point`; conceptually it is intended to be used in a slightly different way. A `Point` is used when we are talking about where something is, and a `Size` is used when we are talking about how big it is.

As an example, think about the rectangle we drew earlier, with top left coordinate (0,0) and size (50,50):

```
Graphics dc = e.Graphics;
Pen BluePen = new Pen(Color.Blue, 3);
dc.DrawRectangle(BluePen, 0,0,50,50);
```

The size of this rectangle is (50,50) and might be represented by a `Size` instance. The bottom right corner is also at (50,50), but that would be represented by a `Point` instance. To see the difference, suppose we drew the rectangle in a different location, so it's top left coordinate was at (10,10).

```
dc.DrawRectangle(BluePen, 10,10,50,50);
```

Now the bottom right corner is at coordinate (60,60), but the size is unchanged – that's still (50,50).

The addition operator has been overloaded for points and sizes, so that it is possible to add a size to a point giving another point:

```
static void Main(string[] args)
{
    Point TopLeft = new Point(10,10);
    Size RectangleSize = new Size(50,50);
    Point BottomRight = TopLeft + RectangleSize;
    Console.WriteLine("TopLeft = " + TopLeft);
    Console.WriteLine("BottomRight = " + BottomRight);
    Console.WriteLine("Size = " + RectangleSize);
}
```

This code, running as a simple console application, produces this output:

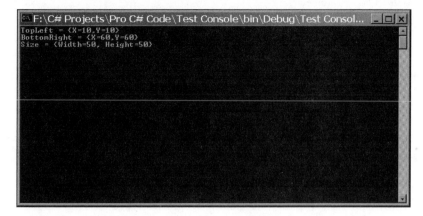

Notice that this output also shows how the `ToString()` method of `Point` and `Size` has been overridden to display the value in {X,Y} format.

Similarly, it is also possible to subtract a `Size` from a `Point` to give a `Point`, and you can add two `Size`s together, giving another `Size`. It is not possible, however, to add a `Point` to another `Point`. Microsoft decided that adding `Point`s doesn't conceptually make sense, so it chose not supply any overload to the + operator that would have allowed that.

You can also explicitly cast a `Point` to a `Size` and vice versa:

```
Point TopLeft = new Point(10,10);
Size S1 = (Size)TopLeft;
Point P1 = (Point)S1;
```

With this cast `S1.Width` is assigned the value of `TopLeft.X`, and `S1.Height` is assigned the value of `TopLeft.Y`. Hence, `S1` contains (10,10). `P1` will end up storing the same values as `TopLeft`.

Rectangle and RectangleF

These structures represent a rectangular region (usually of the screen). Just as with `Point` and `Size`, we'll only consider the `Rectangle` struct here. `RectangleF` is basically identical except that those of its properties that represent dimensions all use `float`, whereas those of `Rectangle` use `int`.

A `Rectangle` can be thought of as composed of a point, representing the top left corner of the rectangle, and a `Size`, which represents how large it is. One of its constructors actually takes a `Point` and a `Size` as its parameters. We can see this by rewriting our earlier code to draw a rectangle:

```
Graphics dc = e.Graphics;
Pen BluePen = new Pen(Color.Blue, 3);
Point TopLeft = new Point(0,0);
Size HowBig = new Size(50,50);
Rectangle RectangleArea = new Rectangle(TopLeft, HowBig);
dc.DrawRectangle(BluePen, RectangleArea);
```

This code also uses an alternative override of Graphics.DrawRectangle(), which takes a Pen and a Rectangle struct, as its parameters.

You can also construct a Rectangle by supplying the top left horizontal coordinate, top left vertical coordinate, width, and height separately, and in that order, as individual numbers:

```
Rectangle RectangleArea = new Rectangle(0, 0, 50, 50)
```

Rectangle makes quite a few read-write properties available to set or extract its dimensions in different combinations:

Property	Description
int Left	x-coordinate of left-hand edge
int Right	x-coordinate of right-hand edge
int Top	y-coordinate of top
int Bottom	y-coordinate of bottom
int X	same as Left
int Y	same as Top
int Width	width of rectangle
int Height	height of rectangle
Point Location	top left corner
Size Size	size of rectangle

Note that these properties are not all independent – for example setting Width will also affect the value of Right.

Region

We'll mention the existence of the System.Drawing.Region class here, though we don't have space to go details in this book. Region represents an area of the screen that has some complex shape. For example the shaded area in the diagram could be represented by Region:

As you can imagine, the process of initializing a Region instance is itself quite complex. Broadly speaking, you can do it by indicating either what component simple shapes make up the region or what path you take as you trace round the edge of the region. If you do need to start working with areas like this, then it's worth looking up the Region class.

A Note about Debugging

We're just about ready to do some more advanced drawing now. First however, I just want to say a few things about debugging. If you have a go at setting break points in the examples in this chapter you will quickly notice that debugging drawing routines isn't quite a simple as debugging other parts of your program. This is because the very fact of entering and leaving the debugger often causes Paint messages to be sent to your application. The result can be that setting a breakpoint in your OnPaint override simply causes your application to keep the painting itself over and over again, so it's unable to do anything else.

A typical scenario is as follows. You want to find out why your application is displaying something incorrectly, so you set a break point in OnPaint. As expected, the application hits the break point and the debugger comes in, at which point your developer environment MDI window comes to the foreground. If you're anything like, me you probably have the developer environments set to full screen display so you can more easily view all the debugging information, which means it always completely hides the application you are debugging.

Moving on, you examine the values of some variables and hopefully find out something useful. Then you hit *F5* to tell the application to continue, so that you can go on to see what happens when the application displays something else, after it's done some processing. Unfortunately, the first thing that happens is that the application comes to the foreground and Windows efficiently detects that the form is visible again and promptly sends it a Paint event. This means, of course, that your break point gets hit again straight away. If that's what you want fine, but more commonly what you really want is to hit the breakpoint *later,* when the application is drawing something more interesting, perhaps after you've selected some menu option to read in a file or in some other way change what is displayed. It looks like you're stuck. Either you don't have a break point in OnPaint at all, or your application can never get beyond the point where it's displaying its initial startup window.

There are a couple of ways around this problem.

If you have a big enough screen the easiest way is simply to keep your developer environment window restored rather than maximized and keep it well away from your application window – so your application never gets hidden in the first place. Unfortunately, in most cases that is not a practicable solution, because that would make your developer environment window too small. An alternative that uses the same principle is to have your application declare itself as the topmost application while you are debugging. You do this by setting a property in the Form class, TopMost, which you can easily do in the InitializeComponent method:

```
private void InitializeComponent()
{
    this.TopMost = true;
```

This means your application can never be hidden by other windows (except other topmost windows). It always remains above other windows even when another application has the focus. This is how the Task Manager behaves.

Even with this technique you have to be careful, because you can never quite be certain when Windows might decide for some reason to raise a `Paint` event. If you really want to trap some problem in that occurs in `OnPaint` for some specific circumstance (for example, the application draws something after you select a certain menu option, and something goes wrong at that point), then the best way to do this is to place some dummy code in `OnPaint` that tests some condition, which will only be true in the specified circumstances – and then place the break point inside the `if` block, like this:

```
protected override void OnPaint( PaintEventArgs e )
{
    // Condition() evaluates to true when we want to break
    if ( Condition() == true)
    {
        int ii = 0;   // <-- SET BREAKPOINT HERE!!!
    }
```

This is a quick-and-easy way of putting in a conditional break point.

Drawing Scrollable Windows

Our earlier `DrawShapes` sample worked very well, because everything we needed to draw fitted into the initial window size. In this section we're going to look at what we need to do if that's not the case.

We shall expand our `DrawShapes` sample to demonstrate scrolling. To make things a bit more realistic, we'll start by creating an example, `BigShapes`, in which we will make the rectangle and ellipse a bit bigger. Also, while we're at it we'll demonstrate how to use the `Point`, `Size`, and `Rectangle` structs by using them define the drawing areas. With these changes, the relevant part of the `Form1` class looks like this:

```
// member fields
private Point rectangleTopLeft = new Point(0, 0);
private Size rectangleSize = new Size(200,200);
private Point ellipseTopLeft = new Point(50, 200);
private Size ellipseSize = new Size(200, 150);
private Pen bluePen = new Pen(Color.Blue, 3);
private Pen redPen = new Pen(Color.Red, 2);

private void InitializeComponent()
{
    this.components = new System.ComponentModel.Container();
    this.Size = new System.Drawing.Size(300,300);
    this.Text = "Scroll Shapes";
    this.BackColor = Color.White;
}
#endregion

protected override void OnPaint( PaintEventArgs e )
{
    Graphics dc = e.Graphics;

    if (e.ClipRectangle.Top < 350 || e.ClipRectangle.Left < 250)
    {
```

```
        Rectangle RectangleArea =
            new Rectangle (RectangleTopLeft, RectangleSize);
        Rectangle EllipseArea =
            new Rectangle (EllipseTopLeft, EllipseSize);
        dc.DrawRectangle(BluePen, RectangleArea);
        dc.DrawEllipse(RedPen, EllipseArea);
    }
    base.OnPaint(e);
}
```

Notice, that we've also turned the Pen objects into member fields – this is more efficient than creating a new Pen every time we need to draw anything, as we have been doing up to now.

The result of running this example looks like this:

We can see a problem instantly. The shapes don't fit in our 300x300 pixel drawing area.

Normally, if a document is too large to display, an application will add scrollbars to let you scroll the window and look at a chosen part of it. This is another area in which, with the kind of user interface that we were dealing with in Chapter 9, we'd let the .NET runtime and the base classes handle everything. If your form has various controls attached to it then the Form instance will normally know where these controls are and it will therefore know if its window becomes so small that scrollbars become necessary. The Form instance will also automatically add the scrollbars for you, and not only that, but it's also able to correctly draw whichever portion of the screen you've scrolled to. In that case there is nothing you need to explicitly do in your code. In this chapter, however, we're taking responsibility for drawing to the screen; therefore, we're going to have to help the Form instance out when it comes to scrolling.

> *In the last paragraph we said,* if a document is too large to display. *This probably made you think in terms of something like a Word or Excel document. With drawing applications, however, it's better to think of the document as whatever data the application is manipulating that it needs to draw. For our current example, the rectangle and ellipse between them constitute the document.*

Getting the scrollbars added is actually very easy. The Form can still handle all that for us – the reason it hasn't in the above ScrollShapes sample is that it doesn't know they are needed – because it doesn't know how big an area we will want to draw in. How big an area is that? More accurately, what we need to figure out is the size of a rectangle that stretches from the top left corner of the document (or equivalently, the top left corner of the client area before we've done any scrolling), and which is just big enough to contain the entire document. In this chapter, we'll refer to this area as the document area. Looking at the diagram of the 'document' we can see that for this example the document area is (250, 350) pixels.

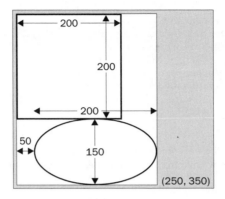

Telling the form how big the document is it is quite easy. We use the relevant property, Form.AutoScrollMinSize. Therefore we write this:

```
private void InitializeComponent()
{
    this.components = new System.ComponentModel.Container();
    this.Size = new System.Drawing.Size(300,300);
    this.Text = "Scroll Shapes";
    this.BackColor = Color.White;
    this.AutoScrollMinSize = new Size(250, 350);
}
```

Notice, that here we've placed MinScrollSize in the InitializeComponent method. That's a good place in this particular application, because we know that is how big the screen area will always be. Our "document" never changes size while this particular application is running. Bear in mind however, that if your application does things like display contents of files or something else for which the area of the screen might change, you will need to set this property at other times.

Setting MinScrollSize is a start, but it's not yet quite enough. To see that, let's look at what ScrollShapes looks like now. Initially we get the screen that correctly displays the shapes:

Notice that, not only has the form correctly set the scrollbars, but it's even correctly sized them to indicate what proportion of the document is currently displayed. You can try resizing the window while the sample is running – you'll find the scrollbars respond correctly, and even disappear if we make the window big enough that they are no longer needed.

However, now look at what happens if we actually use one of the scrollbars and scroll down a bit:

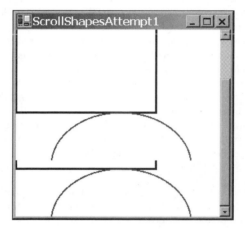

Clearly something has gone wrong!

In fact, what's gone wrong is that we haven't taken into account the position of the scrollbars in the code in our `OnPaint()` override. We can see this very clearly if we force the window to completely repaint itself by minimizing and restoring it. The result looks like this:

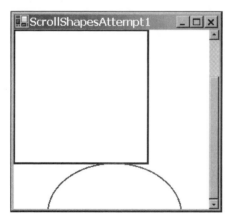

The shapes have been painted, just as before, with the top left corner of the rectangle nestled into the top left corner of the client area – just as if we hadn't moved the scrollbars at all.

Before we go over how to correct this problem, we'll take a closer look at precisely what is happening in these screenshots. Doing so is quite instructive, both because it'll help us to understand exactly how the drawing is done in the presence of scrollbars and because it'll be quite good practice. If you start using GDI+, I promise you that sooner or later, you'll find yourself presented with a strange drawing like one of those above, and having to try to figure out what has gone wrong.

We'll look at the last screenshot first since that one is easy to deal with. The ScrollShapes sample has just been restored so the entire window has just been repainted. Looking back at our code it instructs the graphics instance to draw a rectangle with top left coordinates (0,0) – relative to the top left corner of the client area of the window – which is what has been drawn. The problem is, that the graphics instance by default interprets coordinates as relative to the client window – it doesn't know anything about the scrollbars. Our code as yet does not attempt to adjust the coordinates for the scrollbar positions. The same goes for the ellipse.

Now, we can tackle the earlier screenshot, from immediately after we'd scrolled down. We notice that here the top two-thirds or so of the window look fine. That's because these were drawn when the application first started up. When you scroll windows, Windows doesn't ask the application to redraw what was already on the screen. Windows is smart enough to figure out for itself which bits of what's currently being displayed on the screen can be smoothly moved around to match where the scrollbars now are. That's a much more efficient process, since it may be able to use some hardware acceleration to do that too. The bit in this screenshot that's wrong is the bottom roughly one-third of the window. This part of the window didn't get drawn when the application first appeared, since before we started scrolling it was outside the client area. This means that Windows asks our ScrollShapes application to draw this area. It'll raise a Paint event passing in just this area as the clipping rectangle. And that's exactly what our OnPaint() override has done. This rather strange screenshot results from the application having done exactly what we told it to do!

One way of looking at the problem is that we are at the moment expressing our coordinates relative to the top left corner of the start of the 'document' – we need to convert them to express them relative to the top left corner of the client area instead. The diagram should make this clear. In the diagram the thin rectangles mark the borders of the screen area and of the entire document (to make the diagram clearer we've actually extended the document further downwards and to the right, beyond the boundaries of the screen, but this doesn't change our reasoning. We've also assumed a small horizontal scroll as well as a vertical one). The thick lines mark the rectangle and ellipse that we are trying to draw. P marks some arbitrary point that we are drawing, which we're going to take as an example. When calling the drawing methods we've supplied the graphics instance with the vector from point B to (say) point P, expressed as a Point instance. We actually need to give it the vector from point A to point P.

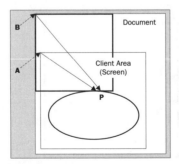

The problem is, that we don't know what the vector from A to P is. We know what B to P is – that's just the coordinates of P relative to the top left corner of the document – the position where we want to draw point P in the document. We also know what the vector from B to A is – that's just the amount we've scrolled by; this is stored in a property of the Form class called AutoScrollPosition. However, we don't know the vector from A to P. Now, if you were good at math at school, you might remember what the solution to this is – you just have to subtract vectors. Say, for example, to get from B to P you move 150 pixels across and 200 pixels down, while to get from B to A you have to move 10 pixels across and 57 pixels down. That means to get from A to P you have to move 140 (=150 minus 10) pixels across and 143 (=200 minus 57) pixels down. In computer terms we just have to do this calculation.

However it's actually a bit easier than that. I've gone through the process in detail, so you know exactly what's going on, but the `Graphics` class actually implements a method that will do these calculations for us. It's called `TranslateTransform`. How it works is that you pass it the horizontal and vertical coordinates that say where the top left of the client area is relative to the top left corner of the document, (our `AutoScrollPosition` property, that is the vector from B to A in the diagram). Then the `Graphics` device will from then on work out all its coordinates taking into account where the client area is relative to the document.

After all that explanation, all we need to do is add this line to our drawing code:

```
dc.TranslateTransform(this.AutoScrollPosition.X, this.AutoScrollPosition.Y);
```

In fact in our example, it's a little more complicated because we are also separately testing whether we need to do any drawing by looking at the clipping region. We need to adjust this test to take the scroll position into account too. When we've done that, the full drawing code for the sample (downloadable from the Wrox Press web site as the `ScrollShapes`) looks like this:

```
protected override void OnPaint( PaintEventArgs e )
{
    Graphics dc = e.Graphics;
    Size ScrollOffset = new Size(this.AutoScrollPosition);
    if (e.ClipRectangle.Top+ScrollOffset.Width < 350 ||
        e.ClipRectangle.Left+ScrollOffset.Height < 250)
    {
        Rectangle RectangleArea = new Rectangle
            (RectangleTopLeft+ScrollOffset, RectangleSize);
        Rectangle EllipseArea = new Rectangle
            (EllipseTopLeft+ScrollOffset, EllipseSize);
        dc.DrawRectangle(BluePen, RectangleArea);
        dc.DrawEllipse(RedPen, EllipseArea);
    }
    base.OnPaint(e);
}
```

Now, we have our scroll code working perfectly, we can at last obtain a correctly scrolled screenshot!

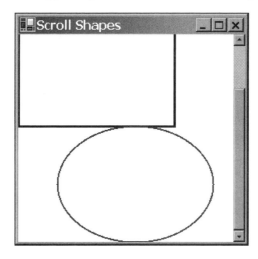

World, Page, and Device Coordinates

The distinction between measuring position relative to the top left corner of the document and measuring it relative to the top left corner of the screen, is so important that GDI+ has special names for them:

❑ **World coordinates** are the position of a point measured in pixels from the top left corner of the document. The name reflects the fact that the entire document can loosely be thought of as the "world" as far as the program is concerned.

❑ **Page coordinates** are the position of a point measured in pixels from the top left corner of the client area. The name comes from thinking of the displayed area as a "page" of displayed output.

Developers familiar with GDI will note that world coordinates correspond to what in GDI were known as logical coordinates. Page coordinates correspond to what used to be known as device coordinates. Those developers should also note that the way you code up conversion between logical and device coordinates has changed in GDI+. In GDI, conversions took place via the device context, using the LPtoDP() and DPtoLP() Windows API functions. In GDI+, it's the Form object that maintains the information needed to carry out the conversion.

GDI+ also distinguishes a third coordinate system, which is now known as **device coordinates**. Device coordinates are similar to page coordinates, except that we do not use pixels as the unit of measurement – instead we use some other unit that can be specified by the user by calling the Graphics.PageUnit property. Possible units, besides the default of pixels, include inches and millimeters. Although we won't use the PageUnit property in this chapter, it can be useful as a way of getting around the different pixel densities of devices. For example, 100 pixels on most monitors will occupy something like an inch. However, laser printers can have anything up to thousands of dpi (dots per inch) – which means that a shape specified to be 100 pixels wide will look a lot smaller when printed on such a laser printer. By setting the units to, say, inches – and specifying that the shape should be 1 inch wide, you can ensure that the shape will look the same size on the different devices.

Colors

In this section, we're going to look at the ways that you can specify what color you want something to be drawn in.

Colors in GDI+ are represented by instances of the System.Drawing.Color struct. Generally, once you've instantiated this struct, you won't do much with the corresponding Color instance – just pass it to whatever other method you are calling that requires a Color. We've encountered this struct once before – when we set the background color of the client area of the window in each of our samples. The Form.BackColor property actually returns a Color instance. In this section, we'll look at this struct in more detail. In particular, we'll examine several different ways that you can construct a Color.

Red-Green-Blue (RGB) Values

The total number of colors that can be displayed by a monitor is huge – over 16 million. To be exact the number is 2 to the power 24, which works out at 16,777,216. Obviously we need some way of indexing those colors so we can indicate which of these is the color we want to display at a given pixel.

The most common way of indexing colors is by dividing them into the red, green, and blue components. This idea is based on the principle that any color that the human eye can distinguish can be constructed from a certain amount of red light, a certain amount of the green light, and a certain amount of blue light. These lights are known as **components**. In practice, it's found that if we divide the amount of each component light into 256 possible intensities that gives a sufficiently fine gradation to be able to display images that are perceived by the human eye to be of photographic quality. We therefore specify colors by giving the amounts of these components on a scale of an 0 to 255 where 0 means that the components is not present and 255 means that it is at its maximum intensity.

We can now see where are quoted figure of 16,777,216 colors comes from, since that number is just 256 cubed.

This gives us our first way of telling GDI+ about a color. You can indicate a color's red, green, and blue values by calling the static function `Color.FromArgb()`. Microsoft has chosen not to supply a constructor to do this task. The reason is that there are other ways, besides the usual RGB components, to indicate a color. Because of this, Microsoft felt that the meaning of parameters passed to any constructor they defined would be open to misinterpretation:

```
Color RedColor = Color.FromArgb (255,0,0);
Color FunnyOrangyBrownColor = Color.FromArgb(255,155,100);
Color BlackColor = Color.FromArgb(0,0,0);
Color WhiteColor = Color.FromArgb(255,255,255);
```

The three parameters are respectively the quantities of red, green, and blue. There are a number of other overloads to this function, some of which also allow you to specify something called an alpha-blend (that's the A in the name of the method, `FromArgb()`). Alpha blending is beyond the scope of this chapter, and allows you paint a color semi-transparently by combining it with whatever color was already on the screen. This can give some beautiful effects and is often used in games.

The Named Colors

Constructing a `Color` using `FromArgb()` is the most flexible technique, since it literally means you can specify any color that the human eye can see. However, if you want a simple, standard, well-known color such as red or blue, it's a lot easier to just be able to name the color you want. Hence Microsoft has also provided a large number of static properties in `Color`, each of which returns a named color. It is one of these properties that we used when we set the background color of our windows to white in our samples:

```
this.BackColor = Color.White;

// has the same effect as:
// this.BackColor = Color.FromArgb(255, 255 , 255);
```

There are several hundred such colors. The full list is given in the MSDN documentation. They include all the simple colors: `Red`, `White`, `Blue`, `Green`, `Black`, and so on, as well as such delights as `MediumAquamarine`, `LightCoral`, and `DarkOrchid`.

Incidentally, although it might look that way, these named colors have not been chosen at random. Each one represents a precise set of RGB values, and they were originally chosen many years ago for use on the Internet. The idea was to provide a useful set of colors right across the spectrum whose names would be recognized by web browsers – thus saving you from having to write explicit RGB values in your HTML code. A few years ago these colors were also important because early browsers couldn't necessarily display very many colors accurately, and the named colors were supposed to provide a set of colors that would be displayed correctly by most browsers. These days that aspect is less important since modern web browsers are quite capable of displaying any RGB value correctly.

Graphics Display Modes and the Safety Palette

Although we've said that in principle monitors can display any of the over 16 million RGB colors, in practice this depends on how you've set the display properties on your computer. You're probably aware that by right-clicking on the backdrop in Windows and selecting **Settings** from the resultant property sheet, you get the option to choose the display color resolution. There are traditionally three main options here (though some machines may provide other options depending on the hardware): true color (24-bit), high color (16-bit), and 256 colors. (On some graphics cards these days, true color is actually marked as 32-bit for reasons to do with optimizing the hardware, though in that case only 24 bits of the 32 bits are used for the color itself.)

Only true-color mode allows you to display all of the RGB colors simultaneously. This sounds the best option, but it comes at a cost: 3 bytes are needed to hold a full RGB value which means 3 bytes of graphics card memory are needed to hold each pixel that is displayed. If graphics card memory is at a premium (a restriction that's less common now than it used to be) you may choose one of the other modes. High color mode gives you two bytes per pixel. That's enough to give 5 bits for each RGB component. So instead of 256 gradations of red intensity you just get 32 gradations; the same for blue and green, which gives a total of 65,536 colors. That is just about enough to give apparent photographic quality on a casual inspection, though areas of subtle shading tend to be broken up a bit.

256-color mode gives you even fewer colors. However, in this mode, you get to choose which colors. What happens is that the system sets up something known as a **palette**. This is a list of 256 colors chosen from the 16 million RGB colors. Once you've specified the colors in the palette, the graphics device will be able to display just those colors. The palette can be changed at any time – but the graphics device can still only display 256 different colors on the screen at any one time. 256-color mode is only really used when high performance and video memory is at a premium. Most games will use this mode – and they can still achieve decent looking graphics because of a very careful choice of palette.

In general, if a display device is in high-color or 256-color mode and it is asked to display a particular RGB color, it will pick the nearest mathematical match from the pool of colors that it is able to display. It's for this reason that it's important to be aware of the color modes. If you are drawing something that involves subtle shading or photographic quality images, and the user does not have 24-bit color mode selected, they may not see the image the same way you intended it. So if you're doing that kind of work with GDI+, you should test your application in different color modes. (It is also possible for your application to programmatically set a given color mode, though we won't go into that in this chapter.)

The Safety Palette

For reference, we'll quickly mention the safety palette here. It is a very commonly used default palette. The way it works is that we set six equally spaced possible values for each color component. Namely, the values 0, 51, 102, 153, 204, and 255. In other words, the red component can have any of these values. So can the green component. So can the blue component. So possible colors from the safety palette include: (0,0,0), black; (153,0,0), a fairly dark shade of red; (0, 255, 102), green with a smattering of blue added; and so on. This gives us a total of 6 cubed = 216 colors. The idea is that this gives us an easy way of having a palette that contains colors from right across the spectrum and of all degrees of brightness, although in practice this doesn't actually work that well because equal mathematical spacing of color components doesn't mean equal perception of color differences by the human eye. Because the safety palette used to be widely used however, you'll still find a fair number of applications and images exclusively use colors from the safety palette.

If you set Windows to 256-color mode, you'll find the default palette you get is the safety palette, with 20 Windows standard colors added to it, and 20 spare colors.

Pens and Brushes

In this section, we'll review two helper classes that are needed in order to draw shapes. We've already encountered the `Pen` class, used to tell the graphics instance how to draw lines. A related class is `System.Drawing.Brush`, which tells it how to fill regions. For example, the `Pen` is needed to draw the outlines of the rectangle and ellipse in our previous samples. If we'd needed to draw these shapes as solid, it would have been a brush that would have been used to specify how to fill them in. One aspect of both of these classes is that you will hardly ever call any methods on them. You simply construct a `Pen` or `Brush` instance with the required color and other properties, and then pass it to drawing methods that require a `Pen` or `Brush`.

We will look at brushes first, then pens.

> *Incidentally, if you've programmed using GDI before you have noticed from the first couple examples that pens are used in a different way in GDI+. In GDI the normal practice was to call a Windows API function, `SelectObject()`, which actually associated a pen with the device context. That pen was then used in all drawing operations that required a pen until you informed of the device context otherwise, by calling `SelectObject()` again. The same principle held for brushes and other objects such as fonts or bitmaps. With GDI+, as mentioned earlier, Microsoft has instead gone for a stateless model in which there is no default pen or other helper object. Rather, you simply specify with each method call the appropriate helper object to be used for that particular method.*

Brushes

GDI+ has several different kinds of brush – more than we have space to go into in this chapter, so we'll just explain the simpler ones to give you an idea of the principles. Each type of brush is represented by an instance of a class derived from `System.Drawing.Brush` (this class is abstract so you can't instantiate `Brush` objects themselves – only objects of derived classes). The simplest brush simply indicates that a region is to be filled with solid color. This kind of brush is represented by an instance of the class `System.Drawing.SolidBrush`, which you can construct as follows:

```
Brush solidBeigeBrush = new SolidBrush(Color.Beige);
Brush solidFunnyOrangyBrownBrush =
                        new SolidBrush(Color.FromArgb(255,155,100));
```

Alternatively, if the brush is one of the Internet named colors you can construct the brush more simply using another class, `System.Drawing.Brushes`. `Brushes` is one of those classes that you never actually instantiate (it's got a private constructor to stop you doing that). It simply has a large number of static properties, each of which returns a brush of a specified color. You'd use `Brushes` like this:

```
Brush solidAzureBrush = Brushes.Azure;
Brush solidChocolateBrush = Brushes.Chocolate;
```

The next level of complexity is a hatch brush, which fills a region by drawing a pattern. This type of brush is considered more advanced so it's in the `Drawing2D` namespace, represented by the class `System.Drawing.Drawing2D.HatchBrush`. The `Brushes` class can't help you with hatch brushes – you'll need to construct one explicitly, by supplying the hatch style and two colors – the foreground color followed by the background color (but you can omit the background color, in which case it defaults to black). The hatch style comes from an enumeration, `System.Drawing.Drawing2D.HatchStyle`. There are a large number of `HatchStyle` values available, so it's easiest to refer to the MSDN documentation for the full list. To give you an idea, typical styles include `ForwardDiagonal`, `Cross`, `DiagonalCross`, `SmallConfetti`, and `ZigZag`. Examples of constructing a hatch brush include:

```
Brush crossBrush = new HatchBrush(HatchStyle.Cross, Color.Azure);

// background color of CrossBrush is black

Brush brickBrush = new HatchBrush(HatchStyle.DiagonalBrick,
                                  Color.DarkGoldenrod, Color.Cyan);
```

Solid and hatch brushes are the only brushes available under GDI. GDI+ has added a couple of new styles of brush:

❑   `System.Drawing.Drawing2D.LinearGradientBrush` fills in an area with a color that varies across the screen

❑   `System.Drawing.Drawing2D.PathGradientBrush` is similar, but in this case the color varies along a path around the region to be filled

We won't go into these brushes in this chapter. We'll note though that both can give some spectacular effects if used carefully. The Bezier example in Chapter 9 uses a linear gradient brush to paint the background of the window.

Pens

Unlike brushes, pens are represented by just one class – `System.Drawing.Pen`. The pen is, however, actually slightly more complex than the brush, because it needs to indicate how thick lines should be (how many pixels wide) and, for a wide line, how to fill the area inside the line. Pens can also specify a number of other properties, which are beyond the scope of this chapter, but which include the `Alignment` property that we mentioned earlier, which indicates where in relation to the border of a shape a line should be drawn, as well as what shape to draw at the end of a line (whether to round off the shape).

The area inside a thick line can be filled with solid color, or it can be filled using a brush. Hence, a `Pen` instance may contain a reference to a `Brush` instance. This is quite powerful, as it means you can draw lines colored using hatching or linear shading. There are four different ways that you can construct a `Pen` instance that you have designed yourself. You can do it by passing a color, or you can do it by passing in a brush. Both of these constructors will produce a pen with a width of one pixel. Alternatively, you can pass in a color or a brush, and additionally a `float`, which represents the width of the pen. (It needs to be a float in case we are using non-default units such as millimeters or inches for the `Graphics` object that will do the drawing – so we can for example specify fractions of an inch.) So for example, you can construct pens like this:

```
Brush brickBrush = new HatchBrush(HatchStyle.DiagonalBrick,
                                  Color.DarkGoldenrod, Color.Cyan);

Pen solidBluePen = new Pen(Color.FromArgb(0,0,255));
Pen solidWideBluePen = new Pen(Color.Blue, 4);
Pen brickPen = new Pen(BrickBrush);
Pen brickWidePen = new Pen(BrickBrush, 10);
```

Additionally, for the quick construction of pens, you can use the class `System.Drawing.Pens` which, like the `Brushes` class simply contains a number of stock pens. These pens all have width one pixel and come in the usual sets of Internet named colors. This allows you to construct pens in this way:

```
Pen SolidYellowPen = Pens.Yellow;
```

Drawing Shapes and Lines

We've almost finished the first part of the chapter, in which we've covered all the basic classes and objects required in order to draw specified shapes and so on to the screen. We'll round off by reviewing some of the drawing methods the `Graphics` class makes available, and presenting a short example that illustrates several brushes and pens.

`System.Drawing.Graphics` has a large number of methods that allow you to draw various lines, outline shapes and solid shapes. Once again there are too many to provide a comprehensive list here, but the following table gives the main ones and should give you some idea of the variety of shapes you can draw.

Method	Typical parameters	What it draws
DrawLine	Pen, start and end points	A single straight line
DrawRectangle	Pen, position, and size	Outline of a rectangle
DrawEllipse	Pen, position, and size	Outline of an ellipse
FillRectangle	Brush, position, and size	Solid rectangle
FillEllipse	Brush, position, and size	Solid ellipse
DrawLines	Pen, array of Points	Series of lines, connecting each point to the next one in the array
DrawBezier	Pen, 4 points	A smooth curve through the two end points, with the remaining two points used to control the shape of the curve
DrawCurve	Pen, array of points	A smooth curve through the points
DrawArc	Pen, rectangle, two angles	Portion of circle within the rectangle defined by the angles
DrawClosedCurve	Pen, array of points	Like `DrawCurve` but also draws a straight line to close the curve
DrawPie	Pen, rectangle, two angles	Wedge-shaped outline within the rectangle
FillPie	Brush, rectangle, two angles	Solid wedge-shaped area within the rectangle
DrawPolygon	Pen, array of points	Like `DrawLines` but also connects first and last points to close the figure drawn

Before we leave the subject of drawing simple objects, we'll round off with a simple example that demonstrates the kinds of visual effect you can achieve by use of brushes. The example is called `ScrollMoreShapes`, and it's essentially a revision of `ScrollShapes`. Besides the rectangle and ellipse, we'll add a thick line and fill the shapes in with various custom brushes. We've already explained the principles of drawing so we'll present the code without too many comments. First, because of our new brushes, we need to indicate we are using the `System.Drawing.Drawing2D` namespace:

```
using System;
using System.Drawing;
using System.Drawing.Drawing2D;
using System.Collections;
using System.ComponentModel;
using System.Windows.Forms;
using System.Data;
```

Next some extra fields in our `Form1` class, which contain details of the locations where the shapes are to be drawn, as well as various pens and brushes we will use:

```
private Rectangle rectangleBounds = new Rectangle(new Point(0,0),
                                                  new Size(200,200));
private Rectangle ellipseBounds = new Rectangle(new Point(50,200),
                                                new Size(200,150));
private Pen BluePen = new Pen(Color.Blue, 3);
private Pen RedPen = new Pen(Color.Red, 2);
private Brush SolidAzureBrush = Brushes.Azure;
private Brush CrossBrush = new HatchBrush(HatchStyle.Cross, Color.Azure);
static private Brush BrickBrush = new HatchBrush(HatchStyle.DiagonalBrick,
                                                 Color.DarkGoldenrod,
                                                 Color.Cyan);
private Pen BrickWidePen = new Pen(BrickBrush, 10);
```

The `BrickBrush` field has been declared as static, so that we can use its value in the initializor for `BrickWidePen` that follows. C# won't let us use one instance field to initialize another instance field, because it's not defined which one will be initialized first, but declaring the field as static solves the problem, since only one instance of the `Form1` class will be instantiated, it is immaterial whether the fields are static or instance fields.

Here is the `OnPaint()` override:

```
        protected override void OnPaint( PaintEventArgs e )
        {
            Graphics dc = e.Graphics;
            Point scrollOffset = this.AutoScrollPosition;
            dc.TranslateTransform(scrollOffset.X, scrollOffset.Y);
            if (e.ClipRectangle.Top+scrollOffset.X < 350 ||
                e.ClipRectangle.Left+scrollOffset.Y < 250)
            {
                dc.DrawRectangle(BluePen, rectangleBounds);
                dc.FillRectangle(CrossBrush, rectangleBounds);
                dc.DrawEllipse(RedPen, ellipseBounds);
                dc.FillEllipse(SolidAzureBrush, ellipseBounds);
                dc.DrawLine(BrickWidePen, rectangleBounds.Location,
                            ellipseBounds.Location+ellipseBounds.Size);
            }
            base.OnPaint(e);
        }
```

Now the results:

Notice that the thick diagonal line has been drawn on top of the rectangle and ellipse, because it was the last item to be painted.

Displaying Images

One of the most common things you may want to do with GDI+ is display an image that already exists in a file. This is actually a lot simpler than drawing your own user interface, because the image is already pre-drawn. Effectively, all you have to do is load the file and instruct GDI+ to display it. The image can be a simple line drawing, an icon, or a complex image such as a photograph. It's also possible to perform some manipulations on the image, such as stretching it or rotating it, and you can choose to display only a portion of it.

In this section, we'll reverse the usual order of things in this chapter: We'll present the example, then we'll discuss some of the issues you need to be aware of when displaying images. We can do this, because the code needed to display an image really is so simple.

The class we need is the .NET base class, `System.Drawing.Image`. An instance of `Image` represents one image – if you like, one picture. Reading in an image takes one line of code:

```
Image MyImage = Image.FromFile("FileName");
```

`FromFile()` is a static member of `Image` and is the usual way of instantiating an image. The file can be any of the commonly supported graphics file formats, including `.bmp`, `.jpg`, `.gif`, and `.png`.

Displaying an image also takes just one line of code, assuming you have a suitable `Graphics` instance to hand:

```
dc.DrawImageUnscaled(MyImage, TopLeft);
```

In this line of code, `dc` is assumed to be a `Graphics` instance, `MyImage` is the `Image` to be displayed, and `TopLeft` is a `Point` struct that stores the device coordinates of where you want the image to be placed.

It could hardly be easier, could it!

Images are probably the area in which developers familiar with GDI will notice the biggest difference with GDI+. In GDI, the API for dealing with images was arcane to say the least. Displaying an image involved several nontrivial steps. If the image was a bitmap, loading it was reasonably simple, but if it was any other file type loading it would involve a sequence of calls to OLE objects. Actually, getting a loaded image onto the screen involved getting a handle to it, selecting it into a memory device context, then performing a block transfer between device contexts. Although the device contexts and handles are still there behind the scenes, and will be needed if you want to start doing sophisticated editing of the images from your code, simple tasks have now been extremely well wrapped up in the GDI+ object model.

We'll illustrate the process of displaying an image with an example called `DisplayImage`. The example simply displays a `.jpg` file in the application's main window. To keep things simple, the path of the `.jpg` file is hard coded into the application (so if you run the sample you'll need to change it to reflect the location of the file in your system). The `.jpg` file we'll display is a group photograph of attendees from a recent COMFest event.

As usual for this chapter, the `DisplayImage` project is a standard C# Visual Studio.NET-generated windows application. We add the following field to our `Form1` class:

```
Image Piccy;
```

We then load the file in our `InitializeComponent` routine:

```
private void InitializeComponent()
{
    this.components = new System.ComponentModel.Container();
    this.Size = new System.Drawing.Size(600, 400);
    this.Text = "Display COMFest Image";
    this.BackColor = Color.White;
    Piccy =
    Image.FromFile(@"c:\ProCSharp\Chapter21\DisplayImage\CF4Group.jpg");
    this.AutoScrollMinSize = Piccy.Size;
}
```

Note that the size in pixels of the image is obtained as its `Size` property, which we use to set the document area. The image is displayed in the `OnPaint()` override:

```
protected override void OnPaint(PaintEventArgs e)
{
    Graphics dc = e.Graphics;
    dc.DrawImageUnscaled(Piccy, this.AutoScrollPosition);
    base.OnPaint(e);
}
```

The choice of `this.AutoScrollPosition` as the device coordinate ensures that the window will scroll correctly, with the image located starting at the top left corner of the client area before any scrolling has taken place.

Finally, we'll take particular note of the modification made to the code wizard-generated `Form1.Dispose()` method:

```
    public override void Dispose()
    {
        base.Dispose();
        if(components != null)
            components.Dispose();
        Piccy.Dispose();
    }
```

Disposing of the image when it's no longer needed is important, because images generally eat a lot of memory while in use. After `Image.Dispose()` has been called the `Image` instance no longer refers to any actual image, and so can no longer be displayed (unless you load a new image).

Running this code produces these results:

By the way if you're wondering, COMFest (www.comfest.co.uk) is an informal group of developers in the United Kingdom who meet to discuss latest technologies, and swap ideas etc. The picture includes all the attendees at COMFest 4 with the exception of the author of this chapter who was (conveniently) taking the picture!

Issues When Manipulating Images

Although displaying images is very simple, it still pays to have some understanding of the underlying technology.

The most important point to understand about images is that they are always rectangular. That's not just a convenience for people, it's because of the underlying technology. It's because all modern graphics cards have hardware built in that can very efficiently copy blocks of pixels from one bit of memory to another bit of memory, provided that the block of pixels represents a rectangular area. This hardware-accelerated operation can occur virtually as one single operation, and as such is extremely fast. Indeed, it is the key to modern high-performance graphics. This operation is known as a **bitmap block transfer** (or **BitBlt** – usually pronounced something like 'BITblert' or 'BITblot'). `Image.DrawImageUnscaled()` internally uses a `BitBlt`, which is why you can see a huge image, perhaps containing as many as a million pixels (the photo in our example has 104,975 pixels) appearing, apparently, instantly. If the computer had to copy the image to the screen individual pixel by individual pixel, you'd see the image gradually being drawn over a period of up to several seconds.

BitBlts are very efficient; therefore almost all drawing and manipulation of images is carried out using them. Even some editing of images will be done by BitBlting portions of images between device contexts that represent areas of memory. In the days of GDI, the Windows 32 API function BitBlt() was arguably the most important and widely used function for image manipulation, though with GDI+ the BitBlt operations are largely hidden by the GDI+ object model.

It's not possible to BitBlt areas of images that are not rectangular; however, similar effects can be easily simulated. One way is to mark a certain color as transparent for the purposes of a BitBlt, so that areas of that color in the source image will not overwrite the existing color of the corresponding pixel in the destination device. It is also possible to specify that in the process of a BitBlt, each pixel of the resultant image will be formed by some logical operation (such as a bitwise AND) on the colors of that pixel in the source image and in the destination device before the BitBlt. Such operations are supported by hardware acceleration, and can be used to give a variety of subtle effects. We're not going to go into details of this here. We'll remark however, that the Graphics object implements another method, DrawImage(). This is similar to DrawImageUnscaled(), but comes in a large number of overloads that allow you to specify more complex forms of BitBlt to be used in the drawing process. DrawImage() also allows you to draw (BitBlt) only a specified part of the image, or to perform certain other operations on it such as scaling it (expanding or reducing it in size) as it is drawn.

Drawing Text

We've left the very important topic of displaying text till later in the chapter because drawing text to the screen is in general more complex than drawing simple graphics. Actually I ought to qualify that statement. Just displaying a line of two of text when you're not that bothered about the appearance is extremely easy – it takes one single call to one method of the Graphics instance, Graphics.DrawString(). However, if you are trying to display a document that has a fair amount of text in it, you rapidly find that things become a lot more complex. This is for two reasons:

❑   First, if you're concerned about getting the appearance just right, you need to understand fonts. Where shape drawing requires brushes and pens as helper objects, the process of drawing text correspondingly requires fonts as helper objects. And understanding fonts is not trivial task. We'll provide a brief introduction to the subject in the next section, but the details of fonts are more complex than those of brushes and pens.

❑   Second, text needs to be very carefully laid out in the window. Users generally expect words to naturally follow one another – to be lined up with clear spaces in between. Doing that is harder than you'd think. For a start, unlike the case for shapes, you don't usually know in advance how much space on the screen a word is going to take up. That has to be calculated (don't worry, you don't have to do that manually – there's a method, Graphics.MeasureString() that will do it). Also, how much space on the screen a word occupies will affect whereabouts on the screen every subsequent word in the document gets placed. If your application does line wrapping then it'll need to carefully assess word sizes before deciding where to place the break. The next time you run Word for Windows, look carefully at the way Word is continually repositioning text as you type, changing fonts, cutting, and pasting, etc. There's a lot of processing going on there, involving some very carefully designed algorithms. Of course, the chances are that any GDI+ application you work on won't be anything like as complex as Word, but if you need to display any text then many of the same considerations still apply. That's why the final part of this chapter is devoted to a sample that allows some simple text manipulation: to give you some idea of the problems that kind of application brings up and the typical solutions you'll probably need to implement.

Having said all that, I don't want to scare you off too much. Good quality text processing is not impossible – it's just tricky to get right. As we've mentioned, the actual process of putting a line of text on the screen, assuming you know the font and where you want it to go, is very simple. Therefore, the next thing we'll do is present a quick example that shows how to display a couple of pieces of text. After that, the plan for the rest of the chapter is to review some of the principles of fonts and font families before moving on to our more realistic text-processing example, the CapsEditor sample, which will demonstrate some of the issues involved when you're trying to control layouts text on-screen and also show how to handle user input.

Simple Text Sample

The sample is our usual Windows Forms effort. This time we've overridden OnPaint() as follows:

```
protected override void OnPaint(PaintEventArgs e)
{
    Graphics dc = e.Graphics;
    Brush blackBrush = Brushes.Black;
    Brush blueBrush = Brushes.Blue;
    Font haettenschweilerFont = new Font("Haettenschweiler", 12);
    Font boldTimesFont = new Font("Times New Roman", 10, FontStyle.Bold);
    Font italicCourierFont = new Font("Courier", 11, FontStyle.Italic |
                                                     FontStyle.Underline);
    dc.DrawString("This is a groovy string", haettenschweilerFont, blackBrush,
                  10, 10);
    dc.DrawString("This is a groovy string " +
                  "with some very long text that will never fit in the box",
                  boldTimesFont, blueBrush,
                  new Rectangle(new Point(10, 40), new Size(100, 40)));
    dc.DrawString("This is a groovy string", italicCourierFont, blackBrush,
                  new Point(10, 100));
    base.OnPaint(e);
}
```

Running this sample produces this:

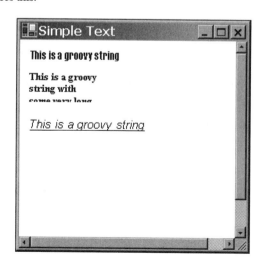

The example demonstrates the use of the `Graphics.DrawString()` method to draw items of text. `DrawString()` comes in a number of overloads, of which we demonstrate three. The different overloads all, however, require parameters that indicate the text to be displayed, the font that the string should be drawn in, and the brush that should be used to construct the various lines and curves that make up each character of text. There are a couple of alternatives for the remaining parameters. In general, however, it is possible to specify either a `Point` (or equivalently, two numbers), or a `Rectangle`. If you specify a `Point`, the text will start with its top left corner at that `Point` and simply stretch out to the right. If you specify a `Rectangle`, then the `Graphics` instance will lay the string out inside that rectangle. If the text doesn't fit into the bounds of the rectangle, then it'll be cut off, as you see from the screenshot. Passing a rectangle to `DrawString()` means that the drawing process will take longer, as `DrawString()` will need to figure out where to put line breaks, but the result may look nicer, if the string fits in the rectangle!

This example also shows a couple of ways of constructing fonts. You always need the name of the font, and its size (height). You can also optionally pass in various styles that modify how the text is to be drawn (bold, underline, etc.).

Fonts and Font Families

We all think intuitively that we have a fairly good understanding of fonts. After all we look at them almost all the time. A font describes exactly how each letter should be displayed, and selection of the appropriate font as well as providing a reasonable variety of fonts within a document is an important factor in improving readability of that document. You just have to look at the pages of this book to see how many fonts have been used to present you with the information. In general, you will need to choose your fonts carefully – because a poor choice of font can badly damage both the attractiveness and the usability of your applications.

Oddly, our intuitive understanding usually isn't quite correct. Most people, if asked to name a font, will say things like 'Arial' or 'Times New Roman' or 'Courier'. In fact, these are not fonts at all – they are **font families**. The font would be something like, say, Arial 9-point italic. Get the idea? The font family tells you in generic terms the visual style of the text. The font family is a key factor in the overall appearance of your application, and most of us will have become used to recognizing the styles of the most common font families, even if we're not consciously aware of this. In casual speech, font families are often mistakenly described simply as fonts. More correctly, a **font** adds more information by specifying the size of the text and also whether any of certain modifications have been applied to the text. For example, whether it is **bold**, *italic,* underlined, or displayed in SMALL CAPS or as a subscript. Such modifications are technically referred to as **styles**, though in some ways the term is misleading, since as we've just noted the visual appearance is determined as much by the font family.

The way the size of the text is measured is by specifying its height. The height is measured in **points** – a traditional unit, which represents 1/72 of an inch (or for people living outside the UK and the USA, a point is 0.351 mm). So for example, letters in a 10-point font are 10/72 of an inch, (or roughly 1/7" or 3.5 mm) high. You might think that this means you'd get seven lines of text that has a font size 10 into one inch of vertical screen or paper space. In fact, you get slightly less than this, because you need to allow for the spacing between the lines as well.

*Strictly speaking, measuring the height isn't quite as simple as that, since there are several different heights that you need to consider. For example, there is the height of tall letters like the A or F (this is the measurement that we really mean when we talk about the height), the additional height occupied by any accents on letters like Å or Ñ (the **internal leading**), and the extra height below the base line needed for the tails of letters like y and g (the **descent**). However, for this chapter we won't worry about that. Once you specify the font family and the main height, these subsidiary heights are determined automatically – you can't independently choose their values.*

Incidentally, when you're dealing with fonts you may also encounter some other terms that are commonly used to describe certain font families.

❑ A **serif** font family is one that has little tick marks at the ends of many of the lines that make up the characters (These ticks are known as serifs). Times New Roman is a classic example of this.

❑ **Sans serif** font families, by contrast, don't have these ticks. Good examples of sans serif fonts are Arial, and Verdana. The lack of tick marks often gives text a blunt, in-your-face appearance, so sans serif fonts are often used for important text.

❑ A **true type** font family is one that is defined by expressing the shapes of the curves that make up the characters in a precise mathematical manner. This means that that the same definition can be used to calculate how to draw fonts of any size within the family. These days, virtually all the fonts you will use are true type fonts. Some older font families from the days of Windows 3.1 were defined by individually specifying the bitmap for each character separately for each font size, but the use of these fonts is now discouraged. (Among other disadvantages, they cause problems when you swap from the screen to a modern printer, where the number of pixels per inch is far greater, so the bitmaps end up looking too small.)

Microsoft has provided two main classes that we need to deal with when selecting or manipulating fonts. These are `System.Drawing.Font` and `System.Drawing.FontFamily`. We have already seen the main use of the `Font` class. When we wish to draw text we instantiate an instance of `Font` and pass it to the `DrawString` method to indicate how the text should be drawn. A `FontFamily` instance is used (surprisingly enough) to represent a family of fonts.

One use of the `FontFamily` class is if you know you want a font of a particular type (Serif, Sans Serif or Monospace), but don't mind which font. The static properties `GenericSerif`, `GenericSansSerif`, and `GenericMonospace` return default fonts that satisfy these criteria:

```
FontFamily sansSerifFont = FontFamily.GenericSansSerif;
```

Generally speaking, however, if you're writing a professional application, you will want to choose your font in a more sophisticated way than this. Most likely, you will implement your drawing code so that it checks what font families are actually installed on the computer and hence what fonts are available. Then it will select the appropriate one, perhaps by taking the first available one on a list of preferred fonts. And if you want your application to be very user-friendly, the first choice on the list will probably be the one that the user selected last time they ran your software. Usually, if you're dealing with the most popular fonts families, such as Arial and Times New Roman, you'll be safe. However, if you do try to display text using a font that doesn't exist the results aren't always predictable and you're quite likely to find the Windows just substitutes the standard system font, which is very easy for the system to draw but it doesn't look very pleasant – and if it does appear in your document it's likely to give the impression of very poor-quality software.

You can find out what fonts are available on your system using a class called `InstalledFontCollection`, which is in the `System.Drawing.Text` namespace. This class implements a property, `Families`, which is an array of all the fonts that are available to use on your system:

```
InstalledFontCollection insFont = new InstalledFontCollection();
FontFamily [] families = insFont.Families;
foreach (FontFamily family in families)
{

    // do processing with this font family

}
```

Example: Enumerating Font Families

In this section, we will work through a quick example, `EnumFontFamilies`, which lists all the font families available on the system and illustrates them by displaying the name of each family using an appropriate font (the 10-point regular version of that font family). When the sample is run it looks like this:

However, note that, depending on what fonts you have installed on your computer, you may get different results when you run it. For this sample we have as usual created a standard C# windows application named `EnumFontFamilies`. We then add the following constant to the `Form1` class:

```
const int margin = 10;
```

The `margin` is the size of the left and top margin between the text and the edge of the document – it stops the text from appearing right at the edge of the client area.

This is designed as a quick-and-easy way of showing off font families; therefore the code is crude and in many cases doesn't do things the way you ought to in a real application. For example, I've just hard coded in a guessed value for the document size instead of calculating how much space we actually need to display the list of font families. (We'll use a more correct approach in the next example.) Hence, our `InitializeComponent()` method looks like this:

```
private void InitializeComponent()
{
    this.components = new System.ComponentModel.Container();
    this.Size = new System.Drawing.Size(300,300);
    this.Text = "EnumFontFamilies";
    this.BackColor = Color.White;
    this.AutoScrollMinSize = new Size(200,500);
}
```

And here is the OnPaint() method:

```
protected override void OnPaint(PaintEventArgs e)
{
    int verticalCoordinate = margin;
    Point topLeftCorner;
    InstalledFontCollection insFont = new InstalledFontCollection();
    FontFamily [] families = insFont.Families;
    e.Graphics.TranslateTransform(AutoScrollPosition.X,
                                  AutoScrollPosition.Y);
    foreach (FontFamily family in families)
    {
        if (family.IsStyleAvailable(FontStyle.Regular))
        {
            Font f = new Font(family.Name, 10);
            topLeftCorner = new Point(margin, verticalCoordinate);
            verticalCoordinate += f.Height;
            e.Graphics.DrawString (family.Name, f,
                                   Brushes.Black, topLeftCorner);
            f.Dispose();
        }
    }
    base.OnPaint(e);
}
```

In this code we start off by using an InstalledFontCollection object to obtain an array that contains details of all the available font families. For each family, we instantiate a font of that family of size 10 point. We use a simple constructor for Font – there are many more that allow more options to be specified. The constructor we've picked takes two parameters: the name of the family and the size of the font:

```
Font f = new Font(family.Name, 10);
```

This constructor constructs a font that has the regular style (that is, it is not underlined, italic, bold, or struckthrough). To be on the safe side, however, we first check that this style is available for each font family before attempting to display anything using that font. This is done using the FontFamily.IsStyleAvailable() method, and this check is important, because not all fonts are available in all styles:

```
if (family.IsStyleAvailable(FontStyle.Regular))
```

FontFamily.IsStyleAvailable() takes one parameter, a FontStyle enumeration. This enumeration contains a number of flags that may be combined with the bitwise OR operator. The possible flags are Bold, Italic, Regular, Strikeout, and Underline.

Finally, note that we use a property of the Font class, Height, which returns the height needed to display text of that font, in order to work out the line spacing,

```
Font f = new Font(family.Name, 10);
topLeftCorner = new Point(margin, verticalCoordinate);
verticalCoordinate += f.Height;
```

Again, to keep things simple, our version of OnPaint() reveals some bad programming practices. For a start, we haven't bothered to check what area of the document actually needs drawing – we just try to display everything. Also, instantiating a Font is, as remarked earlier, a computationally intensive process, so we really ought to save the fonts rather than instantiating new copies every time OnPaint() is called. As a result of the way the code has been designed, you may notice that this example actually takes a noticeable time to paint itself. In order to try to conserve memory and help the garbage collector out we do, however, call Dispose() on each font instance after we have finished with it. If we didn't, then after 10 or 20 paint operations, there'd be a lot of wasted memory storing fonts that
are no longer needed.

Editing a Text Document: The CapsEditor Sample

We now come to our larger example in this chapter. The CapsEditor example is designed to illustrate how the principles of drawing that we've learned up till now need to be applied in a more realistic example. The example won't require any new material, apart from responding to user input via the mouse, but it will show how to manage the drawing of text so the application maintains performance while ensuring that the contents of the client area of the main window are always kept up to date.

The CapsEditor program is functionally quite simple. It allows the user to read in a text file, which is then displayed line by line in the client area. If the user double-clicks on any line, that line will be changed to all uppercase. That's literally all the sample does. Even with this limited set of features, we'll find that the work involved in making sure everything gets displayed in the right place while considering performance issues (such as only displaying what we need to in a given OnPaint() call) is quite complex. In particular, we have a new element here, that the contents of the document can change – either when the user selects the menu option to read a new file or when they double-click to capitalize a line. In the first case we need to update the document size, so the scrollbars still work correctly, and redisplay everything. In the second case, we need to check carefully whether the document size is changed, and what text needs to be redisplayed.

We'll start by reviewing the appearance of CapsEditor. When the application is first run, it has no document loaded, and displays this:

The File menu has two options: **Open** and **Exit**. **Exit** exits the application, while **Open** brings up the standard OpenFileDialog and reads in whatever file the user selects. This screenshot shows CapsEditor being used to view its own source file, Form1.cs. I've also randomly double-clicked on a couple of lines to convert them to uppercase:

```
CapsEditor - F:\C# Projects\Pro C# Code\Ch19_GDIPlus\C...  _ □ ×
File

namespace Wrox.ProfessionalCSharp.Chapter19.CapsEditor
{
        #region using statements
        using System;
        using System.Drawing;
        using System.Collections;
        USING SYSTEM.COMPONENTMODEL;
        using System.Windows.Forms;
        using System.Data;
        using System.IO;
        #ENDREGION
        #REGION TEXTLINEINFORMATION CLASS DEFINITION
        class TextLineInformation
        {
                public string Text;
                public uint Width;

        }
        #endregion

        public class Form1 : System.Windows.Forms.Form
```

The sizes of the horizontal and vertical scrollbars are, by the way, correct. The client area will scroll just enough to view the entire document. (It's a long program, and there are a couple of extremely long code-wizard-generated lines in it, hence the shortness of both scrollbars.) CapsEditor doesn't try to wrap lines of text – the example is already complicated enough without doing that. It just displays each line of the file exactly as it is read in. There are no limits to the size of the file, but we are assuming it is a text file and doesn't contain any non-printable characters.

We'll start off by adding in some fields to the Form1 class that we'll need:

```
#region constant fields
private const string standardTitle = "CapsEditor";
                                            // default text in titlebar
private const uint margin = 10;
                        // horizontal and vertical margin in client area
#endregion
```

```
#region Member fields
private ArrayList documentLines = new ArrayList();   // the 'document'
private uint lineHeight;            // height in pixels of one line
private Size documentSize;          // how big a client area is needed to
                                    // display document
private uint nLines;                // number of lines in document
private Font mainFont;              // font used to display all lines
private Font emptyDocumentFont;     // font used to display empty message
private Brush mainBrush = Brushes.Blue;
                                    // brush used to display document text
private Brush emptyDocumentBrush = Brushes.Red;
                        // brush used to display empty document message
private Point mouseDoubleClickPosition;
    // location mouse is pointing to when double-clicked
private OpenFileDialog fileOpenDialog = new OpenFileDialog();
    // standard open file dialog
private bool documentHasData = false;
    // set to true if document has some data in it
#endregion
```

Most of these fields should be self-explanatory. The `documentLines` field is an `ArrayList` that contains the actual text of the file that has been read in. In a real sense, this is the field that contains the data in the "document". Each element of `DocumentLines` contains information for one line of text that has been read in. It's an `ArrayList`, rather than a plain C# array, so that we can dynamically add elements to it as we read in a file. You'll notice I've also liberally used `#region` preprocessor directives to block up bits of the program to make it easier to edit.

I said each `documentLines` element contains information about a line of text. This information is actually an instance of another class I've defined, `TextLineInformation`:

```
class TextLineInformation
{
    public string Text;
    public uint Width;
}
```

`TextLineInformation` looks like a classic case where you'd normally use a struct rather than a class since it's just there to group together a couple of fields. However its instances are always accessed as elements of an `ArrayList`, which expects its elements to be stored as reference types, so declaring `TextLineInformation` as a class makes things more efficient by saving a lot of boxing and unboxing operations.

Each `TextLineInformation` instance stores a line of text – and that can be thought of as the smallest item that is displayed as a single item. In general, for each such item in a GDI+ application, you'd probably want to store the text of the item, as well as the world coordinates of where it should be displayed and its size. Note: world coordinates, not page coordinates. The page coordinates will change frequently, whenever the user scrolls, whereas world coordinates will normally only change when other parts of the document are modified in some way. In this case we've only stored the `Width` of the item. The reason is because the height in this case is just the height of whatever our selected font is. It's the same for all lines of text so there's no point storing it separately for each one. It's instead stored once, in the `Form1.lineHeight` field. As for the position – well in this case the x coordinate is just equal to the margin, and the y coordinate is easily calculated as:

```
Margin + LineHeight*(however many lines are above this one)
```

If we'd been trying to display and manipulate, say, individual words instead of complete lines, then the x position of each word would have to be calculated using the widths of all the previous words on that line of text, but I wanted to keep it simple here, which is why we're treating each line of text as one single item.

Let's deal with the main menu now. This part of the application is more the realm of Windows Forms – the subject of Chapter 9, than of GDI+. I added the menu options using the design view in Visual Studio.NET, but renamed them as `menuFile`, `menuFileOpen`, and `menuFileExit`. I then modified the code in `InitializeComponent()` to add the appropriate event handlers, as well as perform some other initialization:

```
private void InitializeComponent()
{
    // stuff added by code wizard
    this.menuFileOpen = new System.Windows.Forms.MenuItem();
    this.menuFileExit = new System.Windows.Forms.MenuItem();
    this.mainMenu1 = new System.Windows.Forms.MainMenu();
```

```
      this.menuFile = new System.Windows.Forms.MenuItem();
      this.menuFileOpen.Index = 0;
      this.menuFileOpen.Text = "Open";
      this.menuFileExit.Index = 3;
      this.menuFileExit.Text = "Exit";
      this.mainMenu1.MenuItems.AddRange(new System.Windows.Forms.MenuItem[]
                                              {this.menuFile});
      this.menuFile.Index = 0;
      this.menuFile.MenuItems.AddRange(new System.Windows.Forms.MenuItem[]
                                    {this.menuFileOpen,
                                        this.menuFileExit});
      this.menuFile.Text = "File";

      this.menuFileOpen.Click += new
                          System.EventHandler(this.menuFileOpen_Click);
      this.menuFileExit.Click += new
                          System.EventHandler(this.menuFileExit_Click);
      this.AutoScaleBaseSize = new System.Drawing.Size(5, 13);
      this.BackColor = System.Drawing.Color.White;
      this.Size = new Size(600,400);
      this.Menu = this.mainMenu1;
      this.Text = standardTitle;
      CreateFonts();
      FileOpenDialog.FileOk += new
                      System.ComponentModel.CancelEventHandler(
                                        this.OpenFileDialog_FileOk);
   }
```

We've added event handlers for the **File** and **Exit** menu options, as well as for the file open dialog that gets displayed when the user selects **Open**. `CreateFonts()` is a helper method that sorts out the fonts we intend to use:

```
private void CreateFonts()
{
   mainFont = new Font("Arial", 10);
   lineHeight = (uint)mainFont.Height;
   emptyDocumentFont = new Font("Verdana", 13, FontStyle.Bold);
}
```

The actual definitions of the handlers are pretty standard stuff:

```
protected void OpenFileDialog_FileOk(object Sender, CancelEventArgs e)
{
   this.LoadFile(fileOpenDialog.FileName);
}

protected void menuFileOpen_Click(object sender, EventArgs e)
{
   fileOpenDialog.ShowDialog();
}


protected void menuFileExit_Click(object sender, EventArgs e)
{
   this.Close();
}
```

We'll examine the `LoadFile()` method now. It's the method that handles the opening and reading in of a file (as well as ensuring a `Paint` event gets raised to force a repaint with the new file):

```
private void LoadFile(string FileName)
{
    StreamReader sr = new StreamReader(FileName);
    string nextLine;
    documentLines.Clear();
    nLines = 0;
    TextLineInformation nextLineInfo;
    while ( (nextLine = sr.ReadLine()) != null)
    {
        nextLineInfo = new TextLineInformation();
        nextLineInfo.Text = nextLine;
        documentLines.Add(nextLineInfo);
        ++nLines;
    }
    sr.Close();
    documentHasData = (nLines>0) ? true : false;

    CalculateLineWidths();
    CalculateDocumentSize();

    this.Text = standardTitle + " - " + FileName;
    this.Invalidate();
}
```

Most of this function is just standard file-reading stuff, as covered in Chapter 14. Notice how as the file is read in, we progressively add lines to the `documentLines ArrayList`, so this array ends up containing information for each of the lines in order. After we've read in the file, we set the `documentHasData` flag to indicate whether there is actually anything to display. Our next task is to work out where everything is to be displayed, and, having done that, how much client area we need to display the file – the document size that will be used to set the scrollbars. Finally, we set the title bar text and call `Invalidate()`. `Invalidate()` is an important method supplied by Microsoft, so we'll break for a couple of pages to explain its use, before we examine the code for the `CalculateLineWidths()` and `CalculateDocumentSize()` methods.

The Invalidate() Method

`Invalidate()` is a member of `System.Windows.Forms.Form` that we've not met before. It's an extremely useful method for when you think something needs repainting. Basically it marks an area of the client window as invalid and, therefore, in need of repainting, and then makes sure a `Paint` event is raised. There are a couple of overrides to `Invalidate()`: you can pass it a rectangle that specifies (in page coordinates) precisely which area of the window needs repainting, or if you don't pass any parameters it'll just mark the entire client area as invalid.

You may wonder why we are doing it this way. If we know that something needs painting, why don't we just call `OnPaint()` or some other method to do the painting directly? Occasionally, if there's some very precise small change you want made to the screen you might do that, but generally calling painting routines directly is regarded as bad programming practice – if your code decides it wants some painting done, in general you should call `Invalidate()`.

There are several reasons for this:

❑ Drawing is almost always the most processor-intensive task a GDI+ application will carry out. Doing it in the middle of other work holds up the other work. With our example here, if we'd directly called a method to do the drawing from the LoadFile() method, then the LoadFile() method wouldn't return until that drawing task was complete. During that time, our application can't respond to any other events. On the other hand, by calling Invalidate() we are simply getting Windows to raise a Paint event before immediately returning from LoadFile(). Windows is then free to examine the events that are waiting to be handled. How this works internally is that the events sit as what are known as **messages** in something called a **message queue**. Windows periodically examines the queue and if there are events in it, Windows picks one and calls the corresponding event handler. In all probability, the Paint event will be the only one sitting in the queue, so OnPaint() will get called immediately anyway. However, in a more complex application there may be other events, some of which should get priority. In particular, if the user has decided to quit the application, this will be marked by a message in the queue known as WM_QUIT. Handling this will get priority over everything else. There's no point, for example, doing something like updating the graphics in a window for an application that is just exiting! What this all boils down to, is that using Invalidate() to sort out requests to paint areas means that our application acts like a proper, well-behaved windows application.

❑ Related to the first reason, if you had a more complicated, multithreaded, application, you'll probably want just one thread to handle all the drawing. Using Invalidate() to route all drawing through the message queue provides a good way of ensuring that the same thread (whatever thread is responsible for the message queue – this will be the thread that called Application.Run()) does all the drawing, no matter what other thread requested the drawing operation.

❑ There's an additional performance-related reason. Suppose at about the same time a couple of different requests to draw part of the screen come in. Perhaps, your code has just done something to modify the document and so wants to make sure the updated document is displayed, just as in our example, while at the same time the user has just restored the window or moved another window that was covering part of the client area out of the way. By calling Invalidate(), you are giving windows a chance to notice that this has occurred. Windows can then merge the Paint events if appropriate, combining the invalidated areas, so that the painting is only done once. (Calling a method to do the painting directly from your code might needlessly result in the same area of screen being repainted more than once.)

❑ Finally, the code to do the painting is probably going to be one of the most complex parts of the code in your application, especially if you have a very sophisticated user interface. The guys who have to maintain your code in a couple of years time will thank you for having kept your painting code all in one place and as simple as you reasonably can – something that's easier to do if you don't have too many pathways into it from other parts of the program.

The bottom line from all this, is that it is good practice to keep all your painting in the OnPaint() routine, or in other methods called from that method. Try not to have lots of other places in your code that call up methods to do odd bits of painting, though all aspects of program design have to be balanced against various considerations. If, say, you want to replace just one character or shape on the screen – or add an accent to a letter – and you know perfectly well that it won't effect anything else that you've drawn, then you may decide that it's not worth the overhead of going through Invalidate(), and just write a separate drawing routine.

In a very complicated application, you may even write a full class that takes responsibility for drawing to the screen. A few years ago when MFC was the standard technology for GDI-intensive applications, MFC followed this model, with a C++ class, C<ApplicationName>View *that was responsible for this. However, even in this case, this class had one member function,* OnDraw(), *which was designed to be the entry point for most drawing requests.*

Calculating Item Sizes and Document Size

We'll return to the `CapsEditor` example now and examine the `CalculateLineWidths()` and `CalculateDocumentSize()` methods that are called from `LoadFile()`:

```
private void CalculateLineWidths()
{
    Graphics dc = this.CreateGraphics();
    foreach (TextLineInformation nextLine in documentLines)
    {
        nextLine.Width = (uint)dc.MeasureString(nextLine.Text,
                                                mainFont).Width;
    }
}
```

This method simply runs through each line that has been read in and uses the `Graphics.MeasureString()` method to work out and store how much horizontal screen space the string requires. We store the value, because `MeasureString()` is very computationally intensive. It's not the sort of method we want to call any more times than necessary if we want to keep performance up. If we hadn't made the `CapsEditor` sample so simple that we can easily work out the height and location of each item, this method would almost certainly have needed to be implemented in such a way as to compute all those quantities too.

Now we know how big each item on the screen is, and we can calculate whereabouts each item goes, we are in a position to work out the actual document size. The height is basically the number of lines times the height of each line. The width will need to be worked out by looking through each line to see which one is the longest, and taking the width of that one. For both height and width, we will also want to make an allowance for a small margin around the displayed document, to make the application look more attractive. (We don't want text squeezed up against any corner of the client area.)

Here's the method that calculates the document size:

```
private void CalculateDocumentSize()
{
    if (!documentHasData)
    {
        documentSize = new Size(100, 200);
    }
    else
    {
        documentSize.Height = (int)(nLines*lineHeight) + 2*(int)margin;
        uint maxLineLength = 0;
        foreach (TextLineInformation nextWord in documentLines)
        {
            uint tempLineLength = nextWord.Width + 2*margin;
            if (tempLineLength > maxLineLength)
                maxLineLength = tempLineLength;
        }
        documentSize.Width = (int)maxLineLength;
    }
    this.AutoScrollMinSize = documentSize;
}
```

This method first checks whether there is any data to be displayed. If there isn't we cheat a bit and use a hard-coded document size, which I happen to know is big enough to display the big red <Empty Document> warning. If we'd wanted to really do it properly, we'd have used `MeasureString()` to check how big that warning actually is.

Once we've worked out the document size, we tell the `Form` instance what the size is by setting the `Form.AutoScrollMinSize` property. When we do this, something interesting happens behind the scenes. In the process of setting this property, the client area is invalidated and a `Paint` event is raised, for the very sensible reason that changing the size of the document means scrollbars will need to be added or modified and the entire client area will almost certainly be repainted. Why do I say that's interesting? It perfectly illustrates what I was saying earlier about using the `Form.Invalidate()` method. You see, if you look back at the code for `LoadFile()` you'll realize that our call to `Invalidate()` in that method is actually redundant. The client area will be invalidated anyway when we set the document size. I left the explicit call to `Invalidate()` in the `LoadFile()` implementation to illustrate how in general you should normally do things. In fact in this case, all calling `Invalidate()` again will do is needlessly request a duplicate `Paint` event. However, this in turn illustrates what I was saying about how `Invalidate()` gives Windows the chance to optimize performance. The second `Paint` event won't in fact get raised: Windows will see that there's a `Paint` event already sitting in the queue and will compare the requested invalidated regions to see if it needs to do anything to merge them. In this case both `Paint` events will specify the entire client area, so nothing needs to be done, and Windows will quietly drop the second `Paint` request. Of course, going through that process will take up a little bit of processor time, but it'll be an negligible amount of time compared to how long it takes to actually do some painting.

OnPaint()

Now we've seen how `CapsEditor` loads the file, it's time to look at how the painting is done:

```
protected override void OnPaint(PaintEventArgs e)
{
    Graphics dc = e.Graphics;
    int scrollPositionX = this.AutoScrollPosition.X;
    int scrollPositionY = this.AutoScrollPosition.Y;
    dc.TranslateTransform(scrollPositionX, scrollPositionY);

    if (!documentHasData)
    {
        dc.DrawString("<Empty document>", emptyDocumentFont,
            emptyDocumentBrush, new Point(20,20));
        base.OnPaint(e);
        return;
    }

    // work out which lines are in clipping rectangle
    int minLineInClipRegion =
                    WorldYCoordinateToLineIndex(e.ClipRectangle.Top -
                                            scrollPositionY);
    if (minLineInClipRegion == -1)
        minLineInClipRegion = 0;
    int maxLineInClipRegion =
                    WorldYCoordinateToLineIndex(e.ClipRectangle.Bottom -
                                            scrollPositionY);
    if (maxLineInClipRegion >= this.documentLines.Count ||
```

```
        maxLineInClipRegion == -1)
    maxLineInClipRegion = this.documentLines.Count-1;

    TextLineInformation nextLine;
    for (int i=minLineInClipRegion; i<=maxLineInClipRegion ; i++)
    {
        nextLine = (TextLineInformation)documentLines[i];
        dc.DrawString(nextLine.Text, mainFont, mainBrush,
                    this.LineIndexToWorldCoordinates(i));
    }
    base.OnPaint(e);
}
```

At the heart of this `OnPaint()` override is a loop that goes through each line of the document, calling `Graphics.DrawString()` to paint each one. The rest of this code is mostly to do with optimizing the painting – the usual stuff about figuring out what exactly needs painting instead of rushing in and telling the graphics instance to redraw everything.

We start off by checking if there is any data in the document. If there isn't, we draw a quick message saying so, call the base class's `OnPaint()` implementation, and exit. If there is data, then we start looking at the clipping rectangle. The way we do this is by calling another method that we've written, `WorldYCoordinateToLineIndex()`. We'll examine this method next, but essentially it takes a given y position relative to the top of the document, and works out what line of the document is being displayed at that point.

The first time we call the `WorldYCoordinateToLineIndex()` method, we pass it the coordinate value `e.ClipRectangle.Top - scrollPositionY`. This is just the top of the clipping region, converted to world coordinates. If the return value is –1, we'll play safe and assume we need to start at the beginning of the document (as would be the case if the top of the clipping region was in the top margin).

Once we've done all that, we essentially repeat the same process for the bottom of the clipping rectangle, in order to find the last line of the document that is inside the clipping region. The indices of the first and last lines are respectively stored in `minLineInClipRegion` and `maxLineInClipRegion`, so then we can just run a `for` loop between these values to do our painting. Inside the painting loop, we actually need to do roughly the reverse transformation to the one performed by `WorldYCoordinateToLineIndex()`. We are given the index of a line of text, and we need to check where it should be drawn. This calculation is actually quite simple, but we've wrapped it up in another method, `LineIndexToWorldCoordinates()`, which returns the required coordinates of the top left corner of the item. The returned coordinates are world coordinates, but that's fine, because we have already called `TranslateTransform()` on the `Graphics` object so that we need to pass it world, rather than page, coordinates when asking it to display items.

Coordinate Transforms

In this section, we'll examine the implementation of the helper methods that we've written in the `CapsEditor` sample to help us with coordinate transforms. These are the `WorldYCoordinateToLineIndex()` and `LineIndexToWorldCoordinates()` methods that we referred to in the last section, as well as a couple of other methods.

First, `LineIndexToWorldCoordinates()` takes a given line index, and works out the world coordinates of the top left corner of that line, using the known margin and line height:

```
private Point LineIndexToWorldCoordinates(int index)
{
    Point TopLeftCorner = new Point(
        (int)margin, (int)(lineHeight*index + margin));
    return TopLeftCorner;
}
```

We also used a method that roughly does the reverse transform in `OnPaint()`.
`WorldYCoordinateToLineIndex()` works out the line index, but it only takes into account a vertical world coordinate. This is because it is used to work out the line index corresponding to the top and bottom of the clip region.

```
private int WorldYCoordinateToLineIndex(int y)
{
    if (y < margin)
        return -1;
    return (int)((y-margin)/lineHeight);
}
```

There are three more methods, which will be called from the handler routine that responds to the user double-clicking the mouse. First, we have a method that works out the index of the line being displayed at given world coordinates. Unlike `WorldYCoordinateToLineIndex()`, this method takes into account the x and y positions of the coordinates. It returns −1 if there is no line of text covering the coordinates passed in:

```
private int WorldCoordinatesToLineIndex(Point position)
{
    if (!documentHasData)
        return -1;
    if (position.Y < margin || position.X < margin)
        return -1;
    int index = (int)(position.Y-margin)/(int)this.lineHeight;
    // check position isn't below document
    if (index >= documentLines.Count)
        return -1;
    // now check that horizontal position is within this line
    TextLineInformation theLine =
                        (TextLineInformation)documentLines[index];
    if (position.X > margin + theLine.Width)
        return -1;

    // all is OK. We can return answer
    return index;
}
```

Finally, on occasions we also need to convert between line index and page, rather than world, coordinates. The following methods achieve this:

```
private Point LineIndexToPageCoordinates(int index)
{
    return LineIndexToWorldCoordinates(index) +
                            new Size(AutoScrollPosition);
}

private int PageCoordinatesToLineIndex(Point position)
{
    return WorldCoordinatesToLineIndex(position - new
                        Size(AutoScrollPosition));
}
```

Although these methods by themselves don't look particularly interesting, they do illustrate a general technique that you'll probably often need to use. With GDI+, we'll often find ourselves in a situation where we have been given some coordinates (for example the coordinates of where the user has clicked the mouse) and we'll need to figure out what item is being displayed at that point. Or it could happen the other way round – given a particular display item, whereabouts should it be displayed? Hence, if you are writing a GDI+ application, you'll probably find it useful to write methods that do the equivalent of the coordinate transformation methods illustrated here.

Responding to User Input

So far, with the exception of the File menu in the `CapsEditor` sample, everything we've done in this chapter has been one way: the application has talked to the user, by displaying information on the screen. Almost all software of course works both ways: the user can talk to the software as well. We're now going to add that facility to `CapsEditor`.

Getting a GDI+ application to respond to user input is actually a lot simpler than writing the code to draw to the screen, and indeed we've already covered how handle user input in Chapter 9. Essentially, you override methods from the `Form` class that get called from the relevant event handler – in much the same way that `OnPaint()` is called when a `Paint` event is raised.

For the case of detecting when the user clicks or moves the mouse the functions you may wish to override include:

Method	Called when
`OnClick(EventArgs e)`	mouse is clicked
`OnDoubleClick(EventArgs e)`	mouse is double-clicked
`OnMouseDown(MouseEventArgs e)`	left mouse button pressed
`OnMouseHover(MouseEventArgs e)`	mouse stays still somewhere after moving
`OnMouseMove(MouseEventArgs e)`	mouse is moved
`OnMouseUp(MouseEventArgs e)`	left mouse button is released

If you want to detect when the user types in any text, then you'll probably want to override these methods.

Method	Called when
`OnKeyDown(KeyEventArgs e)`	a key is depressed
`OnKeyPress(KeyPressEventArgs e)`	a key is pressed and released
`OnKeyUp(KeyEventArgs e)`	a pressed key is released

Notice that some of these events overlap. For example, if the user presses a mouse button this will raise the `MouseDown` event. If the button is immediately released again, this will raise the `MouseUp` event and the `Click` event. Also, some of these methods take an argument that is derived from `EventArgs`, and so can be used to give more information about a particular event. `MouseEventArgs` has two properties X and Y, which give the device coordinates of the mouse at the time it was pressed. Both `KeyEventArgs` and `KeyPressEventArgs` have properties that indicate which key or keys the event concerns.

That's all there is to it. It's then up to you to think about the logic of precisely what you want to do. The only point to note is that you'll probably find yourself doing a bit more logic work with a GDI+ application than you would have with a `Windows.Forms` application. That's because in a `Windows.Forms` application you are typically responding to quite high-level events (`TextChanged` for a textbox, for example). By contrast with GDI+, the events tend to be more basic – user clicks the mouse, or hits the key *h*. The action your application takes is likely to depend on a sequence of events rather than a single event. For example, in Word for Windows, in order to select some text the user will normally click the left mouse button, then move the mouse, then release the left mouse button. If the user simply hits, then releases the left mouse button Word doesn't select any text, but simply moves the text caret to the location where the mouse was. So at the point where the user hits the left mouse button, you can't yet tell what the user is going to do. Your application will receive the `MouseDown` event, but assuming you want your application to behave in the same way that Word for Windows does, there's not much you can do with this event except record that the mouse was clicked with the cursor in a certain position. Then, when the `MouseMove` event is received, you'll want to check from the record you've just made whether the left button is currently down, and if so highlight text as the user selects it. When the user releases the left mouse button, your corresponding action (in the `OnMouseUp()` method) will need to check whether any dragging took place while the mouse button was down, and act accordingly. Only at this point is the sequence complete.

Another point to consider is that, because certain events overlap, you will often have a choice of which event you want your code to respond to.

The golden rule really is to think carefully about the logic of every combination of mouse movement or click and keyboard event that the user might initiate, and ensure that your application responds in a way that is intuitive and in accordance with the expected behavior of applications in *every* case. Most of your work here will be in thinking rather than in coding, though the coding you do will be quite fiddly, as you may need to take into account a lot of combinations of user input. For example, what should your application do if the user starts typing in text while one of the mouse buttons is held down? It might sound like an improbable combination, but sooner or later some user is going to try it!

For the `CapsEditor` sample, we are keeping things very simple, so we don't really have any combinations to think about. The only thing we are going to respond to is when the user double-clicks – in which case we capitalize whatever line of text the mouse pointer is hovering over.

This should be a fairly simple task, but there is one snag. We need to trap the `DoubleClick` event, but the table above shows that this event takes an `EventArgs` parameter, not a `MouseEventArgs` parameter. The trouble is that we'll need to know where the mouse is when the user double-clicks, if we are to correctly identify the line of text to be capitalized – and you need a `MouseEventArgs` parameter to do that. There are two workarounds. One is to use a static method that is implemented by the `Form1` object, `Control.MousePosition` to find out the mouse position, like so:

```
protected override void OnDoubleClick(EventArgs e)
{
    Point MouseLocation = Control.MousePosition;
    // handle double click
```

In most cases this will work. However, there could be a problem if your application (or even some other application with a high priority) is doing some computationally intensive work at the moment the user double-clicks. It just might happen in that case that the `OnDoubleClick()` event handler doesn't get called until perhaps half a second later. You don't really want delays like that, because they annoy users really quickly, but even so, such situations do come up occasionally. Half a second is easily enough for the mouse to get moved halfway across the screen – in which case you'll end up executing `OnDoubleClick()` for completely the wrong location!

A better way here is to rely on one of the many overlaps between mouse-event meanings. The first part of double-clicking a mouse involves pressing the left button down. This means that if OnDoubleClick() is called then we know that OnMouseDown() has also just been called, with the mouse at the same location. We can use the OnMouseDown() override to record the position of the mouse, ready for OnDoubleClick(). This is the approach we take in CapsEditor:

```
protected override void OnMouseDown(MouseEventArgs e)
{
    base.OnMouseDown(e);
    this.mouseDoubleClickPosition = new Point(e.X, e.Y);
}
```

Now let's look at our OnDoubleClick() override. There's quite a bit more work to do here:

```
protected override void OnDoubleClick(EventArgs e)
{
    int i = PageCoordinatesToLineIndex(this.mouseDoubleClickPosition);
    if (i >= 0)
    {
        TextLineInformation lineToBeChanged =
                        (TextLineInformation)documentLines[i];
        lineToBeChanged.Text = lineToBeChanged.Text.ToUpper();
        Graphics dc = this.CreateGraphics();
        uint newWidth = (uint)dc.MeasureString(lineToBeChanged.Text,
                                        mainFont).Width;
        if (newWidth > lineToBeChanged.Width)
            lineToBeChanged.Width = newWidth;
        if (newWidth+2*margin > this.documentSize.Width)
        {
            this.documentSize.Width = (int)newWidth;
            this.AutoScrollMinSize = this.documentSize;
        }
        Rectangle changedRectangle = new Rectangle(
                                    LineIndexToPageCoordinates(i),
                                    new Size((int)newWidth,
                                    (int)this.lineHeight));
        this.Invalidate(changedRectangle);
    }
    base.OnDoubleClick(e);
}
```

We start off by calling PageCoordinatesToLineIndex() to work out which line of text the mouse pointer was hovering over when the user double-clicked. If this call returns −1 then we weren't over any text, so there's nothing to do; except, of course, call the base class version of OnDoubleClick() to let Windows do any default processing. You wouldn't ever forget to do that, would you?

Assuming we've identified a line of text, we can use the string.ToUpper() method to convert it to uppercase. That was the easy part. The hard part, is figuring out what needs to be redrawn where. Fortunately, because we kept the sample so simplistic, there aren't too many combinations. We can assume for a start, that converting to uppercase will always either leave the width of the line on the screen unchanged, or increase it. Capital letters are bigger than lowercase letters; therefore, the width will never go down. We also know that since we are not wrapping lines, our line of text won't overflow to the next line and push out other text below. Our action of converting the line to uppercase won't, therefore, actually change the locations of any of the other items being displayed. That's a big simplification!

The next thing the code does is use `Graphics.MeasureString()` to work out the new width of the text. There are now just two possibilities:

❏ First, the new width might make our line the longest line, and cause the width of the entire document to increase. If that's the case then we'll need to set `AutoScrollMinSize` to the new size so that the scrollbars are correctly placed.

❏ Second, the size of the document might be unchanged.

In either case, we need to get the screen redrawn, by calling `Invalidate()`. Only one line has changed; therefore, we don't want to have the entire document repainted. Rather, we need to work out the bounds of a rectangle that contains just the modified line, so that we can pass this rectangle to `Invalidate()`, ensuring that just that line of text will be repainted. That's precisely what the above code does. Our call to `Invalidate()` will result in `OnPaint()` being called, when the mouse event handler finally returns. Bearing in mind our comments earlier in the chapter about the difficulty in setting a break point in `OnPaint()`, if you run the sample and set a break point in `OnPaint()` to trap the resultant painting action, you'll find that the `PaintEventArgs` parameter to `OnPaint()` does indeed contain a clipping region that matches the specified rectangle. And since we've overloaded `OnPaint()` to take careful account of the clipping region, only the one required line of text will be repainted.

Printing

In this chapter we've focused entirely on drawing to the screen. Often, you will also want your application to be able to produce a hard copy of the data too. Unfortunately, in this book we don't have space to go into the details of this process, but we'll briefly review the issues you'll face if you do wish to implement the ability to print your document.

In many ways printing is just the same as displaying to a screen. You will be supplied with a device context (`Graphics` instance) and call all the usual display commands against that instance. However, there are some differences. Printers cannot scroll – instead they have pages. You'll need to make sure you find a sensible way of dividing your document into pages, and draw each page as requested. Also, beware – most users expect the printed output to look very similar to the screen output. This is actually very hard to achieve if you use page coordinates. The problem is that printers have a different number of dots per inch (dpi) from the screen. Display devices have traditionally maintained a standard of around 96 dpi, although some newer monitors have higher resolutions. Printers can have over a thousand dpi. That means, for example, that if you draw shapes or display images sizing them by number of pixels, they will appear too small on the printer. In some cases the same problem can affect text fonts. Luckily, GDI+ allows device coordinates to address this problem. In order to print documents you will almost certainly need to use the `Graphics.PageUnit` property to carry out the painting using some physical units such as inches or millimeters.

.NET does have a large number of classes designed to help with the process of printing. These classes typically allow you to control and retrieve various printer settings and are found mostly in the `System.Drawing.Printing` namespace. There are also predefined dialogs, `PrintDialog` and `PrintPreviewDialog`, available in the `System.Windows.Forms` namespace. The process of printing will initially involve calling the `Show()` method on an instance of one of these classes, after setting some properties.

Summary

In this chapter, we've covered the area of drawing to a display device, where the drawing is done by your code rather than by some predefined control or dialog – the realm of GDI+. GDI+ is a powerful tool, and there are many .NET base classes available to help you draw to a device. We've seen that the process of drawing is actually relatively simple – in most cases you can draw text or sophisticated figures or display images with just a couple of C# statements. However, managing your drawing – the behind the scenes work involving working out what to draw, where to draw it, and what does or doesn't need repainting in any given situation – is far more complex and requires careful algorithm design. For this reason, it is also important to have a good understanding of how GDI+ works, and what actions Windows takes in order to get something drawn. In particular, because of the architecture of Windows, it is important that where possible drawing should be done by invalidating areas of the window and relying on Windows to respond by issuing a `Paint` event.

There are many more .NET classes concerned with drawing than we've had space to cover in this chapter, but if you've worked through it and understood the principles involved in drawing, you'll be in an excellent position to explore them, by looking at their lists of methods in the documentation and instantiating instances of them to see what they do. In the end, drawing, like almost any other aspect of programming, requires logic, careful thought, and clear algorithms. Apply that and you'll be able to write sophisticated user interfaces that don't depend on the standard controls. Your software will benefit hugely in both user-friendliness and visual appearance: There are many applications out there that rely entirely on controls for their user interface. While this can be effective, such applications very quickly end up looking just like each other. By adding some GDI+ code to do some custom drawing you can mark out your software as distinct and make it appear more original – which can only help your sales!

22

Accessing the Internet

We've already seen in Chapters 16-18 how you can use C# to write powerful and efficient dynamic web pages using ASP.NET, as well as web services. For the most part, the clients accessing ASP.NET pages will be users running Internet Explorer or other web browsers. However it sometimes happens that you need your own applications to act as web clients. This might happen for example if you need to add web browsing features to your own applications, or if you need your applications to programmatically obtain information from certain web sites. In this last case, it is usually better for the site to implement a web service – but if you are accessing outside sites you might not have control over how the site is implemented and may therefore have no choice but to programmatically access a site that has been implemented as standard HTML, ASP, or ASP.NET pages.

It is this side of the picture that we will briefly examine in this chapter. In particular we will cover the facilities provided through the .NET base classes for using various network protocols, particularly HTTP, to access networks and the Internet as a client. In particular, we will cover:

- ❑ Requesting data from the web and retrieving the response from servers
- ❑ Sending HTTP POST data
- ❑ Retrieving HTTP header information from server responses

We will also briefly mention the facilities available to access lower-level services directly, such as sending and receiving TCP packets and listening to particular ports.

The `System.Net` and `System.Net.Sockets` namespaces contain most of the .NET base classes that deal with networking from the perspective of the client. The `System.Net` namespace is generally concerned with higher-level operations – for example, downloading and uploading files, and making web requests using the HTTP and other protocols, while `System.NET.Sockets` contains classes that are concerned with lower-level operations. These will be more useful if you want to work directly with sockets or protocols such as TCP/IP, and is largely used simply to wrap the corresponding Windows API functions.

We are going to take a fairly practical approach in this chapter, and work by presenting a number of examples of steadily increasing complexity. We will mix those examples with a discussion of the relevant theory and networking concepts as appropriate.

We will start with the simplest case, when you simply want to send out a request to a server and store or process the information sent back.

The WebClient Class

If all you want to do is carry out a fairly simple operation such as requesting a file from a particular URI, then you'll probably find the easiest .NET class to use is `System.Net.WebClient`. This class is an extremely high-level class designed to perform basic operations with only one or two commands.

Downloading Files

There are two ways of downloading a file from a web site using `WebClient`, depending on whether we want to save the file, or process the contents of the file directly within our application. If we simply want to save the file then we should call the `DownloadFile()` method. This method takes two parameters: the URI of the location from which we want to retrieve the file, and the file name (or path) that we want to save the file to.

```
WebClient Client = new WebClient();
Client.DownloadFile("http://www.Wrox.com/default.htm", "index.htm");
```

More commonly, your application will want to process the data retrieved from the web site. In order to do this, you use the `OpenRead()` method, which returns a `Stream` reference. You can then simply retrieve the data from the stream.

```
WebClient Client = new WebClient();
Stream strm = Client.OpenRead("http://www.Wrox.com/default.htm");
```

Example: Basic Web Client

Our first example will demonstrate using the `WebClient.OpenRead()` method. In this case we will simply display the contents of the downloaded data in a listbox. We create the project as a standard Windows C# application, and add a listbox called `listBox1`, in which we will display the contents of the downloaded file. We then make the following changes to the constructor of the main form.

```csharp
public Form1()
{
    InitializeComponent();

    System.Net.WebClient Client = new WebClient();
    Stream strm = Client.OpenRead("http://www.wrox.com");
    StreamReader sr = new StreamReader(strm);
    string line;
    do
    {
        line = sr.ReadLine();
        listBox1.Items.Add(line);
    }
    while (line != null);
    strm.Close();
}
```

For simplicity, we have hard-coded a URI into the program.

> *If you've not encountered the acronym URI before, it stands for **Uniform Resource Identifier**. It means any short string that refers to some resource. Hence a string like http://www.wrox.com is a URI. In the past the term URL (uniform resource locator) has traditionally been used to identify such addresses, but the term URL is no longer in use in new technical specifications, URI being now preferred. URI has roughly the same meaning as URL, but is a bit more general, since URI doesn't necessarily imply that we are using one of the familiar protocols such as HTTP or FTP.*

Notice how, in this example, we have actually used two streams in succession. We've connected a `StreamReader` to the network stream. This allows us to obtain the data from the stream as text and to use the more useful higher-level methods such as `ReadLine()` that are available with the `StreamReader` class. This is an excellent example of the point we made in Chapter 14, about the benefits of abstracting the concept of moving data into the concept of a stream.

Running this sample produces the following results:

Uploading Files

The `WebClient` class also features `UploadFile()` and `UploadData()` methods. The difference between them is that `UploadFile()` uploads a specified file given the file name, while `UploadData()` uploads binary data, which is supplied as an array of bytes:

```
WebClient client = new WebClient();
client.UploadData("http://www.ourwebsite.com/NewFile.htm",
                  "C:\WebSiteFiles\NewFile.htm");


byte [] image;
// code to initialise image so it contains all the binary data for
// some jpg file
client.UploadData("http://www.ourwebsite.com/NewFile.jpg", image);
```

The WebRequest Classes

Although the `WebClient` class is very simple to use, it has very limited features. In particular, you cannot use it to supply authentication credentials – a particular problem with uploading data is that there are not many sites that will accept uploaded files without authentication! It is possible to add header information to requests and to examine any header information returned, but only in a very generic sense – there is no specific support for any one protocol. The reason for this is that `WebClient` is a very general-purpose class, designed to work with any protocol for which it is possible to send a request and receive a response (HTTP, FTP, etc.). It cannot handle any extra features that are specific to any one protocol, such as cookies, which are specific to HTTP. If you want to take advantage of these features you need to use a family of classes based on two other classes in the `System.Net` namespace: `WebRequest` and `WebResponse`.

We'll start off by showing you how to download a web page using these classes – this is the same example as before, but using `WebRequest` and `WebResponse`. In the process we will explain a bit about the class hierarchy involved, then show how to take advantage of extra HTTP features supported by this hierarchy.

The following code shows modifications we need to make to the `BasicWebClient` sample so that it uses the `WebRequest` and `WebResponse` classes.

```
public Form1()
{
    InitializeComponent();

    WebRequest wrq = WebRequest.Create("http://www.wrox.com");
    WebResponse wrs = wrq.GetResponse();
    Stream strm = wrs.GetResponseStream();
    StreamReader sr = new StreamReader(strm);
    string line;
    while ( (line = sr.ReadLine()) != null)
    {
        listBox1.Items.Add(line);
    }
    strm.Close();
}
```

In this code we start by instantiating an object that represents a web request. Unusually, we don't do this using a constructor, but instead by calling the static `WebRequest.Create()` method; we'll see why in the next section. The `WebRequest` class represents the request for information that we are sending to a particular URI, and so needs to be passed the URI via the `Create()` method. A `WebResponse` represents the data that we get back from the server. By calling the `WebRequest.GetResponse()` method, we actually send the request to the web server and create a `Response` object that we can use to examine the data returned. As with the `WebClient` object, we can obtain a stream that represents this data, but in this case using the method `WebResponse.GetResponseStream()`.

Other WebRequest and WebResponse Features

We'll here quickly mention a couple of the other areas in which good support is provided by `WebRequest` and `WebResponse` and other related classes.

HTTP Header Information

An important part of the HTTP protocol is the ability to send extensive header information with both request and response streams. This information can include GET and POST data, and cookies, as well as the details of the particular browser sending the request. As you'd expect, full support is provided for setting and accessing this data. This support is not part of the WebRequest and WebResponse classes, however, but is implemented by two derived classes: HttpWebRequest and HttpWebResponse. As we will explain soon, when you create a WebRequest using the usual factory mechanism, if the URI you supplied was an HTTP URI, the reference you get back actually refers to an HttpRequest object, and you can cast it to that if you wish. The HttpRequest implementation of GetResponse() actually returns an HttpWebResponse object via a WebResponse reference, so again you can perform a simple cast to access the HTTP-specific features.

Full details of support for this area are in the MSDN documentation for the HttpWebRequest and HttpWebResponse classes.

Asynchronous Page Requests

An extra useful feature of using WebRequest instead of WebClient is that it is possible to request pages asynchronously. This is important since on the Internet there can be quite a long delay between sending a request off to a host and starting to get any data back. Methods like WebClient.DownloadData and WebRequest.GetResponse() won't return until a response has come back from the server. You might not want to have your application tied up waiting for that time. If that's the case then you might prefer to use BeginGetResponse() and EndGetResponse(). These methods work asynchronously. If you call BeginGetResponse() then a request will be fired off to the host, and the method will return immediately, supplying you with a delegate of type AsyncCallback. You can then carry on doing other processing while the server answers the request. We won't go into details here but details of these methods are available on MSDN.

Displaying Output as an HTML Page

Our first example shows that the .NET base classes make it very easy to download and process data from the Internet. However, we have only so far displayed files as plain text. Quite often within your application, you will want to view an HTML file in an Internet Explorer style of interface – so you can see what the web document actually looks like. Unfortunately, at the time of writing the .NET base classes don't include any intrinsic supports for a control that features an Internet Explorer style interface. To do that, you will need to either programmatically call up Internet Explorer, or fall back on the WebBrowser ActiveX control that's been around since pre-.NET days.

> *One situation in which you may wish to display an Internet Explorer user interface is if you are writing a C# application that generates or allows editing of HTML pages, and need to display the pages so generated to the user.*

Programmatically starting an Internet Explorer process that is targeted on a given web page can be done using the Process class in the System.Diagnostics namespace.

```
Process myProcess = new Process();
myProcess.StartInfo.FileName = "iexplore.exe";
myProcess.StartInfo.Arguments = "http://www.wrox.com";
myProcess.Start();
```

However, this starts up IE as a separate window, which isn't really connected to or under the control of your application. Hence although we've given the code here for reference, it's not a technique you're likely to want to use very often.

On the other hand, using the `WebBrowser` control means that the displayed browser can form an integrated part of your application, and your application gets full control over what the browser does. The control is quite sophisticated, featuring a large number of methods, properties, and events.

The easiest way to incorporate this control, using Visual Studio.NET, is to add the control to the toolbox. To do this, right click on the toolbox in Visual Studio.NET and select **Customize Toolbox** from the context menu, which brings up the following dialog. You should select the **COM Components** tab, and check Microsoft Web Browser.

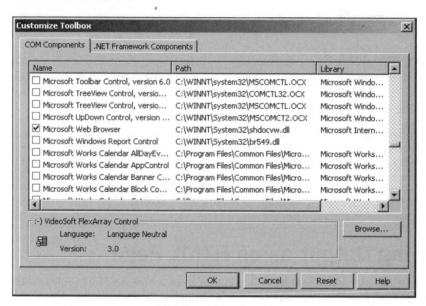

The `WebBrowser` control will now appear in the toolbox and you can click to drop it onto your form in a C# Windows application, just as for any of the .NET Windows Forms controls. Visual Studio.NET will automatically generate all the COM interoperability code required to allow your C# program to act as a client to this control, so that you can just treat it as if it is a .NET control. We will demonstrate this with another very short example, `DisplayWebPage`, in which we display a web page with a hardcoded URI.

We create `DisplayWebPage` as a standard C# Windows application and drop the `WebBrowser` ActiveX control into the form as explained above. By default Visual Studio.NET names the corresponding variable `axWebBrowser1`, and here we'll leave the default name. Then we add this code to the `Form1` constructor:

```
public Form1()
{
    // Required for Windows Form Designer support
    InitializeComponent();
```

```
        int zero = 0;
        object oZero = zero;
        string emptyString = "";
        object oEmptyString = emptyString;
        axWebBrowser1.Navigate("http://www.wrox.com",
                               ref oZero,
                               ref oEmptyString,
                               ref oEmptyString,
                               ref oEmptyString);
    }
```

In this code, we use the `Navigate()` method of the `WebBrowser` control, which actually sends an HTTP request and displays the output from a given URI. The first parameter to this method is a string containing the URL to be navigated to. The remaining parameters respectively allow you to supply various flags, indicate a named frame in which the browser should be displayed, and specify any POST data to be sent with the request and additional HTTP header information. However, the default values of zero and empty strings suffice for our purposes. These parameters are defined in the control as optional parameters, but C# does not support optional parameters, so we need to supply them explicitly. We also need to explicitly declare object references for these variables because they are passed by reference.

Calling `Navigate()` with the parameters as above has basically the same effect as typing the URL into Internet Explorer in order to navigate to the web page. This code is the only code we need to add to the `DisplayWebPage` project manually. If we run the example we get these results (we've also used Visual Studio.NET to change the title text of the main form).

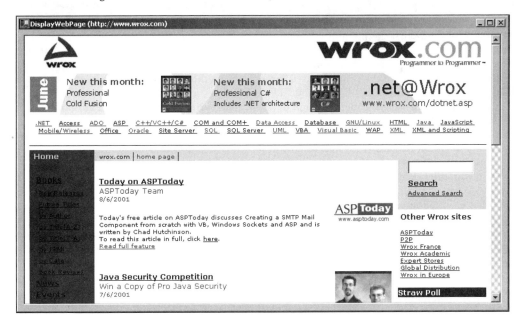

Notice that displaying a web page this way requires only the legacy `WebBrowser` control – we've not needed to use any of the classes in the `System.Net` namespace.

The Web Request and Web Response Hierarchy

In this section we'll take a closer look at the architecture underlying the WebRequest and WebResponse classes.

The inheritance hierarchy of classes involved is shown in the diagram.

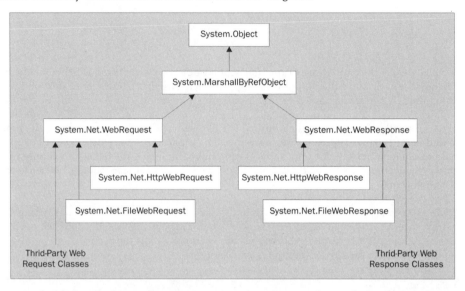

The diagram shows that the hierarchy contains more than the two classes that we've used in our code. In fact the WebRequest and WebResponse classes are both abstract, and so cannot be instantiated. They are there as base classes to provide general functionality for dealing with web requests and responses independent of the protocol used for a given operation. Any given request is always made using a particular protocol (HTTP, Telnet, FTP, SMTP, etc.) and is dealt with using the derived class for that protocol. In our earlier code, although our reference variables were defined as base-class references, WebRequest.Create() actually gave us an HttpWebRequest object, and the GetResponse() method actually returned an HttpWebResponse object. So why didn't we see that explicitly in code? The answer is that Microsoft has provided a factory-based mechanism for hiding details of class hierarchy from client code. The fact that we needed an object specifically capable of dealing with the HTTP protocol is clear from the URI that we supplied to WebRequest.Create(): http://www.wrox.com. WebRequest.Create() examines the protocol specifier in the URI, and uses that to instantiate and return an object of the appropriate class. The intention is that you should never use the constructor to instantiate a WebRequest object; in that way you are, to some extent, freed from having to know anything about the derived classes. Having said that, this theory breaks down somewhat if you need to use any specific features of the protocol you are using that are implemented as methods on the derived class, in which case you'll need to cast your WebRequest or WebResponse reference to the derived class.

In theory, with this architecture we should be able to handle sending requests using any of the common protocols. However Microsoft has only actually written derived classes that cover the HTTP and file:// protocols. If you want to be able to deal with other protocols, for example FTP, Telnet, or SMTP, then you will need to either fall back on the Windows API, write your own classes (which will internally be implemented using the Windows API), or wait for an independent software vendor to write some suitable .NET classes!

Utility Classes

In this section we'll note a couple of utility classes that can make web programming easier when dealing with two common Internet topics – URIs and IP addresses.

URIs

`Uri` and `UriBuilder` are two classes in the `System` (note: not `System.Net`) namespace, and they are both intended to represent a URI. The difference between them is that `UriBuilder` is intended to allow you to build up a URI, given the strings for the component parts, while `Uri` allows you to parse a complete URI.

Since the `Uri` class is really there to let you break down rather than build up a URI, it requires a completed URI string in order to construct it.

```
Uri MSPage = new
            Uri("http://www.Microsoft.com/SomeFolder/SomeFile.htm?Order=true");
```

The class exposes a large number of properties all of which are read-only. A `Uri` object is not intended to be modified once it has been constructed.

```
string Query = MSPage.Query;                        // Order=true;
string AbsolutePath = MSPage.AbsolutePath;          // SomeFolder/SomeFile.htm
string Scheme = MSPage.Scheme;                      // http
int Port = MSPage.Port;                             // 80 (the default for http)
string AbsolutePath = MSPage.AbsolutePath;          // SomeFolder/SomeFile.htm
string Host = MSPage.Host;                          // www.Microsoft.com
bool IsDefaultPort = MSPage.IsDefaultPort;          // true since 80 is default
```

`URIBuilder`, on the other hand, implements fewer properties: just enough to allow you to build up a complete URI. However, these properties are read-write.

You can supply the components to build up a URI to the constructor:

```
Uri MSPage = new
   UriBuilder("http", "www.Microsoft.com", 80, "SomeFolder/SomeFile.htm",
          "Order=true");
```

Or you can build the components up by assigning values to the properties:

```
UriBuilder MSPage = new UriBuilder();
MSPage.Scheme ="http";
MSPage.Host = "www.Microsoft.com";
MSPage.Port = 80;
MSPage.Path = "SomeFolder/SomeFile.htm";
MSPage.Query = "Order=true";
```

Once you have completed initializing the `UriBuilder`, you can obtain the corresponding `Uri` object with the `Uri` property:

```
Uri CompletedUri = MSPage.Uri;
```

The Display Page Sample

We will illustrate the use of `UriBuilder` along with creating an Internet Explorer process with an example, `DisplayPage`. This example allows the user to type in the component parts of a URL. Note that we mean URL, not URI as we assume it's an HTTP request. The user can then click a button marked **View Page**, at which point the application will display the completed URL in a textbox, and display the page using the `WebBrowser` ActiveX control.

The sample is a standard C# Windows application and looks like this:

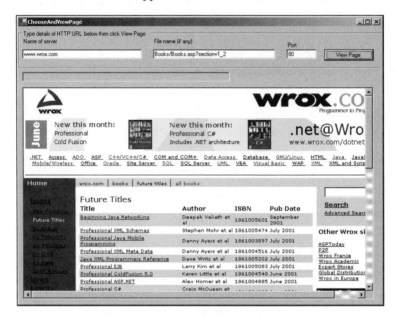

The textboxes are named respectively `textBoxServer`, `textBoxPath`, `textBoxPort`, and `textBoxURI`. The code that has been added for the example is entirely in the `ViewPage` button event handler:

```
private void OnClickViewPage(object sender, System.EventArgs e)
{
    UriBuilder Address = new UriBuilder();
    Address.Host = textBoxServer.Text;
    Address.Port = int.Parse(textBoxPort.Text);
    Address.Scheme = Uri.UriSchemeHttp;
    Address.Path = textBoxFile.Text;

    Uri AddressUri = Address.Uri;

    Process myProcess = new Process();
    myProcess.StartInfo.FileName = "iexplore.exe";
    textBoxURI.Text = AddressUri.ToString();
    myProcess.StartInfo.Arguments = AddressUri.ToString();
    myProcess.Start();
}
```

IP Addresses and DNS Names

On the Internet, servers as well as clients are identified by IP addresses or by hostnames (also referred to as DNS names). Generally the hostname is the human-friendly name that you type in a web browser window, such as www.wrox.com or www.microsoft.com. The IP address on the other hand is the identifier that computers use to identify each other, and is the address that is actually used to ensure that web requests and responses are directed to the appropriate machine.

The IP address is simply a 32-bit integer, which is usually represented in the so-called dotted decimal format as a set of four numbers each between 0 and 255. It is even possible for a computer to have more than one IP address. For example, the computer I'm currently working currently has an IP address of 100.100.100.31 (number changed for obvious security reasons) when talking to other computers on the Internet via its modem, and the address 10.0.0.1 when talking through its network card to the other computers on my home network. Hence, if the other computers on my home network want to send a message to my current machine, they must address it to 10.0.0.1, while computers on the Internet must address it as 100.100.100.31. It is also common for addresses to be dynamically assigned to a computer each time it either boots up (for computers with a permanent intranet connection) or dials up (for computers connected to an ISP via a modem or similar device). That's the case for my computer, so the next time I dial up, I'll have a different IP address. Where a computer uses dynamically assigned IP addresses, its address each time it requires one is assigned from a pool of addresses maintained by its ISP.

Since human beings rarely type in IP addresses directly, or remember the IP addresses of their favorite web sites, but use the more human-friendly DNS names like www.wrox.com, it is necessary whenever you send a network request to first translate the DNS name into an IP address, a task carried out by one of several DNS servers.

The way it works is that some machine that your local computer has a good connection to, by which I mean either a designated machine on your local network, or if you have a modem connection, a machine on the corporate network to which you dial up, will have been designated a DNS server. This machine will store a huge table mapping DNS names to IP addresses for all the computers it knows about – and will also host the IP addresses of other DNS servers that may be able to look up the ones it doesn't know about. Every networked computer must know the IP address of at least one local DNS server (it's one of the pieces of information you or your system administrators need to supply when the networking configuration on a computer is set up. When a request is sent out, your computer will first ask the DNS server to tell it the IP address corresponding to the domain address that you have typed in. Then, armed with the correct IP address, the request can head out. Normally this happens behind the scenes and so is completely transparent to you when you are for example browsing on the Internet.

.NET Classes for IP Addresses

.NET supplies a number of classes that are able to assist with the process of looking up IP addresses and finding out information about host computers.

IPAddress

IPAddress represents an IP address. The address itself is available as the Address property, and may be converted to dotted decimal format with the ToString() method. IPAddress also implements a static Parse() method, which effectively performs the reverse conversion to ToString() – converting from a dotted decimal string to an (integer) IP address.

```
IPAddress ipAddress = IPAddress.Parse("234.56.78.9");
int address = ipAddress.Address;        // address will be assigned 37105130
string ipString = ipAddress.ToString(); // ipString will be assigned
                                        // the text "234.45.54.2"
```

IPAddress also provides a number of constant static fields that return known special IP addresses that have special meanings.

```
// following line will set loopback to "127.0.0.1".
// the loopback address indicates the local host.
string loopback = IPAddress.Loopback.ToString();

// following line will set broadcast to "255.255.255.255".
// the broadcast address is used to send a message to all machines on
// the local network.
string broadcast = IPAddress.Broadcast.ToString();
```

IPHostEntry

The IPHostEntry class encapsulates the information relating to a particular host (computer). It makes the hostname available via the HostName property (which returns a string), and all the IP Addresses via the AddressList property, which returns an array of IPAddress objects. We will see the IPHostEntry class in action in the DNSResolver example that is coming up.

Dns

The Dns class is the class that is able to communicate with your default DNS server in order to retrieve IP addresses. The two important (static) methods here are Resolve(), which uses the DNS server to obtain the details of a host with a given host name, and GetHostByAddress(), which also returns details of the host, but this time using the IP address. Both methods return an IPHostEntry object.

```
HostEntry wroxHost = Dns.Resolve("www.microsoft.com");
HostEntry wroxHostCopy = Dns.GetHostByAddress("234.234.234.234");
```

In this code both HostEntry objects will contain details of the Microsoft.com servers.

The Dns class differs from the IPAddress and IPHostEntry classes in the fact that it encapsulates the ability to actually communicate with servers to obtain information. IPAddress and IPHostEntry by contrast, are little more than data structures that have convenient properties that allow you to access the data contained in them.

Example: DnsLookup

We will illustrate the DNS and IP-related classes with an example that looks up DNS names. This screenshot shows the DnsLookup sample in action:

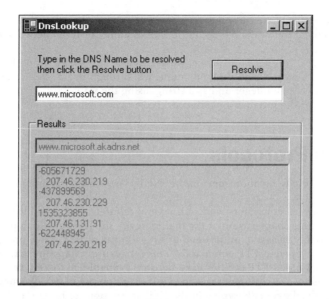

The sample simply invites the user to type in a DNS name in the main textbox. When the user clicks the Resolve button, the sample uses the Dns.Resolve() method to retrieve an IPHostEntry reference and so display the hostname and IP addresses. Note that the hostname displayed may in some cases be different from the name typed in. This can occur if one DNS name (www.microsoft.com) simply acts as a proxy for another DNS name (www.microsoft.akadns.net).

The DnsLookup application is a standard C# Windows application, with the controls added as shown in the screenshot, giving them the respective names textBoxInput, buttonResolve, textBoxHostName, and listboxIPs. Then we simply added the following method to the Form1 class, setting this method up in the Visual Studio.NET properties window as the event handler for the click event for buttonResolve.

```csharp
void OnResolve(object sender, EventArgs e)
{
    try
    {
        IPHostEntry iphost = Dns.Resolve(textBoxInput.Text);
        foreach (IPAddress ip in iphost.AddressList)
        {
            int ipaddress = ip.Address;
            listBoxIPs.Items.Add(ipaddress);
            listBoxIPs.Items.Add("    " + Dns.IpToString(ipaddress));
        }
        textBoxHostName.Text = iphost.HostName;
    }
    catch(Exception ex)
    {
        MessageBox.Show("Unable to process the request because " +
            "the following problem occurred:\n" +
            ex.Message, "Exception occurred");
    }
}
```

Notice how in this code we are careful to trap any exceptions – an exception could easily occur if the user types in something that turns out not to be a DNS name, or if the network is down.

After retrieving the `IPHostEntry` instance, we use its `AddressList` property to obtain an array containing the IP addresses, which we then enumerate through in a `foreach` loop. For each one we display the IP address as an integer and as a string, using the static `Dns.IpToString()` method, which does the same thing as the instance `IPAddress.ToString()` method.

Lower-Level Protocols

In this section we'll briefly mention some of the .NET classes used to communicate at a lower level.

Communication between computers works on several different levels, and the classes we have considered so far in this chapter work at the highest level, the level at which particular commands are specified. It is probably easiest to understand this if we think of FTP, since many developers have at some stage explicitly typed in FTP commands. This is because it happens that, although in recent years a number of good UI-based FTP utilities have become available, until very recently the main tool used for FTP on the Windows environment was the DOS `ftp` command, which worked at the command line, and so using it involved explicitly typing in the FTP instructions to be sent to the server.

FTP is not alone in its reliance on these kinds of commands: HTTP, Telnet, SMTP, POP, and other protocols are based on similar sets of commands – the only difference is that for most of these protocols, you use tools that hide the transmission of the commands from the user, so that you are generally not aware of them. For example, when you type in a URL in a web browser, and the web request goes off, the browser is actually sending a (plain text) GET command to the server, which serves a similar purpose to the FTP `get` command. It may also send a POST command, which indicates that other data is attached to the request.

However, these protocols are not by themselves sufficient to achieve communication between computers. Even if both the client and the server understand, for example, the HTTP protocol, it will still not be possible for them to understand each other unless there is also agreement on exactly how the characters will be transmitted. What binary format will be used, and – even getting down to the lowest level – what voltages will be used to represent 0's and 1's in the binary data? It is because there are so many different items on which some protocol needs to be agreed that developers and hardware engineers who work in the field often refer to a protocol stack. A protocol stack is basically a list of the various protocols, from the topmost level (HTTP, FTP etc.) down to the basic protocols for the voltages etc.

Luckily, for most development work, we don't need to go quite that far down the stack, but if you are writing code that requires efficient communication between computers, it's not unusual to write code that works directly at the level of sending binary data packets between computers. This is the realm of protocols such as TCP, and Microsoft has supplied a number of classes that allow you to conveniently work with binary data at this level. Using these classes you can, for example, send out a multicast message that will be simultaneously received by a number of computers on your network.

Lower-Level Classes

The relevant classes are defined in the `System.Net.Sockets` namespace, and allow you, for example, to directly send out TCP requests or to listen to TCP requests on a particular port. The main classes are:

Class	Purpose
Socket	Low-level class that deals with actually managing connections. This class is used internally by such classes as `WebRequest` and `TcpClient`.
NetworkStream	Derived from `Stream`. Represents a stream of data from the network.
TcpClient	Lets you create connections for listeners.
TcpListener	Lets you listen for incoming connection requests.
UdpClient	Lets you create connections for UDP clients. (UDP is an alternative protocol to TCP, but is much less widely used – mostly on local networks.)

Summary

In this chapter we've very briefly reviewed some of the .NET base classes that deal with opening client connections on the network and Internet and sending requests to and receiving responses from servers – the most obvious use of this being receiving HTML pages.

The .NET classes are at the time of writing admittedly slightly sketchy in their support of many common protocols – and it was noticeable that even to perform a task as basic as displaying an HTML page, we needed to fall back on a legacy COM ActiveX control, the `WebBrowser` control. (Having said that, this isn't so much of a disadvantage since the .NET COM interoperability features and Visual Studio.NET work together to make using such controls almost as easy as using genuine Windows Forms controls.) Nevertheless, the .NET classes that are available do make performing some important tasks simplicity in itself – this is especially true of the process of retrieving a web page into a stream or file.

23

Distributed Applications with .NET Remoting

In Chapter 17, we talked about web services, which allow us to call objects on a remote server. The use of a web server and the SOAP protocol is not always efficient enough for intranet applications. The SOAP protocol causes a lot of overhead when transferring a lot of data. For a fast intranet solution, we could use simple sockets as we've done in the last chapter. In the "old world" however, you've already written programs using DCOM. With DCOM, we are used to calling methods on objects running on a server. The programming model is the same whether objects are used on the server or on the client.

Without DCOM, we have to deal with ports and sockets, pay attention to the target platforms because of possibly different data representations, and build a custom protocol, where messages are sent to the socket so that we finally call some methods. DCOM handles all these issues for us.

The replacement for DCOM is **.NET Remoting**. In contrast to DCOM, .NET Remoting can also be used in Internet solutions. DCOM is not flexible and efficient enough for use in Internet solutions. It's possible to adapt and extend every part of the architecture with .NET Remoting, so it fits for nearly all remoting scenarios.

In this chapter we will look at:

- ❑ The .NET Remoting Architecture
- ❑ Channels, Messages, and Sinks
- ❑ Building clients and servers
- ❑ Remoting properties with configuration files
- ❑ The extension possibilities of the framework
- ❑ Remoting within ASP.NET Applications

Let's begin by finding out what .NET Remoting is.

What is .NET Remoting?

Two expressions can describe .NET Remoting: **Web Services Anywhere** and **CLR Object Remoting**. Let's have a closer look at what these two phrases mean.

Web Services Anywhere

The expression **Web Services Anywhere** is used with .NET Remoting. This means that with .NET Remoting, web services can be used in *any application* over *any transport*, using *any payload encoding*. .NET Remoting is an extremely flexible architecture.

Using SOAP and HTTP together is just one way to call remote objects. The transport channel is pluggable, and can be replaced. We get HTTP and TCP channels represented by the classes `HttpChannel` and `TcpChannel`. We can build transport channels to use UDP, IPX, or a shared memory mechanism – the choice is yours entirely.

The payload encoding can also be replaced. Microsoft delivers SOAP and binary encoding mechanisms. We can use the SOAP formatter using the HTTP channel, but it's also possible to use HTTP using the binary formatter. Of course, both of these formatters can also be used with the TCP channel.

.NET Remoting not only makes it possible to use web services in every .NET application, but also allows us to *offer* web services in *every* application. It doesn't matter if we build a console or a Windows application, a Windows Service, or a COM+ component – web services can be used anywhere!

> *The term **pluggable** is often used with .NET Remoting. Pluggable means that a specific part is designed so that it can be replaced by a custom implementation.*

CLR Object Remoting

CLR Object Remoting sits on top of web services anywhere. CLR Object Remoting makes it easy to use web services. All of the language constructs, such as constructors, delegates, interfaces, methods, properties, and fields, can be used with remote objects. Calling a remote object can be as easy as calling a local object. CLR Object Remoting deals with activation, distributed identities, lifetimes, and call contexts.

.NET Remoting Overview

.NET Remoting can be used for accessing objects in another application domain. .NET Remoting can always be used whether the two objects live inside a single process, in separate processes, or on separate systems.

Remote assemblies can be configured to work locally in the application domain or as a part of a remote application. If the assembly is part of the remote application then the client receives a proxy to talk to instead of the real object. The proxy sends a message into the channel.

.NET applications work within an application domain. An application domain can be seen as a sub-process within a process. Traditionally, processes are used as an isolation boundary. An application running in one process cannot access and destroy memory in another process. For applications to communicate with each other, cross-process communication is needed. With .NET, the application domain is the new safety boundary inside a process, because the CIL code is type-safe and verifiable. Different applications can run inside the same process but within different application domains. Objects inside the same application domain can interact directly; a proxy is needed in order to access objects in a different application domain.

More about application domains can be found in Chapter 10.

Before we look into the internal functionality of .NET Remoting, let's have a look at the major elements of the architecture:

❑ A **remote object** is an object that's running on the server. The client doesn't call methods on this object directly, but uses a proxy instead. With .NET it's easy to differentiate remote objects from local objects: every class that's derived from MarshalByValueObject never leaves its application domain. The client can call methods of the remote object via a proxy.

❑ A **channel** is used for communication between the client and the server. There are client and server parts of the channel. With the .NET Framework, we get two channel types that communicate via TCP or HTTP. We can also create a custom channel that communicates using a different protocol.

❑ **Messages** are sent into the channel. Messages are created for communication between the client and the server. These messages hold the information about the remote object, the method name called, and all of the arguments.

❑ The **formatter** defines how messages are transferred into the channel. With the .NET Framework, we have SOAP and binary formatters. The SOAP formatter can be used to communicate with web services that are not based on the .NET Framework. Binary formatters are much faster and can be used efficiently in an intranet environment. Of course you also have the possibility to create a custom formatter.

❑ A **formatter provider** is used to associate a formatter with a channel. By creating a channel, we can specify what formatter provider to use, and this in turn defines the formatter that will be used to transfer the data into the channel.

❑ The client calls methods on a **proxy** instead of the remote object. There are two types of proxies: the **transparent proxy** and the **real proxy**. The transparent proxy looks like the remote object to the client. The client can call the methods the remote objects implement on the transparent proxy. In turn the transparent proxy calls the Invoke() method on the real proxy. The Invoke() method uses the message sink to pass the message to the channel.

❑ A **message sink** is an interceptor object. We have such interceptors both on the client and on the server. A sink is associated with the channel. The real proxy uses the message sink to pass the message into the channel, so the sink can do some interception before the messages goes into the channel.

❑ The client can use an **activator** to create a remote object on the server or to get a proxy of a server-activated object.

❑ RemotingConfiguration is a utility class to configure remote servers and clients. This class can be used either to read configuration files, or to configure remote objects dynamically.

❑ ChannelServices is a utility class to register channels and then to dispatch messages to them.

To get a better insight into the functionality, let's look at a conceptual picture of how these pieces fit together:

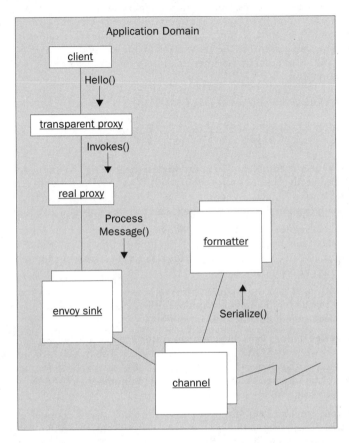

When the client calls methods on a remote object, it actually calls methods on a transparent proxy instead. The transparent proxy looks like the real object – it implements the public methods of the real object. The transparent proxy knows about the public methods by using the reflection mechanism to read the metadata from the assembly.

In turn, the transparent proxy calls the real proxy. The real proxy is responsible for sending the message to the channel. The real proxy is pluggable; we can replace it with a custom implementation. A custom implementation can be used to write a log, to use another way to find a channel, and so on. The default implementation of the real proxy locates the collection (or chain) of envoy sinks and passes the message to the first envoy sink. An envoy sink can intercept and change the message. Examples of such sinks are debugging sinks, security sinks, and synchronization sinks. The last envoy sink sends the message into the channel. How the messages are sent over the wire depends on the formatter. As previously stated, we have SOAP and binary formatters. The formatter however, is also pluggable. The channel is responsible for either connecting to a listening socket on the server or sending the formatted data. With a custom channel you can do something different; just do what's necessary to transfer the data to the other side:

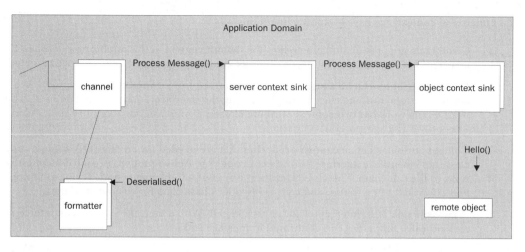

Let's continue with the server side. The channel receives the formatted messages from the client and uses the formatter to unmarshal the SOAP or binary data into messages. Then the channel calls server-context sinks. The server-context sinks are again a chain of sinks, where the last sink in the chain continues the call to the chain of object-context sinks. The last object-context sink then calls the method in the remote object. The object-context sinks are confined to the object context; the server-context sinks are confined to the server context. A single server-context sink can be used to access a number of object sinks.

.NET Remoting is extremely customizable: we can replace the real proxy, add sink objects, or replace the formatter and channel. Of course, we can also use all what's already provided. If you're wondering about the overhead when going through these layers, there's not much overhead if nothing is happening in there. If you add your own functionality, the overhead depends on that.

Contexts

Before we look at using .NET Remoting to build servers and clients that communicate across a network, let's look at the cases where a channel is needed inside an application domain: calling objects across contexts.

If you've written COM+ components, you already know about COM+ contexts. Contexts in .NET are very similar. As you already know, a single process can have multiple application domains. An application domain is something like a sub-process with security boundaries. An application domain can have different contexts. A context is used to group objects with similar execution requirements. Contexts are composed from a set of properties and are used for interception: when a **context-bound object** is accessed from a different context, an **interceptor** can do some work before the call reaches the object.

A class that is derived from `MarshalByRefObject` is bound to the application domain. Outside the application domain a proxy is needed to access the object. A class derived from `ContextBoundObject` is bound to a context. Outside the context, a proxy is needed to access the object. Context-bound objects can have **context attributes**. A context-bound object without context attributes is created in the context of the creator. A context-bound object with context attributes is created in a new context, or in the creator's context if the attributes are compatible.

To understand contexts we have to know some terms:

- ❑ Creating an application domain creates the **default context** in this application domain. If a new object is instantiated that needs different context properties a new context is created.

- ❑ **Context attributes** can be assigned to classes derived from ContextBoundObject. We can create a custom attribute class by implementing the interface IContextAttribute. The .NET Framework has two context attribute classes: SynchronizationAttribute and ThreadAffinityAttribute.

- ❑ Context attributes define **context properties** that are needed for an object. A context property class implements the interface IContextProperty. Active properties contribute message sinks to the call chain. The class ContextAttribute implements both IContextProperty and IContextAttribute, and can be used as a base class for custom attributes.

- ❑ A **message sink** is an interceptor for a method call. With a message sink we can intercept method calls. Properties can contribute to message sinks.

Activation

A new context is created if an instance of a class that's created needs a context different from the calling context. The attribute classes that are associated with the target class are asked if all the properties of the current context are OK. If any of these attribute classes answers that they are not, the runtime asks for all property classes associated with the attribute class and creates a new context. The runtime then asks the property classes for the sinks they want to install. A property class can implement IContributeXXXSink interfaces to contribute sink objects.

Attributes and Properties

A context attribute class primarily is an attribute. You can read more about attributes in Chapter 6. Context attribute classes must implement the interface IContextAttribute. A custom context attribute class can derive from the class ContextAttribute, because this class already has a default implementation of this interface.

With the .NET Framework we have two context attribute classes: System.Runtime.Remoting.Contexts.SynchronizationAttribute and System.Runtime.Remoting.Contexts.ThreadAffinityAttribute. With the ThreadAffinity attribute we can specify that only a single thread can access instance fields, and methods of the context-bound class. That's useful for user interface objects because windows handles are thread-relative. The Synchronization attribute, on the other hand, defines synchronization requirements. Here we can specify that multiple threads cannot access the object concurrently, but the thread accessing the object can change.

With both of these attributes, four values can be set in the constructor:

- ❑ NOT_SUPPORTED defines that the class should not be instantiated in a context that has either thread affinity, or synchronization set

- ❑ With REQUIRED it's specified that we need a context with thread affinity/synchronization

- ❑ With REQUIRES_NEW we always get a new context

- ❑ SUPPORTED means that it doesn't matter what context we get – the object can live in it

Communication between Contexts

So, how does the communication between contexts happen? The client uses a proxy instead of the real object. The proxy creates a message that is transferred to a channel, and sinks can do interception. Does this sound familiar? It ought to. The same mechanism is used for communication across different application domains or different systems. A TCP or HTTP channel is not required for the communication across contexts, but a channel is used here too. `CrossContextChannel` can use the same virtual memory in both the client and server sides of the channel, and formatters are not required for crossing contexts.

Remote Objects, Clients, and Servers

Before we step into the details of the .NET Remoting architecture, let's look briefly at a remote object and a very small, and simple client-server application, that uses that remote object. After that, we will look in more detail at all the required steps and options.

The remote object we implement is called `Hello`, `HelloServer` is the main class of the application on the server, and `HelloClient` is for the client:

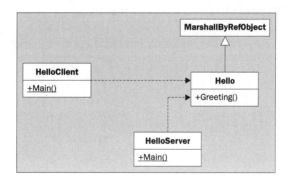

Remote Objects

Remote objects are needed for distributed computing. An object that should be called remotely from a different system must be derived from `System.MarshalByRefObject`. `MarshalByRefObject` objects are **confined to the application domain** in which they were created. This means that they are never passed across application domains; instead a proxy object is used to access the remote object from within another application domain, The other application domain can live inside the same process, in another process, or on another system.

A remote object has **distributed identity**. Because of this, a reference to the object can be passed to other clients, and they will still access the same object. The proxy knows about the identity of the remote object.

The `MarshalByRefObject` class has, in addition to the inherited methods from the `Object` class, methods to initialize and get the lifetime services. The lifetime services define how long the remote object lives. Lifetime services and the leasing features will be dealt with later in this chapter.

To see .NET Remoting in action, we will create a simple Class Library to create a remote object. The class `Hello` derives from `System.MarshalByRefObject`. In the constructor and destructor, a message is written to the console so that we know about the object's lifetime. In addition, we have just a single method, `Greeting()`, that will be called from the client.

In order to easily distinguish between the assembly and the class in the following sections, we have given them different names in the arguments of the method calls used. The name of the assembly is `RemoteHello.dll`, and the class is named `Hello`. The Visual Studio.NET project type used for this class is a Visual C# Class Library:

```
namespace Wrox.ProfessionalCSharp
{
    using System;

    /// <summary>
    ///     Summary description for Class1.
    /// </summary>

    public class Hello : System.MarshalByRefObject
    {
        public Hello()
        {
            Console.WriteLine("Constructor called");
        }
        ~Hello()
        {
            Console.WriteLine("Destructor called");
        }

        public string Greeting(string name)
        {
            Console.WriteLine("Greeting called");
            return "Hello, " + name;
        }
    }
}
```

A Simple Server

For the server we use a C# console application. To use the `TcpServerChannel` class, we have to reference the `System.Runtime.Remoting.dll` assembly. It's also required that we reference the `RemoteHello.dll` assembly that we created earlier.

In the `Main()` method a `System.Runtime.Remoting.Channels.Tcp.TcpServerChannel` is created with the port number 8086. This channel is registered with the `System.Runtime.Remoting.Channels.ChannelServices` class to make it available for remote objects. The remote object type is registered using `System.Runtime.Remoting.RemotingConfiguration.RegisterWellKnownServiceType`. Here we specify the type of the class in the remote object, the URI that is used by the client, and a mode. The mode `WellKnownObject.SingleCall` means that a new instance is created for every method call; we do not hold state in the remote object.

After registration of the remote object, we keep the server running until a key is pressed:

```
using System;
using System.Runtime.Remoting;
using System.Runtime.Remoting.Channels;
using System.Runtime.Remoting.Channels.Tcp;
namespace Wrox.ProfessionalCSharp
{

    /// <summary>
    ///     Summary description for Class1.
    /// </summary>

    public class HelloServer
    {
        public static void Main(string[] args)
        {
            TcpServerChannel channel = new TcpServerChannel(8086);
            ChannelServices.RegisterChannel(channel);
            RemotingConfiguration.RegisterWellKnownServiceType(
                typeof(Hello),
                "Hi",
                WellKnownObjectMode.SingleCall);
            System.Console.WriteLine("hit to exit");
            System.Console.ReadLine();
        }
    }
}
```

A Simple Client

The client is again a C# console application. Here the System.Runtime.Remoting.dll assembly is also referenced so that we can use the TcpClientChannel class. In addition, we also have to reference our RemoteHello.dll assembly. Although we will create the object on the remote server, we need the assembly on the client for the proxy to read the metadata during run time.

In the client program we're creating a TcpClientChannel object that's registered in ChannelServices. For the TcpChannel we are using the default constructor, so a free port is selected. Next the Activator class is used to return a proxy to the remote object. The proxy is of type System.Runtime.Remoting.Proxies.__TransparentProxy. This object looks like the real object. This is done by the reflection mechanism where the metadata of the real object is read. The transparent proxy uses the real proxy to send messages to the channel:

```
using System;
using System.Runtime.Remoting.Channels;
using System.Runtime.Remoting.Channels.Tcp;

namespace Wrox.ProfessionalCSharp
{

    /// <summary>
    ///     Summary description for Class1.
    /// </summary>
```

```
    public class HelloClient
    {
        public static void Main(string[] args)
        {
            ChannelServices.RegisterChannel(new TcpClientChannel());
            Hello obj = (Hello)Activator.GetObject(
                typeof(Hello),
                "tcp://localhost:8086/Hi");
            if (obj == null)
            {
                Console.WriteLine("could not locate server");
                return;
            }
            for (int i=0; i< 5; i++)
            {
                Console.WriteLine(obj.Greeting("Christian"));
            }
        }
    }
}
```

When we start the server and the client program Hello, Christian appears five times in the client console. In the console window of the server application we see a similar output to this window:

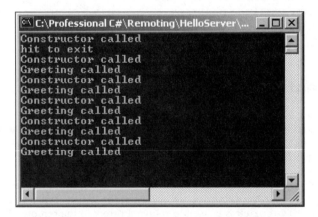

The first constructor is called at the registration time of the remote object. As stated earlier, `RemotingConfiguration.RegisterWellKnownServiceType()` already creates a single instance. Then for every method call a new instance gets created because we selected the `WellKnownObjectMode.SingleCall` activation mode. Depending on timing and resources needed, you may also see some destructor calls. If you start the client a few times you are sure to see some destructor calls.

.NET Remoting Architecture

After we've seen a simple client and server in action, and have got an overview of the .NET architecture, we can go into the details. Based on the previously created program we will look at the details of the architecture and will see mechanisms for extensibility.

Channels

A channel is used to communicate between a .NET client and a server. The .NET framework ships with channel classes that communicate using TCP or HTTP. We can create custom channels for other protocols.

The **HTTP channel** is used by most web services. It uses the HTTP protocol for communication. Because firewalls usually have port 80 opened so that the clients can access web servers and web services, listening to port 80 can be used by these clients too.

It's also possible to use the **TCP channel** on the Internet, but here the firewalls must be configured so that clients can access a specified port that's used by the TCP channel. The TCP channel can be used to communicate more efficiently in an intranet compared to the HTTP channel.

When performing a method call on the remote object, the client channel object sends a message to the remote channel object.

Both the server and the client application must create a channel. This code shows how a `TcpServerChannel` can be created on the server side:

```
using System.Runtime.Remoting.Channels.Tcp;

//...

TcpServerChannel channel = new TcpServerChannel(8086);
```

The port on which the TCP socket is listening is specified in the constructor argument. The server channel must specify a well-known port, and the client must use this port when accessing the server. For creating a `TcpClientChannel` on the client, however, it isn't necessary to specify a well-known port. The default constructor of `TcpClientChannel` chooses an available port, which is passed to the server at connection-time so that the server can send data back to the client.

Creating a new channel instance immediately switches the socket to the listening state, which can be verified typing `netstat -a` at the command line.

The HTTP channels can be used similarly to the TCP channels. We can specify the port where the server can create the listening socket. We also have a constructor where we can specify if a secure HTTP protocol should be used by passing a `Boolean` flag.

A server can listen to multiple channels. Here we are creating both an HTTP and a TCP channel:

```
using System;
using System.Runtime.Remoting;
using System.Runtime.Remoting.Channels;
using System.Runtime.Remoting.Channels.Tcp;
using System.Runtime.Remoting.Channels.Http;

namespace Wrox.ProfessionalCSharp
{

    /// <summary>
    ///     Summary description for Class1.
    /// </summary>
```

```
public class HelloServer
{
    public static void Main(string[] args)
    {
        TcpServerChannel tcpChannel = new TcpServerChannel(8086);
        HttpServerChannel httpChannel = new HttpServerChannel(8085);

        //...
```

A channel class must implement the `IChannel` interface. The `IChannel` interface has these two properties:

❑ `ChannelName` is a read-only property that returns the name of the channel. The name of the channel depends on the type – for example the HTTP channel is named HTTP.

❑ `ChannelPriority` is a read-only property. More than one channel can be used for communication between a client and a server. The priority defines the order of the channel. On the client, the channel with the higher priority is chosen first to connect to the server.

Depending if the channel is a client-channel or a server-channel additonal interfaces are implemented. The server versions of the channels implement the interface `IChannelReceiver`, the client versions implement the interface `IChannelSender`.

The `HttpChannel` and `TcpChannel` classes can be used for both the client and the server. They implement `IChannelSender` and `IChannelReceiver`. These interfaces derive from `IChannel`.

The client-side `IChannelSender` has, in addition to `IChannel`, a single method called `CreateMessageSink()`, which returns an object that implements `IMessageSink`. The `IMessageSink` interface can be used for putting synchronous as well as asynchronous messages into the channel. With the server-side interface `IChannelReceiver`, the channel can be put into listening mode using `StartListening()`, and stopped again with `StopListening()`. We also have a property to access the received data.

We can get information about the configuration of the channels using properties of the channel classes. For both channels, we have a `ChannelName`, a `ChannelPriority`, and a `ChannelData` property. The `ChannelData` property can be used to get information about the URIs that are stored in the `ChannelDataStore` class. With the `HttpChannel` there's also a `Scheme` property. Below is a helper method, `ShowChannelProperties()`, to show this information:

```
protected static void ShowChannelProperties(IChannelReceiver channel)
{
    Console.WriteLine("Name: " + channel.ChannelName);
    Console.WriteLine("Priority: " + channel.ChannelPriority);
    if (channel is HttpChannel)
    {
        HttpChannel httpChannel = channel as HttpChannel;
        Console.WriteLine("Scheme: " + httpChannel.ChannelScheme);
    }
    ChannelDataStore data = (ChannelDataStore)channel.ChannelData;
    foreach (string uri in data.ChannelUris)
    {
        Console.WriteLine("URI: " + uri);
    }
    Console.WriteLine();
}
```

The method ShowChannelProperties() is called after creating the channels:

```
TcpServerChannel tcpChannel = new TcpServerChannel(8086);
ShowChannelProperties(tcpChannel);
HttpServerChannel httpChannel = new HttpServerChannel(8085);
ShowChannelProperties(httpChannel);
```

With our TCP and HTTP channels, we get this information:

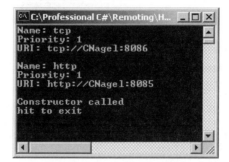

As we can see here, the default name for the TcpServerChannel is tcp, and the HTTP channel is called http. Both channels have a default priority of 1 and I've set the ports 8085 and 8086 in the constructors. The URIs of the channels show the protocol, hostname (in my case CNagel), and port number.

Setting Channel Properties

We can set all the properties of a channel in a list using the constructor TcpServerChannel(IDictionary, IServerChannelSinkProvider). The ListDictionary class implements IDictionary, so I'm setting the Name, Priority, and Port property, with help of this class.

In order to use the ListDictionary class we have to declare the use of the System.Collections.Specialized namespace. In addition to the IDictionary parameter we can pass an IServerChannelSinkProvider parameter. I pass a SoapServerFormatterSinkProvider instead of the BinaryServerFormatterSinkProvider, which is the default of the TcpServerChannel. The default implementation of the SoapServerFormatterSinkProvider class associates a SoapServerFormatterSink class with the channel that uses a SoapFormatter to convert the data for the transfer:

```
ListDictionary properties = new ListDictionary();
properties.Add("Name", "TCP Channel with a SOAP Formatter");
properties.Add("Priority", "20");
properties.Add("Port", "8086");
SoapServerFormatterSinkProvider sinkProvider =
            new SoapServerFormatterSinkProvider();
TcpServerChannel tcpChannel =
            new TcpServerChannel(properties, sinkProvider);
ShowChannelProperties(tcpChannel);
```

The new output we get from our server startup code shows the new properties of the TCP channel:

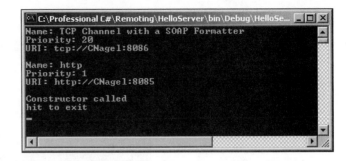

Pluggability of a Channel

A custom channel can be created to send the messages using a transport protocol other than HTTP or TCP, or you can extend the existing channels:

❑ The sending part must implement the interface IChannelSender. The most important part is the CreateMessageSink() method where the client sends a URL, and with this a connection to the server can be instantiated. Here a message sink must be created, which is then used by the proxy to send messages to the channel.

❑ The receiving part must implement the interface IChannelReceiver. We have to start the listening in the ChannelData get property. Then we can wait in a separate thread to receive data from the client. After unmarshaling the message we can use ChannelServices.SyncDispatchMessage() to dispatch the message to the object.

Formatters

The .NET Framework delivers two formatter classes:

❑ System.Runtime.Serialization.Formatters.Binary.BinaryFormatter

❑ System.Runtime.Serialization.Formatters.Soap.SoapFormatter

Formatters are associated with channels through formatter sink objects and formatter sink providers.

Both of these formatter classes implement the interface System.Runtime.Remoting.Messaging.IRemotingFormatter, which defines the methods Serialize() and Deserialize() to transfer the data to and from the channel.

The formatter is also pluggable. When you're writing a custom formatter class an instance must be associated with the channel you want to use. This is done using a formatter sink and a formatter sink provider. The formatter sink provider, for example, SoapServerFormatterSinkProvider, can be passed as an argument when creating a channel as we saw earlier. A formatter sink provider implements the interface IServerChannelSinkProvider for the server, and IClientChannelSinkProvider for the client. Both of these interfaces define a CreateSink() method where a formatter sink must be returned. The SoapServerFormatterSinkProvider returns an instance of the class SoapServerFormatterSink. On the client side, we have the SoapClientFormatterSink class that uses in the SyncProcessMessage() and AsyncProcessMessage() methods of the SoapFormatter class to serialize the message. The SoapServerFormatterSink deserializes the message again using the SoapFormatter.

All these sink and provider classes can be extended and replaced with custom implementations.

ChannelServices and RemotingConfiguration

The `ChannelServices` utility class is used to register channels into the .NET Remoting runtime. With this class we can also access all registered channels. This is extremely useful if configuration files are used to configure the channel, because here the channel is created implicitly, as we will see later.

A channel is registered using the static method `ChannelServices.RegisterChannel()`.

You can see here the server code to register our HTTP and TCP channels:

```
TcpChannel tcpChannel = new TcpChannel(8086);
HttpChannel httpChannel = new HttpChannel(8085);
ChannelServices.RegisterChannel(tcpChannel);
ChannelServices.RegisterChannel(httpChannel);
```

The `ChannelServices` utility class can now be used to dispatch synchronous and asynchronous messages, and to unregister specific channels. The property `RegisteredChannels` returns an `IChannel` array of all the channels we registered. We can also use the `GetChannel()` method to get to a specific channel by its name. With the help of `ChannelServices` we could write a custom administration utility that manages our channels. Here is a small example how the listening mode of a channel can be stopped:

```
HttpServerChannel channel =
    (HttpServerChannel)ChannelServices.GetChannel("http");
channel.StopListening(null);
```

The `RemotingConfiguration` class is another .NET Remoting utility class. On the server side it's used to register remote object types for server-activated objects, and to marshal remote objects to a marshaled object reference class `ObjRef`. `ObjRef` is a serializable representation of an object that's sent over the wire. On the client side `RemotingServices` is used to unmarshal a remote object in order to create a proxy from the object reference.

Here is the server-side code to register a well-known remote object type to the `RemotingServices`:

```
RemotingConfiguration.RegisterWellKnownServiceType(
                typeof(Hello),                      // Type
                "Hi",                               // URI
                WellKnownObjectMode.SingleCall);    // Mode
```

The first argument of `RegisterWellKnownServiceType()`, `Wrox.ProfessionalCSharp.Hello` specifies the type of the remote object. The second argument, `Hi`, is the uniform resource identifier of the remote object that will be used from the client to access the remote object. The last argument is the mode of the remote object. The mode can be a value of the enumeration `WellKnownObjectMode`: `SingleCall` or `Singleton`.

❑ **Single Call** means that the object holds no state. With every call to the remote object a new instance is created. A `SingleCall` object is created from the server with the `RemotingConfiguration.RegisterWellKnownServiceType()` method, and a `WellKnownObjectMode.SingleCall` argument. This is very efficient on the server because it means that we don't need to hold resources for maybe thousands of clients.

❑ With a **Singleton** the object is shared for all clients of the server. Such object types can be used if you want to share some data between all clients. This shouldn't be a problem for read-only data, but with read-write data you have to be aware of locking issues and scalability. A `Singleton` object is created by the server with the `RemotingConfiguration.RegisterWellKnownServiceType()` method and a `WellKnownObjectMode.Singleton` argument. We have to pay attention to locking of resources held by the singleton object. We have to make sure that data can't be corrupted when clients are accessing the singleton concurrently, but we also have to check that the locking is done efficiently enough so that the required scalability is reached.

Server for Client Activated Objects

If a remote object should hold state for a specific client, we can use client-activated objects. In the next section we will look at the client part, more specifically, how to call server-activated as well as client-activated objects. On the server side client-activated objects must be registered in a different way from server-activated objects.

Instead of calling `RemotingConfiguration.RegisterWellKnownType()`, we have to call `RemotingServices.RegisterActivatedServiceType()`. With this method, only the type is specified, and not the URI. The reason for this is that for client-activated objects the clients can instantiate different object types with the same URI. The URI for all client-activated objects must be defined using `RemotingConfiguration.ApplicationName`:

```
RemotingConfiguration.ApplicationName = "HelloServer";
RemotingConfiguration.RegisterActivatedServiceType(typeof(Hello));
```

Object Activation

Clients can use and create remote objects using the `Activator` class. We can get a proxy to a server-activated or well-known remote object using the `GetObject()` method. The `CreateInstance()` method returns a proxy to a client-activated remote object.

Instead of using the `Activator` class the `new` operator can also be used to activate remote objects. To make this possible the remote object must also be configured within the client using the `RemotingConfiguration` class.

Application URL

In all activation scenarios, we have to specify a URL to the remote object. This URL is the same one you'd use when browsing using a web browser. The first part specifies the protocol followed by the server name or IP address, the port number, and a URI that was specified when registering the remote object on the server in this form:

```
protocol://server:port/URI
```

We are continually using two URL examples in our code. We specify the protocols `http` and `tcp`, the server name is `localhost`, the port numbers are `8085` and `8086`, and the URI is `Hi`, as follows:

```
http://localhost:8085/Hi
tcp://localhost:8086/Hi
```

Activating Well-Known Objects

```
using System;
using System.Runtime.Remoting;
using System.Runtime.Remoting.Channels;
using System.Runtime.Remoting.Channels.Tcp;

/// ...

TcpClientChannel channel = new TcpClientChannel();
ChannelServices.RegisterChannel(channel);
```

```
Hello obj = (Hello)Activator.GetObject(typeof(Hello),
                              "tcp://localhost:8086/Hi");
```

GetObject() is a static method of the System.Activator that calls
RemotingServices.Connect() to return a proxy object to the remote object. The first argument
specifies the type of the remote object. The proxy implements all public and protected methods and
properties, so that the client can call these methods as it would call the real object. The second
argument is the URL to the remote object. We are using the string tcp://localhost:8086/Hello.
tcp is the protocol, localhost:8086 is the hostname and the port number, and finally Hello is the
URI of the object that was specified using
RemotingConfiguration.RegisterWellKnownServiceType().

Instead of using Activator.GetObject(), we can also use RemotingServices.Connect() in a
similar way:

```
Hello obj = (Hello)RemotingServices.Connect(typeof(Hello),
                              "tcp://localhost:8086/Hi");
```

If you prefer to do a simple new to activate well-known remote objects, the remote object can be
registered on the client using RemotingConfiguration.RegisterWellKnownClientType(). The
arguments needed here are similar: the type of the remote object and the URI. The new operator can
now be used. new doesn't really create a new remote object, instead it returns a proxy similar to
Activator.GetObject(). If the remote object is registered with a flag
WellKnownObjectMode.SingleCall, the rule always stays the same – the remote object is created
with every method call:

```
RemotingConfiguration.RegisterWellKnownClientType(typeof(Hello),
                              "tcp://localhost:8086/Hi");
Hello obj = new Hello();
```

Activating Client-Activated Objects

Remote objects can hold state for a client. Activator.CreateInstance() creates a client-activated
remote object. Using the Activator.GetObject() method, the remote object is created on a method
call, and is destroyed when the method is finished. The object doesn't hold state on the server. The
situation is different with Activator.CreateInstance(). With the static CreateInstance()
method an activation sequence is started to create the remote object. This object lives until the lease
time is expired and a garbage collection occurs. We will talk about the leasing mechanism later in this
chapter.

Some of the overloaded `Activator.CreateInstance()` methods can only be used to create local objects. To create remote objects a method is needed where it's possible to pass `activationAttributes`. One of these overloaded methods is used in our example. This method accepts two string parameters, the first is the name of the assembly, the second is the type, and the third is an array of objects. In the object array the channel and the object name are specified with the help of a `UrlAttribute`. To use the `UrlAttribute` class the namespace `System.Runtime.Remoting.Activation` must be specified:

```
object[] attrs = {new UrlAttribute("tcp://localhost:8086/Hello") };
ObjectHandle handle = Activator.CreateInstance(
            "RemoteHello", "Wrox.ProfessionalCSharp.Hello", attrs);
if (handle == null)
{
    Console.WriteLine("could not locate server");
    return 0;
}
Hello obj = (Hello)handle.Unwrap();
Console.WriteLine(obj.Greeting("Christian"));
```

Of course for client-activated objects it's again possible to use the new operator instead of the `Activator` class. This way we have to register the client-activated object using `RemotingConfiguration.RegisterActivatedClientType()`. In the architecture of client-activated objects the new operator not only returns a proxy but also creates the remote object:

```
RemotingConfiguration.RegisterActivatedClientType(typeof(Hello),
                            "tcp://localhost:8086/HelloServer");

Hello obj = new Hello();
```

Proxy Objects

The `Activator.GetObject()` and `Activator.CreateInstance()` methods return a proxy to the client. We actually get two proxies, (a transparent proxy and a real proxy). The transparent proxy looks like the remote object – it implements all public methods of the remote object where it calls the `Invoke()` method of the `RealProxy`. The `RealProxy` sends the messages to the channel with the help of message sinks.

With `RemotingServices.IsTransparentProxy()` can check if our object is really a transparent proxy. We can also get to the real proxy using `RemotingServices.GetRealProxy()`. Using the debugger, it's now easy to get all the properties of the real proxy:

```
ChannelServices.RegisterChannel(new TCPChannel());
Hello obj = (Hello)Activator.GetObject(typeof(Hello),
                                "tcp://localhost:8086/Hi");
if (obj == null)
{
    Console.WriteLine("could not locate server");
    return 0;
}
if (RemotingServices.IsTransparentProxy(obj))
{
    Console.WriteLine("Using a transparent proxy");
    RealProxy proxy = RemotingServices.GetRealProxy(obj);

    // proxy.Invoke(message);

}
```

Pluggability of a Proxy

The real proxy can be replaced with a custom proxy. A custom proxy can extend the base class `System.Runtime.Remoting.RealProxy`. We receive the type of the remote object in the constructor of the custom proxy. Calling the constructor of the `RealProxy` creates a transparent proxy in addition to the real proxy. In the constructor, the registered channels can be accessed with the help of the `ChannelServices` class to create a message sink `IChannelSender.CreateMessageSink()`. Besides implementing the constructor, a custom channel has to override the `Invoke()` method. In `Invoke()` a message is received that can be analyzed and sent to the message sink.

Messages

The proxy sends a message into the channel. On the server side, a method call can be made after analyzing the message – so let's look at messages.

We have some message classes for method calls, responses, return messages, and so on. What all the message classes have in common is that they implement the `IMessage` interface. This interface has a single property: `Properties`. This property represents a dictionary where the URI to the object, the called `MethodName`, `MethodSignature`, `TypeName`, `Args`, and the `CallContext` are packaged.

Below is the hierarchy of the message classes and interfaces:

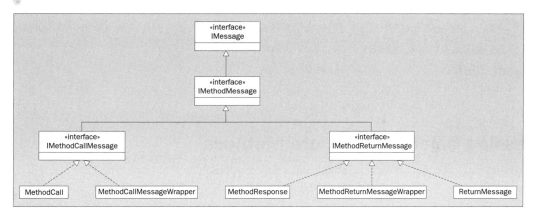

The message that is sent to the real proxy is a `MethodCall`. With the interfaces `IMethodCallMessage` and `IMethodMessage` we have easier access to the properties of the message than through the `IMessage` interface. Instead of using the `IDictionary` interface we have direct access to the method name, the URI, the arguments, and so on. The real proxy returns a `ReturnMessage` to the transparent proxy.

Message Sinks

The `Activator.GetObject()` method calls `RemotingServices.Connect()` to connect to a well known object. In the `Connect()` method, an `Unmarshal()` happens where not only the proxy, but also envoy sinks, are created. The proxy uses a chain of envoy sinks to pass the message to the channel. All the sinks are interceptors that can change the messages and perform some additional actions such as creating a lock, writing an event, performing security checking, and so on.

All message sinks implement the interface IMessageSink. This interface defines one property and two methods:

❑ The property NextSink is used by a sink to get to the next sink and pass the message along.

❑ For synchronous messages SyncProcessMessage() is invoked by a previous sink or by the remoting infrastructure. It has an IMessage parameter to send a message and to return a message.

❑ For asynchronous messages, AsyncProcessMessage() is invoked by a previous sink in the chain, or by the remoting infrastructure. AsyncProcessMessage() has two parameters where a message and a message sink that receives the reply can be passed.

Let's take a look at the three different message sinks available for use.

Envoy Sink

We can get to the chain of envoy sinks by the IEnvoyInfo interface. The marshaled object reference ObjRef has a property, EnvoyInfo, that returns the IEnvoyInfo interface. The envoy list is created from the server context, so the server can inject functionality into the client. Envoys can collect identity information about the client and pass that information to the server.

Server-Context Sink

When the message is received on the server-side of the channel, it is passed to the server-context sinks. The last of the server-context sinks routes the message to the object-sink chain.

Object Sink

The object sink is associated with a particular object. If the object class defines particular context attributes, context sinks are created for the object.

Passing Objects in Remote Methods

The parameter types of remote method calls aren't just limited to basic data types, but can also be classes that we define ourselves. For remoting we have to differentiate between three types of classes:

❑ **Marshal-by-value** classes are serialized through the channel. Classes that should be marshaled must implement either the ISerializable interface, or must be marked using the [Serializable] attribute. Objects of these classes don't have a remote identity, because the complete object is marshaled through the channel, and the object that is serialized to the client is independent of the server object (or the other way around). Marshal-by-value classes are also called **unbound classes** because they don't have data that depends on the application domain.

❑ **Marshal-by-reference** classes do have a remote identity. The objects are not passed across the wire, but instead a proxy is returned. A class that is marshaled by reference must derive from MarshalByRefObject. MarshalByRefObjects are known as **application domain bound objects**. A specialized version of MarshalByRefObject is ContextBoundObject: the abstract class ContextBoundObject is derived from MarshalByRefObject. If a class is derived from ContextBoundObject a proxy is needed even in the same application domain when context boundaries are crossed. Such objects are called **context-bound objects**, and they are only valid in the creation context.

❏   Classes that are not serializable and don't derive from `MarshalByRefObject` are **not remotable**. Classes of these types cannot be used in public methods parameters of remote objects. These classes are bound to the application domain where they are created. Non-remotable classes should be used if the class has a data member that is only valid in the application domain, such as a Win32 file handle.

To see marshaling in action, we will change the remote object to send two objects to the client: the class `MySerialized` will be sent marshal-by-value, the class `MyRemote` marshal-by-reference. In the methods a message is written to the console so that we can verify if the call was made on the client or on the server. In addition, the `Hello` class is changed to return a `MySerialized` and a `MyRemote` instance:

```
using System;

namespace Wrox.ProfessionalCSharp
{
```

```
    [Serializable]
    public class MySerialized
    {
        public MySerialized(int val)
        {
            a = val;
        }
        public void Foo()
        {
            Console.WriteLine("MySerialized.Foo called");
        }
        public int A
        {
            get
            {
                Console.WriteLine("MySerialized.A called");
                return a;
            }
            set
            {
                a = value;
            }
        }
        protected int a;
    }
    public class MyRemote : System.MarshalByRefObject
    {
        public MyRemote(int val)
        {
            a = val;
        }
        public void Foo()
        {
            Console.WriteLine("MyRemote.Foo called");
        }
        public int A
        {
```

```
        get
        {
            Console.WriteLine("MyRemote.A called");
            return a;
        }
        set
        {
            a = value;
        }
    }
    protected int a;
}
```

```
/// <summary>
///     Summary description for Class1.
/// </summary>

public class Hello : System.MarshalByRefObject
{
    public Hello()
    {
        Console.WriteLine("Constructor called");
    }
    ~Hello()
    {
        Console.WriteLine("Destructor called");
    }
    public string Greeting(string name)
    {
        Console.WriteLine("Greeting called");
        return "Hello, " + name;
    }
    public MySerialized GetMySerialized()
    {
        return new MySerialized(4711);
    }
    public MyRemote GetMyRemote()
    {
        return new MyRemote(4712);
    }
}
}
```

The client application also needs to be changed to see the effects when using marshaled-by-value and marshaled-by-reference objects. We are calling the methods GetMySerialized() and GetMyRemote() to receive the new objects. We're also checking if the transparent proxy is used:

```
ChannelServices.RegisterChannel(new TcpChannel());
Hello obj = (Hello)Activator.GetObject(typeof(Hello),
                                    "tcp://localhost:8086/Hi");
if (obj == null)
{
    Console.WriteLine("could not locate server");
    return;
}
```

```
MySerialized ser = obj.GetMySerialized();
if (!RemotingServices.IsTransparentProxy(ser))
{
    Console.WriteLine("ser is not a transparent proxy");
}
ser.Foo();
MyRemote rem = obj.GetMyRemote();
if (RemotingServices.IsTransparentProxy(rem))
{
    Console.WriteLine("rem is a transparent proxy");
}
rem.Foo();
```

In the client console window, we can see that the `ser` object is called on the client. This object is not a transparent proxy because it's serialized to the client. In contrast, the `rem` object on the client *is* a transparent proxy. Methods called on this object are transferred to the server:

In the server output we see that the `Foo()` method is called with the remote object `MyRemote`:

Directional Attributes

Remote objects are never transferred over the wire, whereas value types and serializable classes are transferred. Sometimes we want to send the data only in one direction. This can be especially important when the data is transferred over the network. With COM it was possible to declare directional attributes `[in]`, `[out]`, and `[in, out]` to the arguments if the data should be sent to the server, to the client, or in both directions.

With C# we have similar attributes as part of the language: `ref` and `out` method parameters. The `ref` and `out` method parameters can be used for value types and to reference types that are serializable. Using the `ref` parameter, the argument is marshaled in both directions, `out` goes from the server to the client, and using no method parameter sends the data to the server.

Lifetime Management

How do a client and a server detect if the other side is not available anymore, and what are the problems we get into?

For a client the answer can be short. As soon as the client does a call to a method on the remote object we get an exception of type System.Runtime.Remoting.RemotingException. We just have to handle this exception and do what's necessary, for example perform a retry, write a log, inform the user, and so on.

What about the server? When does the server detect if the client is not around anymore, meaning that the server can clean up resources it's holding for the client? If we wait until the next method call from the client – maybe it never arrives. In the COM area the DCOM protocol used a ping mechanism. The client sent a ping to the server with the information about the object referenced. Because a client can have hundreds of objects referenced on the server to make this mechanism more efficient it wasn't the information about all objects that was sent, but just the difference to the last ping.

This mechanism was efficient on a LAN, but is not suitable for Internet solutions. Think about thousands or millions of clients sending ping information to the server. .NET Remoting has a much more scalable solution for lifetime management: the **Leasing Distributed Garbage Collector (LDGC)**.

This lifetime management is *only active for client-activated objects*. SingleCall objects can be destroyed after every method call because they don't hold state. Client-activated objects do have state and we should be aware of the resources used. For client-activated objects that are referenced outside the application domain a lease is created. A lease has a lease time. When the lease time reaches zero the lease expires and the remote object is disconnected and, finally, is garbage-collected.

For lifetime management we can configure the following values:

- ❑ LeaseTime defines the time until a lease expires.

- ❑ RenewOnCallTime is the time the lease is set on a method call if the current lease time has a lower value.

- ❑ If a sponsor is not available within the SponsorshipTimeout, the remoting infrastructure looks for the next sponsor. If there are no more sponsors, the lease expires.

- ❑ The LeaseManagerPollTime defines the time interval at which the lease manager checks for expired objects.

The default values are listed in this table:

Lease Configuration	Default Value (seconds)
LeaseTime	300
RenewOnCallTime	120
SponsorshipTimeout	120
LeaseManagerPollTime	10

Lease Renewals

As you've seen in the above table, the default lease time for an object is 300 seconds. If the client calls a method on the object when the lease has expired, we get an exception. If we have a client where the remote object could be needed for more than 300 seconds, we have three ways to renew a lease:

❑   An **implicit renewal** of the lease is automatically done when the client calls a method on the remote object. If the current lease time is less than the `RenewOnCallTime` value, the lease is set to `RenewOnCallTime`.

❑   With an **explicit renewal** the client can specify the new lease time. This is done with the `Renew()` method of the `ILease` interface. We can get to the `ILease` interface by calling the `GetLifetimeService()` method of the transparent proxy.

❑   **Sponsoring** is the third possibility to renew leases. The client can create a sponsor that implements the interface `ISponsor` and registers the sponsor in the leasing services using the `Register()` method of the `ILease` interface. The sponsor defines the lease extension time. When a lease expires the sponsor is asked for extension of the lease. The sponsoring mechanism can be used if you want long-lived remote objects on the server.

Classes Used for Lifetime Management

The `ClientSponsor` is one sponsor that implements the `ISponsor` interface. It can be used on the client side for lease-extension. With the `ILease` interface we can get all information about the lease, all the lease properties and the current lease time and state. The state is specified with the `LeaseState` enumeration. With the `LifetimeServices` utility class we can get and set the properties for the lease of all remote objects in the application domain.

Example: Getting Lease Information

In this small code example we are accessing the lease information by calling the `GetLifetimeService()` method of the transparent proxy. For the `ILease` interface we have to open the namespace `System.Runtime.Remoting.Lifetime`:

> Remember, you can use this only for client-activated objects. **SingleCall** objects are instantiated with every method call anyway, so the leasing mechanism doesn't apply.

```
ILease lease = (ILease)obj.GetLifetimeService();
if (lease != null)
{
    Console.WriteLine("Lease Configuration:");
    Console.WriteLine("InitialLeaseTime: " +
                       lease.InitialLeaseTime);
    Console.WriteLine("RenewOnCallTime: " +
                       lease.RenewOnCallTime);
    Console.WriteLine("SponsorshipTimeout: " +
                       lease.SponsorshipTimeout);
    Console.WriteLine(lease.CurrentLeaseTime);
}
```

As a result we see this output in the client console window:

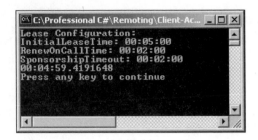

Changing Default Lease Configurations

The server itself can change the default lease configuration *for all remote objects* using the `System.Runtime.Remoting.Lifetime.LifetimeServices` utility class:

```
LifetimeServices.LeaseTime = TimeSpan.FromMinutes(10);
LifetimeServices.RenewOnCallTime = TimeSpan.FromMinutes(2);
```

If you want different default lifetimes depending on the type of the remote object, you can change the lease configuration of the remote object by overriding the `InitializeLifetimeService()` method of the base class `MarshalByRefObject`:

```
public class Hello : System.MarshalByRefObject
{
    public Hello()
    {
        Console.WriteLine("Constructor called");
    }
    ~Hello()
    {
        Console.WriteLine("Destructor called");
    }
    public override Object InitializeLifetimeService()
    {
        ILease lease = (ILease)base.InitializeLifetimeService();
        lease.InitialLeaseTime = TimeSpan.FromMinutes(10);
        lease.RenewOnCallTime = TimeSpan.FromSeconds(40);
        return lease;
    }
}
```

The lifetime services configuration can also be done using a configuration file as we see next.

Configuration Files

Instead of writing the channel and object configuration in the source code, configuration files can be used. This way the channel can be reconfigured, additional channels can be added, and so on, without changing the source code. Like all the other configuration files on the .NET platform, XML is used. The same application and configuration files that you've read about in Chapter 10 are used here, too. We will add security configurations into the same files in Chapter 25. For .NET Remoting, we have some XML elements and attributes to configure the channel and the remote objects. The file should have the same name as the executable followed by `.config`. For the server `HelloServer.exe` the configuration file is `HelloServer.exe.config`. In the code download, you'll find the following example configuration files in the root directory of the examples, under the names `clientactivated.config`, `wellknown.config`, and `wellknownhttp.config`. To use these, they must be renamed as above and placed in the directory containing the executable file.

Here is just one example how such a file could look like. We will walk through all the different configuration options:

```
<configuration>
    <system.runtime.remoting>
        <application name="Hello">
            <service>
                <wellknown mode="SingleCall"
                    type="Wrox.ProfessionalCSharp.Hello, RemoteHello"
                        objectUri="Hi" />
            </service>
            <channels>
                <channel type =
                        "System.Runtime.Remoting.Channels.Tcp.TcpChannel,
                        System.Runtime.Remoting" port="6791" />
                <channel type =
                        "System.Runtime.Remoting.Channels.Http.HttpChannel,
                        System.Runtime.Remoting" port="6792" />
            </channels>
        </application>
    </system.runtime.remoting>
</configuration>
```

`<configuration>` is the XML root element for all .NET configuration files. All the remoting configurations can be found in the sub-element `<system.runtime.remoting>`. `<application>` is a sub-element of `<system.runtime.remoting>`.

Let's look at the main elements and attributes of the parts within `<system.runtime.remoting>`:

❑ With the `<application>` element we can specify the name of the application using the attribute name. On the server side, this is the name of the server, and on the client side it's the name of the client application. An example for a server configuration: `<application name="Hello">` defines the remote application name `Hello`, which is used as part of the URL by the client to access the remote object.

❑ On the server, the element `<service>` is used to specify a collection of remote objects. It can have `<wellknown>` and `<activated>` subelements to specify the type of the remote object as *well known* or *client-activated*.

❑ The client part of the `<service>` element is `<client>`. Like the `<service>` element, it can have `<wellknown>` and `<activated>` subelements to specify the type of the remote object. Unlike the `<service>` counterpart, `<client>` has a `url` attribute to specify the URL to the remote object.

❑ `<wellknown>` is a element that's used on the server and the client to specify well known remote objects. The server part could look like this:

```
<wellknown mode="SingleCall"
    type="Wrox.ProfessionalCSharp.Hello, RemoteHello"
        objectURI="Hi" />
```

❑ While the mode attribute `SingleCall` or `Singleton` can be specified, the type is the type of the remote class including the namespace `Wrox.ProfessionalCSharp.Hello`, followed by the assembly name `RemoteHello`. `objectURI` is the name of the remote object that's registered in the channel.

On the client, the type attribute is the same as for the server version. mode and objectURI are not needed, but instead the url attribute is used to define the path to the remote object: protocol, hostname, port-number, application-name, and the object URI:

```
<wellknown type="Wrox.ProfessionalCSharp.Hello, RemoteHello"
            url="tcp://localhost:6791/Hello/Hi" />
```

❑ The <activated> element is used for client-activated objects. With the type attribute the type and assembly must be defined both for the client and the server application:

```
<activated type="Wrox.ProfessionalCSharp.Hello, RemoteHello" />
```

❑ To specify the channel the <channel> element is used. It's a subelement of <channels> so that a collection of channels can be configured for a single application. Its use is similar for clients and servers. The type attribute is used to specify the type of the channel and the assembly. The port attribute is the port number, which is only needed for the server configuration.:

```
<channels>
   <channel type =
               "System.Runtime.Remoting.Channels.Tcp.TcpChannel,
               System.Runtime.Remoting" port="6791" />
   <channel type =
               "System.Runtime.Remoting.Channels.Http.HttpChannel,
               System.Runtime.Remoting" port="6792" />
</channels>
```

Server Configuration for Well Known Objects

This example file, wellknown.config, has the value Hello for the Name property. We are using the TCP channel to listen on port 6791, and the HTTP channel to listen on port 6792. The remote object class is Wrox.ProfessionalCSharp.Hello in the assembly RemoteHello.dll, the object is called Hi in the channel, and we are using the mode SingleCall:

```
<configuration>
   <system.runtime.remoting>
      <application name="Hello">
         <service>
            <wellknown mode="SingleCall"
                       type="Wrox.ProfessionalCSharp.Hello, RemoteHello"
                       objectUri="Hi" />
         </service>
         <channels>
            <channel type =
                        "System.Runtime.Remoting.Channels.Tcp.TcpChannel,
                        System.Runtime.Remoting" port="6791" />
            <channel type =
                        "System.Runtime.Remoting.Channels.Http.HttpChannel,
                        System.Runtime.Remoting" port="6792" />
         </channels>
      </application>
   </system.runtime.remoting>
</configuration>
```

Client Configuration for Well Known Objects

For well-known objects, we have to specify the assembly and the channel in the client configuration file wellknown.config. The types for the remote object can be found in the RemoteHello.dll assembly, Hi is the name of the object in the channel, and the URI for the remote type Wrox.ProfessionalCSharp.Hello is tcp://localhost:6791/Hi. In the client we are also using a TCP channel, but in the client no port is specified, so a free port is selected:

```
<configuration>
    <system.runtime.remoting>
        <application name="Client">
            <client url="tcp:/localhost:6791/Hello">
                <wellknown type = "Wrox.ProfessionalCSharp.Hello, RemoteHello"
                                  url="tcp://localhost:6791/Hello/Hi" />
            </client>
            <channels>
                <channel type =
                            "System.Runtime.Remoting.Channels.Tcp.TcpChannel,
                            System.Runtime.Remoting" />
            </channels>
        </application>
    </system.runtime.remoting>
</configuration>
```

A small change in the configuration file, and we're using the HTTP channel (as can be seen in wellknownhttp.config):

```
<client url="http:/localhost:6792/Hello">
    <wellknown type="Wrox.ProfessionalCSharp.Hello, RemoteHello"
                      url="http://localhost:6792/Hello/Hi" />
</client>
<channels>
    <channel type =
                "System.Runtime.Remoting.Channels.Http.HttpChannel,
                System.Runtime.Remoting" />
</channels>
```

Server Configuration for Client-Activated Objects

Changing only the configuration file (which can be found in clientactivated.config), we can change the server from server-activated to client-activated objects. Here the <activated> subelement of the <service> element is specified. With the <activated> element for the server configuration just the type attribute must be specified. The name attribute of the application element defines the URI:

```
<configuration>
    <system.runtime.remoting>
        <application name="HelloServer">
            <service>
                <activated type="Wrox.ProfessionalCSharp.Hello, RemoteHello" />
            </service>
            <channels>
                <channel type =
                            "System.Runtime.Remoting.Channels.Http.HttpChannel,
                            System.Runtime.Remoting" ports="6788" />
```

```
                <channel type =
                       "System.Runtime.Remoting.Channels.Tcp.TcpChannel,
                       System.Runtime.Remoting" ports="6789" />
            </channels>
        </application>
    </system.runtime.remoting>
</configuration>
```

Client Configuration for Client-Activated Objects

The clientactivated.config file defines the client-activated remote object using the url attribute of the <client> element and the type attribute of the <activated> element:

```
<configuration>
    <system.runtime.remoting>
        <application>
            <client url="http://localhost:6788/HelloServer">
                <activated type="Wrox.ProfessionalCSharp.Hello, RemoteHello" />
            </client>
            <channels>
                <channel type =
                       "System.Runtime.Remoting.Channels.Http.HttpChannel,
                       System.Runtime.Remoting" />
                <channel type =
                       "System.Runtime.Remoting.Channels.Tcp.TcpChannel,
                       System.Runtime.Remoting" />
            </channels>
        </application>
    </system.runtime.remoting>
</configuration>
```

Server Code Using Configuration Files

In the server code we have to configure remoting using the static method Configure() from the RemotingConfiguration class. Here all the channels that are defined are built up and instantiated. Maybe we also want to know about the channel configurations from the server application. That's why I've created the static methods ShowActivatedServiceTypes() and ShowWellKnownServiceTypes() that are called after loading and starting the remoting configuration:

```
        public static void Main(string[] args)
        {
            RemotingConfiguration.Configure("HelloServer.exe.config");
            Console.WriteLine("Application: " +
                              RemotingConfiguration.ApplicationName);
            ShowActivatedServiceTypes();
            ShowWellKnownServiceTypes();
            System.Console.WriteLine("hit to exit");
            System.Console.ReadLine();
            return;
        }
```

These two functions show configuration information of well known and client-activated types:

```
public static void ShowWellKnownServiceTypes()
{
   WellKnownServiceTypeEntry[] entries =
      RemotingConfiguration.GetRegisteredWellKnownServiceTypes();
   foreach (WellKnownServiceTypeEntry entry in entries)
   {
      Console.WriteLine("Assembly: " + entry.AssemblyName);
      Console.WriteLine("Mode: " + entry.Mode);
      Console.WriteLine("URI: " + entry.ObjectUri);
      Console.WriteLine("Type: " + entry.TypeName);
   }
}
public static void ShowActivatedServiceTypes()
{
   ActivatedServiceTypeEntry[] entries =
      RemotingConfiguration.GetRegisteredActivatedServiceTypes();
   foreach (ActivatedServiceTypeEntry entry in entries)
   {
      Console.WriteLine("Assembly: " + entry.AssemblyName);
      Console.WriteLine("Type: " + entry.TypeName);
   }
}
```

Client Code Using Configuration Files

In the client code, we only have to configure the remoting services using the configuration file client.exe.config. After that, we can use the new operator to create new instances of the Remote class, no matter whether we work with server-activated or client-activated remote objects. Be aware, however – there's a small difference! With client-activated objects it's now possible to use **non-default constructors** with the new operator. This isn't possible for server-activated objects, and it doesn't make sense there: SingleCall objects can have no state because they are destroyed with every call; Singleton objects are created just once. Calling non-default constructors is only useful for client-activated objects because it is only for this kind of objects that the new operator really calls the constructor in the remote object:

```
RemotingConfiguration.Configure("HelloClient.exe.config");
Hello obj = new Hello();
if (obj == null)
{
   Console.WriteLine("could not locate server");
   return 0;
}
for (int i=0; i< 5; i++)
{
   Console.WriteLine(obj.Greeting("Christian"));
}
```

Lifetime Services in Configuration Files

Leasing configuration for remote servers can also be done with the application configuration files. The <lifetime> element has the attributes leaseTime, sponsorshipTimeOut, renewOnCallTime, and pollTime as you see here:

```
<configuration>
    <system.runtime.remoting>
        <application>
            <lifetime leaseTime = "15M" sponsorshipTimeOut = "4M"
                renewOnCallTime = "3M" pollTime = "30s"/>
        </application>
    </system.runtime.remoting>
</configuration>
```

Using configuration files, it is possible to change the remoting configuration by editing files instead of working with source code. We can easily change the channel to use HTTP instead of TCP, change a port, the name of the channel, and so on. With the addition of a single line the server can listen to two channels instead of one.

Tools for Remoting Configuration Files

It's not necessary to start from scratch creating XML configuration files for .NET Remoting. We have some tools to do that:

❑ If you used Beta 1 of .NET Remoting, you will find the sample **convertconfig.exe** in the list of the Framework SDK samples. With this tool it's possible to convert the previously used compact file format to the new XML-based file format.

❑ With the sample **configfilegen.exe**, a configuration file can be created from an assembly. Start this program without options to see all the possible configurations. The following command-line command creates a client-activated (–a) configuration file for the server (–s):

configfilegen –ia:RemoteHello.dll –oc:HelloServer.exe.config –s –a

The System Administrator can use the .NET Admin Tool to reconfigure existing configuration files. The .NET Admin Tool can be started using:

mmc mscorcfg.msc.

With this tool the lifetime values, URIs of remote objects, and channel properties can be changed.

Hosting Applications

Up to this point all our sample servers were running in self-hosted .NET servers. A self-hosted server must be launched manually. A .NET remoting server can also be started in a lot of other application types. In a **Windows Service** the server can be automatically started at boot-time, and in addition the process can run with the credentials of the system account. See Chapter 24 for how to create Windows Services.

Hosting Remote Servers in ASP.NET

There's special support for .NET Remoting servers for ASP.NET. ASP.NET can be used for the automatic startup of remote servers. Contrary to exe-hosted applications, ASP.NET Remoting uses a different file for configuration.

To use the infrastructure from the Internet Information Server and ASP.NET, we just have to create a class that derives from `System.MarshalByRefObject` that has a default constructor. The code used earlier for our server to create and register the channel is no longer necessary; that's done by the ASP.NET runtime. We just have to create a virtual directory on the web server that maps a directory to where we put the configuration file `web.config`. The assembly of the remote class must reside in the `bin` subdirectory.

To configure a virtual directory on the web server we can use the Internet Information Services MMC. Selecting the Default Web Site and opening the Action menu creates a new Virtual Directory.

The configuration file `web.config` on the web server must be put in the home directory of the virtual web site. With the default IIS configuration, the channel that will be used listens to port 80:

```
<configuration>
   <system.runtime.remoting>
      <application>
         <service>
            <wellknown mode="SingleCall"
               type="Wrox.ProfessionalCSharp.Hello, RemoteHello"
               objectUri="HelloService.soap" />
         </service>
      </application>
   </system.runtime.remoting>
</configuration>
```

The client can now connect to the remote object using the following configuration file. The URL that must be specified for the remote object here is the web server `localhost` followed by the web application name `RemoteHello` that was specified when creating the virtual web site, and the URI of the remote object `HelloService.soap` that we defined in the file `web.config`. It's not necessary to specify the port number 80, because that's the default port for the HTTP protocol:

```
<configuration>
   <system.runtime.remoting>
      <application>
         <client url="http:/localhost/RemoteHello">
            <wellknown type="Wrox.ProfessionalCSharp.Hello, RemoteHello"
               url="http://localhost/RemoteHello/HelloService.soap" />
         </client>
         <channels>
            <channel
               type="System.Runtime.Remoting.Channels.Http.HttpChannel,
               System.Runtime.Remoting" />
         </channels>
      </application>
   </system.runtime.remoting>
</configuration>
```

Hosting remote objects in ASP.NET only supports well known objects!

Classes, Interfaces, and SOAPSuds

In the client-server examples we've done until now, we have always referenced a remote object in the client application. This way the CIL code of the remote object is copied, although only the metadata is needed. It's also not possible for the client and server to be programmed independently. A much better way to do this is to use interfaces or the SoapSuds.exe utility instead.

Interfaces

We have a cleaner separation of the client and server code using interfaces. An interface simply defines the methods without implementation. We separate the contract between the client and the server from the implementation. Here are the necessary steps to use an interface:

1. Define an interface that will be placed in an assembly.

2. Implement the interface in the remote object class. To do this, the assembly of the interface must be referenced.

3. On the server side no more changes are required. The server can be programmed and configured in the usual ways.

4. On the client side, reference the assembly of the interface instead of the assembly of the remote class.

5. The client can now use the interface of the remote object rather than the remote object class. The object can be created using the Activator class as we've done earlier. You can't use new in this way, because the interface itself cannot be instantiated.

The interface defines the contract between the client and server. The two applications can now be developed independently of each other. If you also stick to the old COM rules about interfaces (that interfaces should never be changed) you will not have any versioning problems.

SOAPSuds

We can also use the utility soapsuds to get the metadata from an assembly. soapsuds can convert assemblies to XML Schemas, XML Schemas to wrapper classes, and the other directions.

The following command converts the type Hello from the assembly RemoteHello.dll to the assembly HelloWrapper.dll where a transparent proxy gets generated that calls the remote object:

```
soapsuds -types:Wrox.ProfessionalCSharp.Hello,RemoteHello
        -oa:HelloWrapper.dll
```

With soapsuds we can also get the type information directly from a running server:

```
soapsuds -url:http://localhost:6792/hi -oa:HelloWrapper.dll
```

In the client we can now reference the soapsuds-generated assembly instead of the original one. Some of the options are listed in this table:

Option	Description
-url	Retrieve schema from the specified URL
-proxyurl	If a proxy server is required to access the server, specify the proxy with this option
-types	Specify a type and assembly to read the schema information from it
-is	Input schema file
-ia	Input assembly file
-os	Output schema file
-oa	Output assembly file

Tracking Services

For debugging and troubleshooting applications using .NET, remoting tracking services can be used. The `System.Runtime.Remoting.Services.TrackingService` class provides a tracking service to get information about when marshaling and unmarshaling occurred, when remote objects are called and disconnected, and so on:

- With the `TrackingServices` utility class we can register and unregister a handler that implements `ITrackingHandler`.

- The `ITrackingHandler` interface is called when an event happens on a remote object, or a proxy. We can implement three methods in the handler: `MarshaledObject()`, `UnmarshaledObject()`, and `DisconnectedObject()`.

To see tracking services in action in both the client and the server, we create a new class library, `TrackingHandler`. The `TrackingHandler` class implements the `ITrackingHandler` interface. In the methods we receive two arguments: the object itself and `ObjRef`. With `ObjRef` we can get information about the URI, the channel, and the envoy sinks. We can also attach new sinks to add a contributor to all the called methods. In our sample we're writing the URI and information about the channel to the console:

```
using System;
using System.Runtime.Remoting;
using System.Runtime.Remoting.Services;
namespace Wrox.ProfessionalCSharp
{
   public class TrackingHandler : ITrackingHandler
   {
      public TrackingHandler()
      {
      }
      public void MarshaledObject(object obj, ObjRef or)
      {
         Console.WriteLine("--- Marshaled Object " +
                           obj.GetType() + " ---");
         Console.WriteLine("Object URI: " + or.URI);
         object[] channelData = or.ChannelInfo.ChannelData;
```

```
            foreach (object data in channelData)
            {
                ChannelDataStore dataStore = data as ChannelDataStore;
                if (dataStore != null)
                {
                    foreach (string uri in dataStore.ChannelUris)
                    {
                        Console.WriteLine("Channel URI: " + uri);
                    }
                }
            }
            Console.WriteLine("---------");
            Console.WriteLine();
        }
        public void UnmarshaledObject(object obj, ObjRef or)
        {
            Console.WriteLine("Unmarshal");
        }
        public void DisconnectedObject(object obj)
        {
            Console.WriteLine("Disconnect");
        }
    }
}
```

The server program is changed to register the `TrackingHandler`. Just two lines need to be added to register the handler:

```
using System.Runtime.Remoting.Services;

//...

        public static void Main(string[] args)
        {
            TrackingServices.RegisterTrackingHandler(new TrackingHandler());
            TCPChannel channel = new TCPChannel(8086);

            //...
```

When starting the server, a first instance is created during registration of the well-known type and we get the following output. `MarshaledObject()` gets called and displays the type of the object to marshal – `Wrox.ProfessionalCSharp.Hello`. With the object URI we see a GUID that's used internally in the remoting runtime to distinguish different instances and the URI we specified. With the channel URI the configuration of the channel can be verified. In this case the hostname is `Cnagel`:

```
C:\Professional C#\Remoting\TrackingServices\HelloServer\bin\Debug\HelloS...
Constructor called
--- Marshaled Object Wrox.ProfessionalCSharp.Hello ---
Object URI: /3fafce4e_e25d_416a_821d_025afbf5c0b3/Hi
Channel URI: tcp://CNagel:8086
---------

hit to exit
```

Asynchronous Remoting

If server methods take a while to complete and the client needs to do some different work at the same time, it isn't necessary to start a separate thread to do the remote call. Asynchronous calls can be made on a remote object as they are made on a local object.

To make an asynchronous method, we create a delegate, `GreetingDelegate`, with the same argument and return value as the `Greeting()` method of the remote object. The argument of this delegate is a reference to the `Greeting()` method. We start the `Greeting()` call using the `BeginInvoke()` method of the delegate. The second argument of `BeginInvoke()` is an `AsyncCallback` instance that defines the method `HelloClient.Callback()`, which is called when the remote method is finished. In the `Callback()` method the remote call is finished using `EndInvoke()`:

```csharp
using System;
using System.Runtime.Remoting;
namespace Wrox.ProfessionalCSharp
{
    public class HelloClient
    {
        private delegate String GreetingDelegate(String name);
        private static string greeting;
        public static void Main(string[] args)
        {
            RemotingConfiguration.Configure("HelloClient.exe.config");
            Hello obj = new Hello();
            if (obj == null)
            {
                Console.WriteLine("could not locate server");
                return 0;
            }

            // synchronous version
            // string greeting = obj.Greeting("Christian");
            // asynchronous version

            GreetingDelegate d = new GreetingDelegate(obj.Greeting);
            IAsyncResult ar = d.BeginInvoke("Christian", null, null);

            // do some work and then wait

            ar.AsyncWaitHandle.WaitOne();
            if (ar.IsCompleted)
            {
                greeting = d.EndInvoke(ar);
            }

            Console.WriteLine(greeting);
        }
    }
}
```

You can read more about events, delegates, and asynchronous method calls in Chapter 6.

OneWay Attribute

A method that has a void return and only input parameters can be marked with the OneWay attribute. The OneWay attribute makes a method automatically asynchronous, not matter how the client calls it. Adding the method TakeAWhile() to our remote object class RemoteHello creates a **fire-and-forget** method. If the client calls it by the proxy, the proxy immediately returns to the client. On the server the method finishes some time later:

```
[OneWay]
public void TakeAWhile(int ms)
{
    Console.WriteLine("TakeAWhile started");
    System.Threading.Thread.Sleep(ms);
    Console.WriteLine("TakeAWhile finished");
}
```

Remoting and Events

With .NET Remoting not only can the client call methods on the remote object across the network, but the server can also call methods in the client. For this, a mechanism that we already know from the basic language features is used: **delegates and events**.

In principle, the architecture is simple. The server has a remotable object that the client can call, and the client has a remotable object that the server can call:

❑ The remote object in the server must declare an external function (a delegate) with the signature of the method that the client will implement in a handler

❑ The arguments that are passed with the handler function to the client must be marshalable, so all the data sent to the client must be serializable

❑ The remote object also must declare an instance of the delegate function modified with the event keyword; the client will use this to register a handler

❑ The client must create a sink object with a handler method that has the same signature as the delegate defined, and it has to register the sink object with the event in the remote object

To help explain this, let's take a look at an example. To see all the parts of event handling with .NET Remoting we will create five classes. The Server class is a remoting server such as the one we already know. The Server class will create a channel based on information from a configuration file and register the remote object that's implemented in the RemoteObject class in the remoting runtime. The remote object declares the arguments of a delegate and fires events in the registered handler functions. The argument that's passed to the handler function is of type StatusEventArgs. The class StatusEventArgs must be serializable so it can be marshaled to the client.

The Client class represents the client application. This class creates an instance of the EventSink class and registers the method StatusHandler() of this class as a handler for the delegate in the remote object. EventSink must be remotable like the RemoteObject class, because this class will also be called across the network:

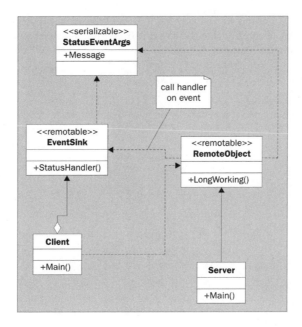

Remote Object

The remote object class is implemented in the file `RemoteObject.cs`. The remote object class must be derived from `MarshalByRefObject`, as we already know from our previous examples. To make it possible that the client can register an event handler that can be called from within the remote object, we have to declare an external function with the `delegate` keyword. We declare the delegate `StatusEvent()` with two arguments: the `sender` (so the client knows about the object that fired the event) and a variable of type `StatusEventArgs`. Into the argument class we can put all the additional information we want to send to the client.

The method that will be implemented in the client has some strict requirements. It may have only input parameters; return types, ref, and out parameters are not allowed; and the argument types must be either `[Serializable]`, or remotable (derived from `MarshalByRefObject`):

```
public delegate void StatusEvent(object sender, StatusEventArgs e);
public class RemoteObject : MarshalByRefObject
{
```

Within the class `RemoteObject` we declare an instance of the delegate function, `Status`, modified with the `event` keyword. The client must add an event handler to the `Status` event to receive status information from the remote object:

```
public class RemoteObject : MarshalByRefObject
{
    public RemoteObject()
    {
        Console.WriteLine("RemoteObject constructor called");
    }
    public event StatusEvent Status;
```

In the `LongWorking()` method we're checking if a event handler is registered before the event is fired with `Status(this, e)`. To verify that the event is fired asynchronously, we fire an event at the start of the method before doing the `Thread.Sleep()`, and after the sleep:

```
public void LongWorking(int ms)
{
    Console.WriteLine("RemoteObject: LongWorking() Started");
    StatusEventArgs e = new StatusEventArgs(
        "Message for Client: LongWorking() Started");

    // fire event

    if (Status != null)
    {
        Console.WriteLine("RemoteObject: Firing Starting Event");
        Status(this, e);
    }
    System.Threading.Thread.Sleep(ms);
    e.Message = "Message for Client: LongWorking() Ending";

    // fire ending event

    if (Status != null)
    {
        Console.WriteLine("RemoteObject: Firing Ending Event");
        Status(this, e);
    }
    Console.WriteLine("RemoteObject: LongWorking() Ending");
}
}
}
```

Event Arguments

As you've seen in the `RemoteObject` class, the class `StatusEventArgs` is used as argument for the delegate. With the `[Serializable]` attribute an instance of this class can be transferred from the server to the client. We are using a simple property of type `string` to send a message to the client:

```
[Serializable]
public class StatusEventArgs
{
    public StatusEventArgs(string m)
    {
        message = m;
    }
    public string Message
    {
        get
        {
            return message;
        }
        set
        {
            message = value;
        }
    }
    private string message;
}
```

Server

The server is implemented within a console application. We are only waiting for a user to end the server after reading the configuration file, and setting up the channel and the remote object:

```
using System;
using System.Runtime.Remoting;
namespace Wrox.ProfessionalCSharp
{
    class Server
    {
        static void Main(string[] args)
        {
            RemotingConfiguration.Configure("Server.exe.config");
            Console.WriteLine("Hit to exit");
            Console.ReadLine();
        }
    }
}
```

Server Configuration File

The server configuration file, `Server.exe.config`, is also created as we've already discussed. There is just one important point. Because the client first registers the event handler and after that calls the remote method, the remote object must keep state for the client. It isn't possible to use `SingleCall` objects with events, so the `RemoteObject` class is configured as a client-activated type:

```
<configuration>
    <system.runtime.remoting>
        <application name="CallbackSample">
            <service>
                <activated type="Wrox.ProfessionalCSharp.RemoteObject,
                               RemoteObject" />
            </service>
            <channels>
                <channel type =
                        "System.Runtime.Remoting.Channels.Http.HttpChannel,
                        System.Runtime.Remoting" port="6791" />
            </channels>
        </application>
    </system.runtime.remoting>
</configuration>
```

Event Sink

The event sink implements the handler `StatusHandler()` that's defined with the delegate. As previously noted, the method can have only input parameters, and only a void return. These are exactly the requirements for `[OneWay]` methods as we've seen earlier with Asynchronous Remoting. `StatusHandler()` will be called asynchronously. The `EventSink` class must also inherit from the class `MarshalByRefObject` to make it remotable because it will be called remotely, from the server:

```
using System;
using System.Runtime.Remoting.Messaging;
namespace Wrox.ProfessionalCSharp
{
    public class EventSink : MarshalByRefObject
```

```
    {
        public EventSink()
        {
        }
        [OneWay]
        public void StatusHandler(object sender, StatusEventArgs e)
        {
            Console.WriteLine("EventSink: Event occurred: " + e.Message);
        }
    }
}
```

Client

The client reads the client configuration file with the RemotingConfiguration class. That's not different from the clients we've seen so far. The client creates an instance of the remotable sink class EventSink locally. The method that should be called from the remote object on the server is passed to the remote object:

```
using System;
using System.Runtime.Remoting;
namespace Wrox.ProfessionalCSharp
{
    class Client
    {
        static void Main(string[] args)
        {
            RemotingConfiguration.Configure("Client.exe.config");
```

The differences start here. We have to create an instance of the remotable sink class EventSink locally. Since this class will not be configured with the <client> element, it's instantiated locally. Next the remote object class RemoteObject is instantiated. This class is configured in the <client> element, so it's instantiated on the remote server:

```
            EventSink sink = new EventSink();
            RemoteObject obj = new RemoteObject();
```

Now can we register the handler method of the EventSink object in the remote object. StatusEvent is the name of the delegate that was defined in the server. The StatusHandler() method has the same arguments as are defined in the StatusEvent.

Calling the method LongWorking() the server will call back into the method StatusHandler() at the beginning and end of the method:

```
            // register client sink in server - subscribe to event

            obj.Status += new StatusEvent(sink.StatusHandler);
            obj.LongWorking(5000);
```

Now are we no longer interested in receiving events from the server and unsubscribe from the event. The next time we call LongWorking() no events will be received:

```
        // unsubscribe to event

        obj.Status -= new StatusEvent(sink.StatusHandler);
        obj.LongWorking(5000);
        Console.WriteLine("Hit to exit");
        Console.ReadLine();
      }
    }
  }
```

Client Configuration File

The configuration file for the client, `client.exe.config`, is nearly the same configuration file for client-activated objects that we've already seen. The difference can be found in defining a port number for the channel. Since the server must reach the client with a known port, we have to define the port number for the channel as an attribute of the `<channel>` element. It isn't necessary to define a `<service>` section for our `EventSink` class, because this class will be instantiated from the client with the new operator locally. The server does not access this object by its name; instead it will receive a marshaled reference to the instance:

```
<configuration>
  <system.runtime.remoting>
    <application name="Client">
      <client url="http://localhost:6791/CallbackSample">
        <activated type="Wrox.ProfessionalCSharp.RemoteObject,
                    RemoteObject" />
      </client>
      <channels>
        <channel type =
                 "System.Runtime.Remoting.Channels.Http.HttpChannel,
                 System.Runtime.Remoting" port="777" />
      </channels>
    </application>
  </system.runtime.remoting>
</configuration>
```

Running Programs

We see the resulting output on the server. The constructor of the remote object is called once because we have a client-activated object. Next, we see the call to `LongWorking()` has started and we are firing the events to the client. The next start of the `LongWorking()` method doesn't fire events, because the client has already unregistered its interest in the event:

In the client output we can see that the events made it across the network:

Call Contexts

Client-activated objects can hold state for a specific client. With client-activated objects, we need resources on the server. With server-activated `SingleCall` objects, a new instance is created for every instance call, and no resources are held on the server; these objects can't hold state for a client. For state management we can keep state on the client side; details of the state of that object are sent with every method call to the server. We don't have to change all method signatures to include an additional parameter that passes the state to the server, because we can use **call contexts**.

A call context flows with a logical thread and is passed with every method call. A **logical thread** is started from the calling thread and flows through all method calls that are started from the calling thread, passing through different contexts, different application domains, and different processes.

We can assign data to the call context using `CallContext.SetData()`. The class of the object that's used as data for the `SetData()` method must implement the interface `ILogicalThreadAffinative`. We can get this data again in the same logical thread (but possibly a different physical thread) using `CallContext.GetData()`.

For the data of the call context I'm creating a new C# class library with the newly created class `CallContextData`. This class will be used to pass some data from the client to the server with every method call. The class that's passed with the call context must implement the interface `System.Runtime.Remoting.Messaging.ILogicalThreadAffinative`. This interface doesn't have a method; it's just a markup for the runtime that defines that instances of this class should flow with a logical thread. The class `CallContextData` must also be marked with the `Serializable` attribute so it can be transferred through the channel:

```csharp
using System;
using System.Runtime.Remoting.Messaging;
namespace Wrox.ProfessionalCSharp
{
    [Serializable]
    public class CallContextData : ILogicalThreadAffinative
    {
        public CallContextData()
        {
        }
        public string Data
        {
            get
            {
                return data;
            }
            set
            {
                data = value;
            }
        }
        protected string data;
    }
}
```

In our `Hello` class, the `Greeting()` method is changed so that we access the call context. For the use of the `CallContextData` class we have to reference the previously created assembly `CallContextData.dll`. To work with the `CallContext` class, the namespace `System.Runtime.Remoting.Messaging` must be opened:

```
public string Greeting(string name)
{
    Console.WriteLine("Greeting started");
    CallContextData cookie =
        (CallContextData)CallContext.GetData("mycookie");
    if (cookie != null)
    {
        Console.WriteLine("Cookie: " + cookie.Data);
    }
    Console.WriteLine("Greeting finished");
    return "Hello, " + name;
}
```

In the client code we pass the call context information:

```
CallContextData cookie = new CallContextData();
cookie.Data = "information for the server";
CallContext.SetData("mycookie", cookie);
for (int i=0; i< 5; i++)
{
    Console.WriteLine(obj.Greeting("Christian"));
}
```

Such a call context can be used to send information about the user, the name of the client system, or simply a unique identifier that's used on the server side to get some state information from a database.

Summary

In this chapter we've seen that .NET Remoting can be used very easily. A remote object just has to inherit form `MarshalByRefObject`. In the server application only a single method is needed to load the configuration file so that the channels and remote objects are both set up and running. Within the client, we load the configuration file and use the new operator to instantiate the remote object.

It's also not that much work even if we don't use configuration files. On the server, we simply create a channel and register a remote object. On the client, we create a channel and use the remote object.

Along with this simplicity we have many mechanisms from other parts of the .NET Framework that work with .NET Remoting as well, such as calling asynchronous methods, performing callbacks using the `delegate` and `event` keywords, and so on.

Although .NET Remoting can be that simple, the architecture is also flexible and can be extended. We can use HTTP and TCP channels, but we can also extend them, or write new channels from scratch. There are SOAP and binary formatters, but we can easily use our own. We also have many interception points where we can add custom functionality to the classes that are delivered with the .NET Framework.

Now let's build on this by exploring Windows Services in our next chapter.

24

Windows Services

In Chapter 22 we had a look at networking and Chapter 23 covered servers using .NET Remoting. The server processes that we've looked at so far must be started manually. However, these programs should be started automatically at boot-time without needing someone to log on to the machine. This is where Windows Services come in handy.

In this chapter we will look at:

- ❑ The architecture of Windows Services; the functionality of a service program, service control program, and service configuration program.

- ❑ How to implement a service with the classes found in the `System.ServiceProcess` namespace.

- ❑ Installation programs to configure the service in the registry.

- ❑ Writing a program to control the service using the `ServiceController` class.

- ❑ How to implement event handling. Because services usually don't have a user interface, errors can't be displayed in a message box. Event handling is a good way to report errors.

- ❑ Implementing a performance category for a service. Performance monitoring can be used to get information about a normal running service.

Now, however, we'll begin with a look at what services actually are.

What are Services?

Windows services are applications that can be automatically started when the operating system boots. They can run without having an interactive user logged on to the system. We can configure a service to be run from a specially configured user; or from the System user – a user that has even more privileges than the system administrator does.

> **Services don't run on Windows 98 or Windows ME. For services, the NT kernel is a requirement. Windows Services do run on Windows NT 4, Windows 2000, and Windows XP.**

Here are few examples of such services:

❑ Simple TCP/IP Services is a service program that hosts some small TCP/IP servers: echo, daytime, quote, and others

❑ World Wide Publishing Service is the service of the Internet Information Server

❑ Event Log is a service to log messages to the event log system

❑ Microsoft Search is a service that creates indexes of data on the disk

We can use the Component Services administrative tool to see all of the services on a system. On a Windows 2000 Server this program can be accessed from Start | Programs | Administrative Tools | Services; on Windows 2000 Professional the program is accessible from Settings | Control Panel | Administrative Tools | Services:

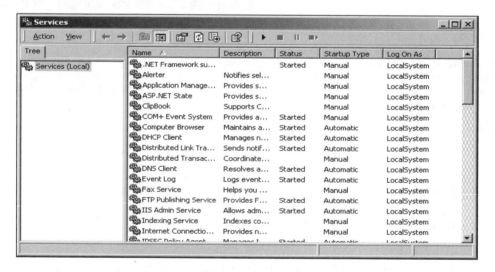

Architecture

Three program types are necessary to operate a service. The service program itself serves the purpose of the real problem we want to solve. In the service program, we have to code the actual functionality. With a service control program, it's possible to send control requests to a service, such as start, stop, pause, and continue. Last, but not least, we need a service configuration program. With a service configuration program a service can be installed, which means that it's not only copied to the file system, but also written into the Registry and configured as a service. While .NET components can be installed by doing an xcopy because they don't need the Registry, installation for services is different because registry configuration is needed here. A service configuration program can also be used to change the configuration of a service later.

Service Program

Before looking at the .NET implementation of a service, let's look at it from an independent viewpoint and discover what the Windows architecture of services looks like, and what the inner functionality of a service is.

The service program implements the functionality of the service. It needs three parts – a **main** function (the entry point of the program), a **service-main** function, and a handler. The **Service Control Manager** (**SCM**) plays a very important part for services. The SCM sends requests to our service to start and stop it. In the service program, we have to register entry points of our service in the SCM so that the SCM can call these entry points in our service.

In the main function of the service program, the entry-points for the service-main functions must be registered in the SCM. The SCM needs the information about the service-main functions so that these functions can be called by the SCM when the service should be started.

A main function may register more than one service-main function. It must register a service-main function for each service it provides. A service program can provide a lot of services in a single program; for example, C:\winnt\system32\services.exe is the service program that includes Alerter, Application Management, Computer Browser, DHCP Client, Distributed Link Tracking Client and Server, DNS Client, Event Log, and some other services.

The second part of the service program is the **service-main function**. This contains the functionality of the service. This function is called by the SCM when the service should start. The World Wide Publishing service starts a thread that listens to port 80, normally, and waits for some HTTP requests. The DHCP client requests, frees, and renews a dynamically assigned IP address. The main functionality of the service lies inside the service-main function. There's one more responsibility of the service-main function in regard to registering another entry point in the SCM: this function must register a handler function in the SCM.

The handler function is the third part of the service program. The handler must respond to events from the SCM. Services can be stopped, suspended, and resumed. The handler must react to these events.

Service Control Manager (SCM)

The service control manager is the part of the operating system that communicates with the service. Let's have a look at how this communication works with a UML sequence diagram:

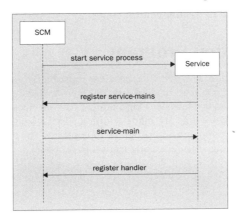

At boot time, each process for which a service is set to automatically start is started, and so the main function of this process gets called. The service has the responsibility to register the main function for each of its services. The SCM now calls the service-main function for each service that should be started. The service-main function is, as previously stated, the main functionality of the service.

One important task this service-main function has is to register a handler with the SCM. Now a service control program can post requests to the SCM to stop, suspend, and resume the service. The service control program is independent of the SCM and the service itself. We get many service control programs with the operating system; one is the MMC Services snap-in that we've seen earlier. We can also write our own service control program. A nice service control program is part of the SQL Server installation. It shows colored buttons to control the SQL Server services:

Service Control Program

As the name suggests, with a service control program we can control the service. For stopping, suspending, and resuming the service, we can send control codes to the service, and the handler should react to these events. It's also possible to ask the service about the actual status, and to implement a custom handler that responds to custom control codes.

Service Configuration Program

We can't use xcopy installation with services. Services must be configured in the Registry. We can set the startup type to automatic, manual, or disabled. We have to configure the user of the service program, and dependencies of the service – for example, the services that must be started before this one can start. All these configurations are made within a service configuration program. The installation program can use the service configuration program to configure the service, but this program can also be used at a later time to change service configuration parameters.

System.ServiceProcess Namespace

In the .NET Framework, we can find service classes in the System.ServiceProcess namespace that implement the three parts of a service:

❑ We inherit from the ServiceBase class to implement a service. The ServiceBase class is used to register the services and answers start and stop requests.

❑ The ServiceController class is used to implement a service control program. With this class we can send requests to services.

❑ The ServiceProcessInstaller and ServiceInstaller classes are, as the names suggest, classes to install and configure service programs.

Let's take a look at how we go about creating a new service.

Create a Service

The service we are creating will host a quote server. With every request made from a client the quote server returns a random quote from a quote file. The first part of the solution will be done with three assemblies, one for the client and two for the server. The assembly QuoteServer holds the actual functionality. We will read the quote file in a memory cache, and answer requests for quotes with the help of a socket server.

The QuoteClient is a Windows Forms rich-client application. This application creates a client socket to communicate with the QuoteServer. The third assembly we will build is the actual service. The QuoteService starts and stops the QuoteServer; the service will control the server:

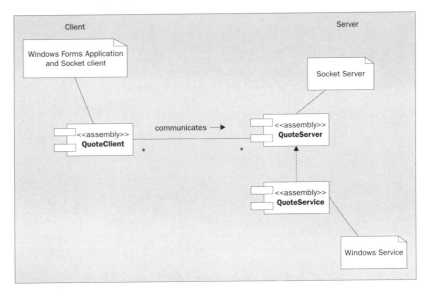

Before creating the service part of our program, we build a simple socket server in an extra C# class library that will be used from our service process.

A Class Library Using Sockets

With a Windows 2000 Server system, the Simple TCP/IP Services can be installed as part of the Windows components. Part of the Simple TCP/IP Services is a "quote of the day" TCP/IP server, short name "qotd". This simple service listens to port 17 and answers every request with a random message from the file `c:\winnt\system32\drivers\etc\quotes`. We will build a similar server here. Our server returns a Unicode string, in contrast to the good old qotd server that returns ASCII code.

Let's start stepping throught the source code of our `QuoteServer` class in the file `QuoteServer.cs`:

```
using System;
using System.IO;
using System.Threading;
using System.Net.Sockets;
using System.Text;
using System.Collections.Specialized;

namespace Wrox.ProfessionalCSharp
{

    /// <summary>
    ///     Socket server sample.
    /// </summary>

    public class QuoteServer
    {
        private TcpListener listener;
        private int port;
        private string filename;
        private StringCollection quotes;
        private Random random;
        private Thread listenerThread;
```

The constructor `QuoteServer()` is overloaded, so that a filename and a port can be passed to the call. The constructor where just the filename is passed uses the default port 7890 for the server. The default constructor defines the default filename for the quotes as `quotes.txt`:

```
        public QuoteServer() : this("quotes.txt")
        {
        }
        public QuoteServer(string filename) : this(filename, 7890)
        {
        }
        public QuoteServer(string filename, int port)
        {
            this.filename = filename;
            this.port = port;
        }
```

`ReadQuotes()` is a helper method that reads all the quotes from a file that was specified in the constructor. All the quotes are added to the `StringCollection quotes`. In addition, we are creating an instance of the `Random` class that will be used to return random quotes:

```
protected void ReadQuotes()
{
    quotes = new StringCollection();
    Stream stream = File.OpenRead(filename);
    StreamReader streamReader = new StreamReader(stream);
    string quote;
    while ((quote = streamReader.ReadLine()) != null)
    {
        quotes.Add(quote);
    }
    streamReader.Close();
    stream.Close();
    random = new Random();
}
```

Another helper method is GetRandomQuoteOfTheDay(). This method returns a random quote from the StringCollection quotes:

```
protected string GetRandomQuoteOfTheDay()
{
    int index = random.Next(0, quotes.Count);
    return quotes[index];
}
```

In the Start() method, the complete file containing the quotes is read in the StringCollection quotes by using the helper function ReadQuotes(). After this a new thread is started, which immediately calls the Listener() method. We are using a thread, because the Start() method may not block and wait for a client; it must return immediately to the caller (SCM). The SCM would assume the start failed if the method didn't return to the caller in a timely fashion:

```
public void Start()
{
    ReadQuotes();
    listenerThread = new Thread(
        new ThreadStart(this.Listener));
    listenerThread.Start();
}
```

The thread function Listener() creates a TCPListener instance. In the AcceptSocket() method, we are waiting for a client to connect. As soon as a client connects AcceptSocket() returns with a socket associated with the client. We're calling GetRandomQuoteOfTheDay() to send the returned random quote to the client using socket.Send():

```
protected void Listener()
{
    listener = new TcpListener(port);
    listener.Start();
    while (true)
    {
        Socket socket = listener.AcceptSocket();
        if (socket == null)
        {
            return;
```

```
        }
        string message = GetRandomQuoteOfTheDay();
        UnicodeEncoding encoder = new UnicodeEncoding();
        byte[] buffer = encoder.GetBytes(message);
        socket.Send(buffer, buffer.Length, 0);
        socket.Close();
    }
}
```

As well as the Start() method, we have some methods to control the service: Stop(),
Suspend(), and Resume():

```
public void Stop()
{
    listener.Stop();
}
public void Suspend()
{
    listenerThread.Suspend();
}
public void Resume()
{
    listenerThread.Resume();
}
```

Another method that will be publicly available, is RefreshQuotes(). If the file containing the quotes
changes we start a reread of the file with this method:

```
public void RefreshQuotes()
{
    ReadQuotes();
}
    }
}
```

Before building a service around our server, it's useful to build a test program that just creates an
instance of the QuoteServer and calls Start(). This way we can test the functionality without the
need to handle service-specific issues; we can concentrate building the functionality we want. This test
server must be started manually, and we can easily walk through the code with a debugger.

The test program is a C# console application. We have to reference the assembly of the QuoteServer
class. The file containing the quotes must be copied to the directory c:\wrox (or you have to change
the argument in the constructor to specify where you copied the file). After calling the constructor, the
Start() method of the QuoteServer instance is called. Start() returns immediately after creating a
thread, so we keep the console application running until Return is pressed:

```
        static void Main(string[] args)
        {
            QuoteServer qs = new QuoteServer(@"c:\wrox\quotes.txt", 4567);
            qs.Start();
            Console.WriteLine("Hit return to exit");
            Console.ReadLine();
            qs.Stop();
        }
```

Note that the QuoteServer will be running on port 4567 on localhost using this program – you will need to use these settings in the client later.

TcpClient Example

The client is a simple Windows application where we can enter the host name and the port number of the server. This application uses the TCPClient class to connect to the running server, and receives the returned message to display it in a Rich Text Box. There's also a status bar at the bottom of the form, which looks like this:

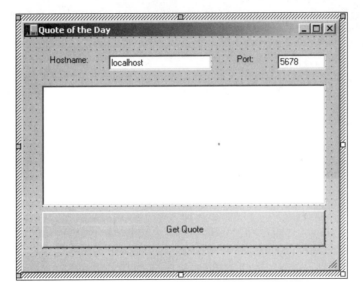

We have to make the following using statements in our code:

```
using System;
using System.Drawing;
using System.Collections;
using System.ComponentModel;
using System.Windows.Forms;
using System.Data;
using System.Net;
using System.Net.Sockets;
using System.Text;
```

We also need to include a reference to the `QuoteServer.dll` file. The remainder of the code is automatically generated by the IDE, so we won't go into it in detail here. The major functionality of the client lies in the handler for the click event of the **Get Quote** button:

```
protected void buttonQuote_Click (object sender, System.EventArgs e)
{
    statusBar.Text = "";
    string server = textBoxHostname.Text;
    try
    {
        int port = Convert.ToInt32(textBoxPortNumber.Text);
    }
    catch (FormatException ex)
    {
        statusBar.Text = ex.Message;
        return;
    }
    TcpClient client = new TcpClient();
    try
    {
        client.Connect(textBoxHostname.Text,
                      Convert.ToInt32(textBoxPortNumber.Text));
        NetworkStream stream = client.GetStream();
        byte[] buffer = new Byte[1024];
        int received = stream.Read(buffer, 0, 1024);
        if (received <= 0)
        {
            statusBar.Text = "Read failed";
            return;
        }
        textBoxQuote.Text = Encoding.Unicode.GetString(buffer);
    }
    catch (SocketException ex)
    {
        statusBar.Text = ex.Message;
    }
    finally
    {
        client.Close();
    }
}
```

After starting the test server and this windows application client, we can test the functionality. A successful run can have this output using the settings in the following screenshot:

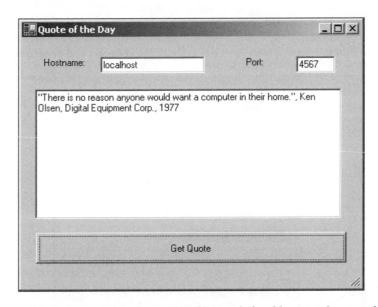

Let's now go on to add what we are here for in this chapter: let's add service functionality to the server. The program is already running, so what more do we need? Well, the server program should be automatically started at boot time without anyone logged on to the system, and we want to control it using service control programs.

Windows Service Project

Using the new project wizard for C# Windows Services, we can now start to create a Windows Service. Pay attention not to select the Web Service project:

Web Services were discussed in Chapter 17.

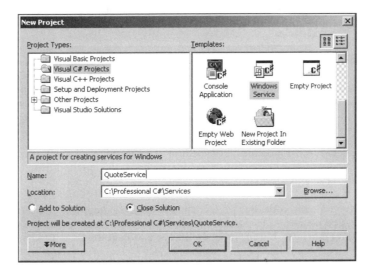

After pressing OK to create the Windows Service application, the designer surface appears as in Windows Forms applications, but you can't insert Windows Forms components. The designer surface will be used to add other components such as performance counters and event logging.

Selecting the properties of this service opens up this properties editor window:

Here, properties of the service can be configured:

- ❏ AutoLog means that events are automatically logged for starting and stopping the service.
- ❏ CanPauseAndContinue, CanShutdown, and CanStop means that the service can handle the specific pause, continue, shutdown, and stop requests.
- ❏ ServiceName is the name of the service that's written to the Registry and is used to control the service.
- ❏ CanHandlePowerEvent is a valid option for services running on a Windows 2000 system. We will talk about the power options later in this chapter.

> The default service name is WinService1 – no matter what the project is named. You can install only a single WinService1 service. If you get installation errors during your testing process, this may be the reason. Make sure, therefore, that you change the name of the service to a more suitable name at the beginning of the service development.

Changing these properties with the properties editor sets the values of our ServiceBase-derived class in the InitalizeComponent() method. You already know this method from the Windows Forms applications. With services it's used in a similar way.

The wizard will generate the code, but we will change the file name to QuoteService.cs, the name of the namespace to Wrox.ProfessionalCSharp, and the class name to QuoteService. We'll take a detailed look at this code later, but for now, we'll have a look at the ServiceBase class.

ServiceBase Class

The ServiceBase class is the base class for all .NET services. Our class QuoteService derives from ServiceBase; this class communicates with the service control manager using an undocumented helper class, System.ServiceProcess.NativeMethods, which is just a wrapper class to the Win32 API calls. The class is private, so we can't use it in our code.

The following sequence diagram shows the interaction of the SCM, our class QuoteService, and the classes from the System.ServiceProcess namespace. In a sequence diagram, we can see the lifelines of objects vertical and communication going on in the horizontal direction. The communication is time-ordered from top to bottom:

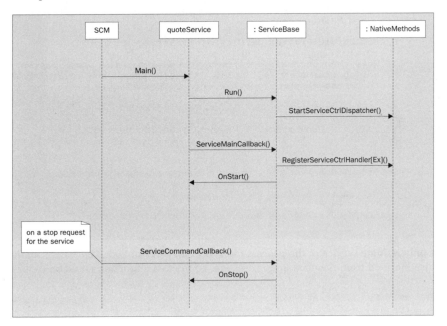

The SCM starts the process of a service that should be started. At startup the Main() method is called. In the Main() method of our service we call the Run() method of the base class ServiceBase. Run() registers the method ServiceMainCallback() using NativeMethods.StartServiceCtrlDispatcher() in the SCM and writes an entry to the event log.

The next step is that the SCM calls the registered method ServiceMainCallback() in our service program. ServiceMainCallback() itself registers the handler using NativeMethods.RegisterServiceCtrlHandler[Ex]() and sets the status of the service in the SCM. Next, the method OnStart() gets called. In OnStart() we have to implement the startup code. If OnStart() was successful the resource value for StartSuccessful is written to the event log.

The handler is implemented in the method ServiceCommandCallback(). The SCM calls this method when changes are requested from the service. The method ServiceCommandCallback() routes the requests further to OnPause(), OnContinue(), OnStop(), OnCustomCommand(), and OnPowerEvent().

1033

Main Function

Let's look into the generated main function of the service process. In the main function an array of `ServiceBase` classes, `ServicesToRun` is declared. One instance of the `QuoteService` class is created and passed as the first element to the `ServicesToRun` array. If more than one service should run inside this service process, it's necessary to add more instances of the specific service classes to the array. This array is then passed to the static `Run()` method of the `ServiceBase` class. With the `Run()` method of `ServiceBase`, we are giving the SCM references to the entry points of our services. The main thread of our service process is now blocked and waits for the service to terminate.

Here's the automatically generated code:

```
// The main entry point for the process
static void Main()
{
    System.ServiceProcess.ServiceBase[] ServicesToRun;

    // More than one user Service may run within the same process. To
    // add another service to this process, change the following line
    // to create a second service object. For example,
    //
    //    ServicesToRun = New System.ServiceProcess.ServiceBase[]
    //    {
    //        new WinService1(), new MySecondUserService()
    //    };
    //

    ServicesToRun = new System.ServiceProcess.ServiceBase[]

        new QuoteService()
    };
    System.ServiceProcess.ServiceBase.Run(ServicesToRun);
}
```

If there's only a single service in the process the array can be removed. The `Run()` method accepts a single object derived from the class `ServiceBase`, so the `Main` function could be reduced to this:

```
System.ServiceProcess.ServiceBase.Run(new QuoteService());
```

If there is more than one service and we need some shared initialization for the services, then this shared initialization must be done before the `Run()` method, because the main thread is blocked until the service process is stopped. Following instructions would not be reached before the end of the service.

The initialization should not take too long: it shouldn't take longer than 30 seconds. If the initialization code would take longer, then the service control manager assumes that the service startup failed. We have to take the slowest machines where this service should run into account when considering this 30 second limit. If the initialization takes longer, we could start the initialization in a different thread so that the main thread calls `Run()` in time. An event object can then be used to signal that the thread completed its work.

Service-Start

At service start the `OnStart()` method is called. Here we can start our socket server. The `QuoteServer.dll` assembly must be referenced for the use of the `QuoteServer`. The thread calling `OnStart()` may not be blocked; this method must return to the caller, which is the `ServiceMainCallback()` method of the `ServiceBase` class. The `ServiceBase` class registers the handler and informs the SCM that the service started successfully after calling `OnStart()`:

```
/// <summary>
///     Set things in motion so your service can do its work.
/// </summary>

protected override void OnStart(string[] args)
{
    quoteServer = new QuoteServer(@"c:\Wrox\quotes.txt", 5678);
    quoteServer.Start();
}
```

The `quoteServer` variable is declared as a private member in the class:

```
namespace Wrox.ProfessionalCSharp
{
    public class QuoteService : System.ServiceProcess.ServiceBase
    {

        /// <summary>
        /// Required designer variable.
        /// </summary>

        private System.ComponentModel.Container components;
        private QuoteServer quoteServer;
```

Handler Methods

When the service is stopped, the `OnStop()` method gets called. We should stop the service functionality in this method:

```
/// <summary>
///     Stop this service.
/// </summary>
protected override void OnStop()
{
    quoteServer.Stop();
}
```

In addition to `OnStart()` and `OnStop()`, we can override the following handlers in our class:

❑   `OnPause()` gets called when the service should be paused.

❑   `OnContinue()` gets called when the service should return to normal operation after being paused. To make it possible for the overridden methods `OnPause()` and `OnContinue()` to be called the `CanPauseAndContinue` property must be set to `true`.

❑   `OnShutdown()` is called when Windows is undergoing system shutdown. Normally, the behavior of this method should be similar to the `OnStop()` implementation; if more time would be needed for a shutdown additional time can be requested. Similar to `OnPause()` and `OnContinue()`, a property must be set to enable this behavior: `CanShutdown` must be set to `true`.

❑   `OnCustomCommand()` is a handler that can serve custom commands. With a custom service control program we can send the service custom commands. How these commands are handled defines our implementation of `OnCustomCommand()`. This method has an `int` argument where we get the custom command number. The value can be in the range 128 to 256; values below 128 are system-reserved values. In our service we are re-reading the quotes-file with the custom command 128:

```
    protected override void OnPause()
    {
        quoteServer.Suspend();
    }
    protected override void OnContinue()
    {
        quoteServer.Resume();
    }
    protected override void OnShutdown()
    {
        OnStop();
    }
    public const int commandRefresh = 128;
    protected override void OnCustomCommand(int command)
    {
        switch (command)
        {
            case commandRefresh:
                quoteServer.RefreshQuotes();
                break;
            default:
                break;
        }
    }
}
```

As before, we'll need to add in a reference to our `QuoteServer.dll` file.

Threading and Services

With services, we have to deal with threads. As we started earlier, the SCM will assume that the service failed if the initialization takes too long. To deal with this, we have to create a thread. The `OnStart()` method in our service class must return in time. If we call a blocking method like the `AcceptSocket()` from the `TcpListener` class we have to start a thread to do this. If we are not waiting inside `AcceptSocket()` the next client requesting our service has to wait until we are there again. This means that if we have to do some work for a client we should use a thread pool.

You can look back in Chapter 6 (*Advanced C# Topics*) for more information on how to work with threads.

Service Installation

A service must be configured in the Registry. All services can be found in `HKEY_LOCAL_MACHINE\System\CurrentControlSetServices`. You can view the Registry entries using `regedit`. The type of the service, display name, path to the executable, startup configuration, and so on are all found here:

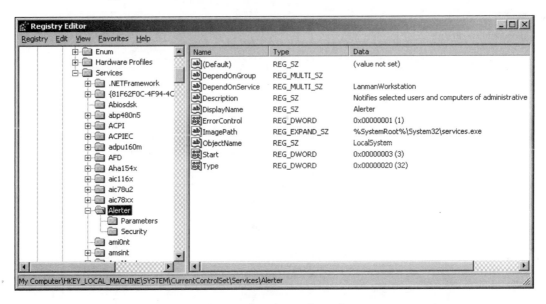

This configuration can be done using the installer classes from the `System.ServiceProcess` namespace.

Installation Program

We can add an installation program to the service by switching to the design view with Visual Studio.NET and then selecting the **Add Installer** option from the context menu. With this option a new `ProjectInstaller` class is created, and a `ServiceInstaller` and a `ServiceProcessInstaller` instance are created:

The class diagram of the installer classes for services should help understanding the generated code from the wizard:

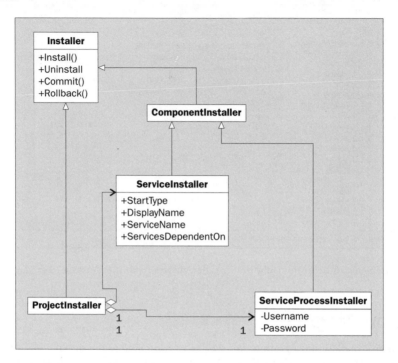

With this diagram in mind, let's go through the source code in the file `ProjectInstaller.cs` that was created with the Add Installer option.

Installer Class

The class `ProjectInstaller` is derived from `System.Configuration.Install.Installer`. `Installer` is the base class for all custom installers. With the `Installer` class, it's possible to build transaction-based installations. With a transaction-based installation it's possible to go back to the previous state if the installation fails. With a rollback all changes done by this installation so far will be undone. The `Installer` class has `Install()`, `Commit()`, `Rollback()`, and `Uninstall()` methods, as you can see in the diagram, which are called from installation programs.

The attribute `RunInstaller(true)` means that the class `ProjectInstaller` should be invoked when installing an assembly. Custom action installers as well as `installutil.exe` (which we will use later) check for this attribute:

```
using System;
using System.Collections;
using System.ComponentModel;
using System.Configuration.Install;

namespace Wrox.ProfessionalCSharp
{
```

```
/// <summary>
///     Summary description for ProjectInstaller.
/// </summary>

[RunInstaller(true)]
public class ProjectInstaller : System.Configuration.Install.Installer
{
```

ServiceProcessInstaller and ServiceInstaller Classes

Similar to Windows Forms applications, InitializeComponent() is called inside the constructor of the ProjectInstaller class. In InitializeComponent() an instance of the ServiceProcessInstaller class and the ServiceInstaller class are created. Both of these classes derive from the class ComponentInstaller that itself is an Installer.

Classes derived from ComponentInstaller can be used as parts within an installation process. Remember that a service process can include more than one service. The ServiceProcessInstaller class is used for the part of the process-installation, and the ServiceInstaller class is for the part of the service, so one instance of ServiceInstaller is needed for every service. If there are three services inside the process, then we have to add additional ServiceInstaller objects – three ServiceInstaller instances are needed in that case:

```
private System.ServiceProcess.ServiceProcessInstaller
            serviceProcessInstaller1;
private System.ServiceProcess.ServiceInstaller serviceInstaller1;

/// <summary>
///     Required designer variable.
/// </summary>

private System.ComponentModel.Container components;
public ProjectInstaller()
{

    // This call is required by the Designer.

    InitializeComponent();

    // TODO: Add any initialization after the InitComponent call

}

/// <summary>
///     Required method for Designer support - do not modify
///     the contents of this method with the code editor.
/// </summary>

private void InitializeComponent()
{
    this.serviceProcessInstaller1 =
            new System.ServiceProcess.ServiceProcessInstaller();
    this.serviceInstaller1 =
            new System.ServiceProcess.ServiceInstaller();

    //
```

1039

```
        // serviceProcessInstaller1
        //

        this.serviceProcessInstaller1.Password = null;
        this.serviceProcessInstaller1.Username = null;

        //
        // serviceInstaller1
        //

        this.serviceInstaller1.ServiceName = "QuoteService";

        //
        // ProjectInstaller
        //

        this.Installers.AddRange(
            new System.Configuration.Install.Installer[]
                {this.serviceProcessInstaller1,
                 this.serviceInstaller1});
        }
    }
}
```

ServiceProcessInstaller installs an executable that implements the class ServiceBase. ServiceProcessInstaller has properties for the complete process, properties shared by all the services inside the process:

Properties for **ServiceProcessInstaller**	
Username, Password	Indicates the user account under which the service runs if the property RunUnderSystemAccount is false
Account	With this property we can specifies whether the service runs under the system account
HelpText	HelpText is a read-only property that returns the help text for setting the user name and password

ServiceInstaller is the class needed for every service; it has properties unique for each service inside a process: StartType, DisplayName, ServiceName, and ServicesDependedOn:

Properties for **ServiceInstaller**	
StartType	The StartType property indicates if the service is manually or automatically started. Possible values: ServiceStartMode.Automatic, ServiceStartMode.Manual, ServiceStartMode.Disabled

Properties for `ServiceInstaller`	
`DisplayName`	`DisplayName` is the friendly name of the service that is displayed to the user. This name is also for many management tools to control and monitor the service.
`ServiceName`	`ServiceName` is the name of the service. This value must be identical with the `ServiceName` property of the `ServiceBase` class in the service program.
`ServicesDependentOn`	Specifies an array of services that must be started before this service can be started. When the service is started, all dependent services are started automatically.

If you change the name of the service in the `ServiceBase`-derived class be sure to also change the `ServiceName` property in the `ServiceInstaller` object!

In the testing phases set the `StartType` to manual. If stopping the service fails, this process can't be killed, because it could be configured as running in the context of the System account. You can change this configuration at a later time when you're sure it works.

ServiceInstallerDialog

Another installer class in the `System.ServiceProcess.Design` namespace is the `ServiceInstallerDialog`. If we want the system administrator to enter the username and password during the installation this class can be used.

If we set the `Username` and `Password` properties of the `ServiceProcessInstaller` class to `null` then this dialog will automatically be displayed at installation time. It's also possible to cancel the installation at this time:

installutil

After adding the installer classes to the project we can now use the `installutil.exe` utility to install and uninstall the service. The command-line inputs for these actions are, respectively:

```
installutil quoteservice.exe
installutil /u quoteservice.exe
```

> If the installation fails be sure to check the installation log files
> `InstallUtil.InstallLog` and `<servicename>.InstallLog`. Often you can find
> very useful information such as "The specified service already exists".

Client

After the service has been successfully installed, and we start the service manually (see next section for further details), we can start our client using the services MMC with the following settings:

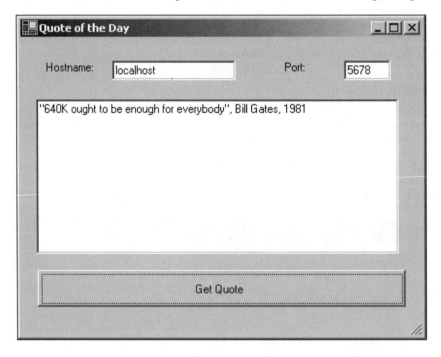

Monitoring and Controlling the Service

To monitor and control services we have some utilities. There's a Services MMC snap-in that's part of the Computer Management administration tool. With every windows system we also get a command-line utility, `net.exe`, which allows us to control services. `sc.exe` is an additional command-line utility that has much more functionality than the `net.exe` command that's part of the Platform SDK. We will also create a small Windows application that makes use of the `System.ServiceProcess.ServiceController` class to monitor and control services.

MMC Computer Management

Using the Services snap-in to the Microsoft Management Console (MMC) we can view the status of all services. It's also possible to send control requests to services to stop, enable, and disable them, as well as change the configuration. The Services snap-in is a service control program as well as a service configuration program:

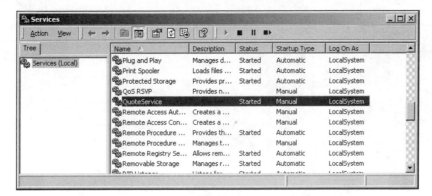

Double-clicking on our QuoteService opens up this dialog. We see the service name, description, and the path to the executable, the startup type, and the status. The service is currently started. The account for the service process can be changed with the Log On tab in this dialog.

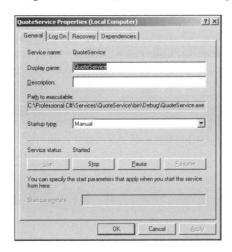

net.exe

The Services snap-in is easy to use, but the system administrator cannot automate it, because it's not usable within an administrative script. A system administrator could prefer to write a Windows Scripting Host program to make his day-by-day activity easier. For this task there is a command-line utility found with every Windows system installed: net.exe. This tool can be used to control services. net start shows all running services, net start *servicename* starts a service, net stop *servicename* sends a stop request to the service. It's also possible to pause and continue a service with net pause and net continue (only if the service allows it, of course).

This console window shows the result of net start:

```
C:\>net start
These Windows 2000 services are started:

   COM+ Event System
   Computer Browser
   DHCP Client
   Distributed Link Tracking Client
   DNS Client
   Event Log
   FTP Publishing Service
   IIS Admin Service
   IPSEC Policy Agent
   Logical Disk Manager
   Machine Debug Manager
   Messenger
   Network Connections
   Plug and Play
   Print Spooler
   Protected Storage
   QuoteService
   Remote Procedure Call (RPC)
   Remote Registry Service
   Removable Storage
   RIP Listener
```

sc.exe

There's a little known utility that's part of the Microsoft Platform SDK: sc.exe. You must install the Microsoft Platform SDK to get to this tool. The Microsoft Platform SDK is not part of the Visual Studio.NET CDs. It's an extra CD part of MSDN, or it can be downloaded from the Internet for MSDN subscribers. The usual installation path for this utility is c:\Program Files\Microsoft Platform SDK\Bin\WinNT.

sc.exe is a great tool to play with services. A lot more can be done with sc.exe compared to the net.exe utility. With sc it's possible to check the actual status of, configure, remove, and add services. This tool helps a lot when de-installation of the service doesn't work the normal way any more:

```
C:\WINNT2\System32\cmd.exe - sc                                        _ □ X

C:\Program Files\Microsoft Platform SDK\Bin\WinNT>sc
DESCRIPTION:
        SC is a command line program used for communicating with the
        NT Service Controller and services.
USAGE:
        sc <server> [command] [service name] <option1> <option2>...

        The option <server> has the form "\\ServerName"
        Further help on commands can be obtained by typing: "sc [command]"
        Commands:
          query-----------Queries the status for a service, or
                           enumerates the status for types of services.
          queryex---------Queries the extended status for a service, or
                           enumerates the status for types of services.
          start-----------Starts a service.
          pause-----------Sends a PAUSE control request to a service.
          interrogate-----Sends an INTERROGATE control request to a service.
          continue--------Sends a CONTINUE control request to a service.
          stop------------Sends a STOP request to a service.
          config----------Changes the configuration of a service (persistant).
          description-----Changes the description of a service.
          failure---------Changes the actions taken by a service upon failure.
          qc--------------Queries the configuration information for a service.
          qdescription----Queries the description for a service.
          qfailure--------Queries the actions taken by a service upon failure.
          delete----------Deletes a service (from the registry).
          create----------Creates a service. (adds it to the registry).
          control---------Sends a control to a service.
          sdshow----------Displays a service's security descriptor.
          sdset-----------Sets a service's security descriptor.
          GetDisplayName--Gets the DisplayName for a service.
          GetKeyName------Gets the ServiceKeyName for a service.
          EnumDepend------Enumerates Service Dependencies.

        The following commands don't require a service name:
        sc <server> <command> <option>
          boot------------<ok | bad> Indicates whether the last boot should
                           be saved as the last-known-good boot configuration
          Lock------------Locks the Service Database .
          QueryLock-------Queries the LockStatus for the SCManager Database
EXAMPLE:
        sc start MyService

Would you like to see help for the QUERY and QUERYEX commands? [ y | n ]:
```

Visual Studio.NET Server Explorer

It's also possible to control services using the Server Explorer within Visual Studio.NET. If you can't see the Server Explorer with your current configuration you can make it visible with the menu View | Server Explorer. By selecting a service and opening the context menu a service can be started and stopped. This context menu can also be used to add a ServiceController class to the project. If you want to control a specific service in your application, drag and drop a service from the Server Explorer to the Designer: a ServiceController instance is added to the application. The properties of this object are automatically set to access the selected service, and the System.ServiceProcess.dll is referenced. You can use this instance to control the service in the same way that we do it in the following section in a generic application to control all services.

ServiceController Class

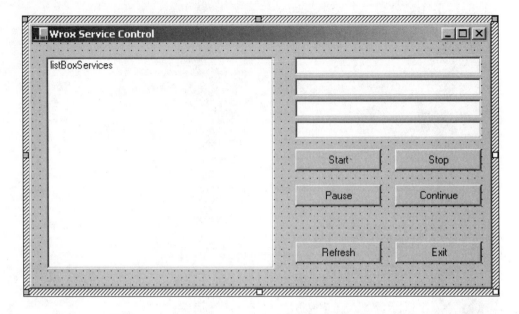

We will create a small Windows application using the `ServiceController` class to monitor and control Windows Services.

The user interface to this application has a listbox to show all services, four textboxes to display the display name, status, type, and name of the service, and four buttons to send control events.

We are using the `System.ServiceProcess.ServiceController` class, so `System.ServiceProcess.dll` must be referenced.

We are implementing the `RefreshServiceList()` method that is called within the constructor of the `ServiceControlForm` class. This method fills a listbox with the display names of all services. `GetServices()` is a static method of the `ServiceController` class, and it returns a `ServiceController` array representing all Windows Services. The `ServiceController` class also has a static method, `GetDevices()`, that returns a `ServiceController` array representing all device drivers.

The listbox is filled using data binding:

```
private System.ServiceProcess.ServiceController[] services;

public ServiceControlForm()
{

    //
    // Required for Windows Form Designer support
```

```
        //
    InitializeComponent();
    RefreshServiceList();
}
protected void RefreshServiceList()
{
    services = ServiceController.GetServices();
    listBoxServices.DisplayMember = "DisplayName";
    listBoxServices.DataSource = services;
}
```

Now, all Windows Services are displayed in the listbox. Next, we must get the information about a service to display it in the textboxes.

Monitoring the Service

Using the `ServiceController` class, we can get the information about each service. The `ServiceController` class has these properties for service information:

ServiceController	Properties
CanPauseAndContinue	If pause and continue requests can be sent to the service, true is returned.
CanShutdown	true if the service has a handler for a system shutdown.
CanStop	true if the service is stoppable.
DependentServices	Returns a collection of dependent services. If the service is stopped all dependent services are stopped beforehand.
ServicesDependentOn	Returns of a collection of the services that this service depends on.
DisplayName	The name that should be displayed for this service.
MachineName	The name of the machine that the service runs on.
ServiceName	Name of the service.
ServiceType	The service can be run inside a shared process where more than one service uses the same process (Win32ShareProcess), or run so there's just one service in a process (Win32OwnProcess). If the service can interact with the desktop the type is InteractiveProcess.
Status	Status of the service. The status can be running, stopped, paused, or in some intermediate mode like start pending, stop pending, and so on.

In our application, we are using the properties DisplayName, ServiceName, ServiceType, and Status to display the service information. Also, CanPauseAndContinue and CanStop are used to enable or disable the **Pause**, **Continue**, and **Stop** buttons.

OnSelectedIndexChanged() is a handler for the listbox. It's called when the user selects a service in the listbox. In OnSelectedIndexChanged() we set the display and service name directly with properties of the ServiceController class. The status and type cannot be set that easily, because a string should be displayed instead of a number, which is what the ServiceController class returns. SetServiceStatus() is a helper function that walks through the enumeration of the Status property to display a string for the status, and also to enable or disable the buttons. GetServiceTypeName() builds up the name of the service type. The ServiceType we get from ServiceController.ServiceType represents a set of flags that can be combined using the bitwise OR operator. The InteractiveProcess bit can be set together with Win32OwnProcess and Win32ShareProcess. First, we check to see that the InteractiveProcess bit is set before we go on to check for the other values:

```
protected string GetServiceTypeName(ServiceType type)
{
    string serviceType = "";
    if ((type & ServiceType.InteractiveProcess) != 0)
    {
        serviceType = "Interactive ";
        type -= ServiceType.InteractiveProcess;
    }
    switch (type)
    {
        case ServiceType.Adapter:
            serviceType += "Adapter";
            break;
        case ServiceType.FileSystemDriver:
        case ServiceType.KernelDriver:
        case ServiceType.RecognizerDriver:
            serviceType += "Driver";
            break;
        case ServiceType.Win32OwnProcess:
            serviceType += "Win32 Service Process";
            break;
        case ServiceType.Win32ShareProcess:
            serviceType += "Win32 Shared Process";
            break;
        default:
            serviceType += "unknown type " + type.ToString();
            break;
    }
    return serviceType;
}
protected void SetServiceStatus(ServiceController controller)
{
    buttonStart.Enabled = true;
    buttonStop.Enabled = true;
    buttonPause.Enabled = true;
    buttonContinue.Enabled = true;
    if (!controller.CanPauseAndContinue)
    {
        buttonPause.Enabled = false;
```

```
                buttonContinue.Enabled = false;
        }
        if (!controller.CanStop)
        {
            buttonStop.Enabled = false;
        }
        ServiceControllerStatus status = controller.Status;
        switch (status)
        {
            case ServiceControllerStatus.ContinuePending:
                textBoxServiceStatus.Text = "Continue Pending";
                buttonContinue.Enabled = false;
                break;
            case ServiceControllerStatus.Paused:
                textBoxServiceStatus.Text = "Paused";
                buttonPause.Enabled = false;
                buttonStart.Enabled = false;
                break;
            case ServiceControllerStatus.PausePending:
                textBoxServiceStatus.Text = "Pause Pending";
                buttonPause.Enabled = false;
                buttonStart.Enabled = false;
                break;
            case ServiceControllerStatus.StartPending:
                textBoxServiceStatus.Text = "Start Pending";
                buttonStart.Enabled = false;
                break;
            case ServiceControllerStatus.Running:
                textBoxServiceStatus.Text = "Running";
                buttonStart.Enabled = false;
                buttonContinue.Enabled = false;
                break;
            case ServiceControllerStatus.Stopped:
                textBoxServiceStatus.Text = "Stopped";
                buttonStop.Enabled = false;
                break;
            case ServiceControllerStatus.StopPending:
                textBoxServiceStatus.Text = "Stop Pending";
                buttonStop.Enabled = false;
                break;
            default:
                textBoxServiceStatus.Text = "Unknown status";
                break;

    }
    protected void OnSelectedIndexChanged (object sender,
                    System.EventArgs e)
    {
        ServiceController controller =
                    (ServiceController)listBoxServices.SelectedItem;
        textBoxDisplayName.Text = controller.DisplayName;
        textBoxServiceType.Text =
                    GetServiceTypeName(controller.ServiceType);
        textBoxServiceName.Text = controller.ServiceName;
        SetServiceStatus(controller);
    }
```

Controlling the Service

With the ServiceController class we can also send control requests to the service.

ServiceController	Methods
Start()	Start() tells the SCM that the service should be started. In our service program OnStart() is called.
Stop()	Stop() calls OnStop() in our service program with the help of the SCM if the property CanStop is true in the service class.
Pause()	Pause() calls OnPause() if the property CanPauseAndContinue is true.
Continue()	Continue calls OnContinue() if the property CanPauseAndContinue is true.
ExecuteCommand()	With ExecuteCommand() it's possible to send a custom command to the service.

The code to control the services follows here. Because the code for starting, stopping, suspending, and pausing is similar , only one handler is used for the four buttons:

```
protected void buttonCommand_Click(object sender, System.EventArgs e)
{
    Cursor.Current = Cursors.WaitCursor;
    ServiceController controller =
                    (ServiceController)listBoxServices.SelectedItem;
    if (sender == this.buttonStart)
    {
        controller.Start();
        controller.WaitForStatus(ServiceControllerStatus.Running);
    }
    else if (sender == this.buttonStop)
    {
        controller.Stop();
        controller.WaitForStatus(ServiceControllerStatus.Stopped);
    }
    else if (sender == this.buttonPause)
    {
        controller.Pause();
        controller.WaitForStatus(ServiceControllerStatus.Paused);
    }
    else if (sender == this.buttonContinue)
    {
        controller.Continue();
        controller.WaitForStatus(ServiceControllerStatus.Running);
    }
    int index =listBoxServices.SelectedIndex;
    RefreshServiceList();
    listBoxServices.SelectedIndex = index;
    Cursor.Current = Cursors.Default;
```

```
    }

    protected void buttonExit_Click(object sender, System.EventArgs e)
    {
        Application.Exit();
    }
    protected void buttonRefresh_Click(object sender, System.EventArgs e)
    {
        RefreshServiceList();
    }
```

As this action can take some time, the cursor is switched to the wait cursor in the first statement. Then a `ServiceController` method is called depending on the pressed button. With the `WaitForStatus()` method we are waiting to see that the service changes the status to the requested value, but we only wait a maximum of 10 seconds. After this time, the information in the listbox is refreshed; and the same service as before is selected so that the new status of this service gets displayed.

The final running application looks like this:

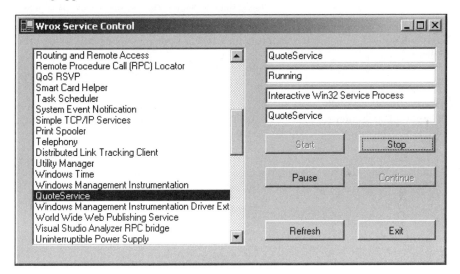

Troubleshooting

Troubleshooting works differently for services from for normal applications. The best way to build services is to first to create an assembly with the desired functionality and a test client, before a service is created. Here, you can do normal debugging and error handling. As soon as the application is running you can build a service using this assembly. Of course, there still can be problems with the service:

❏   In the service don't display errors in a message box (except for interactive services that are running on the client system). Instead, use the event logging service to write errors. Of course, you can display a message box to inform the user about errors in the client application that uses the service.

1051

❑ The service can't be started from within a debugger, but a debugger can be attached to the running service process. Open the solution with the source code of the service and set breakpoints. From the Visual Studio.NET Debug menu select Processes and attach the running process of the service.

❑ The performance monitor can be used to monitor the activity of services. We can add our own performance objects to the service. This can add some useful information for debugging. You can set up an object to give the total number of quotes returned, the time it takes to initialize, and so on.

Interactive Services

For services that are running on the client itself, it can be useful to display message boxes. If a service is meant to run on a client system it can be helpful to display message boxes to the user. If the service should run on a server that can be locked inside a computer room, the service should never display a message box. When you open a message box, and wait for some user input the user input probably won't happen for some days as nobody is looking at the server in the computer room, but it can get even worse than that – if the service isn't configured as interactive service, the message box opens up on a different, hidden, window station. In this case, no one can answer that message box, and the service is blocked.

> **Never open dialogs for services running on a server system. Nobody will answer this dialog.**

In those cases where you really want to interact with the user, an interactive service can be configured. Some examples of such interactive services are the Print Spooler that displays paper-out messages to the user, and the NetMeeting Remote Desktop Sharing service.

To configure an interactive service, the option Allow service to interact with desktop in Computer Management must be set. This changes the type of the service by adding the SERVICE_INTERACTIVE_PROCESS flag to the type:

Event Logging

Services can report errors and other information by adding events to the event log. A service class derived from `ServiceBase` automatically logs events when the `AutoLog` property is set to `true`. The `ServiceBase` class checks this property and writes a log entry at start, stop, pause, and continue requests.

Here's an example of a log entry done by a service:

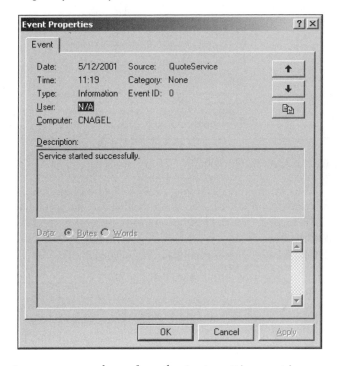

For custom event logging, we can use classes from the `System.Diagnostics` namespace.

Event Logging Architecture

By default the Event Log is stored in three log files: Application, Security, and System. Looking at the registry configuration of the event log service the three entries can be seen at `HKLM\System\CurrentControlSet\Services\EventLog` with configurations pointing to the specific files. The System log file is used from the system and device drivers. Applications and Services write to the Application log. The Security log is a read-only log for applications. The auditing feature of the operating system uses the security log.

We can read these events using the administrator tool Event Viewer. The Event Viewer can be started directly from the Server Explorer of Visual Studio.NET by right-clicking on the Event Logs item, and selecting the Launch Event Viewer entry from the context menu:

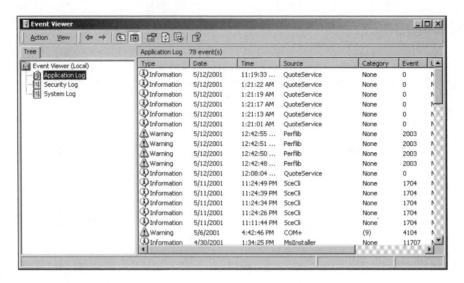

In the Event log we can see this information:

❑ The type can be Information, Warning, or Error. Information is an infrequent successful operation, Warning a problem that's not immediately significant, and Error a major problem. Additional types are FailureAudit and SuccessAudit, but these types are only used for the security log.

❑ Date and Time show the time when the event occurred.

❑ The source is the name of the software that logs the event. The source for the application log is configured in HKLM\System\CurrentControlSet\Services\EventLog\Application. Below this key the value EventMessageFile is configured to point to a resource DLL that holds error messages.

❑ A category can be defined so that event logs can be filtered when using Event View. Categories can be defined by an event source.

❑ The event identifier specifies a particular event message.

Event Logging Classes

The System.Diagnostics namespace has some classes for event logging:

❑ With the EventLog class we can read and write entries to the event log, and establish applications as event sources.

❑ The EventLogEntry is a single entry in the event log. With the EventLogEntryCollection we can iterate through EventLogEntrys.

❑ The EventLogInstaller class is the installer for an EventLog component. EventLogInstaller calls EventLog.CreateEventSource() to create an event source.

❑ With the help of the EventLogTraceListener traces can be written to the event log. This class implements the abstract class TraceListener.

Adding Event Logging

If the `AutoLog` property of the `ServiceBase` class is set to `true` event logging is automatically turned on. The `ServiceBase` class logs an informational event at startup, stop, pause, and continue requests of the service. In the `ServiceInstaller` class an `EventLogInstaller` instance is created so that an event log source is configured. This event log source has the same name as the service. If we want to write events we can use the static `WriteEntry()` method of the `EventLog` class. The `Source` property was already set in the `ServiceBase` class:

```
EventLog.WriteEntry ("event log message");
```

This method logs an informational event. If warning or error events should be created an overloaded method of `WriteEvent()` can be used to specify the type:

```
EventLog.WriteEntry("event log message", EventLogEntryType.Warning);
EventLog.WriteEntry("event log message", EventLogEntryType.Error);
```

Adding Event Logging to Other Application Types

With services the `ServiceBase` class automatically adds event-logging features. If you would like to use event logging within other application types, this can easily be done using Visual Studio.NET.

❑   Use the **Toolbox** to add an **EventLog** component to the designer.

❑   Set the **Log** property of the **EventLog** component to **Application** and the **Source** property to a name you choose. That's typically the name of the application that shows up in the Event View.

❑   Logs can now be written with the `WriteEntry()` method of the `EventLog` instance.

❑   An installer can be added from the **Add Installer** context menu item of the **EventLog** component. This creates the `ProjectInstaller` class that configures the event source in the Registry.

❑   The application can now be registered with the `installutil` command. `installutil` calls the `ProjectInstaller` class and registers the event source.

In the sense of xcopy-installation the last two steps are not really necessary. If the `Source` property of the `EventLog` instance is set, this source is automatically registered when an event log is written the first time. That's really easy to do, but for a real application I would prefer adding the installer: with `installutil /u` the event log configuration gets unregistered. If the application is just deleted, this registry key is left until the end of time if `EventLog.DeleteEventSource()` is not called.

Trace

It's also possible that all your trace messages are redirected to the event log. You shouldn't really do this, because on a normal running system the event log gets overblown with trace messages. The system administrator could miss the really important logs if this happens. Remember, the event log type can be error, warning, or informational. Informational messages are infrequent success information. Turning on trace messages to the event log can be a useful testing feature with problematic services. Tracing is possible with debug as well as with release code.

To send trace messages to the event log an `EventLogTraceListener` object must be created and added to the listener's list of the `Trace` class:

```
EventLogTraceListener listener = new EventLogTraceListener(eventLog1);
Trace.Listeners.Add(listener);
```

Now, all trace messages are sent to the event log:

```
Trace.WriteLine("trace message");
```

For more information about the tracing methods, see Chapter 6.

Creating an Event Log Listener

Now it would be useful if we could write an application that receives an event when something bad happens with a service. We will create a simple Windows application that monitors the events of our Quote service.

This Windows application has just a listbox and an exit button:

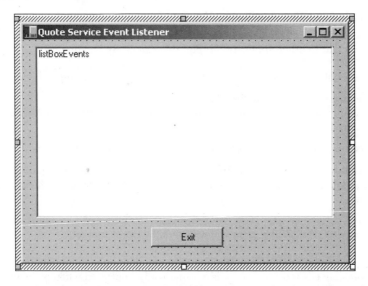

An EventLog component is added to this project by dragging and dropping it from the Toolbox. We set the Log property to Application, and the Source to the source of our service, QuoteService. The EventLog class also has a property, EnableRaisingEvents. Until now, we haven't talked about this property. The default value is false; setting it to true means that an event is generated each time this event occurs, and we can write an event handler for the EntryWritten Windows event.

In the file EventListener.cs the properties are set in InitializeComponent():

```
private void InitializeComponent()
{
    this.eventLogQuote = new System.Diagnostics.EventLog();
    this.buttonExit = new System.Windows.Forms.Button();
    this.listBoxEvents = new System.Windows.Forms.ListBox();
    ((System.ComponentModel.ISupportInitialize)
```

```
                                    (this.eventLogQuote)).BeginInit();
        this.SuspendLayout();

        //
        // eventLogQuote
        //

        this.eventLogQuote.EnableRaisingEvents = true;
        this.eventLogQuote.Log = "Application";
        this.eventLogQuote.Source = "QuoteService";
        this.eventLogQuote.SynchronizingObject = this;
        this.eventLogQuote.EntryWritten +=
                new System.Diagnostics.EntryWrittenEventHandler
                                        (this.OnEntryWritten);

        //...
```

The `OnEntryWritten()` handler receives an `EntryWrittenEventArgs` object as argument where we can get the complete information from an event. With the `Entry` property we get an `EventLogEntry` object with information about the time, event source, type, category, and so on:

```
        protected void OnEntryWritten (object sender,
            System.Diagnostics.EntryWrittenEventArgs e)
        {
            DateTime time = e.Entry.TimeGenerated;
            string message = e.Entry.Message;
            listBoxEvents.Items.Add(time + " " + message);
        }
```

The running application displays all events for the `QuoteService`:

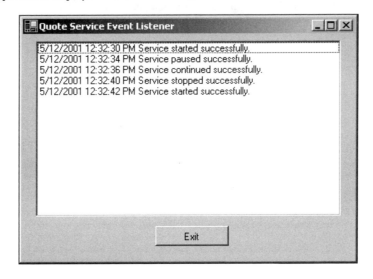

Performance Monitoring

Performance monitoring can be used to get information about the normal running of the service. Performance monitoring is a great tool that helps us to understand the workload of the system, and to observe changes and trends.

Windows 2000 has a lot of performance objects, such as System, Memory, Objects, Process, Processor, Thread, Cache, and so on. Each of these objects has many counts to monitor. For example, with the Process object the user time, handle count, page faults, thread count, and so on, can be monitored for all processes, or for specific process instances. Some applications also add application-specific objects, for example SQL Server.

For our quote service, we could be interested in getting the information about the number of client requests, how big the data is that is sent over the wire, and so on.

Performance Monitoring Classes

The System.Diagnostics namespace has these classes for performance monitoring:

- ❑ PerformanceCounter can be used both to monitor counts as well as to write counts. New performance categories can also be created with this class.

- ❑ With the PerformanceCounterCategory we can walk through all existing categories as well as create new ones. We can programmatically get all the counters of a category.

- ❑ The PerformanceCounterInstaller class is used for the installation of performance counters. The usage is similar to the EventLogInstaller we used previously.

Performance Counter Builder

We can create a new category by selecting the performance counters in the Server Explorer. The category is called Quote Service. Here is a table showing all performance counters of our service:

Name	Description	Type
# of Bytes sent	Total # of bytes sent to the client	NumberOfItems32
# of Bytes sent / sec	# of bytes sent to the client in one second	NumberOfItems32
# of Requests	Total # of requests	NumberOfItems32
# of Requests / sec	# of requests in one second	NumberOfItems32

The Performance Counter Builder writes the configuration to the performance database. This can also be done dynamically using the Create() method of the PerformanceCategory class in the System.Diagnostics namespace. An Installer for other systems can easily be added later using Visual Studio.NET.

The Performance Counter Builder can be started from the Server Explorer by selecting the context menu of the Performance Counters | Create New Category:

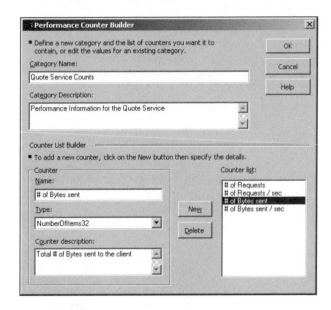

Adding Performance Counts

Next, we want to add the performance counts to the quote server. The `QuoteService` class has no knowledge about the information needed for the performance counts. We want to collect the number of requests, but after the start of the service `QuoteService` receives no requests. The information is completely contained in the `QuoteServer` class we built earlier.

Add Visual Studio.NET Designer Support to the Class Library

We could add instances of the `PerformanceCounter` class manually in the code, or we can use the Visual Studio designer. With the Designer we can drag and drop `PerformanceCounter` components from the toolbox to the designer surface. Designer support can be easily added to a component library by deriving the class from `System.ComponentModel.Component`. The method `InitializeComponent()` that will be used from the Designer to set the properties of the components will be added automatically, but we have to add a call to `InitializeComponent()` in the constructor.

Add PerformanceCounter Components

Now it's possible to add `PerformanceCounter` components from the toolbox. For our service, we add four instances where the `CategoryName` property is set to `"Quote Service Count"` for all objects, and the `CounterName` property is set to one of the values available in the selected category. The `ReadOnly` property must be set to `false`.

The code that was filled into `InitalizeComponent()` by adding the `Components` to the designer and setting the properties:

```
private void InitializeComponent()
{

    //...

    //
```

```
            // performanceCounterRequestsPerSec
            //

            this.performanceCounterRequestsPerSec.CategoryName =
                                "Quote Service Counts";
            this.performanceCounterRequestsPerSec.CounterName =
                                "# of Requests / sec";
            this.performanceCounterRequestsPerSec.ReadOnly = false;

            //
            // performanceCounterBytesSentTotal
            //

            this.performanceCounterBytesSentTotal.CategoryName =
                                "Quote Service Counts";
            this.performanceCounterBytesSentTotal.CounterName =
                                "# of Bytes sent";
            this.performanceCounterBytesSentTotal.ReadOnly = false;

            //
            // performanceCounterBytesSentPerSec
            //

            this.performanceCounterBytesSentPerSec.CategoryName =
                                "Quote Service Counts";
            this.performanceCounterBytesSentPerSec.CounterName =
                                "# of Bytes sent / sec";
            this.performanceCounterBytesSentPerSec.ReadOnly = false;

            //
            // performanceCounterRequestsTotal
            //

            this.performanceCounterRequestsTotal.CategoryName =
                                "Quote Service Counts";
            this.performanceCounterRequestsTotal.CounterName =
                                "# of Requests";
            this.performanceCounterRequestsTotal.ReadOnly = false;

            //...
```

The performance counts that show the total values, are incremented directly in the `Listener()` method of the `QuoteServer` class. `Increment()` increments the count by 1, `IncrementBy()` increments the counter with the value of the argument.

For the performance counts that show the value by seconds just two variables, `requestsPerSec` and `bytessPerSec`, are updated in the `Listener()` method:

```
protected void Listener()
{
    try
    {
        listener = new TCPListener(port);
        listener.Start();
        while (true)
        {
```

```
            Socket socket = listener.Accept();
            if (socket == null)
            {
                return;
            }
            string message = GetRandomQuoteOfTheDay();
            UnicodeEncoding encoder = new UnicodeEncoding();
            byte[] buffer = encoder.GetBytes(message);
            socket.Send(buffer, buffer.Length, 0);
            socket.Close();
            performanceCounterRequestsTotal.Increment();
            performanceCounterBytesSentTotal.IncrementBy(nBytes);
            requestsPerSec++;
            bytesPerSec += nBytes;
        }
    }
    catch (Exception e)
    {
        string message = "Quote Server failed in Listener: "
                         + e.Message;
        eventLog.WriteEntry(message, EventLogEntryType.Error);
    }
}
```

To show updated values every second, we use a `Timer` component. The `OnTimer()` method gets called once per second and sets the performance counts using the `RawValue` property of the `PerformanceCounter` class:

```
protected void OnTimer (object sender, System.EventArgs e)
{
    performanceCounterBytesSentPerSec.RawValue = bytesPerSec;
    performanceCounterRequestsPerSec.RawValue = requestsPerSec;
    bytesPerSec = 0;
    requestsPerSec = 0;
}
```

perfmon.exe

Now we can monitor our service. The Peformance tool can be started from the Administrative Tools | Performance. Pressing the + button in the toolbar, we can add performance counts. the Quote Service shows up as a performance object. All the counters we configured show up in the counter list:

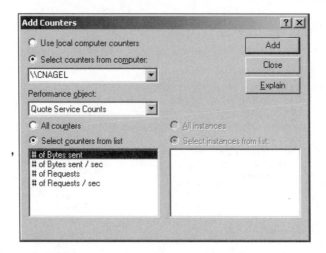

After the counts are added we can see the counts of our service over time. Using this performance tool, we can also create log files to analyze the performance at a later time:

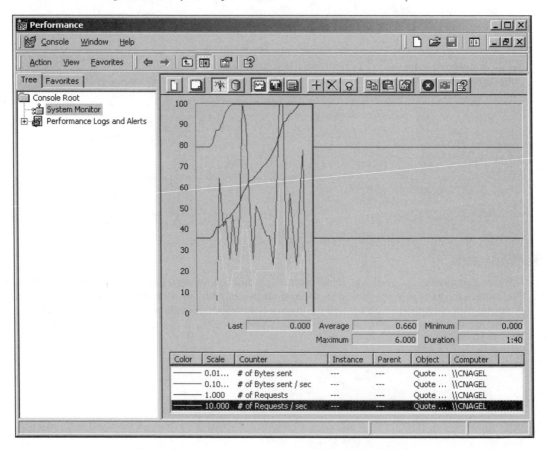

Performance Counter Service

If there's no reference to the performance counter object, and the object is garbage-collected, the count of this object is lost and starts the next time again with 0. To solve this, the state can be kept in a performance counter service. With the .NET Framework a performance counter service is installed on the system. It's just necessary to start the service; you can also configure the service to automatically start at boot time.

Windows 2000 Service Features

Windows 95, 98, and ME don't support Windows Services. Windows Services are supported within Windows NT, Windows 2000, and Windows XP. Windows 2000 has some more features for services than Windows NT had. Let's look into the features of services in Windows 2000.

Network Binding Changes and Power Events

With Windows 2000, it's not necessary that the system must be rebooted as often as it was necessary with Windows NT; for example, it's not necessary to reboot the system when the IP address changes. To make this possible, a service receives events when the address changes and can act accordingly. Windows 2000 sends these control codes to services when the network binding changes:

Control code	Description
SERVICE_CONTROL_NETBINDADD	A new component for binding is available.
SERVICE_CONTROL_NETBINDREMOVE	A component for binding has been removed. It's necessary to re-read the binding information and unbind from the removed component.
SERVICE_CONTROL_NETBINDENABLE	A previously disabled binding is enabled now.
SERVICE_CONTROL_NETBINDDISABLE	A previously enabled binding is disabled now.

If the service is using a binding it's necessary to re-read the binding information and remove the bindings which are no-longer available. The service can react to networking changes so a reboot is not necessary.

Windows 2000 also adds a lot of power management support. There's support to hibernate the system – the memory gets written to disk, so a faster boot is possible. It's also possible to suspend the system in order to reduce the power consumption, but it can automatically be awakened when needed.

For all power events, the service can receive the control code SERVICE_CONTROL_POWEREVENT with additional parameters. In the parameters the reason for the event can be found. The reason code can be battery low, system is going to the suspended state, or a power status change. Depending on the reason code the service should slow down, suspend background threads, close network connections, close files, and so on.

The classes in the System.ServiceProcess namespace have support for these Windows 2000 features, too. In the same way as we can configure a service so that it reacts to pause and continue events with the CanPauseAndContinue property we can also set a property for power management: CanHandlePowerEvent. Windows 2000 services that handle power events are registered in the SCM with the Win32 API method RegisterServiceCtrlHandlerEx().

With a `CanHandlePowerEvent` value of `true` the method:

```
protected virtual bool OnPowerEvent(PowerBroadcastStatus powerStatus);
```

will be called as soon as the power status changes. Some of the values we get from the `PowerBroadcastStatus` enumeration are listed in this table:

Value of **powerStatus**	Description
BatteryLow	The battery power is low. We should reduce the functionality of the service to a minimum.
PowerStatusChange	A switch from battery power to A/C happened, or the battery power slips below a threshold, and so on.
QuerySuspend	The system requests permissions to go into a suspended mode. We could deny the permissions, or prepare to go into the suspended mode by closing files, disconnecting network connections, etc.
QuerySuspendFailed	Change into the suspended mode was denied for the system. We can go on with the functionality as before.
Suspend	Nobody denied the request to go into the suspended mode. The system will be suspended soon.

Recovery

A feature that's just a configuration issue that can be used for all services running on the Windows 2000 system is automatic recovery. If a service process crashes then the service can be automatically restarted, or a special file can be configured to run, or the complete system can be automatically rebooted. There's usually a reason why a service crashes and therefore we don't want to automatically reboot the system continuously; we can differentiate responses to first, second, and subsequent failures.

We can configure the recovery options using the properties in the Computer Management MMC Administrator tool:

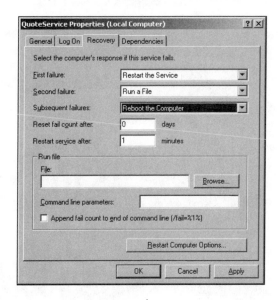

COM+ Applications as Services

Starting with Windows XP (codename Whistler) it's possible that a COM+ application can run as a service. What's the advantage of this? With Windows XP a service can have direct access to COM+ services like transactions, object pooling, thread pools, and so on. If we want to use COM+ Services with Windows 2000 in a Windows Service we have to build two separate applications: one application deals with the service functionality, the second with the COM+ services. Let's look at the advantages this brings us:

❑ It's easier to create a service application. We no longer have to deal with the service-specific installation as this can be done directly from the COM+ configuration.

❑ A COM+ application can act like a service. It can be automatically started at boot time, it can have the rights of the System account, and it can react to service control codes we are sending from a service control program.

❑ The service application that's created as a COM+ application can have direct access to the COM+ services like transaction management, object pooling, thread pools, and so on.

You can read more about COM+ services in Chapter 20.

Summary

In this chapter, we've seen what Windows Services are and how they can be created using the .NET Framework. Applications can start automatically at boot time with Windows Services, and we can use a privileged System account as user of the service. The .NET Framework has great support for services. All the plumbing code that's necessary for building, controlling, and installing services is built into the classes of the .NET Framework in the `System.ServiceProcess` namespace. Also, all the technologies needed for services like event logging and performance monitoring, no matter if you're using it for reading or writing, can be easily accessed using `System.Diagnostics` classes.

25

.NET Security

You're sitting at your machine and you click a button on an application you're using. Behind the scenes, your application responds to the fact that you are attempting to use a feature for which it does not have the relevant module. It connects to the Internet, downloads the module into the Global Assembly Cache and begins executing, and all without you being prompted.

This kind of behind-the-scenes upgrade functionality will become the norm in the not-too-distant future, but clearly there's a concern here over the security implications relating to what's often called **mobile code**. In clear terms, what evidence do we actually have that the code being downloaded can be trusted? How do we know that the module we requested is, in fact, the one that we've received? What does the CLR do behind the scenes to ensure that, for example, a control on a web site isn't reading our e-mails?

.NET enforces a security policy around assemblies. It uses the evidence it has about assemblies, for example where they're from or who they're published by, to split them into groups of code with similar characteristics. For example, all code from the local intranet is placed in a group. It then uses the security policy (normally defined by a system administrator using the caspol.exe command-line utility, or the Microsoft Management Console) to decide what permissions the code should be granted at a very granular level. What do you need to do to enable security on a machine or for a specific application? Nothing – all code automatically runs within the security context of the CLR, although you can turn security off if, for some reason, you need to.

In addition to high levels of confidence that the code we are executing can be trusted, it's also important to be sure that we are permitting the user of our application access to the features they need, but no more. Effective management of users and their roles is something else .NET can help us with by virtue of its role-based security.

In this chapter, we'll look through the features available in .NET to help us manage security, including how we're protected from malicious code, how we administer security policies and how we access the security sub-system programmatically. We'll also take a look at deploying .NET applications securely and see a number of short example applications that will solidify the concepts in this chapter for you.

Code Access Security

Code access security is a feature of .NET that manages code dependent on our trust level of it. If the CLR trusts the code enough to allow it to run, it will begin executing the code. Depending on the permissions provided to the assembly, however, it may run within a restricted environment. If the code is not trusted enough to run, or if it runs but then attempts to perform an action for which it does not have the relevant permissions, a security exception (of type SecurityException, or a subclass of it) is thrown. The code access security system means we can stop malicious code running, but we can also allow code to run within a protected environment where we're confident it can't do any damage.

For example, if a user attempted to run an application that attempted to execute code downloaded from the Internet, the default security policy would raise an exception and the application would fail to start. In a similar way, if the user ran an application from a network drive it would begin executing, but if the application then attempted to access a file on the local drive, an exception would be raised and, depending on the error handling in the application, it would either degrade gracefully or exit.

For most applications, .NET's code access security is a significant benefit but one that sits at the back of the room quietly helping us out. It provides high levels of protection from malicious code, but generally, we do not need to get involved. However, one area we will be involved in is the management of security policy, and this is especially true when configuring desktops to trust code from the locations of software suppliers who are delivering applications to us.

Another area where code access security is more important is where we are building an application that includes an element whose security we want to closely control. For example, if there is a database within your organization containing extremely sensitive data, you would use code access security so that the security policy can be used to state what code is allowed to access that database, and what code must not access it.

It's important to realize that code access security is about protecting resources (local drive, network, user interface) from malicious code; it is not primarily a tool for protecting software from users. For security in relation to users, you will generally use Windows 2000's built-in user security subsystem, or make use of .NET's role-based security, which we'll look at later in the chapter.

Code access security is based upon two high-level concepts; **Code Groups**, and **Permissions**. Let's look at these before we start as they form the foundations of what follows:

❑ **Code Groups** bring together code that has similar characteristics, although the most important property is usually where it came from. For example, code groups include "Internet" (code sourced from the Internet) and "Intranet" (code sourced from the LAN). Information used to place assemblies into code groups is called **evidence**. Other evidence is collected by the CLR, including the publisher of the code, its strong name and (where applicable) the URI from which it was downloaded. Code groups are arranged in a hierarchy, and assemblies are nearly always matched to several code groups. The code group at the root of the hierarchy is called "All Code" and contains all other code groups. The hierarchy is used in deciding which code groups an assembly belongs to; if an assembly does not provide evidence that matches it to a group in the tree, no attempt is made to match it to code groups below.

❑ **Permissions** are the actions that we allow each code group to perform. For example, permissions include "able to access the user interface" and "able to access local storage". The system administrator usually manages permissions, and this can be done at the Enterprise level, the Machine level, and the User level.

The Virtual Execution System within the CLR loads and runs programs. It provides the functionality needed to execute managed code and uses assembly metadata to connect modules together at run time. When the VES loads an assembly, it is matched to one or more of a number of code groups. Each code group is assigned one or more permissions that specify what actions assemblies in those code groups can do. For example, if the MyComputer code group is assigned the permission FileIOPermission, this means that assemblies from the local machine can read and write to the local file system.

Code Groups

Code groups have an entry requirement called a **Membership Condition**. For an assembly to be filed into a code group, it must match the group's membership condition. Membership conditions are things like "the assembly is from the site http://www.microsoft.com" or "the Publisher of this software is Microsoft Corporation".

Each code group has one, and only one, membership condition. Here are the types of code group membership conditions available in .NET:

❑ **Zone** – the region from which the code originated

❑ **Site** – the web site from which the code originated

❑ **Strong name** – a unique, verifiable name for the code, often called a 'shared name'

❑ **Publisher** – the publisher of the code

❑ **URL** – the specific location from which the code originated

❑ **Hash value** – the hash value for the assembly

❑ **Skip verification** – code that requests it bypasses the code verification checks

❑ **Application directory** – the location of the assembly within the application

❑ **All code** – all code fulfills this condition

❑ **Custom** – a user-specified condition

The first type of membership condition in the list is the **Zone** condition, which is one of the most commonly used. A zone is the region of origin of a piece of code and is one of the following: **MyComputer**, **Intranet**, **Trusted** or, **Untrusted**. These zones are managed using the Security Options in Internet Explorer, and we'll see more about these later in the chapter when we look at how to manage security policy. Although the settings are managed within Internet Explorer, they apply to the entire machine. Clearly, these configuration options are not available in non-Microsoft browsers and, in fact, in-page controls written using the .NET Framework will not work in browsers other than Internet Explorer.

Code groups are arranged in a hierarchy, with the All Code membership condition at the root:

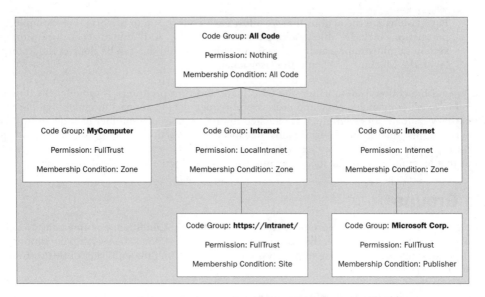

You can see that each code group has a single membership condition and specifies the permissions that the code group has been granted. We'll see more about permissions later. Note that if an assembly does not match the membership condition in a code group, the CLR does not attempt to match code groups below it.

Caspol.exe – Code Access Security Policy Tool

The command-line Code Access Security Policy tool is the one we'll spend the most time looking at in this chapter. It lets us view and manage security policy. To get a list of options for it, just type this command:

```
caspol.exe
```

.NET also includes a snap-in for the Microsoft Management Console to manage code access security; however, we will restrict ourselves to the command-line utility as the examples are easier to follow, and you'll also be in a position to create scripts to alter security policy, which is very useful when applying policy to large numbers of machines.

Let's have a look at the code groups on a machine using `caspol.exe`. The output of the command lists the hierarchical structure of the code groups on the machine, and next to each it gives a description of the code group. Type this command:

```
caspol.exe -listdescription
```

You will see something like this:

```
Microsoft (R) .NET Framework CasPol 1.0.xxxx.xx
Copyright (c) Microsoft Corp 1999-2001. All rights reserved.

Security is ON
```

```
Execution checking is ON
Policy change prompt is ON

Level = Machine

Full Trust Assemblies:

1. All_Code: This code group grants no permissions and forms the root of the code
group tree.
    1.1. My_Computer_Zone: This code group grants full trust to all code
originating on the local machine.
    1.2. LocalIntranet_Zone: This code group grants the intranet permission set to
code from the intranet zone. This permission set grants intranet code the right to
use isolated storage, full UI access, some capability to do reflection and limited
access to environment variables.
        1.2.1. Intranet_Same_Site_Access: All intranet Code gets the right to
connect back to the site of its origin.
        1.2.2. Intranet_Same_Directory_Access: All intranet code gets the right to
read from its install directory.
    1.3. Internet_Zone: This code group grants code from the Internet zone the
Internet permission set. This permission set grants Internet code the right the
use isolated storage and limited UI access.
        1.3.1. Internet_Same_Site_Access: All Internet Code gets the right to
connect back to the site of its origin.
    1.4. Restricted_Zone: Code coming from a restricted zone does not receive any
permissions.
    1.5. Trusted_Zone: Code from a trusted zone is granted the Internet permission
set. This permission set grants the right the use isolated storage and limited UI
access.
        1.5.1. Trusted_Same_Site_Access: All Trusted Code gets the right to connect
back to the site of its origin.
    1.6. Microsoft_Strong_Name: This code group grants code signed with the
Microsoft strong name full trust.
    1.7. Standards_Strong_Name: This code group grants code signed with the
Standards strong name full trust.
Success
```

The .NET security subsystem ensures that code from each code group is allowed to do only certain things. For example, code from the Internet zone will, by default, have much stricter limits than code from the local drive. For example, code from the local drive is normally granted access to data stored on the local drive, but assemblies from the Internet are not granted this permission by default.

Using caspol, and its equivalent in the Microsoft Management Console, we can specify what level of trust we have for each code access group, as well as managing code groups and permissions in a more granular fashion.

Let's take another look at the code access groups, but this time in a slightly more compact view. Make sure you're logged in as a local Administrator, open up a command prompt, and type this command:

```
caspol.exe -listgroups
```

You will see something like this:

```
Microsoft (R) .NET Framework CasPol 1.0.xxxx.x
Copyright (c) Microsoft Corp 1999-2001. All rights reserved.

Security is ON
Execution checking is ON
Policy change prompt is ON

Level = Machine

Code Groups:

1.  All code: Nothing
    1.1.  Zone - MyComputer: FullTrust
    1.2.  Zone - Intranet: FullTrust
       1.2.1.  All code: Same site Socket and Web.
       1.2.2.  All code: Same directory FileIO - Read, PathDiscovery
    1.3.  Zone - Internet: Internet
       1.3.1.  All code: Same site Socket and Web.
    1.4.  Zone - Untrusted: Nothing
    1.5.  Zone - Trusted: Internet
       1.5.1.  All code: Same site Socket and Web.
    1.6.  StrongName -
0024000004800000940000000602000000240000525341310004000001000100007D1FA57C4AED9F0A3
2E84AA0FAEFD0DE9E8FD6AEC8F87FB03766C834C99921EB23BE79AD9D5DCC1DD9AD236132102900B72
3CF980957FC4E177108FC607774F29E8320E92EA05ECE4E821C0A5EFE8F1645C4C0C93C1AB99285D62
2CAA652C1DFAD63D745D6F2DE5F17E5EAF0FC4963D261C8A12436518206DC093344D5AD293:
FullTrust
    1.7.  StrongName - 0000000000000000040000000000000000: FullTrust
Success
```

You'll notice that near the start of the output it says, Security is ON. Later in the chapter, we see that it can be turned off and then back on.

The Execution Checking setting is on by default, which means all assemblies must be granted the permission to execute before they can run. If execution checking is turned off using caspol (caspol.exe –execution on|off), assemblies that do not have the permission to run can execute, although they may well cause security exceptions if they attempt to act contrary to the security policy later in their execution.

The Policy change prompt option specifies whether we see an "Are you sure" warning message when we attempt to alter the security policy.

As code is broken down into these groups, we can manage security at a more granular level, and apply full trust to a much smaller percentage of code. Note that each group has a label (such as "1.2"). These labels are auto-generated by .NET, and can differ between machines. We do not generally manage security for each assembly; we do it using a code group.

You may be curious how caspol.exe operates when a machine has several side-by-side installations of .NET. Under these circumstances, the copy of caspol.exe that you run will only alter the security policy for its associated installation of .NET. To keep security policy management simpler, you may well want to remove previous copies of .NET as you install successive versions.

Viewing an Assembly's Code Groups

Assemblies are matched to code groups dependent upon the membership conditions they match. If we go back to our example code groups and load an assembly from the https://intranet/ web site, it would match code groups like this:

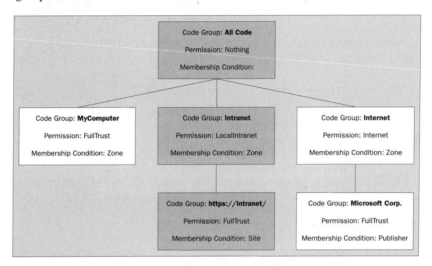

The assembly, as with all others, is a member of the root code group (All Code); as it came from the local network it is also a member of the Intranet code group; but as it was loaded from the specific site https://intranet it is also granted FullTrust, which means it can run unrestricted.

We can easily view the code groups that an assembly is a member of using a command like this:

```
caspol.exe -resolvegroup assembly.dll
```

Running this command on an assembly on the local drive, produces output like this:

```
Microsoft (R) .NET Framework CasPol 1.0.2728.0
Copyright (c) Microsoft Corp 1999-2001. All rights reserved.

Level = Enterprise
Code Groups:
1.  All code: FullTrust

Level = Machine
Code Groups:
1.  All code: Nothing
   1.1.  Zone - MyComputer: FullTrust

Level = User
Code Groups:
1.  All code: FullTrust

Success
```

1073

You'll notice that code groups are listed on three levels – **Enterprise**, **Machine**, and **User**. For now, just stay focused on the Machine level. We'll look at the other two in much more detail later in the chapter. If you are curious about the relationship between the three, the effective permission given to an assembly is the intersection of the permissions from the three levels. For example, if you remove the `FullTrust` permission from the Internet zone at the Enterprise-level policy, all permissions are revoked for code from the Internet zone, and the settings of the other two levels become irrelevant.

Now let's use this command against the same assembly, but across HTTP to a remote server, we'll see the assembly is a member of different groups which have much more restrictive permissions:

```
caspol.exe -resolvegroup http://server/assembly.dll


Microsoft (R) .NET Framework CasPol 1.0.2728.0
Copyright (c) Microsoft Corp 1999-2001. All rights reserved.

Level = Enterprise
Code Groups:
1.  All code: FullTrust

Level = Machine
Code Groups:
1.  All code: Nothing
    1.1.  Zone - Internet: Internet
        1.1.1.  All code: Same site Socket and Web.

Level = User
Code Groups:
1.  All code: FullTrust

Success
```

This time we can see that the intersection of the permissions the assembly grants the `Internet` permissions and the `Same Site Socket` and `Web` permissions.

Let's take a closer look at permissions – the freedom we allow assemblies matched to each code group.

Code Access Permissions & Permissions Sets

Imagine yourself administering security policy on a network of desktop machines in a large enterprise scenario. In this environment it's clearly immensely useful for the CLR to collect evidence on code before it executes it, but equally, you as the administrator must have the opportunity to strictly control what code is allowed to do on the several hundred machines you manage once the CLR knows where it came from. This is where permissions come into the equation.

Once an assembly has been matched to code groups, the CLR looks at the security policy to calculate the permissions it grants to an assembly. This is really much as with Windows 2000 user account security; we generally don't apply permissions to users, we apply permissions to groups. The same is true with assemblies; we apply permissions to code groups rather than individual assemblies, which makes the management of security policy in .NET a much easier task.

The security policy specifies what actions assemblies in a code group are permitted to perform. Let's look at the code access permissions provided by the CLR. As you can see from the following list, there are many of them, giving us a high degree of control over what code is allowed to do or not allowed to do:

- ❑ **DirectoryServicesPermission** – the ability to access Active Directory through the `System.DirectoryServices` classes

- ❑ **DnsPermission** – the ability to use the TCP/IP Domain Name System (DNS)

- ❑ **EnvironmentPermission** – the ability to read and write environment variables

- ❑ **EventLogPermission** – the ability to read and write to the event log

- ❑ **FileDialogPermission** – the ability to access files that have been selected by the user in the Open dialog box

- ❑ **FileIOPermission** – the ability to work with files (reading, writing, and appending to file, as well as creating and altering folders)

- ❑ **IsolatedStorageFilePermission** – the ability to access private virtual file systems

- ❑ **IsolatedStoragePermission** – the ability to access isolated storage: storage that is associated with an individual user and with some aspect of the code's identity, such as its web site, signature, or publisher

- ❑ **MessageQueuePermission** – the ability to use message queues through the Microsoft Message Queue

- ❑ **OleDbPermission** – the ability to access databases with OLE DB

- ❑ **PerformanceCounterPermission** – the ability to make use of performance counters

- ❑ **PrintingPermission** – the ability to print

- ❑ **ReflectionPermission** – the ability to discover information about a type at run time using `System.Reflection`

- ❑ **RegistryPermission** – the ability to read, write, create, or delete registry keys and values

- ❑ **SecurityPermission** – the ability to execute, assert permissions, call into unmanaged code, skip verification, and other rights

- ❑ **ServiceControllerPermission** – the ability to access (running or stopped) Windows Services

- ❑ **SocketPermission** – the ability to make or accept TCP/IP connections on a transport address

- ❑ **SQLClientPermission** – the ability to access SQL databases

- ❑ **UIPermission** – the ability to access the user interface

- ❑ **WebPermission** – the ability to make or accept connections to/from the web

With each of these permission classes, we can often specify an even deeper level of granularity. For example, later in the chapter you'll see an example of requesting not just file access, but a specific level of file access.

In terms of best practice, you are well advised to ensure any attempts to make use of the resources relating to the permissions in this list are enclosed within try-catch error handling blocks, so that your application degrades gracefully should it be running under restricted permissions. The design of your application should specify how your application should act under these circumstances; you should not assume that it will be running under the same security policy under which you develop it. For example, if your application cannot access the local drive, should it exit, or operate in an alternative fashion?

An assembly will be associated with several code groups; the effective permission of an assembly within the security policy is the union of all permissions from all the code groups to which it belongs. That is, each code group that an assembly matches will extend what it is allowed to do. Do note that code groups down the tree will often assign more relaxed permissions than those above.

There is another a set of permissions that are assigned by the CLR on the basis of the identity of the code, which cannot be explicitly granted. These permissions relate directly to the evidence the CLR has collated about the assembly, and are called **Identity Permissions**. Here are the names of the classes for the identity permissions:

- ❏ **PublisherIdentityPermission** – the software publisher's digital signature
- ❏ **SiteIdentityPermission** – the location of the web site from which the code originated
- ❏ **StrongNameIdentityPermission** – the assembly's strong name
- ❏ **URLIdentityPermission** – the URL from which the code came (including the protocol, for example, `https://`)
- ❏ **ZoneIdentityPermission** – the zone from which the assembly originates

Usually, we'll apply permissions in blocks, which is why .NET also gives us **Permission Sets**. These are lists of code access permissions grouped into a named set. Here are the named permission sets we get straight out of the box:

- ❏ **FullTrust** – no permission restrictions.
- ❏ **Execution** – the ability to run, but not to access any protected resources.
- ❏ **Nothing** – no permissions and unable to execute.
- ❏ **LocalIntranet** – the default policy for the local intranet, a subset of the full set of permissions. You can alter this permission set.
- ❏ **Internet** – the default policy for code of unknown origin. The administrator can manage the permissions in this permission set.
- ❏ **Everything** – all the standard permissions, except the permission to skip code verification. The administrator can alter the permissions in this permission set. This is useful where the default policy needs to be tighter.

   Do note that of these you can only change the definitions of the last three – the first three are fixed and cannot be changed.

Identity permissions cannot be included in permission sets because the CLR is the only body able to grant identity permissions to code. For example, if a piece of code is from a specific publisher, it would make little sense for the administrator to give it the identity permissions associated with another publisher. The CLR grants identity permissions where necessary, and we can then make use of them if we wish.

Viewing an Assembly's Permissions

Imagine you're using an application written by Microsoft, and you attempt to use a feature that you have not used before. The application does not have a copy of the code stored locally, so it requests it and the code is then downloaded into the Global Assembly Cache. Under a scenario like this, with code from the Internet published by a named organization that has signed the assembly with a certificate, we'll find the assembly's code group membership looks something like this:

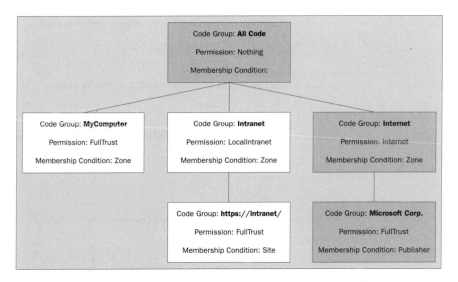

According to our policy in this example, although the All Code and Internet code groups bring only limited permissions, membership of the code group in the bottom right-hand corner grants the assembly the FullTrust permission. The overall effective permission is the **union** of permissions across the matching code groups. When the permissions are merged in this way, the effective permission is that of the highest permissions granted. That is, each code group an assembly belongs to brings additional permissions.

Just as we can look at the code groups an assembly belongs to, we can also look at the permissions assigned to the code groups to which it belongs. When we do this we'll see not only the code access permissions (what the code is allowed to do), but also the code identity permissions that will give us access to the evidence the code presented to the runtime. To see the permissions for an assembly's code groups, we use a command like this:

```
caspol.exe -resolveperm assembly.dll
```

Let's try this on an assembly, and look at the code access and identity permissions it is granted when we access it over a local intranet. If we type the following command we see the code access permissions and then the three identity permissions at the end:

```
caspol.exe -resolveperm http://intranet/assembly.dll
```

```
Microsoft (R) .NET Framework CasPol 1.0.xxxx.x
Copyright (c) Microsoft Corp 1999-2001. All rights reserved.

Resolving permissions for level = Enterprise
Resolving permissions for level = Machine
Resolving permissions for level = User

Grant =
<PermissionSet  class="System.Security.PermissionSet"
                version="1">
```

1077

```
        <IPermission class="System.Security.Permissions.EnvironmentPermission,
                mscorlib,
                Version=1.0.xxxx.x, Culture=neutral,
                PublicKeyToken=b77a5c561934e089"
                version="1"
                Read="USERNAME;TEMP;TMP"/>
        <IPermission class="System.Security.Permissions.FileDialogPermission, mscorlib,
                Version=1.0.xxxx.x, Culture=neutral,
                PublicKeyToken=b77a5c561934e089"
                version="1"
                Unrestricted="true"/>
        <IPermission class="System.Security.Permissions.IsolatedStorageFilePermission,
                mscorlib, Version=1.0.xxxx.x, Culture=neutral,
                PublicKeyToken=b77a5c561934e089"
                version="1"
                Allowed="AssemblyIsolationByUser"
                UserQuota="9223372036854775807"
                Expiry="9223372036854775807"
                Permanent="True"/>
        <IPermission class="System.Security.Permissions.ReflectionPermission, mscorlib,
                Version=1.0.xxxx.x, Culture=neutral,
                PublicKeyToken=b77a5c561934e089"
                version="1"
                Flags="ReflectionEmit"/>
        <IPermission class="System.Security.Permissions.SecurityPermission, mscorlib,
                Version=1.0.xxxx.x, Culture=neutral,
                PublicKeyToken=b77a5c561934e089"
                version="1"
                Flags="Assertion, Execution, RemotingConfiguration"/>
        <IPermission class="System.Security.Permissions.UIPermission, mscorlib,
                Version=1.0.xxxx.x, Culture=neutral,
                PublicKeyToken=b77a5c561934e089"
                version="1"
                Unrestricted="true"/>
        <IPermission class="System.Net.WebPermission, System,
                Version=1.0.xxxx.x, Culture=neutral,
                PublicKeyToken=b77a5c561934e089"version="1">
      <ConnectAccess>
         <URI uri="(https|http)://intranet/.*"/>
      </ConnectAccess>
    </IPermission>
    <IPermission class="System.Net.DnsPermission, System, Version=1.0.xxxx.x,
     Culture=neutral,
                PublicKeyToken=b77a5c561934e089"
                version="1"
                Unrestricted="true"/>
        <IPermission class="System.Drawing.Printing.PrintingPermission, System.Drawing,
                Version=1.0.xxxx.x, Culture=neutral,
                PublicKeyToken=b03f5f7f11d50a3a"
                version="1"
                Level="DefaultPrinting"/>
        <IPermission class="System.Diagnostics.EventLogPermission, System,
                Version=1.0.xxxx.x, Culture=neutral,
                PublicKeyToken=b77a5c561934e089"
                version="1">
      <Machine  name="."
                access="Instrument"/>
    </IPermission>
        <IPermission class="System.Security.Permissions.SiteIdentityPermission,
                mscorlib,
                Version=1.0.xxxx.x, Culture=neutral,
                PublicKeyToken=b77a5c561934e089"
                version="1"
                Site="intranet"/>

 <IPermission class="System.Security.Permissions.UrlIdentityPermission,
                mscorlib,
                Version=1.0.xxxx.x, Culture=neutral,
```

```
        PublicKeyToken=b77a5c561934e089"
                    version="1"
                    Url="http://intranet/assembly.dll"/>
    <IPermission class="System.Security.Permissions.ZoneIdentityPermission,
                    mscorlib,
                    Version=1.0.xxxx.x, Culture=neutral,
                    PublicKeyToken=b77a5c561934e089"
                    version="1"
                    Zone="Intranet"/>
  </PermissionSet>

  Success
```

The output shows each of the permissions in XML, including the class defining the permission, the assembly containing the class, the permission version, and an encryption token. The output suggests it is possible for us to create our own permissions, and you'll see more about that later. We can also see that each of the identity permissions includes more detailed information on, for example, the `UrlIdentityPermission` class, which provides access to the URL from which the code originated.

Note how at the start of the output `caspol.exe` resolved the permissions at the `Enterprise`, `Machine`, and `User` levels and then listed the effective granted permissions. Let's look at these now.

Policy Levels: Machine, User, and Enterprise

Up to now we have looked at security in the context of a single machine. It's often necessary to specify security policies for specific users or for an entire organization, and that is why .NET provides not one, but three levels of code groups:

❑ Machine

❑ Enterprise

❑ User

The code group levels are independently managed and exist in parallel:

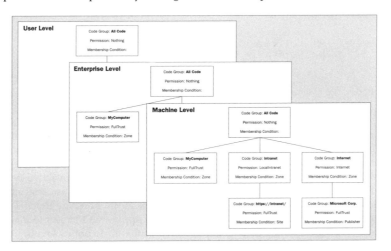

If there are three security policies, how do we know which applies? The effective permission is the **intersection** of the permissions from the three levels. Each of the three levels has the ability to veto the permissions allowed by another – this is clearly good news for administrators as their settings will override user settings.

To work with code groups and permissions on the user or enterprise levels using caspol.exe, add either the –enterprise or –user argument to change the command's mode. caspol.exe works at the Machine level by default and that's how we've been using it up to now. Let's see the code groups listing at the User level:

    caspol.exe –user –listgroups

The output of the command on a default installation looks like this:

```
Security is ON
Execution checking is ON
Policy change prompt is ON

Level = User

Code Groups:

1.  All code: FullTrust
Success
```

Now let's run the same command, but this time to see the code groups at the Enterprise level:

    caspol.exe –enterprise –listgroups

The output of the command looks like this:

```
Security is ON
Execution checking is ON
Policy change prompt is ON

Level = Enterprise

Code Groups:

1.  All code: FullTrust
Success
```

As you can see, by default, both the User level and the Enterprise level are configured to allow FullTrust for the single code group All Code. The result of this is that the default setting for .NET security places no restrictions at the Enterprise or User level, and the enforced policy is dictated solely by the machine-level policy. For example, if we were to assign a more restrictive permission or permission set to either the enterprise or user levels than FullTrust, those restrictions would restrict the overall permissions, and probably override permissions at the Machine level. The effective permissions are intersected, so, for example, if we want to apply FullTrust to a code group, that permission must be assigned to the code group on each of the three policy levels.

When we run `caspol.exe` as an administrator, it defaults to the Machine level, but if we log out and log back in as a user who is not in the Administrator user group, `caspol.exe` will instead default to the User level. In addition, `caspol.exe` will not allow us to alter the security policy in a way that renders the `caspol.exe` utility itself inoperable.

Now we've had a high-level look at the security architecture in .NET, let's look at how we can access its features programmatically.

Support for Security in the Framework

For .NET security to work, we must, as programmers, trust the CLR to enforce the security policy. How does it do this? When a call is made to a method that demands specific permissions (for example, accessing a file on the local drive), the CLR will walk up the stack to ensure that every caller in the call chain has the permissions being demanded.

The word "performance" is probably ringing in your mind at this point, and clearly that is a concern, but to gain the benefits of a managed environment like .NET this is the price we pay. The alternative is that assemblies that are not fully trusted could make calls to trusted assemblies and our system is open to attack.

For reference, the parts of the .NET Framework library namespace most applicable to this chapter are:

❑   `System.Security.Permissions`

❑   `System.Security.Policy`

❑   `System.Security.Principal`

Note that evidence-based code access security works in tandem with Windows logon security. If you attempt to run a .NET desktop application, it must be granted the relevant .NET code access security permissions, but you as the logged-in user must also be running under a Windows account that has the relevant permissions to execute the code. With desktop applications, this means the current user must have been granted the relevant rights to access the relevant assembly files on the drive. For Internet applications, the account under which Internet Information Server is running must have access to the assembly files.

Demanding Permissions

Let's create a Windows Forms application that contains a button that, when clicked, will perform an action that accesses the drive. Let's say, for example, that if the application does not have the relevant permission to access the local drive (`FileIOPermission`), we will mark the button as unavailable (grayed).

In the code that follows, look at the constructor for the form that creates a `FileIOPermission` object, calls its `Demand()` method, and then acts on the result:

```
using System;
using System.Drawing;
using System.Collections;
using System.ComponentModel;
using System.Windows.Forms;
```

```
using System.Data;
using System.Security;
using System.Security.Permissions;

namespace SecurityApp4
{
    public class Form1 : System.Windows.Forms.Form
    {
        private System.Windows.Forms.Button button1;
        private System.ComponentModel.Container components;
        public Form1()
        {
            InitializeComponent();
            try
            {
                FileIOPermission fileioperm = new
                    FileIOPermission(FileIOPermissionAccess.AllAccess,@"C:\");
                fileioperm.Demand();
            }
            catch
            {
                button1.Enabled = false;
            }
        }
        public override void Dispose()
        {
            base.Dispose();
            if(components != null)
                components.Dispose();
        }
        #region Windows Form Designer generated code

        /// <summary>
        /// Required method for Designer support - do not modify
        /// the contents of this method with the code editor.
        /// </summary>

        private void InitializeComponent()
        {
            this.button1 = new System.Windows.Forms.Button();
            this.SuspendLayout();

            //
            // button1
            //

            this.button1.Location = new System.Drawing.Point(48, 104);
            this.button1.Name = "button1";
            this.button1.Size = new System.Drawing.Size(192, 23);
            this.button1.TabIndex = 0;
            this.button1.Text = "Button Requires FileIOPermission";

            //
            // Form1
            //
```

```
            this.AutoScaleBaseSize = new System.Drawing.Size(5, 13);
            this.ClientSize = new System.Drawing.Size(292, 273);
            this.Controls.AddRange(new System.Windows.Forms.Control[]
                                    {this.button1});
            this.Name = "Form1";
            this.Text = "Form1";
            this.ResumeLayout(false);
        }
        #endregion

        /// <summary>
        /// The main entry point for the application.
        /// </summary>

        [STAThread]
        static void Main()
        {
            Application.Run(new Form1());
        }
    }
}
```

You'll notice that FileIOPermission is contained within the System.Security.Permissions namespace, which is home to the full set of permissions, and also provides classes for declarative permission attributes and enumerations for the parameters used to create permissions objects (for example, when creating a FileIOPermission specifying whether we need full access, or read-only).

If we run the application from the local drive where the default security policy allows access to local storage, the application will appear like this:

However, if we copy the executable to a network share and run it again, we're operating within the LocalIntranet permission sets, which blocks access to local storage, and the button will be grayed:

If we implemented the functionality to make the button access the disk when we click it, we would not have to write any security code, as the relevant class in the .NET Framework will demand the file permissions, and the CLR will ensure each caller up the stack has those permissions before proceeding. If we were to run our application from the intranet, and it attempted to open a file on the local disk, we would see an exception unless the security policy had been altered to grant access to the local drive.

If you want to catch exceptions thrown by the CLR when code attempts to act contrary to its granted permissions, you can catch the exception of the type `SecurityException`, which provides access to a number of useful pieces of information including a human-readable stack trace (`SecurityException.StackTrace`) and a reference to the method that threw the exception (`SecurityException.TargetSite`). `SecurityException` even provides us with the `SecurityException.PermissionType` property that returns the type of `Permission` object that caused the security exception to occur. If you're having problems diagnosing security exceptions, this should be one of your first ports of call.

Requesting Permissions

As you saw above, demanding permissions is where you state quite clearly what you need at run time; however, you can configure an assembly so it makes a softer request for permissions right at the start of execution where it states what it needs before it begins executing.

You can request permissions in three ways:

❑ **Minimum** Permissions – the permissions your code must have to run

❑ **Optional** Permissions – the permissions your code can use but is able to run effectively without

❑ **Refused** Permissions – the permissions that you want to ensure are not granted to your code

Why would you want to request permissions when your assembly starts? There are several reasons:

❑ If your assembly needs certain permissions to run, it makes sense to state this at the start of execution rather than during execution

❑ You will only be granted the permissions you request and no more, which reduces the risks of your assembly affecting areas for which it does not have permissions

❑ If you only request a minimum set of permissions, you are increasing the likelihood that your assembly will run

Requesting permissions is likely to be most useful if you're doing more complex deployment, and there is a higher risk that your application will be installed on a machine that does not grant the requisite permissions. It's usually preferable for the application to know right at the start of execution where it not been granted permissions, rather than partway through execution.

To successfully request the permissions your assembly needs, you must keep track of exactly what permissions your assembly is using. In particular, you must be aware of the permission requirements of the calls your assembly is making into other class libraries, including the .NET Framework.

Let's look at three examples from an `AssemblyInfo.cs` file, demonstrating using attributes to request permissions. If you are following this with the code download, these examples can be found in the `SecurityApp9` project. The first attribute requests that the assembly have `UIPermission` granted, which will allow the application access to the user interface. The request is for the minimum permissions, so if this permission is not granted the assembly will fail to start:

```
using System.Security.Permissions;
[assembly:UIPermissionAttribute(SecurityAction.RequestMinimum)]
```

Next, we have a request that the assembly be refused access to the C:\ drive. This attribute's setting means the entire assembly will be blocked from accessing this drive:

```
[assembly:FileIOPermissionAttribute(SecurityAction.RequestRefuse, Read="C:\\")]
```

Finally, here's an attribute that requests our assembly be optionally granted the permission to access unmanaged code:

```
[assembly:SecurityPermissionAttribute(SecurityAction.RequestOptional,
                    Flags = SecurityPermissionFlag.UnmanagedCode)]
```

In this scenario we would add this attribute to an application that accesses unmanaged code in at least one place. In this case, we have specified that this permission is optional, the suggestion being that the application can run without the permission to access unmanaged code. If the assembly is not granted permission to access unmanaged code, and attempts to do so, a SecurityException will be raised, which the application should expect and handle accordingly.

When we are considering the permission requirements of our application, we usually have to decide between one of two options:

❑ Request all the permissions we need at the start of execution, and degrade gracefully or exit if those permissions are not granted

❑ Avoid requesting permissions at the start of execution, but be prepared to handle security exceptions throughout our application

Once an assembly has been configured using permission attributes in this way, we can use the permview.exe utility to view the permissions by aiming it at the assembly file containing the assembly manifest:

permview.exe assembly.dll

The output for an application using the three attributes we have been through looks like this:

```
minimal permission set:
<PermissionSet class="System.Security.PermissionSet"
        version="1">
    <IPermission class="System.Security.Permissions.UIPermission,
        mscorlib, Version=1.0.2411.0, Culture=neutral,
        PublicKeyToken=b77a5c561934e089" version="1" Unrestricted="true"/>
</PermissionSet>
optional permission set:
<PermissionSet class="System.Security.PermissionSet"
        version="1">
    <IPermission class="System.Security.Permissions.SecurityPermission,
        mscorlib, Version=1.0.2411.0, Culture=neutral,
        PublicKeyToken=b77a5c561934e089" version="1"
        Flags="UnmanagedCode"/>
</PermissionSet>
refused permission set:
<PermissionSet class="System.Security.PermissionSet"
        version="1">
    <IPermission class="System.Security.Permissions.FileIOPermission,
        mscorlib, Version=1.0.2411.0, Culture=neutral,
        PublicKeyToken=b77a5c561934e089" version="1" Read="C:\"/>
</PermissionSet>
```

In addition to requesting permissions, we can also request permissions sets, the advantage being that we can request a whole set of permissions all at once. As some permission sets (Internet, LocalIntranet, and Everything) can be altered through the security policy while an assembly is running, they cannot be requested. For example, if an assembly requested at run time that it must be granted all permissions in the LocalIntranet permission set to execute, and the administrator then tightened the LocalIntranet permission set while the application is running, they might be unaware that it is still operating with a wider set of permissions than the policy dictates.

There are three permission sets that cannot be altered while an application is executing; these are the permissions sets that can be requested using attributes:

- ❑ Nothing
- ❑ Execution
- ❑ FullTrust

Here's an example, of how to request a built-in permission set:

```
[assembly:PermissionSetAttribute(SecurityAction.RequestMinimum,
                                 Name = "FullTrust")]
```

In this example the assembly requests that as a minimum it be granted the FullTrust built-in permission set. If it is not granted this set of permissions, the assembly will throw a security exception at run time.

Implicit Permission

When permissions are granted, there is often an implicit statement that we are also granted other permissions. For example, if we are assigned the FileIOPermission for C:\ there is an implicit assumption that we also have access to its subdirectories (Windows account security allowing).

If you want to check whether a granted permission implicitly brings us another permission as a subset, you can do this:

```
// Example from SecurityApp5

class Class1
{
    static void Main(string[] args)
    {
        CodeAccessPermission permissionA =
            new FileIOPermission(FileIOPermissionAccess.AllAccess, @"C:\");
        CodeAccessPermission permissionB =
            new FileIOPermission(FileIOPermissionAccess.Read, @"C:\temp");
        if (permissionB.IsSubsetOf(permissionA))
        {
            Console.WriteLine("PermissionB is a subset of PermissionA");
        }
        else
        {
            Console.WriteLine("PermissionB is NOT a subset of PermissionA");
        }
    }
}
```

The output looks like this:

```
PermissionB is a subset of PermissionA
```

Denying Permissions

There will be circumstances under which we want to perform an action and be absolutely sure that the method we call is acting within a protected environment where it cannot do anything untoward. For example, let's say we want to make a call to a third-party class in a way that we are confident it will not access the local disk.

To do that, we create an instance of the permission we want to ensure the method is not granted, and then call its Deny() method before making the call to the class:

```
using System;
using System.IO;
using System.Security;
using System.Security.Permissions;
namespace SecurityApp6
{
    class Class1
    {
        static void Main(string[] args)
        {
            CodeAccessPermission permission =
                new FileIOPermission(FileIOPermissionAccess.AllAccess,@"C:\");
            permission.Deny();
            UntrustworthyClass.Method();
            CodeAccessPermission.RevertDeny();
        }
    }
    class UntrustworthyClass
    {
        public static void Method()
        {
            try
            {
                StreamReader din = File.OpenText(@"C:\textfile.txt");
            }
            catch
            {
                Console.WriteLine("Failed to open file");
            }
        }
    }
}
```

If you build this code the output will state Failed to open file, as the untrustworthy class does not have access to the local disk.

Note that the Deny() call is made on an instance of the permission object, whereas the RevertDeny() call is made statically. The reason for this is that the RevertDeny() call reverts all deny requests within the current stack frame; this means if you have made several calls to Deny() you only need make one follow-up call to RevertDeny().

Asserting Permissions

Imagine that we have an assembly that has been installed with full trust on a user's system. Within that assembly is a method that saves auditing information to a text file on the local disk. If we later install an application that wants to make use of the auditing feature, it will be necessary for the application to have the relevant `FileIOPermission` permissions to save the data to disk.

This seems excessive, however, as really all we want to do is perform a highly restricted action on the local disk. At times like these, it would be useful if assemblies with limiting permissions could make calls to more trusted assemblies, which can temporarily increase the scope of the permissions on the stack, and perform operations on behalf of the caller that it does not have the permissions to do itself.

To achieve this, assemblies with high enough levels of trust can assert permissions that they require. If the assembly has the permissions it needs to assert additional permissions, it removes the need for callers up the stack to have such wide-ranging permissions.

The code below contains a class called `AuditClass` that implements a method called `Save()`, which takes a string and saves audit data to `C:\audit.txt`. The `AuditClass` method asserts the permissions it needs to add the audit lines to the file. To test it out, the `Main()` method for the application explicitly denies the file permission that the `Audit` method needs:

```
using System;
using System.IO;
using System.Security;
using System.Security.Permissions;
namespace SecurityApp7
{
    class Class1
    {
        static void Main(string[] args)
        {
            CodeAccessPermission permission =
                    new FileIOPermission(FileIOPermissionAccess.Append,
                    @"C:\audit.txt");
            permission.Deny();
            AuditClass.Save("some data to audit");
            CodeAccessPermission.RevertDeny();
        }
    }
    class AuditClass
    {
        public static void Save(string value)
        {
            try
            {
                FileIOPermission permission =
                    new FileIOPermission(FileIOPermissionAccess.Append,
                    @"C:\audit.txt");
                permission.Assert();
                FileStream stream = new FileStream(@"C:\audit.txt",
                    FileMode.Append, FileAccess.Write);

                // code to write to audit file here...
```

```
            CodeAccessPermission.RevertAssert();
            Console.WriteLine("Data written to audit file");
        }
        catch
        {
            Console.WriteLine("Failed to write data to audit file");
        }
    }
  }
}
```

When this code is executed, you'll find the call to the `AuditClass` method does not cause a security exception, even though when it was called it did not have the required permissions to carry out the disk access.

As with `RevertDeny()`, `RevertAssert()` is a static method, and it reverts all assertions within the current frame.

It's important to be very careful when using assertions. We are explicitly assigning permissions to a method that has been called by code that may well not have those permissions. For example, in the auditing example, even if the security policy dictated that installed applications cannot write to the local disk, our application would be able to if the auditing functionality had been installed with full trust.

Creating Code Access Permissions

The .NET Framework implements code access security permissions that provide protection for the resources that it exposes. There may be occasions when you want to create your own permissions, however, and in that event you can do so by subclassing `CodeAccessPermission`. Deriving from this class gives you the benefits of the .NET code access security system, including stack walking and policy management.

Here are two examples of cases where you might want to roll your own code access permissions:

❑ **Protecting a resource not already protected by the Framework**. For example, you have developed a .NET application for home automation that is implemented using an onboard hardware device. By creating your own code access permissions, you have a highly granular level of control over the access given to the home automation hardware.

❑ **Providing a finer degree of management than existing permissions**. For example, although the .NET Framework provides permissions that allow granular control over access to the local file system, you may have an application where you want to control access to a specific file or folder much more tightly. In this scenario, you may find it useful to create a code access permission that relates specifically to that file or folder, and without that permission no managed code can access that area of the disk.

Declarative Security

You can deny, demand, and assert permissions by calling classes in the .NET Framework, but you can also use attributes and specify permission requirements declaratively.

The main benefit of using declarative security is that the settings are accessible via reflection. (It's also easier on the fingers as there's less to type!) Being able to access this information through reflection can be of enormous benefit to system administrators, who will often want to view the security requirements of applications.

For example, we can specify that a method must have permission to read from C:\ to execute:

```
using System;
using System.Security.Permissions;
namespace SecurityApp8
{
    class Class1
    {
        static void Main(string[] args)
        {
            MyClass.Method();
        }
    }

    [FileIOPermission(SecurityAction.Assert, Read="C:\\")]
    class MyClass
    {
        public static void Method()
        {

            // implementation goes here

        }
    }
}
```

Be aware that if you use attributes to assert or demand permissions, you cannot catch any exceptions that are raised if the action fails, as there is no imperative code around which you can place a try-catch-finally clause.

For more information on the attributes available to you, take a look at the System.Security.Permissions.SecurityAction enumeration.

Role-Based Security

As we have seen, code access security gives the CLR the ability to make intelligent decisions behind the scenes as to whether code should run or not and with what permissions based on the evidence it presents. In addition to this, .NET provides role-based security that specifies whether code can perform actions on the basis of evidence about the user and their role, rather than just the code. You'll probably be glad to hear that it does this without walking the stack!

Role-based security is especially useful in situations where access to resources is an issue, the primary example being the finance industry, where employees' roles define what information they can access and what actions they can perform.

Role-based security is also ideal for use in conjunction with Windows 2000 accounts, Microsoft Passport, or a custom user directory to manage access to web-based resources. For example, a web site could restrict access to its content until a user registers their details with the site, and then additionally provide access to special content only if the user is a paying subscriber. In many ways, ASP.NET makes role-based security easier because much of the code is based on the server.

For example, if we want to implement a web service that requires authentication, we could use Windows 2000's accounts subsystem and write the web method in such a way that it ensures the user is a member of a specific Windows 2000 user group before allowing access to the method's functionality.

The Principal

.NET gives the current thread easy access to the our application user, which it refers to as a `Principal`. The principal is at the core of the role-based security that .NET provides, and through it, we can access the user's `Identity`, which will usually map to a user account of one of these types:

❑ Windows account

❑ Passport account

❑ ASP.NET cookie-authenticated user

As an added bonus, the role-based security in .NET has been designed so that you can create your own principals by implementing the `IPrincipal` interface. If you are not relying on Windows authentication, Passport, or simple cookie authentication, you should look at creating your own using a custom `principal` class.

With access to the principal we can make security decisions based on the principal's identity and roles. A role is a collection of users who have the same security permissions, and is the unit of administration for users. For example, if we're using Windows authentication to authenticate our users, we will use the `WindowsIdentity` type as our choice of `Identity`. We can use that type to find out whether the user is a member of a specific Windows user account group, and we can then use that information to decide whether to grant or deny access to code and resources.

You'll generally find that it's much easier to manage security if you allow access to resources and functionality on the basis of permissions rather than roles. Imagine a scenario where you have three methods that each provide access to a feature over which you need tight control to ensure only authorized personnel can access it. If the application had, say, four users, we could quite easily specify within each method which users can and which users cannot access the method. However, imagine a time in the future where the number of features has extended to nine; to allow access to an additional user potentially requires changing every one of the nine methods even though this is an administrative task! Even worse, as users move between roles in the company we would need to change the code each time that happens too. If we had instead implemented the system using roles, we could then simply add and remove users from roles, rather than adding and removing individual users from the application. This simplifies the application, as for each method we simply request that the user be a member of a specific role. It also simplifies the management of roles, as the administrator can do it rather than the application developer. Put simply, the developer should be concerned with ensuring that, for example, Managers but not Secretaries can access a method, not that Julie and Bob can, but not Conrad.

.NET's role-based security builds on that provided in MTS and COM+ 1.0, and provides a flexible framework that can be used to build fences around sections of the application that need to be protected. If COM+ 1.0 is installed on a machine, its role-based security will interoperate with .NET; however, COM is not required for .NET's role-based security to function.

Windows Principal

Let's create a console application that gives us access to our principal in an application, where we want access to the underlying Windows account. We'll need to reference the System.Security.Principal and System.Threading namespaces. First of all, we must specify that we want .NET to automatically hook up our principal with the underlying Windows account, as .NET does not automatically do this for security reasons. We do that like this:

```
using System;
using System.Security.Principal;
using System.Security.Permissions;
using System.Threading;

namespace SecurityApplication2
{
    class Class1
    {
        static void Main(string[] args)
        {
            AppDomain.CurrentDomain.SetPrincipalPolicy(
                                    PrincipalPolicy.WindowsPrincipal);
```

It's possible to use WindowsIdentity.GetCurrent() to access the Windows account details; however, that method is best used when you're only going to look at the principal once. If you want to access the principal a number of times it is more efficient to set the policy so the current thread provides access to the principal for you. When we use the SetPrincipalPolicy method we are specifying that the principal in the current thread should hold a WindowsIdentity object for us.

Let's add some code to access the principal's properties from the Thread object:

```
            WindowsPrincipal principal =
                            (WindowsPrincipal)Thread.CurrentPrincipal;
            WindowsIdentity identity = (WindowsIdentity)principal.Identity;
            Console.WriteLine("IdentityType:" + identity.ToString());
            Console.WriteLine("Name:" + identity.Name);
            Console.WriteLine("'Users'?:" +
                            principal.IsInRole("BUILTIN\\Users"));
            Console.WriteLine("'Administrators'?:" +
                        principal.IsInRole(WindowsBuiltInRole.Administrator));
            Console.WriteLine("Authenticated:" + identity.IsAuthenticated);
            Console.WriteLine("AuthType:" + identity.AuthenticationType);
            Console.WriteLine("Anonymous?:" + identity.IsAnonymous);
            Console.WriteLine("Token:" + identity.Token);
        }
    }
}
```

The output from this console application will look something like this depending on your machine configuration and the roles associated with the account under which you're signed in:

```
IdentityType:System.Security.Principal.WindowsIdentity
Name:MACHINE\alaric
'Users'?:True
'Administrators'?:True
Authenticated:True
AuthType:NTLM
Anonymous?:False
Token:256
```

Clearly, it is enormously beneficial to be able to access details about the current user and their roles so easily, and using this information we can make decisions about what actions to permit and to deny. The ability to make use of roles and Windows user groups provides the added benefit that administration can be done using standard user administration tools, and we can usually avoid altering the code when user roles change. Let's look at roles in more detail.

Roles

Imagine a scenario where we have an intranet application relying on Windows accounts. The system has a group called Manager and one called Assistant; users are assigned to these groups dependent upon their role within the organization. Let's say our application contains a feature that displays information about employees that we only want those in the Managers group to access. We can easily use code that checks whether the current user is a member of the Managers group and permit or deny access based on this.

However, if we later decide to rearrange our account groups and introduce a group called Personnel that also has access to employee details, we have a problem. We have to go through all the code and update it to include rules for this new group.

A better solution would be to create a permission called something like ReadEmployeeDetails and assign it to groups where necessary. If our code applies a check for the ReadEmployeeDetails permission, to update the application to allow those in the Personnel group access to employee details is simply a matter of creating the group, placing the users in it, and assigning the ReadEmployeeDetails permission.

Declarative Role-Based Security

Just as with code access security, we can implement role-based security requests ("the user must be in the Administrators group") using imperative requests (as you saw in the preceding section), or using attributes. We can state permission requirements declaratively at the class level like this:

```
using System;
using System.Security;
using System.Security.Principal;
using System.Security.Permissions;

namespace SecurityApp3
{
    class Class1
    {
        static void Main(string[] args)
        {
AppDomain.CurrentDomain.SetPrincipalPolicy(PrincipalPolicy.WindowsPrincipal);
            try
            {
                ShowMessage();
            }
            catch (SecurityException exception)
            {
                Console.WriteLine("Security exception caught (" +
                                            exception.Message + ")");
```

```
                Console.WriteLine("The current principal must be in the local"
                                                    + "Users group");
        }
    }

    [PrincipalPermissionAttribute(SecurityAction.Demand, Role =
                                            "BUILTIN\\Users")]
    static void ShowMessage()
    {
        Console.WriteLine("The current principal is logged in locally ");
        Console.WriteLine("(they are a member of the local Users group)");
    }
  }
}
```

The ShowMessage() method will throw an exception unless we execute the application in the context of a user in the Windows 2000 local Users group. For a web application, the account under which the ASP.NET code is running must be in the group, although in a real-world example you would certainly avoid adding this account to the administrators group!

If you run the code above using an account in the local Users group, the output will look like this:

```
The current principal is logged in locally
(they are a member of the local Users group)
```

For more information on role-based security in .NET, your first stop should be the MSDN documentation for the System.Security.Principal namespace.

Managing Security Policy

Although .NET's security features are wide ranging and far in advance of anything seen before on Windows, there are some limitations that we should be aware of:

❑ .NET security policy does not enforce security on unmanaged code (although it provides some protection against calls to unmanaged code).

❑ If a user copies an assembly to their local machine, the assembly has FullTrust and security policy is effectively bypassed. To work around this, we can limit the permissions granted to local code.

❑ .NET security policy provides very little help in dealing with script-based viruses and malicious Win32 .EXE files, which Microsoft is dealing with in different ways. For example, recent versions of Outlook do no allow you to run executable files from e-mails – the user is warned they may contain a virus and forced to save them to disk where there are opportunities for administrative restraints to be installed, including blocking access to the local drive and providing an opportunity for anti-virus software to act.

However, .NET helps enormously in assisting the operating system in making intelligent decisions about how much trust to give to code, whether it is from an intranet application, a control on a web page, or a Windows Forms application downloaded from a software supplier on the Internet.

The Security Configuration File

As we've seen already, the glue that connects together code groups, permissions, and permission sets is our three levels of security policy (Enterprise, Machine, and User). Security configuration information in .NET is stored in XML configuration files that are protected by Windows security. For example, the Machine-level security policy is only accessible to users in the Administrator, Power User, and SYSTEM Windows 2000 groups.

On Windows 2000, the files that store the security policy are located in the following places:

Enterprise policy Configuration

C:\WinNT\Microsoft.NET\Framework\v1.0.xxxx\Config\enterprise.config

Machine policy configuration

C:\WinNT\Microsoft.NET\Framework\v1.0.xxxx\Config\security.config

User policy configuration

%USERPROFILE%\application data\Microsoft\CLR security config\vxx.xx\security.config

The version number marked with several 'x's will vary depending on the version of the .NET framework you have on your machine. If necessary, it's possible to manually edit these configuration files, for example, if an administrator needs to configure policy for a user without logging into their account. However, in general it's recommended to use caspol.exe or the MMC snap-in to manage security policy.

A Simple Example

Given everything you've read so far, let's create a simple application that accesses the local drive, the kind of behavior we're likely to want to manage carefully. The application is a C# Windows Forms application with a listbox and a button. If you click the button, the listbox is populated from a file called animals.txt in the root of the C:\ drive:

The application was created using Visual Studio.NET and the only changes were to add the listbox and
Load Data button to the form and to add an event to the button that looks like this:

```
// Example from SecurityApp1

private void button1_Click(object sender, System.EventArgs e)
{
    StreamReader stream = File.OpenText(@"C:\animals.txt");
    String str;
    while ((str=stream.ReadLine()) != null)
    {
        listBox1.Items.Add(str);
    }
}
```

It opens a simple text file from the root of the C:\ drive, which contains a list of animals on separate
lines, and loads each line into a string which it then uses to create each item in the listbox.

If we run the application from our local machine and click the button, we'll see the data loaded from the
root of the C:\ drive and displayed in the listbox as we'd expect. Behind the scenes the runtime has
granted our assembly the permission it needs to execute, access the user interface, and read data from
the local disk:

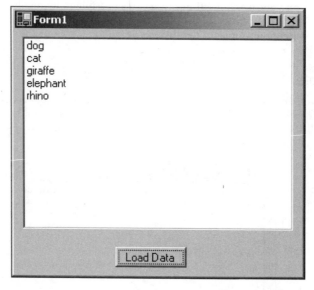

You may remember that the permissions on the intranet zone code group are more restrictive than on
the local machine, in particular, they do not allow access to the local disk (except in the folder from
which the application runs). If we run the application again, but this time from a network share, it will
run just as before as it is granted the permissions to execute and access the user interface, however, if we
now click the **Load Data** button on the form, a security exception is thrown:

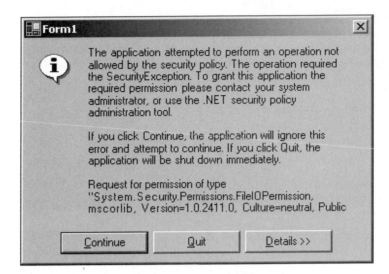

You'll see in the exception message text that it mentions the
System.Security.Permissions.FileIOPermission object; this is the permission that our
application was not granted that was demanded by the class in the Framework that we are using to load
the data from the file on the local disk.

By default, the Intranet code group is granted the LocalIntranet permission set; let's change the
permission set to FullTrust so any code from the intranet zone can run completely unrestricted using
this command:

```
caspol.exe -chggroup 1.2 FullTrust
```

If we now run the application from the network share again and click the button, we'll see that the
listbox is populated from the file in the root of the C:\ drive and no exception occurs:

In scenarios like these where we're making use of resources that are governed by permissions, it is advisable to extend the code so security exceptions are caught, so that the application can degrade gracefully. For example, in our application we can add a try-catch block around the file access code and if a `SecurityException` is thrown we display a line in the listbox saying, "Permission denied accessing file":

```
// Code from SecurityApp1

private void button1_Click(object sender, System.EventArgs e)
{
    try
    {
        StreamReader din = File.OpenText(@"C:\animals.txt");
        String str;
        while ((str=din.ReadLine()) != null)
        {
            listBox1.Items.Add(str);
        }
    }
    catch (SecurityException exception)
    {
        listBox1.Items.Add("Permission denied accessing file");
    }
}
```

In reality, if we wanted to run a specific application from a network share, we'd most likely opt for a solution that didn't open up our client machine to all code on the intranet. Instead, we would use code groups and membership conditions to tightly control the requirements of the application – perhaps using its location on the intranet, a strong name, or a certificate proving the identity of the publisher.

Managing Code Groups and Permissions

In managing security on .NET, we find that if an assembly is failing with a security exception we usually have three choices:

❑ Ease the policy permissions

❑ Move the assembly

❑ Apply a strong name to the assembly

When making these kinds of decisions you must take care to take into account your trust level of the assembly.

Turning Security On and Off

By default .NET security is enabled. If, for any reason, you need to turn it off, you can do it like this:

```
caspol.exe -security off
```

To turn security back on, use this:

```
caspol.exe -security on
```

Generally, the security risks inherent in opening a machine up by turning off security mean that it's only necessary to turn off security for testing and debugging. Something you should be aware of is that the command above does not need administrative privileges; this means any user (or a virus) could turn off .NET security. You are well advised to alter the Windows file security on the `caspol` utility to guard against malicious or misinformed usage.

Resetting Security Policy

If you need to revert the security configuration to its original state, you can type this command:

```
caspol.exe -reset
```

This command resets the security policy to the installation default.

Creating a Code Group

We can create our own code groups and then apply specific permissions to them. For example, we could specify that we want to trust all code from the web site www.wrox.com and give it full access to our system (without trusting code from any other web site). First, we need to get the numeric label of the code group within which our new code group will live:

```
caspol.exe -listgroups
```

This will output something like this:

```
Code Groups:
1.  All code: Nothing
    1.1.  Zone - MyComputer: FullTrust
    1.2.  Zone - Intranet: LocalIntranet
        1.2.1.  All code: Same site Socket and Web.
        1.2.2.  All code: Same directory FileIO - Read, PathDiscovery
    1.3.  Zone - Internet: Internet
        1.3.1.  All code: Same site Socket and Web.
    1.4.  Zone - Untrusted: Nothing
    1.5.  Zone - Trusted: Internet
        1.5.1.  All code: Same site Socket and Web.
...
```

Using the fact that Zone: Internet is labeled 1.3, we then type this command:

```
caspol.exe -addgroup 1.3 -site www.wrox.com FullTrust
```

Note that this command will ask for confirmation as we are attempting to explicitly alter the security policy on the machine. If we now run the caspol.exe -listgroups command again, we'll see the new code group has been added and assigned FullTrust:

```
Code Groups:
1.  All code: Nothing
    1.1.  Zone - MyComputer: FullTrust
    1.2.  Zone - Intranet: LocalIntranet
        1.2.1.  All code: Same site Socket and Web.
        1.2.2.  All code: Same directory FileIO - Read, PathDiscovery
    1.3.  Zone - Internet: Internet
        1.3.1.  All code: Same site Socket and Web.
        1.3.2.  Site - www.wrox.com: FullTrust
    1.4.  Zone - Untrusted: Nothing
    1.5.  Zone - Trusted: Internet
        1.5.1.  All code: Same site Socket and Web.
....
```

Let's look at another example. Let's say we want to create a code group under the Intranet code group (1.2) that grants FullTrust to all applications running from a specific network share:

```
caspol.exe -addgroup 1.2 -url file:///\\intranetserver/sharename/* FullTrust
```

Deleting a Code Group

To remove a code group we have created, we can type a command like this:

```
caspol.exe -remgroup 1.3.2
```

It will ask for confirmation that you want to alter the security policy, and if you give positive confirmation it will state that the group has been removed.

Be aware that although you cannot delete the code group `All Code`, it is possible to delete code groups at the level below, including the groups for `Internet`, `MyComputer`, and `LocalIntranet`.

Changing a Code Group's Permissions

To ease or restrict the permissions assigned to a code group, we can use `caspol.exe` again. Let's say we want to apply `FullTrust` to the `Intranet` zone, first we need to get the label that represents the `Intranet` code group:

```
caspol.exe -listgroups
```

The output shows the `Intranet` code group:

```
Code Groups:
1.  All code: Nothing
    1.1.   Zone - MyComputer: FullTrust
    1.2.   Zone - Intranet: LocalIntranet
        1.2.1.  All code: Same site Socket and Web.
        1.2.2.  All code: Same directory FileIO - Read, PathDiscovery
    1.3.   Zone - Internet: Internet
        1.3.1.  All code: Same site Socket and Web.
    1.4.   Zone - Untrusted: Nothing
    1.5.   Zone - Trusted: Internet
        1.5.1.  All code: Same site Socket and Web.
....
```

Once we have the `Intranet` code group's label, `1.2`, we enter a second command to alter the code group's permissions:

```
caspol.exe -chggroup 1.2 FullTrust
```

The command will ask us to confirm the change to the security policy, and if we now run the `caspol.exe -listgroups` command again, we can see the permission on the end of the `Intranet` line has changed to `FullTrust`:

```
Code Groups:
1.  All code: Nothing
    1.1.   Zone - MyComputer: FullTrust
    1.2.   Zone - Intranet: FullTrust
        1.2.1.  All code: Same site Socket and Web.
        1.2.2.  All code: Same directory FileIO - Read, PathDiscovery
    1.3.   Zone - Internet: Internet
        1.3.1.  All code: Same site Socket and Web.
    1.4.   Zone - Untrusted: Nothing
    1.5.   Zone - Trusted: Internet
        1.5.1.  All code: Same site Socket and Web.
....
```

Creating and Applying Permissions Sets

We can create new permission sets using a command like this:

```
caspol.exe -addpset CustomPermissionSet permissionset.xml
```

This command specifies that we are creating a new permissions set called `CustomPermissionSet`, and basing it on the contents of the specified XML file. The XML file must contain a standard format specifying a `PermissionSet`. For reference, here's the permission set file for the `Everything` permission set, which you can trim down to the permission set you want to create:

```xml
<PermissionSet class="NamedPermissionSet" version="1" Name="Everything"
        Description="Allows unrestricted access to all resources covered
        by built in permissions">
  <IPermission class="EnvironmentPermission" version="1"
        Unrestricted="true"/>
  <IPermission class="FileDialogPermission" version="1"
        Unrestricted="true"/>
  <IPermission class="FileIOPermission" version="1"
        Unrestricted="true"/>
  <IPermission class="IsolatedStorageFilePermission" version="1"
        Unrestricted="true"/>
  <IPermission class="ReflectionPermission" version="1"
        Unrestricted="true"/>
  <IPermission class="RegistryPermission" version="1"
        Unrestricted="true"/>
  <IPermission class="SecurityPermission" version="1"
        Flags="Assertion, UnmanagedCode, Execution, ControlThread,
        ControlEvidence, ControlPolicy, SerializationFormatter,
        ControlDomainPolicy, ControlPrincipal, ControlAppDomain,
        RemotingConfiguration, Infrastructure"/>
  <IPermission class="UIPermission" version="1"
        Unrestricted="true"/>
  <IPermission class="DnsPermission" version="1"
        Unrestricted="true"/>
  <IPermission class="PrintingPermission" version="1"
        Unrestricted="true"/>
  <IPermission class="EventLogPermission" version="1"
        Unrestricted="true"/>
  <IPermission class="SocketPermission" version="1"
        Unrestricted="true"/>
  <IPermission class="WebPermission" version="1"
        Unrestricted="true"/>
  <IPermission class="PerformanceCounterPermission"
        version="1" Unrestricted="true"/>
  <IPermission class="DirectoryServicesPermission"
        version="1" Unrestricted="true"/>
  <Permission class="MessageQueuePermission"
        version="1" Unrestricted="true"/>
  <IPermission class="ServiceControllerPermission"
        version="1" Unrestricted="true"/>
</PermissionSet>
```

To view all permission sets in XML format, you can use this command:

```
caspol.exe -listpset
```

If you want to apply an XML `PermissionSet` configuration file to an existing permission set, you can use this command:

```
caspol.exe -chgpset permissionset.xml CustomPermissionSet
```

Distributing Code Using a Strong Name

.NET provides the ability for us to match an assembly to a code group when the assembly's identity and integrity have been confirmed using a strong name. This scenario is very common when assemblies are being deployed across networks, for example, distributing software over the Internet.

If you are a software company, and you want to provide code to your customers via the Internet, you build an assembly and give it a strong name. The strong name ensures that the assembly can be uniquely identified, and also provides protection against tampering. Your customers can incorporate this strong name into their code access security policy; an assembly that matches this unique strong name can then be assigned permissions explicitly. As you saw in the chapter on assemblies, the strong name includes checksums for hashes of all the files within an assembly, so we have strong evidence that the assembly has not been altered since the publisher created the strong name.

Note that, if your application uses an installer, the installer will install assemblies that have already been given a strong name. The strong name is generated once for each distribution before being sent to customers; the installer does not run these commands. The reason for this is that the strong name provides an assurance that the assembly has not been modified since it left your company; a common way to achieve this is to give your customer not only the application code, but also, separately, a copy of the strong name for the assembly. You may find it beneficial to pass the strong name to your customer using a secure form (perhaps fax or encrypted e-mail) to guard against the assembly being tampered with en-route.

Let's look at an example where we want to create an assembly with a strong name that we can distribute in such a way that the recipient of the assembly can use the strong name to grant the `FullTrust` permission to the assembly.

First, we need to create a key pair, as strong names make use of public key encryption. The public and private key are stored in the file we specify, and are used to sign the strong name. To create a key pair, we use the Strong Name Tool (sn.exe), which in addition to helping us create key pairs can also be used to manage keys and strong names. Let's create a key; do this by typing the following command:

```
sn.exe -k key.snk
```

We then place the keyfile (`key.snk` in our case) in the folder where Visual Studio builds our output file (normally the **Debug** folder) and add the key to our code using an assembly attribute. Once we have added this attribute to `AssemblyInfo.cs`, we just rebuild the assembly. The recompilation ensures the hash is recalculated and the assembly is protected against malicious modifications:

```
[assembly: AssemblyKeyFileAttribute("key.snk")]
```

1103

Our assembly has now been compiled and signed; it has a unique identifying strong name. We can now create a new code group on the machine where we want the assembly to execute, which has a membership condition that requires a match for the strong name of our assembly.

The following command states that we want to create a new code group using the strong name from the specified assembly manifest file, that we do not mind which version of the assembly is used, and that we want the code group to be granted the FullTrust permissions:

```
caspol.exe -addgroup 1 -strong -file \bin\debug\SecurityApp10.exe
           -noname -noversion FullTrust
```

The application in this example will now run from any zone, even the Internet zone, because the strong name provides powerful evidence that the assembly can be trusted. If we look at our code groups using caspol.exe -listgroups, we'll see the new code group (1.8) and its associated public key (in hexadecimal):

```
1.  All code: Nothing
    1.1.  Zone - MyComputer: FullTrust
    1.2.  Zone - Intranet: LocalIntranet
        1.2.1.  All code: Same site Socket and Web.
        1.2.2.  All code: Same directory FileIO - Read, PathDiscovery
    1.3.  Zone - Internet: Internet
        1.3.1.  All code: Same site Socket and Web.
    1.4.  Zone - Untrusted: Nothing
    1.5.  Zone - Trusted: Internet
        1.5.1.  All code: Same site Socket and Web.
    1.6.  StrongName -
0240000048000000940000000602000000240000525341310004000001000100007D1FA57C4AED9F0A32
E84AA0FAEFD0DE9E8FD6AEC8F87FB03766C834C99921EB23BE79AD9D5DCC1DD9AD236132102900B723
CF980957FC4E177108FC607774F29E8320E92EA05ECE4E821C0A5EFE8F1645C4C0C93C1AB99285D622
CAA652C1DFAD63D745D6F2DE5F17E5EAF0FC4963D261C8A12436518206DC093344D5AD293:
FullTrust
    1.7.  StrongName - 00000000000000000400000000000000: FullTrust
    1.8.  StrongName -
0024000004800000940000000602000000240000525341310004000001000100075 08D0780C56AF85BA
1BAD6D88E2C653E0A836286682C18134CC988546C1143252795A791F042238040F5627CCC1590ECEA3
0A9CD4780F5F0B29B55C375D916A33FD46B14582836E346A316BA27CD555B8F715377422EF589770E5
A5346A00BAABB70EF36774DFBCB17A30B67C913384E62A1C762CF40AFE6F1F605CCF406ECF:
FullTrust
Success
```

If you want to access the strong name in an assembly you can use the secutil.exe tool against the assembly manifest file. Let's use secutil.exe to view the strong name information for our assembly. We'll add the -hex option, so the public key is shown in hexadecimal (like caspol.exe) and then the -strongname argument that specifies that we want to view the strong name. Type this command, and you'll see a listing containing the strong name public key, the assembly name, and the assembly version:

```
secutil.exe -hex -strongname securityapp10.exe
```

```
Microsoft (R) .NET Framework SecUtil 1.0.xxxx.x
Copyright (c) Microsoft Corp 1999-2001. All rights reserved.
```

```
Public Key =
0x002400000480000094000000060200000024000052534131300040000010001007508D0780C56AF85
BA1BAD6D88E2C653E0A836286682C18134CC988546C1143252795A791F042238040F5627CCC1590ECE
A30A9CD4780F5F0B29B55C375D916A33FD46B14582836E346A316BA27CD555B8F715377422EF589770
E5A5346A00BAABB70EF36774DFBCB17A30B67C913384E62A1C762CF40AFE6F1F605CCF406ECF
Name = SecurityApp10
Version = 1.0.513.28751
Success
```

The curious among you may be wondering what the two strong name code groups installed by default refer to. One is a strong name key for Microsoft code, and the other strong name key is for the parts of .NET that have been submitted to the ECMA for standardization, which Microsoft will have much less control over.

Distributing Code Using Certificates

In the last section, we looked at how we can apply a unique strong name to an assembly so system administrators can explicitly grant permissions to assemblies that match that strong name using a code access group. Although this method of security policy management can be very effective, it's sometimes necessary to work at a higher level, where the administrator of the security policy grants permissions on the basis of the publisher of the software, rather than each individual software component. You'll probably have seen a similar method used before when you have downloaded executables from the Internet that have been Authenticode signed.

To provide information about the software publisher, we make use of digital certificates, and sign assemblies so that consumers of the software can verify the identity of the software publisher. In a commercial environment we would obtain a certificate from a company such as Verisign or Thawte.

The benefit of purchasing a certificate from a supplier such as this, rather than creating your own, is that it provides high levels of trust in its authenticity; the supplier acts as a trusted third-party. For test purposes however .NET includes a command-line utility we can use to create a test certificate. The process of creating certificates and using them to publish software is complex, but to give you a picture of what's involved we'll walk through an example without going into too much detail; if we did this chapter would be twice as long!

Let's imagine we're a company called ABC Corporation, and let's create a certificate for our software product "ABC Suite". First off, we need to create a test certificate; type the following command:

```
makecert -sk ABC -n "CN=ABC Corporation" abccorptest.cer
```

The command creates a test certificate under the name "ABC Corporation" and saves it to a file called abccorptest.cer. The -sk ABC argument creates a key container location, which is used by the public key cryptography.

To sign our assembly with the certificate, we use the signcode.exe utility on the assembly file containing the assembly manifest. Often the easiest way to sign an assembly is to use the signcode.exe in its wizard mode; to start the wizard, just type signcode.exe with no parameters:

If we click Next, we're asked to specify where the file is that we wish to sign. For an assembly, we sign the file containing the manifest:

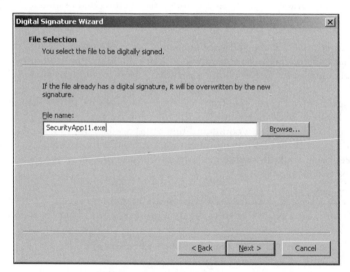

If we click Next and select the Custom option on the next screen, we're then asked to specify the certificate we want to use to sign the assembly. If we click Select from File and browse to the abccorptest.cer file, we'll see this confirmation screen:

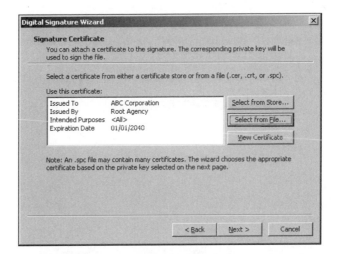

The following screen then appears, which asks us for our private key file. This key file was created by the `makecert` utility, so we can select the options as shown in the below screenshot. The cryptographic service provider is an application that implements the cryptographic standards. Public key cryptography was covered in Chapter 10:

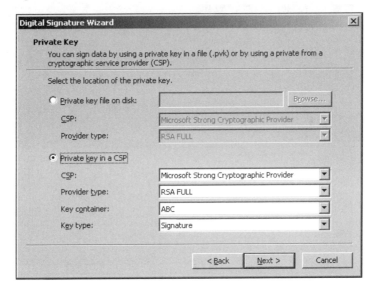

We're then asked a series of question about the way the signing is performed, including this screen, which asks us to specify the encryption algorithm:

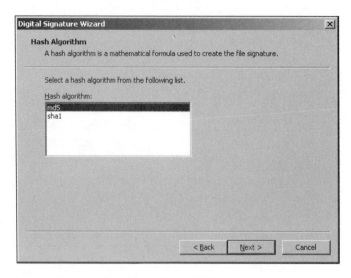

Next, we specify the name of our application and the URL for a web page that gives more information about it:

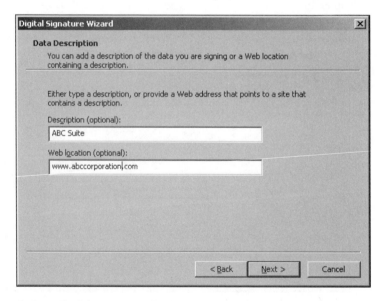

That's pretty much the end of the process; the last screen confirms the details of the certificate and the fact that the assembly has been successfully signed:

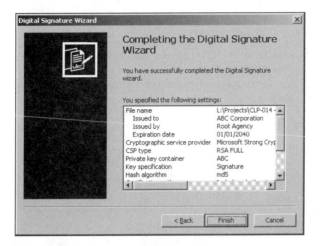

As our executable is now signed with the certificate, a recipient of the assembly has access to strong evidence as to who published the software; the runtime can examine the certificate and match the publisher of the assembly to a code group with high levels of confidence as to the identity of the code, because the trusted third-party certifies the publisher's identity.

Let's look at the signed assembly in a bit more detail. Although we're using a test certificate, we can temporarily configure .NET to treat test certificates more like trusted certificates issued by a trusted third-party using `setreg.exe`, which lets us configure public key and certificate settings in the Registry. If we enter the following command, our machine will be configured to trust the test root certificate, which gives us a more meaningful test environment:

```
setreg.exe 1 true
```

Let's check out our assembly and verify its trust level using the `chktrust.exe` utility:

```
chktrust.exe securityapp11.exe
```

This command will pop up a window like this:

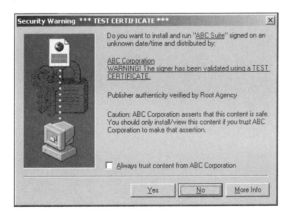

Note that `chktrust.exe` has successfully confirmed the publisher of the software using the certificate, but also reminded us that although the certificate has been verified it is still a test certificate.

Let's now turn our attention to a machine that we want to configure to trust software from the ABC Corporation. To do this we can create a new code access group that matches this software from ABC Corporation. To do that we grab a hexadecimal representation of the certificate from the assembly using this the `secutil.exe` tool:

```
secutil.exe -hex -x securityapp11.exe
```

The command will output something like this:

```
Microsoft (R) .NET Framework SecUtil 1.0.xxxx.x
Copyright (c) Microsoft Corp 1999-2001. All rights reserved.

X.509 Certificate =
0x3082017B30820125A0030201020210D69BE8D88D8FF9B54A9C689A71BB7E33300D06092A864886F7
0D0101040500301631143012060355040313 0B526F6F74204167656E6379301E170D30313035323831
38333133305A170D333931323331323335393539 5A301A311830160603550403130F41424320436F72
706F726174696F6E305C300D06092A864886F70D010101 0500034B003048024100ECBEFB348C1364B0
A3AE14FA9805F893AD180C7B2E57ADABBBE7EF94694A1E92BC5B4B59EF76FBDAC8D04D3DF2140B7616
550FE2D5AE5F15E03CBB54932F5CBB0203010001A34B304930470603551D010440303E801012E4092D
061D1D4F008D6121DC166463A11830163114301206035504 03130B526F6F74204167656E6379821006
376C00AA00648A11CFB8D4AA5C35F4300D06092A864886F70D0 1010405000341001D1B5F6FBB0C4C0E
85A9BB5FDA5FEC1B8D9C229BB0FB8A7CBE3340A527A5B25EAA2A70205DD71571607291272D5A81981C
73028AB849FF273465FAEF2F4C7174
Success
```

Let's now create the new code group and apply the `FullTrust` permission to assemblies published by the ABC Corporation using this (rather long) command:

```
caspol -addgroup 1. -pub -hex
3082017B30820125A0030201020210D69BE8D88D8FF9B54A9C689A71BB7E33300D06092A864886F70D
0101040500301631143012060355040313 0B526F6F74204167656E6379301E170D3031303532383138
333133305A170D333931323331323335393539 5A301A311830160603550403130F41424320436F7270
6F726174696F6E305C300D06092A864886F70D010101 0500034B003048024100ECBEFB348C1364B0A3
AE14FA9805F893AD180C7B2E57ADABBBE7EF94694A1E92BC5B4B59EF76FBDAC8D04D3DF2140B761655
0FE2D5AE5F15E03CBB54932F5CBB0203010001A34B304930 470603551D010440303E801012E4092D06
1D1D4F008D6121DC166463A1183016311430120603550403130B526F6F74204167656E637982100637
6C00AA00648A11CFB8D4AA5C35F4300D06092A86
4886F70D01010405000341001D1B5F6FBB0C4C0E85A9BB5FDA5FEC1B8D9C229BB0FB8A7CBE3340A527
A5B25EAA2A70205DD71571607291272D5A81981C73028AB849FF273465FAEF2F4C7174 FullTrust
```

The parameters specify that the code group should be added at the top level (`1.`), and that the code group membership condition is of the type `Publisher`, and the last parameter specifies the permission set to grant (`FullTrust`). The command will ask for confirmation:

```
Microsoft (R) .NET Framework CasPol 1.0.xxxx.x
Copyright (c) Microsoft Corp 1999-2001. All rights reserved.

The operation you are performing will alter security policy.
Are you sure you want to perform this operation? (yes/no) y
Added union code group with "-pub" membership condition to the Machine level.
Success
```

Our machine is now configured to trust fully all assemblies that have been signed with the certificate from ABC Corporation. To confirm that, we can run a `caspol.exe -lg` command which lists the new code access group (1.8):

```
Security is ON
Execution checking is ON
Policy change prompt is ON

Level = Machine

Code Groups:

1.  All code: Nothing
    1.1.   Zone - MyComputer: FullTrust
    1.2.   Zone - Intranet: LocalIntranet
        1.2.1.  All code: Same site Socket and Web.
        1.2.2.  All code: Same directory FileIO - Read, PathDiscovery
    1.3.   Zone - Internet: Internet
        1.3.1.  All code: Same site Socket and Web.
    1.4.   Zone - Untrusted: Nothing
    1.5.   Zone - Trusted: Internet
        1.5.1.  All code: Same site Socket and Web.
    1.6.   StrongName - 00240000048000009400000006020000002400005253413100004000001
00010007D1FA57C4AED9F0A32E84AA0FAEFD0DE9E8FD6AEC8F87FB03766C834C99921EB23BE79AD9D5
DCC1DD9AD236132102900B723CF980957FC4E177108FC607774F29E8320E92EA05ECE4E821C0A5EFE8
F1645C4C0C93C1AB99285D622CAA652C1DFAD63D745D6F2DE5F17E5EAF0FC4963D261C8A1243651820
6DC093344D5AD293: FullTrust
    1.7.   StrongName - 0000000000000000000400000000000000: FullTrust
    1.8.   Publisher -
3048024100ECBEFB348C1364B0A3AE14FA9805F893AD180C7B2E57ADABBBE7EF94694A1E92BC5B4B59
EF76FBDAC8D04D3DF2140B7616550FE2D5AE5F15E03CBB54932F5CBB0203010001: FullTrust
Success
```

As another check, let's ask `caspol.exe` to tell us what code groups our assembly matches:

caspol.exe -resolvegroup securityapp11.exe

```
Level = Enterprise
Code Groups:
1.  All code: FullTrust

Level = Machine
Code Groups:
1.  All code: Nothing
    1.1.   Zone - Intranet: LocalIntranet
        1.1.1.  All code: Same site Socket and Web.
        1.1.2.  All code: Same directory FileIO - Read, PathDiscovery
    1.2.   Publisher - 3048024100ECBEFB348C1364B0A3AE14FA9805F893AD180C7B2E57ADABB
BE7EF94694A1E92BC5B4B59EF76FBDAC8D04D3DF2140B7616550FE2D5AE5F15E03CBB54932F5CBB0
203010001: FullTrust

Level = User
Code Groups:
1.  All code: FullTrust

Success
```

In the center of the results we can see that the assembly has been successfully matched to our new code group and granted the `FullTrust` permission set.

Managing Zones

Earlier we talked about the zones that Windows provides and that we manage using Internet Explorer's security tools. The four zones we manage in this way are:

❑   `Intranet` – all web sites that are on your organization's intranet

❑   `Trusted Sites` – web sites that you trust not to damage your data

❑   `Restricted Sites` – web sites that could potentially damage your computer

❑   `Internet` – all web sites you haven't placed in other zones

These settings are managed from within Internet Explorer because they apply to sites visited using the browser that access .NET code (whether downloaded, or in page controls). If you are using a non-Microsoft browser, it will most likely not support .NET code, and so there will be no options to manage the associated zones.

Any user on a machine can alter the zone settings; however, the security settings for the zones that they specify only apply to their account. That is, it is not possible for one user to alter another user's zone settings. That said, there is a risk here as a user might alter the zone settings without understanding what they are doing and inadvertently open their machine up to attack.

To alter the settings associated with each zone, open Internet Explorer and open the **Options** dialogue box from the **Tools** menu. In the **Options** box, move to the **Security** tab:

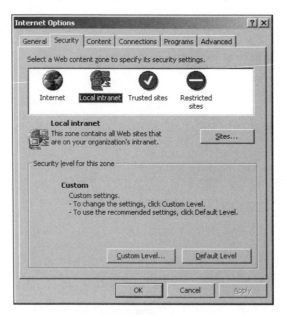

At the top you can see the four zones, and having selected one of the zones by clicking on its icon, you can use the Sites... button to specify sites that you want included in that zone. For example, if you want to configure the Local intranet zone, you will use this dialogue box:

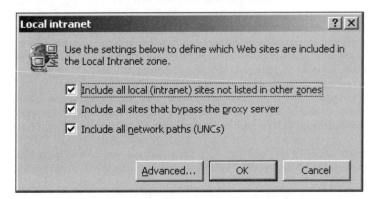

The options here give us enough scope to accurately define what constitutes the 'intranet' in our organization. In addition, the Advanced button gives us access to a dialogue box where we can specify URI's for particular sites we want included in the Local intranet zone:

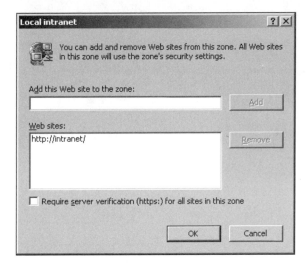

Note the option at the bottom of this dialogue box, which is provided for each of the zones except the Internet zone. It allows you to specify that you only trust sites in this zone when they are accessed over secure HTTP using Secure Sockets Layer (SSL) encryption. If you trust a site that is accessed over an unencrypted connection, you are potentially risking an attack as your traffic may be intercepted. If you want to verify that a site is held within a specific zone, visit the site and look at the bottom right hand corner of the Internet Explorer window, which will display the name of the zone for the web address you are currently viewing.

As well as being able to specify the scope of the zone by detailing sites you trust or do not trust, you can also specify what actions are permitted within each zone using the security-level settings. These specify things like whether a prompt should be given for ActiveX controls, and whether cookies are accepted.

Summary

In this chapter, we've covered how assemblies are matched to code groups, and how those code groups are assigned permissions by the security policy at the user, enterprise, and machine levels, and we've seen how we can use tools to manage this policy. We've also seen how, for an assembly to execute, it must have the relevant permissions at the three policy levels, as well as the correct role-based permissions and the relevant Windows account permissions. We've also looked at the options available to us in distributing code using strong names and digital certificates.

Clearly, there are more security checks in place with .NET than we have seen before on Windows, and much of the security comes "for free" as we do not need to do much to make use of it at the basic level. However, when we do want to extend it we are provided with the classes and frameworks to do that.

Security is an ongoing challenge, and although Microsoft has not solved all the problems, the managed security environment provided by .NET is a significant step forwards as it provides a framework within which code is challenged before it executes.

It's no coincidence that these developments are occurring at a time when Microsoft is moving towards distributing its products over the web, as a secure distribution method for that is essential.

C# for C++ Developers

Introduction

This appendix is intended for developers who are already very familiar with C++, and wish to see what the differences are between C++ and C#. We will survey the C# language, noting specifically those areas in which it is different from C++. Because the two languages do have a large amount of syntax and methodology in common, advanced C++ programmers may find they can use this appendix as a shortcut to learning C#.

It should be made clear that C# is a distinct language from C++. Whereas C++ was designed for general object-oriented programming in the days when the typical computer was a standalone machine running a command line-based user interface, C# is designed specifically to work with .NET, and is geared to the modern environment of Windows and mouse-controlled user interfaces, networks, and the Internet. However, it is also undeniable that the two languages are very similar both in their syntax and in that they are both designed to facilitate the same paradigm of programming, in which code is based around hierarchies of inherited classes. This similarity is not surprising given that, as we have remarked often in this book, C# was designed to a large extent as an object-oriented language that took the good points of earlier object-oriented languages but learned from the poorer design features of these languages – of which C++ has been arguably the most successful example up to now.

Because of the similarities between the two languages, developers who are fluent in C++ may find that the easiest way to learn C# is to treat it as C++ with a few differences and learn what those differences are. This appendix is designed to help you do that. We will start off with a broad overview that mentions in general terms what the main differences between the two languages are, and also indicates what areas they have in common. We follow this by comparing what the standard 'Hello, World' program looks like in each of the two languages. Then the bulk of the appendix is given over to a topic by topic analysis that looks at each of the main language areas and gives a detailed comparison between C# and C++. Inevitably, an appendix of this size cannot be completely comprehensive, but it is designed to cover all the main differences between the languages that you will notice in the course of everyday programming. We will point out, however, that C# relies very heavily on support from the .NET base class library in a large number of areas. In this appendix we will largely restrict our attention to the C# language itself, and not extensively cover the base classes.

For the purposes of comparison, we are taking ANSI C++ as our reference point. Microsoft has added numerous extensions to C++, and the Windows C++ compiler has a few incompatibilities with the ANSI standard, which we'll occasionally point out, but we will not normally use these when comparing the two languages.

Conventions for this Appendix

Note that in this appendix we adopt an additional convention when displaying code. C# code is always displayed as in the rest of the book, with gray shading:

```
// this is C# code
class MyClass : MyBaseClass
{
```

If we want to highlight any new or important C# code, it will be displayed in bold:

```
// this is C# code
class MyClass : MyBaseClass          // we've already seen this bit
{
    int X;                           // this is interesting
```

C++ code presented for comparison is presented like this:

```
// this is C++ code
class CMyClass : public CMyBaseClass
{
```

In the sample code in this appendix we have also taken account of the most common naming conventions when using the two languages under Windows. Hence class names in the C++ examples begin with C while the corresponding names in the C# examples do not. Also, Hungarian notation is often used for variable names in the C++ samples only.

Terminology

You should be aware that a couple of language constructs have a different terminology in C# from that in C++. Member variables in C++ are known as **fields** in C# while functions in C++ are known as **methods** in C#. In C#, the term **function** has a more general meaning, and refers to any member of a class that contains code. This means that "function" covers methods, properties, constructors, destructors, indexers, and operator overloads. In C++, "function" and "method" are often used interchangeably in casual speech, though strictly a C++ method is a virtual member function.

If this all sounds confusing, the following table should help:

Meaning	C++ Term	C# Term
Variable that is a member of a class	Member Variable	Field
Any item in a class that contains instructions	Function (or member function)	Function
Item in a class that contains instructions and is callable by name with the syntax `DoSomething(/*parameters*/).`	Function (or member function)	Method
Virtual function that is defined as a member of a class	Method	Virtual Method

You should also be aware of a couple of other different terms:

C++ Term	C# Term
Compound Statement	Block Statement
lvalue	Variable Expression

In this appendix we will, where possible, use the terminology appropriate to the language we are discussing.

A Comparison of C# and C++

In this section we'll briefly summarize the overall differences and similarities between the two languages.

Differences

The main areas in which C# differs from C++ are as follows:

❑ **Compile Target** – C++ code usually compiles to assembly language. C# by contrast compiles to **intermediate language** (**IL**), which has some similarities to Java bytecode. The IL is subsequently converted to native executable code by a process of Just-In-Time compilation. The emitted IL code is stored in a file or set of files known as an assembly. An **assembly** essentially forms the unit in which IL code is packaged, corresponding to a DLL or executable file that would be created by a C++ compiler.

❑ **Memory management** – C# is designed to free the developer from bookkeeping tasks to do with memory management. This means that in C# you do not have to explicitly delete memory that was allocated dynamically on the heap, as you would in C++. Rather, the garbage collector periodically cleans up memory that is no longer needed. In order to facilitate this, C# does impose certain restrictions on how you can use variables that are stored on the heap, and is stricter about type safety than C++.

❑ **Pointers** – Pointers may be used in C# just as in C++, but *only* in blocks of code that you have specifically marked for pointer use. For the most part, C# relies on VB/Java-style references for instances of classes, and the language has been designed in such a way that pointers are not required nearly as often as they are in C++.

❑ **Operator Overloads** – C# does not allow you to explicitly overload as many operators as C++. This is largely because the C# compiler automates this task to some extent by using any available custom overloads of elementary operators (like =) to work out overloads of combined operators (+=) automatically.

❑ **Library** – Both C++ and C# rely on the presence of an extensive library. For ANSI C++ this is the standard library. C# relies on a set of classes known as the .NET base classes. The .NET base classes are based on single inheritance, whereas the standard library is based on a mixture of inheritance and templates. Also, whereas ANSI C++ keeps the library largely separate from the language itself, the interdependence in C# is much closer, and the implementation of many C# keywords is directly dependent on particular base classes.

❑ **Target Environments** – C# is specifically designed to target programming needs in GUI-based environments (not necessarily just Windows, although the language happens to be only available for Windows at the present time), as well as background services such as web services. This doesn't really affect the language itself, but is reflected in the design of the base class library. C++ by contrast was designed for more general use in the days when command-line user interfaces were dominant. Neither C++ nor the standard library include any support for GUI elements. On Windows, C++ developers have had to rely directly or indirectly on the Windows API for this support.

❑ **Preprocessor Directives** – C# has some preprocessor directives, which follow the same overall syntax as in C++. But in general there are far fewer preprocessor directives in C#, since other C# language features make these less important.

❑ **Enumerators** – These are present in C#, but are much more versatile than their C++ equivalents, since they are syntactically fully fledged structs in their own right, supporting various properties and methods. Note that this support exists in source code only – when compiled to native executable, enumerators are still implemented as primitive numeric types, so there is no performance loss.

❑ **Destructors** – C# cannot guarantee when class destructors are called. In general, you should not use the programming paradigm of placing code in C# class destructors, as you can in C++, unless there are specific external resources to be cleaned up, such as file or database connections. Since the garbage collector cleans up all dynamically allocated memory, destructors are not so important in C# as they are in C++. For cases in which it is important to clean up external resources as soon as possible, C# implements an alternative mechanism involving the IDisposable interface.

❑ **Classes versus Structs** – C# formalizes the difference between classes (typically used for large objects with many methods) and structs (typically used for small objects that comprise little more than collections of variables). Among other differences, classes and structs are stored differently, and structs do not support inheritance.

Similarities

Areas in which C# and C++ are very similar include:

- **Syntax** – The overall syntax of C# is very similar to that of C++, although there are numerous minor differences.

- **Execution Flow** – C++ and C# both have roughly the same statements to control flow of execution, and these generally work in the same way in the two languages.

- **Exceptions** – Support for these in C# is essentially the same as in C++, except that C# allows `finally` blocks and imposes some restrictions on the type of object that can be thrown.

- **Inheritance Model** – Classes are inherited in the same way in C# as in C++. Related concepts such as abstract classes and virtual functions are implemented in the same way, although there are some differences in syntax. Also, C# supports only single inheritance of classes. The similarity in class hierarchy incidentally means that C# programs will normally have a very similar overall architecture to corresponding C++ programs.

- **Constructors**. Constructors work in the same way in C# as in C++, though again there are some differences in syntax.

New Features

C# introduces a number of new concepts that are not part of the ANSI C++ specification (although most of these have been introduced by Microsoft as non-standard extensions supported by the Microsoft C++ compiler). These are:

- **Delegates** – C# does not support function pointers. However, a similar effect is achieved by wrapping references to methods in a special form of class known as a delegate. Delegates can be passed around between methods, and used to call the methods to which they contain references, in the same way that function pointers can be in C++. What is significant about delegates is that they incorporate an object reference as well as a method reference. This means that, unlike a function pointer, a delegate contains sufficient information to call an instance method in a class.

- **Events** – Events are similar to delegates, but are specifically designed to support the callback model, in which a client notifies a server that it wishes to be informed when some action takes place. C# uses events as a wrapper around Windows messages in the same way that VB does.

- **Properties** – This idea, used extensively in VB and in COM, has been imported into C#. A property is a method or get/set pair of methods in a class that have been dressed up syntactically so they look to the outside world like a field. They allow you to write code like `MyForm.Height = 400` instead of `MyForm.SetHeight(400)`.

- **Interfaces** – An interface can be thought of as an abstract class, whose purpose is to define a set of methods or properties that classes can agree to implement. The idea originated in COM. C# interfaces are not the same as COM interfaces – they are simply lists of methods etc., whereas COM interfaces have other associated features such as GUIDs, but the principle is very similar. This means that C# formally recognizes the principle of interface inheritance, whereby a class inherits the definitions of functions, but not any implementations.

- **Attributes** – C# allows you to decorate classes, methods, parameters, and other items in code with meta-information known as attributes. Attributes can be accessed at runtime and used to determine the actions taken by your code.

New Base Class Features

The following features are new to C# and have no counterparts in the C++ language. However, support for these features comes almost entirely from the base classes, with little or no support from the C# language syntax itself, and so we will not cover them in this appendix. Full details are in Chapter 7.

❑ **Threading** – The C# language includes some support for thread synchronization, via the `lock` statement. (C++ has no inbuilt support for threads and you have to call functionality in code libraries.)

❑ **Reflection** – C# allows code to obtain information dynamically about the definitions of classes in compiled assemblies (libraries and executables). You can actually write a program in C# that displays information about the classes and methods that it is made up from!

Unsupported Features

The following parts of the C++ language do not have any equivalent in C#:

❑ **Multiple implementation inheritance of classes** – Classes support multiple inheritance only for interfaces.

❑ **Templates** – These are not part of the C# language at present, although Microsoft has stated that it is investigating the possibility of template support for future versions of C#.

The Hello World Example

Writing a 'Hello World' application in the world of programming is about as unoriginal as it is possible to get. But a direct comparison of 'Hello World' in C++ and C# can be quite instructive for illustrating some of the differences between the two languages. In this comparison we've tried to innovate a bit (and demonstrate more features) by displaying `"Hello World!"` both at the command-line and in a message box. We've also made a slight change to the text of the message in the C++ version, in a move which we emphasize should be interpreted as a bit of fun rather than a serious statement.

The C++ version looks like this:

```
#include <iostream>
#include <Windows.h>

using namespace std;

int main(int argc, char *argv)
{
    cout << "Goodbye, World!";
    MessageBox(NULL, "Goodbye, World!", "", MB_OK);
    return 0;
}
```

Here's the C# version:

```
using System;
using System.Windows.Forms;

namespace Console1
{
    class Class1
    {
        static int Main(string[] args)
        {
            Console.WriteLine("Hello, World!");
            MessageBox.Show("Hello, World!");
            return 0;
        }
    }
}
```

Comparing the two programs tells us that the syntax of the two languages is quite similar. In particular, code blocks are marked off with braces { }, and semicolons are used as statement delimiters. Like C++, C# ignores all excess whitespace between statements.

We'll go through the samples line by line, examining the features they demonstrate.

#include Statements

The C++ version of "Hello World" starts with a couple of preprocessor directives to include some header files:

```
#include <iostream>
#include <Windows.h>
```

These are absent from the C# version, something which illustrates an important point about the way that C# accesses libraries. In C++ we need to include header files in order for the compiler to be able to recognize the relevant symbols in your code. We need to instruct the linker separately to reference the libraries – something that is achieved via command-line parameters passed to the linker. C# doesn't really separate out compiling and linking in the way that C++ does. In C# the command-line parameters are all that is required (and only then if you are accessing anything beyond the basic core library). These by themselves will allow the compiler to find all the class definitions; hence explicit references in the source code are unnecessary. This is actually a much simpler way of doing it – and indeed once you've got used to the C# model, the C++ version, in which everything needs to be referred to twice, starts to look rather strange and cumbersome.

One other point we should note is that of the two #include statements in the above C++ code, the first accesses an ANSI standard library (the iostream part of the standard library). The second is a Windows-specific library, and is referenced in order that we can display the message box. C++ code on Windows often needs to access the Windows API because the ANSI standard doesn't have any windowing facilities. By contrast, the .NET base classes – the C# equivalent of the ANSI standard template library – do include windowing facilities, and only the .NET base classes are used here. Our C# code requires no non-standard features. (Although arguably, this point is balanced by the fact that 'standard' C# is only available on Windows, at present.)

Although the C# code above happens not to have any #include directives, it's worth noting that some preprocessor directives (though not #include) are available in C#, and do retain the # syntax.

Namespaces

The C# "Hello World" program starts with a namespace declaration, which is scoped by the curly braces to include the entire program. Namespaces work in exactly the same way in C# as they do in C++, providing ways to remove possible ambiguity from the names of symbols in the program. Placing items in a namespace is optional in both languages, but in C# the convention is that all items should be in a namespace. Hence, while it is very common to see C++ code that is not contained in a namespace, it is extremely rare to see such code in C#.

For the next part of the code, C# and C++ versions are very similar – in both we use the statement using to indicate the namespace in which any symbols should be searched for. The only difference is a syntactical one: The statement in C# is just using, whereas in C++ it is using namespace.

Many C++ developers will be used to the old C++ library, which meant including the file iostream.h rather than iostream – in which case the using namespace std statement is unnecessary. The old C++ library is officially deprecated and will no longer be supported from Visual Studio 8 (the version that will follow Visual Studio .NET). The above example demonstrates how you really should be accessing the iostream library in C++ code.

Entry Point: Main() versus main()

The next items in our "Hello World" samples are the program entry points. In the C++ case this is a global function named main(). C# does roughly the same thing, although in C# the name is Main(). However, whereas in C++ main() is defined outside of any class, the C# version is defined as a static member of a class. This is because C# requires all functions and variables to be members of a class or struct. C# will not allow any top-level items in your program except classes and structs. To that extent C# can be regarded as enforcing stricter object-oriented practices than C++ does. Relying extensively on global and static variables and functions in C++ code tends to be regarded as poor program design anyway.

Of course, requiring that everything should be a member of a class does lead to the issue of where the program entry point should be. The answer is that the C# compiler will look for a static member method called Main(). This can be a member of any class in the source code, but only one class should normally have such a method. (If more than one class defines this method, a compiler switch will need to be used to indicate to the compiler which should be the program entry point.) Like its C++ counterpart, Main() can return either a void or an int, though int is the more usual. Also like its C++ equivalent, Main() takes the same arguments – either the set of any command-line parameters passed to the program, as an array of strings, or no parameters. But as you can see from the code, strings are defined in a slightly more intuitive manner in C# than they are in C++. (In fact, the word string is a keyword in C#, and it maps to a class defined in the .NET base class library, System.String.) Also, arrays are more sophisticated in C# than in C++. Each array stores the number of elements it contains as well as the elements themselves, so there is no need to pass in the number of strings in the array separately in the C# code, as C++ does via the argc parameter.

Displaying the Message

Finally we get to the lines that actually write our message – first to the console, then to a message box. In both cases these lines of code rely on calling up features from the supporting libraries for the two languages. The classes in the standard library are obviously designed very differently from those in the .NET base class library, so the details of the method calls in these code samples are different. In the C# case both calls are made as calls to static methods on base classes, whereas to display a message box C++ has to rely on a non-standard Windows API function, `MessageBox()`, which is not object-oriented.

The base classes are designed to be highly intuitive – arguably more so than the standard library. Without any knowledge of C#, it's immediately obvious what `Console.WriteLine()` does. If you didn't already know, you'd have a hard time figuring out what `cout <<` means, although I suspect that the unique artistic style of `cout <<` will be missed by more than just a few developers. But in the commercial world of programming, being easy to understand is usually worth more than being artistic.

`MessageBox.Show()` takes fewer parameters than its C++ equivalent in this example, because it is overloaded. Other overloads that take additional parameters are available.

Also, one point that could be easy to miss is that the above code demonstrates that C# uses the period, or full stop, symbol (`.`) rather than two colons (`::`) for scope resolution. `Console` and `MessageBox` are the names of classes rather than class instances! In order to access static members of classes, C# always requires the syntax `<ClassName>.<MemberName>` whereas C++ gives you a choice between `<ClassName>::<MemberName>` and `<InstanceName>.<MemberName>` (if an instance of the class exists and is in scope).

Topic-by-Topic Comparison

The above example has given a quick flavor of some of the differences you'll see. For the remainder of this appendix we will compare the two languages in detail, working systematically through the various language features of C++ and C#.

Program Architecture

In this section we'll look in very broad terms at how the features of the two languages affect the overall architecture of programs.

Program Objects

In C++ any program will consist of an entry point (in ANSI C++ this is the `main()` function, though for Windows applications this is usually named `WinMain()`), as well as various classes, structs, and global variables or functions that are defined outside of any class. Although many developers would regard good object-oriented design as meaning that as far as possible the topmost-level items in your code are objects, C++ does not enforce this. As we've just seen, C# does enforce that idea. It lays down a more exclusively object-oriented paradigm by requiring that everything is a member of a class. In other words the only top-level objects in your program are classes (or other items that can be regarded as special types of classes: enumerations, delegates, and interfaces). To that extent you'll find that your C# code is forced to be even more object-oriented than would be required in C++.

File Structure

In C++ the syntax by which your program is built up is very much based around the file as a unit of source code. You have for example source files (.cpp files), which will each contain #include preprocessor directives to include relevant header files. The compilation process involves compiling each source file individually, after which these objects files are linked to generate the final executable. Although the final executable will not contain any information about the original source or object files, C++ has been designed in a way that requires the developer to explicitly code around the chosen source code file structure.

With C#, the compiler takes care of the details of matching up individual source files for you. You can put your source code either in a single file or in several files, but that's immaterial for the compiler and there's no need for any file to explicitly refer to other files. In particular, there is no requirement for items to be defined before they are referenced in any individual file, as there is in C++. The compiler will happily locate the definition of each item wherever it happens to be. As a side effect of this, there isn't really any concept of linking up your own code in C#. The compiler simply compiles all your source files into an assembly (though you can specify other options such as a module – a unit which will form part of an assembly). Linking does take place in C#, but this is really confined to linking your code with any existing library code in assemblies. There is no such thing as a header file in C#.

Program Entry Point

In standard ANSI C++, the program entry point is by default at a function called main(), which normally has the signature:

```
int main(int argc, char *argv)
```

Where argc indicates the number of arguments passed to the program, and argv is an array of strings giving these arguments. The first argument is always the command used to run the program itself. Windows somewhat modifies this. Windows applications traditionally start with an entry point called WinMain(), and DLLs with DllMain(). These methods also take different sets of parameters.

In C#, the entry point follows similar principles. However, due to the requirement that all C# items are part of a class, the entry point can no longer be a global function. Instead, the requirement is that one class must have a static member method called Main(), as we saw earlier.

Language Syntax

C# and C++ share virtually identical syntaxes. Both languages, for example, ignore whitespace between statements, and use the semicolon to separate statements and braces to block statements together. This all means that, at first sight, programs written in either language look very much alike. However, note the following differences:

❑   C++ requires a semicolon after a class definition. C# does not.

❑   C++ permits expressions to be used as statements even if they have no effect, for example:

```
i+1;
```

In C# this would be flagged as an error.

We should also note that, like C++, C# is case-sensitive. However, because C# is designed to be interoperable with VB.NET (which is case-insensitive), you are strongly advised not to use names that differ only by case for any items that will be visible to code outside your project (in other words, names of public members of classes in library code). If you do use public names that differ only by case, you'll prevent VB.NET code from being able to access your classes. (Incidentally if you write any managed C++ code for the .NET environment, the same advice applies.)

Forward Declarations

Forward declarations are neither supported nor required in C#, since the order in which items are defined in the source files is immaterial. It's perfectly OK for one item to refer to another item that is only actually defined later in that file or in a different file – as long as it is defined somewhere. This contrasts with C++, in which symbols and so on can only be referred to in any one source file if they have already been declared in the same file or an included file.

No Separation of Definition and Declaration

Something that is related to the lack of forward declarations in C# is that there is never any separation of declaration and definition of any item in C#. For example, in C++ it's common to write out a class something like this in the header file, where only signatures of the member functions are given, and the full definitions are specified elsewhere:

```
class CMyClass
{
public:
    void MyMethod();    // definition of this function is in the C++ file,
                        // unless MyMethod() is inline
// etc.
```

This is not done in C#. The methods are always defined in full in the class definition:

```
class MyClass
{
    public void MyMethod()
    {
        // implementation here
```

You might at first sight think that this leads to code that is less easy to read. The beauty of the C++ way of doing it was, after all, that you could just scan through the header file to see what public functions a class exposed, without having to see the implementations of those functions. However, this facility is no longer needed in C#, partly because of modern editors (the Visual Studio .NET editor is a folding editor, which allows you to collapse method implementations) and partly because C# has a facility to generate documentation in XML format for your code automatically.

Program Flow

Program flow is similar in C# to C++. In particular, the following statements work in exactly the same way in C# as they do in C++, and have exactly the same syntax:

❑   for

❑   return

❑   goto

❑   break

❑   continue

There are a couple of syntactical differences for the if, while, do ... while, and switch statements, and C# provides an additional control flow statement, foreach.

if...else

The if statement works in exactly the same way and has exactly the same syntax in C# as in C++, apart from one point. The condition in each if or else clause must evaluate to a bool. For example, assuming x is an integer data type, not a bool, the following C++ code would generate a compilation error in C#:

```
if (x)
{
```

The correct C# syntax is:

```
if (x != 0)
{
```

since the != operator returns a bool.

This requirement is a good illustration of how the additional type safety in C# traps errors early. Run-time errors in C++ caused by writing if (a = b) when you meant to write if (a == b) are commonplace. In C# these errors will be caught at compile time.

Note that in C# it is not possible to convert numeric variables to or from bool.

while and do...while

Just as for if, these statements have exactly the same syntax and purpose in C# as they do in C++, except that the condition expression must evaluate to a bool:

```
int x;
while (x) { /* statements */ }             // wrong
while (x != 0) { /* statements */ }        // OK
```

switch

The `switch` statement serves the same purpose in C# as it does in C++. It is, however, more powerful in C#, since you can use a string as the test variable, something that is not possible in C++:

```
string myString;
// initialize myString
switch (myString)
{
    case "Hello":
        // do something
        break;
    case "Goodbye":
        // etc.
```

The syntax in C# is slightly different in that each `case` clause must explicitly exit. It is not permitted for one `case` to fall through to another `case`, unless the first `case` is empty. If you want to achieve this effect you'll need to use the `goto` statement:

```
switch (myString)
{
    case "Hello":
        // do something;
        goto case "Goodbye";   // Will go on to execute the statements
                               // in the "Goodbye" clause
    case "Goodbye":
        // do something else
        break;
    case "Black":              // OK for this to fall through since it's empty
    case "White":
    // do something else        // This is executed if myString contains
                               // either "Black" or "White"
        break;
    default:
        int j = 3;
        break;
}
```

Microsoft has decided to enforce use of the `goto` statement in this context in order to prevent bugs in which code in switch statements falls through to the next `case` clause when the intention was actually to break.

foreach

C# provides an additional flow control statement, `foreach`. A `foreach` loop iterates through all items in an array or collection without requiring explicit specification of the indices.

A `foreach` loop on an array might look as follows. In this example we assume that `MyArray` is an array of `doubles`, and we want to output each value to the console window. To do this you would use the following code:

```
foreach (double someElement in myArray)
{
    Console.WriteLine(someElement);
}
```

Note that in this loop `someElement` is the name we choose to assign to the variable used to iterate through the loop – it is not a keyword and we can choose any name here, as long as it doesn't clash with any other variable names.

We could alternatively write the above loop as:

```
foreach (double someElement in myArray)
   Console.WriteLine(someElement);
```

since block statements in C# work in the same way as compound statements in C++.

This loop would have exactly the same effect as:

```
for (int i=0; i<myArray.Length; i++)
{
   Console.WriteLine(myArray[i]);
}
```

(We note that the second version also illustrates how to obtain the number of elements in an array in C#! We'll cover how to declare an array in C# later in the appendix.)

Note however that, unlike array element access, the `foreach` loop provides read-only access to its elements. Hence the following code will not compile:

```
foreach (double someElement in MyArray)
   someElement *= 2;                 // Wrong - someElement cannot be assigned to
```

We mentioned that the `foreach` loop can be used for arrays or collections. A collection is something that has no counterpart in C++, though the concept has become common in Windows through its use in VB and COM. Essentially a collection is a class that implements the interface `IEnumerable`. Because this involves support from the base classes, we explain collections in Chapter 7.

Variables

Variable definitions follow basically the same pattern in C# as they do in C++:

```
int nCustomers, Result;
double distanceTravelled;
double height = 3.75;
const decimal balance = 344.56M;
```

However, as you'd expect, some of the types are different. Also, as remarked earlier, variables may only be declared locally in a method or as members of a class. C# has no equivalent to global or static (that is scoped to a file) variables in C++. As noted earlier, variables that are members of a class are termed **fields** in C#.

Note that C# also rigidly distinguishes between data types which are stored on the stack (value data types) and those which are stored on the heap (reference data types). We'll examine this issue in more detail later on.

Basic Data Types

As with C++, C# has a number of predefined data types, and you can define your own types as classes or structs.

The data types that are predefined in C# differ somewhat from those in C++. The types available in C# are:

Name	Contains	Symbol
sbyte	Signed 8-bit integer	
byte	Unsigned 8-bit integer	
short	Signed 16-bit integer	
ushort	Unsigned 16-bit integer	
int	Signed 32-bit integer	
uint	Unsigned 32-bit integer	U
long	Signed 64-bit integer	L
ulong	Unsigned 64-bit integer	UL
float	Signed 32-bit floating point value	F
double	Signed 64-bit floating point value	D
bool	True or false	
char	16-bit Unicode character	' '
decimal	Floating point number with 28 significant digits	M
string	Set of Unicode characters of variable length	" "
object	Used where you choose not to specify the type. The nearest C++ equivalent is void*, except that object is not a pointer.	

In the above table the symbol in the third column refers to the letter that may be placed after a number to indicate its type in situations for which it is desirable to indicate the type explicitly, for example, 28UL means the number 28 stored as an unsigned long. As with C++, single quotes are used to denote characters, double quotes for strings. However, in C#, characters are always Unicode characters, and strings are a defined reference type, not simply an array of characters.

The data types in C# are more tightly defined than they are in C++. For example, in C++, the traditional expectation was that an int would occupy 2 bytes (16 bits), but the ANSI C++ definition allowed this to be platform-dependent. Hence, on Windows, a C++ int occupies 4 bytes, the same as a long. This obviously causes quite a few compatibility problems when transferring C++ programs between platforms. On the other hand, in C# each predefined data type (except string and object, obviously!) has its total storage specified explicitly.

Because the size of each of the primitive types is fixed in C# (a primitive type is any of the above types, except `string` and `object`), there is less need for the `sizeof` operator, though it does exist in C#, but is only permitted in unsafe code (as described later).

Although many C# names are similar to C++ names and there is a fairly obvious intuitive mapping between many of the corresponding types, some things have changed syntactically. In particular `signed` and `unsigned` are not recognized keywords in C#. In C++ you could use these keywords, as well as `long` and `short` to modify other other types (for example, `unsigned long`, `short int`). Such modifications are not permitted in C#, so the above table literally is the complete list of predefined data types.

Basic Data Types As Objects

Unlike C++ (but like Java), the basic data types in C# may also be treated as objects so that you may call some methods on them. For example, in C# you can convert an integer to a string like this.

```
int i = 10;
string y = i.ToString();
```

You can even write:

```
string y = 10.ToString();
```

The fact that we can treat the basic data types as objects reflects the close association between C# and the .NET base class library. C# actually compiles the basic data types by mapping each one onto one of the base classes, for example `string` maps to `System.String`, `int` to `System.Int32`, etc. So in a real sense in C#, everything is an object. However, note that this only applies for syntactical purposes. In reality, when your code is executed, these types are implemented as the underlying Intermediate Language types, so there is no performance loss associated with treating basic types as objects.

We won't list all the methods available to the basic data types here, as details are in MSDN. We will however note the following:

❑   All types have a `ToString()` method. For the basic data types this returns a string representation of their value.

❑   `char` has a large number of properties that give information about its contents (`IsLetter`, `IsNumber`, etc.) as well as methods to perform conversions (`ToUpper()`, `ToLower()`).

❑   `string` has a very large number of methods and properties available. We'll treat strings separately.

A number of static member methods and properties are also available. These include:

❑   Integer types have `MinValue` and `MaxValue` to indicate the minimum and maximum values that may be contained in the type.

❑   The `float` and `double` types also have a property, `Epsilon`, which indicates the smallest possible value greater than zero that may be stored.

❑   Separate values, `NaN` (not a number; that is, undefined), `PositiveInfinity`, and `NegativeInfinity` are defined for `float` and `double`. Results of computations will return these values as appropriate (for example, dividing a positive number by zero will give `PositiveInfinity`, while dividing zero by zero will give `NaN`). These values are available as static properties.

❑   Many types, including all the numeric types, have a static `Parse()` method that allows you to convert from a string: `double D = double.Parse("20.5")`.

Note that static methods in C# are called by specifying the name of the type: `int.MaxValue` and `float.Epsilon`.

Casting between the Basic Data Types

Casting is the process of converting a value stored in a variable of one data type to a value of another data type. In C++ this can be done either implicitly or explicitly:

```
float f1 = 40.0;
long l1 = f1;              // implicit
short s1 = (short) l1;     // explicit, old C style
short s2 = short (f1);     // explicit, new C++ style
```

If the cast is specified explicitly then this means that you have explicitly indicated the name of the destination data type in your code. C++ allows you to write explicit casts in either of two styles – the old C style in which the name of the data type was enclosed in brackets, or new style in which the name of the variable is enclosed in brackets. Both styles are demonstrated above, and are syntactical preferences – the choice of style has no effect on the code. In C++ it is legal to convert between any of the basic data types. However, if there is a risk of a loss of data because the destination data type has a smaller range than the source data type, then the compiler may issue a warning, depending on your warning level settings. In the above example, the implicit cast may cause loss of data so will normally cause the compiler to issue a warning. Explicitly specifying the conversion is really a way of telling the compiler that you know what you are doing – as a result this will normally suppress any warnings.

Because C# is designed to be more type-safe than C++, it is less flexible about converting between the data types. It also formalizes the notion of explicit and implicit casts. Certain conversions are defined as implicit casts, which means that you are allowed to perform them using either the implicit or the explicit syntax. Other conversions can only be done using explicit casts, which means the compiler will generate an error (not a warning, as in C++!) if you try to carry out the cast implicitly.

The rules in C# concerning which of the basic numeric data types can be converted to which other types are quite logical. Implicit casts are the ones that involve no risk of loss of data – for example, `int` to `long` or `float` to `double`. Explicit casts are ones where there may be data loss, due to an overflow error, sign error, or loss of the fractional part of a number, for example, `float` to `int`, `int` to `uint`, or `short` to `ulong`. In addition, because `char` is considered somewhat distinct from the other integer types, you can only convert explicitly to or from a `char`.

For example, the following lines all count as valid C# code:

```
float f1 = 40.0F;
long l1 = (long)f1;        // explicit due to possible rounding error
short s1 = (short) l1;     // explicit due to possible overflow error
int i1 = s1;               // implicit - no problems
uint i2 = (uint)i1;        // explicit due to possible sign error
```

Note that in C#, explicit casts are always done using the old C-style syntax. The new C++ syntax cannot be used:

```
uint i2 = uint(i1);        // wrong syntax - this won't compile
```

1133

Checked Casting

C# offers the ability to perform casting and other arithmetic operations in a checked context. This means that the .NET runtime will detect if any overflows occur and throw an exception (specifically an OverFlowException) if any overflows do occur. This feature has no counterpart in C++.

```
checked
{
    int i1 = -3;
    uint i2 = (uint)i1;
}
```

Because of the checked context, the second line will throw an exception. If we had not specified checked, no exception would be thrown and the variable i2 would contain garbage.

Strings

String handling is far easier in C# than it ever was in C++. This is because of the existence of string as a basic data type that is recognized by the C# compiler. There is no need to treat strings as arrays of characters in C#.

The closest equivalent to C#'s string data type in C++ is the string class in the standard library. However, C# string differs from C++ string in the following main ways.

- ❏ C# string contains Unicode, not ANSI, characters.
- ❏ C# string has many more methods and properties than the C++ version does.
- ❏ In C++ the standard library string class is no more than a class supplied by the library, whereas in C# the language syntax specifically supports the string class as part of the language.

Escape Sequences

C# uses the same method of escaping special characters as C++ – using a backslash. The complete list is:

Escape sequence	Character name	Unicode encoding
\'	Single quote	0x0027
\"	Double quote	0x0022
\\	Backslash	0x005C
\0	Null	0x0000
\a	Alert	0x0007
\b	Backspace	0x0008
\f	Form feed	0x000C
\n	Newline	0x000A
\r	Carriage return	0x000D
\t	Horizontal tab	0x0009
\v	Vertical tab	0x000B

This basically means that the codes used in C# are the same as those used in C++, except that C# doesn't recognize \?.

There are a couple of differences between escape characters in C++ and C#:

❑ The escape sequence \0 is recognized in C#. However, it is not used as string terminator in C# and so can be embedded in strings. C# strings work by separately storing their lengths so no character is used as a terminator. Hence C# strings really can contain any Unicode character.

❑ C# has an additional escape sequence \uxxxx (or equivalently \Uxxxx) where xxxx represents a 4-digit hexadecimal number. \uxxxx represents the Unicode character xxxx, for example \u0065 represents 'e'. However, unlike the other escape sequences, \uxxxx can be used in variable names as well as in character and string constants. For example, the following is valid C# code:

```
int r\u0065sult;      // has the same effect as int result;
result = 10;
```

According to the documentation, this escape sequence is case-insensitive: \uxxxx and \Uxxxx are both equivalent. However, we found when writing this book that only the lowercase version successfully compiled with the current version of .NET.

C# also has an alternative method for expressing strings that is more convenient for strings that contain special characters. Placing an @ symbol in front of the string prevents any characters from being escaped. These strings are known as verbatim strings. For example, to represent the string C:\Book\Chapter2, we could write either "C:\\Book\\Chapter2", or @"C:\Book\Chapter2". Interestingly, this also means we can include carriage returns in verbatim strings without escaping them:

```
string Message = @"This goes on the first line
and this goes on the next line";
```

Value Types and Reference Types

C# divides all data types into two types: value types and reference types. This distinction has no equivalent in C++, where variables always implicitly contain values, unless a variable is specifically declared as a reference to another variable.

In C#, a value type actually contains its value. All the predefined data types in C# are value types, except for object and string. If you define your own structs or enumerations, these will also be value types. This means that the simple data types in C# generally work in exactly the same way as in C++ when you assign values to them:

```
int i = 10;
long j = i;    // creates another copy of the value 10
i = 15;        // has no effect on j
```

A reference type, as its name implies, contains only a reference to where the data is kept in memory. Syntactically, this works the same way as references in C++, but in terms of what is actually happening, C# references are closer to C++ pointers. In C#, object and string are reference types, as are any classes that you define yourself. C# references can be reassigned to point to different data items, in much the same way that C++ pointers can. Also, C# references can be assigned the value null to indicate that they don't refer to anything. For example, suppose we have a class called MyClass, which has a public property, Width.

```
MyClass My1 = new MyClass();  // In C#, new simply calls a constructor.
My1.Width = 20;
MyClass My2 = My1;            // My2 now points to the same memory
                             // location as My1.

My2.Width = 30;              // Now My1.Width = 30 too because My1 and My2
                             // point to the same location.
My2 = null;                  // Now My2 doesn't refer to anything.
                             // My1 still refers to the same object.
```

It is not possible in C# to declare a particular variable programmatically as a value or as a reference type – that is determined exclusively by the data type of the variable.

Value and reference types have implications for memory management, since reference types are always stored on the heap, whereas value types are usually on the stack. This is covered in more detail in the next section, on memory management.

Initialization of Variables

In C++ variables are never initialized unless you explicitly initialize them (or in the case of classes, supply constructors). If you don't, then variables will contain whatever random data happened to previously be in the memory location now assigned to that variable – this reflects the emphasis on performance in C++. C# put more emphasis on avoiding runtime bugs, and is therefore stricter about initializing variables. The rules in C# are as follows:

❑   Variables that are member fields are by default initialized by being zeroed out if you do not explicitly initialize them. This means that numeric value types will contain zero, `bool`s will contain `false`, and all reference types (including `string` and `object`) will contain the null reference). Structs will have each of their members zeroed out.

❑   Variables that are local to methods are not initialized by default. However, the compiler will raise an error if a local variable is used before it is initialized. You can, if you wish, initialize a variable by calling its default constructor (which zeros out the memory):

```
// variables that are local to a method
int x1;            // At this point x1 contains random data
//int y = x1;      // This commented out line would produce a compilation error
                   // as x1 is used before it is initialized
x1 = new int();    // Now x1 will contain zero and is initialized
```

Boxing

In some cases you might wish to treat a value type as if it were a reference type. This is achieved by a process known as boxing. Syntactically this just means casting the variable to an object:

```
int j = 10;
object boxedJ = (object) j;
```

Boxing acts like any other cast, but you should be aware that it means that the contents of the variable will be copied to the heap and a reference created (since the object `boxedJ` is a reference type).

The usual reason for boxing a value is in order to pass it to a method that expects a reference type as a parameter. You can also unbox a boxed value, simply by casting it back to its original type:

```
int j = 10;
object boxedJ = (object) j;
int k = (int) boxedJ;
```

Note that the process of unboxing will raise an exception if you attempt to cast to the wrong type and no cast is available for you to do the conversion.

Memory Management

In C++, variables (including instances of classes or structs) may be stored on the stack or the heap. In general, a variable is stored on the heap if it, or some containing class, has been allocated with new, and it is placed on the stack otherwise. This means that through your choice of whether to allocate memory for a variable dynamically using new, you have complete freedom to choose whether a variable should be stored on the stack or the heap. (But obviously, due to the way the stack works, data stored on the stack will only exist as long as the corresponding variable is in scope.)

C# works very differently in this regard. One way to understand the situation in C# is by thinking of two common scenarios in C++. Look at these two C++ variable declarations:

```
int j = 30;
CMyClass *pMine = new CMyClass;
```

Here the contents of j are stored on the stack. This is exactly the situation that exists with C# value types. Our MyClass instance is, however, stored on the heap, and a pointer to it is on the stack. This is basically the situation with C# reference types, except that in C# the syntax dresses the pointer up as a reference. The equivalent in C# is:

```
int J = 30;
MyClass Mine = new MyClass();
```

This code has pretty much the same effect in terms of where the objects are stored as does the above C++ code – the difference is that MyClass is syntactically treated as a reference rather than a pointer.

The big difference between C++ and C# is that C# does not allow you to choose how to allocate memory for a particular instance. For example, in C++ you could if you wished do this:

```
int* pj = new int(30);
CMyClass Mine;
```

This will cause the int to be allocated on the heap, and the CMyClass instance to be allocated on the stack. You cannot do this in C# because C# deems that an int is a value type, while any class is always a reference type.

The other difference is that there is no equivalent to C++'s delete operator in C#. Instead, with C# the .NET garbage collector periodically comes in and scans through the references in your code in order to identify which areas of the heap are currently in use by your program. It is then automatically able to remove all the objects that are no longer in use. This technique effectively saves you from having to free up any memory yourself on the heap.

In C# the following are always value types:

- ❑ All simple predefined types (except `object` and `string`)
- ❑ All structs
- ❑ All enumerations

The following are always reference types:

- ❑ `object`
- ❑ `string`
- ❑ All classes

The new operator

The new operator has a very different meaning in C# compared to C++. In C++, new indicates a request for memory on the heap. In C#, new simply means that you are calling the constructor of a variable. However, the action is similar to the extent that if the variable is a reference type, calling its constructor will implicitly mean that memory for it is allocated on the heap. For example, suppose we have a class, `MyClass`, and a struct, `MyStruct`. In accordance with the rules of C#, `MyClass` instances will always be stored on the heap and `MyStruct` instances on the stack.

```
MyClass Mine;              // Just declares a reference. Similar to declaring
                           // an uninitialized pointer in C++.

Mine = new MyClass();      // Creates an instance of MyClass. Calls no-
                           // parameter constructor. In the process, allocates
                           // memory on the heap.

MyStruct Struct;           // Creates a MyStruct instance but does not call
                           // any constructor. Fields in MyStruct will be
                           // uninitialized.

Struct = new MyStruct();   // Calls constructor, so initializing fields.
                           // But doesn't allocate any memory because Struct
                           // already exists on stack.
```

It is possible to use new to call the constructor for predefined data types, too:

```
int x = new int();
```

This has the same effect as:

```
int x = 0;
```

Note that this is not the same as:

```
int x;
```

This latter statement leaves x uninitialized (if x is a local variable).

Methods

Methods in C# are defined in the same way as functions in C++, apart from the fact that C# methods must always be members of a class, and the definition and declaration are always merged in C#:

```
class MyClass
{
    public int MyMethod()
    {
        // implementation
```

One restriction, however, is that member methods may not be declared as const in C#. The C++ facility for methods to be explicitly declared as const (in other words, not modifying their containing class instance) looked originally like a good compile-time check for bugs, but tended to cause problems in practice. This was because it's common for methods that do not alter the public state of the class to alter the values of private member variables (for example, for variables that are set on first access). It's not uncommon in C++ code to find the const_cast operator being used to circumvent a method having been declared as const. In view of these problems, Microsoft decided not to allow const methods in C#.

Method Parameters

As in C++, parameters are by default passed to methods by value. If you wish to modify this, you can use the keywords ref to indicate that a parameter is passed by reference, and out to indicate that it is an output parameter (always passed by reference). If you do this, you need to indicate the fact both in the method definition and when the method is called:

```
public void MultiplyByTwo(ref double d, out double square)
{
    d *= 2;
    square = d * d;
}

// Later on, when calling method:
double value, square;
value = 4.0;
MultiplyByTwo(ref value, out square);
```

Passing by reference means that the method can modify the value of the parameter. You might also pass by reference in order to improve performance when passing large structs, since, just as in C++, passing by reference means that only the address gets copied. Note however, that, if you are passing by reference for performance reasons, the called method will still be able to modify the value of the parameter: C# does not permit the const modifier to be attached to parameters in the way that C++ does.

Out parameters work in much the same way as reference parameters, except that they are intended for cases in which the called method supplies the value of the parameter rather than modifying it. Hence the requirements when a parameter is initialized are different. C# requires that a ref parameter is initialized before being passed to a method, but requires that an out parameter is initialized within the called method before being used.

Method Overloads

Methods may be overloaded in the same way as in C++. However, C# does not permit default parameters to methods. This must be simulated with overloads:

In C++, you can do this:

```
double DoSomething(int someData, bool Condition = true)
{
    // etc.
```

Whereas in C#, you have to do this:

```
double DoSomething(int someData)
{
    DoSomething(someData, true);
}

double DoSomething(int someData, bool condition)
{
    // etc.
```

Properties

Properties have no equivalent in ANSI C++, though they have been introduced as extensions in Microsoft Visual C++. A property is a method or pair of methods that are dressed syntactically to appear to calling code as if they were a field. They exist for the situation in which it is more intuitive for a method to be called with the syntax of a field – an obvious example being the case of a private field that is to be encapsulated by being wrapped by public accessor methods. Suppose a class has such a field, length, of type int. In C++ we would encapsulate it with methods GetLength() and SetLength(), and we would need to access it from outside the class like this:

```
// MyObject is an instance of the class in question
MyObject.SetLength(10);
int length = MyObject.GetLength();
```

In C# we could implement these methods instead as get and set accessors of a property named Length. Then we could write:

```
// MyObject is an instance of the class in question
MyObject.Length = 10;
int Length = MyObject.Length;
```

To define these accessors we would define the property as shown:

```
class MyClass
{
    private int length;

    public int Length
    {
        get
        {
            return length;
        }
        set
        {
            Length = value;
        }
    }
}
```

Although we have implemented the `get` and `set` accessors here to simply return or set the length field, we can put any other C# code we wish in these accessors, just as we could for a method. For example, we might add some data validation to the set accessor. Notice that the set accessor returns void and takes an extra implicit parameter, which has the name `value`.

It is possible to omit either the `get` or `set` accessor from the property definition, in which case the corresponding property respectively becomes either write-only or read-only.

Operators

The meanings and syntaxes of operators is much the same in C# as in C++. The following operators by default have the same meaning and syntax in C# as in C++:

- ❑ The binary arithmetic operators +, -, *, /, %
- ❑ The corresponding arithmetic assignment operators +=, -=, *=, /=, %=
- ❑ The unary operators ++ and -- (both prefix and postfix versions)
- ❑ The comparison operators !=, ==, <, <=, >, >=
- ❑ The shift operators >> and <<
- ❑ The logical operators &, |, &&, ||, ~, ^, !
- ❑ The assignment operators corresponding to the logical operators: >>=, <<=, &=, |=, ^=
- ❑ The ternary (conditional) operator ? :

The symbols (), [], and , (comma) also have broadly the same effect in C# as they do in C++.

You'll need to be careful of the following operators as they work differently in C# from in C++:

- ❑ Assignment (=), new, this.

Scope resolution in C# is represented by ., not by :: (:: has no meaning in C#). Also, the `delete` and `delete[]` operators do not exist in C#. They are not necessary since the garbage collector automatically handles cleaning up of memory on the heap. However, C# also supplies three other operators that do not exist in C++: is, as, and `typeof`. These operators are related to obtaining type information for an object or class.

Assignment Operator (=)

For simple data types, = simply copies the data. However, when you define your own classes, C++ regards it as largely the responsibility of the developer to indicate the meaning of = for your classes. By default in C++ = causes a shallow memberwise copy of any variable, class, or struct to be made. However, programmers overload this operator to carry out more complex assignment operations.

In C#, the rules governing what the assignment operator means are much simpler; it also does not permit you to overload = at all – its meaning is defined implicitly in all situations.

The situation in C# is as follows:

- ❑ For simple data types, = simply copies the values as in C++.
- ❑ For structs, = does a shallow copy of the struct – a direct memory copy of the data in the struct instance. This is similar to its behavior in C++.
- ❑ For classes, = copies the reference; that is, the address and not the object. This is **not** the behavior in C++.

If you want to be able to copy instances of classes, the usual way in C# is to override a method, MemberwiseCopy(), which all classes in C# by default inherit from the class System.Object, the grandfather class from which all C# classes implicitly derive.

this

The this operator has the same meaning as in C++, but it is a reference rather than a pointer. For example, in C++ you can do this:

```
this->m_MyField = 10;
```

However, in C#, you must do this:

```
this.MyField = 10;
```

this is used in the same way in C# as in C++. For example, you can pass it as a parameter in method calls, or use it to make it explicit that you are accessing a member field of a class. In C#, there are a couple of other situations that syntactically require use of this, which we'll mention in the section on classes.

new

As mentioned earlier, the new operator has a very different meaning in C#, being interpreted as a constructor, to the extent that if forces an object to initialize, rather than as a request for dynamic memory allocation.

Classes and Structs

In C++, classes and structs are extremely similar. Formally, the only difference is that members of a struct are by default public, while members of a class are by default private. In practice, however, many programmers prefer to use structs and classes in different ways, reserving use of structs for data objects, which contain only member variables (in other words, no member functions or explicit constructors).

C# reflects this traditional difference of usage. In C# a class is a very different type of object from a struct, so you'll need to consider carefully whether a given object is best defined as a class or as a struct. The most important differences between C# classes and C# structs are:

❑ Structs do not support inheritance, other than the fact that they derive from System.ValueType. It is not possible to inherit from a struct, nor can a struct inherit from another struct or class.

❑ Structs are value types. Classes are always reference types.

❑ Structs allow you to organize the way that fields are laid out in memory, and to define the equivalent of C++ unions.

❑ The default (no-parameter) constructor of a struct is always supplied by the compiler and cannot be replaced.

Because classes and structs are so different in C#, we'll treat them separately in this appendix.

Classes

Classes in C# follow much the same principles as in C++, though there are a few differences in both features and syntax. We'll go over the differences between C++ classes and C# classes in this section.

Definition of a Class

Classes are defined in C# using what at first sight looks like much the same syntax as in C++:

```
class MyClass : MyBaseClass
{
   private string SomeField;
   public int SomeMethod()
   {
      return 2;
   }
}
```

Behind this initial similarity, there are numerous differences in the detail:

❑ There is no access modifier on the name of the base class. Inheritance is always public.

❑ A class can only be derived from one base class (though it may also be derived from any number of interfaces). If no base class is explicitly specified, then the class will automatically be derived from System.Object, which will give the class all the functionality of System.Object, the most commonly used of which is ToString().

❑ Each member is explicitly declared with an access modifier. There is no equivalent to the C++ syntax in which one access modifier can be applied to several members:

```
public:   // you can't use this syntax in C#
   int MyMethod();
   int MyOtherMethod();
```

❑ Methods cannot be declared as inline. This is because C# is compiled to Intermediate Language (IL). Any inlining will happen at the second stage of compilation – when the Just-In-Time compiler will convert from IL to native machine code. The JIT compiler has access to all the information in the IL to determine which methods may suitably be inlined without any need for guidance from the developer in the source code.

❑ The implementation of methods is always placed with the definition. There is no ability to write the implementation outside the class, as C++ allows.

❑ Whereas in ANSI C++, the only types of class member are variables, functions, constructors, destructors, and operator overloads, C# also permits delegates, events, and properties.

❑ The access modifiers public, private, and protected have the same meaning as in C++, but there are two additional access modifiers available:

   ❑ internal restricts access to other code within the same assembly.

   ❑ protected internal restricts access to derived classes that are within the same assembly.

❑ Initialization of variables is permitted in the class definition in C#.

❑ C++ requires a semicolon after the closing brace at the end of a class definition. This is not required in C#.

Initialization of Member Fields

The syntax used to initialize member fields in C# is very different from that in C++, although the end effect is identical.

Instance Members

In C++, instance member fields are usually initialized in the constructor initialization list:

```
MyClass::MyClass()
    : m_MyField(6)
{
// etc.
```

In C# this syntax is wrong. The only things that can be placed in the constructor initializor (which is C#'s equivalent of the C++ constructor initialization list) is another constructor. Instead, the initialized value is marked with the definition of the member in the class definition:

```
class MyClass
{
    private int MyField = 6;
```

Note that in C++, this would be an error because C++ uses roughly this syntax to define pure virtual functions. In C# this is fine, as C# does not use the =0 syntax for this purpose (it uses the abstract keyword instead).

Static Fields:

In C++ static fields are initialized via a separate definition outside the class:

```
int MyClass::MyStaticField = 6;
```

Indeed in C++, even if you do not wish to initialize a static field, you must include this statement in order to avoid a link error. By contrast, C# does not expect a statement like this, since in C# variables are only declared in one place:

```
class MyClass
{
    private static int MyStaticField = 6;
```

Constructors

The syntax for declaring constructors in C# is the same as that for inline constructors defined in the class definition in C++:

```
class MyClass
{
    public MyClass()
    {
        // construction code
    }
```

As with C++, you may define as many constructors as you wish, provided they take different numbers or types of parameters. (Note that, as with methods, default parameters are not permitted – you must simulate this with multiple overloads.)

For derived classes in a hierarchy, constructors work in C# in basically the same way as in C++. By default, the constructor at the top of the hierarchy (this is always `System.Object`) is executed first, followed in order by constructors down the tree.

Static Constructors

C# also allows the concept of a static constructor, which is executed once only, and may be used to initialize static variables. The concept has no direct equivalent in C++.

```
class MyClass
{
    static MyClass()
    {
        // static construction code
    }
}
```

Static constructors are very useful in that they allow static fields to be initialized with values that are determined at runtime (for example, they may be set to values that are read in from a database). This kind of effect is possible in C++ but takes a fair bit of work, and the solution normally looks messy. The most common way would be to have a function that accesses the static member variable, and implement the function so that it sets the value of the variable the first time it is called.

Note that a static constructor has no access specifier – it is not declared as public, private, or anything else. An access specifier would be meaningless since the static constructor is only ever called by the .NET runtime, when the class definition is loaded. It cannot be called by any other C# code.

C# does not specify exactly when a static constructor will be executed, except that it will be after any static fields have been initialized but before any objects of the class are instantiated or static methods on the class are actually used.

Default Constructors

As in C++, C# classes normally have a no-parameter default constructor, which simply calls the no-parameter constructor of the immediate base class and then initializes all fields to their default parameters. Also as in C++, the compiler will generate this default constructor only if you have not supplied any constructors explicitly in your code. If any constructors are present in the class definition, whether or not a no-parameter constructor is included, then these constructors will be the only ones available.

As in C++ it is possible to prevent instantiation of a class by declaring a private constructor as the only constructor:

```
class MyClass
{
    private MyClass()
    {
    }
}
```

This also prevents instantiation of any derived classes. However, if a class or any methods in it are declared abstract this prevents instantiation of that class but not necessarily of any derived classes.

Constructor Initialization Lists

C# constructors may have something that looks like a C++ constructor initialization list. However, in C# this list can only contain at most one member and is known as a **constructor initializer**. The item in the initializer must either be a constructor of the immediate base class, or another constructor of the same class. The syntax for these two options use the keywords base and this respectively:

```
class MyClass : MyBaseClass
{
    MyClass(int X)
    : base(X)        // executes the MyBaseClass 1-parameter constructor
    {
        // other initialization here
    }

    MyClass()
    : this(10)    // executes the 1-parameter MyClass constructor
                  // passing in the value of 10
    {
        // other initialization here
    }
```

If you do not explicitly supply any constructor initialization list, then the compiler will implicitly supply one that consists of the item base(). In other words, the default initializer calls the default base class constructor. This behavior mirrors that of C++.

Unlike C++, you cannot place member variables in a constructor initialization list. However, that is just a matter of syntax – the C# equivalent is to mark their initial values in the class definition.

A more serious difference is the fact that you can only place one other constructor in the list. This will affect the way you plan out your constructors, though this is arguably beneficial since it forces you into a well defined and effective paradigm for arranging your constructors. This paradigm is indicated in the above code: the constructors all follow a single path for the order in which various constructors are executed.

Destructors

C# implements a very different programming model for destructors compared to C++. This is because the garbage collection mechanism in C# implies that:

❑   There is less need for destructors, since dynamically allocated memory will get removed automatically.

❑   Since it is not possible to predict when the garbage collector will actually destroy a given object, if you do supply a destructor for a class, it is not possible to predict precisely when that destructor will be executed.

Because memory is cleaned up behind the scenes in C#, you will find that only a small proportion of your classes actually requires destructors. For those that do (this will be classes that maintain external unmanaged resources such as file and database connections), C# has a two-stage destruction mechanism:

1. The class should derive from the IDisposable interface, and implement a method, Dispose(). This method is intended to be called explicitly by client code to indicate it has finished with an object, and needs to clean up resources. (We'll cover interfaces later in this appendix.)

2. The class should separately implement a destructor, which is viewed as a reserve mechanism, in case a client does not call Dispose().

The usual implementation of Dispose() looks like this:

```
public void Dispose()
{
    // clean up resources
    System.GC.SuppressFinalize(this);
}
```

System.GC is a base class that represents the garbage collector. SuppressFinalize() is a method that informs the garbage collector that there is no need to call the destructor for the object that it is destroying. Calling SuppressFinalize() is important, because there is a performance hit if the object has a destructor that needs to be called while the garbage collector is doing its job; the consequence of this is that the actual freeing of that object's managed memory resources will be considerably delayed.

The syntax for the actual destructor is basically the same in C# as in C++. Note that in C# there is no need to declare the destructor as virtual – the compiler will assume it is. You should also not supply an access modifier:

```
class MyClass
{
    ~MyClass()
    {
        // clean up resources
    }
```

Although the Dispose() method is normally called explicitly by clients, C# does allow an alternative syntax that ensures that the compiler will arrange for it to be called. If the variable is declared inside a using() block, then it will be scoped to the using block and its Dispose() method will be called on exiting the block:

```
using (MyClass MyObject = new MyClass())
{
    // code
}   // MyObject.Dispose() will be implicitly called on leaving this block
```

Note that the above code will only compile successfully if MyClass derives from IDisposable and implements Dispose(). If you don't wish to use the using syntax then you are at liberty to omit either or both of the two steps involved in the destructor sequence (implementing Dispose() and implementing a destructor), but normally you would implement both steps. You can also implement Dispose() without deriving from IDisposable, but if you do this then again it will not be possible to use the using syntax to have Dispose() automatically called for instances of that class.

Inheritance

Inheritance works in basically the same way in C# as in C++, with the exception that multiple implementation inheritance is not supported. Microsoft believes that multiple inheritance leads to code that is less well structured and harder to maintain, and so made a decision to omit this feature from C#.

```
class MyClass : MyBaseClass
{
    // etc.
```

In C++, a pointer to a class can additionally point to an instance of a derived class. (Virtual functions do after all depend on this fact!) In C#, classes are accessed via references, but the equivalent rule holds. A reference to a class can refer to instances of that class or to instances of any derived class.

```
MyBaseClass Mine;
Mine = new MyClass();    //OK if MyClass is derived from MyBaseClass
```

If you want a reference to be able to refer to anything (the equivalent of void* in C++), you can define it as object in C#, since C# maps object to the System.Object class, from which all other classes are derived.

```
object Mine2 = new MyClass();
```

Virtual and non-Virtual Functions

Virtual functions are supported in C# in the same way as in C++. However, there are some syntactical differences in C#, which are designed to eliminate certain potential ambiguities in C++. This means that certain types of error, which only appear at runtime in C++, will be identified at compile time in C#.

Also note that in C#, classes are always accessed through a reference (equivalent to access through a pointer in C++).

In C++, if you require a function to be virtual, all you need to do is to specify the virtual keyword in both the base and derived class. By contrast, in C# you need to declare the function as virtual in the base class and as override in any derived class versions:

```
class MyBaseClass
{
    public virtual void DoSomething(int X)
    {
        // etc.
    }
    // etc.
}

class MyClass : MyBaseClass
{
    public override void DoSomething(int X)
    {
        // etc.
    }
    // etc.
}
```

The point of this syntax is that it explicit to the compiler how you want your function to be interpreted, and it means that there is no risk of any bugs where, for example, you type in a slightly incorrect method signature in an override version, and therefore end up defining a new function when you intended to override an existing one. The compiler will flag an error if a function is marked as an override and the compiler cannot identify a version of it in any base class.

If the function is not virtual, you can still define versions of that method in the derived class, in which case the derived class version is said to hide the base class version. In this case, which method gets called depends solely on the type of the reference used to access the class, just as it depends on the pointer type used to access a class in C++.

In C# if the version of the function in the derived class hides a corresponding function in the base class, you can explicitly indicate this with the new keyword:

```
class MyBaseClass
{
    public void DoSomething(int X)
    {
        // etc.
    }
    // etc.
}

class MyClass : MyBaseClass
{
    public new void DoSomething(int X)
    {
        // etc.
    }
    // etc.
}
```

If you do not mark the new version of the class explicitly as new, the code will still compile but the compiler will flag a warning. This warning is intended to guard against any subtle run-time bugs in which, for example, a new version of the base class is written, in which a method has been added that happens to have the same name as an existing method in the derived class.

You can declare abstract functions in C# just as you can in C++ (in C++ these are also termed pure virtual functions). The syntax, however, is different in C#: instead of using =0 at the end of the definition we use the keyword abstract.

C++:
```
public:
    virtual void DoSomething(int X) = 0;
```

C#:
```
    public abstract void DoSomething(int X);
```

As in C++, you can only instantiate a class if it contains no abstract methods itself, and it provides implementations of any abstract methods that have been defined in any of its base classes.

Structs

The syntax for defining structs in C# follows that for defining classes.

```
struct MyStruct
{
    private SomeField;
    public int SomeMethod()
    {
        return 2;
    }
}
```

Inheritance, and the associated concepts, virtual and abstract functions, are not permitted. Otherwise, the basic syntax is identical to classes except that the keyword struct replaces class in the definition.

There are, however, a couple of differences between structs and classes when it comes to construction. In particular, structs always have a default constructor that zeros out all the fields, and this constructor is still present even if you define other constructors of your own. Also, it is not possible to define a no-parameter constructor explicitly to replace the default one. You may only define constructors that take parameters. In this respect, structs in C# differ from their C++ counterparts.

Unlike classes in C#, structs are value types. This means that a statement such as:

```
MyStruct Mine;
```

actually creates an instance of MyStruct on the stack, just as the same statement in C# would. However, in C#, this instance is uninitialized unless you explicitly call the constructor:

```
MyStruct Mine = new MyStruct();
```

If the member fields of MyStruct are all public, you can alternatively initialize it by initializing each member field separately.

Constants

The C++ keyword const has quite a large variety of uses. For example, you can declare variables as const, which indicates that their values are usually set at compile time and cannot be modified by any assignment statement at run-time (although there is a tiny bit of flexibility since the value of a const member variable can be set in a constructor initialization list, which implies that in this case the value can be calculated at run time). You can also apply const to pointers and references to prevent those pointers or references from being used to modify the data to which they point, and you can also use the const keyword to modify the definitions of parameters passed to functions. Here, const indicates that a variable that has been passed by reference or via a pointer should not be modified by the function. Also, as mentioned earlier, member functions themselves can be declared as const to indicate that they do not change their containing class instance.

C# also allows use of the const keyword to indicate that a variable cannot be changed. In many ways, however, use of const is far more restrictive in C# than in C++. In C#, the *only* use of const is to fix the value of a variable (or of the referent of a reference) at compile time. It cannot be applied to methods or parameters. On the other hand, C# is more flexible than C++, to the extent that the syntax in C# does allow a little more flexibility for initializing const fields at runtime than C++ does.

The syntax for declaring constants is very different in C# from C++, so we'll go over it in some detail. The C# syntax makes use of two keywords, const and readonly. The const keyword implies that a value is set at compile time, while readonly implies it is set once at runtime, in a constructor.

Since everything in C# must be a member of a class or struct, there is of course no direct equivalent in C# to global constants in C++. This functionality must be obtained using either enumerations or static member fields of a class.

Constants that are Associated with a Class (Static Constants)

The usual way of defining a static constant in C++ is as a static const member of a class. C# approaches this in broadly the same way, but with a simpler syntax:

C++ syntax:

```
int CMyClass :: MyConstant = 2;

class CMyClass
{
public:
    static const int MyConstant;
```

C# syntax:

```
class MyClass
{
    public const int MyConstant = 2;
```

Note that in C# we do not explicitly declare the constant as static – doing so would give a compilation error. It is, of course, implicitly static, because there is no point storing a constant value more than once, and hence it must always be accessed as a static field.

```
int SomeVariable = MyClass.MyConstant;
```

Things get a bit more interesting when you want your static constant to be initialized with some value that is calculated at runtime. C++ simply has no facility to allow this. If you want to achieve that effect, then you will have to find some means of initializing the variable the first time it is accessed, which means you will not be able to declare it as const in the first place. In this case, C# scores easily over C++, since static constants initialized at runtime are easy to define in C++. You define the field as readonly, and initialize it in the static constructor:

```
class MyClass
{
    public static readonly int MyConstant;

    static MyClass()
    {
        // work out and assign the initial value of MyConstant here
    }
```

Instance Constants

Constants that are associated with class instances are always initialized with values calculated at runtime. (If their values were calculated at compile time that would, by definition, make them static.)

In C++, such constants must be initialized in the initialization list of a class constructor. This restricts your flexibility, to some extent, in calculating the values of these constants since the initial value must be something that you can write down as an expression in the constructor initialization list.

```
class CMyClass
{
public:
    const int MyConstInst;

    CMyClass()
        : MyConstInst(45)
    {
```

In C# the principle is similar, but the constant is declared as `readonly` rather than `const`. This means that its value is set in the body of the constructor giving you a bit more flexibility, since you can use any C# statements in the process of calculating its initial value. (Recall that you cannot set the values of variables in constructor initializers in C# – you can only call one other constructor.)

```
class MyClass
{
    public readonly int MyConstInst;

    MyClass()
    {
        // work out and initialize MyConstInst here
```

In C#, if a field is declared as `readonly`, then it may be assigned to only in constructors.

Operator Overloading

Operator overloading follows similar principles in C# to C++, but there are some differences. Most notably, C++ allows the vast majority of its operators to be overloaded. C# has more restrictions. For many compound operators, C# automatically works out the meaning of the operator from the meanings of the constituent operators, where C++ allows direct overload. For example, in C++, you can overload + and separately overload +=. In C# you can only overload +. The compiler will always use your overload of + to automatically work out the meaning of += for that class or struct.

The following operators can be overloaded in C# as well as C++:

- ❑ The binary arithmetic operators + - * /%
- ❑ The unary operators ++ and -- (prefix version only)
- ❑ The comparison operators !=, == <, <=, >, >=
- ❑ The bitwise operators &, |, ~, ^, !
- ❑ The Boolean values true and false

The following operators, which you will be used to overloading in C++, cannot be overloaded in C#:

❑ The arithmetic assignment operators *=, /=, +=, -=, %=. (These are worked out by the compiler from the corresponding arithmetic operator and the assignment operator, which cannot be overloaded.) The postfix increment operators. These are worked out by the compiler from the overloads of the corresponding prefix operators. (They are implemented by calling the corresponding prefix operator overload, but returning the original value of the operand instead of the new value.)

❑ The bitwise assignment operators &=, |=, ^=, >>=, and <<=.

❑ The Boolean operators &&, ||. (These are worked out by the compiler from the corresponding bitwise operators.)

❑ The assignment operator =. The meaning of this operator in C# is fixed.

There is also a restriction that the comparison operators must be overloaded in pairs – in other words, if you overload == you must overload != and vice versa. Similarly, if you overload one of < or <=, you must overload both operators, and similarly for > and >=. The reason for this is to ensure consistent support for any database types which may have the value null, and for which therefore, for example, == does not necessarily have the opposite effect to !=.

Once you have established that the operator you wish to overload is one that you can overload in C#, the syntax for actually defining the overload is much easier than the corresponding syntax in C++. The only points that you need to be careful of in overloading C# operators is that they must always be declared as static members of a class. This contrasts with the situation in C++ in which you can choose to define your operator either as a static member of the class, as an instance member of the class but taking one parameter fewer, or as a function that is not a member of a class at all.

The reason that defining operator overloads is so much simpler in C# has actually got nothing to do with the operator overloads themselves. It is because of the way that C# memory management naturally works to help you out. Defining operator overloads in C++ is an area that is filled with traps to catch the unwary. Consider, for example, an attempt to overload the addition operator for class in C++. (We'll assume for this that CMyClass has a member, x, and adding instances means adding the x members.) The code might look something like this (assuming the overload is inline):

```
static CMyClass operator + (const CMyClass &lhs, const CMyClass &rhs)
{
    CMyClass Result;
    Result.x = lhs.x + rhs.x;
    return Result;
}
```

Notice that the parameters are both declared as const and passed by reference, in order to ensure optimum efficiency. This by itself isn't too bad. However, in this case we need to create a temporary CMyClass instance inside the operator overload in order to return a result. The final return Result statement looks innocuous, but it will only compile if an assignment operator is available to copy Result out of the function, and works in an appropriate way. If you've defined your own copy constructor for CMyClass, you may need to define the assignment operator yourself too, to make sure assignment behaves appropriately. That in itself is not a trivial task, since if you don't use references correctly when defining it, it's very easy to accidentally define one that recursively calls itself until you get a stack overflow! Bluntly, overloading operators in C++ is not a task for inexperienced programmers! It's not hard to see why Microsoft decided to make certain operators not overloadable in C#.

In C# the picture is very different. There's no need to explicitly pass by reference, since C# classes are reference variables anyway (and for structs, passing by reference tends to degrade rather than help performance). And returning a value is a breeze. Whether it's a class or a struct, you simply return the value of the temporary result, and the C# compiler will ensure that either the member fields in the result get copied (for value types) or the address is copied (for reference types). The only disadvantage is you can't use the const keyword to get the extra compiler check that makes sure that the operator overload doesn't modify the parameters for a class. Also, C# doesn't give you the inline performance enhancements of C++.

```
static MyClass operator + (MyClass lhs, CMyClass rhs)
{
    MyClass Result = new MyClass();
    Result.x = lhs.x + rhs.x;
    return Result;
}
```

Indexers

C# doesn't strictly permit [ ] to be overloaded. However, it does permit you to define something called an indexer for a class, which gives the same effect.

The syntax for defining an indexer is very similar to that for a property. Suppose that we want to be able to treat instances of MyClass as an array, where each element is indexed with an int and returns a long. Then you would write:

```
class MyClass
{
    public long this[int x]
    {
        get
        {
            // code to get element
        }
        set
        {
            // code to set element. eg. X = value;
        }
    }
// etc.
```

The code inside the get block is executed whenever the expression Mine[x] appears on the right-hand side of an expression (assuming Mine is an instance of MyClass and x is an int), while the set block is executed whenever Mine[x] appears on the left side of an expression. The set block cannot return anything, and uses the value keyword to indicate the quantity that appears on the right-hand side of the expression. The get block must return the same data type as that of the indexer.

It is possible to overload indexers to take any data type in the square brackets, or any number of arguments – allowing the effect of multi-dimensional arrays.

User-Defined Casts

Just as for indexers and [ ], C# does not formally regard ( ) as an operator that can be overloaded. However, it does permit the definition of user-defined casts, which have the same effect. For example, suppose you have two classes (or structs) called MySource and MyDest, and you wish to define a cast from MySource to MyDest. The syntax looks like this:

```
public static implicit operator MyDest (MySource Source)
{
    // code to do cast. Must return a MyDest instance
}
```

The cast must be defined as a static member of either the MyDest or the MySource class. It must also be declared as either implicit or explicit. If you declare it as implicit, then the cast may be used implicitly, like this:

```
MySource Source = new MySource();
MyDest Dest = MySource;
```

If you declare it as explicit then the cast may only be used explicitly:

```
MySource Source = new MySource();
MyDest Dest = (MyDest) MySource;
```

You should define implicit casts for conversions that will always work, and explicit casts for conversions that might fail by losing data or causing an exception to be thrown.

Just as in C++, if the C# compiler is faced with a request to convert between data types for which no direct cast exists, it will seek to find the 'best' route using the casts it has available. The same issues as in C++ apply concerning ensuring that your casts are intuitive, and that different routes to achieve any conversion don't give incompatible results.

C# does not permit you to define casts between classes that are derived from each other. Such casts are already available – implicitly from a derived class to a base class and explicitly from a base class to a derived class.

Note that if you attempt to cast from a base class reference to a derived class reference, and the object in question is not an instance of the derived class (or anything derived from it) then an exception will be thrown. In C++, it is not difficult to cast a pointer to an object to the 'wrong' class of object. That is simply not possible in C# using references. For this reason, casting in C# is considered safer than in C++.

```
// assume MyDerivedClass is derived from MyBaseClass
MyBaseClass MyBase = new MyBaseClass();
MyDerivedClass MyDerived = (MyDerivedClass) MyBase;    // this will result
                                                       // in an exception being thrown
```

If you don't want to try to cast something to a derived class, but don't want an exception to be thrown you can use the as keyword. Using as, if the cast fails then it will simply return null.

```
// assume MyDerivedClass is derived from MyBaseClass
MyBaseClass MyBase = new MyBaseClass();
MyDerivedClass MyDerived as (MyDerivedClass) MyBase;    // this will
                                                        // return null
```

Arrays

Arrays are one area in which a superficial similarity in syntax between C++ and C# hides the fact that what is actually going on behind the scenes is very different in the two languages. In C++, an array is essentially a set of variables packed together in memory and accessed via a pointer. In C#, on the other hand, an array is an instance of the base class `System.Array`, and is therefore a full-blown object stored on the heap under the control of the garbage collector. C# uses a C++-type syntax to access methods on this class in a way that gives the illusion of accessing arrays. The downside to this approach is that the overhead for arrays is greater than that for C++ arrays, but the advantage is that C# arrays are more flexible and easier to code around. As an example, C# arrays all have a property, `Length`, that gives the number of elements in the array, saving you from having to store this separately. C# arrays are also much safer to use – for example, the index bounds checking is performed automatically.

If you do want a simple array with none of the overhead of the `System.Array` class, it is still possible to do this in C#, but you'll need to use pointers and unsafe code blocks.

One-Dimensional Arrays

For one-dimensional arrays (C# terminology: arrays of **rank** 1), the syntax to access an array in the two languages is identical, with square brackets used to indicate elements of arrays. Arrays are also zero-indexed in both languages.

For example, to multiply each element in an array of `floats` by 2:

```
// array declared as an array of floats
// this code works in C++ and C# without any changes
for (int i=0; i<10; i++)
    Array[i] *= 2.0f;
```

As mentioned earlier, however, C# arrays support the property `Length`, which can be used to find out how many elements are in it:

```
// Array declared as an array of floats
// this code compiles in C# only
for (int i=0; i<Array.Length; i++)
    Array[i] *= 2.0f;
```

In C# we can also use the `foreach` statement to access elements of an array, as discussed earlier.

The syntax for declaring arrays is slightly different in C#, however, since C# arrays are always declared as reference objects:

```
double [] Array;            // Simply declares a reference without actually
                            // instantiating an array.
Array = new double[10];     // Actually instantiates a System.Array object,
                            // and gives it size 10.
```

Or combining these statements, we might write:

```
double [] Array = new double[10];
```

Notice that the array is only sized with its instance. The declaration of the reference simply uses the square brackets to indicate that the dimension (rank) of the array is one. In C#, rank is considered part of the type of the array, whereas the number of elements is not.

The nearest C++ equivalent to the above definition would be

```
double *pArray = new double[10];
```

This C++ statement actually gives a fairly close analogy, since both C++ and C# versions are allocated on the heap. Note that the C++ version is just an area of memory that contains ten doubles, while the C# version instantiates a full-blown object. The simpler stack version of C++:

```
double pArray[10];
```

doesn't have a C# counterpart that uses actual C# arrays, though the C# stackalloc statement can achieve the equivalent to this statement using pointers. This is discussed later in the section on unsafe code.

Arrays in C# can be explicitly initialized when instantiated:

```
double [] Array = new double[10]
                  {1.0, 2.0, 3.0, 4.0, 5.0, 6.0, 7.0, 8.0, 9.0, 10.0);
```

A shortened form exists too:

```
double [] Array = {1.0, 2.0, 3.0, 4.0, 5.0, 6.0, 7.0, 8.0, 9.0, 10.0);
```

If an array is not explicitly initialized, the default constructor will automatically be called on each of its elements. (Elements of arrays are formally regarded as member fields of a class.) This behavior is very different from C++, which does not allow any kind of automatic initialization of arrays allocated with new on the heap (though C++ does allow this for stack-based arrays).

Multidimensional Arrays

C# departs significantly from C++ in multidimensional arrays, since C# supports both rectangular and jagged arrays.

A rectangular array is a true grid of numbers. In C#, this is indicated by a syntax in which commas separate the number of elements in each dimension. Hence, for example, a two-dimensional rectangular array might be defined like this:

```
int [,] MyArray2d;
MyArray2d = new int[2,3]  { {1, 0}, {3, 6}, {9, 12} };
```

The syntax here is a fairly intuitive extension of the syntax for one-dimensional arrays. The initialization list in the above code could be absent. For example:

```
int [,,] MyArray3d = new int[2,3,2];
```

This will cause the default constructor to be called on each element, initializing each int to zero. In this particular example, we are illustrating the creation of a three-dimensional array. The total number of elements in this array is 2 x 3 x 2 = 12. A characteristic of rectangular arrays is that each row has the same number of elements.

Elements of rectangular arrays are accessed using a similar syntax:

```
int x = MyArray3d[1,2,0] + MyArray2d[0,1];
```

C# rectangular arrays have no direct counterpart in C++. C# jagged arrays, however, correspond fairly directly to multidimensional C++ arrays. For example, if you declare an array like this in C++:

```
int MyCppArray[3][5];
```

what you are actually declaring is not really a 3x5 array, but an array of arrays – an array of size 3, each element of which is an array of size 5. This is perhaps clearer if we try to do the same thing dynamically – we'd need to write:

```
int pMyCppArray = new int[3];
for (int i=0; i<3; i++)
   pMyCppArray[i] = new int[5];
```

It should be clear from this code that now there is no reason for each row to contain the same number of elements (though it happens to do so in this example). As an example of a jagged array in C++, which really does have different numbers of elements in each row, you might write:

```
int pMyCppArray = new int[3];
for (int i=0 ; i<3 ; i++)
   pMyCppArray[i] = new int[2*i + 2];
```

The respective rows of this array have dimensions 2, 4, and 6.

C# achieves the same thing in much the same manner, though in the C# case, the syntax indicates the numbers of dimensions more explicitly:

```
int [][] MyJaggedArray = new int[3][];
for (int i=0; i<3; i++)
   MyJaggedArray[i] = new int[2*i + 2];
```

Accessing members of a jagged array follows exactly the same syntax as for C++:

```
int x = MyJaggedArray[1][3];
```

Here we've shown a jagged array with rank 2. Just as in C++, however, you can define a jagged array with whatever rank you wish – you just need to add more square brackets to its definition.

Bounds Checking

One area in which the object nature of C# arrays becomes apparent is bounds checking. If you ever attempt to access an array element in C# by specifying an index that is not within the array bounds, this will be detected at runtime, and an `IndexOutOfBoundsException` will be thrown. In C++, this does not happen, and subtle run-time bugs can result. Once again, C# goes for extra checking against bugs at the expense of performance. Although you might expect this to give a loss in performance, it does have the benefit that the .NET runtime is able to check through code to ensure that it is safe, in the sense that it will not attempt to access any memory beyond that allocated for its variables. This allows performance benefits, since different applications may for example be run in the same process and we can still be certain that those applications will be isolated from each other. There are also security benefits, since it is possible to predict more accurately what a given program will or won't attempt to do.

On the other hand, it's not uncommon now for C++ programmers to use any of the various array wrapper classes in the standard library or in MFC in preference to raw arrays, in order to gain the same bounds checking and various other features – although in this case without the performance and security benefits associated with being able to analyze the program before it is executed.

Resizing Arrays

C# arrays are dynamic in the sense that you can specify the number of elements in each dimension at compile time (just as with dynamically allocated arrays in C++). However, it is not possible to resize them after they have been instantiated. If you need that kind of functionality, you'll need to look at some of the other related classes in the `System.Collections` namespace in the base class library, such as `System.Collections.ArrayList`. However, to that extent C# is no different from C++. Raw C++ arrays do not allow resizing, but a number of standard library classes exist that do provide for that feature.

Enumerations

In C#, it is possible to define an enumeration using the same syntax as in C++:

```
// valid in C++ or C#
enum TypeOfBuilding {Shop, House, OfficeBlock, School};
```

Note, however, that the trailing semicolon in C# is optional, since an enumeration definition in C# is effectively a struct definition, and struct definitions do not need trailing semicolons:

```
// valid in C# only
enum TypeOfBuilding {Shop, House, OfficeBlock, School}
```

However, in C# the enumeration must be named, whereas in C++, providing a name for the enumeration is optional. Just as in C++, C# numbers the elements of the array upwards from zero, unless you specify that an element should have a particular value:

```
enum TypeOfBuilding {Shop, House=5, OfficeBlock, School=10}
// Shop will have value 0, OfficeBlock will have value 6
```

The way that you access the values of the elements is different in C#, since in C# you must specify the name of the enumeration:

C++ syntax:

```
TypeOfBuilding MyHouse = House;
```

C# syntax:

```
TypeOfBuilding MyHouse = TypeOfBuilding.House;
```

You might regard this as a disadvantage because the syntax is more cumbersome, but this actually reflects the fact that enumerations are far more powerful in C#. In C#, each enumeration is a fully-fledged struct in its own right (derived from System.Enum), and therefore has certain methods available. In particular, for any enumerated value, it is possible to do this:

```
TypeOfBuilding MyHouse = TypeOfBuilding.House;
string Result = MyHouse.ToString();    // Result will contain "House"
```

This is something that is almost impossible to achieve in C++.

You can also go the other way in C#, using the static Parse() method of the System.Enum class, although the syntax is a little more awkward:

```
TypeOfBuilding MyHouse = (TypeOfBuilding)Enum.Parse(typeof(TypeOfBuilding),
                                            "House", true);
```

Enum.Parse() returns an object reference, and so must be explicitly cast (unboxed) back to the appropriate enum type. The first parameter to Parse() is a System.Type object that describes which enumeration the string should represent. The second parameter is the string, and the third parameter indicates whether the case should be ignored. A second overload omits the third parameter, and does not ignore the case.

C# also permits you to select the underlying data type used to store an enum:

```
enum TypeOfBuilding : short {Shop, House, OfficeBlock, School};
```

If you do not specify a type, the compiler will assume a default of int.

Exceptions

Exceptions are used in the same way in C# as in C++, apart from the following two differences:

- ❑ C# defines the finally block, which contains code that is always executed at the end of the try block, irrespective of whether any exception was thrown. The lack of this feature in C++ has been a common cause of complaint among C++ developers. The finally block is executed as soon as control leaves a catch or try block, and typically contains clean-up code for resources allocated in the try block.

- ❑ In C++ the class thrown in the exception may be any class. C#, however, requires that the exception be a class derived from System.Exception.

The rules for program flow through `try` and `catch` blocks are identical in C++ and C#. The syntax used is also identical, except for one difference – in C# a `catch` block that does not specify a variable to receive the exception object is denoted by the `catch` statement on its own.

C++ syntax:

```
catch (...)
{
```

C# syntax:

```
catch
{
```

In C#, this kind of `catch` statement can be useful to catch exceptions that are thrown by code written in other languages (and which therefore might not be derived from `System.Exception` – the C# compiler will flag an error if you attempt to define an exception object that isn't, but that isn't the case for other languages!).

The full syntax for `try ... catch ... finally` in C# looks like this:

```
try
{
   // normal code
}
catch (MyException e)        // MyException derived from System.Exception
{
   // error handling code
}
// optionally further catch blocks
finally
{
   // clean up code
}
```

Note that the `finally` block is optional. It is also permitted to have no `catch` blocks – in which case the `try ... finally` construct simply serves as a way of ensuring that the code in the `finally` block is always executed when the `try` block exits. This could be useful for example if the `try` block contains several `return` statements and you want some cleaning up of resources to be done before the method actually returns.

Pointers and Unsafe Code

Pointers may be declared in C# and they are used in much the same way as in C++. However, they may be declared and used only in an unsafe code block.

You can declare any method as unsafe:

```
public unsafe void MyMethod()
{
```

You can alternatively declare any class or struct as unsafe:

```
unsafe class MyClass
{
```

Declaring a class or struct as unsafe means that all members are regarded as unsafe. You can also declare any member field (but not local variables) as unsafe, if you have a member field of a pointer type:

```
private unsafe int* pX;
```

It is also possible to mark a block statement as unsafe:

```
unsafe
{
    // statements that use pointers
}
```

The syntax for declaring, accessing, de-referencing, and performing arithmetic operations on pointers is the same as in C++:

```
// This code would compile in C++ or C#, and has the same effect in both
// languages
int X = 10, Y = 20;
int *pX = &X;
*pX = 30;
pX = &Y;
++pX;     // adds sizeof(int) to pX
```

Note the following points, however:

❑ In C# it is not permitted to de-reference void* pointers, nor can you perform pointer arithmetic operations on void* pointers. The void* pointer syntax has been retained for backwards compatibility, to call external API functions that are not .NET-aware and which require void* pointers as parameters.

❑ Pointers cannot point to reference types (classes or arrays). Nor can they point to structs that contain embedded reference types as members. This is really an attempt to protect data that is used by the garbage collector and by the .NET runtime (though in C#, just as in C++, once you start using pointers you can almost always find a way around any restriction by performing arithmetic operations on pointers and then de-referencing).

❑ Besides declaring the relevant parts of your code as unsafe, you also need to specify the /unsafe flag to the compiler when compiling code that contains pointers.

❑ Pointers cannot point to any variables that are embedded in reference data types (for example, members of classes) unless declared inside a fixed statement.

Fixing Data on the Heap

It is permitted to assign the address of a value type to a pointer even if that value type is embedded as a member field in a reference type. However, such a pointer must be declared inside a `fixed` statement. The reason for this is that reference types may at any time be moved around on the heap by the garbage collector. The garbage collector is aware of C# references and can update them as necessary, but it is not aware of pointers. Hence, if a pointer points to a class member on the heap and the garbage collector moves the entire class instance, then the pointer will end up pointing to the wrong address. The `fixed` statement prevents the garbage collector from moving the specified class instance for the duration of the `fixed` block, ensuring the integrity of pointer values:

```
class MyClass
{
    public int X;
    // etc.
}

// Elsewhere in your code ...
MyClass Mine = new MyClass();

// Do processing

fixed(int *pX = Mine.X)
{
    // Can use pX in this block.
}
```

It is possible to nest `fixed` blocks in order to declare more than one pointer. You can also declare more than one pointer in a single `fixed` statement, provided both pointers have the same referent type.

```
fixed(int *pX = Mine.X, *pX2 = Mine2.X)
{
```

Declaring Arrays on the Stack

C# provides an operator called `stackalloc`, which can be used in conjunction with pointers to declare a low-overhead array on the stack. The array so allocated is not a full C#-style `System.Array` object, but is a simple array of numbers exactly analogous to a one-dimensional C++ array. The elements of this array are not initialized and are accessed using the same syntax as in C++ by applying square brackets to the pointer.

The `stackalloc` operator requires specification of the data type and the number of elements for which space is required.

C++ syntax:

```
unsigned long pMyArray[20];
```

C# syntax:

```
ulong *pMyArray = stackalloc ulong [20];
```

Note, however, that although these arrays are exactly analogous, the C# version allows the size to be determined at runtime:

```
int X;
// Initialize X
ulong *pMyArray = stackalloc ulong [X];
```

Interfaces

Interfaces are an aspect of C# with no direct equivalent in ANSI C++, although Microsoft has introduced interfaces in C++ with a Microsoft-specific keyword. The idea of an interface evolved from COM interfaces, which are intended as contracts that indicate which methods and properties an object implements.

An interface in C# is not quite the same as a COM interface, since it does not have an associated GUID, does not derive from IUnknown, and does not have associated registry entries (although it is possible to map a C# interface onto a COM interface). A C# interface is simply a set of definitions for functions and properties. It can be considered analogous to an abstract class and is defined using a similar syntax to a class:

```
interface IMyInterface
{
    void MyMethod(int X);
}
```

You'll notice, however, the following syntactical differences from a class definition:

- ❑ The methods do not have access modifiers.
- ❑ Methods can never be implemented in an interface.
- ❑ Methods may not be declared as virtual or explicitly as an abstract. The choice of how to implement methods is the responsibility of any class that implements this interface.

A class implements an interface by deriving from it. Although a class can only be derived from one other class, it can also derive from as many interfaces as you want. If a class implements an interface, it must supply implementations of all methods defined by that interface.

```
class MyClass : MyBaseClass, IMyInterface, IAnotherInterface // etc
{
    public virtual void MyMethod(int X)
    {
        // implementation
    }
    // etc.
```

In this example, we've chosen to implement MyMethod as a virtual method with public access.

Interfaces can also derive from other interfaces, in which case the derived interface contains its own methods as well as those of the base interface:

```
interface IMyInterface : IBaseInterface
```

You can check that an object implements an interface either by using the `is` operator or by using the `as` operator to cast it to that interface. Alternatively, you can cast it directly, but in that case you'll get an exception if the object doesn't implement the interface, so that approach is only advisable if you know the cast will succeed. You can use the interface reference so obtained to call methods on that interface (the implementation being supplied by the class instance):

```
IMyInterface MyInterface;
MyClass Mine = new MyClass();
MyInterface = Mine as IMyInterface;
if (MyInterface != null)
   MyInterface.MyMethod(10);
```

The main uses of interfaces are:

❑ For interoperability and backwards compatibility with COM components.

❑ To serve as contracts for other .NET classes. An interface can be used to indicate that a class implements certain features. For example, the C# `foreach` loop works internally by checking that the class to which it is applied implements the `IEnumerable` interface, and by then calling methods that are defined by that interface.

Delegates

A delegate in C# has no direct equivalent in C++, and performs the same task as a C++ function pointer. The idea of a delegate is that the method pointer is wrapped in a specialized class, along with a reference to the object against which the method is to be called (for an instance method, or the null reference for a static method). This means that, unlike a C++ function pointer, a C# delegate contains enough information to call an instance method.

Formally, a delegate is a class that is derived from the class `System.Delegate`. Hence instantiating a delegate involves two stages: defining this derived class, then declaring a variable of the appropriate type. The definition of a delegate class includes details of the full signature (including the return type) of the method that the delegate wraps.

The main use for delegates is for passing around and invoking references to methods. References to methods cannot be passed around directly, but they can be passed around inside the delegate. The delegate ensures type safety, by preventing a method with the wrong signature from being invoked. The method contained by the delegate can be invoked by syntactically invoking the delegate. The following code shows the general principles.

First, we need to define the delegate class:

```
// Define a delegate class that represents a method that takes an int and
// returns void
delegate void MyOp(int X);
```

Next, for the purposes of our example we will declare a class that contains the method to be invoked:

```
// Later - a class definition
class MyClass
{
    void MyMethod(int X)
    {
        // etc.
    }
}
```

Then, later on, perhaps in the implementation of some other class, we have the method that is to be passed a method reference via a delegate:

```
void MethodThatTakesDelegate(MyOp Op)
{
    // call the method passing in value 4
    Op(4);
}
// etc.
```

And finally, the code that actually uses the delegate:

```
MyClass Mine = new MyClass();

// Instantiate a MyOp delegate. Set it to point to the MyMethod method
// of Mine.
MyOp DoIt = new MyOp(Mine.MyMethod);
```

Once this delegate variable is declared, we can invoke the method via the delegate:

```
DoIt();
```

Or pass it to another method:

```
MethodThatTakesDelegate(DoIt);
```

In the particular case that a delegate represents a method that returns a void, that delegate is a multicast delegate, and can simultaneously represent more than one method. Invoking the delegate causes all the methods it represents to be invoked in turn. The + and += operators can be used to add a method to a delegate, and – and –= can be used to remove a method that is already in the delegate. Delegates are explained in more detail in Chapter 6 on *Advanced C# Topics*.

Events

Events are specialized forms of delegates that are used to support the callback event notification model. An event is a delegate that has this signature:

```
delegate void EventClass(obj Sender, EventArgs e);
```

This is the signature any event handler that is called back must have. Sender is expected to be a reference to the object that raised the event, whereas System.EventArgs (or any class derived from EventArgs – this is also permitted as a parameter) is the class used by the .NET runtime to pass generic information concerning the details of an event.

The special syntax for declaring an event is this:

```
public event EventClass OnEvent;
```

Clients use the += syntax of multicast delegates to inform the event that they wish to be notified:

```
// EventSource refers to the class instance that contains the event
EventSource.OnEvent += MyHandler;
```

The event source then simply invokes the event when required, using the same syntax as we demonstrated above for delegates. Since the event is a multicast delegate, all the event handlers will be called in the process. Events are explained in more detail in Chapter 6.

```
OnEvent(this, new EventArgs());
```

Attributes

Attributes are a concept that has no equivalent in ANSI C++, though they are supported by Microsoft's C++ compiler as a Windows-specific extension. In the C# version, they are .NET classes that are derived from `System.Attribute`. They may be applied to various elements in C# code (classes, enums, methods, parameters, etc.) to generate extra documentation information in the compiled assembly. In addition, certain attributes are recognized by the C# compiler and will have an effect on the compiled code. These include:

Attribute	Description
`DllImport`	Indicates that a method is defined in an external DLL.
`StructLayout`	Permits the contents of a struct to be laid out in memory. Allows the same functionality as a C++ union.
`Obsolete`	Generates a compiler error or warning if this method is used.
`Conditional`	Forces a conditional compilation. This method and all references to it will be ignored unless a particular preprocessor symbol is present.

There are a large number of other attributes, and it is also possible to define your own custom ones. Use of attributes is discussed in Chapters 6 and 7.

The syntax of attributes is that they appear immediately before the object to which they apply, in square brackets. This is the same syntax as for Microsoft C++ attributes:

```
[Conditional("Debug")]
void DisplayValuesOfImportantVariables()
{
    // etc.
```

Preprocessor Directives

C# supports preprocessor directives in the same way as C++, except that there are far fewer of them. In particular, C# does not support the commonly used `#include` of C++. (It's not needed because C# does not require forward declarations.)

The syntax for preprocessor directives is the same in C# as in C++. The directives supported by C# are:

Directive	Meaning
`#define`/`#undef`	Same as C++, except that they must appear at the start of the file, before C# code.
`#if`/`#elif`/`#else`/`#endif`	Same as C++ `#ifdef`/`#elif`/`#else`/`#endif`.
`#line`	Same as C++ `#line`.
`#warning`/`#error`	Same as C++ `#warning`/`#error`.
`#region`/`#endregion`	Marks off a block of code as a region. Regions are recognized by certain editors (such as the folding editors of Visual Studio .NET) and so can be used to improve the layout of code presented to the user while editing.

B

C# for Java Developers

In *The Art of War* Sun Tzu claims that "one should regard things of great importance with little effort, and things of little importance with great effort". This might sound strange to hear, but I think the point the author is trying to make is that if you take care of the little things, the big things will then of take care of themselves. So how does this apply to C# and Java?

Looking at C# code initially, you might find it not very exciting because of what might appear to be a distinct similarity between it and Java. However, if what you're expecting is something dramatic, the truth is that there's just not that much of a syntactic difference. Where you will find the path of the two languages splitting is in the inner subtleties: things such as operator overloading, indexers, delegates, properties, and type safe enumerations. On closer examination, you will realize that there is a major difference between them after all. (The above topics will be discussed later on in this appendix).

The focus of this appendix will primarily be on identifying to a Java developer how to use his or her much-loved Java tricks with C#, and highlighting things that C# adds to the picture, or things that C# cannot do. (I assure you, however, that you won't find many of those). Because I am assuming the reader is a professional Java developer I am not going to go into too much detail in describing the Java language, except to elaborate on some differences that are present.

The Basics

One of the major differences between C# and Java lies not in the languages themselves, but in the platforms on top of which they are implemented. Java programs need a runtime environment, the **Java Runtime Environment** (**JRE**), to execute code. Similarly C#, and indeed all of the .NET framework are executed in an environment called the **Common Language Runtime** (**CLR**).

Most of the features of the CLR, internal memory management, framework consistency, scalability, and underlying platform independence are mirrored by Java's JRE. Whereas the JRE is bound exclusively to one language, Java, CLR provides multiple language support and integration through the use of **VOS** (**Virtual Object System**), which provides a rich type system that is intended to support the implementation of many different types of programming languages. Java source code can be compiled into an intermediate state known as **bytecode**. This can then be executed using a supplied virtual machine. Conversely, CLR does not provide a virtual machine. C# code does also compile to an intermediate state, conveniently named **Intermediate Language** (**IL**). But IL code is passed to the CLR-managed execution processes or the CLR JIT compilers, commonly referred to as JITters, which compile sections of the IL to native code on demand.

Let's take a look at the infamous "Hello World!" example in Java:

```
public class Hello
{
    public static void main (String args [])
    {
        System.out.println ("Hello world! This is Java Code!");
    }
}
```

The corresponding C# code for this is as follows:

```
public class Hello
{
    public static void Main (string [] args)
    {
        System.Console.WriteLine ("Hello world! This is C# code!");
    }
}
```

The first thing that you'll notice is that the two appear to be very similar – for the most part, the differences are small (such as the capitalization of string and Main, and the use of System.Console.WriteLine instead of System.out.println). It is, on the other hand, still case-sensitive.

Another thing to bring to light is the string type, which in C# can also be written with a capital "S" as String. Hence the above code could have been written as:

```
public class Hello
{
    public static void Main (String [] args)
    {
        System.Console.WriteLine ("Hello world! This is C# code!");
    }
}
```

You will notice that the array rank specifier, [], has been shifted from in front of the args variable in the Java example, to between the String type and args variable in the C# sample. In C#, the array rank specifier must appear before the variable name because an array in actually a type of its own indicated by type []:

```
//C#

int [] x;     //array of integers in c#

//java sample

int [] x;     //array of integers in java
int x[];      //array of integers in java
```

The same C# code can also be presented as follows:

```
using System;
class Hello
{
    public static int Main()
    {
        Console.WriteLine("Hello world! This is C# code!");
        return 0;
    }
}
```

As you can see, a few things have changed. The `string [] args` declaration in the method signature is optional in C# (although the brackets must appear before the parameter name), as is the use of `public` when declaring the method. The `using` keyword is similar in concept to the `include` keyword in Java, and while `System` is a default inclusion in C#, the first line allows us to drop the `System` that was in front of `Console.WriteLine`. Because we're using `int` instead of `void` in this example, we need to include the `return 0;` line.

C# code blocks are enclosed by braces just as in Java. You can tell that the `Main()` method is part of the class because it is enclosed in the braces. The entry point to a C# application is the static `Main()` method, as required by the compiler. You should note that Java uses a lowercase `main()`. Also note that only one class in the application can have a `Main()`. The public access modifier (discussed later) declares the method accessible to code consumers outside the class, package, or application, and is required make the method visible. The compiler also requires it. Similarly in Java, the `static` keyword allows for the method to be called without creating an instance of the class first. For the `Main()` method you have the choice of either a `void` or `int` return type. `void` specifies that the method does not return a value and `int` specifies that it returns an integer type.

Identifiers

Keywords, discussed in the next section, may not be identifiers either in Java or C#; however, in C# one may use keywords as identifiers by prefixing the identifier with "@". Note that this exception is only with keywords and does not allow the breaking of any other rules. Both languages are case-sensitive, so identifiers must have a consistent capitalization. Although identifiers may have letters and numbers, the first letter of the identifier in both C# and Java must not be a number. Java does not allow any symbols except for "$", and C# does not allow any symbols:

```
int 7x;     //invalid, number cannot start identifier
int x7;     //valid, number may be part of identifier
int x;      //valid
int x$;     //invalid, no symbols allowed
int @7k;    //invalid, @ only works for keywords
int @class; //valid, @ prefixing keyword allows it to be used as an
            // identifier
```

Naming Standard

One major difference that may not be obvious at first glance, and that is not tied specifically to the C# language, is the syntax with which identifiers are written. Java practices **camel** notation, meaning that method and identifiers are small letter for the first letter in the name and capital letter for the first letter of every other word in the name. The general syntax you would find most programmers following in Java is given below:

```
int id;
int idName;
int id_name;                      //practiced also
final int CONSTANT_NAME;          //widely adopted
int reallyLongId;

public class ClassName            //every first letter capitalized
public interface _InterfaceName   //preceded by underscore

public void method(){}
public void methodName(){}
public void longMethodName(){}
public void reallyLongMethodName(){}
```

Based on the library classes provided by Microsoft for C#, it is safe to make certain assumptions about the C# naming standards. A documented naming guideline for C# was not provided at the time of this writing. Each first letter of all method and property identifier names is capitalized, as is each first letter of all class and namespace (discussed latter) names. Interfaces are preceded with an I. Some examples are given below:

```
int id;
int idName;

public class ClassName            //every first letter capitalized
public interface IInterfaceName   //interface name preceded by I

public void Method(){}            // first letter always capitalized
public void MethodName(){}        // first letter of all other words
                                  // capitalized
public void LongMethodName(){}
public void ReallyLongMethodName(){}
```

Keywords

A keyword is simply a special reserved word of a language. So far, you have been exposed to a number of them: declaring a variable as an integer by preceding it with int, for example. Other examples of keywords are the public, class, static, and void associated with the code listings earlier on in this appendix.

Keywords can be broken into a number of categories based on their purpose. In this section, we will highlight and define each category as well as identify the keywords associated with it. The actual keywords will be identified by their Java versions so that this section is easier to navigate. The C# equivalent (if any) will then be given. For those keywords that are only present in Java, a reference to a best fit will be provided. Keywords present in C# and not Java will be addressed in their own category with an associated best fit for Java (if any is available).

Primitive Keywords: byte, char, short, int, long, float, double, and boolean

Primitive types in either language refer to the low level value types of the language. Of course, the value ranges of the indicated types may be different from one language to another. Boolean values in C# are identified with the `bool` keyword as opposed to `boolean` in Java. Below is a tabular listing of the Java types and their C# counterparts:

Java Type	Description	C# Type equiv.	Description
byte	signed 8-bit	sbyte	signed 8-bit
short	signed 16-bit	short	signed 16-bit
int	signed 32-bit	int	signed 32-bit
long	signed 64-bit	long	signed 64-bit
float	signed 32-bit floating point	float	signed 32-bit floating point
double	signed 64-bit floating point	double	signed 64-bit floating point
boolean	true/false	bool	true/false
char	unicode 2-byte	char	unicode 2-byte

There are also a number of types supported by C# that Java does not use. The table below highlights these types:

Unique C# Type	Description
Byte	8-bit unsigned integer
ushort	16-bit unsigned integer
Uint	32-bit unsigned integer
ulong	64-bit unsigned integer
decimal	128-bit

Variable Keywords: this, void, and super

These are keywords that are themselves variables. Java and C# both have three keywords that fall into this category. The keywords `this` and `void` have the same functionality in both languages.

The `Super` reference variable is used to signify the immediate parent class. In C# the equivalent is `base`. Take a class `SuperEX` that provides the ability to resolve the power of a number given the number and the power to resolve to (provided an overflow does not occur):

```
public class SuperEX
{
    int power;
```

```java
    public SuperEX(int power){
        this.power = power;
    }

    public int aMethod(int x){
        int total = 1;
        for(int i = 0; i < power; i ++){
            total *= x;
        }

        return total;
    }
    public static void main(String args[]){
        SuperEX x = new SuperEX (Integer.parseInt (args [0]));
        int tot = x.aMethod(Integer.parseInt(args[1]));
        System.out.println (tot);
    }
}
```

A child class of this could access aMethod with the call super.aMethod(<int value>), the variable power with the call super.power = <int value> , and even the constructor with the call super(<int value>) where <int value> can be any integer literal, variable, or constant.

Similarly, in C# a child class of this could access aMethod with the call super.aMethod(<int value>), and the variable power with the call super.power = <int value> . Making a call to the base constructor is also possible, the syntax; however, is different. The example below is the C# equivalent of SuperEX:

```csharp
namespace SuperEX
{
    using System;
    public class SuperEX {
        internal int power;
        public SuperEX(int power){
            this.power = power;
        }
        public int aMethod(int x){
            int total = 1;
            for(int i = 0; i < power; i ++){
                total *= x;
            }
            return total;
        }
        public static void Main(String[] args){
            SuperEX x = new SuperEX(int.Parse(args[0]));
            int tot = x.aMethod(int.Parse(args[1]));
            Console.WriteLine(tot);
        }
    }
    public class Child : SuperEX{
        public Child(): base(55){
        }
    }
}
```

As you can see from the child class Child, the call to a base class's constructor is a part of the child class constructor's declaration. The programmer is free to specify the parameter list of the child class's constructor, but the reference to the base class constructor must match the argument list required by the base class. In our example the child constructor could take the form <child constructor>: base constructor (<int value>) where <int value> can be any integer literal, variable, or constant and <child constructor> represents any child constructor that wants to make use of the base class's constructor. A more generalized version of how to access a base class's constructor is given below:

```
ChildConstructor (argument_list): BaseConstructor (argument_list)
```

Package Control Keywords: import, and package

Just as in Java the import statements give access to packages and classes in your code without full qualification; the using directive can be utilized to make components of a namespace visible to a C# class without full qualification. There is no package statement equivalent in C#. To make a class a part of a namespace, simply enclose the class in the namespace declaration. Namespaces will be discussed in more detail later on in this chapter.

Control Flow and Iteration Keywords: break, case, continue, default, do, else, for, if, instanceof, return, switch, and while

Most of the aforementioned keywords have the same name, syntax, and functionality in C# and Java. The exception is Java's instanceof operator used to determine if an object is an instance of a class or any subclass of the class. C# provides the same functionality with the is keyword. Some examples of how statements work in C# is given below. You will find that much of the code is exactly the same as in Java:

```
public static void Main(string[] args)
{
    int option = int.Parse(arg[0]);
    if(option == 1)
    {

        //do something

    }
    else if(option == 2)
    {

      //do something else

    }

    switch(option)
    {
        case 1:

            //do something

            break;
        case 2:

            //do something else
```

```
        default:
        break;
    }
}
```

C# introduces a foreach statement, used specifically to iterate through, and not change collection or array entries to get the desired information. Changing the contents may have unpredictable side effects. The foreach statement usually takes the form supplied below:

```
foreach (ItemType item in TargetCollection)
```

ItemType represents the data type stored in the collection or array and TargetCollection represents the actual array or collection. There are two sets of requirements that a collection you want to iterate through using the foreach statement must meet. The first set is to do with the composition of the collection itself. They are as follows:

❑ The collection type must be an interface, class, or struct.

❑ The collection type must include a GetEnumerator() method for returning an enumerator type. An enumerator type is basically an object that allows you to step through a collection item by item.

The second set of requirements deal with the composition of the enumerator type returned by the GetEnumerator() method mentioned above. The list of requirements is given below:

❑ The enumerator should provide a boolean method MoveNext().

❑ MoveNext() should return true if there are more items in the collection.

❑ MoveNext() should increment the item counter at each invocation.

❑ The enumerator type must provide a property named Current that returns an ItemType (or a type that can be converted to ItemType).

❑ The property accessor Current should return the current element of the collection.

The following example uses foreach to iterate through a Hashtable:

```
Hashtable t = new Hashtable();
t["a"] = "hello";
t["b"] = "world";
t["c"] = "of";
t["d"] = "c-sharp";
foreach(DictionaryEntry b in t)
{
    Console.WriteLine( b.Value );
}
```

Access Modifying Keywords: private, protected, public, and (default package)

The private keyword is used to make methods and variables accessible only from within elements of the containing class. It serves the same function in both languages. The public modifier allows for entities outside the package to access the internal elements. Of course, for C# it would be entities outside the namespace, not packages.

C# and Java differ in the way `protected` and `default` are handled. While in Java, `protected` makes the method or variable accessible to classes in the same package or subclasses of the class, in C# `protected` makes code only visible to that class and subclasses that inherit from it.

C# also introduces a new access modifier: `internal`. The `internal` keyword modifies data members so that they are visible to all code within the entire component but not clients of that component. The difference between no modifier in Java (which signifies an element that is accessible only to elements within the package) and `internal` is that `internal` is accessible to all elements of the assembly, which can span multiple namespaces. Assemblies and namespaces will be discussed later in the appendix.

Modifiers: abstract, class, extends, final, implements, interface, native, new, static, synchronized, transient, and volatile

The `abstract` modifier is the same in form and syntax in both languages. So is the `class` keyword. C# does not have the `extends` or `implements` modifier. To derive from a class or implement an interface, use the `":"` operator. When a class base list contains a base class and interfaces, the base class comes first in the list. The `interface` keyword is used to declare an interface. Examples of the concepts we have discussed to this point are given below:

```
class ClassA: BaseClass, Iface1, Iface2
{
    // class members
}
Public interface IfruitHaver
{
    Public void Fruit();
}
public class Plant: IfruitHaver
{
    public Plant()
    {
    }
    public void Fruit()
    {
    }
}
class Tree : Plant{
    public Tree()
    {
    }
}
```

The `final` keyword in Java is difficult to categorize. Part of the reason is that it provides a kind of two-in-one functionality that makes it difficult to nail it down to any one purpose. Declaring a class as `final` seals it, making it impossible to extend. Declaring a method as `final` also seals it, making it impossible to override. Declaring a variable as `final` is essentially making it read-only. I say read-only and not constant because it is possible to set a `final` value to the value of a variable. The value of constants must be known at compile time so constants may only be set equal to other constants.

In contrast, C# provides specific techniques to address each individual issue. By default a subclass should not be able to re-implement a public method that is already implemented in the superclass. C# introduces a new concept, **method hiding**, which allows the programmer to redefine superclass members in the child class and hide the base class implementation; C# uses *new* as a modifier to accomplish this.

Prepending new to the method declaration does this. The benefit of hiding members from the base class versions is that you can selectively determine which implementation to use. An example of this concept is highlighted in the code below:

```
namespace Fona
    {
    using System;
    public class Plant
        {
        public Plant(){}
        public void BearFruit()
        {
            Console.WriteLine("Generic plant fruit");
        }
    }
    class Tree : Plant
    {
        public Tree(){}

        //new keyword used explicitly here to hide the Base version

        new public void BearFruit()
        {
            Console.WriteLine("Tree fruit is:->Mango");
        }
    }
    public class PlantEX
    {
        public PlantEX(){}
        public static void Main(String[] args)
        {
            Plant p = new Plant();
            p.BearFruit();  //calls base class implementation
            Tree t = new Tree();
            t.BearFruit();  //calls child class implementation
            ((Plant)t).BearFruit();  //calls base class implementation
                                     //using child
        }
    }
}
```

Running this example will produce the output listed below:

```
Generic plant fruit
Tree fruit is:->Mango
Generic plant fruit
```

One thing to note is the difference between method hiding and regular polymorphism. The latter will always expose you the most derived method for calling.

Note: At the time of writing, I found that method hiding compiled without error or warning even when the new keyword was not introduced.

To provide overriding functionality, the modifiers `virtual` and `override` are used in tandem. All methods in the base class that you expect will be overridden must utilize the `virtual` keyword. To actually override them use the `override` keyword in the child class. Below is the `Tree` class example modified to display override functionality:

```
class Tree : Plant
{
    public Tree(){}
    public override void Fruit()
    {
        Console.WriteLine("Tree fruit is:->Mango");
    }
}
```

Compiling and running this will produce the output listed below:

```
Generic plant fruit
Tree fruit is:->Mango
Tree fruit is:->Mango
```

As you can see the most derived `Fruit()` method is called, irrespective of our use of the casting strategy `((Plant)t).BearFruit();` we previously utilized to reference the base class's `Fruit()` method. The `new` modifier can also be used to hide any other type of inherited members from base class members of a similar signature.

To prevent accidental inheritance of a class the `sealed` keyword can be used. In the above example, you could change the `Plant` declaration to `public sealed class Plant`, in which case `Tree` would no longer be able to inherit from it.

C# does not have a `native` modifier. In Java, using `native` indicates that the method is implemented in a platform-dependent language. It requires that the method be abstract since the implementation is to be found elsewhere. The closest relative to this type of functionality is the `extern` modifier. Using `extern` implies that the code is implemented externally (by some native DLL for example). Unlike Java, however, there is no need to use the `abstract` keyword in association with it. In fact doing this would be an error since they mean two similar, but very different things. Below, the `Plant` class from earlier displays an example of how `extern` can be used:

```
public class Plant: IfruitHaver
    {
    public extern int See();
    public Plant(){}
    public void Fruit()
    {
        Console.WriteLine("Generic plant fruit");
    }
}
```

This doesn't make much sense without using the `DllImport` attribute to specify the external implementation. Attributes will be discussed in more detail later on in the appendix. The code overleaf makes the appropriate modifications, assuming there was a `See` function exported by the `User32.dll` resource:

```
public class Plant: IfruitHaver
{
    [System.Runtime.InteropServices.DllImport ("User32.dll")]
    public static extern int See();
    public Plant(){}
    public void Fruit()
    {
        Console.WriteLine("Generic plant fruit");
    }
}
```

If you haven't already noticed, I have now marked See() as static. The DllImport attribute requires this of the methods it is used on.

There is no C# version of transient, volatile, or synchronized at the time of writing. There are, however, a number of ways provided by the .NET SDK to mimic some of this functionality. C# uses the NonSerialized attribute, tied to the class's fields, to provide mechanisms similar in functionality to Java's transient modifier; this attribute is deprecated, however, and so is subject to change in future releases.

Synchronization in C# is somewhat complicated (perhaps robust is a better word) compared to Java. In general, any thread can access all members of an object by default. There are, however, a number of ways to synchronize code depending on the needs of the developer through the use of various tools. Monitors provide the ability to take and release sync block locks on objects. SyncBlocks contain the lock used to implement synchronized methods and blocks of code, and contain a list of waiting threads used to implement monitor functionality. ReaderWriterLock defines a single writer multiple reader pattern. Mutex defines synchronization primitives, which provide inter process synchronization. System.Threading.Interlocked can be used to provide synchronized access to variables shared across multiple threads.

The first step to synchronization in C# is referencing the System.EnterpriseServices.dll assembly. The lock keyword, whose syntax is:

```
lock (<expression>){// block of code}
```

is the only synchronization-associated keyword in C#. It can be used, much as in Java, to gain a mutually exclusive access to the object <ref>'s lock. All attempts to access <expression> will block until the thread with the lock releases it. Typically, an expression will use either this or a System.Type corresponding to the present object and Type. Using this will protect instance variables of the expression while using System.Type will protect static ones.

Error Handling Keywords: catch, finally, throw, throws, and try

These modifiers are the same in both languages with the exception of the throws statement, which is not present in C#. The awesome thing about Java's throws statement is that it allows, with relatively simple syntax, component consumers to use the component without knowledge of what exceptions the component may be throwing. One can rest assured that compiled code is handling all relevant exceptions because the compile will fail otherwise, and inform you of any uncaught exceptions. This type of functionality is not present in C# at this time. Providing a method for consumers of your assembly to know when exceptions are raised will have to fall to good documentation practices or some nifty attribute programming.

Performing calculations can lead to the scenario where your computed result exceeds the range of the result variable's data type. In Java, when integral types reach their limits, they have the nasty habit of flowing over to the opposite bound. To illustrate this examine the code in the following class:

```
//OverflowEX.java

public class OverflowEX
{
    public static void main(String args[])
    {
        byte x = 0;
        for (int i = 0; i < 130; i++)
        {
            x++;
            System.out.println(x);
        }
    }
}
```

As you will no doubt remember, the Java byte is 8-bits and signed. This means that the range of a byte is from −128 to 127. The result of adding one to either limit of a given integer type's range is the other limit of the integer type's range. So in our example adding 1 to 127 would produce −128. Therefore, if you were to compile and run this program, the last five numbers displayed by the console would be as follows:

```
126
127
-128
-127
-126
```

As you can imagine, this could be a major problem, especially since neither a warning nor an exception is raised to allow you to handle such an event (perhaps by saving the value to a larger type). By default, C# also silently handles overflow situations, but the language and compiler do provide tools for explicitly handling or notifying the programmer in the event of an overflow.

The programmatic approach: to battle this type of silent error, C# introduces the concept of checked and unchecked statements. The checked keyword is used to control the overflow-checking context for integral-type arithmetic operations and conversions such as the one we saw above. It can be used as an operator or a statement. The checked/unchecked statements follow the syntax below:

```
checked {block_of_code }
unchecked{block_of_code}
```

They are meant to enclose a number of statements that may generate overflows. The checked/unchecked operation syntax is shown here:

```
checked (expression)
unchecked(expression)
```

The checked operation focuses on checking overflows for a single expression. block_of_code contains the code that the checked/unchecked statement is watching for overflows on, and expression represents the expression that checked/unchecked is observing for overflows in its final value. The example overleaf illustrates the use of checked/unchecked:

1181

```
//OverflowEX.cs

public class OverflowEX
{
    public static void Main(String[] args)
    {
        sbyte x = 0; //remember that you need to change byte to sbyte
        for (int i = 0; i < 130; i++)
        {
            checked
            {   //could have also used checked(x++)
                x++;
                Console.WriteLine(x);
            }
        }
    }
}
```

The compiler switch approach: for overflow checking of the entire application the compiler setting /checked+ can be used. To illustrate this we will remove the checked statement from the above example and attempt to compile it using the /checked+ flag. You can toggle arithmetic overflow checking on and off from the Configuration Properties section of the Project Properties page. Setting the value to true turns overflow checking on.

With overflow checking on we can briefly talk about the unchecked statement. Essentially, it provides functionality to arbitrarily exclude checking on expressions or statement blocks while application-wide checking is enabled. In the example below we have replaced the previous checked statement with an unchecked statement. Compiling and running this will produce output similar to that of OverflowEX.java:

```
//OverflowEX.cs

public class OverflowEX
{
    public static void Main(String[] args)
    {
        sbyte x = 0;
        for (int i = 0; i < 130; i++)
        {
            unchecked
            {   //could have also used unchecked(x++)
                x++;
                Console.WriteLine(x);
            }
        }
    }
}
```

Input and Output

Being able to collect input from the command prompt and display output on the command prompt is an integral part of Java's input/output functionality. Usually in Java one would have to create an instance of a java.io.BufferedReader object using the System.in field in order to retrieve an input from the command prompt. Below we have a simple Java class, JavaEcho, which takes input from the console and echoes it back, to illustrate the use of the Java.io package to gather and format input and output:

```
//JavaEcho.java

import java.io.*;
public class JavaEcho
{
   public static void main(String[] args)throws IOException
   {
      BufferedReader stdin = new BufferedReader(new
                                      InputStreamReader(System.in));
      String userInput = stdin.readLine ();
      System.out.println ("You said: " + userInput);
   }
}
```

The System.Console class provides methods in C# that can provide similar functionality for reading and writing from and to the command prompt. There is no need for any extra objects; the Console class provides methods that can read whole lines, read character by character, and even expose the underlying stream being read from. It is important to note that it is the System.Console provides this functionality without an instantiated Console object. In fact you will find that you cannot instantiate an instance of the Console object. The members of Console are briefly described in the tables below:

Public Static (Shared) Properties	Description
Error	Gets the system's standard error output stream.
In	Gets the system's standard input stream.
Out	Gets the system's standard output stream.

Public Static (Shared) Methods	Description
OpenStandardError	Overloaded. Returns the standard error stream.
OpenStandardInput	Overloaded. Returns the standard input stream.
OpenStandardOutput	Overloaded. Returns the standard output stream.
Read	Reads the next character from the standard input stream.
ReadLine	Reads the next line of characters from Console.In, which is set to the system's standard input stream by default.
SetError	Redirects the Error property to use the specified TextWriter stream.
SetIn	Redirects the In property to use the specified TextReader stream.
SetOut	Redirects the Out property to use the specified TextWriter stream.
Write	Overloaded. Writes the specified information to Console.Out.
WriteLine	Overloaded. Writes information followed by a line terminator to Console.Out.

As you can see, all of the `Console` members are static. `static` is an example of a C# modifier. It shares the same meaning as its Java counterpart – that is, it makes the specified variable or method belong to the entire class and not any one instance of the class. We will discuss modifiers in more detail later on in the appendix.

Using the powerful methods of the `Console` class we could write an equivalent of the `JavaEcho` class in C# as follows:

```
class CSEchoer
{
    static void Main(string[] args)
    {
        string userInput = System.Console.ReadLine();
        System.Console.WriteLine ("You said : " + userInput);
    }
}
```

The above code is much shorter and easier to digest in comparison with its Java counterpart. One useful thing you'll get with the `Console.WriteLine` static method is the ability to use formatted strings. The flexibility of formatted strings can be illustrated by writing a simple game where user input is used to generate a story. The code for `EchoGame` is listed below:

```
class EchoGame
{
    static void Main(string[] args)
    {
        System.Console.WriteLine("Once upon a time in a far away" + "?");
        string userInput1 = System.Console.ReadLine();
        System.Console.WriteLine("a young prince ?");
        string userInput2 = System.Console.ReadLine();
        System.Console.WriteLine("One day while ?");
        string userInput3 = System.Console.ReadLine();
        System.Console.WriteLine("He came accross a ?");
        string userInput4 = System.Console.ReadLine();
        System.Console.WriteLine("The prince ?");
        string userInput5 = System.Console.ReadLine();
        System.Console.WriteLine("Once  upon a time in a far away"
                        + " {0}, a young prince {1}. \n  One day" +
                        " while {2}, He came accross a {3}. \n The " +
                        + "prince {4} ! ", userInput1, userInput2,
                        userInput3, userInput4, userInput5 );
    }
}
```

The insertion points are replaced by the supplied arguments starting from the index `{0}`, which corresponds to the leftmost variable (in this case `userInput1`). You are not limited to supplying only string variables, nor are you confined to using just variables, or even using variables of the same type. Any type that the method `WriteLine` can display may be supplied as an argument including string literals or actual values. There is also no limit to the number of insertion points that can be added to the string, as long as it is less than the overall number of arguments. Note that omitting insertion points from the string will cause the variable not to be displayed. You must, however, have an argument for each insertion point you specify whose index in the argument list corresponds to the index of the insertion point. In the following listing for example, removing `{1}` is fine as long as there are still three arguments. In this case `{0}` matches up with `strA` and `{2}` matches up with `strC`:

```
Console.WriteLine("hello {0} {1} {2}", strA, strB, strC);
```

Compilation

In describing some differences between Java's JRE and C#'s CLR, I briefly went into some detail on how code written in the respective languages is compiled and run. As you will recall, although code from both languages is compiled into some intermediate form, the Java version, bytecode, is never recompiled into native machine instructions (unless you use a native compiler). Instead, the bytecode requires a runtime environment, specifically a virtual machine, to execute. The name of the compiled file is bound to the name of the file your code is written in, which is in turn bound to the name of the public class within that file. In the case where multiple classes are defined in the same file, every class definition will produce a class file that matches the name of the defined class. For example, take the source file Test.java with code as follows:

```
//Test.java

class x
{
}
class y
{
}
class Z
{
}
```

Compiling this file will produce three class files: x.class, y.class, and Z.class. One (and only one for each source file), of these classes may be declared as public as follows:

```
//Test.java

public class x
{
}
class y
{
}
class Z
{
}
```

In the above example, the source file name, Test.java, would have to be changed to match the name of the resident public class. Test.java would therefore have to become x.java for the code to compile.

In contrast, C# code compiled to IL is run by the **VES** (**Virtual Execution System**), which provides support for IL, loading managed code, and JITters (which convert managed code in the form of intermediate language to native code). The filename Hello.cs is not bound to the name of the final executable, and it can be changed at compile time with the /out option. If an output filename is not specified, an exe will take the name of whatever source code file contains the main method and a DLL will take the name of the first source code file specified. In fact, the name of the file is not even bound to whatever class definitions are provided inside the file. A class, Hello, may be defined in a file, Goodbye.cs, which was compiled into an unrelated MisterHanky.exe.

The .NET SDK comes with a C# compiler so you won't have to worry about getting specific compilers for this application. Just open the command prompt, switch to the directory where you saved `hello.cs` and type:

```
csc hello.cs
```

The file will be compiled to `hello.exe`. Although most Java programmers are familiar with this form of low level compilation, it is important to note that Visual Studio.NET provides similar functionality integrated into its IDE. For example, changing the executable filename can be easily achieved by augmenting the **Assembly Name** property. To do this, right-click on your project name from the **Solution Explorer** bar and select **Properties**, or click **Project** from the menu while your project name is highlighted and select the **Properties** menu item. Under the **Common Properties** folder, the **General Properties** page should be selected; if no,t select it and modify the **Assembly Name** property. You should see the read-only property **Output File** change to reflect the new name of your assembly.

Types of Compilations

All Java files are compiled into a bytecode file with a `.class` extension that can be run by the virtual machine. Within the source code one must provide the appropriate functionality to create one type of application as opposed to another. For example, the code specified below will produce a window much like a windows `Form`. The second source file, `AddLib.java`, is a helper class used to perform the addition of two integers. You will notice that they are included in separate packages and that the `JavaFrame` imports the `AddLib` class. The packages and their C# equivalent will be discussed in the next section:

```
//code for JavaFrame.java

Package com.javaapp;
import java.awt.*;
import java.io.*;
import com.javalib.AddLib;
public class JavaFrame extends java.awt.Frame
{
    public static void main (String[] args)
    {
        JavaFrame jfrm = new JavaFrame();
        jfrm.setSize(100,100);
        jfrm.setVisible(true);
        AddLib lib = new AddLib();
        jfrm.setTitle("Frame Version " + lib.operationAdd(12,23) );
    }
}
```

```
//code for AddLib.java

Package com.javalib;
public class AddLib
{
    public AddLib()
    {
    }
    public int operationAdd(int a, int b)
```

```
    {
        return a + b;
    }
}
```

Java provides a two-step process for generating executable or library compilation units: compile the file(s), and make the file available by providing the compiler with the path to the folder where the files reside (one could write a batch file that would do this in one step). Making the class available entails using the −classpath switch of the compiler to set where the compiler may look to resolve symbols undefined in the source code (different compilers may have different names for this switch). Your system also has a classpath environment variable. If the −classpath switch is not specified the compiler will look there. If the switch is specified, it overrides whatever classpath entries may exist in the environment for that specific compilation.

Classes can also be bundled together into a JAR file, which would then need to be made available in the same manner as the folder containing the class is. Classes inside or outside a JAR file may or may not be part of zero or more packages. In the above example, JavaFrame and AddLib would need to be compiled into class files. The path to these class files could then be added to the CLASSPATH environment variable. Once the classpath is set any classes in the package can be run from any directory in the system by passing the fully qualified name of the class to the virtual machine. With JDK1.3, making the call:

```
java javalib.JavaFrame
```

would run the JavaFrame program and create a Frame with the title bar displaying Java Frame Version 35.

Code in C# is always automatically bundled in one type of component or another after compilation. Compilation units may contain as many files and class definitions as required. Again, the path to using this functionality is split between using the command line and using an IDE (specifically Visual Studio.NET). Creating a new project with VS.NET mandates that you specify the type of project you want created. You have the ability to create console applications, Windows applications, and class libraries among other things. You may even create an empty project and specify the output type later. The process of specifying the output type of a project using VS.NET is described later on in this section. As to the command line, using the /target: <target-type> option, where <target type> can be one of the strings:

- ❑ Exe
- ❑ Library
- ❑ Winexe

will allow you to change the output type. Any number of files may also be added as space delimited arguments:

```
csc /target:<target-type> <file1> <file2> <filen>
```

Adding multiple files to a compilation unit using VS.NET is just a matter of adding the individual files to the project. Modifying the output file type can easily be achieved by changing the Output Type property from the project's General Properties page.

Namespaces

My intention is to provide a C# version of the JavaFrame and AddLib source code files and to look in detail at the build process for C# code. As these two classes utilize packaging and importing, it is necessary to discuss the C# equivalents I promised earlier.

Java classes, as shown above, may reside in logical divisions referred to as **packages**. A package can simply be defined as an entity that groups classes together. Packages can make it easy to import other programmer's code into yours, and more importantly help to specify access restrictions to variables and methods.

Namespaces in C# provide a similar mechanism for grouping managed classes together but are much more powerful and flexible. I say "managed classes" and not specifically C# classes because classes in a namespace may be from any CLS-compliant language (remember that the CLR is language independent). However, packages and namespaces differ dramatically in their implementation. A Java class that you want to make part of the com.samples package, for example, must have Package com.samples; as the first line of code in the file. This is, of course, excluding any comments. Any code within that file automatically becomes a part of the specified package. Also, a Java package name is associated with the folder containing the class file in that they must have the same name. The com.samples package must therefore be in a file that exists in the com\samples folder. Lets take a look at some examples of how packages work:

```
//package_samples.java

package samples.on;    //maps directly to folder where class file is
public class Packaging
{
    int x;
    public class Internal
    {   //is in same package automatically
    }
    public static void main(String args[])
    {
    }
}
class Internal
{   //is in same package automatically
}
```

Examples of how the above code could be referenced or executed are given below. This assumes that the class file has been made available to the JRE:

❑   From the command line:

java samples.on.Packaging

❑   As a direct reference in the code:

```
//Referencer.java

public class Referencer
{
    samples.on.Packaging pack = new samples.on.two.three.Packaging();
```

❑ By utilizing the `import` directive one could omit fully qualified package names, so `Referencer` could also be written as:

```
//Referencer.java

import samples.on.*;
public class Referencer{
    Packaging pack = new Packaging();
}
```

Wrapping a class in a namespace is achieved in C# by using the `namespace` keyword with an identifier, and enveloping the target class in brackets. Here is an example:

```
//namespace_samples.cs

namespace Samples.On
{
    using System;
    public class Example
    {
        public Example()
        {
        }
    }
}
```

The advantage of using the brackets to explicitly delimit the namespace is that it restricts the user defined type to the actual class defined in the file and not the file itself. In Java, files and folders indirectly represent language structures because they are analogous to classes and the packages containing those classes. In C#, because files are not forcibly bound to anything, files as a whole become merely a place where the definition of a class resides and not a part of any language structure. Namespaces are also not bound to folders. Consequently, multiple namespaces may be introduced in the same file with no restriction. We could, for example, add the definition of a new class and place it in a new namespace in the same file and still not be outside the bounds of the language:

```
//namespace_samples.cs
namespace Samples.On
{
    using System;
    public class Example
    {
        public Example()
        {
        }
    }
}
namespace Com.Cslib
{
    using System;
    using System.Collections;
    public class AddLib
    {
```

```
      public AddLib()
      {
      }
      public int operationAdd(int a, int b)
      {
         return a + b;
      }
   }
}
```

Namespaces are introduced with the using <namespace name> directive, where <namespace name> is the namespace name. There is no "*" needed in C# – applying the using directive implicitly imports all elements of the specified namespace. Another benefit is that namespaces can be exclusively included into your class. Although the classes Example and AddLib above are defined in the file namespace_samples.cs, Example does not have access to the System.Collections namespace even though AddLib does. Java's import statement, however, is not class-specific. It clumsily imports the specified item(s) into the file as a whole. Let us take another look at x.java, which we examined in the compilation section. If you recall, the code was as follows:

```
//x.java

public class x
{
}
class y
{
}
class Z
{
}
```

If we were to add an import statement such as import java.util.Hashtable, all classes defined within this file would have access to the Hashtable class. The code below would compile:

```
//x.java

package samples;
import java.util.Hashtable ;
public class x
{
   Hashtable hash = new Hashtable();
}
class y
{
   Hashtable hash = new Hashtable();
}
class Z
{
   Hashtable hash = new Hashtable();
}
```

Namespaces may also be defined within other namespaces. This type of flexibility is impossible in Java without having to create a subdirectory. The above Com.Cslib namespace could be extended as follows:

```
namespace Com.Cslib
{
   using System;
   public class AddLib
   {
       public AddLib()
       {
       }
       public int operationAdd(int a, int b)
       {
          return a + b;
       }
   }
   namespace Ext
   {
       public class AddLib
       {
          public AddLib()
          {
          }
          public int operationAdd(int a, int b)
          {
             return a + b;
          }
       }
   }
}
```

The Java package com.javalib can be extended to mirror the above code by creating a new folder \EXT under com\javalib. In this folder we create a source file AddLib.java as follows:

```
package com.javalib.ext;
public class AddLib
{
   public AddLib()
   {
   }
   public int operationAdd(int a, int b)
   {
      return a + b;
   }
}
```

Notice that the package name has been extended to com.javalib.ext to for this class.

Internal namespaces and sub-packages are accessed using the dot operator "."; hence, we could retrieve the extended AddLib with the notation Com.Cslib.Ext.AddLib in C#. In Java we would use com.javalib.ext.AddLib.

The above example brings to light one similarity between Java packages and C# namespaces. Even if not used for external presentation, namespaces as well as packages provide a great way to create globally unique types; it's your own sandbox in the world of third-party and other assemblies. As far as C# is concerned, Com.Cslib.AddLib is not the same class as Com.Cslib.Ext.AddLib.

Java classes are part of a package whether they like it or not. All classes created without specifying one imply inclusion in the default package. C# mimics this functionality. Even if you do not declare one, a default namespace is created for you. It is present in every file, and available for use in named namespaces. Just as in Java you cannot change package information, namespaces cannot be modified. Packages can span multiple files in the same folder; namespaces can span multiple files in any number of folders, and even multiple assemblies (assemblies will be discussed in the next section). Two classes wrapped by namespace A that are defined in separate files that exist in separate folders are still both part of namespace A.

To access an element in a namespace, you must either use the type's fully qualified name (in the above example this would be Com.Cslib.AddLib) or import the namespace element into your current namespace by utilizing the using directive. Note that the default accessibility for types inside a namespace is internal. You must explicitly mark types as public if you want them available without full qualification but I would strongly recommend against such a strategy. No other access modifiers are allowed. In Java, internal package types may also be marked as final or abstract or not marked at all (this default access makes them available only to consumers inside the package). Access modifiers will be discussed later on in this appendix.

One final attribute namespaces have that is not available to packages is that they may be given a using alias. using aliases make it very easy to qualify an identifier to a namespace or class. The syntax is simple. Suppose you had a namespace Very.Very.Long.NameSpace.Name. You could define and use a using alias for the namespace as follows:

```
using VVLNN = Very.Very.Long.Namespace.Name;
```

Of course the name you give as an alias is arbitrary, as long as it follows the C# variable naming rules.

Creating and Adding Libraries to a Compilation

Earlier on when we discussed compilation and compilation units, we touched briefly on the concept of libraries for your code. Once you a have produced a library, the next step is to make it accessible to all potential consumers. In Java, adding the path to the folder containing your library classes to the classpath environment variable does this. Of course to make things simpler you could just add the class files in that folder to a JAR and place the path to the .jar file in the classpath. In any case, it is the job of the class loader to locate any unresolved links and the classpath is where it will look.

C# provides a very different mechanisms for packaging classes together into a library. By default all C# files in a project will become part of the compilation unit when using VS.NET. If you are using the command line, you will have to explicitly add each file you want to be part of the unit as described earlier.

Code libraries are compiled into a **PE** (**Portable Executable**) type file. I want to make the distinction at this point between the code libraries we are talking about and a C# Class Library project that can be created using the VS.NET IDE. By code library I mean simply a reusable set of C# files bundled together into some compilation unit, hence the reference to a PE file and not an actual DLL or EXE. A code library of this sort is more frequently referred to as an **assembly**, so I will use this name from now on to avoid any confusion.

Just like a JAR file, an assembly has a manifest that describes its contents. The C# assembly manifest does much more than that, however. It contains all the metadata (a collection of data that describes how the elements in an assembly relate) needed to specify the version requirements, security identity, and all information needed to define the scope of the assembly and resolve references to resources and classes. The assembly manifest can be stored either in a PE file (an EXE or DLL) with IL code, or as a stand-alone file that contains only assembly manifest information. In .NET, namespaces contained within an assembly are exposed to the outside world (that is, anything that can consume the assembly, such as other assemblies) via type metadata information stored in the assembly manifest.

The classes in namespace_samples.cs can be compiled into a library with the command:

```
csc /target:library /out:FirstLibrary.dll namespace_samples.cs
```

Two compiler options can be used to make type information from one assembly available to another: /addmodule and /reference. They are essentially the same except that /reference is for assemblies with an assembly manifest while /addmodule is for assemblies without an assembly manifest (a module does not have an assembly manifest). The syntax for adding external references from the command line is:

```
csc /reference: <lib.dll>; <libn.cs> <filename.exe>
```

or:

```
csc /addmodule: <lib.dll>; <libn.cs> <filename.exe>
```

To do this using VS.NET, right-click on your project's **References** folder in the **Solution Explorer** and select **Add Reference**. A dialog containing a number of available references that allows you to browse the file system for a reference is displayed. You can also get at this dialog by selecting the **Add Reference** option from your **Project** menu while the desired project is highlighted.
Adding a reference to your current assembly typically copies the referenced file to the project folder where the new assembly being created will reside.

Let us now create a consumer for the AddLib library that is similar in form and functionality to the JavaFrame class we produced earlier:

```
//LibConsumer.cs

namespace Com.CSapp
{
    using System;
    using System.Windows.Forms;
    using Com.CsLib;
    public class Form1 : System.Windows.Forms.Form
    {
        public Form1()
        {
            AddLib al = new AddLib();
            this.Text = "C# Form Version " + al.operationAdd(12,23);
        }
        public override void Dispose()
        {
            base.Dispose();
```

```
        }
        static void Main(string[] args)
        {
            Form1 f1 = new Form1();
            Application.Run(f1);
        }
    }
}
```

This code can be compiled at the command line to reference `FirstLibrary.dll` by typing:

```
csc /reference: FirstLibrary.dll /target:exe /out:EmptyForm.exe
    LibConsumer.cs
```

Using VS.NET, you would first need to reference `FirstLibrary.dll` as described earlier, and then simply build the application. Once the application has been successfully built, execute it. It should produce a Windows Form with title C# form Version 35.

Location and Resolution

We have already discussed how the JRE resolves references to other classes using the class loader to probe your `classpath` environment variable at runtime. The CLR also goes through a number of steps, often referred to as **probing**, when attempting to locate an assembly and resolve an assembly reference. Attempting to execute `EmptyForm.exe` sets a number of things into motion. By default, all managed code is loaded into the application domain and to be run by a particular operation system thread. Referenced assemblies, meaning assemblies whose types are used in the application domain code, must also be loaded before they can be run. The CLR must go through several steps to locate and bind to a specified assembly.

Because assembly-binding behavior can be configured based on the application configuration file, the publisher configuration file, and the machine/administrator configuration file, the CLR must retrieve this configuration information to ensure that the appropriate version of the specified assembly is retrieved. These files are all XML-based and follow a similar syntax. They provide information such as binding redirects, the location of code, and binding modes for particular assemblies. Usually the correct assembly version is determined by some combination of the three configuration files and the assembly's own manifest.

The CLR first looks to see if the application configuration file information overrides the information stored in the calling assembly's assembly manifest. Next, the CLR examines the publisher configuration file. This file is present only when an application has been updated with new versions of one or more application components. It is primarily used to override information in the application configuration file so the new version of the component is to be picked up by the application. CLR then examines the machine/administrator configuration file. Although it is looked at last, whatever settings are present in this file take precedent over all other configuration settings. Essentially, administrators use `admin.cfg` to specify binding restrictions local to a given machine.

The CLR then needs to locate the assembly. In Java, JRE will look in the current directory and the classpath to find a class needed to resolve a reference. The CLR relies on the `<codeBase>` element associated with the aforementioned configuration files to determine the location of a given assembly. If one is not supplied, the CLR probes for the file under the application root directory, under all directories listed in the configuration file's `<probing>` element, and under any subdirectory of the application root that has the same name as the assembly being probed. These elements are always relative to the application's root directory (you load assemblies outside the application's root directory using probing). Note that the CLR always searches for the assembly name concatenated with the two valid PE file extensions, `.exe` and `.dll`.

Finally, if the reference is to an assembly with a strong name, the CLR will look in the global assembly cache. Strong names and the global assembly cache will be discussed in more detail in the next section.

Strong Names and the Global Cache

A strong name makes an assembly globally unique. It consists of the assembly's identity, a public key, and digital signature. Because an assembly generated with one private key has a different name from an assembly generated with another private key, the uniqueness of your assembly name is guaranteed. One cannot modify an assembly with a strong name without having access to the private key used to generate it; consequently, a strong name ensures that no one can produce different versions of your assembly. Strong names also provide a strong integrity check. Creating a strong name is a two-step process. First, you must generate or have a key pair. Generating a key-pair can be done at the command line with the command:

```
sn -k <key file name>
```

For example to create the key file `examplekey.key` you would type:

```
sn -k examplekey.key
```

Once you have a key file, it can be used to assign a strong name for your assembly in two ways. From the command line you can use the `alink` utility as follows:

```
al /keyfile: <key file name> <assembly name>
```

In our case to give `FirstLibrary.dll` a strong name we could execute:

```
al  /keyfile:examplekey.key FirstLibrary.dll
```

Or in VS.NET we could modify the `[assembly: AssemblyKeyFile ("")]` attribute in the `AssemblyInfo.cs` file. Simple replace the empty string with a string representing the key file name. Our `FirstLibrary.dll` assembly could then be associated with a key by changing the `AssemblyKeyFile` attribute to `[assembly: AssemblyKeyFile ("examplekey.key")]`. Whichever method is used, the end result is the same. The CLR will install the key in the file with the **Crypto Service Provider** (CSP). The workings of the CSP are outside the scope of this appendix.

All assemblies in the global assembly cache must have a strong name. The global assembly cache is used to store assemblies specifically designated for sharing by several applications on the machine. There are several ways to deploy an assembly into the global assembly cache. You can use an installer designed to work with the global assembly cache; .NET Framework SDK provides one called `gacutil.exe`. To drop `FirstLibrary.dll` in the global assembly cache we would use the command:

```
gacutil -i FirstLibrary.dll
```

You can use Windows Explorer to drag and drop assemblies into the cache. Note that you must have administrator privileges on a machine to install assemblies into the global assembly cache regardless of which approach you take.

Types

Types in Java and C# can be grouped into two main categories: **value** types and **reference** types. There is only one category of value type in Java. All value types are by default the primitive data types of the language. C# offers a more robust assortment. Value types can be broken into three main categories:

- ❏ Simple types
- ❏ Enumeration types
- ❏ Structures

Let's take a look at each of these in turn.

Simple Types

Earlier on in the *Keywords* section we made some detailed comparisons between the Java primitive types and their C# equivalents (in size at least). We also introduced a number of value types present in C# that Java did not have. These were the 8-bit unsigned `byte` (different from Java's `byte` which is signed and maps to C#'s `sbyte`), the unsigned `short` `ushort`, unsigned `int` `uint`, unsigned `long` `ulong`, and finally the high precision `decimal`.

Integer Values

When an integer has no suffix the type to which its value can be bound is evaluated in the order `int`, `uint`, `long`, `ulong`, `decimal`. Integer values may be represented as decimal or hexadecimal literals. In the code below the result is 52 for both values:

```
int dec = 52;
int hex = 0x34;
Console.WriteLine("decimal {0}, hexadecimal {1}",dec, hex);
```

Character Values

`char` represents a single two byte long Unicode character. C# extends the flexibility of character assignment by allowing assignment via the hexadecimal escape sequence prefixed by `\x` and Unicode representation via the `\u`. You will also find that you will not be able to convert characters to integers implicitly. All other common Java language escape sequences are fully supported.

Boolean Values

The `bool` type in Java, is used to represent the values `true` and `false` directly, or as the result of an equation as shown below:

```
bool first_time = true;
bool second_time = (counter < 0);
```

Decimal Values

C# introduces the decimal type, which is a 128-bit data type that represents values ranging from approximately 1.0×10^{28} to 7.9×10^{28}. They are primarily intended for financial and monetary calculations where precision is of the utmost importance. When assigning the decimal type a value, m must be appended to the literal value. Otherwise, the compiler treats the value as a double. Because decimal cannot be implicitly converted to a double, omitting the m requires an explicit cast:

```
decimal precise = 1.234m;
decimal precise = (decimal)1.234;
```

Floating-point Values

Floating-point values can either be doubles or floats. In calculations, all other simple value types will be implicitly converted to the appropriate floating-point type, if the floating-point type is present.

A real numeric literal on the right hand-side of an assignment operator is treated as a double by default. Because there is no implicit conversion from float to double you may be taken aback when a compiler error occurs. The example below illustrates this problem:

```
float f = 5.6;
Console.WriteLine(x);
```

This example will produce the compiler error message listed below.

```
C:\_wrox\c# for java developers\code\SuperEX\Class1.cs(15): Literal of type double
cannot be implicitly converted to type 'float'; use an 'F' suffix to create a
literal of this type
```

There are two ways to solve this problem. We could cast our literal to float, but the compiler itself offers a more reasonable alternative. Using the suffix F tells the compiler this is a literal of type float and not double. Although it is not necessary, you can use a D suffix to signify a double type literal.

Enumeration Types

An **enumeration** is a distinct type consisting of a set of named constants. In Java you can achieve this by using static final variables. In this sense, the enumerations may actually be part of the class that is using them. Another alternative is to define the enumeration as an interface. The example below illustrates this concept:

```
interface Color
{
    static int RED = 0;
    static int GREEN = 1;
    static int BLUE = 2;
}
```

Of course, the problem with this approach is that it is not type safe. Any integer read in or calculated can be used as a color. It is possible, however, to programmatically implement a type safe enumeration in Java by utilizing a variation of the Singleton pattern, which limits the class to a predefined number of instances. The code overleaf illustrates how this can be done:

1197

```
final class Day
{   // final so it cannot be sub-classed
   private String internal;
   private Day(String Day) {internal = Day;}    //private constructor
   public static final Day MONDAY = new Day("MONDAY");
   public static final Day TUESDAY = new Day("TUESDAY");
   public static final Day WEDNESDAY = new Day("WEDNESDAY");
   public static final Day THURDAY = new Day("THURSDAY");
   public static final Day FRIDAY = new Day("FRIDAY");
}
```

As you can see from the above example, the enumerated constants are not tied to primitive types, but to object references. Also, because the class is defined as final, it can't be sub-classed, so no other classes can be created from it. The constructor is marked as private, so other methods can't use the class to create new objects. The only objects that will ever be created with this class are the static objects the class creates for itself the first time the class is referenced.

Although the concept is pretty simple, the workaround involves advanced techniques that may not be immediately apparent to a novice – after all, we just want a readily available list of constants. C#, in contrast, provides inbuilt enumeration support, which also ensures type safety. To declare an enumeration in C# the enum keyword is used. In its simple form an enum could look something like the code below:

```
public enum Status
{
    Working,
    Complete,
    BeforeBegin
}
```

In the above case, the first value is 0 and the enum counts upwards from there, Complete being 1 and so on. If for some reason you are interested in having the enum represent different values you can do so simply be assigning them as follows:

```
public enum Status
{
    Working = 131,
    Complete = 129,
    BeforeBegin = 132
}
```

You also have the choice of using a different numerical integral type by 'inheriting' from long, short, or byte. int is always the default type. This concept is illustrated below:

```
public enum Status : int
{
    Working,
    Complete,
    BeforeBegin
}
public enum SmallStatus : byte
{
    Working,
```

```
      Complete,
      BeforeBegin
   }
public enum BigStatus : long
{
   Working,
   Complete,
   BeforeBegin
}
```

It may not be immediately apparent but there is a big difference between these three enumerations, tied directly to the size of the type they inherit from. The C# `byte`, for example, can contain one byte of memory. It means the `SmallStatus` cannot have more than 255 constants or set the value of any of its constants to more than 255. The following listing displays how we can use the `sizeof()` operator to identify the differences between the different versions of `Status`:

```
int x = sizeof(Status);
int y = sizeof(SmallStatus);
int z = sizeof(BigStatus);
Console.WriteLine("Regular size:\t{0}\nSmall size:\t{1}\nLarge size:\t{2}",
                  x, y, z);
```

Compiling the listing will produce the results shown below:

```
Regular size:    4
Small size:      1
Large size:      8
```

Structures

One of the major differences between a C# structure (identified with the keyword `struct`) and a class is that, by default, the `struct` is passed by value, while an object is passed by reference. As you well know, objects are created in the heap while the variables that reference them are kept in the stack. Structures on the other hand are created and stored on the stack. There is no analogue in Java to structures. Structures have constructors and, methods; they can have indexers, properties, operators, and even nested types. By using `structs` we can create types that behave in the same way as, and share similar benefits to, the built-in types. Below is an example of how a structure can be used:

```
public struct WroxInt
{
   int internalVal;
   private WroxInt(int x)
   {
      internaVal = x;
   }
   public override string ToString()
   {
      return int.ToString(internalVal);
   }
   public static implicit operator WroxInt(int x)
   {
      return new WroxInt(x);
   }
}
```

```
public static void UseWroxInt()
{
    WroxInt wi = 90;
    Console.WriteLine(wi);
}
```

The example above highlights the types of power structures possess. WroxInt can be used in much the same way as the built-in int type. As you well know, there is no way to do something like this in Java. There are a number of other benefits and limitations associated with using structures. These are listed below:

❏ A struct cannot inherit from other struct or from classes.

❏ A struct cannot act as the base for a class.

❏ Although a struct may declare constructors, those constructors *must* take at least one argument.

❏ The struct members cannot have initializers.

❏ A struct can be instantiated without the use of the new keyword.

❏ A struct can implement interfaces.

Attributes can be used with structures to add more power and flexibility to them. The StructLayout attribute in the System.Runtime.InteropServices namespace, for example, can be used to define the layout of fields in the struct. It is possible to use this feature to create a structure similar in functionality to a C/C++ union. A union is a data type whose members share the same memory block. It is can be used to store values of different types in the same memory block. In the event that one does not know what type the values to be received will be, a union is a great way to go. Of course there is no actual conversion happening; in fact there are no underlying checks on the validity of the data. The same bit pattern is simply interpreted in a different way. An example of how a union could be created using a struct is listed below:

```
[StructLayout(LayoutKind.Explicit)]
public struct Variant
{
    [FieldOffset(0)]public int intVal;
    [FieldOffset(0)]public string strinVal;
    [FieldOffset(0)]public decimal decVal;
    [FieldOffset(0)]public float floatVal;
    [FieldOffset(0)]public char charVal;
}
```

The FieldOffset attribute applied to the fields is used to set the physical location of the specified field. Setting the starting point of each field to 0 ensures that any data store in one field will overwrite to a certain extent whatever data may have been stored there. It follows then that the total size of the fields will be the size of the largest field, in this case decimal.

Reference Types

All a reference type stores is the reference to data that exists on the heap. Only the memory addresses of the stored objects are kept in the stack. The object type, arrays, interfaces, class type, and delegates are all reference types. Objects, classes, and the relationship between the two do not differ between Java and C#. You will also find that interfaces, and how they are used, are not very different in the two languages. One major difference which you probably have already seen is that C# does not have the extends or implements keywords. The colon operator (:) replaces both Java keywords, and as we saw earlier, the using directive is similar to Java's import statement. Strings can also be used the same way in either C# or Java. C# also introduces a new type of reference type called a **delegate**. Delegates represent a type safe version of function pointers. We will discuss them later on in this chapter.

Arrays

C# supports "jagged" arrays and adds multidimensional arrays. This is something that you might find confusing, considering that Java does not make a distinction between the two:

```
int[] x = new int[20];   //same as in Java except [] must be next to type
int[,] y = new int[12,3]; //same as int y[][] = new int[12][3];
int[][] z = new int[5][];   //same as int x[][] = new int[5][];
```

Note: The int [] keyword denotes an actual type so it must be written syntactically as such. You cannot, as with Java, place the double brackets before or after the variable. Before we go into more detail on reference types and discuss such concepts as classes, let's talk a little bit about operations. The next section goes into more detail on operators.

Operators

In Java, the result of applying an operator to one or more operands is a new value for one or more of the operands involved. C# provides similar functionality. However, you will see from the sections below that there are certain minor differences between C# and Java even in this area. This section will cover the different groups of operators in C# and bring to light what differences exist between C# and Java for each group.

Assignment

C# and Java both use the "=" sign for assigning values to variables. As with Java, variables assigned to objects in C# only contain a reference or "address" to that object, and not the whole object. Assigning one reference variable to another then simply copies that "address" to the new variable. Hence, both variables now have the ability to reference the same object. This concept can easily be illustrated with an example. Examine the class EXOperators below:

```
public class EXOperators
{
    internal int p;
    public EXOperators()
    {
    }
    public static void Main()
    {
        EXOperators one = new EXOperators();
        one.p = 200;
        EXOperators two;
```

```
        two = one;
        two.p = 100;
        Console.WriteLine(two.p);
        Console.WriteLine(one.p);
    }
}
```

For now, ignore the `internal` keyword in front of the variable p. It is an access modifier, and C# access modifiers will be discussed later on in this chapter. Suffice it to say that it makes the variable p visible to our `Main()` method. The above example creates an instance of the object EXOperators and saves it to a local variable one. This variable is then assigned to another variable, two. Next, the value of p in the object being referenced by two is changed to 100. Finally, we display the value of the p variable in both referenced objects. Compiling and running this will produce the result 100 twice, signifying that changing two.p was the same as changing the value of one.p.

Comparison

Comparison operators are generally equal in form and functionality in both languages. The four main operators are "<", which represents less than, ">", which represents grater than, "<=", which represents less than or equal to, and ">=", which represents greater than or equal to.

To determine whether an object belongs to a given class or any of the parent classes Java uses the `instanceof` operator. A simple example of this is provided in the listing below:

```
String y = "a string";
Object x = y;
if(x instanceof String)
{
    System.out.println("x is a string");
}
```

The C# equivalent of `instanceof` is the `is` operator. It returns `true` if the runtime type of the given class is compatible with the specified type. A C# version of the above code would take the following form:

```
string y = "a string";
object x = y;
if(x is System.String)
{
    System.Console.WriteLine("x is a string");
}
```

Equality, Arithmetic, Conditional, Bitwise, Bitwise Complement, and Shift Operators

In both languages, these operators can be used to test numbers, characters, Boolean primitives, and reference variables, and generally work the same way.

Conversion and Casting

Conversion in Java consists of implicit or explicit narrow and wide casting, using the "()" operator as needed. It is generally possible to perform similar type conversions in C#. C# also introduces a number of powerful features built into the language. These include **boxing** and **unboxing**.

Because value types are nothing more than memory blocks of a certain size, they are great to use for speed reasons. Sometimes, however, the convenience of objects is good to have for a value type. Boxing and unboxing provide a mechanism that forms a binding link between value types and reference types by allowing them to be converted to and from the object type.

Boxing an object means implicitly converting any value type to type `Object`. An instance of `Object` is created and allocated, and the value in the value type is copied to the new object. Below is an example of how boxing works in C#:

```
//BoxEX.cs

public class OverflowEX
{
   public static void Main(String[] args)
   {
      int x = 10;
      Object obj = (Object) x;
      Console.WriteLine(obj);
   }
}
```

This type of functionality is not available in Java. The code listed below would not compile because primitives cannot be converted to reference types:

```
//BoxEX.java

public class BoxEX
{
   public static void main(String args[])
   {
      int x = 10;
      object obj = (object) x;
      System.out.println(obj);
   }
}
```

Unboxing is simply the casting of the `Object` type containing the value back to the appropriate value type. Again, this functionality is not available in Java. We can modify the code above to illustrate this concept. You will immediately notice that while boxing is an implicit cast, Unboxing requires as explicit one. Here is the new implementation of `BoxEX.cs`:

```
//BoxEX.cs

public class OverflowEX
{
   public static void Main(String[] args)
   {
```

```
        int x = 10;
        Object obj = (Object) x;
        Console.WriteLine(obj);
        int y = (int) obj;
        Console.WriteLine(y);
    }
}
```

Another powerful feature of C# dealing with casting is the ability to define custom conversion operators. User-defined conversions are from type to type, not instance to instance, and so must be static operations. You can use the `implicit` keyword to declare user-defined conversions from one type to another that do not require a cast and the `explicit` keyword to declare user-defined conversions from one type to another that do require a cast. Let us say we have two classes, Man and Car, which are completely unrelated. We could for some reason create a user-defined conversion that allows us to convert from one to the other. Below is the listing for `Man.cs`:

```
public class Man
{
    int arms, legs;
    string name;
    public Man(){}
    public int Arms
    {
        set
        {
            arms = value;
        }
        get
        {
            return arms;
        }
    }
    public string Name{
        set
        {
            name = value;
        }
        get
        {
            return name;
        }
    }
    public int Legs
    {
        set
        {
            legs = value;
        }
        get
        {
            return legs;
        }
    }
}
```

As you can see from the above, the Man class has three properties: you can set or get the Legs, Arms, or Name. The listing below is for the Car class:

```
public class Car
{
    int wheels, doors, headlights;
    public Car(int wheels, int doors, int headlights)
    {
        this.wheels = wheels;
        this.doors = doors;
        this.headlights = headlights;
    }
}
```

There are really no defined rules on what to include in the implementation of a custom conversion. However, you should try to mach up as many field data pairs as possible between the two operands. In the case of our example, we will match Car.wheel field with Man.legs and Car.doors with Man.arms. There is no field in Car to represent something like Man.Name but that does not prevent us from using it. We could, for example, match Car.headlights with the length of the string stored in Man.name. Any implementation that makes sense to the programmer is acceptable. In this case we will not match Man.name with Car.headlights, instead we will hard code the value 2 for headlights whenever the conversion is made, and discard Man.name. The code below contains the modifications to the Car class:

```
public class Car
{
    int wheels, doors, headlights;
    public Car(int wheels, int doors, int headlights)
    {
        this.wheels = wheels;
        this.doors = doors;
        this.headlights = headlights;
    }
    public static implicit operator Car(Man man)
    {
        return new Car(man.Legs,man.Arms,2);
    }
    public static explicit operator Man(Car car)
    {
        Man man = new Man();
        man.Arms = car.doors;
        man.Legs = car.wheels;
        man.Name = "john";
        return man;
    }
}
```

We will also add overrides for the ToString() methods of both classes so that we can display the contents of the Car object. Adding the following line to the classes will do this:

```
//for Man.cs

public override string ToString()
{
    return "[arms:" + arms + "|legs:" + legs + "|name:" + name + "]";
}

//for Car.cs

public override string ToString()
{
    return "[wheels:" + wheels + "|doors:" + doors + "|headlights:" +
            headlights + "]";
}
```

The code listing below displays the use of the custom conversion:

```
//BoxEX.cs

public class OverflowEX
{
    public static void Main(String[] args)
    {
        Car car = new Car(4,5,2);
        Man man = (Man) car;    //use of explicit custom converter
        Console.WriteLine("Man - ");
        Console.WriteLine(man);
        Console.WriteLine();
        Car car2 = man;         //use of implicit custom converter
        Console.WriteLine("Car - ");
        Console.WriteLine(car2);
    }
}
```

Compiling and executing this will produce the results displayed below:

```
Man -
[arms:5|legs:4|name:john]

Car -
[wheels:4|doors:5|headlights:2]
```

Overloading

Before we begin it is important note that operator overloading is not defined in CLS. It is, however, addressed by the CLS in such a way that languages that provide this functionality do so in a way that other languages can understand. In this way, languages that do not support operator overloading still have access to the underlying functionality. Java is a prime example of a language that does not support operator overloading; none of the concepts discussed in this section are possible using it. Should you decide to use operator overloading, the .NET framework specification includes a number of guidelines to follow when using operator overloading:

❑ Define operators on value types that are logically a built-in language type (such as `System.Decimal`)

❑ Provide operator-overloading methods only involving the class the methods are defined on.

❑ Use the names and signature conventions described in the CLS.

❑ Operator overloading is useful in the cases where it is immediately obvious what the result of the operation would be.

❑ Provide alternative signatures. Not all languages support calling overloaded operators. It is therefore a good idea to always include a secondary method with an appropriate domain-specific name that has equivalent functionality.

As with user-defined conversions, operator overloading is type and not instance related. What this means is that they are bound to the entire type and not any one instance of an object. What this ultimately means to the programmer is that the operation must always be `static` and `public`.

In the example below, we create a value type `Wheels`, which can perform overloaded addition with itself. You will notice heavy use of comments and XML-type tags within the comments; they are used for documentation. C# documentation will be discussed in greater detail later on in the appendix:

```
public struct Wheels
{
    int wheel;

    //load an initial value to a wheel

    private Wheels(int initVal)
    {
        wheel = initVal;
    }

    /// <summary>
    /// exposes the internal number of wheels
    /// </summary>

    internal int Number
    {
        set
        {
            wheel = value;
        }
        get
        {
            return wheel;
        }
    }

    /// <summary>
    /// returns the internal number. If this
    /// method is not overridden the type
    /// Two.Wheels would be the string returned
    /// </summary>
    /// <returns></returns>
```

```
    public override string ToString()
    {
       return wheel.ToString();
    }


    /// <summary>
    /// Performs addition operation on two wheels
    /// </summary>
    /// <param name="w1"></param>
    /// <param name="w2"></param>
    /// <returns></returns>

    public static Wheels operator +(Wheels w1, Wheels w2)
    {
       w1.wheel += w2.wheel;
       return w1;
    }


    /// <summary>
    /// provides alternative add functionality.
    /// note that the second add operations alternative
    /// is not in this struct but in the car class
    /// </summary>
    /// <param name="w"></param>
    /// <returns></returns>

    public Wheels AddWheel(Wheels w)
    {
       this.wheel+=w.wheel;
       return this;
    }


    /// <summary>
    /// so integer literals can be implicitly cast to wheel
    /// </summary>
    /// <param name="x"></param>
    /// <returns></returns>

    public static implicit operator Wheels(int x)
    {
       return new Wheels(x);
    }
}
```

You will notice the use of an `AddWheel()` method; this satisfies the alternative signatures guideline. A CLS language that does not support operator overloading could access the same add functionality by using this method. The code snippet below displays how this value type can be used:

```
public static void Main(String[] args)
{
   Wheels front = 2;            //implicit conversion
   Wheels back = 4;             //implicit conversion
   Wheels total = front + back; //addition overload
   Console.WriteLine(total);
}
```

Compiling and running the above will produce the result 6. We can also modify the Car type to allow addition and subtraction of Wheels from it. The code below displays the modifications made to the Car class:

```csharp
public class Car
{
    int wheels, doors, headlights;
    public Car(int wheels, int doors, int headlights)
    {
        this.wheels = wheels;
        this.doors = doors;
        this.headlights = headlights;
    }
    public Car AddWheel(Two.Wheels w)
    {
        this.wheels += w.Number;
        return this;
    }
    internal int Wheels
    {
        set
        {
            wheels = value;
        }
        get
        {
            return wheels;
        }
    }

    /// <summary>
    /// performs addition operation on Wheel and Car
    /// </summary>
    /// <param name="c1">car</param>
    /// <param name="w1">wheel</param>
    /// <returns></returns>

    public static Car operator +(Car c1, Wheels w1)
    {
        c1.Wheels += w1.Number;
        return c1;
    }

    /// <summary>
    /// performs subtraction operation on Wheel and Car
    /// </summary>
    /// <param name="c1">car</param>
    /// <param name="w1">wheel</param>
    /// <returns></returns>

    public static Car operator -(Car c1, Wheels w1)
    {
        c1.Wheels -= w1.Number;
        return c1;
    }
    public override string ToString()
```

```
        {
            return "[wheels = " + wheels + "|  doors = " + doors + "|"
                + " headlights = " + headlights + "]";
        }


    }
```

An AddWheel method has also been to Car. The code snippet below tests the functionality we just added to Car:

```
public static void Main(String[] args)
{
    Wheels front = 2;
    Wheels back = 4;
    Wheels total = front + back;
    Car greenFordExpedition = new Car(0,4,2);
    Console.WriteLine("initial:\t" + greenFordExpedition);
    greenFordExpedition += total;
    Console.WriteLine("after add:\t" + greenFordExpedition);
    greenFordExpedition -= front;
    Console.WriteLine("after subtract:\t" + greenFordExpedition);
}
```

Compiling and executing the above code would produce the results listed below:

```
initial:        CAR-[wheels = 0|  doors = 4| headlights = 2]
after add:      CAR-[wheels = 6|  doors = 4| headlights = 2]
after subtract: CAR-[wheels = 4|  doors = 4| headlights = 2]
```

sizeof and typeof

Since Java has no value types other than the primitives whose size is always known, there is no real use for a sizeof operator. In C#, value types range from primitives to structs to enums. As with Java, the size of the primitives is known. There is a need, however, to know how much space a struct type or enum type occupies. This is what the sizeof operator is for. The syntax is quite simple: sizeof(<ValueType>), where <Value Type> is the struct or enum. One thing to note when using the sizeof operator; sizeof may only be used in an unsafe context. The sizeof operator cannot be overloaded.

The typeof operator is used to get an instance of a type's System.Type object without having to create an instance of the type. In Java, every type has a public static class variable that returns a handle to the Class object associated with that class. The typeof operator provides this type of functionality. Just as we saw with sizeof, the syntax is very simple. The statement typeof(<Type>) where <Type> is any user defined type will return you the type object of that type.

Delegates

Delegates are namespace members that encapsulate a reference to a method inside a delegate object. The delegate object can then be passed to code, which can call the referenced method, without having to know at compile time which method will be invoked. The beauty, power, and flexibility of delegates can only be highlighted through example. Let us look at an example of how delegates work:

```
namespace Samples
{
    using System;
    using System.Collections;
    public delegate void TestDelegate(string k);   //defines a delegate that
                                               // takes a string as an argument.

    public class Sample
    {
        public Sample()
        {
        }
        public void test(string i)
        {
            Console.WriteLine(i + " has been invoked.");
        }
        public void test2(string j)
        {
            Console.WriteLine("this is another way to invoke {0}" + j);
        }
        public static void Main(string[] args)
        {
            Sample sm = new Sample();
            TestDelegate aDelegate = new TestDelegate(sm.test);
            TestDelegate anotherDelegate = new TestDelegate(sm.test2);
            aDelegate("test");
            anotherDelegate("test2");
        }
    }
}
```

The first step to using delegates is to define one. Our test delegate is defined with the line `public delegate void TestDelegate(string k);`. Next we simply define a class with methods that have signatures similar to the delegate. The final step is to instantiate the delegate. Instantiating a delegate is the same as instantiating a class. It is done using the `new` operator. The only difference is that the target method name is passed as an argument to the delegate. Next invoke the delegate. In the example we invoke the `aDelegate` instance with the call `aDelegate("test");`.

Classes in Detail

In both C# and Java, a class is a skeleton that contains methods but no data. It is the declaration of the framework of a potential object. Instantiating a class creates an object based on that framework. There are various keywords and concepts associated with classes that were discussed earlier. A recap of these keywords and an introduction to some new keywords is provided in this section.

Modifiers

As with Java, modifiers in C# are used to modify type and member declarations. Overleaf is a list of the C# modifiers. You will find that a more detailed definition of the meaning of some of these identifiers is given in the keywords section of this appendix. Some of the modifiers listed, however, are new and will be discussed in later sections.

Class Modifiers	Description
Abstract	Abstract classes cannot be instantiated. Derived classes that extend them must implement all the abstract methods of the class, and the sealed modifier cannot be applied to them.
Sealed	Used to prevent accidental inheritance because a class defined as sealed cannot be inherited from.

Member Modifiers	Target	Java Equivalent	Description
virtual	methods, accessors	n/a	Allows target members to be overridden by an inherited class.
static	all	static	Target member marked as static belongs to class and not instance of class. There is therefore no need to instantiate the class in order to gain access to it
event	fields, properties	n/a	Used to bind client code to events of the class, the event modifier allows you to specify a delegate that will be called when some "event" in your code occurs. Note that it is the job of the class programmer to define when and where the event is raised, and the job of the subscriber to choose how to handle the it.
abstract	methods, accessors	abstract	Indicates that the target member is implicitly virtual, and has no implementation code. The derived class must provide this implementation and the implemented method must be marked as override.
const	fields, local variables	final	Indicates that the target member cannot be modified. Java also has a const keyword, which at the time of this writing is simply a reserved word.
readonly	fields	n/a	Indicates that the target member can only be assigned values in its declaration or in the constructor of its containing class.
Extern	methods	n/a	Indicates that the target member is implemented externally. This modifier is typically used with the DllImport attribute.
override	methods	n/a	Indicates that the target member provides a new implementation of a member inherited from a base class.

Access Modifiers	Target	Java Equivalent	Description	Default
public	all	public	No restrictions.	members of enum and interface, as well as namespaces
private	all	private	Accessible only to the declaring class.	members of class and struct
internal	all	n/a	Accessible to files in the same assembly.	
protected	all	n/a	Accessible to the declaring class, and any subclass of the declaring class. In C# protected is more restrictive than in Java. Protected access will not allow other files in the same assembly to access the member.	
protected internal	all	protected	Accessible to assembly files and subclasses of declaring class.	

Constructors

The first method to be invoked in your class when an object is being instantiated is the constructor. This is true for Java, C++, and C# among others. In fact, even if you do not specifically write your own constructor, a default one is provided. In C#, making a call to a parent object or another constructor is handled quite differently from in Java:

```
public class Parent
{
}
public class Sample: Parent
{
    private string internalVal;
    private string newVal;
    public Sample():base()
    {
    }
    public Sample(String s)
    {
        internalVal = s;
    }
    public Sample(String s, String t):this(s)
    {
        newVal = t;
    }
}
```

As you can see from the above example, making a call to a parent constructor, or even another constructor, can be achieved by extending it with the ":" symbol. In the case of a parent constructor, the base keyword is used to identify the source as coming from the parent object, while this is used to identify the source as coming from another constructor of the object. Applying the proper signature to base will invoke the appropriate parent constructor just as applying the correct signature to this invokes the correct internal constructor. We will highlight this by making some modifications to the Sample class:

```
public class Parent
{
   protected Parent(string a)
   {
      Console.WriteLine(a);
   }
   protected Parent()
   {
      Console.WriteLine("This is the base constructor");
   }
}
public class Sample: Parent
{
   public Sample()
   {
   }
   public Sample(String s):base(s)
   {
   }
   public Sample(String s, String t):this(s)
   {
      Console.WriteLine(t);
   }
}
```

C# introduces the concept of destructors, borrowed from C++. They work similarly to finalizers in Java; their syntax, however, is very different. With destructors, a logical not sign (~) prefixes the class name:

```
~Sample()
{
}
```

A word of advice concerning code in the destructor: the garbage collector in .NET is not invoked immediately after a variable goes out of scope. Indeed, there are certain intervals or memory conditions that bring the thread to life. Since there is a possibility that it may be triggered at low memory situations, consider making code in the destructor as short and sweet as possible. It is also a good idea to call close() on resource-intensive objects before destroying the controllers that use them.

Methods

Java and C# differ extensively in syntax and ideology regarding the way methods are handled by an object. For one thing, not all reference data type parameters are passed as references and not all simple data types have to be passed by value. You have the option to pass arguments by value as an in parameter (this is the default way parameters are passed) by reference as a ref parameter, or as an out parameter. The following code:

```
public static void Main(string[] args)
{
    int a = 10;
    Console.WriteLine(a);
    Add(a);
    Console.WriteLine(a);
}
public static void Add(int a)
{
    a++;
}
```

would produce the output below in both C# and Java:

```
10
10
```

Because a is passed by value, the value that is passed is not tied to the value a in Main().
Consequently, incrementing a in the Add() method does not affect the a in Main(). With the
flexibility of being able to pass simple data types as references, the code above can be modified to:

```
public static void Main(string[] args)
{
    int a = 10;
    Console.WriteLine(a);
    Add(ref a);
    Console.WriteLine(a);
}
public static void Add(ref int a)
{
    a++;
}
```

and will produce:

```
10
11
```

To use a reference parameter, precede the parameter type with the ref keyword. In contrast to the two
other parameter types, out parameters do not need to be initialized before they are passed as
arguments, they are used to pass values back from a method. The following code will produce the result
100:

```
public static void Main(string[] args)
{
    int a;
    Add(out a);
    Console.WriteLine(a);
}
public static void Add(out int a)
{
    a = 100;
}
```

Another useful feature of C# is **method hiding**. The concept of method hiding was discussed earlier in this appendix. It allows you to have the same signature as a base class method without having to override the base method. This is achieved by preceding the method implementation with the `new` keyword. As described earlier, omitting the `new` keyword in this instance will still result in the same behavior and will not cause a compiler error – it will only generate a warning. However, it's a good idea to use it, at least so that you know where you have those method signature clashes. An example of method hiding is given below:

```
namespace Samples
{
    using System;
    public class SuperHider
    {
        public string Test()
        {
            return "parent test";
        }
    }
    public class Hider: SuperHider
    {
        public Hider()
        {
        }
        new public string Test()
        {
            return "child test";
        }
    }
}
```

The following listing shows how either versions of the `Test()` method can be invoked:

```
Hider hider = new Hider();
Console.WriteLine(hider.Test());
Console.WriteLine(((SuperHider)h).Test() );
```

The result of the above will be:

```
Child test
Parent test
```

Method hiding is very different from method overriding. In C#, method overriding is a very explicit procedure. This is quite different from the Java approach, where overriding is the default behavior when the signature of a super class member is the same as the signature of its subclass. In order for you to be able to override a base class method in C# it must be marked as `virtual`. Fortunately, you cannot simply change the hider class to the example given below:

```
namespace Samples
{
    using System;
    public class SuperHider
    {
        public string Test()
```

```
        {
            return "parent test";
        }
    }
    public class Hider: SuperHider
    {
        public Hider()
        {
        }
        public override string Test()
        {
            return "child test";
        }
    }
}
```

This will not compile. You must first inform the compiler that the specified method, in this case `SuperHider.test()` can be overridden by child classes. This is done in C# with the `virtual` keyword and the methods this modifier is applied to are referred to as **virtual methods**. An example of the proper way to perform method overriding is shown below:

```
namespace Samples
{
    using System;
    public class SuperHider
    {
        public virtual string Test()
        {
            return "parent test";
        }
    }
    public class Hider: SuperHider
    {
        public Hider()
        {
        }
        public override string Test()
        {
            return "child test";
        }
    }
}
```

The benefit of using method overriding is that you are guaranteed that the most derived method will be called. Take a look at the invoking code listed below, the same code that in the method hiding sample produced two different values:

```
Hider hider = new Hider();
Console.WriteLine(hider.Test());
Console.WriteLine( ((SuperHider)hider).Test()    );
```

Because we are guaranteed `Hider`'s version of `test` is always called we know compiling and executing the code will always produce the results below:

```
Child test
Child test
```

The only difference between abstract classes in Java and C# syntactically is the placement of the `abstract` keyword. As with Java, defining abstract methods in C# mandates that the class be abstract.

Properties and Indexers

C# does not use `get()` and `set()` methods to access an object's internal attributes. It introduces the concept of **accessors** that provide a safe and flexible way of getting at internal fields. There are two types of accessor. The **get** accessor allows reading of internal fields of an object, and the **set** accessor allows you to change the value of an internal field. The `value` keyword represents the new value to the right of the equals sign at assignment time. Not including the appropriate accessor in the property declaration will make the property either read-only (no `set`), or write only (no `get`):

```
namespace Samples
{
    using System;
    public class Properties
    {
        private int age;
        private string name;
        public Properties(string name)
        {
            this.name = name;
        }
        public int Age
        {
            get
            {
                return age;
            }
            set
            {
                age = value;
            }
        }
        public string Name
        {
            get
            {
                return name;
            }
        }
    }
}
```

In the above example, the property `Age` has a `get` and `set` accessor so you may read or write to the property. `Name`, however, is created once when you create a new instance of the properties object, after which you can only read the value of the `Name` property. `Properties` are accessed as if they are public fields:

```
Properties props = new Properties("john");
props.Age = 21;
Console.WriteLine("My name is {0}, and I am {1} years old.", props.Name,
                   props.Age);
```

The result of the above code will be:

```
My name is john, and I am 21 years old.
```

Note that property names must be unique.

As the name implies, **indexers** allow us to index the attributes of our objects easily. Suppose, for example, you wanted to provide similar functionality without having to create two separate properties. You could index the fields you have so that they can be accessible via some key (the value used to access an index; for arrays, the key is an integer value). We could take out the two property declarations in the above example and replace them with:

```
public string this[string a]
{
    get
    {
        if(a.Equals("Age"))
        {
            return int.ToString(age);
        }
        else if(a.Equals("Name"))
        {
            return name;
        }
        else
        {
        throw new Exception("can only accept 'name' or 'age' key");
        }
    }
    set
    {
        if(a.Equals("Age"))
        {
            age = int.Parse(value);
        }
        else
        {
            throw new Exception(a + " is read only or does not exist");
        }
    }
}
```

We could then access the properties attributes as below:

```
Properties props = new Properties("john");
props["Age"] = "21";
Console.WriteLine("my name is {0}, I am {1} years old.", props["Name"],
                   props["Age"]);
```

The result will be:

```
My name is john, and I am 21 years old.
```

Events

C# events provide a much more robust and flexible observer pattern than is present in Java. What's more, they can be declared as either fields or properties. Creating an event is a three-part process. First, you create a delegate. Next, you create the event associated with that delegate, and finally you invoke the event when some action happens.

We will illustrate this by removing the exceptions that we have in the Properties class and using events instead. One of the things I love most about events is the flexibility we are afforded by using the delegate model. Essentially, you can use whatever custom signature you want to associate with an event and it is then up to the event subscriber to provide a target method that matches the required parameter list. Creating this custom signature starts with defining the delegate in your namespace code. For the Properties class we need it to raise string events similar to the exceptions we need thrown:

```
public delegate void ObservableDelegate(string message);
```

Next, declare the delegate as an event field in the class:

```
public event ObservableDelegate ExceptionEventListener;
```

Finally, we can rewrite the indexer implementation to trigger the listener event every time an exception condition occurs:

```
public string this[string a]
{
   get
   {
      if(a.Equals("Age"))
      {
         return int.ToString(age);
      }
      else if(a.Equals("Name"))
      {
         return name;
      }
      else
      {
         ExceptionEventListener("can only accept 'name' or 'age' key");
         return null; //program flow continues after our event is
                      //raised so we must return a value.
                      //In this case since the key is invalid
                      //key in invalid (not 'name' or 'age') null
                      //is returned signifying no value
      }
   }
   set
   {
      if(a.Equals("Age"))
```

```
        {
            age = int.Parse(value);
        }
        else
        {
            listener(a+ " is read only or does not exist");
        }
    }
}
```

The `delegate` bound to the event listener is never instantiated. This is because the instantiation actually happens at the client that consumes this event. To the client, the event appears as a public field but don't be fooled into thinking it is unrestricted. The only actions possible on an event field are:

❑   Composing new delegate instances on the event

❑   Removing delegate instances from the event

C# uses the "+=" and "-=" operators respectively for adding and removing delegate instances from events. Both operators are the same in C# and Java. You are not allowed to set the event equal to any one delegate instance. Rather, you have the flexibility to add as many delegates as necessary to the event. This loosely translates to having as many event listeners for a single event as needed; the example below shows how this can be achieved:

```
public delegate void TestEvent();
public class  Tester
{
    public event TestEvent testEvent;
    Tester()
    {
    }
    public void Perform()
    {
        testEvent();
    }
    public class Client
    {
    Client()
    {
        Tester tester = new Tester();
        TestEvent a = new TestEvent(Callback1);     //create delegate first
        tester.testEvent  += a;                      //then add it
        tester.testEvent  += new Test(CallBack2);    //or you can do
                                                      //it all in one go

        tester.testEvent  += new Test(Callback3);
        tester.testEvent  += new Test(Callback4);
        tester.Perform();
    }
    public void CallBack1()
    { //notify by email  }
    public void CallBack2()
    { //send faxes  }
    public void CallBack3()
    { //send wireless messages  }
    public void CallBack4()
    { //save to log  }
}
```

As you can see from the above example, to use a class's event(s) we must first create a method in our subscriber class to handle the event (similarly to how delegates function), then add the event handling method(s) to the event. We will create a static method, `Notify()`:

```
public static void Notify(string i)
{
    Console.WriteLine(i);
}
```

As you can see, this method shares the same signature as the `Properties` class's event listener. In the `Main()` method we can register our `Notify()` method and fake an error condition to test our event:

```
Properties props = new Properties("hello");

//register our event handler

props.ExceptionEventListener += new ExceptionEventListener(test);
p["Aged"] = "35";    //wrong key used to simulate error
```

Exceptions

Exceptions in C#, at least on the surface, are the same as in Java. The C# statements `try...catch` and `try...catch...finally` work along similar lines to their Java counterparts (see the *Keywords* section). However, in C# you cannot use the `throws` statement so it is not possible to indicate to a caller that some code in your method may throw an exception. Also there is a `try...finally`, which does not suppress thrown exceptions, but offers the `finally` block, which executes after the exception is raised to clean up.

Throwing exceptions is achieved by using the `throw` statement. For example to throw a `SystemException` you would use the code `throw new SystemException (<arg_list>);`. This is similar to how exceptions are thrown in Java. All you need is the `throws` statement and an appropriate exception class. Below is a list of some of the standard exception classes provided by the .NET runtime. Just as in Java, their functionality is reflected in the names given to them:

❑   `Exception` is the base class for all exception objects.

❑   `SystemException` is the base class for all errors generated at runtime.

❑   `IndexOutOfRangeException` is thrown when an array index is out of range at runtime.

❑   `NullReferenceException` is raised when a null reference is referenced at runtime.

❑   `InvalidOperationException` is thrown by certain methods when the call to the method is invalid for the object's current state.

❑   `ArgumentException` is the base class of all argument exceptions.

❑   `ArgumentNullException` is thrown when an argument is `null` where not allowed.

❑   `InteropException` is the base class for exceptions that occur or are targeted at environments outside the CLR .

One exception that may occur whether you throw it or not is the `System.OverflowException` associated with computed results exceeding the value range of a result variable's data type. The `checked` and `unchecked` statements can raise or suppress exceptions associated with that. Refer to the keywords section of this appendix for more information on `checked` and `unchecked`.

Conditional Compilation

The pre-processor in C# is emulated. It runs as a separate process before the compiler begins its work. The directives supported here are more similar to C++ than to any other language. There is certainly no pure Java equivalent to the functionality described in this section. You are allowed to define symbols, against which you test using simple conditional directives. Those that evaluate `true` are included and compiled. Otherwise, the code is ignored. Defining a symbol can happen in two ways. First of all, you can use the compiler option `/define` followed by a colon and the symbol you are defining, as follows:

```
csc /define:TEST_TEST samples.cs
```

From the configuration properties page of your project properties symbols may also be defined by adding them to the semicolon delimited conditional compilation constants list. You can also programmatically define symbols using the `#define` directive. In this case, the directive must appear before anything else, and applies to all tokens in the scope of the file. The conditional directives allowed are listed below:

❑ `#if`: used to test the existence of a symbol

❑ `#elif`: allows you to add multiple branches to the `#if` statement

❑ `#else`: provides final alternative condition to `#if` and `#elif`

❑ `#endif`: closes the `#if` statement

```
namespace Samples
{
    using System;
    #if EXAMPLE
    public class Example
    {
        public Example()
        {
        }
    }
    #elif TEST_TEST
    public class Test
    {
        public Test()
        {
        }
    }
    #else
    public class None
    {
        public None()
        {
        }
    }
    #endif
}
```

Adding the statement #define TEST_TEST will make class Test visible to compilation. Adding #define EXAMPLE will make class Example visible to compilation. If neither is added, class none will be compiled. Two other directives, #warning and #error are available to the C# pre-processor for producing compiler errors and warnings. They must be enclosed in the #if conditional. Try adding the line below to the #else statement above:

```
#warning I wouldn't try to instantiate the example object if I were you
```

C# also supports conditional functionality. In the code below, adding the conditional attribute to AMethod() makes it compile only when the Test symbol is defined:

```
[conditional("TEST_TEST")]
public void AMethod()
{
    string s = "I am available only when Test is defined";
}
```

Security Issues

Code these days can come from many different sources. In Java, prior to Java 2, there was an assumption that all applications should be completely trusted and allowed to use all features of the language. Recent experiences have shown us that this approach can be quite dangerous. Java now provides security policy services via the java.policy file. Applications are held to the same security scrutiny as applets. The security policy can be edited directly or via policytool to create applications that are more limited. The .NET framework addresses this threat with code-access security. Code-access security controls access to protected resources and operations. Below is a list of the most notable functions of code-access security:

❑ Code can demand that a caller must have specific permissions.

❑ Code execution is restricted by the runtime, in which case checks are performed that verify the granted permissions of a caller match the required permissions for the operations.

❑ Code can request the permissions it requires to run and the permission that would be useful, as well as explicitly state which permissions it must never have.

❑ Permissions are defined that that represents certain rights to access various system resources.

❑ Administrators can define security policies that assign certain permissions to defined groups of code.

❑ Code-access security grants permissions when a component is loaded. This granting is based on the requests by code, as well as the permitted operations defined by the security.

Enforcement of a security policy is what makes .NET Framework-managed code safe. This is because every assembly that loads is subject to a security policy that grants code permissions based on trust, with trust based on evidence about that code. .NET security allows code to use protected resources only if it has "permission" to do so. To enforce this, permissions, which represent the right for code to access protected resources, are utilized. Code requests the permissions it needs, and the security policy applied by .NET determines which permissions the code is actually granted. The .NET framework provides C# code access permission classes, each of which encapsulates the ability to access a particular resource. Associated with each permissions class is a permission flag enumeration used to specify the access flag for the permissions object. You use these permissions to indicate to .NET what your code needs to be allowed to do and to indicate what your code's callers must be authorized to do. Policy also uses these objects to determine what permissions to grant to code. Following is a list of the standard permissions:

- ❏ EnvironmentPermission. Defines access permissions to environment variables. There are two types of access that are possible: read-only and write access. The write access also provides permissions to create and delete environment variables.

- ❏ FileIOPermission. There are three possible types of file I/O: read, write, and append. Read and write are self-explanatory; append limits you to appending you cannot read other bits.

- ❏ ReflectionPermission. Controls the ability to read type information of non-public members of a type. Also controls the use of Reflection.Emit.

- ❏ RegistryPermission. Controls reading, writing, and creation in the registry.

- ❏ Securitypermission. Controls, collection of permission flags used by the security system.

- ❏ UIPermission. Controls access to different aspects of the user interface.

- ❏ FileDialogPermission. Controls access to files based on the system file dialog.

- ❏ IsolatedStroragePermission. Controls access to isolated storage.

There are two ways to modify the current security permissions in C#: using calls to permission classes in the .NET frameworks, or using security permission attributes.

Summary

Microsoft describes C# as a simple, modern language derived from C and C++. Because Java is also a modernization of C++, much of the syntax and inbuilt features present in C# are also available in Java.

C# uses the .NET framework, and so offers built-in, type safe, object-oriented code that is interoperable with any language that supports the CTS (Common Type System). Java does offer interoperability with C and C++, but it is not type safe. Moreover, it is highly complex. In a similar vein, C# provides operator overloading while Java does not.

C# filenames are not bound to the classes within them as they are in Java, nor are namespace names bound to folders as package names are in Java. C# introduces the concept of delegates, function pointers that can be used to encapsulate a method with a certain signature. C# also provides a rich set of built-in value types including type safe enumerations, structures, and the inbuilt primitives that offer a robust alternative to Java's primitives.

C# provides bi-directional conversion between reference and value types called boxing and unboxing. This functionality is not supported in Java. C# supports the use of classes, complete with fields, constructors, and methods, as a template for describing types, and provides the ability to define destructors, methods called just before the class is garbage collected. C# also provides three approaches to method parameters. They may be in, out, or ref with in being the default.

C# also introduces the concept of method hiding, as well as supporting explicit overriding via the virtual and override keywords. C# provides properties as an alternative to get() and set() methods as a way to safely access internal fields. In addition, C# allows the creation of indexers to provide indexed access to internal fields of an object. Unlike Java, however, C# does not provide a way of declaring that a method might throw exceptions.

C# namespaces provide a much more flexible way of grouping related classes together. C# provides pre-processor emulation. Code can be conditionally included or excluded based on the existence of defined symbols. C# provides a permission-based security model that can be controlled programmatically.

C

C# for VB 6 Developers

In this appendix we will present a brief introduction to the C# language, specifically aimed at those developers whose experience up until now has been mostly or entirely with Visual Basic 6.

> *Note that throughout this appendix, references to VB indicate VB 6. On those few occasions when we mention VB.NET, we will explicitly name it as such.*

C# and Visual Basic are very different languages, both in their syntactical style and in the fundamental concepts that they are based on. This means that Visual Basic developers will find they have quite a steep learning curve to climb in order to become familiar with C#, even at a basic level. The aim of this appendix is to make that learning curve easier by providing a tutorial introduction to C#, which specifically presumes knowledge of VB, and focuses on the main conceptual differences between the two languages. Our approach through much of the appendix will be to compare how you would code up the solution to a problem in VB and in C#, presenting C# and corresponding VB code together.

This does mean that our coverage of the C# language will be restricted to a basic level. We are not going to cover the more advanced features of the language – you'll need to look at the tutorial chapters in the early part of this book for that. The emphasis will be on showing you the different methodologies involved in writing code using the C# language.

Differences Between C# and VB

Beyond the obvious syntactical differences between the languages, there are really two main concepts that you need to become familiar with in order to progress from VB to C#:

1. The concept of the complete flow of execution of a program from start to finish: Visual Basic hides this aspect of programs from you, so that the only part of a VB program you code up is the event handlers and any methods and so on in class modules. C# makes the complete program available to you as sourcecode. The reasaon for this is to do with the fact that C# can be seen, philosophically, as next-generation C++, and the roots of C++ go back to the 1960s. C++ predates windowed user interfaces and sophisticated operating systems. C++ evolved as a low-level, close-to-the-machine, all-purpose language. To write GUI apps with C++ meant that you needed to explicitly invoke the system calls to create and interact with the windowed forms. C# builds upon this heritage while simplifying and modernizing C++, with the aim being that the low-level performance benefits of C++ can be roughly achieved with coding not being much harder than it is in VB. VB, on the other hand, is a young language designed specifically for rapid application development of Windows GUI applications. For this reason, in VB all the GUI boilerplate code is hidden, and all the VB programmer implements are the event handlers. In C# on the other hand, this boilerplate code is exposed as part of your sourcecode.

2. Classes and inheritance: C# is much more object-oriented than VB, requiring all code to be a part of a class. It also includes extensive support for implementation inheritance. Indeed, most well-designed C# programs will be very much designed around this form of inheritance, which is completely absent in VB.

The bulk of this appendix will be devoted to developing two samples, for which we will code up versions in both VB and C#. The first example is a simple form that asks the user for a number and displays the square root and sign of the number. By comparing the VB and C# versions of the sample in some detail, we will learn basic C# syntax and also understand the concepts behind the flow of execution of a program.

Next we will present a VB class module that stores information about employees, and its C# equivalent. However, in this case we will start to see the real power of C#, since as we add features to the samples, we will rapidly discover that VB simply doesn't support the concepts we need to develop the class module according to the requirements we will set ourselves, and we will have to proceed in C# alone.

We will then finish off the appendix with a short tour of some of the remaining differences between VB and C# not illustrated by the examples.

Before we start, however, we need to clarify a couple of concepts: classes, compilation, and the .NET base classes. Let's take a look at each of these in turn.

Classes

Throughout the appendix we will be using C# classes quite extensively. C# classes represent precisely defined objects, which we explain in detail Chapters 4 and 5. However, for our purposes, we are better off thinking of them as the C# equivalent to VB class modules, because they are quite similar entities: Like a VB class module, a C# class implements properties and methods, and contains member variables. Like a VB class module, you can create objects of a given C# class (class instances) using the operator new. Behind these similarities, however, there are many differences. For example, a VB class module is really a COM class. C# classes, by contrast, are not usually COM classes, but they are always integrated into the .NET framework. C# classes are also more lightweight than their VB/COM counterparts, in the sense that they are more defined for performance and give a smaller performance hit when instantiated. However, these differences will largely not affect our discussion of the C# language here.

Compilation

You are almost certainly well aware that the computer never directly executes code in any high level-language, whether it is VB, C++, C, or any other language. Instead, all sourcecode is first translated into native executable code, a process usually known as **compilation**. When you are debugging, VB offers the option of just running the code straight away (meaning that each line of VB code is compiled – or in this case, we speak of the code as being **interpreted** – as the computer comes to execute that line), or of doing a full compile (meaning that the entire program is first translated into executable code, and then execution starts). Performing a full compile first means that any syntax errors are discovered by the compiler before the program starts running. It also leads to much higher performance when running, and is therefore the only option permitted in C#.

In C#, compilation is done in two stages, with the first stage being into the so-called Intermediate Language (IL). This is the stage that we will informally refer to as compilation. The second stage, converting into native executable code, may be done at run time, but is a much simpler stage so it doesn't lead to such significant performance problems. It's also not the same as interpreting. Entire portions of code are converted from IL to assembly language at a time and the resultant native executable is then stored so it doesn't need to be recompiled the next time that portion of code is executed. Combined with various optimizations, Microsoft believes that this will ultimately lead to code that is actually faster to execute than with the previous system of compiling direct from sourcecode to native executable. Although the existence of IL is something that you need to bear in mind, it won't affect any of our discussion in this appendix, as it doesn't really affect C# language syntax.

The .NET Base Classes

VB doesn't just consist of the language itself. There are also a large number of associated functions around, such as the conversion functions CInt, CStr, and so on, the file system functions, date-time functions, and many more. VB also relies on the presence of ActiveX controls to provide the standard controls that you put on your form – listboxes, buttons, textboxes, and so on.

C# also relies on extensive support for these sorts of areas – but in the C# case, the support comes from a very large set of classes known as the .NET base classes. These classes provide support for almost every aspect of Windows development. There are classes that represent all the normal controls, classes that perform conversions, classes that perform date-time and file system access, classes that access the Internet, and many more. We won't go into the .NET base-class library in detail here, but we will frequently refer to it. Indeed, C# is so well integrated into the .NET base classes that we will find that many C# keywords just provide wrappers around particular base classes. In particular, all the basic C# data types that are used to represent integers, floating-point numbers, strings, and so on are actually base classes.

One important difference between VB 6 and C# in this respect is that VB's system functions are specific to VB, whereas the .NET base classes are accessible to any .NET-aware language.

Conventions

In this appendix we will frequently be comparing code in C# and Visual Basic. In order to make it easier to identify code in the two languages, we will present C# code in this format:

```
// C# code that we have already seen
// C# code that we want to draw attention to or which is new
```

However, all VB code will be presented in this format:

```
' VB code is presented with a white background
```

Example: The Square Root Form

In this section, we are going to examine a simple application called SquareRoot, which we have developed in both Visual Basic and C#. The application is a simple dialog box, which invites the user to type in a number, and then, when the user clicks a button, displays the sign and square root of that number. If the number is negative, then the square root needs to be displayed as a complex number – which simply means taking the square root of minus the number and adding 'i' after it. The C# version of the example looks like this. The VB version is pretty much identical in appearance except that it has a standard VB icon in place of the .NET windows forms icon in the top left corner:

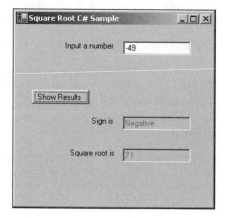

SquareRoot VB Version

To get this application working in Visual Basic, we simply need to add an event handler for the event of clicking the button. We have given the button the name cmdShowResults, and the textboxes have the intuitive names of txtNumber, txtSign, and txtResult. With these names, the event handler looks like this:

```
Option Explicit
Private Sub cmdShowResults_Click()
    Dim NumberInput As Single
    NumberInput = CSng(Me.txtNumber.Text)
    If (NumberInput < 0) Then
        Me.txtSign.Text = "Negative"
        Me.txtResult.Text = CStr(Sqr(-NumberInput)) & " i"
    ElseIf (NumberInput = 0) Then
        txtSign.Text = "Zero"
        txtResult.Text = "0"
    Else
        Me.txtSign.Text = "Positive"
        Me.txtResult.Text = CStr(Sqr(NumberInput))
    End If
End Sub
```

That is the only bit of VB code that we need to write.

SquareRoot C# Version

In C# we also need to write an event handler for the event of the button being clicked. We have kept the same names for the button and the textboxes, but in C# the code looks like this:

```
// Event handler for user clicking Show Results button.
// Displays square root and sign of number

private void OnClickShowResults(object sender, System.EventArgs e)
{
    float NumberInput = float.Parse(this.txtNumber.Text);
    if (NumberInput < 0)
    {
        this.txtSign.Text = "Negative";
        this.txtResult.Text = Math.Sqrt(-NumberInput).ToString() + " i";
    }
    else if (NumberInput == 0)
    {
        txtSign.Text = "Zero";
        txtResult.Text = "0";
    }
    else
    {
        this.txtSign.Text = "Positive";
        this.txtResult.Text = Math.Sqrt(NumberInput).ToString ();
    }
}
```

Comparing these two code samples, you can almost certainly see the similarity in the code structure, and even without any knowledge of C#, you can probably get some idea of what is going on. It is also evident that there are a huge number of differences in the syntax between the two languages. Over the next couple of pages, we are going to compare these samples to see what we can learn about C# syntax in the process. In the process, we will also uncover some of the differences between the basic methodologies of C# and VB.

Basic Syntax

In this section we will examine the two SquareRoot programs to see what they teach us about C# syntax.

C# Requires All Variables to be Declared

If we start with the first line of VB code, we encounter the Option Explicit declaration. This statement has no counterpart in C#. The reason is that in C# variables must always be declared before they are used. It's as if C# always runs with Option Explicit turned on and doesn't allow you to switch it off. Hence there's no need to declare Option Explicit explicitly.

The point of this restriction is that C# has been very carefully designed to make it difficult for you to accidentally introduce bugs into your code. Standard advice in VB is always to use Option Explicit because it prevents hard-to-find bugs caused by misspelled variable names. Generally, you will find that C# doesn't allow you to do things that have a high risk of causing bugs.

Comments

Since commenting code is always important, the next thing we do in both samples (or the first thing in the C# sample!) is add a comment:

```
// Event handler for user clicking Show Results button.
// Displays square root and sign of number

private void OnClickShowResults(object sender, System.EventArgs e)
{
```

In VB we use an apostrophe to denote the start of a comment, and the comment lasts until the end of the line. Our C# comments in the code work the same way, except they start with two forward slashes: //. Just as for VB comments, we can use an entire line for a comment, or append a comment to the end of a line:

```
// This code works out the results

    int Result = 10*Input;    // get result
```

However, C# is more flexible in its comments, because it allows two other ways of indicating comments, which each have a slightly different effect.

A comment may be also be delimited by the sequences /* and */. In other words, if the compiler sees a /* sequence, it assumes all the following text is a comment until it sees a */ sequence. This allows you to have long comments that stretch over several lines:

```
/* this text is a really long
long
long
long
comment */
```

Short comments within a line are very useful if you just want to temporarily swap something in a line while you are debugging:

```
X = /*20*/  15;
```

The third way is very similar to the first way. However, now we use three forward slashes:

```
///  <summary>
///  Event handler for user clicking Show Results button.
///  Displays square root and sign of number
///  </summary>
///  <param name="sender"></param>
///  <param name="e"></param>

private void OnClickShowResults(object sender, System.EventArgs e)
```

If you use three forward slashes instead of two, the comment still lasts until the end of that line. However, this comment now has an additional effect: The C# compiler is actually capable of using comments that start with three slashes in order to automatically generate documentation for your sourcecode, as a separate XML file. That's why the example above appears to have a fairly formal structure to the actual comment text: The structure is ready to be placed into an XML file. We won't go into the details of this process here (it's covered in Chapter 3). We will, however, say that this means that by commenting each method of your code you can have complete documentation automatically generated and updated when you modify your code. The compiler will even check that the documentation matches the method signatures and so on.

Statement Separation and Grouping

The most visible difference between the above C# and VB codes will almost certainly be the presence of all the semicolons and the curly braces in the C# code. Although this can make C# code look daunting, the principle is actually very simple. Visual Basic uses carriage returns to indicate the ends of statements, whereas C# uses semicolons for the same purpose. In fact, the C# compiler completely ignores all excess whitespace – including carriage returns. These features of C# syntax can combine to give you a lot of freedom in laying out your code. For example, the following (reformatted from part of the above sample) is also perfectly valid C# code:

```
        this.txtSign.Text =

   "Negative"; this.txtResult.Text = Math.Sqrt
   (-NumberInput) + " i";
```

Although obviously, if you want other people to be able to read your code, you will opt for the first coding style, and Visual Studio.NET will automatically lay out your code in that style for you anyway.

The braces are used to group statements together into what are known as **block statements** (or sometimes as **compound statements**). This is a concept that doesn't really exist in VB. You can group together any statements by placing braces around them. The group is now regarded as one single block statement, and can be used anywhere in C# where a single statement is expected.

Block statements are used a lot in C#. For example, in the C# code above there is no explicit indication of the end of the method (C# has methods where VB has functions and subs). VB needs an `End Sub` statement at the end of any sub because a sub can contain as many statements as you want – so a specific marker is the only way that VB knows where you intend the sub to end. C# works differently. In C# a method is formed from exactly one compound statement. Because of this, the method ends with the closing curly brace matching the opening one at the start of the method.

You find this a lot in C#: where Visual Basic uses some keyword to mark the end of a block of code, C# simply organizes the block into one compound statement. The `if` statement in the above samples illustrates the same point. In VB, we need an `EndIf` statement to mark where the `if` block ends. In C#, the rule is simply that an `if` clause always contains exactly one statement, and the `else` clause also contains one statement. If we want to put more than one statement into either clause, as is the case in the above example, we use a compound statement.

Capitalization

One other point you may notice about the syntax is that all the keywords – `if`, `else`, `int`, and so on – in the C# code are in lowercase. Unlike VB, C# is case-sensitive. If you write `If` instead of `if`, then the compiler won't understand your code. One advantage of being case-sensitive, however, is that you can have two variables whose names differ only in case, such as `Name` and `name`. We'll encounter this in the second example later in the appendix.

If you are used to VB's case-insensitivity, you might find the idea of having different variable names that differ only by case quite strange at first. But once you've got used to it, you will find the extra freedom it gives you in naming your variables does come in really useful.

In general, you'll find that all C# keywords are entirely lowercase.

Methods

Let's compare the syntax that VB and C# use to declare the part of the code that will handle the event: In VB:

```
Private Sub cmdShowResults_Click()
```

and in C#:

```
private void OnClickShowResults(object sender, System.EventArgs e)
```

The first point we should make is that the VB version declares a sub, whereas the C# version declares a method. In Visual Basic, code is traditionally grouped into subs and functions, with the concept of a procedure being either. Additionally, VB class objects have what are known as methods, which for all practical purposes means the same thing as procedures except that they are part of a class module.

C#, by contrast, only has methods (this is connected with the fact that, as we will see later, everything in C# is part of a class). In C# there is no separate concept of functions and subroutines – those terms don't even exist in the C# language specification. In VB, the only real difference between a sub and a function is that a sub never returns a value. In C#, if a method does not need to return a value, it is declared as returning `void` (as the `OnClickShowResults()` method illustrated here).

The syntax for declaring a method is similar in the two languages, at least to the extent that the parameters follow the method name in brackets. Note, however, that whereas in VB we indicated that we were declaring a sub with the word `Sub`, there is no corresponding word in the C# version. In C#, the return type (`void` in this case), followed by the method name, followed by the opening bracket is sufficient to tell the compiler that we are declaring a method, since no other construct in C# has this syntax (arrays in C# are marked with square rather than round brackets so there is no risk of confusion with arrays).

Like the VB Sub, the C# method declaration above is preceded by the keyword private. This has roughly the same meaning as in VB – it prevents outside code from being able to see the method. We'll examine just what exactly we mean by 'outside code' later.

There are two other differences to remark on about the method declaration: the C# version takes two parameters, and it has a different name to the VB event handler.

We'll tackle the name first. The name of the event handler in VB is supplied for you by the VB IDE. The reason that VB knows that the Sub is the event handler for when the button gets clicked is because of the name, cmdShowResults_Click. If you renamed the sub, then it wouldn't get called when you clicked the button. However, C# doesn't use the name in this way. In C#, as we'll see soon, there is some other code that tells the compiler which method is the event handler for this event. That means that we can give the handler whatever name we want. However, something starting with On for an event handler is traditional, and in C#, common practice is to name methods (and for that matter most other items) with something called **Pascal** casing, which means that words are joined together with their first letters capitalized. Using underscores in names in C# is not recommended, and we've chosen a name in accordance with these guidelines: OnClickShowResults().

Now for the parameters. We won't worry about the details of these parameters in this appendix, but we'll just say that all event handlers in C# are required to take two parameters similar to these, and these parameters can provide some useful extra information about the event concerned (for example, for a mouse move event they might indicate the location of the mouse pointer).

Variables

The SquareRoot sample can tell us quite a lot about the differences between the variable declarations in C# and VB. In the VB version we declare a floating-point number and set up its value as follows:

```
Dim NumberInput As Single
NumberInput = CSng(Me.txtNumber.Text)
```

The C# version looks like this:

```
float NumberInput = float.Parse(this.txtNumber.Text);
```

As you'd expect, the data types in C# aren't exactly the same as in VB. float is C#'s equivalent to Single. It's probably easier for us to understand what's going on if we split up the C# version into two lines. The following C# code has exactly the same effect as the line above:

```
float NumberInput;
NumberInput = float.Parse(this.txtNumber.Text);
```

Now we can compare the declaration and initialization of the variable separately.

Declarations

The obvious syntactical difference between C# and VB, as far as variable declarations are concerned, is that in C#, the data type precedes rather than follows the name of the variable, with no other keywords. This gives C# declarations a more compact format than their VB counterparts.

You'll notice that this idea of a declaration consisting only of a type followed by a name is used elsewhere too. Look again at the method declaration in C#:

```
private void OnClickShowResults(object sender, System.EventArgs e)
```

The type (void) precedes the name of the method, with no other keywords to indicate what we are declaring – that's obvious from the context. The same is also true for the parameters. The types of the parameters are object and System.EventArgs. The object type in C#, incidentally, plays a similar role to Object in VB – it indicates something for which we are choosing not to specify its type. However, C#'s object is much more powerful than VB's Object. In C#, object also replaces VB's Variant data type. We'll look at object later on. We won't really cover System.EventArgs in any detail in this appendix. It's a .NET base class, and it has no equivalent in VB.

In the case of variables, the declaration syntax used in C# allows you to combine the declaration with the setting of an initial value for the variable. In the code sample NumberInput is initialized to quite a complicated-looking expression, which we will examine soon. But to take two simpler examples:

```
int X = 10;       // int is similar to Long in VB
string Message = "Hello World";    // string is similar to String in VB
```

While we are on the subject, we ought to mention a couple of other points about variables.

No Suffixes in C#

VB allows you to attach suffixes to variables to indicate their data types, with $ for String, % for Int, and & for Long:

```
Dim Message$    ' will be a string
```

This syntax is not supported in C#. Variable names may contain only letters, numbers, and the underscore character, and you must always explicitly indicate the data type.

No Default Values for Local Variables

In the VB code sample, the variable NumberInput will be assigned the default value of 0 when it is declared. This is actually a waste of processor time since we immediately assign it a new value in the next statement. C# is a little more performance-conscious, and does not bother putting any default values in local variables when they are declared. Instead, it requires that you always initialize such variables yourself before you use them. The C# compiler will raise a compilation error if you attempt to read the value in any local variable before you have set it.

Assigning Values to Variables

Assigning values to variables in C# is done with the same syntax as in VB. You simply put an = sign after the variable name, followed by the value you are assigning to it. However, one point to watch out for is that this is the **only** syntax used in C#. In some cases in VB we use Let, while for objects VB always uses the Set keyword:

```
Set MyListBox = new ListBox
```

C# does not use a separate syntax for assigning to object references. The C# equivalent of the above is:

```
MyListBox = new ListBox();
```

> Remember that in C#, variables are always assigned using the syntax
> `<VariableName>=<Expression>;`

Classes

Now we come to look at what's going on in the expression used to initalize the variable NumberInput in the SquareRoot sample. The C# and VB examples are both actually doing exactly the same thing: grabbing the text from the txtNumber textbox; but the syntax to do this looked rather different in the two languages:

```
NumberInput = CSng(Me.txtNumber.Text)
```

and:

```
float NumberInput = float.Parse(this.txtNumber.Text);
```

Getting the value out of the textboxes is quite similar in both cases. The only difference for that part of the process is the purely syntactical one that VB uses the keyword Me while C# uses the keyword this, which has exactly the same meaning (in fact, in C# you can omit this if you want, just as you can omit Me in VB). In C# we could equally well have written:

```
float NumberInput = float.Parse(txtNumber.Text);
```

The more interesting part is how the string retrieved from the textbox is converted to a float (or single), because this illustrates a fundamental point of the C# language, which we've hinted briefly at earlier:

> Everything in C# is part of a class.

In VB, the conversion is carried out by a function, CSng. However, C# does not have functions in the way that VB has. C# is totally object-oriented, and will only allow you to declare methods that are part of a class.

In C#, the conversion from string to float is carried out by the Parse() method. However, because Parse() is part of a class, it has to be preceded by the name of the class. The class against which we need to call the Parse() method is float. Yes, I did say that right. Up until now we have treated float as simply being C#'s equivalent to VB's Single. However, it is actually a class as well. In C#, all data types are classes as well, which means even things like int, float, and string have methods and properties that you can call (although we should point out that int and float are special types of class known in C# as **structs**. The difference is not important for our code here, but we will explain it later).

If you are looking really carefully at the code above, you might notice a slight apparent problem with the analogy with VB class modules. In VB, you call methods by specifying the name of a variable not the name of the class module, but we've called Parse *by specifying the name of the class,* float, *instead of the name of a variable.* Parse() *is actually a special type of method known as a* static *method. There is no equivalent in VB, and a* static *method can be called without creating an instance of a class. Hence we specify the class name,* float, *rather than a variable name.* static *by the way, confusingly, does not have the same meaning in C# as it does in VB. There is no equivalent in C# to VB static variables – there is no need for these in C#'s object-oriented programming methodology, because you will use C# fields instead for this purpose.*

Also, to be strictly accurate, we should point out that the name of the class is actually System.Single, *not* float. System.Single *is one of the .NET base classes, and C# uses the keyword* float *to indicate this class.*

If Statements

Next we come to the main part of the event handler. The if statement. Recall that the VB version looks like this:

```
If (NumberInput < 0) Then
    Me.txtSign.Text = "Negative"
    Me.txtResult.Text = CStr(Sqr(-NumberInput)) & " i"
ElseIf (NumberInput = 0) Then
    txtSign.Text = "Zero"
    txtResult.Text = "0"
Else
    Me.txtSign.Text = "Positive"
    Me.txtResult.Text = CStr(Sqr(NumberInput))
End If
```

while this is the C# version:

```
if (NumberInput < 0)
{
   this.txtSign.Text = "Negative";
   this.txtResult.Text = Math.Sqrt(-NumberInput).ToString() + " i";
}
else if (NumberInput == 0)
{
   txtSign.Text = "Zero";
   txtResult.Text = "0";
}
else
{
   this.txtSign.Text = "Positive";
   this.txtResult.Text = Math.Sqrt(NumberInput).ToString();
}
```

In fact, we have already explained the biggest syntactical difference here: that each part of the if statement in C# must be a single statement, hence, if we need to conditionally execute more than one statement we must combine them into a single block statement. In C#, if there is only one statement to be conditionally executed, we don't need to form a block statement. For example, if we skipped setting the text in the txtSign textbox in the above code we could have written:

```
   if (NumberInput < 0)
       this.txtResult.Text = Math.Sqrt(-NumberInput) + " i";
   else if (NumberInput == 0)
       txtSign.Text = "Zero";
   else
       this.txtResult.Text = Math.Sqrt(NumberInput).ToString();
```

There are some other differences in syntax that we should remark on. In C#, the brackets around the condition to be tested in an `if` statement are compulsory. In VB we could have written:

```
   If NumberInput < 0 Then
```

Trying the same trick in C# would result in a compilation error immediately. In general, C# is much more precise about the syntax expected than VB. Also, notice that when we test whether `NumberInput` is zero, we use two equal signs in succession for the comparison:

```
   else if (NumberInput == 0)
```

In VB, the symbol = doubles up for two purposes: it is used for assigning values to variables, and it is used for comparing values. C# formally recognizes these as two very different types of operation, and so uses different symbols: = for assignment and == for comparison.

There is one other important difference that you should be aware of, because this one can easily catch you out when making the transition from VB to C#:

> `else if` is two words in C# whereas it is one word in VB: `ElseIf`.

Calculating Square Roots: Another Class Method

Given our earlier comments about everything in C# being a member of the class, you won't be surprised to learn that C#'s equivalent of the VB's `Sqr` function, which calculates square roots, is also a method that is a member of a class. In this case it is the `Sqrt()` method, which is a static member of another .NET base class, `System.Math`, which we can abbreviate to just `Math` in our code.

You'll have also noticed that, in the sample code, when dealing with the condition of the number input being exactly zero, we don't specify the `this` keyword in the C# code:

```
   txtSign.Text = "Zero";
   txtResult.Text = "0";
```

and in the corresponding VB code we don't specify `Me` explicitly either. In C#, just as in VB, you don't have to explicitly specify `this` (`Me`) unless, for any reason, the context is unclear. We've chosen not to do so here just to illustrate the point.

Strings

When we display the square root of a negative number, we have our first bit of string processing:

```
this.txtResult.Text = Math.Sqrt(-NumberInput).ToString() + " i";
```

You will notice from this code that in C# concatenation of strings is done using the symbol + rather than &. You will also notice that we convert from a `float` to a `String` by calling a method on the `float` object. The method is called `ToString()`, and this method is not static, so it is called using the same syntax as in VB when you call methods on objects: by prefixing the name of the method with the name of the variable that represents the object, followed by a dot. One useful thing to remember about C# is that every object (and hence every variable) implements the `ToString()` method.

Extra Code in C#

We have now completed comparing the event handler routines in C# and VB. In the process, we've learned a lot about the syntactical differences between the languages. In fact, we have now learned most of the basic syntax that C# uses to string statements together. We have also had our first brush with the fact that everything in C# is a class. However, if you have downloaded the sample code for these samples from the Wrox Press web site, and looked at the code, you will have almost certainly noticed that we have carefully avoided any discussion of the most obvious difference between the samples: there is actually a lot more code in the C# sample than simply an event handler. For the VB version of the `SquareRoot` sample, the code for the event handler that we have presented here represents the complete total of all the sourcecode in the project. However, in the C# version of the project, this event handler is just one method in a huge sourcecode file that contains a very large amount of other code.

The reason why there is so much additional code in the C# project is to do with the fact that the Visual Basic IDE hides a lot of what's going on in your program from you. In Visual Basic, all we needed to write was the event handler, but in fact the sample is doing a lot more. It needs to start up, display the form on the screen, send information to Windows regarding what it wants to do with events, and shut it down when you have finished. In Visual Basic, you don't have access to any of the code that does this. By contrast, C# takes a completely different philosophy, and leaves all this code in the open. That might make your sourcecode look more complicated, but it does have the advantage that if the code is available, then you can edit it, which means you gain much more flexibility in deciding how your application should behave.

In fact, so successful is Visual Basic at hiding almost everything that goes on in your program from you, that is very easy to become highly proficient in Visual Basic, and to be able to code up quite sophisticated complex applications, without actually having any understanding of the full structure of a computer program! In the next section we will have a look at what really goes on in any computer program, and then we will be ready to have a look at all the extra code you get in the C# version of `SquareRoot`.

What Happens When You Run a Program

Any program involves a precise sequence of execution. When an application is launched there will be an identifiable location in the executable code that the computer knows is where it has to start running the code from. In other words, an instruction that it executes first. It will then carry on executing the next instruction, and the next, and the next, and so on. Some of these these commands will tell the computer to jump to a different instruction, perhaps depending on the values contained in certain variables. Very often the computer will jump back and execute the same instructions again. However, there is always this continuous sequence of executing the next instruction until the computer hits a command that tells it to terminate execution of the code. This linear sequence is true of any program. Some programs may be multithreaded, in which case there are several sequences of execution (threads) but each thread still follows this sequence from an initial instruction through to termination of the program.

Of course, this sequence is not what you see when you write a VB executable program. In VB 6, what you write is essentially a set of event handlers – a set of subs, each of which you know will be called when the user does something. There's no single start to the program, although the Form_Load event handler comes close to that in concept. Even so, Form_Load is really only another event handler. It just happens to be the handler for the event that gets raised when the form is loaded, which means it'll be the first event that runs. Similarly, if, instead of an executable, you are writing a control or a class object, you don't have a start point. You simply write a class and add lots of methods and properties to it. Each method or property will execute if and when the client code chooses to call it.

> *Actually the above paragraph isn't quite true. In VB, Sub Main() does exist, and acts as the entry point to a program, but it's not very commonly used. Since we are comparing a typical C# program with a typical VB program, our point that VB programs really only show the code for events is generally still valid.*

In order to see how we can relate the two programming ideas, let's look at what actually happens when any Visual Basic application – or for that matter any Windows GUI application, no matter what language it is written in – executes. This is a bit more restrictive than the applications we mentioned before, as now we are confining our attention to Windows GUI apps (in other words, not consoles, services, and so on).

As usual, execution starts at some well-defined point. The commands executed will probably involve the creation of some Windows and controls, and displaying those controls on the screen. At that point, the program then does something that is known as **entering a message loop**. What effectively happens is that the program puts itself to sleep and tells Windows to wake it up when something interesting happens that it needs to know about. These "interesting" things are the events that you have written handlers for, and also a good few events that you haven't written your own event handlers for, because even if you don't write a handler for a particular event, the VB IDE may quietly supply one for you. A good example of this is the handlers that deal with resizing a form. You never see the sourcecode for this in VB, but a VB application is still able to respond correctly when the user attempts to resize it because the VB IDE has invisibly added event handlers to your project that correctly handle this situation.

Whenever an event occurs, Windows wakes the application up and calls the relevant event handler – that's when the code that you wrote might start executing. When the event handler subroutine exits, the application will put itself to sleep again, once again telling Windows to wake it up when another interesting event happens. Finally, assuming nothing goes disastrously wrong, at some point Windows will wake up the application and inform it that it needs to shut down. At that point, the application will take any appropriate action – for example, displaying a message box asking the user if they want to save a file – and will then quietly terminate itself. Again, most of the code to do this has been quietly added to your project behind the scenes by the VB IDE, and you never get to see it.

The thread of execution in a typical Windows GUI application looks rather like this:

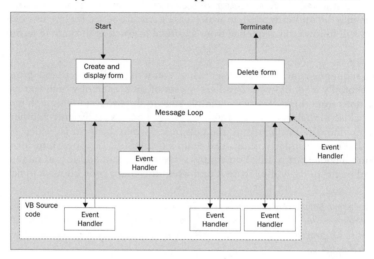

In this diagram, the box with a dashed border indicates the part of execution that the VB IDE lets you get access to, and for which you can write sourcecode: some of the event handlers. The rest of the code is inaccessible to you, though you can to some extent specify it through your choice of type of application when you first ask VB to create a project. Recall that when you create a new project in VB, you get a dialog box asking you what type of application you want to create – Standard EXE, ActiveX EXE, ActiveX DLL, and so on. Well, what happens when you make that selection is that the VB IDE uses your choice to generate all the appropriate code for the part of the program that is outside the dashed box in the above diagram. The diagram shows the situation when you choose to create a Standard EXE project, and will differ for other types of project (for example, an ActiveX DLL doesn't have a message loop at all but relies on clients to call the methods instead), but it should give you a rough idea of what's going on.

Now, I said earlier that in C# you get access to all the code that does everything but I should qualify that. All the nitty-gritty details of things, like what's going on inside the message loop, are well hidden inside various DLLs that Microsoft has written, but you do get to see the high-level methods that call up the various bits of processing. So, for example, you have access to the code that starts the whole program running, the call to a library method that makes your program enter the message loop and puts it to sleep, and so on. You also get access to the sourcecode that instantiates all the various controls you place on your form, makes them visible, and sorts out their initial positions and sizes, and all the rest. One other point I should stress is that you don't need to write any of this code yourself. When you use Visual Studio.NET to create a C# project, you will still get a dialog box asking you which type of project you want to create, and Visual Studio.NET will still write all the background code for you. The difference is that Visual Studio.NET writes this background code as source C# code, which then becomes code that you can edit directly.

Doing things this way does, as we've remarked, mean that your sourcecode is much longer and more complex. However, the huge advantage is that you have much more flexibility in what your program does and how it behaves. It also means that you can write many more types of project in C#. Whereas in Visual Basic, the only things you can write are different kinds of form, and COM components, in C# you can write any of the different types of program that run on Windows. This includes, for example, console (command-line) applications and ASP.NET (the successor to ASP) pages, which are impossible to write in VB 6 (though, admittedly, you can use VBScript for ASP pages). In this appendix however, we will concentrate exclusively on classic Windows GUI applications.

The C# Code for the Rest of the Program

In this section, we will examine the rest of the code for the `SquareRoot` sample. In the process we will learn a bit more about classes in C#.

> *The C# `SquareRoot` sample was created in Visual Studio.NET, and the VB one was created in the VB 6 IDE. However, the code presented here isn't quite what Visual Studio.NET generated for us. Apart from adding the event handler, I've made a couple of other tweaks to the code in order to better illustrate the principles of C# programming. However, it will still give you a good idea of the sort of work that Visual Studio.NET does when it creates a project for you.*

The full text of the sourcecode is quite long. We present it here for completeness, but you're probably better off skipping to the following explanation, and referring back to this sourcecode as necessary:

```csharp
using System;
using System.Drawing;
using System.Collections;
using System.ComponentModel;
using System.Windows.Forms;
using System.Data;

namespace Wrox.ProfessionalCSharp.AppendixC.SquareRootSample
{

    /// <summary>
    /// The Form that forms the main window for the app.
    /// </summary>

    public class SquareRootForm : System.Windows.Forms.Form
    {
        private System.Windows.Forms.TextBox txtNumber;
        private System.Windows.Forms.TextBox txtSign;
        private System.Windows.Forms.TextBox txtResult;
        private System.Windows.Forms.Button cmdShowResults;
        private System.Windows.Forms.Label label1;
        private System.Windows.Forms.Label label2;
        private System.Windows.Forms.Label label3;
        private System.Windows.Forms.Label label4;

        /// <summary>
        /// Required designer variable.
        /// </summary>
```

```csharp
    private System.ComponentModel.Container components;
    public SquareRootForm()
    {
        InitializeComponent();
    }
    public override void Dispose()
    {
        base.Dispose();
        if(components != null)
            components.Dispose();
    }

    #region Windows Form Designer generated code

    /// <summary>
    /// Required method for Designer support - do not modify
    /// the contents of this method with the code editor.
    /// </summary>

    private void InitializeComponent()
    {
        this.txtNumber = new System.Windows.Forms.TextBox();
        this.txtSign = new System.Windows.Forms.TextBox();
        this.cmdShowResults = new System.Windows.Forms.Button();
        this.label3 = new System.Windows.Forms.Label();
        this.label4 = new System.Windows.Forms.Label();
        this.label1 = new System.Windows.Forms.Label();
        this.label2 = new System.Windows.Forms.Label();
        this.txtResult = new System.Windows.Forms.TextBox();
        this.SuspendLayout();

        //
        // txtNumber
        //

        this.txtNumber.Location = new System.Drawing.Point(160, 24);
        this.txtNumber.Name = "txtNumber";
        this.txtNumber.TabIndex = 0;
        this.txtNumber.Text = "";

        //
        // txtSign
        //

        this.txtSign.Enabled = false;
        this.txtSign.Location = new System.Drawing.Point(160, 136);
        this.txtSign.Name = "txtSign";
        this.txtSign.TabIndex = 1;
        this.txtSign.Text = "";

        //
        // cmdShowResults
        //

        this.cmdShowResults.Location = new System.Drawing.Point(24, 96);
        this.cmdShowResults.Name = "cmdShowResults";
```

```
this.cmdShowResults.Size = new System.Drawing.Size(88, 23);
this.cmdShowResults.TabIndex = 3;
this.cmdShowResults.Text = "Show Results";
this.cmdShowResults.Click += new
                    System.EventHandler(this.OnClickShowResults);

//
// label3
//

this.label3.Location = new System.Drawing.Point(72, 24);
this.label3.Name = "label3";
this.label3.Size = new System.Drawing.Size(80, 23);
this.label3.TabIndex = 6;
this.label3.Text = "Input a number";

//
// label4
//

this.label4.Location = new System.Drawing.Point(80, 184);
this.label4.Name = "label4";
this.label4.Size = new System.Drawing.Size(80, 16);
this.label4.TabIndex = 7;
this.label4.Text = "Square root is";

//
// label1
//

this.label1.Location = new System.Drawing.Point(112, 136);
this.label1.Name = "label1";
this.label1.Size = new System.Drawing.Size(40, 23);
this.label1.TabIndex = 4;
this.label1.Text = "Sign is";

//
// label2
//

this.label2.Location = new System.Drawing.Point(48, 184);
this.label2.Name = "label2";
this.label2.Size = new System.Drawing.Size(8, 8);
this.label2.TabIndex = 5;

//
// txtResult
//

this.txtResult.Enabled = false;
this.txtResult.Location = new System.Drawing.Point(160, 184);
this.txtResult.Name = "txtResult";
this.txtResult.TabIndex = 2;
this.txtResult.Text = "";

//
```

```
        // Form1
        //

        this.AutoScaleBaseSize = new System.Drawing.Size(5, 13);
        this.ClientSize = new System.Drawing.Size(292, 269);
        this.Controls.AddRange(new System.Windows.Forms.Control[]
                                {this.label4,
                                 this.label3,
                                 this.label2,
                                 this.label1,
                                 this.cmdShowResults,
                                 this.txtResult,
                                 this.txtSign,
                                 this.txtNumber});
        this.Name = "Form1";
        this.Text = "Square Root C# Sample";
        this.ResumeLayout(false);
    }

    #endregion

    /// <summary>
    /// Event handler for user clicking Show Results button.
    /// Displays square root and sign of number
    /// </summary>
    /// <param name="sender"></param>
    /// <param name="e"></param>

    private void OnClickShowResults(object sender, System.EventArgs e)
    {
        float NumberInput = float.Parse(this.txtNumber.Text);
        if (NumberInput < 0)
        {
            this.txtSign.Text = "Negative";
            this.txtResult.Text = Math.Sqrt(-NumberInput) + " I";
        }
        else if (NumberInput == 0)
        {
            txtSign.Text = "Zero";
            txtResult.Text = "0";
        }
        else
        {
            this.txtSign.Text = "Positive";
            this.txtResult.Text = Math.Sqrt(NumberInput).ToString();
        }
    }
}
class MainEntryClass
{

    /// <summary>
    /// The main entry point for the application.
    /// </summary>

    [STAThread]
```

```
        static void Main()
        {
            SquareRootForm TheMainForm = new SquareRootForm();
            Application.Run(TheMainForm);
        }
    }
}
```

Namespaces

The main part of the C# `SquareRoot` sourcecode begins with a couple of namespace declarations and a class declaration:

```
namespace Wrox.ProfessionalCSharp.AppendixC.SquareRootForm
{
    public class SquareRootForm : System.Windows.Forms.Form
    {
```

The `SquareRootForm` class is going to hold almost all the code – all the methods and so on, with a small amount of code being contained in another class called `MainEntryClass`. Remember that it's easiest here to think of a class as being like a VB class object – though we can see here one difference is that we actually see the sourcecode that begins the declaration of the class. In VB, the VB IDE just gives you a separate window with the contents of the class in it.

A namespace is something that doesn't really have an analogy in VB, and the easiest way to think of it is as a way of organizing the names of your classes in much the same way as a file system organizes the names of your files. For example, you have almost certainly got a large number of files on your hard drive all called `ReadMe.Txt`. If that name, `ReadMe.Txt`, were the only information you had about each file, then you'd have no way of distinguishing between them all. However, you can distinguish between them using their full pathnames; for example, on my computer one of them is actually `C:\Program Files\ReadMe.txt` and another is `G:\Program Files\HTML Help Workshop\ReadMe.txt`.

Namespaces work in same way, but without all the overhead of having an actual file system – they are basically no more than labels. You don't have to formally do anything to create a namespace, other than just declare it in your code in the way we've done in our sample above. The code presented above means that the full name of the class we have defined is not `SquareRootForm`, but `Wrox.ProfessionalCSharp.AppendixC.SquareRootForm`. It is extremely unlikely that anyone else will write a class with that full name. On the other hand, if we didn't have the namespace, there would be more risk of confusion because someone else might conceivably write a class called `SquareRootForm`.

Avoiding clashes in this way is important in C#, because the .NET environment uses only these names to identify classes, whereas the ActiveX controls created by VB used a complex mechanism involving GUIDs to avoid name clashes. Microsoft has opted for the simpler concept of namespaces because of concerns that some of the complexities of COM, such as GUIDs, were making it unnecessarily difficult for developers to write good Windows applications.

In C#, although namespaces are not strictly required, it is strongly advised that you place all your classes in a namespace in order to prevent any possible name clashes with other software. In fact it is extremely rare to see C# code that does not start with a namespace declaration.

Namespaces can be nested. For example, the namespace code:

```
namespace Wrox.ProfessionalCSharp.AppendixC.SquareRootSample
{
    public class SquareRootForm : System.Windows.Forms.Form
    {

    // and so on

    }
}
```

could have been written like this:

```
namespace Wrox
{
    namespace ProfessionalCSharp
    {
        namespace AppendixC
        {
            namespace SquareRootSample
            {
                public class SquareRootForm : System.Windows.Forms.Form
                {

                    // and so on

                }
            }
        }
    }
}
```

In this code we have added the closing curly braces just to emphasize that they always have to match up. Curly braces are used to mark the boundaries of namespaces and classes just as they are used to mark the boundaries of methods and compound statements.

The using Statement

The final part of the above code that begins the SquareRoot project consists of using statements:

```
using System;
using System.Drawing;
using System.Collections;
using System.ComponentModel;
using System.Windows.Forms;
using System.Data;

namespace Wrox.ProfessionalCSharp.AppendixC.SquareRootSample
{
```

These using statements are here to simplify the code. Full names of classes, including the namespace names, are long. For example, later in this code we will be defining a couple of textboxes. A textbox is represented by the class System.Windows.Forms.TextBox. If we had to write that in our code every time we wanted to refer to a TextBox, our code would look very messy. Instead, the statement using System.Windows.Forms; instructs the compiler to look in this namespace for any classes that are not in the current namespace, and for which we have not specified a namespace. Now we can simply write TextBox whenever we want to refer to that class. It is usual to start any C# program with a number of using statements that bring in all the namespaces we are going to be using into the set of namespaces searched by the compiler. The namespaces specified in the above code are all namespaces that cover various parts of the .NET base-class library, and so allow us to conveniently use various .NET base classes.

The Class Definition: Inheritance

Now we come to the definition of the SquareRootForm class. The definition itself is fairly simple:

```
public class SquareRootForm : System.Windows.Forms.Form
{
```

The keyword class tells the compiler that we are about to define a class. The interesting part is the colon after the name of the class, which is followed by another name, Form. This is the point at which we need to bring in that other important concept that we mentioned earlier you need to learn in order to understand C# programming: **inheritance**.

What the above syntax does is tell the compiler that our SquareRootForm class inherits from the class Form (actually System.Windows.Forms.Form). What this means is that our class gets not only any methods, properties, etc. that we define; it also gets everything that was in Form. Form is an extremely powerful .NET base class, which gives you all the features of a basic form. It contains methods that get the form to display itself, and a large number of properties including Height, Width, Desktop Location, and BackColor (the background color of the form), which control the appearance of the form on the screen. By inheriting from this class, our own class gets all these features straight away, and is therefore already a fully-fledged form. The class you inherit from is known as the **base class**, and the new class is known as the **derived class**.

If you have used interfaces much before, inheritance will not be new to you, since you will know that interfaces can inherit from each other. What we have here, however, is much more powerful than interface inheritance. When a COM interface inherits from another interface, all it gets is the names and signatures of the methods and properties. That is, after all, all that an interface contains. However, a class contains all the code that implements these methods and so on as well, just as in VB a class object does. This means that SquareRootForm gets all the implementations of just about everything in Form, as well as the method names. This kind of inheritance is known as **implementation inheritance**, and is not new to C#: It has been a fundamental concept of classic object-oriented programming (OOP) for decades. C++ programs, in particular, normally use the concept extensively, but it was not supported in VB. (Implementation inheritance does have similarities to subclassing.) As you get used to writing C# programs, you will find that the entire architecture of a typical C# program is almost invariably based around implementation inheritance.

But implementation inheritance is even more powerful than that. As we will see later on, when a class inherits from another class, it doesn't have to take **all** the implementations of everything in the base class. If you want, you can modify the implementations of particular methods and properties using a technique called **overriding**. This means that you can create a class that is very similar to an existing class, but has some differences in how it works or what it does. That makes it very easy for you to reuse code that other people have written, thereby saving yourself a lot of development time. It is also important to understand that you don't need access to the sourcecode of the base class in order to derive from it. For obvious commercial reasons, Microsoft is keeping the sourcecode of Form to itself. The fact that the compiled library is available in the form of an assembly is sufficient for us to be able to inherit from the class, taking those methods we want and overriding those that we don't.

Program Entry Point

We will now jump to near the bottom of the code for the example, to examine the main program entry point. That is the Main() function, reproduced below:

```
class MainEntryClass
{

    /// <summary>
    /// The main entry point for the application.
    /// </summary>

    [STAThread]
    static void Main()
    {
        SquareRootForm TheMainForm = new SquareRootForm();
        Application.Run(TheMainForm);
    }
}
```

This doesn't look at first sight like a very obvious program entry point, but it is. The rule in C# is that program execution starts at a method called Main(). This method must be defined as a static method in some class. There should normally be only one method throughout all the classes in the sourcecode that answers this description in the program – otherwise the compiler won't know which one to choose. Main() here is defined as not taking any parameters and returning void (in other words, not returning anything). This isn't the only possible signature for the method, but it is the usual one for a Windows application (command-line applications may take parameters; these are any command-line arguments you specify).

As we mentioned earlier, VB code can have a Main() method, but this is rarely used and is optional. In C#, the Main() method must be present as the main program entry point.

Since Main() has to be in a class, we've put it in one: a class called MainEntryClass. This class doesn't contain anything else, but that's not necessarily the case – it's quite legitimate for a class that contains the main entry point to contain other methods as well. The fact that Main() is a static method is important. Recall that we said earlier that static methods are special methods that can be run without actually creating an object of the class first. Well, since the very first thing that happens when the program is run is that Main() is called, there aren't yet any instances of any classes – we haven't yet executed any code to create them! That's why the entry point has to be static.

Apart from the static keyword, the definition of Main() looks much like the earlier method definition we examined. However, it is prefixed by the word [STAThread] in square brackets. STAThread is an example of an **attribute** – another concept that has no parallel in VB sourcecode.

An attribute is something that provides extra information to the compiler about some item in the code, and always takes the form of a word (possibly with some parameters as well, though not in this case) in square brackets, immediately before the item to which it applies. This particular attribute tells the compiler about the threading model that the code needs to run in. We won't go into details of threading models here, but we will say that writing [STAThread] in the C# sourcecode has a similar effect to selecting the threading model under **Project Properties** in the VB IDE, although in VB you can only do this for ActiveX DLL and ActiveX Control projects. Also, note that the analogy is only approximate, because the C# attribute selects a .NET threading model, not a COM threading model.

Incidentally, this comparison shows once again the different philosophy of C# compared to VB. In VB, the threading model is there and needs to be specified, but it is all but hidden by the VB IDE, so you can't get to it in the VB sourcecode – hence in VB you have to access it through the project settings.

Instantiating Classes

Now let's examine the code inside the Main() method. The first thing we need to do is create the form – in other words, instantiate a SquareRootForm object. This is dealt with by the first line of code:

```
SquareRootForm TheMainForm = new SquareRootForm();
```

We obviously can't compare this with the corresponding VB code, since the corresponding VB commands aren't available as sourcecode, but we can do a comparison – if we imagine that in some VB code we are going to create a dialog box. In VB, the way you would do that would look something like this:

```
Dim SomeDialog As MyDialogClass
Set SomeDialog = New MyDialogClass
```

In this VB code, we first declare a variable that is an object reference: SomeDialog will refer to a MyDialogClass instance. Then we actually instantiate an object using VB's New keyword, and set our variable to refer to it.

That's exactly what is going on in the C# code too: we declare a variable called TheMainForm, which is a reference to a SquareRootForm object, then we use the C#'s new keyword to create an instance of SquareRootForm, and set our variable to refer to it. The main syntactical difference is that C# allows us to combine both operations into one statement, in the same way that we were previously able to declare and initialize the NumberInput variable in one go. You will also notice the parentheses after the new expression. That is a requirement of C#. When creating objects, you always have to write these brackets in. The reason is that C# treats creating an object a bit like a method call, to the extent that you can even sometimes pass parameters into the call to new, to indicate how you want the new object to be initialized. In this case, we don't pass in any parameters, but we still need the parentheses.

C# Classes

Up until now we've said that C# classes are similar to class modules in VB. We've already seen one difference in that C# classes allow static methods. The code for the Main() method above now highlights another difference. If we were doing something like this in VB, we would also need to set the object created to Nothing when we'd finished with it. However, nothing like that appears in our C# code, because in C# it is not necessary to do this.

The reason for this difference is to do with the fact that C# classes are more efficient and lightweight than their corresponding VB counterparts are. VB class objects are really COM objects, which means they each include some sophisticated code that checks how many references to the object are being held, so that each object can destroy itself when it detects it is no longer needed. In VB, if you don't set your object reference to Nothing when you've finished with the object, this is considered bad practice because it means the object does not know that it is no longer needed, so it can hang around in memory, possibly until the whole process ends.

However, for performance reasons, C# objects don't perform this kind of checking. Instead, C# uses a mechanism called **garbage collection**. What happens is that, instead of each object checking whether it should still be alive, every so often the .NET runtime hands control to something called the garbage collector. The garbage collector examines the state of memory, uses a very efficient algorithm to identify those objects that are no longer referenced by your code, and removes them. Because of this mechanism, it is not considered important that you reset references when you have finished with them – it is normally sufficient to simply wait until the variable goes out of scope.

If, however, you do want to set reference variables not to refer to anything, then the relevant C# keyword is null, which means the same thing as Nothing in VB. Hence where in VB you would write:

```
Set SomeDialog = Nothing
```

in C# you would write:

```
TheMainForm = null;
```

Note, however, that this doesn't by itself really achieve much in C# unless the variable TheMainForm still has a substantial lifetime left, as the object still won't be destroyed until the garbage collector is called up.

Entering the Message Loop

We will now consider the final statement in the main method:

```
Application.Run(TheMainForm);
```

This statement is the one that enters the message loop. What we are actually doing is calling a static method of the class System.Windows.Forms.Application. The method in question is the Run() method. This method handles the message loop. It puts the application (or strictly speaking, the thread) to sleep and requests Windows to wake it up whenever an interesting event occurs. The Run() method can take one parameter, which is a reference to the form that will handle all events. Run() exits when an event instructing the form to terminate has occurred and been handled.

Once the Run() method has exited, there is nothing else to be done, so the Main() method returns. Since this method was the entry point to the program, when it returns execution of the entire process stops.

One piece of syntax in the above statements that you might find surprising is that we use parentheses when calling the Run() method, even though we are not using any return value from this method, and hence we are doing the equivalent of calling a VB sub. In this situation, VB does not require parentheses, but the rule is that in C# you *always* use parentheses when calling any method.

> Always use parentheses in C# when calling any method, whether or not you are going to use any return value.

The SquareRootForm Class

We have now seen how C# enters a message loop, but we have not yet seen the process of displaying and creating the form itself, and we have also been rather vague about the calling of the event handlers. We have indicated that Windows calls event handlers, such as our OnClickButtonResults() method. But how does Windows know that that is the method to be called? We can find the answers to those questions in the SquareRootForm class definition, and in its base class, Form.

First we note that the SquareRootForm class has quite a number of member fields. (Member field is C# parlance for a variable that is defined as a member of a class. You can think of it as being like a VB variable that has form scope, or alternatively as being like a VB variable that is defined as a member of a class module. Each such variable is associated with a particular instance of a class – a particular object – and stays in scope for as long as its containing object remains alive.)

```
public class SquareRootForm : System.Windows.Forms.Form
{
    private System.Windows.Forms.TextBox txtNumber;
    private System.Windows.Forms.TextBox txtSign;
    private System.Windows.Forms.TextBox txtResult;
    private System.Windows.Forms.Button cmdShowResults;
    private System.Windows.Forms.Label label1;
    private System.Windows.Forms.Label label2;
    private System.Windows.Forms.Label label3;
    private System.Windows.Forms.Label label4;
```

These fields each correspond to one of the controls. We can see clearly the three textboxes and the button. There are also four labels, corresponding to the areas of text on the form. We won't be doing anything with these labels so we haven't bothered to give them more user-friendly names.

However, each of these variables is just a reference to an object, so the fact that these variables exist doesn't imply any instances of these objects exist – the objects have to be instantiated separately. The process of instantiating these controls is done in something called a constructor. A constructor in C# is a bit analogous to such VB subs as Form_Load(), Form_Initialize(), Class_Load(), and Class_Initialize(). It is a special method that is automatically called whenever an instance of the class is created, and it contains whatever code is needed to initialize the instance.

We can spot the constructor in the class because a constructor always has the same name as the class itself. In this case we just look for a method called SquareRootForm:

```
public SquareRootForm()
{
    InitializeComponent();
}
```

Notice that because this is a constructor rather than a method that you can call, it doesn't have any return type specified. It does, however, have parentheses after its name just like a method. You can use these parentheses to specify parameters to be passed to the constructor (recall that earlier we said that you can pass parameters in the parentheses after the new clause when creating a variable – well that will be these parameters, if we specify any). The definition of the constructor indicates if any parameters are needed to create an instance of the object. However, we don't have any parameters here – we will see examples of constructors that take parameters in the Employee code sample later in the appendix.

In this case the constructor just calls a method, InitializeComponent(). This is really because of Visual Studio.NET. Visual Studio.NET has all the same kinds of features as the VB 6 IDE for manipulating controls graphically – clicking to place controls on the form and so on. However, because now with C# the definitions of all the controls are set out in the sourcecode, Visual Studio.NET has to be able to read the sourcecode to find out what controls are around on your form. It does this by looking for an InitializeComponent() method, and seeing what controls are instantiated there.

InitializeComponent() is a huge method, so we won't look at it all, but it starts off like this:

```
private void InitializeComponent()
{
    this.txtNumber = new System.Windows.Forms.TextBox();
    this.txtSign = new System.Windows.Forms.TextBox();
    this.cmdShowResults = new System.Windows.Forms.Button();
    this.label3 = new System.Windows.Forms.Label();
    this.label4 = new System.Windows.Forms.Label();
    this.label1 = new System.Windows.Forms.Label();
    this.label2 = new System.Windows.Forms.Label();
    this.txtResult = new System.Windows.Forms.TextBox();
```

The above code is a set of calls to actually instantiate all the controls on the form. This bit of code doesn't really contain any new pieces of C# syntax that we haven't already encountered. The next part of the code starts setting properties on the controls:

```
//
// txtNumber
//
this.txtNumber.Location = new System.Drawing.Point(160, 24);
this.txtNumber.Name = "txtNumber";
this.txtNumber.TabIndex = 0;
this.txtNumber.Text = "";

//
// txtSign
//
this.txtSign.Enabled = false;
this.txtSign.Location = new System.Drawing.Point(160, 136);
this.txtSign.Name = "txtSign";
this.txtSign.TabIndex = 1;
this.txtSign.Text = "";
```

This code sets up the start positions and initial text of two of the controls, the input textbox and the textbox that displays the sign of the number input. One new bit of code is that the location relative to the top left corner of the screen is specified using a `Point`. `Point` is a .NET base class (strictly, a struct) that stores x and y coordinates. The syntax for the two lines above that set the `Location` is instructive. The `TextBox.Location` property is just a reference to a `Point`, so in order to set it to a value we need to create and initialize a `Point` object that holds the correct coordinates. This is the first time that we've seen a constructor that takes parameters – in this case the horizontal and vertical coordinates of the `Point`, and hence of the control. If we'd wanted to translate one of these lines into VB, assuming we'd defined some VB class module called `Point`, and we had a class that had such a property, the best we would be able to do would look something like this:

```
Dim Location As Point
Set Location = New Point
Location.X = 160
Location.Y = 24
SomeObject.Location = Location
```

Compare this to the C# code:

```
someObject.Location = new System.Drawing.Point(160, 24);
```

The relative compactness of the equivalent C# statement should be obvious!

Now we will look at the same commands for the button. In this case, we see the same kinds of properties being set up, but here there is one other thing that needs to be done: we need to tell Windows to call our event handler when the button is clicked. The line that does this is highlighted:

```
this.cmdShowResults.Name = "cmdShowResults";
this.cmdShowResults.Size = new System.Drawing.Size(88, 23);
this.cmdShowResults.TabIndex = 3;
this.cmdShowResults.Text = "Show Results";
this.cmdShowResults.Click += new
                       System.EventHandler(this.OnClickShowResults);
```

What's going on here is this. The button, which is referred to by the `cmdShowResults` button object, contains an event, `Click`, which will be raised when the user clicks on it. We need to add our event handler to this event. Now C# doesn't allow us to pass names of methods around directly – instead we have to wrap them up into something called a delegate. The details of this are beyond the scope of this appendix – they are covered in Chapter 6 of this book, but this is done to ensure type safety, and is the reason for the new `System.EventHandler()` text in the code. Once we've wrapped the name of the event handler up, we add it to the event using an operator +=, which we will discuss next.

Arithmetic-Assignment Operators

The += symbol represents what is known as the addition-assignment operator in C#. It provides a convenient shorthand for cases where you want to add some quantity to another quantity. How it works is this. Say, in VB you had declared two Integers, A and B, and you were going to write:

```
B = B + A
```

In C# the equivalent type is `int`, and you can write something very similar:

```
B = B + A;
```

However, in C#, there is an alternative shorthand for this:

```
B += A;
```

`+=` really means "add the expression on the right to the variable on the left", and it works for all the numeric data types, not just `int`. Not only that but there are other similar operators, `*=`, `/=`, and `-=` which respectively multiply, divide, and subtract the quantity on the left by the one on the right. So for example, to divide a number by 2, and assign the result back to `B`, you'd write:

```
B /= 2;
```

Although we won't go into the details in this appendix, C# has other operators that represent bitwise operations, as well as one that takes the remainder on division – and almost all of these have corresponding operation-assignment operators. Details of these operators are in Chapter 3.

In the `SquareRootForm` sample, we have simply applied the addition-assignment operator to an event; the line:

```
this.cmdShowResults.Click += new
                    System.EventHandler(this.OnClickShowResults);
```

simply means "add this handler to the event". You might be a bit surprised at seeing an operator like `+=` being applied to something that isn't a simple numeric type like `int` or `float`, but this actually illustrates an important point about operators in C# compared to ones in VB:

> Operators like +, -, *, and so on in VB only really have a meaning when applied to numeric data. But in C#, they can be applied to any type of object.

The above statement needs to be qualified a bit. In order to be able to apply these operators to other types of object, you have to first tell the compiler what these operators mean for other types of object – a process known as **operator overloading**. It works a bit like this. Suppose you wanted to write a class that represented a mathematical vector. Something that in VB you would code up as a class module, and would then let you write:

```
Dim V1 As Vector
Set V1 = New Vector
```

In mathematics, it's possible to add vectors together, which is where operator overloading would come in. But VB 6 doesn't support operator overloading, so instead in VB 6 you'd probably define a method, `Add`, on the `Vector`, so you could do this:

```
' V1, V2, and V3 are Vectors

Set V3 = V1.Add(V2)
```

In VB, that's the best you could do. However, in C#, if you defined a `Vector` class you could add an operator overload for + to it. The operator overload is basically a method that has the name `operator +`, and which the compiler will call up if it sees + applied to a `Vector`. That means that in C# you would be able to write:

```
// V1, V2 and V3 are Vectors

V3 = V1 + V2;
```

Obviously you wouldn't want to define operator overloads for all classes. For most classes that you write, it wouldn't make sense to do things like add or multiply objects together. However, for the classes for which it does make sense to do this, operator overloads can go a long way towards making your code easier to read. That's what has happened with events. Because it makes sense to talk about adding a handler to an event, an operator overload has been supplied to let us do this using the intuitive syntax using the + (and +=) operators. You can also use − or −= to remove a handler from an event.

Summing Up

We've really got as far as we can go with the `SquareRootForm` code samples. There is a lot more C# code that we haven't examined in the C# version of this application, but this extra code is largely to do with setting up the various other controls on the form, and doesn't introduce any new principles, so we're not going to examine it further.

Up to now, we've got a flavor of the syntax of C#. We've seen how it lets you write statements in a way that is often much shorter than the corresponding VB code. We have also seen the way that C# places all the code in the source file, unlike VB, where much of the background code is hidden from you – something that makes your code simpler at the cost of reducing your flexibility in the kinds of applications you can write. We've also had our first hints at the concepts behind inheritance.

However, what we have not yet seen is a real example of some code that you can write in C#, where it would be extremely hard to write VB code to do the same sort of thing. We are going to see an example of this in the next code sample, in which we write a couple of classes that illustrate the kinds of things we can do with inheritance.

Example: Employees and Managers

For this example, we are going to assume that we are writing an application that does some sort of processing on data that pertains to company employees. We are not really going to worry about what sort of processing this involves – we are more interested in the fact that this means it will be quite useful to write a C# class (or a VB class module) that represents employees. We are assuming that this will form part of a software package that we can sell to companies to help them with their salary payments and so on.

The VB Employee Class Module

The following code represents our attempt to code up an `Employee` class module in VB. The class module exposes two public properties, the `EmployeeName` and the `Salary`, as well as a public method, `GetMonthlyPayment()`, which returns the amount the company needs to pay the employee each month. This isn't the same as the salary, partly because the salary is assumed to be the salary per year, and partly because later on we want to allow for the possibility of other things getting added on to what the company pays its employees (like performance-related bonuses):

```
'local variable(s) to hold property value(s)

Private mStrEmployeeName As String 'local copy
Private mCurSalary As Currency 'local copy
Public Property Let Salary(ByVal curData As Currency)
    mCurSalary = curData
End Property

Public Property Get Salary() As Currency
    Salary = mCurSalary
End Property

Public Property Get EmployeeName() As String
    EmployeeName = mStrEmployeeName
End Property

Public Sub Create(sEmployeeName As String, curSalary As Currency)
    mStrEmployeeName = sEmployeeName
    mCurSalary = curSalary
End Sub

Public Function GetMonthlyPayment() As Currency
    GetMonthlyPayment = mCurSalary/12
End Function
```

In real life we'd probably be writing something more complex than this, but this class will be sufficient to illustrate the concepts I want to cover. In fact, we already have a problem with this VB class module. Most people's names do not change very often, which is why we have made the EmployeeName property read-only. That still leaves us needing to set up the name in the first place. For that, we've had to add a Create method, which sets the name and the salary. That means that the process of creating an employee object is going to look like this:

```
Dim Britney As Employee
Set Britney = New Employee
Britney.Create "Britney Spears", 20000
```

This is workable but messy. The problem with initializing the Employee object is that, although VB does provide the Class_Load and class_Initialize methods for this purpose, Class_Load cannot take any parameters. This means that we can't do any initialization that's particular to this instance of Employee in it – so we just have to write a separate initialization method, Create, instead, and hope that everyone writing client code will always remember to call it. This solution is awkward, because it doesn't make any sense to have an Employee object lying around that doesn't have a name and a salary set – but that is exactly what we have in the above code for the brief instant between instantiating Britney and initializing the object in the code above. As long as you always remember to call Create, you are fine, but there is a potential source of bugs here.

In C# the situation is completely different. In C# we are able to supply parameters to constructors (the C# equivalent to the Class_Load method). All we need to do is make sure that when we define our C# Employee class, the constructor takes the name and salary as parameters. Then in C# we will be able to write:

```
Employee Britney = new Employee("Britney Spears", 20000.00M);
```

which is a lot neater and less prone to bugs. Notice by the way, the 'M' appended to the salary. This is because the C# equivalent to VB's Currency type is something called decimal, and 'M' appended to a number in C# indicates we want the number interpreted as a decimal. We don't have to supply it, but it makes for a useful extra compile-time check.

The C# Employee Class

Bearing in mind the above comments, we can now present our first definition of the C# version of Employee (note that here we have just shown the class definition, not the containing namespace definition):

```csharp
class Employee
{
    private readonly string name;
    private decimal salary;
    public Employee(string name, decimal salary)
    {
        this.name = name;
        this.salary = salary;
    }
    public string Name
    {
        get
        {
            return name;
        }
    }
    public virtual decimal Salary
    {
        get
        {
            return salary;
        }
        set
        {
            salary = value;
        }
    }
    public decimal GetMonthlyPayment()
    {
        return salary/12;
    }
    public override string ToString()
    {
        return "Name: " + name + ", Salary: $" + salary.ToString();
    }
}
```

Working through this code, we first see a couple of private variables, the so-called member fields corresponding to the member variables in the VB class module. The field name is marked readonly. We'll see what exactly this means soon. Roughly speaking, it ensures that this field must be set when an Employee object is created and cannot subsequently be modified. In C# it isn't usual to use Hungarian notation for the names of variables, so they are called simply name and salary, rather than mStrEmployeeName and mCurSalary. Hungarian notation means that we prefix the names of variables with some letters that indicate their type (mStr, mCur and so on). It's not considered as important nowadays because editors are more sophisticated and can supply automatic information about data types, Hence the recommendation is not to use Hungarian notation in C# programs.

There is also a constructor in our `Employee` class, a couple of properties, `Name` and `Salary`, and two methods, `GetMonthlyPayment()` and `ToString()`. We will examine all of these next.

Notice by the way, that the names of the properties `Name` and `Salary` differ only in case from the names of their corresponding fields. This isn't a problem, because C# is case-sensitive. The way we've named the properties and fields here corresponds to the usual convention in C# and shows how we can actually take advantage of case sensitivity.

The Employee Constructor

After the field declarations in the above code, we get to a "method" that has the same name as the class, `Employee`, which tells us that it is a constructor. However, this constructor takes parameters, and does the same thing as the `Create` method in the VB version. It uses the parameters to initialize the member fields:

```
public Employee(string name, decimal salary)
{
    this.name = name;
    this.salary = salary;
}
```

There's a potential syntax problem, because the obvious names for the parameters are the same as the names of the fields – `name` and `salary`. But we've resolved this using the `this` reference to mark the fields. We could have given the parameters different names instead, but the way we've done it is still clear enough, and means that the parameters keep the obvious simple names that correspond to their meanings. It's also the conventional way of dealing with this situation in C#.

We can now explain the precise meaning of the `readonly` qualifier on the name field:

```
private readonly string name;
```

If a field is marked as `readonly` then the only place in which it may be assigned to is in the constructor to the class. The compiler will raise an error if it finds any code in which we attempt to modify the value of a `readonly` variable anywhere except in a constructor. This provides a very good way of guaranteeing that a variable cannot be modified once it has been set. It wouldn't be possible to do anything like this in VB because VB doesn't have constructors that take parameters, so class-level variables in VB have to be initialized via methods or properties that are called after the object has been instantiated.

Incidentally, this constructor doesn't just allow us to supply parameters to initialize an `Employee` object: it actually forces us to do so. If we tried to write code like this:

```
Employee Britney = new Employee();    // wrong
```

then this code would actually not compile. The compiler would raise an error because, in C#, a constructor must always be called when a new object is created. However, we have not supplied any parameters, and the only constructor available requires two parameters. Therefore, it is simply not possible to create an `Employee` object without supplying any parameters. This provides a good guarantee against bugs caused by uninitialized `Employee` objects!

It is possible to supply more than one constructor to a class so that you get a choice of what sets of parameters you want to pass in when you create a new object of that class. We'll see how to do this later in the chapter. However, for this particular class, our one constructor is quite adequate.

Properties of Employee

We next come to the properties Name and Salary. The C# syntax for declaring a property is very different from the corresponding VB syntax, but the basic principles are unchanged. We need to define two **accessors** to respectively get and set the values of the property. In VB, these are syntactically treated like methods, but in C# we declare the property as a whole, then define the accessors within the definition of the property:

```
public decimal Salary
{
   get
   {
      return salary;
   }
   set
   {
      salary = value;
   }
}
```

In VB, the compiler knows that we are defining a property, because we use the keyword Property. In C# this information is conveyed by the fact that the name of the property is followed immediately by an opening brace. If we were defining a method, this would be an opening parenthesis signaling the start of the parameter list, while for a field this would be a semicolon, marking the end of the definition.

One other point to note is that the definitions of the get and set accessors do not contain any parameter lists. There's no point – we know from the fact that Salary is a decimal that the get accessor will return a decimal and take no parameters, while the set accessor will take one decimal parameter and return void. For the set accessor, this parameter is not explicitly declared, but the compiler always interprets the word value as referring to it.

> *Once again, the syntax for defining properties shows how C# syntax is more compact, and can save you a fair bit of typing!*

Just as with VB, if you want to make a property read-only, you simply omit the set accessor, as we have done for the Name property:

```
public string Name
{
   get
   {
      return name;
   }
}
```

Methods of Employee

There are also two methods: GetMonthlySalary() and ToString().

GetMonthlySalary() needs little comment, since we have covered most of relevant C# syntax already. It simply takes the salary, divides it by 12 to convert from annual to monthly salary, and returns the result:

```
public decimal GetMonthlyPayment()
{
    return salary/12;
}
```

The only new piece of syntax here is the `return` statement. In VB, we specify a return value from a method by setting a dummy variable that has the same name as the function to the required value:

```
GetMonthlyPayment = mCurSalary/12
```

In C#, we achieve the same result by appending a parameter to a `return` statement (without parentheses). `return` in C# also specifies that we are exiting from the function, so the C# statement:

```
return salary/12;
```

is actually equivalent to the following VB code:

```
GetMonthlyPayment = mCurSalary/12
Exit Function
```

`ToString()` is slightly more interesting. In most cases, when you write a C# class, it is a good idea to write a `ToString()` method that can be used to get a quick view of the contents of an object. As mentioned before, `ToString()` is already available because all classes inherit it from `System.Object`. However, the version in `System.Object` simply displays the name of the class – not any data in the class instance. Microsoft has already overridden this method for all the numeric data types (`int`, `float`, and so on) to display the actual value of the variable, and it's quite useful for us to do the same thing in our classes. If nothing else, it can be a useful way of seeing the contents of an object when you are debugging:

```
public override string ToString()
{
    return "Name: " + name + ", Salary: $" + salary.ToString();
}
```

Our override here simply displays the name and the salary of the employee. One new piece of syntax is that we have specifically declared the method as `override`. C# requires that you explicitly mark method overrides in this way, and will raise a compilation error if you don't. This eliminates the risk of any potential bugs where, for example you accidentally override a method without realizing it, perhaps because you didn't realize that a method of that name was already present in the base class.

We have now completed writing the `Employee` class in both VB and C# – and so far, although there is a bit of awkwardness about constructing and initializing an `Employee` instance in the VB version, both languages have coped reasonably well with our requirements. However, one of the aims of this appendix is to show you why C# can be so much more powerful than VB 6 in some situations. So it's about time we started demonstrating some useful C# code where it would be very difficult or impossible to do the same thing in VB 6. That's what's going to happen from now on. We're going to start adding some features to the C# version of our sample, which are going to leave the VB version way behind and quite unable to catch up. Let's start with a `static` field and property.

Static Members

We have mentioned a few times that in C# classes can have special methods referred to as static methods, which can be called without instantiating any objects. These methods do not have any counterpart in VB. In fact, not only methods, but also fields, properties, or any other class member can be static.

> The term static has a very different meaning in C# from its meaning in VB.

To illustrate how static members work and why you would use them we are going to imagine that we would like our `Employee` class to support retrieving the name of the company that each employee works for. Now there is an important difference here between the company name and the employee name, in that each employee object represents a different employee, and therefore needs to store a different employee's name. This is the usual behavior for variables in class modules in VB, and the default behavior for fields in C#. However, if your organization has just purchased the software that contains the `Employee` class, obviously all of the employees will have the same company name. This means that it would be wasteful to store the company name separately for each employee. You'd just be duplicating the string unnecessarily. Instead, what we want is just to store the company name once, and then have every employee object access the same data. This is how a static field works. Lets declare such a field, `companyName`:

```
class Employee
{
    private string name;
    private decimal salary;
    private static readonly string companyName;
```

In this code, we have simply declared another field, but by marking it as `static` we have instructed the compiler to store this variable only once, no matter how many `Employee` objects get created. In a real sense, this static field is associated with the class as a whole, rather than with any one object.

We have also declared this field as read-only. This makes sense because, like the employee's name, the company name should not be changed once the program is running.

Of course, merely declaring this field isn't quite enough. We also need to make sure it is initialized with the correct data. Where should we do that? Well, clearly not in our constructor – the constructor gets called every time we create an `Employee` object, whereas we only want to initialize `companyName` once. The answer is that C# provides another construct for this purpose, known as the **static constructor**. The static constructor acts like any other constructor, but it works for the class as a whole, not for any particular object. If you define a static constructor for a class, then it will be executed just once. It's not guaranteed exactly when it will execute, but it will be before the first time any client code attempts to access the class. This will normally be when the program first starts up. Let's add a static constructor to the `Employee` class:

```
static Employee()
{
    companyName = "Wrox Press Pop Stars";
}
```

As usual, we identify the constructor because it has the same name as the class. This one is also identified as `static`, hence it is the static constructor. It is not marked as either `public` or `private` because it will not be called by any other C# code, but by the .NET runtime. So, just for the static constructor, we don't need any access modifier.

In our example, we have implemented the static constructor by hard-coding in a company name. More realistically, we might read a registry entry or a file, or connect to a database to find out the company name. Incidentally, because the `companyName` field has been declared as both static and read-only, the static constructor is the only place in which we can legally assign a value to it. We have one last thing to do, which is to define a public property that lets us access the company name.

```
public static string CompanyName
{
    get
    {
        return companyName;
    }
}
```

The `CompanyName` property has also been declared as static, and we can now see the real significance of a static method or property: a method or property can be declared as static if it accesses only static fields, and does not access any data that is associated with a particular object.

As we have already seen, the syntax for calling static members of the class from outside the class is slightly different from that used for other members. Because a static member is associated with the class rather than with any object, we use the class name rather than the name of a variable to call it:

```
string Company = Employee.CompanyName;
```

The concept of static members is very powerful, and provides a very useful means for a class to implement any functionality that is the same for every object of that class. The only way that you can achieve anything like this in VB is by defining global variables. If you do that, though, the global variables have the disadvantage that they are not associated with any class – which also leads to name conflict issues.

Other examples where you might use static class members are:

❑ You might choose to implement a `MaximumLength` property for our `Employee` class, or for that matter for any other class that contains a name, where you might need to specify the maximum length of the name.

❑ In C#, most of the numeric data types have static properties that indicate their maximum possible values. For example, in order to find out the biggest values that can be stored in an `int` and a `float`, you could write:

```
int MaxIntValue = int.MaxValue;
float MaxFloatValue = float.MaxValue;
```

Inheritance

We are now going to look in a bit more detail at how implementation inheritance works, using an example. We are going to suppose that, a year or so after we have shipped our software package, it's time for the next version. One point that our customers have commented on is that some of their employees are actually managers, and managers usually get profit-related bonuses as well as regular salaries. This means that our `GetMonthlyPayment()` method doesn't give the complete information for managers. The practical upshot of this is that there is a need to add some way of dealing with managers, too.

For the purposes of our example we will assume the bonus is some constant figure, that can be specified when we create a manager. We don't want to get bogged down in doing profit-related calculations here.

If we were coding in VB, how would we set about upgrading our software? There are two possible approaches, but both of them have severe disadvantages.

- ❑ We could write a new class, `Manager`
- ❑ We could modify the `Employee` class

Writing a new class is probably the approach that what would give us the least amount of work, since we'd probably start by simply copying and pasting all the code for the `Employee` class module and then modifying our copy of the code. The trouble is that `Employee` and `Manager` have an awful lot of code in common, such as all of the code around the `Name`, `CompanyName`, and `Salary` properties. Having the same code duplicated is dangerous. What happens if, at some point in the future, some reason turns up why you need to modify the code? Some poor developer is going to have to remember to make exactly the same changes to both classes. That is just asking for bugs to creep in. Another problem is that there are now two unrelated classes that client code will have to deal with, which is likely to make it harder for the people writing the code that uses `Employee` and `Manager`. (Although you could get around this by wrapping the common properties into an interface and having both `Employee` and `Manager` implement this interface).

A slightly different alternative is to write a `Manager` class, and put an `Employee` object inside it as a class-scoped variable. This solves the problem of duplicating code, but still leaves us with two separate objects, as well as an awkward, indirect, syntax for calling employee methods and properties (`objManager.objEmployee.Name` and so on).

If we opt for modifying the `Employee` class module, then we would presumably add an extra field, a `Boolean`, that indicates whether this `Employee` is a manager or not. Then, at relevant parts of the code, we would test this `Boolean` in an `If` statement, to check what to do. This solves the problem of having two unrelated classes – we are back to just one class. However, it introduces a new difficulty: I specifically said earlier that we decide a **year or so later** to add manager support. This means that the `Employee` class module has presumably been shipped, tested, fully debugged, and is known to be working correctly. Do we really want to have to dive in and start pulling working code to bits, with all the associated risk of introducing new bugs?

Bluntly, we have reached a point at which VB cannot offer any satisfactory solutions. From the title of this section you won't be surprised to learn that C# does offer a way round this problem, through inheritance.

We have already seen that inheritance involves adding or replacing features of classes. In our previous example, our `SquareRootForm` class added stuff to the .NET class, `System.Windows.Forms.Form`. It defined the controls to go on the `SquareRootForm` as member fields, and also added an event handler. In the `Employee` example we are going to demonstrate both adding and replacing features of a base class. We will define a `Manager` class, which is derived from `Employee`. We will add a field and property that represent the bonus, and replace the `GetMonthlyPayment()` method (for completeness, we'll also replace `ToString()` so that it displays the bonus as well as the name and salary). This all means that we will get a separate class. But we won't need to duplicate any code, and we won't need to make any big changes to the `Employee` class either. You might think that we still have a problem of two different classes – which makes it more difficult to write client code, but as we will see later, C# has got an answer for this is as well.

Inheriting from the Employee Class

Before we define the `Manager` class we need to make one small change to `Employee`:

```
public virtual decimal GetMonthlyPayment()
{
    return salary/12;
}
```

The change we have made is to make the `GetMonthlyPayment()` method `virtual`. Roughly speaking, this is C#'s way of saying that this is a method that in principle can be overridden.

> *You might think that this means we are changing the base class, which knocks out our argument about not needing to change the base class. However, adding a* `virtual` *keyword isn't really the sort of major change that carries a risk of new bugs – with the VB approach we were going to have to actually rewrite the implementations of several methods. Besides, usually when you write classes in C#, you plan in advance for what methods are suitable candidates for overriding. If this was a real-life example,* `GetMonthlyPayment()` *would almost certainly have been declared virtual in the first place, so then we really would have been able to add the* `Manager` *class without making any changes whatsoever to the* `Employee` *class.*

The Manager Class

We can now define the `Manager` class:

```
class Manager : Employee
{
    private decimal bonus;
    public Manager(string name, decimal salary, decimal bonus)
        :   base(name, salary)
    {
        this.bonus = bonus;
    }
    public Manager(string name, decimal salary)
        :   this(name, salary, 100000M)
    {
    }
    public decimal Bonus
    {
```

```
        get
        {
            return bonus;
        }
    }
    public override string ToString()
    {
        return base.ToString() + ", bonus: " + bonus;
    }
    public override decimal GetMonthlyPayment()
    {
        return base.GetMonthlyPayment() + bonus/12;
    }
  }
}
```

Besides the near-complete implementation of the Employee class that we have inherited, Manager contains the following members:

- ❏ A field, bonus, which will be used to store the manager's bonus, and a corresponding property, Bonus
- ❏ The overloaded GetMonthlyPayment() method, as well as a new overload of ToString()
- ❏ Two constructors

The bonus field and corresponding Bonus property shouldn't need any further discussion. However, we will look in detail at the overridden methods and the new constructors, as these will illustrate important language features of C#.

Method Overrides

Our override of GetMonthlyPayment() is reasonably simple. Notice that we have marked it with the keyword override to tell the compiler that we are overriding a base-class method, as we did with Employee.ToString():

```
public override decimal GetMonthlyPayment()
{
    return base.GetMonthlyPayment() + bonus/12;
}
```

Our override also contains a call to the base-class version of this method. This uses a new keyword, base. base works in the same way as this, except that it specifically indicates that we want to grab a method, or property etc, from the definition in the base class. If we had wanted, we could alternatively have implemented our override of GetMonthlyPayment() like this:

```
public override decimal GetMonthlyPayment()
{
    return (Salary + bonus)/12;
}
```

but I wanted to show off the base keyword, so I chose not to do it this way! Incidentally, one thing that we could not do is this:

```
public override decimal GetMonthlyPayment()
{
    return (salary + bonus)/12;    // wrong
}
```

This code looks almost exactly like the previous version, except that we are hitting the salary field directly instead of going through the `Salary` property. You might think that this looks like a more efficient solution, because we are saving what is effectively a method call. The trouble is that the compiler will raise an error because the `salary` field has been declared as `private`. That means that nothing outside the `Employee` class is allowed to see this field. Even derived classes are not aware of `private` fields in base classes.

If you do want derived classes to be able to see a field, but not unrelated classes, C# provides an alternative level of protection, `protected`:

```
protected decimal salary;    // we could have done this
```

If a member of a class is declared as protected then it is visible only in that class and in derived classes. However, in general, you are strongly advised to keep all fields private for exactly the same reason that you are advised to keep variables private in VB class modules: because by hiding the implementation of a class (or class module) you are making it easier to carry out future maintenance of that class. Usually, you will use the `protected` modifier for properties and methods that are intended purely to allow derived classes access to certain features of the base-class definition.

The Manager Constructors

We need to add at least one constructor to the `Manager` class for two reasons:

❑   There is now an extra piece of information, the manager's bonus, which we need to specify when we create a `Manager` instance

❑   Unlike methods, properties, and fields, constructors are not inherited by derived classes

In fact, we have added two constructors. This is because we have decided to assume that the manager's bonus normally defaults to $100,000 if it is not explicitly specified. In VB we can specify default parameters to methods, but C# doesn't allow us to do that directly. Instead, C# offers a more powerful technique that can achieve the same effect, **method overloads**. Defining two constructors here will allow us to illustrate this technique.

The first `Manager` constructor takes three parameters:

```
public Manager(string name, decimal salary, decimal bonus)
    :   base(name, salary)
{
    this.bonus = bonus;
}
```

The first thing we notice about this constructor is a call to the base class constructor using a slightly strange syntax. The syntax is known as a **constructor initializor**. What happens is that any constructor is allowed to call one other constructor before it executes. This call is made in a constructor initializor with the syntax shown above. It is permitted for a constructor to call either another constructor in the same class, or a constructor in the base class. This might sound restrictive, but it is done for good reasons in terms of imposing a well-designed architecture on the constructors. These issues are discussed in Chapter 5. The syntax for the constructor initializor requires a colon, followed by one of the keywords `base` or `this` to specify which class we are calling the second constructor from, followed by the parameters we are passing on to the second constructor.

The constructor shown above takes three parameters. However, two of these parameters, name and salary, are really there in order to initialize base class fields in Employee. These parameters are really the responsibility of the Employee class rather than the Manager class, so what we do is simply pass them on to the Employee constructor for it to deal with – that's what the call to base(name, salary) achieves. And as we saw earlier, the Employee constructor will simply use these parameters to initialize the name and salary fields. Finally, we take the bonus parameter, which *is* the responsibility of the Manager class, and use it to initialize the bonus field. The second Manager constructor that we've supplied also uses a constructor initialization list:

```
public Manager(string name, decimal salary)
    :   this(name, salary, 100000M)
{
}
```

In this case, what is happening is that we set up the value of the default parameter, and then pass everything on to the three-parameter constructor. Of course, in turn, the three-parameter constructor will call the base-class constructor to deal with the name and salary parameters. You might wonder why we haven't used the following alternative way of implementing the two-parameter constructor:

```
public Manager(string name, decimal salary,)
    :   base(name, salary)     // not so good
{
    this.bonus = 100000M;
}
```

The reason is that this involves some potential duplication of code. The two constructors each separately initialize the bonus field, and this might cause problems in the future in terms of both constructors needing separately to be modified if for example, in some future version of Manager we change how we store the bonus. In general, in C# just as in VB, you should avoid duplicating code if you can. For this reason, the previous implementation of the two-parameter constructor would be considered better.

Method Overloading

The fact that we have supplied two constructors for the Manager class illustrates the principle of method overloading in C#. All that method overloading involves is that a class has more than one method that have the same name, but have different numbers of parameters. We have illustrated overloading for constructors, but exactly the same principles apply for all methods.

> **Don't confuse the terms *method overloading* and *method overriding*. Despite the similar names, they are different, and completely unrelated, concepts!**

When the compiler encounters a call to a method that has been overloaded, it examines the parameters you are attempting to pass in, in order to figure out which method is the one that should be called. In the case of creating a manager object, since one constructor takes three parameters and the other only takes two, the first thing the compiler will examine is the number of parameters. Hence if you write:

```
Manager SomeManager = new Manager ("Name", 300000.00M);
```

the compiler will arrange for a `Manager` object to be instantiated, with the two-parameter constructor being called – which means that the bonus will be given its default value of 100000M. If, on the other hand, you write this:

```
Manager SomeManager = new Manager ("Name", 300000.00M, 50000.00M);
```

the compiler will arrange for the three-parameter constructor to be called, so `bonus` will now be given the specified value of `50000.00M`. If there are several overloads available, but the compiler is unable to find one that is suitable, it will raise a compilation error. For example, if you wrote:

```
Manager SomeManager = new Manager (100, 300000.00M, 50000.00M);   // wrong
```

you would get a compilation error because both of the available `Manager` constructors require a string, and not a numeric type, as the first parameter. The C# compiler can arrange for some type conversions between the different numeric types to be done automatically, but it will not convert automatically from a numeric value to a string.

Finally, we will note that, as previously remarked, C# does not allow methods to take default parameters in the way VB does. However, it is very easy to achieve the same effect using method overloads, as we have done in this example. The usual way is simply to have the overloads that have fewer parameters simply supply default values for the remaining parameters and then call the other overloads.

Using the Employee and Manager Classes

Now that we have completed defining the `Employee` and `Manager` classes, we can write some code that uses them. In fact, if you download the sourcecode for this project from the Wrox Press web site, you will find that we defined these two classes as part of a standard Windows Forms project, quite similar to the `SquareRoot` sample. In this case, however, the main form just has one control – a listbox. We use the constructor of the main form class (a class called `MainForm`) to instantiate a couple of instances of `Employee` and `Manager` objects, then display data for these objects in the listbox. The results look like this:

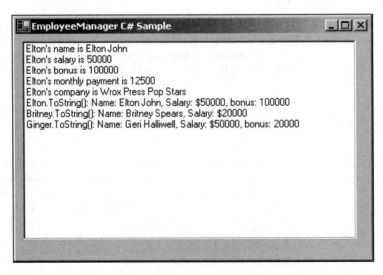

The code used to generate these results is this:

```
public MainForm()
{
    InitializeComponent();
    Employee Britney = new Employee("Britney Spears", 20000.00M);
    Employee Elton = new Manager("Elton John", 50000.00M);
    Manager Ginger = new Manager("Geri Halliwell", 50000.00M,
                                          20000.00M);
    this.listBox1.Items.Add("Elton's name is $" + Elton.Name);
    this.listBox1.Items.Add("Elton's salary is $" + Elton.Salary);
    this.listBox1.Items.Add("Elton's bonus is " +
                                      ((Manager)Elton).Bonus);
    this.listBox1.Items.Add("Elton's monthly payment is $" +
                                  Elton.GetMonthlyPayment());
    this.listBox1.Items.Add("Elton's company is " +
                                  Employee.CompanyName);
    this.listBox1.Items.Add("Elton.ToString(): " + Elton.ToString());
    this.listBox1.Items.Add("Britney.ToString(): " +
                                  Britney.ToString());
    this.listBox1.Items.Add("Ginger.ToString(): " + Ginger.ToString());
}
```

This code should be self-explanatory, based on the C# that we have learned up to now, apart from one little oddity, that one of the Manager objects, Elton, is being referred to by an Employee reference instead of a Manager reference. Will explain how this works next.

References to Derived Classes

Let's have a closer look at that Manager class that is referenced by a variable declared as a reference to Employee:

```
Employee Elton = new Manager("Elton John", 50000.00M);
```

This is actually perfectly legal C# syntax. The rule is quite simple: if you declare a reference to some type B, then that reference is permitted to refer to instances of B or to instances of any class derived from B. This works because any class derived from B must also implement any methods or properties and so on that B implements. So in the above example, we call Elton.Name, Elton.Salary, and Elton.GetMonthlyPayment(). This is fine. The fact that Employee implements all these members guarantees that any class derived from Employee will too. So it doesn't matter if a reference points to a derived class – we can still use the reference to call up any member of the class the reference is defined as and be confident that that method exists in the derived class.

On the other hand, notice the syntax that we use when we call the Bonus property against Elton: ((Manager)Elton).Bonus. In this case, we need to explicitly convert Elton to a Manager reference because Bonus is not implemented by Employee. The compiler knows this, and would raise a compilation error if we tried to call Bonus through an Employee reference. That line of code is really a shorthand way of writing:

```
Manager ManagerElton = (Manager) Elton;
this.listBox1.Items.Add("Elton's bonus is " + ManagerElton.Bonus);
```

As in VB, conversion between data types in C# is known as casting. We can see from the code above that the syntax for casting involves placing the name of the destination data type in parentheses before the name of the variable we are attempting to cast. Of course, the object being referred to must be of the correct type in the first place. If with this example, we wrote:

```
Manager ManagerBritney = (Manager) Britney;
```

the code would compile correctly, but when we ran it, we would get an error, because the .NET runtime would see that `Britney` is just an `Employee` instance, not a `Manager`. References are permitted to refer to instances of derived classes, but not to instances of base classes of their native type. It's not permitted for a `Manager` reference to refer to an `Employee` object. (We can't permit it because if we did, what would happen if we attempted to call the `Bonus` property through such a reference?)

Incidentally I've not said anything about what raising an error at run time involves. In fact, C# has a very sophisticated mechanism for this, known as exceptions, which we will briefly look at later in this appendix.

Because VB doesn't support implementation inheritance, there is no direct parallel in VB for C#'s support for references referring to objects of derived classes. However, this is some similarity with the fact that in VB you can declare an interface reference, and then it does not matter what type of object that interface refers to, as long as the object in question implements that interface. If we were coding the `Employee` and `Manager` classes in VB, we might well have done so by defining an `IEmployee` interface that both class modules implement, and then accessing the `Employer` features through this interface.

Arrays of Objects

One important benefit of having references able to refer to derived class instances is that we can form arrays of object references, where the different objects in the array might be of different types. This is analogous to the situation in Visual Basic where we could form arrays of interface references and not care about the fact these interface references might be implemented by completely different classes of object.

We haven't yet seen how C# deals with arrays, so we will take a chance now and rewrite the test harness code for the `Employee` and `Manager` classes so that it forms an array of object references. This revised code is also downloadable from the Wrox Press web site as the `EmployeeManagerWithArrays` sample. The new code looks like this:

```
public MainForm()
{
    InitializeComponent();

    Employee Britney = new Employee("Britney Spears", 20000.00M);
    Employee Elton = new Manager("Elton John", 50000.00M);
    Manager Ginger = new Manager("Geri Halliwell", 50000.00M,
                                 20000.00M);
    Employee [] Employees = new  Employee[3];
    Employees[0] = Britney;
    Employees[1] = Elton;
    Employees[2] = Ginger;
```

```
        for (int I=0 ; I<3 ; I++)
        {
            this.listBox1.Items.Add(Employees[I].Name);
            this.listBox1.Items.Add(Employees[I].ToString());
            this.listBox1.Items.Add("");
        }
    }
```

We simply call up the `Name` property and the `ToString()` method of each element of the array. Running this code gives these results:

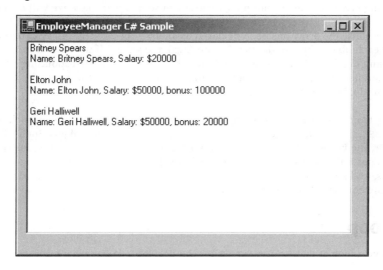

From this we can see that C# uses square brackets for dealing with arrays. This means that, unlike in VB, there is no danger of any confusion about whether we're talking about an array or a method or function call. The syntax for declaring an array looks like this:

```
Employee [] Employees = new Employee[3];
```

We see that we declare an array of variables of a certain type by putting square brackets after the name of the type. An array in C# always counts as a reference object (even if its elements are simple types like `int` or `double`) so there are actually two stages: declaring the reference, and instantiating the array. To make this clearer we could have split the above line of code up like this:

```
Employee [] Employees;
Employees = new Employee[3];
```

There is no difference between what we're doing here and how we instantiate objects, except that we are using square brackets to indicate that this is an array. Also note that the size of the array is established when we instantiate the object – the reference itself doesn't contain details of the size of the array – only its dimension. The dimension is specified by any commas in the array declaration, so for example, if we wanted to declare a two-dimensional, 3x4 array of doubles, we would write this:

```
double [,] DoubleArray = new double[3,4];
```

There are a couple of other slightly different syntaxes for declaring arrays but we will stick to this one here. Once we have the array we simply assign values to its elements in the usual way. Notice, however, that one difference between C# and VB is that arrays in C# always start at element 0. In VB we have the option to change this to element 1 using the `Option Base` statement. Also in VB, you can specify any lower boundary you like for any particular array. But this feature doesn't really add any benefits, and it can hurt performance, because it means that whenever you access an element in an array in VB, the code has to do some extra checking to find out what of the lower bound of that array is. C# does not support changing the base of an array in this way.

In the above code, once we have initialized the elements of the array, we just loop through them. The strange-looking syntax of the `for` loop may cause you some headache – we will examine that soon.

Notice that because the array has been declared as an array of `Employee`, we can only access those members of each object that are defined for the `Employee` class. If we wanted to access the `Bonus` property of any object in the array, we would first have to cast the corresponding reference to a `Manager` reference, which would mean checking whether the object was actually a `Manager`. That is not difficult to do, but is beyond the scope of this appendix.

On the other hand, although we are using `Employee` references, we do always pick up the correct version of `ToString()`. If the object we're referring to is a `Manager` object, then when we call `ToString()`, the version of `ToString()` defined in the `Manager` class is the one that is executed for that object. That is the beauty of overriding methods in C#. You can replace some method in the derived class, and know that no matter what reference type this object is accessed through, you will always run the correct method for that object.

The for Loop

Now let's have a look at that strange syntax for the `for` loop. What we are doing is the C# equivalent of this VB code:

```
Integer I
For I = 1 To 3
    listBox1.Items.Add "Details of the Employee"
Next
```

The idea of the `For` loop in VB is that you start off by initializing some variable – the **loop control variable** – and each time you go round the loop, you add something to the loop control variable until it exceeds a final value. This is quite useful, but gives you almost no flexibility in how the loop works. Although you can change the value of the increment, or even make the increment negative, by using the `Step` facility, the loop always works by counting, and the test of whether the loop exits is always whether the variable has hit some minimum or maximum value.

In C# the `for` loop generalizes this concept. The basic idea of the `for` loop in C# is this. At the beginning of the loop you do something, at each step of the loop you do something in order to move to the next iteration, and in order to determine when to exit from the loop, you perform some test. Comparing the Visual Basic and C# versions of `for`, the situation looks like this:

	VB	C#
At start of loop	Initialize loop control variable	Do something
To test whether to exit loop	Has loop control variable exceeded some value?	Test some condition
At end of each iteration	Increment loop control variable	Do something

This might look a bit vague, but it does give you a lot of flexibility! For example in C#, instead of adding a quantity to the loop control variable at each iteration, you might multiply its value by some number. Or instead of adding on a fixed amount you might add some number that you've read in from a file and which changes with each iteration. The test doesn't have to be a test of the value of the loop control variable – it could be a test of, for example, whether you have reached the end of the file. What this adds up to is that, by a suitable choice of the start action, test, and action at the end of each iteration, the for loop can effectively perform the same task as any of the loops in VB – For, Foreach, Do, and While, or alternatively the loop can work in some exotic manner for which there is no simple equivalent in VB. The C# for loop really gives you complete freedom to control the loop in whatever manner is appropriate to the task at hand.

> *We should point out, however, that C# also does support* foreach, do, *and* while, *for the situations where that is what you need.*

So let's get down to some precise syntax. Recall that the C# version of the above for loop looks like this:

```
for (int I=0 ; I<3 ; I++)
{
    this.listBox1.Items.Add(Employees[I].Name);
    this.listBox1.Items.Add(Employees[I].ToString());
    this.listBox1.Items.Add("");
}
```

As you can see, the for statement itself takes three different items inside the associated parentheses. These items are separated by semicolons:

❑ The first item is the action that is performed right at the start of the loop in order to initialize the loop. In this case here we declare and initialize the loop control variable.

❑ The next item is the condition that will be evaluated to determine whether the loop should exit. In this case our condition is that I must be less than 3. The loop continues as long as this condition is true and exits as soon as the condition evaluates to false. The condition will be evaluated at the beginning of each iteration, so that if it turns out to be false right at the start, the statement inside the loop will not get executed at all.

❑ In the third item is the statement that will be executed at the end of each iteration of the loop. Visual Basic loops always works by incrementing some number, and this is exactly what we do in this case.

The syntax looks unfamiliar, but once you've got used to it, it means that you can use the `for` loop in very powerful ways. For example, suppose we wanted to display all the integer powers of 2 that are less than 4000 in a listbox. We could write this:

```
for (int I = 2 ; I<4000 ; I*=2)
    listBox1.Items.Add(I.ToString);
```

This kind of effect is possible to achieve in VB, but slightly harder – for this particular loop, we would probably opt for a `while` loop in VB.

Other C# Features

We have now completed examining the code samples. The remainder of his appendix will briefly examine a couple of features of C# that you need to be aware of when making the transition from VB to C#, and which we haven't yet discussed – in particular some of the C# concepts relating to data types and operators.

Data Types

As we have indicated, the data types available in C# do differ in detail from those available in Visual Basic. Not only that, all data types in C# have features that you would normally associate with an object. For example, as we have seen, every type, even simple types such as `int` and `float`, supports the calling of methods (incidentally this feature does not cause any loss of performance).

Although the types available in C# are slightly different from VB types, most of the types that you are familiar with in VB do have direct equivalents types in C#. For example, in place of VB's `Double`, C# has `double`. Where VB has the `Date`, C# has a .NET base class, `DateTime`, which implements a huge number of methods and properties to allow you to extract or set the date using different formats.

One exception, however, is `Variant`, for which there is no direct equivalent in C#. The `Variant` type in VB is a very generic type, which to some extent exists only in order to support scripting languages that are not aware of any other data types. The philosophy of C#, however, is that the language is strongly typed. The idea is that if, at each point in the program, you have to explicitly indicate the data type you are referring to, at least one major source of run-time bugs is eliminated. Because of this, a `Variant` type isn't really appropriate to C#. However, there are still some situations in which you do need to refer to a variable without indicating what type that variable is, and for those cases C# does have the `object`type. C#'s `object` is a very much analogous to `Object` in VB. However, in VB, `Object` specifically refers to a COM object, and therefore can only be used to refer to objects, which in VB terms effectively means to reference data types. You cannot use an object reference, for example, to refer to an `Integer` or to a `Single`. In C#, by contrast, objects can be used to refer to any .NET data type, and since in C# all data types are .NET data types, this means that you can legitimately convert anything to an object, including `int`, `float`, and all the predefined data types. To this extent, `object` in C# does perform a similar role to `Variant` in VB.

Value and Reference Types

In Visual Basic there is a sharp distinction between value types and reference types. Value types include most of the predefined data types: Integer, Single, Double, and even Variant (though strictly speaking Variant can also contain a reference). Reference types are any object, including class modules that you define and ActiveX objects. As you will have noticed through the samples in this appendix, C# also makes the distinction between value and reference types. However, C# allows a little more flexibility to the extent that it permits you, when defining a class, to specify that that class should be a value type. You do this by declaring the class as something called a **struct**. As far as C# is concerned, a struct is basically a special type of class that is represented as a value rather than a reference. The overhead involved in instantiating structs and destroying them when we have finished with them is less than that involved when instantiating and destroying classes. However, C# does restrict the features supported by structs. In particular, you cannot derive classes or other structs from structs. The reasoning here is that structs are intended to be used for really lightweight, simple objects, for which inheritance isn't really appropriate. In fact, all the predefined classes in C#, such as int, long, float, and double are actually .NET structs, which is why we can call methods such as ToString() against them. The data type string, however, is a reference type and so is really a class.

Operators

We need to say a couple of words about operators in C#, because they do work in a somewhat different way from VB operators, and this can catch you out if you are used to the VB way of working. In VB there are really two types of operator:

❑   The assignment operator, =, which assigns values to variables

❑   All the other operators, such as +, -,*, and /, which each return some value

There is an important distinction here in that none of the operators, apart from = has any effect in terms of modifying any value. On the other hand, = assigns a value but does not return anything. There are no operators that do both.

In C#, this categorization simply does not exist. The rule in C# is that **all** operators return a value, and some operators have an additional side effect of assigning some value to a variable as well. In fact we have already seen an example of this when we examined the addition-assignment operator, +=:

```
int A=5, B=15;
A+=B;    // performs an arithmetic operation AND assigns result (20) to A
```

In fact, += returns a value as well as assigning the value. It returns the new value that has been assigned. Because of this we could actually write:

```
int A=5, B=15;
int C = (A+=B);
```

This will have the results that both A and C will be assigned the value 20. The assignment operator, =, also returns a value. It returns the value that is just been assigned to the variable on the left side of the expression. This means that you can write code like this:

```
C = (A = B);
```

This code sets A equal to whatever value is in B, then sets C to this same value too. You can also write this statement more simply as:

```
C = A = B;
```

A common use of this type of syntax is to evaluate some condition inside an if statement, and simultaneously set a variable of type bool (the C# equivalent of VB's Boolean) to the result of this condition, so we can reuse this value later:

```
// assume X and Y are some other variables that have been initialized

bool B;
if ( B = (X==Y) )
   DoSomething();
```

This code looks daunting at first sight but it is quite logical. Let's break it down. The first thing the computer will do is check the condition X==Y. Depending on whether X and Y contain the same data, this will either return true or false and this value will be assigned to the variable B. However, since the assignment operator also returns the value that it is just assigned, the complete expression B = (X==Y) will also return this same value (true or false). This return value will then be used by the if clause to determine whether to execute the conditional DoSomething() statement. The results of this code is that the condition X==Y gets tested to determine whether the conditional statements should be executed, and at the same time we have stored the results of this test in the variable B.

The Ternary Operator

We do not have space in this appendix to go over all the various operators are available in C#. They are detailed in Chapters 3-6. However, we will mention the ternary operator (also known as the conditional operator) because it has a very unusual syntax. The ternary operator is formed from the two symbols ? and :. It takes three parameters, and is actually equivalent to an If statement in VB. It is used syntactically like this:

```
// B, X and Y are some variables or expressions. B is a Boolean.

B ? X : Y
```

The way it works is that the first expression – the one before the ? symbol – is evaluated. If it evaluates to true, then the result of the second expression is returned, but if it evaluates to false then the result of the third expression is returned instead. This provides an extremely compact syntax for conditionally setting the value of variable. For example, we could write:

```
int Z = (X==Y) ? 5 : 8;
```

which would achieve exactly the same effect as:

```
int Z;
if (X == Y)
   Z = 5;
else
   Z = 8;
```

Summary

In this appendix, we have presented a brief introduction to C# from the point of view of comparing it with Visual Basic. We have found quite a few differences in syntax. In general, C# syntax allows most statements to be expressed in a more compact way. We have also found many similarities between the languages – for example in their use of classes (or class modules in VB), value and reference types, and many of the syntactical structures. However, we have also seen how C# supports many powerful features, particularly those related to inheritance and classic object-oriented programming, that are not available in VB.

Making the transfer from VB to C# does require a fair bit of learning, but is well worth it because the methodology of C# allows you to simply code up not only any application that you could have done in VB, but also a wide range of other applications that would be difficult or impossible to design in a good, well-structured, and maintainable manner in VB. With C# you also get the added bonus of the .NET runtime and all the associated benefits.

D

C# Compilation Options

This appendix lists the various C# compiler options that you may use if you have to compile your C# projects without the benefit of Visual Studio.NET, or if you want to carry out compiler operations not supported by Visual Studio.NET. They have been arranged as a series of tables according to category.

The first table shows the various file formats that can be output by the compiler:

Option	Purpose
`/doc:<filename>`	Processes XML documentation comments (marked with three slashes, `///`) and outputs to the specified XML file.
`/nooutput`	Compiles code but does not create an output file; useful for debugging purposes as the console will show warnings and errors.
`/out:<filename>`	Specifies the name of the output file. If this is not specified the compiler generates a standard `.exe` file with the same name as the source file (minus the extension).
`/target:<option>` `/t:<option>`	Specifies the format of the output file. The four options are: `exe`: produces a standard executable (the default setting). `library`: produces a code library (DLL). `module`: produces a code module (assembly with no manifest), which is later added to an assembly (using `/addmodule`). `winexe`: creates a Windows executable.

Unless the /target:module option is specified the compiler will add a manifest to the EXE that is created (or the first DLL if no EXE is created). Note that /target can be abbreviated to /t.

The next table explains the command-line option for determining compiler optimizations.

Option	Purpose
/optimize<+ | -> /o<+ | ->	Enables or disables optimizations carried out by the compiler to produce smaller, faster, and more efficient output. This is disabled by default. To enable, use the syntax: /optimize or /optimize+ To disable, use this syntax: /optimize-

The following table describes options that are used when creating and referring to .NET assemblies:

Option	Purpose
/addmodule:<module>	Specifies one or more modules to be included in the specified assembly. If more than one module is specified, they are separated by semicolons. This option is not available in Visual Studio.NET.
/nostdlib<+ | ->	Specifies whether or not to import the standard library (mscorlib.dll), which is imported by default. If you want to implement your own System namespace and classes, you may want the compiler *not* to load the standard library. The syntax for doing this is: /nostdlib or /nostdlib+ The syntax for importing it is: /nostdlib-
/reference:<assembly> /r:<assembly>	Imports metadata from an assembly file. You can specify the full path to the assembly, or anywhere specified by the PATH environment variable, or a relative path starting at the current project. If more than one file is specified, they are separated by semicolons.

The following table explains the options that apply to debugging and error checking:

Option	Purpose
`/bugreport:<filename>`	Creates the specified file that contains any bug information produced by the compiler. The contents of the file include: ❑ A copy of all source code ❑ A listing of compiler options ❑ Information on the compiler version, operating system etc. ❑ Any compiler output ❑ Description of problem and possible solution (optional) This option is not available in Visual Studio.NET

`/checked<+ | ->`	Specifies whether integer overflows raise a run-time error. This applies only to code outside of the scope of `checked` and `unchecked` blocks. This is disabled by default. The syntax for overflow checking is:
	
	 `/checked` or `/checked+`
	
	 To disable overflow checking use this syntax:
	
	 `/checked-`

`/debug<+ | ->`
 `/debug:<option>`
	Generates debugging information. To enable this use the syntax:
	
	 `/debug` or `/debug+`
	
	 To disable use this:
	
	 `/debug-`
	
	 Debugging is disabled by default. If you specify that debugging information should be output, then you have two options regarding the type of debugging information that is produced:
	
	 `/debug:full`: enables the attaching of a debugger to the operating program
	
	 `/debug:pdbonly`: allows source code debugging when the program is started in the debugger but will only display assembler when the running program is attached to the debugger.

`/fullpaths`	Specifies the full path to the file containing the error. This option is not available in Visual Studio.NET.

Table continued on following page

1283

Option	Purpose
/nowarn:<number>	Suppresses the compiler's ability to generate specified warnings. The <number> option specifies which warning number to suppress. If more than one is specified, they are separated by commas. This option is not available in Visual Studio.NET.
/warn:<option> /w:<option>	Sets the minimum warning level that you want to display. The options are: 0: Suppresses all warnings. 1: Displays only severe warnings. 2: Displays severe warnings plus warnings of medium severity. 3: Displays severe warnings plus warnings of medium and low severity. 4: Displays all warnings including informational warnings.
/warnaserror<+ | ->	Treats all warnings as errors. To enable, this use this syntax: /warnaserror or /warnaserror+ To disable use this syntax: /warnaserror- This is disabled by default.

This table show how to set preprocessor directives:

Option	Purpose
/define:<name> /d:<name>	Defines preprocessor symbol specified by <name>.

This table explains the options associated with including external resources:

Option	Purpose
/linkresource:<filename> /linkres:<filename>	Creates a link to the specified .NET resource. Two optional additional parameters (delimited by commas) are: identifier: The logical name for the resource; the name used to load the resource (the default is the filename) mimetype: A string representing the media type for the resource (the default is none) This option is not available in Visual Studio.NET.

Option	Purpose
`/resource:<filename>` `/res:<filename>`	Embeds a .NET-specified resource into the output file. Two optional additional parameters (delimited by commas) are: `identifier`: The logical name for the resource; the name used to load the resource (the default is the filename). `mimetype`: A string representing the media type for the resource (the default is none).
`/win32icon:<filename>`	Inserts the specified Win32 icon (`.ico`) file into the output file.
`/win32res:<filename>`	Inserts the specified Win32 resource (`.res`) file into the output file. This option is not available in Visual Studio.NET.

The final table lists various miscellaneous compiler options:

Option	Purpose
`@<filename>`	Specifies a file that contains all the compiler options and source files which will be processed by the compiler as if they had been entered at the command line.
`/baseaddress:<address>`	Specifies the preferred base address at which to load a DLL. The value of `<address>` can be decimal, hexadecimal, or octal.
`/codepage:<id>`	Specifies the code page (value passed as the `<id>` option) to use for all source code files in the compilation. Use this option if you use a character set in the C# files which isn't the default for your system. This option is not available in Visual Studio.NET.
`/help` `/?`	Lists compiler options to standard output. This option is not available in Visual Studio.NET.

`/incremental<+ | ->`
`/incr<+ | ->`
	Allows incremental compilation of source code files, that is, it compiles only those functions that have been altered since the previous compilation. Information about the state of the previous compilation is stored in two files, a `.dbg` file (or `.pdb` if `/debug` has been specified) to hold debug information and a `.incr` file to hold state information. To enable this use either syntax:
	
	`/incremental` or `/incremental+`
	
	To disable use this syntax:
	
	`/incremental-`
	
	This is disabled by default.

Table continued on following page

Option	Purpose
`/main:<class>`	Specifies the location of the `Main()` method, if more than one exists in the source code.
`/nologo`	Suppresses the output of the compiler banner information. This option is not available in Visual Studio.NET.
`/recurse:<dir\file>`	Searches subdirectories for source files to compile. There are two options: `dir` (optional): the directory or subdirectory to start the search from. If not specified, it is the directory of the current project. `file`: the file or files to search for. You can use wildcards.
`/unsafe`	Allows the compilation of code that uses the `unsafe` keyword.

Index

A Guide to the Index

The index is arranged hierarchically, in alphabetical order, with symbols preceding the letter A. Most second-level entries and many third-level entries also occur as first-level entries. This is to ensure that users will find the information they require however they choose to search for it.

Z

Building An Online Shopping Cart Using C#

Introduction

As web developers we are required to face a wide variety of application needs. Each web site developed is unique and furnished according to each client's specific needs. The fact is that websites are indeed fabricated for each client with different specifications but every site shares some common characteristics. Those parts of the site that share functionality features can be treated as separate applications to be reused.

In this case we will address the development cycle for one of the common blocks in today's websites – an Online Shopping Cart.

We will analyze the development of a shopping cart as a group of components described clearly before we implement them, thus allowing us to use this knowledge in areas other than ASP.NET. After a description of each component the implementation will be explained using C#.

The application will be designed to work with a SQLServer database for storage. Application logic will be done within the Web Form and presented to the user through the web browser. Core logic will reside in a separate C# component using the code behind technique. It will also be .NET framework Beta 2 compliant.

It is assumed that you have regular knowledge of the C# language, web development knowledge and database design basics.

Setting up the basis

First we will take some time to understand how a simple shopping cart works. From this knowledge we will draw some conclusions and state our requirements. From these requirements the database design will emerge.

After these steps we will have a clear path of development and be ready to implement our online shopping cart in the C# language.

Digging in the Online Shopping Cart Model

We will first take a look at a simplified diagram of an Online Shopping Cart. These are the functionality blocks to be discussed.

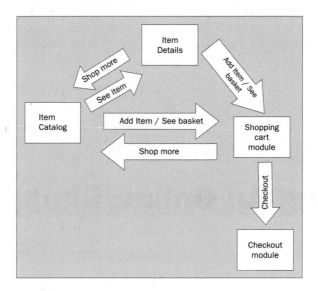

We then have four basic modules:

- **Item Catalog** – Here we display the options to our clients in an organized way.
- **Item Details** – Here we show the client as much info as we can to show off our product.
- **Shopping Cart** – Here we manage the user's selected items.
- **Checkout System** – Here we save the items selected and the client's information to close the transaction.

These are the basic blocks to be implemented in our online store. It includes the indispensable functionality that will be described in detail later. These blocks could be enriched further with more features, which will be covered in later articles.

Defining requirements

As in every software development cycle, we need to define our requirements first so we can design software capable of giving satisfaction to our customers.

Our online shopping cart application should do the following:

- Have a list of categories and subcategories.
- Items should be arranged in its corresponding subcategory.
- Items could be selected for category and home promotion.
- Each product should have an id, name, short and long descriptions, small and large images, stock and price.
- Users should be able to add products to the basket and remove them.

The user should be given an order number and will be able to track it through an order tracking system.

Generating our database model

From our requirements we define the database schema. The tables are shown as a conceptual model, with all tables used in this version of the shopping cart.

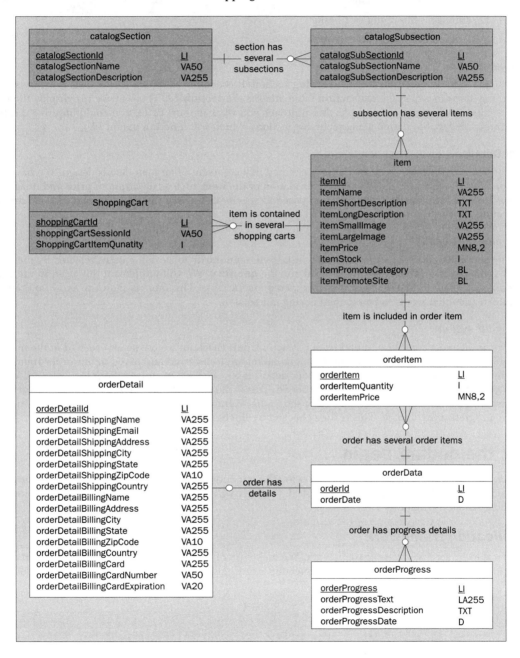

The tables are grouped as follows:

- ❑ Green – The catalog part of our application.
- ❑ Sky blue – Item details.
- ❑ Orange – Shopping cart basket.
- ❑ Yellow – The checkout system.

Catalog Section

The green part corresponds to the **catalog** section. It is composed of two tables. This is a very simple arrangement in which the **subsection** table inherits the **section Id**. This way we can display the items in a section/subsection approach. As this approach will work in most cases, you could improve this to a completely flexible design using recursive sections, which will inherit a parent Id.

Item Details

The item details part of our model is a trimmed down version of an item details design. We have only one table in which we save the vital information of the **item** such as description, price and images. We have a couple of Boolean values that are used to specify if the item should be displayed as a home or section item.

Shopping cart basket

The shopping basket is a simple table that is used temporarily to store the items selected by the user. We just save the **session Id**, the **item id** and the **quantity**. We will implement this as an **in-memory data table** and hold our selected items in a session variable. This table is shown to show you're the information that needs to be retained during our session.

Checkout system

This is the most complicated part or our system. Upon checkout we create an order Id in the order table. Then the items stored in the shopping basket are transferred and saved in our order Items table. The user information is stored in the order details table. These two tables inherit the order Id. We have a fourth table which also inherits the order Id. This is the order Progress table and it is used for order tracking. As progress is done, the online shop administrator should add a record to this table indicating the progress done to date. This is then checked by the buyer.

Let the coding begin

As our design basis is done, we are all set to start our coding. The architecture will be based on simple Web Forms calling custom User Controls. Core logic will be done in separate components using the code behind technique.

Application framework

We start by setting our basic framework. We make use of our **web.config** file to save important application information such as our connection string. This is how our configuration file will look:

```
<configuration>
  <appSettings>
    <add key="connString"
value="server=(local)\NetSDK;database=ShoppingCart;Trusted_Connection=yes" />
  </appSettings>
</configuration>
```

1316

To retrieve this information we use the following code snippet.

```
String connString = ConfigurationSettings.AppSettings["connString"];
```

As you can see, this is a very easy and convenient way to store application wise data.

Category List Block

All being set, we have our first task which is to display a list of products which will be filtered by section and subsection if selected.

The first task is to set up the workspace of our Web Forms. We set up our language and add the appropriate namespaces for our code to work.. We set C# as our language and import the **System** namespace for general purposes. We then add the **System.Data** and **System.Data.OleDb** since we will be using SQLServer as our database engine. We should set the debug flag to false once we deliver this application to the real world.

```
<%@ Page Language="C#" Debug="true" %>
<%@ Import Namespace="System" %>
<%@ Import Namespace="System.Data" %>
<%@ Import Namespace="System.Data.SqlClient " %>
```

We now set our references to our custom **User Controls**.

```
<%@ Register TagPrefix="SC" TagName="Site" Src="uc_header.ascx" %>
<%@ Register TagPrefix="SC" TagName="Section" Src="uc_catalog_section.ascx" %>
<%@ Register TagPrefix="SC" TagName="SubSection" Src="uc_catalog_subsection.ascx"
%>
<%@ Register TagPrefix="SC" TagName="ProductList"
Src="uc_catalog_product_list.ascx" %>
```

We reference our controls by embedding them into the aspx file.

```
<SC:Site runat="server" />
```

This will be our complete catalog WebForm, the **catalog.aspx** file.

```
<%@ Page Language="C#" Debug="true" %>
<%@ Register TagPrefix="SC" TagName="Site" Src="uc_header.ascx" %>
<%@ Register TagPrefix="SC" TagName="Section" Src="uc_catalog_section.ascx" %>
<%@ Register TagPrefix="SC" TagName="SubSection" Src="uc_catalog_subsection.ascx"
%>
<%@ Register TagPrefix="SC" TagName="ProductList"
Src="uc_catalog_product_list.ascx" %>
<html>
<head>
<title>Shopping Cart in C# - Catalog</title>
<link rel="stylesheet" href="style.css">
```

```
</head>
<body>
<form runat=server>
<SC:Site runat="server" />
<table width="800" cellspacing="0" cellpadding="3" border="0" style="border-
color:Black;border-width:1px;border-style:solid;">
<tr>
<td width="800" align="right" bgcolor="#CCCCCC"><span class="itemTitle">Item
Catalog</span></td>
</tr>
</table>
<table width="800" cellspacing="0" cellpadding="0" border="0">
<tr>
<td width="200" height="100%" rowspan="2" valign="top"><SC:Section runat="server"
/></td>
<td width="600" height="10" valign="top"><SC:SubSection runat="server" /></td>
</tr>
<tr>
<td width="600" height="100%"><SC:ProductList runat="server" /></td>
</tr>
</table>
</form>
</body>
</html>
```

We have used four custom user controls in our first Web Form. We shall now go towards implementing these custom controls, most of which, will be reused through out the site.

Lets start by implementing the simplest of our user controls, **uc_header.ascx**. This file contains the "logo" of the site and a couple of links. We encapsulate this into a control since it will be repeated through the whole site. This is the code:

```
<table width="800" cellspacing="0" cellpadding="3" border="0" style="border-
color:Black;border-width:1px;border-style:solid;">
<tr>
<td width="400"><a href="catalog.aspx"><span class="mainTitle">Shopping Cart
Site</span></a></td>
<td width="400" align="right"><a href="cart.aspx">View Cart</a><span
class="mainText"> | </span><a href="tracking.aspx">Track your order</a></td>
</tr>
</table>
```

As you can see this is just a static table, reminiscent of old style include files. Next we code a more complex user control, **uc_catalog_section.ascx** which displays the list of sections available on the site. This is done by binding a data retrieval codebehind class to the user control.

This is our User Control Code:

```
<%@ Control Language="C#" Debug="true" Inherits="CodeBehind.UcSection" %>
<%@ Import Namespace="System.Data" %>
<%@ Import Namespace="System.Data.SqlClient" %>
```

```html
<html>
<head>
    <title></title>
    <script language="C#" runat="server"></script>
</head>
<body>

    <font face="Verdana" size="-1">
        <asp:DataList id="MySectionList" runat="server"
            BorderColor="black"
            BorderWidth="1"
            GridLines="Both"
            CellPadding="3"
            Font-Name="Verdana"
            Font-Size="8pt"
            Width="200px"
            HeaderStyle-BackColor="#aaaadd"
            SelectedItemStyle-BackColor="Gainsboro"
            >
            <HeaderTemplate>
              Sections
            </HeaderTemplate>
            <ItemTemplate>
            <a href="catalog.aspx?sectionId=<%#
DataBinder.Eval(Container.DataItem,"catalogSectionId") %>

&sectionIndex=<%#Container.ItemIndex%>">
                                  <%# DataBinder.Eval(Container.DataItem,
"catalogSectionName") %></a>
            </ItemTemplate>
            <SelectedItemTemplate>
               <%# DataBinder.Eval(Container.DataItem, "catalogSectionName") %>
            </SelectedItemTemplate>
        </asp:DataList>
    </font>

</body>
</html>
```

We place some more html into the control and we drop a DataList object to handle the rendering of the information. The `<%# DataBinder.Eval(Container.DataItem, "catalogSectionName") %>` code is used to select specific information from the bound data and put it in place.

In our codebehind class we first have to declare our DataList as protected. We then do some database work. Once we have the information we need ready from our database, we bind this data to our Web Control, the DataList.

Our User Control inherits the code behind class and that way they can work together. It is important to declare your shared variables (such as Web Form Controls) as protected so that the can be reached within the code behind class.

1319

```
public class UcSection : UserControl {
  protected DataList MySectionList;
  protected Label MyLabel;

  protected void Page_Load(object sender, EventArgs e) {
    if (!IsPostBack) {
      Bind_MySectionList();
    }

    if (Request.QueryString["sectionIndex"] != null) {
      MySectionList.SelectedIndex =
Int32.Parse(Request.QueryString["sectionIndex"]);
    }
  }

  protected void Bind_MySectionList() {
    String connString = ConfigurationSettings.AppSettings["connString"];
    SqlConnection myConnection = new SqlConnection(connString);
    SqlDataAdapter myCommand = new SqlDataAdapter("SELECT catalogSectionId,
catalogSectionName
                              FROM catalogSection ORDER BY catalogSectionName",
myConnection);
    DataSet ds = new DataSet();
    myCommand.Fill(ds, "catalogSection");

    MySectionList.DataSource = new DataView(ds.Tables[0]);
    MySectionList.DataBind();
  }
}
```

We then have to implement our **subsection user control**. This control will do a similar task to the section control. We will just add a filter to the Query applied to the database. We will select subsections corresponding to the selected section. The rest is pretty much the same.

```
"SELECT catalogSubSectionId, catalogSubSectionName FROM catalogSubSection WHERE
catalogSectionId= " +
                                            sectionId + " ORDER BY
catalogSubSectionName"
```

We then need to display our product list. We have three types of products:

❑   Site Products: These are shown if no section is selected

❑   Section Products: These are shown if a section is selected but no subsection is selected.

❑   Normal Products: These are products that belong to the selected subsection.

We need to filter the three possibilities and create the proper query. This is done in the blah class with this code. After we have our query we bind it to a DataGrid Web Control to display the items in a table arrangement.

```
string SQLQuery = "SELECT itemId, itemName, itemShortDescription, itemSmallImage,
itemPrice, itemStock
                                          FROM item WHERE itemPromoteSite=1
ORDER BY itemName";


int mysectionId = 0;
if (Request.QueryString["sectionId"] != null) {
  mysectionId = Int32.Parse(Request.QueryString["sectionId"]);
}
if (mysectionId != 0) {
  //If we have a section selected we filter products for this section
  SQLQuery = "SELECT item.itemId, item.itemName, item.itemShortDescription,
item.itemSmallImage, item.itemPrice, item.itemStock
      FROM (catalogSection INNER JOIN catalogSubSection ON
catalogSection.catalogSectionId = catalogSubSection.catalogSectionId)
                                          INNER JOIN item ON
catalogSubSection.catalogSubSectionId = item.catalogSubSectionId
                        WHERE (((catalogSection.catalogSectionId)=" +
mysectionId + ") AND ((item.itemPromoteCategory)=1))";
}

int mysubsectionId = 0;
if (Request.QueryString["subsectionId"] != null) {
  mysubsectionId = Int32.Parse(Request.QueryString["subsectionId"]);
}
if (mysubsectionId != 0) {
  //If we have a subsection selected we filter products for this subsection
  SQLQuery = "SELECT itemId, itemName, itemShortDescription, itemSmallImage,
itemPrice, itemStock FROM item WHERE catalogSubSectionId=" + mysubsectionId + "
ORDER BY itemName";
}
```

This concludes our catalog presentation layer which consists of four main user controls.

❑   The first control is responsible for displaying a list of sections.

❑   The second control is responsible for the subsection list.

❑   The third control is responsible for displaying a grid of items. This list of items is retrieved from one of three sql queries depending on the situation.

❑   A final control renders the top of the page.

All the controls work together to form **catalog.aspx**. The user controls make use of codebehind classes for database access and bind the DataLists in our page.

Our `catalog.aspx` file should yield something like this:

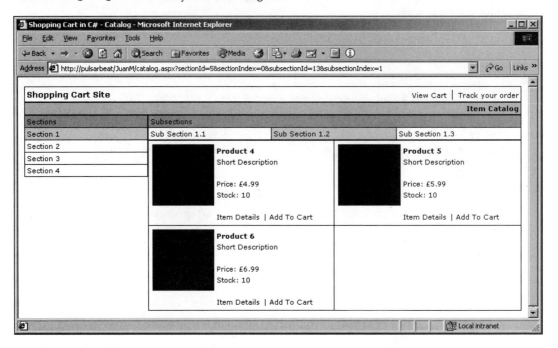

Item Details

Our next step in building our shopping cart is to show off the item details. We first will use some of the code done for the catalog presentation before. We will take the basic html framework and three user controls. We will reuse the header, section and subsection control.

The difference here will be to replace the **item list** control with a **new item details** control. We will use a data list Web Control to display the items characteristics as well as its corresponding class in our code behind repository.

The code to do this simple task is as follows for the user control:

```
<%@ Control Language="C#" Debug="true" Inherits="CodeBehind.UcItemDetails" %>
<%@ Import Namespace="System.Data" %>
<%@ Import Namespace="System.Data.SqlClient" %>

<script language="C#" runat="server"></script>
<font face="Verdana" size="-1">
<asp:DataList id="MyItemDetails" runat="server"
  BorderColor="black"
  BorderWidth="1"
  GridLines="Both"
  CellPadding="3"
  Font-Name="Verdana"
  Font-Size="8pt"
  Width="600px"
```

```
   HeaderStyle-BackColor="#aaaadd"
   SelectedItemStyle-BackColor="Gainsboro"
   RepeatDirection = "Horizontal"
   RepeatColumns = "1"
   >
   <ItemTemplate>
     <table>
     <tr>
     <td valign="top">
       <img src="images/<%# DataBinder.Eval(Container.DataItem, "itemLargeImage")
%>" width="200" height="200">
     </td>
     <td valign="top">
       <span class="itemTitle"><%# DataBinder.Eval(Container.DataItem, "itemName")
%></span>
       <br>
       <span class="itemText"><%# DataBinder.Eval(Container.DataItem,
"itemLongDescription") %></span>
       <br><br>
       <span class="itemText">Price: <%# (DataBinder.Eval(Container.DataItem,
"itemPrice", "{0:c}")) %></span>
       <br>
       <span class="itemText">Stock: <%# DataBinder.Eval(Container.DataItem,
"itemStock") %></span>
       <br><br>
       <a
href="catalog.aspx?sectionId=<%=sectionId%>&sectionIndex=<%=sectionIndex%>&subsect
ionId=<%=subsectionId%>

&subsectionIndex=<%=subsectionIndex%>">Keep On Shopping!</a>
       <span class="itemText"> | </span>
       <a href="cart.aspx?cartAction=1&itemId=<%#
DataBinder.Eval(Container.DataItem, "itemId") %>">Add To Cart</a>
     </td>
     </tr>
     </table>
   </ItemTemplate>
   </asp:DataList>
</font>
```

And our code behind class:

```
protected void Bind_ItemDetails() {
  int myItemId = 0;
  if (Request.QueryString["itemId"] != null) {
    myItemId = Int32.Parse(Request.QueryString["itemId"]);
  }
  string SQLQuery = "SELECT itemId, itemName, itemLongDescription, itemLargeImage,
itemPrice, itemStock
                                                    FROM item WHERE
itemId = " + myItemId;
  String connString = ConfigurationSettings.AppSettings["connString"];
  SqlConnection myConnection = new SqlConnection(connString);
```

```
    SqlDataAdapter myCommand = new SqlDataAdapter(SQLQuery, myConnection);
    DataSet ds = new DataSet();
    myCommand.Fill(ds, "item");

    MyItemDetails.DataSource = new DataView(ds.Tables[0]);
    MyItemDetails.DataBind();
}
```

Further enhancements can be done to this simple module. This form shows the stored details of the item and can be enriched with user reviews and related item lists.

Our resulting screen should look as follows:

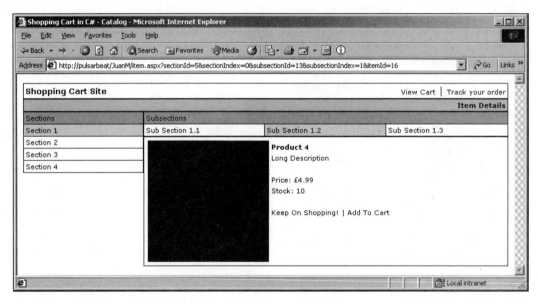

Shopping cart basket

The shopping cart basket implements the majority of the functionality. It should provide ways to add, edit and delete items from it. The basket is merely a temporal storage area for the user to group the items of interest. We then need some session management to be able to recognize which items belong to each client in its own session.

ASP.NET, as in previous asp applications, provides the necessary objects to work with sessions. In this case we will take advantage of the **Session** object. We will store a **DataTable** object as a Session variable therefore all shopping cart basket operations are done in memory. This is a very fast approach but will need to be provided with enough memory to handle concurrent clients.

The shopping basket module comprises two fundamental parts. The first involves managing the items that the user wants to have in the basket. The second is in charge of displaying the items currently in the basket. We will see the details now.

❑ We instruct our Web Form to add an item to the cart with querystring variables. We just add an item to the DataTable. To implement the update and delete methods we bind the DataTable to the DataList Web Control and perform the operations.

```csharp
void Page_Load(Object Sender, EventArgs E) {
    if (Request.QueryString["cartAction"] != null) {
        this.cartAction = Int32.Parse(Request.QueryString["cartAction"]);
    }

    if (Session["ShoppingCart"] == null) {
        Cart = new DataTable();
        Cart.Columns.Add(new DataColumn("ItemId", typeof(string)));
        Cart.Columns.Add(new DataColumn("Item", typeof(string)));
        Cart.Columns.Add(new DataColumn("Qty", typeof(string)));
        Cart.Columns.Add(new DataColumn("Price", typeof(string)));
        Session["ShoppingCart"] = Cart;
    }
    else {
        Cart = (DataTable)Session["ShoppingCart"];
    }

    CartView = new DataView(Cart);
    CartView.Sort = "Item";

    if (!IsPostBack) {
        //Add new entry to the shopping cart
        int myCartAction = 0;
        if (Request.QueryString["cartAction"] != null) {
            myCartAction = Int32.Parse(Request.QueryString["cartAction"]);
        }
        if (myCartAction==1) {
            //Take the items details from the database
            string myItemId = "0";
            if (Request.QueryString["itemId"] != null) {
                myItemId = Request.QueryString["itemId"];
            }
            string SQLQuery = "SELECT itemName, itemPrice FROM item WHERE itemId = "
 + myItemId;
            String connString = ConfigurationSettings.AppSettings["connString"];

            SqlConnection myConnection = new SqlConnection(connString);
                SqlCommand myCommand = new SqlCommand(SQLQuery, myConnection);
            myConnection.Open();
            SqlDataReader dr2 = myCommand.ExecuteReader();

            if (dr2.Read()) {
                DataRow dr = Cart.NewRow();
                dr[0] = myItemId;
                dr[1] = dr2.GetString(0);
                dr[2] = "1";
                dr[3] = dr2.GetSqlMoney(1).ToString();
                Cart.Rows.Add(dr);
            }
        }

        BindCartList();
        BindTotalList();
    }
}
```

The functions to update and delete data are as follows:

```csharp
    protected void DataCartList_DeleteCommand1(Object Sender,
DataListCommandEventArgs e) {
        string item = ((Label)e.Item.FindControl("Label4")).Text;
    CartView.RowFilter = "Item='"+item+"'";
        if (CartView.Count > 0) //item exists in cart
            CartView.Delete(0);
        CartView.RowFilter = "";

        CartList.EditItemIndex = -1;
        BindCartList();
    BindTotalList();
    }


    protected void DataCartList_EditCommand1(Object Sender,
DataListCommandEventArgs e) {
        CartList.EditItemIndex = (int)e.Item.ItemIndex;
        BindCartList();
    BindTotalList();
    }

    protected void DataCartList_CancelCommand1(Object Sender,
DataListCommandEventArgs e) {
        CartList.EditItemIndex = -1;
        BindCartList();
    BindTotalList();
    }

    protected void DataCartList_UpdateCommand1(Object Sender,
DataListCommandEventArgs e) {
    string itemId = ((Label)e.Item.FindControl("Label1")).Text;
        string item = ((Label)e.Item.FindControl("Label2")).Text;
        string qty = ((TextBox)e.Item.FindControl("Text1")).Text;
        string price = ((Label)e.Item.FindControl("Label3")).Text;

        // with a database, we'd use an update command.  Since we're using an in-
memory
        // DataTable, we'll delete the old row and replace it with a new one
        //remove old entry
        CartView.RowFilter = "Item='"+item+"'";
        if (CartView.Count > 0) //item exists in cart
            CartView.Delete(0);
        CartView.RowFilter = "";

        //add new entry
        DataRow dr = Cart.NewRow();
        dr[0] = itemId;
        dr[1] = item;
        dr[2] = qty;
    dr[3] = price;
        Cart.Rows.Add(dr);

        CartList.EditItemIndex = -1;
        BindCartList();
    BindTotalList();
    }
```

Finally we need to calculate the subtotal, tax and total cost of the order. We use the
BindTotalList() function to generate content and bind it to another Web Control in our page.

```
protected void BindTotalList() {
    double mySubTotal = 0;
    double myTaxRate = 0.15;
    double myTax = 0;
    double myTotal = 0;

    DataTable CartTable = (DataTable)Session["ShoppingCart"];
    foreach(DataRow myRow in CartTable.Rows) {
        Double tempPrice = Double.Parse(myRow[3].ToString());
        Int32 tempQty = Int32.Parse(myRow[2].ToString());
        mySubTotal += tempPrice * tempQty;
    }

    myTax = mySubTotal * myTaxRate;
    myTotal = mySubTotal + myTax;

    CartTotal = new DataTable();
        CartTotal.Columns.Add(new DataColumn("SubTotal", typeof(string)));
        CartTotal.Columns.Add(new DataColumn("Tax", typeof(string)));
        CartTotal.Columns.Add(new DataColumn("Total", typeof(string)));

    DataRow drTotal = CartTotal.NewRow();
        drTotal[0] = mySubTotal.ToString();
        drTotal[1] = myTax.ToString();
        drTotal[2] = myTotal.ToString();
    CartTotal.Rows.Add(drTotal);

    CartTotalView = new DataView(CartTotal);
    CartTotalList.DataSource = CartTotalView;
    CartTotalList.DataBind();
}
```

The shopping cart screen looks like this:

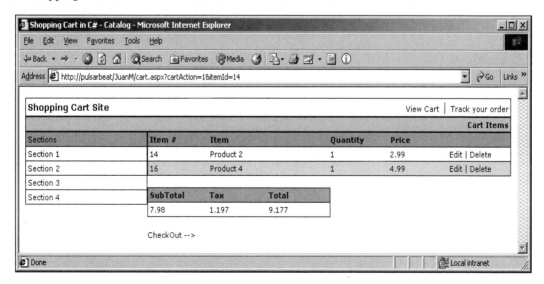

Checkout System

The checkout system has the responsibility of saving the client info and selected items for processing. We use three tables to save the client info. These are the following:

- ❑ orderData – Stores the date of the order and generates the order Id.
- ❑ orderItem – List of items bought, it also saves the price at the time of purchase.
- ❑ orderDetail – Saves shipping and billing information for the order.

We divide our process into three steps:

- ❑ Shipping and Billing Information – Here we get the shipping information. With this info we can calculate the shipping costs. This should be done accordingly to each store's necessities. We validate credit card information also. This should be done using a specific provider like paypal.
- ❑ Confirmation – Here we present a summary of the information received and show the list of items to be bought, as well as the grand total of the order. The user is asked to submit the information if it is correct.
- ❑ Summary – We finish the transaction and show the user the order number.

We post the info from the first to the second step. We then use Web Form Controls to ask for confirmation. If the info is correct, then we register the order for our client.

We do need to implement some form validation before posting the information and implement some credit card validation through an external provider or your own software.

Tracking your order

The final part of our online shopping cart application is the tracking system. We will implement a basic tracking system which will ask the user for their email and order number. The system will then show a list of milestones registered in the tracking database.

We use a single table to save the tracking information. It consists of the order id and the information of the goals achieved. Upon valid email and order number we display the list of events below.

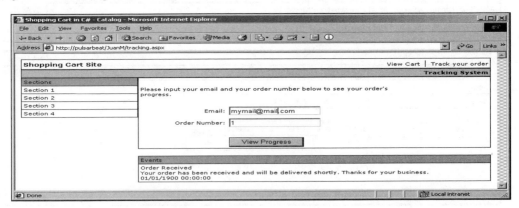

This is the code required:

```csharp
protected void ButtonView_Click(object Source, EventArgs e) {
    //Look for order id with provided email and order number
    String connString = ConfigurationSettings.AppSettings["connString"];
    string strSelect = "SELECT orderId FROM orderDetail WHERE orderId=" +
orderIdBox.Text + " AND orderDetailShippingEmail='" + emailBox.Text + "'";
    SqlConnection myConnection = new SqlConnection(connString);
    SqlCommand myCommand = new SqlCommand(strSelect, myConnection);

    myConnection.Open();
    SqlDataReader dr = myCommand.ExecuteReader();
    int newOrderId = 0;
    if (dr.Read()) {
        //emailBox.Text = "Encontramos!!!";
        Bind_TrackingList();
    }
    myConnection.Close();
}

protected void Bind_TrackingList() {
    string SQLQuery = "SELECT orderProgressText, orderProgressDescription,
orderProgressDate FROM orderProgress WHERE orderId = " + orderIdBox.Text;
    String connString = ConfigurationSettings.AppSettings["connString"];

    SqlConnection myConnection = new SqlConnection(connString);
    SqlDataAdapter myCommand = new SqlDataAdapter(SQLQuery, myConnection);

    DataSet ds = new DataSet();
    myCommand.Fill(ds, "orderProgress");

    MyTrackingList.DataSource = new DataView(ds.Tables[0]);
    MyTrackingList.DataBind();
}
```

Deployment of the site

Deployment of this particular application is very simple.

❑ Create a **new database** in SQLServer

❑ Once we have created the database we need to run the **database creation script** provided.

❑ Create a **new site** in your IIS administration program

❑ Copy the **web.config** file to the wwwroot folder.

❑ Copy the **Web Forms** and **User controls** to the wwwroot folder.

❑ Copy the **codebehind.dll** into your wwwroot/bin directory (no registration required!).

Improvements to our online shopping cart application

The shopping cart we just made takes a basic approach to the application providing the central framework of an online shopping cart. Further enhancements can be made and will be the responsibility of the reader. These enhancements should be made to enrich the shopping cart application give a better service to the online community. Some ideas are presented here.

Feature improvements

- ❏ Recursive sections for n levels of profundity
- ❏ Item reviews
- ❏ Item related items
- ❏ User accounts and management
- ❏ Mailing list to customers
- ❏ Specific shipping costs calculations

Technical improvements

- ❏ Build based on components for performance and possible code reuse
- ❏ Migrate to SQL Server database using stored procedures for performance
- ❏ Implement SSL in your server (a must but out of scope!)
- ❏ Implement real time credit card processing and charging.

Conclusions

The system presented shows the basis of a working online shopping cart. It involves the main aspects of an online store which are the catalog of items, the item detail module, the shopping cart basket and the checkout module. Every shopping cart online today must implement these basic parts to be functional. Hopefully this article has given you the knowledge to build your own with ease and to add new functionality to meet your needs as ideas for improvement have been given.

In future articles, we will cover some of the important requirements of a real – world shopping cart that have been left out of this article for the sake of brevity – a management console to add, modify and delete categories, items and orders; item reviews; SSL for credit card payments; and a discussion of working with a credit card processing provider.